CRIME IN THE UNITED STATES

CONTENTS

SECTION I

SUMMARY OF THE UNIFORM CRIME REPORTING (UCR) PROGRAM

SUMMARY OF THE UNIFORM CRIME REPORTING (UCR) PROGRAM

Bernan Press is proud to present its eighth edition of *Crime in the United States*. This title was formerly published by the Federal Bureau of Investigation (FBI), but is no longer available in printed form from the government. This edition contains final data from 2012, the most current year for which data is available.

This section describes the history of the UCR program, which collects the data used in *Crime in the United States,* and it examines the best way to use the data in this publication.

About the UCR program

The UCR program's primary objective is to generate reliable information for use in law enforcement administration, operation, and management; however, over the course of the program, its data has stood as one of the country's leading social indicators.

The UCR program is a nationwide, cooperative statistical effort of more than 18,000 city, university and college, county, state, tribal, and federal law enforcement agencies voluntarily reporting data on crimes brought to their attention. Since 1930, the FBI has administered the UCR program and continued to assess and monitor the nature and type of crime in the nation. Criminologists, sociologists, legislators, municipal planners, the media, and other students of criminal justice use the data for varied research and planning purposes. In 2012, law enforcement agencies active in the UCR program represented more than 308 million United States inhabitants—98.1 percent of the total population. The coverage amounted to 98.9 percent of the population in metropolitan statistical areas, 93.3 percent of the population in cities outside metropolitan areas, and 94.2 percent of the population in nonmetropolitan counties.

Note for Users

It is important for UCR data users to remember that the FBI's primary objective is to generate a reliable set of crime statistics for use in law enforcement administration, operation, and management. The FBI does not provide a ranking of agencies; instead, it provides alphabetical tabulations of states, metropolitan statistical areas, cities with over 10,000 inhabitants, suburban and rural counties, and selected colleges and universities. Law enforcement officials use these data for their designed purposes. Additionally, the public relies on these data for information about the fluctuations in levels of crime from year to year, while criminologists, sociologists, legislators, city planners, media outlets, and other students of criminal justice use them for a variety of research and planning purposes. Since crime is a sociological phenomenon influenced by a variety of factors, the FBI discourages data users from ranking agencies and using the data as a measurement of the effectiveness of law enforcement.

To ensure that data are uniformly reported, the FBI provides contributing law enforcement agencies with a handbook that explains how to classify and score offenses and provides uniform crime offense definitions. Acknowledging that offense definitions may vary from state to state, the FBI cautions agencies to report offenses according to the guidelines provided in the handbook, rather than by local or state statutes. Most agencies make a good faith effort to comply with established guidelines.

The UCR program publishes the statistics most commonly requested by data users. More information regarding the availability of UCR program data is available by telephone at (304) 625-4995, by fax at (304) 625-5394, or by e-mail at cjis_comm@leo.gov. Data requests via e-mail cannot be processed without the requester's full name, mailing address, and contact telephone number.

Variables Affecting Crime: Caution Against Ranking

Until data users examine all the variables that affect crime in a town, city, county, state, region, or college or university, they can make no meaningful comparisons. In each edition of *Crime in the United States*, many entities—including news media, tourism agencies, and other organizations with an interest in crime in the nation—use reported figures to compile rankings of cities and counties. However, these rankings are merely a quick choice made by that data user; they provide no insight into the many variables that mold the crime in a particular town, city, county, state, or region. Consequently, these rankings may lead to simplistic and/or incomplete analyses, which can create misleading perceptions and thus adversely affect cities and counties, along with their residents.

Considering other Characteristics of a Jurisdiction

To assess criminality and law enforcement's response from jurisdiction to jurisdiction, data users must consider many variables, some of which (despite having significant impact on crime) are not readily measurable or applicable among all locales. Geographic and demographic factors specific to each jurisdiction must be considered and applied in order to make an accurate and complete assessment of crime in that jurisdiction. Several sources of information are available to help the researcher explore the variables that affect crime in a particular locale. The U.S. Census Bureau data, for example, can help the user better understand the makeup of a locale's population. The transience of the population, its racial and ethnic makeup, and its composition by age and gender, educational levels, and prevalent family structures are all key factors in assessing and understanding crime.

Local chambers of commerce, planning offices, and similar entities provide information regarding the economic and cultural makeup of cities and counties. Understanding a jurisdiction's industrial/economic base, its dependence upon neighboring jurisdictions, its transportation system, its economic dependence on nonresidents (such as tourists and convention attendees), and its proximity to military installations, correctional institutions, and other types of facilities all contribute to accurately gauging and interpreting the crime known to and reported by law enforcement.

The strength (including personnel and other resources) and aggressiveness of a jurisdiction's law enforcement agency are also key factors in understanding the nature and extent of crime occurring in that area. Although information pertaining to the number of sworn and civilian employees can be found in this publication, it cannot be used alone as an assessment of the emphasis that a community places on enforcing the law. For example, one city may report more crime than another comparable city because its law enforcement agency identifies more offenses. Attitudes of citizens toward crime and their crime reporting practices—especially for minor offenses—also have an impact on the volume of crimes known to police.

Making Valid Crime Assessments

It is essential for all data users to become as well educated as possible about understanding and quantifying the nature and extent of crime in the United States and in the jurisdictions represented by law enforcement contributors to the UCR program. Valid assessments are possible only with careful study and analysis of the various unique conditions that affect each local law enforcement jurisdiction.

Some factors that are known to affect the volume and type of crime occurring from place to place are:

- Population density and degree of urbanization
- Variations in composition of population, particularly in the concentration of youth
- Stability of the population with respect to residents' mobility, commuting patterns, and transient factors
- Modes of transportation and highway systems
- Economic conditions, including median income, poverty level, and job availability
- Cultural factors and educational, recreational, and religious characteristics
- Family conditions, with respect to divorce and family cohesiveness
- Climate
- Effective strength of law enforcement agencies
- Administrative and investigative emphases of law enforcement
- Policies of other components of the criminal justice system (that is, prosecutorial, judicial, correctional, and probational policies)
- Residents' attitudes toward crime
- Crime reporting practices of residents

Although many of the listed factors equally affect the crime of a particular area, the UCR program makes no attempt to relate them to the data presented. **The data user is therefore cautioned against comparing statistical data of individual reporting units from cities, counties, metropolitan areas, states, or colleges or universities solely on the basis on their population coverage or student enrollment.** Until data users examine all the variables that affect crime in a town, city, county, state, region, or college or university, they can make no meaningful comparisons.

Historical Background

Since 1930, the FBI has administered the UCR program; the agency continues to assess and monitor the nature and type of crime in the nation. Data users look to the UCR program for various research and planning purposes.

Recognizing a need for national crime statistics, the International Association of Chiefs of Police (IACP) formed the Committee on Uniform Crime Records in the 1920s to develop a system of uniform crime statistics. After studying state criminal codes and making an evaluation of the recordkeeping practices in use, the committee completed a plan for crime reporting that became the foundation of the UCR program in 1929. The plan included standardized offense definitions for seven main offense classifications known as Part I crimes to gauge fluctuations in the overall volume and rate of crime. Developers also instituted the Hierarchy Rule as the main reporting procedure for what is now known as the Summary Reporting System of the UCR program.

Seven main offense classifications, known as Part I crimes, were chosen to gauge the state of crime in the nation. These seven offense classifications included the violent crimes of murder and nonnegligent manslaughter, forcible rape, robbery, and aggravated assault; also included were the property crimes of burglary, larceny-theft, and motor vehicle theft. By congressional mandate, arson was added as the eighth Part I offense category. Data collection for arson began in 1979.

During the early planning of the program, it was recognized that the differences among criminal codes precluded a mere aggregation of state statistics to arrive at a national total. Also, because of the variances in punishment for the same offenses in different states, no distinction between felony and misdemeanor crimes was possible. To avoid these problems and provide nationwide uniformity in crime reporting, standardized offense definitions were developed. Law enforcement agencies use these to submit data without regard for local statutes. UCR program offense definitions can be found in Appendix II.

In January 1930, 400 cities (representing 20 million inhabitants in 43 states) began participating in the UCR program. Congress enacted Title 28, Section 534, of the *United States Code* that same year, which authorized the attorney general to gather crime information. The attorney general, in turn, designated the FBI to serve as the national clearinghouse for the collected crime data. Since then, data based on uniform classifications and procedures for reporting have been obtained annually from the nation's law enforcement agencies.

Advisory Groups

Providing vital links between local law enforcement and the FBI for the UCR program are the Criminal Justice Information Systems Committees of the IACP and the National Sheriffs' Association (NSA). The IACP represents the thousands of police departments nationwide, as it has since the program began. The NSA encourages sheriffs throughout the country to participate fully in the program. Both committees serve the program in advisory capacities.

In 1988, a Data Providers' Advisory Policy Board was established. This board operated until 1993, when it combined with the National Crime Information Center Advisory Policy Board to form a single Advisory Policy Board (APB) to address all FBI criminal justice information services. The current APB works to ensure continuing emphasis on UCR-related issues. The Association of State Uniform Crime Reporting Programs (ASUCRP) focuses on UCR issues within individual state law enforcement associations and also promotes interest in the UCR program. These organizations foster widespread and responsible use of uniform crime statistics and lend assistance to data contributors.

Redesign of UCR

Although UCR data collection was originally conceived as a tool for law enforcement administration, the data were widely used by other entities involved in various forms of social planning by the 1980s. Recognizing the need for more detailed crime statistics, law enforcement called for a thorough evaluative study to modernize the UCR program. The FBI formulated a comprehensive three-phase redesign effort. The Bureau of Justice Statistics (BJS) agency in the Department of Justice responsible for funding criminal justice information projects, agreed to underwrite the first two phases. These phases were conducted by an independent contractor and structured to determine what, if any, changes should be made to the current program. The third phase would involve implementation of the changes identified.

The final report, the Blueprint for the Future of the Uniform Crime Reporting Program, was released in the summer of 1985. It specifically outlined recommendations for an expanded, improved UCR program to meet future informational needs. There were three recommended areas of enhancement to the UCR program:

- Offenses and arrests would be reported using an incident-based system
- Data would be collected on two levels. Agencies in level one would report important details about those offenses comprising the Part I crimes, their victims, and arrestees. Level two would consist of law enforcement agencies covering populations of more than 100,000 and a sampling of smaller agencies that would collect expanded detail on all significant offenses
- A quality assurance program would be introduced

In January 1986, Phase III of the redesign effort began, guided by the general recommendations set forth in the *Blueprint*. The FBI selected an experimental site to implement the redesigned program, while contractors developed new data guidelines and system specifications. Upon selecting the South Carolina Law Enforcement Division (SLED), which enlisted the cooperation of nine local law enforcement agencies, the FBI developed automated data capture specifications to adapt the SLED's state system to the national UCR program's standards, and the BJS funded the revisions. The pilot demonstration ran from March 1 through September 30, 1987, and resulted in further refinement of the guidelines and specifications.

From March 1 through March 3, 1988, the FBI held a national UCR conference to present the new system to law enforcement and to obtain feedback on its acceptability. Attendees of the conference passed three overall recommendations without dissent: first, that there be established a new, incident-based national crime reporting system; second, that the FBI manage this program, and third, that an Advisory Policy Board composed of law enforcement executives be formed to assist in directing and implementing the new program. Furthermore, attendees recommended that the implementation of national incident-based reporting proceed at a pace commensurate with the resources and limitations of contributing law enforcement agencies.

Establishing the NIBRS

From March 1988 through January 1989, the FBI developed and assumed management of the UCR program's National Incident-Based Reporting System (NIBRS), and by April 1989, the first test of NIBRS data was submitted to the national UCR program. Over the next few years, the national lUCR program published information about the redesigned program in five documents:

- *Uniform Crime Reporting Handbook*, NIBRS Edition (1992) provides a nontechnical program overview focusing on definitions, policies, and procedures of the IBRS
- *Data Submission Specifications* (May 1992) is used by local and state systems personnel, who are responsible for preparing magnetic media for submission to the FBI
- *Approaches to Implementing an Incident-Based System* (July 1992) is a guide for system designers
- *Error Message Manual* (revised December 1999) contains designations of mandatory and optional data elements, data element edits, and error messages
- *Data Collection Guidelines* (revised August 2000) contains a system overview and descriptions of the offense codes, reports, data elements, and data values used in the system

As more agencies inquired about the NIBRS, the FBI, in May 2002, made the *Handbook for Acquiring a Records Management System (RMS) That Is Compatible with the NIBRS* available to agencies considering or developing automated incident-based records management systems. The handbook, developed under the sponsorship of the FBI and the BJS, provides instructions for planning and conducting a system acquisition and offers guidelines on preparing an agency for conversion to the new system and to the NIBRS.

The National UCR Program staff has also presented additional documents, including the *National Incident-Based Reporting System (NIBRS) Technical Specification* (Version 1.0, dated April 16, 2012) and the *National Incident-Based Reporting System (NIBRS) User Manual* (Version dated January 17, 2013.)

Originally designed with 52 data elements, the redesigned NIBRS captures up to 57 data elements via 6 types of data segments: administrative, offense, victim property, offender, and arrestee. Although, in the late 1980s, the FBI committed to hold all changes to the NIBRS in abeyance until a substantial amount of contributors implemented the system, modifications have been necessary. The system's flexibility has allowed the collection of four additional pieces of information to be captured within an incident: bias-motivated offenses (1990), the presence of gang activity (1997), data for law enforcement officers killed and assaulted (2003), and data on cargo theft (2005). The system has also allowed the addition of new codes to further specify location types and property types (2010).

The FBI began accepting NIBRS data from a handful of agencies in January 1989. As more contributing law enforcement agencies become educated about the rich data available through incident-based reporting and as resources permit, more agencies are implementing the NIBRS. Based on the 2012 data submissions, 15 states submit all their data via the NIBRS and 32 state UCR Programs are certified for NIBRS participation.

Suspension of the *Crime Index* and the *Modified Crime Index*

In June 2004, the CJIS APB approved discontinuing the use of the *Crime Index* in the UCR program and its publications and directed the FBI to publish a violent crime total and a property crime total. The *Crime Index*, first published in *Crime in the United States* in 1960, was the title used for a simple aggregation of the seven main offense classifications (Part I offenses) in the Summary Reporting System. The Modified Crime Index was the number of Crime Index offenses plus arson.

For several years, the CJIS Division studied the appropriateness and usefulness of these indices and brought the matter before many advisory groups including the UCR Subcommittee of the CJIS APB, the ASUCRP, and a meeting of leading criminologists and sociologists hosted by the BJS. In short, the *Crime Index* and the *Modified Crime Index* were not true indicators of the degrees of criminality because they were always driven upward by the offense with the highest number, typically larceny-theft. The sheer volume of those offenses overshadowed more serious but less frequently committed offenses, creating a bias against a jurisdiction with a high number of larceny-thefts but a low number of other serious crimes such as murder and forcible rape.

Recent Developments in UCR Program

In the fall of 2011, the APB recommended, and FBI Director Robert Mueller III approved, changing the definition of rape. Since 1929, in the SRS, forcible rape had been defined as "the carnal knowledge of a female forcibly and against her will," (*UCR Handbook*, 2004, p.19). Beginning with the 2013 data collection, the SRS definition for the violent crime of rape will be: "Penetration, no matter how slight, of the vagina or anus with any body part or object, or oral penetration by a sex organ of another person, without the consent of the victim." This definition can be found in the *Summary Reporting System [SRS] User Manual*, Version 1.0, dated June 20, 2013. The FBI is developing reporting options for law enforcement agencies to meet this requirement, which will be built into the redeveloped data collection system.

In addition to approving the new definition of rape for the SRS, the APB and Director Mueller approved removing the word "forcible" from the name of the offense and also replacing the phrase "against the person's will" with "without the consent of the victim" in other sex-related offenses in the SRS, the NIBRS, the Hate Crime Statistics Program, and Cargo Theft.

In response to a directive by the U.S. Government's Office of Management and Budget, the national UCR Program has expanded its data collection categories for race from four (White, Black, American Indian or Alaska Native, and Asian or Other Pacific Islander) to five (White, Black or African American, American Indian or Alaska Native, Asian, and Native Hawaiian or Other Pacific Islander). Also, the ethnicity categories have changed from "Hispanic" to "Hispanic or Latino" and from "Non-Hispanic" to "Not Hispanic or Latino." These changes are reflected in data presented for 2012.

The national UCR Program staff continues to develop data collection methods to comply with both the William Wilberforce Trafficking Victims Protection Reauthorization Act of 2008 and the Matthew Shepard and James Byrd, Jr. Hate Crime Prevention Act of 2009. As a result, the FBI will begin accepting data on human trafficking as well as data on crimes motivated by "gender and gender identity" bias and "crimes committed by, and crimes directed against, juveniles" from contributors in January 2013.

UCR Redevelopment Project Update

To streamline the program's database management and quality control activities, the FBI created the UCR Redevelopment Project (UCRRP). The UCRRP's goal is to improve the efficiency, usability, and maintainability of the UCR Program's submission processes, databases, and quality control activities. Through the UCRRP, the UCR Program will improve customer service by decreasing the time it takes to analyze data and by decreasing the time needed to release and publish crime data. The program will also enhance its external data query tool so that the public can view and analyze more published UCR data from the Internet.

Another major goal of the UCRRP is to reduce, to the point of elimination, the exchange of printed materials between submitting agencies and the FBI. Beginning with the 2013 data collections, all data was to be submitted electronically, and after July 2013, the UCR Program no longer accepted paper submissions or the electronic submission of documents (for example, Portable Document Format files). The UCRRP has begun working with agencies to help them adopt electronic submissions via the NIBRS, electronic SRS, or Extensible Markup Language.

Expanded Offense Tables

Expanded offense data are the details of the various offenses that the Uniform Crime Reporting Program collects beyond the count of how many crimes law enforcement agencies report. These details may include the type of weapon used in a crime, the type or value of items stolen, and so forth. Expanded homicide data provide supplemental details about murders such as the age, sex, and race of both the victim and the offender, the weapon used in the homicide, the circumstances surrounding the offense, and the relationship of the victim to the offender. In addition, expanded data includes trends (for example, 2-year comparisons) and rates per 100,000 inhabitants.

Expanded offense data, including expanded homicide data, are information collected in addition to the reports of the number of crimes known. As a result, law enforcement agencies can report an offense without providing the supplemental data about that offense. These additional tables can be found at www.fbi.gov/about-us/cjis/ucr/crime-in-the-u.s/2012/crime-in-the-u.s.-2012/offenses-known-to-law-enforcement/expanded-offense-data.

About the Editor

Gwenavere W. Dunn is a research editor for Bernan Press. She holds a Master of Science degree in Human Resource Management from Trinity Washington University and is a former senior editor with the Board of Governors of the Federal Reserve System and managing editor of the Board's *Federal Reserve Bulletin*. At Bernan, she is the editor of *Employment, Hours, and Earnings*; and assistant editor of the *State and Metropolitan Area Data Book*; *Race and Employment in America*, *Almanac of American Education,* and the *Who, What, and Where of America*.

SECTION II

OFFENSES KNOWN TO POLICE

VIOLENT CRIME

- **MURDER**
- **FORCIBLE RAPE**
- **ROBBERY**
- **AGGRAVATED ASSAULT**

PROPERTY CRIME

- **BURGLARY**
- **LARCENY-THEFT**
- **MOTOR VEHICLE THEFT**
- **ARSON**

VIOLENT CRIME

Figure II-1. Violent Crime Rates, by Offense and Region, 2012

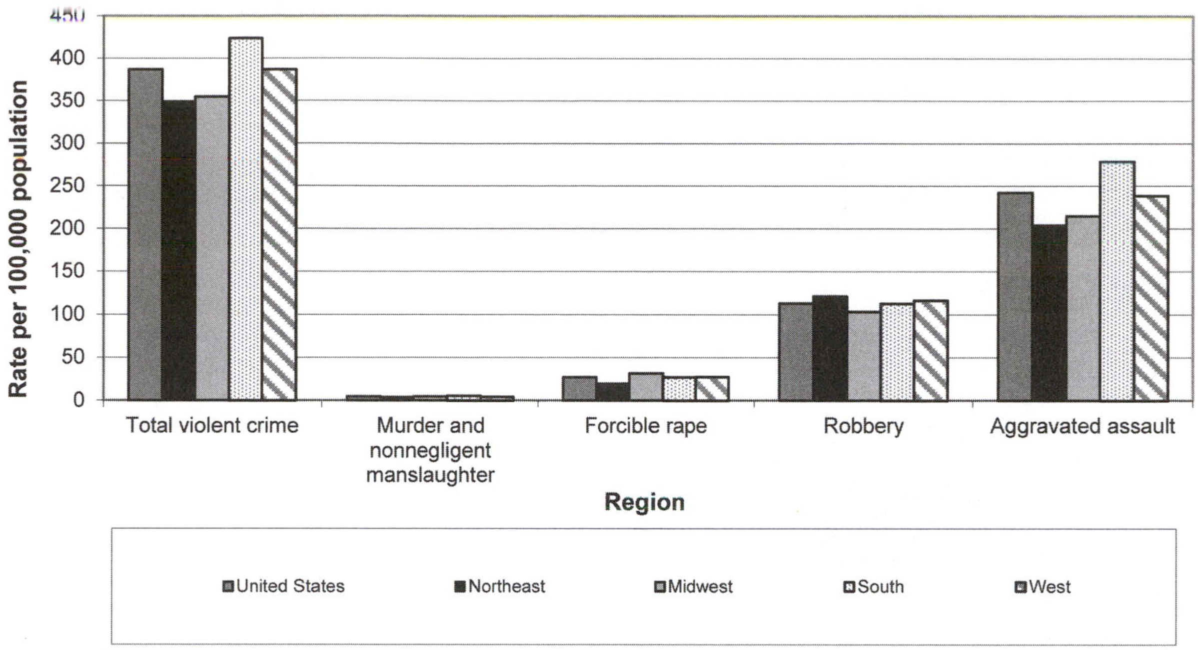

Source: Table 4

Definition

Violent crime consists of four offenses: murder and nonnegligent manslaughter, forcible rape, robbery, and aggravated assault. According to the Uniform Crime Reporting (UCR) program, run by the Federal Bureau of Investigation (FBI), violent crimes involve either the use of force or the threat of force.

Data Collection

The data presented in *Crime in the United States* reflect the Hierarchy Rule, which counts only the most serious offense in a multiple-offense criminal incident. In descending order of severity, the violent crimes are murder and nonnegligent manslaughter, forcible rape, robbery, and aggravated assault; these are followed by the property crimes of burglary, larceny-theft, and motor vehicle theft. Arson is also considered a property crime, but the Hierarchy Rule does not apply to the arson offense. In cases in which arson occurs in conjunction with another violent or property crime, the arson and the additional crime are reported. More information on the expanded violent crime tables (which are available online but not included in this publication) can be found in Section I.

National Volume, Trends, and Rate

In 2012, an estimated 1,214,462 violent crimes occurred in the United States, showing an increase of 0.7 percent from the 2011 estimate. An estimated 386.9 violent crimes were committed per 100,000 inhabitants in 2012, a change of only 0.3 since 2011. Aggravated assaults accounted for 62.6 percent of violent crimes, the highest percentage of violent crimes reported to law enforcement. Robbery accounted for 29.2 percent of violent crimes, forcible rape accounted for 6.9 percent of violent crimes (representing no change from 2011), and murder accounted for 1.2 percent of violent crimes (a proportion that has not changed since 2009). (Table 1)

Occurrences in three of the four violent crime categories increased from 2011 to 2012, a change in the trend from the previous year. Murder increased 1.1 percent, forcible rape increased 0.2 percent, and aggravated assault increased 1.1 percent. Robbery, however, decreased 0.1 percent. The 2012 murder rate of 4.7 offenses per 100,000 inhabitants was a 0.4 percent increase from the 2011 rate. (Tables 1 and 1B)

In longer-term trends, the 2012 estimated violent crime total was 12.9 percent below the 2008 level and 12.2 percent below the 2003 level. The 5-year and 10-year trend data also showed that the violent crime rate decreased 15.6 percent between

2008 and 2012 and decreased 18.7 percent between 2003 and 2012. (Tables 1 and 1B)

In 2012, offenders used firearms in 69.3 percent of the nation's murders, 41.0 percent of robberies, and 21.8 percent of aggravated assaults. Although the largest percentage of murders and robberies were committed with firearms, weapons such as clubs and blunt objects accounted for the majority (32.6 percent) of aggravated assaults. (Weapons data are not collected for forcible rape offenses.) (Expanded Homicide Table 7, Expanded Offense Robbery Table 3, and Expanded Aggravated Assault Table; see http://www.fbi.gov/about-us/cjis/ucr/crime-in-the-u.s/2012/crime-in-the-u.s.-2012/offenses-known-to-law-enforcement/expanded-offense/expandedoffensemain for more information)

Many violent crimes are committed by people in known relationships. Figure 2 shows the number of murder victims who knew their offender. In the figure, the relationship categories of husband and wife include common-law and ex-spouses. The categories of mother, father, sister, brother, son, and daughter include stepparents, stepchildren, and stepsiblings. The category of "acquaintance" includes homosexual relationships and the composite category of other known-to-victim offenders.

Regional Offense Trends and Rate

The UCR program divides the United States into four regions: the Northeast, the South, the Midwest, and the West. (More details concerning geographic regions are provided in Appendix IV) The population distribution of the regions can be found in Table 3, and the estimated volume and rate of violent crime by region are provided in Table 4.

THE NORTHEAST

The Northeast accounted for an estimated 17.8 percent of the nation's population in 2012 and an estimated 16.0 percent of its violent crimes. The estimated number of violent crimes decreased 1.2 percent from 2011 to 2012. Murder decreased 3.1 percent in the Northeast. Forcible rape increased 1.1 percent. Aggravated assaults decreased 1.0 percent from 2011. In 2012, there were an estimated 349.0 violent crimes per 100,000 inhabitants. (Tables 3 and 4)

THE MIDWEST

With an estimated 21.4 percent of the total population of the United States, the Midwest accounted for 19.7 percent of the nation's estimated number of violent crimes in 2012. The region had a 1.5 percent increase in violent crime from 2011 to 2012. The estimated number of aggravated assaults incrcreatedd3.5 percent and the estimated number of robberies fell 2.4 percent, while the number of murders rose 2.8 percent and the estimated number of forcible rapes rose 1.4 percent. The rate of violent crime per 100,000 inhabitants in the Midwest was 354.6, an increase of 1.3 percent from 2011 to 2012. (Tables 3 and 4)

THE SOUTH

The South, the nation's most populous region, accounted for 37.4 percent of the nation's population in 2012. Almost 41 percent (40.9 percent) of violent crimes in 2012 occurred in the South. Violent crime decreased 0.3 percent, while the estimated number of forcible rapes fell 0.2 percent. Robberies had the largest decline (0.8 percent) of the four violent crime offenses, followed by aggravated assault and forcible rape (each decreased 0.2 percent). The number of murders, increased 1.6 percent. The estimated rate of violent crime in the South was 423.7 incidents per 100,000 inhabitants in 2012. (Tables 3 and 4)

THE WEST

With 23.4 percent of the nation's population in 2012, the West also accounted for an estimated 23.9 percent of the nation's violent crime. Violent crime in the West increased 3.2 percent from 2011 to 2012. All four violent offense categories increased in number from 2011 to 2012, except for forcible rape, which went down 0.7 percent; aggravated assault increased 3.0 percent, robbery increased 4.6 percent, and murder increased 1.7 percent. The region's violent crime rate in 2012 was 386.5 per 100,000 inhabitants, a 2.1 percent increase from the 2011 rate. (Tables 3 and 4)

Community Types

The UCR program aggregates crime data into three community types: metropolitan statistical areas (MSAs), cities outside MSAs, and nonmetropolitan counties outside MSAs. Appendix IV provides additional information regarding community types. In 2012 84.9 percent of the nation's population lived in MSAs. Residents of cities outside MSAs continued to account for 6.1 percent of the country's population, and residents living in nonmetropolitan counties continued to account for 8.9 percent of the population. (Table 2)

In the areas reporting violent crimes to the UCR Program, approximately 89.3 percent of these crimes occurred in MSAs, while 5.6 percent occurred in cities outside MSAs and 3.9 percent occurred in nonmetropolitan counties. By community type, the violent crime rates were estimated at

409.4 incidents per 100,000 inhabitants in MSAs, 380.4 incidents per 100,000 inhabitants in cities outside MSAs, and 177.0 incidents per 100,000 inhabitants in nonmetropolitan counties. (Table 2)

Population Groups: Trends and Rates

In the UCR program, data are also aggregated into population groups; these groups are described in more detail in Appendix IV. The nation's cities had an overall increase of 0.7 percent in the estimated number of violent crimes from 2011 to 2012. By city population group, cities with 25,000 to 49,999 (Group V) and those with 10,000 to 24,999 (Group VI) inhabitants had the largest percentage decline in the estimated number of violent crimes (both declined 1.6 percent). (Table 12)

The law enforcement agencies in the nation's cities collectively reported a rate of 468.5 violent crimes per 100,000 inhabitants in 2012. Law enforcement agencies in the subset of cities with 500,000 to 999,999 inhabitants reported the highest violent crime rate, 869.2 violent crimes per 100,000 inhabitants; the violent crime rate for all cities with 250,000 or more inhabitants was 777.3 per 100,000 inhabitants. Agencies in cities with 10,000 to 24,999 inhabitants reported the lowest violent crime rate (273.5 incidents per 100,000 inhabitants). Law enforcement agencies in the nation's metropolitan counties reported a collective violent crime rate of 258.6 per 100,000 inhabitants, while agencies in nonmetropolitan counties reported a collective rate of 179.2 violent crimes per 100,000 inhabitants. (Table 16)

MURDER

Figure II-2. Murder Victim, Known Relationship to Offender, 2012

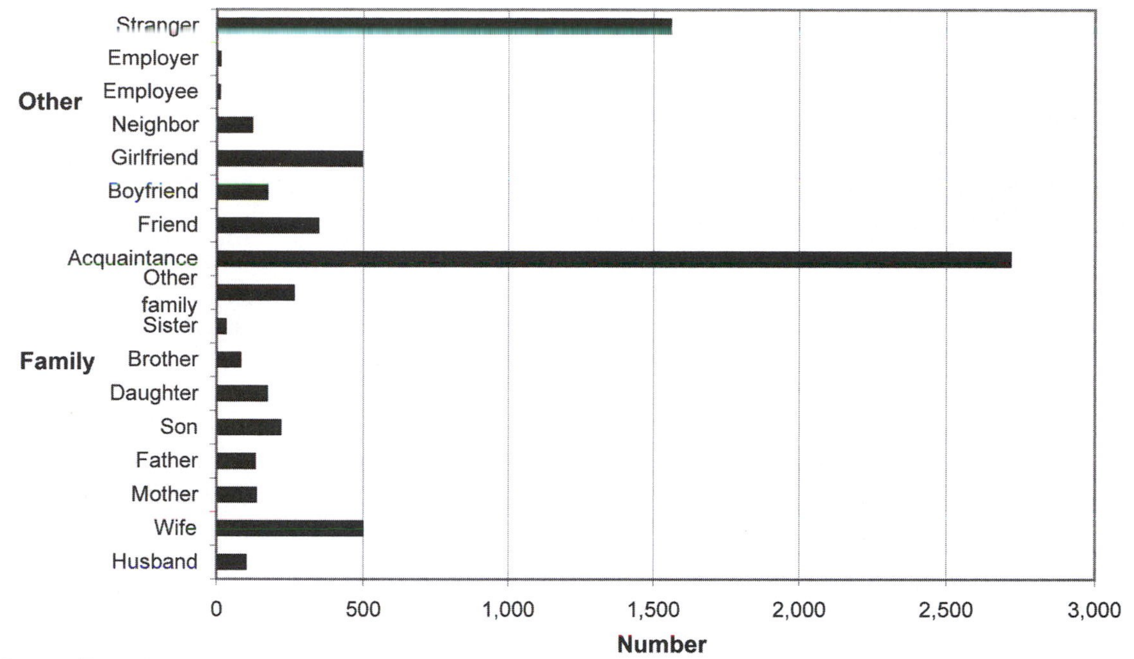

Source: Expanded Homicide Table 10

Definition

The UCR program defines murder and non-negligent manslaughter as the willful (non-negligent) killing of one human being by another. The classification of this offense is based solely on police investigation, rather than on the determination of a court, medical examiner, coroner, jury, or other judicial body. The UCR program does not include the following situations under this offense classification: deaths caused by negligence, suicide, or accident; justifiable homicides; and attempts to murder or assaults to murder, which are considered aggravated assaults.

Data Collection/Supplementary Homicide Reports (SHR)

The UCR program's *Supplementary Homicide Report* (SHR) provides information about murder victims and offenders by age, sex, and race; the types of weapons used in the murders; the relationships of the victims to the offenders; and the circumstances surrounding the incident. Law enforcement agencies are asked to complete an SHR for each murder reported to the UCR program. Data from SHRs can be viewed in the Expanded Homicide Data section, found on the FBI web site: http://www.fbi.gov/about-us/cjis/ucr/crime-in-the-u.s/2012/crime-in-the-u.s.-2012/offenses-known-to-law-enforcement. More information on these reports and the expanded homicide tables can be found in Section I. Highlights from these tables have been included below.

National Volume, Trends, and Rates

An estimated 14,827 persons were murdered nationwide in 2012. This number was a 1.1 percent increase from the 2011 estimate, a 9.9 percent decrease from the 2008 figure, and a 10.3 percent decrease from the 2003 estimate. The 2012 murder rate, 4.7 offenses per 100,000 inhabitants, was a 0.4 percent increase from the 2011 rate. Murder accounted for 1.2 percent of the overall estimated number of violent crimes in 2012, a percentage it has maintained for 4 years. (Tables 1 and 1B)

Regional Offense Trends and Rates

The UCR program divides the United States into four regions: the Northeast, the South, the Midwest, and the West. (More details concerning geographic regions are provided in Appendix IV.) In 2012, nearly 44 percent (43.6 percent) of murders were reported in the South, the country's most populous region. The West reported 21.0 percent of murders,

21.1 percent of murders were reported in the Midwest, and 14.2 percent of murders were reported in the Northeast.

THE NORTHEAST

In 2012, the Northeast accounted for an estimated 17.8 percent of the nation's population and 14.2 percent of its estimated number of murders. With an estimated 2,106 murders, the Northeast saw a 3.1 percent decrease from its 2011 figure. The offense rate for the Northeast was 3.8 murders per 100,000 inhabitants, a continued decline from 4.2 murders per 100,000 inhabitants in 2010; 3.9 in 2011. (Tables 3 and 4)

THE MIDWEST

The Midwest accounted for an estimated 21.4 percent of the nation's total population and 21.1 percent of the country's estimated number of murders in 2012. The Midwest reported an estimated 3,134 murders in 2012. The region experienced a rate of 4.7 murders per 100,000 inhabitants in 2012, slightly above its 2011 rate. (Tables 3 and 4)

THE SOUTH

The South accounted for an estimated 37.4 percent of the nation's population in 2012 and 43.6 percent of the nation's murders, the highest proportion among the four regions. The estimated 6,466 murders represented a 1.6 percent increase from the 2011 figure. The region's estimated rate of 5.5 murders per 100,000 inhabitants represented an increase of 0.5 percent from the estimated rate for 2011. (Tables 3 and 4)

THE WEST

The West again accounted for an estimated 23.4 percent of the nation's population and 21.0 percent of the estimated number of murders in 2012. The West experienced an estimated 3,021 murders, a 1.7 percent increase from the 2011 estimate. The region's murder rate was 4.2 per 100,000 inhabitants. (Tables 3 and 4)

Community Types

The UCR program aggregates data for three community types: metropolitan statistical areas (MSAs), cities outside MSAs, and nonmetropolitan counties outside MSAs. (See Appendix IV for definitions.) In 2012, MSAs accounted for 84.9 percent of the nation's population and 88.9 percent of the estimated total number of murders. With 13,175 estimated homicides, MSAs again experienced a rate of 4.9 murders per 100,000 inhabitants in 2012, unchanged from 2011. Cities outside MSAs accounted for 6.1 percent of the U.S. population and (with an estimated 720 murders) accounted for 4.9 percent of the estimated murders in the nation. The murder rate for cities outside MSAs was 3.8 per 100,000 inhabitants. In2012, approximately 9.0 percent of the nation's population lived in nonmetropolitan counties outside MSAs. An estimated 932 murders took place in these counties, accounting for 6.3 percent of the nation's estimated total. (Table 2)

Population Groups: Trends and Rates

The UCR program uses the following population group designations in its data presentations: cities (grouped according to population size) and counties (classified as either metropolitan or nonmetropolitan). A breakdown of these classifications is provided in Appendix IV.

From 2011 to 2012, the nation's cities experienced a 1.3 percent increase in homicides. Four city groups experienced increases (4.3 percent in cities with 250,000 or more inhabitants, 0.2 percent in cities with 100,000 to 249,999 inhabitants, 1.9 percent in cities with 50,000 to 99,999 inhabitants, and 7.3 percent in cities with 25,000 to 49,999 inhabitants). The city groups with decreases in homicides werecities with fewer than 10,000 inhabitants (7.5 percent decrease) and cities with 10,000 to 24,999 inhabitants (2.7 percent decrease). Metropolitan counties experienced a decrease in homicides of 5.2 percent from 2011 to 2012, while nonmetropolitan counties experienced a increase of 4.7 percent. (Table 12)

In 2012, cities collectively had a rate of 5.6 murders per 100,000 inhabitants. Cities with 250,000 to 499,999 inhabitants had the highest murder rate (11.8 murders per 100,000 inhabitants). Cities with fewer than 10,000 inhabitants had the lowest murder rate, with 2.7 murders per 100,000 inhabitants. The homicide rate for metropolitan counties was 3.2 murders per 100,000 inhabitants, and for nonmetropolitan counties, it was 3.4 murders per 100,000 inhabitants. Suburban areas had a homicide rate of 2.8 per 100,000 inhabitants. (Table 16)

Supplementary Homicide Reports Data

VICTIMS/OFFENDERS

Based on 2012 supplemental homicide data (where the ages, sexes, or races of the murder victims were identified), 90.5 percent of victims were over 18 years of age, 22.3 percent were under 22 years of age 2, 8.6 percent were under 18 years of age, and the age of 0.9 percent of the victims was unknown. Of the 12,765 murder victims represented in the 2012 expanded tables whose gender was identified, 77.7 percent were male. Concerning race, 45.9 percent of victims were White, 50.6 percent were Black, and 5.6 percent were of other races. Race was unknown for 130 victims. For murders in which the gender of the offender was identified, 64.6 percent were males; the sex of offenders for 27.8 percent of homicides was unknown. For the offenders for whom race was identified, 37.9 percent were Black, 31.42 percent were White, and 2.5 percent were other races; 4,228 offenders were of unknown race. (Expanded Homicide Data Tables 1, 2, and 3)

VICTIM-OFFENDER RELATIONSHIPS

For incidents in which the victim-offender relationship was specified (including the designation of "unknown"), 12.5 percent of victims were slain by family members, 12.2 percent were murdered by strangers, and 30.2 percent were killed by acquaintances (neighbor, friend, boyfriend, employer, etc.). (Expanded Homicide Data Table 10)

CIRCUMSTANCES/WEAPONS

Concerning the known circumstances surrounding murders, and including murders with unknown circumstances, 26.1 percent of victims were murdered during arguments (including romantic triangles) in 2012. Felony circumstances (rape, robbery, burglary, etc.) accounted for 14.4 percent of murders. Circumstances were unknown for 35.9 percent of reported homicides. Of the homicides for which the type of weapon was specified, 69.4 percent involved the use of firearms. Of the identified firearms used, handguns comprised 71.9 percent of the total. (Expanded Homicide Data Tables 8 and 12)

Justifiable Homicide

Certain willful killings must be reported as justifiable, or excusable, homicide. In the UCR program, justifiable homicide is defined as, and is limited to, the following:

- The killing of a felon by a peace officer in the line of duty
- The killing of a felon, during the commission of a felony, by a private citizen

Because these killings are determined by law enforcement investigation to be justifiable, they are tabulated separately from murder and nonnegligent manslaughter. Law enforcement reported 720 justifiable homicides in 2012. Of those, law enforcement officers justifiably killed 410 individuals, and private citizens justifiably killed 310 individuals. (Expanded Homicide Data Tables 14 and 15)

FORCIBLE RAPE

Figure II-3. Number of Forcible Rapes and Rape Rate, 1992–2012

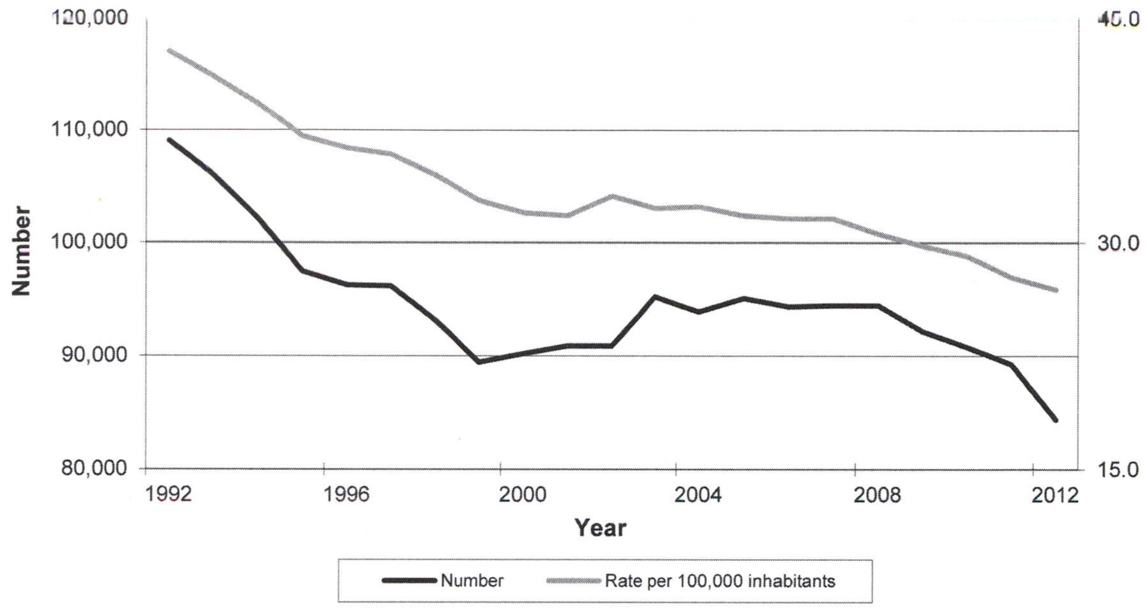

Source: Table 1

Definition

Forcible rape is the carnal knowledge of a female forcibly and against her will. Assaults and attempts to commit rape by force or threat of force are included; however, statutory rape (without force) and other sex offenses are excluded.

Data Collection

The UCR program counts one offense for each female victim of a forcible rape, attempted forcible rape, or assault with intent to rape, regardless of the victim's age. A rape by force involving a female victim and a familial offender is counted as a forcible rape, not as an act of incest. The program collects only arrest statistics concerning all other crimes of a sexual nature. The offense of statutory rape, in which no force is used but the female victim is under the age of consent, is included in the arrest total for the sex offenses category. Sexual attacks on males are counted as aggravated assaults or sex offenses, depending on the circumstances and the extent of any injuries.

National Volume, Trends, and Rates

In 2012, the estimated number of forcible rapes (84,376) increased 0.2 percent from the 2011 estimate. The estimated volume of rapes in 2012 was 7.0 percent lower than in 2008 and 10.1 percent lower than in 2003. (Tables 1 and 1B)

Of the forcible rapes known to law enforcement agencies in 2012, rapes by force made up 81.4 percent of reported rape offenses, and assaults to rape-attempts accounted for 5.9 percent of reported rape offenses. (Tables 1 and 19)

Regional Offense Trends and Rates

The UCR program divides the United States into four regions: the Northeast, the South, the Midwest, and the West. (More details concerning geographic regions are provided in Appendix IV) Regional analysis offers estimates of the volume of female rapes, the percent change from the previous year's estimate, and the rate of rape per 100,000 female inhabitants in each region.

THE NORTHEAST

The Northeast made up 17.8 percent of the U.S. population in 2012. An estimated 11,001 forcible rapes of females—13.0 percent of the national total—occurred in the Northeast. This was a increase of 1.1 percent from the 2011 estimated figure. (Tables 3 and 4)

THE MIDWEST

The Midwest accounted for 21.4 percent of the U.S. population in 2012. Of all the forcible rapes in the nation, 31.7 percent occurred in the Midwest in 2012. The 2012 estimate (21,344 forcible rapes) represented an increase of 1.4 percent from the 2011 estimate. (Tables 3 and 4)

THE SOUTH

The South, the nation's most populous region, accounted for an estimated 37.4 percent of the nation's population in 2012; the region also accounted for an estimated 37.6 percent of the nation's estimated number of forcible rapes. An estimated 31,760 female victims reported forcible rape in the South in 2012, down 0.2 percent from the 31,834 forcible rapes reported in 2011. (Tables 3 and 4)

THE WEST

The West accounted for 23.4 percent of the nation's population in 2012. The region also accounted for 24.0 percent of the nation's total number of estimated forcible rapes with an estimated 20,271 offenses. The West saw a 0.7 percent decline in forcible rapes from 2011 to 2012. (Tables 3 and 4)

Community Types

Using the U.S. Office of Management and Budget's designations, the UCR program aggregates crime data by type of community in which the offenses occur: metropolitan statistical areas (MSAs), cities outside MSAs, and nonmetropolitan counties outside MSAs. (Appendix IV provides more detailed information about community types.)

MSAS

In 2012, MSAs accounted for 85.05 percent of the nation's population and 83.5 percent of the nation's estimated number of forcible rapes. An estimated 70,482 females were forcibly raped in metropolitan areas. (Table 2)

CITIES OUTSIDE MSAS

Cities outside MSAs are mostly incorporated areas that are served by city law enforcement agencies. Although accounting for only 6.1 percent of the U.S. population in 2012, cities outside MSAs accounted for 9.3 percent of the nation's estimated forcible rapes (7,879 offenses). (Table 2)

NONMETROPOLITAN COUNTIES

In 2012, approximately 9.0 percent of the nation's population lived in nonmetropolitan counties outside MSAs (counties made up of mostly non-incorporated areas that are served by noncity law enforcement agencies). Collectively, these areas had an estimated 6,015 forcible rapes, representing 7.1 percent of the nation's estimated total. (Table 2)

Population Groups: Trends and Rates

The UCR program uses the following population group designations in its data presentations: cities (grouped according to population size) and counties (classified as either metropolitan or nonmetropolitan). A breakdown of these classifications is provided in Appendix IV.

From 2011 to 2012, the nation's cities experienced a 0.1 percent decrease in forcible rapes. Cities with 25,000 to 49,999 in habitanats and those with 100,000 to 249,999 inhabitants experienced the greatest declines (3.2 percent and 1.2 percent, respectively). Metropolitan counties experienced a decrease in forcible rapes of 1.1 percent from 2011 to 2012, while nonmetropolitan counties experienced a increase of 1.7 percent. (Table 12)

In 2012, cities collectively had a rate of 29.7 forcible rapes per 100,000 inhabitants. Cities with 250,000 to 499,999 inhabitants had the highest rate of forcible rape (42.7 forcible rapes per 100,000 inhabitants). Cities with 10,000 to 24,999 inhabitants had the lowest rate, with 25.1 forcible rapes per 100,000 inhabitants. The forcible rape rate for metropolitan counties was 20.0 per 100,000 inhabitants, and for nonmetropolitan counties, it was 22.0 per 100,000 inhabitants. Suburban areas had a forcible rape rate of 20.5 per 100,000 inhabitants. (Table 16)

ROBBERY

Figure II-4. Robberies by Location and Percent, 2012

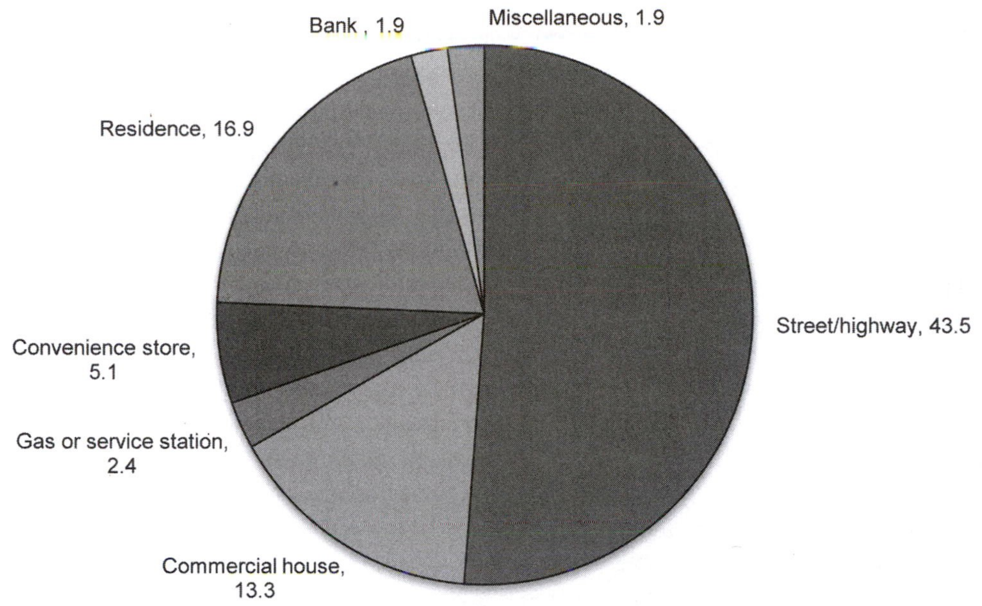

Source: Table 23

Definition

The UCR program defines robbery as the taking or attempt to take anything of value from the care, custody, or control of a person or persons by force or threat of force or violence and/or by putting the victim in fear.

National Volume, Trends, and Rates

In 2012, the estimated robbery total (354,520) decreased 0.1 percent from the 2011 estimate. The 5-year robbery trend (2008 data compared with 2012 data) showed a decrease of 20.1 percent. The 2012 estimated robbery rate (112.9 per 100,000 inhabitants) showed a decrease of 0.8 percent when compared with the 2011 rate. (Tables 1 and 1B)

Regional Offense Trends and Rates

The UCR program divides the United States into four regions: the Northeast, the South, the Midwest, and the West. (More details concerning geographic regions are provided in Appendix IV.)

THE NORTHEAST

The Northeast, with an estimated 17.8 percent of the nation's population in 2012, accounted for 19.1 percent of the nation's estimated number of robberies. The estimated number of robberies decreased 1.9 percent from 2011. The rate for this region was 121.4 robberies per 100,000 inhabitants, down from 124.0 robberies per 100,000 inhabitants in 2011. (Tables 3 and 4)

THE MIDWEST

The Midwest accounted for 21.4 percent of the total population of the United States and 19.6 percent of its estimated number of robberies in 2012. An estimated 69,498 robberies occurred in the Midwest in 2012, a 2.4 percent decrease from the estimated figure from 2011. The region's robbery rate was 103.2 robberies per 100,000 inhabitants in 2012. (Tables 3 and 4)

THE SOUTH

The South, the nation's most highly populated region, accounted for an estimated 37.4 percent of the nation's population and 37.2 percent of the nation's estimated number of robberies in 2012. Robberies accounted for an estimated 131,862 violent crimes in this region in 2012, representing a 0.8 percent decrease from the 2011 figure. The 2012 robbery rate in the South was 112.5 per 100,000 inhabitants, down 1.8 percent from 2011. (Tables 3 and 4)

THE WEST

The West was home to an estimated 23.4 percent of the nation's population and accounted for 24.1 percent of the nation's estimated number of robberies in 2012. The estimated number of robberies (85,480) in the region in 2012 represented a 4.6 percent decrease from the 2011 figure. The rate of robberies per 100,000 inhabitants in the West was 116.2, a 3.6 percent decrease from the 2011 rate. (Tables 3 and 4)

Community Types

The UCR program aggregates data for three community types: metropolitan statistical areas (MSAs), cities outside MSAs, and nonmetropolitan counties outside MSAs. MSAs include a central city or urbanized area with at least 50,000 inhabitants, as well as the county that contains the principal city and other adjacent counties that have, as defined by the U.S. Office of Management and Budget, a high degree of social and economic integration as measured through commuting. Cities outside MSAs are mostly incorporated areas, and nonmetropolitan counties are made up of mostly unincorporated areas served by non-city law enforcement.

In 2012, MSAs were home to an estimated 85.0 percent of the nation's population, and 96.2 percent of the nation's estimated number of robberies took place in these areas. Robberies in MSAs occurred at a rate of 127.9 per 100,000 inhabitants. Cities outside MSAs accounted for 6.1 percent of the U.S. population and accounted for 2.8 percent of the estimated number of robberies in the nation. The robbery rate for cities outside MSAs was 51.6 per 100,000 inhabitants. Nonmetropolitan counties made up 9.0 percent of the nation's estimated population and 1.0 percent of the nation's estimated robberies, at a rate of 12.6 robberies per 100,000 inhabitants. (Table 2)

Population Groups: Trends and Rates

The national UCR program aggregates data by various population groups, which include cities, metropolitan counties, and nonmetropolitan counties. A definition of these groups can be found in Appendix IV. The number of robberies in cities as a whole increased by less than 1 percent between 2011 and 2012. Among the population groups labeled *city*, those cities with 10,000 to 24,999 inhabitants had the greatest decrease in the number of robberies (3.5 percent). Nonmetropolitan counties had a 0.5 percent decrease in the estimated number of robberies, and metropolitan counties showed a 1.9 percent decrease. The number of robberies in suburban areas fell 1.8 percent. (Table 12)

Among the population groups, the nation's cities collectively had a rate of 150.6 robberies per 100,000 inhabitants. Of the population groups and subsets designated *city*, those 250,000 to 499,999 inhabitants had the highest rate (298.6 per 100,000 inhabitants), while those with fewer than 10,000 inhabitants had the lowest rate (47.1 per 100,000 inhabitants) of robberies. Of the two county groups, metropolitan counties had a rate of 54.7 robberies per 100,000 inhabitants, a slight increase from 2011; while nonmetropolitan counties had a rate of 12.7 robberies per 100,000 inhabitants, a slight decrease from 2011. Suburban areas had a robbery rate of 57.8 per 100,000 inhabitants, virtually unchanged from the 2011 rate. (Table 16)

Offense Analysis

The UCR program collects supplemental data about robberies to document the use of weapons, the dollar loss associated with the offense, and the location types.

ROBBERY BY WEAPON

Firearms were used in 41.0 percent of robberies in 2012. Strong-arm robberies accounted for 42.5 percent of the total. Offenders used knives or cutting instruments in 7.8 percent of these crimes. In the remaining 8.8 percent of the robberies, the offenders used other types of weapons. (Table 19)

LOSS BY DOLLAR VALUE

Based on the supplemental reports from law enforcement agencies, robberies cost victims, collectively, an estimated $414 million in 2012. The average loss per robbery was $1,167. Average dollar losses were the highest for banks, which suffered an average loss of $3,810 per offense, although this is almost $1,000 less per offense than the rate in 2011. Gas and service stations lost an average of $943 per offense. Commercial houses, which include supermarkets, department stores, and restaurants, had average losses of $1,754 per offense. An average of $1,631 was taken from residences. An average of $706 was lost in each offense against convenience stores. (Tables 1 and 23)

ROBBERY TRENDS BY LOCATION

Among the location types, bank robberies had the greatest percentage decrease from 2011 to 2012, declining 5.5 percent. Robberies that occurred at convenience stores decreased 0.4 percent; those that occurred on streets and highways decreased 0.5 percent; and those that occurred at residences decreased 1.0 percent. The number of robberies that occurred at commercial houses went up 1.9 percent, while those that occurred at gas or service stations increased 1.4 percent. (Table 23)

By location type, the greatest proportion of robberies in 2012 occurred on streets and highways (43.5 percent). Robbers targeted commercial houses in 13.3 percent of offenses and struck residences in 16.9 percent of offenses. Convenience stores accounted for 5.1 percent of robberies, followed by gas and service stations (2.4 percent) and banks (1.9 percent). (Table 23)

AGGRAVATED ASSAULT

Figure II-5. Number and Rate of Aggravated Assaults, 1992–2012

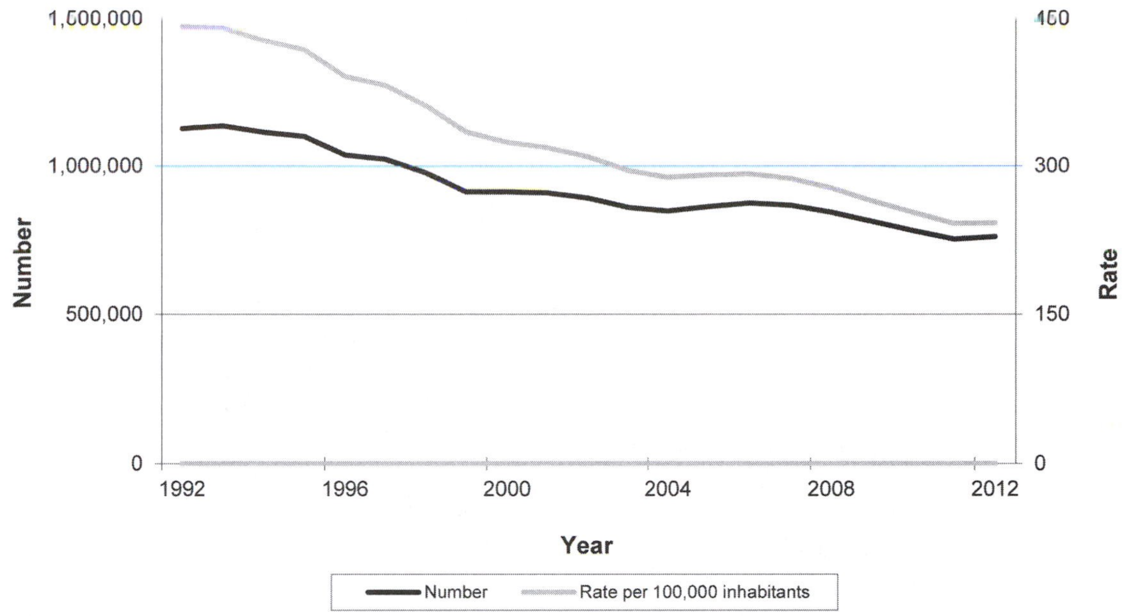

Source: Table 1

Definition

The UCR program defines aggravated assault as an unlawful attack by one person upon another for the purpose of inflicting severe or aggravated bodily injury. This type of assault is usually accompanied by the use of a weapon or by other means likely to produce death or great bodily harm. Attempted aggravated assaults that involve the display or threat of a gun, knife, or other weapon are included in this crime category because serious personal injury would likely result if these assaults were completed. When aggravated assault and larceny-theft occur together, the offense falls under the category of robbery.

National Volume, Trends, and Rates

In 2012, estimated occurrences of aggravated assaults totaled 760,739, a 1.1 percent increase from the 2011 figure but an 18.0 percent decline when compared with the estimate for 2003. The 2012 data also show an increase for the first time in five years in the rate of aggravated assaults per 100,000 U.S. inhabitants. This rate, estimated at 242.3, represents a 0.4 percent increase from the 2011 rate. However, it also represents a 12.7 percent decrease from the 2008–2012 (5-year trend) rate and an 18.0 percent decrease from the 2003–2012 (10-year trend) rate. (Tables 1 and 1B)

Among the four types of violent crime offenses (murder, forcible rape, robbery, and aggravated assault), aggravated assault typically has the highest rate of occurrence. This trend continued in 2012 with aggravated assault accounting for 62.6 percent of all violent crimes. (Table 1)

Regional Offense Trends and Rates

The UCR program divides the United States into four regions: the Northeast, the South, the Midwest, and the West. (More details concerning geographic regions are provided in Appendix IV.)

THE NORTHEAST

The region with the smallest proportion of the nation's population (an estimated 17.8 percent in 2012) also accounted for the smallest proportion of the nation's estimated number of aggravated assaults (15.0 percent). Occurrences of aggravated assault decreased 1.0 percent from 2011 to 2012, dropping to an estimated 113,830 incidents. However, the region continued to have the lowest aggravated assault rate in the nation, at 204.1 incidents per 100,000 inhabitants. (Tables 3 and 4)

THE MIDWEST

With 21.4 percent of the nation's total population in 2012, the Midwest accounted for approximately 19.0 percent of the nation's estimated number of aggravated assaults. Occurrences of this offense increased 3.5 percent from the estimated total for 2011, climbing to an estimated 144,736 incidents. The region's aggravated assault rate, at 215.0 incidents per 100,000 inhabitants, represented a 3.3 percent increase from the 2011 rate. (Tables 3 and 4)

THE SOUTH

The South, the nation's most highly populated region, accounted for an estimated 37.2 percent of the nation's population in 2012 and the largest amount of the nation's estimated number of aggravated assaults (42.9 percent, a slight decrease from the rate in 2011). From 2011 to 2012, the estimated number of aggravated assaults decreased 0.2 percent, to a total of 325,685 incidents. The rate of aggravated assaults decreased to 278.6 per 100,000 inhabitants. (Tables 3 and 4)

THE WEST

In 2012, the West was home again to an estimated 23.4 percent of the nation's population. The region accounted for 23.1 percent of the nation's estimated number of aggravated assaults. From 2011 to 2012, the estimated number of offenses increased 3.0 percent to 175,488 incidents. The rate, estimated at 238.5 offenses per 100,000 inhabitants, represented a drop of 1.9 percent from the rate of 2011. (Tables 3 and 4)

Community Types

The UCR program aggregates data for three community types: metropolitan statistical areas (MSAs), cities outside MSAs, and nonmetropolitan counties outside MSAs. MSAs include a central city or urbanized area with at least 50,000 inhabitants, as well as the county that contains the principal city and other adjacent counties that have a high degree of social and economic integration as measured through commuting. Cities outside MSAs are mostly incorporated areas, and nonmetropolitan counties are made up of mostly unincorporated areas. (For additional information about community types, see Appendix IV.)

In 2012, 85.0 percent of the nation's population lived in MSAs, where the rate of aggravated assault was an estimated 250.2 per 100,000 inhabitants. Cities outside MSAs (with 6.1 percent of the U.S. population) had the highest rate of aggravated assault at 283.9 offenses per 100,000 inhabitants. Nonmetropolitan counties accounted for 9.0 percent of the U.S. population and had an offense rate of 139.7 aggravated assaults per 100,000 inhabitants. (Table 2)

Population Groups: Trends and Rates

From 2011 to 2012, the number of aggravated assaults increased slightly for all cities. Cities with 500,000 to 999,999 inhabitants experienced the greatest increase (5.9 percent), followed by cities with 100,000 to 249,999 and 250,000 to 499,999, both which increased 2.1 percent. In metropolitan counties, the number of aggravated assaults slid down 0.1 percent; in nonmetropolitan counties, this number decreased bit more by 2.6 percent. Aggravated assaults in suburban areas decreased 0.8 percent from 2011 to 2012. (Table 12)

Aggravated assault occurred at an estimated rate of 246.5 offenses per 100,000 inhabitants nationwide. The collective rate for cities was 282.6 aggravated assaults per 100,000 inhabitants. Among city population groups, rates ranged from a high of 521.6 offenses per 100,000 inhabitants (in cities with 500,000 to 999,999 inhabitants) to a low of 185.3 offenses per 100,000 inhabitants (in cities with 10,000 to 24,999 inhabitants). The aggravated assault rate was 180.6 in metropolitan counties and 414.0 in nonmetropolitan counties. It was 171.4 in suburban areas. (Table 16)

Offense Analysis

AGGRAVATED ASSAULT BY WEAPON

Of the aggravated assault offenses for which law enforcement agencies provided expanded data in 2012, 32.6 percent were committed with blunt objects or other dangerous weapons; 26.8 percent involved personal weapons such as hands, fists, and/or feet; 21.8 percent were committed with firearms; and 18.8 percent involved knives or other cutting instruments. (Table 19)

Figure II-6. Percent Change of Property Crimes, 1992–2012

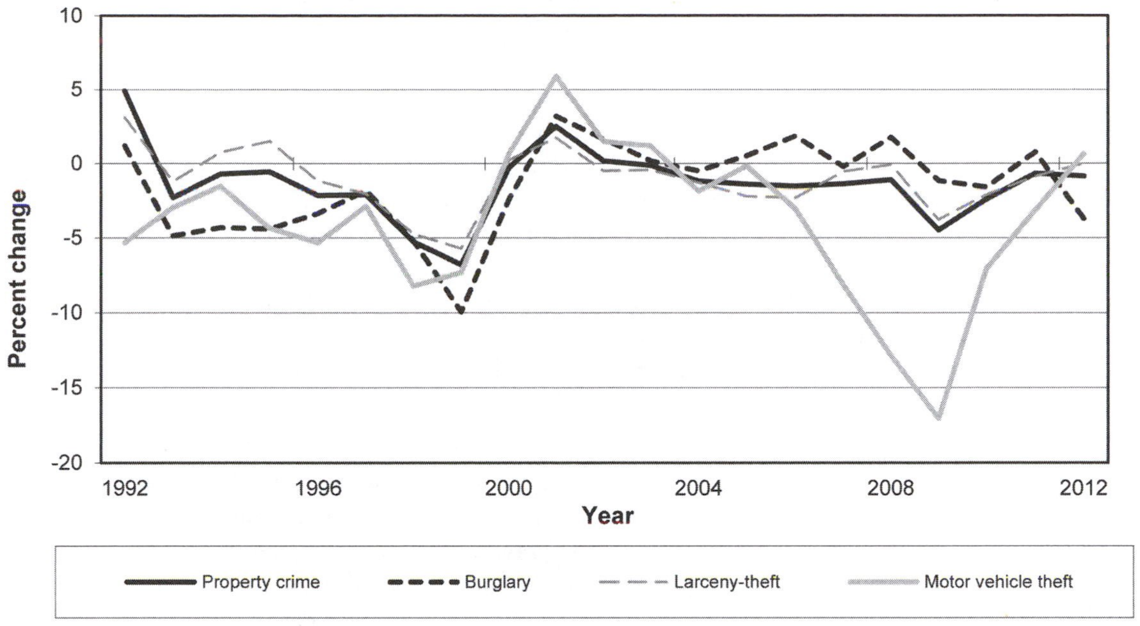

Source: Table 1

Definition

The UCR program's definition of property crime includes the offenses of burglary, larceny-theft, motor vehicle theft, and arson. The object of theft-type offenses is the taking of money or property without the use of force or threat of force against the victims. Property crime includes arson because the offense involves the destruction of property; however, arson victims may be subjected to force. Because of limited participation and the varying collection procedures conducted by local law enforcement agencies, only limited data are available for arson. Arson statistics are included in the trend, clearance, and arrest tables in *Crime in the United States*, but they are not included in any estimated volume data. More information on the expanded arson tables (which are available online but not included in this publication) can be found in Section I.

Data Collection

The data presented in *Crime in the United States* reflect the Hierarchy Rule, which counts only the most serious offense in a multiple-offense criminal incident. In descending order of severity, the violent crimes are murder and nonnegligent manslaughter, forcible rape, robbery, and aggravated assault; these are followed by the property crimes of burglary, larceny-theft, and motor vehicle theft. The Hierarchy Rule does not apply to the offense of arson.

National Volume, Trends, and Rates

An estimated 8,975,438 property crimes were committed in the United States in 2012, representing a 0.9 percent decrease from the 2011 (2-year trend) estimate, a 8.2 percent decrease from the 2008 (5-year trend) estimate, and a 14.1 percent decrease from the 2003 (10-year trend) estimate. (Tables 1 and 1B)

From 2011 to 2012, motor vehicle theft increased 0.6 percent. Larceny-theft decreased 12.5 percent from 2003 to 2012 and 6.6 percent from 2008 to 2012, but remained mostly static from the 2011 estimate. Burglary declined 2.4 percent from 2003, 5.6 percent from 2008, and 3.7 percent from 2011. (Tables 1 and 1B)

The estimated property crime rate per 100,000 inhabitants in 2012 was 2,859.2, a 1.6 percent decrease from the 2011 rate, an 11.1 percent decrease from the 2008 rate, and a 20.4 percent decrease from the 2003 rate. The rate of burglaries fell 9.6 percent from 2003 to 2012. The motor vehicle theft rates per 100,000 residents fell 42.8 percent from 2003 to 2012. (Tables 1 and 1B)

Regional Offense Trends and Rates

The UCR program separates the United States into four regions: the Northeast, the Midwest, the South, and the West. (Geographic breakdowns can be found in Appendix IV.) Property crime data collected by the UCR program and aggregated by region reflected the following results.

THE NORTHEAST

The Northeast region accounted for 17.8 percent of the nation's population in 2012. The region also accounted for 12.9 percent of the nation's estimated number of property crimes in 2012. Law enforcement in the Northeast saw a 1.7 percent decrease in the estimated number of property crimes from 2011 to 2012. The property crime rate for the Northeast, estimated at 2,080.5 incidents per 100,000 inhabitants, was 2.0 percent less than the 2011 rate. (Tables 3 and 4)

THE MIDWEST

The Midwest, with 21.4percent of the U.S. population in 2012, accounted for 20.7 percent of the nation's estimated number of property crimes. Law enforcement in the Midwest saw the number of property crimes decrease almost 2 percent from 2011 to 2012. The rate of property crime in the Midwest in 2012, estimated at 2,764.8 incidents per 100,000 inhabitants, represented a 2.2 percent decrease from the 2011 rate. (Tables 3 and 4)

THE SOUTH

The South, the nation's most populous region, accounted for 37.4percent of the U.S. population in 2012. The region also accounted for an estimated 42.2 percent of the nation's property crimes. The South experienced a 3.3 percent decrease in its estimated number of property crimes from 2011 to 2012. The 2012 property crime rate, an estimated 3,226.8 incidents per 100,000 inhabitants, dropped 4.3 percent from the 2011 rate. (Tables 3 and 4)

THE WEST

In 2012, the West accounted for 23.4 percent of the nation's population. The West also accounted for 24.2 percent of the nation's estimated number of property crimes. From 2011 to 2012, the estimated number of property crimes in this region increased 5.2 percent. The estimated property crime rate in the West in 2012, 2,949.8 incidents per 100,000 inhabitants, was a 4.1 increase over the 2011 rate. (Tables 3 and 4)

Community Types

The UCR program aggregates data by three community types: metropolitan statistical areas (MSAs), cities outside metropolitan areas, and nonmetropolitan counties. (Additional in-depth information regarding community types can be found in Appendix IV.) In 2012, 85.0 percent of the U.S. population lived in MSAs. The property crime rate for MSAs was 2,949.8 per 100,000 inhabitants. Cities outside metropolitan areas, which accounted for 6.1 percent of the total population in 2012, had a property crime rate of 3,534.6 per 100,000 inhabitants. Nonmetropolitan counties, with 9.0 percent of the nation's population in 2012, had a property crime rate of 1,539.3 per 100,000 inhabitants. (Table 2)

Population Groups: Trends and Rates

The UCR program organizes the agencies that contribute data into population groups, which include cities, metropolitan counties, and nonmetropolitan counties. (Appendix IVprovides further details about these groups.) From 2011 to 2012, law enforcement in the nation's cities collectively reported a 0.4 percent decrease in the number of property crimes. Most city groups experienced decreases in the number of property crimes; cities with 1 million or more inhabitants had the largest decline at 1.0 percent. Metropolitan counties experienced a decrease of 3.1 percent from 2011 to 2012, while property crime in nonmetropolitan counties dropped 3.2 percent. (Table 12)

The nation's cities collectively had a property crime rate of 2,873.8 incidents per 100,000 inhabitants in 2012. Nonmetropolitan counties had a rate of 1,552.2 incidents per 100,000 inhabitants, and metropolitan counties had a rate of 2,056.4 incidents per 100,000 inhabitants. The rate was 2,336.5 in suburban areas. (Table 16)

Offense Analysis

The estimated dollar loss attributing to property crimes, not including arson, in 2012 was $13.3 billion. Among the individual property crime categories, the dollar losses were an estimated $4.1 billion for burglary, $5.3 billion for larceny-theft, and $3.8 billion for motor vehicle theft. In 2012, the average dollar value per motor vehicle stolen in the United States was $6,1019. The average dollar value of property taken during burglaries was $2,2230, and during larceny-thefts, $987. (Tables 1 and 23) Arson had an average dollar loss of $12,796. Arsons of "other commercial" structures had the highest average dollar loss ($46,933), followed by industrial/manufacturing structures. (Expanded Arson Table 2)

BURGLARY

Figure II-7. Burglary, By Location and Time, 2012

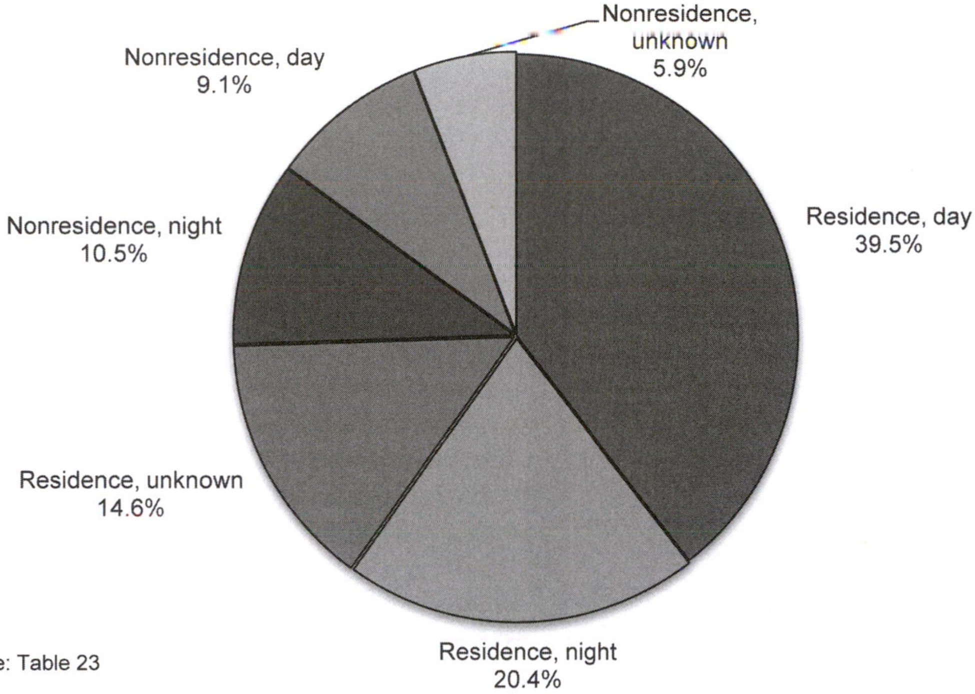

Source: Table 23

Definition

The UCR program defines burglary as the unlawful entry of a structure to commit a felony or theft. To classify an offense as a burglary, the use of force to gain entry need not have occurred. The program has three subclassifications for burglary: forcible entry, unlawful entry where no force is used, and attempted forcible entry. The UCR definition of "structure" includes, but is not limited to, apartments, barns, house trailers or houseboats (when used as permanent dwellings), offices, railroad cars (but not automobiles), stables, and vessels (such as ships).

National Volume, Trends, and Rate

In 2012, there were an estimated 2,103,787 burglaries—a decrease of 3.7 percent when compared with 2011 data. There was a decrease of 5.6 percent in the number of burglaries in 2012 when compared with the 2008 estimate, and a decrease of 2.4 percent when compared with the 2003 estimate. Burglary accounted for 23.2 percent of the estimated number of property crimes committed in 2012. The burglary rate for the United States in 2012 was 670.2 incidents per 100,000 inhabitants, a 4.4 percent decrease from the 2011 rate. (Tables 1 and 1B)

Regional Offense Trends and Rates

The UCR program divides the United States into four regions: the Northeast, the Midwest, the South, and the West. (Details regarding these regions can be found in Appendix IV.) An analysis of burglary data by region showed the following details.

THE NORTHEAST

In 2012, 17.8 percent of the nation's population lived in the Northeast. This region accounted for 11.2 percent of the estimated total number of burglary offenses in the nation in 2012. The region's burglary rate, an estimated 422.9 offenses per 100,000 inhabitants, represented a decrease of 3.3 percent from the 2011 rate. (Tables 3 and 4)

THE MIDWEST

The Midwest accounted for 21.4 percent of the nation's population in 2012. This region accounted for 20.6 percent of the nation's estimated number of burglaries. In this region, the estimated number of burglaries dropped 5.5 percent from 2011 to 2012. The Midwest had a decreased burglary rate of 644.5 offenses per 100,000 inhabitants, a 5.7 percent decrease from the 2011 rate. (Tables 3 and 4)

THE SOUTH

The South, the nation's most highly populated region, had the most burglaries in 2012 (an estimated 946,081); however, this represented a considerable drop from its estimate in 2011. With 37.4 percent of the nation's population, this region accounted for 45.0 percent of all burglaries in the United States. The estimated rate of burglary in the South was 806.8 incidents per 100,000 inhabitants, an 8.0 percent decrease from the 2011 rate. (Tables 3 and 4)

THE WEST

The West accounted for 23.4 percent of the nation's population in 2012. This region accounted for an estimated 23.2 percent of the nation's burglaries. The region's burglary rate was 663.3, a 3.7 percent increase from the 2011 rate. The total number of burglaries (488,065) represented a 4.8 percent increase from the 2011 estimate. (Tables 3 and 4)

Community Types

The UCR program aggregates data by three community types: metropolitan statistical areas (MSAs), cities outside MSAs, and nonmetropolitan counties. (See Appendix IV for more information regarding community types.) In 2012, 85.0 percent of the U.S. population lived in MSAs, and an estimated 85.7 percent of all burglaries occurred in this type of community. Inhabitants of cities outside MSAs accounted for 6.1percent of the total population in 202 and 7.2 percent of the estimated number of burglaries; nonmetropolitan counties, with 9.0 percent of the U.S. population, accounted for 7.1 percent of all burglaries. The burglary rates per 100,000 inhabitants were 676.2 in MSAs, 792.1 in cities outside MSAs, and 530.0 in nonmetropolitan counties. (Table 2)

Population Groups: Trends and Rates

In addition to analyzing data by region and community type, the UCR program aggregates crime statistics by population groups. Cities are categorized into six groups based on the number of inhabitants; counties are categorized into two groups, metropolitan and nonmetropolitan. (Appendix IV offers further details regarding these population groups.)

An examination of data from law enforcement agencies showed that the nation's cities again experienced a collective 3.9 percent decrease in burglaries from 2011 to 2012. Burglaries decreased in all city groups, with cities of 250,000 to 499,999 posting the greatest decrease (7.0 percent). The volume of burglaries decreased 4.7 percent in metropolitan counties, 3.9 percent in suburban areas, and 3.8 percent in nonmetropolitan counties. (Table 12)

The UCR program calculates burglary rates for population groups from the information provided by participating agencies that submitted all 12 months of offense data for the year. In 2012, the nation's cities had 670.5 offenses per 100,000 inhabitants. Cities with 500,000 to 999,999 inhabitants had the highest burglary rate at 1,041.3 incidents per 100,000 inhabitants. Cities with 10,000 to 24,999 inhabitants had the lowest burglary rate—588.9 incidents per 100,000 inhabitants. Metropolitan counties had a rate of 567.7 per 100,000 inhabitants, and nonmetropolitan counties had a rate of 534.2 per 100,000 inhabitants. The rate in suburban areas was 545.7 per 100,000 inhabitants. (Table 16)

Offense Analysis

The UCR program requests that participating law enforcement agencies provide details regarding the nature of burglaries in their jurisdictions, such as type of entry, type of structure, time of day, and dollar loss associated with each offense.

Of all burglaries in 2012, 59.7 percent involved forcible entry, 33.9 percent were unlawful entries (without force), and the remainder (6.3 percent) comprised forcible entry attempts. (Table 19)

Victims of burglary offenses suffered an estimated $4.1 billion in lost property in 2012; overall, the average dollar loss per burglary offense was $1,965. (Tables 1 and 23)

As in the past, burglars targeted residences more often than nonresidential structures. In 2012, burglaries of residential properties accounted for 74.5 percent of all burglary offenses. Law enforcement agencies were unable to determine the time of day for 20.5 percent of all reported burglaries. However, of the burglaries for which time of day could be established, most burglaries of residences (39.5 percent of all reported burglaries) occurred during the day, while most burglaries of nonresidential structures (10.5 percent of all reported burglaries) occurred at night. (Table 23)

LARCENY-THEFT

Figure II-8. Larceny Theft Distribution, 2012

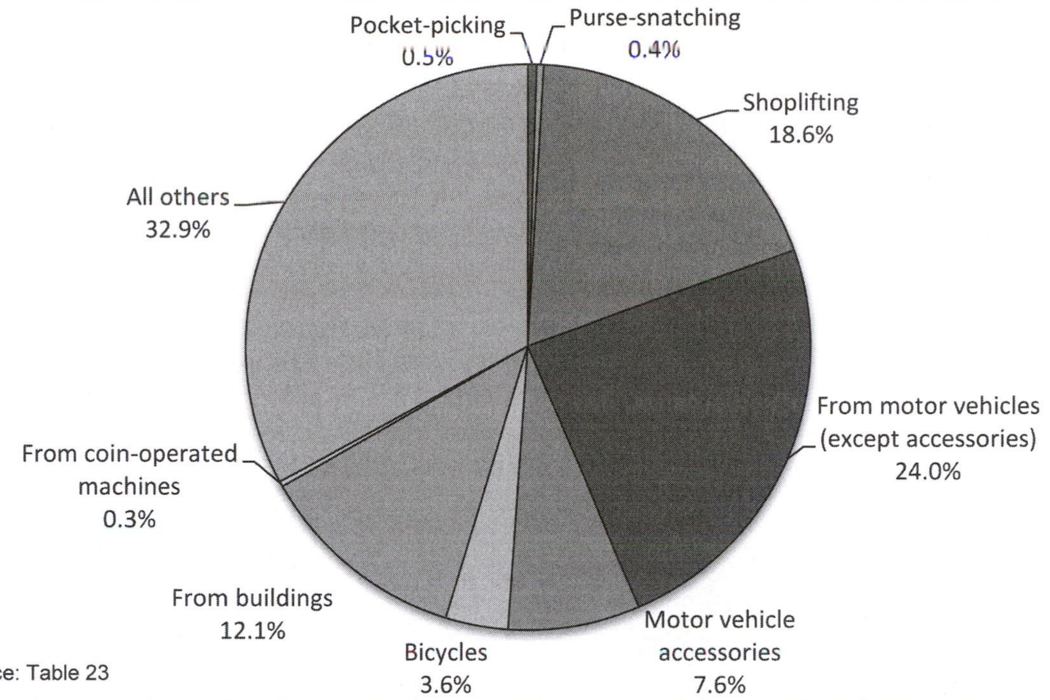

Source: Table 23

Definition

The UCR program defines larceny-theft as the unlawful taking, carrying, leading, or riding away of property from the possession or constructive possession of another. Examples are thefts of bicycles, motor vehicle parts and accessories, shoplifting, pocket picking, or the stealing of any property or article not taken by force and violence or by fraud. Attempted larcenies are included. Embezzlement, confidence games, forgery, check fraud, and so on, are excluded from this category.

National Volume, Trends, and Rates

Larceny-thefts accounted for an estimated 68.5 percent of property crimes in 2012—an estimated 6,150,598 larceny-thefts nationwide. The estimated number of larceny-thefts changed less than one-tenth of one percent from 2011 to 2012. The 2012 estimate showed a 12.5 percent decline compared with the 2003 estimate. The trend data also showed decreases in the larceny-theft rates per 100,000 inhabitants during these periods. The rate of larceny-thefts declined 0.7 percent from 2011 to 2012 and 18.9 percent from 2003 to 2012. (Tables 1 and 1B)

Regional Offense Trends and Rates

The UCR program defines four regions within the United States: the Northeast, the Midwest, the South, and the West. (See Appendix IV for a geographical description of each region.)

THE NORTHEAST

The Northeast was the region with the smallest proportion (17.8 percent) of the U.S. population in 2012. The region also experienced the fewest larceny-thefts in the country, accounting for only 13.9 percent of all larceny-thefts. The estimated number of offenses in 2012 (854,688) represented a 0.8 percent decline from 2011, and the estimated rate—1,532.8 incidents per 100,000 inhabitants—represented a 1.1 percent decline. (Tables 3 and 4)

THE MIDWEST

With 21.4 percent of the U.S. population in 2012, the Midwest accounted for an estimated 21.0 percent of the nation's larceny-thefts. The estimated number of offenses (1,293,237) declined 0.5 percent compared with the 2011 data, and the estimated rate of occurrences (1,921.1 incidents per 100,000 inhabitants) declined 0.8 percent. (Tables 3 and 4)

THE SOUTH

With more than one-third of the U.S. population in 2012 (37.4 percent), the South had the nation's highest proportion of larceny-theft offenses: an estimated 42.1 percent. (Estimated offenses in this region totaled 2,586,999, a 1.8 percent decrease from the 2011 estimate. The South's larceny-theft rate—estimated at 2,206.3 offenses per 100,000 inhabitants—decreased 2.8 percent from the 2011 estimate. (Tables 3 and 4)

THE WEST

In 2012, an estimated 23.4 percent of the U.S. population lived in the West. This region was also where 23.0 percent of the nation's estimated number of larceny-thefts took place. Occurrences of larceny-theft increased 4.5 percent from 2011 to 2012, to an estimated total of 1,415,674 offenses. The region's larceny-theft rate, estimated at 1,924.0 offenses per 100,000 inhabitants, was an increase of 3.4 percent from the 2011 rate. (Tables 3 and 4)

Community Types

The UCR program aggregates data for three community types: metropolitan statistical areas (MSAs), cities outside MSAs, and nonmetropolitan counties outside MSAs. MSAs include a central city or urbanized area with at least 50,000 inhabitants, as well as the county that contains the principal city and other adjacent counties that share a high degree of social and economic integration as measured through commuting. Cities outside MSAs are mostly incorporated areas, and nonmetropolitan counties are composed of unincorporated areas. (See Appendix IV for more information regarding community types.)

In 2012, MSAs were home to an estimated 85.0 percent of the nation's population and again experienced 87.7 percent of the nation's larceny-theft incidents. Cities outside MSAs accounted for 6.1 percent of the U.S. population and 8.1 percent of larceny-theft offenses. Nonmetropolitan counties, which were home to 9.0 percent of the nation's population, accounted for 4.2 percent of the estimated number of larceny-theft offenses. (Table 2)

Population Groups: Trends and Rates

In cities, collectively, occurrences of larceny-theft increased 0.5 percent between 2011 and 2012. Cities with 250,000 to 499,999 inhabitants experienced the greatest increase (2.3 percent). However, larceny thefts continued to show decline in counties and suburban areas—nonmentropolitan counties experienced the greatest drop in larceny thefts, decreasing 3.0 percent, followed by metropolitan counties, with larceny theft decreasing 2.8 percent, and suburban areas, with a decrease of1.2 percent. (Table 12)

Based on reports of larceny-theft offenses from U.S. law enforcement agencies that submitted 12 months of complete data for 2012, this offense occurred at a rate of 1,968.6offenses per 100,000 inhabitants. The collective rate for cities was 2,323.7 offenses per 100,000 inhabitants. Among city population groups, cities with 500,000 to 999,000 inhabitants had the highest larceny-theft rate, 2,958.9 incidents per 100,000 inhabitants. Cities with 1 million or more inhabitants had the lowest rate, at 2,053.0. In metropolitan counties, the rate was 1,322.4 incidents per 100,000 inhabitants; in nonmetropolitan counties, the rate was 921.9 incidents per 100,000 inhabitants. The rate in suburban areas was 1,635.5 incidents per 100,000 inhabitants. (Table 16)

Offense Analysis

DISTRIBUTION

Table 23 provides a further breakdown of larceny-theft offenses, including shoplifting, thefts from buildings, thefts of motor vehicle accessories, thefts of bicycles, thefts from coin-operated machines, purse snatching, and pocket picking. The "all other" category, which includes the less-defined types of larceny-theft, accounted for 32.9 percent of all offenses in 2012.

LOSS BY DOLLAR VALUE

Larceny-theft offenses cost victims an estimated $5.3 billion dollars in 2012. The average value of property stolen was $987per offense, $1 less than in 2011. Larceny-theft from buildings had the highest average dollar loss per offense at $1,479. Thefts from motor vehicles (except accessories) had an average dollar loss of $751 per offense; thefts of motor vehicle accessories, $5730; purse snatching, $468; pocket picking, $627; thefts from coin-operated machines, $412; thefts of bicycles, $384; and shoplifting, $202. (Tables 1 and 23)

Offenses in which the stolen property was valued at more than $200 accounted for 46.6 percent of all larceny-thefts in 2012, up 0.3 percent from 2011. Table 23 provides further analysis, including the average dollar value per offense of all offenses in the overall category of property crime. (Table 23)

MOTOR VEHICLE THEFT

Figure II-9. Number and Rate of Motor Vehicle Thefts, 1992–2012

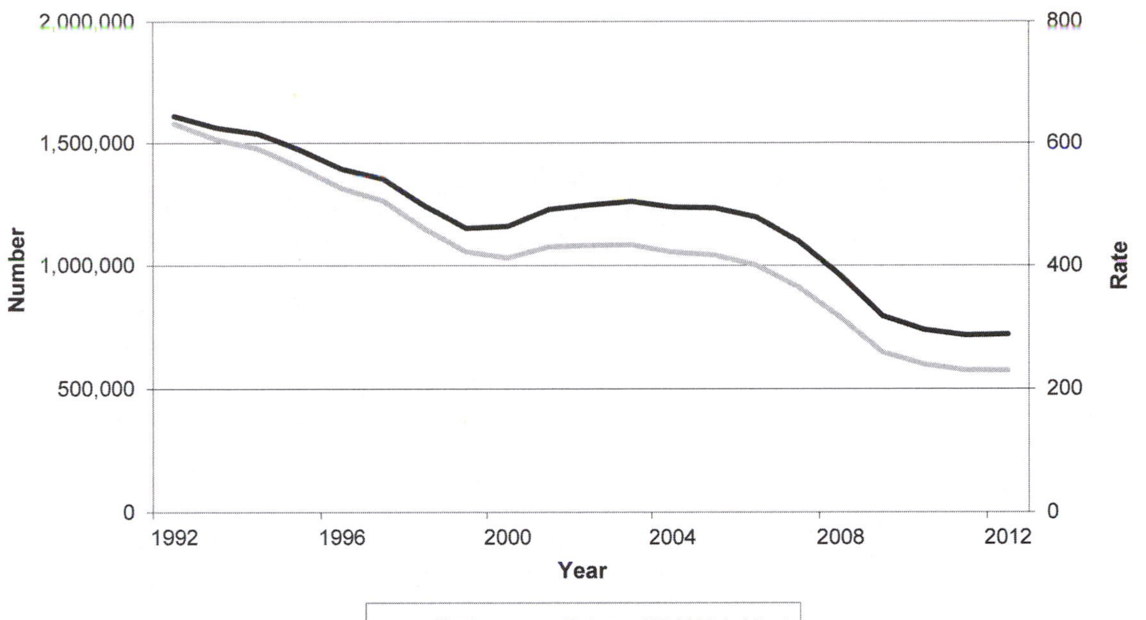

Source: Table 1

Definition

The UCR program defines motor vehicle theft as the theft or attempted theft of a motor vehicle. The offense includes the stealing of automobiles, trucks, buses, motorcycles, snowmobiles, etc. The taking of a motor vehicle for temporary use by a person or persons with lawful access is excluded.

National Volume, Trends, and Rates

In 2012, an estimated 721.053 motor vehicle thefts took place in the United States. The estimated number of motor vehicle thefts increased 0.6 percent when compared with data from 2011, decreased 24.8 percent when compared with 2008 figures, and decreased 42.8 percent when compared with 2003 figures. (Tables 1 and 1B)

The estimated rate of motor vehicle theft in 2012 was 229.7incidents per 100,000 inhabitants. In the 2-year, 5-year, and 10-year trend data, this rate showed decline: the 2012 rate was 0.1 percent lower than the 2011 rate, 27.2 percent lower than the 2008 rate, and 47.0 percent lower than the 2003 rate. (Tables 1 and 1B)

Regional Offense Trends and Rates

In order to analyze crime by geographic area, the UCR program divides the United States into four regions: the Northeast, the Midwest, the South, and the West. (Appendix IV provides a map delineating the regions.) This section provides a regional overview of motor vehicle theft.

THE NORTHEAST

The Northeast accounted for an estimated 17.8 percent of the nation's population in 2012. The region also accounted for an estimated 9.7 percent of its motor vehicle thefts. An estimated 69,619 motor vehicle thefts occurred in the Northeast in 2012, an 8.5 percent drop in occurrences from 2011. The estimated rate of 124.9 motor vehicle thefts per 100,000 inhabitants in the Northeast in 2012 represented an 8.8 percent decline from the 2011 rate. (Tables 3 and 4)

THE MIDWEST

An estimated 21.4 percent of the country's population resided in the Midwest in 2012. The region accounted for 18.6 percent of the nation's motor vehicle thefts. The Midwest had an estimated 134,124 motor vehicle thefts in 2012, a decrease of 3.2 percent from the previous year's total. The motor vehicle theft rate was estimated at 199.2 motor vehicles stolen per 100,000 inhabitants, adecrease of 3.4 percent from the 2011 rate. (Tables 3 and 4)

THE SOUTH

The South, the nation's most populous region, was home to an estimated 37.4 percent of the U.S. population in 2012 and accounted for 34.8 percent of the nation's motor vehicle thefts. The estimated 250,603 motor vehicle thefts in the South was down 3.6 percent from the 2011 estimate. Motor vehicles in the South were stolen at an estimated rate of 213.7 offenses per 100,000 inhabitants in 2012, a rate that was 4.6 percent lower than the 2011 rate. (Tables 3 and 4)

THE WEST

With approximately 23.4 percent of the U.S. population in 2012, the West accounted for the highest percentage (37.0 percent) of all motor vehicle thefts in the nation in 2012. An estimated 266,707 motor vehicle thefts occurred in this region. This number represented a 10.3 percent increase from the previous year's estimate. The motor vehicle theft rate for the West was also higher in 2012 than in 2011; the 2012 rate of 362.5 motor vehicles stolen per 100,000 inhabitants was 9.1 percent higher than the 2011 rate. (Tables 3 and 4)

Community Types

The UCR program aggregates data by three community types: metropolitan statistical areas (MSAs), cities outside MSAs, and nonmetropolitan counties. MSAs are areas that include a principal city or urbanized area with at least 50,000 inhabitants and the county that contains the principal city and other adjacent counties that have, as defined by the U.S. Office of Management and Budget, a high degree of economic and social integration.

In 2012, the vast majority (85.0 percent) of the U.S. population resided in MSAs, where approximately 92.7 percent of motor vehicle thefts occurred. For 2012, the UCR program estimated an overall rate of 250.7 motor vehicles stolen per 100,000 MSA inhabitants. Cities outside MSAs accounted for 3.6 percent of motor vehicle thefts, and nonmetropolitan counties accounted for 3.7 percent of motor vehicle thefts. The UCR program estimated a 2012 rate of 136.0 motor vehicles stolen for every 100,000 inhabitants in cities outside MSAs, and a rate of 93.8 motor vehicles stolen per 100,000 inhabitants in nonmetropolitan counties. (Table 2)

Population Groups: Trends and Rates

The UCR program aggregates data by various population groups, which include cities, metropolitan counties, and nonmetropolitan counties. (A definition of these groups can be found in Appendix IV.)

In cities, collectively, the number of motor vehicle thefts increased 1.0 percent from 2011 to 2012. The number of motor vehicle thefts decreased in four of the six city groups. Cities with one million or more inhabitants experienced the greatest decline—5.1 percent; however cities with 250,000 to 499,999 inhabitants show an increase in motor vehicle theft of 4.8 percent, followed closely by cities with 100,000 to 249,999 inhabitants showing an increase of 4.2 percent Nonmetropolitan counties experienced a decrease of 2.1 percent, suburban areas experienced a decrease of 0.3 percent, although metropolitan counties experienced an increase of 0.5 percent. (Table 12)

In 2012, cities had a collective motor vehicle theft rate of 275.7 per 100,000 inhabitants. Among the population groups, cities with 500,000 to 999,999 inhabitants experienced the highest rate of motor vehicle thefts with 538.5 motor vehicle thefts per 100,000 inhabitants. Conversely, the nation's smallest cities, those with populations under 10,000, had the lowest rate of motor vehicle theft with 128.8 incidents per 100,000 in population. Within the county groups, metropolitan counties had a rate of 166.3 motor vehicles stolen per 100,000 inhabitants, while nonmetropolitan counties had a rate of 96.1 incidents per 100,000 inhabitants. Suburban areas had a rate of 155.3 per 100,000 inhabitants. (Table 16)

Offense Analysis

Based on the reports of law enforcement agencies, the UCR program estimated the combined value of motor vehicles stolen nationwide in 2012 at approximately $4.3 billion. In 2012, the average dollar value per motor vehicle stolen in the United States was $6,019. (Tables 1 and 23) Automobiles were, by far, the most frequently stolen vehicles, accounting for 73.9 percent of all vehicles stolen. Trucks and buses accounted for 15.2 percent of stolen vehicles, and other vehicles accounted for 10.9 percent of stolen vehicles. (Expanded Motor Vehicle Theft Table)

By type of vehicle, automobiles were stolen at a rate of 176.7 cars per 100,000 inhabitants in 2012. Trucks and buses were stolen at a rate of 36.3 vehicles per 100,000 inhabitants, and other types of vehicles were stolen at a rate of 26.1 vehicles per 100,000 inhabitants. (Table 19)

ARSON

Figure II-10. Average Dollar Amount of Arson Damage by Property Type, 2012

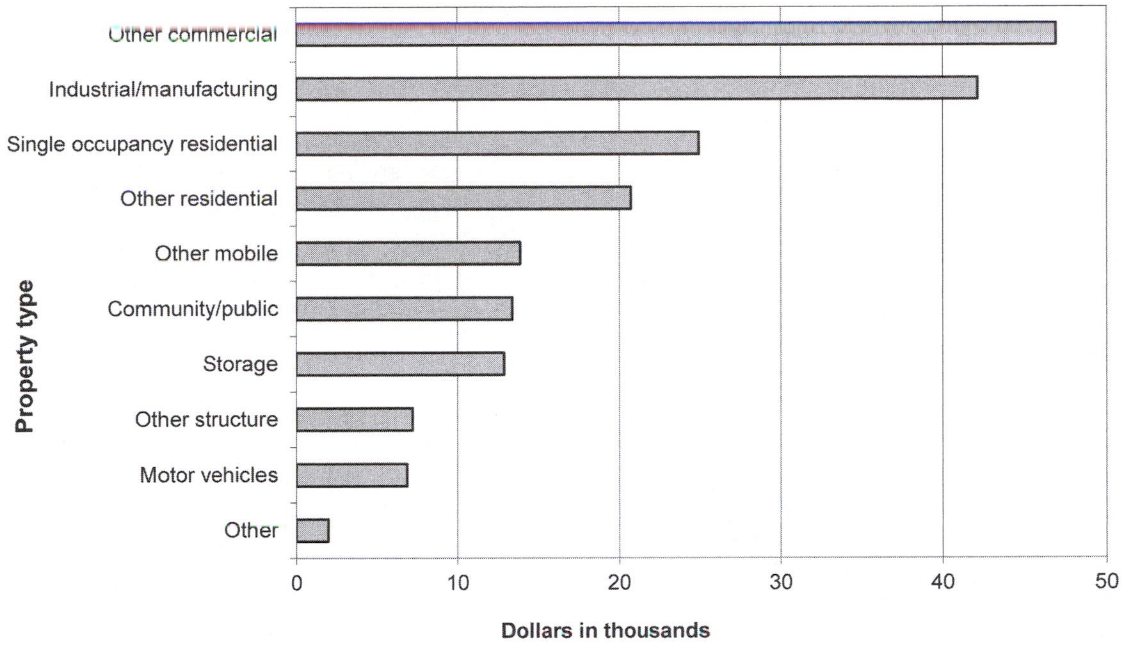

Source: Expanded Arson Table 2

Definition

The UCR program defines arson as any willful or malicious burning or attempt to burn (with or without intent to defraud) a dwelling house, public building, motor vehicle, aircraft, or personal property of another, etc.

Data Collection

Only fires that investigators determined were willfully set (not fires labeled as "suspicious" or "of unknown origin") are included in this arson data collection. Points to consider regarding arson statistics include:

National offense rates per 100,000 inhabitants (found in Tables 1, 2, and 4) do not include arson data; the FBI presents rates for arson separately. Arson rates are calculated based upon data received from all law enforcement agencies that provide the UCR program with data for 12 complete months.

Arson data collection does not include estimates for arson, because the degree of reporting arson offenses varies from agency to agency. Because of this unevenness of reporting, arson offenses are excluded from Tables 1 through 7, all of which contain offense estimations.

The number of arsons reported by individual law enforcement agencies is available in Tables 8 through 11. Arson trend data (which indicate year-to-year changes) can be found in Tables 12 through 15.

Population Groups: Trends and Rates

The number of arsons reported in 2012 was within one-tenth of one percent of the number reported in 2011. Law enforcement agencies in the nation's cities collectively reported a 1.4 percent increase in the number of arsons from the 2011 figure. Among the population groups labeled city, the subset with 500,000 to 999,999 inhabitants had the largest year-to-year decrease in reported arsons, 8.5 percent. Agencies in the nation's metropolitan counties reported a 5.8 percent decrease in the number of arsons, while those in nonmetropolitan counties reported a 0.5 percent increase. Those in suburban areas reported a 2.4 percent decline. (Table 12)

Arson rates were based on information received from 13,151 agencies that provided 12 months of complete arson data to the UCR program. An examination of data indicated that in 2012, the highest rate among non-subset city groups—30.5 arsons per 100,000 inhabitants—was reported in cities with 250,000 or more inhabitants. Among cities with 250,000 or more inhabitants, those with a population of 250,000 to 499,999 had the highest rate at 36.4 offenses per 100,000 inhabitants. Cities with 10,000 to 24,999 inhabitants had the lowest rate of arson at 13.2 per 100,000 inhabitants. Metropolitan counties had 13.2 arsons per 100,000 inhabitants, and nonmetropolitan counties had 13.0 arsons per 100,000 inhabitants, the lowest of all the population groups. The rate in suburban areas was 13.4 per 100,000 inhabitants. (Expanded Arson Table 1)

Offense Analysis

The UCR program breaks down arson offenses into three property categories: structural, mobile, and other. In addition, the structural property type is broken down into seven types of structures, and the mobile property type consists of two subgroupings. The program also collects information on the estimated dollar value of the damaged property.

Property Type

The total number of arsons increased in 2012. Arsons for the structural property type increased 3.2 percent and other arsons rose 5.2 percent, while arsons for the mobile property type dropped 3.3 percent from 2011 to 2012. (Table 15)

DISTRIBUTION BY PROPERTY TYPE

Arsons involving structures (residential, storage, public, etc.) accounted for 46.8 percent of the total number of arson offenses in 2012; arsons involving mobile property accounted for 23.1 percent; and other types of property (such as crops, timber, fences, etc.) accounted for 30.1 percent of reported arsons. Of the arsons involving structures, 64.9 percent involved residential properties. Of the residential arsons, 74.6 percent were single-occupancy residences. Approximately 16.5 percent of structures were not in use when the arson occurred. Mobile arsons accounted for 23.1 percent of all arsons. Within this category, 93.8 percent of offenses involved the burning of motor vehicles. (Expanded Arson Table 2)

DOLLAR LOSS

In monetary terms, the average dollar loss in 2012 for arson was $12,796. The average dollar loss for a structural arson was $22,477. Within the structural arson category, the “other commercial” subcategory had the highest average dollar loss at $46,933. Within that same category, single-occupancy dwellings had an average dollar loss of $24,993. Mobile property had an average dollar loss of $7,281. Other property types had an average dollar loss of $1,974. (Expanded Arson Table 2)

Table 1. Violent Crime in the United States, by Volume and Rate per 100,000 Inhabitants, 1993–2012

(Number, rate per 100,000 population)

Year	Population[1]	Violent crime		Murder and nonnegligent manslaughter		Forcible rape		Robbery		Aggravated assault	
		Number	Rate	Number	Rate	Number	Rate	Number	Rate	Number	Rate
1993	257,782,608	1,926,017	747.1	24,526	9.5	106,014	41.1	659,870	256.0	1,135,607	440.5
1994	260,327,021	1,857,670	713.6	23,326	9.0	102,216	39.3	618,949	237.8	1,113,179	427.6
1995	262,803,276	1,798,792	684.5	21,606	8.2	97,470	37.1	580,509	220.9	1,099,207	418.3
1996	265,228,572	1,688,540	636.6	19,645	7.4	96,252	36.3	535,594	201.9	1,037,049	391.0
1997	267,783,607	1,636,096	611.0	18,208	6.8	96,153	35.9	498,534	186.2	1,023,201	382.1
1998	270,248,003	1,533,887	567.6	16,974	6.3	93,144	34.5	447,186	165.5	976,583	361.4
1999	272,690,813	1,426,044	523.0	15,522	5.7	89,411	32.8	409,371	150.1	911,740	334.3
2000	281,421,906	1,425,486	506.5	15,586	5.5	90,178	32.0	408,016	145.0	911,706	324.0
2001 [2]	285,317,559	1,439,480	504.5	16,037	5.6	90,863	31.8	423,557	148.5	909,023	318.6
2002	287,973,924	1,423,677	494.4	16,229	5.6	95,235	33.1	420,806	146.1	891,407	309.5
2003	290,788,976	1,383,676	475.8	16,528	5.7	93,883	32.3	414,235	142.5	859,030	295.4
2004	293,656,842	1,360,088	463.2	16,148	5.5	95,089	32.4	401,470	136.7	847,381	288.6
2005	296,507,061	1,390,745	469.0	16,740	5.6	94,347	31.8	417,438	140.8	862,220	290.8
2006	299,398,484	1,435,123	479.3	17,309	5.8	94,472	31.6	449,246	150.0	874,096	292.0
2007	301,621,157	1,422,970	471.8	17,128	5.7	92,160	30.6	447,324	148.3	866,358	287.2
2008	304,059,724	1,394,461	458.6	16,465	5.4	90,750	29.8	443,563	145.9	843,683	277.5
2009	307,006,550	1,325,896	431.9	15,399	5.0	89,241	29.1	408,742	133.1	812,514	264.7
2010 [3]	309,330,219	1,251,248	404.5	14,722	4.8	85,593	27.7	369,089	119.3	781,844	252.8
2011	311,587,816	1,206,005	387.1	14,661	4.7	84,175	27.0	354,746	113.9	752,423	241.5
2012	313,914,040	1,214,462	386.9	14,827	4.7	84,376	26.9	354,520	112.9	760,739	242.3

1 Populations are U.S. Census Bureau provisional estimates as of July 1 for each year except 2000 and 2010, which are decennial census counts. 2 The murder and nonnegligent homicides that occurred as a result of the events of September 11, 2001, are not included in this table. 3 The crime figures have been adjusted.

Table 1A. Property Crime in the United States, by Volume and Rate per 100,000 Inhabitants, 1993–2012

(Number, rate per 100,000 population)

Year	Property crime		Burglary		Larceny-theft		Motor vehicle theft	
	Number	Rate	Number	Rate	Number	Rate	Number	Rate
1993	12,218,777	4,740.0	2,834,808	1,099.7	7,820,909	3,033.9	1,563,060	606.3
1994	12,131,873	4,660.2	2,712,774	1,042.1	7,879,812	3,026.9	1,539,287	591.3
1995	12,063,935	4,590.5	2,593,784	987.0	7,997,710	3,043.2	1,472,441	560.3
1996	11,805,323	4,451.0	2,506,400	945.0	7,904,685	2,980.3	1,394,238	525.7
1997	11,558,475	4,316.3	2,460,526	918.8	7,743,760	2,891.8	1,354,189	505.7
1998	10,951,827	4,052.5	2,332,735	863.2	7,376,311	2,729.5	1,242,781	459.9
1999	10,208,334	3,743.6	2,100,739	770.4	6,955,520	2,550.7	1,152,075	422.5
2000	10,182,584	3,618.3	2,050,992	728.8	6,971,590	2,477.3	1,160,002	412.2
2001 [2]	10,437,189	3,658.1	2,116,531	741.8	7,092,267	2,485.7	1,228,391	430.5
2002	10,455,277	3,630.6	2,151,252	747.0	7,057,379	2,450.7	1,246,646	432.9
2003	10,442,862	3,591.2	2,154,834	741.0	7,026,802	2,416.5	1,261,226	433.7
2004	10,319,386	3,514.1	2,144,446	730.3	6,937,089	2,362.3	1,237,851	421.5
2005	10,174,754	3,431.5	2,155,448	726.9	6,783,447	2,287.8	1,235,859	416.8
2006	10,019,601	3,346.6	2,194,993	733.1	6,626,363	2,213.2	1,198,245	400.2
2007	9,882,212	3,276.4	2,190,198	726.1	6,591,542	2,185.4	1,100,472	364.9
2008	9,774,152	3,214.6	2,228,887	733.0	6,586,206	2,166.1	959,059	315.4
2009	9,337,060	3,041.3	2,203,313	717.7	6,338,095	2,064.5	795,652	259.2
2010 [3]	9,112,625	2,945.9	2,168,459	701.0	6,204,601	2,005.8	739,565	239.1
2011	9,052,743	2,905.4	2,185,140	701.3	6,151,095	1,974.10	716,508	230.0
2012	8,975,438	2,859.2	2,103,787	670.2	6,150,598	1,959.30	721,053	229.7

1 Populations are U.S. Census Bureau provisional estimates as of July 1 for each year except 2000 and 2010, which are decennial census counts. 2 The murder and nonnegligent homicides that occurred as a result of the events of September 11, 2001, are not included in this table. 3 The crime figures have been adjusted.

Table 1B. Violent Crime in the United States, Percent Change in Volume and Rate per 100,000 Inhabitants for 2 Years, 5 Years, and 10 Years, 2003–2012

(Percent change)

Year	Violent crime		Murder and nonnegligent manslaughter		Forcible rape		Robbery		Aggravated assault	
	Number	Rate	Number	Rate	Number	Rate	Number	Rate	Number	Rate
2003–2012	[illegible]	[illegible]	[illegible]	[illegible]	[illegible]	[illegible]	[illegible]	[illegible]	[illegible]	[illegible]
2008–2012	-12.9	-15.6	-9.9	-12.8	-7.0	-9.9	-20.1	-22.6	-9.8	-12.7
2011–2012	0.7	*	1.1	0.4	0.2	-0.5	-0.1	-0.8	1.1	0.4

* = Less than one-tenth of 1 percent.

Table 1C. Property Crime in the United States, Percent Change in Volume and Rate per 100,000 Inhabitants for 2 Years, 5 Years, and 10 Years, 2003–2012

(Percent change)

Year	Property crime		Burglary		Larceny-theft		Motor vehicle theft	
	Number	Rate	Number	Rate	Number	Rate	Number	Rate
2003–2012	-14.1	-20.4	-2.4	-9.6	-12.5	-18.9	-42.8	-47.0
2008–2012	-8.2	-11.1	-5.6	-8.6	-6.6	-9.5	-24.8	-27.2
2011–2012	-0.9	-1.6	-3.7	-4.4	*	-0.7	0.6	-0.1

* = Less than one-tenth of 1 percent.

Table 2. Crime in the United States, by Community Type, 2012

(Number, percent, rate per 100,000 population)

Area	Population[1]	Violent crime	Murder and nonnegligent manslaughter	Forcible rape	Robbery	Aggravated assault	Property crime	Burglary	Larceny-theft	Motor vehicle theft
United States	313,914,040	1,214,464	14,827	84,376	354,522	760,739	8,975,438	2,103,787	6,150,598	721,053
Rate per 100,000 inhabitants		386.9	4.7	26.9	112.9	242.3	2,859.2	670.2	1,959.3	229.7
Metropolitan Statistical Areas	266,700,731									
Area actually reporting (percent)[2]	98.9%	1,084,765	13,157	68,419	339,791	663,398	7,801,507	1,788,702	5,347,372	665,433
Estimated total (percent)	100.0%	1,092,001	13,175	70,482	341,122	667,222	7,867,268	1,803,461	5,395,107	668,700
Rate per 100,000 inhabitants		409.4	4.9	26.4	127.9	250.2	2,949.8	676.2	2,022.9	250.7
Cities Outside Metropolitan Areas	19,114,670									
Area actually reporting (percent)[2]	93.0%	67,985	668	7,217	9,143	50,957	629,593	140,630	464,661	24,302
Estimated total (percent)	100.0%	72,715	720	7,879	9,859	54,257	675,635	151,406	498,229	26,000
Rate per 100,000 inhabitants		380.4	3.8	41.2	51.6	283.9	3,534.6	792.1	2,606.5	136.0
Nonmetropolitan Counties	28,098,639									
Area actually reporting (percent)[2]	94.2%	47,145	881	5,608	3,375	37,281	410,634	140,927	244,547	25,160
Estimated total (percent)	100.0%	49,748	932	6,015	3,541	39,260	432,535	148,920	257,262	26,353
Rate per 100,000 inhabitants		177.0	3.3	21.4	12.6	139.7	1,539.3	530.0	915.6	93.8

Note: Although arson data are included in the trend and clearance tables, sufficient data are not available to estimate totals for this offense. Therefore, no arson data are published in this table. 1 Population figures are U.S. Census Bureau provisional estimates as of July 1, 2012. 2 The percentage reported under "Area actually reporting" is based on the population covered by agencies providing 3 months or more of crime reports to the FBI.

Table 3. Crime in the United States, Population and Offense Distribution, by Region, 2012

(Percent distribution)

Region	Population	Violent crime	Murder and nonnegligent manslaughter	Forcible rape	Robbery	Aggravated assault	Property crime	Burglary	Larceny-theft	Motor vehicle theft
United States [1]	100.0	100.0	100.0	100.0	100.0	100.0	100.0	100.0	100.0	100.0
Northeast	17.8	16.0	14.2	13.0	19.1	15.0	12.9	11.2	13.9	9.7
Midwest	21.4	19.7	21.1	25.3	19.6	19.0	20.7	20.6	21.0	18.6
South	37.4	40.9	43.6	37.6	37.2	42.9	42.2	45.0	42.1	34.8
West	23.4	23.4	21.0	24.0	24.1	23.1	24.2	23.2	23.0	37.0

Note: Although arson data are included in the trend and clearance tables, sufficient data are not available to estimate totals for this offense. Therefore, no arson data are published in this table. 1 Because of rounding, the percentages may not add to 100.0.

Table 4. Crime, by Region, Geographic Division, and State, 2011–2012

Area	Population[1]	Violent crime		Murder and nonnegligent manslaughter		Forcible rape		Robbery	
		Number	Rate	Number	Rate	Number	Rate	Number	Rate
United States [2, 3, 4, 5]									
2011	311,587,816	1,206,031	387.1	14,661	4.7	84,175	27.0	354,772	113.9
2012	313,914,040	1,214,464	386.9	14,827	4.7	84,376	26.9	354,522	112.9
Percent change		0.7	*	1.1	0.4	0.2	-0.5	-0.1	-0.8
Northeast [3]									
2011	55,597,646	196,989	354.3	2,174	3.9	10,879	19.6	68,958	124.0
2012	55,761,091	194,609	349.0	2,106	3.8	11,001	19.7	67,672	121.4
Percent change		-1.2	-1.5	-3.1	-3.4	1.1	0.8	-1.9	-2.2
New England									
2011	14,517,309	46,134	317.8	386	2.7	3,783	26.1	12,179	83.9
2012	14,562,704	44,769	307.4	349	2.4	3,791	26.0	11,959	82.1
Percent change		-3.0	-3.3	-9.6	-9.9	0.2	-0.1	-1.8	-2.1
Connecticut									
2011	3,586,717	9,889	275.7	129	3.6	689	19.2	3,689	102.9
2012	3,590,347	10,160	283.0	146	4.1	919	25.6	3,687	102.7
Percent change		2.7	2.6	13.2	13.1	33.4	33.2	-0.1	-0.2
Maine									
2011	1,328,544	1,638	123.3	26	2.0	394	29.7	370	27.9
2012	1,329,192	1,631	122.7	25	1.9	372	28.0	423	31.8
Percent change		-0.4	-0.5	-3.8	-3.9	-5.6	-5.6	14.3	14.3
Massachusetts									
2011	6,607,003	28,232	427.3	184	2.8	1,654	25.0	6,768	102.4
2012	6,646,144	26,953	405.5	121	1.8	1,642	24.7	6,552	98.6
Percent change		-4.5	-5.1	-34.2	-34.6	-0.7	-1.3	-3.2	-3.8
New Hampshire									
2011	1,317,807	2,864	217.3	16	1.2	581	44.1	509	38.6
2012	1,320,718	2,481	187.9	15	1.1	449	34.0	472	35.7
Percent change		-13.4	-13.6	-6.3	-6.5	-22.7	-22.9	-7.3	-7.5
Rhode Island									
2011	1,050,646	2,586	246.1	20	1.9	319	30.4	744	70.8
2012	1,050,292	2,651	252.4	34	3.2	288	27.4	713	67.9
Percent change		2.5	2.5	70.0	70.1	-9.7	-9.7	-4.2	-4.1
Vermont									
2011	626,592	925	147.6	11	1.8	146	23.3	99	15.8
2012	626,011	893	142.6	8	1.3	121	19.3	112	17.9
Percent change		-3.5	-3.4	-27.3	-27.2	-17.1	-17.0	13.1	13.2
Middle Atlantic [3]									
2011	41,080,337	150,855	367.2	1,788	4.4	7,096	17.3	56,779	138.2
2012	41,198,387	149,840	363.7	1,757	4.3	7,210	17.5	55,713	135.2
Percent change		-0.7	-1.0	-1.7	-2.0	1.6	1.3	-1.9	-2.2
New Jersey									
2011	8,834,773	27,203	307.9	380	4.3	1,006	11.4	12,209	138.2
2012	8,864,590	25,727	290.2	388	4.4	1,035	11.7	11,385	128.4
Percent change		-5.4	-5.7	2.1	1.8	2.9	2.5	-6.7	-7.1
New York[3]									
2011	19,501,616	77,463	397.2	769	3.9	2,751	14.1	28,405	145.7
2012	19,570,261	79,610	406.8	684	3.5	2,848	14.6	28,655	146.4
Percent change		2.8	2.4	-11.1	-11.4	3.5	3.2	0.9	0.5
Pennsylvania									
2011	12,743,948	46,189	362.4	639	5.0	3,339	26.2	16,165	126.8
2012	12,763,536	44,503	348.7	685	5.4	3,327	26.1	15,673	122.8
Percent change		-3.7	-3.8	7.2	7.0	-0.4	-0.5	-3.0	-3.2

Table 4. Crime, by Region, Geographic Division, and State, 2011–2012— continued

Area	Population[1]	Violent crime		Murder and nonnegligent manslaughter		Forcible rape		Robbery	
		Number	Rate	Number	Rate	Number	Rate	Number	Rate
Midwest [4]									
2011	67,145,089	235,138	350.2	3,050	4.5	21,039	31.3	71,231	106.1
2012	67,316,297	238,712	354.6	3,134	4.7	21,344	31.7	69,498	103.2
Percent change		1.5	1.3	2.8	2.5	1.4	1.2	-2.4	-2.7
East North Central									
2011	46,503,756	169,359	364.2	2,342	5.0	14,001	30.1	58,048	124.8
2012	46,566,572	171,586	368.5	2,411	5.2	14,703	31.6	56,360	121.0
Percent change		1.3	1.2	2.9	2.8	5.0	4.9	-2.9	-3.0
Illinois									
2011	12,859,752	54,523	424.0	781	6.1	3,030	23.6	20,217	157.2
2012	12,875,255	53,403	414.8	744	5.8	3,570	27.7	19,471	151.2
Percent change		-2.1	-2.2	-4.7	-4.9	17.8	17.7	-3.7	-3.8
Indiana									
2011	6,516,353	21,619	331.8	306	4.7	1,758	27.0	6,977	107.1
2012	6,537,334	22,602	345.7	310	4.7	1,667	25.5	6,598	100.9
Percent change		4.5	4.2	1.3	1.0	-5.2	-5.5	-5.4	-5.7
Michigan									
2011	9,876,801	43,731	442.8	617	6.2	4,344	44.0	10,263	103.9
2012	9,883,360	44,922	454.5	689	7.0	4,589	46.4	10,434	105.6
Percent change		2.7	2.7	11.7	11.6	5.6	5.6	1.7	1.6
Ohio									
2011	11,541,007	35,218	305.2	500	4.3	3,679	31.9	15,991	138.6
2012	11,544,225	34,595	299.7	495	4.3	3,658	31.7	15,235	132.0
Percent change		-1.8	-1.8	-1.0	-1.0	-0.6	-0.6	-4.7	-4.8
Wisconsin									
2011	5,709,843	14,268	249.9	138	2.4	1,190	20.8	4,600	80.6
2012	5,726,398	16,064	280.5	173	3.0	1,219	21.3	4,622	80.7
Percent change		12.6	12.3	25.4	25.0	2.4	2.1	0.5	0.2
West North Central[4]									
2011	20,641,333	65,779	318.7	708	3.4	7,038	34.1	13,183	63.9
2012	20,749,725	67,126	323.5	723	3.5	6,641	32.0	13,138	63.3
Percent change		2.0	1.5	2.1	1.6	-5.6	-6.1	-0.3	-0.9
Iowa									
2011	3,064,097	7,883	257.3	44	1.4	866	28.3	824	26.9
2012	3,074,186	8,112	263.9	45	1.5	871	28.3	962	31.3
Percent change		2.9	2.6	2.3	1.9	0.6	0.2	16.7	16.4
Kansas									
2011	2,870,386	10,209	355.7	111	3.9	1,122	39.1	1,448	50.4
2012	2,885,905	10,232	354.6	84	2.9	1,053	36.5	1,500	52.0
Percent change		0.2	-0.3	-24.3	-24.7	-6.1	-6.7	3.6	3.0
Minnesota[4]									
2011	5,347,299	12,323	230.5	75	1.4	2,113	39.5	3,385	63.3
2012	5,379,139	12,419	230.9	99	1.8	1,638	30.5	3,475	64.6
Percent change		0.8	0.2	32.0	31.2	-22.5	-22.9	2.7	2.1
Missouri									
2011	6,008,984	26,888	447.5	366	6.1	1,469	24.4	6,275	104.4
2012	6,021,988	27,155	450.9	389	6.5	1,511	25.1	5,782	96.0
Percent change		1.0	0.8	6.3	6.1	2.9	2.6	-7.9	-8.1
Nebraska									
2011	1,842,234	4,672	253.6	68	3.7	699	37.9	993	53.9
2012	1,855,525	4,814	259.4	53	2.9	711	38.3	1,130	60.9
Percent change		3.0	2.3	-22.1	-22.6	1.7	1.0	13.8	13.0
North Dakota									
2011	684,740	1,699	248.1	24	3.5	266	38.8	91	13.3

Table 4. Crime, by Region, Geographic Division, and State, 2011–2012— continued

Area	Population[1]	Violent crime		Murder and nonnegligent manslaughter		Forcible rape		Robbery	
		Number	Rate	Number	Rate	Number	Rate	Number	Rate
2012	699,628	1,712	244.7	28	4.0	272	38.9	131	18.7
Percent change		0.8	-1.4	16.7	14.2	2.3	0.1	44.0	40.9
South Dakota									
2011	823,593	2,105	255.6	20	2.4	503	61.1	167	20.3
2012	833,354	2,682	321.8	25	3.0	585	70.2	158	19.0
Percent change		27.4	25.9	25.0	23.5	16.3	14.9	-5.4	-6.5
South [3,5]									
2011	116,022,230	498,306	429.5	6,367	5.5	31,834	27.4	132,877	114.5
2012	117,257,221	496,773	423.7	6,466	5.5	31,760	27.1	131,862	112.5
Percent change		-0.3	-1.4	1.6	0.5	-0.2	-1.3	-0.8	-1.8
South Atlantic [5]									
2011	60,545,194	259,180	428.1	3,297	5.4	14,619	24.1	74,188	122.5
2012	61,188,567	254,911	416.6	3,293	5.4	14,634	23.9	71,446	116.8
Percent change		-1.6	-2.7	-0.1	-1.2	0.1	-0.9	-3.7	-4.7
Delaware									
2011	908,137	5,144	566.4	48	5.3	307	33.8	1,558	171.6
2012	917,092	5,020	547.4	57	6.2	243	26.5	1,492	162.7
Percent change		-2.4	-3.4	18.8	17.6	-20.8	-21.6	-4.2	-5.2
District of Columbia[5]									
2011	619,020	7,433	1,200.8	108	17.4	173	27.9	4,094	661.4
2012	632,323	7,864	1,243.7	88	13.9	236	37.3	4,036	638.3
Percent change		5.8	3.6	-18.5	-20.2	36.4	33.5	-1.4	-3.5
Florida									
2011	19,082,262	98,198	514.6	984	5.2	5,273	27.6	25,622	134.3
2012	19,317,568	94,087	487.1	1,009	5.2	5,260	27.2	23,889	123.7
Percent change		-4.2	-5.4	2.5	1.3	-0.2	-1.5	-6.8	-7.9
Georgia									
2011	9,812,460	36,762	374.6	549	5.6	2,066	21.1	12,266	125.0
2012	9,919,945	37,591	378.9	581	5.9	2,124	21.4	12,463	125.6
Percent change		2.3	1.1	5.8	4.7	2.8	1.7	1.6	0.5
Maryland									
2011	5,839,572	28,817	493.5	399	6.8	1,200	20.5	10,342	177.1
2012	5,884,563	28,055	476.8	369	6.3	1,235	21.0	10,141	172.3
Percent change		-2.6	-3.4	-7.5	-8.2	2.9	2.1	-1.9	-2.7
North Carolina									
2011	9,651,103	33,421	346.3	498	5.2	1,959	20.3	9,448	97.9
2012	9,752,073	34,464	353.4	479	4.9	1,984	20.3	9,392	96.3
Percent change		3.1	2.1	-3.8	-4.8	1.3	0.2	-0.6	-1.6
South Carolina									
2011	4,673,348	27,894	596.9	320	6.8	1,678	35.9	4,631	99.1
2012	4,723,723	26,397	558.8	324	6.9	1,679	35.5	4,489	95.0
Percent change		-5.4	-6.4	1.3	0.2	0.1	-1.0	-3.1	-4.1
Virginia									
2011	8,104,384	16,014	197.6	304	3.8	1,591	19.6	5,425	66.9
2012	8,185,867	15,564	190.1	314	3.8	1,452	17.7	4,706	57.5
Percent change		-2.8	-3.8	3.3	2.3	-8.7	-9.6	-13.3	-14.1
West Virginia									
2011	1,854,908	5,497	296.3	87	4.7	372	20.1	802	43.2
2012	1,855,413	5,869	316.3	72	3.9	421	22.7	838	45.2
Percent change		6.8	6.7	-17.2	-17.3	13.2	13.1	4.5	4.5
East South Central [3]									
2011	18,547,747	77,535	418.0	1,062	5.7	5,827	31.4	19,189	103.5

Table 4. Crime, by Region, Geographic Division, and State, 2011–2012— continued

Area	Population[1]	Violent crime		Murder and nonnegligent manslaughter		Forcible rape		Robbery	
		Number	Rate	Number	Rate	Number	Rate	Number	Rate
2012	18,643,607	80,781	433.3	1,145	6.1	5,422	29.1	19,008	102.0
Percent change		4.2	3.7	7.8	7.3	-7.0	-7.4	-0.9	-1.5
Alabama[3]									
2011	4,803,689	20,166	419.8	299	6.2	1,370	28.5	4,906	102.1
2012	4,822,023	21,693	449.9	342	7.1	1,296	26.9	5,020	104.1
Percent change		7.6	7.2	14.4	13.9	-5.4	-5.8	2.3	1.9
Kentucky									
2011	4,366,814	10,465	239.6	151	3.5	1,499	34.3	3,705	84.8
2012	4,380,415	9,752	222.6	195	4.5	1,272	29.0	3,535	80.7
Percent change		-6.8	-7.1	29.1	28.7	-15.1	-15.4	-4.6	-4.9
Mississippi									
2011	2,977,457	8,009	269.0	232	7.8	863	29.0	2,496	83.8
2012	2,984,926	7,786	260.8	220	7.4	822	27.5	2,284	76.5
Percent change		-2.8	-3.0	-5.2	-5.4	-4.8	-5.0	-8.5	-8.7
Tennessee									
2011	6,399,787	38,895	607.8	380	5.9	2,095	32.7	8,082	126.3
2012	6,456,243	41,550	643.6	388	6.0	2,032	31.5	8,169	126.5
Percent change		6.8	5.9	2.1	1.2	-3.0	-3.9	1.1	0.2
West South Central									
2011	36,929,289	161,591	437.6	2,008	5.4	11,388	30.8	39,500	107.0
2012	37,425,047	161,081	430.4	2,028	5.4	11,704	31.3	41,408	110.6
Percent change		-0.3	-1.6	1.0	-0.3	2.8	1.4	4.8	3.4
Arkansas									
2011	2,938,582	14,173	482.3	160	5.4	1,230	41.9	2,357	80.2
2012	2,949,131	13,835	469.1	173	5.9	1,247	42.3	2,320	78.7
Percent change		-2.4	-2.7	8.1	7.7	1.4	1.0	-1.6	-1.9
Louisiana									
2011	4,574,766	25,373	554.6	506	11.1	1,262	27.6	5,235	114.4
2012	4,601,893	22,868	496.9	495	10.8	1,158	25.2	5,475	119.0
Percent change		-9.9	-10.4	-2.2	-2.8	-8.2	-8.8	4.6	4.0
Oklahoma									
2011	3,784,163	17,311	457.5	212	5.6	1,410	37.3	3,288	86.9
2012	3,814,820	17,902	469.3	216	5.7	1,588	41.6	3,231	84.7
Percent change		3.4	2.6	1.9	1.1	12.6	11.7	-1.7	-2.5
Texas									
2011	25,631,778	104,734	408.6	1,130	4.4	7,486	29.2	28,620	111.7
2012	26,059,203	106,476	408.6	1,144	4.4	7,711	29.6	30,382	116.6
Percent change		1.7	*	1.2	-0.4	3.0	1.3	6.2	4.4
West [3]									
2011	72,822,851	275,598	378.4	3,070	4.2	20,423	28.0	81,706	112.2
2012	73,579,431	284,370	386.5	3,121	4.2	20,271	27.5	85,490	116.2
Percent change		3.2	2.1	1.7	0.6	-0.7	-1.8	4.6	3.6
Mountain [3]									
2011	22,345,433	82,979	371.3	981	4.4	8,410	37.6	17,981	80.5
2012	22,617,874	85,645	378.7	880	3.9	8,233	36.4	19,141	84.6
Percent change		3.2	2.0	-10.3	-11.4	-2.1	-3.3	6.5	5.2
Arizona									
2011	6,467,315	26,789	414.2	397	6.1	2,499	38.6	7,145	110.5
2012	6,553,255	28,108	428.9	358	5.5	2,277	34.7	7,386	112.7
Percent change		4.9	3.5	-9.8	-11.0	-8.9	-10.1	3.4	2.0
Colorado									
2011	5,116,302	16,085	314.4	155	3.0	2,285	44.7	3,299	64.5
2012	5,187,582	16,023	308.9	162	3.1	2,113	40.7	3,395	65.4

Table 4. Crime, by Region, Geographic Division, and State, 2011–2012— continued

Area	Population[1]	Violent crime		Murder and nonnegligent manslaughter		Forcible rape		Robbery	
		Number	Rate	Number	Rate	Number	Rate	Number	Rate
Percent change		-0.4	-1.8	4.5	3.1	-7.5	-8.8	2.9	1.5
Idaho									
2011	1,583,744	3,202	202.2	35	2.2	444	28.0	188	11.9
2012	1,595,728	3,318	207.9	29	1.8	479	30.0	243	15.2
Percent change		3.6	2.8	-17.1	-17.8	7.9	7.1	29.3	28.3
Montana[3]									
2011	997,667	2,755	276.1	29	2.9	366	36.7	171	17.1
2012	1,005,141	2,736	272.2	27	2.7	379	37.7	191	19.0
Percent change		-0.7	-1.4	-6.9	-7.6	3.6	2.8	11.7	10.9
Nevada									
2011	2,720,028	15,452	568.1	139	5.1	913	33.6	4,308	158.4
2012	2,758,931	16,763	607.6	124	4.5	931	33.7	4,918	178.3
Percent change		8.5	7.0	-10.8	-12.0	2.0	0.5	14.2	12.5
New Mexico									
2011	2,078,674	11,904	572.7	158	7.6	856	41.2	1,720	82.7
2012	2,085,538	11,660	559.1	116	5.6	957	45.9	1,847	88.6
Percent change		-2.0	-2.4	-26.6	-26.8	11.8	11.4	7.4	7.0
Utah									
2011	2,814,347	5,547	197.1	50	1.8	901	32.0	1,079	38.3
2012	2,855,287	5,876	205.8	50	1.8	943	33.0	1,100	38.5
Percent change		5.9	4.4	0.0	-1.4	4.7	3.2	1.9	0.5
Wyoming									
2011	567,356	1,245	219.4	18	3.2	146	25.7	71	12.5
2012	576,412	1,161	201.4	14	2.4	154	26.7	61	10.6
Percent change		-6.7	-8.2	-22.2	-23.4	5.5	3.8	-14.1	-15.4
Pacific									
2011	50,477,418	192,619	381.6	2,089	4.1	12,013	23.8	63,725	126.2
2012	50,961,557	198,725	390.0	2,241	4.4	12,038	23.6	66,349	130.2
Percent change		3.2	2.2	7.3	6.3	0.2	-0.7	4.1	3.1
Alaska									
2011	723,860	4,416	610.1	30	4.1	436	60.2	576	79.6
2012	731,449	4,412	603.2	30	4.1	583	79.7	630	86.1
Percent change		-0.1	-1.1	0.0	-1.0	33.7	32.3	9.4	8.2
California									
2011	37,683,933	154,943	411.2	1,792	4.8	7,665	20.3	54,291	144.1
2012	38,041,430	160,944	423.1	1,884	5.0	7,837	20.6	56,521	148.6
Percent change		3.9	2.9	5.1	4.1	2.2	1.3	4.1	3.1
Hawaii									
2011	1,378,129	3,465	251.4	20	1.5	353	25.6	994	72.1
2012	1,392,313	3,330	239.2	29	2.1	285	20.5	1,040	74.7
Percent change		-3.9	-4.9	45.0	43.5	-19.3	-20.1	4.6	3.6
Oregon[2]									
2011	3,868,229	9,643	249.3	84	2.2	1,239	32.0	2,237	57.8
2012	3,899,353	9,653	247.6	92	2.4	1,140	29.2	2,413	61.9
Percent change		0.1	-0.7	9.5	8.6	-8.0	-8.7	7.9	7.0
Washington									
2011	6,823,267	20,152	295.3	163	2.4	2,320	34.0	5,627	82.5
2012	6,897,012	20,386	295.6	206	3.0	2,193	31.8	5,745	83.3
Percent change		1.2	0.1	26.4	25.0	-5.5	-6.5	2.1	1.0

Table 4. Crime, by Region, Geographic Division, and State, 2011–2012

(Number, rate per 100,000 population, percent)

Area	Aggravated assault		Property crime		Burglary		Larceny-theft	
	Number	Rate	Number	Rate	Number	Rate	Number	Rate
United States [2, 3, 4, 5]								
2011	752,423	241.5	9,052,743	2,905.4	2,185,140	701.3	6,151,095	1,974.1
2012	760,739	242.3	8,975,438	2,859.2	2,103,787	670.2	6,150,598	1,959.3
Percent change	1.1	0.4	-0.9	-1.6	-3.7	-4.4	*	-0.7
Northeast [3]								
2011	114,978	206.8	1,180,679	2,123.6	243,085	437.2	861,511	1,549.5
2012	113,830	204.1	1,160,127	2,080.5	235,820	422.9	854,688	1,532.8
Percent change	-1.0	-1.3	-1.7	-2.0	-3.0	-3.3	-0.8	-1.1
New England								
2011	29,786	205.2	335,681	2,312.3	76,654	528.0	236,480	1,629.0
2012	28,670	196.9	326,010	2,238.7	72,070	494.9	233,178	1,601.2
Percent change	-3.7	-4.0	-2.9	-3.2	-6.0	-6.3	-1.4	-1.7
Connecticut								
2011	5,382	150.1	77,205	2,152.5	15,468	431.3	55,067	1,535.3
2012	5,408	150.6	76,834	2,140.0	14,711	409.7	55,674	1,550.7
Percent change	0.5	0.4	-0.5	-0.6	-4.9	-5.0	1.1	1.0
Maine								
2011	848	63.8	33,829	2,546.3	7,865	592.0	24,886	1,873.2
2012	811	61.0	33,361	2,509.9	7,461	561.3	24,905	1,873.7
Percent change	-4.4	-4.4	-1.4	-1.4	-5.1	-5.2	0.1	*
Massachusetts								
2011	19,626	297.0	148,829	2,252.6	36,403	551.0	101,644	1,538.4
2012	18,638	280.4	143,089	2,153.0	34,540	519.7	99,317	1,494.4
Percent change	-5.0	-5.6	-3.9	-4.4	-5.1	-5.7	-2.3	-2.9
New Hampshire								
2011	1,758	133.4	32,756	2,485.6	6,244	473.8	25,398	1,927.3
2012	1,545	117.0	30,693	2,324.0	5,444	412.2	24,226	1,834.3
Percent change	-12.1	-12.3	-6.3	-6.5	-12.8	-13.0	-4.6	-4.8
Rhode Island								
2011	1,503	143.1	27,976	2,662.7	6,836	650.6	18,765	1,786.0
2012	1,616	153.9	27,017	2,572.3	5,949	566.4	18,440	1,755.7
Percent change	7.5	7.6	-3.4	-3.4	-13.0	-12.9	-1.7	-1.7
Vermont								
2011	669	106.8	15,086	2,407.6	3,838	612.5	10,720	1,710.8
2012	652	104.2	15,016	2,398.7	3,965	633.4	10,616	1,695.8
Percent change	-2.5	-2.5	-0.5	-0.4	3.3	3.4	-1.0	-0.9
Middle Atlantic [3]								
2011	85,192	207.4	844,998	2,056.9	166,431	405.1	625,031	1,521.5
2012	85,160	206.7	834,117	2,024.6	163,750	397.5	621,510	1,508.6
Percent change	*	-0.3	-1.3	-1.6	-1.6	-1.9	-0.6	-0.8
New Jersey								
2011	13,608	154.0	189,719	2,147.4	43,238	489.4	129,066	1,460.9
2012	12,919	145.7	181,481	2,047.3	42,338	477.6	122,662	1,383.7
Percent change	-5.1	-5.4	-4.3	-4.7	-2.1	-2.4	-5.0	-5.3
New York [3]								
2011	45,538	233.5	371,837	1,906.7	65,227	334.5	287,361	1,473.5
2012	47,423	242.3	376,140	1,922.0	64,553	329.9	294,239	1,503.5
Percent change	4.1	3.8	1.2	0.8	-1.0	-1.4	2.4	2.0
Pennsylvania								
2011	26,046	204.4	283,442	2,224.1	57,966	454.9	208,604	1,636.9
2012	24,818	194.4	276,496	2,166.3	56,859	445.5	204,609	1,603.1
Percent change	-4.7	-4.9	-2.5	-2.6	-1.9	-2.1	-1.9	-2.1
Midwest [4]								
2011	139,818	208.2	1,897,790	2,826.4	459,064	683.7	1,300,212	1,936.4
2012	144,736	215.0	1,861,182	2,764.8	433,821	644.5	1,293,237	1,921.1
Percent change	3.5	3.3	-1.9	-2.2	-5.5	-5.7	-0.5	-0.8
East North Central								
2011	94,968	204.2	1,322,297	2,843.4	338,113	727.1	885,874	1,905.0
2012	98,112	210.7	1,280,542	2,749.9	315,744	678.0	872,604	1,873.9
Percent change	3.3	3.2	-3.2	-3.3	-6.6	-6.7	-1.5	-1.6
Illinois								

Table 4. Crime, by Region, Geographic Division, and State, 2011–2012— continued

(Number, rate per 100,000 population, percent)

Area	Aggravated assault		Property crime		Burglary		Larceny-theft	
	Number	Rate	Number	Rate	Number	Rate	Number	Rate
2011	30,495	237.1	344,468	2,678.7	77,719	604.4	237,362	1,845.8
2012	29,618	230.0	332,013	2,578.7	71,101	552.2	235,222	1,826.9
Percent change	-2.9	-3.0	-3.6	-3.7	-8.5	-8.6	-0.9	-1.0
Indiana								
2011	12,578	193.0	206,016	3,161.5	50,571	776.1	140,630	2,158.1
2012	14,027	214.6	198,032	3,029.2	47,612	728.3	136,759	2,092.0
Percent change	11.5	11.2	-3.9	-4.2	-5.9	-6.2	-2.8	-3.1
Michigan								
2011	28,507	288.6	251,329	2,544.6	69,755	706.3	156,666	1,586.2
2012	29,210	295.5	250,101	2,530.5	65,665	664.4	159,321	1,612.0
Percent change	2.5	2.4	-0.5	-0.6	-5.9	-5.9	1.7	1.6
Ohio								
2011	15,048	130.4	380,572	3,297.6	112,901	978.3	246,744	2,138.0
2012	15,207	131.7	359,883	3,117.4	103,421	895.9	236,950	2,052.5
Percent change	1.1	1.0	-5.4	-5.5	-8.4	-8.4	-4.0	-4.0
Wisconsin								
2011	8,340	146.1	139,912	2,450.4	27,167	475.8	104,472	1,829.7
2012	10,050	175.5	140,513	2,453.8	27,945	488.0	104,352	1,822.3
Percent change	20.5	20.2	0.4	0.1	2.9	2.6	-0.1	-0.4
West North Central [4]								
2011	44,850	217.3	575,493	2,788.1	120,951	586.0	414,338	2,007.3
2012	46,624	224.7	580,640	2,798.3	118,077	569.1	420,633	2,027.2
Percent change	4.0	3.4	0.9	0.4	-2.4	-2.9	1.5	1.0
Iowa								
2011	6,149	200.7	72,043	2,351.2	17,573	573.5	50,472	1,647.2
2012	6,234	202.8	69,839	2,271.8	17,096	556.1	48,720	1,584.8
Percent change	1.4	1.0	-3.1	-3.4	-2.7	-3.0	-3.5	-3.8
Kansas								
2011	7,528	262.3	88,655	3,088.6	18,712	651.9	63,259	2,203.8
2012	7,595	263.2	90,710	3,143.2	18,767	650.3	65,165	2,258.0
Percent change	0.9	0.3	2.3	1.8	0.3	-0.2	3.0	2.5
Minnesota[4]								
2011	6,750	126.2	136,183	2,546.8	25,681	480.3	102,354	1,914.1
2012	7,207	134.0	138,152	2,568.3	25,378	471.8	104,316	1,939.3
Percent change	6.8	6.1	1.4	0.8	-1.2	-1.8	1.9	1.3
Missouri								
2011	18,778	312.5	199,085	3,313.1	44,875	746.8	138,879	2,311.2
2012	19,473	323.4	199,590	3,314.4	42,466	705.2	140,816	2,338.4
Percent change	3.7	3.5	0.3	*	-5.4	-5.6	1.4	1.2
Nebraska								
2011	2,912	158.1	50,894	2,762.6	8,725	473.6	38,060	2,066.0
2012	2,920	157.4	51,118	2,754.9	8,735	470.8	38,236	2,060.7
Percent change	0.3	-0.4	0.4	-0.3	0.1	-0.6	0.5	-0.3
North Dakota								
2011	1,318	192.5	13,334	1,947.3	2,458	359.0	9,891	1,444.5
2012	1,281	183.1	14,063	2,010.1	2,377	339.8	10,535	1,505.8
Percent change	-2.8	-4.9	5.5	3.2	-3.3	-5.4	6.5	4.2
South Dakota								
2011	1,415	171.8	15,299	1,857.6	2,927	355.4	11,423	1,387.0
2012	1,914	229.7	17,168	2,060.1	3,258	391.0	12,845	1,541.4
Percent change	35.3	33.7	12.2	10.9	11.3	10.0	12.4	11.1
South [3,5]								
2011	327,228	282.0	3,911,383	3,371.2	1,017,157	876.7	2,634,208	2,270.4
2012	326,685	278.6	3,783,683	3,226.8	946,081	806.8	2,586,999	2,206.3
Percent change	-0.2	-1.2	-3.3	-4.3	-7.0	-8.0	-1.8	-2.8
South Atlantic [5]								
2011	167,076	276.0	1,999,058	3,301.8	507,261	837.8	1,358,090	2,243.1
2012	165,538	270.5	1,924,730	3,145.6	470,185	768.4	1,327,951	2,170.3
Percent change	-0.9	-2.0	-3.7	-4.7	-7.3	-8.3	-2.2	-3.2
Delaware								
2011	3,231	355.8	31,163	3,431.5	7,617	838.8	22,001	2,422.7
2012	3,228	352.0	30,639	3,340.9	7,371	803.7	21,832	2,380.6
Percent change	-0.1	-1.1	-1.7	-2.6	-3.2	-4.2	-0.8	-1.7

Table 4. Crime, by Region, Geographic Division, and State, 2011–2012— continued

(Number, rate per 100,000 population, percent)

Area	Aggravated assault		Property crime		Burglary		Larceny-theft	
	Number	Rate	Number	Rate	Number	Rate	Number	Rate
District of Columbia[5]								
2011	3,058	494.0	29,654	4,790.5	3,850	622.0	21,347	3,448.5
2012	3,504	554.1	30,736	4,860.8	3,519	556.5	23,556	3,725.3
Percent change	14.6	12.2	3.6	1.5	-8.6	-10.5	10.3	8.0
Florida								
2011	66,319	347.5	671,200	3,517.4	170,171	891.8	461,408	2,418.0
2012	63,929	330.9	632,988	3,276.7	153,563	794.9	442,095	2,288.6
Percent change	-3.6	-4.8	-5.7	-6.8	-9.8	-10.9	-4.2	-5.4
Georgia								
2011	21,881	223.0	357,235	3,640.6	96,014	978.5	231,543	2,359.7
2012	22,423	226.0	338,329	3,410.6	86,789	874.9	223,004	2,248.0
Percent change	2.5	1.4	-5.3	-6.3	-9.6	-10.6	-3.7	-4.7
Maryland								
2011	16,876	289.0	166,846	2,857.2	35,823	613.5	114,951	1,968.5
2012	16,310	277.2	162,031	2,753.5	33,732	573.2	113,274	1,924.9
Percent change	-3.4	-4.1	-2.9	-3.6	-5.8	-6.6	-1.5	-2.2
North Carolina								
2011	21,516	222.9	337,806	3,500.2	105,534	1,093.5	215,453	2,232.4
2012	22,609	231.8	328,594	3,369.5	99,323	1,018.5	213,151	2,185.7
Percent change	5.1	4.0	-2.7	-3.7	-5.9	-6.9	-1.1	-2.1
South Carolina								
2011	21,265	455.0	183,243	3,921.0	47,351	1,013.2	122,255	2,616.0
2012	19,905	421.4	180,550	3,822.2	45,086	954.5	122,263	2,588.3
Percent change	-6.4	-7.4	-1.5	-2.5	-4.8	-5.8	*	-1.1
Virginia								
2011	8,694	107.3	182,902	2,256.8	30,656	378.3	142,476	1,758.0
2012	9,092	111.1	176,985	2,162.1	29,511	360.5	138,398	1,690.7
Percent change	4.6	3.5	-3.2	-4.2	-3.7	-4.7	-2.9	-3.8
West Virginia								
2011	4,236	228.4	39,009	2,103.0	10,245	552.3	26,656	1,437.1
2012	4,538	244.6	43,878	2,364.9	11,291	608.5	30,378	1,637.3
Percent change	7.1	7.1	12.5	12.5	10.2	10.2	14.0	13.9
East South Central [3]								
2011	51,457	277.4	612,938	3,304.6	177,421	956.6	399,104	2,151.8
2012	55,206	296.1	582,274	3,123.2	161,325	865.3	387,105	2,076.3
Percent change	7.3	6.7	-5.0	-5.5	-9.1	-9.5	-3.0	-3.5
Alabama[3]								
2011	13,591	282.9	173,192	3,605.4	51,119	1,064.2	111,411	2,319.3
2012	15,035	311.8	168,878	3,502.2	47,481	984.7	111,523	2,312.8
Percent change	10.6	10.2	-2.5	-2.9	-7.1	-7.5	0.1	-0.3
Kentucky								
2011	5,110	117.0	119,037	2,725.9	32,750	750.0	79,586	1,822.5
2012	4,750	108.4	111,826	2,552.9	29,587	675.4	75,571	1,725.2
Percent change	-7.0	-7.3	-6.1	-6.3	-9.7	-9.9	-5.0	-5.3
Mississippi								
2011	4,418	148.4	89,809	3,016.3	30,722	1,031.8	54,179	1,819.6
2012	4,460	149.4	83,906	2,811.0	28,076	940.6	51,508	1,725.6
Percent change	1.0	0.7	-6.6	-6.8	-8.6	-8.8	-4.9	-5.2
Tennessee								
2011	28,338	442.8	230,900	3,607.9	62,830	981.8	153,928	2,405.2
2012	30,961	479.6	217,664	3,371.4	56,181	870.2	148,503	2,300.1
Percent change	9.3	8.3	-5.7	-6.6	-10.6	-11.4	-3.5	-4.4
West South Central								
2011	108,695	294.3	1,299,387	3,518.6	332,475	900.3	877,014	2,374.8
2012	105,941	283.1	1,276,679	3,411.3	314,571	840.5	871,943	2,329.8
Percent change	-2.5	-3.8	-1.7	-3.0	-5.4	-6.6	-0.6	-1.9
Arkansas								
2011	10,426	354.8	110,430	3,757.9	34,016	1,157.6	70,645	2,404.1
2012	10,095	342.3	107,941	3,660.1	31,890	1,081.3	70,327	2,384.7
Percent change	-3.2	-3.5	-2.3	-2.6	-6.3	-6.6	-0.5	-0.8
Louisiana								
2011	18,370	401.6	168,529	3,683.9	46,242	1,010.8	113,174	2,473.9
2012	15,740	342.0	162,936	3,540.6	42,140	915.7	112,915	2,453.7

Table 4. Crime, by Region, Geographic Division, and State, 2011–2012— continued

(Number, rate per 100,000 population, percent)

Area	Aggravated assault		Property crime		Burglary		Larceny-theft	
	Number	Rate	Number	Rate	Number	Rate	Number	Rate
Percent change	-14.3	-14.8	-3.3	-3.9	-8.9	-9.4	-0.2	-0.8
Oklahoma								
2011	12,401	327.7	127,618	3,372.4	36,462	963.5	80,064	2,115.8
2012	12,867	337.3	129,743	3,401.0	35,731	936.6	82,440	2,161.3
Percent change	3.8	2.9	1.7	0.8	-2.0	-2.8	3.0	2.2
Texas								
2011	67,498	263.3	892,810	3,483.2	215,755	841.7	613,131	2,392.1
2012	67,239	258.0	876,059	3,361.8	204,810	785.9	606,253	2,326.4
Percent change	-0.4	-2.0	-1.9	-3.5	-5.1	-6.6	-1.1	-2.7
West [3]								
2011	170,399	234.0	2,062,891	2,832.8	465,834	639.7	1,355,164	1,860.9
2012	175,488	238.5	2,170,446	2,949.8	488,065	663.3	1,415,674	1,924.0
Percent change	3.0	1.9	5.2	4.1	4.8	3.7	4.5	3.4
Mountain [3]								
2011	55,607	248.9	660,023	2,953.7	147,477	660.0	457,278	2,046.4
2012	57,391	253.7	680,071	3,006.8	148,743	657.6	474,961	2,099.9
Percent change	3.2	2.0	3.0	1.8	0.9	-0.4	3.9	2.6
Arizona								
2011	16,748	259.0	229,896	3,554.7	54,695	845.7	155,400	2,402.9
2012	18,087	276.0	231,930	3,539.2	52,934	807.8	159,838	2,439.1
Percent change	8.0	6.6	0.9	-0.4	-3.2	-4.5	2.9	1.5
Colorado								
2011	10,346	202.2	132,781	2,595.3	25,725	502.8	96,054	1,877.4
2012	10,353	199.6	139,270	2,684.7	26,157	504.2	101,021	1,947.4
Percent change	0.1	-1.3	4.9	3.4	1.7	0.3	5.2	3.7
Idaho								
2011	2,535	160.1	32,875	2,075.8	6,915	436.6	24,629	1,555.1
2012	2,567	160.9	31,651	1,983.5	7,186	450.3	23,101	1,447.7
Percent change	1.3	0.5	-3.7	-4.4	3.9	3.1	-6.2	-6.9
Montana[3]								
2011	2,189	219.4	23,885	2,394.1	3,347	335.5	19,089	1,913.4
2012	2,139	212.8	25,970	2,583.7	3,894	387.4	20,387	2,028.3
Percent change	-2.3	-3.0	8.7	7.9	16.3	15.5	6.8	6.0
Nevada								
2011	10,092	371.0	70,075	2,576.3	20,342	747.9	40,156	1,476.3
2012	10,790	391.1	77,510	2,809.4	22,120	801.8	45,372	1,644.6
Percent change	6.9	5.4	10.6	9.1	8.7	7.2	13.0	11.4
New Mexico								
2011	9,170	441.1	73,549	3,538.3	21,419	1,030.4	46,730	2,248.1
2012	8,740	419.1	75,094	3,600.7	21,384	1,025.3	48,247	2,313.4
Percent change	-4.7	-5.0	2.1	1.8	-0.2	-0.5	3.2	2.9
Utah								
2011	3,517	125.0	84,084	2,987.7	13,170	468.0	64,727	2,299.9
2012	3,783	132.5	85,424	2,991.8	12,943	453.3	66,482	2,328.4
Percent change	7.6	6.0	1.6	0.1	-1.7	-3.1	2.7	1.2
Wyoming								
2011	1,010	178.0	12,878	2,269.8	1,864	328.5	10,493	1,849.5
2012	932	161.7	13,222	2,293.8	2,125	368.7	10,513	1,823.9
Percent change	-7.7	-9.2	2.7	1.1	14.0	12.2	0.2	-1.4
Pacific								
2011	114,792	227.4	1,402,868	2,779.2	318,357	630.7	897,886	1,778.8
2012	118,097	231.7	1,490,375	2,924.5	339,322	665.8	940,713	1,845.9
Percent change	2.9	1.9	6.2	5.2	6.6	5.6	4.8	3.8
Alaska								
2011	3,374	466.1	19,094	2,637.8	2,852	394.0	14,854	2,052.1
2012	3,169	433.2	20,037	2,739.4	2,950	403.3	15,565	2,128.0
Percent change	-6.1	-7.1	4.9	3.8	3.4	2.4	4.8	3.7
California								
2011	91,195	242.0	973,822	2,584.2	230,075	610.5	596,905	1,584.0
2012	94,702	248.9	1,049,465	2,758.7	245,767	646.1	635,090	1,669.5
Percent change	3.8	2.9	7.8	6.8	6.8	5.8	6.4	5.4
Hawaii								
2011	2,098	152.2	43,874	3,183.6	8,165	592.5	31,240	2,266.8

Table 4. Crime, by Region, Geographic Division, and State, 2011–2012— continued

(Number, rate per 100,000 population, percent)

Area	Aggravated assault		Property crime		Burglary		Larceny-theft	
	Number	Rate	Number	Rate	Number	Rate	Number	Rate
2012	1,976	141.9	42,817	3,075.2	7,979	573.1	31,233	2,243.2
Percent change	-5.8	-6.8	-2.4	-3.4	-2.3	-3.3	*	-1.0
Oregon[2]								
2011	6,083	157.3	121,869	3,150.5	20,704	535.2	92,059	2,379.9
2012	6,008	154.1	125,723	3,224.2	21,901	561.7	93,619	2,400.9
Percent change	-1.2	-2.0	3.2	2.3	5.8	4.9	1.7	0.9
Washington								
2011	12,042	176.5	244,209	3,579.1	56,561	828.9	162,828	2,386.4
2012	12,242	177.5	252,333	3,658.6	60,725	880.5	165,206	2,395.3
Percent change	1.7	0.6	3.3	2.2	7.4	6.2	1.5	0.4

Note: Although arson data are included in the trend and clearance tables, sufficient data are not available to estimate totals for this offense. Therefore, no arson data are published in this table. * = Less than one-tenth of 1 percent. 1 Populations are U.S. Census Bureau provisional estimates as of July 1, 2012. 2 The crime figures have been adjusted. 3 Because of changes in the state's reporting practices, figures are not comparable to previous years' data. 4 The data collection methodology for the offense of forcible rape used by the Minnesota state Uniform Crime Reporting (UCR) Program (with the exception of Minneapolis and St. Paul, Minnesota) does not comply with national UCR Program guidelines. Consequently, its figures for forcible rape and violent crime (of which forcible rape is a part) are not published in this table. 5 Includes offenses reported by the Zoological Police and the Metro Transit Police.

Table 5. Crime, by State and Area, 2012

(Number, percent, rate per 100,000 population)

Area	Population	Violent crime	Murder and nonnegligent manslaughter	Forcible rape	Robbery	Aggravated assault	Property crime	Burglary	Larceny-theft	Motor vehicle theft
Alabama										
Metropolitan statistical area	3,650,288									
Area actually reporting	98.9%	16,842	283	981	4,517	11,061	133,153	37,131	88,221	7,801
Estimated total	100.0%	17,034	285	990	4,562	11,197	134,817	37,524	89,402	7,891
Cities outside metropolitan areas	530,240									
Area actually reporting	94.1%	2,813	28	177	364	2,244	22,441	5,530	15,765	1,146
Estimated total	100.0%	2,972	30	186	380	2,376	23,541	5,817	16,518	1,206
Nonmetropolitan counties	641,495									
Area actually reporting	99.2%	1,674	27	119	77	1,451	10,438	4,108	5,559	771
Estimated total	100.0%	1,687	27	120	78	1,462	10,520	4,140	5,603	777
State total	4,822,023	21,693	342	1,296	5,020	15,035	168,878	47,481	111,523	9,874
Rate per 100,000 inhabitants		449.9	7.1	26.9	104.1	311.8	3502.2	984.7	2312.8	204.8
Alaska										
Metropolitan statistical area	348,132									
Area actually reporting	100.0%	2,726	18	336	535	1,837	12,893	1,384	10,518	991
Cities outside metropolitan areas	127,551									
Area actually reporting	96.5%	699	4	103	56	536	3,645	422	2,979	244
Estimated total	100.0%	724	4	107	58	555	3,777	437	3,087	253
Nonmetropolitan counties	255,766									
Area actually reporting	100.0%	962	8	140	37	777	3,367	1,129	1,960	278
State total	731,449	4,412	30	583	630	3,169	20,037	2,950	15,565	1,522
Rate per 100,000 inhabitants		603.2	4.1	79.7	86.1	433.2	2739.4	403.3	2128.0	208.1
Arizona										
Metropolitan statistical area	6,202,680									
Area actually reporting	99.8%	25,286	324	1,733	7,251	15,978	219,952	49,185	153,015	17,752
Estimated total	100.0%	25,312	324	1,735	7,257	15,996	220,275	49,249	153,254	17,772
Cities outside metropolitan areas	125,367									
Area actually reporting	78.9%	1,909	25	417	88	1,379	7,424	2,259	4,199	966
Estimated total	100.0%	2,418	32	528	111	1,747	9,405	2,862	5,319	1,224
Nonmetropolitan counties	225,208									
Area actually reporting	100.0%	378	2	14	18	344	2,250	823	1,265	162
State total	6,553,255	28,108	358	2,277	7,386	18,087	231,930	52,934	159,838	19,158
Rate per 100,000 inhabitants		428.9	5.5	34.7	112.7	276.0	3539.2	807.8	2439.1	292.3
Arkansas										
Metropolitan statistical area	1,782,720									
Area actually reporting	92.5%	9,710	118	801	1,894	6,897	71,252	19,357	48,012	3,883
Estimated total	100.0%	10,163	122	853	1,913	7,275	73,787	20,322	49,371	4,094
Cities outside metropolitan areas	510,920									
Area actually reporting	98.7%	2,273	33	231	342	1,667	21,509	7,274	13,549	686
Estimated total	100.0%	2,303	33	234	347	1,689	21,796	7,371	13,730	695
Nonmetropolitan counties	655,491									
Area actually reporting	89.0%	1,217	16	142	53	1,006	10,995	3,734	6,429	832
Estimated total	100.0%	1,369	18	160	60	1,131	12,358	4,197	7,226	935
State total	2,949,131	13,835	173	1,247	2,320	10,095	107,941	31,890	70,327	5,724
Rate per 100,000 inhabitants		469.1	5.9	42.3	78.7	342.3	3,660.1	1,081.3	2,384.7	194.1
California										
Metropolitan statistical area	37,191,572									
Area actually reporting	99.9%	157,689	1,852	7,562	56,074	92,201	1,028,710	239,283	622,803	166,624

Table 5. Crime, by State and Area, 2012— continued

(Number, percent, rate per 100,000 population)

Area	Population	Violent crime	Murder and nonnegligent manslaughter	Forcible rape	Robbery	Aggravated assault	Property crime	Burglary	Larceny-theft	Motor vehicle theft
Estimated total	100.0%	157,749	1,852	7,565	56,094	92,238	1,029,164	239,392	623,083	166,689
Cities outside metropolitan areas	277,160									
Area actually reporting	100.0%	1,573	9	118	268	1,178	10,573	2,727	7,078	768
Nonmetropolitan counties	572,698									
Area actually reporting	100.0%	1,622	23	154	159	1,286	9,728	3,648	4,929	1,151
State total	38,041,430	160,944	1,884	7,837	56,521	94,702	1,049,465	245,767	635,090	168,608
Rate per 100,000 inhabitants		423.1	5.0	20.6	148.6	248.9	2,758.7	646.1	1,669.5	443.2
Colorado										
Metropolitan statistical area	4,492,292									
Area actually reporting	99.2%	14,734	145	1,936	3,297	9,356	126,058	23,715	90,810	11,533
Estimated total	100.0%	14,813	145	1,948	3,309	9,411	127,022	23,859	91,563	11,600
Cities outside metropolitan areas	329,576									
Area actually reporting	91.4%	723	7	104	72	540	8,366	1,278	6,801	287
Estimated total	100.0%	792	8	114	79	591	9,152	1,398	7,440	314
Nonmetropolitan counties	365,714									
Area actually reporting	88.7%	370	8	45	6	311	2,745	798	1,789	158
Estimated total	100.0%	418	9	51	7	351	3,096	900	2,018	178
State total	5,187,582	16,023	162	2,113	3,395	10,353	139,270	26,157	101,021	12,092
Rate per 100,000 inhabitants		308.9	3.1	40.7	65.4	199.6	2,684.7	504.2	1,947.4	233.1
Connecticut										
Metropolitan statistical area	2,933,569									
Area actually reporting	100.0%	9,680	108	828	3,609	5,135	69,896	13,021	50,840	6,035
Cities outside metropolitan areas	118,014									
Area actually reporting	100.0%	124	2	37	19	66	2,326	378	1,848	100
Nonmetropolitan counties	538,764									
Area actually reporting	100.0%	356	36	54	59	207	4,612	1,312	2,986	314
State total	3,590,347	10,160	146	919	3,687	5,408	76,834	14,711	55,674	6,449
Rate per 100,000 inhabitants		283.0	4.1	25.6	102.7	150.6	2,140.0	409.7	1,550.7	179.6
Delaware										
Metropolitan statistical area	917,092									
Area actually reporting	100.0%	5,020.0	57.0	243.0	1,492.0	3,228.0	30,639.0	7,371.0	21,832.0	1,436.0
Cities outside metropolitan areas	None									
Area actually reporting	None									
State total	917,092	5,020.0	57.0	243.0	1,492.0	3,228.0	30,639.0	7,371.0	21,832.0	1,436.0
Rate per 100,000 inhabitants		547.4	6.2	26.5	162.7	352.0	3,340.9	803.7	2,380.6	156.6
District of Columbia [1]										
Metropolitan statistical area	632,323									
Area actually reporting	100.0%	7,864	88	236	4,036	3,504	30,736	3,519	23,556	3,661
Cities outside metropolitan areas	None									
Nonmetropolitan counties	None									
District total	632,323	7,864	88	236	4,036	3,504	30,736	3,519	23,556	3,661
Rate per 100,000 inhabitants		1243.7	13.9	37.3	638.3	554.1	4860.8	556.5	3725.3	579.0
Florida										
Metropolitan statistical area	18,601,449									
Area actually reporting	99.9%	90,584	986	5,012	23,480	61,106	613,039	146,949	429,515	36,575
Estimated total	100.0%	90,694	986	5,017	23,513	61,178	613,951	147,151	430,173	36,627

Table 5. Crime, by State and Area, 2012— continued

(Number, percent, rate per 100,000 population)

Area	Population	Violent crime	Murder and nonnegligent manslaughter	Forcible rape	Robbery	Aggravated assault	Property crime	Burglary	Larceny-theft	Motor vehicle theft
Cities outside metropolitan areas	146,081									
Area actually reporting	98.5%	1,066	7	60	189	810	6,429	1,710	4,514	205
Estimated total	100.0%	1,082	7	61	192	822	6,526	1,736	4,582	208
Nonmetropolitan counties	570,038									
Area actually reporting	100.0%	2,311	16	182	184	1,929	12,511	4,676	7,340	495
State total	19,317,568	94,087	1,009	5,260	23,889	63,929	632,988	153,563	442,095	37,330
Rate per 100,000 inhabitants		487.1	5.2	27.2	123.7	330.9	3,276.7	794.9	2,288.6	193.2
Georgia										
Metropolitan statistical area	8,122,687									
Area actually reporting	99.5%	31,515	492	1,712	11,396	17,915	281,144	71,871	182,887	26,386
Estimated total	100.0%	31,675	492	1,721	11,453	18,009	282,825	72,230	184,075	26,520
Cities outside metropolitan areas	663,946									
Area actually reporting	92.6%	3,180	37	215	750	2,178	29,697	7,137	21,745	815
Estimated total	100.0%	3,434	40	232	810	2,352	32,074	7,708	23,486	880
Nonmetropolitan counties	1,133,312									
Area actually reporting	96.2%	2,388	47	165	192	1,984	22,544	6,592	14,859	1,093
Estimated total	100.0%	2,482	49	171	200	2,062	23,430	6,851	15,443	1,136
State total	9,919,945	37,591	581	2,124	12,463	22,423	338,329	86,789	223,004	28,536
Rate per 100,000 inhabitants		378.9	5.9	21.4	125.6	226.0	3,410.6	874.9	2,248.0	287.7
Hawaii										
Metropolitan statistical area	1,134,635									
Area actually reporting	100.00%	2,675	25	204	939	1,507	34,679	6,039	25,607	3,033
Cities outside metropolitan areas	None									
Nonmetropolitan counties	257,678									
Area actually reporting	100.00%	655	4	81	101	469	8,138	1,940	5,626	572
State total	1392313.0	3,330	29	285	1,040	1,976	42,817	7,979	31,233	3,605
Rate per 100,000 inhabitants		239.2	2.1	20.5	74.7	141.9	3075.2	573.1	2243.2	258.9
Idaho										
Metropolitan statistical area	1,046,821									
Area actually reporting	99.9%	2,241	11	319	189	1,722	23,187	4,920	17,332	935
Estimated total	100.0%	2,242	11	319	189	1,723	23,198	4,922	17,341	935
Cities outside metropolitan areas	249,143									
Area actually reporting	100.0%	679	6	94	47	532	5,316	1,191	3,905	220
Nonmetropolitan counties	299764.0									
Area actually reporting	100.0%	397	12	66	7	312	3137	1073	1855	209
State total	1595728.0	3,318	29	479	243	2,567	31,651	7,186	23,101	1,364
Rate per 100,000 inhabitants		207.9	1.8	30.0	15.2	160.9	1983.5	450.3	1447.7	85.5
Illinois										
Metropolitan statistical area	11,351,574									
Area actually reporting	96.7%	49,174	718	3,047	19,031	26,378	296,052	62,951	208,470	24,631
Estimated total	100.0%	49,982	726	3,139	19,245	26,872	303,879	64,538	214,378	24,963
Cities outside metropolitan areas	833,251									
Area actually reporting	87.8%	2,323	10	290	182	1,841	18,413	3,761	14,233	419
Estimated total	100.0%	2,644	11	330	207	2,096	20,960	4,281	16,202	477
Nonmetropolitan counties	690,430									
Area actually reporting	94.3%	733	7	95	18	613	6,768	2,153	4,379	236
Estimated total	100.0%	777	7	101	19	650	7,174	2,282	4,642	250
State total	12,875,255	53,403	744	3,570	19,471	29,618	332,013	71,101	235,222	25,690

Table 5. Crime, by State and Area, 2012— continued

(Number, percent, rate per 100,000 population)

Area	Population	Violent crime	Murder and nonnegligent manslaughter	Forcible rape	Robbery	Aggravated assault	Property crime	Burglary	Larceny-theft	Motor vehicle theft
Rate per 100,000 inhabitants		414.8	5.8	27.7	151.2	230.0	2578.7	552.2	1826.9	199.5
Indiana										
Metropolitan statistical area	5,054,644									
Area actually reporting	89.5%	19,898	267	1,322	6,228	12,081	158,421	38,510	108,199	11,712
Estimated total	100.0%	20,537	275	1,396	6,323	12,543	167,343	40,612	114,459	12,272
Cities outside metropolitan areas	524,374									
Area actually reporting	86.2%	1,015	10	140	184	681	17,092	3,082	13,224	786
Estimated total	100.0%	1,177	12	162	213	790	19,832	3,576	15,344	912
Nonmetropolitan counties	958,316									
Area actually reporting	78.6%	699	18	86	49	546	8,538	2,693	5,470	375
Estimated total	100.0%	888	23	109	62	694	10,857	3,424	6,956	477
State total	6,537,334	22,602	310	1,667	6,598	14,027	198,032	47,612	136,759	13,661
Rate per 100,000 inhabitants		345.7	4.7	25.5	100.9	214.6	3029.2	728.3	2092.0	209.0
Iowa										
Metropolitan statistical area	1,773,013									
Area actually reporting	98.4%	5,356	31	625	829	3,871	48,220	11,157	34,135	2,928
Estimated total	100.0%	5,394	31	631	830	3,902	48,560	11,259	34,349	2,952
Cities outside metropolitan areas	604,442									
Area actually reporting	89.7%	1,799	11	167	110	1,511	14,660	3,600	10,434	626
Estimated total	100.0%	2,005	12	186	123	1,684	16,339	4,012	11,629	698
Nonmetropolitan counties	696,731									
Area actually reporting	86.0%	613	2	46	8	557	4,249	1,570	2,358	321
Estimated total	100.0%	713	2	54	9	648	4,940	1,825	2,742	373
State total	3,074,186	8,112	45	871	962	6,234	69,839	17,096	48,720	4,023
Rate per 100,000 inhabitants		263.9	1.5	28.3	31.3	202.8	2,271.8	556.1	1,584.8	130.9
Kansas										
Metropolitan statistical area	1,923,596									
Area actually reporting	99.2%	7,207	67	689	1,297	5,154	63,939	12,207	46,230	5,502
Estimated total	100.0%	7,239	67	693	1,301	5,178	64,300	12,269	46,505	5,526
Cities outside metropolitan areas	620,655									
Area actually reporting	96.1%	2,233	9	277	178	1,769	20,552	4,470	15,223	859
Estimated total	100.0%	2,323	9	288	185	1,841	21,384	4,651	15,839	894
Nonmetropolitan counties	341,654									
Area actually reporting	97.6%	654	8	70	14	562	4,904	1,802	2,753	349
Estimated total	100.0%	670	8	72	14	576	5,026	1,847	2,821	358
State total	2,885,905	10,232	84	1,053	1,500	7,595	90,710	18,767	65,165	6,778
Rate per 100,000 inhabitants		354.6	2.9	36.5	52.0	263.2	3,143.2	650.3	2,258.0	234.9
Kentucky										
Metropolitan statistical area	2,530,495									
Area actually reporting	99.6%	7,289	101	656	2,925	3,607	79,535	18,970	55,714	4,851
Estimated total	100.0%	7,313	101	660	2,937	3,615	79,876	19,048	55,961	4,867
Cities outside metropolitan areas	530,844									
Area actually reporting	95.7%	936	17	146	363	410	16,643	3,617	12,404	622
Estimated total	100.0%	979	18	153	379	429	17,398	3,781	12,967	650
Nonmetropolitan counties	1,319,076									
Area actually reporting	97.4%	1,422	74	447	213	688	14,173	6,582	6,470	1,121
Estimated total	100.0%	1,460	76	459	219	706	14,552	6,758	6,643	1,151
State total	4,380,415	9,752	195	1,272	3,535	4,750	111,826	29,587	75,571	6,668
Rate per 100,000 inhabitants		222.6	4.5	29.0	80.7	108.4	2,552.9	675.4	1,725.2	152.2

Table 5. Crime, by State and Area, 2012— continued

(Number, percent, rate per 100,000 population)

Area	Population	Violent crime	Murder and nonnegligent manslaughter	Forcible rape	Robbery	Aggravated assault	Property crime	Burglary	Larceny-theft	Motor vehicle theft
Louisiana										
Metropolitan statistical area	[illegible]									
Area actually reporting	96.6%	18,739	450	908	4,972	12,409	136,314	35,438	93,929	6,947
Estimated total	100.0%	19,200	456	934	5,059	12,751	140,631	36,395	97,127	7,109
Cities outside metropolitan areas	279,709									
Area actually reporting	77.4%	1,744	17	75	251	1,401	10,168	2,717	7,222	229
Estimated total	100.0%	2,254	22	97	324	1,811	13,140	3,511	9,333	296
Nonmetropolitan counties	498,607									
Area actually reporting	88.5%	1,250	15	112	81	1,042	8,110	1,977	5,712	421
Estimated total	100.0%	1,414	17	127	92	1,178	9,165	2,234	6,455	476
State total	4,601,893	22,868	495	1,158	5,475	15,740	162,936	42,140	112,915	7,881
Rate per 100,000 inhabitants		496.9	10.8	25.2	119.0	342.0	3,540.6	915.7	2,453.7	171.3
Maine										
Metropolitan statistical area	777,579									
Area actually reporting	100.0%	982	15	200	324	443	20,607	4,179	15,819	609
Cities outside metropolitan areas	272,036									
Area actually reporting	100.0%	402	4	114	75	209	8,280	1,683	6,382	215
Nonmetropolitan counties	279,577									
Area actually reporting	100.0%	247	6	58	24	159	4,474	1,599	2,704	171
State total	1,329,192	1,631	25	372	423	811	33,361	7,461	24,905	995
Rate per 100,000 inhabitants		122.7	1.9	28.0	31.8	61.0	2,509.9	561.3	1,873.7	74.9
Maryland										
Metropolitan statistical area	5,729,173									
Area actually reporting	100.0%	27,531	364	1,188	10,040	15,939	158,189	32,580	110,726	14,883
Cities outside metropolitan areas	52,943									
Area actually reporting	100.0%	321	2	31	74	214	1,934	438	1,442	54
Nonmetropolitan counties	102,447									
Area actually reporting	100.0%	203	3	16	27	157	1,908	714	1,106	88
State total	5,884,563	28,055	369	1,235	10,141	16,310	162,031	33,732	113,274	15,025
Rate per 100,000 inhabitants		476.8	6.3	21.0	172.3	277.2	2,753.5	573.2	1,924.9	255.3
Massachusetts										
Metropolitan statistical area	6,546,761									
Area actually reporting	98.0%	26,233	120	1,590	6,432	18,091	138,322	33,264	96,045	9,013
Estimated total	100.0%	26,648	120	1,620	6,516	18,392	140,839	33,874	97,803	9,162
Cities outside metropolitan areas	91,869									
Area actually reporting	87.2%	245	1	19	31	194	1,963	581	1,321	61
Estimated total	100.0%	281	1	22	36	222	2250	666	1514	70
Nonmetropolitan counties	7,514									
Area actually reporting	100.0%	24	0	0	0	24	0	0	0	0
State total	6,646,144	26,953	121	1,642	6,552	18,638	143,089	34,540	99,317	9,232
Rate per 100,000 inhabitants		405.5	1.8	24.7	98.6	280.4	2,153.0	519.7	1,494.4	138.9
Michigan										
Metropolitan statistical area	8,069,120									
Area actually reporting	98.7%	40,674	659	3,365	10,225	26,425	212,949	57,129	132,041	23,779
Estimated total	100.0%	40,963	660	3,398	10,292	26,613	215,518	57,671	133,871	23,976
Cities outside metropolitan areas	609,654									
Area actually reporting	87.0%	1,381	8	376	70	927	15,020	2,244	12,359	417
Estimated total	100.0%	1,587	9	432	80	1,066	17,268	2,580	14,209	479

Table 5. Crime, by State and Area, 2012— continued

(Number, percent, rate per 100,000 population)

Area	Population	Violent crime	Murder and nonnegligent manslaughter	Forcible rape	Robbery	Aggravated assault	Property crime	Burglary	Larceny-theft	Motor vehicle theft
Nonmetropolitan counties	1,204,586									
Area actually reporting	89.8%	2,131	18	682	56	1,375	15,550	4,862	10,095	593
Estimated total	100.0%	2,372	20	759	62	1,531	17,315	5,414	11,241	660
State total	9,883,360	44,922	689	4,589	10,434	29,210	250,101	65,665	159,321	25,115
Rate per 100,000 inhabitants		454.5	7.0	46.4	105.6	295.5	2,530.5	664.4	1,612.0	254.1
Minnesota [2]										
Metropolitan statistical area	4,129,414									
Area actually reporting	100.0%		84		3,360	5,716	113,606	20,487	85,803	7,316
Cities outside metropolitan areas	491,959									
Area actually reporting	100.0%		5		95	996	15,178	2,300	12,291	587
Nonmetropolitan counties	757,766									
Area actually reporting	100.0%		10		20	495	9,368	2,591	6,222	555
State total	5,379,139	12,419	99	1,638	3,475	7,207	138,152	25,378	104,316	8,458
Rate per 100,000 inhabitants		230.9	1.8	30.5	64.6	134.0	2568.3	471.8	1939.3	157.2
Mississippi										
Metropolitan statistical area	1,346,110									
Area actually reporting	87.3%	3,582	105	398	1,374	1,705	39,268	11,667	25,114	2,487
Estimated total	100.0%	3,803	111	429	1,421	1,842	42,480	12,719	27,092	2,669
Cities outside metropolitan areas	589,064									
Area actually reporting	77.5%	1,753	43	186	544	980	20,580	6,820	13,051	709
Estimated total	100.0%	2,261	55	240	702	1,264	26,539	8,795	16,830	914
Nonmetropolitan counties	1,049,752									
Area actually reporting	54.1%	932	29	83	87	733	8,058	3,552	4,106	400
Estimated total	100.0%	1,722	54	153	161	1,354	14,887	6,562	7,586	739
State total	2,984,926	7,786	220	822	2,284	4,460	83,906	28,076	51,508	4,322
Rate per 100,000 inhabitants		260.8	7.4	27.5	76.5	149.4	2,811.0	940.6	1,725.6	144.8
Missouri										
Metropolitan statistical area	4,459,490									
Area actually reporting	99.9%	22,444	366	1,236	5,480	15,362	158,787	32,998	111,426	14,363
Cities outside metropolitan areas	100.0%	22,415	336	1,236	5,480	15,363	158,804	33,001	111,439	14,364
Area actually reporting	663,032									
Estimated total	99.8%	2,799	14	147	246	2,392	26,657	4,628	21,053	976
Nonmetropolitan counties	100.0%	2,805	14	147	247	2,397	26,718	4,639	21,101	978
Area actually reporting	899,466									
Estimated total	100.0%	1,935	39	128	55	1,713	14,068	4,826	8,276	966
State total	6,021,988	27,155	389	1,511	5,782	19,473	199,590	42,466	140,816	16,308
Rate per 100,000 inhabitants		450.9	6.5	25.1	96.0	323.4	3,314.4	705.2	2,338.4	270.8
Montana										
Metropolitan statistical area	355,392									
Area actually reporting	100.0%	971	3	100	133	735	12,486	1,851	9,838	797
Cities outside metropolitan areas	203,868									
Area actually reporting	97.5%	894	11	180	39	664	7,149	935	5,795	419
Estimated total	100.0%	917	11	185	40	681	7,335	959	5,946	430
Nonmetropolitan counties	445,881									
Area actually reporting	98.8%	838	13	93	18	714	6,074	1,071	4,547	456
Estimated total	100.0%	848	13	94	18	723	6,149	1,084	4,603	462
State total	1,005,141	2,736	27	379	191	2,139	25,970	3,894	20,387	1,689
Rate per 100,000 inhabitants		272.2	2.7	37.7	19.0	212.8	2,583.7	387.4	2,028.3	168.0

Table 5. Crime, by State and Area, 2012— continued

(Number, percent, rate per 100,000 population)

Area	Population	Violent crime	Murder and nonnegligent manslaughter	Forcible rape	Robbery	Aggravated assault	Property crime	Burglary	Larceny-theft	Motor vehicle theft
Nebraska										
Metropolitan statistical area	1,177,981									
Area actually reporting	97.9%	4,028	46	494	1,077	2,411	38,218	6,183	28,160	3,605
Estimated total	100.0%	4,044	46	498	1,078	2,422	38,569	6,551	28,391	3,627
Cities outside metropolitan areas	343,307									
Area actually reporting	88.9%	532	3	157	40	332	8,423	1,324	6,784	315
Estimated total	100.0%	599	3	177	45	374	9,477	1,490	7,633	354
Nonmetropolitan counties	334,237									
Area actually reporting	81.4%	139	3	29	6	101	2,501	565	1,801	135
Estimated total	100.0%	171	4	36	7	124	3,072	694	2,212	166
State total	1,855,525	4,814	53	711	1,130	2,920	51,118	8,735	38,236	4,147
Rate per 100,000 inhabitants		259.4	2.9	38.3	60.9	157.4	2,754.9	470.8	2,060.7	223.5
Nevada										
Metropolitan statistical area	2,487,122									
Area actually reporting	100.0%	15,754	107	824	4,852	9,971	71,770	20,521	41,708	9,541
Cities outside metropolitan areas	46,956									
Area actually reporting	100.0%	305	12	39	19	235	1,815	469	1,187	159
Nonmetropolitan counties	224,853									
Area actually reporting	100.0%	704	5	68	47	584	3,925	1,130	2,477	318
State total	2758931.0	16,763	124	931	4,918	10,790	77,510	22,120	45,372	10,018
Rate per 100,000 inhabitants		607.6	4.5	33.7	178.3	391.1	2809.4	801.8	1644.6	363.1
New Hampshire										
Metropolitan statistical area	823,334									
Area actually reporting	94.6%	1,571	10	265	360	936	17,792	3,033	14,131	628
Estimated total	100.0%	1,610	10	274	365	961	18,391	3,126	14,617	648
Cities outside metropolitan areas	444,509									
Area actually reporting	87.6%	675	4	143	94	434	9,999	1,763	7,954	282
Estimated total	100.0%	770	5	163	107	495	11,416	2,013	9,081	322
Nonmetropolitan counties	52,875									
Area actually reporting)	4.4%	20	0	2	0	18	102	36	62	4
Estimated total	100.0%	101	0	12	0	89	886	305	528	53
State total	1,320,718	2,481	15	449	472	1,545	30,693	5,444	24,226	1,023
Rate per 100,000 inhabitants		187.9	1.1	34.0	35.7	117.0	2,324.0	412.2	1,834.3	77.5
New Jersey										
Metropolitan statistical area	8,864,590									
Area actually reporting	99.9%	25,707	388	1,034	11,377	12,908	181,293	42,296	122,529	16,468
Estimated total	100.0%	25727	388	1035	11385	12919	181481	42338	122662	16481
Cities outside metropolitan areas	None									
Nonmetropolitan counties	None									
State total	8,864,590	25,727	388	1,035	11,385	12,919	181,481	42,338	122,662	16,481
Rate per 100,000 inhabitants		290.2	4.4	11.7	128.4	145.7	2,047.3	477.6	1,383.7	185.9
New Mexico										
Metropolitan statistical area	1,388,294									
Area actually reporting	99.3%	7,858	72	621	1,507	5,658	52,207	14,091	33,866	4,250
Estimated total	100.0%	7,906	72	625	1,511	5,698	52,507	14,161	34,072	4,274
Cities outside metropolitan areas	397,656									
Area actually reporting	99.0%	2,941	36	265	282	2,358	17,422	4,810	11,835	777
Estimated total	100.0%	2,970	36	268	285	2,381	17,589	4,856	11,949	784

Table 5. Crime, by State and Area, 2012— continued

(Number, percent, rate per 100,000 population)

Area	Population	Violent crime	Murder and nonnegligent manslaughter	Forcible rape	Robbery	Aggravated assault	Property crime	Burglary	Larceny-theft	Motor vehicle theft
Nonmetropolitan counties	299,588									
Area actually reporting	84.0%	659	7	54	43	555	4,197	1,988	1,869	340
Estimated total	100.0%	784	8	64	51	661	4,998	2,367	2,226	405
State total	2,085,538	11,660.0	116.0	957.0	1,847.0	8,740.0	75,094.0	21,384.0	48,247.0	5,463.0
		559.1	5.6	45.9	88.6	419.1	3,600.7	1,025.3	2,313.4	261.9
New York [3]										
Metropolitan statistical area	18,146,686									
Area actually reporting	99.2%	77,229	666	2,518	28,297	45,748	344,885	57,785	270,535	16,565
Estimated total	100.0%	77,445	668	2,533	28,361	45,883	347,280	58,219	272,403	16,658
Cities outside metropolitan areas	528,831									
Area actually reporting	97.5%	1,194	4	144	215	831	15,505	2,910	12,298	297
Estimated total	100.0%	1,224	4	148	220	852	15,894	2,983	12,607	304
Nonmetropolitan counties	894,744									
Area actually reporting	100.0%	941	12	167	74	688	12,966	3,351	9,229	386
State total	19570261.0	79,610	684	2,848	28,655	47,423	376,140	64,553	294,239	17,348
Rate per 100,000 inhabitants		406.8	3.5	14.6	146.4	242.3	1922.0	329.9	1503.5	88.6
North Carolina										
Metropolitan statistical area	7,523,905									
Area actually reporting	99.2%	26,943	329	1,513	7,833	17,268	252,494	72,337	167,235	12,922
Estimated total	100.0%	27,088	329	1,522	7,868	17,369	254,349	72,825	168,531	12,993
Cities outside metropolitan areas	642,467									
Area actually reporting	91.8%	3,642	59	179	934	2,470	33,453	9,006	23,277	1,170
Estimated total	100.0%	3,966	64	195	1,017	2,690	36,434	9,809	25,351	1,274
Nonmetropolitan counties	1,585,701									
Area actually reporting	97.7%	3,330	84	261	495	2,490	36,926	16,298	18,818	1,810
Estimated total	100.0%	3,410	86	267	507	2,550	37,811	16,689	19,269	1,853
State total	9,752,073	34,464	479	1,984	9,392	22,609	328,594	99,323	213,151	16,120
Rate per 100,000 inhabitants		353.4	4.9	20.3	96.3	231.8	3,369.5	1,018.5	2,185.7	165.3
North Dakota										
Metropolitan statistical area	343,667									
Area actually reporting	100.0%	1,063	6	164	105	788	8,129	1388	6244	497
Cities outside metropolitan areas	161,463									
Area actually reporting	94.1%	452	13	79	20	340	3,861	527	2,938	396
Estimated total	100.0%	480	14	84	21	361	4,104	560	3,123	421
Nonmetropolitan counties	194,498									
Area actually reporting	99.4%	168	8	24	5	131	1,819	426	1,161	232
Estimated total	100.0%	169	8	24	5	132	1,830	429	1,168	233
State total	699,628	1,712	28	272	131	1,281	14,063	2,377	10,535	1,151
Rate per 100,000 inhabitants		244.7	4.0	38.9	18.7	183.1	2010.1	339.8	1505.8	164.5
Ohio										
Metropolitan statistical area	9,153,765									
Area actually reporting	93.4%	30,974	446	3,052	14,314	13,162	284,666	84,284	183,037	17,345
Estimated total	100.0%	31,824	454	3,183	14,629	13,558	300,466	87,578	195,002	17,886
Cities outside metropolitan areas	1,039,632									
Area actually reporting	80.0%	1,302	12	233	368	689	30,130	6,707	22,769	654
Estimated total	100.0%	1,627	15	291	460	861	37,668	8,385	28,465	818
Nonmetropolitan counties	1,350,828									
Area actually reporting	97.6%	1,116	25	180	142	769	21,225	7,278	13,158	789
Estimated total	100.0%	1,144	26	184	146	788	21,749	7,458	13,483	808
State total	11,544,225	34,595	495	3,658	15,235	15,207	359,883	103,421	236,950	19,512

Table 5. Crime, by State and Area, 2012— continued

(Number, percent, rate per 100,000 population)

Area	Population	Violent crime	Murder and nonnegligent manslaughter	Forcible rape	Robbery	Aggravated assault	Property crime	Burglary	Larceny-theft	Motor vehicle theft
Rate per 100,000 inhabitants		299.7	4.3	31.7	132.0	131.7	3,117.4	895.9	2,052.5	169.0
Oklahoma										
Metropolitan statistical area	2,465,038									
Area actually reporting	100.0%	13,374	171	1,124	2,858	9,221	94,951	26,135	59,466	9,350
Cities outside metropolitan areas	722,935									
Area actually reporting	99.9%	3,541	25	348	334	2,834	26,958	6,760	18,703	1,495
Estimated total	100.0%	3,544	25	348	334	2,837	26,989	6,768	18,724	1,497
Nonmetropolitan counties	626,847									
Area actually reporting	100.0%	984	20	116	39	809	7,803	2,828	4,258	717
State total	3,814,820	17,902	216	1,588	3,231	12,867	129,743	35,731	82,448	11,564
Rate per 100,000 inhabitants		469.3	5.7	41.6	84.7	337.3	3,401.0	936.6	2,161.3	303.1
Oregon										
Metropolitan statistical area	3,241,382									
Area actually reporting	99.9%	8,356	73	965	2,216	5,102	106,863	17,850	79,987	9,026
Estimated total	100.0%	8,363	73	966	2,218	5,106	106,966	17,866	80,066	9,034
Cities outside metropolitan areas	306,270									
Area actually reporting	89.2%	837	12	107	143	575	11,997	2,247	9,115	635
Estimated total	100.0%	938	13	120	160	645	13,451	2,519	10,220	712
Nonmetropolitan counties	351,701									
Area actually reporting	98.4%	346	6	53	34	253	5,221	1,492	3,279	450
Estimated total	100.0%	352	6	54	35	257	5,306	1,516	3,333	457
State total	3,899,353	9,653	92	1,140	2,413	6,008	125,723	21,901	93,619	10,203
Rate per 100,000 inhabitants		247.6	2.4	29.2	61.9	154.1	3,224.2	561.7	2,400.9	261.7
Pennsylvania										
Metropolitan statistical area	11,253,278									
Area actually reporting	99.4%	41,344	648	2,800	15,353	22,543	250,881	50,686	186,047	14,148
Estimated total	100.0%	41,463	649	2,807	15,387	22,620	252,060	50,881	186,992	14,187
Cities outside metropolitan areas	684,242									
Area actually reporting	97.2%	1,835	7	127	171	1,530	12,595	2,200	10,096	299
Estimated total	100.0%	1,888	7	131	176	1,574	12,956	2,263	10,385	308
Nonmetropolitan counties	826,016									
Area actually reporting	100.0%	1,152	29	389	110	624	11,480	3,715	7,232	533
State total	12,763,536	44,503	685	3,327	15,673	24,818	276,496	56,859	204,609	15,028
Rate per 100,000 inhabitants		348.7	5.4	26.1	122.8	194.4	2,166.3	445.5	1,603.1	117.7
Rhode Island										
Metropolitan statistical area	1,050,292									
Area actually reporting	100.0%	2,628	32	281	713	1,602	26,928	5,947	18,419	2,562
Cities outside metropolitan areas	None									
Nonmetropolitan counties	None									
Area actually reporting	100.0%	23	2	7	0	14	89	2	21	66
State total	1,050,292	2,651	34	288	713	1,616	27,017	5,949	18,440	2,628
Rate per 100,000 inhabitants		252.4	3.2	27.4	67.9	153.9	2,572.3	566.4	1,755.7	250.2
South Carolina										
Metropolitan statistical area	3,956,484									
Area actually reporting	99.8%	21,468	260	1,423	3,852	15,933	149,317	35,981	102,169	11,167
Estimated total	100.0%	21,497	260	1,425	3,857	15,955	149,576	36,027	102,369	11,180
Cities outside metropolitan areas	211,649									

Table 5. Crime, by State and Area, 2012— continued

(Number, percent, rate per 100,000 population)

Area	Population	Violent crime	Murder and nonnegligent manslaughter	Forcible rape	Robbery	Aggravated assault	Property crime	Burglary	Larceny-theft	Motor vehicle theft
Area actually reporting	98.0%	2,193	20	92	379	1,702	12,872	3,389	8,985	498
Estimated total	100.0%	2,238	20	94	387	1,737	13,138	3,459	9,171	508
Nonmetropolitan counties	555,590									
Area actually reporting	100.0%	2,662	44	160	245	2,213	17,836	5,600	10,723	1,513
State total	4,723,723	26,397	324	1,679	4,489	19,905	180,550	45,086	122,263	13,201
Rate per 100,000 inhabitants		558.8	6.9	35.5	95.0	421.4	3,822.2	954.5	2,588.3	279.5
South Dakota										
Metropolitan statistical area	388,098									
Area actually reporting	99.3%	1,248	6	300	125	817	10,297	1,901	7,776	620
Estimated total	100.0%	1,252	6	301	125	820	10,336	1,906	7,808	622
Cities outside metropolitan areas	219,788									
Area actually reporting	77.7%	1,179	10	232	28	909	5,231	956	3,948	327
Estimated total	100.0%	1,238	11	244	29	954	5,492	1,004	4,145	343
Nonmetropolitan counties	225,468									
Area actually reporting	77.7%	149	6	31	3	109	1,041	270	693	78
Estimated total	100.0%	192	8	40	4	140	1,340	348	892	100
State total	833,354	2,682	25	585	158	1,914	17,168	3,258	12,845	1,065
Rate per 100,000 inhabitants		321.8	3.0	70.2	19.0	229.7	2,060.1	391.0	1,541.4	127.8
Tennessee										
Metropolitan statistical area	4,953,032									
Area actually reporting	100.0%	35,306	327	1,701	7,678	25,600	175,516	44,094	120,691	10,731
Cities outside metropolitan areas	516,983									
Area actually reporting	100.0%	3,261	17	185	360	2,699	23,311	5,195	17,271	845
Nonmetropolitan counties	986,228									
Area actually reporting	100.0%	2,983	44	146	131	2,662	18,837	6,892	10,541	1,404
State total	6,456,243	41,550	388	2,032	8,169	30,961	217,664	56,181	148,503	12,980
Rate per 100,000 inhabitants		643.6	6.0	31.5	126.5	479.6	3,371.4	870.2	2,300.1	201.0
Texas										
Metropolitan statistical area	22,993,976									
Area actually reporting	99.9%	97,603	1,016	6,791	29,625	60,171	805,325	184,006	559,621	61,698
Estimated total	100.0%	97,633	1,016	6,794	29,632	60,191	805,678	184,076	559,884	61,718
Cities outside metropolitan areas	1,427,466									
Area actually reporting	99.0%	5,747	58	583	605	4,501	45,308	11,193	32,545	1,570
Estimated total	100.0%	5,796	59	588	608	4,541	45,684	11,288	32,817	1,579
Nonmetropolitan counties	1,637,761									
Area actually reporting	98.3%	2,995	68	323	140	2,464	24,276	9,285	13,321	1,670
Estimated total	100.0%	3,047	69	329	142	2,507	24,697	9,446	13,552	1,699
State total	26,059,203	106,476	1,144	7,711	30,382	67,239	876,059	204,810	606,253	64,996
Rate per 100,000 inhabitants		408.6	4.4	29.6	116.6	258.0	3,361.8	785.9	2,326.4	249.4
Utah										
Metropolitan statistical area	2,545,653									
Area actually reporting	99.9%	5,226	36	833	1,071	3,286	78,305	11,682	60,984	5,639
Estimated total	100.0%	5,231	36	834	1,072	3,289	78,406	11,697	61,064	5,645
Cities outside metropolitan areas	135,463									
Area actually reporting	92.2%	297	9	53	19	216	3,677	611	2,913	153
Estimated total	100.0%	322	10	57	21	234	3,986	662	3,158	166
Nonmetropolitan counties	174,171									
Area actually reporting	95.6%	310	4	50	7	249	2,899	558	2,161	180
Estimated total	100.0%	323	4	52	7	260	3,032	584	2,260	188

Table 5. Crime, by State and Area, 2012— continued

(Number, percent, rate per 100,000 population)

Area	Population	Violent crime	Murder and nonnegligent manslaughter	Forcible rape	Robbery	Aggravated assault	Property crime	Burglary	Larceny-theft	Motor vehicle theft
State total	2,855,287	5,876	50	943	1,100	3,783	85,424	12,943	66,482	5,999
Rate per 100,000 inhabitants		205.8	1.8	33.0	38.5	132.5	2,991.8	453.3	2,328.4	210.1
Vermont										
Metropolitan statistical area	212,393									
Area actually reporting	100.0%	344	1	45	51	247	6,035	1,374	4,524	137
Cities outside metropolitan areas	205,469									
Area actually reporting	98.5%	359	3	50	47	259	5,337	1,125	4,065	147
Nonmetropolitan counties	100.0%	365	3	51	48	263	5,417	1,142	4,126	149
Area actually reporting	208,149									
Estimated total	100.0%	184	4	25	13	142	3,564	1,449	1,966	149
State total	626,011	893	8	121	112	652	15,016	3,965	10,616	435
Rate per 100,000 inhabitants		142.6	1.3	19.3	17.9	104.2	2398.7	633.4	1695.8	69.5
Virginia										
Metropolitan statistical area	7,105,199									
Area actually reporting	100.0%	13,912	270	1,247	4,432	7,963	157,319	24,903	124,181	8,235
Cities outside metropolitan areas	267,746									
Area actually reporting	100.0%	614	14	76	145	379	8,592	1,478	6,852	262
Nonmetropolitan counties	812922.0									
Area actually reporting	100.0%	1,038	30	129	129	750	11,074	3,130	7,365	579
State total	8185867.0	15,564	314	1,452	4,706	9,092	176,985	29,511	138,398	9,076
Rate per 100,000 inhabitants		190.1	3.8	17.7	57.5	111.1	2,162.1	360.5	1,690.7	110.9
Washington										
Metropolitan statistical area	6,179,551									
Area actually reporting	100.0%	18,830	180	1,927	5,543	11,180	231,017	54,547	151,575	24,895
Cities outside metropolitan areas	296,203									
Area actually reporting	97.7%	912	11	169	147	585	13,080	3,121	9,084	875
Estimated total	100.0%	934	11	173	151	599	13,394	3,196	9,302	896
Nonmetropolitan counties	421,258									
Area actually reporting	100.0%	622	15	93	51	463	7922	2982	4329	611
State total	6,897,012	20,386	206	2,193	5,745	12,242	252,333	60,725	165,206	26,402
Rate per 100,000 inhabitants		295.6	3.0	31.8	83.3	177.5	3658.6	880.5	2395.3	382.8
West Virginia										
Metropolitan statistical area	1,135,886									
Area actually reporting	93.4%	3,725	43	280	668	2,734	30,063	7,721	20,890	1,452
Estimated total	100.0%	3,929	44	295	698	2,892	32,190	8,152	22,506	1,532
Cities outside metropolitan areas	190,838									
Area actually reporting	77.8%	582	6	32	61	483	3,543	732	2,717	94
Estimated total	100.0%	748	8	41	78	621	4,554	941	3,492	121
Nonmetropolitan counties	528,689									
Area actually reporting	90.7%	1,080	18	77	56	929	6,469	1,993	3,972	504
Estimated total	100.0%	1,192	20	85	62	1,025	7,134	2,198	4,380	556
State total	1,855,413	5,869	72	421	838	4,538	43,878	11,291	30,378	2,209
Rate per 100,000 inhabitants		316.3	3.9	22.7	45.2	244.6	2,364.9	608.5	1,637.3	119.1
Wisconsin										
Metropolitan statistical area	4,213,426									
Area actually reporting	98.8%	14,089	162	950	4,486	8,491	110,111	21,625	81,274	7,212
Estimated total	100.0%	14,151	163	955	4,503	8,530	111,286	21,784	82,261	7,241

Table 5. Crime, by State and Area, 2012— continued

(Number, percent, rate per 100,000 population)

Area	Population	Violent crime	Murder and nonnegligent manslaughter	Forcible rape	Robbery	Aggravated assault	Property crime	Burglary	Larceny-theft	Motor vehicle theft
Cities outside metropolitan areas	636,932									
Area actually reporting	97.1%	1,038	5	127	83	823	18,047	2,495	15,133	419
Estimated total	100.0%	1,068	5	131	85	847	18,581	2,569	15,581	431
Nonmetropolitan counties	876,040									
Area actually reporting	97.3%	822	5	129	33	655	10,358	3,495	6,334	529
Estimated total	100.0%	845	5	133	34	673	10,646	3,592	6,510	544
State total	5,726,398	16,064	173	1,219	4,622	10,050	140,513	27,945	104,352	8,216
Rate per 100,000 inhabitants		280.5	3.0	21.3	80.7	175.5	2,453.8	488.0	1,822.3	143.5
Wyoming										
Metropolitan statistical area	171,501									
Area actually reporting	100.0%	379	5	40	39	295	5,062	899	3,886	277
Cities outside metropolitan areas	242,167									
Area actually reporting	96.5%	567	8	93	12	454	6,422	830	5,375	217
Estimated total	100.0%	586	8	96	12	470	6,652	860	5,567	225
Nonmetropolitan counties	162,744									
Area actually reporting	92.6%	182	1	17	9	155	1,397	339	982	76
Estimated total	100.0%	196	1	18	10	167	1,508	366	1,060	82
State total	576,412	1,161	14	154	61	932	13,222	2,125	10,513	584
Rate per 100,000 inhabitants		201.4	2.4	26.7	10.6	161.7	2,293.8	368.7	1,823.9	101.3

Note: Although arson data are included in the trend and clearance tables, sufficient data are not available to estimate totals for this offense. Therefore, no arson data are published in this table. 1 Includes offenses reported by the Zoological Police and the Metro Transit Police. 2 The data collection methodology for the offense of forcible rape used by the Minnesota state Uniform Crime Reporting (UCR) Program (with the exception of Minneapolis and St. Paul, Minnesota) does not comply with national UCR Program guidelines. Consequently, its figures for forcible rape and violent crime (of which forcible rape is a part) are not published in this table. 3 Because of changes in the state's/local agency's reporting practices, figures are not comparable to previous years' data.

Table 6. Crime, by Selected Metropolitan Statistical Area, 2012

(Number, percent, rate per 100,000 population)

Area	Population	Violent crime	Murder and nonnegligent manslaughter	Forcible rape	Robbery	Aggravated assault	Property crime	Burglary	Larceny-theft	Motor vehicle theft
Abilene, TX M.S.A.	168,908									
Includes Callahan, Jones, and Taylor Counties										
City of Abilene	119,886	472	3	38	127	304	4,393	1,037	3,185	171
Total area actually reporting	100.0%	555	3	45	136	371	5,080	1,245	3,631	204
Rate per 100,000 inhabitants		328.6	1.8	26.6	80.5	219.6	3,007.6	737.1	2,149.7	120.8
Akron, OH M.S.A.	701,412									
Includes Portage and Summit Counties										
City of Akron	198,390	1,759	24	167	577	991	10,034	3,429	5,884	721
Total area actually reporting	91.6%	2,144	26	265	700	1,153	19,709	5,389	13,287	1,033
Estimated total	1.0	2,227	27	278	732	1,190	21,287	5,708	14,492	1,087
Rate per 100,000 inhabitants		317.5	3.8	39.6	104.4	169.7	3,034.9	813.8	2,066.1	155.0
Albany, GA M.S.A.	159,370									
Includes Baker, Dougherty, Lee, Terrell, and Worth Counties										
City of Albany	78,512	813	4	27	224	558	5,001	1,408	3,369	224
Total area actually reporting	97.8%	1,054	9	35	253	757	7,129	2,062	4,741	326
Estimated total	100.0%	1,068	9	36	258	765	7,276	2,090	4,849	337
Rate per 100,000 inhabitants		670.1	5.6	22.6	161.9	480.0	4,565.5	1,311.4	3,042.6	211.5
Albany-Schenectady-Troy, NY M.S.A. [1]	876,182									
Includes Albany, Rensselaer, Saratoga, Schenectady, and Schoharie Counties										
City of Albany[1]	98,187	802	4	43	249	506	4,340	887	3,299	154
City of Schenectady[1]	66,631	626	7	32	199	388	2,828	810	1,876	142
City of Troy[1]	50,391	335	7	15	111	202	2,372	593	1,677	102
Total area actually reporting	99.6%	2,332	23	159	696	1,454	21,517	4,194	16,665	658
Estimated total	100.0%	2,338	23	159	698	1,458	21,586	4,205	16,721	660
Rate per 100,000 inhabitants		266.8	2.6	18.1	79.7	166.4	2,463.6	479.9	1,908.4	75.3
Albuquerque, NM M.S.A. [2]	900,072									
Includes Bernalillo, Sandoval, Torrance, and Valencia[2] Counties										
City of Albuquerque	553,684	4,151	41	278	1,092	2,740	29,718	6,677	20,298	2,743
Total area actually reporting	99.1%	5,769	53	368	1,226	4,122				3,427
Estimated total	100.0%	5,806	53	371	1,229	4,153				3,446
Rate per 100,000 inhabitants		645.1	5.9	41.2	136.5	461.4				382.9
Alexandria, LA M.S.A. [2]	155,419									
Includes Grant and Rapides[2] Parishes										
City of Alexandria	48,449	815	9	14	142	650	3,630	974	2,472	184
Total area actually reporting	94.9%		9	44	169			1,820	4,386	
Estimated total	100.0%		9	46	175			1,879	4,636	
Rate per 100,000 inhabitants			5.8	29.6	112.6			1,209.0	2,982.9	
Allentown-Bethlehem-Easton, PA-NJ M.S.A. [1]	826,611									
Includes Warren County, NJ and Carbon, Lehigh, and Northampton Counties, PA										
City of Allentown, PA[1]	119,334	653	15	54	374	210	4,603	1,248	2,987	368
City of Bethlehem, PA	75,388	238	2	19	121	96	1,948	377	1,488	83
Total area actually reporting	99.3%	1,732	34	155	701	842	18,195	3,507	13,819	869
Estimated total	1.0	1,743	34	156	704	849	18,304	3,525	13,906	873

Table 6. Crime, by Selected Metropolitan Statistical Area, 2012— continued

(Number, percent, rate per 100,000 population)

Area	Population	Violent crime	Murder and nonnegligent manslaughter	Forcible rape	Robbery	Aggravated assault	Property crime	Burglary	Larceny-theft	Motor vehicle theft
Rate per 100,000 inhabitants		210.9	4.1	18.9	85.2	102.7	2,214.3	426.4	1,682.3	105.6
Altoona, PA M.S.A.	127,305									
Includes Blair County										
City of Altoona	46,404	163	2	31	32	98	903	226	641	36
Total area actually reporting	100.0%	321	6	44	38	233	2,113	387	1,647	79
Rate per 100,000 inhabitants		252.2	4.7	34.6	29.8	183.0	1,659.8	304.0	1,293.7	62.1
Amarillo, TX M.S.A.	259,729									
Includes Armstrong, Carson, Oldham, Potter, and Randall Counties										
City of Amarillo	196,576	1,278	10	110	278	880	8,900	2,087	6,184	629
Total area actually reporting	100.0%	1,366	11	118	280	957	9,716	2,346	6,685	685
Rate per 100,000 inhabitants		525.9	4.2	45.4	107.8	368.5	3,740.8	903.2	2,573.8	263.7
Ames, IA M.S.A.	90,011									
Includes Story County										
City of Ames	59,271	78	0	32	7	39	1,454	291	1,132	31
Total area actually reporting	100.0%	132	0	46	8	78	2,031	448	1,534	49
Rate per 100,000 inhabitants		146.6	0.0	51.1	8.9	86.7	2,256.4	497.7	1,704.2	54.4
Anchorage, AK M.S.A. [1]	313,529									
Includes Anchorage Municipality and Matanuska-Susitna Borough										
City of Anchorage	299,143	2,479	15	303	488	1,673	10,543	1,158	8,554	831
Total area actually reporting	1.0	2,543	15	307	496	1,725	11,344	1,236	9,235	873
Rate per 100,000 inhabitants		811.1	4.8	97.9	158.2	550.2	3,618.2	394.2	2,945.5	278.4
Ann Arbor, MI M.S.A.	348,215									
Includes Washtenaw County										
City of Ann Arbor	115,008	227	1	35	50	141	2,726	714	1,898	114
Total area actually reporting	1.0	1,026	5	148	187	686	8,487	2,334	5,713	440
Rate per 100,000 inhabitants		294.6	1.4	42.5	53.7	197.0	2,437.3	670.3	1,640.7	126.4
Anniston-Oxford-Jacksonville, AL M.S.A.	118,270									
Includes Calhoun County										
City of Anniston	23,051	504	5	14	92	393	2,484	912	1,501	71
City of Oxford	17,170	62	1	7	23	31	1,007	179	791	37
City of Jacksonville	12,532	43	0	1	11	31	484	138	327	19
Total area actually reporting	100.0%	678	6	37	131	504	5,339	1,710	3,482	147
Rate per 100,000 inhabitants		573.3	5.1	31.3	110.8	426.1	4,514.2	1,445.8	2,944.1	124.3
Appleton, WI M.S.A.	227,986									
Includes Calumet and Outagamie Counties										
City of Appleton	73,431	213	0	28	22	163	1,392	254	1,111	27
Total area actually reporting	100.0%	351	1	40	37	273	3,519	516	2,920	83
Rate per 100,000 inhabitants		154.0	0.4	17.5	16.2	119.7	1,543.5	226.3	1,280.8	36.4
Asheville, NC M.S.A.	433,267									
Includes Buncombe, Haywood, Henderson, and Madison Counties										
City of Asheville	85,295	423	6	33	141	243	4,910	742	3,832	336
Total area actually reporting	99.2%	965	20	98	233	614	12,010	3,199	7,995	816
Estimated total	100.0%	976	20	99	236	621	12,143	3,229	8,093	821
Rate per 100,000 inhabitants		225.3	4.6	22.8	54.5	143.3	2,802.7	745.3	1,867.9	189.5

Table 6. Crime, by Selected Metropolitan Statistical Area, 2012— continued

(Number, percent, rate per 100,000 population)

Area	Population	Violent crime	Murder and nonnegligent manslaughter	Forcible rape	Robbery	Aggravated assault	Property crime	Burglary	Larceny-theft	Motor vehicle theft
Athens-Clarke County, GA M.S.A.	195,380									
Includes Clarke, Madison, Oconee, and Oglethorpe Counties										
City of Athens-Clarke County	117,457	455	5	48	158	244	4,601	1,149	3,210	242
Total area actually reporting	0.994	621	6	69	177	369	6,602	1,559	4,699	344
Estimated total	1.0	626	6	69	179	372	6,650	1,568	4,734	348
Rate per 100,000 inhabitants		320.4	3.1	35.3	91.6	190.4	3,403.6	802.5	2,423.0	178.1
Atlanta-Sandy Springs-Roswell, GA M.S.A.	5,434,540									
Includes Barrow, Bartow, Butts, Carroll, Cherokee, Clayton, Cobb, Coweta, Dawson, DeKalb, Douglas, Fayette, Forsyth, Fulton, Gwinnett, Haralson, Heard, Henry, Jasper, Lamar, Meriwether, Morgan, Newton, Paulding, Pickens, Pike, Rockdale, Spalding, and Walton Counties										
City of Atlanta	437,041	6,027	83	113	2,276	3,555	28,554	6,192	17,212	5,150
City of Sandy Springs	97,890	187	3	5	98	81	2,750	709	1,871	170
City of Roswell	92,141	132	1	7	63	61	1,721	399	1,228	94
City of Alpharetta	60,031	42	1	6	18	17	1,230	127	1,076	27
Cit of Marietta	57,969	474	1	12	132	329	2,548	496	1,865	187
Total area actually reporting	99.9%	22,181	333	1,091	8,373	12,384	183,592	47,331	115,896	20,365
Estimated total	100.0%	22,207	333	1,093	8,382	12,399	183,871	47,384	116,101	20,386
Rate per 100,000 inhabitants		408.6	6.1	20.1	154.2	228.2	3,383.4	871.9	2,136.4	375.1
Atlantic City-Hammonton, NJ M.S.A. [3]	275,689									
Includes Atlantic County										
City of Atlantic City	39,722	699	19	35	322	323	2,453	481	1,884	88
City of Hammonton	14,852	15	0	0	1	14	186	60	118	8
Total area actually reporting	96.6%		30	73	469		8,226	1,751	6,186	289
Estimated total	100.0%		30	74	477		8,404	1,791	6,312	301
Rate per 100,000 inhabitants			10.9	26.8	173.0		3,048.4	649.6	2,289.5	109.2
Auburn-Opelika, AL M.S.A.	144,044									
Includes Lee County										
City of Auburn	54,785	132	3	13	25	91	1,919	418	1,450	51
City of Opelika	27,201	207	5	11	43	148	1,681	428	1,204	49
Total area actually reporting	100.0%	372	8	26	77	261	4,023	954	2,941	128
Rate per 100,000 inhabitants		258.3	5.6	18.1	53.5	181.2	2,792.9	662.3	2,041.7	88.9
Augusta-Richmond County, GA-SC M.S.A.	575,582									
Includes Burke, Columbia, Lincoln, McDuffie, and Richmond Counties, GA and Aiken and Edgefield Counties, SC										
Total area actually reporting	97.7%	1,757	47	161	699	850	22,565	5,735	14,885	1,945
Estimated total	100.0%	1,802	47	164	715	876	23,040	5,844	15,212	1,984
Rate per 100,000 inhabitants		313.1	8.2	28.5	124.2	152.2	4,002.9	1,015.3	2,642.9	344.7
Austin-Round Rock, TX M.S.A.	1,810,230									
Includes Bastrop, Caldwell, Hays, Travis, and Williamson Counties										
City of Austin	832,901	3,405	31	209	978	2,187	43,472	7,244	33,913	2,315
City of Round Rock	106,232	141	0	32	45	64	2,636	336	2,222	78
Total area actually reporting	100.0%	5,299	39	453	1,195	3,612	62,113	11,173	47,929	3,011

Table 6. Crime, by Selected Metropolitan Statistical Area, 2012— continued

(Number, percent, rate per 100,000 population)

Area	Population	Violent crime	Murder and nonnegligent manslaughter	Forcible rape	Robbery	Aggravated assault	Property crime	Burglary	Larceny-theft	Motor vehicle theft
Rate per 100,000 inhabitants		292.7	2.2	25.0	66.0	199.5	3,431.2	617.2	2,647.7	166.3
Bakersfield, CA M.S.A.	859,608									
Includes Kern County										
City of Bakersfield	355,696	1,929	34	57	697	1,141	17,754	4,994	9,540	3,220
Total area actually reporting	100.0%	4,976	65	174	1,313	3,424	34,761	10,931	17,584	6,246
Rate per 100,000 inhabitants		578.9	7.6	20.2	152.7	398.3	4,043.8	1,271.6	2,045.6	726.6
Baltimore-Columbia-Towson, MD M.S.A.	2,755,459									
Includes Anne Arundel, Baltimore, Carroll, Harford, Howard, and Queen Anne's Counties and Baltimore City										
City of Baltimore	625,474	8,789	218	315	3,605	4,651	29,149	7,770	17,397	3,982
Total area actually reporting	100.0%	17,117	262	671	5,901	10,283	82,232	17,483	57,582	7,167
Rate per 100,000 inhabitants		621.2	9.5	24.4	214.2	373.2	2,984.3	634.5	2,089.7	260.1
Bangor, ME M.S.A.	153,902									
Includes Penobscot County										
City of Bangor	33,036	76	6	7	40	23	1,842	253	1,543	46
Total area actually reporting	100.0%	139	8	19	61	51	4,623	912	3,573	138
Rate per 100,000 inhabitants		90.3	5.2	12.3	39.6	33.1	3,003.9	592.6	2,321.6	89.7
Barnstable Town, MA M.S.A.	217,689									
Includes Barnstable County										
City of Barnstable	45,570	283	1	22	29	231	1,269	378	847	44
Total area actually reporting	100.0%	901	1	62	78	760	5,835	2,224	3,455	156
Rate per 100,000 inhabitants		413.9	0.5	28.5	35.8	349.1	2,680.4	1,021.6	1,587.1	71.7
Baton Rouge, LA M.S.A. [2]	813,022									
Includes Ascension[2], East Baton Rouge, East Feliciana, Iberville, Livingston, Pointe Coupee, St. Helena, West Baton Rouge, and West Feliciana[2] Parishes										
City of Baton Rouge	231,500	2,507	66	64	1,033	1,344	12,059	3,826	7,751	482
Total area actually reporting	98.3%		95	134	1,449			8,039	22,520	
Estimated total	100.0%		96	137	1,460			8,142	22,952	
Rate per 100,000 inhabitants			11.8	16.9	179.6			1,001.4	2,823.0	
Bay City, MI M.S.A.	107,188									
Includes Bay County										
City of Bay City	34,742	215	1	42	29	143	791	199	553	39
Total area actually reporting	100.0%	321	1	68	41	211	2,090	441	1,560	89
Rate per 100,000 inhabitants		299.5	0.9	63.4	38.3	196.9	1949.8	411.4	1455.4	83
Beaumont-Port Arthur, TX M.S.A.	411,053									
Includes Hardin, Jefferson, Newton, and Orange Counties										
City of Beaumont	120,323	1,242	13	76	408	745	5,824	1,828	3,717	279
City of Port Arthur	54,745	344	4	19	121	200	2,406	854	1,428	124
Total area actually reporting	100.0%	2,175	24	137	613	1,401	13,352	4,037	8,516	799
Rate per 100,000 inhabitants		529.1	5.8	33.3	149.1	340.8	3,248.2	982.1	2,071.8	194.4
Beckley, WV M.S.A.	124,829									
Includes Fayette and Raleigh Counties										

Table 6. Crime, by Selected Metropolitan Statistical Area, 2012— continued

(Number, percent, rate per 100,000 population)

Area	Population	Violent crime	Murder and nonnegligent manslaughter	Forcible rape	Robbery	Aggravated assault	Property crime	Burglary	Larceny-theft	Motor vehicle theft
City of Beckley	17,675	189	6	21	55	107	1588	335	1221	32
Total area actually reporting	95.7%	477	14	45	120	298	4352	1336	2831	185
Estimated total	100.0%	[illegible]	[illegible]	[illegible]	[illegible]	[illegible]	[illegible]	[illegible]	[illegible]	[illegible]
Rate per 100,000 inhabitants		394.1	11.2	36.9	98.5	247.5	3631.4	1095.1	2384.1	152.2
Bellingham, WA M.S.A.	205,660									
Includes Whatcom County										
City of Bellingham	82,665	220	0	29	53	138	3,975	614	3,223	138
Total area actually reporting	100.0%	488	4	101	65	318	6,318	1,332	4,751	235
Rate per 100,000 inhabitants		237.3	1.9	49.1	31.6	154.6	3,072.1	647.7	2,310.1	114.3
Billings, MT M.S.A.	162,082									
Includes Carbon, Golden Valley, and Yellowstone Counties										
City of Billings	106,371	370	3	38	68	261	4,812	793	3,608	411
Total area actually reporting	100.0%	461	3	43	69	346	5,755	999	4,262	494
Rate per 100,000 inhabitants		284.4	1.9	26.5	42.6	213.5	3,550.7	616.4	2,629.5	304.8
Binghamton, NY M.S.A. [1]	251,424									
Includes Broome and Tioga Counties[1]										
City of Binghamton[1]	47,250	315	3	15	81	216	2,336	558	1,732	46
Total area actually reporting	100.0%	632	7	59	142	424	6,851	1,400	5,310	141
Rate per 100,000 inhabitants		251.4	2.8	23.5	56.5	168.6	2,724.9	556.8	2,112.0	56.1
Birmingham-Hoover, AL M.S.A.	1,136,805									
Includes Bibb, Blount, Chilton, Jefferson, St. Clair, Shelby, and Walker Counties										
City of Birmingham	213,266	3,237	67	152	983	2,035	14,788	4,704	9,042	1,042
City of Hoover	82,332	86	2	13	46	25	2,180	393	1,702	85
Total area actually reporting	97.7%	6,301	105	357	1,741	4,098	42,101	12,503	27,199	2,399
Estimated total	100.0%	6,424	107	363	1,769	4,185	43,172	12,756	27,958	2,458
Rate per 100,000 inhabitants		565.1	9.4	31.9	155.6	368.1	3,797.7	1,122.1	2,459.3	216.2
Bismarck, ND M.S.A.	119,673									
Includes Burleigh,Morton, Oliver, and Sioux Counties										
City of Bismarck	64,103	218	1	31	16	170	1,945	320	1,522	103
Total area actually reporting	100.0%	424	4	60	27	333	2,897	515	2,180	202
Rate per 100,000 inhabitants		354.3	3.3	50.1	22.6	278.3	2,420.8	430.3	1,821.6	168.8
Blacksburg-Christiansburg-Radford, VA M.S.A.	179,827									
Includes Floyd, Giles, Montgomery, and Pulaski Counties and Radford City										
City of Blacksburg	43,070	39	0	12	11	16	475	80	377	18
City of Christiansburg	21,262	30	0	7	4	19	675	87	576	12
City of Radford	16,595	78	1	9	9	59	457	102	336	19
Total area actually reporting	100.0%	297	2	57	36	202	3,914	734	3,052	128
Rate per 100,000 inhabitants		165.2	1.1	31.7	20.0	112.3	2,176.5	408.2	1,697.2	71.2
Bloomington, IL M.S.A.	187,221									
Includes DeWitt and McLean Counties										
City of Bloomington	77,107	372	1	42	45	284	1,797	357	1,396	44
Total area actually reporting	91.1%	565	1	74	85	405	3,689	778	2,823	88
Estimated total	100.0%	602	1	78	95	428	4,052	849	3,100	103
Rate per 100,000 inhabitants		321.5	0.5	41.7	50.7	228.6	2,164.3	453.5	1,655.8	55.0

Table 6. Crime, by Selected Metropolitan Statistical Area, 2012— continued

(Number, percent, rate per 100,000 population)

Area	Population	Violent crime	Murder and nonnegligent manslaughter	Forcible rape	Robbery	Aggravated assault	Property crime	Burglary	Larceny-theft	Motor vehicle theft
Bloomington, IN M.S.A.	161,803									
Includes Monroe and Owen Counties										
City of Bloomington	81,636	243	3	18	42	180	3,244	622	2,471	151
Total area actually reporting	86.7%	372	4	53	53	262	4,846	942	3,653	251
Estimated total	100.0%	392	4	56	55	277	5,142	1,022	3,850	270
Rate per 100,000 inhabitants		242.3	2.5	34.6	34.0	171.2	3,177.9	631.6	2,379.4	166.9
Bloomsburg-Berwick, PA M.S.A.	85,911									
Includes Columbia and Montour Counties										
City of Bloomsburg Town	15,135	20	0	1	2	17	266	51	211	4
City of Berwick	10,480	25	0	9	6	10	490	148	335	7
Total area actually reporting	96.2%	134	2	31	10	91	1,738	365	1,342	31
Estimated total	100.0%	140	2	31	12	95	1,800	375	1,392	33
Rate per 100,000 inhabitants		163.0	2.3	36.1	14.0	110.6	2,095.2	436.5	1,620.3	38.4
Boise City, ID M.S.A.	631,917									
Includes Ada, Boise, Canyon, Gem, and Owyhee Counties										
City of Boise	211,569	567	1	75	64	427	5,342	913	4,272	157
Total area actually reporting	99.9%	1,334	7	193	117	1,017	12,450	2,627	9,396	427
Estimated total	100.0%	1,335	7	193	117	1,018	12,461	2,629	9,405	427
Rate per 100,000 inhabitants		211.3	1.1	30.5	18.5	161.1	1,971.9	416.0	1,488.3	67.6
Boston-Cambridge-Newton, MA-NH M.S.A. [1]	4,629,025									
Includes the Metropolitan Divisions of Boston, MA; Cambridge-Newton-Framingham, MA; and Rockingham County-Strafford County, NH										
City of Boston, MA	630,648	5,266	57	249	1,910	3,050	18,349	3,325	13,400	1,624
City of Cambridge, MA	106,981	431	1	20	135	275	3,091	502	2,482	107
City of Newton, MA	86,710	76	0	5	17	54	894	185	693	16
City of Framingham, MA[1]	69,605	154	0	7	21	126	1,238	254	884	100
City of Waltham, MA	61,725	146	0	12	24	110	849	191	610	48
Total area actually reporting	97.6%	16,085	95	1,010	4,241	10,739	89,455	17,892	65,570	5,993
Estimated total	100.0%	16,444	95	1,039	4,312	10,998	91,833	18,439	67,269	6,125
Rate per 100,000 inhabitants		355.2	2.1	22.4	93.2	237.6	1,983.9	398.3	1,453.2	132.3
Boston, MA M.D. [1]	*1,920,886*									
Includes Norfolk, Plymouth, and Suffolk Counties										
Total area actually reporting	97.7%	9,389	71	499	2,840	5,979	40,999	8,495	29,629	2,875
Estimated total	100.0%	9,532	71	509	2,869	6,083	41,866	8,705	30,235	2,926
Rate per 100,000 inhabitants		496.2	3.7	26.5	149.4	316.7	2,179.5	453.2	1,574.0	152.3
Cambridge-Newton-Framingham, MA M.D. [1]	*2,287,271*									
Includes Essex and Middlesex Counties										
Total area actually reporting	97.4%	6,104	15	385	1,315	4,389	39,674	8,055	28,791	2,828
Estimated total	100.0%	6,298	15	399	1,354	4,530	40,850	8,340	29,612	2,898
Rate per 100,000 inhabitants		275.3	0.7	17.4	59.2	198.1	1,786.0	364.6	1,294.6	126.7
Rockingham County-Strafford County, NH M.D.	*420,868*									
Includes Rockingham and Strafford Counties										
Total area actually reporting	95.0%	592	9	126	86	371	8,782	1,342	7,150	290

Table 6. Crime, by Selected Metropolitan Statistical Area, 2012— continued

(Number, percent, rate per 100,000 population)

Area	Population	Violent crime	Murder and nonnegligent manslaughter	Forcible rape	Robbery	Aggravated assault	Property crime	Burglary	Larceny-theft	Motor vehicle theft
Estimated total	100.0%	614	9	131	89	385	9,117	1,394	7,422	301
Rate per 100,000 inhabitants		145.9	2.1	31.1	21.1	91.5	2,166.2	331.2	1,763.5	71.5
Boulder, CO M.S.A.	303,520									
Includes Boulder County										
City of Boulder	100,257	249	0	32	48	169	2,937	472	2,337	128
Total area actually reporting	93.3%	567	0	66	95	406	6,583	1,091	5,200	292
Estimated total	100.0%	611	0	73	102	436	7,107	1,169	5,609	329
Rate per 100,000 inhabitants		201.3	0.0	24.1	33.6	143.6	2,341.5	385.1	1,848.0	108.4
Bowling Green, KY M.S.A.	160,980									
Includes Allen, Butler, Ed-monson, and Warren Counties										
City of Bowling Green	59,043	189	4	36	75	74	3,025	547	2,322	156
Total area actually reporting	100.0%	231	4	45	83	99	4,003	909	2,887	207
Rate per 100,000 inhabitants		143.5	2.5	28.0	51.6	61.5	2,486.6	564.7	1,793.4	128.6
Bremerton-Silverdale, WA M.S.A.	257,130									
Includes Kitsap County										
City of Bremerton	39,434	230	1	38	44	147	2,123	444	1,487	192
Total area actually reporting	100.0%	696	5	105	110	476	8,127	2,080	5,421	626
Rate per 100,000 inhabitants		270.7	1.9	40.8	42.8	185.1	3,160.7	808.9	2,108.3	243.5
Bridgeport-Stamford-Norwalk, CT M.S.A.	910,707									
Includes Fairfield County										
City of Bridgeport	146,030	1,760	22	388	606	744	5,153	1,377	2,908	868
City of Stamford	124,201	351	5	25	145	176	1,932	290	1,472	170
City of Norwalk	86,693	272	3	9	68	192	1,713	250	1,352	111
City of Danbury	81,891	109	1	23	45	40	1,562	287	1,201	74
City of Stratford	52,041	104	0	15	28	61	1,413	245	1,070	98
Total area actually reporting	100.0%	2,736	33	482	946	1,275	16,256	3,205	11,536	1,515
Rate per 100,000 inhabitants		300.4	3.6	52.9	103.9	140.0	1,785.0	351.9	1,266.7	166.4
Brownsville-Harlingen, TX M.S.A.	420,325									
Includes Cameron County										
City of Brownsville	181,102	473	3	38	125	307	8,337	1,145	6,986	206
City of Harlingen	67,112	271	4	23	62	182	3,272	606	2,555	111
Total area actually reporting	100.0%	1,080	13	98	237	732	16,754	3,092	13,186	476
Rate per 100,000 inhabitants		256.9	3.1	23.3	56.4	174.2	3,986.0	735.6	3,137.1	113.2
Brunswick, GA M.S.A.	114,128									
Includes Brantley, Glynn, and McIntosh Counties										
City of Brunswick	15,691	220	4	3	61	152	1,113	294	788	31
Total area actually reporting	98.3%	519	8	22	134	355	4,630	1,332	3,163	135
Estimated total	100.0%	527	8	22	137	360	4,713	1,348	3,224	141
Rate per 100,000 inhabitants		461.8	7.0	19.3	120.0	315.4	4,129.6	1,181.1	2,824.9	123.5
Buffalo-Cheektowaga-Niagara Falls, NY M.S.A. [1]	1,140,160									
Includes Erie and Niagara Counties[1]										
City of Buffalo[1]	262,434	3,382	48	138	1,388	1,808	13,454	3,976	8,371	1,107
City of Cheektowaga Town[1]	79,178	175	0	19	66	90	2,821	338	2,396	87
City of Niagara Falls[1]	50,356	619	3	26	171	419	2,963	750	2,083	130
Total area actually reporting	100.0%	5,045	54	258	1,811	2,922	33,364	7,461	24,194	1,709

Table 6. Crime, by Selected Metropolitan Statistical Area, 2012— continued

(Number, percent, rate per 100,000 population)

Area	Population	Violent crime	Murder and nonnegligent manslaughter	Forcible rape	Robbery	Aggravated assault	Property crime	Burglary	Larceny-theft	Motor vehicle theft
Rate per 100,000 inhabitants		442.5	4.7	22.6	158.8	256.3	2,926.3	654.4	2,122.0	149.9
Burlington, NC M.S.A.	154,810									
Includes Alamance County										
City of Burlington	51,430	406	2	17	105	282	2,792	671	1,998	123
Total area actually reporting	100.0%	674	4	35	138	497	5,218	1,438	3,530	250
Rate per 100,000 inhabitants		435.4	2.6	22.6	89.1	321.0	3,370.6	928.9	2,280.2	161.5
California-Lexington Park, MD M.S.A.	108,522									
Includes St. Mary's County										
Total area actually reporting	100.0%	257.0	0	12	51	194	2,778	753	1,938	87
Rate per 100,000 inhabitants		236.8	0.0	11.1	47.0	178.8	2,559.8	693.9	1,785.8	80.2
Canton-Massillon, OH M.S.A.	403,843									
Includes Carroll and Stark Counties										
City of Canton	72,914	729	10	64	414	241	4,722	1,590	2,671	461
City of Massillon	32,104	66	0	14	31	21	1,097	353	713	31
Total area actually reporting	98.6%	1,189	13	121	586	469	11,805	3,698	7,377	730
Estimated total	100.0%	1,197	13	122	589	473	11,957	3,729	7,493	735
Rate per 100,000 inhabitants		296.4	3.2	30.2	145.8	117.1	2,960.8	923.4	1,855.4	182.0
Cape Coral-Fort Myers, FL M.S.A.	639,944									
Includes Lee County										
City of Cape Coral	159,625	229	4	16	41	168	3,521	860	2,547	114
City of Fort Myers	64,379	754	24	26	172	532	2,346	507	1,639	200
Total area actually reporting	100.0%	2,234	45	109	553	1,527	15,021	4,171	9,927	923
Rate per 100,000 inhabitants		349.1	7.0	17.0	86.4	238.6	2,347.2	651.8	1,551.2	144.2
Cape Girardeau, MO-IL M.S.A.	97,195									
Includes Alexander County, IL, and Bollinger and Cape Girardeau Counties, MO										
City of Cape Girardeau, MO	38,474	243	3	12	66	162	2,628	500	2,052	76
Total area actually reporting	1.0	424	5	18	73	328	3,721	812	2,790	119
Rate per 100,000 inhabitants		436.2	5.1	18.5	75.1	337.5	3,828.4	835.4	2,870.5	122.4
Carson City, NV M.S.A.	56,164									
Includes Carson City										
Total area actually reporting	100.0%	132	0	0	14	118	1,107	298	731	78
Rate per 100,000 inhabitants		235.0	0.0	0.0	24.9	210.1	1,971.0	530.6	1,301.5	138.9
Casper, WY M.S.A.	77,475									
Includes Natrona County										
City of Casper	56,801	86	3	2	12	69	1,968	363	1,501	104
Total area actually reporting	100.0%	152	3	7	12	130	2,346	474	1,739	133
Rate per 100,000 inhabitants		196.2	3.9	9.0	15.5	167.8	3,028.1	611.8	2,244.6	171.7
Cedar Rapids, IA M.S.A. 3	261,586									
Includes Benton, Jones, and Linn Counties										
City of Cedar Rapids	128,401	356	3	43	97	213	4,723	966	3,503	254
Total area actually reporting	94.7%	445	4	67	101	273			4,415	321
Estimated total	100.0%	464	4	70	102	288			4,512	333

Table 6. Crime, by Selected Metropolitan Statistical Area, 2012— continued

(Number, percent, rate per 100,000 population)

Area	Population	Violent crime	Murder and nonnegligent manslaughter	Forcible rape	Robbery	Aggravated assault	Property crime	Burglary	Larceny-theft	Motor vehicle theft
Rate per 100,000 inhabitants		177.4	1.5	26.8	39.0	110.1			1,724.9	127.3
Chambersburg-Waynesboro, PA M.S.A.	151,055									
Includes Franklin County										
City of Chambersburg	20,458	82	2	8	31	41	804	120	661	23
City of Waynesboro	10,670	18	0	1	4	13	220	33	179	8
Total area actually reporting	100.0%	212	5	34	47	126	2,508	497	1,931	80
Rate per 100,000 inhabitants		140.3	3.3	22.5	31.1	83.4	1,660.3	329.0	1,278.3	53.0
Champaign-Urbana, IL M.S.A.	232,445									
Includes Champaign, Ford, and Piatt Counties										
City of Champaign	81,329	741	3	51	135	552	2,700	722	1,897	81
City of Urbana	41,537	148	0	20	68	60	1,443	416	974	53
Total area actually reporting	97.7%	1,200	4	143	225	828	6,039	1,685	4,180	174
Estimated total	100.0%	1,211	4	144	228	835	6,155	1,708	4,268	179
Rate per 100,000 inhabitants		521.0	1.7	62.0	98.1	359.2	2,647.9	734.8	1,836.1	77.0
Charleston, North Charleston, SC M.S.A.	688,607									
Includes Berkeley, Charleston, and Dorchester Counties										
City of Charleston	123,856	296	12	19	104	161	3,373	374	2,764	235
City of North Charleston	100,676	737	13	61	212	451	5,757	854	4,363	540
Total area actually reporting	99.5%	2,890	48	197	615	2,030	22,350	4,345	16,158	1,847
Estimated total	100.0%	2,907	48	198	618	2,043	22,508	4,373	16,280	1,855
Rate per 100,000 inhabitants		422.2	7.0	28.8	89.7	296.7	3,268.6	635.1	2,364.2	269.4
Charlottesville, VA M.S.A.	223,598									
Includes Albemarle, Buckingham, Fluvanna, Greene, and Nelson Counties and Charlottesville City										
City of Charlottesville	43,991	198	2	17	50	129	1,502	162	1,246	94
Total area actually reporting	100.0%	381	6	56	73	246	4,380	823	3,351	206
Rate per 100,000 inhabitants		170.4	2.7	25.0	32.6	110.0	1,958.9	368.1	1,498.7	92.1
Cheyenne, WY M.S.A.	94,026									
Includes Laramie County										
City of Cheyenne	60,969	140	0	21	21	98	2,081	255	1,730	96
Total area actually reporting	100.0%	227	2	33	27	165	2,716	425	2,147	144
Rate per 100,000 inhabitants		241.4	2.1	35.1	28.7	175.5	2,888.6	452.0	2,283.4	153.1
Chicago-Naperville, Elgin, IL-IN-WI M.S.A. [4]	9,511,421									
Includes the Metropolitan Divisions of Chicago-Naperville, Arlington Heights, IL; Elgin IL; Gary, IN; and Lake County-Kenosha County, IL-WI										
City of Chicago, IL[4]	2,708,382		500		13,476	12,272	112,466	22,748	72,717	17,001
City of Naperville, IL	142,840	119	3	7	24	85	2,044	255	1,748	41
City of Elgin, IL	109,155	257	2	67	76	112	1,982	357	1,546	79
City of Gary, IN	80,472	728	37	56	275	360	4,475	1,634	2,066	775
City of Arlington Heights, IL	75,463	41	1	7	8	25	978	140	821	17
City of Evanston, IL	74,820	228	3	4	79	142	2,054	421	1,570	63
City of Schaumburg, IL	74,585	68	0	13	18	37	2,487	199	2,226	62
City of Skokie, IL	65,096	134	0	17	37	80	1,577	284	1,232	61
City of Des Plaines, IL	58,644	65	0	4	13	48	941	137	757	47
City of Hoffman Estates, IL	52,148	66	0	13	26	27	710	129	560	21

Table 6. Crime, by Selected Metropolitan Statistical Area, 2012— continued

(Number, percent, rate per 100,000 population)

Area	Population	Violent crime	Murder and nonnegligent manslaughter	Forcible rape	Robbery	Aggravated assault	Property crime	Burglary	Larceny-theft	Motor vehicle theft
Total area actually reporting	98.0%		675		17,417	19,033	250,691	49,976	176,674	24,041
Estimated total	100.0%		679		17,518	19,272	254,619	50,771	179,630	24,218
Rate per 100,000 inhabitants			7.1		184.2	202.6	2,677.0	533.8	1,888.6	254.6
Chicago-Naperville-Arlington Heights, IL M.D. [4]	*7,300,952*									
Includes Cook, DuPage, Grundy, Kendall, McHenry, and Will Counties										
Total area actually reporting	98.0%		594		16,119	16,202	201,675	39,772	140,717	21,186
Estimated total	100.0%		598		16,207	16,397	204,797	40,385	143,093	21,319
Rate per 100,000 inhabitants			8.2		222.0	224.6	2,805.1	553.1	1,959.9	292.0
Elgin, IL M.D.	*625305*									
Includes DeKalb and Kane Counties										
Total area actually reporting	98.9%	1,131.0	7.0	188.0	217.0	719.0	10,171.0	1,948.0	7,939.0	284.0
Estimated total	100.0%	1,146.0	7.0	190.0	221.0	728.0	10,322.0	1,978.0	8,054.0	290.0
Rate per 100,000 inhabitants		183.3	1.1	30.4	35.3	116.4	1,650.7	316.3	1,288.0	46.4
Gary, IN M.D.	*710,891*									
Includes Jasper, Lake, Newton, and Porter Counties										
Total area actually reporting	95.6%	2,238	66	145	701	1,326	21,917	4,910	14,889	2,118
Estimated total	100.0%	2,274	66	150	706	1,352	22,426	5,033	15,243	2,150
Rate per 100,000 inhabitants		319.9	9.3	21.1	99.3	190.2	3,154.6	708.0	2,144.2	302.4
Lake County-Kenosha County, IL-WI M.D.	*874,273*									
Includes Lake County, IL, and Kenosha County, WI										
Total area actually reporting	99.2%	1,389	8	215	380	786	16,928	3,346	13,129	453
Estimated total	100.0%	1,404	8	217	384	795	17,074	3,375	13,240	459
Rate per 100,000 inhabitants		160.6	0.9	24.8	43.9	90.9	1,952.9	386.0	1,514.4	52.5
Chico, CA M.S.A.	222,309									
Includes Butte County										
City of Chico	87,090	282	1	46	95	140	2,291	778	1,259	254
Total area actually reporting	100%	684	11	75	167	431	5,659	1,919	3,147	593
Rate per 100,000 inhabitants		307.7	4.9	33.7	75.1	193.9	2,545.6	863.2	1,415.6	266.7
Cincinnati, OH-KY-IN M.S.A. [1]	2,123,695									
Includes Dearborn, Ohio, and Union Counties, IN; Boone, Bracken, Campbell, Gallatin, Grant, Kenton, and Pendleton Counties, KY; and Brown, Butler, Clermont, Hamilton,[1] and Warren Counties, OH										
City of Cincinnati, OH	296,204	2,887	46	188	1,725	928	18,173	5,483	11,590	1,100
Total area actually reporting	96.2%	5,935	74	666	2,760	2,435	68,513	16,457	49,306	2,750
Estimated total	100.0%	6,042	75	683	2,798	2,486	70,483	16,869	50,790	2,824
Rate per 100,000 inhabitants		284.5	3.5	32.2	131.8	117.1	3,318.9	794.3	2,391.6	133.0
Clarksville, TN-KY M.S.A.	266,196									
Includes Christian and Trigg Counties, KY, and Montgomery County, TN										
City of Clarksville, TN	137,356	875	10	46	99	720	3,741	976	2,598	167
Total area actually reporting	99.40%	1,171	17	84	172	898	6,909	1,835	4,746	328
Estimated total	100.00%	1,175	17	85	174	899	6,966	1,848	4,787	331

Table 6. Crime, by Selected Metropolitan Statistical Area, 2012— continued

(Number, percent, rate per 100,000 population)

Area	Population	Violent crime	Murder and nonnegligent manslaughter	Forcible rape	Robbery	Aggravated assault	Property crime	Burglary	Larceny-theft	Motor vehicle theft
Rate per 100,000 inhabitants		441.4	6.4	31.9	65.4	337.7	2,616.9	694.2	1,798.3	124.3
Cleveland, TN M.S.A.	117,700									
Includes Bradley and Polk Counties										
City of Cleveland	42,068	371	0	29	39	303	2,225	398	1,751	76
Total area actually reporting	100.0%	642	5	36	55	546	3,567	788	2,580	199
Rate per 100,000 inhabitants		545.0	4.2	30.6	46.7	463.5	3,028.0	668.9	2,190.2	168.9
Coeur d'Alene, ID M.S.A.	142,089									
Includes Kootenai County										
City of Coeur d'Alene	45,267	260	0	26	14	220	1,978	431	1,395	152
Total area actually reporting	100.0%	417	1	53	22	341	4,522	1,165	3,084	273
Rate per 100,000 inhabitants		293.5	0.7	37.3	15.5	240.0	3,182.5	819.9	2,170.5	192.1
College Station-Bryan, TX M.S.A.	235,092									
Includes Brazos, Burleson, and Robertson Counties										
City of College Station	96,567	491	3	34	38	416	2,398	576	1,762	60
City of Bryan	78,749	312	1	31	69	211	2,473	496	1,889	88
Total area actually reporting	100.0%	934	6	77	116	735	6,304	1,474	4,641	189
Rate per 100,000 inhabitants		397.3	2.6	32.8	49.3	312.6	2,681.5	627.0	1,974.1	80.4
Colorado Springs, CO M.S.A. [3]	669,453									
Includes El Paso[3] and Teller Counties										
City of Colorado Springs	432,287	1,968	18	358	523	1,069	17,899	3,641	12,456	1,802
Total area actually reporting	99.9%	2,529	20	447	567	1,495			14,934	2,077
Estimated total	100.0%	2,530	20	447	567	1,496			14,950	2,078
Rate per 100,000 inhabitants		377.9	3.0	66.8	84.7	223.5			2,233.2	310.4
Columbia, MO M.S.A.	165,938									
Includes Boone County										
City of Columbia	110,646	476	3	41	162	270	4,221	784	3,294	143
Total area actually reporting	100.0%	623	3	46	180	394	5,544	1,023	4,321	200
Rate per 100,000 inhabitants		375.4	1.8	27.7	108.5	237.4	3,341.0	616.5	2,604.0	120.5
Columbus, GA-AL M.S.A.	304,291									
Includes Russell County, AL, and Chattahoochee, Harris, Marion, and Muscogee Counties, GA										
City of Columbus, GA	196,178	994	17	31	423	523	11,266	2,709	7,711	846
Total area actually reporting	97.3%	1,306	19	58	497	732	14,289	3,616	9,592	1,081
Estimated total	100.0%	1,331	19	59	506	747	14,541	3,685	9,753	1,103
Rate per 100,000 inhabitants		437.4	6.2	19.4	166.3	245.5	4,778.6	1,211.0	3,205.2	362.5
Columbus, IN M.S.A.	78,114									
Includes Bartholomew County										
City of Columbus	44,817	83	1	12	22	48	2,210	262	1,768	180
Total area actually reporting	99.5%	134	1	18	25	90	2,754	382	2,138	234
Estimated total	100.0%	135	1	18	25	91	2,767	384	2,148	235
Rate per 100,000 inhabitants		172.8	1.3	23.0	32.0	116.5	3,542.3	491.6	2,749.8	300.8
Corpus Christi, TX M.S.A. [3]	437,841									
Includes Aransas, Nueces, and San Patricio Counties										
City of Corpus Christi	312,565	2,057	16	184	375	1,482	14,061	2,452	11,166	443

Table 6. Crime, by Selected Metropolitan Statistical Area, 2012— continued

(Number, percent, rate per 100,000 population)

Area	Population	Violent crime	Murder and nonnegligent manslaughter	Forcible rape	Robbery	Aggravated assault	Property crime	Burglary	Larceny-theft	Motor vehicle theft
Total area actually reporting	100.0%	2,458	23	240	412	1,783			13,925	588
Rate per 100,000 inhabitants		561.4	5.3	54.8	94.1	407.2			3,180.4	134.3
Corvallis, OR M.S.A.	86,538									
Includes Benton County										
City of Corvallis	55,062	67	1	11	15	40	1,418	235	1,153	30
Total area actually reporting	100.0%	96	1	19	18	58	1,841	322	1,460	59
Rate per 100,000 inhabitants		110.9	1.2	22.0	20.8	67.0	2,127.4	372.1	1,687.1	68.2
Crestview-Fort Walton Beach-Destin, FL M.S.A.	242,539									
Includes Okaloosa and Walton Counties										
City of Crestview	21,574	186	1	14	38	133	933	167	728	38
City of Fort Walton Beach	20,063	48	1	4	7	36	772	143	586	43
Total area actually reporting	100.0%	1,116	3	86	126	901	6,453	1,295	4,869	289
Rate per 100,000 inhabitants		460.1	1.2	35.5	52.0	371.5	2,660.6	533.9	2,007.5	119.2
Cumberland, MD-WV M.S.A.	103,606									
Includes Allegany County, MD, and Mineral County, WV										
City of Cumberland, MD	20,939	166	0	15	27	124	1,415	317	1,068	30
Total area actually reporting	0.992	344	4	29	48	263	2,949	697	2,165	87
Estimated total	100.0%	346	4	29	48	265	2,979	702	2,189	88
Rate per 100,000 inhabitants		334.0	3.9	28.0	46.3	255.8	2,875.3	677.6	2,112.8	84.9
Dallas-Fort Worth-Arlington, TX M.S.A.	6,680,025									
Includes the Metropolitan Divisions of Dallas-Plano-Irving and Fort Worth-Arlington										
City of Dallas	1,241,549	8,380	154	486	4,093	3,647	54,300	16,090	31,148	7,062
City of Fort Worth	770,101	4,524	44	391	1,280	2,809	32,514	8,442	21,648	2,424
City of Arlington	379,295	1,909	17	135	532	1,225	15,109	3,543	10,616	950
City of Plano	273,816	358	1	55	110	192	6,453	1,095	5,043	315
City of Irving	224,007	507	3	27	135	342	6,307	1,277	4,466	564
City of Denton	118,942	369	1	86	82	200	3,262	632	2,473	157
City of Richardson	103,266	171	2	27	80	62	3,004	698	2,175	131
Total area actually reporting	99.9%	23,017	277	1,892	8,004	12,844	212,023	52,309	142,089	17,625
Estimated total	100.0%	23,028	277	1,893	8,007	12,851	212,153	52,335	142,186	17,632
Rate per 100,000 inhabitants		344.7	4.1	28.3	119.9	192.4	3,175.9	783.5	2,128.5	264.0
Dallas-Plano-Irving, TX M.D.	4,405,585									
Includes Collin, Dallas, Denton, Ellis, Hunt, Kaufman, and Rockwall Counties										
Total area actually reporting	99.9%	14,371	194	1,119	5,763	7,295	136,399	34,226	89,510	12,663
Estimated total	100.0%	14,378	194	1,120	5,765	7,299	136,479	34,242	89,570	12,667
Rate per 100,000 inhabitants		326.4	4.4	25.4	130.9	165.7	3,097.9	777.2	2,033.1	287.5
Fort Worth-Arlington, TX M.D.	2,274,440									
Includes Hood, Johnson, Parker, Somerville, Tarrant, and Wise Counties										
Total area actually reporting	99.9%	8,646	83	773	2,241	5,549	75,624	18,083	52,579	4,962
Estimated total	100.0%	8,650	83	773	2,242	5,552	75,674	18,093	52,616	4,965
Rate per 100,000 inhabitants		380.3	3.6	34.0	98.6	244.1	3,327.1	795.5	2,313.4	218.3
Dalton, GA M.S.A.	144,264									

Table 6. Crime, by Selected Metropolitan Statistical Area, 2012— continued

(Number, percent, rate per 100,000 population)

Area	Population	Violent crime	Murder and nonnegligent manslaughter	Forcible rape	Robbery	Aggravated assault	Property crime	Burglary	Larceny-theft	Motor vehicle theft
Includes Murray and Whitfield Counties										
City of Dalton	33,668	88	2	8	26	52	1,250	229	984	37
Total area actually reporting	98.3%	365	4	26	41	294	3,887	950	2,766	171
Estimated total	100.0%	375	4	27	44	300	3,990	970	2,841	179
Rate per 100,000 inhabitants		259.9	2.8	18.7	30.5	208.0	2,765.8	672.4	1,969.3	124.1
Danville, IL M.S.A.	81,547									
Includes Vermilion County										
City of Danville	32,997	328	3	42	80	203	1,980	659	1,247	74
Total area actually reporting	98.4%	451	4	63	87	297	3,028	949	1,956	123
Estimated total	100.0%	454	4	63	88	299	3,057	955	1,978	124
Rate per 100,000 inhabitants		556.7	4.9	77.3	107.9	366.7	3,748.8	1,171.1	2,425.6	152.1
Daphne-Fairhope-Foley, AL M.S.A.	187,467									
Includes Baldwin County										
City of Daphne	22,198	40	1	4	2	33	514	77	421	16
City of Fairhope	15,766	43	1	2	5	35	649	131	503	15
City of Foley	15,049	54	0	4	15	35	665	87	549	29
Total area actually reporting	100.0%	446	8	30	76	332	4,988	967	3,829	192
Rate per 100,000 inhabitants		237.9	4.3	16.0	40.5	177.1	2,660.7	515.8	2,042.5	102.4
Davenport-Moline-Rock Island, IA-IL M.S.A.	382,090									
Includes Henry, Mercer, and Rock Island Counties, IL, and Scott County, IA										
City of Davenport, IA	101,193	604	4	40	151	409	4,088	890	2,912	286
City of Moline, IL	43,509	176	0	16	23	137	1,354	204	1,095	55
City of Rock Island, IL	39,038	222	4	6	39	173	1,124	217	856	51
Total area actually reporting	97.6%	1,402	10	115	239	1,038	9,677	1,936	7,292	449
Estimated total	100.0%	1,422	10	117	245	1,050	9,879	1,976	7,446	457
Rate per 100,000 inhabitants		372.2	2.6	30.6	64.1	274.8	2,585.5	517.2	1,948.8	119.6
Dayton, OH M.S.A.	803,255									
Includes Greene, Miami, and Montgomery Counties										
City of Dayton	142,139	1,384	24	112	633	615	8,385	3,043	4,649	693
Total area actually reporting	98.8%	2,330	31	300	1,011	988	27,040	7,205	18,382	1,453
Estimated total	100.0%	2,343	31	302	1,016	994	27,287	7,255	18,571	1,461
Rate per 100,000 inhabitants		291.7	3.9	37.6	126.5	123.7	3,397.1	903.2	2,312.0	181.9
Decatur, AL M.S.A.	154,689									
Includes Lawrence and Morgan Counties										
City of Decatur	56,126	240	2	9	80	149	2,913	821	1,964	128
Total area actually reporting	99.6%	403	2	20	92	289	4,492	1,320	2,957	215
Estimated total	100.0%	406.0	2.0	20.0	93.0	291.0	4,518.0	1,326.0	2,976.0	216.0
Rate per 100,000 inhabitants		262.5	1.3	12.9	60.1	188.1	2,920.7	857.2	1,923.9	139.6
Decatur, IL M.S.A.	110,782									
Includes Macon County										
City of Decatur	76,131	352	6	26	106	214	2,448	921	1,445	82
Total area actually reporting	100.0%	427	6	39	111	271	2,963	1,090	1,776	97
Rate per 100,000 inhabitants		385.4	5.4	35.2	100.2	244.6	2,674.6	983.9	1,603.1	87.6
Deltona-Daytona Beach-Ormond Beach, FL M.S.A.	600,260									
Includes Flagler and Volusia Counties										
City of Daytona Beach	61,861	715	4	23	179	509	3,869	799	2,724	346

Table 6. Crime, by Selected Metropolitan Statistical Area, 2012— continued

(Number, percent, rate per 100,000 population)

Area	Population	Violent crime	Murder and nonnegligent manslaughter	Forcible rape	Robbery	Aggravated assault	Property crime	Burglary	Larceny-theft	Motor vehicle theft
City of Ormond Beach	38,674	122	2	9	15	96	1,301	199	1,045	57
Total area actually reporting	99.7%	2,417	20	104	460	1,833	19,155	4,531	13,504	1,120
Estimated total	100.0%	2,424	20	104	462	1,838	19,223	4,546	13,553	1,124
Rate per 100,000 inhabitants		403.8	3.3	17.3	77.0	306.2	3,202.4	757.3	2,257.9	187.3
Denver-Aurora-Broomfield, CO M.S.A. [1]	2,635,467									
Includes Adams, Arapahoe, Broomfield, Clear Creek, Denver, Douglas,[1] Elbert, Gilpin, Jefferson, and Park Counties										
City of Denver	628,545	3,871	39	376	1,165	2,291	23,343	5,129	14,544	3,670
City of Aurora	336,952	1,433	29	179	483	742	10,059	1,791	7,370	898
City of Lakewood	146,404	676	2	94	148	432	6,705	917	5,180	608
City of Broomfield	58,145	30	1	7	6	16	1,213	90	1,076	47
Total area actually reporting	99.9%	8,893	103	1,150	2,224	5,416	72,354	13,158	51,376	7,820
Estimated total	100.0%	8,895	103	1,150	2,224	5,418	72,387	13,163	51,402	7,822
Rate per 100,000 inhabitants		337.5	3.9	43.6	84.4	205.6	2,746.6	499.5	1,950.4	296.8
Des Moines-West Des Moines, IA M.S.A. [3]	582,506									
Includes Dallas, Guthrie, Madison, Polk, and Warren Counties										
City of Des Moines	207,400	1,094	7	100	250	737	10,210	2,514	6,914	782
City of West Des Moines	58,134	95	0	16	8	71	1,825	213	1,562	50
Total area actually reporting	98.2%	1,673	8	176	284	1,205			12,035	1,077
Estimated total	100.0%	1,685	8	178	284	1,215			12,093	1,086
Rate per 100,000 inhabitants		289.3	1.4	30.6	48.8	208.6			2,076.0	186.4
Detroit-Warren-Livonia, MI M.S.A.	4,288,943									
Includes the Metropolitan Divisions of Detroit-Dearborn-Livonia and Warren-Troy-Farmington Hills										
City of Detroit	707,096	15,011	386	441	4,843	9,341	40,956	13,488	15,968	11,500
City of Warren	134,340	715	0	91	148	476	3,787	999	2,049	739
City of Dearborn	97,215	322	1	24	107	190	3,282	462	2,463	357
City of Livonia	96,028	146	3	19	32	92	2,124	323	1,601	200
City of Troy	81,567	60	2	9	13	36	1,664	181	1,376	107
City of Farmington Hills	80,316	74	1	15	12	46	1,264	231	907	126
City of Southfield	72,253	352	2	34	136	180	2,549	625	1,530	394
City of Taylor	62,534	303	1	31	60	211	2,398	563	1,581	254
City of Novi	55623	37	0	4	9	24	1,048	72	937	39
Total area actually reporting	99.7%	24,602	469	1,464	7,005	15,664	116,772	29,806	67,672	19,294
Estimated total	100.0%	24,637	469	1,468	7,013	15,687	117,088	29,873	67,897	19,318
Rate per 100,000 inhabitants		574.4	10.9	34.2	163.5	365.8	2,730.0	696.5	1,583.1	450.4
	1,803,403									
Detroit-Livonia-Dearborn, MI M.D.										
Includes Wayne County	99.5%	18,906	430	796	5,881	11,799	70,165	19,997	34,902	15,266
Total area actually reporting	100.0%	18,932	430	799	5,887	11,816	70,402	20,047	35,071	15,284
Rate per 100,000 inhabitants		1,049.8	23.8	44.3	326.4	655.2	3,903.8	1,111.6	1,944.7	847.5
Warren-Troy-Farmington Hills, MI M.D.	2,485,540									
Includes Lapeer, Livingston, Macomb, Oakland, and St. Clair Counties										
Total area actually reporting	99.9%	5,696	39	668	1,124	3,865	46,607	9,809	32,770	4,028
Estimated total	100.0%	5,705	39	669	1,126	3,871	46,686	9,826	32,826	4,034
Rate per 100,000 inhabitants		229.5	1.6	26.9	45.3	155.7	1,878.3	395.3	1,320.7	162.3

Table 6. Crime, by Selected Metropolitan Statistical Area, 2012— continued

(Number, percent, rate per 100,000 population)

Area	Population	Violent crime	Murder and nonnegligent manslaughter	Forcible rape	Robbery	Aggravated assault	Property crime	Burglary	Larceny-theft	Motor vehicle theft
Dothan, AL M.S.A.	147,151									
Includes Geneva, Henry, and Houston Counties										
City of Dothan	65,389	316	5	30	99	182	2,895	874	1,893	128
Total area actually reporting	99.6%	564	11	54	118	381	4,567	1,391	2,942	234
Estimated total	100.0%	567	11	54	119	383	4,589	1,396	2,958	235
Rate per 100,000 inhabitants		385.3	7.5	36.7	80.9	260.3	3,118.6	948.7	2,010.2	159.7
Dover, DE M.S.A.	166,643									
Includes Kent County										
City of Dover	36,961	280	1	13	61	205	2,189	116	2,008	65
Total area actually reporting	100.0%	901	4	47	161	689	6,172	1,226	4,735	211
Rate per 100,000 inhabitants		540.7	2.4	28.2	96.6	413.5	3,703.7	735.7	2,841.4	126.6
Dubuque, IA M.S.A. [3]	95,015									
Includes Dubuque County										
City of Dubuque	58,460	128	2	20	22	84			1,160	46
Total area actually reporting	95.5%	146	2	23	23	98			1,267	73
Rate per 100,000 inhabitants	100.0%	153.0	2.0	24.0	23.0	104.0			1,322.0	76.0
		161.0	2.1	25.3	24.2	109.5			1,391.4	80.0
Duluth, MN-WI M.S.A. [4]	281,439									
Includes Carlton and St. Louis Counties, MN[4] and Douglas County, WI										
City of Duluth, MN[4]	86,830		2		90	213	3,861	642	3,047	172
Total area actually reporting	100.0%		4		133	447	8,836	1,640	6,787	409
Rate per 100,000 inhabitants			1.4		47.3	158.8	3,139.6	582.7	2,411.5	145.3
Durham-Chapel Hill, NC M.S.A.	518,062									
Includes Chatham, Durham, Orange, and Person Counties										
City of Durham	235,563	1,710	21	63	615	1,011	10,279	3,284	6,291	704
City of Chapel Hill	58,586	87	2	10	30	45	1,493	452	969	72
Total area actually reporting	100.0%	2,214	27	110	725	1,352	17,821	5,673	11,162	986
Rate per 100,000 inhabitants		427.4	5.2	21.2	139.9	261.0	3,439.9	1,095.0	2,154.6	190.3
East Stroudsburg, PA M.S.A.	170,157									
Includes Monroe County										
Total area actually reporting	100.0%	666	4	50	95	517	4,486	1,202	3,185	99
Rate per 100,000 inhabitants		391	2	29	56	304	2,636	706	1,872	58
El Centro, CA M.S.A.	178,699									
Includes Imperial County										
City of El Centro	43,643	166	2	7	40	117	2,477	734	1,572	171
Total area actually reporting	95.6%	492	3	20	111	358	6,263	2,037	3,508	718
Estimated total	100.0%	519	3	21	120	375	6,471	2,087	3,636	748
Rate per 100,000 inhabitants		290.4	1.7	11.8	67.2	209.9	3,621.2	1,167.9	2,034.7	418.6
Elizabethtown-Fort Knox, KY M.S.A.	151,716									
Includes Hardin, Larue, and Meade Counties										
City of Elizabethtown	29,118	37	1	9	9	18	1,083	133	911	39
Total area actually reporting	100.0%	115	1	25	44	45	2,160	471	1,613	76
Rate per 100,000 inhabitants		75.8	0.7	16.5	29.0	29.7	1,423.7	310.4	1,063.2	50.1
Elmira, NY M.S.A. [1]	89,320									
Includes Chemung County										

Table 6. Crime, by Selected Metropolitan Statistical Area, 2012— continued

(Number, percent, rate per 100,000 population)

Area	Population	Violent crime	Murder and nonnegligent manslaughter	Forcible rape	Robbery	Aggravated assault	Property crime	Burglary	Larceny-theft	Motor vehicle theft
City of Elmira	29,362	104	2	1	40	61	1,192	250	923	19
Total area actually reporting	100.0%	222	4	2	46	170	2,212	398	1,768	46
Rate per 100,000 inhabitants		248.5	4.5	2.2	51.5	190.3	2,476.5	445.6	1,979.4	51.5
El Paso, TX M.S.A.	836,557									
Includes El Paso and Hudspeth Counties										
City of El Paso	675,536	2,859	23	184	471	2,181	16,411	1,826	13,425	1,160
Total area actually reporting	100.0%	3,319	28	220	508	2,563	19,361	2,380	15,623	1,358
Rate per 100,000 inhabitants		396.7	3.3	26.3	60.7	306.4	2,314.4	284.5	1,867.5	162.3
Erie, PA M.S.A.	281,440									
Includes Erie County										
City of Erie	101,972	458	8	64	172	214	3,510	1,095	2,311	104
Total area actually reporting	100.0%	693	11	93	223	366	7,345	1,808	5,326	211
Rate per 100,000 inhabitants		246.2	3.9	33.0	79.2	130.0	2,609.8	642.4	1,892.4	75.0
Eugene, OR M.S.A.	355,926									
Includes Lane County										
City of Eugene	158,043	430	0	72	196	162	8,004	1,515	6,054	435
Total area actually reporting	99.1%	835	7	125	259	444	13,435	2,605	9,976	854
Estimated total	100.0%	842	7	126	261	448	13,538	2,621	10,055	862
Rate per 100,000 inhabitants		236.6	2.0	35.4	73.3	125.9	3,803.6	736.4	2,825.0	242.2
Fairbanks, AK M.S.A.	34,603									
Includes Fairbanks North Star Borough										
City of Fairbanks	32,423	169	3	29	37	100	1,379	130	1,137	112
Total area actually reporting	100.0%	183	3	29	39	112	1,549	148	1,283	118
Rate per 100,000 inhabitants		528.9	8.7	83.8	112.7	323.7	4,476.5	427.7	3,707.8	341.0
Fargo, ND-MN M.S.A. [4]	216,055									
Includes Clay County, MN,[4] and Cass County, ND										
City of Fargo, ND	109,813	394	2	69	46	277	2,835	451	2,229	155
Total area actually reporting	100.0%		2		59	401	4,729	799	3,694	236
Rate per 100,000 inhabitants			0.9		27.3	185.6	2,188.8	369.8	1,709.7	109.2
Farmington, NM M.S.A.	128,404									
Includes San Juan County										
City of Farmington	45,328	481	4	81	39	357	1,866	332	1,430	104
Total area actually reporting	100.0%	849	6	132	56	655	3,175	677	2,315	183
Rate per 100,000 inhabitants		661.2	4.7	102.8	43.6	510.1	2,472.7	527.2	1,802.9	142.5
Fayetteville, NC M.S.A.	377,864									
Includes Cumberland and Hoke Counties										
City of Fayetteville	205,966	1,186	22	70	560	534	13,163	4,109	8,298	756
Total area actually reporting	100.0%	1,893	30	95	753	1,015	20,252	6,905	12,330	1,017
Rate per 100,000 inhabitants		501.0	7.9	25.1	199.3	268.6	5,359.6	1,827.4	3,263.1	269.1
Fayetteville-Springdale-Rogers, AR-MO M.S.A.	475,585									
Includes Benton, Madison, and Washington Counties, AR and McDonald County, MO										
City of Fayetteville, AR	75387	388	1	58	40	289	3,043	504	2,406	133
City of Springdale, AR	71668	332	1	57	30	244	2,692	457	2,089	146
City of Rogers, AR	57757	202	0	43	11	148	2,091	362	1,675	54
City of Bentonville, AR	36433	82	2	15	5	60	740	153	561	26

Table 6. Crime, by Selected Metropolitan Statistical Area, 2012— continued

(Number, percent, rate per 100,000 population)

Area	Population	Violent crime	Murder and nonnegligent manslaughter	Forcible rape	Robbery	Aggravated assault	Property crime	Burglary	Larceny-theft	Motor vehicle theft
Total area actually reporting	99.5%	1,768	11	253	102	1,402	11,996	2,647	8,814	535
Estimated total	100.0%	1,781	11	254	104	1,412	12,089	2,675	8,875	539
Rate per 100,000 inhabitants		374.5	2.3	53.4	21.9	296.9	2,541.9	562.5	1,866.1	113.3
Flagstaff, AZ M.S.A.	135,979									
Includes Coconino County										
City of Flagstaff	66,633	262	0	28	45	189	2,834	242	2,533	59
Total area actually reporting	100.0%	456	4	47	56	349	4,268	555	3,596	117
Rate per 100,000 inhabitants		335.3	2.9	34.6	41.2	256.7	3,138.7	408.2	2,644.5	86.0
Flint, MI M.S.A.	422,387									
Includes Genesee County										
City of Flint	101,632	2,774	63	108	673	1,930	5,645	2,979	2,207	459
Total area actually reporting	99.7%	3,830	69	243	979	2,539	15,345	6,111	8,297	937
Rate per 100,000 inhabitants	100.0%	3,833.0	69.0	243.0	980.0	2,541.0	15,376.0	6,118.0	8,319.0	939.0
		907.5	16.3	57.5	232.0	601.6	3,640.3	1,448.4	1,969.5	222.3
Florence, SC M.S.A.	208121									
Includes Darlington and Florence Counties										
City of Florence	37,681	328	3	25	83	217	2,897	566	2,190	141
Total area actually reporting	100.0%	1,132	16	53	205	858	9,880	2,641	6,664	575
Rate per 100,000 inhabitants		543.9	7.7	25.5	98.5	412.3	4,747.2	1,269.0	3,202.0	276.3
Florence-Muscle Shoals, AL M.S.A.	147,885									
Includes Colbert and Lauderdale Counties										
City of Florence	39,512	165	2	19	45	99	1,740	454	1,223	63
City of Muscle Shoals	13,228	76	0	4	16	56	647	148	473	26
Total area actually reporting	99.1%	507	5	44	89	369	4,399	1,247	2,937	215
Estimated total	100.0%	513	5	44	90	374	4,454	1,260	2,976	218
Rate per 100,000 inhabitants		346.9	3.4	29.8	60.9	252.9	3,011.8	852.0	2,012.4	147.4
Fond du Lac, WI M.S.A.	102,340									
Includes Fond du Lac County										
City of Fond du Lac	43,319	183	0	35	11	137	1,210	118	1,057	35
Total area actually reporting	100.0%	225	0	41	13	171	1,784	251	1,479	54
Rate per 100,000 inhabitants		219.9	0.0	40.1	12.7	167.1	1,743.2	245.3	1,445.2	52.8
Fort Collins-Loveland, CO M.S.A.	309,752									
Includes Larimer County										
City of Fort Collins	148,792	391	2	44	40	305	4,119	598	3,379	142
Total area actually reporting	100.0%	710	3	86	75	546	7,605	1,100	6,254	251
Rate per 100,000 inhabitants		229.2	1.0	27.8	24.2	176.3	2,455.2	355.1	2,019.0	81.0
Fort Smith, AR-OK M.S.A.	283,329									
Includes Crawford, Franklin, and Sebastian Counties, AR and Le Flore and Sequoyah Counties, OK										
City of Fort Smith, AR	87,483	687	5	69	95	518	4,771	1,064	3,524	183
Total area actually reporting	100.0%	1,161	8	115	110	928	8,475	2,240	5,872	363
Rate per 100,000 inhabitants		409.8	2.8	40.6	38.8	327.5	2,991.2	790.6	2,072.5	128.1
Fort Wayne, IN M.S.A.	420,767									
Includes Allen, Wells, and Whitley Counties										
City of Fort Wayne	256,625	931	22	93	447	369	9,515	2,025	7,073	417

Table 6. Crime, by Selected Metropolitan Statistical Area, 2012— continued

(Number, percent, rate per 100,000 population)

Area	Population	Violent crime	Murder and nonnegligent manslaughter	Forcible rape	Robbery	Aggravated assault	Property crime	Burglary	Larceny-theft	Motor vehicle theft
Total area actually reporting	94.5%	1,057	24	109	470	454	11,800	2,453	8,806	541
Estimated total	100.0%	1,078	24	112	472	470	12,116	2,538	9,016	562
Rate per 100,000 inhabitants		256.2	5.7	26.6	112.2	111.7	2,879.5	603.2	2,142.8	133.6
Fresno, CA M.S.A.	951,648									
Includes Fresno County										
City of Fresno	506,011	2,748	51	54	1,015	1,628	25,737	5,902	15,534	4,301
Total area actually reporting	99.0%	5,104	76	170	1,410	3,448	41,853	10,493	24,451	6,909
Estimated total	100.0%	5,137	76	172	1,421	3,468	42,099	10,552	24,603	6,944
Rate per 100,000 inhabitants		539.8	8.0	18.1	149.3	364.4	4,423.8	1,108.8	2,585.3	729.7
Gadsden, AL M.S.A. [1]	104,722									
Includes Etowah County[1]										
City of Gadsden[1]	36,961	372	1	33	113	225	3,000	835	1,969	196
Total area actually reporting	92.5%	530	2	45	125	358	4,177	1,233	2,652	292
Estimated total	100.0%	568	2	47	134	385	4,504	1,310	2,884	310
Rate per 100,000 inhabitants		542.4	1.9	44.9	128.0	367.6	4,300.9	1,250.9	2,754.0	296.0
Gainesville, FL M.S.A.	270,003									
Includes Alachua and Gilchrist Counties										
City of Gainesville	127,036	851	6	74	171	600	5,201	1,009	3,953	239
Total area actually reporting	100.0%	1,567	10	138	254	1,165	8,852	2,011	6,468	373
Rate per 100,000 inhabitants		580.4	3.7	51.1	94.1	431.5	3,278.5	744.8	2,395.5	138.1
Gainesville, GA M.S.A.	185,005									
Includes Hall County										
City of Gainesville	34,789	113	3	15	49	46	1,497	240	1,172	85
Total area actually reporting	100.0%	323	7	36	95	185	4,323	923	3,076	324
Rate per 100,000 inhabitants		174.6	3.8	19.5	51.3	100.0	2,336.7	498.9	1,662.7	175.1
Gettysburg, PA M.S.A.	101,598.0									
Includes Adams County										
City of Gettysburg	7,634.0	27	1	5	1	20	182	24	155	3
Total area actually reporting	100.0%	112	5	14	6	87	1,211	263	898	50
		110.2	4.9	13.8	5.9	85.6	1,192.0	258.9	883.9	49.2
Glens Falls, NY M.S.A. [1]	129,692									
Includes Warren and Washington Counties										
City of Glens Falls	14,807	43	1	3	2	37	372	51	315	6
Total area actually reporting	100.0%	200	7	29	16	148	2,178	403	1,719	56
Rate per 100,000 inhabitants		154.2	5.4	22.4	12.3	114.1	1,679.4	310.7	1,325.4	43.2
Goldsboro, NC M.S.A.	124,923									
Includes Wayne County										
City of Goldsboro	37,107	312	13	3	73	223	2,357	584	1,648	125
Total area actually reporting	97.7%	524	20	8	108	388	4,820	1,576	2,981	263
Estimated total	100.0%	533	20	9	110	394	4,930	1,601	3,062	267
Rate per 100,000 inhabitants		426.7	16.0	7.2	88.1	315.4	3,946.4	1,281.6	2,451.1	213.7
Grand Forks, ND-MN M.S.A. [4]	99,784									
Includes Polk County, MN,[4] and Grand Forks County, ND										
City of Grand Forks, ND	53,839	146	0	24	23	99	1,409	228	1,091	90
Total area actually reporting	100.0%		1		27	155	2,232	394	1,715	123
Rate per 100,000 inhabitants			1.0		27.1	155.3	2,236.8	394.9	1,718.7	123.3

Table 6. Crime, by Selected Metropolitan Statistical Area, 2012— continued

(Number, percent, rate per 100,000 population)

Area	Population	Violent crime	Murder and nonnegligent manslaughter	Forcible rape	Robbery	Aggravated assault	Property crime	Burglary	Larceny-theft	Motor vehicle theft
Grand Junction, CO M.S.A.	149,118									
Includes Mesa County										
City of Grand Junction	59,516	252	2	52	29	169	2,733	308	2,295	130
Total area actually reporting	99.5%	467	5	107	44	311	4,291	573	3,456	262
Estimated total	100.0%	468	5	107	44	312	4,309	576	3,470	263
Rate per 100,000 inhabitants		313.8	3.4	71.8	29.5	209.2	2,889.7	386.3	2,327.0	176.4
Great Falls, MT M.S.A.	82,406									
City of Great Falls	59,360	151	1	10	25	115	2,788	320	2,338	130
Total area actually reporting	100.0%	190	1	16	26	147	3,115	391	2,567	157
Rate per 100,000 inhabitants		230.6	1.2	19.4	31.6	178.4	3,780.1	474.5	3,115.1	190.5
Greeley, CO M.S.A.	262,216									
Includes Weld County										
City of Greeley	96,276	426	1	40	64	321	3,243	542	2,560	141
Total area actually reporting	94.5%	737	6	59	89	583	5,365	971	4,112	282
Estimated total	100.0%	768	6	64	94	604	5,734	1,026	4,400	308
Rate per 100,000 inhabitants		292.9	2.3	24.4	35.8	230.3	2,186.7	391.3	1,678.0	117.5
Green Bay, WI M.S.A.	310,262									
Includes Brown, Kewaunee, and Oconto Counties										
City of Green Bay	106,080	514	1	44	87	382	2,978	659	2,210	109
Total area actually reporting	100.0%	717	7	68	100	542	5,857	1,265	4,392	200
Rate per 100,000 inhabitants		231.1	2.3	21.9	32.2	174.7	1,887.8	407.7	1,415.6	64.5
Greensboro-High Point, NC M.S.A.	738,208									
Includes Guilford, Randolph, and Rockingham Counties										
City of Greensboro	276,134	1,555	21	70	556	908	12,064	3,345	8,153	566
City of High Point	106,801	556	5	19	185	347	4,417	1,188	2,943	286
Total area actually reporting	99.9%	2,726	44	137	856	1,689	26,186	7,402	17,556	1,228
Estimated total	100.0%	2,726	44	137	856	1,689	26,195	7,404	17,563	1,228
Rate per 100,000 inhabitants		369.3	6.0	18.6	116.0	228.8	3,548.5	1,003.0	2,379.1	166.3
Greenville, NC M.S.A.										
Includes Pitt County										
City of Greenville	86,869	455	7	23	169	256	3,845	1,130	2,596	119
Total area actually reporting	98.60%	696	11	36	207	442	5,933	1,763	3,982	188
Estimated total	100.00%	704	11	37	209	447	6,030	1,785	4,054	191
Rate per 100,000 inhabitants		407.3	6.4	21.4	120.9	258.6	3,489.0	1,032.8	2,345.7	110.5
Greenville-Anderson-Mauldin, SC M.S.A.	843,836									
Includes Anderson, Greenville, Laurens, and Pickens Counties										
City of Greenville	60,953	509	1	21	104	383	3,223	603	2,411	209
City of Anderson	27,127	250	7	10	38	195	1,970	386	1,458	126
City of Mauldin	23,631	48	0	5	6	37	461	84	345	32
City of Easley	20,249	106	3	10	12	81	1,329	224	1,048	57
Total area actually reporting	100.0%	4,814	54	305	703	3,752	33,066	8,158	22,368	2,540
Rate per 100,000 inhabitants		570.5	6.4	36.1	83.3	444.6	3,918.5	966.8	2,650.8	301.0
Hagerstown-Martinsburg, MD-WV M.S.A.	255,387									
Includes Washington County, MD and Berkeley County, WV										
City of Hagerstown, MD	40,275	197	3	11	75	108	1,456	310	1,020	126

Table 6. Crime, by Selected Metropolitan Statistical Area, 2012— continued

(Number, percent, rate per 100,000 population)

Area	Population	Violent crime	Murder and nonnegligent manslaughter	Forcible rape	Robbery	Aggravated assault	Property crime	Burglary	Larceny-theft	Motor vehicle theft
City of Martinsburg, WV	17,487	89	0	3	33	53	886	127	732	27
Total area actually reporting	100.0%	628	7	40	170	411	5,890	1,488	4,050	352
Rate per 100,000 inhabitants		245.9	2.7	15.7	66.6	160.9	2,306.3	582.6	1,585.8	137.8
Hammond, LA M.S.A.	123,296									
Includes Tangipahoa Parish										
City of Hammond	20,355	332	4	15	103	210	2,440	993	1,446	1
Total area actually reporting	96.6%	1,168	11	63	180	914	6,958	2,635	4,111	212
Estimated total	100.0%	1,185	11	64	183	927	7,127	2,666	4,243	218
Rate per 100,000 inhabitants		961.1	8.9	51.9	148.4	751.8	5,780.4	2,162.3	3,441.3	176.8
Hanford-Corcoran, CA M.S.A	155,191									
Includes Kings County										
City of Hanford	54,787	309	2	24	59	224	1,711	337	1,176	198
City of Corcoran	25,119	89	0	4	5	80	328	83	209	36
Total area actually reporting	100.0%	767	4	55	106	602	3,440	813	2,222	405
Rate per 100,000 inhabitants		494.2	2.6	35.4	68.3	387.9	2,216.6	523.9	1,431.8	261.0
Harrisburg-Carlisle, PA M.S.A.	553,808									
Includes Cumberland, Dauphin, and Perry Counties										
City of Harrisburg	49,753	727	11	56	388	272	2,426	613	1,655	158
City of Carlisle	19,103	48	0	15	19	14	610	60	547	3
Total area actually reporting	99.7%	1,656	18	176	607	855	11,799	2,327	9,079	393
Estimated total	100.0%	1,659	18	176	608	857	11,835	2,333	9,108	394
Rate per 100,000 inhabitants		299.6	3.3	31.8	109.8	154.7	2,137.0	421.3	1,644.6	71.1
Harrisonburg, VA M.S.A.	127,957									
Includes Rockingham County and Harrisonburg City										
City of Harrisonburg	50,524	110	1	14	25	70	1,067	152	888	27
Total area actually reporting	1.0	169	1	27	29	112	1,799	356	1,367	76
Rate per 100,000 inhabitants		132.1	0.8	21.1	22.7	87.5	1,405.9	278.2	1,068.3	59.4
Hartford-West Hartford-East Hartford, CT M.S.A.	1,023,883									
Includes Hartford, Middlesex, and Tolland Counties										
City of Hartford	125,203	1,655	23	27	640	965	5,319	1,050	3,467	802
City of West Hartford	63,487	46	0	2	35	9	1,695	243	1,348	104
City of East Hartford	51,431	192	2	26	83	81	1,573	362	1,029	182
City of Middletown	47,878	72	1	1	25	45	900	156	661	83
Total area actually reporting	100.0%	2,926	37	157	1,194	1,538	25,096	4,764	18,154	2,178
Rate per 100,000 inhabitants		285.8	3.6	15.3	116.6	150.2	2,451.1	465.3	1,773.1	212.7
Hattiesburg, MS M.S.A.	145741									
Includes Forrest, Lamar, and Perry Counties										
City of Hattiesburg	46726	118.0	5.0	13.0	66.0	34.0	2,668.0	375.0	2,183.0	110.0
Total area actually reporting	91.6%	160.0	5.0	23.0	78.0	54.0	3,701.0	946.0	2,630.0	125.0
Estimated total	100.0%	172.0	5.0	25.0	80.0	62.0	3,905.0	1,019.0	2,748.0	138.0
Rate per 100,000 inhabitants		118.0	3.4	17.2	54.9	42.5	2,679.4	699.2	1,885.5	94.7
Hickory-Lenoir-Morganton, NC M.S.A.	368,179									
Includes Alexander, Burke, Caldwell, and Catawba Counties										
City of Hickory	40,361	265	3	22	81	159	2,640	475	2,003	162

Table 6. Crime, by Selected Metropolitan Statistical Area, 2012— continued

(Number, percent, rate per 100,000 population)

Area	Population	Violent crime	Murder and nonnegligent manslaughter	Forcible rape	Robbery	Aggravated assault	Property crime	Burglary	Larceny-theft	Motor vehicle theft
City of Lenoir	18,270	51	0	1	17	33	935	231	662	42
City of Morganton	17,085	52	1	3	17	31	562	156	389	17
Total area actually reporting	0.995	815	20	57	198	540	12,120	3,690	7,866	564
Estimated total	1.0	821	20	57	200	544	12,204	3,716	7,921	567
Rate per 100,000 inhabitants		223.0	5.4	15.5	54.3	147.8	3,314.7	1,009.3	2,151.4	154.0
Hilton Head Island-Bluffton-Beaufort, SC M.S.A.	191,685									
Includes Beaufort and Jasper Counties										
City of Bluffton	12,855	39	0	5	15	19	461	72	372	17
City of Beaufort	12,653	139	2	4	29	104	824	147	656	21
Total area actually reporting	100.0%	996	21	60	171	744	5,826	1,497	4,050	279
Rate per 100,000 inhabitants		519.6	11.0	31.3	89.2	388.1	3,039.4	781.0	2,112.8	145.6
Hinesville, GA M.S.A.	81,447									
Includes Liberty and Long Counties										
City of Hinesville	34,887	153	2	18	33	100	1,479	389	1,049	41
Total area actually reporting	100.0%	275	4	38	44	189	2,457	758	1,600	99
Rate per 100,000 inhabitants		337.6	4.9	46.7	54.0	232.1	3,016.7	930.7	1,964.5	121.6
Homosassa Spring, FL M.S.A.	141,942									
Includes Citrus County										
Total area actually reporting	97.8%	451	5	26	57	363	2,837	737	1,971	129
Estimated total	100.0%	465	5	27	61	372	2,954	763	2,055	136
Rate per 100,000 inhabitants		327.6	3.5	19.0	43.0	262.1	2,081.1	537.5	1,447.8	95.8
Holland-Grand Haven, MI M.S.A.	263,602									
Includes Ottawa County										
City of Holland	26,015	93	0	19	8	66	852	174	664	14
City of Grand Haven	10,404	19	0	12	1	6	292	39	252	1
Total area actually reporting	100.0	401	2	127	26	246	4,842	967	3,764	111
Rate per 100,000 inhabitants	X	152.1	0.8	48.2	9.9	93.3	1,836.9	366.8	1,427.9	42.1
Houma-Thibodaux, LA M.S.A.	209,817									
Includes Lafourche and Terrebonne Parishes										
City of Houma	33,945	210	2	7	59	142	1,768	281	1,423	64
City of Thibodaux	14,701	65	1	1	13	50	581	74	498	9
Total area actually reporting	100.0%	611	9	28	131	443	6,855	1,464	5,071	320
Rate per 100,000 inhabitants		291.2	4.3	13.3	62.4	211.1	3,267.1	697.8	2,416.9	152.5
Houston-The Woodlands-Sugar Land, TX M.S.A. [3]	6,150,496									
Includes Austin, Brazoria, Chambers, Fort Bend, Galveston, Harris, Liberty, Montgomery, and Waller Counties										
City of Houston	2,177,273	21,610	217	665	9,385	11,343	107,678	26,630	67,978	13,070
City of Sugar Land	82,924	109	0	4	37	68	1,541	289	1,217	35
City of Baytown	74,420	247	5	15	97	130	3,684	939	2,438	307
City of Conroe	59,856	221	2	13	74	132	2,061	447	1,501	113
Total area actually reporting	99.90%	34,534	349	1,498	13,524	19,163			141,407	23,271
Estimated total	100.00%	34,535	349	1,498	13,524	19,164			141,416	23,272
Rate per 100,000 inhabitants		561.5	5.7	24.4	219.9	311.6			2,299.3	378.4
Huntsville, AL M.S.A.	427,189									

Table 6. Crime, by Selected Metropolitan Statistical Area, 2012— continued

(Number, percent, rate per 100,000 population)

Area	Population	Violent crime	Murder and nonnegligent manslaughter	Forcible rape	Robbery	Aggravated assault	Property crime	Burglary	Larceny-theft	Motor vehicle theft
Includes Limestone and Madison Counties										
City of Huntsville	183,691	1,696	14	72	456	1,154	9,261	2,165	6,386	710
Total area actually reporting	100.0%	2,228	22	109	548	1,549	14,292	3,615	9,702	975
Rate per 100,000 inhabitants		521.5	5.1	25.5	128.3	362.6	3,345.6	846.2	2,271.1	228.2
Idaho Falls, ID M.S.A.	135,809									
Includes Bonneville, Butte, and Jefferson Counties										
City of Idaho Falls	58,037	139	0	26	13	100	1,705	276	1,361	68
Total area actually reporting	100.0%	223	0	46	15	162	2,559	456	1,997	106
Rate per 100,000 inhabitants		164.2	0.0	33.9	11.0	119.3	1,884.3	335.8	1,470.4	78.1
Indianapolis-Carmel-Anderson, IN M.S.A.	1,915,784									
Includes Boone, Brown, Hamilton, Hancock, Hendricks, Johnson, Madison, Marion, Morgan, Putnam, and Shelby Counties										
City of Indianapolis	838,650	9,942	97	436	3,442	5,967	46,898	14,774	27,525	4,599
City of Carmel	81,819	11	0	2	6	3	808	113	649	46
City of Anderson	56,132	270	1	54	75	140	2,860	641	2,012	207
Total area actually reporting	85.2%	11,111	108	563	3,694	6,746	65,243	17,804	41,925	5,514
Estimated total	100.0%	11,485	114	602	3,755	7,014	70,358	18,955	45,572	5,831
Rate per 100,000 inhabitants		599.5	6.0	31.4	196.0	366.1	3,672.5	989.4	2,378.8	304.4
Iowa City, IA M.S.A.	155,494									
Includes Johnson and Washington Counties										
City of Iowa City	69,214	185	1	29	31	124	1,842	387	1,394	61
Total area actually reporting	100.0%	412	2	54	47	309	3,058	635	2,321	102
Rate per 100,000 inhabitants		265.0	1.3	34.7	30.2	198.7	1,966.6	408.4	1,492.7	65.6
Jackson, MS M.S.A.	574,517									
Includes Copiah, Hinds, Madison, Rankin, Simpson, and Yazoo Counties										
City of Jackson	175,939	1,668	63	135	799	671	11,568	4,124	6,308	1,136
Total area actually reporting	88.4%	2,116	74	180	901	961	17,691	5,840	10,392	1,459
Estimated total	100.0%	2,224	77	194	926	1,027	19,112	6,267	11,313	1,532
Rate per 100,000 inhabitants		387.1	13.4	33.8	161.2	178.8	3,326.6	1,090.8	1,969.1	266.7
Jackson, TN M.S.A.	131,023									
Includes Chester, Crockett, and Madison Counties										
City of Jackson	65,725	972	11	22	191	748	3,246	972	2,139	135
Total area actually reporting	100.0%	1,256	13	45	199	999	4,594	1,481	2,912	201
Rate per 100,000 inhabitants		958.6	9.9	34.3	151.9	762.5	3,506.3	1,130.3	2,222.5	153.4
Jacksonville, FL M.S.A.	1,378,810									
Includes Baker, Clay, Duval, Nassau, and St. Johns Counties										
City of Jacksonville	840,660	5,189	93	341	1,371	3,384	34,674	7,632	25,403	1,639
Total area actually reporting	100.0%	7,079	110	426	1,610	4,933	47,687	10,259	35,335	2,093
Rate per 100,000 inhabitants		513.4	8.0	30.9	116.8	357.8	3,458.6	744.0	2,562.7	151.8
Janesville-Beloit, WI M.S.A.	160,502									
Includes Rock County										
City of Janesville	63,642	179	2	21	35	121	2,463	339	2,059	65
City of Beloit	37,008	119	1	8	38	72	1,294	299	946	49

Table 6. Crime, by Selected Metropolitan Statistical Area, 2012— continued

(Number, percent, rate per 100,000 population)

Area	Population	Violent crime	Murder and nonnegligent manslaughter	Forcible rape	Robbery	Aggravated assault	Property crime	Burglary	Larceny-theft	Motor vehicle theft
Total area actually reporting	100.0%	384	3	44	96	241	4,771	884	3,738	149
Rate per 100,000 inhabitants		239.2	1.9	27.4	59.8	150.2	2,972.5	550.8	2,328.9	92.8
Jefferson City, MO M.S.A.	150,764									
Includes Callaway, Cole, Moniteau, and Osage Counties										
City of Jefferson City	43,413	261	2	12	39	208	1,586	235	1,311	40
Total area actually reporting	100.0%	469	3	24	59	383	3,577	773	2,661	143
Rate per 100,000 inhabitants		311.1	2.0	15.9	39.1	254.0	2,372.6	512.7	1,765.0	94.9
Johnson City, TN M.S.A.	201,468									
Includes Carter, Unicoi, and Washington Counties										
City of Johnson City	64,342	319	1	14	51	253	2,875	540	2,238	97
Total area actually reporting	100.0%	631	5	24	68	534	6,000	1,494	4,245	261
Rate per 100,000 inhabitants		313.2	2.5	11.9	33.8	265.1	2,978.1	741.6	2,107.0	129.5
Johnstown, PA M.S.A.	143,961									
Includes Cambria County										
City of Johnstown	22,360	131	1	6	31	93	822	285	499	38
Total area actually reporting	98.4%	316	6	30	47	233	2,529	650	1,787	92
Estimated total	100.0%	320	6	30	48	236	2,572	657	1,822	93
Rate per 100,000 inhabitants		222.3	4.2	20.8	33.3	163.9	1,786.6	456.4	1,265.6	64.6
Jonesboro, AR M.S.A.	123,295									
Includes Craighead and Poinsett Counties										
City of Jonesboro	68,807	295	4	21	78	192	3,157	1,166	1,889	102
Total area actually reporting	100.0%	403	6	47	88	262	4,309	1,574	2,610	125
Rate per 100,000 inhabitants		326.9	4.9	38.1	71.4	212.5	3,494.9	1,276.6	2,116.9	101.4
Joplin, MO M.S.A.	177,182									
Includes Jasper and Newton Counties										
City of Joplin	50,654	288	2	27	70	189	3,838	653	2,920	265
Total area actually reporting	100.0%	634	6	73	86	469	7,545	1,506	5,528	511
Rate per 100,000 inhabitants		357.8	3.4	41.2	48.5	264.7	4,258.3	850.0	3,120.0	288.4
Kahului-Wailuku-Lahaina, HI M.S.A.	158760									
Includes Kalawao and Maui Counties										
Total area actually reporting	100.0%	411	5	44	115	247	6,003	1,067	4,419	517
Rate per 100,000 inhabitants		258.9	3.1	27.7	72.4	155.6	3,781.2	672.1	2,783.4	325.6
Kalamazoo-Portage, MI M.S.A.										
Includes Kalamazoo and Van Buren Counties										
City of Kalamazoo	74,797	657	9	77	165	406	3,120	835	2,135	150
City of Portage	46,658	76	0	23	15	38	1,643	184	1,418	41
Total area actually reporting	98.9%	1,168	12	199	240	717	9,149	2,040	6,698	411
Estimated total	100.0%	1,178	12	200	242	724	9,239	2,059	6,762	418
Rate per 100,000 inhabitants		358.7	3.7	60.9	73.7	220.4	2,813.0	626.9	2,058.8	127.3
Kankakee, IL M.S.A.	113,751									
Includes Kankakee and Van Buren Counties										
City of Kankakee	27,609	237	6	26	71	134	1,201	348	809	44
Total area actually reporting	91.2%	365	8	47	81	229	2,937	658	2,184	95

Table 6. Crime, by Selected Metropolitan Statistical Area, 2012— continued

(Number, percent, rate per 100,000 population)

Area	Population	Violent crime	Murder and nonnegligent manslaughter	Forcible rape	Robbery	Aggravated assault	Property crime	Burglary	Larceny-theft	Motor vehicle theft
Estimated total	100.0%	387	8	49	87	243	3,155	701	2,350	104
Rate per 100,000 inhabitants		340.2	7.0	43.1	76.5	213.6	2,773.6	616.3	2,065.9	91.4
Kansas City, MO-KS M.S.A. [1]	2,033,239									
Includes Johnson, Leavenworth, Linn, Miami, and Wyandotte Counties, KS, and Bates, Caldwell, Cass, Clay, Clinton, Jackson, Lafayette, Platte, and Ray Counties, MO										
City of Kansas City, MO	464,073	5,862	105	246	1,647	3,864	25,642	6,964	15,088	3,590
City of Overland Park, KS	177,085	285	2	40	42	201	4,079	517	3,238	324
City of Kansas City, KS	147,201	877	15	85	277	500	7,538	1,772	4,558	1,208
Total area actually reporting	99.9%	9,920	156	686	2,420	6,658	70,600	15,298	47,426	7,876
Estimated total	100.0%	9,926	156	687	2,421	6,662	70,667	15,310	47,477	7,880
Rate per 100,000 inhabitants		488.2	7.7	33.8	119.1	327.7	3,475.6	753.0	2,335.0	387.6
Kennewick-Richland, WA M.S.A.	266,723									
Includes Benton and Franklin Counties										
City of Kennewick	76,971	229	1	33	35	160	2,372	450	1,795	127
City of Richland	50,057	82	0	20	11	51	1,270	187	1,019	64
Total area actually reporting	100.0%	624	2	81	99	442	6,400	1,379	4,583	438
Rate per 100,000 inhabitants		234.0	0.7	30.4	37.1	165.7	2,399.5	517.0	1,718.3	164.2
Killeen-Temple, TX M.S.A. [3]	417,760									
Includes Bell, Coryell, and Lampasas Counties										
City of Killeen	131,965	851	12	82	236	521	4,986	1,498	3,296	192
City of Temple[3]	68,194	202	1	22	74	105			1,433	89
Total area actually reporting	99.5%	1,495	20	165	375	935			7,711	361
Estimated total	100.0%	1,501	20	166	376	939			7,763	365
Rate per 100,000 inhabitants		359.3	4.8	39.7	90.0	224.8			1,858.2	87.4
Kingsport-Bristol-Bristol, TN-VA M.S.A.	312,616									
Includes Hawkins and Sullivan Counties, TN, and Scott and Washington Counties and Bristol City, VA										
City of Kingsport, TN	49,639	367	2	31	50	284	2,950	431	2,387	132
City of Bristol, TN	27,024	143	0	12	9	122	1,102	184	850	68
City of Bristol, VA	17,946	60	2	5	17	36	653	117	505	31
Total area actually reporting	100.0%	1,188	9	98	109	972	9,310	1,926	6,885	499
Rate per 100,000 inhabitants		380.0	2.9	31.3	34.9	310.9	2,978.1	616.1	2,202.4	159.6
Kingston, NY M.S.A. [1]	183,433									
Includes Ulster County										
City of Kingston	24,016	70	0	4	20	46	772	114	648	10
Total area actually reporting	100.0%	279	1	31	38	209	3,671	731	2,863	77
Rate per 100,000 inhabitants		152.1	0.5	16.9	20.7	113.9	2,001.3	398.5	1,560.8	42.0
Knoxville, TN M.S.A.	850,421									
Includes Anderson, Blount, Campbell, Grainger, Knox, Loudon, Morgan, Roane, and Union Counties										
City of Knoxville	182,254	1,774	18	119	528	1,109	12,169	2,882	8,373	914
Total area actually reporting	100.0%	3,584	34	271	759	2,520	29,675	7,676	19,995	2,004
Rate per 100,000 inhabitants		421.4	4.0	31.9	89.2	296.3	3,489.4	902.6	2,351.2	235.6
Kokomo, IN M.S.A.	83,059									

Table 6. Crime, by Selected Metropolitan Statistical Area, 2012— continued

(Number, percent, rate per 100,000 population)

Area	Population	Violent crime	Murder and nonnegligent manslaughter	Forcible rape	Robbery	Aggravated assault	Property crime	Burglary	Larceny-theft	Motor vehicle theft
Includes Howard County										
City of Kokomo	45,636	177	4	15	61	97	1,857	462	1,294	101
Total area actually reporting	100.0%	221	4	19	63	135	2,368	682	1,574	107
Rate per 100,000 inhabitants		266.1	4.8	22.9	75.8	162.5	2,845.0	821.1	1,895.0	128.8
La Crosse-Onalaska, WI-MN M.S.A. [4]	134,905									
Includes Houston County, MN[4] and La Crosse County, WI										
City of La Crosse, WI	51,851	154	4	21	38	91	1,954	404	1,501	49
City of Onalaska, WI	17,945	10	0	1	2	7	504	61	439	4
Total area actually reporting	100.0%		4		43	141	3,266	678	2,506	82
Rate per 100,000 inhabitants			3.0		31.9	104.5	2,421.0	502.6	1,857.6	60.8
Lafayette, LA M.S.A. [2]	473,751									
Includes Acadia, Iberia,[2] Lafayette, St. Martin, and Vermilion Parishes										
City of Lafayette	122,852	779	11	11	202	555	6,815	1,330	5,244	241
Total area actually reporting	89.7%		31	79	404			3,496	10,348	
Estimated total	100.0%		34	88	436			3,858	11,483	
Rate per 100,000 inhabitants			7.2	18.6	92.0			814.4	2,423.8	
Lafayette, West Lafayette, IN M.S.A.	204,246									
Includes Benton, Carroll, and Tippecanoe Counties										
City of Lafayette	68,160	407	1	36	69	301	3,293	713	2,382	198
City of West Lafayette	30,015	78	0	8	11	59	487	80	379	28
Total area actually reporting	96.5%	570	1	69	88	412	5,412	1,143	3,967	302
Estimated total	100.0%	577	1	70	89	417	5,522	1,170	4,043	309
Rate per 100,000 inhabitants		282.5	0.5	34.3	43.6	204.2	2,703.6	572.8	1,979.5	151.3
Lake Havasu City-Kingman, AZ M.S.A.	204,559									
Includes Mohave County										
City of Lake Havasu City	53,513	58	2	10	7	39	1,356	256	1,012	88
City of Kingman	28,588	93	0	9	8	76	1,775	406	1,269	100
Total area actually reporting	100.0%	367	12	31	57	267	7,073	1,790	4,839	444
Rate per 100,000 inhabitants		179.4	5.9	15.2	27.9	130.5	3,457.7	875.1	2,365.6	217.1
Lakeland-Winter Haven, FL M.S.A.	617,808									
Includes Polk County										
City of Lakeland	99,934	465	10	33	144	278	5,216	1,296	3,735	185
City of Winter Haven	34,759	245	5	8	59	173	1,812	489	1,267	56
Total area actually reporting	100.0%	2,170	39	126	421	1,584	19,088	5,796	12,467	825
Rate per 100,000 inhabitants		351.2	6.3	20.4	68.1	256.4	3,089.6	938.2	2,017.9	133.5
Lancaster, PA M.S.A.	524,442									
Includes Lancaster County										
City of Lancaster	60,155	465	7	37	208	213	2,900	439	2,351	110
Total area actually reporting	100.0%	878	15	113	331	419	10,294	1,720	8,227	347
Rate per 100,000 inhabitants		167.4	2.9	21.5	63.1	79.9	1,962.8	328.0	1,568.7	66.2
Lansing-East Lansing, MI M.S.A.	465,476									
Includes Clinton, Eaton, and Ingham Counties										
City of Lansing	114,688	1,078	13	92	203	770	3,774	1,307	2,203	264
City of East Lansing	48,701	116	0	17	19	80	993	215	695	83

Table 6. Crime, by Selected Metropolitan Statistical Area, 2012— continued

(Number, percent, rate per 100,000 population)

Area	Population	Violent crime	Murder and nonnegligent manslaughter	Forcible rape	Robbery	Aggravated assault	Property crime	Burglary	Larceny-theft	Motor vehicle theft
Total area actually reporting	94.9%	1,587	15	207	278	1,087	9,748	2,536	6,690	522
Estimated total	100.0%	1,656	16	215	294	1,131	10,348	2,662	7,118	568
Rate per 100,000 inhabitants		355.8	3.4	46.2	63.2	243.0	2,223.1	571.9	1,529.2	122.0
Laredo, TX M.S.A.	260,337									
Includes Webb County										
City of Laredo	245,558	1,036	8	81	183	764	10,685	1,718	8,586	381
Total area actually reporting	100.0%	1,127	8	86	187	846	11,080	1,825	8,845	410
Rate per 100,000 inhabitants		432.9	3.1	33.0	71.8	325.0	4,256.0	701.0	3,397.5	157.5
Las Cruces, NM M.S.A.	213,938									
Includes Dona Ana County										
City of Las Cruces	99,824	394	5	56	70	263	4,419	991	3,214	214
Total area actually reporting	98.9%	712	7	96	87	522	6,446	1,695	4,375	376
Estimated total	100.0%	723	7	97	88	531	6,511	1,710	4,420	381
Rate per 100,000 inhabitants		337.9	3.3	45.3	41.1	248.2	3,043.4	799.3	2,066.0	178.1
Las Vegas-Henderson-Paradise, NV M.S.A.	1,995,735									
Includes Clark County										
City of Las Vegas Metropolitan Police Department	1,479,393	11,598	76	596	3,824	7,102	46,427	14,220	25,522	6,685
City of Henderson	263,469	445	4	61	172	208	5,295	1,408	3,386	501
Total area actually reporting	100.0%	13,901	95	739	4,422	8,645	59,193	17,539	33,435	8,219
Rate per 100,000 inhabitants		696.5	4.8	37.0	221.6	433.2	2,966.0	878.8	1,675.3	411.8
Lawrence, KS M.S.A.	112,784									
Includes Douglas County										
City of Lawrence	89,180	370	0	52	53	265	3,997	604	3,190	203
Total area actually reporting	100.0%	416	0	58	57	301	4,548	740	3,590	218
Rate per 100,000 inhabitants		368.8	0.0	51.4	50.5	266.9	4,032.5	656.1	3,183.1	193.3
Lawton, OK M.S.A.	132,806									
Includes Comanche and Cotton Counties										
City of Lawton	98,781	920	13	38	173	696	5,208	1,560	3,349	299
Total area actually reporting	100.0%	959	13	42	174	730	5,675	1,710	3,635	330
Rate per 100,000 inhabitants		722.1	9.8	31.6	131.0	549.7	4,273.2	1,287.6	2,737.1	248.5
Lebanon, PA M.S.A.	134,529									
Includes Lebanon County										
City of Lebanon	25,662	99	2	6	48	43	696	123	544	29
Total area actually reporting	97.9%	281	3	24	64	190	2,515	377	2,060	78
Estimated total	100.0%	287	3	24	66	194	2,570	386	2,104	80
Rate per 100,000 inhabitants		213.3	2.2	17.8	49.1	144.2	1,910.4	286.9	1,564.0	59.5
Lewiston, ID-WA M.S.A.	61,959									
Includes Nez Perce County, ID and Asotin County, WA										
City of Lewiston, ID	32,337	55	0	7	10	38	1,280	289	934	57
Total area actually reporting	100.0%	112	0	13	16	83	2,135	419	1,622	94
Rate per 100,000 inhabitants		180.8	0.0	21.0	25.8	134.0	3,445.8	676.3	2,617.9	151.7
Lewiston-Auburn, ME M.S.A.	107,479									
Includes Androscoggin County										
City of Lewiston	36,519	80	0	15	43	22	1,387	328	1,018	41
City of Auburn	23,002	47	0	15	18	14	1,123	179	913	31

Table 6. Crime, by Selected Metropolitan Statistical Area, 2012— continued

(Number, percent, rate per 100,000 population)

Area	Population	Violent crime	Murder and nonnegligent manslaughter	Forcible rape	Robbery	Aggravated assault	Property crime	Burglary	Larceny-theft	Motor vehicle theft
Total area actually reporting	100.0%	157	0	44	66	47	3,271	768	2,400	103
Rate per 100,000 inhabitants		146.1	0.0	40.9	61.4	43.7	3,043.4	714.6	2,233.0	95.8
Lexington-Fayette, KY M.S.A. [1]	480,457									
Includes Bourbon, Clark, Fayette, Jessamine, Scott, and Woodford Counties										
City of Lexington[1]	302,332	1,066	12	102	606	346	13,399	2,854	9,641	904
Total area actually reporting	99.7%	1,429	18	161	700	550	19,633	4,315	14,183	1,135
Estimated total	100.0%	1,432	18	161	702	551	19,682	4,326	14,219	1,137
Rate per 100,000 inhabitants		298.0	3.7	33.5	146.1	114.7	4,096.5	900.4	2,959.5	236.6
Lima, OH M.S.A.	106,087									
Includes Allen County										
City of Lima	38,691	466	6	51	101	308	2,080	618	1,382	80
Total area actually reporting	97.4%	554	8	72	119	355	3,768	1,027	2,611	130
Estimated total	100.0%	558	8	73	120	357	3,843	1,042	2,668	133
Rate per 100,000 inhabitants		526.0	7.5	68.8	113.1	336.5	3,622.5	982.2	2,514.9	125.4
Lincoln, NE M.S.A.	308,646									
Includes Lancaster and Seward Counties										
City of Lincoln	264,175	1,050	3	182	197	668	10,171	1,616	8,244	311
Total area actually reporting	100.0%	1,092	4	196	201	691	10,938	1,780	8,825	333
Rate per 100,000 inhabitants		353.8	1.3	63.5	65.1	223.9	3,543.9	576.7	2,859.3	107.9
Little Rock-North Little Rock-Conway, AR M.S.A.	712,592									
Includes Faulkner, Grant, Lonoke, Perry, Pulaski, and Saline Counties										
City of Little Rock	196,055	2,579	45	137	807	1,590	15,804	4,244	10,465	1,095
City of North Little Rock	63,125	449	8	9	177	255	5,471	1,204	3,894	373
City of Conway	60,700	252	1	29	76	146	2,539	410	2,028	101
Total area actually reporting	90.1%	4,505	63	297	1,193	2,952	35,401	9,334	23,794	2,273
Estimated total	100.0%	4,739	65	324	1,202	3,148	36,701	9,833	24,485	2,383
Rate per 100,000 inhabitants		665.0	9.1	45.5	168.7	441.8	5,150.4	1,379.9	3,436.0	334.4
Logan, UT-ID M.S.A.	129,186									
Includes Franklin County, ID and Cache County, UT										
City of Logan, UT	49,672	32	0	1	3	28	1,047	206	805	36
Total area actually reporting	100.0%	69	0	23	4	42	2,034	397	1,568	69
Rate per 100,000 inhabitants		53.4	0.0	17.8	3.1	32.5	1,574.5	307.3	1,213.8	53.4
Longview, TX M.S.A.	219,910									
Includes Gregg, Rusk, and Upshur Counties										
City of Longview	80,637	452	7	27	128	290	4,115	928	2,878	309
Total area actually reporting	99.5%	948	8	96	178	666	7,996	1,970	5,502	524
Estimated total	100.0%	951	8	96	179	668	8,032	1,977	5,529	526
Rate per 100,000 inhabitants		432.4	3.6	43.7	81.4	303.8	3,652.4	899.0	2,514.2	239.2
Longview, WA M.S.A.	103,483									
Includes Cowlitz County										
City of Longview	37,032	156	1	26	55	74	2,211	468	1,604	139
Total area actually reporting	100.0%	304	4	73	66	161	3,785	853	2,701	231
Rate per 100,000 inhabitants		293.8	3.9	70.5	63.8	155.6	3,657.6	824.3	2,610.1	223.2

Table 6. Crime, by Selected Metropolitan Statistical Area, 2012— continued

(Number, percent, rate per 100,000 population)

Area	Population	Violent crime	Murder and nonnegligent manslaughter	Forcible rape	Robbery	Aggravated assault	Property crime	Burglary	Larceny-theft	Motor vehicle theft
Los Angeles-Long Beach-Nanheim, CA M.S.A.	13,064,838									
Includes the Metropolitan Divisions of Anaheim-Santa Ana-Irvine and Los Angeles-Long Beach-Glendale										
City of Los Angeles	3,855,122	18,547	299	936	8,983	8,329	87,478	16,388	56,006	15,084
City of Long Beach	469,893	2,705	32	115	1,239	1,319	14,131	3,799	7,702	2,630
City of Anaheim	344,526	1,279	15	82	440	742	10,070	1,605	7,025	1,440
City of Santa Ana	332,482	1,334	11	55	541	727	7,389	1,032	4,779	1,578
City of Irvine	217,528	110	2	8	29	71	3,304	570	2,599	135
City of Glendale	194,902	233	0	6	108	119	3,043	516	2,218	309
City of Torrance	147,851	190	4	17	92	77	2,690	529	1,823	338
City of Pasadena	139,382	433	5	21	172	235	3,379	891	2,238	250
City of Orange	139,692	135	4	8	54	69	2,833	500	2,044	289
City of Costa Mesa	112,635	254	4	32	83	135	4,079	668	3,050	361
City of Burbank	105,057	243	2	24	111	106	2,493	383	1,911	199
City of Carson	93,233	520	7	14	142	357	2,709	601	1,558	550
City of Santa Monica	91,215	395	2	23	151	219	3,398	586	2,634	178
City of Newport Beach	87,286	101	1	11	27	62	2,151	445	1,611	95
City of Tustin	77,400	114	0	11	36	67	1,653	240	1,282	131
City of Monterey Park	61,270	75	4	1	42	28	1,022	249	551	222
City of Gardena	59,802	287	0	13	167	107	1,321	297	716	308
City of Arcadia	57,295	57	0	1	22	34	1,388	339	975	74
City of Fountain Valley	56,674	106	1	7	17	81	1,469	299	1,063	107
Total area actually reporting	100.0%	51,345	651	2,374	21,055	27,265	300,087	60,926	191,503	47,658
Rate per 100,000 inhabitants		393.0	5.0	18.2	161.2	208.7	2,296.9	466.3	1,465.8	364.8
Anaheim-Santa Ana-Irvine, CA M.D.	3,084,081									
Includes Orange County										
Total area actually reporting	100.0%	6,789	51	398	2,132	4,208	67,821	11,819	48,899	7,103
Rate per 100,000 inhabitants		220.1	1.7	12.9	69.1	136.4	2,199.1	383.2	1,585.5	230.3
Los Angeles-Long Beach-Glendale, CA M.D.	9,980,757									
Includes Los Angeles County										
Total area actually reporting	100.0%	44,556	600	1,976	18,923	23,057	232,266	49,107	142,604	40,555
Rate per 100,000 inhabitants		446.4	6.0	19.8	189.6	231.0	2,327.1	492.0	1,428.8	406.3
Louisville/Jefferson County, KY-IN M.S.A.	1,248,616									
Includes Clark, Floyd, Harrison, Scott, and Washington Counties, IN, and Bullitt, Henry, Jefferson, Oldham, Shelby, Spencer, and Trimble Counties, KY										
City of Louisville Metro, KY	666,200	3,989	62	183	1,394	2,350	28,606	7,008	19,411	2,187
Total area actually reporting	96.4%	5,251	77	268	1,700	3,206	42,585	10,294	29,295	2,996
Estimated total	100.0%	5,310	78	275	1,711	3,246	43,390	10,482	29,863	3,045
Rate per 100,000 inhabitants		425.3	6.2	22.0	137.0	260.0	3,475.0	839.5	2,391.7	243.9
Lubbock, TX M.S.A.	300,321									
Includes Crosby, Lubbock, Lynn Counties										
City of Lubbock	237,241	1,962	11	104	325	1,522	12,273	3,099	8,429	745
Total area actually reporting	100.0%	2,163	12	144	329	1,678	13,582	3,452	9,298	832
Rate per 100,000 inhabitants		720.2	4.0	47.9	109.5	558.7	4,522.5	1,149.4	3,096.0	277.0
Lynchburg, VA M.S.A.	256,973									

Table 6. Crime, by Selected Metropolitan Statistical Area, 2012— continued

(Number, percent, rate per 100,000 population)

Area	Population	Violent crime	Murder and nonnegligent manslaughter	Forcible rape	Robbery	Aggravated assault	Property crime	Burglary	Larceny-theft	Motor vehicle theft
Includes Amherst, Appomattox, Bedford, and Campbell Counties and Bedford and Lynchburg Cities										
City of Lynchburg	77,347	267	3	34	46	184	2,093	365	1,659	69
Total area actually reporting	100.0%	400	6	62	61	271	4,591	951	3,461	179
Rate per 100,000 inhabitants		155.7	2.3	24.1	23.7	105.5	1,786.6	370.1	1,346.8	69.7
Macon, GA M.S.A.	235,405									
Includes Bibb, Crawford, Jones, Monroe, and Twiggs Counties										
City of Macon	92,836	583	21	41	242	279	6,699	1,828	4,371	500
Total area actually reporting	99.5%	933	26	60	311	536	11,037	2,884	7,372	781
Estimated total	100.0%	938	26	60	313	539	11,089	2,894	7,410	785
Rate per 100,000 inhabitants		398.5	11.0	25.5	133.0	229.0	4,710.6	1,229.4	3,147.8	333.5
Madera, CA M.S.A.	154,343									
Includes Madera County										
City of Madera	62,796	466	2	19	114	331	1,621	653	622	346
Total area actually reporting	100.0%	934	2	35	139	758	4,017	1,654	1,715	648
Rate per 100,000 inhabitants		605.1	1.3	22.7	90.1	491.1	2,602.6	1,071.6	1,111.2	419.8
Madison, WI M.S.A.	614,928									
Includes Columbia, Dane, Green, and Iowa Counties										
City of Madison	237,508	897	3	114	241	539	7,753	1,601	5,898	254
Total area actually reporting	99.6%	1,270	15	174	296	785	14,866	2,735	11,684	447
Estimated total	100.0%	1,273	15	174	297	787	14,919	2,742	11,729	448
Rate per 100,000 inhabitants		207.0	2.4	28.3	48.3	128.0	2,426.1	445.9	1,907.4	72.9
Manchester-Nashua, NH M.S.A.	402,466									
Includes Hillsborough County										
City of Manchester	110,040	624	1	72	205	346	3,848	849	2,848	151
City of Nashua	86,870	204	0	37	48	119	2,361	375	1,902	84
Total area actually reporting	94.2%	979	1	139	274	565	9,010	1,691	6,981	338
Estimated total	100.0%	996	1	143	276	576	9,274	1,732	7,195	347
Rate per 100,000 inhabitants		247.5	0.2	35.5	68.6	143.1	2,304.3	430.3	1,787.7	86.2
Manhattan, KS M.S.A.	95,402									
Includes Geary, Pottawatomie, and Riley Counties										
Total area actually reporting	94.6%	219	1	29	25	164	1,759	318	1,381	60
Estimated total	100.0%	229	1	30	26	172	1,876	338	1,470	68
Rate per 100,000 inhabitants		240.0	1.0	31.4	27.3	180.3	1,966.4	354.3	1,540.8	71.3
Mankato-North Mankato, MN M.S.A. [4]	97,827									
Includes Blue Earth and Nicollet Counties										
City of Mankato[4]	39,782		0		29	90	1,912	346	1,508	58
City of North Mankato[4]	13,523		0		1	4	219	28	185	6
Total area actually reporting	100.0%		0		33	119	2,733	489	2,154	90
Rate per 100,000 inhabitants			0.0		33.7	121.6	2,793.7	499.9	2,201.8	92.0
Mansfield, OH M.S.A.	123,502									
Includes Richland County										
City of Mansfield	47,480	178	1	27	93	57	3,205	1,016	2,104	85
Total area actually reporting	99.2%	240	3	44	115	78	5,807	1,819	3,838	150
Estimated total	100.0%	242	3	44	116	79	5,832	1,824	3,857	151

Table 6. Crime, by Selected Metropolitan Statistical Area, 2012— continued

(Number, percent, rate per 100,000 population)

Area	Population	Violent crime	Murder and nonnegligent manslaughter	Forcible rape	Robbery	Aggravated assault	Property crime	Burglary	Larceny-theft	Motor vehicle theft
Rate per 100,000 inhabitants		195.9	2.4	35.6	93.9	64.0	4,722.2	1,476.9	3,123.0	122.3
McAllen-Edinburg-Mission, TX M.S.A.	809,759									
Includes Hidalgo County										
City of McAllen	135,745	166	1	3	56	106	5,465	503	4,751	211
City of Edinburg	80,332	357	1	29	50	277	4,732	857	3,666	209
City of Mission	80,557	104	3	6	46	49	2,370	423	1,788	159
Total area actually reporting	100.0%	2,585	30	202	474	1,879	30,517	6,465	22,631	1,421
Rate per 100,000 inhabitants		319.2	3.7	24.9	58.5	232.0	3,768.7	798.4	2,794.8	175.5
Medford, OR M.S.A.	206,276									
Includes Jackson County										
City of Medford	76,037	425	2	39	64	320	4,418	477	3,764	177
Total area actually reporting	100.0%	673	4	74	82	513	7,776	1,014	6,449	313
Rate per 100,000 inhabitants		326.3	1.9	35.9	39.8	248.7	3,769.7	491.6	3,126.4	151.7
Memphis, TN-MS-AR M.S.A.	1,343,608									
Includes Crittenden County, AR; DeSoto, Marshall, Tate, and Tunica Counties; MS, and Fayette, Shelby, and Tipton Counties, TN										
City of Memphis	657,436	11,507	133	420	3,382	7,572	41,503	12,575	25,959	2,969
Total area actually reporting	95.7%	14,141	153	595	3,828	9,565	57,738	17,174	36,834	3,730
Estimated total	100.0%	14,199	155	604	3,839	9,601	58,680	17,511	37,380	3,789
Rate per 100,000 inhabitants		1,056.8	11.5	45.0	285.7	714.6	4,367.3	1,303.3	2,782.1	282.0
Merced, CA M.S.A.	262,308									
Includes Merced County										
City of Merced	80,976	810	9	25	215	561	4,111	955	2,721	435
Total area actually reporting	100.0%	1,833	23	54	331	1,425	10,091	2,686	6,047	1,358
Rate per 100,000 inhabitants		698.8	8.8	20.6	126.2	543.3	3,847.0	1,024.0	2,305.3	517.7
Miami-Fort Lauderdale-West Pompano Beach, FL M.S.A.	5,747,489									
Includes the Metropolitan Divisions of Fort Lauderdale-Pompano Beach-Deerfield Beach, Miami-Miami Beach-Kendall, and West Palm Beach-Boca Raton-Delray\ Beach										
City of Miami	414,327	4,856	69	65	2,096	2,626	22,271	4,255	15,305	2,711
City of Fort Lauderdale	170,827	1,543	16	48	835	644	9,960	2,951	6,419	590
City of Pompano Beach	103,003	1,060	5	37	419	599	5,562	1,283	3,876	403
City of West Palm Beach	102,422	821	17	31	334	439	5,404	1,289	3,801	314
City of Miami Beach	91,066	941	5	42	407	487	9,028	1,048	7,536	444
City of Boca Raton	86,493	164	0	12	62	90	2,557	491	1,965	101
City of Deerfield Beach	77,431	360	4	17	149	190	2,458	594	1,680	184
City of Delray Beach	62,044	457	6	26	157	268	2,950	565	2,230	155
City of Jupiter	56,674	115	0	11	37	67	1,196	235	918	43
Total area actually reporting	99.9%	32,461	364	1,355	11,314	19,428	225,642	48,808	160,350	16,484
Estimated total	100.0%	32,487	364	1,356	11,322	19,445	225,857	48,856	160,505	16,496
Rate per 100,000 inhabitants		565.2	6.3	23.6	197.0	338.3	3,929.7	850.0	2,792.6	287.0
Fort Lauderdale-Pompano Beach-Deerfield Beach, FL M.D.	1,804,461									
Includes Broward County										
Total area actually reporting	100.0%	8,720	80	404	3,425	4,811	67,932	17,469	46,079	4,384
Rate per 100,000 inhabitants		483.2	4.4	22.4	189.8	266.6	3,764.7	968.1	2,553.6	243.0

Table 6. Crime, by Selected Metropolitan Statistical Area, 2012— continued

(Number, percent, rate per 100,000 population)

Area	Population	Violent crime	Murder and nonnegligent manslaughter	Forcible rape	Robbery	Aggravated assault	Property crime	Burglary	Larceny-theft	Motor vehicle theft
Miami-Miami Beach-Kendall, FL M.D.	2,589,623									
Includes Miami-Dade County										
Total area actually reporting	100.0%	17,173	210	570	6,006	10,387	113,692	21,109	83,124	9,459
Rate per 100,000 inhabitants		663.1	8.1	22.0	231.9	401.1	4,390.3	815.1	3,209.9	365.3
West Palm Beach-Boca Raton-Delray Beach, FL M.D.	1,353,405									
Includes Palm Beach County										
Total area actually reporting	99.6%	6,568	74	381	1,883	4,230	44,018	10,230	31,147	2,641
Rate per 100,000 inhabitants	100.0%	6,594.0	74.0	382.0	1,891.0	4,247.0	44,233.0	10,278.0	31,302.0	2,653.0
		487.2	5.5	28.2	139.7	313.8	3,268.3	759.4	2,312.8	196.0
Michigan City-La Porte, IN M.S.A.	111,723									
Includes La Porte County										
City of Michigan City	31,551	120	3	11	56	50	1,725	325	1,339	61
City of La Porte	22,102	28	0	4	9	15	1,079	188	855	36
Total area actually reporting	96.9%	183	3	22	72	86	3,639	825	2,668	146
Estimated total	100.0%	193	3	23	74	93	3,755	843	2,759	153
Rate per 100,000 inhabitants		172.7	2.7	20.6	66.2	83.2	3,361.0	754.5	2,469.5	136.9
Midland, MI M.S.A.	84,124									
Includes Midland County										
City of Midland	42,106	38	1	15	5	17	457	56	400	1
Total area actually reporting	100.0%	102	2	47	7	46	941	209	719	13
Rate per 100,000 inhabitants		121.2	2.4	55.9	8.3	54.7	1,118.6	248.4	854.7	15.5
Midland, TX M.S.A.	147,417									
Includes Martin and Midland Counties										
City of Midland	115,637	398	4	21	52	321	3,008	559	2,313	136
Total area actually reporting	100.0%	464	5	23	54	382	3,705	714	2,773	218
Rate per 100,000 inhabitants		314.8	3.4	15.6	36.6	259.1	2,513.3	484.3	1,881.1	147.9
Milwaukee-Waukesha-West Allis, WI M.S.A.	1,566,214									
Includes Milwaukee, Ozaukee, Washington, and Waukesha Counties										
City of Milwaukee	599,395	7,759	91	230	3,027	4,411	30,228	6,977	18,448	4,803
City of Waukesha	71,049	107	1	26	24	56	1,304	233	1,039	32
City of West Allis	60,870	191	0	11	97	83	2,918	552	2,234	132
Total area actually reporting	97.3%	8,962	107	321	3,432	5,102	51,366	9,903	36,083	5,380
Estimated total	100.0%	9,015	108	326	3,446	5,135	52,377	10,040	36,932	5,405
Rate per 100,000 inhabitants		575.6	6.9	20.8	220.0	327.9	3,344.2	641.0	2,358.0	345.1
Minneapolis-St. Paul-Bloomington, MN-WI M.S.A. [3,4]	3,408,532									
Includes Anoka, Carver, Chisago, Dakota, Hennepin, Isanti, Le Sueur, Mille Lacs, Ramsey, Scott, Sherburne, Sibley, Washington, and Wright Counties, MN[4] and Pierce and St. Croix Counties, WI										
City of Minneapolis, MN	390,240	3,872	39	403	1,719	1,711	19,359	4,782	12,760	1,817
City of St. Paul, MN	290,700	2,101	13	168	658	1,262	11,893	3,150	6,938	1,805
City of Bloomington, MN[4]	84,596		0		59	63	3,212	227	2,908	77
City of Plymouth, MN[4]	72,020		0		14	19	1,198	258	909	31
City of Eagan, MN[4]	65,180		0		11	15	1,526	181	1,301	44
City of Eden Prairie, MN[4]	62,052		0		3	11	963	107	836	20

Table 6. Crime, by Selected Metropolitan Statistical Area, 2012— continued

(Number, percent, rate per 100,000 population)

Area	Population	Violent crime	Murder and nonnegligent manslaughter	Forcible rape	Robbery	Aggravated assault	Property crime	Burglary	Larceny-theft	Motor vehicle theft
Total area actually reporting	100%		76		3,083	4,818			71,575	6,599
Estimated total	100%		76		3,084	4,820			71,629	6,601
Rate per 100,000 inhabitants			2.2		90.5	141.4			2,101.5	193.7
Missoula, MT M.S.A.	110,904									
Includes Missoula County										
City of Missoula	67,758	221	0	25	33	163	3,041	378	2,558	105
Total area actually reporting	100.0%	321	0	41	38	242	3,616	461	3,009	146
Rate per 100,000 inhabitants		289.4	0.0	37.0	34.3	218.2	3,260.5	415.7	2,713.2	131.6
Mobile, AL M.S.A. [5]	414,233									
Includes Mobile County										
City of Mobile[5]	251,516	1,314	32	45	460	777	12,103	2,796	8,755	552
Total area actually reporting	100.0%	2,287	46	87	661	1,493	17,807	4,458	12,315	1,034
Rate per 100,000 inhabitants		552.1	11.1	21.0	159.6	360.4	4,298.8	1,076.2	2,973.0	249.6
Modesto, CA M.S.A.	523,330									
Includes Stanislaus County										
City of Modesto	204,631	1,590	20	59	450	1,061	11,276	2,571	6,906	1,799
Total area actually reporting	100.0%	2,875	38	129	788	1,920	22,061	5,551	12,425	4,085
Rate per 100,000 inhabitants		549.4	7.3	24.6	150.6	366.9	4,215.5	1,060.7	2,374.2	780.6
Monroe, LA M.S.A.	178,701									
Includes Ouachita and Union Parishes										
City of Monroe	49,474	490	5	18	137	330	3,775	1,172	2,525	78
Total area actually reporting	96.2%	786	11	30	177	568	7,833	2,233	5,410	190
Estimated total	100.0%	814	11	32	182	589	8,104	2,283	5,622	199
Rate per 100,000 inhabitants		455.5	6.2	17.9	101.8	329.6	4,534.9	1,277.6	3,146.0	111.4
Monroe, MI M.S.A.	151,670									
Includes Monroe County										
City of Monroe	20,687	108	1	10	25	72	831	234	560	37
Total area actually reporting	94.4%	396	5	67	92	232	3,867	1,043	2,594	230
Estimated total	100.0%	421	5	70	98	248	4,080	1,088	2,746	246
Rate per 100,000 inhabitants		277.6	3.3	46.2	64.6	163.5	2,690.1	717.3	1,810.5	162.2
Montgomery, AL M.S.A.	380,129									
Includes Autauga, Elmore, Lowndes, and Montgomery Counties										
City of Montgomery	209,018	827	44	41	459	283	12,058	3,409	7,548	1,101
Total area actually reporting	99.3%	1,328	53	86	551	638	16,794	4,876	10,554	1,364
Estimated total	100.0%	1,341	53	87	554	647	16,908	4,903	10,635	1,370
Rate per 100,000 inhabitants		352.8	13.9	22.9	145.7	170.2	4,448.0	1,289.8	2,797.7	360.4
Morgantown, WV M.S.A.	132,255									
Includes Monongalia and Preston Counties										
City of Morgantown	30,294	107	1	4	26	76	823	175	632	16
Total area actually reporting	93.8%	358	3	28	44	283	2,276	472	1,703	101
Estimated total	100.0%	381	3	30	48	300	2,553	519	1,925	109
Rate per 100,000 inhabitants		288.1	2.3	22.7	36.3	226.8	1,930.4	392.4	1,455.5	82.4
Morristown, TN M.S.A.	115,676									
Includes Hamblen and Jefferson Counties										
City of Morristown	29,617	203	0	13	45	145	1,798	191	1,522	85
Total area actually reporting	100.0%	455	3	29	85	338	3,898	799	2,917	182

Table 6. Crime, by Selected Metropolitan Statistical Area, 2012— continued

(Number, percent, rate per 100,000 population)

Area	Population	Violent crime	Murder and nonnegligent manslaughter	Forcible rape	Robbery	Aggravated assault	Property crime	Burglary	Larceny-theft	Motor vehicle theft
Rate per 100,000 inhabitants		393.3	2.6	25.1	73.5	292.2	3,369.8	690.7	2,521.7	157.3
Mount Vernon-Anacortes, WA M.S.A.	119,267									
Includes Skagit County										
City of Mount Vernon	32,384	79	1	13	21	44	1,552	315	1,155	82
City of Anacortes	16,097	16	0	1	2	13	577	157	386	34
Total area actually reporting	100.0%	232	2	38	46	146	5,008	1,275	3,478	255
Rate per 100,000 inhabitants		194.5	1.7	31.9	38.6	122.4	4,199.0	1,069.0	2,916.1	213.8
Muncie, IN M.S.A.	118,029									
Includes Delaware County										
City of Muncie	70,300	258	1	9	99	149	2,934	690	2,041	203
Total area actually reporting	100.0%	308	1	11	104	192	3,776	914	2,630	232
Rate per 100,000 inhabitants		261.0	0.8	9.3	88.1	162.7	3,199.2	774.4	2,228.3	196.6
Napa, CA M.S.A.	139,368									
Includes Napa County										
City of Napa	78,589	216	2	17	39	158	1,643	349	1,073	221
Total area actually reporting	100.0%	485	2	30	71	382	2,863	658	1,895	310
Rate per 100,000 inhabitants		348.0	1.4	21.5	50.9	274.1	2,054.3	472.1	1,359.7	222.4
Naples-Immokalee-Marco Island, FL M.S.A.	332,611									
Includes Collier County										
City of Naples	20,211	32	0	1	5	26	537	96	431	10
City of Marco Island	16,985	12	0	1	0	11	216	36	178	2
Total area actually reporting	100.0%	829	6	41	151	631	5,531	1,356	3,932	243
Rate per 100,000 inhabitants		249.2	1.8	12.3	45.4	189.7	1,662.9	407.7	1,182.2	73.1
Nashville-Davidson--Murfreesboro--Franklin, TN M.S.A.	1,712,682									
Includes Cannon, Cheatham, Davidson, Dickson, Hickman, Macon, Maury, Robertson, Rutherford, Smith, Sumner, Trousdale, Williamson, and Wilson Counties										
City of Nashville	620,886	7,550	62	311	1,724	5,453	26,052	5,736	18,885	1,431
City of Murfreesboro	112,247	701	3	55	134	509	4,006	923	2,899	184
City of Franklin	64,848	93	1	11	11	70	1,033	90	902	41
Total area actually reporting	100.0%	11,405	87	566	2,184	8,568	50,076	10,975	36,505	2,596
Rate per 100,000 inhabitants		665.9	5.1	33.0	127.5	500.3	2,923.8	640.8	2,131.5	151.6
New Bern, NC M.S.A.	129,271									
Includes Craven, Jones, and Pamlico Counties										
City of New Bern	30,195	163	3	10	36	114	1,861	745	1,066	50
Total area actually reporting	92.2%	359	3	26	66	264	4,517	1,974	2,392	151
Estimated total	100.0%	376	3	27	69	277	4,738	2,054	2,523	161
Rate per 100,000 inhabitants		290.9	2.3	20.9	53.4	214.3	3,665.2	1,588.9	1,951.7	124.5
New Haven-Milford, CT M.S.A.	809,772									
Includes New Haven County										
City of New Haven	129,934	1,870	17	55	844	954	6,516	1,451	4,351	714
City of Milford	52,817	46	0	2	33	11	1,586	150	1,371	65
Total area actually reporting	100.0%	3,352	33	134	1,349	1,836	24,254	4,188	17,972	2,094
Rate per 100,000 inhabitants		413.9	4.1	16.5	166.6	226.7	2,995.2	517.2	2,219.4	258.6
New Orleans-Metairie, LA M.S.A.	1,220,047									

Table 6. Crime, by Selected Metropolitan Statistical Area, 2012— continued

(Number, percent, rate per 100,000 population)

Area	Population	Violent crime	Murder and nonnegligent manslaughter	Forcible rape	Robbery	Aggravated assault	Property crime	Burglary	Larceny-theft	Motor vehicle theft
Includes Jefferson, Orleans, Plaquemines, St. Bernard, St. Charles, St. James, St. John the Baptist, and St. Tammany Parishes										
City of New Orleans	362,874	2,958	193	136	1,065	1,564	13,689	3,423	8,051	2,215
Total area actually reporting	96.8%	5,774	249	278	1,699	3,548	38,573	8,540	26,402	3,631
Estimated total	100.0%	5,894	251	285	1,722	3,636	39,672	8,827	27,168	3,677
Rate per 100,000 inhabitants		483.1	20.6	23.4	141.1	298.0	3,251.7	723.5	2,226.8	301.4
New York-Newark-Jersey City, NY-NJ-PA M.S.A. [1]	19,791,750									
Includes the Metropolitan Divisions of Dutchess County-Putnam County, NY; Nassau County-Suffolk County, NY; Newark, NJ-PA; and New York-Jersey City-White Plains, NY-NJ										
City of New York, NY[1]	8,289,415	52,993	419	1,162	20,201	31,211	142,760	18,635	115,935	8,190
City of Newark, NJ	278,906	3,220	96	55	1,976	1,093	10,199	2,144	4,093	3,962
City of Jersey City, NJ	251,554	1,847	11	45	880	911	5,479	1,426	3,291	762
City of White Plains, NY	57,567	92	1	3	31	57	1,386	82	1,279	25
City of New Brunswick, NJ	55,717	382	8	24	216	134	1,511	557	871	83
City of Lakewood Township, NJ	93,742	110	2	1	46	61	1,103	274	785	44
Total area actually reporting	99.9%		748	2,124	31,768		336,211	57,572	254,023	24,616
Estimated total	100.0%		749	2,132	31,798		337,353	57,780	254,913	24,660
Rate per 100,000 inhabitants			4	11	161		1,705	292	1,288	125
Dutchess County-Putnam County, NY M.D. [1]	400,079									
Includes Dutchess and Putnam Counties[1]										
Total area actually reporting	98.4%	717	5	37	169	506	5,992	1,084	4,730	178
Estimated total	100.0%	730	5	38	173	514	6,119	1,104	4,833	182
Rate per 100,000 inhabitants		182.5	1.2	9.5	43.2	128.5	1,529.4	275.9	1,208.0	45.5
Nassau County-Suffolk County, NY M.D. [1]	2,858,599									
Includes Nassau and Suffolk Counties[1]										
Total area actually reporting	99.9%	4,575	51	124	1,836	2,564	43,537	7,101	34,253	2,183
Estimated total	100.0%	4,578	51	124	1,837	2,566	43,566	7,106	34,276	2,184
Rate per 100,000 inhabitants		160.1	1.8	4.3	64.3	89.8	1,524.0	248.6	1,199.0	76.4
Newark, NJ-PA M.D.	2,489,919									
Includes Essex, Hunterdon, Morris, Somerset, Sussex, and Union Counties, NJ and Pike County, PA										
Total area actually reporting	100.0%	7,860	162	281	4,152	3,265	46,566	10,743	27,611	8,212
Rate per 100,000 inhabitants		315.7	6.5	11.3	166.8	131.1	1,870.2	431.5	1,108.9	329.8
New York-Jersey City-White Plains, NY-NJ M.D. [1,3]	14,043,153									
Includes Bergen, Hudson, Middlesex, Monmouth, Ocean, and Passaic Counties, NJ and Bronx, Kings, New York, Orange, Queens, Richmond, Rockland, and Westchester Counties, NY[1]										
Total area actually reporting	99.5%		530	1,682	25,611		240,116	38,644	187,429	14,043
Estimated total	100.0%		531	1,689	25,636		241,102	38,827	188,193	14,082

Table 6. Crime, by Selected Metropolitan Statistical Area, 2012— continued

(Number, percent, rate per 100,000 population)

Area	Population	Violent crime	Murder and nonnegligent manslaughter	Forcible rape	Robbery	Aggravated assault	Property crime	Burglary	Larceny-theft	Motor vehicle theft
Rate per 100,000 inhabitants			3.8	12.0	182.6		1,716.9	276.5	1,340.1	100.3
North Port-Sarasota-Bradenton, FL M.S.A.	719,024									
Includes Manatee and Sarasota Counties										
City of North Port	58,568	130	2	20	12	96	1,074	278	770	26
City of Sarasota	53,055	425	4	25	136	260	2,897	705	2,093	99
City of Bradenton	50,878	341	4	23	94	220	2,026	511	1,440	75
City of Venice	21,182	40	0	3	6	31	418	99	308	11
Total area actually reporting	100.0%	3,241	43	212	676	2,310	21,843	5,461	15,600	782
Rate per 100,000 inhabitants		450.7	6.0	29.5	94.0	321.3	3,037.8	759.5	2,169.6	108.8
Norwich-New London, CT M.S.A.	146,391									
Includes New London County										
City of Norwich	40,517	99	1	18	35	45	963	274	639	50
City of New London	27,643	366	3	10	45	308	764	183	515	66
Total area actually reporting	100.0%	594	5	44	99	446	3,461	670	2,617	174
Rate per 100,000 inhabitants		405.8	3.4	30.1	67.6	304.7	2,364.2	457.7	1,787.7	118.9
Ocala, FL M.S.A.	337,066									
Includes Marion County										
City of Ocala	57,288	375	6	42	92	235	3,097	606	2,431	60
Total area actually reporting	100.0%	1,616	21	166	162	1,267	7,311	1,989	5,080	242
Rate per 100,000 inhabitants		479.4	6.2	49.2	48.1	375.9	2,169.0	590.1	1,507.1	71.8
Ocean City, NJ M.S.A.	97,077									
Includes Cape May County										
City of Ocean City	11,676	15	0	1	1	13	478	88	388	2
Total area actually reporting	100.0%	254	2	12	53	187	4,411	1,054	3,273	84
Rate per 100,000 inhabitants		261.6	2.1	12.4	54.6	192.6	4,543.8	1,085.7	3,371.6	86.5
Odessa, TX M.S.A.	142,209									
Includes Ector County										
City of Odessa	103,635	1,103	5	43	141	914	3,717	770	2,565	382
Total area actually reporting	100.0%	1,168	5	44	163	956	5,177	1,090	3,571	516
Rate per 100,000 inhabitants		821.3	3.5	30.9	114.6	672.2	3,640.4	766.5	2,511.1	362.8
Ogden-Clearfield, UT M.S.A.	614,396									
Includes Box Elder, Davis, Morgan, and Weber Counties										
City of Ogden	85,083	353	2	25	96	230	4,001	734	3,051	216
City of Clearfield	31,032	51	0	9	6	36	735	92	626	17
Total area actually reporting	99.5%	856	4	186	146	520	14,813	2,444	11,716	653
Estimated total	100.0%	861.0	4.0	187.0	147.0	523.0	14,902.0	2,457.0	11,787.0	658.0
Rate per 100,000 inhabitants		140.1	0.7	30.4	23.9	85.1	2,425.5	399.9	1,918.5	107.1
Oklahoma City, OK M.S.A.	1,285,907									
Includes Canadian, Cleveland, Grady, Lincoln, Logan, McClain, and Oklahoma Counties										
City of Oklahoma City	595,607	5,474	85	389	1,209	3,791	35,390	9,854	21,162	4,374
Total area actually reporting	100.0%	7,054	103	596	1,479	4,876	56,160	14,924	35,430	5,806
Rate per 100,000 inhabitants		548.6	8.0	46.3	115.0	379.2	4,367.3	1,160.6	2,755.3	451.5
Olympia-Tumwater, WA M.S.A.	259,107									

Table 6. Crime, by Selected Metropolitan Statistical Area, 2012— continued

(Number, percent, rate per 100,000 population)

Area	Population	Violent crime	Murder and nonnegligent manslaughter	Forcible rape	Robbery	Aggravated assault	Property crime	Burglary	Larceny-theft	Motor vehicle theft
Includes Thurston County										
City of Olympia	47,729	150	5	45	37	63	2,085	468	1,504	113
City of Tumwater	17,844	46	0	11	9	26	627	158	440	29
Total area actually reporting	100.0%	552	10	98	89	355	7,590	2,137	5,013	440
Rate per 100,000 inhabitants		213.0	3.9	37.8	34.3	137.0	2,929.3	824.8	1,934.7	169.8
Omaha-Council Bluffs, NE-IA M.S.A.	882,865									
Includes Harrison, Mills, and Pottawattamie Counties, IA and Cass, Douglas, Sarpy, Saunders, and Washington Counties, NE										
City of Omaha, NE	417,970	2,485	41	187	815	1,442	19,178	3,311	13,120	2,747
City of Council Bluffs, IA	62,708	744	1	67	81	595	4,290	970	2,847	473
Total area actually reporting	98.5%	3,585	43	333	938	2,271	29,578	5,459	20,348	3,771
Estimated total	100.0%	3,594	43	335	939	2,277	29,742	5,496	20,464	3,782
Rate per 100,000 inhabitants		407.1	4.9	37.9	106.4	257.9	3,368.8	622.5	2,317.9	428.4
Orlando-Kissimmee-Sanford, FL M.S.A.	2,200,987									
Includes Lake, Orange, Osceola, and Seminole Counties										
City of Orlando	246,513	2,508	24	103	603	1,778	16,304	3,778	11,222	1,304
City of Kissimmee	62,183	563	2	34	121	406	3,112	822	2,150	140
City of Sanford	54,662	323	3	21	166	133	2,964	822	1,986	156
Total area actually reporting	100.0%	12,019	109	676	2,673	8,561	76,705	21,316	50,130	5,259
Rate per 100,000 inhabitants		546.1	5.0	30.7	121.4	389.0	3,485.0	968.5	2,277.6	238.9
Oshkosh-Neenah, WI M.S.A.	168,129									
Includes Winnebago County										
City of Oshkosh	66,514	191	0	13	18	160	1,722	340	1,345	37
City of Neenah	25,681	35	0	2	2	31	495	76	404	15
Total area actually reporting	100.0%	321	0	28	24	269	3,386	675	2,621	90
Rate per 100,000 inhabitants		190.9	0.0	16.7	14.3	160.0	2,013.9	401.5	1,558.9	53.5
Owensboro, KY M.S.A.	115,625									
Includes Daviess, Hancock, and McLean Counties										
City of Owensboro	57,751	125	0	28	45	52	2,518	469	1,928	121
Total area actually reporting	99.3%	144	0	32	47	65	3,113	633	2,334	146
Estimated total	100.0%	146	0	32	48	66	3,139	639	2,353	147
Rate per 100,000 inhabitants		126.3	0.0	27.7	41.5	57.1	2,714.8	552.6	2,035.0	127.1
Oxnard-Thousand Oaks-Ventura, CA M.S.A.	839,484									
Includes Ventura County										
City of Oxnard	201,797	603	9	8	304	282	4,071	848	2,677	546
City of Thousand Oaks	129,171	157	0	23	46	88	1,838	278	1,470	90
City of Ventura	108,511	310	1	24	140	145	3,885	778	2,825	282
City of Camarillo	66,506	61	0	5	21	35	955	139	767	49
Total area actually reporting	100.0%	1,664	21	100	617	926	15,921	3,113	11,404	1,404
Rate per 100,000 inhabitants		198.2	2.5	11.9	73.5	110.3	1,896.5	370.8	1,358.5	167.2
Palm Bay-Melbourne-Titusville, FL M.S.A.	550,983									
Includes Brevard County										
City of Palm Bay	104,635	553	3	19	78	453	2,457	719	1,601	137
City of Melbourne	77,133	658	6	48	133	471	3,374	648	2,607	119
City of Titusville	44,374	294	4	26	77	187	1,765	519	1,001	245

Table 6. Crime, by Selected Metropolitan Statistical Area, 2012— continued

(Number, percent, rate per 100,000 population)

Area	Population	Violent crime	Murder and nonnegligent manslaughter	Forcible rape	Robbery	Aggravated assault	Property crime	Burglary	Larceny-theft	Motor vehicle theft
Total area actually reporting	100.0%	2,963	30	199	505	2,229	16,659	3,945	11,867	847
Rate per 100,000 inhabitants		537.8	5.4	36.1	91.7	404.5	3,023.5	716.0	2,153.8	153.7
Panama City, FL M.S.A.	188,234									
Includes Bay County										
City of Panama City	37,187	285	3	9	75	198	2,307	434	1,743	130
City of Lynn Haven	100.0%	939	10	74	173	682	7,658	1,683	5,672	303
City of Panama City Beach		498.8	5.3	39.3	91.9	362.3	4,068.3	894.1	3,013.3	161.0
Parkersburg-Vienna, WV M.S.A.	92,884									
Includes Wirt and Wood Counties										
City of Parkersburg	31,558	146	1	17	22	106	1,698	433	1,199	66
City of Vienna	10,770	13	0	1	3	9	294	19	271	4
Total area actually reporting	96.9%	305	1	29	33	242	2,602	639	1,846	117
Estimated total	100.0%	313	1	30	34	248	2,701	656	1,925	120
Rate per 100,000 inhabitants		337.0	1.1	32.3	36.6	267.0	2,907.9	706.3	2,072.5	129.2
Pensacola-Ferry Pass-Brent, FL M.S.A.	459,402									
Includes Escambia and Santa Rosa Counties										
City of Pensacola	52,909	473	7	30	89	347	3,032	711	2,201	120
Total area actually reporting	100.0%	2,687	22	187	529	1,949	16,745	4,496	11,469	780
Rate per 100,000 inhabitants		584.9	4.8	40.7	115.1	424.2	3,645.0	978.7	2,496.5	169.8
Peoria, IL M.S.A.	379,733									
Includes Marshall, Peoria, Stark, Tazewell, and Woodford Counties										
City of Peoria	115,288	919	10	25	324	560	5,022	1,420	3,370	232
Total area actually reporting	92.4%	1,497	17	90	385	1,005	9,750	2,597	6,795	358
Estimated total	100.0%	1,562	18	97	403	1,044	10,379	2,721	7,273	385
Rate per 100,000 inhabitants		411.3	4.7	25.5	106.1	274.9	2,733.2	716.6	1,915.3	101.4
Philadelphia-Camden-Wilmington, PA-NJ-DE-MD M.S.A. [1,6]	6,012,363									
Includes the Metropolitan Divisions of Camden, NJ; Montgomery County-Bucks County-Chester County, PA; Philadelphia, PA; and Wilmington, DE-MD-NJ										
City of Philadelphia, PA	1,538,957	17,853	331	880	7,984	8,658	56,997	12,004	38,592	6,401
City of Camden, NJ	77,665	1,993	67	74	755	1,097	4,007	1,089	2,214	704
City of Wilmington, DE	72,088	1,228	26	34	474	694	3,824	1,212	2,247	365
Total area actually reporting	99.9%		517	1,667	12,651		160,263	33,846	114,487	11,930
Estimated total	100.0%		517	1,667	12,651		160,273	33,848	114,494	11,931
Rate per 100,000 inhabitants			8.6	27.7	210.4		2,665.7	563.0	1,904.3	198.4
Camden, NJ M.D.	1,258,086									
Includes Burlington, Camden, and Gloucester Counties										
Total area actually reporting	99.9%	4,263	80	231	1,596	2,356	32,329	7,691	22,595	2,043
Estimated total	100.0%	4,264	80	231	1,596	2,357	32,339	7,693	22,602	2,044
Rate per 100,000 inhabitants		338.9	6.4	18.4	126.9	187.3	2,570.5	611.5	1,796.5	162.5
Montgomery County-Bucks County-Chester County, PA M.D.	1,892,483									
Includes Bucks, Chester, and Montgomery Counties										

Table 6. Crime, by Selected Metropolitan Statistical Area, 2012— continued

(Number, percent, rate per 100,000 population)

Area	Population	Violent crime	Murder and nonnegligent manslaughter	Forcible rape	Robbery	Aggravated assault	Property crime	Burglary	Larceny-theft	Motor vehicle theft
Total area actually reporting	100.0%	2,800	26	289	875	1,610	33,268	5,620	26,478	1,170
Rate per 100,000 inhabitants		148.0	1.4	15.3	46.2	85.1	1,757.9	297.0	1,399.1	61.8
Philadelphia, PA M.D. **[1,6]**	2,144,972									
Includes Delaware and Philadelphia Counties										
Total area actually reporting	100.0%		361	972	8,851		71,230	14,542	49,637	7,051
Rate per 100,000 inhabitants			16.8	45.3	412.6		3,320.8	678.0	2,314.1	328.7
Wilmington, DE-MD-NJ M.D.	716,822									
Includes New Castle County, DE; Cecil County, MD; and Salem County, NJ										
Total area actually reporting	100.0%	3,905	50	175	1,329	2,351	23,436	5,993	15,777	1,666
Rate per 100,000 inhabitants		544.8	7.0	24.4	185.4	328.0	3,269.4	836.1	2,201.0	232.4
Phoenix-Mesa-Scottsdale, AZ M.S.A. [1,2]	4,309,766									
Includes Maricopa and Pinal[2] Counties										
City of Phoenix	1,485,509	9,458	123	556	3,516	5,263	60,777	17,912	35,678	7,187
City of Mesa	451,391	1,804	14	172	469	1,149	14,140	2,681	10,572	887
City of Scottsdale	223,432	329	3	42	115	169	6,047	1,255	4,551	241
City of Tempe	166,061	878	11	44	253	570	7,824	1,250	6,085	489
Total area actually reporting	99.9%	17,521	228	1,187	5,485	10,621		35,307	98,322	
Estimated total	100.0%	17,534	228	1,188	5,488	10,630		35,341	98,449	
Rate per 100,000 inhabitants		406.8	5.3	27.6	127.3	246.6		820.0	2,284.3	
Pine Bluff, AR M.S.A.	99,299									
Includes Cleveland, Jefferson, and Lincoln Counties										
City of Pine Bluff	48,522	625	14	32	135	444	3,312	1,124	2,008	180
Total area actually reporting	100.0%	725	14	45	143	523	4,218	1,544	2,406	268
Rate per 100,000 inhabitants		730.1	14.1	45.3	144.0	526.7	4,247.8	1,554.9	2,423.0	269.9
Pittsburgh, PA M.S.A. [6]	2,363,571									
Includes Allegheny, Armstrong, Beaver, Butler, Fayette, Washington, and Westmoreland Counties										
City of Pittsburgh	312,112	2,347	41	47	1,134	1,125	10,691	2,537	7,610	544
Total area actually reporting	98.7%		99	355	2,108		44,323	9,321	33,216	1,786
Estimated total	100.0%		100	359	2,125		44,920	9,420	33,694	1,806
Rate per 100,000 inhabitants			4.2	15.2	89.9		1,900.5	398.5	1,425.6	76.4
Pittsfield, MA M.S.A.	131,619									
Includes Berkshire County										
City of Pittsfield	44,868	191	0	34	38	119	1,166	372	751	43
Total area actually reporting	94.3%	434	0	66	55	313	2,903	900	1,900	103
Estimated total	100.0%	458	0	68	60	330	3,049	935	2,002	112
Rate per 100,000 inhabitants		348.0	0.0	51.7	45.6	250.7	2,316.5	710.4	1,521.1	85.1
Pocatello, ID M.S.A.	84,258									
Includes Bannock County										
City of Pocatello	55,166	141	1	10	22	108	1,502	262	1,192	48
Total area actually reporting	100.0%	195	3	14	25	153	2,155	328	1,761	66
Rate per 100,000 inhabitants		231.4	3.6	16.6	29.7	181.6	2,557.6	389.3	2,090.0	78.3
Portland-South Portland, ME M.S.A.	516,198									

Table 6. Crime, by Selected Metropolitan Statistical Area, 2012— continued

(Number, percent, rate per 100,000 population)

Area	Population	Violent crime	Murder and nonnegligent manslaughter	Forcible rape	Robbery	Aggravated assault	Property crime	Burglary	Larceny-theft	Motor vehicle theft
Includes Cumberland, Sagadahoc, and York Counties										
City of Portland	66,413	173	1	33	82	57	2,632	411	2,139	82
City of South Portland	25,087	49	0	3	11	35	966	108	847	11
Total area actually reporting	100.0%	686	7	137	197	345	12,713	2,499	9,846	368
Rate per 100,000 inhabitants		132.9	1.4	26.5	38.2	66.8	2,462.8	484.1	1,907.4	71.3
Portland-Vancouver-Hillsboro, OR-WA M.S.A.	2,279,873									
Includes Clackamas, Columbia, Multnomah, Washington, and Yamhill Counties, OR and Clark and Skamania Counties, WA										
City of Portland, OR	598,037	3,093	20	231	950	1,892	30,454	4,471	22,398	3,585
City of Vancouver, WA	166,375	592	5	72	172	343	6,478	1,044	4,343	1,091
City of Hillsboro, OR	94,119	180	2	34	52	92	2,154	323	1,716	115
City of Beaverton, OR	92,276	141	0	21	36	84	1,471	196	1,165	110
Total area actually reporting	100.0%	6,076	54	724	1,780	3,518	72,141	12,057	52,421	7,663
Rate per 100,000 inhabitants		266.5	2.4	31.8	78.1	154.3	3,164.3	528.8	2,299.3	336.1
Port St. Lucie, FL M.S.A.	433,712									
Includes Martin and St. Lucie Counties										
City of Port St. Lucie	168,416	395	4	47	55	289	3,031	816	2,124	91
Total area actually reporting	100.0%	1,527	11	140	311	1,065	10,170	2,722	7,042	406
Rate per 100,000 inhabitants		352.1	2.5	32.3	71.7	245.6	2,344.9	627.6	1,623.7	93.6
Prescott, AZ M.S.A.	214,201									
Includes Yavapai County										
City of Prescott	40,420	168	2	14	19	133	1,104	197	883	24
Total area actually reporting	100.0%	700	12	45	47	596	4,442	948	3,268	226
Rate per 100,000 inhabitants		326.8	5.6	21.0	21.9	278.2	2,073.8	442.6	1,525.7	105.5
Providence-Warwick, RI-MA M.S.A.	1,604,098									
Includes Bristol County, MA and Bristol, Kent, Newport, Providence, and Washington Counties RI										
City of Providence, RI	177,882	1,133	17	84	362	670	7,977	1,929	4,884	1,164
City of Warwick RI	82,282	102	1	15	29	57	2,117	334	1,688	95
Total area actually reporting	100.0%	5,449	38	466	1,407	3,538	40,028	9,606	27,000	3,422
Rate per 100,000 inhabitants		339.7	2.4	29.1	87.7	220.6	2,495.4	598.8	1,683.2	213.3
Provo-Orem, UT M.S.A.	548,142									
Includes Juab and Utah Counties										
City of Provo	116,879	149	0	36	19	94	2,465	301	2,051	113
City of Orem	91,953	41	2	11	21	7	2,168	203	1,887	78
Total area actually reporting	100.0%	388	4	83	68	233	10,189	1,315	8,506	368
Rate per 100,000 inhabitants		70.8	0.7	15.1	12.4	42.5	1,858.8	239.9	1,551.8	67.1
Pueblo, CO M.S.A.	162,766									
Includes Pueblo County										
City of Pueblo	109,065	797	8	21	199	569	7,030	1,895	4,642	493
Total area actually reporting	100.0%	831	8	21	203	599	8,114	2,087	5,478	549
Rate per 100,000 inhabitants		510.5	4.9	12.9	124.7	368.0	4,985.1	1,282.2	3,365.6	337.3
Punta Gorda, FL M.S.A.	162,701									
Includes Charlotte County										
City of Punta Gorda	16,925	11	0	0	4	7	278	49	223	6

Table 6. Crime, by Selected Metropolitan Statistical Area, 2012— continued

(Number, percent, rate per 100,000 population)

Area	Population	Violent crime	Murder and nonnegligent manslaughter	Forcible rape	Robbery	Aggravated assault	Property crime	Burglary	Larceny-theft	Motor vehicle theft
Total area actually reporting	100.0%	399	1	24	37	337	3,507	910	2,475	122
Rate per 100,000 inhabitants		245.2	0.6	14.8	22.7	207.1	2,155.5	559.3	1,521.2	75.0
Racine, WI M.S.A.	195,888									
Includes Racine County										
City of Racine	79,055	374	4	31	211	128	3,181	1,101	1,950	130
Total area actually reporting	100.0%	484	6	40	226	212	5,290	1,430	3,673	187
Rate per 100,000 inhabitants		247.1	3.1	20.4	115.4	108.2	2,700.5	730.0	1,875.1	95.5
Raleigh, NC M.S.A.	1,175,043									
Includes Franklin, Johnston, and Wake Counties										
City of Raleigh	420,594	1,780	17	113	665	985	13,779	3,036	9,812	931
Total area actually reporting	99.8%	2,895	21	205	891	1,778	28,938	7,219	20,147	1,572
Estimated total	100.0%	2,902	21	205	893	1,783	29,032	7,240	20,217	1,575
Rate per 100,000 inhabitants		247.0	1.8	17.4	76.0	151.7	2,470.7	616.1	1,720.5	134.0
Rapid City, SD M.S.A.	138,237									
Includes Meade and Pennington Counties										
City of Rapid City	69,979	425	4	111	55	255	3,555	591	2,734	230
Total area actually reporting	100.0%	529	4	142	55	328	4,371	753	3,347	271
Rate per 100,000 inhabitants		382.7	2.9	102.7	39.8	237.3	3,162.0	544.7	2,421.2	196.0
Reading, PA M.S.A.	413,447									
Includes Berks County										
City of Reading	88,557	828	15	44	382	387	3,612	1,447	1,629	536
Total area actually reporting	99.1%	1,368	19	92	480	777	9,231	2,444	6,002	785
Estimated total	100.0%	1,376	19	93	482	782	9,305	2,456	6,062	787
Rate per 100,000 inhabitants		332.8	4.6	22.5	116.6	189.1	2,250.6	594.0	1,466.2	190.4
Redding, CA M.S.A.	179,423									
Includes Shasta County										
City of Redding	90,974	705	3	66	131	505	4,380	1,088	2,790	502
Total area actually reporting	100.0%	1,298	7	97	165	1,029	6,280	1,754	3,623	903
Rate per 100,000 inhabitants		723.4	3.9	54.1	92.0	573.5	3,500.1	977.6	2,019.3	503.3
Reno, NV M.S.A.	435,223									
Includes Storey and Washoe Counties										
City of Reno	230,486	1,192	7	33	327	825	7,423	1,633	4,909	881
Total area actually reporting	100.0%	1,721	12	85	416	1,208	11,470	2,684	7,542	1,244
Rate per 100,000 inhabitants		395.4	2.8	19.5	95.6	277.6	2,635.4	616.7	1,732.9	285.8
Richmond, VA M.S.A.	1,232,458									
Includes Amelia, Caroline, Charles City, Chesterfield, Dinwiddie, Goochland, Hanover, Henrico, King William, New Kent, Powhatan, Prince George, and Sussex Counties and Colonial Heights, Hopewell, Petersburg, and Richmond Cities										
City of Richmond	207,799	1,348	42	38	633	635	9,103	2,030	6,138	935
Total area actually reporting	100.0%	3,000	84	160	1,165	1,591	31,592	6,301	23,242	2,049
Rate per 100,000 inhabitants		243.4	6.8	13.0	94.5	129.1	2,563.3	511.3	1,885.8	166.3
Riverside-San Bernardino-Ontario, CA M.S.A.	4,344,917									
Includes Riverside and San Bernardino Counties										
City of Riverside	313,532	1,389	16	76	517	780	10,818	2,247	7,095	1,476

Table 6. Crime, by Selected Metropolitan Statistical Area, 2012— continued

(Number, percent, rate per 100,000 population)

Area	Population	Violent crime	Murder and nonnegligent manslaughter	Forcible rape	Robbery	Aggravated assault	Property crime	Burglary	Larceny-theft	Motor vehicle theft
City of San Bernardino	214,987	2,022	47	56	803	1,116	10,510	2,809	4,991	2,710
City of Ontario	167,933	534	3	36	266	229	5,056	1,058	3,019	979
City of Corona	157,342	210	1	17	102	90	4,143	861	2,766	516
City of Victorville	118,687	676	6	40	222	408	4,465	1,837	1,981	647
City of Temecula	103,414	97	0	10	53	34	2,440	588	1,640	212
City of Chino	79,792	291	1	9	52	229	2,116	562	1,319	235
City of Redlands	70,399	221	2	15	75	129	2,992	608	1,984	400
Total area actually reporting	100.0%	16,021	178	744	5,272	9,827	131,275	37,893	72,682	20,700
Rate per 100,000 inhabitants		368.7	4.1	17.1	121.3	226.2	3,021.3	872.1	1,672.8	476.4
Roanoke, VA M.S.A.	312,265									
Includes Botetourt, Craig, Franklin, and Roanoke Counties and Roanoke and Salem Cities										
City of Roanoke	97,780	542	9	40	141	352	4,771	940	3,583	248
Total area actually reporting	100.0%	794	11	75	166	542	8,027	1,575	6,069	383
Rate per 100,000 inhabitants		254.3	3.5	24.0	53.2	173.6	2,570.6	504.4	1,943.5	122.7
Rochester, MN M.S.A. [4]	209,826									
Includes Dodge, Fillmore, Olmsted, and Wabasha Counties[4]										
City of Rochester[4]	108,582		2		55	104	2,721	495	2,137	89
Total area actually reporting	100.0%		3		59	165	3,697	777	2,773	147
Rate per 100,000 inhabitants			1.4		28.1	78.6	1,761.9	370.3	1,321.6	70.1
Rochester, NY M.S.A. [1]	1,086,565									
Includes Livingston, Monroe, Ontario, Orleans, Wayne, and Yates Counties[1]										
City of Rochester[1]	211,993	2,069	36	112	817	1,104	11,283	2,978	7,683	622
Total area actually reporting	100.0%	3,090	44	256	1,060	1,730	28,745	6,304	21,341	1,100
Rate per 100,000 inhabitants		284.4	4.0	23.6	97.6	159.2	2,645.5	580.2	1,964.1	101.2
Rockford, IL M.S.A.	348,522									
Includes Boone and Winnebago Counties										
City of Rockford	152,293	2,083	9	124	499	1,451	7,608	2,224	5,003	381
Total area actually reporting	80.8%	2,450	11	191	554	1,694	10,819	2,937	7,387	495
Estimated total	100.0%	2,578	12	208	583	1,775	12,039	3,217	8,274	548
Rate per 100,000 inhabitants		739.7	3.4	59.7	167.3	509.3	3,454.3	923.0	2,374.0	157.2
Rocky Mount, NC M.S.A.	153,664									
Includes Edgecombe and Nash Counties										
City of Rocky Mount	58,002	749	8	13	128	600	3,383	1,046	2,192	145
Total area actually reporting	99.0%	940	14	31	161	734	5,391	1,860	3,282	249
Estimated total	100.0%	944	14	31	162	737	5,448	1,873	3,324	251
Rate per 100,000 inhabitants		614.3	9.1	20.2	105.4	479.6	3,545.4	1,218.9	2,163.2	163.3
Rome, GA M.S.A.	97,013									
Includes Floyd County										
City of Rome	36,567	190	2	15	45	128	2,241	490	1,667	84
Total area actually reporting	100.0%	353	5	26	57	265	3,877	941	2,786	150
Rate per 100,000 inhabitants		363.9	5.2	26.8	58.8	273.2	3,996.4	970.0	2,871.8	154.6
Sacramento—Roseville—Arden-Arcade, CA M.S.A.	2,196,416									
Includes El Dorado, Placer, Sacramento, and Yolo Counties										
City of Sacramento	476,557	3,520	34	125	1,211	2,150	19,967	4,474	12,147	3,346

Table 6. Crime, by Selected Metropolitan Statistical Area, 2012— continued

(Number, percent, rate per 100,000 population)

Area	Population	Violent crime	Murder and nonnegligent manslaughter	Forcible rape	Robbery	Aggravated assault	Property crime	Burglary	Larceny-theft	Motor vehicle theft
City of Roseville	122,896	293	2	15	84	192	3,288	519	2,536	233
City of Folsom	73,678	85	0	7	24	54	1,277	235	963	79
Total area actually reporting	100.0%	9,688	84	530	2,919	6,155	64,260	15,279	39,256	9,725
Rate per 100,000 inhabitants		441.1	3.8	24.1	132.9	280.2	2,925.7	695.6	1,787.3	442.8
Saginaw, MI M.S.A.	199,233									
Includes Saginaw County										
City of Saginaw	51,267	1,211	27	65	167	952	1,765	1,042	618	105
Total area actually reporting	100.0%	1,627	30	120	242	1,235	4,662	1,746	2,690	226
Rate per 100,000 inhabitants		816.6	15.1	60.2	121.5	619.9	2,340.0	876.4	1,350.2	113.4
Salem, OR M.S.A.	397,669									
Includes Marion and Polk Counties										
City of Salem	157,353	564	7	40	138	379	6,731	1,043	4,958	730
Total area actually reporting	100.0%	942	13	89	200	640	12,771	2,185	9,313	1,273
Rate per 100,000 inhabitants		236.9	3.3	22.4	50.3	160.9	3,211.5	549.5	2,341.9	320.1
Salinas, CA M.S.A.	425,810									
Includes Monterey County										
City of Salinas	154,413	1,027	21	41	488	477	4,906	1,218	2,606	1,082
Total area actually reporting	100.0%	1,866	45	94	706	1,021	10,298	2,912	5,612	1,774
Rate per 100,000 inhabitants		438.2	10.6	22.1	165.8	239.8	2,418.4	683.9	1,318.0	416.6
Salisbury, MD M.S.A.	381,281									
Includes Sussex County, DE and Somerset, Wicomico, and Worcester Counties, MD										
City of Salisbury, MD	30,778	366	1	18	118	229	1,859	336	1,470	53
Total area actually reporting	100.0%	1,758	15	127	356	1,260	12,589	3,184	9,046	359
Rate per 100,000 inhabitants		461.1	3.9	33.3	93.4	330.5	3,301.8	835.1	2,372.5	94.2
Salt Lake City, UT M.S.A.	1,123,286									
Includes Salt Lake and Tooele Counties										
City of Salt Lake City	192,465	1,300	8	122	316	854	14,357	1,824	10,827	1,706
Total area actually reporting	99.9%	3,679	25	502	823	2,329	48,604	7,047	37,136	4,421
Estimated total	100.0%	3,679	25	502	823	2,329	48,616	7,049	37,145	4,422
Rate per 100,000 inhabitants		327.5	2.2	44.7	73.3	207.3	4,328.0	627.5	3,306.8	393.7
San Antonio-New Braunfels, TX M.S.A.	2,227,800									
Includes Atascosa, Bandera, Bexar, Comal, Guadalupe, Kendall, Medina, and Wilson Counties										
City of San Antonio	1,380,123	6,943	89	549	1,864	4,441	82,668	15,668	60,633	6,367
City of New Braunfels	60,482	115	1	19	27	68	2,110	300	1,718	92
Total area actually reporting	99.9%	8,700	114	811	2,117	5,658	104,406	20,590	76,254	7,562
Estimated total	100.0%	8,703	114	811	2,118	5,660	104,441	20,597	76,280	7,564
Rate per 100,000 inhabitants		390.7	5.1	36.4	95.1	254.1	4,688.1	924.5	3,424.0	339.5
San Diego-Carlsbad, CA M.S.A.	3,169,187									
Includes San Diego County										
City of San Diego	1,338,477	5,529	47	304	1,517	3,661	31,700	5,902	19,188	6,610
City of Carlsbad	107,879	265	2	26	55	182	2,109	497	1,463	149
Total area actually reporting	100.0%	11,839	107	692	3,200	7,840	69,624	14,076	43,412	12,136
Rate per 100,000 inhabitants		373.6	3.4	21.8	101.0	247.4	2,196.9	444.2	1,369.8	382.9

Table 6. Crime, by Selected Metropolitan Statistical Area, 2012— continued

(Number, percent, rate per 100,000 population)

Area	Population	Violent crime	Murder and nonnegligent manslaughter	Forcible rape	Robbery	Aggravated assault	Property crime	Burglary	Larceny-theft	Motor vehicle theft
San Francisco-Oakland-Hayward, CA M.S.A.[2,3]	4,431,755									
Includes the Metropolitan Divisions of Oakland-Hayward-Berkeley, San Francisco-Redwood City-South San Francisco, and San Rafael										
City of San Francisco	820,363	5,777	69	108	3,484	2,116	38,898	5,317	28,242	5,339
City of Oakland	399,487	7,963	127	271	4,338	3,227	26,342	6,168	13,198	6,976
City of Hayward	147,424	613	6	46	342	219	4,792	1,109	2,227	1,456
City of Berkeley	114,961	487	5	39	335	108	5,696	971	4,084	641
City of San Leandro	86,869	437	2	15	271	149	3,585	699	2,094	792
City of Redwood City	78,466	208	0	13	88	107	1,800	526	1,121	153
City of San Ramon	74,013	45	0	3	13	29	850	146	633	71
City of Pleasanton	71,875	49	1	4	18	26	1,279	165	995	119
City of Walnut Creek	65,816	84	0	3	19	62	2,050	446	1,463	141
City of South San Francisco	65,006	111	0	12	29	70	1,321	351	782	188
City of San Rafael	58,854	191	0	14	84	93	1,785	360	1,132	293
Total area actually reporting	100.0%	24,411	288	892	12,040	11,191				27,833
Rate per 100,000 inhabitants		550.8	6.5	20.1	271.7	252.5				628.0
Oakland-Hayward-Berkeley, CA M.D.[3]	2,620,044									
Includes Alameda and Contra Costa Counties										
Total area actually reporting	100.0%	16,283	209	646	7,822	7,606		21,801		20,302
Rate per 100,000 inhabitants		621.5	8.0	24.7	298.5	290.3		832.1		774.9
San Francisco-Redwood City-South San Francisco, CA M.D.	1,554,315									
Includes San Francisco and San Mateo Counties										
Total area actually reporting	100.0%	7,638	79	216	4,062	3,281	54,471	8,674	38,850	6,947
Rate per 100,000 inhabitants		491.4	5.1	13.9	261.3	211.1	3,504.5	558.1	2,499.5	446.9
San Rafael, CA M.D.[2]	257,396									
Includes Marin County										
Total area actually reporting	100.0%	490.0	0.0	30.0	156.0	304.0				584.0
Rate per 100,000 inhabitants		190.4	0.0	11.7	60.6	118.1				226.9
San Jose-Sunnyvale-Santa Clara, CA M.S.A.	1,882,748									
Includes San Benito and Santa Clara Counties										
City of San Jose	976,459	3,547	45	280	1,208	2,014	28,463	5,206	14,498	8,759
City of Sunnyvale	143,606	170	3	14	71	82	2,555	524	1,696	335
City of Santa Clara	119,360	221	0	10	61	150	3,306	584	2,273	449
City of Mountain View	75,933	155	0	5	34	116	1,419	178	1,127	114
City of Milpitas	68,433	81	1	11	34	35	2,023	332	1,350	341
City of Palo Alto	66,019	53	0	4	26	23	1,409	327	1,034	48
City of Cupertino	59,769	58	0	6	23	29	797	175	569	53
Total area actually reporting	100.0%	5,159	56	417	1,672	3,014	49,015	9,297	28,617	11,101
Rate per 100,000 inhabitants		274.0	3.0	22.1	88.8	160.1	2,603.4	493.8	1,520.0	589.6
San Luis Obispo-Paso Robles-Arroyo Grande, CA M.S.A.	274,491									
Includes San Luis Obispo County										
City of San Luis Obispo	45,947	119	1	20	19	79	1,971	414	1,476	81
City of Paso Robles	30,344	91	1	6	6	78	777	152	578	47
City of Arroyo Grande	17,568	60	0	1	1	58	358	123	210	25
Total area actually reporting	100.0%	906	6	69	78	753	6,252	1,568	4,266	418

Table 6. Crime, by Selected Metropolitan Statistical Area, 2012— continued

(Number, percent, rate per 100,000 population)

Area	Population	Violent crime	Murder and nonnegligent manslaughter	Forcible rape	Robbery	Aggravated assault	Property crime	Burglary	Larceny-theft	Motor vehicle theft
Rate per 100,000 inhabitants		330.1	2.2	25.1	28.4	274.3	2,277.7	571.2	1,554.1	152.3
Santa Cruz-Watsonville, CA M.S.A.	266,749									
Includes Santa Cruz County										
City of Santa Cruz	60,902	433	3	34	83	313	3,585	527	2,794	264
City of Watsonville	52,064	252	2	15	87	148	1,585	265	1,024	296
Total area actually reporting	100.0%	1,041	10	76	220	735	8,709	1,633	6,104	972
Rate per 100,000 inhabitants		390.3	3.7	28.5	82.5	275.5	3,264.9	612.2	2,288.3	364.4
Santa Fe, NM M.S.A.	145,880									
Includes Santa Fe County										
City of Santa Fe	68,751	331	2	15	109	205	3,897	1,907	1,816	174
Total area actually reporting	100.0%	528	6	25	138	359	5,445	2,715	2,466	264
Rate per 100,000 inhabitants		361.9	4.1	17.1	94.6	246.1	3,732.5	1,861.1	1,690.4	181.0
Santa Maria-Santa Barbara, CA M.S.A.	430,836									
Includes Santa Barbara County										
City of Santa Maria	101,207	690	0	21	145	524	2,430	712	1,318	400
City of Santa Barbara	89,871	363	0	53	95	215	3,115	558	2,424	133
Total area actually reporting	100.0%	1,643	6	146	311	1,180	10,164	2,430	6,933	801
Rate per 100,000 inhabitants		381.4	1.4	33.9	72.2	273.9	2,359.1	564.0	1,609.2	185.9
Santa Rosa, CA M.S.A.	492,642									
Includes Sonoma County										
City of Santa Rosa	170,862	636	2	67	126	441	3,818	725	2,777	316
Total area actually reporting	100.0%	1,792	4	152	232	1,404	8,514	1,826	5,982	706
Rate per 100,000 inhabitants		363.8	0.8	30.9	47.1	285.0	1,728.2	370.7	1,214.3	143.3
Savannah, GA M.S.A.	359,371									
Includes Bryan, Chatham, and Effingham Counties										
City of Savannah-Chatham Metropolitan	231,285	878	23	25	491	339	8,325	2,083	5,583	659
Total area actually reporting	100.0%	1,177	25	60	555	537	11,256	2,773	7,666	817
Rate per 100,000 inhabitants		327.5	7.0	16.7	154.4	149.4	3,132.1	771.6	2,133.2	227.3
Scranton—Wilkes-Barre—Hazleton, PA M.S.A.	564,136									
Includes Lackawanna, Luzerne, and Wyoming Counties										
City of Scranton	76,118	252	0	23	129	100	2,553	641	1,796	116
City of Wilkes-Barre	41,532	172	3	30	76	63	1,243	271	869	103
City of Hazleton	25,358	114	3	19	46	46	600	210	344	46
Total area actually reporting	98.1%	1,370	13	126	389	842	12,638	2,714	9,366	558
Estimated total	100.0%	1,390	13	127	395	855	12,841	2,748	9,528	565
Rate per 100,000 inhabitants		246.4	2.3	22.5	70.0	151.6	2,276.2	487.1	1,689.0	100.2
Seattle-Tacoma-Bellevue, WA M.S.A. [2]	3,534,349									
Includes the Metropolitan Divisions of Seattle-Bellevue-Everett and Tacoma-Lakewood										
City of Seattle	626,865	3,746	23	119	1,421	2,183	31,931	6,523	21,852	3,556
City of Tacoma	202,646	1,615	12	93	486	1,024	12,866	2,965	7,995	1,906
City of Bellevue	126,022	161	2	26	67	66	3,503	685	2,649	169
City of Everett	105,318	481	1	46	182	252	6,416	1,165	4,281	970
City of Kent	122,102	543	2	68	194	279	5,468	1,239	3,365	864
City of Renton	93,722	283	2	27	115	139	4,562	897	3,048	617

Table 6. Crime, by Selected Metropolitan Statistical Area, 2012— continued

(Number, percent, rate per 100,000 population)

Area	Population	Violent crime	Murder and nonnegligent manslaughter	Forcible rape	Robbery	Aggravated assault	Property crime	Burglary	Larceny-theft	Motor vehicle theft
City of Auburn	72,218	248	6	23	110	109	3,985	984	2,415	586
City of Lakewood	59,416	465	1	39	108	317	2,893	715	1,960	218
City of Redmond	55,770	36	0	8	11	17	1,192	172	971	49
Total area actually reporting	100.0%	11,904	104	1,015	3,913	6,872			88,216	16,023
Rate per 100,000 inhabitants		336.8	2.9	28.7	110.7	194.4			2,496.0	453.4
Seattle-Bellevue-Everett, WA M.D.	2,718,523									
Includes King and Snohomish Counties										
Total area actually reporting	100.0%	8,394	72	729	2,998	4,595	102,194	22,872	67,364	11,958
Rate per 100,000 inhabitants		308.8	2.6	26.8	110.3	169.0	3,759.2	841.3	2,478.0	439.9
Tacoma-Lakewood, WA M.D.[2]	815,826									
Includes Pierce County										
Total area actually reporting	100.0%	3,510	32	286	915	2,277			20,852	4,065
Rate per 100,000 inhabitants		430.2	3.9	35.1	112.2	279.1			2,555.9	498.3
Sebastian-Vero Beach, FL M.S.A.	140,789									
Includes Indian River County										
City of Sebastian	22,368	48	0	1	5	42	606	130	461	15
City of Vero Beach	15,527	56	0	1	17	38	586	132	440	14
Total area actually reporting	100.0%	438	1	17	64	356	3,783	851	2,830	102
Rate per 100,000 inhabitants		311.1	0.7	12.1	45.5	252.9	2,687.0	604.5	2,010.1	72.4
Sebring, FL M.S.A.	99,976									
Includes Highlands County										
City of Sebring	10617	51.0	0.0	4.0	22.0	25.0	461.0	136.0	318.0	7.0
Total area actually reporting	91.1%	265.0	3.0	24.0	65.0	173.0	2,472.0	840.0	1,527.0	105.0
Estimated total	100.0%	306.0	3.0	26.0	77.0	200.0	2,806.0	914.0	1,768.0	124.0
Rate per 100,000 inhabitants		306.1	3.0	26.0	77.0	200.0	2,806.7	914.2	1,768.4	124.0
Sheboygan, WI M.S.A.	115,444									
Includes Sheboygan County										
City of Sheboygan	49,261	170	4	19	21	126	1,517	262	1,212	43
Total area actually reporting	100.0%	195	5	25	23	142	2,452	408	1,964	80
Rate per 100,000 inhabitants		168.9	4.3	21.7	19.9	123.0	2,124.0	353.4	1,701.3	69.3
Sherman-Denison, TX M.S.A.	123,237									
Includes Grayson County										
City of Sherman	39,269	139	2	3	28	106	1,542	372	1,077	93
City of Denison	23,125	94	1	10	15	68	1,081	251	767	63
Total area actually reporting	100.0%	311	3	32	48	228	3,760	1,013	2,510	237
Rate per 100,000 inhabitants		252.4	2.4	26.0	38.9	185.0	3,051.0	822.0	2,036.7	192.3
Shreveport-Bossier City, LA M.S.A. [2]										
Includes Bossier,2 Caddo,2 De Soto, and Webster Parishes										
City of Shreveport	202,164	1,550	17	92	433	1,008	9,862	2,425	6,973	464
City of Bossier City	63,116	236	2	19	52	163	2,435	417	1,949	69
Total area actually reporting	99.1%		24	134	526			3,464	10,980	
Estimated total	100.0%		24	135	529			3,494	11,106	
Rate per 100,000 inhabitants			5.4	30.2	118.2			780.8	2,481.7	

Table 6. Crime, by Selected Metropolitan Statistical Area, 2012— continued

(Number, percent, rate per 100,000 population)

Area	Population	Violent crime	Murder and nonnegligent manslaughter	Forcible rape	Robbery	Aggravated assault	Property crime	Burglary	Larceny-theft	Motor vehicle theft
Sierra Vista-Douglas, AZ M.S.A.										
Includes Cochise County										
City of Sierra Vista	46,612	130	0	24	28	78	1,541	246	1,217	78
City of Douglas	17,743	199	1	2	5	191	614	92	487	35
Total area actually reporting	99.0%	764	4	40	52	668	3,570	713	2,660	197
Estimated total	100.0%	768	4	40	53	671	3,619	723	2,696	200
Rate per 100,000 inhabitants		570.0	3.0	29.7	39.3	498.0	2,685.8	536.6	2,000.8	148.4
Sioux City, IA-NE-SD M.S.A	169,806									
Includes Plymouth and Woodbury Counties, IA; Dakota and Dixon Counties, NE; and Union County, SD										
City of Sioux City, IA	83,289	274	2	30	46	196	3,470	621	2,645	204
Total area actually reporting	98.3%	357	4	40	51	262	4,530	852	3,418	260
Estimated total	100.0%	361	4	41	51	265	4,569	857	3,450	262
Rate per 100,000 inhabitants		212.6	2.4	24.1	30.0	156.1	2,690.7	504.7	2,031.7	154.3
Sioux Falls, SD M.S.A.	235,045									
Includes Lincoln, McCook, Minnehaha, and Turner Counties										
City of Sioux Falls	158,354	631	2	139	70	420	5,041	899	3,843	299
Total area actually reporting	100.0%	713	2	158	70	483	5,816	1,130	4,342	344
Rate per 100,000 inhabitants		303.3	0.9	67.2	29.8	205.5	2,474.4	480.8	1,847.3	146.4
South Bend-Mishawaka, IN-MI M.S.A.	319,561									
Includes St. Joseph County, IN and Cass County, MI										
City of South Bend, IN	101,398	622	18	55	316	233	4,827	1,744	2,798	285
City of Mishawaka, IN	48,363	160	3	22	55	80	2,797	501	2,138	158
Total area actually reporting	95.9%	963	24	113	390	436	9,815	2,969	6,292	554
Estimated total	100.0%	999	24	117	398	460	10,147	3,038	6,530	579
Rate per 100,000 inhabitants		312.6	7.5	36.6	124.5	143.9	3,175.3	950.7	2,043.4	181.2
Spartanburg, SC M.S.A.	318,548									
Includes Spartanburg County										
City of Spartanburg	37,689	537	2	20	120	395	2,694	479	2,120	95
Total area actually reporting	100.0%	1,407	12	98	270	1,027	10,591	2,695	7,241	655
Rate per 100,000 inhabitants		441.7	3.8	30.8	84.8	322.4	3,324.8	846.0	2,273.1	205.6
Spokane-Spokane Valley, WA M.S.A.	535,393									
Includes Pend Oreille, Spokane, and Stevens Counties										
City of Spokane	212,163	1,369	13	81	537	738	18,522	3,827	12,600	2,095
City of Spokane Valley	91,164	196	1	31	67	97	4,805	889	3,484	432
Total area actually reporting	100.0%	1,859	21	149	662	1,027	29,653	6,634	20,009	3,010
Rate per 100,000 inhabitants		347.2	3.9	27.8	123.6	191.8	5,538.5	1,239.1	3,737.3	562.2
Springfield, IL M.S.A.	211,646									
Includes Menard and Sangamon Counties										
City of Springfield	117,131	1,138	10	76	260	792	6,945	1,670	5,033	242
Total area actually reporting	89.3%	1,378	13	105	290	970	8,301	2,056	5,957	288
Estimated total	100.0%	1,430	14	111	304	1,001	8,793	2,153	6,331	309
Rate per 100,000 inhabitants		675.7	6.6	52.4	143.6	473.0	4,154.6	1,017.3	2,991.3	146.0

Table 6. Crime, by Selected Metropolitan Statistical Area, 2012— continued

(Number, percent, rate per 100,000 population)

Area	Population	Violent crime	Murder and nonnegligent manslaughter	Forcible rape	Robbery	Aggravated assault	Property crime	Burglary	Larceny-theft	Motor vehicle theft
Springfield, MA M.S.A.	627,135									
Includes Franklin, Hampden, and Hampshire Counties										
City of Springfield	154,518	1,606	11	39	542	1,014	7,024	2,317	3,947	760
Total area actually reporting	98.7%	3,108	13	220	819	2,056	18,790	5,215	12,265	1,310
Estimated total	100.0%	3,134	13	222	824	2,075	18,949	5,254	12,376	1,319
Rate per 100,000 inhabitants		499.7	2.1	35.4	131.4	330.9	3,021.5	837.8	1,973.4	210.3
Springfield, MO M.S.A.	440,970									
Includes Christian, Dallas, Greene, Polk, and Webster Counties										
City of Springfield	160,962	1,596	16	141	353	1,086	14,504	2,215	11,238	1,051
Total area actually reporting	100%	2,123	22	187	376	1,538	20,386	3,735	15,248	1,403
Rate per 100,000 inhabitants		481.4	5.0	42.4	85.3	348.8	4,623.0	847.0	3,457.8	318.2
Springfield, OH M.S.A.	137,682									
Includes Clark County										
City of Springfield	60,329	373	5	38	178	152	4,337	1,420	2,746	171
Total area actually reporting	100%	403	5	45	182	171	5,635	1,748	3,677	210
Estimated total	100%	403	5	45	182	171	5,643	1,750	3,683	210
Rate per 100,000 inhabitants		292.7	3.6	32.7	132.2	124.2	4,098.6	1,271.0	2,675.0	152.5
State College, PA M.S.A.	154,973									
Includes Centre County										
City of State College	57,020	53	1	11	12	29	787	115	658	14
Total area actually reporting	100.0%	151	1	32	27	91	2,199	355	1,800	44
Rate per 100,000 inhabitants		97.4	0.6	20.6	17.4	58.7	1,419.0	229.1	1,161.5	28.4
Staunton-Waynesboro, VA M.S.A.	119,937									
Includes Augusta County and Staunton and Waynesboro Cities										
City of Staunton	24,031	42	0	8	11	23	527	62	456	9
City of Waynesboro	21546	70	0	11	9	50	744	88	617	39
Total area actually reporting	100.0%	198	2	26	22	148	2,119	281	1,750	88
Rate per 100,000 inhabitants		165.1	1.7	21.7	18.3	123.4	1,766.8	234.3	1,459.1	73.4
St. George, UT M.S.A.	143,580									
Includes Washington County										
City of St. George	75,780	155	0	27	23	105	1,561	307	1,167	87
Total area actually reporting	100.0%	244	3	43	30	168	2,773	502	2,141	130
Rate per 100,000 inhabitants		169.9	2.1	29.9	20.9	117.0	1,931.3	349.6	1,491.2	90.5
St. Joseph, MO-KS M.S.A.	127,840									
Includes Doniphan County, KS and Andrew, Buchanan, and De Kalb Counties, MO										
City of St. Joseph, MO	77,330	323	1	22	91	209	4,708	993	3,344	371
Total area actually reporting	100.0%	402	2	25	93	282	5,473	1,201	3,851	421
Rate per 100,000 inhabitants		314.5	1.6	19.6	72.7	220.6	4,281.1	939.5	3,012.4	329.3
St. Louis, MO-IL M.S.A.	2,798,017									
Includes Bond, Calhoun, Clinton, Jersey, Macoupin, Madison, Monroe, and St. Clair Counties, IL and Franklin, Jefferson, Lincoln, St. Charles, St. Louis, and Warren Counties and St. Louis City, MO										

Table 6. Crime, by Selected Metropolitan Statistical Area, 2012— continued

(Number, percent, rate per 100,000 population)

Area	Population	Violent crime	Murder and nonnegligent manslaughter	Forcible rape	Robbery	Aggravated assault	Property crime	Burglary	Larceny-theft	Motor vehicle theft
City of St. Louis, MO	318,667	5,661	113	199	1,778	3,571	21,995	4,986	13,520	3,489
City of St. Charles, MO	66,723	101	1	7	23	70	1,949	222	1,663	64
Total area actually reporting	98.5%	12,880	202	749	3,097	8,832	79,753	16,800	56,025	6,928
Estimated total	100.0%	12,971	203	759	3,121	8,888	80,634	16,980	56,689	6,965
Rate per 100,000 inhabitants		463.6	7.3	27.1	111.5	317.7	2,881.8	606.9	2,026.0	248.9
Stockton-Lodi, CA M.S.A.	702,670									
Includes San Joaquin County										
City of Stockton	299,105	4,630	71	90	1,556	2,913	15,258	4,416	8,339	2,503
City of Lodi	63,718	280	2	12	86	180	2,599	754	1,508	337
Total area actually reporting	100.0%	6,249	89	152	1,992	4,016	29,264	8,019	16,847	4,398
Rate per 100,000 inhabitants		889.3	12.7	21.6	283.5	571.5	4,164.7	1,141.2	2,397.6	625.9
Sumter, SC M.S.A.	108,482									
Includes Sumter County										
City of Sumter	40,911	403	7	8	65	323	2,147	599	1,409	139
Total area actually reporting	100.0%	827	12	28	104	683	4,645	1,604	2,696	345
Rate per 100,000 inhabitants		762.3	11.1	25.8	95.9	629.6	4,281.8	1,478.6	2,485.2	318.0
Syracuse, NY M.S.A. [1]	666,129									
Includes Madison, Onondaga, and Oswego Counties[1]										
City of Syracuse[1]	145,934	1,372	14	75	454	829	5,976	1,896	3,698	382
Total area actually reporting	99.6%	2,021	15	154	574	1,278	16,737	4,039	11,973	725
Estimated total	100.0%	2,026	15	154	576	1,281	16,784	4,046	12,011	727
Rate per 100,000 inhabitants		304.1	2.3	23.1	86.5	192.3	2,519.6	607.4	1,803.1	109.1
Tallahassee, FL M.S.A.	374,804									
Includes Gadsden, Jefferson, Leon, and Wakulla Counties										
City of Tallahassee	185,461	1,582	12	115	525	930	8,617	2,630	5,463	524
Total area actually reporting	99.8%	2,296	22	165	611	1,498	13,026	4,074	8,238	714
Estimated total	100.0%	2,299	22	165	612	1,500	13,050	4,079	8,256	715
Rate per 100,000 inhabitants		613.4	5.9	44.0	163.3	400.2	3,481.8	1,088.3	2,202.8	190.8
Tampa-St. Petersburg-Clearwater, FL M.S.A.	2,863,265									
Includes Hernando, Hillsborough, Pasco, and Pinellas Counties										
City of Tampa	350,758	2,162	23	43	573	1,523	9,947	2,476	6,864	607
City of St. Petersburg	248,340	2,239	15	94	585	1,545	12,451	2,933	8,642	876
City of Clearwater	109,255	727	3	59	206	459	4,264	919	3,169	176
City of Largo	78,783	394	1	43	114	236	3,117	574	2,413	130
Total area actually reporting	100.0%	11,718	111	701	2,711	8,195	81,969	19,377	58,203	4,389
Rate per 100,000 inhabitants		409.3	3.9	24.5	94.7	286.2	2,862.8	676.7	2,032.7	153.3
Terre Haute, IN M.S.A.	173,204									
Includes Clay, Sullivan, Vermillion, and Vigo Counties										
City of Terre Haute	61,152	191	4	29	85	73	3,730	1,035	2,412	283
Total area actually reporting	86.7%	299	8	41	92	158	6,021	1,512	4,116	393
Estimated total	100.0%	328	8	44	97	179	6,420	1,604	4,398	418
Rate per 100,000 inhabitants		189.4	4.6	25.4	56.0	103.3	3,706.6	926.1	2,539.2	241.3
Texarkana, TX-AR M.S.A.	151,153									
Includes Little River and Miller Counties, AR and Bowie County, TX										

Table 6. Crime, by Selected Metropolitan Statistical Area, 2012— continued

(Number, percent, rate per 100,000 population)

Area	Population	Violent crime	Murder and nonnegligent manslaughter	Forcible rape	Robbery	Aggravated assault	Property crime	Burglary	Larceny-theft	Motor vehicle theft
City of Texarkana, TX	37,048	392	5	16	71	300	2,506	616	1,761	129
Total area actually reporting	100.0%	1,039	8	51	135	845	6,292	1,622	4,293	377
Rate per 100,000 inhabitants		687.4	5.3	33.7	89.3	559.0	4,162.7	1,073.1	2,840.2	249.4
The Villages, FL M.S.A.	99,090									
Includes Sumter County										
Total area actually reporting	95.8%	152	0	16	17	119	925	321	559	45
Estimated total	100.0%	171	0	17	23	131	1,079	355	670	54
Rate per 100,000 inhabitants		172.6	0.0	17.2	23.2	132.2	1,088.9	358.3	676.2	54.5
Toledo, OH M.S.A. [6]	608,831									
Includes Fulton, Lucas, Ottawa, and Wood Counties										
City of Toledo[3]	286,020	3,352	39	172	1,126	2,015		6,729		1,334
Total area actually reporting	89.9%	3,648	42	211	1,206	2,189		8,129		1,566
Estimated total	100.0%	3,735	43	225	1,239	2,228		8,460		1,622
Rate per 100,000 inhabitants		613.5	7.1	37.0	203.5	365.9		1,389.5		266.4
Topeka, KS M.S.A.	235,846									
Includes Jackson, Jefferson, Osage, Shawnee, and Wabaunsee Counties										
City of Topeka	128,843	772	15	39	237	481	6,841	1,277	4,967	597
Total area actually reporting	97.8%	972	18	49	245	660	8,930	1,848	6,345	737
Estimated total	100.0%	982	18	50	246	668	9,047	1,868	6,434	745
Rate per 100,000 inhabitants		416.4	7.6	21.2	104.3	283.2	3,836.0	792.0	2,728.1	315.9
Trenton-Ewing, NJ M.S.A.	368,870									
Includes Mercer County										
City of Trenton	85,317	1,251	24	23	577	627	2,746	1,291	986	469
Total area actually reporting	100.0%	1,645	26	50	758	811	8,200	2,447	5,039	714
Rate per 100,000 inhabitants		446.0	7.0	13.6	205.5	219.9	2,223.0	663.4	1,366.1	193.6
Tucson, AZ M.S.A. [6]	1,000,369									
Includes Pima County										
City of Tucson[6]	531,535	3,851	43	234	1,260	2,314		5,021		2,499
Total area actually reporting	100.0%	4,771	57	342	1,481	2,891		8,323		3,613
Rate per 100,000 inhabitants		476.9	5.7	34.2	148.0	289.0		832.0		361.2
Tulsa, OK M.S.A.	952,785									
Includes Creek, Okmulgee, Osage, Pawnee, Rogers, Tulsa, and Wagoner Counties										
City of Tulsa	398,904	3,949	42	316	1,062	2,529	20,807	6,235	12,162	2,410
Total area actually reporting	100.0%	5,171	54	470	1,200	3,447	31,461	8,972	19,371	3,118
Rate per 100,000 inhabitants		542.7	5.7	49.3	125.9	361.8	3,302.0	941.7	2,033.1	327.3
Tuscaloosa, AL M.S.A.	232,913									
Includes Greene, Hale, and Tuscaloosa Counties										
City of Tuscaloosa	91,973	478	4	37	170	267	4,349	1,182	2,965	202
Total area actually reporting	99.7%	929	13	61	237	618	7,674	2,072	5,216	386
Estimated total	100.0%	932	13	61	238	620	7,699	2,078	5,234	387
Rate per 100,000 inhabitants		400.1	5.6	26.2	102.2	266.2	3,305.5	892.2	2,247.2	166.2
Tyler, TX M.S.A.	216,577									
Includes Smith County										
City of Tyler	100,040	536	3	45	92	396	4,506	1,025	3,350	131
Total area actually reporting	100.0%	847	6	91	115	635	6,894	1,894	4,679	321

Table 6. Crime, by Selected Metropolitan Statistical Area, 2012— continued

(Number, percent, rate per 100,000 population)

Area	Population	Violent crime	Murder and nonnegligent manslaughter	Forcible rape	Robbery	Aggravated assault	Property crime	Burglary	Larceny-theft	Motor vehicle theft
Rate per 100,000 inhabitants		391.1	2.8	42.0	53.1	293.2	3,183.2	874.5	2,160.4	148.2
Utica-Rome, NY M.S.A. [1]	300,058									
Includes Herkimer and Oneida Counties[1]										
City of Utica[1]	62,445	411	1	23	126	261	2,704	591	2,014	99
City of Rome[1]	33,842	46	0	8	21	17	468	133	310	25
Total area actually reporting	98.0%	727	4	53	168	502	6,938	1,472	5,212	254
Estimated total	100.0%	739	4	54	172	509	7,054	1,490	5,306	258
Rate per 100,000 inhabitants		246.3	1.3	18.0	57.3	169.6	2,350.9	496.6	1,768.3	86.0
Valdosta, GA M.S.A.	143,826									
Includes Brooks, Echols, Lanier, and Lowndes Counties										
City of Valdosta	56,617	248	3	38	88	119	2,324	655	1,592	77
Total area actually reporting	99.1%	482	5	60	111	306	4,082	1,121	2,803	158
Estimated total	100.0%	487	5	60	113	309	4,137	1,132	2,843	162
Rate per 100,000 inhabitants		338.6	3.5	41.7	78.6	214.8	2,876.4	787.1	1,976.7	112.6
Vallejo-Fairfield, CA M.S.A.	420,333									
Includes Solano County										
City of Vallejo	117,912	878	14	44	380	440	5,844	2,688	1,681	1,475
City of Fairfield	107,110	454	8	30	139	277	3,317	676	2,144	497
Total area actually reporting	100.0%	1,850	28	115	660	1,047	13,227	4,342	6,451	2,434
Rate per 100,000 inhabitants		440.1	6.7	27.4	157.0	249.1	3,146.8	1,033.0	1,534.7	579.1
Victoria, TX M.S.A.	96,207									
Includes Calhoun, Goliad, and Victoria Counties										
City of Victoria	64,076	405	5	31	47	322	2,584	594	1,887	103
Total area actually reporting	100.0%	500	6	49	52	393	3,207	799	2,275	133
Rate per 100,000 inhabitants		519.7	6.2	50.9	54.1	408.5	3,333.4	830.5	2,364.7	138.2
Vineland-Bridgeton, NJ M.S.A.	157,869									
Includes Cumberland County										
City of Vineland	61,252	225	1	7	66	151	2,541	694	1,804	43
City of Bridgeton	25,378	322	2	4	140	176	1,108	484	582	42
Total area actually reporting	100.0%	866	7	32	315	512	6,756	2,033	4,559	164
Rate per 100,000 inhabitants		548.6	4.4	20.3	199.5	324.3	4,279.5	1,287.8	2,887.8	103.9
Virginia Beach-Norfolk-Newport News, VA-NC M.S.A.	1,703,542									
Includes Currituck and Gates Counties, NC and Gloucester, Isle of Wight, James City, Mathews, and York Counties and Chesapeake, Hampton, Newport News, Norfolk, Poquoson, Portsmouth, Suffolk, Virginia Beach, and Williamsburg Cities, VA										
City of Virginia Beach, VA	447,588	758	21	58	326	353	11,717	1,573	9,662	482
City of Norfolk, VA	245,303	1,332	34	75	491	732	11,391	2,261	8,403	727
City of Newport News, VA	181,591	754	20	50	271	413	5,722	1,029	4,431	262
City of Hampton, VA	137,905	314	9	16	146	143	4,657	758	3,637	262
City of Portsmouth, VA	96,739	461	11	41	182	227	4,821	1,218	3,392	211
Total area actually reporting	99.3%	5,104	116	348	1,739	2,901	52,597	8,989	41,134	2,474
Estimated total	100.0%	5,124	116	350	1,742	2,916	52,842	9,084	41,271	2,487
Rate per 100,000 inhabitants		300.8	6.8	20.5	102.3	171.2	3,101.9	533.2	2,422.7	146.0

Table 6. Crime, by Selected Metropolitan Statistical Area, 2012— continued

(Number, percent, rate per 100,000 population)

Area	Population	Violent crime	Murder and nonnegligent manslaughter	Forcible rape	Robbery	Aggravated assault	Property crime	Burglary	Larceny-theft	Motor vehicle theft
Visalia-Porterville, CA M.S.A.	453,419									
Includes Tulare County										
City of Visalia	127,604	544	5	44	134	361	5,531	1,227	3,778	526
City of Porterville	55,533	200	3	10	63	124	1,807	595	1,014	198
Total area actually reporting	100.0%	2,164	37	117	415	1,595	15,488	4,375	9,265	1,848
Rate per 100,000 inhabitants		477.3	8.2	25.8	91.5	351.8	3,415.8	964.9	2,043.4	407.6
Waco, TX M.S.A.	260,350									
Includes Falls and McLennan Counties										
City of Waco	128,595	635	6	63	182	384	5,844	1,550	4,139	155
Total area actually reporting	99.1%	1,051	10	119	222	700	9,061	2,307	6,466	288
Rate per 100,000 inhabitants	100.0%	1,057.0	10.0	120.0	223.0	704.0	9,131.0	2,321.0	6,518.0	292.0
		406.0	3.8	46.1	85.7	270.4	3,507.2	891.5	2,503.6	112.2
Walla Walla, WA M.S.A.	64262									
Includes Columbia and Walla Walla Counties										
City of Walla Walla	32463	113.0	0.0	16.0	18.0	79.0	1,446.0	274.0	1,101.0	71.0
Total area actually reporting	100.0%	147.0	1.0	22.0	22.0	102.0	2,266.0	496.0	1,664.0	106.0
Rate per 100,000 inhabitants		228.8	1.6	34.2	34.2	158.7	3,526.2	771.8	2,589.4	164.9
Warner Robins, GA M.S.A.	185,441									
Includes Houston, Peach, and Pulaski Counties										
City of Warner Robins	69,231	366	6	21	141	198	3,979	781	3,050	148
Total area actually reporting	97.3%	707	8	35	187	477	6,824	1,508	5,054	262
Estimated total	100.0%	727	8	36	194	489	7,035	1,548	5,209	278
Rate per 100,000 inhabitants		392.0	4.3	19.4	104.6	263.7	3,793.7	834.8	2,809.0	149.9
Washington-Arlington-Alexandria, DC-VA-MD-WV M.S.A.	5,826,080									
Includes the Metropolitan Divisions of Silver Spring-Frederick-Rockville, MD and Washington-Arlington-Alexandria, DC-VA-MD-WV										
City of Washington, D.C.	632,323	7,448	88	236	3,725	3,399	29,264	3,519	22,196	3,549
City of Alexandria, VA	145,892	243	0	9	138	96	2,990	281	2,383	326
City of Frederick, MD	66,808	381	1	26	106	248	1,899	245	1,527	127
Total area actually reporting	99.9%	19,369	210	982	8,771	9,406	132,807	18,167	101,930	12,710
Estimated total	100.0%	19,381	210	983	8,773	9,415	132,959	18,193	102,052	12,714
Rate per 100,000 inhabitants		332.7	3.6	16.9	150.6	161.6	2,282.1	312.3	1,751.6	218.2
Silver Spring-Frederick-Rockville, MD M.D.	1,238,384									
Includes Frederick and Montgomery Counties										
Total area actually reporting	100.0%	2,497	15	156	1,009	1,317	21,372	3,360	16,741	1,271
Rate per 100,000 inhabitants		201.6	1.2	12.6	81.5	106.3	1,725.8	271.3	1,351.8	102.6
Washington-Arlington-Alexandria, DC-VA-MD-WV M.D.	4,587,696									
Includes District of Columbia; Calvert, Charles, and Prince George's Counties, MD; Arlington, Clarke, Culpeper, Fairfax, Fauquier, Loudoun, Prince William, Rapppahannock, Spotsylvania, Stafford, and Warren Counties and Alexandria, Fairfax, Falls Church, Fredericksburg, Manassas, and Manassas Park Cities, VA; and Jefferson County, WV										

Table 6. Crime, by Selected Metropolitan Statistical Area, 2012— continued

(Number, percent, rate per 100,000 population)

Area	Population	Violent crime	Murder and nonnegligent manslaughter	Forcible rape	Robbery	Aggravated assault	Property crime	Burglary	Larceny-theft	Motor vehicle theft
Total area actually reporting	99.9%	16,872	195	826	7,762	8,089	111,435	14,807	85,189	11,439
Estimated total	100.0%	16,884	195	827	7,764	8,098	111,587	14,833	85,311	11,443
Rate per 100,000 inhabitants		368.0	4.3	18.0	169.2	176.5	2,432.3	323.3	1,859.6	249.4
Waterloo-Cedar Falls, IA M.S.A.	168,941									
Includes Black Hawk, Bremer, and Grundy Counties										
City of Waterloo	68,919	470	4	64	69	333	2,514	828	1,590	96
City of Cedar Falls	39,540	47	0	15	4	28	647	104	520	23
Total area actually reporting	100.0%	616	6	91	76	443	3,836	1,115	2,577	144
Rate per 100,000 inhabitants		364.6	3.6	53.9	45.0	262.2	2,270.6	660.0	1,525.4	85.2
Watertown-Fort Drum, NY M.S.A. [1]	118546									
Includes Jefferson County[1]										
City of Watertown1	27571	154.0	0.0	12.0	20.0	122.0	1,576.0	269.0	1,183.0	124.0
Total area actually reporting	96.1%	213.0	1.0	14.0	24.0	174.0	2,683.0	458.0	2,071.0	154.0
Estimated total	100.0%	221.0	1.0	14.0	27.0	179.0	2,773.0	472.0	2,144.0	157.0
Rate per 100,000 inhabitants		186.4	0.8	11.8	22.8	151.0	2,339.2	398.2	1,808.6	132.4
Wausau, WI M.S.A.	134,744									
Includes Marathon County										
City of Wausau	39,313	120	1	21	21	77	1,079	241	806	32
Total area actually reporting	98.6%	165	2	28	24	111	2,238	486	1,681	71
Rate per 100,000 inhabitants	100.0%	168.0	2.0	28.0	25.0	113.0	2,284.0	492.0	1,720.0	72.0
		124.7	1.5	20.8	18.6	83.9	1,695.1	365.1	1,276.5	53.4
Wheeling, WV-OH M.S.A.	147,195									
Includes Belmont County, OH and Marshall and Ohio Counties, WV										
City of Wheeling, WV	28,356	245	0	17	42	186	767	265	455	47
Total area actually reporting	96.2%	412	0	33	54	325	2,717	721	1,878	118
Estimated total	100.0%	426	0	34	57	335	2,896	752	2,021	123
Rate per 100,000 inhabitants		289.4	0.0	23.1	38.7	227.6	1,967.5	510.9	1,373.0	83.6
Wichita, KS M.S.A.	636,615									
Includes Butler, Harvey, Kingman, Sedgewick, and Sumner Counties										
City of Wichita	386,409	2,869	23	228	495	2,123	21,070	3,919	15,331	1,820
Total area actually reporting	99.5%	3,361	24	287	525	2,525	26,550	5,227	19,232	2,091
Estimated total	100.0%	3,368	24	288	526	2,530	26,627	5,240	19,291	2,096
Rate per 100,000 inhabitants		529.0	3.8	45.2	82.6	397.4	4,182.6	823.1	3,030.2	329.2
Wichita Falls, TX M.S.A.	152,511									
Includes Archer, Clay, and Wichita Counties										
City of Wichita Falls	105,488	475	5	36	150	284	5,021	1,259	3,532	230
Total area actually reporting	100.0%	584	7	46	156	375	5,854	1,527	4,043	284
Rate per 100,000 inhabitants		382.9	4.6	30.2	102.3	245.9	3,838.4	1,001.2	2,651.0	186.2
Williamsport, PA M.S.A.	116,936									
Includes Lycoming County										
City of Williamsport	29,582	111	2	5	62	42	1,235	266	926	43
Total area actually reporting	100.0%	211	2	27	81	101	2,530	515	1,935	80
Rate per 100,000 inhabitants		180.4	1.7	23.1	69.3	86.4	2,163.6	440.4	1,654.8	68.4
Wilmington, NC M.S.A.	262,160									

Table 6. Crime, by Selected Metropolitan Statistical Area, 2012— continued

(Number, percent, rate per 100,000 population)

Area	Population	Violent crime	Murder and nonnegligent manslaughter	Forcible rape	Robbery	Aggravated assault	Property crime	Burglary	Larceny-theft	Motor vehicle theft
Includes New Hanover and Pender Counties										
City of Wilmington	109,370	618	8	23	261	326	5,910	1,694	3,843	373
Total area actually reporting	99.1%	959	10	57	314	578	9,947	2,653	6,751	543
Estimated total	100.0%	966	10	57	316	583	10,041	2,674	6,821	546
Rate per 100,000 inhabitants		368.5	3.8	21.7	120.5	222.4	3,830.1	1,020.0	2,601.8	208.3
Winchester, VA-WV M.S.A.	131,237									
Includes Frederick County and Winchester City, VA and Hampshire County, WV										
City of Winchester, VA	26,880	59	0	9	17	33	1,194	161	1,004	29
Total area actually reporting	100.0%	247	2	40	30	175	3,035	548	2,355	132
Rate per 100,000 inhabitants		188.2	1.5	30.5	22.9	133.3	2,312.6	417.6	1,794.5	100.6
Winston-Salem, NC M.S.A.	651,110									
Includes Davidson, Davie, Forsyth, Stokes, and Yadkin Counties										
City of Winston-Salem	234,687	1,556	6	74	428	1,048	13,701	4,529	8,490	682
Total area actually reporting	99.3%	2,607	13	133	579	1,882	24,723	7,910	15,678	1,135
Estimated total	100.0%	2,621	13	134	583	1,891	24,896	7,949	15,806	1,141
Rate per 100,000 inhabitants		402.5	2.0	20.6	89.5	290.4	3,823.6	1,220.8	2,427.5	175.2
Worcester, MA-CT M.S.A.	851,171									
Includes Windham County, CT and Worcester County, MA										
City of Worcester, MA	183,247	1,758	8	33	419	1,298	6,432	2,040	3,927	465
Total area actually reporting	99.0%	3,548	14	184	652	2,698	17,850	4,910	11,985	955
Estimated total	100.0%	3,576	14	186	658	2,718	18,019	4,951	12,103	965
Rate per 100,000 inhabitants		420.1	1.6	21.9	77.3	319.3	2,117.0	581.7	1,421.9	113.4
Yakima, WA M.S.A.	249,564									
Includes Yakima County										
City of Yakima	93,419	566	11	52	152	351	5,774	1,573	3,106	1,095
Total area actually reporting	100.0%	872	18	73	211	570	10,230	3,039	5,511	1,680
Rate per 100,000 inhabitants		349.4	7.2	29.3	84.5	228.4	4,099.1	1,217.7	2,208.3	673.2
York-Hanover, PA M.S.A.	437,478									
Includes York County										
City of York	43,955	587	11	44	189	343	1,582	433	1,050	99
City of Hanover	15,373	31	0	6	13	12	609	30	573	6
Total area actually reporting	100.0%	1,095	16	103	303	673	8,659	1,309	7,058	292
Rate per 100,000 inhabitants		250.3	3.7	23.5	69.3	153.8	1,979.3	299.2	1,613.3	66.7
Youngstown-Warren-Boardman, OH-PA M.S.A.	562,899									
Includes Mahoning and Trumbull Counties, OH and Mercer County, PA										
City of Youngstown, OH	66,567	684	22	39	244	379	3,636	1,739	1,621	276
City of Warren, OH	41,355	279	4	16	102	157	2,010	812	1,086	112
City of Boardman, OH	40,608	43	1	6	31	5	1,698	273	1,371	54
Total area actually reporting	97.2%	1,584.0	32.0	132.0	549.0	871.0	17,183.0	5,649.0	10,764.0	770.0
Estimated total	100.0%	1,605.0	32.0	135.0	557.0	881.0	17,599.0	5,733.0	11,082.0	784.0
Rate per 100,000 inhabitants		285.1	5.7	24.0	99.0	156.5	3,126.5	1,018.5	1,968.7	139.3
Yuba City, CA M.S.A.	169,050									

Table 6. Crime, by Selected Metropolitan Statistical Area, 2012— continued

(Number, percent, rate per 100,000 population)

Area	Population	Violent crime	Murder and nonnegligent manslaughter	Forcible rape	Robbery	Aggravated assault	Property crime	Burglary	Larceny-theft	Motor vehicle theft
Includes Sutter and Yuba Counties										
City of Yuba City	65,653	247	4	22	43	178	1,982	501	1,297	184
Total area actually reporting	100.0%	603	11	53	84	455	4,845	1,370	2,934	541
Rate per 100,000 inhabitants		356.7	6.5	31.4	49.7	269.2	2,866.0	810.4	1,735.6	320.0
Yuma, AZ M.S.A.	203,062									
Includes Yuma County										
City of Yuma	95,568	508	5	27	61	415	3,353	955	2,162	236
Total area actually reporting	98.5%	707	7	41	73	586	5,026	1,549	3,083	394
Estimated total	100.0%	716	7	42	75	592	5,128	1,569	3,159	400
Rate per 100,000 inhabitants		352.6	3.4	20.7	36.9	291.5	2,525.3	772.7	1,555.7	197.0

1 Because of changes in the state/local agency's reporting practices, figures are not comparable to previous years' data. 2 The FBI determined that the agency's data were underreported. Consequently, those data are not included in this table. 3 The FBI determined that the agency's data were overreported. Consequently, affected data are not included in this table. 4 The data collection methodology for the offense of forcible rape used by Chicago, Illinois, and the Minnesota state Uniform Crime Reporting (UCR) Program (with the exception of Minneapolis and St. Paul, Minnesota) does not comply with national UCR Program guidelines. Consequently, its figures for forcible rape and violent crime (of which forcible rape is a part) are not published in this table. 5 The population for the city of Mobile, Alabama, includes 55,819 inhabitants from the jurisdiction of the Mobile County Sheriff's Department. 6 The FBI determined that the agency did not follow national Uniform Crime Reporting Program guidelines for reporting an offense. Consequently, this figure is not included in this table.

Table 7. Offense Analysis, United States, 2008–2012

(Number)

Classification	2008	2009	2010	2011[1]	2012
Murder	16,465	15,399	14,722	14,661	14,827
Forcible rape	90,750	89,241	85,593	84,175	84,376
Robbery [2]	443,563	408,742	369,089	354,746	354,520
By location					
Street/highway	191,050	174,886	159,307	155,218	154,058
Commercial house	61,207	55,980	48,804	46,156	47,081
Gas or service station	11,468	9,881	8,549	8,539	8,647
Convenience store	24,394	21,983	19,282	18,108	18,152
Residence	72,217	69,280	63,779	60,138	59,889
Bank	8,996	8,829	8,034	7,038	6,656
Miscellaneous	74,231	67,903	61,333	59,549	60,036
Burglary [2]	2,228,887	2,203,313	2,168,459	2,185,140	2,103,787
By location					
Residence (dwelling)	1,567,682	1,599,047	1,602,056	1,628,656	1,567,058
Residence, night	438,323	445,983	445,480	442,390	428,411
Residence, day	807,617	819,725	825,163	859,299	830,518
Residence, unknown	321,742	333,339	331,414	326,967	308,128
Nonresidence (store, office, etc.)	661,205	604,266	566,403	556,484	536,729
Nonresidence, night	276,743	255,147	233,765	227,446	220,141
Nonresidence, day	223,303	200,924	192,985	196,461	192,401
Nonresidence, unknown	161,159	148,195	139,652	132,577	124,187
Larceny-theft (except motor vehicle theft) [2]	6,586,206	6,338,095	6,204,601	6,151,095	6,150,598
By type					
Pocket-picking	27,140	26,631	24,231	26,518	29,462
Purse-snatching	33,314	30,493	28,137	27,082	26,329
Shoplifting	1,067,655	1,149,406	1,064,608	1,077,791	1,144,279
From motor vehicles (except accessories)	1,714,745	1,727,583	1,638,670	1,523,950	1,476,403
Motor vehicle accessories	642,964	573,270	549,905	497,980	465,984
Bicycles	221,846	212,362	206,677	216,987	223,123
From buildings	753,450	704,184	699,599	728,050	743,031
From coin-operated machines	26,899	26,085	20,309	19,536	17,189
All others	2,098,192	1,888,080	1,972,464	2,033,200	2,024,798
By value					
Under $50	2,155,372	2,060,325	1,971,705	1,901,309	1,891,938
$50 to $200	1,465,002	1,443,919	1,421,342	1,399,484	1,394,725
Over $200	2,965,832	2,833,851	2,811,555	2,850,302	2,863,935
Motor vehicle theft	959,059	795,652	739,565	716,508	721,053

1 The crime figures have been adjusted. 2 Because of rounding, the number of offenses may not add to the total.

Table 8. Offenses Known to Law Enforcement, by Selected State and City, 2012

(Number)

State/city	Population	Violent crime	Murder and nonnegligent manslaughter	Forcible rape	Robbery	Aggravated assault	Property crime	Burglary	Larceny-theft	Motor vehicle theft	Arson[1]
Alabama [2]											
Abbeville	2,715	22	0	1	3	18	57	16	38	3	
Adamsville	4,543	28	0	1	7	20	292	49	223	20	
Addison	757	7	0	0	0	7	29	5	18	6	
Alabaster	30,923	49	0	2	6	41	683	65	585	33	
Alexander City	14,936	95	2	2	15	76	688	125	536	27	
Aliceville	2,448	9	0	0	0	9	60	19	39	2	
Anniston	23,051	504	5	14	92	393	2,484	912	1,501	71	
Arab	8,180	50	0	6	5	39	695	191	469	35	
Ashford	2,176	2	0	0	0	2	68	23	41	4	
Ashland	2,036	7	0	0	1	6	50	9	40	1	
Ashville	2,241	9	0	0	4	5	37	8	28	1	
Athens	22,681	31	1	1	14	15	850	166	666	18	
Atmore	10,188	63	1	2	7	53	343	82	242	19	
Auburn	54,785	132	3	13	25	91	1,919	418	1,450	51	
Bay Minette	8,249	49	2	2	8	37	354	47	297	10	
Bayou La Batre	2,565	47	0	0	5	42	228	77	123	28	
Bessemer	27,585	582	4	20	164	394	3,329	873	2,218	238	
Birmingham	213,266	3,237	67	152	983	2,035	14,788	4,704	9,042	1,042	117
Blountsville	1,703	9	0	2	0	7	88	18	66	4	
Brent	4,945	17	1	0	1	15	64	16	46	2	
Brewton	5,398	67	0	1	7	59	296	56	224	16	
Bridgeport	2,431	21	0	1	0	20	35	7	25	3	
Brundidge	2,085	2	0	0	0	2	33	3	30	0	
Butler	1,870	8	1	0	0	7	43	13	27	3	
Camp Hill	1,019	21	0	1	0	20	45	25	16	4	
Carbon Hill	2,017	9	0	0	0	9	139	19	108	12	
Carrollton	1,006	1	0	0	0	1	23	7	16	0	
Cedar Bluff	1,832	22	0	1	0	21	185	64	110	11	
Centre	3,512	20	1	1	1	17	271	51	208	12	
Centreville	2,769	5	0	0	3	2	45	6	38	1	
Chatom	1,277	3	0	0	0	3	34	9	21	4	
Chickasaw	6,124	61	0	1	8	52	364	86	261	17	
Childersburg	5,163	3	0	0	1	2	115	45	68	2	
Citronelle	3,917	19	0	1	1	17	216	50	149	17	
Clanton	8,701	51	0	5	7	39	517	84	420	13	
Coaling	1,691	10	0	1	1	8	72	20	43	9	
Collinsville	1,997	7	0	1	1	5	46	9	34	3	
Columbiana	4,276	13	0	0	0	13	139	24	112	3	
Cordova	2,092	18	0	1	2	15	127	42	80	5	
Creola	1,932	3	0	0	0	3	85	12	69	4	
Dadeville	3,243	42	0	0	0	42	144	32	102	10	
Daleville	5,294	13	1	2	3	7	115	33	75	7	
Daphne	22,198	40	1	4	2	33	514	77	421	16	
Dauphin Island	1,242	1	0	0	0	1	106	34	71	1	
Decatur	56,126	240	2	9	80	149	2,913	821	1,964	128	
Demopolis	7,393	38	0	5	8	25	313	54	253	6	
Dora	2,022	20	1	2	2	15	136	45	73	18	
Dothan	66,275	319	5	30	100	184	2,934	886	1,918	130	
Double Springs	1,080	2	0	0	0	2	41	15	25	1	
Douglas	757	7	0	0	1	6	96	47	41	8	
East Brewton	2,472	26	0	1	1	24	127	37	85	5	
Eclectic	1,017	5	0	0	1	4	46	8	37	1	
Elba	3,998	31	0	0	0	31	113	42	67	4	
Elberta	1,541	1	0	0	0	1	64	23	39	2	
Enterprise	26,971	110	2	4	12	92	861	177	631	53	
Eutaw	2,907	41	0	0	7	34	76	26	45	5	
Evergreen	3,923	43	0	3	4	36	225	52	154	19	
Excel	717	3	0	1	0	2	35	2	29	4	
Fairfield	11,169	153	2	7	61	83	1,337	462	800	75	
Fairhope	15,766	43	1	2	5	35	649	131	503	15	
Falkville	1,288	2	0	0	1	1	43	12	30	1	
Fayette	4,622	11	0	1	2	8	67	11	53	3	

Table 8. Offenses Known to Law Enforcement, by Selected State and City, 2012— continued

(Number)

State/city	Population	Violent crime	Murder and nonnegligent manslaughter	Forcible rape	Robbery	Aggravated assault	Property crime	Burglary	Larceny-theft	Motor vehicle theft	Arson[1]
Flomaton	1,438	24	0	0	2	22	34	7	26	1	
Florala	2,003	4	0	1	0	3	33	11	21	1	
Florence	39,512	165	2	19	45	99	1,740	454	1,223	63	
Foley	15,049	54	0	4	15	35	665	87	549	29	
Fort Payne	14,219	22	0	5	2	15	470	90	354	26	
Fultondale	8,421	20	0	1	6	13	287	56	221	10	
Gadsden	36,961	372	1	33	113	225	3,000	835	1,969	196	
Gardendale	13,960	27	0	1	7	19	642	91	533	18	
Geneva	4,473	19	0	0	2	17	112	22	80	10	
Geraldine	906	0	0	0	0	0	28	2	26	0	
Glencoe	5,175	8	0	1	1	6	114	36	65	13	
Grant	911	6	0	0	0	6	36	8	20	8	
Greenville	8,047	48	2	1	8	37	311	46	258	7	
Grove Hill	1,566	7	0	0	1	6	42	16	24	2	
Guin	2,377	12	0	0	0	12	64	15	39	10	
Gulf Shores	10,022	46	0	3	7	36	761	133	603	25	
Guntersville	8,327	44	0	3	18	23	766	144	594	28	
Hackleburg	1,517	4	0	0	0	4	25	7	16	2	
Haleyville	4,163	18	0	8	0	10	174	33	134	7	
Hamilton	6,890	8	0	1	0	7	160	41	114	5	
Hanceville	2,999	15	0	1	0	14	93	27	59	7	
Hartford	2,634	10	0	0	0	10	137	27	103	7	
Hartselle	14,380	21	0	2	3	16	400	78	306	16	
Headland	4,556	14	2	1	1	10	132	52	76	4	
Heflin	3,463	18	0	0	2	16	86	18	67	1	
Helena	17,076	11	0	1	1	9	174	24	140	10	
Henagar	2,362	3	0	0	0	3	36	15	21	0	
Hokes Bluff	4,298	3	0	0	1	2	67	29	28	10	
Hoover	82,332	86	2	13	46	25	2,180	393	1,702	85	
Hueytown	16,181	43	2	5	10	26	637	136	485	16	
Huntsville	183,691	1,696	14	72	456	1,154	9,261	2,165	6,386	710	20
Ider	728	5	0	0	0	5	34	14	11	9	
Irondale	12,407	53	0	4	19	30	500	122	346	32	
Jackson	5,217	34	0	6	3	25	229	49	175	5	
Jacksonville	12,532	43	0	1	11	31	484	138	327	19	
Jasper	14,365	123	0	8	40	75	1,141	242	855	44	
Jemison	2,611	18	0	2	1	15	179	52	115	12	
Killen	1,120	3	0	1	0	2	43	3	38	2	
Kinston	549	2	0	0	0	2	11	5	5	1	
Lafayette	2,992	23	0	0	2	21	101	27	70	4	
Lanett	6,442	103	1	2	13	87	565	158	365	42	
Leeds	11,844	58	1	3	20	34	422	66	333	23	
Leesburg	1,033	4	0	0	0	4	57	18	37	2	
Level Plains	2,078	7	0	0	0	7	39	16	23	0	
Lincoln	6,242	37	0	4	1	32	351	78	241	32	
Littleville	1,016	2	0	0	0	2	17	1	11	5	
Lockhart	522	1	0	0	0	1	17	6	10	1	
Loxley	1,679	14	0	3	4	7	129	25	88	16	
Luverne	2,809	18	0	2	0	16	53	10	39	4	
Madison	43,860	90	0	4	20	66	1,068	219	805	44	
Maplesville	715	6	0	0	1	5	39	11	22	6	
Margaret	4,485	1	0	0	0	1	30	6	22	2	
Midfield	5,392	42	3	1	18	20	320	130	171	19	
Midland City	2,347	8	0	0	0	8	55	15	37	3	
Millbrook	14,868	81	0	8	19	54	608	175	415	18	
Mobile[2]	251,516	1,314	32	45	460	777	12,103	2,796	8,755	552	66
Monroeville	6,459	81	0	7	7	67	422	68	339	15	
Montevallo	6,429	23	0	1	2	20	186	49	127	10	
Montgomery	209,018	827	44	41	459	283	12,058	3,409	7,548	1,101	64
Moody	11,889	18	1	0	2	15	179	34	134	11	
Morris	1,867	5	0	0	2	3	30	11	16	3	
Moulton	3,463	8	0	0	3	5	78	14	59	5	
Moundville	2,413	7	0	1	1	5	61	12	47	2	
Mountain Brook	20,511	8	0	0	3	5	303	72	225	6	

Table 8. Offenses Known to Law Enforcement, by Selected State and City, 2012— continued

(Number)

State/city	Population	Violent crime	Murder and nonnegligent manslaughter	Forcible rape	Robbery	Aggravated assault	Property crime	Burglary	Larceny-theft	Motor vehicle theft	Arson[1]
Mount Vernon	1,575	25	0	1	1	23	74	14	54	6	
Muscle Shoals	13,228	76	0	4	16	56	647	148	473	26	
Napier Field	354	1	0	0	0	1	19	5	12	2	
New Brockton	1,165	8	0	0	0	8	48	21	23	4	
New Hope	2,866	14	0	0	1	13	78	19	49	10	
Newton	1,511	4	0	0	1	3	44	12	30	2	
Northport	23,742	135	2	3	24	106	821	222	565	34	
Notasulga	959	2	0	0	0	2	96	38	46	12	
Odenville	3,636	12	0	1	0	11	52	7	42	3	
Oneonta	6,633	23	0	0	3	20	193	25	157	11	
Opelika	27,201	207	5	11	43	148	1,681	428	1,204	49	
Orange Beach	5,598	23	1	1	3	18	289	38	247	4	
Owens Crossroads	1,551	3	0	0	0	3	20	5	15	0	
Oxford	21,306	76	1	9	28	38	1,250	222	982	46	
Ozark	14,908	103	0	2	21	80	793	173	590	30	
Pelham	21,756	36	2	7	8	19	471	50	402	19	
Pell City	12,863	61	1	4	9	47	523	74	420	29	
Phenix City	33,940	248	2	17	71	158	2,284	696	1,377	211	
Piedmont	4,865	23	0	3	0	20	304	80	215	9	
Pine Hill	962	18	0	0	2	16	24	4	18	2	
Pleasant Grove	10,158	17	0	2	0	15	150	53	92	5	
Powell	963	1	0	0	0	1	29	8	18	3	
Prattville	34,525	60	3	6	31	20	1,317	274	990	53	
Prichard	22,728	527	6	13	143	365	1,444	494	757	193	
Ragland	1,660	4	1	1	0	2	35	6	25	4	
Rainbow City	9,630	28	0	1	7	20	243	61	171	11	
Rainsville	4,987	15	0	1	1	13	107	19	84	4	
Red Bay	3,190	6	0	2	0	4	76	23	52	1	
Reform	1,676	6	0	1	0	5	56	15	41	0	
Riverside	2,239	13	3	0	0	10	42	12	27	3	
Roanoke	6,065	23	0	2	3	18	227	40	176	11	
Robertsdale	5,424	19	0	1	2	16	267	44	212	11	
Rogersville	1,259	7	0	0	2	5	48	8	34	6	
Russellville	9,924	76	0	3	10	63	368	90	257	21	
Samson	1,948	27	0	3	2	22	90	29	60	1	
Saraland	13,470	35	1	2	9	23	549	53	462	34	
Sardis City	1,708	1	0	0	1	0	53	9	39	5	
Satsuma	6,187	11	1	0	2	8	114	21	83	10	
Scottsboro	14,855	65	0	7	1	57	594	128	451	15	
Selma	20,611	274	5	21	61	187	1,778	539	1,117	122	
Sheffield	9,090	101	0	3	14	84	639	211	401	27	
Silverhill	726	5	0	0	0	5	36	9	27	0	
Slocomb	1,988	4	0	0	0	4	55	23	27	5	
Snead	844	11	0	1	0	10	85	19	54	12	
Southside	8,434	9	0	1	0	8	104	38	57	9	
Spanish Fort	7,095	12	0	1	3	8	326	27	296	3	
Springville	4,137	10	0	0	1	9	80	22	57	1	
Sulligent	1,902	8	0	2	1	5	66	13	50	3	
Sumiton	2,511	19	1	0	5	13	244	37	192	15	
Summerdale	888	8	0	0	0	8	54	9	43	2	
Sylvania	1,852	1	0	0	0	1	13	0	13	0	
Talladega	15,631	107	1	9	21	76	1,272	373	838	61	
Tallassee	4,871	65	1	2	3	59	291	82	197	12	
Tarrant	6,427	15	0	1	8	6	395	172	217	6	
Thorsby	2,001	3	0	0	0	3	28	8	14	6	
Town Creek	1,098	7	0	0	0	7	33	11	20	2	
Triana	507	11	0	0	0	11	35	15	16	4	
Trinity	2,110	5	0	1	0	4	56	16	35	5	
Troy	18,097	115	3	5	18	89	890	251	592	47	
Tuscaloosa	91,973	478	4	37	170	267	4,349	1,182	2,965	202	
Tuscumbia	8,469	43	1	3	2	37	390	116	249	25	
Tuskegee	9,792	120	2	8	17	93	683	290	336	57	
Valley	9,486	60	0	5	8	47	590	156	386	48	
Vestavia Hills	34,195	22	0	0	10	12	505	101	384	20	

Table 8. Offenses Known to Law Enforcement, by Selected State and City, 2012— continued

(Number)

State/city	Population	Violent crime	Murder and nonnegligent manslaughter	Forcible rape	Robbery	Aggravated assault	Property crime	Burglary	Larceny-theft	Motor vehicle theft	Arson[1]
Warrior	3,192	14	0	1	1	12	83	23	57	3	
Weaver	3,017	20	0	2	2	16	140	40	92	8	
Wetumpka	6,618	47	0	1	10	36	377	69	298	10	
Winfield	4,720	15	0	2	1	12	134	35	93	6	
Woodstock	1,416	3	0	0	3	0	85	14	67	4	
York	2,495	26	0	1	2	23	74	25	46	3	
Alaska											
Anchorage	299,143	2,479	15	303	488	1,673	10,543	1,158	8,554	831	97
Bethel	6,294	49	1	14	2	32	135	39	58	38	4
Bristol Bay Borough	1,042	1	0	0	0	1	44	5	32	7	0
Cordova	2,297	4	0	0	0	4	45	4	36	5	0
Craig	1,254	5	0	0	0	5	26	3	20	3	0
Dillingham	2,419	47	0	18	1	28	74	12	55	7	0
Fairbanks	32,423	169	3	29	37	100	1,379	130	1,137	112	3
Haines	2,585	4	0	0	0	4	28	2	25	1	0
Homer	5,146	54	0	1	3	50	189	11	166	12	0
Juneau	32,553	115	0	9	16	90	1,099	94	975	30	9
Kenai	7,305	25	0	1	0	24	340	37	295	8	2
Ketchikan	8,217	29	0	9	4	16	323	31	284	8	1
Kodiak[3]	6,332	121	0	8	10	103	254	23	200	31	3
Kotzebue	3,334	78	0	23	12	43	210	46	126	38	2
Nome	3,776	23	0	3	2	18	44	12	23	9	2
North Pole	2,180	8	0	0	0	8	73	15	53	5	1
North Slope Borough	9,618	70	1	14	3	52	106	36	59	11	1
Palmer	6,196	18	0	2	2	14	126	16	103	7	6
Petersburg	3,003	12	0	0	0	12	106	15	85	6	0
Seward	2,759	2	0	0	1	1	76	6	68	2	0
Sitka	9,060	12	0	1	1	10	143	17	120	6	0
Skagway	946	2	0	0	0	2	19	0	19	0	0
Soldotna	4,282	15	0	1	0	14	175	7	164	4	1
Unalaska	4,385	13	1	1	1	10	61	8	43	10	0
Valdez	4,081	14	0	0	0	14	111	7	99	5	0
Wasilla[3]	8,190	43	0	2	6	35	490	61	408	21	2
Wrangell	2,411	3	0	0	0	3	37	7	27	3	0
Arizona											
Apache Junction	36,986	130	1	13	21	95	1,025	236	719	70	1
Avondale	78,364	233	7	4	72	150	3,682	685	2,752	245	10
Benson	5,219	9	0	6	0	3	136	25	105	6	0
Bisbee	5,694	79	1	0	2	76	171	3	160	8	0
Buckeye	52,213	54	3	1	11	39	1,372	374	924	74	1
Bullhead City	40,277	86	5	0	26	55	1,626	330	1,195	101	2
Camp Verde	11,033	21	1	0	0	20	276	44	221	11	4
Casa Grande	50,132	211	3	4	46	158	2,857	767	1,934	156	
Chandler[3]	242,721	628	4	64	149	411	6,571	1,147	5,168	256	78
Chino Valley	10,981	77	2	3	1	71	219	45	162	12	
Clarkdale	4,158	6	0	0	0	6	83	23	55	5	0
Clifton	3,414	5	0	0	0	5	33	12	20	1	0
Coolidge	12,206	70	2	5	10	53	656	117	507	32	8
Cottonwood	11,434	51	0	0	7	44	411	37	357	17	14
Douglas	17,743	199	1	2	5	191	614	92	487	35	3
Eagar	5,008	4	1	0	0	3	136	37	95	4	0
El Mirage	32,685	86	3	7	18	58	946	292	582	72	3
Eloy	17,149	84	1	7	9	67	569	179	358	32	22
Flagstaff	66,633	262	0	28	45	189	2,834	242	2,533	59	23
Florence	25,795	29	0	0	1	28	224	47	169	8	0
Fredonia	1,328	4	0	0	0	4	12	4	7	1	0
Gilbert	214,264	205	5	19	59	122	3,386	726	2,496	164	25
Glendale	232,997	1,145	12	54	413	666	14,934	2,847	10,863	1,224	78
Goodyear	67,033	103	0	12	24	67	1,774	479	1,188	107	13
Holbrook	5,105	58	1	2	1	54	334	85	231	18	0
Jerome	451	7	0	0	0	7	24	8	13	3	0
Kingman	28,588	93	0	9	8	76	1,775	406	1,269	100	4
Lake Havasu City	53,513	58	2	10	7	39	1,356	256	1,012	88	4

Table 8. Offenses Known to Law Enforcement, by Selected State and City, 2012— continued

(Number)

State/city	Population	Violent crime	Murder and nonnegligent manslaughter	Forcible rape	Robbery	Aggravated assault	Property crime	Burglary	Larceny-theft	Motor vehicle theft	Arson[1]
Mammoth	1,473	7	0	0	0	7	37	15	21	1	0
Marana	35,617	35	0	0	13	22	1,157	126	936	95	2
Maricopa	44,881	58	1	9	12	36	844	155	634	55	1
Mesa	451,391	1,804	14	172	469	1,149	14,140	2,681	10,572	887	97
Miami	1,833	17	0	0	0	17	89	41	41	7	10
Nogales	21,177	45	1	0	10	34	497	75	375	47	0
Oro Valley	41,786	21	1	4	3	13	679	95	553	31	2
Page	7,331	71	2	2	7	60	494	59	399	36	1
Paradise Valley	13,177	9	2	3	0	4	256	129	119	8	1
Parker	3,107	29	0	0	2	27	195	51	129	15	1
Payson	15,337	48	1	0	7	40	421	134	270	17	1
Peoria	158,347	296	9	24	77	186	4,673	929	3,478	266	7
Phoenix	1,485,509	9,458	123	556	3,516	5,263	60,777	17,912	35,678	7,187	306
Pima	2,408	2	0	0	0	2	39	10	27	2	0
Pinetop-Lakeside	4,327	38	0	0	1	37	215	33	181	1	1
Prescott	40,420	168	2	14	19	133	1,104	197	883	24	9
Prescott Valley	39,407	89	4	1	8	76	750	95	622	33	3
Sahuarita	25,736	11	0	2	2	7	374	49	311	14	14
San Luis	28,168	29	0	6	1	22	582	158	352	72	4
Scottsdale	223,432	329	3	42	115	169	6,047	1,255	4,551	241	27
Sedona	10,173	20	0	4	4	12	219	50	161	8	0
Show Low	10,773	87	0	4	6	77	569	107	450	12	0
Sierra Vista	46,612	130	0	24	28	78	1,541	246	1,217	78	5
Snowflake-Taylor	9,803	27	0	0	0	27	117	33	82	2	2
Somerton	14,687	18	0	0	0	18	224	70	143	11	0
South Tucson	5,757	159	0	5	40	114	1,003	140	829	34	2
Springerville	2,008	10	0	0	0	10	67	23	42	2	0
Surprise	120,793	162	3	8	62	89	2,488	519	1,851	118	14
Tempe	166,061	878	11	44	253	570	7,824	1,250	6,085	489	25
Thatcher	4,908	3	0	0	0	3	134	29	104	1	0
Tolleson	6,728	54	1	2	13	38	638	226	372	40	1
Tucson[4]	531,535	3,851	43	234	1,260	2,314		5,021		2,499	198
Wickenburg	6,538	15	0	3	3	9	185	65	104	16	4
Willcox	3,837	8	0	0	1	7	244	48	188	8	6
Winslow	9,757	101	2	2	3	94	630	76	539	15	1
Yuma	95,568	508	5	27	61	415	3,353	955	2,162	236	35
Arkansas											
Alma	5,439	15	0	3	1	11	302	99	195	8	1
Arkadelphia	10,698	48	5	5	3	35	407	111	290	6	1
Ashdown	4,680	19	0	4	1	14	160	32	125	3	0
Atkins	3,057	1	0	0	0	1	85	30	51	4	0
Austin	2,076	3	0	1	0	2	33	20	13	0	0
Bald Knob	2,950	13	0	0	1	12	129	36	83	10	0
Barling	4,718	15	0	1	0	14	66	12	53	1	0
Bay	1,845	2	0	0	0	2	31	12	19	0	1
Bearden	961	4	0	1	1	2	28	13	14	1	0
Beebe	7,449	34	0	2	0	32	241	64	164	13	1
Bella Vista	27,310	25	1	1	0	23	187	90	94	3	0
Benton	31,486	116	0	13	23	80	1,373	250	1,036	87	6
Bentonville	36,433	82	2	15	5	60	740	153	561	26	5
Berryville	5,389	21	0	8	0	13	266	71	178	17	0
Blytheville	15,506	196	8	9	39	140	1,173	482	638	53	2
Booneville	3,993	13	0	2	1	10	114	30	81	3	0
Bradford	774	2	0	0	0	2	19	3	15	1	0
Brinkley	3,171	25	0	2	5	18	108	44	61	3	2
Bryant	17,129	16	0	5	11	0	911	187	689	35	0
Bull Shoals	1,947	4	0	0	0	4	33	5	28	0	0
Cabot	24,212	61	0	5	6	50	1,027	501	484	42	1
Caddo Valley	632	6	0	0	1	5	45	15	30	0	0
Camden	12,118	70	1	0	9	60	590	178	405	7	1
Cammack Village	779	0	0	0	0	0	34	24	10	0	0
Carlisle	2,254	6	0	1	2	3	53	24	28	1	0
Cave City	1,923	4	0	0	0	4	37	9	28	0	0

Table 8. Offenses Known to Law Enforcement, by Selected State and City, 2012— continued

(Number)

State/city	Population	Violent crime	Murder and nonnegligent manslaughter	Forcible rape	Robbery	Aggravated assault	Property crime	Burglary	Larceny-theft	Motor vehicle theft	Arson[1]
Cave Springs	1,785	1	0	0	0	1	22	13	9	0	0
Charleston	2,492	4	0	1	1	2	28	9	19	0	0
Cherokee Village	4,735	4	0	1	0	3	122	46	72	4	1
Clarendon	1,655	2	1	0	0	1	33	7	23	3	0
Clarksville	9,286	16	0	3	0	13	508	123	383	2	0
Clinton	2,580	0	0	0	0	0	60	16	41	3	0
Conway	60,700	252	1	29	76	146	2,539	410	2,028	101	9
Corning	3,348	3	0	0	1	2	41	22	17	2	0
Crossett	5,487	20	1	1	6	12	296	115	176	5	4
Danville	2,405	1	0	0	0	1	19	6	12	1	0
Dardanelle	4,738	28	0	3	6	19	184	98	83	3	0
Decatur	1,752	4	0	0	0	4	34	19	12	3	1
De Queen	6,708	20	0	3	1	16	198	56	141	1	1
De Witt	3,282	19	0	3	2	14	107	32	74	1	1
Diaz	1,313	3	0	0	0	3	23	10	9	4	0
Dumas	4,635	24	0	3	5	16	124	60	56	8	1
Earle	2,405	11	0	0	1	10	103	41	60	2	5
El Dorado	18,860	197	1	2	29	165	1,009	430	545	34	7
Elkins	2,718	2	0	0	0	2	15	4	10	1	0
Eudora	2,261	2	0	1	1	0	20	1	19	0	0
Eureka Springs	2,082	3	0	2	0	1	91	20	69	2	0
Fairfield Bay	2,319	5	0	0	0	5	37	17	20	0	1
Farmington	6,133	30	0	2	0	28	108	29	78	1	0
Fayetteville	75,387	388	1	58	40	289	3,043	504	2,406	133	7
Flippin	1,354	6	0	2	1	3	68	19	49	0	0
Fordyce	4,295	39	2	4	7	26	197	68	124	5	1
Forrest City	15,295	122	4	6	38	74	1,227	356	839	32	6
Fort Smith	87,483	687	5	69	95	518	4,771	1,064	3,524	183	10
Gassville	2,087	3	0	2	0	1	32	5	26	1	0
Gentry	3,260	5	0	1	0	4	33	9	20	4	0
Glenwood	2,228	1	0	0	0	1	58	21	37	0	0
Gravette	2,400	6	0	0	0	6	51	6	38	7	0
Green Forest	2,779	24	0	7	2	15	94	34	59	1	0
Greenland	1,292	5	0	0	0	5	23	9	12	2	0
Greenwood	9,086	19	0	0	0	19	86	37	48	1	0
Greers Ferry	892	1	0	0	0	1	27	8	19	0	0
Gurdon	2,205	14	0	1	0	13	42	17	21	4	0
Guy	732	3	0	0	0	3	15	7	7	1	0
Hamburg	2,883	16	1	0	1	14	43	16	27	0	1
Hampton	1,273	8	1	1	0	6	25	5	18	2	0
Hardy	780	5	0	2	1	2	53	14	36	3	0
Harrisburg	2,292	9	0	1	1	7	104	43	59	2	1
Harrison	13,043	60	1	11	1	47	672	157	489	26	6
Heber Springs	7,173	19	0	7	0	12	289	109	169	11	0
Helena-West Helena	12,152	165	1	8	26	130	932	470	431	31	11
Highfill	604	0	0	0	0	0	7	3	4	0	0
Highland	1,056	4	0	0	0	4	22	10	12	0	1
Hope	10,103	96	1	10	13	72	678	229	420	29	4
Horseshoe Bend	2,146	3	0	1	0	2	35	16	18	1	0
Hot Springs	35,722	164	9	10	55	90	3,067	622	2,330	115	2
Jacksonville	28,733	246	2	21	33	190	1,693	416	1,210	67	4
Jonesboro	68,807	295	4	21	78	192	3,157	1,166	1,889	102	12
Kensett	1,678	5	0	1	0	4	36	9	23	4	0
Lakeview	745	2	0	0	0	2	5	0	5	0	0
Lake Village	2,567	60	0	1	7	52	115	38	75	2	1
Lepanto	1,895	8	0	2	0	6	58	24	33	1	1
Lewisville	1,272	2	0	0	0	2	27	10	17	0	0
Lincoln	2,308	0	0	0	0	0	39	18	21	0	0
Little Flock	2,667	5	0	1	0	4	28	4	21	3	0
Little Rock	196,055	2,579	45	137	807	1,590	15,804	4,244	10,465	1,095	87
Lonoke	4,319	18	0	0	2	16	185	40	142	3	2
Lowell	7,565	10	0	0	1	9	192	55	125	12	1
Luxora	1,169	2	0	0	0	2	6	2	4	0	0
Magnolia	11,554	27	0	3	4	20	486	240	224	22	1

Table 8. Offenses Known to Law Enforcement, by Selected State and City, 2012— continued

(Number)

State/city	Population	Violent crime	Murder and nonnegligent manslaughter	Forcible rape	Robbery	Aggravated assault	Property crime	Burglary	Larceny-theft	Motor vehicle theft	Arson[1]
Marianna	4,084	7	0	0	6	1	186	69	108	9	2
Marion	12,300	63	0	5	10	48	437	171	245	21	5
Marmaduke	1,132	14	0	1	0	13	57	21	35	1	0
Maumelle	17,391	28	1	1	5	21	361	52	302	7	3
Mayflower	2,307	4	0	1	1	2	72	24	42	6	0
McGehee	4,157	28	0	3	3	22	159	43	111	5	2
McRae	696	1	0	0	0	1	29	13	16	0	0
Mena	5,745	17	1	5	2	9	362	108	245	9	2
Mineral Springs	1,221	2	0	0	0	2	18	10	7	1	0
Monticello	9,482	38	0	3	4	31	428	111	310	7	0
Morrilton	6,792	19	0	2	0	17	304	36	262	6	0
Mountain Home	12,501	7	0	6	0	1	548	32	505	11	0
Mountain View	2,804	12	0	4	0	8	95	21	70	4	1
Mulberry	1,660	9	0	2	1	6	76	33	43	0	0
Murfreesboro	1,644	2	0	0	0	2	10	0	10	0	0
Nashville	4,678	19	0	2	1	16	267	66	200	1	0
Newport	7,862	21	0	5	13	3	590	156	414	20	3
North Little Rock	63,125	449	8	9	177	255	5,471	1,204	3,894	373	10
Osceola	7,702	102	0	9	5	88	498	204	285	9	4
Ozark	3,683	19	0	5	1	13	171	46	121	4	0
Pangburn	611	0	0	0	0	0	29	8	20	1	0
Paragould	26,602	89	2	10	16	61	1,560	577	898	85	6
Paris	3,535	6	0	0	0	6	152	75	70	7	0
Parkin	1,103	8	0	0	0	8	33	23	10	0	2
Pea Ridge	4,948	24	0	1	1	22	93	36	55	2	1
Perryville	1,461	1	0	0	0	1	29	3	25	1	0
Piggott	3,813	4	0	0	0	4	72	40	32	0	1
Pine Bluff	48,522	625	14	32	135	444	3,312	1,124	2,008	180	39
Plummerville	830	11	0	2	0	9	10	3	7	0	0
Pocahontas	6,650	4	0	0	0	4	8	2	6	0	0
Pottsville	2,877	6	0	1	0	5	42	29	12	1	0
Prairie Grove	4,497	10	1	0	0	9	73	12	60	1	0
Prescott	3,317	17	0	1	4	12	140	42	93	5	4
Quitman	764	0	0	0	0	0	25	1	21	3	1
Redfield	1,280	1	0	0	0	1	38	14	20	4	0
Rison	1,349	2	0	0	1	1	32	22	9	1	0
Rogers	57,757	202	0	43	11	148	2,091	362	1,675	54	5
Russellville	28,267	94	0	18	6	70	1,127	262	803	62	3
Sheridan	4,655	18	1	1	1	15	154	55	97	2	0
Sherwood	29,914	122	0	3	12	107	1,029	259	719	51	3
Siloam Springs	15,497	49	0	10	4	35	446	108	321	17	3
Springdale	71,668	332	1	57	30	244	2,692	457	2,089	146	16
Stamps	1,671	2	0	1	0	1	35	20	15	0	1
Star City	2,258	5	0	1	1	3	21	13	8	0	0
Swifton	794	0	0	0	0	0	1	0	1	0	0
Texarkana	30,231	393	1	3	46	343	1,996	438	1,456	102	2
Trumann	7,250	56	2	10	6	38	445	134	302	9	2
Van Buren	22,877	70	1	13	6	50	783	196	554	33	0
Vilonia	3,939	5	0	2	0	3	69	35	33	1	0
Waldron	3,644	10	0	4	1	5	231	87	137	7	1
Walnut Ridge	4,842	10	0	2	1	7	75	19	55	1	0
Ward	4,143	23	0	3	3	17	148	66	76	6	1
Warren	6,013	28	1	1	9	17	168	113	52	3	1
West Fork	2,385	5	0	1	0	4	53	29	23	1	1
West Memphis	26,153	653	6	29	137	481	2,394	1,090	1,166	138	16
White Hall	5,456	5	0	0	0	5	95	33	56	6	0
California											
Adelanto	32,520	199	1	18	45	135	924	397	380	147	15
Agoura Hills	20,667	12	0	2	1	9	236	62	158	16	1
Alameda	75,467	160	1	9	80	70	1,892	296	1,301	295	18
Albany	18,960	35	0	2	26	7	537	116	346	75	4
Alhambra	84,469	149	0	2	66	81	1,919	325	1,339	255	9
Aliso Viejo	48,999	43	0	0	6	37	415	102	300	13	0

Table 8. Offenses Known to Law Enforcement, by Selected State and City, 2012— continued

(Number)

State/city	Population	Violent crime	Murder and nonnegligent manslaughter	Forcible rape	Robbery	Aggravated assault	Property crime	Burglary	Larceny-theft	Motor vehicle theft	Arson[1]
Alturas	2,802	36	1	4	3	28	62	22	38	2	3
American Canyon	19,873	64	0	8	26	30	616	119	448	49	1
Anaheim	344,526	1,279	15	82	440	742	10,070	1,605	7,025	1,440	27
Anderson	10,056	87	0	6	11	70	606	144	368	94	1
Antioch	105,009	1,068	10	29	372	657	4,757	1,741	1,920	1,096	51
Apple Valley	70,823	221	3	7	65	146	1,874	694	977	203	20
Arcadia	57,295	57	0	1	22	34	1,388	339	975	74	1
Arcata	17,408	54	0	2	20	32	754	165	515	74	7
Arroyo Grande	17,568	60	0	1	1	58	358	123	210	25	6
Artesia	16,793	60	1	1	27	31	262	70	164	28	1
Arvin	19,761	165	3	5	14	143	671	267	317	87	21
Atascadero	28,825	192	0	21	10	161	658	160	451	47	9
Atherton	7,060	6	0	0	3	3	124	27	97	0	0
Atwater	28,891	180	2	8	32	138	1,400	440	773	187	8
Auburn	13,787	44	0	5	8	31	249	61	156	32	1
Avalon	3,795	13	0	0	3	10	64	11	41	12	0
Avenal	15,704	53	1	4	5	43	132	54	66	12	1
Azusa	47,111	220	1	6	41	172	1,204	306	737	161	4
Bakersfield	355,696	1,929	34	57	697	1,141	17,754	4,994	9,540	3,220	208
Baldwin Park	76,644	261	2	5	73	181	1,585	335	861	389	3
Banning	30,541	148	2	5	26	115	708	382	251	75	0
Barstow	23,188	207	0	17	45	145	843	265	394	184	5
Bear Valley	5,282	1	0	0	1	0	92	24	66	2	0
Beaumont	38,072	103	0	7	16	80	1,342	192	1,061	89	7
Bell	36,062	225	1	9	95	120	662	177	394	91	0
Bellflower	77,886	304	6	11	135	152	1,802	417	886	499	12
Bell Gardens	42,769	125	3	2	67	53	728	111	308	309	3
Belmont	26,389	24	0	4	5	15	408	92	270	46	2
Belvedere	2,109	0	0	0	0	0	20	2	18	0	0
Benicia	27,459	37	0	3	14	20	390	156	180	54	8
Berkeley	114,961	487	5	39	335	108	5,696	971	4,084	641	15
Beverly Hills	34,677	89	1	7	35	46	1,081	258	790	33	2
Big Bear Lake	5,141	42	1	3	4	34	313	125	170	18	0
Biggs	1,724	19	0	0	0	19	34	10	20	4	1
Bishop	3,900	16	0	0	0	16	137	31	102	4	0
Blythe	21,323	73	1	3	16	53	759	265	491	3	13
Bradbury	1,067	0	0	0	0	0	10	6	4	0	0
Brawley	25,570	59	0	5	16	38	1,176	395	709	72	6
Brea	40,253	74	0	2	23	49	1,292	191	1,052	49	1
Brentwood	52,811	99	1	4	42	52	1,185	240	835	110	11
Brisbane	4,374	6	0	1	0	5	142	17	110	15	3
Broadmoor	4,264	13	0	0	7	6	62	20	31	11	1
Buellton	4,908	3	0	1	0	2	93	28	56	9	0
Buena Park	82,505	206	1	13	77	115	2,066	342	1,415	309	8
Burbank	105,057	243	2	24	111	106	2,493	383	1,911	199	10
Burlingame	29,427	61	0	5	8	48	707	133	518	56	5
Calabasas	23,442	13	1	5	3	4	238	62	165	11	0
Calexico	39,527	108	1	2	37	68	1,538	499	680	359	2
California City	14,460	90	3	3	10	74	517	260	234	23	0
Calimesa	8,136	13	1	0	2	10	202	61	122	19	0
Calistoga	5,266	4	0	0	1	3	64	22	38	4	1
Camarillo	66,506	61	0	5	21	35	955	139	767	49	7
Campbell	40,339	90	0	18	32	40	1,649	371	1,103	175	18
Canyon Lake	10,905	11	0	0	0	11	209	53	129	27	0
Capitola	10,085	47	0	2	15	30	541	47	474	20	2
Carlsbad	107,879	265	2	26	55	182	2,109	497	1,463	149	7
Carmel	3,822	7	0	0	1	6	99	27	69	3	0
Carpinteria	13,257	17	0	3	1	13	305	51	228	26	0
Carson	93,233	520	7	14	142	357	2,709	601	1,558	550	12
Cathedral City	52,867	204	2	10	68	124	1,576	626	653	297	10
Ceres	46,167	183	0	15	55	113	1,940	394	1,185	361	11
Cerritos	49,856	120	0	7	67	46	1,870	441	1,253	176	10
Chico	87,090	282	1	46	95	140	2,291	778	1,259	254	49
Chino	79,792	291	1	9	52	229	2,116	562	1,319	235	5

Table 8. Offenses Known to Law Enforcement, by Selected State and City, 2012— continued

(Number)

State/city	Population	Violent crime	Murder and nonnegligent manslaughter	Forcible rape	Robbery	Aggravated assault	Property crime	Burglary	Larceny-theft	Motor vehicle theft	Arson[1]
Chino Hills	76,632	64	0	2	22	40	956	350	541	65	3
Chowchilla	19,221	115	0	2	6	107	446	207	208	31	3
Chula Vista	249,830	581	8	33	227	313	5,081	926	3,153	1,002	26
Citrus Heights	85,112	329	2	13	100	214	3,117	625	2,017	475	6
City of Angels	3,826	14	0	1	3	10	86	43	37	6	1
Claremont	35,469	40	0	5	19	16	901	227	611	63	7
Clayton	11,179	9	0	3	2	4	104	31	67	6	1
Clearlake	15,311	170	2	20	26	122	675	273	319	83	18
Cloverdale	8,775	6	0	2	3	1	157	34	106	17	1
Clovis	97,828	219	3	34	57	125	4,025	955	2,685	385	11
Coachella	42,034	265	5	9	67	184	1,547	424	780	343	10
Coalinga	13,669	188	0	9	7	172	476	146	293	37	28
Colma	1,832	7	0	0	5	2	287	64	214	9	0
Colton	53,431	189	0	10	84	95	1,907	526	1,027	354	8
Colusa	6,065	11	1	2	5	3	170	71	92	7	0
Commerce	13,035	112	1	2	53	56	1,010	130	616	264	4
Compton	98,057	1,218	21	33	428	736	2,399	574	1,006	819	40
Concord	125,205	402	0	19	153	230	4,182	829	2,694	659	17
Corcoran	25,119	89	0	4	5	80	328	83	209	36	2
Corning	7,751	51	0	4	7	40	281	68	184	29	1
Corona	157,342	210	1	17	102	90	4,143	861	2,766	516	30
Coronado	19,345	20	3	3	0	14	504	117	367	20	3
Costa Mesa	112,635	254	4	32	83	135	4,079	668	3,050	361	24
Cotati	7,398	54	0	3	4	47	85	37	39	9	0
Covina	48,588	151	2	13	55	81	1,651	393	1,070	188	8
Crescent City	7,723	51	0	0	9	42	215	54	143	18	1
Cudahy	24,201	151	0	1	57	93	347	50	219	78	4
Culver City	39,528	179	0	6	96	77	1,760	193	1,465	102	0
Cupertino	59,769	58	0	6	23	29	797	175	569	53	12
Cypress	48,976	56	0	2	17	37	1,018	183	771	64	3
Daly City	103,311	216	0	9	76	131	1,803	395	1,151	257	21
Dana Point	34,172	65	0	5	13	47	604	129	444	31	2
Danville	43,121	16	0	0	2	14	442	94	331	17	0
Davis	66,628	95	0	20	31	44	1,476	390	999	87	17
Delano	54,318	274	0	6	53	215	1,437	545	552	340	34
Del Mar	4,263	15	0	2	0	13	211	54	144	13	0
Del Rey Oaks	1,668	2	0	0	1	1	37	7	30	0	0
Desert Hot Springs	27,929	344	6	12	67	259	1,157	571	432	154	3
Diamond Bar	56,470	55	0	1	17	37	952	354	525	73	4
Dinuba	21,999	181	0	4	32	145	919	341	424	154	5
Dixon	18,708	53	0	5	20	28	315	96	181	38	1
Dorris	939	1	0	1	0	0	23	7	15	1	0
Dos Palos	5,079	59	1	2	1	55	162	44	99	19	0
Downey	113,628	381	6	20	190	165	3,537	670	1,908	959	4
Duarte	21,673	71	0	5	17	49	507	121	317	69	0
Dublin	47,004	84	0	4	20	60	731	155	522	54	7
Dunsmuir	1,650	5	0	0	1	4	41	16	25	0	0
East Palo Alto	28,766	333	7	11	85	230	587	321	128	138	0
Eastvale	55,439	41	0	1	15	25	1,007	256	641	110	3
El Cajon	101,864	365	2	24	147	192	2,414	493	1,527	394	15
El Centro	43,643	166	2	7	40	117	2,477	734	1,572	171	9
El Cerrito	24,156	128	0	2	79	47	1,022	239	635	148	1
Elk Grove	156,344	512	1	20	95	396	3,292	674	2,406	212	26
El Monte	115,356	395	4	14	203	174	2,230	571	1,081	578	14
El Segundo	16,931	38	0	1	15	22	595	156	389	50	5
Emeryville	10,309	175	3	4	100	68	1,735	170	1,390	175	1
Encinitas	60,960	150	1	12	23	114	1,296	291	929	76	3
Escalon	7,314	24	0	2	2	20	227	72	144	11	7
Escondido	147,386	628	5	38	206	379	3,887	764	2,365	758	14
Etna	737	1	0	0	0	1	2	0	2	0	0
Eureka	27,469	159	0	17	71	71	1,956	347	1,430	179	26
Exeter	10,596	28	0	3	1	24	306	89	191	26	1
Fairfax	7,590	10	0	3	0	7	133	32	93	8	1
Fairfield	107,110	454	8	30	139	277	3,317	676	2,144	497	14

Table 8. Offenses Known to Law Enforcement, by Selected State and City, 2012— continued

(Number)

State/city	Population	Violent crime	Murder and nonnegligent manslaughter	Forcible rape	Robbery	Aggravated assault	Property crime	Burglary	Larceny-theft	Motor vehicle theft	Arson[1]
Farmersville	10,860	34	1	1	4	28	227	65	129	33	0
Ferndale	1,385	3	0	0	0	3	17	4	12	1	0
Fillmore	15,298	24	2	0	4	18	198	27	148	23	0
Firebaugh	7,724	29	0	1	5	23	141	50	00	20	1
Folsom	73,678	85	0	7	24	54	1,277	235	963	79	13
Fontana	200,874	850	5	31	291	523	4,494	1,099	2,389	1,006	12
Fort Bragg	7,317	34	1	3	1	29	367	95	261	11	2
Fort Jones	841	0	0	0	0	0	14	6	7	1	0
Fortuna	12,050	46	0	7	8	31	442	74	339	29	4
Foster City	31,230	18	0	0	3	15	345	83	239	23	1
Fountain Valley	56,674	106	1	7	17	81	1,469	299	1,063	107	4
Fowler	5,698	48	0	0	0	48	213	44	135	34	4
Fremont	218,927	306	2	14	132	158	4,259	1,176	2,502	581	16
Fresno	506,011	2,748	51	54	1,015	1,628	25,737	5,902	15,534	4,301	134
Fullerton	138,455	452	0	31	137	284	3,937	742	2,872	323	12
Galt	24,163	59	1	2	7	49	470	148	267	55	11
Gardena	59,802	287	0	13	167	107	1,321	297	716	308	7
Garden Grove	175,079	439	1	16	135	287	4,017	761	2,655	601	21
Gilroy	50,042	159	3	7	68	81	1,788	339	1,217	232	7
Glendale	194,902	233	0	6	108	119	3,043	516	2,218	309	13
Glendora	50,903	59	0	8	27	24	1,293	202	1,018	73	7
Goleta	30,384	50	0	4	8	38	523	129	368	26	0
Gonzales	8,404	36	0	1	15	20	102	40	51	11	0
Grand Terrace	12,333	29	1	1	8	19	285	105	138	42	0
Grass Valley	12,959	65	0	5	8	52	639	136	452	51	9
Greenfield	16,765	120	5	1	32	82	306	102	165	39	4
Gridley	6,654	78	1	4	3	70	220	66	128	26	3
Grover Beach	13,398	32	0	3	5	24	306	91	192	23	4
Guadalupe	7,198	10	0	1	1	8	57	12	36	9	2
Gustine	5,663	24	0	1	2	21	120	39	65	16	3
Hanford	54,787	309	2	24	59	224	1,711	337	1,176	198	12
Hawaiian Gardens	14,493	69	1	2	21	45	193	41	100	52	1
Hawthorne	85,692	637	7	26	307	297	2,181	575	1,138	468	9
Hayward	147,424	613	6	46	342	219	4,792	1,109	2,227	1,456	34
Healdsburg	11,458	18	0	1	3	14	271	69	189	13	0
Hemet	81,213	406	1	21	146	238	3,486	1,052	1,955	479	4
Hercules	24,682	43	1	1	17	24	298	98	144	56	2
Hermosa Beach	19,830	54	0	9	18	27	678	138	494	46	0
Hesperia	92,383	402	6	17	69	310	2,502	917	1,185	400	16
Hidden Hills	1,887	0	0	0	0	0	4	1	3	0	0
Highland	54,403	296	4	5	92	195	1,616	629	689	298	10
Hillsborough	11,060	1	0	0	1	0	86	31	54	1	1
Hollister	35,766	162	1	12	26	123	724	281	379	64	12
Holtville	6,088	11	0	0	3	8	98	31	59	8	1
Hughson	6,754	10	0	0	2	8	144	58	73	13	1
Huntington Beach	194,677	313	3	31	83	196	5,470	797	4,352	321	39
Huntington Park	59,079	373	4	9	243	117	1,917	241	1,018	658	17
Huron	6,901	69	1	2	29	37	301	105	152	44	8
Imperial	15,126	7	0	0	2	5	73	17	50	6	0
Imperial Beach	26,956	147	2	12	25	108	471	122	261	88	0
Indian Wells	5,120	2	0	0	1	1	203	58	141	4	0
Indio	78,501	450	2	22	153	273	2,791	836	1,466	489	7
Industry	222	68	0	1	34	33	1,110	111	785	214	2
Inglewood	111,488	780	14	27	373	366	2,673	646	1,389	638	24
Ione	7,977	10	0	1	0	9	109	22	83	4	0
Irvine	217,528	110	2	8	29	71	3,304	570	2,599	135	22
Irwindale	1,447	15	0	0	5	10	243	50	152	41	1
Jackson	4,677	38	0	0	4	34	136	41	85	10	1
Jurupa Valley	97,577	312	1	12	93	206	3,174	731	1,779	664	9
Kensington	5,185	4	1	0	3	0	85	30	45	10	2
Kerman	13,854	42	0	3	16	23	608	126	353	129	3
King City	13,214	54	3	4	8	39	332	183	108	41	2
Kingsburg	11,644	38	1	6	6	25	432	111	230	91	2
La Canada Flintridge	20,584	12	0	1	4	7	324	129	179	16	2

Table 8. Offenses Known to Law Enforcement, by Selected State and City, 2012— continued

(Number)

State/city	Population	Violent crime	Murder and nonnegligent manslaughter	Forcible rape	Robbery	Aggravated assault	Property crime	Burglary	Larceny-theft	Motor vehicle theft	Arson[1]
Lafayette	24,510	21	0	2	7	12	419	101	292	26	0
Laguna Beach	23,283	57	1	6	7	43	548	123	399	26	4
Laguna Hills	31,090	29	1	4	12	12	620	85	502	33	1
Laguna Niguel	64,533	47	0	6	16	25	764	188	541	35	2
Laguna Woods	16,590	4	0	0	2	2	148	20	121	7	0
La Habra	61,731	147	2	7	45	93	1,150	255	789	106	3
La Habra Heights	5,413	6	0	0	0	6	44	24	18	2	3
Lake Elsinore	53,912	130	2	3	57	68	1,932	537	1,141	254	3
Lake Forest	79,166	107	0	8	20	79	1,088	227	798	63	4
Lakeport	4,772	16	0	1	3	12	324	63	251	10	0
Lake Shastina	2,460	0	0	0	0	0	0	0	0	0	0
Lakewood	81,382	227	1	13	102	111	2,062	371	1,381	310	6
La Mesa	58,444	224	2	11	88	123	1,732	351	1,180	201	9
La Mirada	49,312	98	2	4	20	72	776	170	503	103	4
Lancaster	159,155	859	8	54	313	484	3,498	1,043	2,051	404	64
La Palma	15,954	18	0	1	7	10	340	85	227	28	1
La Puente	40,479	121	3	6	42	70	521	110	253	158	4
La Quinta	38,690	150	0	5	45	100	1,669	541	1,033	95	1
La Verne	31,575	50	0	8	15	27	823	142	637	44	3
Lawndale	33,312	167	2	4	51	110	397	135	164	98	3
Lemon Grove	25,932	137	1	11	48	77	434	85	248	101	2
Lemoore	24,904	131	0	9	18	104	698	127	494	77	11
Lincoln	44,378	14	0	1	5	8	506	203	253	50	0
Lindsay	12,068	49	0	1	12	36	321	84	182	55	5
Livermore	82,800	301	0	15	32	254	1,805	310	1,319	176	9
Livingston	13,394	74	2	3	12	57	306	120	146	40	4
Lodi	63,718	280	2	12	86	180	2,599	754	1,508	337	11
Loma Linda	23,819	43	1	3	11	28	626	173	299	154	2
Lomita	20,591	95	1	1	30	63	391	81	264	46	0
Lompoc	43,120	222	3	16	27	176	1,166	312	787	67	14
Long Beach	469,893	2,705	32	115	1,239	1,319	14,131	3,799	7,702	2,630	104
Los Alamitos	11,728	27	0	2	12	13	357	80	253	24	0
Los Altos	29,704	6	0	0	5	1	299	94	197	8	3
Los Altos Hills	8,121	5	0	0	1	4	45	19	23	3	0
Los Angeles	3,855,122	18,547	299	936	8,983	8,329	87,478	16,388	56,006	15,084	1,262
Los Banos	36,897	142	1	0	24	117	1,210	340	776	94	5
Los Gatos	30,161	38	0	5	6	27	629	123	464	42	9
Lynwood	70,908	541	9	24	211	297	1,373	350	503	520	8
Madera	62,796	466	2	19	114	331	1,621	653	622	346	0
Malibu	12,854	15	0	4	5	6	329	78	232	19	0
Mammoth Lakes	8,373	38	0	3	9	26	196	54	140	2	1
Manhattan Beach	35,719	62	0	7	29	26	855	183	631	41	1
Manteca	68,887	265	0	11	83	171	2,681	454	1,844	383	19
Marina	20,227	41	0	6	12	23	498	151	316	31	0
Martinez	36,729	70	1	9	18	42	930	174	567	189	0
Marysville	12,254	88	0	9	19	60	502	176	240	86	11
Maywood	27,850	175	1	6	56	112	286	66	139	81	7
McFarland	13,010	57	0	4	7	46	218	80	85	53	16
Menifee	80,047	87	1	4	24	58	1,942	507	1,109	326	0
Mendota	11,270	53	0	0	20	33	344	81	226	37	15
Menlo Park	32,713	53	2	2	23	26	625	165	432	28	2
Merced	80,976	810	9	25	215	561	4,111	955	2,721	435	58
Mill Valley	14,181	12	0	1	6	5	175	47	107	21	0
Milpitas	68,433	81	1	11	34	35	2,023	332	1,350	341	6
Mission Viejo	95,599	73	0	3	28	42	1,197	216	936	45	6
Modesto	204,631	1,590	20	59	450	1,061	11,276	2,571	6,906	1,799	54
Monrovia	37,199	81	0	2	36	43	948	120	714	114	3
Montague	1,443	2	0	0	0	2	6	0	6	0	0
Montclair	37,556	197	0	13	67	117	1,703	239	1,092	372	5
Montebello	63,538	146	3	4	67	72	1,775	718	622	435	48
Monterey	28,508	153	1	10	27	115	1,016	274	704	38	8
Monterey Park	61,270	75	4	1	42	28	1,022	249	551	222	2
Monte Sereno	3,426	3	1	1	0	1	35	11	22	2	1
Moorpark	35,102	41	0	6	6	29	330	77	228	25	0

Table 8. Offenses Known to Law Enforcement, by Selected State and City, 2012— continued

(Number)

State/city	Population	Violent crime	Murder and nonnegligent manslaughter	Forcible rape	Robbery	Aggravated assault	Property crime	Burglary	Larceny-theft	Motor vehicle theft	Arson[1]
Moraga	16,401	6	0	1	0	5	152	30	111	11	1
Moreno Valley	199,673	706	5	25	331	345	6,371	2,018	3,456	897	8
Morgan Hill	38,834	50	0	11	13	26	695	157	464	74	18
Morro Bay	10,423	21	0	0	4	17	140	44	92	4	2
Mountain View	75,933	155	0	5	34	116	1,419	178	1,127	114	7
Mount Shasta	3,396	5	0	0	0	5	79	18	56	5	0
Murrieta	106,839	70	1	8	21	40	1,715	408	1,177	130	15
Napa	78,589	216	2	17	39	158	1,643	349	1,073	221	8
National City	59,920	371	4	18	165	184	1,863	366	1,090	407	30
Needles	4,963	23	0	6	6	11	213	96	90	27	7
Nevada City	3,092	12	0	2	1	9	172	65	90	17	0
Newark	43,539	169	1	14	69	85	1,349	390	811	148	5
Newman	10,402	25	0	2	6	17	194	41	113	40	0
Newport Beach	87,286	101	1	11	27	62	2,151	445	1,611	95	6
Norco	27,850	56	1	5	24	26	580	163	344	73	4
Norwalk	107,295	433	11	13	171	238	2,609	539	1,537	533	15
Novato	52,942	96	0	5	26	65	956	241	624	91	13
Oakdale	21,031	58	2	10	13	33	934	240	596	98	0
Oakland	399,487	7,963	127	271	4,338	3,227	26,342	6,168	13,198	6,976	188
Oakley	36,348	85	1	7	11	66	477	120	257	100	4
Oceanside	171,141	728	8	48	175	497	4,289	841	3,003	445	19
Ojai	7,607	13	0	0	1	12	162	24	133	5	1
Ontario	167,933	534	3	36	266	229	5,056	1,058	3,019	979	30
Orange	139,692	135	4	8	54	69	2,833	500	2,044	289	26
Orinda	18,098	7	1	0	1	5	216	77	132	7	0
Orland	7,361	27	0	0	2	25	210	63	110	37	7
Oroville	15,707	107	1	11	45	50	991	326	563	102	8
Oxnard	201,797	603	9	8	304	282	4,071	848	2,677	546	40
Pacifica	38,041	42	1	5	9	27	578	148	382	48	3
Pacific Grove	15,437	27	0	4	7	16	249	97	147	5	1
Palmdale	155,294	812	6	37	224	545	3,393	1,035	2,068	290	29
Palm Desert	50,021	104	0	6	49	49	2,322	727	1,477	118	5
Palm Springs	45,996	302	3	18	104	177	2,232	883	1,112	237	18
Palo Alto	66,019	53	0	4	26	23	1,409	327	1,034	48	12
Palos Verdes Estates	13,661	6	0	1	0	5	136	48	80	8	1
Paradise	26,492	66	0	5	6	55	479	241	214	24	0
Paramount	54,997	244	3	7	129	105	1,536	272	810	454	9
Parlier	14,828	119	0	7	16	96	431	175	147	109	8
Pasadena	139,382	433	5	21	172	235	3,379	891	2,238	250	52
Paso Robles	30,344	91	1	6	6	78	777	152	578	47	5
Patterson	20,769	53	1	1	24	27	734	279	314	141	2
Perris	70,616	240	3	6	94	137	2,081	488	1,118	475	0
Petaluma	58,995	167	1	25	29	112	822	149	622	51	9
Pico Rivera	63,988	261	1	6	92	162	1,780	349	1,063	368	5
Piedmont	10,909	13	0	0	6	7	333	134	151	48	0
Pinole	18,864	91	0	8	39	44	674	161	400	113	3
Pismo Beach	7,798	36	0	7	7	22	305	79	214	12	3
Pittsburg	64,890	152	3	6	83	60	2,107	741	824	542	4
Placentia	51,778	107	1	4	29	73	906	183	627	96	2
Placerville	10,479	55	0	2	8	45	194	65	109	20	3
Pleasant Hill	34,001	73	1	3	40	29	1,621	319	1,183	119	5
Pleasanton	71,875	49	1	4	18	26	1,279	165	995	119	5
Pomona	151,511	1,021	17	63	377	564	5,055	901	3,044	1,110	19
Porterville	55,533	200	3	10	63	124	1,807	595	1,014	198	1
Port Hueneme	22,142	65	0	8	11	46	467	107	307	53	2
Poway	48,968	94	0	6	27	61	559	137	389	33	3
Rancho Cordova	66,214	393	9	28	112	244	2,107	421	1,364	322	3
Rancho Cucamonga	169,276	321	4	16	112	189	4,362	1,460	2,427	475	13
Rancho Mirage	17,778	23	0	7	4	12	726	282	411	33	2
Rancho Palos Verdes	42,335	35	0	1	6	28	498	167	306	25	4
Rancho Santa Margarit	49,038	27	0	2	10	15	319	69	240	10	1
Red Bluff	14,236	112	0	8	21	83	811	249	531	31	4
Redding	90,974	705	3	66	131	505	4,380	1,088	2,790	502	5

Table 8. Offenses Known to Law Enforcement, by Selected State and City, 2012— continued

(Number)

State/city	Population	Violent crime	Murder and nonnegligent manslaughter	Forcible rape	Robbery	Aggravated assault	Property crime	Burglary	Larceny-theft	Motor vehicle theft	Arson[1]
Redlands	70,399	221	2	15	75	129	2,992	608	1,984	400	20
Redondo Beach	67,856	190	4	6	51	129	1,596	266	1,223	107	3
Redwood City	78,466	208	0	13	88	107	1,800	526	1,121	153	9
Reedley	24,747	173	0	6	15	152	570	199	249	122	2
Rialto	101,595	509	4	17	201	287	3,571	898	1,798	875	17
Richmond	106,357	1,162	18	36	391	717	5,018	1,537	1,615	1,866	24
Ridgecrest	28,273	108	2	4	16	86	602	234	327	41	12
Rio Dell	3,403	8	0	1	0	7	95	20	73	2	0
Rio Vista	7,485	39	0	0	1	38	145	41	86	18	2
Ripon	14,662	6	0	1	1	4	297	49	229	19	2
Riverbank	23,070	57	0	5	19	33	761	252	389	120	1
Riverside	313,532	1,389	16	76	517	780	10,818	2,247	7,095	1,476	65
Rocklin	58,865	49	0	5	16	28	917	243	612	62	9
Rohnert Park	41,716	192	1	11	21	159	770	112	599	59	10
Rolling Hills	1,891	0	0	0	0	0	27	9	17	1	0
Rolling Hills Estates	8,202	9	0	0	1	8	129	36	90	3	1
Rosemead	54,656	143	0	4	54	85	913	184	511	218	0
Roseville	122,896	293	2	15	84	192	3,288	519	2,536	233	13
Ross	2,465	2	0	0	1	1	23	13	10	0	0
Sacramento	476,557	3,520	34	125	1,211	2,150	19,967	4,474	12,147	3,346	130
Salinas	154,413	1,027	21	41	488	477	4,906	1,218	2,606	1,082	29
San Anselmo	12,584	13	0	0	2	11	172	55	110	7	3
San Bernardino	214,987	2,022	47	56	803	1,116	10,510	2,809	4,991	2,710	48
San Bruno	42,002	85	0	11	29	45	961	128	690	143	0
San Clemente	65,089	75	0	6	24	45	839	175	603	61	3
Sand City	343	7	1	1	2	3	76	2	68	6	0
San Diego	1,338,477	5,529	47	304	1,517	3,661	31,700	5,902	19,188	6,610	183
San Dimas	33,923	51	0	2	14	35	668	141	471	56	3
San Fernando	24,039	77	3	2	25	47	380	70	220	90	1
San Francisco	820,363	5,777	69	108	3,484	2,116	38,898	5,317	28,242	5,339	207
San Gabriel	40,376	88	0	3	34	51	550	143	346	61	1
Sanger	24,827	269	3	13	30	223	1,041	260	646	135	3
San Jacinto	45,637	137	3	5	51	78	1,479	421	863	195	3
San Jose	976,459	3,547	45	280	1,208	2,014	28,463	5,206	14,498	8,759	176
San Juan Capistrano	35,449	59	0	3	13	43	519	102	380	37	8
San Leandro	86,869	437	2	15	271	149	3,585	699	2,094	792	14
San Luis Obispo	45,947	119	1	20	19	79	1,971	414	1,476	81	48
San Marcos	85,810	227	2	11	57	157	1,502	366	907	229	3
San Marino	13,364	13	0	0	3	10	183	68	111	4	0
San Mateo	99,303	261	0	13	81	167	1,876	285	1,448	143	6
San Pablo	29,884	277	7	7	145	118	1,459	375	575	509	3
San Rafael	58,854	191	0	14	84	93	1,785	360	1,132	293	19
San Ramon	74,013	45	0	3	13	29	850	146	633	71	10
Santa Ana	332,482	1,334	11	55	541	727	7,389	1,032	4,779	1,578	36
Santa Barbara	89,871	363	0	53	95	215	3,115	558	2,424	133	12
Santa Clara	119,360	221	0	10	61	150	3,306	584	2,273	449	17
Santa Clarita	179,248	342	1	30	96	215	2,742	616	1,822	304	18
Santa Cruz	60,902	433	3	34	83	313	3,585	527	2,794	264	21
Santa Fe Springs	16,492	99	2	3	42	52	1,272	207	855	210	1
Santa Maria	101,207	690	0	21	145	524	2,430	712	1,318	400	9
Santa Monica	91,215	395	2	23	151	219	3,398	586	2,634	178	10
Santa Paula	29,899	91	1	4	28	58	590	103	422	65	3
Santa Rosa	170,862	636	2	67	126	441	3,818	725	2,777	316	22
Santee	54,700	154	2	9	30	113	1,109	183	794	132	0
Saratoga	30,683	9	0	1	2	6	231	69	155	7	2
Sausalito	7,202	7	0	0	2	5	254	56	189	9	0
Scotts Valley	11,775	16	0	4	2	10	325	53	261	11	0
Seal Beach	24,764	17	0	1	5	11	545	135	387	23	1
Seaside	33,887	109	2	4	27	76	499	126	335	38	5
Sebastopol	7,512	8	0	0	2	6	170	40	122	8	2
Selma	23,753	208	2	14	45	147	1,218	312	606	300	4
Shafter	17,391	49	0	5	13	31	576	193	296	87	12
Sierra Madre	11,098	4	0	0	1	3	112	30	76	6	0
Signal Hill	11,198	43	1	3	15	24	536	87	362	87	2

Table 8. Offenses Known to Law Enforcement, by Selected State and City, 2012— continued

(Number)

State/city	Population	Violent crime	Murder and nonnegligent manslaughter	Forcible rape	Robbery	Aggravated assault	Property crime	Burglary	Larceny-theft	Motor vehicle theft	Arson[1]
Simi Valley	126,686	141	3	7	36	95	1,916	398	1,394	124	13
Solana Beach	13,181	24	0	0	5	19	313	79	210	24	0
Soledad	26,253	80	5	3	23	49	284	129	116	39	4
Solvang	5,332	5	0	0	2	3	63	15	46	2	0
Sonoma	10,841	27	0	0	3	24	193	51	142	0	1
Sonora	4,911	20	0	3	5	12	311	82	224	5	5
South El Monte	20,452	88	2	3	38	45	399	104	184	111	3
South Gate	95,966	553	9	15	265	264	2,545	410	1,217	918	10
South Lake Tahoe	21,586	148	0	10	27	111	544	152	360	32	0
South Pasadena	26,045	27	0	6	13	8	443	118	277	48	6
South San Francisco	65,006	111	0	12	29	70	1,321	351	782	188	23
Stallion Springs	2,540	6	0	0	0	6	9	3	5	1	0
Stanton	39,124	104	1	3	46	54	630	121	381	128	5
St. Helena	5,939	3	0	1	0	2	86	34	50	2	0
Stockton	299,105	4,630	71	90	1,556	2,913	15,258	4,416	8,339	2,503	68
Suisun City	28,593	57	2	6	18	31	558	116	372	70	6
Sunnyvale	143,606	170	3	14	71	82	2,555	524	1,696	335	22
Susanville	17,849	96	1	5	9	81	320	104	203	13	4
Sutter Creek	2,513	7	0	1	0	6	62	23	34	5	0
Taft	9,552	54	0	1	3	50	365	92	244	29	0
Tehachapi	14,766	59	1	4	9	45	472	210	233	29	0
Temecula	103,414	97	0	10	53	34	2,440	588	1,640	212	2
Temple City	36,148	38	0	2	16	20	354	116	201	37	4
Thousand Oaks	129,171	157	0	23	46	88	1,838	278	1,470	90	20
Tiburon	9,142	10	0	1	1	8	95	13	79	3	0
Torrance	147,851	190	4	17	92	77	2,690	529	1,823	338	5
Tracy	85,047	145	4	8	66	67	2,158	284	1,587	287	18
Truckee	16,304	22	0	4	2	16	232	61	157	14	1
Tulare	60,848	376	6	10	71	289	2,400	716	1,352	332	13
Tulelake	1,010	1	0	0	0	1	5	2	3	0	0
Turlock	69,730	445	2	20	97	326	2,486	624	1,353	509	35
Tustin	77,400	114	0	11	36	67	1,653	240	1,282	131	9
Twentynine Palms	25,612	81	0	11	11	59	463	196	224	43	14
Twin Cities[5]	21,606	37	0	3	8	26				63	2
Ukiah	16,172	108	0	6	15	87	481	171	278	32	4
Union City	71,089	235	0	9	103	123	1,808	430	1,071	307	6
Upland	75,531	148	0	8	67	73	2,328	633	1,329	366	6
Vacaville	93,951	246	3	24	73	146	2,031	319	1,540	172	11
Vallejo	117,912	878	14	44	380	440	5,844	2,688	1,681	1,475	65
Ventura	108,511	310	1	24	140	145	3,885	778	2,825	282	15
Vernon	114	27	1	1	16	9	311	26	199	86	0
Victorville	118,687	676	6	40	222	408	4,465	1,837	1,981	647	25
Villa Park	5,956	2	0	0	0	2	87	22	62	3	0
Visalia	127,604	544	5	44	134	361	5,531	1,227	3,778	526	10
Vista	96,087	465	1	25	144	295	1,885	438	1,118	329	5
Walnut	29,658	37	0	2	10	25	382	141	209	32	6
Walnut Creek	65,816	84	0	3	19	62	2,050	446	1,463	141	5
Waterford	8,604	31	0	3	4	24	205	59	101	45	1
Watsonville	52,064	252	2	15	87	148	1,585	265	1,024	296	9
Weed	2,970	18	1	1	5	11	125	38	68	19	0
West Covina	107,861	281	2	11	108	160	3,224	546	2,135	543	2
West Hollywood	34,971	338	0	12	134	192	1,642	331	1,194	117	9
Westlake Village	8,406	3	0	1	1	1	154	36	106	12	0
Westminster	91,908	284	2	9	88	185	2,875	466	2,086	323	7
Westmorland	2,282	2	0	0	1	1	9	7	1	1	0
West Sacramento	49,500	190	0	26	73	91	1,458	379	913	166	23
Wheatland	3,509	2	0	1	0	1	36	6	25	5	2
Whittier	86,740	247	0	10	81	156	2,502	449	1,758	295	10
Wildomar	33,227	53	1	2	14	36	707	208	392	107	0
Williams	5,200	9	0	1	5	3	76	22	39	15	1
Willits	4,917	32	0	0	5	27	71	19	42	10	2
Willows	6,223	26	0	1	4	21	234	68	149	17	0
Windsor	27,293	67	0	6	2	59	318	59	248	11	1
Winters	6,726	6	0	0	0	6	84	27	49	8	0

Table 8. Offenses Known to Law Enforcement, by Selected State and City, 2012— continued

(Number)

State/city	Population	Violent crime	Murder and nonnegligent manslaughter	Forcible rape	Robbery	Aggravated assault	Property crime	Burglary	Larceny-theft	Motor vehicle theft	Arson[1]
Woodlake	7,466	48	1	2	4	41	211	60	127	24	4
Woodland	56,323	177	0	10	47	120	1,735	361	1,172	202	54
Yorba Linda	65,820	53	0	3	11	39	787	223	532	32	3
Yountville	2,984	7	0	0	1	6	56	16	38	2	1
Yreka	7,768	42	1	7	6	28	293	65	220	8	2
Yuba City	65,653	247	4	22	43	178	1,982	501	1,297	184	14
Yucaipa	52,622	119	0	5	35	79	944	271	559	114	11
Yucca Valley	21,204	90	0	5	19	66	560	190	304	66	6
Colorado											
Arvada	109,029	158	0	22	29	107	2,605	390	2,014	201	20
Aspen	6,734	12	0	4	0	8	308	23	280	5	2
Ault	1,577	3	0	0	0	3	2	0	1	1	0
Aurora	336,952	1,433	29	179	483	742	10,059	1,791	7,370	898	72
Avon	6,453	22	1	7	0	14	96	9	86	1	1
Basalt	3,889	14	0	0	4	10	43	4	33	6	0
Berthoud	5,278	2	0	0	0	2	62	10	50	2	0
Black Hawk	120	4	0	0	0	4	170	6	159	5	0
Blue River	860	0	0	0	0	0	3	0	3	0	0
Boulder	100,257	249	0	32	48	169	2,937	472	2,337	128	26
Bow Mar	894	1	0	0	1	0	7	0	7	0	0
Broomfield	58,145	30	1	7	6	16	1,213	90	1,076	47	6
Brush	5,365	1	0	0	1	0	49	11	36	2	0
Buena Vista	2,674	0	0	0	0	0	1	0	1	0	0
Burlington	4,130	21	0	3	0	18	72	9	59	4	0
Campo	111	0	0	0	0	0	0	0	0	0	0
Canon City	16,727	93	0	23	4	66	539	75	445	19	4
Carbondale	6,501	7	0	1	1	5	144	21	114	9	0
Castle Rock	50,038	45	1	12	7	25	666	102	538	26	7
Cedaredge	2,247	1	0	0	0	1	55	15	38	2	0
Centennial	104,022	157	1	40	33	83	1,439	277	1,085	77	16
Center	2,311	7	0	0	0	7	43	15	26	2	1
Cherry Hills Village	6,206	3	0	1	0	2	94	25	65	4	0
Colorado Springs	432,287	1,968	18	358	523	1,069	17,899	3,641	12,456	1,802	76
Columbine Valley	1,302	0	0	0	0	0	5	2	3	0	0
Commerce City	47,590	170	7	27	17	119	1,420	295	1,001	124	6
Cortez	8,568	26	0	0	3	23	297	18	265	14	0
Craig	9,357	14	1	4	0	9	261	37	217	7	4
Crested Butte	1,517	3	0	0	1	2	28	9	13	6	0
Cripple Creek	1,206	17	0	0	0	17	74	9	63	2	0
Dacono	4,308	5	0	1	0	4	4	2	2	0	0
De Beque	512	0	0	0	0	0	6	1	5	0	0
Del Norte	1,706	1	0	0	0	1	17	8	9	0	0
Delta	8,890	19	0	2	5	12	320	54	255	11	10
Denver	628,545	3,871	39	376	1,165	2,291	23,343	5,129	14,544	3,670	97
Dillon	927	0	0	0	0	0	31	8	23	0	1
Durango	17,305	53	1	3	6	43	418	47	357	14	3
Eagle	6,555	7	0	2	0	5	70	8	61	1	0
Eaton	4,529	4	0	0	0	4	2	0	2	0	0
Elizabeth	1,381	4	0	0	1	3	32	7	25	0	0
Empire	284	0	0	0	0	0	2	0	1	1	0
Englewood	31,358	61	0	12	27	22	1,800	220	1,402	178	8
Erie	18,761	9	0	0	1	8	107	23	82	2	0
Estes Park	6,059	11	0	1	3	7	96	17	79	0	0
Evans	19,236	79	0	2	10	67	386	55	304	27	2
Federal Heights	11,886	81	1	19	11	50	667	86	508	73	2
Firestone	10,529	4	0	1	0	3	97	12	74	11	2
Florence	3,960	4	0	0	0	4	70	9	59	2	0
Fort Collins	148,792	391	2	44	40	305	4,119	598	3,379	142	15
Fort Lupton	7,655	8	0	0	1	7	55	5	42	8	1
Fort Morgan	11,586	14	0	0	2	12	324	57	259	8	1
Fountain	26,841	68	0	11	12	45	711	121	554	36	3
Fowler	1,201	1	0	0	1	0	8	1	7	0	0
Frederick	9,007	3	0	0	1	2	113	18	93	2	0

Table 8. Offenses Known to Law Enforcement, by Selected State and City, 2012— continued

(Number)

State/city	Population	Violent crime	Murder and nonnegligent manslaughter	Forcible rape	Robbery	Aggravated assault	Property crime	Burglary	Larceny-theft	Motor vehicle theft	Arson[1]
Frisco	2,717	4	0	1	0	3	34	6	27	1	1
Fruita	12,852	17	0	1	2	14	246	38	195	13	1
Georgetown	1,039	4	0	0	0	4	4	3	1	0	0
Glenwood Springs	9,727	33	0	3	3	27	500	70	101	20	2
Golden	19,298	31	0	3	4	24	471	55	397	19	2
Granby	1,852	5	0	1	1	3	45	6	39	0	0
Grand Junction	59,516	252	2	52	29	169	2,733	308	2,295	130	18
Greeley	96,276	426	1	40	64	321	3,243	542	2,560	141	33
Green Mountain Falls	664	1	0	1	0	0	0	0	0	0	0
Greenwood Village	14,434	28	1	1	4	22	538	91	424	23	3
Gunnison	5,967	28	0	5	1	22	234	16	214	4	0
Haxtun	950	1	0	0	0	1	2	0	2	0	0
Hayden	1,814	1	0	0	0	1	19	4	15	0	0
Holyoke	2,322	0	0	0	0	0	10	3	6	1	0
Idaho Springs	1,726	7	0	0	1	6	71	10	57	4	1
Ignacio	721	0	0	0	0	0	0	0	0	0	0
Johnstown	10,259	7	0	0	0	7	88	9	72	7	0
Kersey	1,509	5	0	1	0	4	21	3	14	4	1
Kiowa	736	2	0	1	0	1	10	3	7	0	0
Lafayette	25,209	54	0	7	11	36	403	70	317	16	5
La Junta	7,187	20	0	4	2	14	188	49	132	7	2
Lakeside	8	1	0	0	0	1	18	4	14	0	0
Lakewood	146,404	676	2	94	148	432	6,705	917	5,180	608	15
Lamar	8,035	9	0	0	2	7	292	55	227	10	0
La Salle	2,030	2	0	0	0	2	37	5	31	1	0
La Veta	788	1	0	1	0	0	14	8	6	0	1
Leadville	2,680	8	0	2	1	5	37	4	32	1	0
Limon	1,900	7	0	0	0	7	16	0	14	2	0
Littleton	43,229	56	4	20	15	17	1,248	256	911	81	3
Lone Tree	11,488	6	0	0	0	6	597	33	554	10	0
Longmont	88,925	188	0	11	30	147	2,169	359	1,705	105	57
Loveland	69,147	145	0	22	22	101	1,798	227	1,525	46	20
Mancos	1,348	1	0	0	0	1	1	1	0	0	0
Manitou Springs	5,184	14	0	1	2	11	150	21	119	10	0
Mead	3,532	2	0	0	1	1	34	5	25	4	2
Meeker	2,554	2	0	0	0	2	27	9	17	1	0
Minturn	1,037	1	0	0	0	1	17	1	15	1	0
Monte Vista	4,495	13	2	1	5	5	206	60	143	3	1
Montrose	19,274	42	1	0	3	38	693	112	555	26	3
Monument	5,744	2	0	1	0	1	196	73	114	9	0
Morrison	437	3	0	0	3	0	4	1	2	1	0
Mount Crested Butte	817	6	0	0	0	6	6	1	5	0	0
New Castle	4,570	7	0	0	0	7	56	7	44	5	0
Northglenn	37,094	102	1	32	7	62	1,015	173	708	134	11
Ouray	996	1	0	0	0	1	25	2	23	0	0
Pagosa Springs	1,741	10	0	1	1	8	94	22	71	1	0
Palisade	2,735	4	0	0	0	4	3	2	1	0	1
Palmer Lake	2,512	3	0	1	0	2	11	4	6	1	0
Parachute	1,098	5	0	0	0	5	45	25	18	2	0
Parker	47,004	59	0	11	3	45	449	103	325	21	4
Pueblo	109,065	797	8	21	199	569	7,030	1,895	4,642	493	43
Rangely	2,438	5	0	1	1	3	14	3	8	3	0
Rocky Ford	4,019	1	0	0	0	1	39	15	22	2	0
Salida	5,347	7	0	0	0	7	194	24	169	1	0
Severance	3,284	2	0	2	0	0	5	0	3	2	0
Sheridan	5,871	35	0	0	10	25	390	53	288	49	1
Silt	2,965	3	0	2	0	1	79	14	59	6	0
Silverthorne	3,930	2	0	1	0	1	83	2	79	2	2
Snowmass Village	2,857	0	0	0	0	0	48	2	46	0	0
South Fork	382	0	0	0	0	0	1	1	0	0	0
Springfield	1,474	1	0	0	0	1	5	0	5	0	0
Steamboat Springs	12,116	35	0	8	4	23	322	45	259	18	2
Sterling	14,929	31	1	3	3	24	431	110	310	11	1
Stratton	676	0	0	0	0	0	9	2	7	0	0

Table 8. Offenses Known to Law Enforcement, by Selected State and City, 2012— continued

(Number)

State/city	Population	Violent crime	Murder and nonnegligent manslaughter	Forcible rape	Robbery	Aggravated assault	Property crime	Burglary	Larceny-theft	Motor vehicle theft	Arson[1]
Telluride	2,401	6	0	0	0	6	115	8	105	2	0
Thornton[3]	123,115	332	1	58	41	232	3,257	476	2,431	350	24
Timnath	647	2	0	0	0	2	26	2	23	1	1
Trinidad	8,939	18	0	1	7	10	166	41	120	5	0
Vail	5,343	22	0	2	0	20	280	22	252	6	0
Walsenburg	3,021	25	0	3	6	16	125	36	87	2	0
Walsh	556	1	0	0	0	1	3	0	3	0	0
Westminster	109,461	284	2	29	51	202	2,830	395	2,146	289	11
Wheat Ridge	30,886	117	2	19	24	72	1,204	182	930	92	12
Windsor	19,330	2	0	0	0	2	222	37	182	3	2
Woodland Park	7,301	10	0	2	0	8	90	15	68	7	1
Wray	2,387	1	0	0	0	1	4	2	2	0	0
Yuma	3,593	4	0	3	0	1	23	4	18	1	0
Connecticut											
Ansonia	19,271	29	0	4	15	10	455	80	317	58	1
Avon	18,162	5	0	2	2	1	169	25	143	1	0
Berlin	19,935	21	0	0	5	16	309	55	243	11	2
Bethel	18,822	6	0	3	2	1	321	48	263	10	2
Bloomfield	20,557	31	0	5	8	18	505	69	404	32	0
Branford	28,055	21	0	0	10	11	675	56	595	24	1
Bridgeport	146,030	1,760	22	388	606	744	5,153	1,377	2,908	868	25
Bristol	60,688	93	3	9	51	30	1,590	355	1,123	112	7
Brookfield	16,662	2	0	0	0	2	191	36	149	6	0
Canton	10,328	1	0	1	0	0	88	7	78	3	0
Cheshire	29,295	4	0	0	4	0	265	48	210	7	0
Clinton	13,326	27	0	16	3	8	302	53	241	8	1
Coventry	12,451	2	0	2	0	0	170	67	101	2	0
Cromwell	14,075	11	0	1	6	4	290	44	233	13	0
Danbury	81,891	109	1	23	45	40	1,562	287	1,201	74	6
Darien	20,998	2	0	0	1	1	99	13	85	1	0
Derby	12,917	28	1	8	10	9	397	92	271	34	2
East Hampton	13,024	5	1	1	1	2	148	34	109	5	0
East Hartford	51,431	192	2	26	83	81	1,573	362	1,029	182	11
East Haven	29,288	32	1	6	15	10	875	166	642	67	4
Easton	7,584	0	0	0	0	0	40	17	22	1	0
East Windsor	11,200	18	0	7	6	5	338	61	268	9	4
Enfield	44,806	30	0	0	12	18	820	198	591	31	5
Fairfield	60,122	33	0	2	13	18	1,301	231	1,000	70	1
Farmington	25,429	24	0	2	17	5	629	50	549	30	1
Glastonbury	34,547	22	0	3	9	10	326	55	258	13	1
Granby	11,321	2	0	0	1	1	96	5	91	0	0
Greenwich	61,948	23	0	2	6	15	368	45	301	22	4
Groton	10,397	17	0	4	3	10	157	8	139	10	3
Groton Long Point	518	0	0	0	0	0	14	3	9	2	0
Groton Town	29,231	48	0	8	8	32	610	72	515	23	6
Guilford	22,400	24	0	3	7	14	293	51	235	7	0
Hamden	61,032	322	2	3	39	278	1,382	196	1,089	97	2
Hartford	125,203	1,655	23	27	640	965	5,319	1,050	3,467	802	88
Madison	18,288	2	0	0	1	1	116	25	89	2	1
Manchester	58,444	111	1	12	46	52	1,797	288	1,417	92	7
Meriden	60,934	222	5	25	76	116	1,812	421	1,223	168	9
Middlebury	7,583	4	0	2	1	1	70	20	45	5	0
Middletown	47,878	72	1	1	25	45	900	156	661	83	3
Milford	52,817	46	0	2	33	11	1,586	150	1,371	65	4
Monroe	19,728	3	0	1	1	1	159	41	115	3	0
Naugatuck	31,896	30	0	7	11	12	632	92	498	42	2
New Britain	73,458	317	3	5	179	130	2,917	775	1,749	393	0
New Canaan	19,992	6	1	0	2	3	130	14	114	2	0
New Haven	129,934	1,870	17	55	844	954	6,516	1,451	4,351	714	15
Newington	30,668	28	1	8	14	5	784	99	636	49	4
New London	27,643	366	3	10	45	308	764	183	515	66	10
New Milford	28,047	21	0	9	1	11	363	4	335	24	1
Newtown	27,904	7	0	5	0	2	185	32	151	2	1

Table 8. Offenses Known to Law Enforcement, by Selected State and City, 2012— continued

(Number)

State/city	Population	Violent crime	Murder and nonnegligent manslaughter	Forcible rape	Robbery	Aggravated assault	Property crime	Burglary	Larceny-theft	Motor vehicle theft	Arson[1]
North Branford	14,422	5	1	1	1	2	201	34	160	7	0
North Haven	24,119	12	0	0	11	1	578	63	478	37	0
Norwalk	86,693	272	3	9	68	192	1,713	250	1,352	111	4
Norwich	40,517	99	1	18	35	45	963	274	639	50	15
Old Saybrook	10,293	9	0	0	0	9	162	7	152	3	0
Orange	13,971	7	0	2	5	0	376	33	332	11	4
Plainfield	15,410	14	0	3	5	6	121	36	72	13	1
Plainville	17,778	44	0	0	4	40	665	145	482	38	0
Plymouth	12,202	8	0	4	0	4	210	38	157	15	2
Portland	9,556	10	0	0	2	8	76	21	52	3	0
Putnam	9,588	29	0	6	3	20	200	51	142	7	3
Redding	9,275	0	0	0	0	0	59	8	47	4	0
Ridgefield	24,952	1	0	0	1	0	88	10	77	1	1
Rocky Hill	19,776	3	0	2	1	0	276	33	234	9	0
Seymour	16,558	10	0	2	2	6	161	45	106	10	1
Shelton	40,062	22	0	7	12	3	432	134	265	33	0
Simsbury	23,591	7	1	0	2	4	176	25	147	4	0
Southington	43,219	28	1	5	11	11	751	130	585	36	7
South Windsor	25,798	9	0	3	2	4	372	48	307	17	0
Stamford	124,201	351	5	25	145	176	1,932	290	1,472	170	10
Stonington	18,556	11	0	3	1	7	330	66	257	7	1
Stratford	52,041	104	0	15	28	61	1,413	245	1,070	98	9
Suffield	15,789	4	0	1	0	3	131	25	105	1	0
Thomaston	7,859	4	0	0	0	4	138	58	72	8	0
Torrington	36,264	51	0	18	11	22	842	111	711	20	4
Trumbull	36,474	14	0	0	11	3	531	52	449	30	0
Vernon	29,217	46	0	5	7	34	311	65	237	9	2
Wallingford	45,183	15	0	2	10	3	914	161	728	25	2
Waterbury	110,486	328	5	7	185	131	4,713	662	3,538	513	8
Waterford	19,529	45	1	0	6	38	515	55	451	9	0
Watertown	22,437	25	2	4	3	16	520	86	412	22	0
West Hartford	63,487	46	0	2	35	9	1,695	243	1,348	104	2
West Haven	55,626	319	1	1	58	259	1,447	197	1,076	174	1
Weston	10,309	3	0	0	0	3	41	11	30	0	0
Westport	26,728	11	0	0	2	9	318	40	271	7	0
Wethersfield	26,762	23	0	1	11	11	410	62	328	20	1
Willimantic	17,818	27	0	1	13	13	433	104	276	53	4
Wilton	18,291	2	1	0	0	1	93	17	75	1	0
Winchester	11,205	15	0	2	4	9	253	81	161	11	1
Windsor	29,145	15	0	4	7	4	429	55	361	13	0
Windsor Locks	12,541	10	0	2	4	4	225	49	166	10	0
Wolcott	16,697	6	0	1	5	0	318	78	226	14	0
Woodbridge	9,000	8	0	1	2	5	107	23	77	7	0
Delaware											
Bethany Beach	1,089	1	0	0	0	1	121	17	103	1	0
Blades	1,275	7	0	1	3	3	31	7	22	2	0
Bridgeville	2,104	17	0	2	2	13	70	14	52	4	1
Camden	3,558	17	0	1	5	11	295	18	275	2	0
Cheswold	1,416	2	0	0	0	2	17	3	14	0	0
Clayton	2,999	13	0	1	0	12	41	8	33	0	0
Dagsboro	822	0	0	0	0	0	24	5	17	2	0
Delaware City	1,725	3	0	0	2	1	38	11	27	0	0
Delmar	1,648	10	0	2	3	5	64	26	37	1	0
Dewey Beach	351	7	0	0	1	6	76	9	63	4	0
Dover	36,961	280	1	13	61	205	2,189	116	2,008	65	10
Ellendale	390	0	0	0	0	0	4	4	0	0	0
Elsmere	6,240	64	0	0	17	47	169	40	117	12	0
Felton	1,334	8	0	0	0	8	28	4	24	0	0
Fenwick Island	388	0	0	0	0	0	35	7	28	0	0
Frankford	871	2	0	1	0	1	8	3	5	0	0
Georgetown	6,596	60	0	4	23	33	308	67	230	11	1
Greenwood	1,001	4	0	1	1	2	23	9	13	1	0
Harrington	3,659	28	0	2	2	24	191	57	129	5	0

Table 8. Offenses Known to Law Enforcement, by Selected State and City, 2012— continued

(Number)

State/city	Population	Violent crime	Murder and nonnegligent manslaughter	Forcible rape	Robbery	Aggravated assault	Property crime	Burglary	Larceny-theft	Motor vehicle theft	Arson[1]
Laurel	3,810	44	0	3	10	31	238	72	159	7	1
Lewes	2,820	9	0	1	1	7	64	11	51	2	1
Middletown	19,203	59	0	3	22	34	468	60	387	21	1
Milford	9,816	124	1	6	34	83	771	150	613	8	3
Millsboro	3,985	23	0	0	6	17	145	28	112	5	0
Milton	2,650	10	0	0	0	10	89	32	56	1	0
Newark	31,965	130	0	8	43	79	1,017	177	806	34	6
New Castle	5,378	17	0	0	6	11	295	39	249	7	0
Newport	1,074	8	0	0	3	5	59	15	38	6	0
Ocean View	1,933	1	0	0	0	1	42	22	20	0	0
Rehoboth Beach	1,364	10	0	1	1	8	160	39	121	0	0
Seaford	7,113	80	1	3	20	56	576	70	502	4	0
Selbyville	2,216	7	0	2	1	4	131	28	100	3	0
Smyrna	10,292	39	0	1	17	21	325	63	254	8	0
South Bethany	461	0	0	0	0	0	12	1	11	0	0
Wilmington	72,088	1,228	26	34	474	694	3,824	1,212	2,247	365	1
Wyoming	1,349	1	0	0	0	1	27	12	14	1	0
District of Columbia											
Washington	632,323	7,448	88	236	3,725	3,399	29,264	3,519	22,196	3,549	50
Florida											
Alachua	9,264	40	0	3	4	33	231	66	159	6	0
Altamonte Springs	42,296	142	1	9	35	97	1,293	181	1,042	70	3
Altha	548	0	0	0	0	0	4	2	2	0	0
Apalachicola	2,273	3	0	1	0	2	24	15	8	1	0
Apopka	43,046	146	1	13	59	73	1,316	279	977	60	4
Arcadia	7,747	65	1	4	16	44	194	85	106	3	2
Astatula	1,861	3	0	1	0	2	23	11	9	3	0
Atlantic Beach	12,925	55	0	2	12	41	312	62	245	5	1
Atlantis	2,057	5	0	1	0	4	1	1	0	0	0
Auburndale	13,862	46	0	5	17	24	865	171	671	23	4
Aventura	37,110	51	0	0	21	30	2,082	82	1,965	35	0
Bal Harbour Village	2,609	1	0	0	0	1	76	3	73	0	0
Bartow	17,740	116	1	6	21	88	994	228	740	26	3
Bay Harbor Islands	5,841	7	0	2	1	4	64	28	30	6	0
Belleair	3,925	2	0	1	0	1	118	26	88	4	0
Belleair Beach	1,582	1	0	0	0	1	35	7	26	2	0
Belleair Bluffs	2,060	9	0	0	2	7	70	18	48	4	1
Belle Glade	17,908	366	4	11	35	316	696	272	387	37	5
Belle Isle	6,194	12	0	0	2	10	160	48	105	7	0
Belleview	4,571	16	1	2	5	8	204	68	121	15	0
Biscayne Park	3,169	4	0	0	1	3	32	19	13	0	0
Blountstown	2,557	3	0	1	0	2	42	7	34	1	0
Boca Raton	86,493	164	0	12	62	90	2,557	491	1,965	101	0
Bonifay	2,834	5	0	1	0	4	41	22	17	2	0
Bowling Green	2,987	11	0	0	1	10	70	19	51	0	0
Boynton Beach	69,937	399	5	8	127	259	2,988	627	2,210	151	3
Bradenton	50,878	341	4	23	94	220	2,026	511	1,440	75	5
Bradenton Beach	1,203	5	0	0	1	4	53	9	42	2	0
Brooksville	7,841	78	0	6	22	50	459	65	382	12	1
Bunnell	2,754	44	0	1	4	39	115	39	69	7	1
Cape Coral	159,625	229	4	16	41	168	3,521	860	2,547	114	7
Carrabelle	2,823	2	0	0	0	2	18	7	11	0	0
Casselberry	26,747	161	4	9	42	106	1,070	205	822	43	2
Cedar Key	702	3	0	0	0	3	37	11	25	1	0
Center Hill	1,052	9	0	2	1	6	13	5	7	1	0
Chattahoochee	3,686	40	0	1	1	38	80	36	40	4	0
Chiefland	2,239	2	0	0	0	2	223	102	118	3	0
Chipley	3,660	22	0	1	3	18	145	27	117	1	2
Clearwater	109,255	727	3	59	206	459	4,264	919	3,169	176	21
Clermont	29,523	88	0	9	15	64	728	164	533	31	1
Clewiston	7,244	32	0	0	13	19	305	106	194	5	1
Cocoa	17,381	312	2	18	71	221	1,343	351	919	73	4
Cocoa Beach	11,388	90	0	5	21	64	828	109	694	25	1

Table 8. Offenses Known to Law Enforcement, by Selected State and City, 2012— continued

(Number)

State/city	Population	Violent crime	Murder and nonnegligent manslaughter	Forcible rape	Robbery	Aggravated assault	Property crime	Burglary	Larceny-theft	Motor vehicle theft	Arson[1]
Coconut Creek	54,651	107	1	10	32	64	1,622	270	1,265	87	4
Cooper City	29,473	48	0	0	9	39	666	120	518	28	2
Coral Gables	48,435	79	3	4	22	50	2,277	409	1,757	111	2
Coral Springs	125,021	229	1	10	78	140	2,820	572	2,098	150	9
Crescent City	1,592	23	0	0	0	23	84	34	50	0	0
Crestview	21,574	186	1	14	38	133	933	167	728	38	0
Cross City	1,759	7	0	0	0	7	36	10	26	0	0
Cutler Bay	41,799	124	1	5	35	83	1,856	240	1,521	95	1
Dade City	6,549	60	1	5	10	44	338	80	246	12	3
Dania	30,595	213	1	12	64	136	1,494	300	1,053	141	1
Davenport	2,971	3	0	0	0	3	61	21	36	4	0
Davie	94,952	369	5	23	74	267	3,473	667	2,565	241	7
Daytona Beach	61,861	715	4	23	179	509	3,869	799	2,724	346	4
Daytona Beach Shores	4,311	20	0	0	2	18	187	46	134	7	0
Deerfield Beach	77,431	360	4	17	149	190	2,458	594	1,680	184	6
De Funiak Springs	5,320	53	1	3	11	38	284	70	207	7	0
Deland	27,410	128	2	1	37	88	1,284	281	954	49	0
Delray Beach	62,044	457	6	26	157	268	2,950	565	2,230	155	7
Doral	47,427	84	0	5	16	63	2,363	234	1,969	160	1
Dunedin	35,836	110	2	19	19	70	892	205	655	32	1
Dunnellon	1,764	10	0	0	3	7	24	22	1	1	0
Eatonville	2,229	32	1	0	4	27	114	45	61	8	0
Edgewater	21,044	40	0	2	11	27	526	138	360	28	0
Edgewood	2,590	3	0	0	0	3	70	16	50	4	0
El Portal	2,412	6	0	0	3	3	82	38	43	1	0
Eustis	19,062	50	1	6	19	24	646	164	466	16	3
Fellsmere	5,300	11	0	0	4	7	105	33	71	1	0
Fernandina Beach	11,783	41	0	4	8	29	333	74	248	11	0
Flagler Beach	4,625	9	1	2	0	6	147	35	108	4	0
Florida City	11,668	242	3	6	84	149	1,154	230	860	64	1
Fort Lauderdale	170,827	1,543	16	48	835	644	9,960	2,951	6,419	590	39
Fort Myers	64,379	754	24	26	172	532	2,346	507	1,639	200	8
Fort Pierce	42,566	472	3	31	137	301	2,325	705	1,528	92	5
Fort Walton Beach	20,063	48	1	4	7	36	772	143	586	43	1
Fruitland Park	4,188	10	0	0	0	10	190	60	127	3	0
Gainesville	127,036	851	6	74	171	600	5,201	1,009	3,953	239	9
Golden Beach	953	0	0	0	0	0	10	5	5	0	0
Graceville	2,289	3	0	0	0	3	51	24	25	2	0
Greenacres City	38,528	234	0	13	58	163	1,185	327	766	92	5
Green Cove Springs	7,053	72	0	5	7	60	224	47	172	5	0
Gretna	1,472	22	0	0	0	22	15	10	5	0	0
Groveland	8,967	11	0	0	2	9	133	46	80	7	0
Gulf Breeze	5,950	5	0	1	0	4	142	27	114	1	0
Gulfport	12,205	49	0	4	12	33	570	187	363	20	11
Gulf Stream	806	0	0	0	0	0	24	5	17	2	0
Haines City	21,091	78	1	10	15	52	701	161	512	28	0
Hallandale	38,316	287	4	11	98	174	1,863	456	1,264	143	0
Havana	1,767	16	1	2	1	12	41	8	32	1	0
Hialeah	233,107	810	4	40	260	506	7,194	1,048	5,409	737	10
Hialeah Gardens	22,561	28	0	0	10	18	933	95	782	56	0
Highland Beach	3,629	0	0	0	0	0	44	12	30	2	0
High Springs	5,465	30	0	4	5	21	165	44	113	8	2
Hillsboro Beach	1,936	0	0	0	0	0	31	9	21	1	0
Holly Hill	11,822	66	1	3	12	50	635	133	433	69	0
Hollywood	145,313	643	5	38	278	322	7,713	1,958	5,095	660	17
Holmes Beach	3,941	9	0	0	1	8	143	47	95	1	0
Homestead	62,785	1,045	4	33	315	693	3,216	877	2,151	188	16
Howey-in-the-Hills	1,133	0	0	0	0	0	5	2	3	0	0
Hypoluxo	2,654	2	0	0	2	0	46	16	29	1	0
Indialantic	2,758	6	0	0	2	4	64	8	53	3	0
Indian Creek Village	89	0	0	0	0	0	1	0	1	0	0
Indian Harbour Beach	8,340	10	0	3	3	4	162	27	129	6	0
Indian River Shores	3,978	1	0	0	0	1	20	4	16	0	0

Table 8. Offenses Known to Law Enforcement, by Selected State and City, 2012— continued

(Number)

State/city	Population	Violent crime	Murder and nonnegligent manslaughter	Forcible rape	Robbery	Aggravated assault	Property crime	Burglary	Larceny-theft	Motor vehicle theft	Arson[1]
Indian Rocks Beach	4,173	19	0	1	1	17	134	22	104	8	0
Indian Shores	1,440	4	0	0	0	4	69	17	49	3	0
Inglis	1,322	6	0	0	0	6	50	10	39	1	0
Interlachen	1,415	7	0	0	0	7	79	26	52	1	0
Jacksonville	840,660	5,189	93	341	1,371	3,384	34,674	7,632	25,403	1,639	80
Jacksonville Beach	21,817	196	1	11	43	141	1,018	147	828	43	5
Jasper	4,590	6	0	0	1	5	61	27	34	0	1
Jennings	881	0	0	0	0	0	19	9	9	1	0
Juno Beach	3,257	9	0	1	1	7	76	11	63	2	0
Jupiter	56,674	115	0	11	37	67	1,196	235	918	43	5
Jupiter Inlet Colony	410	0	0	0	0	0	7	2	5	0	0
Jupiter Island	834	0	0	0	0	0	10	6	4	0	0
Kenneth City	5,052	25	0	2	5	18	190	28	157	5	0
Key Biscayne	12,809	3	0	0	0	3	285	8	261	16	0
Key Colony Beach	817	0	0	0	0	0	14	4	10	0	0
Key West	25,249	208	1	21	51	135	1,546	290	1,161	95	3
Kissimmee	62,183	563	2	34	121	406	3,112	822	2,150	140	6
Lady Lake	14,304	29	0	0	2	27	306	59	229	18	0
Lake Alfred	5,146	24	1	1	1	21	153	66	82	5	0
Lake City	12,190	179	3	6	26	144	1,004	253	734	17	3
Lake Clarke Shores	3,462	12	0	1	4	7	110	36	68	6	0
Lake Hamilton	1,264	4	0	0	0	4	60	17	36	7	2
Lake Helen	2,661	9	0	1	0	8	63	20	39	4	0
Lakeland	99,934	465	10	33	144	278	5,216	1,296	3,735	185	4
Lake Mary	14,090	21	0	3	1	17	291	50	231	10	0
Lake Park	8,361	98	1	2	43	52	815	107	684	24	1
Lake Placid	2,249	11	0	1	3	7	103	15	86	2	1
Lake Wales	14,595	46	2	4	10	30	468	161	288	19	1
Lake Worth	35,788	461	8	35	194	224	1,728	487	1,113	128	11
Lantana	10,687	60	0	7	23	30	491	108	374	9	1
Largo	78,783	394	1	43	114	236	3,117	574	2,413	130	10
Lauderdale-by-the-Sea	6,252	23	0	1	6	16	152	27	116	9	0
Lauderdale Lakes	33,644	336	6	12	151	167	1,676	638	931	107	7
Lauderhill	69,046	587	8	19	242	318	2,934	1,238	1,511	185	8
Leesburg	20,668	186	3	10	36	137	1,049	222	779	48	5
Lighthouse Point	10,680	12	0	0	6	6	327	69	241	17	0
Live Oak	7,012	61	0	0	12	49	317	166	144	7	0
Longboat Key	7,048	2	0	0	1	1	123	17	106	0	0
Longwood	13,919	92	1	3	12	76	436	127	294	15	0
Lynn Haven	18,861	59	1	3	2	53	560	64	483	13	0
Madeira Beach	4,325	36	1	3	2	30	188	36	146	6	0
Madison	2,865	39	0	2	7	30	196	54	140	2	2
Maitland	16,295	24	0	2	3	19	445	150	269	26	1
Manalapan	417	0	0	0	0	0	24	2	22	0	0
Mangonia Park	1,936	59	0	0	30	29	256	76	170	10	1
Marco Island	16,985	12	0	1	0	11	216	36	178	2	0
Margate	55,010	144	3	6	42	93	1,113	309	743	61	3
Marianna	6,125	59	0	3	15	41	182	55	127	0	4
Mascotte	5,246	23	0	4	2	17	160	62	91	7	0
Medley	869	11	1	0	0	10	219	22	171	26	0
Melbourne	77,133	658	6	48	133	471	3,374	648	2,607	119	15
Melbourne Beach	3,144	3	0	0	2	1	53	36	15	2	0
Melbourne Village	672	0	0	0	0	0	19	3	14	2	0
Mexico Beach	1,093	6	0	0	1	5	40	4	35	1	0
Miami	414,327	4,856	69	65	2,096	2,626	22,271	4,255	15,305	2,711	89
Miami Beach	91,066	941	5	42	407	487	9,028	1,048	7,536	444	3
Miami Gardens	111,177	931	25	16	369	521	4,784	1,290	3,081	413	28
Miami Lakes	30,467	54	1	2	15	36	733	90	585	58	0
Miami Shores	10,866	49	1	2	25	21	557	131	401	25	1
Miami Springs	14,322	38	0	0	11	27	433	98	305	30	0
Milton	9,107	25	0	0	4	21	332	79	242	11	1
Minneola	9,661	14	0	2	3	9	166	48	112	6	0
Miramar	125,998	537	2	31	163	341	2,984	862	1,901	221	11

Table 8. Offenses Known to Law Enforcement, by Selected State and City, 2012— continued

(Number)

State/city	Population	Violent crime	Murder and nonnegligent manslaughter	Forcible rape	Robbery	Aggravated assault	Property crime	Burglary	Larceny-theft	Motor vehicle theft	Arson[1]
Monticello	2,521	16	0	0	2	14	36	27	6	3	0
Mount Dora	12,705	67	0	4	9	54	441	88	336	17	4
Naples	20,211	32	0	1	5	26	537	96	431	10	1
Neptune Beach	7,187	11	0	0	2	9	225	31	190	4	0
New Port Richey	15,165	118	0	4	33	81	637	232	385	20	3
New Smyrna Beach	22,788	110	0	1	22	87	1,042	253	757	32	3
Niceville	13,118	14	0	2	2	10	198	20	172	6	1
North Bay Village	7,405	25	1	2	6	16	198	29	149	20	0
North Lauderdale	42,352	192	3	14	67	108	1,187	396	720	71	3
North Miami	60,964	521	3	21	214	283	2,973	784	1,890	299	7
North Miami Beach	43,084	279	2	27	130	120	1,988	702	1,163	123	2
North Palm Beach	12,319	19	0	2	13	4	239	78	150	11	1
North Port	58,568	130	2	20	12	96	1,074	278	770	26	11
North Redington Beach	1,437	4	0	0	0	4	28	5	20	3	0
Oakland	2,625	13	0	0	3	10	69	23	44	2	0
Oakland Park	42,701	335	0	16	135	184	2,259	699	1,442	118	6
Ocala	57,288	375	6	42	92	235	3,097	606	2,431	60	7
Ocean Ridge	1,831	2	0	0	0	2	72	25	46	1	1
Ocoee	36,816	140	1	10	34	95	1,508	315	1,074	119	4
Okeechobee	5,718	14	0	1	7	6	304	32	259	13	0
Oldsmar	13,804	37	2	5	6	24	428	63	351	14	0
Opa Locka	15,792	439	4	9	108	318	1,267	372	746	149	2
Orange City	10,870	44	0	0	11	33	891	88	779	24	0
Orange Park	8,592	42	2	11	8	21	268	63	199	6	2
Orlando	246,513	2,508	24	103	603	1,778	16,304	3,778	11,222	1,304	36
Ormond Beach	38,674	122	2	9	15	96	1,301	199	1,045	57	0
Oviedo	33,985	76	0	4	8	64	525	104	397	24	4
Pahokee	5,790	58	0	3	9	46	129	43	82	4	2
Palatka	10,657	130	0	9	22	99	687	143	530	14	3
Palm Bay	104,635	553	3	19	78	453	2,457	719	1,601	137	17
Palm Beach	8,560	4	0	0	1	3	189	29	152	8	0
Palm Beach Gardens	49,679	75	0	11	30	34	1,584	242	1,291	51	3
Palm Beach Shores	1,171	0	0	0	0	0	36	9	26	1	0
Palmetto	12,948	135	4	9	21	101	431	137	272	22	2
Palmetto Bay	24,291	54	2	2	16	34	912	212	666	34	2
Palm Springs	19,457	131	2	10	35	84	1,173	320	775	78	6
Panama City	37,187	285	3	9	75	198	2,307	434	1,743	130	11
Panama City Beach	12,257	102	0	10	25	67	1,292	200	1,090	2	1
Parker	4,402	22	0	0	3	19	123	47	69	7	2
Parkland	24,737	20	0	1	4	15	235	52	171	12	0
Pembroke Park	6,299	48	0	2	20	26	487	117	318	52	0
Pembroke Pines	159,744	238	2	14	83	139	4,238	846	3,175	217	8
Pensacola	52,909	473	7	30	89	347	3,032	711	2,201	120	9
Perry	7,126	99	2	7	5	85	174	63	102	9	2
Pinellas Park	49,821	228	5	13	48	162	2,745	471	2,148	126	14
Plantation	87,705	278	4	11	127	136	3,443	702	2,552	189	12
Plant City	36,306	141	1	12	34	94	1,414	289	1,043	82	4
Pompano Beach	103,003	1,060	5	37	419	599	5,562	1,283	3,876	403	16
Ponce Inlet	3,075	0	0	0	0	0	60	8	49	3	0
Port Orange	57,300	62	2	1	12	47	1,429	301	1,064	64	2
Port Richey	2,718	23	0	0	8	15	239	45	185	9	0
Port St. Joe	3,487	18	0	1	2	15	41	15	25	1	2
Port St. Lucie	168,416	395	4	47	55	289	3,031	816	2,124	91	6
Punta Gorda	16,925	11	0	0	4	7	278	49	223	6	1
Quincy	8,041	65	1	2	12	50	487	166	312	9	2
Redington Beaches	1,447	6	0	1	0	5	33	8	24	1	0
Riviera Beach	33,309	440	11	9	86	334	1,624	520	983	121	5
Rockledge	25,275	57	1	10	5	41	630	149	466	15	4
Royal Palm Beach	35,004	118	1	9	30	78	968	181	761	26	1
Safety Harbor	17,132	41	0	7	6	28	315	72	233	10	1
Sanford	54,662	323	3	21	166	133	2,964	822	1,986	156	1
Sanibel	6,692	3	0	0	0	3	111	29	76	6	0
Sarasota	53,055	425	4	25	136	260	2,897	705	2,093	99	6

Table 8. Offenses Known to Law Enforcement, by Selected State and City, 2012— continued

(Number)

State/city	Population	Violent crime	Murder and nonnegligent manslaughter	Forcible rape	Robbery	Aggravated assault	Property crime	Burglary	Larceny-theft	Motor vehicle theft	Arson[1]
Satellite Beach	10,251	44	0	2	1	41	172	44	126	2	0
Sea Ranch Lakes	691	0	0	0	0	0	13	0	12	1	0
Sebastian	22,368	48	0	1	5	42	606	130	461	15	0
Sebring	10,617	51	0	4	22	25	461	136	318	7	2
Seminole	17,485	46	0	2	10	34	531	69	444	18	2
Sewall's Point	2,040	0	0	0	0	0	28	13	15	0	0
Shalimar	738	1	0	0	0	1	13	2	9	2	0
Sneads	1,855	6	0	1	0	5	23	4	19	0	1
South Bay	4,978	27	0	2	3	22	86	28	54	4	1
South Daytona	12,425	41	0	1	9	31	522	140	345	37	3
South Miami	12,095	90	0	2	39	49	841	136	680	25	0
South Palm Beach	1,201	1	0	0	0	1	9	2	7	0	0
South Pasadena	5,036	16	0	0	4	12	153	8	142	3	0
Southwest Ranches	7,582	8	0	0	0	8	174	46	112	16	0
Springfield	9,076	55	2	7	10	36	355	107	227	21	0
Starke	5,463	41	0	1	4	36	213	16	184	13	0
St. Augustine	13,518	89	1	7	12	69	880	116	739	25	1
St. Augustine Beach	6,453	14	0	0	3	11	189	47	136	6	0
St. Cloud	36,656	143	1	8	23	111	981	239	720	22	1
St. Pete Beach	9,483	38	0	6	7	25	343	57	277	9	0
St. Petersburg	248,340	2,239	15	94	585	1,545	12,451	2,933	8,642	876	69
Stuart	15,932	55	0	5	10	40	623	79	521	23	1
Sunny Isles Beach	21,618	26	0	3	5	18	473	46	405	22	0
Sunrise	87,168	230	1	19	94	116	3,229	799	2,287	143	5
Surfside	5,959	15	0	1	2	12	152	23	120	9	0
Sweetwater	20,703	54	0	2	13	39	1,010	83	846	81	1
Tallahassee	185,461	1,582	12	115	525	930	8,617	2,630	5,463	524	9
Tamarac	62,382	191	5	13	74	99	1,572	611	863	98	2
Tampa	350,758	2,162	23	43	573	1,523	9,947	2,476	6,864	607	84
Tarpon Springs	23,828	141	3	6	33	99	592	98	475	19	2
Tavares	14,326	54	1	0	3	50	282	81	184	17	0
Temple Terrace	25,659	93	1	12	27	53	653	172	444	37	1
Titusville	44,374	294	4	26	77	187	1,765	519	1,001	245	10
Treasure Island	6,803	12	0	1	3	8	275	29	235	11	0
Trenton	2,032	5	0	0	1	4	39	15	21	3	0
Umatilla	3,551	6	0	0	1	5	85	5	77	3	0
Valparaiso	5,164	7	0	0	1	6	49	11	35	3	0
Venice	21,182	40	0	3	6	31	418	99	308	11	5
Vero Beach	15,527	56	0	1	17	38	586	132	440	14	0
Village of Pinecrest	18,912	26	0	3	11	12	741	133	586	22	2
Virginia Gardens	2,464	0	0	0	0	0	24	2	20	2	0
Waldo	1,037	11	0	0	0	11	50	26	22	2	0
Wauchula	5,122	11	0	1	2	8	161	62	94	5	0
Welaka	708	0	0	0	0	0	6	3	2	1	0
Wellington	57,943	144	0	10	28	106	1,445	234	1,104	107	4
West Melbourne	18,613	60	1	1	11	47	556	78	454	24	1
West Miami	6,188	17	0	0	2	15	147	42	99	6	0
Weston	67,452	62	2	5	14	41	661	148	493	20	5
West Palm Beach	102,422	821	17	31	334	439	5,404	1,289	3,801	314	21
West Park	14,614	132	0	2	35	95	564	233	273	58	0
White Springs	779	5	0	0	2	3	11	5	6	0	0
Wildwood	7,139	26	0	1	4	21	124	47	69	8	1
Williston	2,763	14	0	0	2	12	108	17	84	7	1
Wilton Manors	12,005	77	0	3	32	42	596	136	433	27	2
Windermere	2,548	2	0	0	0	2	36	0	36	0	0
Winter Garden	35,768	196	0	11	30	155	1,275	233	992	50	3
Winter Haven	34,759	245	5	8	59	173	1,812	489	1,267	56	2
Winter Park	28,785	83	0	1	26	56	1,167	384	743	40	1
Winter Springs	33,925	47	3	0	7	37	348	89	245	14	2
Zephyrhills	13,519	52	0	1	15	36	1,035	225	790	20	0
Georgia											
Abbeville	2,946	3	0	2	0	1	23	14	9	0	0
Acworth	20,932	11	0	0	4	7	416	43	347	26	0

Table 8. Offenses Known to Law Enforcement, by Selected State and City, 2012— continued

(Number)

State/city	Population	Violent crime	Murder and nonnegligent manslaughter	Forcible rape	Robbery	Aggravated assault	Property crime	Burglary	Larceny-theft	Motor vehicle theft	Arson[1]
Adairsville	4,710	22	0	1	2	19	87	21	59	7	0
Adel	5,368	26	0	8	4	14	163	74	84	5	0
Alapaha	679	1	0	0	0	1	15	4	11	0	1
Albany	78,512	813	4	27	224	558	5,001	1,408	3,369	224	13
Alma	3,540	44	0	7	12	25	161	43	113	5	
Alpharetta	60,031	42	1	6	18	17	1,230	127	1,076	27	2
Alto	1,185	0	0	0	0	0	10	5	4	1	0
Americus	16,988	219	0	0	38	181	1,220	630	562	28	0
Aragon	1,257	5	0	0	0	5	32	3	25	4	0
Arcade	1,829	1	0	0	1	0	31	4	26	1	0
Arlington	1,496	31	0	0	7	24	60	12	45	3	0
Ashburn	4,169	39	0	5	4	30	130	19	96	15	1
Athens-Clarke County	117,457	455	5	48	158	244	4,601	1,149	3,210	242	20
Atlanta	437,041	6,027	83	113	2,276	3,555	28,554	6,192	17,212	5,150	103
Attapulgus	451	0	0	0	0	0	1	0	1	0	0
Auburn	7,017	1	0	0	0	1	37	17	15	5	0
Austell	6,743	57	0	2	5	50	176	41	125	10	0
Avondale Estates	3,027	3	0	0	2	1	123	25	93	5	0
Bainbridge	12,764	89	2	2	9	76	681	151	520	10	
Baldwin	3,322	5	0	1	0	4	146	44	99	3	0
Ball Ground	1,475	2	0	1	0	1	14	3	11	0	0
Barnesville	6,661	35	3	7	6	19	232	29	187	16	0
Barwick	386	0	0	0	0	0	0	0	0	0	0
Baxley	4,445	11	1	1	2	7	269	77	188	4	0
Berlin	598	0	0	0	0	0	12	6	6	0	0
Blackshear	3,485	27	0	3	14	10	130	46	82	2	0
Blairsville	654	0	0	0	0	0	17	3	14	0	0
Blakely	5,019	38	0	2	2	34	157	61	93	3	0
Bloomingdale	2,808	1	0	0	0	1	59	8	45	6	0
Blue Ridge	1,305	14	0	0	0	14	82	29	43	10	
Blythe	732	0	0	0	0	0	27	8	19	0	0
Boston	1,329	23	0	2	1	20	40	10	29	1	0
Bowdon	2,074	10	0	1	1	8	76	14	60	2	0
Braselton	7,728	6	0	2	1	3	117	21	88	8	0
Bremen	6,258	13	0	0	1	12	165	41	114	10	0
Brooklet	1,466	1	0	0	0	1	15	1	12	2	0
Brunswick	15,691	220	4	3	61	152	1,113	294	788	31	6
Buchanan	1,110	14	0	3	1	10	71	6	62	3	0
Buena Vista	2,172	4	0	0	0	4	76	18	56	2	0
Butler	1,951	15	0	0	0	15	26	9	15	2	0
Byron	4,583	39	0	1	2	36	205	67	118	20	1
Cairo	9,805	19	0	7	3	9	328	85	234	9	0
Calhoun	15,941	35	0	3	6	26	765	131	616	18	0
Camilla	5,409	18	0	0	5	13	183	27	145	11	0
Canton	23,629	18	0	4	7	7	415	65	326	24	0
Carrollton	24,774	156	2	11	42	101	1,093	225	838	30	2
Cartersville	19,993	51	2	6	12	31	933	166	699	68	6
Cave Spring	1,208	0	0	0	0	0	30	8	20	2	0
Cedartown	9,695	96	2	2	37	55	920	224	670	26	0
Centerville	7,436	20	0	1	9	10	271	50	212	9	0
Chatsworth	4,340	7	0	1	1	5	104	17	81	6	0
Chattahoochee Hills	2,480	3	0	0	0	3	57	13	37	7	0
Chickamauga	3,130	6	0	1	0	5	119	40	77	2	0
Clarkesville	1,761	5	0	0	1	4	48	6	41	1	0
Clarkston	7,723	58	0	2	45	11	224	51	130	43	0
Claxton	2,786	4	0	0	1	3	120	34	81	5	0
Clayton	2,065	21	0	0	1	20	96	60	31	5	
Cleveland	3,462	18	0	1	1	16	194	27	162	5	0
Climax	282	0	0	0	0	0	0	0	0	0	0
Cochran	5,251	10	0	1	4	5	199	53	145	1	1
College Park	14,513	293	5	25	142	121	1,775	398	1,028	349	1
Colquitt	2,017	12	0	1	1	10	83	18	60	5	0
Columbus	196,178	994	17	31	423	523	11,266	2,709	7,711	846	28

Table 8. Offenses Known to Law Enforcement, by Selected State and City, 2012— continued

(Number)

State/city	Population	Violent crime	Murder and nonnegligent manslaughter	Forcible rape	Robbery	Aggravated assault	Property crime	Burglary	Larceny-theft	Motor vehicle theft	Arson[1]
Commerce	6,696	14	0	1	0	13	128	27	99	2	0
Conyers	15,455	66	0	1	27	38	1,007	161	759	87	2
Coolidge	530	0	0	0	0	0	8	7	1	0	0
Cordele	11,397	91	3	9	36	43	991	257	709	25	4
Cornelia	4,229	14	0	3	0	11	174	13	158	3	0
Covington	13,367	58	1	12	19	26	824	168	609	47	0
Cumming	5,668	17	0	1	6	10	382	55	319	8	0
Cuthbert	3,834	5	0	0	2	3	48	12	36	0	0
Dallas	11,762	21	0	1	7	13	253	51	174	28	0
Dalton	33,668	88	2	8	26	52	1,250	229	984	37	7
Danielsville	561	2	0	0	0	2	10	2	7	1	0
Dawson	4,644	18	0	0	0	18	60	60	0	0	0
Decatur	19,764	39	0	0	25	14	652	92	498	62	0
Dillard	344	1	0	0	0	1	7	1	5	1	
Doerun	788	4	1	0	0	3	37	4	30	3	0
Donalsonville	2,696	11	0	0	2	9	93	29	60	4	0
Doraville	8,519	31	0	0	19	12	268	43	196	29	0
Douglas	11,665	114	1	18	42	53	1,091	231	836	24	0
Douglasville	31,506	190	0	5	40	145	1,995	231	1,679	85	7
Dublin	16,215	115	0	2	46	67	1,071	230	806	35	
Duluth	27,549	35	0	1	14	20	556	80	453	23	0
Dunwoody	47,308	45	1	4	28	12	1,927	271	1,544	112	0
East Dublin	2,443	14	0	0	1	13	108	21	86	1	0
East Ellijay	552	10	0	1	0	9	142	10	131	1	
Eastman	5,037	37	0	1	4	32	569	97	464	8	0
East Point	35,155	421	12	13	268	128	3,819	1,029	2,018	772	3
Eatonton	6,588	43	0	5	10	28	143	41	97	5	
Edison	1,562	1	0	0	0	1	10	4	6	0	0
Elberton	4,638	43	0	1	2	40	306	77	222	7	0
Ellaville	1,835	4	0	0	0	4	30	8	22	0	0
Ellijay	1,636	0	0	0	0	0	0	0	0	0	0
Emerson	1,489	5	0	0	0	5	54	8	38	8	0
Enigma	1,348	0	0	0	0	0	13	7	6	0	0
Ephesus	429	0	0	0	0	0	0	0	0	0	0
Eton	919	1	0	0	0	1	10	3	5	2	0
Euharlee	4,191	6	0	3	0	3	51	13	36	2	0
Fairmount	734	0	0	0	0	0	10	5	5	0	1
Fayetteville	16,296	25	0	1	8	16	398	45	327	26	0
Fitzgerald	9,172	63	0	12	9	42	356	145	200	11	
Flowery Branch	5,853	4	0	0	3	1	127	21	104	2	0
Folkston	2,509	3	0	0	1	2	86	17	68	1	0
Forest Park	18,815	143	2	3	65	73	1,021	229	684	108	4
Forsyth	3,858	14	0	0	5	9	130	13	115	2	0
Fort Oglethorpe	9,442	36	2	2	4	28	693	63	606	24	2
Fort Valley	9,959	116	0	1	13	102	480	126	348	6	0
Franklin	998	8	0	2	0	6	37	0	35	2	0
Franklin Springs	956	0	0	0	0	0	10	0	10	0	0
Gainesville	34,789	113	3	15	49	46	1,497	240	1,172	85	1
Garden City	9,097	118	0	4	18	96	420	162	219	39	3
Glennville	3,636	7	0	2	0	5	117	32	80	5	0
Gordon	2,011	0	0	0	0	0	38	4	34	0	0
Gray	3,295	3	0	0	0	3	35	3	32	0	0
Greensboro	3,402	28	0	0	2	26	171	34	132	5	0
Greenville	873	2	0	0	2	0	28	11	15	2	0
Griffin	23,880	202	2	7	53	140	1,676	303	1,335	38	3
Grovetown	11,713	7	0	2	2	3	257	51	195	11	0
Guyton	1,715	3	0	0	1	2	13	1	12	0	0
Hagan	1,014	0	0	0	0	0	4	1	3	0	0
Hahira	2,834	1	0	1	0	0	39	19	20	0	0
Hampton	7,180	10	0	3	1	6	126	33	88	5	0
Hapeville	6,648	41	0	0	22	19	538	96	335	107	
Harlem	2,782	2	0	0	0	2	41	4	35	2	0
Harrison	493	0	0	0	0	0	0	0	0	0	0
Hartwell	4,533	31	0	0	2	29	394	59	330	5	0

Table 8. Offenses Known to Law Enforcement, by Selected State and City, 2012— continued

(Number)

State/city	Population	Violent crime	Murder and nonnegligent manslaughter	Forcible rape	Robbery	Aggravated assault	Property crime	Burglary	Larceny-theft	Motor vehicle theft	Arson[1]
Hazlehurst	4,297	5	0	0	0	5	214	50	163	1	0
Helen	518	8	1	0	0	7	61	8	50	3	0
Helena	[illegible]	6	0	1	0	5	19	9	10	0	
Hiawassee	901	1	0	0	1	0	54	14	39	1	0
Hinesville	34,887	153	2	18	33	100	1,479	389	1,049	41	6
Hiram	3,614	12	0	0	2	10	342	14	324	4	0
Hoboken	534	0	0	0	0	0	3	0	3	0	0
Hogansville	3,128	34	0	1	2	31	110	31	76	3	0
Holly Springs	9,462	5	0	1	1	3	104	37	60	7	0
Homeland	917	0	0	0	0	0	1	0	0	1	0
Homerville	2,475	31	2	0	6	23	181	55	124	2	0
Jackson	5,066	25	0	1	3	21	153	22	124	7	0
Jefferson	9,656	1	0	0	1	0	158	27	127	4	0
Jesup	10,388	71	3	0	17	51	785	110	666	9	0
Johns Creek	80,037	43	0	3	16	24	526	104	406	16	0
Jonesboro	4,798	25	1	3	6	15	225	69	141	15	0
Kennesaw	30,518	30	0	1	9	20	499	105	369	25	
Kingsland	16,083	80	0	3	7	70	519	104	401	14	1
Lagrange	30,221	126	3	8	65	50	1,785	464	1,247	74	6
Lake City	2,659	6	0	1	4	1	126	15	97	14	0
Lakeland	3,507	21	0	2	4	15	85	38	39	8	0
Lavonia	2,156	27	0	3	0	24	104	18	81	5	0
Lawrenceville	29,559	70	0	4	50	16	1,061	214	804	43	0
Leary	630	0	0	0	0	0	2	0	2	0	0
Leslie	407	0	0	0	0	0	0	0	0	0	0
Lilburn	12,079	46	0	3	22	21	789	99	656	34	2
Lincolnton	1,557	4	0	0	3	1	52	16	36	0	0
Lithonia	1,967	10	0	0	5	5	87	25	58	4	0
Locust Grove	5,553	15	0	1	1	13	344	58	274	12	0
Loganville	10,714	15	0	1	4	10	297	35	243	19	0
Lookout Mountain	1,617	0	0	0	0	0	17	6	11	0	0
Ludowici	1,799	5	0	2	1	2	28	7	20	1	1
Lumber City	1,301	3	0	0	0	3	30	9	20	1	0
Lumpkin	2,731	2	0	0	0	2	0	0	0	0	
Macon	92,836	583	21	41	242	279	6,699	1,828	4,371	500	56
Madison	4,042	16	0	1	8	7	207	49	152	6	
Manchester	4,238	21	0	0	1	20	215	33	168	14	1
Marietta	57,969	474	1	12	132	329	2,548	496	1,865	187	1
Maysville	1,823	9	0	0	0	9	12	6	6	0	0
McCaysville	1,068	2	0	0	2	0	50	9	39	2	0
McDonough	22,686	60	0	9	27	24	723	131	555	37	0
McIntyre	649	2	0	1	1	0	28	5	23	0	0
McRae	5,672	23	0	0	1	22	58	14	42	2	0
Meigs	1,045	7	0	1	0	6	34	9	24	1	0
Metter	4,267	28	0	1	9	18	200	61	139	0	0
Midville	274	0	0	0	0	0	0	0	0	0	0
Midway	2,208	7	0	1	0	6	76	22	45	9	0
Milledgeville	17,686	52	0	7	10	35	726	193	522	11	3
Milton	34,071	15	1	2	6	6	352	48	304	0	0
Montezuma	3,408	18	1	0	3	14	150	44	99	7	0
Morrow	6,564	34	0	1	24	9	1,063	60	946	57	0
Moultrie	14,311	84	2	8	39	35	1,032	237	763	32	9
Mountain City	1,100	0	0	0	0	0	6	0	5	1	0
Mount Zion	1,725	0	0	0	0	0	9	5	4	0	0
Nahunta	1,062	1	0	0	0	1	19	14	5	0	0
Nashville	5,014	27	0	1	7	19	239	96	139	4	0
Nelson	1,338	0	0	0	0	0	9	5	4	0	0
Newington	272	1	0	0	1	0	11	0	11	0	0
Newnan	34,085	125	2	4	35	84	1,147	246	840	61	2
Newton	591	7	0	0	0	7	11	3	8	0	0
Nicholls	3,510	3	0	0	2	1	35	16	18	1	0
Norcross	9,440	79	5	6	36	32	618	183	394	41	2
Norman Park	991	2	0	0	1	1	21	3	16	2	0
Oakwood	4,089	17	0	0	6	11	291	30	252	9	0

Table 8. Offenses Known to Law Enforcement, by Selected State and City, 2012— continued

(Number)

State/city	Population	Violent crime	Murder and nonnegligent manslaughter	Forcible rape	Robbery	Aggravated assault	Property crime	Burglary	Larceny-theft	Motor vehicle theft	Arson[1]
Ocilla	3,606	23	0	6	0	17	141	25	109	7	2
Oglethorpe	1,308	5	0	0	1	4	37	10	23	4	
Omega	1,276	0	0	0	0	0	0	0	0	0	0
Oxford	2,170	1	0	0	1	0	49	13	36	0	0
Palmetto	4,674	23	0	2	1	20	99	33	52	14	0
Patterson	738	2	0	0	2	0	7	0	7	0	0
Pavo	630	0	0	0	0	0	2	1	1	0	0
Peachtree City	35,128	15	0	2	6	7	457	36	366	55	5
Pearson	2,150	18	1	1	2	14	62	21	39	2	0
Pelham	3,935	15	0	1	5	9	175	29	137	9	0
Pembroke	2,303	4	0	0	0	4	72	21	51	0	0
Perry	14,367	47	0	3	8	36	324	82	220	22	3
Pine Lake	746	0	0	0	0	0	8	3	4	1	0
Pine Mountain	1,327	7	0	1	1	5	107	17	89	1	
Pooler	19,850	27	1	4	11	11	510	112	367	31	1
Porterdale	1,457	34	0	1	1	32	103	31	68	4	0
Port Wentworth	5,551	14	0	1	4	9	112	26	78	8	1
Poulan	870	3	0	0	0	3	93	30	63	0	0
Powder Springs	14,284	77	0	0	17	60	401	169	214	18	0
Quitman	3,806	66	0	1	9	56	251	33	209	9	0
Ray City	1,106	0	0	0	0	0	0	0	0	0	0
Register	183	0	0	0	0	0	0	0	0	0	0
Remerton	1,163	4	0	3	1	0	43	7	35	1	0
Reynolds	1,070	0	0	0	0	0	0	0	0	0	0
Richland	1,441	0	0	0	0	0	0	0	0	0	0
Richmond Hill	9,731	9	0	3	4	2	246	45	183	18	0
Rincon	9,001	4	0	0	4	0	258	25	229	4	0
Ringgold	3,652	12	0	0	0	12	186	40	139	7	0
Riverdale	15,414	119	1	1	45	72	914	291	541	82	0
Roberta	1,014	5	0	0	2	3	34	7	26	1	0
Rockmart	4,230	23	0	4	7	12	301	75	219	7	0
Rome	36,567	190	2	15	45	128	2,241	490	1,667	84	27
Rossville	4,145	49	0	1	23	25	274	65	186	23	1
Roswell	92,141	132	1	7	63	61	1,721	399	1,228	94	3
Royston	2,594	0	0	0	0	0	73	0	73	0	0
Sandersville	5,952	19	0	1	8	10	264	59	200	5	0
Sandy Springs	97,890	187	3	5	98	81	2,750	709	1,871	170	5
Sardis	1,019	6	0	0	0	6	31	11	20	0	0
Savannah-Chatham Metropolitan	231,285	878	23	25	491	339	8,325	2,083	5,583	659	34
Screven	781	1	0	0	0	1	6	1	5	0	0
Senoia	3,402	3	0	0	1	2	41	10	30	1	0
Shiloh	453	0	0	0	0	0	4	2	1	1	0
Sky Valley	275	0	0	0	0	0	10	4	6	0	0
Smyrna	52,537	161	3	12	68	78	1,392	366	898	128	7
Snellville	18,885	34	0	3	9	22	860	70	760	30	1
Social Circle	4,349	9	2	0	4	3	114	19	81	14	1
Sparks	2,062	3	0	0	0	3	70	23	46	1	0
Sparta	1,388	7	0	0	2	5	48	24	22	2	0
Springfield	2,899	4	0	2	1	1	50	8	39	3	0
Statesboro	29,713	86	2	16	48	20	1,307	297	964	46	2
Statham	2,451	11	0	0	0	11	138	38	97	3	0
Stillmore	536	0	0	0	0	0	42	1	41	0	0
St. Marys	17,281	76	2	3	10	61	534	152	363	19	3
Stone Mountain	5,934	115	1	5	6	103	304	69	197	38	0
Summerville	4,529	0	0	0	0	0	64	4	60	0	0
Suwanee	15,902	22	0	4	7	11	336	64	259	13	0
Swainsboro	7,346	130	2	6	8	114	675	146	507	22	2
Sycamore	717	0	0	0	0	0	0	0	0	0	0
Sylvania	2,941	20	0	0	11	9	127	25	99	3	0
Sylvester	6,323	48	1	1	5	41	343	132	200	11	0
Talbotton	964	4	0	0	0	4	19	6	11	2	0
Tallapoosa	3,189	14	0	2	1	11	119	23	78	18	0
Tallulah Falls	170	0	0	0	0	0	1	0	0	1	0

Table 8. Offenses Known to Law Enforcement, by Selected State and City, 2012— continued

(Number)

State/city	Population	Violent crime	Murder and nonnegligent manslaughter	Forcible rape	Robbery	Aggravated assault	Property crime	Burglary	Larceny-theft	Motor vehicle theft	Arson[1]
Temple	4,297	35	0	3	7	25	220	38	167	15	0
Tennille	1,549	8	0	0	0	8	80	21	58	1	0
Thomaston	9,209	28	1	2	9	16	476	106	367	3	0
Thomasville	18,603	77	2	7	22	46	1,195	353	791	51	3
Thunderbolt	2,755	4	0	0	2	2	104	21	73	10	0
Tifton	17,049	123	0	9	33	81	1,205	216	955	34	8
Tignall	542	0	0	0	0	0	7	3	4	0	0
Toccoa	8,511	66	1	2	12	51	501	39	458	4	0
Toomsboro	472	1	0	0	0	1	0	0	0	0	0
Trenton	2,316	0	0	0	0	0	44	6	36	2	0
Trion	1,825	3	0	0	0	3	37	10	24	3	0
Tunnel Hill	870	2	0	0	1	1	32	3	27	2	0
Twin City	1,759	6	0	0	6	0	15	13	0	2	0
Tybee Island	3,096	4	0	0	0	4	115	14	98	3	0
Tyrone	7,033	2	0	0	0	2	106	23	78	5	0
Union City	20,293	166	5	5	72	84	1,642	458	927	257	5
Union Point	1,638	2	0	0	2	0	75	27	44	4	0
Uvalda	600	3	0	2	0	1	5	2	2	1	0
Valdosta	56,617	248	3	38	88	119	2,324	655	1,592	77	10
Vidalia	10,664	56	2	3	13	38	710	166	526	18	0
Vienna	3,952	31	0	1	0	30	97	27	69	1	0
Villa Rica	14,197	31	0	5	8	18	550	134	391	25	0
Wadley	2,053	23	0	1	9	13	84	18	63	3	
Warm Springs	422	0	0	0	0	0	8	3	5	0	0
Warner Robins	69,231	366	6	21	141	198	3,979	781	3,050	148	18
Warwick	433	0	0	0	0	0	14	5	9	0	0
Washington	4,103	48	0	0	1	47	154	41	108	5	0
Watkinsville	2,910	3	0	0	0	3	54	9	42	3	0
Waverly Hall	749	3	0	0	0	3	2	0	1	1	0
Waycross	14,875	61	2	3	32	24	910	115	777	18	8
Waynesboro	5,875	23	0	1	11	11	162	53	98	11	0
West Point	3,546	37	0	3	6	28	203	54	142	7	0
Whigham	480	0	0	0	0	0	0	0	0	0	0
Whitesburg	598	2	0	0	0	2	23	4	17	2	
Willacoochee	1,412	2	0	0	1	1	52	21	31	0	0
Winder	14,361	46	0	2	13	31	554	117	415	22	1
Winterville	1,139	3	0	0	0	3	12	0	10	2	0
Woodbury	955	8	0	0	1	7	40	15	25	0	0
Woodstock	24,606	42	0	5	7	30	601	61	527	13	0
Wrens	2,175	10	0	0	5	5	84	23	57	4	
Wrightsville	2,216	7	0	1	2	4	70	25	43	2	0
Zebulon	1,178	6	0	0	2	4	30	4	26	0	0
Idaho											
Aberdeen	2,023	0	0	0	0	0	13	1	12	0	0
American Falls	4,458	6	0	1	0	5	59	6	47	6	0
Bellevue	2,283	15	1	0	0	14	24	11	10	3	0
Blackfoot	12,068	26	0	7	3	16	411	117	277	17	1
Boise	211,569	567	1	75	64	427	5,342	913	4,272	157	56
Bonners Ferry	2,524	3	0	0	0	3	36	10	25	1	0
Buhl	4,191	5	0	2	0	3	90	29	59	2	1
Caldwell	47,223	121	1	7	7	106	1,151	266	837	48	9
Challis	1,079	0	0	0	0	0	11	5	5	1	1
Chubbuck	14,162	39	0	2	3	34	568	39	513	16	3
Coeur d'Alene	45,267	260	0	26	14	220	1,978	431	1,395	152	15
Cottonwood	916	0	0	0	0	0	11	1	10	0	0
Emmett	6,581	19	0	5	0	14	80	23	56	1	3
Filer	2,551	2	0	0	0	2	5	2	1	2	0
Fruitland	4,715	5	0	0	0	5	83	27	54	2	2
Garden City	11,293	57	1	11	3	42	476	89	370	17	3
Gooding	3,593	9	0	1	1	7	62	14	43	5	2
Grangeville	3,198	1	0	0	0	1	35	15	19	1	0
Hagerman	879	2	0	0	0	2	7	1	5	1	0
Hailey	7,946	33	0	4	0	29	65	21	34	10	1

Table 8. Offenses Known to Law Enforcement, by Selected State and City, 2012— continued

(Number)

State/city	Population	Violent crime	Murder and nonnegligent manslaughter	Forcible rape	Robbery	Aggravated assault	Property crime	Burglary	Larceny-theft	Motor vehicle theft	Arson[1]
Heyburn	3,121	3	0	1	0	2	37	19	16	2	3
Idaho Falls	58,037	139	0	26	13	100	1,705	276	1,361	68	6
Jerome	11,115	45	0	7	6	32	197	67	118	12	6
Kamiah	1,304	2	0	0	0	2	11	3	6	2	0
Ketchum	2,712	13	0	0	0	13	62	11	47	4	0
Kimberly	3,320	5	0	0	1	4	37	8	26	3	2
Lewiston	32,337	55	0	7	10	38	1,280	289	934	57	1
McCall	2,944	15	0	5	0	10	106	22	82	2	0
Meridian	77,270	92	0	13	9	70	1,230	220	990	20	13
Montpelier	2,622	3	0	1	0	2	68	12	56	0	0
Moscow	24,243	32	0	3	4	25	671	91	558	22	3
Mountain Home	13,935	53	0	7	3	43	218	35	178	5	9
Nampa	83,316	203	2	44	20	137	2,180	510	1,590	80	20
Orofino	3,145	5	0	0	0	5	59	31	26	2	0
Parma	2,026	3	0	0	0	3	45	18	21	6	0
Payette	7,529	31	0	3	0	28	214	47	163	4	3
Pocatello	55,182	141	1	10	22	108	1,502	262	1,192	48	4
Ponderay	1,143	2	0	2	0	0	126	15	106	5	0
Post Falls	28,294	52	0	6	4	42	964	205	718	41	8
Preston	5,265	8	0	3	0	5	82	22	58	2	0
Priest River	1,759	1	1	0	0	0	23	5	15	3	0
Rathdrum	7,016	14	0	3	1	10	147	55	83	9	1
Rexburg	25,879	9	0	2	1	6	216	21	191	4	2
Rigby	4,015	5	0	3	0	2	84	14	68	2	0
Rupert	5,616	7	0	4	2	1	108	23	79	6	0
Salmon	3,145	7	0	0	0	7	30	10	19	1	0
Sandpoint	7,404	7	0	0	1	6	361	91	258	12	1
Shelley	4,474	2	0	1	1	0	49	12	34	3	0
Shoshone	1,464	3	0	1	1	1	5	4	1	0	0
Soda Springs	3,029	11	0	0	0	11	11	1	10	0	0
Spirit Lake	1,995	3	0	0	0	3	24	2	17	5	0
St. Maries	2,398	13	0	0	1	12	22	9	13	0	0
Sun Valley	1,404	1	0	0	0	1	14	3	9	2	0
Twin Falls	44,866	169	0	20	17	132	1,264	207	1,001	56	4
Weiser	5,575	2	0	0	0	2	21	5	14	2	0
Wendell	2,803	4	0	0	0	4	124	94	28	2	0
Wilder	1,568	4	0	1	1	2	14	5	7	2	0
Illinois											
Addison	37,215	74	0	14	18	42	722	117	574	31	16
Albany	889	0	0	0	0	0	12	0	12	0	0
Albers	1,197	0	0	0	0	0	2	1	1	0	0
Albion	1,959	2	0	0	0	2	17	4	12	1	0
Algonquin	30,159	29	0	4	7	18	502	56	435	11	1
Alsip	19,371	36	0	6	15	15	712	158	502	52	1
Altamont	2,323	3	0	0	0	3	31	11	19	1	0
Alton	27,794	125	3	14	40	68	1,230	326	861	43	10
Amboy	2,459	8	1	0	0	7	38	5	33	0	1
Anna	4,422	17	1	0	0	16	130	20	109	1	0
Antioch	14,495	15	0	0	4	11	212	22	189	1	0
Arcola	2,895	4	0	1	1	2	34	11	21	2	0
Arlington Heights	75,463	41	1	7	8	25	978	140	821	17	5
Armington	343	1	0	0	0	1	4	3	1	0	0
Arthur	2,277	5	0	1	0	4	40	6	33	1	0
Ashland	1,327	0	0	0	0	0	13	5	8	0	0
Atwood	1,219	2	0	0	0	2	14	5	9	0	1
Aurora	199,765	563	0	65	125	373	3,565	944	2,495	126	29
Aviston	1,956	1	0	0	0	1	2	0	2	0	0
Bannockburn	1,587	1	0	0	0	1	39	6	33	0	0
Barrington	10,376	1	0	1	0	0	147	18	125	4	3
Barrington Hills	4,225	2	1	0	0	1	40	9	31	0	0
Barry	1,317	2	0	1	1	0	3	0	2	1	0
Bartlett	41,477	31	0	4	9	18	317	29	278	10	1
Bartonville	6,486	25	0	5	3	17	203	44	149	10	0

Table 8. Offenses Known to Law Enforcement, by Selected State and City, 2012— continued

(Number)

State/city	Population	Violent crime	Murder and nonnegligent manslaughter	Forcible rape	Robbery	Aggravated assault	Property crime	Burglary	Larceny-theft	Motor vehicle theft	Arson[1]
Batavia	26,310	33	1	6	6	20	479	61	410	8	6
Beardstown	6,099	23	0	0	0	23	22	5	15	2	0
Beecher	4,386	2	0	0	1	1	42	4	37	1	0
Belgium	404	0	0	0	0	0	1	1	0	0	0
Bellwood	19,165	138	2	9	53	74	655	164	428	63	6
Benld	1,554	1	0	0	0	1	4	2	1	1	1
Benton	7,102	8	0	1	2	5	260	64	190	6	0
Berkeley	5,234	10	0	0	0	10	90	17	72	1	2
Berwyn	56,933	113	1	20	44	48	1,431	435	892	104	10
Bethalto	9,495	59	0	16	0	43	184	39	141	4	0
Blandinsville	650	0	0	0	0	0	2	0	2	0	0
Bloomingdale	22,177	13	0	3	6	4	656	46	601	9	4
Bloomington	77,107	372	1	42	45	284	1,797	357	1,396	44	12
Blue Island	23,820	89	3	2	51	33	535	161	285	89	0
Blue Mound	1,158	4	0	0	0	4	29	6	21	2	0
Bolingbrook	73,836	180	1	16	50	113	1,139	162	940	37	13
Bradley	15,939	54	0	8	6	40	746	71	663	12	7
Braidwood	6,231	12	0	3	0	9	115	23	91	1	1
Breese	4,467	6	0	2	0	4	38	0	38	0	0
Bridgeview	16,527	43	0	3	12	28	529	43	452	34	2
Brighton	2,250	0	0	0	0	0	9	2	7	0	0
Broadview	7,970	28	1	6	12	9	423	87	309	27	0
Brookfield	19,070	29	0	8	8	13	313	57	248	8	0
Buffalo Grove	41,687	5	0	0	3	2	372	37	333	2	1
Burbank	29,065	52	1	4	18	29	575	74	466	35	5
Burnham	4,226	11	1	3	5	2	160	46	75	39	1
Burr Ridge	10,629	2	0	1	0	1	155	18	133	4	0
Byron	3,728	0	0	0	0	0	54	11	43	0	1
Cahokia	15,258	73	4	6	30	33	756	222	534	0	5
Cairo	2,760	108	1	1	4	102	211	67	138	6	1
Cambridge	2,154	1	0	0	0	1	13	4	9	0	0
Campton Hills	11,244	6	0	1	0	5	44	32	12	0	0
Canton	14,673	44	0	11	5	28	357	67	281	9	2
Carbondale	25,972	260	0	29	36	195	1,092	246	798	48	12
Carlinville	5,912	21	0	0	1	20	159	28	128	3	2
Carlyle	3,307	7	0	0	0	7	70	0	70	0	0
Carol Stream	40,008	36	0	3	6	27	480	70	395	15	15
Carpentersville	38,080	31	1	2	11	17	533	136	390	7	6
Carrollton	2,469	19	0	1	0	18	40	16	24	0	0
Carthage	2,595	0	0	0	0	0	49	21	27	1	0
Cary	18,290	8	0	0	1	7	216	25	188	3	0
Casey	2,742	31	0	2	0	29	33	8	22	3	0
Caseyville	4,250	40	0	3	3	34	107	48	48	11	0
Catlin	2,038	2	0	0	0	2	38	5	32	1	0
Central City	1,169	2	0	0	0	2	35	6	27	2	0
Champaign	81,329	741	3	51	135	552	2,700	722	1,897	81	17
Channahon	12,625	2	0	0	0	2	88	9	75	4	0
Charleston	21,862	50	0	7	3	40	127	35	86	6	1
Chebanse	1,055	0	0	0	0	0	2	2	0	0	0
Chenoa	3,240	1	0	0	0	1	40	13	26	1	0
Cherry Valley	3,153	7	0	0	1	6	308	25	279	4	0
Chester	8,573	9	0	0	1	8	35	8	26	1	1
Chicago[6]	2,708,382		500		13,476	12,272	112,466	22,748	72,717	17,001	
Chicago Heights	30,422	252	3	26	115	108	1,099	480	531	88	42
Chicago Ridge	14,373	29	1	5	8	15	617	50	531	36	0
Chillicothe	6,111	21	0	1	1	19	126	21	99	6	1
Cicero	84,300	379	5	18	183	173	2,221	711	1,225	285	22
Clayton	710	0	0	0	0	0	2	0	2	0	0
Coal City	5,598	2	0	0	0	2	131	19	111	1	0
Coal Valley	3,744	3	0	1	0	2	40	7	32	1	0
Cobden	1,151	3	0	0	0	3	13	3	10	0	0
Colchester	1,398	1	0	0	0	1	11	1	10	0	0
Colfax	1,066	0	0	0	0	0	32	9	22	1	0
Collinsville	25,525	41	1	8	10	22	758	162	580	16	7

Table 8. Offenses Known to Law Enforcement, by Selected State and City, 2012— continued

(Number)

State/city	Population	Violent crime	Murder and nonnegligent manslaughter	Forcible rape	Robbery	Aggravated assault	Property crime	Burglary	Larceny-theft	Motor vehicle theft	Arson[1]
Columbia	9,816	10	0	5	0	5	92	16	76	0	0
Cortland	4,254	3	0	0	0	3	34	4	29	1	0
Country Club Hills	16,623	62	1	14	26	21	472	102	351	19	0
Countryside	5,923	8	0	0	2	6	240	22	205	13	0
Crest Hill	20,953	33	1	1	9	22	378	90	257	31	0
Crestwood	11,002	16	0	4	7	5	548	31	493	24	1
Crete	8,311	16	0	0	5	11	187	42	133	12	1
Crystal Lake	40,785	62	0	7	10	45	804	61	727	16	7
Danville	32,997	328	3	42	80	203	1,980	659	1,247	74	21
Darien	22,251	13	1	1	4	7	311	67	233	11	1
Davis	674	0	0	0	0	0	0	0	0	0	0
Decatur	76,131	352	6	26	106	214	2,448	921	1,445	82	30
Deer Creek	705	1	0	0	0	1	31	2	29	0	1
Deerfield	18,305	3	0	2	0	1	211	27	182	2	0
De Kalb	43,722	196	0	34	28	134	1,304	209	1,071	24	21
Delavan	1,692	2	0	0	1	1	50	19	31	0	1
De Pue	1,821	4	0	0	1	3	18	5	13	0	0
De Soto	1,594	2	0	0	0	2	10	5	5	0	0
Des Plaines	58,644	65	0	4	13	48	941	137	757	47	3
Diamond	2,532	0	0	0	0	0	48	0	48	0	0
Divernon	1,182	4	0	0	0	4	7	1	6	0	0
Dixon	15,518	17	0	8	2	7	372	63	303	6	0
Dolton	23,264	113	2	1	98	12	1,426	330	972	124	0
Downers Grove	48,185	29	0	4	12	13	994	157	819	18	4
Dupo	4,143	32	0	1	0	31	97	17	77	3	1
Du Quoin	6,087	10	0	1	0	9	102	26	68	8	0
Dwight	4,254	2	0	0	0	2	55	5	49	1	0
Earlville	1,696	1	0	0	0	1	50	11	38	1	0
East Alton	6,285	15	0	4	2	9	282	37	239	6	0
East Dubuque	1,707	9	0	2	0	7	27	4	20	3	0
East Dundee	2,888	1	0	0	0	1	60	2	58	0	0
East Moline	21,313	87	0	14	12	61	553	111	433	9	1
Easton	316	0	0	0	0	0	1	0	0	1	0
East Peoria	23,459	84	1	10	8	65	946	308	626	12	11
East St. Louis	27,040	1,350	17	60	198	1,075	1,827	869	569	389	37
Edwardsville	24,231	20	0	1	5	14	438	55	372	11	1
Effingham	12,345	25	0	8	2	15	420	48	358	14	4
Elburn	5,662	3	0	0	0	3	38	13	25	0	0
Eldorado	4,135	16	0	0	0	16	177	40	123	14	0
Elgin	109,155	257	2	67	76	112	1,982	357	1,546	79	12
Elizabeth	761	2	0	0	0	2	2	1	1	0	0
Elk Grove Village	33,288	21	0	6	5	10	683	108	524	51	1
Elmhurst	44,460	32	0	5	16	11	622	112	483	27	2
Elmwood	2,103	8	0	0	0	8	72	8	60	4	0
Elmwood Park	25,005	29	0	0	9	20	448	78	323	47	2
El Paso	2,825	6	0	0	0	6	56	4	51	1	0
Elwood	2,293	4	0	0	0	4	37	1	32	4	1
Eureka	5,321	5	0	0	1	4	56	8	47	1	0
Evanston	74,820	228	3	4	79	142	2,054	421	1,570	63	17
Evergreen Park	19,949	34	0	2	27	5	573	76	479	18	1
Fairbury	3,751	3	0	0	0	3	83	11	67	5	0
Fairfield	5,125	34	0	3	1	30	167	48	117	2	0
Fairmont City	2,639	7	0	1	1	5	47	10	36	1	0
Fairmount	641	0	0	0	0	0	2	0	2	0	0
Fairview Heights	17,099	45	2	3	3	37	1,030	78	924	28	0
Farmington	2,441	12	0	1	0	11	60	23	36	1	0
Fayetteville	366	0	0	0	0	0	14	8	6	0	0
Findlay	678	0	0	0	0	0	16	3	12	1	0
Fithian	484	0	0	0	0	0	0	0	0	0	0
Flora	5,043	4	0	1	0	3	158	6	151	1	0
Flossmoor	9,508	9	0	1	5	3	154	23	128	3	3
Forest Park	14,235	53	0	2	27	24	739	86	608	45	1
Forest View	700	0	0	0	0	0	38	12	16	10	0
Fox Lake	10,625	26	0	5	6	15	280	58	209	13	0

Table 8. Offenses Known to Law Enforcement, by Selected State and City, 2012— continued

(Number)

State/city	Population	Violent crime	Murder and nonnegligent manslaughter	Forcible rape	Robbery	Aggravated assault	Property crime	Burglary	Larceny-theft	Motor vehicle theft	Arson[1]
Fox River Grove	4,797	2	0	0	1	1	100	28	72	0	0
Frankfort	17,894	10	0	0	1	9	194	28	159	7	0
Franklin Grove	1,004	0	0	0	0	0	9	3	5	1	1
Franklin Park	18,424	27	0	4	5	18	370	91	237	42	2
Freeburg	4,357	10	0	0	0	10	45	7	38	0	0
Freeport	25,571	37	2	5	14	16	940	221	712	7	4
Fulton	3,476	4	0	0	0	4	42	13	28	1	0
Galena	3,437	2	0	1	0	1	34	6	27	1	1
Galesburg	32,208	123	2	18	14	89	1,098	237	844	17	4
Geneseo	6,569	4	0	1	0	3	96	8	85	3	2
Geneva	21,717	2	0	0	0	2	266	40	223	3	8
Genoa	5,175	8	0	4	0	4	58	10	46	2	0
Georgetown	3,470	18	0	2	2	14	63	27	33	3	2
Germantown	1,279	0	0	0	0	0	9	4	5	0	0
Gibson City	3,383	5	0	2	0	3	40	12	28	0	0
Gifford	977	1	0	0	0	1	1	0	1	0	0
Gilberts	6,952	3	0	2	0	1	30	4	22	4	0
Gillespie	3,315	6	0	0	0	6	65	11	51	3	0
Girard	2,100	21	0	0	0	21	10	2	8	0	0
Glasford	1,024	6	0	0	0	6	0	0	0	0	0
Glen Carbon	12,899	8	0	1	1	6	73	12	57	4	0
Glencoe	8,764	0	0	0	0	0	94	9	85	0	0
Glendale Heights	34,461	27	0	10	5	12	590	67	503	20	1
Glen Ellyn	27,661	16	0	5	6	5	363	37	321	5	4
Glenview	44,909	39	0	9	7	23	479	115	354	10	2
Glenwood	9,012	22	0	0	12	10	247	61	181	5	0
Godfrey	17,960	22	0	4	5	13	272	37	230	5	0
Godley	605	3	0	0	0	3	13	3	10	0	0
Goodfield	863	0	0	0	0	0	60	1	59	0	0
Grafton	672	0	0	0	0	0	16	1	15	0	0
Grandview	1,452	4	0	0	1	3	44	16	27	1	2
Granite City	29,772	172	7	17	29	119	840	311	509	20	16
Grantfork	335	0	0	0	0	0	0	0	0	0	0
Grant Park	1,335	0	0	0	0	0	14	0	13	1	0
Granville	1,418	0	0	0	0	0	10	1	9	0	1
Grayslake	21,052	32	0	9	8	15	410	67	338	5	5
Greenfield	1,064	1	0	0	0	1	10	1	9	0	0
Greenup	1,521	17	0	0	0	17	31	7	24	0	7
Greenville	6,990	2	0	0	1	1	119	25	90	4	1
Gurnee	31,439	27	0	5	8	14	1,446	103	1,312	31	1
Hampshire	5,619	10	0	1	2	7	77	15	59	3	0
Hampton	1,864	5	1	1	0	3	26	13	13	0	0
Hanover	845	3	0	1	0	2	9	2	7	0	0
Hanover Park	38,205	45	0	4	13	28	439	64	361	14	1
Harrisburg	9,043	53	0	3	4	46	186	127	55	4	2
Hartford	1,424	2	0	0	1	1	29	1	27	1	0
Harvard	9,457	12	0	2	1	9	132	19	113	0	0
Harvey	25,404	349	10	9	205	125	1,483	597	666	220	14
Harwood Heights	8,653	8	0	1	3	4	127	19	102	6	0
Havana	3,263	29	0	7	1	21	76	16	55	5	0
Hawthorn Woods	7,700	0	0	0	0	0	50	8	42	0	0
Hazel Crest	14,169	58	2	6	35	15	581	185	349	47	3
Henning	252	0	0	0	0	0	0	0	0	0	0
Herrin	12,576	161	0	0	3	158	425	213	201	11	0
Herscher	1,596	1	0	0	0	1	12	1	10	1	2
Heyworth	2,860	12	0	2	1	9	33	6	27	0	0
Hickory Hills	14,115	15	0	2	6	7	245	48	182	15	0
Highland	9,896	9	0	2	2	5	126	25	101	0	0
Highland Park	29,896	36	0	13	2	21	362	35	319	8	0
Highwood	5,429	7	0	3	0	4	57	2	54	1	0
Hillsboro	6,170	6	0	0	1	5	76	11	58	7	2
Hinsdale	16,931	2	0	0	1	1	181	29	150	2	0
Hodgkins	1,905	6	0	0	0	6	275	9	262	4	0
Hoffman Estates	52,148	66	0	13	26	27	710	129	560	21	4

Table 8. Offenses Known to Law Enforcement, by Selected State and City, 2012— continued

(Number)

State/city	Population	Violent crime	Murder and nonnegligent manslaughter	Forcible rape	Robbery	Aggravated assault	Property crime	Burglary	Larceny-theft	Motor vehicle theft	Arson[1]
Homer	1,197	1	0	0	0	1	7	0	7	0	0
Homer Glen	24,376	6	0	0	1	5	186	43	141	2	0
Hometown	4,370	2	0	0	2	0	62	3	55	4	0
Homewood	19,415	25	0	1	17	7	707	101	585	21	1
Hoopeston	5,345	31	0	3	2	26	205	40	162	3	0
Hopedale	866	0	0	0	0	0	7	1	6	0	0
Hudson	1,851	2	0	1	1	0	6	2	4	0	0
Huntley	24,369	6	1	0	1	4	214	33	181	0	0
Indian Head Park	3,827	6	0	0	0	6	29	5	22	2	5
Indianola	277	0	0	0	0	0	0	0	0	0	0
Inverness	7,436	0	0	0	0	0	34	17	17	0	0
Irving	491	0	0	0	0	0	11	4	7	0	0
Irvington	652	0	0	0	0	0	16	9	7	0	0
Island Lake	8,101	7	0	0	3	4	188	38	135	15	1
Itasca	8,714	2	0	0	1	1	91	10	77	4	0
Jacksonville	19,454	57	0	5	7	45	371	52	316	3	3
Jerseyville	8,441	30	0	12	0	18	295	49	242	4	0
Joliet	148,471	506	11	30	104	361	3,835	954	2,723	158	78
Justice	12,988	16	0	1	3	12	139	36	90	13	0
Kankakee	27,609	237	6	26	71	134	1,201	348	809	44	25
Kenilworth	2,524	0	0	0	0	0	30	7	22	1	0
Kewanee	12,882	41	0	12	0	29	492	41	444	7	2
Kildeer	3,985	0	0	0	0	0	32	8	23	1	0
Kincaid	1,510	4	0	0	0	4	6	1	4	1	0
Kingston	1,160	0	0	0	0	0	8	3	5	0	0
Knoxville	2,911	7	0	0	0	7	44	12	32	0	0
Lacon	1,921	3	0	0	0	3	19	5	14	0	0
La Grange	15,624	14	0	3	2	9	165	27	135	3	2
La Grange Park	13,642	4	1	1	0	2	107	1	98	8	0
Lake Bluff	5,748	0	0	0	0	0	63	12	51	0	0
Lake Forest	19,457	14	0	0	0	14	41	10	29	2	0
Lake Villa	8,778	10	0	0	0	10	93	13	77	3	1
Lakewood	3,855	0	0	0	0	0	31	6	25	0	0
Lake Zurich	19,718	8	0	0	1	7	282	28	253	1	3
Lansing	28,471	93	1	30	27	35	1,332	238	1,023	71	2
La Salle	9,580	6	0	0	1	5	191	25	160	6	3
Lawrenceville	4,322	7	1	0	0	6	95	19	71	5	5
Leland	973	6	0	0	0	6	11	3	8	0	0
Lemont	16,083	14	0	2	1	11	236	24	206	6	0
Libertyville	20,405	5	0	0	0	5	313	49	259	5	0
Lincoln	14,426	58	0	8	7	43	417	103	310	4	3
Lincolnshire	7,306	2	0	0	0	2	83	8	75	0	0
Lincolnwood	12,652	11	0	2	4	5	745	69	659	17	1
Lindenhurst	14,529	6	0	1	1	4	88	13	72	3	0
Lisle	22,550	18	0	4	5	9	256	25	218	13	1
Litchfield	6,880	11	0	2	1	8	219	27	185	7	1
Loami	750	0	0	0	0	0	12	3	9	0	0
Lockport	24,999	15	1	4	4	6	317	44	264	9	0
Lombard	43,482	54	1	2	18	33	1,142	118	1,008	16	3
Loves Park	23,915	55	0	14	7	34	811	131	655	25	1
Lovington	1,129	2	0	0	0	2	16	7	8	1	0
Lyons	10,780	18	0	4	4	10	191	35	142	14	2
Machesney Park	23,403	76	1	15	7	53	599	108	480	11	6
Macomb	19,289	48	0	9	2	37	418	66	344	8	0
Mahomet	7,285	4	0	0	0	4	98	30	63	5	2
Malta	1,159	0	0	0	0	0	10	3	6	1	0
Manhattan	7,096	5	0	0	0	5	57	18	37	2	1
Maple Park	1,316	2	0	0	0	2	7	0	6	1	0
Marine	958	2	0	0	0	2	5	2	3	0	0
Maroa	1,802	2	0	0	0	2	12	5	7	0	2
Marseilles	5,101	5	0	0	1	4	43	7	36	0	0
Martinsville	1,154	1	0	0	0	1	48	16	31	1	3
Maryville	7,468	12	0	0	0	12	38	14	23	1	0
Mascoutah	7,492	1	0	0	0	1	85	4	79	2	0

Table 8. Offenses Known to Law Enforcement, by Selected State and City, 2012— continued

(Number)

State/city	Population	Violent crime	Murder and nonnegligent manslaughter	Forcible rape	Robbery	Aggravated assault	Property crime	Burglary	Larceny-theft	Motor vehicle theft	Arson[1]
Matteson	19,102	35	0	0	23	12	775	103	617	55	0
Mattoon	18,579	65	2	12	9	42	364	84	276	4	16
Maywood	24,207	238	7	18	94	119	988	397	465	126	9
McCook	229	10	0	0	0	10	33	6	22	5	0
McHenry	27,023	35	0	17	2	16	417	28	383	6	1
McLean	834	0	0	0	0	0	5	2	3	0	0
Melrose Park	25,536	58	2	9	18	29	500	93	327	80	1
Mendota	7,349	13	0	0	0	13	157	70	87	0	6
Meredosia	1,045	2	0	0	0	2	23	10	13	0	0
Merrionette Park	1,909	4	0	0	2	2	55	10	42	3	0
Metropolis	6,557	55	0	11	3	41	262	22	233	7	0
Midlothian	14,891	42	0	4	25	13	272	76	182	14	3
Milan	5,101	11	0	1	2	8	151	35	114	2	0
Milledgeville	1,018	0	0	0	0	0	22	7	15	0	0
Millstadt	4,016	1	0	0	0	1	32	17	15	0	0
Minooka	10,963	4	0	0	0	4	146	6	140	0	0
Mokena	18,863	11	0	1	4	6	217	45	165	7	10
Moline	43,509	176	0	16	23	137	1,354	204	1,095	55	11
Momence	3,320	4	0	1	0	3	59	11	45	3	0
Monee	5,181	2	0	0	2	0	69	23	40	6	0
Monmouth	9,504	71	0	4	2	65	509	95	405	9	3
Montgomery	18,697	18	0	4	3	11	366	67	292	7	3
Monticello	5,533	7	0	1	0	6	33	15	17	1	0
Morris	13,660	23	1	1	1	20	505	77	427	1	5
Morrison	4,183	9	0	4	1	4	48	8	40	0	0
Morton	16,308	22	1	1	2	18	172	41	130	1	0
Morton Grove	23,384	4	0	1	0	3	408	85	315	8	2
Mount Carmel	7,219	22	0	2	0	20	234	35	191	8	1
Mount Carroll	1,694	0	0	0	0	0	32	4	28	0	0
Mount Morris	2,978	3	0	0	0	3	34	5	29	0	0
Mount Olive	2,103	2	0	0	0	2	16	5	11	0	0
Mount Prospect	54,428	32	0	0	6	26	745	83	632	30	2
Mount Pulaski	1,556	2	0	0	0	2	5	0	5	0	0
Mount Sterling	2,002	4	0	0	0	4	21	6	15	0	1
Mount Vernon	15,243	190	0	19	26	145	896	218	661	17	9
Mount Zion	5,833	6	0	0	0	6	42	17	23	2	0
Moweaqua	1,819	3	0	0	0	3	18	7	11	0	0
Mundelein	31,201	26	1	7	1	17	337	49	282	6	2
Murphysboro	7,994	48	0	1	6	41	456	74	382	0	6
Naperville	142,840	119	3	7	24	85	2,044	255	1,748	41	16
Neoga	1,643	3	0	0	0	3	19	7	11	1	0
New Athens	2,057	4	0	1	0	3	32	9	23	0	0
New Lenox	24,549	19	0	2	1	16	302	29	268	5	5
Newton	2,856	22	0	0	0	22	36	7	29	0	0
Niles	29,945	24	0	3	13	8	750	66	645	39	0
Nokomis	2,238	13	0	0	0	13	71	20	51	0	0
Normal	52,797	114	0	19	34	61	1,306	265	1,016	25	9
Norridge	14,642	20	0	0	13	7	791	49	714	28	1
Norris City	1,276	4	0	0	2	2	7	3	3	1	0
North Aurora	16,930	31	2	8	5	16	278	36	237	5	2
Northbrook	33,327	10	0	2	1	7	533	58	473	2	1
North Chicago	32,697	80	0	6	20	54	191	78	110	3	4
Northfield	5,446	2	0	0	1	1	71	9	61	1	0
Northlake	12,381	13	2	0	4	7	357	28	319	10	2
North Riverside	6,702	8	0	0	3	5	602	30	551	21	0
Norwood	479	0	0	0	0	0	0	0	0	0	0
Oak Brook	7,941	3	0	0	2	1	602	14	578	10	1
Oakbrook Terrace	2,150	5	0	2	1	2	116	20	92	4	0
Oak Forest	28,097	29	1	3	14	11	449	108	330	11	2
Oak Lawn	56,964	82	0	9	31	42	1,137	113	970	54	4
Oakwood	1,595	1	0	1	0	0	11	2	8	1	0
Oakwood Hills	2,085	7	0	1	0	6	14	1	13	0	0
Oblong	1,470	11	0	0	0	11	20	12	8	0	0
O'Fallon	28,372	31	0	10	7	14	665	114	535	16	2

Table 8. Offenses Known to Law Enforcement, by Selected State and City, 2012— continued

(Number)

State/city	Population	Violent crime	Murder and nonnegligent manslaughter	Forcible rape	Robbery	Aggravated assault	Property crime	Burglary	Larceny-theft	Motor vehicle theft	Arson[1]
Oglesby	3,779	6	0	3	0	3	93	15	75	3	1
Okawville	1,418	1	0	0	1	0	21	6	15	0	0
Olney	9,125	35	0	10	1	24	296	51	238	7	7
Olympia Fields	5,012	7	0	0	3	4	110	16	88	6	0
Oquawka	1,346	7	0	1	0	6	29	11	18	0	0
Orion	1,856	0	0	0	0	0	11	0	11	0	0
Orland Park	57,043	16	1	1	4	10	1,359	45	1,298	16	3
Oswego	30,870	16	0	5	1	10	502	50	448	4	0
Ottawa	18,708	25	0	0	2	23	428	63	363	2	2
Palatine	68,890	29	1	6	8	14	891	33	837	21	5
Palestine	1,373	5	0	0	0	5	12	0	12	0	0
Palos Heights	12,573	6	0	2	1	3	124	9	113	2	0
Palos Hills	17,569	6	0	0	3	3	140	19	110	11	1
Palos Park	4,871	4	1	0	1	2	40	4	34	2	0
Pana	5,860	5	0	0	0	5	107	31	66	10	0
Park Forest	22,086	66	1	8	27	30	698	366	307	25	4
Park Ridge	37,660	22	1	0	12	9	459	118	328	13	7
Pawnee	2,760	0	0	0	0	0	14	3	11	0	0
Paxton	4,443	4	0	0	0	4	56	17	37	2	0
Pekin	34,176	176	1	19	19	137	915	164	728	23	8
Peoria	115,288	919	10	25	324	560	5,022	1,420	3,370	232	52
Peoria Heights	6,170	18	1	1	2	14	208	50	155	3	2
Peotone	4,169	7	0	2	0	5	49	1	43	5	0
Peru	10,262	10	0	0	4	6	229	20	200	9	0
Phoenix	1,973	11	0	1	2	8	38	20	13	5	0
Pierron	599	0	0	0	0	0	1	0	1	0	0
Pinckneyville	5,637	10	0	3	0	7	23	8	15	0	0
Pingree Grove	4,578	4	0	0	0	4	22	2	19	1	0
Pittsfield	4,571	0	0	0	0	0	1	0	1	0	0
Plainfield	39,859	35	0	4	13	18	499	59	425	15	5
Plano	11,040	5	0	0	2	3	136	23	111	2	2
Pleasant Hill	965	0	0	0	0	0	18	6	12	0	0
Pleasant Plains	808	0	0	0	0	0	5	0	5	0	0
Polo	2,340	3	0	0	0	3	37	8	29	0	0
Pontoon Beach	5,821	3	0	0	3	0	113	19	85	9	0
Posen	6,016	13	0	1	8	4	161	43	97	21	1
Potomac	749	0	0	0	0	0	6	2	4	0	0
Princeton	7,585	13	0	0	1	12	176	31	144	1	0
Prospect Heights	16,335	14	0	3	2	9	142	42	89	11	0
Quincy	40,684	188	0	26	16	146	1,304	224	1,054	26	8
Raleigh	351	1	0	0	0	1	8	2	6	0	0
Ramsey	1,036	3	0	0	0	3	20	5	15	0	0
Rankin	560	1	0	0	0	1	4	2	2	0	0
Rantoul	12,990	112	0	17	9	86	270	106	157	7	3
Raymond	995	3	0	0	0	3	2	0	2	0	0
Red Bud	3,685	15	0	0	1	14	30	5	24	1	0
Richmond	1,877	0	0	0	0	0	36	11	24	1	0
Richton Park	13,711	47	0	7	22	18	353	118	213	22	2
Ridge Farm	879	1	0	0	1	0	9	2	7	0	0
Riverdale	13,615	178	1	15	101	61	492	226	238	28	2
River Forest	11,224	17	0	2	8	7	302	49	249	4	1
River Grove	10,277	9	0	1	2	6	226	52	159	15	2
Riverside	8,919	2	0	0	1	1	139	20	116	3	0
Riverton	3,482	16	1	0	1	14	106	20	83	3	1
Riverwoods	3,676	1	0	0	0	1	23	4	18	1	2
Robinson	7,730	32	0	6	0	26	144	25	114	5	4
Rockdale	1,989	2	0	0	0	2	27	7	18	2	0
Rock Falls	9,253	29	0	2	3	24	446	74	355	17	1
Rockford	152,293	2,083	9	124	499	1,451	7,608	2,224	5,003	381	72
Rock Island	39,038	222	4	6	39	173	1,124	217	856	51	13
Rockton	7,656	9	0	0	1	8	120	20	99	1	1
Rolling Meadows	24,216	21	0	3	6	12	361	51	303	7	3
Romeoville	39,931	30	0	2	11	17	830	94	721	15	0
Roselle	22,923	12	0	2	4	6	306	73	225	8	1

Table 8. Offenses Known to Law Enforcement, by Selected State and City, 2012— continued

(Number)

State/city	Population	Violent crime	Murder and nonnegligent manslaughter	Forcible rape	Robbery	Aggravated assault	Property crime	Burglary	Larceny-theft	Motor vehicle theft	Arson[1]
Rosemont	4,224	7	0	0	4	3	226	9	205	12	0
Round Lake	18,374	28	0	4	3	21	184	43	137	4	0
Round Lake Beach	28,302	35	0	9	7	19	758	122	628	8	1
Round Lake Park	7,540	0	0	0	0	0	8	1	7	0	0
Roxana	1,539	7	0	1	0	6	46	8	38	0	0
Ruma	316	1	0	0	0	1	3	1	2	0	0
Rushville	3,181	1	0	0	0	1	55	5	49	1	0
Salem	7,465	8	0	1	3	4	341	56	280	5	4
Sauget	160	14	1	7	4	2	83	5	67	11	0
Sauk Village	10,558	96	1	12	36	47	536	349	160	27	13
Schaumburg	74,585	68	0	13	18	37	2,487	199	2,226	62	4
Schiller Park	11,850	11	0	3	5	3	222	42	158	22	1
Seneca	2,364	14	0	0	0	14	64	8	56	0	0
Sherman	4,178	2	0	0	0	2	20	0	20	0	0
Shiloh	12,699	23	0	8	3	12	220	60	160	0	0
Shorewood	15,715	9	0	2	2	5	190	38	143	9	2
Sidell	616	1	0	0	0	1	1	0	1	0	1
Silvis	7,487	20	0	0	1	19	277	30	247	0	0
Skokie	65,096	134	0	17	37	80	1,577	284	1,232	61	8
Sleepy Hollow	3,339	2	0	0	0	2	32	1	31	0	0
Smithton	3,700	0	0	0	0	0	20	1	19	0	0
South Barrington	4,588	1	0	0	1	0	100	20	79	1	4
South Beloit	7,860	17	0	2	6	9	163	34	122	7	1
South Chicago Heights	4,160	10	1	0	4	5	162	19	135	8	1
South Elgin	22,208	36	0	1	3	32	321	24	291	6	2
South Holland	22,133	76	0	2	60	14	514	178	295	41	1
South Pekin	1,148	5	0	1	1	3	16	8	8	0	0
Sparta	4,288	5	0	2	0	3	157	36	119	2	0
Springfield	117,131	1,138	10	76	260	792	6,945	1,670	5,033	242	41
Spring Grove	5,785	1	0	0	0	1	51	10	40	1	0
Spring Valley	5,502	7	0	2	0	5	113	27	85	1	2
St. Anne	1,263	2	1	0	0	1	32	13	18	1	0
St. Charles	33,302	18	0	5	3	10	502	55	429	18	9
Steger	9,626	14	0	1	3	10	337	69	259	9	1
Sterling	15,417	43	0	17	4	22	603	85	503	15	0
Stockton	1,865	9	0	0	0	9	23	6	17	0	0
Stone Park	4,968	12	0	1	1	10	94	17	60	17	0
Stonington	933	1	0	0	0	1	8	1	6	1	0
Streamwood	40,050	34	0	6	11	17	703	123	568	12	1
Streator	13,665	8	0	0	3	5	430	51	378	1	2
Stronghurst	867	0	0	0	0	0	2	2	0	0	0
Sugar Grove	9,090	3	0	1	0	2	52	16	35	1	0
Summit	11,109	60	1	0	23	36	319	83	186	50	5
Swansea	13,446	15	0	8	3	4	280	59	205	16	0
Sycamore	17,454	13	1	0	0	12	253	23	222	8	0
Taylorville	11,273	32	0	4	0	28	226	51	164	11	9
Teutopolis	1,532	0	0	0	0	0	10	3	7	0	0
Thomasboro	1,130	7	0	5	0	2	26	11	15	0	0
Thornton	2,349	5	0	0	0	5	52	11	39	2	0
Tilton	2,720	11	0	3	2	6	55	19	32	4	0
Tinley Park	56,992	43	1	6	11	25	839	108	710	21	3
Tolono	3,461	4	0	1	0	3	62	17	43	2	0
Tonica	765	1	0	0	0	1	5	4	1	0	0
Tower Lakes	1,288	0	0	0	0	0	7	0	7	0	0
Tuscola	4,449	25	0	0	0	25	69	30	38	1	0
Urbana	41,537	148	0	20	68	60	1,443	416	974	53	13
Valmeyer	1,276	0	0	0	0	0	10	3	7	0	0
Vandalia	7,043	31	0	6	0	25	210	52	151	7	0
Vernon Hills	25,223	18	0	7	1	10	576	36	532	8	0
Vienna	1,443	4	0	1	0	3	42	3	38	1	0
Villa Park	22,067	40	0	5	17	18	454	73	360	21	3
Virden	3,482	11	0	3	0	8	63	6	54	3	2
Virginia	1,604	0	0	0	0	0	0	0	0	0	0

Table 8. Offenses Known to Law Enforcement, by Selected State and City, 2012— continued

(Number)

State/city	Population	Violent crime	Murder and nonnegligent manslaughter	Forcible rape	Robbery	Aggravated assault	Property crime	Burglary	Larceny-theft	Motor vehicle theft	Arson[1]
Warrensburg	1,210	5	0	0	0	5	13	5	8	0	0
Warrenville	13,238	5	0	2	1	2	155	20	132	3	0
Warsaw	1,602	0	0	0	0	0	32	3	28	1	0
Washington	15,172	22	0	3	3	16	155	40	109	6	0
Washington Park	4,201	130	2	7	40	81	151	34	80	37	2
Waterloo	9,922	0	0	0	0	0	59	3	56	0	0
Watseka	5,212	6	0	1	1	4	159	34	122	3	2
Wauconda	13,662	10	0	1	1	8	156	19	131	6	0
Waukegan	89,468	420	2	47	160	211	2,688	625	1,999	64	27
Waverly	1,308	2	0	0	0	2	9	4	5	0	0
Wayne	2,450	0	0	0	0	0	15	6	7	2	0
Westchester	16,798	15	1	3	5	6	242	81	154	7	2
West Chicago	27,286	24	0	8	5	11	349	61	264	24	6
West City	663	11	0	0	2	9	57	15	40	2	0
West Dundee	7,405	4	0	0	2	2	250	9	234	7	0
Western Springs	13,039	1	0	0	0	1	49	5	42	2	2
West Frankfort	8,196	25	0	4	5	16	119	46	63	10	0
Westmont	24,867	27	0	4	15	8	389	62	300	27	4
Westville	3,199	8	0	2	0	6	53	12	36	5	0
Wheaton	53,263	12	1	1	3	7	580	96	474	10	4
Wheeling	37,830	31	0	2	8	21	540	102	425	13	6
White Hall	2,505	17	0	0	0	17	38	12	26	0	1
Willisville	630	1	0	0	0	1	6	4	1	1	0
Willowbrook	8,602	16	0	0	5	11	185	14	160	11	0
Willow Springs	5,551	4	0	0	2	2	37	10	25	2	0
Wilmette	27,219	11	0	1	5	5	420	99	320	1	0
Wilmington	5,760	20	0	8	1	11	122	15	105	2	0
Winfield	9,149	0	0	0	0	0	54	9	44	1	0
Winnebago	3,088	3	0	1	0	2	60	8	52	0	0
Winnetka	12,247	4	0	0	1	3	169	34	132	3	0
Winthrop Harbor	6,773	15	0	5	2	8	100	15	82	3	0
Witt	896	0	0	0	0	0	3	1	2	0	0
Wood Dale	13,871	6	0	0	0	6	222	45	169	8	0
Woodhull	810	0	0	0	0	0	4	4	0	0	0
Woodridge	33,215	38	1	7	15	15	523	50	442	31	4
Wood River	10,630	29	1	4	6	18	444	53	376	15	0
Woodstock	24,797	37	0	3	5	29	381	41	337	3	2
Worth	10,840	5	0	0	0	5	121	27	87	7	0
Yorkville	17,206	22	1	13	1	7	258	32	225	1	1
Zeigler	1,805	85	0	0	0	85	64	27	37	0	0
Zion	24,519	145	1	33	24	87	1,037	418	585	34	5
Indiana											
Alexandria	5,144	10	0	2	1	7	206	42	160	4	0
Anderson	56,132	270	1	54	75	140	2,860	641	2,012	207	35
Angola	8,605	4	0	0	2	2	491	40	449	2	1
Attica	3,250	4	1	0	0	3	40	12	27	1	1
Auburn	12,842	13	0	4	3	6	409	40	355	14	0
Avon	12,707	45	0	1	8	36	556	56	486	14	2
Bargersville	6,054	10	0	0	0	10	0	0	0	0	0
Batesville	6,528	17	0	1	2	14	140	31	104	5	1
Bedford	13,466	38	0	8	4	26	556	75	459	22	0
Beech Grove	14,364	32	0	8	19	5	585	119	417	49	1
Berne	4,010	1	0	1	0	0	60	12	44	4	1
Bloomington	81,636	243	3	18	42	180	3,244	622	2,471	151	25
Bluffton	9,960	2	0	1	0	1	416	63	344	9	0
Boonville	6,326	45	0	4	1	40	232	29	196	7	5
Brazil	8,098	15	0	1	1	13	253	45	190	18	0
Bremen	4,601	1	0	0	0	1	92	15	68	9	3
Brownsburg	21,729	23	0	1	4	18	327	46	269	12	0
Brownstown	2,995	7	0	1	1	5	177	23	151	3	0
Burns Harbor	1,169	1	0	0	0	1	33	2	29	2	0
Carmel	81,819	11	0	2	6	3	808	113	649	46	2
Cedar Lake	11,585	15	1	2	0	12	296	61	225	10	3

Table 8. Offenses Known to Law Enforcement, by Selected State and City, 2012— continued

(Number)

State/city	Population	Violent crime	Murder and nonnegligent manslaughter	Forcible rape	Robbery	Aggravated assault	Property crime	Burglary	Larceny-theft	Motor vehicle theft	Arson[1]
Charlestown	7,702	4	0	1	3	0	274	68	198	8	0
Chesterfield	2,550	7	0	0	0	7	78	6	69	3	0
Chesterton	[illegible]	11	0	1	0	11	211	40	150	15	0
Clarksville	22,057	120	1	6	21	92	1,597	188	1,352	57	1
Clinton	4,913	8	0	0	1	7	102	30	67	5	1
Columbia City	8,802	12	0	1	1	10	181	23	148	10	0
Columbus	44,817	83	1	12	22	48	2,210	262	1,768	180	5
Corydon	3,130	0	0	0	0	0	44	4	35	5	1
Crawfordsville	16,092	41	0	3	4	34	589	147	417	25	0
Crown Point	27,890	7	0	2	2	3	514	56	435	23	4
Culver	1,357	4	1	0	1	2	24	2	20	2	0
Cumberland	5,227	27	1	2	6	18	187	34	145	8	3
Danville	9,187	25	0	0	0	25	102	20	77	5	0
Decatur	9,431	7	0	0	2	5	66	14	49	3	0
Delphi	2,886	7	0	3	1	3	90	15	70	5	0
Dyer	16,427	7	2	0	3	2	291	24	249	18	0
East Chicago	29,764	220	3	9	88	120	1,754	560	1,025	169	2
Ellettsville	6,492	29	0	0	2	27	110	32	70	8	0
Elwood	8,613	28	0	0	9	19	284	74	197	13	6
Evansville	118,194	560	8	56	199	297	6,083	1,132	4,531	420	76
Fairmount	2,950	2	0	0	0	2	31	17	13	1	0
Fishers	79,375	14	0	1	9	4	821	101	693	27	2
Fort Wayne	256,625	931	22	93	447	369	9,515	2,025	7,073	417	57
Fowler	2,325	10	0	1	0	9	51	16	35	0	0
Frankfort	16,416	61	0	7	12	42	760	109	618	33	1
Franklin	24,115	60	0	0	13	47	1,062	126	920	16	1
Garrett	6,343	6	0	2	0	4	153	43	104	6	0
Gary	80,472	728	37	56	275	360	4,475	1,634	2,066	775	82
Gas City	5,959	1	0	0	0	1	165	16	149	0	0
Goshen	32,034	47	1	13	22	11	1,143	200	876	67	11
Greendale	4,539	7	0	0	0	7	112	13	97	2	0
Greenfield	20,819	19	1	0	10	8	398	60	318	20	0
Greensburg	11,617	33	0	0	1	32	115	8	105	2	3
Greenwood	51,746	191	1	3	19	168	1,809	207	1,543	59	3
Hagerstown	1,786	2	0	0	0	2	39	18	21	0	0
Hammond	81,010	665	6	18	192	449	3,448	936	2,143	369	29
Hartford City	6,155	9	0	0	3	6	199	40	155	4	0
Hebron	3,764	0	0	0	0	0	3	1	2	0	0
Highland	23,779	25	1	2	10	12	713	98	571	44	5
Hobart	29,122	51	0	6	21	24	1,447	110	1,253	84	7
Huntingburg	6,120	20	0	2	0	18	95	14	81	0	0
Huntington	17,486	31	0	10	4	17	467	65	388	14	3
Indianapolis	838,650	9,942	97	436	3,442	5,967	46,898	14,774	27,525	4,599	409
Jasper	15,193	6	0	0	0	6	160	27	122	11	0
Jeffersonville	45,640	436	2	2	36	396	1,946	410	1,394	142	2
Kendallville	9,896	10	0	2	2	6	398	51	336	11	1
Knox	3,689	2	0	0	0	2	80	8	70	2	0
Kokomo	45,636	177	4	15	61	97	1,857	462	1,294	101	1
Lafayette	68,160	407	1	36	69	301	3,293	713	2,382	198	11
Lake Station	12,599	26	1	5	8	12	549	101	406	42	14
La Porte	22,102	28	0	4	9	15	1,079	188	855	36	3
Lawrenceburg	5,064	5	0	0	3	2	135	8	123	4	0
Ligonier	4,421	2	0	0	0	2	28	5	22	1	0
Linton	5,386	0	0	0	0	0	191	5	183	3	0
Logansport	18,387	12	0	6	3	3	984	149	784	51	2
Lowell	9,298	10	0	0	0	10	148	20	125	3	1
Marion	29,931	83	3	9	50	21	1,329	257	983	89	10
Martinsville	11,960	17	1	3	3	10	997	131	802	64	2
Merrillville	35,325	106	4	6	39	57	1,390	143	1,125	122	2
Michigan City	31,551	120	3	11	56	50	1,725	325	1,339	61	17
Mishawaka	48,363	160	3	22	55	80	2,797	501	2,138	158	15
Monticello	5,406	26	1	1	2	22	152	20	123	9	0
Mooresville	9,432	14	0	1	1	12	357	43	292	22	1
Mount Vernon	6,660	8	0	1	3	4	417	105	289	23	2

Table 8. Offenses Known to Law Enforcement, by Selected State and City, 2012— continued

(Number)

State/city	Population	Violent crime	Murder and nonnegligent manslaughter	Forcible rape	Robbery	Aggravated assault	Property crime	Burglary	Larceny-theft	Motor vehicle theft	Arson[1]
Muncie	70,300	258	1	9	99	149	2,934	690	2,041	203	35
Munster	23,657	30	0	2	10	18	419	52	337	30	0
Nappanee	6,712	4	0	1	2	1	164	14	141	9	0
New Albany	36,685	138	4	23	38	73	2,168	367	1,632	169	5
New Castle	18,094	11	0	5	5	1	1,285	242	995	48	1
New Haven	14,968	32	0	4	8	20	446	80	336	30	6
New Whiteland	5,569	8	0	0	3	5	56	6	47	3	0
North Judson	1,766	16	0	1	0	15	73	9	62	2	1
North Liberty	1,901	4	0	0	0	4	22	3	18	1	0
North Manchester	6,087	2	0	2	0	0	141	15	126	0	0
Oakland City	2,437	1	0	1	0	0	39	7	29	3	0
Plainfield	28,164	55	0	7	8	40	774	99	629	46	2
Portage	37,213	69	2	4	8	55	1,023	165	812	46	5
Porter	4,910	9	0	2	0	7	80	15	52	13	1
Portland	6,260	15	0	0	0	15	254	32	207	15	0
Rushville	6,323	6	0	0	2	4	318	68	239	11	0
Russiaville	1,099	3	0	0	1	2	45	12	33	0	0
Scottsburg	6,715	37	0	3	3	31	330	49	271	10	0
Sellersburg	6,221	41	0	0	5	36	115	25	80	10	0
Seymour	18,340	79	0	4	6	69	1,190	143	976	71	3
Shelbyville	19,209	4	0	1	1	2	836	28	771	37	0
South Bend	101,398	622	18	55	316	233	4,827	1,744	2,798	285	34
Speedway	11,954	30	3	0	21	6	697	128	518	51	1
St. John	14,885	8	0	1	1	6	139	18	116	5	0
Tell City	7,302	6	0	2	0	4	166	33	125	8	4
Terre Haute	61,152	191	4	29	85	73	3,730	1,035	2,412	283	47
Tipton	5,075	0	0	0	0	0	202	48	152	2	0
Valparaiso	32,042	28	1	7	5	15	841	153	644	44	2
Walkerton	2,149	0	0	0	0	0	22	6	15	1	1
Warsaw[7]	13,599		0	5	6		584	64	493	27	4
Washington	11,648	47	0	2	2	43	593	164	409	20	1
Waterloo	2,262	8	0	0	0	8	72	12	52	8	1
Westfield	31,068	28	0	5	3	20	507	54	423	30	2
West Lafayette	30,015	78	0	8	11	59	487	80	379	28	0
West Terre Haute	2,251	9	0	1	0	8	127	34	83	10	0
Westville	5,869	11	0	2	0	9	38	7	26	5	1
Whitestown	2,920	10	0	0	1	9	84	13	68	3	0
Whiting	5,008	4	1	0	2	1	195	31	145	19	0
Winchester	4,938	4	0	0	0	4	247	39	197	11	1
Winona Lake	4,921	3	0	0	0	3	35	6	25	4	0
Zionsville	23,742	0	0	0	0	0	46	10	35	1	0
Iowa											
Adel	3,879	16	1	0	0	15	84	38	44	2	0
Albia	3,820	12	0	0	0	12	78	21	55	2	0
Algona	5,529	10	0	1	0	9	50	15	34	1	0
Altoona	14,830	24	0	1	4	19	533	74	438	21	3
Ames	59,271	78	0	32	7	39	1,454	291	1,132	31	5
Anamosa	5,547	3	0	0	0	3	86	27	57	2	0
Ankeny	46,482	34	0	8	7	19	644	142	483	19	2
Atlantic	7,068	12	0	1	0	11	128	55	68	5	2
Audubon	2,155	4	0	0	0	4	22	7	14	1	0
Bettendorf	33,729	91	0	8	5	78	497	78	405	14	1
Bloomfield	2,658	0	0	0	0	0	6	1	4	1	0
Blue Grass	1,476	0	0	0	0	0	2	1	1	0	0
Boone	12,684	67	0	12	1	54	326	110	213	3	3
Buffalo	1,289	4	0	0	0	4	6	1	5	0	0
Burlington	25,663	174	1	4	18	151	1,037	253	737	47	14
Camanche	4,457	14	0	0	0	14	63	14	44	5	0
Carlisle	3,933	3	0	2	0	1	29	11	18	0	0
Carroll	10,165	8	0	1	1	6	130	24	99	7	0
Carter Lake	3,816	23	0	4	1	18	185	49	105	31	3
Cedar Falls	39,540	47	0	15	4	28	647	104	520	23	1
Cedar Rapids	128,401	356	3	43	97	213	4,723	966	3,503	254	30

Table 8. Offenses Known to Law Enforcement, by Selected State and City, 2012— continued

(Number)

State/city	Population	Violent crime	Murder and nonnegligent manslaughter	Forcible rape	Robbery	Aggravated assault	Property crime	Burglary	Larceny-theft	Motor vehicle theft	Arson[1]
Centerville	5,513	29	0	4	0	25	244	82	153	9	5
Chariton	4,312	26	0	1	1	24	144	31	99	14	1
Charles City	7,573	26	0	4	0	22	154	30	117	7	2
Cherokee	5,272	18	0	2	0	16	59	20	36	3	1
Clarinda	5,610	11	0	1	0	10	162	48	101	13	1
Clarion	2,826	6	0	3	0	3	23	2	21	0	0
Clinton	26,934	171	0	14	20	137	1,211	276	879	56	4
Clive	15,920	27	0	5	1	21	341	49	276	16	6
Coralville	19,294	32	1	4	10	17	533	76	446	11	3
Council Bluffs	62,708	744	1	67	81	595	4,290	970	2,847	473	43
Cresco	3,883	0	0	0	0	0	36	9	25	2	0
Davenport	101,193	604	4	40	151	409	4,088	890	2,912	286	17
Decorah	8,149	6	0	3	0	3	82	3	78	1	0
Denison	8,416	7	0	0	0	7	46	8	35	3	0
Des Moines	207,400	1,094	7	100	250	737	10,210	2,514	6,914	782	51
De Witt	5,331	14	0	2	0	12	61	13	45	3	4
Dubuque[7]	58,460	128	2	20	22	84			1,160	46	32
Eagle Grove	3,553	11	0	0	0	11	28	11	16	1	1
Eldora	2,726	5	0	1	0	4	43	7	33	3	0
Eldridge	5,739	8	0	0	0	8	46	13	32	1	1
Emmetsburg	3,918	7	0	0	0	7	16	10	4	2	1
Estherville	6,263	16	0	2	1	13	111	42	68	1	0
Evansdale	4,787	17	0	3	2	12	102	32	65	5	1
Forest City	4,141	8	0	1	1	6	47	12	34	1	1
Fort Dodge	25,078	134	0	23	18	93	1,167	207	902	58	10
Fort Madison	11,023	60	0	7	2	51	272	98	165	9	3
Glenwood	5,268	23	0	2	1	20	119	43	72	4	0
Grinnell	9,205	26	0	3	1	22	163	42	109	12	6
Grundy Center	2,717	1	0	0	0	1	9	1	7	1	0
Hampton	4,499	6	0	1	0	5	22	9	11	2	0
Hawarden	2,572	2	0	0	0	2	19	3	16	0	0
Hiawatha	7,141	3	0	0	0	3	77	30	46	1	0
Humboldt	4,701	2	0	0	1	1	32	3	26	3	0
Iowa City	69,214	185	1	29	31	124	1,842	387	1,394	61	3
Iowa Falls	5,227	6	0	1	1	4	151	13	137	1	0
Jefferson	4,340	2	0	0	0	2	27	4	21	2	0
Johnston	17,620	18	0	3	0	15	208	34	166	8	0
Keokuk	10,748	111	0	2	3	106	599	114	432	53	11
Le Claire	3,824	8	0	0	0	8	18	2	16	0	1
Le Mars	9,829	6	0	1	0	5	178	41	128	9	3
Leon	1,942	1	0	0	0	1	2	0	2	0	0
Lisbon	2,187	0	0	0	0	0	28	14	13	1	0
Manchester	5,168	19	2	1	1	15	82	14	64	4	0
Maquoketa	6,148	17	0	8	1	8	187	73	110	4	1
Marengo	2,533	4	0	0	0	4	10	2	4	4	0
Marion	35,349	37	0	11	4	22	633	127	484	22	7
Marshalltown	27,883	142	1	0	6	135	910	284	593	33	11
Mason City	28,052	40	2	6	3	29	1,376	344	979	53	6
Mount Pleasant	8,756	14	0	3	0	11	189	34	153	2	5
Mount Vernon	4,567	1	0	0	0	1	76	23	52	1	0
Muscatine	23,013	156	0	27	4	125	808	165	616	27	11
Nevada	6,833	32	0	3	0	29	106	29	72	5	1
New Hampton	3,587	2	0	0	0	2	36	13	23	0	0
Newton	15,189	35	1	0	1	33	524	107	393	24	5
North Liberty	13,661	47	0	1	0	46	87	20	61	6	1
Norwalk	9,079	12	0	1	0	11	103	17	80	6	1
Ogden	2,049	8	1	0	0	7	16	4	11	1	0
Orange City	6,058	6	0	1	1	4	58	19	39	0	1
Osage[7]	3,636	4	0	1	0	3			18	0	1
Osceola	4,985	3	0	1	0	2	101	18	78	5	1
Ottumwa	24,977	70	1	7	17	45	960	263	662	35	17
Perry	8,114	20	0	1	0	19	126	25	99	2	1
Pleasant Hill	8,960	14	0	0	2	12	161	57	93	11	3
Polk City	3,485	0	0	0	0	0	31	6	24	1	0

Table 8. Offenses Known to Law Enforcement, by Selected State and City, 2012— continued

(Number)

State/city	Population	Violent crime	Murder and nonnegligent manslaughter	Forcible rape	Robbery	Aggravated assault	Property crime	Burglary	Larceny-theft	Motor vehicle theft	Arson[1]
Prairie City	1,671	0	0	0	0	0	21	11	10	0	0
Princeton	898	0	0	0	0	0	1	0	1	0	0
Red Oak	5,710	12	0	3	0	9	166	57	103	6	1
Sergeant Bluff	4,256	16	0	1	0	15	94	18	75	1	2
Sioux City	83,289	274	2	30	46	196	3,470	621	2,645	204	17
Spencer	11,224	2	1	0	0	1	252	94	147	11	0
Spirit Lake	4,926	2	0	0	0	2	113	14	98	1	0
State Center	1,487	1	0	0	0	1	7	4	2	1	0
Storm Lake	10,715	48	0	2	0	46	250	57	182	11	2
Story City	3,449	0	0	0	0	0	39	13	24	2	0
Tipton	3,215	4	0	0	0	4	33	0	33	0	1
Toledo	2,342	22	0	1	0	21	23	1	21	1	0
Urbandale	40,467	57	0	3	2	52	688	107	548	33	7
Vinton[7]	5,280	8	0	3	0	5			50	6	0
Walcott	1,654	4	0	1	0	3	12	2	10	0	0
Washington	7,343	53	0	5	1	47	84	27	54	3	0
Waterloo	68,919	470	4	64	69	333	2,514	828	1,590	96	26
Waukee	14,540	9	0	0	0	9	145	33	108	4	1
Waverly	9,914	33	0	2	0	31	139	32	103	4	0
Webster City	8,031	31	0	0	3	28	195	39	140	16	1
West Branch	2,319	0	0	0	0	0	1	0	1	0	0
West Burlington	2,967	11	1	1	2	7	261	27	230	4	0
West Des Moines	58,134	95	0	16	8	71	1,825	213	1,562	50	6
West Union	2,507	3	0	0	0	3	33	14	18	1	1
Wilton	2,818	6	0	1	0	5	41	14	25	2	0
Windsor Heights	4,957	11	0	3	2	6	283	42	239	2	0
Winterset[7]	5,242	6	0	1	0	5			85	5	0
Kansas											
Abilene	6,874	13	0	4	1	8	213	31	178	4	0
Altamont	1,081	1	0	0	0	1	12	5	7	0	0
Andover	11,839	13	0	3	1	9	281	14	254	13	1
Anthony	2,265	5	0	1	0	4	52	9	40	3	0
Arkansas City	12,464	70	0	7	2	61	534	126	385	23	4
Arma	1,492	1	1	0	0	0	22	4	17	1	1
Assaria	418	0	0	0	0	0	0	0	0	0	0
Atchison	10,999	49	0	2	6	41	443	91	333	19	3
Augusta	9,312	25	0	2	1	22	327	61	257	9	1
Baldwin City	4,592	2	0	1	0	1	88	18	69	1	2
Basehor	4,716	1	0	0	1	0	38	5	31	2	2
Baxter Springs	4,216	2	0	0	0	2	117	37	77	3	1
Bel Aire	6,841	3	0	1	0	2	48	18	27	3	1
Belle Plaine	1,665	5	0	0	0	5	13	8	4	1	0
Beloit	3,808	12	0	1	0	11	49	13	34	2	1
Benton	883	0	0	0	0	0	6	0	5	1	0
Bonner Springs	7,384	20	0	2	3	15	275	30	219	26	5
Buhler	1,335	0	0	0	0	0	13	0	11	2	0
Burden	537	0	0	0	0	0	9	3	4	2	0
Burlington	2,668	7	0	0	0	7	31	3	26	2	0
Chanute	9,131	29	0	6	4	19	501	218	273	10	5
Chapman	1,401	0	0	0	0	0	13	3	9	1	0
Chase	478	0	0	0	0	0	0	0	0	0	0
Cheney	2,117	4	0	0	0	4	17	6	11	0	0
Chetopa	1,126	2	0	0	1	1	15	7	6	2	1
Clay Center	4,376	8	0	2	0	6	126	39	83	4	2
Clearwater	2,509	3	0	0	0	3	41	15	26	0	1
Coffeyville	10,189	109	0	7	12	90	532	130	387	15	6
Colby	5,466	12	0	3	2	7	134	24	99	11	0
Columbus	3,295	15	0	0	0	15	72	22	48	2	0
Concordia	5,329	30	0	7	0	23	231	59	166	6	2
Council Grove	2,180	2	0	1	0	1	28	8	19	1	0
Derby	22,393	24	0	2	3	19	522	98	399	25	4
Dodge City	28,064	101	2	20	15	64	1,053	240	777	36	4
Edwardsville	4,382	15	1	2	3	9	96	24	63	9	1

Table 8. Offenses Known to Law Enforcement, by Selected State and City, 2012— continued

(Number)

State/city	Population	Violent crime	Murder and nonnegligent manslaughter	Forcible rape	Robbery	Aggravated assault	Property crime	Burglary	Larceny-theft	Motor vehicle theft	Arson[1]
El Dorado	13,074	57	0	7	3	47	458	127	302	29	2
Ellinwood	2,154	5	0	3	1	1	54	16	35	3	1
Ellsworth	3,129	3	0	1	0	2	56	20	34	2	0
Elwood	1,229	10	0	1	0	9	32	12	15	5	0
Emporia	25,099	57	0	24	7	26	831	132	673	26	1
Eudora	6,249	17	0	3	0	14	79	20	57	2	2
Fairway	3,965	2	0	1	1	0	28	5	22	1	0
Fort Scott	8,031	51	0	5	1	45	344	79	246	19	3
Frontenac	3,463	8	0	2	0	6	75	30	39	6	0
Galena	3,070	17	0	2	1	14	187	56	121	10	0
Garden City	27,017	115	0	10	9	96	764	85	655	24	13
Gardner	19,532	35	0	5	2	28	343	68	258	17	4
Garnett	3,419	8	0	0	0	8	109	26	80	3	2
Girard	2,810	6	0	1	0	5	51	9	41	1	1
Goddard	4,389	3	0	0	1	2	94	20	72	2	1
Grandview Plaza	1,611	7	0	1	0	6	41	7	29	5	1
Great Bend	16,174	95	0	6	6	83	725	140	553	32	3
Halstead	2,106	3	0	0	0	3	41	20	21	0	1
Haven	1,247	1	0	1	0	0	18	4	11	3	0
Hays	20,823	98	0	6	6	86	621	66	521	34	3
Haysville	10,939	43	0	14	2	27	293	66	213	14	4
Herington	2,538	3	0	0	0	3	50	17	28	5	0
Hesston	3,744	4	0	0	1	3	66	13	51	2	0
Hiawatha	3,197	1	0	0	0	1	97	8	86	3	0
Hoisington	2,737	5	0	0	0	5	62	20	38	4	1
Holcomb	2,123	0	0	0	0	0	42	9	33	0	0
Holton	3,339	5	0	0	0	5	101	16	81	4	0
Horton	1,789	6	0	2	0	4	43	14	27	2	0
Hugoton	3,849	2	0	0	0	2	13	1	11	1	0
Hutchinson	42,357	262	1	26	24	211	2,519	502	1,893	124	21
Inman	1,387	1	0	0	0	1	16	4	12	0	0
Iola	5,716	28	0	5	1	22	296	41	250	5	1
Junction City	24,138	162	1	9	13	139	621	150	446	25	5
Kansas City	147,201	877	15	85	277	500	7,538	1,772	4,558	1,208	69
Kingman	3,192	10	0	0	0	10	51	16	32	3	0
Kiowa	1,036	1	0	1	0	0	7	2	3	2	1
La Cygne	1,150	2	0	0	0	2	3	1	1	1	0
Lansing	11,443	21	0	2	2	17	68	28	38	2	1
Larned	4,101	22	0	5	0	17	112	30	78	4	1
Lawrence	89,180	370	0	52	53	265	3,997	604	3,190	203	26
Leavenworth	35,857	248	0	15	30	203	1,163	242	845	76	9
Leawood	32,554	18	1	4	5	8	460	81	370	9	0
Lebo	937	0	0	0	0	0	0	0	0	0	0
Lenexa	49,222	58	1	9	5	43	944	93	753	98	14
Liberal	20,968	67	0	8	7	52	576	153	405	18	0
Lindsborg	3,483	4	0	1	1	2	56	13	43	0	1
Louisburg	4,327	0	0	0	0	0	48	9	38	1	0
Maize	3,455	13	0	0	0	13	69	10	58	1	0
Marion	1,918	3	0	0	0	3	21	10	11	0	0
Marysville	3,278	9	0	1	0	8	75	14	58	3	0
McPherson	13,249	32	1	5	1	25	590	256	316	18	2
Merriam	11,237	55	2	8	12	33	563	59	426	78	0
Minneapolis	2,052	2	0	1	1	0	38	6	29	3	0
Mission	9,523	22	1	4	6	11	347	42	264	41	0
Mission Hills	3,572	1	0	0	1	0	25	6	18	1	0
Moran	560	0	0	0	0	0	0	0	0	0	0
Mulvane	6,158	8	0	0	2	6	125	19	96	10	0
Neodesha	2,470	6	0	1	0	5	61	11	49	1	1
Newton	19,328	108	0	7	4	97	672	140	505	27	2
North Newton	1,774	0	0	0	0	0	17	4	13	0	0
Norton	2,923	4	0	2	0	2	60	11	46	3	0
Olathe	128,560	191	0	38	24	129	2,480	315	1,988	177	16
Onaga	717	0	0	0	0	0	2	1	1	0	0
Osage City	2,960	11	0	0	0	11	94	18	73	3	2

Table 8. Offenses Known to Law Enforcement, by Selected State and City, 2012— continued

(Number)

State/city	Population	Violent crime	Murder and nonnegligent manslaughter	Forcible rape	Robbery	Aggravated assault	Property crime	Burglary	Larceny-theft	Motor vehicle theft	Arson[1]
Osawatomie	4,460	24	0	8	0	16	126	13	105	8	0
Oswego	1,830	1	0	0	0	1	30	9	16	5	0
Ottawa	12,684	37	0	9	2	26	304	52	244	8	5
Overland Park	177,085	285	2	40	42	201	4,079	517	3,238	324	27
Paola	5,619	13	0	3	0	10	235	31	197	7	2
Park City	7,373	13	0	1	4	8	263	105	143	15	1
Parsons	10,507	62	0	6	4	52	464	111	343	10	4
Prairie Village	21,906	13	0	3	3	7	243	50	179	14	2
Pratt	6,885	25	0	2	1	22	215	43	157	15	1
Rose Hill	3,948	4	0	1	0	3	62	3	58	1	1
Rossville	1,163	4	0	0	0	4	5	1	2	2	0
Russell	4,520	18	0	1	0	17	87	26	52	9	1
Sabetha	2,568	5	0	1	0	4	31	10	17	4	0
Salina	48,155	161	1	19	23	118	2,353	445	1,801	107	23
Scott City	3,815	12	0	2	0	10	49	10	36	3	0
Sedgwick	1,712	1	0	1	0	0	8	3	4	1	0
Shawnee	63,542	85	0	11	12	62	1,060	152	769	139	11
South Hutchinson	2,474	6	1	0	0	5	95	20	73	2	0
Spring Hill	5,511	10	0	0	1	9	77	18	57	2	1
Stafford	1,032	3	0	1	0	2	9	3	6	0	0
Sterling	2,338	2	0	0	0	2	27	10	17	0	1
St. Marys	2,678	4	0	0	0	4	30	15	14	1	1
Tonganoxie	5,091	11	0	2	0	9	114	51	57	6	0
Topeka	128,843	772	15	39	237	481	6,841	1,277	4,967	597	7
Udall	749	1	0	0	0	1	7	3	3	1	0
Ulysses	6,299	21	0	0	1	20	93	36	52	5	2
Valley Center	6,896	8	0	1	0	7	138	40	90	8	3
Wa Keeney	1,827	2	0	1	0	1	18	2	15	1	1
Wathena	1,374	6	0	0	0	6	29	9	18	2	0
Waverly	590	1	0	0	0	1	2	2	0	0	0
Wellington	8,098	27	0	7	1	19	428	85	332	11	1
Wellsville	1,862	3	0	1	1	1	32	12	19	1	0
Westwood	1,539	0	0	0	0	0	39	10	26	3	0
Wichita	386,409	2,869	23	228	495	2,123	21,070	3,919	15,331	1,820	134
Yates Center	1,417	4	0	0	0	4	19	6	13	0	0
Kentucky											
Alexandria	8,557	3	0	2	0	1	197	26	161	10	0
Anchorage	2,372	1	0	0	0	1	35	5	30	0	0
Ashland	21,707	56	0	4	30	22	1,298	274	992	32	4
Auburn	1,340	1	0	0	0	1	12	3	8	1	2
Audubon Park	1,490	1	0	0	0	1	69	20	46	3	0
Augusta	1,197	1	0	1	0	0	28	7	21	0	1
Barbourville	3,178	3	0	0	1	2	45	11	31	3	0
Bardstown	11,869	22	0	6	8	8	469	125	319	25	1
Bardwell	717	0	0	0	0	0	2	1	1	0	0
Beattyville	1,299	2	0	1	0	1	9	3	6	0	0
Beaver Dam	3,454	1	0	0	0	1	52	8	44	0	0
Bellevue	6,011	12	0	1	5	6	234	62	161	11	2
Benham	498	0	0	0	0	0	0	0	0	0	0
Benton	4,341	5	0	1	1	3	105	22	80	3	0
Berea	13,798	16	0	1	4	11	444	149	267	28	1
Bloomfield	852	0	0	0	0	0	2	2	0	0	0
Bowling Green	59,043	189	4	36	75	74	3,025	547	2,322	156	5
Brandenburg	2,733	4	0	0	1	3	26	3	21	2	0
Brownsville	833	2	0	0	0	2	5	4	1	0	0
Burkesville	1,520	0	0	0	0	0	6	3	2	1	0
Burnside	620	3	1	1	0	1	31	5	23	3	0
Cadiz	2,557	9	0	1	2	6	103	21	78	4	0
Calvert City	2,561	4	0	3	0	1	31	7	22	2	0
Campbellsville	9,209	26	3	0	15	8	314	84	224	6	2
Carlisle	1,999	2	0	0	1	1	21	8	11	2	0
Carrollton	4,021	7	1	2	0	4	81	31	46	4	2
Catlettsburg	1,859	3	0	1	0	2	45	14	30	1	0

Table 8. Offenses Known to Law Enforcement, by Selected State and City, 2012— continued

(Number)

State/city	Population	Violent crime	Murder and nonnegligent manslaughter	Forcible rape	Robbery	Aggravated assault	Property crime	Burglary	Larceny-theft	Motor vehicle theft	Arson[1]
Cave City	2,252	5	0	1	0	4	48	19	24	5	0
Centertown	429	0	0	0	0	0	1	0	1	0	0
Central City	5,955	3	0	0	0	3	86	5	76	5	0
Clarkson	883	0	0	0	0	0	1	0	1	0	0
Clay City	1,082	0	0	0	0	0	11	6	5	0	0
Clinton	1,361	0	0	0	0	0	5	1	4	0	0
Cloverport	1,168	0	0	0	0	0	0	0	0	0	0
Coal Run Village	1,707	1	0	0	1	0	53	9	42	2	1
Cold Spring	5,968	2	0	0	2	0	208	13	192	3	0
Columbia	4,468	4	0	1	3	0	47	20	24	3	0
Corbin	7,351	16	1	3	7	5	301	87	206	8	4
Cumberland	2,226	4	0	2	0	2	29	16	11	2	0
Cynthiana	6,396	16	0	2	6	8	372	60	297	15	1
Danville	16,314	48	2	6	21	19	594	139	442	13	3
Dawson Springs	2,769	2	0	0	0	2	31	11	17	3	1
Dayton	5,388	17	0	4	6	7	297	108	176	13	2
Dry Ridge	2,210	0	0	0	0	0	12	0	11	1	0
Earlington	1,416	0	0	0	0	0	1	0	0	1	0
Eddyville	2,559	0	0	0	0	0	51	5	45	1	0
Edgewood	8,633	3	0	1	0	2	129	10	109	10	0
Edmonton	1,595	0	0	0	0	0	6	2	4	0	0
Elizabethtown	29,118	37	1	9	9	18	1,083	133	911	39	11
Elkton	2,067	3	0	1	0	2	38	18	16	4	0
Elsmere	8,509	25	0	4	8	13	211	60	141	10	0
Eminence	2,508	1	0	0	0	1	43	10	33	0	0
Erlanger	22,034	26	1	6	11	8	600	88	481	31	1
Evarts	959	1	0	0	0	1	16	9	7	0	1
Falmouth	2,152	4	0	0	3	1	57	23	33	1	0
Ferguson	934	0	0	0	0	0	2	0	2	0	0
Flatwoods	7,431	2	0	0	1	1	53	31	18	4	1
Flemingsburg	2,693	1	0	0	0	1	55	11	42	2	1
Florence	30,765	89	0	15	48	26	1,629	191	1,369	69	8
Fort Mitchell	8,264	3	0	0	2	1	180	38	137	5	0
Fort Thomas	16,478	2	0	1	1	0	196	43	145	8	1
Fort Wright	5,764	9	0	0	8	1	332	29	295	8	1
Frankfort3	25,648	132	1	13	63	55	1,267	334	875	58	6
Franklin	8,453	22	1	5	10	6	333	86	236	11	1
Fulton	2,428	7	0	2	4	1	106	22	82	2	1
Gamaliel	377	0	0	0	0	0	0	0	0	0	0
Georgetown[3]	29,765	171	0	21	29	121	1,089	213	829	47	0
Glasgow	14,095	26	0	10	5	11	313	68	234	11	3
Graymoor-Devondale	2,897	2	0	0	1	1	35	12	22	1	0
Grayson	4,210	6	0	0	2	4	65	24	36	5	0
Greensburg	2,162	2	0	1	0	1	53	9	41	3	0
Greenup	1,190	0	0	0	0	0	2	0	1	1	0
Greenville	4,294	0	0	0	0	0	16	5	10	1	0
Guthrie	1,423	2	0	0	1	1	13	3	9	1	0
Hardinsburg	2,369	2	0	2	0	0	7	3	3	1	1
Harlan	1,735	7	0	0	2	5	77	11	64	2	0
Harrodsburg	8,342	12	0	1	5	6	179	70	94	15	1
Hartford	2,707	4	0	2	0	2	10	4	4	2	1
Hawesville	947	0	0	0	0	0	0	0	0	0	0
Hazard	4,474	19	0	2	7	10	314	59	251	4	2
Henderson	28,926	73	0	16	34	23	841	142	651	48	1
Heritage Creek	1,087	0	0	0	0	0	5	2	2	1	0
Highland Heights[3]	6,978	1	1	0	0	0	75	18	52	5	1
Hillview	8,279	7	0	1	3	3	215	63	145	7	0
Hodgenville	3,239	2	0	0	1	1	13	5	4	4	0
Hopkinsville	31,499	134	2	14	56	62	1,383	391	936	56	7
Horse Cave	2,321	1	0	0	0	1	6	4	2	0	0
Hurstbourne Acres	1,831	0	0	0	0	0	5	3	2	0	0
Independence	24,927	19	0	5	6	8	302	79	204	19	2
Indian Hills	2,898	2	0	0	2	0	36	16	20	0	0
Inez	708	0	0	0	0	0	2	0	2	0	0

Table 8. Offenses Known to Law Enforcement, by Selected State and City, 2012— continued

(Number)

State/city	Population	Violent crime	Murder and nonnegligent manslaughter	Forcible rape	Robbery	Aggravated assault	Property crime	Burglary	Larceny-theft	Motor vehicle theft	Arson[1]
Irvine	2,720	0	0	0	0	0	18	6	9	3	0
Irvington	1,195	0	0	0	0	0	3	3	0	0	0
Jackson	2,231	2	0	0	1	1	55	21	32	2	0
Jamestown	1,804	0	0	0	0	0	13	1	11	1	0
Jeffersontown	26,874	39	0	4	27	8	592	169	386	37	0
Jenkins	2,203	0	0	0	0	0	1	0	1	0	0
La Center	1,012	0	0	0	0	0	4	0	4	0	0
La Grange	8,149	5	0	1	3	1	137	27	103	7	2
Lakeside Park-Crestview Hills	5,856	1	0	1	0	0	143	15	121	7	0
Lancaster	3,445	5	0	0	1	4	97	43	53	1	2
Lawrenceburg	10,642	4	0	0	1	3	96	26	64	6	0
Lebanon	5,601	12	0	4	0	8	171	55	108	8	0
Lebanon Junction	1,837	0	0	0	0	0	34	11	18	5	1
Leitchfield	6,766	8	0	3	0	5	165	34	124	7	2
Lewisburg	811	0	0	0	0	0	2	1	1	0	0
Lewisport	1,677	1	0	0	0	1	6	0	6	0	0
Lexington[3]	302,332	1,066	12	102	606	346	13,399	2,854	9,641	904	60
Liberty	2,168	1	0	0	1	0	5	2	3	0	0
London	8,078	13	1	0	8	4	393	54	320	19	0
Louisa	2,500	1	0	0	0	1	46	14	32	0	0
Louisville Metro	666,200	3,989	62	183	1,394	2,350	28,606	7,008	19,411	2,187	223
Loyall	1,454	0	0	0	0	0	12	2	10	0	0
Ludlow	4,438	5	0	3	1	1	224	84	125	15	1
Lynnview	923	0	0	0	0	0	5	4	1	0	0
Madisonville	19,637	35	0	13	9	13	602	110	468	24	2
Manchester	1,261	4	0	0	1	3	49	7	38	4	0
Marion	3,053	2	0	0	1	1	75	17	57	1	0
Martin	631	2	0	0	2	0	19	5	11	3	0
Mayfield	10,155	17	0	1	3	13	163	56	98	9	1
Maysville	9,117	16	0	3	5	8	411	72	327	12	2
Meadow Vale	745	0	0	0	0	0	6	1	5	0	0
Middlesboro	10,358	23	0	0	17	6	785	86	673	26	1
Monticello	6,240	9	1	0	4	4	181	60	115	6	0
Morehead	6,914	4	0	2	1	1	134	19	108	7	0
Morganfield	3,308	0	0	0	0	0	44	9	35	0	1
Morgantown	2,425	2	0	0	1	1	41	10	27	4	0
Mortons Gap	865	0	0	0	0	0	4	1	3	0	0
Mount Sterling	6,977	21	0	2	11	8	440	71	353	16	2
Mount Vernon	2,486	2	0	0	1	1	52	27	23	2	1
Mount Washington	9,237	6	0	2	2	2	189	76	108	5	0
Muldraugh	981	2	0	0	1	1	17	9	7	1	0
Munfordville	1,621	0	0	0	0	0	12	3	9	0	0
Murray	17,938	30	2	3	6	19	623	161	441	21	3
Newport	15,412	85	1	13	50	21	1,265	273	931	61	12
Nicholasville	28,366	63	0	15	28	20	1,322	357	932	33	3
Northfield	1,030	0	0	0	0	0	7	0	7	0	0
Oak Grove	7,469	20	1	4	7	8	285	78	186	21	3
Olive Hill	1,596	0	0	0	0	0	50	15	34	1	0
Owensboro	57,751	125	0	28	45	52	2,518	469	1,928	121	12
Owenton	1,332	0	0	0	0	0	27	10	15	2	0
Owingsville	1,554	1	0	0	0	1	20	4	16	0	0
Paducah	25,199	78	2	14	40	22	1,280	143	1,091	46	6
Paintsville	3,473	3	0	0	2	1	89	12	71	6	0
Paris	8,580	19	1	3	5	10	341	95	224	22	2
Park Hills	2,991	2	0	0	1	1	89	38	46	5	1
Pewee Valley	1,467	0	0	0	0	0	4	1	2	1	0
Pikeville	6,909	9	1	1	2	5	439	46	385	8	1
Pineville	1,884	1	0	0	0	1	63	11	52	0	2
Pioneer Village	2,057	0	0	0	0	0	7	2	5	0	0
Powderly	741	0	0	0	0	0	14	1	12	1	0
Prestonsburg	3,246	4	0	0	1	3	72	13	57	2	0
Princeton	6,339	16	0	4	3	9	145	49	87	9	1
Prospect	4,747	1	0	0	1	0	11	3	7	1	0

Table 8. Offenses Known to Law Enforcement, by Selected State and City, 2012— continued

(Number)

State/city	Population	Violent crime	Murder and nonnegligent manslaughter	Forcible rape	Robbery	Aggravated assault	Property crime	Burglary	Larceny-theft	Motor vehicle theft	Arson[1]
Providence	3,213	2	0	0	0	2	28	13	15	0	0
Raceland	2,426	3	0	0	0	3	35	7	27	1	0
Radcliff	22,148	51	0	13	27	11	621	153	457	11	2
Ravenna	606	0	0	0	0	0	14	0	0	0	0
Richmond	31,890	87	0	8	50	29	1,721	377	1,290	54	6
Russell	3,385	2	0	1	1	0	68	10	58	0	1
Russell Springs	2,453	4	0	0	2	2	64	12	49	3	0
Russellville	6,968	18	0	4	2	12	269	65	199	5	1
Sadieville	309	0	0	0	0	0	1	0	1	0	0
Salyersville	1,870	0	0	0	0	0	4	3	1	0	0
Science Hill	702	0	0	0	0	0	7	3	4	0	0
Scottsville	4,275	1	0	0	1	0	25	15	10	0	0
Shelbyville	14,425	37	1	3	16	17	353	135	204	14	1
Shepherdsville	11,372	24	0	3	11	10	349	104	223	22	2
Shively	15,422	84	6	7	55	16	658	221	382	55	0
Silver Grove	1,112	1	0	0	1	0	42	13	28	1	0
Simpsonville	2,550	0	0	0	0	0	14	6	8	0	0
Smiths Grove	728	0	0	0	0	0	6	2	4	0	0
Somerset	11,325	36	0	9	15	12	621	86	517	18	5
South Shore	1,124	0	0	0	0	0	1	1	0	0	0
Springfield	2,554	3	0	0	1	2	28	14	9	5	1
Stamping Ground	659	0	0	0	0	0	5	1	4	0	0
Stanford	3,498	1	0	0	0	1	79	13	64	2	0
Stanton	2,748	2	0	0	0	2	46	19	26	1	0
St. Matthews	17,651	40	0	4	30	6	713	127	565	21	1
Strathmoor Village	656	0	0	0	0	0	4	2	2	0	0
Sturgis	1,911	0	0	0	0	0	5	3	2	0	0
Taylor Mill	6,650	8	0	0	3	5	99	32	57	10	0
Taylorsville	780	2	0	2	0	0	34	9	24	1	0
Tompkinsville	2,402	0	0	0	0	0	4	2	2	0	0
Trenton	385	0	0	0	0	0	0	0	0	0	0
Uniontown	1,009	0	0	0	0	0	18	5	12	1	0
Vanceburg	1,530	1	0	0	0	1	12	7	5	0	0
Versailles	8,593	29	0	9	6	14	688	167	495	26	5
Villa Hills	7,540	0	0	0	0	0	42	4	33	5	0
Vine Grove	4,616	5	0	1	2	2	65	12	51	2	0
Warsaw	1,623	1	0	0	0	1	20	11	6	3	0
West Liberty	3,444	1	0	0	0	1	24	4	16	4	0
West Point	813	0	0	0	0	0	28	8	20	0	0
Wheelwright	775	0	0	0	0	0	0	0	0	0	0
Whitesburg	2,135	0	0	0	0	0	1	1	0	0	0
Wilder	3,064	4	0	1	1	2	77	12	61	4	0
Williamsburg	5,281	5	0	0	0	5	124	41	78	5	2
Williamstown	3,957	2	0	0	0	2	88	26	60	2	0
Wilmore	3,720	1	0	0	0	1	111	33	76	2	0
Winchester[3]	18,374	53	4	8	15	26	973	168	769	36	5
Worthington	1,612	0	0	0	0	0	9	4	4	1	0
Louisiana											
Abbeville	12,389	118	6	3	19	90	541	191	332	18	
Addis	3,666	4	1	0	0	3	6	0	6	0	0
Alexandria	48,449	815	9	14	142	650	3,630	974	2,472	184	
Baker	14,017	11	0	1	6	4	374	81	288	5	
Bastrop	11,280	170	0	3	33	134	1,105	304	751	50	6
Baton Rouge	231,500	2,507	66	64	1,033	1,344	12,059	3,826	7,751	482	187
Berwick	4,934	3	0	0	0	3	65	14	47	4	0
Blanchard	2,939	0	0	0	0	0	30	7	20	3	0
Bogalusa	12,296	122	4	10	32	76	709	250	425	34	2
Bossier City	63,116	236	2	19	52	163	2,435	417	1,949	69	
Breaux Bridge	8,301	17	1	0	1	15	225	32	190	3	
Broussard	8,351	24	1	1	3	19	301	115	171	15	
Brusly	2,640	0	0	0	0	0	3	1	2	0	0
Bunkie	4,177	77	0	1	8	68	214	97	110	7	0
Carencro	7,668	57	1	1	10	45	301	93	199	9	0

Table 8. Offenses Known to Law Enforcement, by Selected State and City, 2012— continued

(Number)

State/city	Population	Violent crime	Murder and nonnegligent manslaughter	Forcible rape	Robbery	Aggravated assault	Property crime	Burglary	Larceny-theft	Motor vehicle theft	Arson[1]
Clarence	501	0	0	0	0	0	0	0	0	0	0
Clinton	1,651	3	1	0	0	2	8	3	5	0	0
Coushatta	1,934	14	0	0	1	13	50	9	41	0	0
Covington	8,933	44	0	2	5	37	469	100	359	10	0
Denham Springs	10,451	76	0	3	26	47	913	125	770	18	0
De Quincy	3,277	0	0	0	0	0	31	6	21	4	
De Ridder	10,774	69	0	3	2	64	200	45	155	0	0
Epps	857	0	0	0	0	0	0	0	0	0	0
Erath	2,136	16	0	0	5	11	17	2	15	0	0
Eunice	10,481	116	1	7	7	101	594	201	379	14	0
Farmerville	3,884	22	0	0	2	20	235	65	164	6	0
Ferriday	3,540	29	0	2	2	25	123	62	59	2	0
Florien	645	0	0	0	0	0	0	0	0	0	0
Folsom	729	0	0	0	0	0	21	4	15	2	0
Franklin	7,645	73	0	1	9	63	413	108	304	1	
Franklinton	3,877	19	0	2	1	16	156	39	114	3	0
French Settlement	1,142	4	0	0	0	4	15	6	9	0	0
Georgetown	325	0	0	0	0	0	0	0	0	0	0
Glenmora	1,358	3	0	0	0	3	16	7	9	0	
Golden Meadow	2,121	2	0	1	0	1	2	1	1	0	0
Gonzales[5]	10,095		0	2	11		727	72	650	5	
Grambling	4,987	18	0	0	1	17	86	83	2	1	
Gramercy	3,581	16	0	2	1	13	79	10	66	3	0
Greenwood	3,264	19	0	0	1	18	61	17	39	5	0
Gretna	17,844	76	0	3	21	52	585	99	433	53	3
Hammond	20,355	332	4	15	103	210	2,440	993	1,446	1	0
Harahan	9,334	14	1	1	3	9	119	27	86	6	2
Haughton	3,557	3	0	0	0	3	3	1	2	0	0
Houma	33,945	210	2	7	59	142	1,768	281	1,423	64	5
Independence	1,695	20	0	1	4	15	100	29	62	9	0
Iowa	3,035	65	1	0	5	59	61	7	47	7	2
Jeanerette	5,575	9	0	0	0	9	120	21	92	7	0
Jena	3,439	7	0	0	0	7	0	0	0	0	0
Jennings[5]	10,477		0	1	9		305	55	250	0	
Jonesville	2,258	21	0	0	2	19	62	16	45	1	0
Kaplan	4,649	7	0	3	1	3	93	17	76	0	
Kenner	67,110	139	2	12	61	64	2,509	387	1,973	149	6
Kentwood	2,238	7	0	1	3	3	154	36	115	3	0
Kinder	2,491	6	0	0	0	6	85	0	79	6	
Lafayette	122,852	779	11	11	202	555	6,815	1,330	5,244	241	32
Lake Arthur	2,762	4	0	1	1	2	24	8	16	0	
Lake Providence	3,937	31	0	0	3	28	57	25	32	0	0
Leesville	6,623	30	0	3	1	26	285	8	274	3	0
Livonia	1,443	3	0	0	0	3	6	2	4	0	0
Lutcher	3,529	14	0	0	1	13	36	7	29	0	0
Mamou	3,253	4	0	1	3	0	102	20	82	0	
Mandeville	11,777	26	0	5	2	19	342	52	282	8	1
Mansfield	5,059	80	1	4	10	65	313	79	228	6	0
Many	2,901	28	0	1	3	24	189	30	158	1	0
Marion	770	7	0	1	0	6	29	8	21	0	0
Marksville	5,715	89	1	2	5	81	447	105	327	15	
Monroe	49,474	490	5	18	137	330	3,775	1,172	2,525	78	0
Moreauville	930	3	0	0	0	3	8	0	8	0	0
Morgan City	12,376	46	0	7	11	28	387	66	311	10	
Napoleonville	657	0	0	0	0	0	0	0	0	0	0
Natchitoches	18,378	157	1	6	19	131	1,108	384	713	11	4
New Orleans	362,874	2,958	193	136	1,065	1,564	13,689	3,423	8,051	2,215	
Norwood	321	0	0	0	0	0	0	0	0	0	0
Oil City	1,023	0	0	0	0	0	8	4	3	1	0
Opelousas	16,767	280	6	15	50	209	1,234	334	864	36	3
Patterson	6,099	19	1	0	1	17	24	1	23	0	0
Pearl River	2,553	11	0	1	0	10	80	18	54	8	0
Pineville	14,721	126	0	6	13	107	810	161	631	18	
Plaquemine[5]	7,122		0	2	5		464	51	409	4	

Table 8. Offenses Known to Law Enforcement, by Selected State and City, 2012— continued

(Number)

State/city	Population	Violent crime	Murder and nonnegligent manslaughter	Forcible rape	Robbery	Aggravated assault	Property crime	Burglary	Larceny-theft	Motor vehicle theft	Arson[1]
Pollock	469	2	0	1	0	1	9	3	6	0	0
Ponchatoula	6,680	72	0	2	17	53	510	189	312	9	0
Port Allen[5]	5,281		0	0	1			6		1	
Port Vincent	757	6	0	0	0	6	17	4	11	2	0
Ruston	22,046	106	2	5	26	73	869	200	654	15	0
Scott	8,776	21	0	1	2	18	222	30	177	15	0
Shreveport	202,164	1,550	17	92	433	1,008	9,862	2,425	6,973	464	79
Slidell	27,581	106	2	13	17	74	1,633	178	1,414	41	0
Springhill	5,310	13	1	0	1	11	97	5	90	2	
St. Francisville	1,746	12	0	1	0	11	57	14	43	0	1
St. Gabriel	6,700	26	0	1	3	22	99	45	51	3	0
St. Martinville	6,236	43	0	0	1	42	119	32	84	3	0
Stonewall	1,836	3	0	0	0	3	14	3	10	1	0
Sulphur	20,671	159	0	7	19	133	983	271	693	19	2
Thibodaux	14,701	65	1	1	13	50	581	74	498	9	1
Tickfaw	707	5	0	0	0	5	30	4	25	1	0
Vidalia	4,336	30	0	0	1	29	105	18	87	0	0
Vinton	3,254	0	0	0	0	0	75	25	50	0	
Walker	6,279	44	0	0	9	35	389	54	322	13	0
West Monroe	13,250	47	0	3	9	35	1,040	155	868	17	3
Westwego	8,586	34	1	5	4	24	170	43	121	6	0
Wilson	593	0	0	0	0	0	0	0	0	0	0
Winnfield	4,787	45	1	0	8	36	205	71	129	5	1
Zachary	15,092	37	0	4	0	33	403	26	368	9	0
Zwolle	1,791	18	0	1	3	14	85	43	42	0	0
Maine											
Ashland	1,296	1	0	0	0	1	15	8	7	0	0
Auburn	23,002	47	0	15	18	14	1,123	179	913	31	4
Augusta	19,117	88	1	16	27	44	1,186	241	914	31	12
Baileyville	1,511	4	0	0	0	4	30	18	6	6	2
Bangor	33,036	76	6	7	40	23	1,842	253	1,543	46	3
Bar Harbor	5,253	1	0	0	0	1	89	28	61	0	0
Bath	8,499	10	0	2	3	5	285	21	260	4	1
Belfast	6,665	0	0	0	0	0	205	58	138	9	0
Berwick	7,291	7	0	0	3	4	149	31	108	10	7
Biddeford	21,402	95	2	5	13	75	1,208	189	995	24	3
Boothbay Harbor	2,153	1	0	0	0	1	58	19	39	0	3
Brewer	9,481	6	0	1	2	3	285	26	254	5	1
Bridgton	5,228	3	0	0	0	3	74	15	56	3	0
Brownville	1,243	0	0	0	0	0	5	1	4	0	0
Brunswick	20,343	20	0	6	3	11	595	99	470	26	4
Bucksport	4,945	17	0	1	2	14	131	53	74	4	1
Buxton	8,083	3	0	1	0	2	104	32	70	2	0
Calais	3,105	7	0	3	1	3	172	55	117	0	1
Camden	4,850	4	0	1	2	1	86	7	71	8	0
Cape Elizabeth	9,045	2	0	1	1	0	115	33	77	5	1
Caribou	8,150	5	0	0	1	4	164	26	134	4	0
Carrabassett Valley	779	1	0	0	0	1	40	5	35	0	0
Clinton	3,483	3	0	0	0	3	41	17	23	1	1
Cumberland	7,236	2	0	0	0	2	38	10	25	3	0
Damariscotta	2,206	3	0	0	0	3	38	3	35	0	0
Dexter	3,894	1	0	0	0	1	118	33	80	5	0
Dixfield	2,547	4	0	2	0	2	73	23	44	6	0
Dover-Foxcroft	4,189	16	0	1	0	15	99	23	74	2	1
East Millinocket	3,071	1	0	1	0	0	42	12	29	1	0
Eastport	1,323	1	0	0	0	1	17	9	8	0	0
Eliot	6,243	0	0	0	0	0	29	7	21	1	1
Ellsworth	7,770	7	0	1	3	3	247	30	214	3	0
Fairfield	6,714	8	1	0	2	5	261	44	212	5	1
Falmouth	11,221	3	0	0	0	3	167	26	141	0	0
Farmington	7,765	9	0	2	2	5	194	28	162	4	0
Fort Fairfield	3,480	7	0	1	0	6	46	5	37	4	0
Fort Kent	4,078	1	0	0	0	1	14	1	13	0	0

Table 8. Offenses Known to Law Enforcement, by Selected State and City, 2012— continued

(Number)

State/city	Population	Violent crime	Murder and nonnegligent manslaughter	Forcible rape	Robbery	Aggravated assault	Property crime	Burglary	Larceny-theft	Motor vehicle theft	Arson[1]
Freeport	7,906	8	0	0	1	7	177	24	152	1	0
Fryeburg	3,442	2	0	0	1	1	48	13	33	2	2
Gardiner	5,793	10	0	5	2	3	172	30	140	2	1
Gorham	16,432	22	0	4	7	11	212	46	156	10	8
Gouldsboro	1,743	0	0	0	0	0	17	4	12	1	0
Greenville	1,636	6	0	0	0	6	39	13	24	2	0
Hallowell	2,379	0	0	0	0	0	91	16	72	3	0
Hampden	7,254	3	1	1	0	1	101	32	67	2	1
Holden	3,076	2	0	0	1	1	82	19	63	0	0
Houlton	6,095	10	0	3	3	4	152	24	124	4	0
Islesboro	565	0	0	0	0	0	8	7	0	1	0
Jay	4,848	8	0	3	0	5	162	40	116	6	1
Kennebunk	10,864	10	0	7	0	3	155	43	111	1	0
Kennebunkport	3,496	1	0	0	0	1	48	8	40	0	0
Kittery	9,548	10	0	1	3	6	172	15	157	0	0
Lewiston	36,519	80	0	15	43	22	1,387	328	1,018	41	10
Limestone	2,306	2	0	1	0	1	23	7	16	0	0
Lincoln	5,084	4	0	1	1	2	240	50	183	7	0
Lincolnville	2,164	0	0	0	0	0	28	6	22	0	0
Lisbon	8,993	9	0	5	1	3	162	53	101	8	1
Livermore Falls	3,180	1	0	1	0	0	111	19	89	3	0
Machias	2,209	1	0	0	0	1	51	13	38	0	0
Madawaska	4,017	1	0	0	1	0	41	4	35	2	0
Madison[3]	4,840	1	0	1	0	0	121	36	81	4	0
Mechanic Falls	3,025	2	0	0	0	2	44	11	31	2	0
Mexico	2,677	7	0	5	0	2	189	45	138	6	0
Milbridge	1,344	0	0	0	0	0	0	0	0	0	0
Millinocket	4,502	2	0	0	0	2	90	22	64	4	0
Milo	2,327	9	0	1	0	8	49	11	36	2	1
Monmouth	4,096	1	0	0	0	1	60	18	38	4	1
Mount Desert	2,061	0	0	0	0	0	47	5	40	2	0
Newport	3,275	2	0	0	2	0	92	20	72	0	0
North Berwick	4,607	3	0	0	1	2	46	20	22	4	0
Norway	5,006	4	0	1	0	3	156	43	110	3	2
Oakland	6,233	8	0	5	0	3	137	22	108	7	0
Ogunquit	898	0	0	0	0	0	56	18	37	1	0
Old Orchard Beach	8,678	17	2	9	3	3	292	80	206	6	6
Old Town	7,839	7	0	1	3	3	262	42	210	10	2
Orono	10,364	3	0	0	2	1	205	27	175	3	1
Oxford	4,103	7	0	6	0	1	192	20	170	2	0
Paris	5,175	5	0	4	1	0	78	18	57	3	0
Phippsburg	2,212	0	0	0	0	0	31	7	24	0	0
Pittsfield	4,202	4	0	1	3	0	84	12	69	3	0
Portland	66,413	173	1	33	82	57	2,632	411	2,139	82	10
Presque Isle	9,648	11	0	6	2	3	354	53	299	2	0
Rangeley	1,175	0	0	0	0	0	13	3	9	1	0
Richmond	3,406	0	0	0	0	0	50	8	41	1	0
Rockland	7,297	10	0	2	3	5	314	23	282	9	4
Rockport	3,331	1	0	0	0	1	33	7	25	1	0
Rumford	5,831	8	0	5	0	3	228	61	165	2	2
Sabattus	4,866	3	0	0	1	2	65	21	42	2	1
Saco	18,595	24	1	4	10	9	471	93	365	13	3
Sanford	20,925	64	0	26	16	22	794	144	618	32	12
Scarborough	18,982	10	0	6	4	0	500	65	425	10	1
Searsport	2,614	1	0	0	1	0	55	7	44	4	0
Skowhegan	8,562	25	0	14	5	6	539	105	419	15	6
South Berwick	7,265	5	0	3	0	2	57	17	39	1	0
South Portland	25,087	49	0	3	11	35	966	108	847	11	0
Southwest Harbor	1,771	0	0	0	0	0	62	11	51	0	0
Swan's Island	333	0	0	0	0	0	0	0	0	0	0
Thomaston	2,781	0	0	0	0	0	70	12	57	1	0
Topsham	8,770	6	0	3	2	1	219	33	182	4	1
Van Buren	2,161	2	0	0	0	2	4	1	2	1	0
Veazie	1,918	1	0	0	1	0	46	12	32	2	0

Table 8. Offenses Known to Law Enforcement, by Selected State and City, 2012— continued

(Number)

State/city	Population	Violent crime	Murder and nonnegligent manslaughter	Forcible rape	Robbery	Aggravated assault	Property crime	Burglary	Larceny-theft	Motor vehicle theft	Arson[1]
Waldoboro	5,044	3	1	0	1	1	76	12	62	2	1
Washburn	1,679	2	0	1	0	1	47	11	36	0	0
Waterville	15,709	43	1	15	9	18	758	154	589	15	4
Wells	[illegible]	1	0	0	0	1	161	[illegible]	[illegible]	7	0
Westbrook	17,553	33	0	7	15	11	608	66	532	10	4
Wilton	4,115	7	0	3	1	3	83	20	59	4	0
Windham	17,054	17	0	3	5	9	325	65	251	9	4
Winslow	7,787	4	0	3	1	0	145	16	123	6	0
Winter Harbor	518	0	0	0	0	0	6	1	5	0	0
Winthrop	6,086	2	0	0	0	2	129	20	106	3	0
Wiscasset	3,711	3	0	0	1	2	79	27	51	1	0
Yarmouth	8,376	4	0	2	1	1	78	21	56	1	0
York	12,608	2	0	1	1	0	245	58	184	3	0
Maryland											
Aberdeen	15,208	75	0	7	34	34	464	92	338	34	4
Annapolis	39,255	177	2	4	54	117	1,042	185	775	82	8
Baltimore	625,474	8,789	218	315	3,605	4,651	29,149	7,770	17,397	3,982	242
Baltimore City Sheriff		0	0	0	0	0	0	0	0	0	0
Bel Air	10,285	40	1	1	4	34	366	27	331	8	2
Berlin	4,534	8	0	1	2	5	119	28	90	1	0
Berwyn Heights	3,181	10	1	0	5	4	49	13	34	2	0
Bladensburg	9,322	93	2	3	47	41	469	106	266	97	0
Boonsboro	3,386	0	0	0	0	0	15	3	12	0	1
Bowie	55,765	79	1	0	38	40	906	175	678	53	5
Brentwood	3,104	4	0	0	1	3	30	11	16	3	0
Brunswick	6,014	5	0	0	1	4	104	16	87	1	2
Cambridge	12,454	128	1	9	33	85	706	126	554	26	7
Capitol Heights	4,419	10	0	0	1	9	58	14	35	9	0
Centreville	4,376	2	0	0	1	1	42	11	29	2	1
Chestertown	5,305	35	0	1	14	20	140	26	109	5	0
Cheverly	6,291	23	0	0	10	13	120	17	83	20	0
Chevy Chase Village	2,008	0	0	0	0	0	53	4	47	2	1
Colmar Manor	1,431	7	0	0	3	4	30	4	18	8	0
Cottage City	1,329	8	0	1	5	2	45	10	23	12	0
Crisfield	2,736	13	2	0	4	7	38	7	31	0	0
Cumberland	20,939	166	0	15	27	124	1,415	317	1,068	30	8
Delmar	3,047	11	1	1	2	7	68	20	43	5	1
Denton	4,450	16	0	3	6	7	177	47	123	7	1
District Heights	5,948	15	3	0	4	8	141	33	83	25	0
Easton	16,202	56	0	7	13	36	449	95	348	6	0
Edmonston	1,471	3	0	0	2	1	66	15	45	6	1
Elkton	15,681	195	2	11	48	134	1,265	234	1,000	31	12
Fairmount Heights	1,523	1	0	0	1	0	11	3	8	0	0
Federalsburg	2,758	44	1	4	1	38	88	30	57	1	0
Forest Heights	2,495	4	0	0	3	1	38	25	12	1	0
Frederick	66,808	381	1	26	106	248	1,899	245	1,527	127	
Frostburg	9,049	14	0	1	5	8	244	67	173	4	0
Fruitland	4,937	19	0	2	1	16	251	35	214	2	0
Glenarden	6,113	5	1	0	0	4	98	20	71	7	0
Greenbelt	23,506	115	1	6	69	39	1,035	247	651	137	0
Greensboro	1,945	4	0	1	1	2	61	22	37	2	0
Hagerstown	40,275	197	3	11	75	108	1,456	310	1,020	126	24
Hampstead	6,393	4	0	1	1	2	73	12	60	1	2
Hancock	1,568	3	0	1	1	1	22	7	14	1	1
Havre de Grace	13,166	31	0	3	8	20	367	73	281	13	
Hurlock	2,113	10	0	1	3	6	97	53	42	2	0
Hyattsville	17,889	100	0	5	74	21	1,179	138	973	68	0
Landover Hills	1,720	6	0	1	3	2	69	9	53	7	0
La Plata	8,982	37	0	0	9	28	254	33	216	5	1
Laurel	25,591	134	0	1	48	85	811	125	594	92	0
Lonaconing	1,220	1	0	0	0	1	0	0	0	0	0
Luke	65	0	0	0	0	0	0	0	0	0	0
Manchester	4,859	2	0	0	0	2	44	7	35	2	2

Table 8. Offenses Known to Law Enforcement, by Selected State and City, 2012— continued

(Number)

State/city	Population	Violent crime	Murder and nonnegligent manslaughter	Forcible rape	Robbery	Aggravated assault	Property crime	Burglary	Larceny-theft	Motor vehicle theft	Arson[1]
Morningside	2,047	10	0	0	5	5	89	14	67	8	0
Mount Rainier	8,234	73	1	1	39	32	277	62	149	66	0
New Carrollton	12,366	30	0	0	21	9	212	55	135	22	1
North East	3,719	9	0	1	5	3	166	18	138	10	0
Oakland	1,941	3	0	0	0	3	31	1	30	0	0
Ocean City	7,179	93	0	12	21	60	1,407	211	1,180	16	4
Ocean Pines	11,935	14	0	0	1	13	83	40	41	2	0
Oxford	661	0	0	0	0	0	4	1	3	0	0
Perryville	4,429	8	0	1	5	2	129	20	101	8	0
Pocomoke City	4,230	15	0	1	1	13	187	35	151	1	2
Princess Anne	3,301	28	0	4	0	24	167	47	117	3	0
Ridgely	1,650	9	0	0	2	7	80	17	60	3	0
Rising Sun	2,824	2	0	0	1	1	72	10	62	0	1
Riverdale Park	7,087	38	1	0	16	21	178	27	125	26	0
Rock Hall	1,324	1	0	0	0	1	23	10	13	0	0
Salisbury	30,778	366	1	18	118	229	1,859	336	1,470	53	8
Seat Pleasant	4,628	44	2	1	10	31	173	34	107	32	0
Smithsburg	3,020	1	0	0	0	1	32	7	25	0	0
Snow Hill	2,124	8	0	0	0	8	47	13	32	2	1
St. Michaels	1,045	9	0	2	1	6	59	9	49	1	0
Sykesville	4,482	3	0	0	1	2	44	9	35	0	2
Takoma Park	17,185	64	0	1	42	21	491	73	364	54	4
Taneytown	6,801	7	0	0	1	6	101	10	91	0	1
Thurmont	6,320	7	0	0	1	6	51	15	35	1	1
Trappe	1,095	6	0	3	0	3	19	1	17	1	0
University Park	2,595	0	0	0	0	0	47	10	34	3	0
Upper Marlboro	644	1	0	0	1	0	13	2	11	0	0
Westminster	18,786	122	0	0	23	99	784	106	664	14	5
Massachusetts											
Abington	16,215	41	0	1	6	34	358	97	244	17	1
Acton	22,349	23	0	4	1	18	241	37	202	2	0
Acushnet	10,408	13	0	0	1	12	139	72	57	10	2
Adams	8,508	41	0	11	4	26	189	49	135	5	3
Agawam	28,708	34	0	5	5	24	272	108	140	24	0
Amesbury	16,557	44	0	6	5	33	256	48	192	16	1
Amherst	38,112	79	0	26	4	49	343	92	242	9	2
Andover	33,753	23	0	1	2	20	290	50	226	14	0
Arlington	43,675	51	0	3	9	39	515	100	404	11	7
Ashburnham	6,155	10	0	0	1	9	59	20	36	3	1
Ashby	3,134	2	0	0	0	2	32	23	8	1	0
Ashfield	1,757	1	0	1	0	0	10	2	8	0	0
Ashland	16,916	14	0	3	3	8	143	56	74	13	1
Athol	11,727	46	0	8	8	30	255	88	162	5	5
Attleboro	44,033	142	0	19	23	100	1,062	245	753	64	6
Auburn	16,389	48	0	3	3	42	587	74	493	20	4
Avon	4,427	9	0	1	0	8	155	29	124	2	
Ayer	7,568	28	0	3	4	21	169	76	89	4	2
Barnstable	45,570	283	1	22	29	231	1,269	378	847	44	10
Barre	5,464	13	0	0	0	13	80	24	51	5	0
Bedford	13,575	7	0	1	0	6	76	19	56	1	0
Belchertown	14,751	19	0	1	1	17	156	50	97	9	1
Belmont	25,209	19	0	3	4	12	291	114	168	9	1
Berkley	6,475	7	0	2	0	5	75	36	36	3	0
Berlin	2,903	1	0	0	0	1	43	1	41	1	0
Bernardston	2,154	4	0	0	0	4	28	13	15	0	0
Beverly	40,150	83	0	8	13	62	630	116	503	11	3
Billerica	41,016	56	1	10	7	38	468	89	356	23	4
Blackstone	9,138	15	0	0	2	13	124	12	102	10	2
Blandford	1,245	0	0	0	0	0	14	10	4	0	
Bolton	4,959	10	0	1	0	9	47	19	25	3	0
Boston	630,648	5,266	57	249	1,910	3,050	18,349	3,325	13,400	1,624	
Bourne	19,921	76	0	8	8	60	542	267	249	26	5
Boxborough	5,094	1	0	0	0	1	48	4	44	0	1

Table 8. Offenses Known to Law Enforcement, by Selected State and City, 2012— continued

(Number)

State/city	Population	Violent crime	Murder and nonnegligent manslaughter	Forcible rape	Robbery	Aggravated assault	Property crime	Burglary	Larceny-theft	Motor vehicle theft	Arson[1]
Boxford	8,099	0	0	0	0	0	37	7	26	4	0
Braintree	36,310	30	0	2	15	13	700	133	530	37	2
Brewster	9,902	15	0	0	2	13	168	47	117	4	1
Brimfield	3,643	6	0	1	0	5	32	6	26	0	0
Brockton	95,156	1,088	6	48	225	809	3,071	815	2,046	210	33
Brookline	59,658	82	0	4	31	47	803	148	637	18	0
Burlington	24,975	39	1	5	7	26	631	58	557	16	0
Cambridge	106,981	431	1	20	135	275	3,091	502	2,482	107	8
Canton	21,903	35	0	1	5	29	259	50	185	24	1
Carver	11,676	27	0	2	2	23	292	85	196	11	2
Charlton	13,142	19	0	2	4	13	172	47	117	8	2
Chatham	6,176	18	0	2	0	16	169	32	134	3	1
Chelmsford	34,460	25	0	0	5	20	547	69	463	15	0
Chelsea	35,966	666	2	41	253	370	1,377	288	910	179	5
Cheshire	3,245	1	0	0	0	1	11	5	5	1	
Chesterfield	1,230	0	0	0	0	0	7	2	4	1	0
Chicopee	55,825	258	0	27	72	159	1,679	634	925	120	7
Clinton	13,774	9	0	0	1	8	60	9	42	9	0
Concord	17,995	13	0	2	1	10	170	20	149	1	0
Dalton	6,774	21	0	0	3	18	66	27	34	5	2
Danvers	26,934	58	0	3	6	49	753	57	673	23	2
Dartmouth	34,368	73	0	9	11	53	1,011	193	802	16	2
Dedham	25,116	19	0	0	8	11	623	60	536	27	0
Deerfield	5,186	8	0	0	0	8	84	37	44	3	0
Dennis	14,325	49	0	0	6	43	527	256	267	4	2
Dighton	7,157	10	0	0	0	10	49	16	27	6	0
Douglas	8,576	11	0	4	0	7	50	25	23	2	1
Dover	5,677	3	0	3	0	0	45	10	33	2	0
Dracut	30,032	14	0	2	8	4	311	77	212	22	0
Dudley	11,528	39	0	3	1	35	73	39	33	1	1
Duxbury	15,276	3	0	0	0	3	95	45	47	3	0
East Bridgewater	13,989	24	0	1	2	21	217	53	158	6	3
East Brookfield	2,209	3	0	0	0	3	37	14	22	1	0
Eastham	4,997	8	0	1	0	7	126	24	98	4	0
Easthampton	16,166	35	1	7	1	26	200	52	138	10	0
East Longmeadow	15,871	25	0	1	6	18	359	79	274	6	2
Easton	23,342	31	0	5	6	20	259	81	162	16	0
Egremont	1,229	3	0	0	0	3	18	4	13	1	
Erving	1,822	11	0	0	0	11	37	7	29	1	0
Essex	3,562	0	0	0	0	0	27	4	22	1	
Everett	42,476	170	2	11	66	91	986	249	602	135	2
Fairhaven	16,033	50	1	2	11	36	421	83	323	15	0
Fall River	89,753	954	2	52	262	638	2,706	774	1,659	273	27
Falmouth	31,794	129	0	11	16	102	1,064	559	472	33	3
Fitchburg	40,809	319	1	21	47	250	1,086	307	734	45	6
Framingham[3]	69,605	154	0	7	21	126	1,238	254	884	100	1
Franklin	32,134	11	0	0	9	2	135	43	90	2	0
Freetown	8,960	12	0	0	2	10	200	75	111	14	1
Gardner	20,474	88	0	7	8	73	523	142	366	15	1
Gill	1,518	0	0	0	0	0	19	10	9	0	0
Gloucester	29,272	27	0	4	0	23	416	40	372	4	0
Goshen	1,062	0	0	0	0	0	4	3	1	0	0
Grafton	17,986	22	0	1	1	20	116	40	69	7	2
Granby	6,282	7	0	1	0	6	91	23	62	6	1
Granville	1,581	0	0	0	0	0	13	4	9	0	
Greenfield	17,667	115	1	8	22	84	574	230	330	14	4
Groton	10,851	7	0	0	1	6	104	46	54	4	0
Groveland	6,567	2	0	0	0	2	45	2	40	3	0
Hadley	5,288	14	0	0	4	10	238	26	209	3	0
Halifax	7,627	19	0	2	2	15	75	22	46	7	1
Hamilton	7,896	5	0	0	1	4	55	11	40	4	0
Hampden	5,188	5	0	0	0	5	36	14	22	0	0
Hanover	14,078	3	0	0	1	2	268	36	230	2	0
Hanson	10,357	29	0	3	1	25	112	33	73	6	0

Table 8. Offenses Known to Law Enforcement, by Selected State and City, 2012— continued

(Number)

State/city	Population	Violent crime	Murder and nonnegligent manslaughter	Forcible rape	Robbery	Aggravated assault	Property crime	Burglary	Larceny-theft	Motor vehicle theft	Arson[1]
Hardwick	3,027	11	0	0	0	11	55	8	43	4	0
Harvard	6,595	3	0	1	0	2	50	32	18	0	0
Harwich	12,345	28	0	4	0	24	249	119	126	4	1
Haverhill	61,897	418	2	12	52	352	1,439	393	920	126	8
Hingham	22,475	17	0	0	3	14	362	89	261	12	1
Holbrook	10,963	42	0	0	20	22	226	80	144	2	
Holden	17,562	8	0	3	1	4	98	20	75	3	1
Holliston	13,811	8	0	0	0	8	106	23	78	5	0
Holyoke	40,260	382	0	33	87	262	2,509	444	1,955	110	16
Hopedale	5,985	17	0	0	0	17	49	10	35	4	2
Hopkinton	15,214	2	0	0	1	1	94	0	92	2	0
Hubbardston	4,436	11	0	3	0	8	53	20	31	2	0
Hudson	19,435	8	0	0	0	8	235	19	205	11	0
Hull	10,441	34	0	2	0	32	109	35	68	6	0
Ipswich	13,397	5	0	2	1	2	107	27	77	3	0
Kingston	12,809	17	0	2	4	11	260	57	195	8	3
Lakeville	10,754	12	0	1	1	10	221	70	145	6	1
Lancaster	8,148	9	0	0	1	8	82	34	46	2	1
Lawrence	77,661	785	2	25	223	535	1,965	536	743	686	
Lee	5,960	15	0	4	1	10	129	39	89	1	1
Leicester	11,106	18	0	4	1	13	171	42	119	10	1
Lenox	5,039	5	0	0	0	5	122	31	78	13	1
Leominster	41,262	271	0	13	45	213	1,316	267	1,000	49	8
Lexington	32,000	13	0	0	0	13	226	36	190	0	0
Lincoln	6,487	8	0	0	0	8	45	17	28	0	0
Littleton	9,097	11	0	0	1	10	113	35	73	5	1
Longmeadow	15,936	11	0	1	6	4	194	26	163	5	1
Lowell	108,539	585	0	37	174	374	3,125	849	1,981	295	27
Ludlow	21,304	28	0	2	12	14	361	115	233	13	3
Lunenburg	10,212	27	0	1	1	25	227	51	167	9	0
Lynn	91,846	754	2	48	170	534	2,589	698	1,614	277	8
Lynnfield	11,791	7	0	0	1	6	106	30	70	6	1
Malden	60,605	280	1	19	75	185	1,203	281	794	128	7
Manchester-by-the-Sea	5,222	4	0	0	0	4	26	2	24	0	0
Marblehead	20,142	27	0	2	2	23	222	43	171	8	1
Marion	4,976	6	0	1	0	5	69	21	46	2	0
Marlborough	39,241	117	0	12	6	99	698	112	547	39	4
Marshfield	25,496	38	0	4	1	33	294	56	224	14	0
Mashpee	14,123	47	0	4	7	36	293	60	226	7	3
Mattapoisett	6,133	7	0	1	1	5	104	32	70	2	0
Maynard	10,303	24	0	3	1	20	139	13	119	7	0
Medfield	12,216	16	0	2	1	13	69	13	56	0	0
Medway	12,956	12	2	1	0	9	118	23	94	1	0
Melrose	27,506	38	0	1	6	31	313	82	216	15	5
Mendon	5,913	5	0	2	0	3	44	14	26	4	1
Merrimac	6,446	7	0	1	0	6	58	19	37	2	0
Methuen	48,051	78	0	1	14	63	870	142	658	70	1
Middleboro	23,448	73	0	1	7	65	515	140	353	22	4
Middleton	9,130	14	0	0	0	14	82	3	77	2	1
Milford	28,346	79	1	8	14	56	525	93	412	20	0
Millbury	13,425	40	0	6	2	32	298	55	233	10	1
Millville	3,228	1	0	0	0	1	42	15	26	1	0
Milton[3]	27,424	28	0	0	5	23	278	90	181	7	
Monson	8,641	20	0	3	0	17	145	69	69	7	2
Montague	8,540	38	0	7	1	30	214	81	127	6	2
Monterey	965	4	0	0	0	4	3	2	1	0	0
Nahant	3,467	6	0	0	0	6	34	9	25	0	1
Nantucket	10,232	15	0	2	1	12	327	37	279	11	0
Natick	33,646	61	0	4	7	50	792	83	683	26	2
Needham	29,342	2	0	0	0	2	276	48	220	8	0
New Bedford	96,031	1,030	2	54	272	702	3,180	929	1,950	301	29
Newburyport	17,708	21	0	1	2	18	235	35	188	12	1
Newton	86,710	76	0	5	17	54	894	185	693	16	2

Table 8. Offenses Known to Law Enforcement, by Selected State and City, 2012— continued

(Number)

State/city	Population	Violent crime	Murder and nonnegligent manslaughter	Forcible rape	Robbery	Aggravated assault	Property crime	Burglary	Larceny-theft	Motor vehicle theft	Arson[1]
Norfolk	11,390	1	0	0	1	0	56	19	34	3	1
North Adams	13,753	97	0	5	6	86	595	187	390	18	2
Northampton	28,755	115	0	8	16	91	858	137	696	25	5
North Attleboro	29,001	0	0	0	0	0	438	26	407	5	0
Northborough	14,329	16	1	0	0	15	180	36	142	2	0
Northbridge	15,901	32	0	5	2	25	446	112	316	18	2
North Brookfield	4,737	16	0	0	0	16	46	28	14	4	0
Northfield	3,069	1	0	0	0	1	42	13	28	1	0
North Reading	15,182	15	0	1	5	9	148	40	101	7	0
Norton	19,222	9	0	1	1	7	129	70	55	4	0
Norwell	10,656	9	0	0	2	7	100	27	69	4	0
Norwood	29,057	28	0	5	7	16	509	82	392	35	3
Oak Bluffs	4,631	14	0	0	2	12	147	22	117	8	0
Oakham	1,926	1	0	0	0	1	20	11	8	1	0
Orleans	5,939	17	0	0	0	17	178	38	138	2	0
Oxford	13,880	47	1	4	11	31	215	43	161	11	3
Palmer	12,257	47	0	4	3	40	259	116	126	17	3
Paxton	4,864	3	0	1	0	2	36	16	19	1	0
Peabody	52,113	121	0	11	12	98	1,102	155	893	54	3
Pelham	1,329	0	0	0	0	0	7	2	5	0	0
Pepperell	11,719	18	0	1	3	14	177	50	121	6	0
Pittsfield	44,868	191	0	34	38	119	1,166	372	751	43	5
Plainville	8,396	8	0	2	3	3	155	26	125	4	0
Plympton	2,862	2	0	0	0	2	73	34	38	1	2
Princeton	3,454	1	0	0	0	1	43	28	14	1	0
Provincetown	2,966	27	0	0	0	27	117	13	104	0	0
Quincy	93,736	401	0	31	84	286	1,554	495	943	116	13
Randolph	32,624	125	1	8	18	98	552	150	379	23	4
Raynham	13,518	19	0	2	5	12	339	48	272	19	0
Reading	25,223	10	0	0	6	4	189	44	136	9	0
Rehoboth	11,724	14	0	1	0	13	181	46	129	6	1
Revere	52,926	269	1	12	72	184	1,245	230	844	171	2
Rochester	5,308	6	0	0	1	5	62	23	37	2	0
Rockport	7,068	3	0	0	0	3	15	2	12	1	0
Rowley	5,955	4	0	0	0	4	17	7	9	1	0
Rutland	8,073	19	0	6	0	13	61	31	28	2	0
Salem[3]	42,025	159	0	7	17	135	955	148	754	53	
Salisbury	8,422	36	0	5	1	30	226	47	165	14	0
Sandwich	20,848	39	0	5	3	31	315	115	193	7	1
Saugus	27,075	84	2	5	24	53	796	113	641	42	1
Scituate	18,395	23	0	2	1	20	208	34	169	5	6
Seekonk	13,862	34	0	4	6	24	396	53	323	20	3
Sharon	17,892	15	0	0	2	13	109	43	62	4	0
Shelburne	1,915	1	0	0	0	1	16	6	10	0	0
Sherborn	4,199	2	0	0	0	2	28	9	18	1	0
Shirley	7,337	18	0	3	0	15	42	23	18	1	1
Shrewsbury	36,048	6	1	0	2	3	273	75	185	13	1
Somerset	18,349	35	0	1	6	28	298	69	217	12	2
Somerville	77,200	269	0	23	82	164	1,724	348	1,248	128	3
Southampton	5,832	3	0	1	0	2	67	16	49	2	0
Southborough	9,887	3	0	0	0	3	69	32	37	0	0
Southbridge	16,924	63	0	2	13	48	428	183	234	11	5
South Hadley	17,642	42	1	10	2	29	334	90	235	9	2
Southwick	9,594	15	0	1	0	14	147	56	83	8	0
Spencer	11,832	23	1	3	0	19	212	48	159	5	2
Springfield	154,518	1,606	11	39	542	1,014	7,024	2,317	3,947	760	68
Sterling	7,904	14	0	0	0	14	89	31	56	2	1
Stockbridge	1,953	6	0	1	0	5	54	23	29	2	0
Stoneham	21,852	29	0	1	9	19	259	111	138	10	0
Stoughton	27,392	89	0	2	16	71	603	100	459	44	4
Stow	6,717	2	0	0	0	2	63	26	33	4	0
Sturbridge	9,383	29	0	1	3	25	177	30	140	7	0
Sudbury	18,002	1	0	0	0	1	75	24	50	1	0
Sutton	9,075	10	0	1	1	8	115	55	51	9	0

Table 8. Offenses Known to Law Enforcement, by Selected State and City, 2012— continued

(Number)

State/city	Population	Violent crime	Murder and nonnegligent manslaughter	Forcible rape	Robbery	Aggravated assault	Property crime	Burglary	Larceny-theft	Motor vehicle theft	Arson[1]
Swansea	16,025	42	0	7	6	29	382	89	275	18	3
Taunton	56,438	268	0	18	62	188	851	380	437	34	2
Templeton	8,111	11	0	1	1	9	69	29	36	4	0
Tewksbury	29,518	98	0	15	9	74	615	152	428	35	1
Tisbury	4,040	7	0	0	1	6	113	12	90	11	2
Truro	2,020	4	0	0	0	4	40	10	29	1	0
Upton	7,636	8	0	2	0	6	75	21	53	1	0
Uxbridge	13,623	19	0	4	1	14	150	51	90	9	1
Wakefield	25,415	67	0	3	8	56	309	70	223	16	0
Wales	1,855	1	0	0	0	1	5	0	5	0	0
Walpole	24,450	13	0	6	1	6	374	37	326	11	0
Waltham	61,725	146	0	12	24	110	849	191	610	48	1
Ware	9,942	41	0	3	2	36	194	46	145	3	6
Wareham	22,136	152	1	15	26	110	893	244	629	20	6
Watertown	32,535	56	0	3	6	47	528	66	442	20	0
Wayland	13,248	8	0	0	1	7	50	17	29	4	0
Webster	16,974	112	0	6	23	83	554	111	418	25	4
Wellesley	28,402	12	0	1	1	10	211	46	161	4	0
Wellfleet	2,772	6	0	0	1	5	53	19	32	2	1
Wenham	4,948	3	0	0	0	3	33	4	27	2	0
Westborough	18,496	18	0	5	3	10	200	42	148	10	1
West Boylston	7,759	6	0	0	1	5	102	25	76	1	1
West Bridgewater	7,016	9	0	0	2	7	149	31	110	8	1
Westfield	41,485	76	0	8	14	54	770	201	551	18	2
Westford	22,378	11	0	2	1	8	160	32	121	7	1
Westminster	7,367	10	0	0	2	8	140	16	124	0	0
West Newbury	4,306	11	0	0	0	11	24	5	18	1	1
Weston	11,472	1	0	0	0	1	51	15	34	2	0
Westport	15,688	20	1	2	1	16	264	129	122	13	0
West Springfield	28,663	156	0	16	33	107	1,365	267	989	109	7
West Tisbury	2,803	2	0	0	0	2	17	4	13	0	0
Westwood	14,852	27	0	5	2	20	136	36	95	5	0
Weymouth	54,597	188	0	9	42	137	805	210	551	44	9
Whately	1,514	0	0	0	0	0	23	5	18	0	0
Whitman	14,699	43	0	2	7	34	189	31	150	8	0
Wilbraham	14,356	25	0	2	4	19	251	70	165	16	2
Williamsburg	2,499	2	0	0	0	2	32	11	20	1	0
Wilmington	22,758	28	0	2	3	23	275	58	213	4	3
Winchendon	10,427	34	0	4	1	29	258	24	223	11	0
Winchester	21,786	12	0	1	3	8	202	40	154	8	1
Winthrop	17,895	39	0	2	6	31	184	41	125	18	2
Woburn	38,863	96	0	4	19	73	668	105	544	19	0
Worcester	183,247	1,758	8	33	419	1,298	6,432	2,040	3,927	465	6
Wrentham	11,125	6	0	0	1	5	85	8	71	6	0
Yarmouth	23,991	147	0	5	6	136	724	287	422	15	7
Michigan											
Allegan	4,994	15	0	6	0	9	142	17	122	3	0
Allen Park	27,941	45	2	4	16	23	717	139	504	74	1
Alma	9,319	20	0	8	1	11	211	32	176	3	2
Almont	2,669	4	0	1	0	3	59	17	37	5	0
Ann Arbor	115,008	227	1	35	50	141	2,726	714	1,898	114	23
Argentine Township	6,857	1	0	0	0	1	31	18	12	1	0
Armada	1,734	0	0	0	0	0	8	1	5	2	0
Auburn Hills	21,559	45	0	8	13	24	830	102	700	28	2
Augusta	892	0	0	0	0	0	6	0	5	1	0
Bad Axe	3,092	8	0	5	0	3	129	7	120	2	0
Bancroft	538	0	0	0	0	0	3	1	2	0	0
Bangor	1,882	10	0	1	0	9	79	5	70	4	3
Baroda-Lake Township	3,851	4	0	1	0	3	53	6	45	2	0
Barry Township	3,360	2	0	0	0	2	21	7	14	0	0
Bath Township	11,621	22	1	1	3	17	103	28	67	8	7
Bay City	34,742	215	1	42	29	143	791	199	553	39	10
Beaverton	1,078	2	0	0	0	2	19	8	11	0	0

Table 8. Offenses Known to Law Enforcement, by Selected State and City, 2012— continued

(Number)

State/city	Population	Violent crime	Murder and nonnegligent manslaughter	Forcible rape	Robbery	Aggravated assault	Property crime	Burglary	Larceny-theft	Motor vehicle theft	Arson[1]
Belding	5,768	12	0	4	1	7	140	14	123	3	3
Bellaire	1,076	0	0	0	0	0	13	1	12	0	0
Belleville	3,951	10	0	0	1	0	107	32	71	1	0
Benton Harbor	10,054	236	1	14	53	168	864	396	439	29	8
Berkley	15,078	9	0	2	3	4	132	24	99	9	1
Berrien Springs-Oronoko Township	9,206	16	0	5	0	11	122	21	97	4	1
Beverly Hills	10,341	8	0	0	1	7	107	22	81	4	0
Big Rapids	10,703	27	0	7	0	20	247	28	214	5	1
Birch Run	1,547	3	0	0	1	2	93	5	86	2	0
Birmingham	20,250	20	0	1	7	12	331	62	254	15	2
Blissfield	3,326	1	0	1	0	0	58	9	44	5	2
Bloomfield Hills	3,895	5	0	1	0	4	37	5	32	0	0
Bloomfield Township	41,367	22	1	2	4	15	452	106	329	17	0
Boyne City	3,749	9	0	4	0	5	69	11	58	0	0
Breckenridge	1,318	0	0	0	0	0	23	2	21	0	0
Bridgeport Township	10,465	39	0	5	2	32	158	83	66	9	1
Bridgman	2,294	5	0	1	0	4	46	2	42	2	3
Brighton	7,480	6	0	0	2	4	155	11	144	0	0
Bronson	2,349	2	1	1	0	0	43	6	37	0	0
Brown City	1,312	3	0	2	0	1	31	4	26	1	0
Buena Vista Township	8,635	85	1	9	15	60	339	142	183	14	3
Burr Oak	828	5	0	0	0	5	26	0	25	1	0
Burton	29,758	144	1	14	55	74	1,562	443	1,061	58	25
Calumet	728	1	0	0	0	1	27	6	20	1	0
Cambridge Township	5,710	2	0	0	1	1	36	1	35	0	0
Capac	1,874	4	0	0	0	4	50	5	42	3	0
Carleton	2,339	10	0	3	1	6	49	11	35	3	1
Caro	4,211	17	0	2	0	15	220	27	191	2	0
Carrollton Township	6,073	17	0	2	5	10	115	39	73	3	1
Caseville	767	3	0	1	0	2	34	1	33	0	0
Cass City	2,417	4	0	2	0	2	49	2	46	1	0
Cassopolis	1,765	1	0	0	0	1	38	12	22	4	1
Cedar Springs	3,546	28	0	4	6	18	133	28	104	1	1
Center Line	8,275	30	0	1	5	24	265	45	178	42	1
Central Lake	942	0	0	0	0	0	14	2	12	0	0
Charlevoix	2,520	5	0	2	0	3	115	11	103	1	0
Charlotte	9,106	31	0	17	2	12	291	68	214	9	1
Cheboygan	4,830	5	0	3	1	1	183	21	158	4	0
Chelsea	4,995	6	0	1	0	5	93	23	68	2	1
Chesaning	2,382	7	0	0	0	7	22	5	16	1	0
Chesterfield Township	43,474	121	0	7	14	100	889	129	713	47	4
Chocolay Township	5,966	2	0	2	0	0	70	11	57	2	0
Clare	3,130	4	0	3	0	1	86	14	71	1	0
Clawson	11,909	13	0	1	4	8	114	15	89	10	0
Clayton Township	7,438	6	0	0	2	4	134	72	60	2	0
Clay Township	8,994	8	0	1	1	6	121	20	98	3	2
Clinton	2,326	1	0	0	0	1	25	5	19	1	0
Clinton Township	97,001	291	0	38	58	195	2,230	477	1,572	181	8
Clio	2,625	7	0	0	0	7	115	21	93	1	2
Coleman	1,250	5	0	1	2	2	36	4	32	0	0
Coloma Township	6,515	7	0	2	0	5	91	17	73	1	1
Colon	1,171	2	0	1	0	1	25	2	23	0	0
Columbia Township	7,401	11	0	0	2	9	85	12	71	2	1
Constantine	2,073	9	0	5	0	4	87	9	75	3	0
Corunna	3,462	8	0	0	1	7	47	7	39	1	1
Covert Township	2,886	14	0	1	0	13	97	43	48	6	0
Croswell	2,420	12	0	4	0	8	108	13	93	2	1
Crystal Falls	1,467	1	0	0	0	1	19	3	16	0	0
Davison	5,132	6	0	1	1	4	96	14	79	3	2
Davison Township	19,415	38	0	7	4	27	347	83	256	8	0
Dearborn	97,215	322	1	24	107	190	3,282	462	2,463	357	20
Dearborn Heights	57,228	193	3	15	43	132	1,260	375	666	219	9

Table 8. Offenses Known to Law Enforcement, by Selected State and City, 2012— continued

(Number)

State/city	Population	Violent crime	Murder and nonnegligent manslaughter	Forcible rape	Robbery	Aggravated assault	Property crime	Burglary	Larceny-theft	Motor vehicle theft	Arson[1]
Decatur	1,816	7	0	1	1	5	70	9	60	1	0
Denton Township	5,553	2	0	1	0	1	103	13	86	4	0
Detroit	707,096	15,011	386	441	4,843	9,341	40,956	13,488	15,968	11,500	562
Dewitt	4,514	4	0	0	1	3	19	5	14	0	0
Dryden Township	4,758	6	0	2	0	4	33	10	23	0	0
East Jordan	2,358	2	0	1	0	1	42	8	34	0	0
East Lansing	48,701	116	0	17	19	80	993	215	695	83	60
Eastpointe	32,511	203	0	13	48	142	972	268	492	212	8
Eaton Rapids	5,233	4	0	2	0	2	104	14	88	2	2
Eau Claire	626	0	0	0	0	0	16	1	15	0	1
Elk Rapids	1,624	1	0	1	0	0	43	3	40	0	0
Elkton	798	1	0	0	0	1	11	4	7	0	0
Elsie	968	0	0	0	0	0	14	4	8	2	0
Emmett Township	11,722	59	1	7	15	36	550	63	481	6	3
Escanaba	12,636	55	0	10	4	41	784	66	699	19	2
Essexville	3,459	11	0	0	0	11	60	18	40	2	0
Evart	1,902	8	0	1	0	7	70	10	56	4	0
Farmington	10,446	16	0	2	0	14	151	20	123	8	0
Farmington Hills	80,316	74	1	15	12	46	1,264	231	907	126	8
Fenton	11,662	17	0	7	4	6	338	47	277	14	0
Ferndale	20,045	83	0	1	19	63	516	112	321	83	1
Flat Rock	9,785	20	0	2	4	14	202	41	148	13	0
Flint	101,632	2,774	63	108	673	1,930	5,645	2,979	2,207	459	226
Flint Township	31,677	307	2	24	127	154	2,158	642	1,393	123	12
Flushing	8,322	6	0	1	1	4	132	35	94	3	0
Forsyth Township	6,230	7	0	3	0	4	123	32	86	5	1
Fowlerville	2,900	9	0	5	1	3	139	15	122	2	0
Frankenmuth	4,936	4	0	2	1	1	107	16	86	5	0
Frankfort	1,281	4	0	0	0	4	33	1	32	0	0
Franklin	3,173	4	0	1	3	0	50	14	35	1	0
Fraser	14,512	28	0	4	10	14	380	48	308	24	1
Fremont	4,081	3	0	2	0	1	141	10	127	4	1
Fruitport	1,088	22	0	6	2	14	679	62	605	12	2
Garden City	27,428	73	1	8	14	50	608	177	367	64	2
Gaylord	3,635	16	0	3	2	11	290	45	236	9	0
Genesee Township	21,407	94	0	4	13	77	699	398	255	46	10
Gerrish Township	2,991	1	0	0	0	1	24	3	20	1	0
Gibraltar	4,611	9	0	0	2	7	71	13	56	2	1
Gladstone	4,982	9	0	2	1	6	96	11	81	4	0
Gladwin	2,952	18	0	2	0	16	129	22	100	7	1
Grand Beach	272	0	0	0	0	0	6	0	6	0	0
Grand Blanc	8,210	19	0	1	3	15	159	53	102	4	2
Grand Blanc Township	37,206	88	0	17	14	57	746	167	528	51	4
Grand Haven	10,519	18	0	8	2	8	354	31	321	2	3
Grand Ledge	7,814	4	0	0	0	4	143	27	112	4	5
Grand Rapids	189,953	1,465	16	46	462	941	6,618	1,917	4,433	268	90
Grandville	15,538	12	1	4	3	4	640	88	547	5	5
Grayling	1,877	11	0	4	0	7	49	0	49	0	1
Green Oak Township	17,561	19	0	7	3	9	203	42	155	6	0
Greenville	8,466	37	0	8	6	23	493	64	424	5	1
Grosse Ile Township	10,271	1	0	0	0	1	88	11	76	1	0
Grosse Pointe	5,369	6	0	1	2	3	102	20	78	4	1
Grosse Pointe Farms	9,389	5	0	0	2	3	114	25	81	8	0
Grosse Pointe Park	11,444	18	1	2	5	10	291	60	188	43	2
Grosse Pointe Shores	2,981	1	0	0	0	1	17	7	9	1	0
Grosse Pointe Woods	15,981	5	0	1	3	1	254	33	168	53	1
Hamburg Township	21,269	10	0	3	0	7	107	28	71	8	1
Hampton Township	9,601	7	0	2	1	4	268	31	231	6	0
Hamtramck	22,214	236	2	5	105	124	764	251	325	188	16
Hancock	4,638	4	0	0	1	3	42	8	33	1	0
Harbor Beach	1,682	1	0	0	0	1	25	8	16	1	0
Harbor Springs	1,200	0	0	0	0	0	29	2	26	1	0
Harper Woods	14,102	131	1	4	53	73	1,075	150	716	209	6

Table 8. Offenses Known to Law Enforcement, by Selected State and City, 2012— continued

(Number)

State/city	Population	Violent crime	Murder and nonnegligent manslaughter	Forcible rape	Robbery	Aggravated assault	Property crime	Burglary	Larceny-theft	Motor vehicle theft	Arson[1]
Hart	2,124	7	1	2	0	4	108	15	93	0	0
Hartford	2,686	6	0	0	0	6	55	9	45	1	0
Hastings	[illegible]	27	0	7	1	[illegible]	[illegible]	14	[illegible]	2	0
Hazel Park	16,542	86	0	2	19	65	494	116	283	95	1
Highland Park	11,672	230	6	8	96	120	648	172	277	199	16
Hillsdale	8,284	12	0	2	1	9	232	43	184	5	1
Holland	33,294	136	0	31	19	86	1,276	208	1,033	35	7
Holly	6,128	21	1	5	3	12	120	23	94	3	2
Houghton	7,716	5	0	1	0	4	149	9	140	0	0
Howard City	1,805	3	0	0	0	3	67	22	42	3	1
Hudson	2,298	6	0	4	0	2	54	3	48	3	1
Huntington Woods	6,285	1	0	0	1	0	47	7	39	1	0
Huron Township	15,728	25	0	8	2	15	245	80	151	14	2
Imlay City	3,590	15	0	9	1	5	103	19	82	2	2
Inkster	25,129	381	10	32	84	255	1,013	465	408	140	19
Ionia	11,410	15	0	7	0	8	198	25	166	7	1
Iron River	3,027	3	0	2	0	1	114	29	67	18	0
Ironwood	5,339	7	0	1	0	6	150	12	138	0	1
Ishpeming	6,536	9	1	4	1	3	97	7	87	3	0
Ishpeming Township	3,551	0	0	0	0	0	10	1	9	0	0
Jonesville	2,252	6	0	0	0	6	81	8	72	1	0
Kalamazoo	74,797	657	9	77	165	406	3,120	835	2,135	150	33
Kalamazoo Township	23,909	60	1	14	15	30	570	153	380	37	8
Kalkaska	2,023	1	0	1	0	0	44	1	43	0	1
Keego Harbor	2,992	4	0	1	0	3	53	8	42	3	0
Kingston	439	0	0	0	0	0	25	8	15	2	0
Kinross Township	7,595	2	0	0	0	2	16	3	13	0	0
Lake Odessa	2,023	6	0	0	0	6	26	6	19	1	0
Lake Orion	2,994	3	0	1	0	2	45	4	41	0	0
Lansing	114,688	1,078	13	92	203	770	3,774	1,307	2,203	264	39
Lapeer	8,825	30	0	7	2	21	393	41	346	6	0
Lapeer Township	5,047	0	0	0	0	0	27	2	24	1	0
Lathrup Village	4,104	5	0	1	1	3	52	14	27	11	0
Laurium	1,978	3	0	2	0	1	20	2	16	2	0
Lawton	1,897	5	0	2	0	3	52	9	43	0	1
Leslie	1,857	2	0	1	1	0	27	8	19	0	0
Lincoln Park	37,779	222	1	10	54	157	1,549	384	972	193	7
Lincoln Township	14,714	8	0	5	2	1	183	13	168	2	0
Linden	3,960	2	0	1	0	1	46	1	43	2	0
Litchfield	1,366	2	0	0	0	2	21	4	17	0	0
Livonia	96,028	146	3	19	32	92	2,124	323	1,601	200	13
Lowell	3,822	10	0	1	0	9	138	13	125	0	1
Luna Pier	1,434	2	0	0	0	2	53	7	44	2	0
Mackinac Island	489	1	0	1	0	0	258	2	255	1	0
Mackinaw City	808	1	0	1	0	0	37	2	34	1	0
Madison Heights	29,909	77	1	7	30	39	946	153	659	134	9
Madison Township	8,599	2	0	0	0	2	103	10	92	1	0
Mancelona	1,376	4	0	2	0	2	44	2	40	2	0
Manistique	3,100	8	0	5	1	2	91	18	72	1	2
Marenisco Township	1,722	0	0	0	0	0	7	5	2	0	0
Marine City	4,215	16	0	4	0	12	124	14	106	4	0
Marlette	1,855	14	0	4	0	10	36	5	31	0	0
Marquette	21,540	21	0	9	0	12	432	31	392	9	0
Marshall	7,058	9	0	0	0	9	194	19	173	2	1
Marysville	9,881	3	0	1	0	2	163	14	143	6	3
Mason	8,278	9	0	4	0	5	118	20	96	2	0
Mattawan	1,994	0	0	0	0	0	43	5	36	2	1
Mayville	945	0	0	0	0	0	9	1	8	0	0
Melvindale	10,612	40	0	4	12	24	392	88	253	51	3
Meridian Township	39,824	64	0	12	13	39	927	164	725	38	9
Metamora Township	4,241	4	0	1	0	3	51	13	34	4	0
Midland	42,106	38	1	15	5	17	457	56	400	1	3
Milan	5,870	16	1	1	1	13	143	22	114	7	2
Milford	15,848	7	0	3	1	3	152	35	110	7	1

Table 8. Offenses Known to Law Enforcement, by Selected State and City, 2012— continued

(Number)

State/city	Population	Violent crime	Murder and nonnegligent manslaughter	Forcible rape	Robbery	Aggravated assault	Property crime	Burglary	Larceny-theft	Motor vehicle theft	Arson[1]
Monroe	20,687	108	1	10	25	72	831	234	560	37	8
Montague	2,350	2	0	0	0	2	77	8	69	0	1
Montrose Township	7,818	7	0	0	2	5	135	56	75	4	0
Morenci	2,211	4	0	1	0	3	57	7	39	11	0
Mount Morris	3,061	17	0	1	3	13	139	37	96	6	3
Mount Morris Township	21,326	152	2	15	57	78	1,128	550	519	59	21
Mundy Township	14,960	23	0	6	6	11	342	101	222	19	1
Munising	2,331	3	0	0	0	3	36	4	30	2	0
Muskegon Heights	10,806	200	1	15	52	132	692	274	359	59	15
Napoleon Township	6,759	3	0	1	0	2	41	8	33	0	0
Nashville	1,619	2	0	0	0	2	33	4	27	2	0
Negaunee	4,615	9	0	2	0	7	115	17	91	7	0
Newaygo	1,975	4	0	2	0	2	115	15	94	6	2
New Baltimore	12,109	10	0	1	0	9	56	10	42	4	0
New Buffalo	1,885	3	0	2	0	1	63	13	48	2	1
New Era	450	0	0	0	0	0	11	2	9	0	0
New Haven	4,650	14	0	3	1	10	85	23	59	3	0
North Branch	1,031	7	0	1	0	6	9	3	6	0	0
Northfield Township	8,329	21	0	2	0	19	137	30	93	14	0
North Muskegon	3,769	6	0	0	1	5	110	5	103	2	0
Northville	5,968	2	0	1	0	1	78	11	65	2	1
Norton Shores	23,884	52	0	10	11	31	818	139	657	22	2
Novi	55,623	37	0	4	9	24	1,048	72	937	39	2
Oak Park	29,532	162	1	10	59	92	704	199	401	104	8
Olivet	1,609	1	0	1	0	0	10	0	9	1	0
Orchard Lake	2,391	1	0	1	0	0	34	7	27	0	0
Oscoda Township	6,907	18	0	4	1	13	270	109	159	2	1
Otsego	3,953	7	0	4	0	3	67	13	53	1	0
Ovid	1,607	1	0	0	0	1	14	5	9	0	0
Owendale	238	0	0	0	0	0	7	0	7	0	0
Owosso	15,035	61	1	13	4	43	500	90	400	10	4
Oxford	3,462	0	0	0	0	0	42	8	31	3	0
Paw Paw	3,532	7	0	0	1	6	142	14	126	2	0
Pentwater	856	3	0	3	0	0	9	0	9	0	0
Petoskey	5,700	4	0	1	0	3	83	9	70	4	0
Pinckney	2,439	5	0	0	1	4	27	4	23	0	0
Pinconning	1,300	1	0	0	1	0	18	7	11	0	0
Pittsfield Township	35,020	55	0	8	19	28	931	169	702	60	1
Plainwell	3,802	4	1	1	0	2	62	9	52	1	0
Pleasant Ridge	2,545	1	0	0	0	1	19	4	14	1	0
Plymouth	9,047	11	0	2	0	9	100	22	74	4	0
Portage	46,658	76	0	23	15	38	1,643	184	1,418	41	7
Port Austin	655	4	0	0	0	4	20	4	16	0	0
Potterville	2,627	3	0	0	0	3	64	10	54	0	0
Prairieville Township	3,387	1	0	1	0	0	12	2	10	0	0
Raisin Township	7,529	2	0	0	1	1	26	7	18	1	0
Reading	1,075	0	0	0	0	0	7	2	5	0	0
Reed City	2,425	10	0	1	0	9	68	6	62	0	1
Reese	1,447	0	0	0	0	0	6	3	3	0	0
Richfield Township, Genessee County	8,659	9	0	5	0	4	112	46	61	5	0
Richfield Township, Roscommon County	3,728	7	0	2	0	5	55	9	43	3	0
Richland	758	0	0	0	0	0	7	2	5	0	0
Richland Township, Saginaw County	4,124	0	0	0	0	0	32	15	14	3	1
Richmond	5,747	28	0	1	0	27	71	3	66	2	1
Riverview	12,371	11	0	0	5	6	92	10	78	4	0
Rochester	12,802	9	0	1	2	6	132	24	101	7	1
Rockwood	3,257	8	0	0	1	7	64	8	50	6	0
Rogers City	2,783	2	0	0	0	2	57	10	44	3	0
Romeo	3,605	0	0	0	0	0	45	3	40	2	1
Roseville	47,400	227	0	32	59	136	1,935	281	1,451	203	5
Rothbury	431	1	0	0	1	0	32	5	26	1	0

Table 8. Offenses Known to Law Enforcement, by Selected State and City, 2012— continued

(Number)

State/city	Population	Violent crime	Murder and nonnegligent manslaughter	Forcible rape	Robbery	Aggravated assault	Property crime	Burglary	Larceny-theft	Motor vehicle theft	Arson[1]
Royal Oak	57,649	72	0	9	12	51	1,008	179	742	87	4
Saginaw	51,267	1,211	27	65	167	952	1,765	1,042	618	105	26
Saginaw Township	40,642	85	1	6	33	45	820	119	678	23	9
Saline	8,899	18	0	1	3	14	148	22	121	5	1
Sand Lake	504	0	0	0	0	0	7	2	5	0	0
Sandusky	2,652	7	0	2	1	4	62	14	46	2	0
Saugatuck-Douglas	2,156	9	0	2	1	6	79	20	56	3	1
Sebewaing	1,736	2	0	1	0	1	20	3	16	1	1
Shelby Township	73,960	86	0	20	9	57	1,048	163	841	44	9
Shepherd	1,524	3	0	2	0	1	37	2	35	0	0
Somerset Township	4,609	0	0	0	0	0	27	5	22	0	0
Southfield	72,253	352	2	34	136	180	2,549	625	1,530	394	9
Southgate	29,761	82	1	4	24	53	1,193	153	930	110	6
South Haven	4,399	24	0	3	7	14	326	33	280	13	0
South Lyon	11,408	4	0	2	1	1	116	21	92	3	1
South Rockwood	1,676	4	0	0	1	3	34	7	26	1	0
Sparta	4,183	11	0	6	0	5	97	5	89	3	0
Spring Arbor Township	8,250	1	0	0	1	0	36	4	32	0	0
Springfield	5,238	23	0	1	3	19	124	28	87	9	1
Spring Lake-Ferrysburg	5,269	3	0	1	0	2	89	14	73	2	0
St. Charles	2,043	6	0	0	0	6	31	14	17	0	0
St. Clair	5,442	8	0	2	0	6	55	13	42	0	0
St. Clair Shores	59,841	151	0	20	13	118	1,185	281	815	89	4
Sterling Heights	129,974	232	4	16	30	182	2,578	357	2,059	162	9
St. Ignace	2,437	6	0	1	0	5	55	6	48	1	0
St. Johns	7,879	5	0	2	0	3	112	29	80	3	0
St. Joseph Township	10,043	15	0	1	3	11	147	32	111	4	0
Stockbridge	1,222	2	0	1	0	1	38	4	34	0	0
Sumpter Township	9,457	12	0	2	1	9	170	53	106	11	1
Suttons Bay	611	0	0	0	0	0	13	0	13	0	0
Swartz Creek	5,712	6	0	0	2	4	105	29	70	6	0
Sylvan Lake	1,732	2	0	0	1	1	30	7	23	0	0
Tawas	4,580	7	0	4	2	1	121	20	100	1	0
Taylor	62,534	303	1	31	60	211	2,398	563	1,581	254	27
Tecumseh	8,487	9	0	4	0	5	107	18	86	3	2
Thetford Township	6,991	10	1	0	0	9	40	21	15	4	0
Thomas Township	11,927	14	0	3	1	10	216	28	180	8	0
Tittabawassee Township	9,688	4	0	1	0	3	82	13	68	1	0
Trenton	18,676	21	0	3	4	14	229	57	162	10	1
Troy	81,567	60	2	9	13	36	1,664	181	1,376	107	14
Tuscarora Township	3,013	4	0	0	0	4	136	7	128	1	0
Unadilla Township	3,383	3	0	0	0	3	50	19	27	4	0
Union City	1,598	1	0	1	0	0	60	5	55	0	0
Utica	4,766	14	0	0	4	10	259	32	219	8	2
Van Buren Township	28,548	107	1	19	10	77	801	170	559	72	1
Vassar	2,685	2	0	0	0	2	26	2	24	0	0
Vicksburg	2,929	3	0	0	0	3	95	19	74	2	1
Walker	23,783	46	1	5	7	33	819	75	724	20	2
Walled Lake	7,049	12	0	2	0	10	104	18	83	3	1
Warren	134,340	715	0	91	148	476	3,787	999	2,049	739	53
Waterford Township	72,224	141	0	19	32	90	1,341	298	948	95	11
Watervliet	1,737	7	0	2	0	5	34	2	31	1	0
Wayne	17,427	119	0	18	23	78	557	141	341	75	9
West Bloomfield Township	65,157	36	2	2	9	23	690	148	530	12	4
West Branch	2,129	7	0	2	0	5	80	9	68	3	0
Westland	83,299	338	1	61	80	196	2,410	575	1,505	330	20
White Cloud	1,407	8	0	2	0	6	66	13	51	2	0
Whitehall	2,694	7	0	3	2	2	64	12	50	2	1
White Lake Township	30,236	24	0	6	2	16	434	57	359	18	2
White Pigeon	1,519	2	0	2	0	0	18	1	16	1	0
Williamston	3,868	4	0	2	1	1	29	7	21	1	0

Table 8. Offenses Known to Law Enforcement, by Selected State and City, 2012— continued

(Number)

State/city	Population	Violent crime	Murder and nonnegligent manslaughter	Forcible rape	Robbery	Aggravated assault	Property crime	Burglary	Larceny-theft	Motor vehicle theft	Arson[1]
Wixom	13,597	39	0	4	4	31	328	43	254	31	1
Wolverine Lake	4,343	1	0	0	1	0	33	8	25	0	1
Woodhaven	12,752	16	0	2	4	10	235	15	201	19	0
Woodland Township	2,037	0	0	0	0	0	0	0	0	0	0
Wyandotte	25,637	36	0	4	7	25	733	129	542	62	2
Ypsilanti	19,610	171	2	19	41	109	968	373	557	38	15
Zeeland	5,560	11	0	4	0	7	102	39	61	2	2
Zilwaukee	1,650	0	0	0	0	0	16	2	13	1	0
Minnesota[6]											
Albany	2,601		0		0	0	26	2	24	0	1
Albert Lea	18,082		0		1	25	494	55	425	14	6
Alexandria	11,192		0		2	14	320	47	257	16	0
Annandale	3,292		0		0	5	80	11	66	3	0
Anoka	17,367		0		15	16	747	74	634	39	6
Appleton	1,401		0		0	3	20	6	14	0	0
Apple Valley	49,827		2		16	18	1,116	109	981	26	4
Arden Hills	9,704		0		1	2	156	32	108	16	1
Aurora	1,693		0		0	0	0	0	0	0	0
Austin	24,993		0		11	46	712	154	540	18	1
Avon	1,411		0		0	0	13	2	11	0	0
Babbitt	1,484		0		0	3	37	3	33	1	1
Baxter	7,691		0		0	8	504	8	493	3	1
Bayport	3,518		0		0	0	43	5	34	4	0
Becker	4,609		0		0	5	43	10	32	1	0
Belgrade	748		0		0	0	0	0	0	0	0
Belle Plaine	6,836		0		0	4	100	4	95	1	0
Bemidji	13,745		1		7	35	1,332	98	1,203	31	7
Benson	3,214		0		0	9	110	25	79	6	0
Big Lake	10,222		0		0	12	144	18	124	2	0
Blackduck	804		0		0	1	23	0	23	0	0
Blaine	57,953		0		11	29	1,922	200	1,666	56	3
Blooming Prairie	2,007		0		0	0	0	0	0	0	0
Bloomington	84,596		0		59	63	3,212	227	2,908	77	21
Blue Earth	3,365		1		0	4	47	9	37	1	0
Brainerd	13,734		0		2	36	695	103	575	17	1
Breckenridge	3,417		0		2	2	78	22	54	2	0
Brooklyn Center	30,725		1		54	49	1,571	249	1,196	126	5
Brooklyn Park	77,346		4		91	122	2,629	493	2,001	135	17
Brownton	762		0		0	0	2	0	2	0	0
Buffalo	15,765		0		1	12	423	53	363	7	3
Burnsville	61,218		0		17	86	1,810	202	1,536	72	4
Caledonia	2,868		0		0	2	34	5	28	1	0
Cambridge	8,262		0		0	1	318	27	285	6	0
Cannon Falls	4,112		0		0	3	112	23	85	4	0
Centennial Lakes	10,903		0		0	13	130	15	108	7	0
Champlin	23,568		0		2	10	382	66	312	4	4
Chaska	24,344		0		3	10	339	36	300	3	4
Chisholm	5,008		0		0	2	107	8	94	5	0
Cloquet	12,226		1		3	17	539	66	455	18	2
Cold Spring	5,508		1		0	1	43	4	37	2	0
Columbia Heights	19,758		0		18	38	595	132	438	25	1
Coon Rapids	62,301		1		16	42	1,917	194	1,663	60	10
Corcoran	5,491		0		0	6	47	5	38	4	0
Cottage Grove	35,277		1		3	13	651	110	520	21	15
Crookston	7,907		1		2	16	165	35	120	10	1
Crosby	2,410		0		0	1	54	8	43	3	0
Crystal	22,607		1		18	15	720	116	572	32	3
Dawson	1,536		0		0	1	18	4	14	0	0
Dayton	4,766		0		0	7	54	20	27	7	0
Deephaven-Woodland	4,163		0		0	0	24	9	14	1	0
Dilworth	4,108		0		0	9	187	13	173	1	1
Duluth	86,830		2		90	213	3,861	642	3,047	172	54
Eagan	65,180		0		11	15	1,526	181	1,301	44	6

Table 8. Offenses Known to Law Enforcement, by Selected State and City, 2012— continued

(Number)

State/city	Population	Violent crime	Murder and nonnegligent manslaughter	Forcible rape	Robbery	Aggravated assault	Property crime	Burglary	Larceny-theft	Motor vehicle theft	Arson[1]
Eagle Lake	2,453		0		0	3	22	7	14	1	0
East Grand Forks	8,615		0		0	10	197	25	163	9	0
Eden Prairie	[illegible]		0		0	11	[illegible]	107	[illegible]	20	0
Edina	48,932		0		5	8	871	112	741	18	1
Elk River	23,335		0		3	15	564	58	498	8	3
Elmore	666		0		0	4	14	5	9	0	0
Ely	3,482		0		0	2	75	4	67	4	0
Eveleth	3,742		0		1	6	135	27	97	11	2
Fairmont	10,657		0		1	12	284	36	241	7	1
Falcon Heights	5,416		0		1	3	137	24	103	10	0
Faribault	23,600		0		9	41	790	138	635	17	11
Farmington	21,403		0		2	12	203	33	155	15	2
Fergus Falls	13,209		0		3	22	464	91	355	18	4
Floodwood	531		0		0	6	41	1	39	1	0
Forest Lake	18,738		0		3	6	428	46	349	33	1
Fridley	27,574		0		17	36	1,238	165	1,004	69	3
Gilbert	1,810		0		0	0	1	1	0	0	0
Glencoe	5,634		1		0	2	108	14	93	1	0
Glenwood	2,557		0		0	3	27	9	18	0	0
Golden Valley	20,787		0		9	9	518	100	399	19	3
Goodview	4,055		0		0	2	84	16	66	2	0
Grand Rapids	10,932		0		1	20	482	35	433	14	0
Granite Falls	2,882		0		0	5	35	5	28	2	0
Hallock	979		0		0	0	0	0	0	0	0
Hastings	22,502		0		4	20	702	106	570	26	3
Hermantown	9,476		0		0	1	332	46	281	5	0
Hibbing	16,469		0		3	16	90	6	82	2	0
Hilltop	755		0		0	5	92	10	81	1	1
Hokah	579		0		0	1	13	1	12	0	0
Houston	979		0		0	2	19	4	13	2	0
Hoyt Lakes	2,031		0		0	0	0	0	0	0	0
Hutchinson	14,183		0		1	13	419	30	377	12	5
International Falls	6,417		0		0	11	186	37	143	6	0
Inver Grove Heights	34,394		0		16	43	843	161	608	74	0
Janesville	2,286		0		0	0	16	5	10	1	0
Jordan	5,619		0		0	4	67	3	64	0	0
Kasson	6,016		0		1	3	39	9	30	0	0
Kimball	771		0		0	1	1	0	1	0	0
La Crescent	4,864		0		0	0	0	0	0	0	0
Lake City	5,080		0		1	1	80	13	63	4	0
Lake Crystal	2,582		0		0	1	52	11	40	1	0
Lakes Area	9,473		0		1	10	84	19	61	4	0
Lakeville	56,805		0		1	9	756	123	620	13	4
Lauderdale	2,423		0		2	2	42	5	31	6	2
Lester Prairie	1,732		0		0	4	15	3	11	1	0
Le Sueur	4,076		0		1	2	78	18	56	4	0
Lewiston	1,627		0		0	2	3	0	3	0	0
Lino Lakes	20,478		0		0	11	188	21	164	3	2
Litchfield	6,758		0		1	4	118	24	87	7	0
Little Canada	9,956		0		5	21	256	50	152	54	9
Little Falls	8,403		0		0	13	175	10	156	9	0
Long Prairie	3,473		0		0	3	77	6	70	1	0
Mankato	39,782		0		29	90	1,912	346	1,508	58	8
Maple Grove	62,840		0		11	13	1,280	158	1,097	25	2
Mapleton	1,777		0		0	3	20	4	15	1	2
Maplewood	38,719		0		21	38	2,477	288	1,992	197	2
Marshall	13,788		0		0	25	403	124	270	9	3
Medina	4,995		0		0	0	99	14	84	1	1
Melrose	3,637		0		0	1	41	11	30	0	0
Mendota Heights	11,240		0		1	5	329	54	258	17	0
Milaca	2,953		0		0	0	23	0	23	0	0
Minneapolis	390,240	3,872	39	403	1,719	1,711	19,359	4,782	12,760	1,817	117
Minnetonka	50,758		0		5	15	836	185	629	22	11
Minnetrista	8,846		1		0	0	89	11	76	2	0

Table 8. Offenses Known to Law Enforcement, by Selected State and City, 2012— continued

(Number)

State/city	Population	Violent crime	Murder and nonnegligent manslaughter	Forcible rape	Robbery	Aggravated assault	Property crime	Burglary	Larceny-theft	Motor vehicle theft	Arson[1]
Montevideo	5,365		1		0	11	99	7	92	0	2
Montgomery	2,969		0		1	3	54	8	45	1	0
Moorhead	38,813		0		5	43	865	145	688	32	16
Moose Lake	2,771		0		0	4	96	1	93	2	0
Morris	5,299		0		1	2	141	10	130	1	1
Mound	9,239		0		0	5	142	24	113	5	2
Mounds View	12,384		2		5	25	408	69	312	27	2
Mountain Iron	2,887		0		0	0	0	0	0	0	0
Mountain Lake	2,117		0		0	0	0	0	0	0	0
New Brighton	21,854		0		10	14	584	104	441	39	3
New Hope	20,748		0		10	19	589	88	474	27	5
Newport	3,503		0		1	3	173	25	137	11	0
New Prague	7,448		0		1	6	108	14	92	2	1
New Richland	1,220		0		0	0	0	0	0	0	0
New Ulm	13,526		0		0	4	235	61	171	3	0
North Branch	10,196		1		2	16	331	35	271	25	11
Northfield	20,213		0		7	5	391	53	321	17	8
North Mankato	13,523		0		1	4	219	28	185	6	0
North Oaks	4,552		0		0	0	30	7	23	0	0
North St. Paul	11,675		0		2	2	292	35	234	23	0
Oakdale	27,921		0		10	35	1,238	184	978	76	6
Oak Park Heights	4,417		0		0	1	222	16	204	2	0
Orono	11,646		0		0	6	133	43	89	1	0
Ortonville	1,917		0		0	0	1	0	1	0	0
Osakis	1,757		0		1	3	23	3	19	1	0
Osseo	2,479		0		0	0	0	0	0	0	0
Owatonna	25,734		0		1	22	612	82	509	21	4
Park Rapids	3,710		0		0	6	228	34	183	11	1
Paynesville	2,459		0		0	3	64	9	53	2	0
Plainview	3,350		0		0	0	0	0	0	0	0
Plymouth	72,020		0		14	19	1,198	258	909	31	6
Princeton	4,706		0		5	3	146	17	122	7	0
Prior Lake	23,410		0		4	7	455	45	388	22	0
Proctor	3,078		0		0	3	87	10	70	7	2
Ramsey	23,988		0		2	7	532	68	456	8	3
Red Wing	16,578		0		6	26	655	95	529	31	2
Redwood Falls	5,260		0		1	18	177	35	137	5	2
Richfield	35,953		1		31	32	928	189	691	48	7
Robbinsdale	14,239		1		17	13	443	92	316	35	0
Rochester	108,582		2		55	104	2,721	495	2,137	89	13
Rogers	8,945		0		1	2	124	7	111	6	2
Roseau	2,635		0		0	1	44	2	41	1	0
Rosemount	22,206		0		0	6	262	41	214	7	2
Roseville	34,276		0		11	25	1,491	162	1,230	99	2
Sartell	16,056		0		1	3	384	24	356	4	0
Sauk Centre	4,367		0		1	3	95	8	84	3	0
Sauk Rapids	12,928		0		2	8	129	39	82	8	0
Savage	27,635		0		2	19	666	90	561	15	4
Shakopee	38,057		0		9	54	1,141	146	969	26	7
Shoreview	25,513		0		1	10	282	61	204	17	5
Silver Bay	1,893		0		0	2	9	5	3	1	0
Silver Lake	836		0		0	1	6	2	4	0	0
Slayton	2,145		0		0	0	12	5	7	0	0
Sleepy Eye	3,600		0		0	0	7	3	3	1	0
South Lake Minnetonka	11,901		0		1	12	139	36	101	2	0
South St. Paul	20,465		0		6	39	542	120	365	57	12
Springfield	2,152		0		0	0	0	0	0	0	0
Spring Grove	1,330		0		0	0	0	0	0	0	0
Spring Lake Park	6,498		0		6	19	344	41	282	21	0
St. Anthony	8,388		1		2	5	335	44	277	14	0
Staples	2,993		0		1	7	83	18	60	5	0
St. Charles	3,752		0		0	0	36	4	28	4	2
St. Francis	7,315		0		1	8	167	26	131	10	0

Table 8. Offenses Known to Law Enforcement, by Selected State and City, 2012— continued

(Number)

State/city	Population	Violent crime	Murder and nonnegligent manslaughter	Forcible rape	Robbery	Aggravated assault	Property crime	Burglary	Larceny-theft	Motor vehicle theft	Arson[1]
Stillwater	18,582		1		1	8	478	86	370	22	4
St. James	4,637		0		0	5	113	15	96	2	2
St. Louis Park	46,176		0		16	15	1,490	247	1,192	51	6
St. Paul	290,700	2,101	13	168	658	1,262	11,893	3,150	6,938	1,805	135
St. Paul Park	5,384		0		0	4	206	36	154	16	1
St. Peter	11,295		0		3	7	255	28	225	2	1
Thief River Falls	8,716		0		1	7	242	32	202	8	1
Tracy	2,180		0		0	0	0	0	0	0	0
Two Harbors	3,754		0		0	0	16	1	15	0	0
Vadnais Heights	12,533		0		5	15	396	46	298	52	7
Virginia	8,769		0		9	28	517	53	449	15	2
Wabasha	2,529		0		0	2	73	16	54	3	1
Waite Park	6,790		0		5	18	656	41	604	11	0
Warroad	1,781		0		0	3	34	3	30	1	0
Waseca	9,538		0		3	12	200	24	170	6	0
Wayzata	3,764		0		0	2	120	15	103	2	0
Wells	2,351		0		0	0	17	2	15	0	0
West Hennepin	5,380		0		0	0	60	13	44	3	0
West St. Paul	19,834		0		17	35	931	103	737	91	1
Wheaton	1,419		0		0	0	15	2	11	2	1
White Bear Lake	24,241		0		6	28	790	174	539	77	4
White Bear Township	11,155		0		1	3	154	30	112	12	3
Willmar	19,708		0		8	34	593	73	502	18	3
Windom	4,676		0		0	5	88	31	52	5	2
Winnebago	1,442		0		0	0	37	11	24	2	1
Winona	27,731		0		7	21	498	91	380	27	0
Winsted	2,357		0		0	2	34	5	27	2	0
Woodbury	63,190		0		7	11	1,448	193	1,207	48	4
Worthington	12,858		0		2	18	206	45	150	11	1
Wyoming	7,847		0		0	2	89	15	63	11	2
Zumbrota	3,277		0		0	4	57	13	36	8	2
Mississippi											
Aberdeen	5,571	19	0	0	10	9	187	54	128	5	0
Ackerman	1,490	0	0	0	0	0	9	4	3	2	0
Amory	7,261	8	0	1	1	6	293	86	203	4	0
Bay St. Louis	9,428	26	4	4	11	7	384	77	290	17	3
Belzoni	2,225	3	0	0	0	3	11	0	11	0	0
Biloxi	45,037	188	1	30	85	72	2,267	732	1,420	115	7
Brandon	22,079	6	0	3	2	1	235	111	110	14	3
Brookhaven	12,547	14	1	0	7	6	227	58	165	4	1
Byhalia	1,289	3	0	0	2	1	50	11	35	4	0
Byram	11,653	7	0	0	4	3	268	52	188	28	0
Carthage	5,037	12	0	0	3	9	48	17	30	1	0
Charleston	2,184	11	0	0	10	1	70	27	43	0	0
Cleveland	12,228	51	0	4	28	19	848	127	698	23	0
Clinton	25,573	30	0	8	12	10	650	169	432	49	0
Columbia	6,534	24	0	4	7	13	222	76	146	0	0
Columbus	23,650	100	1	4	16	79	1,145	336	773	36	3
Como	1,278	8	0	1	2	5	31	10	20	1	0
Crystal Springs	5,022	16	1	0	1	14	122	50	66	6	2
D'Iberville	9,711	26	0	3	12	11	666	88	560	18	0
Eupora	2,217	6	0	0	1	5	35	13	21	1	0
Florence	4,214	4	0	1	0	3	48	28	20	0	0
Flowood	7,956	41	0	6	4	31	474	93	375	6	0
Fulton	3,962	3	0	0	2	1	85	7	78	0	0
Gautier	18,643	61	2	5	16	38	640	199	399	42	2
Greenwood	15,010	109	1	23	36	49	871	286	577	8	0
Hattiesburg	46,726	118	5	13	66	34	2,668	375	2,183	110	3
Heidelberg	708	1	0	0	0	1	11	3	6	2	0
Holly Springs	7,654	94	1	2	21	70	293	98	185	10	0
Horn Lake	26,576	24	1	2	14	7	686	155	505	26	4
Indianola	10,641	99	2	5	26	66	808	266	538	4	0
Itta Bena	2,022	11	1	1	4	5	237	159	77	1	1

Table 8. Offenses Known to Law Enforcement, by Selected State and City, 2012— continued

(Number)

State/city	Population	Violent crime	Murder and nonnegligent manslaughter	Forcible rape	Robbery	Aggravated assault	Property crime	Burglary	Larceny-theft	Motor vehicle theft	Arson[1]
Iuka	3,037	12	0	4	1	7	104	43	55	6	0
Jackson	175,939	1,668	63	135	799	671	11,568	4,124	6,308	1,136	63
Kosciusko	7,381	18	1	0	4	13	137	57	80	0	0
Laurel	18,665	61	0	3	28	30	959	325	608	26	3
Leakesville	894	0	0	0	0	0	0	0	0	0	0
Leland	4,427	14	0	0	3	11	158	86	72	0	0
Lexington	1,699	12	1	0	0	11	22	15	5	2	0
Long Beach	15,143	5	0	1	1	3	325	69	246	10	3
Louisville	6,599	14	0	1	4	9	84	29	53	2	1
Lucedale	2,962	4	0	0	1	3	69	9	58	2	0
Madison	24,648	14	0	0	3	11	212	8	202	2	0
McComb	12,818	71	0	3	23	45	727	173	525	29	0
Meridian	41,347	234	10	33	124	67	2,139	734	1,226	179	8
Moss Point	13,756	104	0	12	29	63	736	314	368	54	2
Natchez	15,706	58	3	11	26	18	845	185	651	9	11
Newton	3,346	0	0	0	0	0	5	4	0	1	0
Ocean Springs	17,510	34	2	2	5	25	549	106	419	24	1
Olive Branch	34,141	70	1	12	17	40	999	402	562	35	1
Oxford	19,435	8	0	1	3	4	210	50	147	13	0
Pascagoula	22,477	86	0	31	33	22	1,339	268	991	80	11
Pass Christian	4,722	9	1	3	1	4	168	51	108	9	1
Pearl	25,530	33	0	10	2	21	629	172	446	11	0
Petal	10,610	2	0	0	1	1	73	32	38	3	0
Philadelphia	7,529	52	0	4	11	37	319	144	164	11	0
Picayune	10,877	29	0	3	9	17	410	97	294	19	4
Poplarville	2,896	0	0	0	0	0	100	44	52	4	0
Ridgeland	24,541	38	2	0	10	26	699	65	612	22	1
Ripley	5,386	3	0	0	1	2	98	52	41	5	0
Saltillo	4,834	3	0	0	0	3	96	34	59	3	0
Southaven	49,938	146	0	24	22	100	1,325	189	1,078	58	2
Summit	1,708	3	0	0	3	0	48	29	19	0	0
Vaiden	722	0	0	0	0	0	0	0	0	0	0
Vicksburg	23,700	174	2	21	29	122	1,381	293	1,037	51	5
West Point	11,245	63	3	8	8	44	375	119	253	3	0
Wiggins	4,407	14	0	3	0	11	120	45	74	1	0
Winona	5,030	10	0	0	0	10	34	8	24	2	0
Yazoo City	11,347	78	1	7	16	54	514	252	239	23	0
Missouri											
Adrian	1,677	8	0	0	0	8	53	18	31	4	0
Advance	1,342	0	0	0	0	0	25	2	23	0	1
Alma	401	0	0	0	0	0	0	0	0	0	0
Alton	883	18	0	0	0	18	37	13	22	2	1
Anderson	1,958	15	0	1	0	14	65	14	49	2	0
Appleton City	1,111	6	0	0	0	6	26	10	14	2	0
Arbyrd	510	0	0	0	0	0	0	0	0	0	0
Archie	1,178	0	0	0	0	0	11	4	4	3	0
Arnold	20,920	30	1	3	8	18	725	53	648	24	0
Ashland	3,784	7	0	1	0	6	50	6	43	1	1
Aurora	7,528	69	0	1	2	66	336	56	251	29	1
Auxvasse	987	5	0	0	0	5	59	22	36	1	1
Ava	2,969	6	0	0	1	5	147	34	108	5	0
Ballwin	30,454	18	0	1	1	16	216	52	154	10	1
Bates City	218	0	0	0	0	0	2	0	2	0	0
Battlefield	5,645	2	0	0	2	0	86	28	56	2	2
Bella Villa	730	4	0	0	0	4	5	4	1	0	0
Belle	1,549	5	0	0	0	5	19	8	10	1	0
Bellefontaine Neighbors	10,877	59	0	1	17	41	432	155	202	75	0
Bellerive	188	0	0	0	0	0	1	1	0	0	0
Bellflower	395	1	0	0	0	1	0	0	0	0	0
Bel-Nor	1,501	3	0	2	0	1	24	6	15	3	0
Bel-Ridge	2,741	49	0	1	7	41	133	57	69	7	0
Belton	23,295	71	0	7	10	54	656	101	524	31	6
Berkeley	8,993	261	1	7	23	230	516	226	234	56	10

Table 8. Offenses Known to Law Enforcement, by Selected State and City, 2012— continued

(Number)

State/city	Population	Violent crime	Murder and nonnegligent manslaughter	Forcible rape	Robbery	Aggravated assault	Property crime	Burglary	Larceny-theft	Motor vehicle theft	Arson[1]
Bernie	1,952	2	0	0	0	2	23	6	16	1	1
Bethany	3,265	2	0	0	0	2	58	15	36	7	0
Beverly Hills	575	9	0	0	1	8	29	20	9	0	0
Billings	1,052	1	0	0	1	0	25	8	15	2	0
Birch Tree	679	9	0	0	0	9	14	4	7	3	0
Bismarck	1,554	2	0	1	0	1	4	3	1	0	2
Blackburn	247	0	0	0	0	0	0	0	0	0	0
Bloomfield	1,932	10	0	0	0	10	34	11	23	0	0
Blue Springs	52,848	128	4	12	20	92	1,767	260	1,378	129	5
Bolivar	10,353	47	0	2	1	44	346	71	271	4	1
Bonne Terre	6,891	4	0	0	1	3	60	15	33	12	0
Boonville	8,362	26	0	1	0	25	268	39	224	5	1
Bowling Green	5,356	6	0	1	0	5	162	23	135	4	1
Branson	10,759	165	0	2	20	143	1,297	149	1,103	45	1
Branson West	480	6	0	0	0	6	52	3	48	1	0
Braymer	869	0	0	0	0	0	10	5	5	0	0
Breckenridge Hills	4,753	15	0	1	4	10	187	76	103	8	0
Brentwood	8,068	13	0	0	8	5	252	14	232	6	1
Bridgeton	11,569	76	1	3	18	54	1,118	88	989	41	1
Brookfield	4,482	3	0	0	1	2	124	49	70	5	0
Bucklin	460	1	0	0	0	1	5	3	2	0	0
Buckner	3,092	7	0	4	1	2	65	21	39	5	0
Buffalo	3,086	4	0	0	0	4	155	37	118	0	0
Butler	4,217	5	0	0	1	4	202	31	158	13	1
Butterfield Village	468	0	0	0	0	0	5	2	3	0	0
Byrnes Mill	2,796	5	0	0	0	5	33	0	31	2	0
Cabool	2,144	3	0	1	0	2	41	12	26	3	1
California	4,312	14	0	3	6	5	84	13	64	7	0
Calverton Park	1,294	3	0	1	1	1	16	6	8	2	0
Camden Point	483	0	0	0	0	0	1	1	0	0	0
Camdenton	3,698	22	0	1	0	21	269	29	233	7	0
Cameron	9,943	31	0	0	1	30	216	49	161	6	1
Campbell	1,998	4	0	0	0	4	90	34	52	4	0
Canalou	335	0	0	0	0	0	1	0	0	1	0
Canton	2,370	4	0	0	0	4	69	9	56	4	0
Cape Girardeau	38,474	243	3	12	66	162	2,628	500	2,052	76	16
Cardwell	715	1	0	0	0	1	8	4	3	1	0
Carl Junction	7,525	2	0	0	0	2	166	29	132	5	1
Carterville	1,912	4	0	1	1	2	12	1	10	1	1
Carthage	14,529	26	1	4	3	18	450	65	366	19	3
Caruthersville	6,139	105	0	3	14	88	283	98	176	9	2
Cassville	3,243	20	0	1	1	18	342	33	304	5	1
Center	515	0	0	0	0	0	10	2	8	0	0
Centralia	4,111	8	0	0	2	6	103	19	81	3	1
Chaffee	2,958	5	0	1	0	4	39	15	22	2	1
Charlack	1,365	5	1	1	2	1	39	9	26	4	0
Charleston	5,941	75	2	4	5	64	144	32	108	4	6
Chesterfield	47,560	23	0	2	7	14	755	68	667	20	1
Chillicothe	9,462	14	0	2	2	10	304	66	221	17	2
Clarkton	1,290	9	0	0	0	9	33	6	24	3	1
Claycomo	1,454	6	0	3	0	3	43	4	36	3	0
Clayton	15,966	24	0	3	6	15	270	59	192	19	0
Cleveland	666	1	0	1	0	0	2	2	0	0	0
Clever	2,175	13	0	1	0	12	4	1	2	1	0
Clinton	9,003	47	0	1	2	44	433	97	309	27	1
Cole Camp	1,126	3	0	1	0	2	19	6	10	3	0
Columbia	110,646	476	3	41	162	270	4,221	784	3,294	143	14
Concordia	2,443	4	0	1	0	3	57	22	33	2	0
Conway	791	0	0	0	0	0	7	1	6	0	0
Cool Valley	1,197	5	0	0	3	2	59	11	48	0	0
Corder	403	0	0	0	0	0	0	0	0	0	0
Cottleville	3,121	0	0	0	0	0	79	4	75	0	0
Country Club Hills	1,275	10	0	1	6	3	66	20	42	4	0
Country Club Village	2,442	7	0	0	0	7	20	3	14	3	0

Table 8. Offenses Known to Law Enforcement, by Selected State and City, 2012— continued

(Number)

State/city	Population	Violent crime	Murder and nonnegligent manslaughter	Forcible rape	Robbery	Aggravated assault	Property crime	Burglary	Larceny-theft	Motor vehicle theft	Arson[1]
Crane	1,468	1	0	1	0	0	33	11	22	0	0
Creighton	351	0	0	0	0	0	0	0	0	0	0
Crestwood	11,931	11	0	0	2	9	281	11	264	6	0
Creve Coeur	17,863	17	0	4	4	9	270	46	218	6	1
Crocker	1,136	10	0	1	1	8	44	12	28	4	1
Crystal City	4,879	18	0	2	2	14	217	25	190	2	0
Cuba	3,376	8	0	1	0	7	149	29	114	6	0
Delta	446	0	0	0	0	0	0	0	0	0	0
Desloge	5,082	5	0	0	1	4	290	19	265	6	0
De Soto	6,433	25	0	0	3	22	312	39	253	20	2
Des Peres	8,388	13	0	3	5	5	457	26	430	1	0
Dexter	7,838	25	0	1	4	20	318	59	246	13	1
Diamond	909	4	0	1	0	3	9	2	6	1	0
Dixon	1,583	3	0	0	0	3	61	10	48	3	1
Doniphan	2,007	18	0	1	1	16	201	29	167	5	1
Doolittle	629	4	0	0	0	4	6	1	5	0	0
Drexel	971	3	0	2	0	1	15	6	9	0	0
Duenweg	1,133	3	0	1	1	1	25	12	11	2	1
Duquesne	1,781	5	0	0	0	5	57	14	39	4	1
East Prairie	3,170	14	0	0	0	14	157	27	124	6	0
Edgar Springs	207	0	0	0	0	0	2	1	1	0	0
Edmundson	836	8	0	1	2	5	33	5	23	5	0
Eldon	4,580	11	0	0	1	10	248	56	185	7	2
El Dorado Springs	3,590	30	0	1	4	25	208	48	158	2	2
Ellington	974	2	0	0	0	2	2	1	0	1	1
Ellisville	9,148	6	0	0	0	6	109	19	85	5	0
Ellsinore	455	4	0	1	0	3	1	1	0	0	0
Elsberry	1,956	11	0	0	0	11	27	10	16	1	1
Eminence	600	0	0	0	0	0	5	2	3	0	0
Emma	232	0	0	0	0	0	0	0	0	0	0
Eureka	10,206	11	0	1	1	9	248	21	212	15	0
Excelsior Springs	11,255	29	0	3	2	24	495	96	367	32	2
Exeter	765	0	0	0	0	0	0	0	0	0	0
Fair Grove	1,407	0	0	0	0	0	18	9	9	0	0
Fair Play	476	0	0	0	0	0	3	0	3	0	0
Fairview	385	0	0	0	0	0	0	0	0	0	0
Farmington	16,317	52	0	3	3	46	788	45	722	21	0
Fayette	2,706	4	0	1	0	3	12	1	10	1	0
Ferguson	21,238	80	2	3	38	37	1,041	247	699	95	0
Ferrelview	460	4	0	0	0	4	14	6	8	0	0
Festus	11,665	40	0	4	4	32	291	35	247	9	2
Flordell Hills	824	5	0	0	2	3	49	17	28	4	0
Florissant	52,243	79	0	3	29	47	1,170	244	787	139	2
Foley	163	1	0	0	0	1	1	0	1	0	0
Fordland	807	3	0	0	0	3	20	7	12	1	1
Foristell	508	2	0	0	0	2	25	4	20	1	0
Forsyth	2,303	5	0	0	0	5	87	15	66	6	0
Fredericktown	3,983	5	0	1	1	3	170	18	146	6	1
Freeman	487	0	0	0	0	0	0	0	0	0	0
Frontenac	3,766	3	0	0	1	2	59	12	45	2	0
Fulton	12,833	36	0	2	9	25	463	69	379	15	1
Gallatin	1,764	2	0	0	0	2	12	4	8	0	0
Garden City	1,654	4	0	0	1	3	30	16	13	1	0
Gerald	1,355	2	0	1	0	1	37	12	24	1	0
Gideon	1,085	7	0	0	0	7	0	0	0	0	0
Gladstone	25,832	73	5	3	13	52	726	125	526	75	8
Glasgow	1,112	1	0	0	0	1	9	3	6	0	0
Glendale	5,936	3	2	0	0	1	84	7	75	2	0
Glen Echo Park	160	1	1	0	0	0	4	2	2	0	0
Goodman	1,245	2	0	2	0	0	21	7	11	3	1
Gower	1,531	0	0	0	0	0	15	7	6	2	0
Grain Valley	12,922	30	0	5	2	23	231	42	167	22	1
Granby	2,150	2	0	0	0	2	11	3	7	1	0
Grandin	246	1	0	0	0	1	0	0	0	0	0

Table 8. Offenses Known to Law Enforcement, by Selected State and City, 2012— continued

(Number)

State/city	Population	Violent crime	Murder and nonnegligent manslaughter	Forcible rape	Robbery	Aggravated assault	Property crime	Burglary	Larceny-theft	Motor vehicle theft	Arson[1]
Grandview[3]	24,601	90	0	5	38	47	798	209	504	85	3
Greendale	652	2	0	0	0	2	16	2	12	2	0
Greenfield	1,361	2	0	0	0	2	14	3	9	2	1
Greenville	496	2	0	0	0	2	10	3	7	0	0
Greenwood	5,249	5	0	0	2	3	56	15	36	5	0
Hallsville	1,524	3	0	0	0	3	18	3	15	0	0
Hamilton	1,790	3	0	0	0	3	43	11	30	2	0
Hannibal	17,914	59	0	5	10	44	1,107	165	901	41	1
Hardin	562	0	0	0	0	0	3	0	3	0	0
Harrisonville	10,095	24	0	4	1	19	463	46	396	21	0
Hartville	611	2	0	0	0	2	6	0	6	0	0
Hawk Point	677	0	0	0	0	0	15	3	12	0	0
Hayti	2,924	15	0	2	3	10	187	21	164	2	0
Hayti Heights	624	0	0	0	0	0	2	0	2	0	0
Hazelwood	25,743	88	2	3	23	60	995	178	737	80	4
Henrietta	367	2	0	0	0	2	5	2	3	0	0
Herculaneum	3,486	2	0	0	0	2	73	10	59	4	1
Hermann	2,427	2	0	0	0	2	71	13	58	0	0
Higginsville	4,783	2	0	2	0	0	120	26	85	9	1
Highlandville	927	0	0	0	0	0	0	0	0	0	0
Hillsboro	2,833	10	0	3	1	6	74	10	61	3	3
Hillsdale	1,480	35	1	1	1	32	46	19	23	4	0
Holcomb	637	0	0	0	0	0	0	0	0	0	0
Holden	2,294	15	0	0	0	15	132	18	103	11	0
Hollister	4,525	24	0	2	2	20	131	37	89	5	1
Holt	453	1	0	0	1	0	6	0	4	2	0
Holts Summit	3,260	22	1	1	0	20	48	18	27	3	0
Houston	2,079	5	0	0	0	5	146	15	128	3	0
Howardville	381	0	0	0	0	0	0	0	0	0	0
Humansville	1,051	2	0	0	0	2	9	1	7	1	0
Huntsville	1,564	7	0	0	0	7	28	9	19	0	0
Hurley	178	0	0	0	0	0	1	0	1	0	0
Iberia	737	0	0	0	0	0	2	1	1	0	0
Independence	117,433	537	5	43	127	362	7,152	1,253	5,116	783	33
Indian Point	530	0	0	0	0	0	7	4	2	1	0
Iron Mountain Lake	741	2	1	0	0	1	3	0	3	0	0
Ironton	1,467	0	0	0	0	0	32	7	23	2	1
Jackson	13,964	27	0	2	0	25	338	69	257	12	0
Jasper	942	3	0	0	0	3	18	5	12	1	0
Jefferson City	43,413	261	2	12	39	208	1,586	235	1,311	40	10
Jennings	14,735	144	3	2	34	105	903	307	465	131	7
Jonesburg	771	3	0	2	1	0	29	6	23	0	0
Joplin	50,654	288	2	27	70	189	3,838	653	2,920	265	28
Kahoka	2,048	4	0	0	0	4	15	0	13	2	0
Kansas City	464,073	5,862	105	246	1,647	3,864	25,642	6,964	15,088	3,590	262
Kearney	8,520	3	1	0	1	1	176	18	150	8	0
Kennett	10,960	26	0	1	9	16	656	153	479	24	3
Kimberling City	2,411	2	0	0	0	2	35	8	26	1	0
Kimmswick	157	0	0	0	0	0	0	0	0	0	0
King City	1,021	0	0	0	0	0	9	5	1	3	0
Kinloch	299	8	1	0	1	6	9	5	2	2	2
Kirksville	17,502	50	0	1	2	47	507	88	411	8	4
Kirkwood	27,586	34	0	2	2	30	535	54	472	9	4
Knob Noster	2,760	6	0	1	1	4	87	18	68	1	1
Ladue	8,536	5	0	0	1	4	126	21	104	1	0
La Grange	927	0	0	0	0	0	0	0	0	0	0
Lake Ozark	1,589	10	0	0	0	10	60	18	42	0	0
Lakeshire	1,434	2	0	0	0	2	16	9	7	0	0
Lake St. Louis	14,764	15	0	1	3	11	319	22	291	6	0
Lake Tapawingo	733	0	0	0	0	0	5	1	4	0	0
Lake Waukomis	888	1	0	1	0	0	12	0	12	0	0
Lake Winnebago	1,141	1	0	0	0	1	5	3	2	0	0
Lamar	4,512	10	1	5	0	4	158	30	118	10	2
La Monte	1,141	2	0	0	0	2	10	2	8	0	0

Table 8. Offenses Known to Law Enforcement, by Selected State and City, 2012— continued

(Number)

State/city	Population	Violent crime	Murder and nonnegligent manslaughter	Forcible rape	Robbery	Aggravated assault	Property crime	Burglary	Larceny-theft	Motor vehicle theft	Arson[1]
La Plata	1,372	0	0	0	0	0	7	2	5	0	0
Lathrop	2,094	8	0	2	0	6	27	10	17	0	1
Laurie	943	3	0	0	0	3	27	9	17	1	0
Lawson	2,454	5	0	3	0	2	82	15	65	2	0
Leadington	424	1	0	1	0	0	2	0	1	1	0
Leadwood	1,289	21	0	1	0	20	33	10	21	2	0
Leasburg	341	0	0	0	0	0	1	0	1	0	0
Lebanon	14,527	70	0	2	5	63	699	86	592	21	0
Lee's Summit	91,840	109	0	13	24	72	2,127	263	1,756	108	6
Leeton	577	0	0	0	0	0	6	0	5	1	0
Liberal	755	0	0	0	0	0	6	3	3	0	0
Liberty	29,613	57	0	9	7	41	589	113	400	76	9
Licking	3,126	4	0	0	0	4	97	7	87	3	0
Lincoln	1,196	0	0	0	0	0	18	6	11	1	0
Linn	1,466	4	0	0	0	4	25	9	15	1	0
Linn Creek	242	1	0	0	0	1	2	1	1	0	0
Lone Jack	1,055	0	0	0	0	0	22	4	17	1	0
Louisiana	3,382	0	0	0	0	0	14	1	13	0	0
Lowry City	632	0	0	0	0	0	2	2	0	0	0
Macon	5,490	22	0	0	0	22	222	50	162	10	0
Malden	4,285	8	0	0	1	7	75	27	44	4	0
Manchester	18,124	9	0	1	1	7	333	40	283	10	0
Mansfield	1,292	3	1	1	0	1	72	15	57	0	0
Maplewood	8,059	32	1	2	10	19	587	40	528	19	2
Marble Hill	1,479	5	0	1	0	4	46	9	37	0	0
Marceline	2,202	20	1	2	0	17	58	14	41	3	0
Marionville	2,230	4	0	1	1	2	167	22	128	17	1
Marshall	13,037	28	1	3	3	21	330	64	257	9	0
Marshfield	6,690	38	0	1	1	36	278	36	233	9	0
Marthasville	1,139	0	0	0	0	0	4	0	4	0	0
Martinsburg	305	0	0	0	0	0	0	0	0	0	0
Maryland Heights	27,518	58	0	5	11	42	592	74	489	29	1
Maryville	12,039	12	1	0	2	9	216	27	183	6	0
Matthews	623	1	0	0	0	1	22	6	14	2	0
Maysville	1,102	0	0	0	0	0	9	3	6	0	0
Memphis	1,820	0	0	0	0	0	28	7	21	0	0
Merriam Woods	1,802	0	0	0	0	0	0	0	0	0	0
Mexico	11,583	38	0	5	4	29	296	49	246	1	4
Milan	1,948	0	0	0	0	0	9	1	7	1	0
Miller	701	8	0	2	0	6	15	2	13	0	0
Miner	984	25	0	0	3	22	81	10	69	2	1
Moberly	13,966	26	0	1	7	18	584	85	476	23	5
Moline Acres	2,446	23	1	1	3	18	127	25	97	5	0
Monett	8,841	21	0	1	4	16	479	118	337	24	4
Monroe City	2,509	5	0	1	0	4	45	9	34	2	0
Montgomery City	2,848	8	0	0	0	8	55	15	38	2	0
Morehouse	967	0	0	0	0	0	8	2	4	2	1
Morley	697	0	0	0	0	0	0	0	0	0	0
Mosby	192	3	0	0	0	3	3	1	2	0	0
Moscow Mills	2,539	6	0	0	0	6	39	10	28	1	0
Mound City	1,139	3	0	0	0	3	22	5	17	0	0
Mountain View	2,741	19	0	2	0	17	127	20	106	1	0
Mount Vernon	4,586	24	0	1	2	21	211	23	180	8	0
Napoleon	221	0	0	0	0	0	6	3	1	2	0
Naylor	635	0	0	0	0	0	9	7	2	0	1
Neosho	11,916	33	0	6	2	25	515	95	397	23	3
Nevada	8,328	49	0	3	9	37	868	140	684	44	2
New Bloomfield	671	0	0	0	0	0	1	0	1	0	0
Newburg	470	0	0	0	0	0	1	0	1	0	1
New Florence	772	0	0	0	0	0	28	3	24	1	0
New Franklin	1,099	2	0	0	0	2	4	1	3	0	0
New Haven	2,101	6	0	0	1	5	37	5	31	1	0
New London	987	0	0	0	0	0	25	4	21	0	0
New Madrid	3,093	0	0	0	0	0	42	0	42	0	0

Table 8. Offenses Known to Law Enforcement, by Selected State and City, 2012— continued

(Number)

State/city	Population	Violent crime	Murder and nonnegligent manslaughter	Forcible rape	Robbery	Aggravated assault	Property crime	Burglary	Larceny-theft	Motor vehicle theft	Arson[1]
New Melle	481	1	0	0	0	1	9	1	8	0	0
Niangua	409	0	0	0	0	0	0	0	0	0	0
Nixa	19,339	23	0	5	1	17	357	64	287	6	0
Noel	1,825	8	0	0	0	8	31	4	27	0	0
Normandy	5,015	27	0	1	3	23	121	28	83	10	1
North Kansas City	4,279	13	0	0	6	7	333	31	263	39	0
Northmoor	332	1	0	0	0	1	17	1	11	5	0
Northwoods	4,233	28	0	0	7	21	147	54	78	15	0
Norwood	662	3	0	0	0	3	8	2	6	0	0
Oak Grove	7,834	8	0	2	2	4	223	26	188	9	1
Oakland	1,383	1	0	0	0	1	2	0	2	0	0
Odessa	5,283	9	1	0	2	6	134	25	101	8	0
O'Fallon	80,670	74	2	5	4	63	1,246	125	1,100	21	3
Old Monroe	269	0	0	0	0	0	0	0	0	0	2
Olivette	7,751	9	0	2	1	6	144	28	107	9	2
Oran	1,295	1	0	0	0	1	11	4	7	0	0
Oregon	843	0	0	0	0	0	4	3	1	0	0
Oronogo	2,968	0	0	0	0	0	22	2	20	0	0
Orrick	829	1	0	0	0	1	15	2	8	5	1
Osage Beach	4,330	32	0	2	2	28	295	28	259	8	0
Osceola	934	10	0	0	0	10	29	6	16	7	0
Overland	16,089	54	1	7	21	25	697	182	492	23	6
Owensville	2,672	4	0	0	0	4	48	2	45	1	0
Ozark	18,116	44	0	2	4	38	618	108	491	19	1
Pacific	7,041	24	0	1	2	21	177	36	127	14	0
Pagedale	3,308	27	2	3	6	16	139	52	76	11	3
Palmyra	3,594	5	0	0	0	5	79	11	66	2	0
Parkville	5,658	5	0	0	2	3	122	17	104	1	0
Parma	708	9	0	0	1	8	12	2	9	1	1
Pasadena Park	471	0	0	0	0	0	14	4	10	0	1
Peculiar	4,645	11	0	1	2	8	99	19	76	4	0
Perry	702	1	0	0	0	1	9	2	7	0	0
Perryville	8,272	16	0	1	2	13	193	36	153	4	2
Pevely	5,512	14	0	0	2	12	122	25	91	6	3
Piedmont	1,977	3	0	0	0	3	40	9	28	3	0
Pierce City	1,295	1	0	1	0	0	24	12	10	2	0
Pilot Grove	772	2	0	0	0	2	18	3	15	0	0
Pilot Knob	745	0	0	0	0	0	4	2	2	0	0
Pine Lawn	3,279	36	0	4	7	25	108	49	50	9	3
Pineville	793	0	0	0	0	0	0	0	0	0	0
Platte City	4,782	7	0	1	1	5	97	5	88	4	16
Platte Woods	393	2	0	0	1	1	10	2	8	0	0
Plattsburg	2,328	7	0	2	1	4	67	9	53	5	1
Pleasant Hill	8,176	6	0	1	0	5	96	14	81	1	1
Pleasant Hope	616	1	0	0	0	1	5	2	3	0	1
Pleasant Valley	3,008	2	0	1	0	1	53	20	33	0	0
Polo	568	0	0	0	0	0	8	1	5	2	0
Poplar Bluff	17,167	138	1	7	28	102	1,344	265	1,036	43	9
Portageville	3,203	1	0	0	1	0	22	0	22	0	0
Potosi	2,652	5	0	0	1	4	204	28	170	6	0
Purcell	414	0	0	0	0	0	0	0	0	0	0
Purdy	1,091	1	0	0	1	0	29	12	16	1	0
Puxico	878	1	0	0	0	1	3	1	1	1	1
Queen City	592	0	0	0	0	0	0	0	0	0	0
Qulin	463	0	0	0	0	0	25	3	21	1	1
Randolph	52	0	0	0	0	0	6	1	4	1	0
Raymore	19,354	19	0	1	5	13	393	35	346	12	3
Raytown	29,678	111	1	11	45	54	1,305	276	906	123	5
Reeds Spring	915	2	0	0	0	2	8	4	4	0	2
Republic	14,892	67	0	1	0	66	494	55	424	15	0
Rich Hill	1,396	5	0	0	0	5	40	8	31	1	1
Richland	1,900	4	0	1	0	3	48	11	36	1	0
Richmond	5,744	10	2	2	0	6	295	57	227	11	2
Richmond Heights	8,617	35	0	3	14	18	647	41	582	24	0

Table 8. Offenses Known to Law Enforcement, by Selected State and City, 2012— continued

(Number)

State/city	Population	Violent crime	Murder and nonnegligent manslaughter	Forcible rape	Robbery	Aggravated assault	Property crime	Burglary	Larceny-theft	Motor vehicle theft	Arson[1]
Risco	344	0	0	0	0	0	0	0	0	0	0
Riverside	2,994	11	0	1	0	10	171	12	150	9	0
Riverview	2,860	31	1	2	6	22	166	50	82	34	0
Rockaway Beach	860	2	0	1	1	0	6	4	2	0	0
Rock Hill	4,642	7	0	0	2	5	47	19	26	2	0
Rock Port	1,294	8	0	0	0	8	16	1	15	0	0
Rogersville	3,101	4	1	0	0	3	96	13	79	4	3
Rolla	19,543	55	1	4	10	40	781	108	648	25	3
Rosebud	408	0	0	0	0	0	0	0	0	0	0
Salem	4,965	14	0	2	1	11	184	18	161	5	0
Salisbury	1,600	1	0	0	0	1	19	10	9	0	3
Sarcoxie	1,344	5	0	1	0	4	55	9	43	3	0
Savannah	5,038	2	0	2	0	0	42	8	30	4	0
Scott City	4,565	15	0	1	0	14	119	29	86	4	0
Sedalia	21,416	101	0	5	15	81	1,612	378	1,173	61	8
Seligman	841	4	0	0	0	4	15	5	9	1	0
Senath	1,772	27	0	14	0	13	23	10	11	2	1
Seneca	2,352	1	0	0	0	1	82	20	56	6	0
Seymour	1,937	6	0	0	2	4	54	16	38	0	0
Shelbina	1,682	5	0	4	0	1	5	3	0	2	0
Shrewsbury	6,265	2	0	1	1	0	67	11	51	5	0
Sikeston	16,319	394	2	5	22	365	943	149	769	25	6
Silex	189	0	0	0	0	0	3	2	1	0	0
Slater	1,851	1	0	0	0	1	31	9	22	0	0
Smithville	8,563	16	0	3	0	13	102	19	78	5	0
Southwest City	967	4	0	0	0	4	9	2	7	0	0
Sparta	1,786	4	0	0	1	3	26	7	18	1	0
Springfield	160,962	1,596	16	141	353	1,086	14,504	2,215	11,238	1,051	61
St. Ann	13,040	85	0	5	6	74	399	75	272	52	2
St. Charles	66,723	101	1	7	23	70	1,949	222	1,663	64	16
St. Clair	4,754	38	1	3	4	30	328	46	270	12	0
Steele	2,162	43	0	0	1	42	78	22	51	5	0
Steelville	1,652	6	0	1	1	4	62	5	51	6	0
Ste. Genevieve	4,412	12	1	0	1	10	118	12	99	7	0
St. James	4,212	10	0	2	0	8	108	3	102	3	0
St. John	6,528	21	0	1	4	16	252	75	161	16	0
St. Joseph	77,330	323	1	22	91	209	4,708	993	3,344	371	25
St. Louis	318,667	5,661	113	199	1,778	3,571	21,995	4,986	13,520	3,489	196
St. Marys	361	0	0	0	0	0	3	0	3	0	0
Stover	1,093	2	0	0	0	2	41	11	28	2	0
St. Peters	53,364	119	0	6	14	99	1,389	114	1,249	26	9
Strafford	2,379	4	0	0	1	3	118	11	104	3	0
Strasburg	141	0	0	0	0	0	0	0	0	0	0
St. Robert	4,440	24	0	2	6	16	370	61	298	11	1
Sturgeon	890	0	0	0	0	0	0	0	0	0	0
Sugar Creek	3,362	10	0	3	0	7	205	54	133	18	0
Sullivan	7,135	15	0	4	4	7	413	61	334	18	0
Summersville	502	0	0	0	0	0	12	2	10	0	0
Sunset Hills	8,510	7	1	0	2	4	155	15	130	10	0
Sweet Springs	1,482	0	0	0	0	0	15	2	12	1	2
Tarkio	1,555	0	0	0	0	0	20	7	13	0	0
Terre du Lac	2,332	6	0	0	0	6	34	11	18	5	0
Thayer	2,274	0	0	0	0	0	19	2	16	1	0
Tipton	3,282	0	0	0	0	0	27	5	20	2	0
Town and Country	10,833	3	0	0	1	2	97	20	76	1	0
Tracy	212	0	0	0	0	0	6	0	6	0	0
Trenton	5,993	10	0	1	0	9	174	43	121	10	1
Trimble	649	3	0	0	0	3	6	2	4	0	1
Troy	10,661	14	0	1	7	6	369	23	335	11	0
Truesdale	733	0	0	0	0	0	12	3	9	0	0
Union	10,277	36	0	0	4	32	542	60	473	9	1
Unionville	1,867	0	0	0	0	0	24	3	19	2	0
University City	35,428	143	8	5	56	74	1,499	295	1,108	96	12
Uplands Park	446	6	0	0	0	6	18	8	8	2	0

Table 8. Offenses Known to Law Enforcement, by Selected State and City, 2012— continued

(Number)

State/city	Population	Violent crime	Murder and nonnegligent manslaughter	Forcible rape	Robbery	Aggravated assault	Property crime	Burglary	Larceny-theft	Motor vehicle theft	Arson[1]
Urbana	417	3	0	0	0	3	7	1	6	0	0
Van Buren	834	0	0	0	0	0	10	0	9	1	0
Vandalia	3,910	3	0	1	0	2	62	13	47	2	1
Velda City	1,422	15	0	0	0	15	40	21	17	2	0
Velda Village Hills	1,056	13	0	0	2	11	30	19	9	2	0
Verona	620	1	0	0	0	1	11	4	5	2	0
Viburnum	696	2	0	0	0	2	11	7	4	0	1
Vienna	611	2	0	0	0	2	25	3	22	0	0
Vinita Park	1,883	7	0	1	1	5	43	11	31	1	0
Walnut Grove	671	0	0	0	0	0	3	0	3	0	0
Wardell	424	0	0	0	0	0	5	4	1	0	0
Warrensburg	19,146	33	1	4	7	21	625	95	497	33	5
Warrenton	7,906	33	0	1	2	30	456	48	396	12	1
Warsaw	2,137	18	0	0	1	17	150	24	122	4	0
Warson Woods	1,965	2	0	0	1	1	10	2	8	0	0
Washburn	433	0	0	0	0	0	3	3	0	0	0
Washington	14,071	19	0	1	4	14	489	77	399	13	3
Waverly	846	0	0	0	0	0	14	2	11	1	0
Waynesville	4,938	18	0	0	2	16	102	34	67	1	1
Weatherby Lake	1,757	1	0	0	0	1	20	2	18	0	0
Webb City	11,116	11	0	5	2	4	587	64	492	31	0
Webster Groves	23,032	21	0	3	5	13	264	59	195	10	1
Wellington	809	0	0	0	0	0	0	0	0	0	0
Wellston	2,316	155	0	6	49	100	232	80	110	42	5
Wellsville	1,222	3	0	0	0	3	15	7	7	1	0
Wentzville	29,506	57	0	11	9	37	602	51	523	28	4
Weston	1,673	5	0	0	0	5	27	7	20	0	0
West Plains	12,086	58	0	3	2	53	841	134	676	31	0
Wheaton	690	0	0	0	0	0	8	4	4	0	0
Willard	5,337	3	0	1	0	2	96	11	83	2	0
Willow Springs	2,203	20	0	1	1	18	105	35	69	1	0
Winfield	1,419	2	0	0	0	2	7	1	6	0	1
Winona	1,337	13	0	0	0	13	52	11	38	3	0
Wood Heights	709	2	0	0	0	2	10	7	2	1	0
Woodson Terrace	4,069	16	0	3	4	9	145	37	70	38	2
Wright City	3,125	18	0	0	2	16	79	22	56	1	0
Montana											
Baker	1,792	0	0	0	0	0	21	3	18	0	0
Belgrade	7,601	18	0	5	1	12	227	28	190	9	5
Billings	106,371	370	3	38	68	261	4,812	793	3,608	411	14
Boulder	1,189	2	0	0	0	2	8	0	8	0	0
Bozeman	38,289	98	1	30	8	59	1,326	134	1,136	56	7
Bridger	709	1	0	0	0	1	7	2	5	0	0
Colstrip	2,264	2	0	0	0	2	14	1	12	1	0
Columbia Falls	4,740	4	0	0	0	4	131	4	124	3	1
Columbus	1,909	8	0	0	1	7	38	4	32	2	0
Conrad	2,634	8	0	0	0	8	35	1	32	2	0
Cut Bank	2,939	15	0	2	0	13	104	30	72	2	0
Dillon	4,142	4	0	0	0	4	43	5	34	4	0
East Helena	2,055	1	0	0	0	1	16	1	11	4	0
Ennis	841	0	0	0	0	0	2	0	2	0	0
Eureka	1,038	1	0	1	0	0	28	2	24	2	0
Fort Benton	1,470	5	0	0	0	5	11	0	9	2	0
Glasgow	3,324	6	0	3	0	3	42	4	33	5	0
Glendive	4,981	13	1	1	0	11	192	29	154	9	3
Great Falls	59,360	151	1	10	25	115	2,788	320	2,338	130	15
Hamilton	4,404	29	1	3	0	25	229	21	200	8	3
Havre	9,667	62	0	15	1	46	434	28	381	25	8
Helena	28,791	127	0	26	12	89	1,015	122	861	32	11
Hot Springs	549	3	0	0	0	3	17	1	16	0	0
Joliet	597	0	0	0	0	0	0	0	0	0	0
Kalispell	20,147	69	1	17	7	44	894	90	770	34	0
Laurel	6,861	11	0	1	0	10	185	17	152	16	3

Table 8. Offenses Known to Law Enforcement, by Selected State and City, 2012— continued

(Number)

State/city	Population	Violent crime	Murder and nonnegligent manslaughter	Forcible rape	Robbery	Aggravated assault	Property crime	Burglary	Larceny-theft	Motor vehicle theft	Arson[1]
Lewistown	5,899	17	0	3	0	14	81	5	69	7	1
Libby	2,630	4	0	0	0	4	65	7	55	3	0
Livingston	7,017	24	0	3	1	20	142	15	118	9	1
Manhattan	1,564	0	0	0	0	0	18	3	14	1	1
Miles City	8,497	22	0	3	0	19	200	15	173	12	2
Missoula	67,758	221	0	25	33	163	3,041	378	2,558	105	10
Plains	1,057	2	0	0	0	2	10	0	9	1	0
Polson	4,555	23	0	3	0	20	263	25	224	14	3
Red Lodge	2,129	12	0	2	0	10	68	9	55	4	2
Ronan City	1,896	20	0	2	1	17	100	11	83	6	0
Sidney	5,474	25	0	1	2	22	144	32	100	12	0
Stevensville	1,833	8	0	1	0	7	21	4	14	3	1
St. Ignatius	855	2	0	0	0	2	14	1	13	0	0
Thompson Falls	1,326	0	0	0	0	0	26	7	18	1	1
Troy	939	2	0	1	0	1	31	5	26	0	0
West Yellowstone	1,307	2	0	0	0	2	7	0	7	0	0
Whitefish	6,428	17	0	4	1	12	175	14	152	9	0
Wolf Point	2,664	23	0	5	1	17	199	40	155	4	2
Nebraska											
Ashland	2,479	2	0	0	0	2	7	0	6	1	0
Auburn	3,499	4	0	4	0	0	19	3	13	3	0
Aurora	4,484	7	0	1	0	6	46	21	24	1	0
Beatrice	12,388	37	0	9	2	26	452	104	342	6	1
Bellevue	51,678	55	1	20	13	21	1,142	155	890	97	8
Bennington	1,491	0	0	0	0	0	12	2	9	1	0
Blair	8,069	7	0	2	2	3	124	19	92	13	0
Broken Bow	3,571	2	0	1	0	1	61	8	49	4	0
Central City	2,912	0	0	0	0	0	60	5	52	3	0
Chadron	5,901	7	0	3	2	2	164	16	140	8	1
Columbus	22,537	20	0	7	2	11	475	68	389	18	1
Cozad	4,014	1	0	0	0	1	41	8	30	3	0
Crete	7,077	10	0	2	2	6	217	62	148	7	3
Emerson	845	0	0	0	0	0	5	1	4	0	0
Falls City	4,346	4	0	0	0	4	46	9	36	1	0
Fremont	26,641	29	0	10	1	18	693	104	555	34	6
Gering	8,578	3	0	0	0	3	138	23	109	6	0
Gordon	1,600	12	0	2	0	10	31	2	28	1	0
Gothenburg	3,608	6	0	3	0	3	70	5	61	4	1
Grand Island	49,583	162	0	40	21	101	2,305	367	1,859	79	17
Hastings	24,961	57	0	24	10	23	911	149	726	36	2
Holdrege	5,531	3	0	1	0	2	119	10	104	5	0
Imperial	2,110	2	0	1	0	1	11	0	11	0	0
Kearney	31,392	42	1	15	3	23	867	118	733	16	9
La Vista	16,242	10	0	5	3	2	262	36	192	34	0
Lexington	10,329	16	0	7	0	9	306	79	219	8	1
Lincoln	264,175	1,050	3	182	197	668	10,171	1,616	8,244	311	26
Lyons	851	3	0	0	0	3	7	2	5	0	0
Madison	2,458	1	0	0	0	1	18	5	13	0	0
McCook	7,735	8	0	3	1	4	236	38	186	12	3
Milford	2,099	1	0	1	0	0	30	8	22	0	0
Minden	2,985	2	0	1	0	1	108	21	85	2	0
Mitchell	1,717	1	0	1	0	0	26	13	12	1	0
Nebraska City	7,366	4	0	2	1	1	200	37	152	11	2
Norfolk	24,418	28	0	18	0	10	820	108	675	37	3
North Platte	24,806	65	0	19	7	39	1,118	121	953	44	9
Ogallala	4,732	5	0	1	2	2	113	10	100	3	0
Omaha	417,970	2,485	41	187	815	1,442	19,178	3,311	13,120	2,747	73
O'Neill	3,719	1	0	0	0	1	23	4	19	0	0
Papillion	19,466	8	0	2	1	5	444	36	388	20	4
Plainview	1,247	1	0	0	0	1	1	0	1	0	0
Plattsmouth	6,534	4	0	3	1	0	180	14	153	13	1
Ralston	6,077	7	0	0	3	4	216	35	141	40	0
Scottsbluff	15,174	19	0	4	3	12	576	77	480	19	2

Table 8. Offenses Known to Law Enforcement, by Selected State and City, 2012— continued

(Number)

State/city	Population	Violent crime	Murder and nonnegligent manslaughter	Forcible rape	Robbery	Aggravated assault	Property crime	Burglary	Larceny-theft	Motor vehicle theft	Arson[1]
Scribner	865	0	0	0	0	0	0	0	0	0	0
Seward	6,995	6	0	2	0	4	94	10	79	5	0
Sidney	6,789	9	2	0	0	7	100	16	81	3	0
South Sioux City	13,386	21	0	3	5	13	369	50	299	20	0
Superior	1,961	3	0	0	0	3	11	6	5	0	0
Valentine	2,779	13	0	2	0	11	25	2	17	6	0
Valley	1,915	4	0	1	1	2	66	4	57	5	0
Wahoo	4,560	1	0	1	0	0	59	9	48	2	0
Wilber	1,888	0	0	0	0	0	16	2	13	1	0
Wymore	1,449	0	0	0	0	0	22	2	20	0	0
York	7,857	4	0	0	3	1	208	27	176	5	1
Nevada											
Boulder City	15,364	12	0	0	3	9	218	94	117	7	6
Carlin	2,431	7	0	0	0	7	30	7	16	7	0
Elko	18,788	118	5	26	7	80	836	209	541	86	0
Fallon	8,633	23	0	1	6	16	362	60	278	24	0
Henderson	263,469	445	4	61	172	208	5,295	1,408	3,386	501	30
Las Vegas Metropolitan Police Department	1,479,393	11,598	76	596	3,824	7,102	46,427	14,220	25,522	6,685	216
Lovelock	1,906	32	0	0	1	31	45	16	27	2	0
Mesquite	15,625	17	0	4	3	10	302	72	216	14	0
North Las Vegas	221,884	1,695	14	73	389	1,219	5,534	1,557	3,022	955	14
Reno	230,486	1,192	7	33	327	825	7,423	1,633	4,909	881	29
Sparks	92,387	234	1	32	68	133	2,559	609	1,710	240	14
West Wendover	4,530	20	0	6	1	13	173	45	114	14	1
Winnemucca	7,587	10	1	0	2	7	133	42	79	12	2
Yerington	3,081	12	0	2	0	10	96	28	67	1	1
New Hampshire											
Alexandria	1,612	2	0	0	0	2	52	21	29	2	0
Alstead	1,936	0	0	0	0	0	9	2	7	0	0
Alton	5,274	1	0	0	1	0	100	24	75	1	1
Amherst	11,251	4	0	3	0	1	220	18	201	1	2
Antrim	2,649	4	0	3	0	1	69	7	51	11	0
Ashland	2,075	2	0	0	1	1	39	10	28	1	1
Atkinson	6,787	0	0	0	0	0	33	11	22	0	0
Auburn	4,980	5	0	0	1	4	114	28	85	1	1
Barnstead	4,615	3	0	0	0	3	70	26	41	3	0
Barrington	8,647	1	0	0	0	1	97	22	70	5	0
Bartlett	2,783	1	0	1	0	0	42	9	31	2	0
Bedford	21,297	8	0	1	1	6	393	43	343	7	2
Belmont	7,385	15	0	6	1	8	197	37	152	8	2
Bennington	1,482	1	0	0	0	1	66	19	44	3	5
Berlin	9,964	14	0	5	2	7	169	49	117	3	2
Bethlehem	2,525	2	0	1	0	1	32	12	17	3	0
Boscawen	3,975	4	0	0	2	2	82	3	73	6	0
Bow	7,539	1	0	0	0	1	77	13	61	3	0
Bradford	1,654	0	0	0	0	0	15	5	9	1	0
Brentwood	4,508	5	0	2	0	3	38	8	29	1	0
Bristol	3,053	5	0	1	0	4	103	42	58	3	0
Campton	3,331	2	0	0	0	2	85	25	57	3	2
Candia	3,931	2	0	0	0	2	59	12	46	1	0
Canterbury	2,360	0	0	0	0	0	20	2	17	1	1
Carroll	756	1	0	0	0	1	55	5	50	0	0
Center Harbor	1,101	0	0	0	0	0	33	13	19	1	0
Charlestown	5,092	4	0	0	0	4	56	13	36	7	2
Claremont	13,293	39	1	6	2	30	477	66	397	14	3
Colebrook	2,278	2	0	1	1	0	49	6	43	0	0
Concord	42,815	92	0	22	19	51	1,272	182	1,063	27	15
Conway	10,096	45	0	6	9	30	438	59	370	9	5
Dalton	969	4	1	1	0	2	12	2	9	1	0
Danville	4,409	2	0	0	0	2	72	14	53	5	0
Deerfield	4,303	1	0	1	0	0	54	13	41	0	0
Deering	1,920	0	0	0	0	0	21	6	14	1	1

Table 8. Offenses Known to Law Enforcement, by Selected State and City, 2012— continued

(Number)

State/city	Population	Violent crime	Murder and nonnegligent manslaughter	Forcible rape	Robbery	Aggravated assault	Property crime	Burglary	Larceny-theft	Motor vehicle theft	Arson[1]
Derry	33,284	60	0	8	5	47	793	182	574	37	18
Dover	30,226	36	1	8	9	18	623	87	528	8	14
Dublin	1,596	1	0	0	0	1	18	6	12	0	0
Dunbarton	2,766	4	0	0	0	4	18	6	12	0	0
Durham	14,712	21	0	5	0	16	116	18	96	2	2
Effingham	1,463	2	0	0	0	2	40	17	21	2	0
Enfield	4,578	5	0	0	0	5	55	18	36	1	0
Epping	6,443	11	0	3	1	7	222	23	195	4	4
Epsom	4,580	8	0	1	2	5	62	18	38	6	1
Exeter	14,380	16	0	8	1	7	155	19	129	7	5
Farmington	6,840	16	2	7	1	6	209	71	131	7	2
Fitzwilliam	2,395	1	0	0	0	1	32	10	18	4	1
Franconia	1,104	1	0	1	0	0	38	11	26	1	0
Fremont	4,305	6	0	1	0	5	59	15	44	0	0
Gilford	7,156	16	0	5	0	11	214	38	170	6	0
Gilmanton	3,791	1	0	0	0	1	45	24	18	3	1
Goffstown	17,723	8	0	1	2	5	244	48	194	2	0
Grantham	2,972	1	1	0	0	0	21	4	17	0	0
Greenland	3,569	4	2	1	0	1	70	12	58	0	0
Hampstead	8,567	2	0	0	0	2	119	35	72	12	1
Hampton	15,510	25	0	7	1	17	318	40	261	17	1
Hampton Falls	2,246	0	0	0	0	0	32	12	20	0	0
Hancock	1,661	0	0	0	0	0	8	1	7	0	0
Hanover	11,265	11	0	8	0	3	230	16	212	2	3
Haverhill	4,696	8	0	0	1	7	99	23	73	3	1
Henniker	4,849	10	0	3	0	7	83	13	67	3	3
Hillsborough	6,038	11	0	4	1	6	115	10	97	8	1
Hinsdale	4,044	8	0	0	2	6	137	8	127	2	1
Hooksett	13,489	22	0	5	5	12	431	49	376	6	1
Hopkinton	5,606	10	0	0	0	10	55	4	51	0	0
Hudson	24,574	30	0	6	5	19	423	68	335	20	4
Jaffrey	5,451	1	0	1	0	0	77	25	51	1	0
Keene	23,399	61	0	6	13	42	831	114	688	29	4
Kingston	6,058	5	0	2	0	3	70	17	45	8	0
Laconia	16,016	60	0	10	8	42	714	120	575	19	5
Lancaster	3,476	7	1	1	3	2	135	18	114	3	0
Lebanon	13,145	39	0	10	8	21	432	43	384	5	8
Lee	4,366	3	0	0	0	3	33	5	26	2	1
Lincoln	1,661	7	0	1	0	6	110	22	86	2	2
Lisbon	1,594	0	0	0	0	0	23	7	15	1	0
Litchfield	8,307	6	0	1	1	4	78	25	51	2	2
Londonderry	24,257	25	0	3	3	19	407	71	320	16	5
Loudon	5,333	3	0	0	0	3	150	20	126	4	1
Madison	2,496	1	0	1	0	0	28	6	22	0	0
Manchester	110,040	624	1	72	205	346	3,848	849	2,848	151	55
Marlborough	2,060	0	0	0	0	0	29	11	17	1	0
Meredith	6,267	9	0	2	0	7	189	38	147	4	0
Merrimack	25,606	6	0	0	1	5	223	33	181	9	0
Middleton	1,798	7	0	0	0	7	22	10	12	0	1
Milford	15,181	32	0	3	8	21	333	43	275	15	2
Milton	4,636	14	0	4	0	10	89	30	53	6	3
Mont Vernon	2,420	2	0	1	0	1	16	4	10	2	1
Moultonborough	4,037	6	0	4	0	2	81	29	51	1	0
Nashua	86,870	204	0	37	48	119	2,361	375	1,902	84	31
New Boston	5,345	2	0	0	0	2	45	20	24	1	2
Newbury	2,078	0	0	0	0	0	22	11	11	0	0
New Durham	2,659	4	0	0	0	4	46	18	28	0	0
Newfields	1,688	0	0	0	0	0	18	7	11	0	0
New Hampton	2,174	1	0	1	0	0	68	8	59	1	0
Newington	756	1	0	0	1	0	241	7	234	0	0
New Ipswich	5,123	0	0	0	0	0	22	7	14	1	2
New London	4,407	0	0	0	0	0	38	9	28	1	0
Newport	6,476	17	0	6	0	11	289	58	219	12	0
Newton	4,628	1	0	0	0	1	70	11	57	2	0

Table 8. Offenses Known to Law Enforcement, by Selected State and City, 2012— continued

(Number)

State/city	Population	Violent crime	Murder and nonnegligent manslaughter	Forcible rape	Robbery	Aggravated assault	Property crime	Burglary	Larceny-theft	Motor vehicle theft	Arson[1]
Northfield	4,842	9	0	2	1	6	121	22	90	9	2
North Hampton	4,323	4	0	1	1	2	73	10	63	0	1
Northumberland	2,264	2	0	0	0	2	36	12	23	1	2
Northwood	4,263	10	0	2	0	8	95	18	65	12	0
Nottingham	4,811	4	0	1	0	3	49	11	34	4	0
Orford	1,235	1	0	0	0	1	14	3	10	1	0
Ossipee	4,338	7	0	1	2	4	105	5	91	9	0
Pelham	12,954	11	0	1	1	9	217	40	168	9	1
Pembroke	7,137	7	0	1	1	5	99	16	82	1	2
Peterborough	6,310	6	0	0	0	6	113	20	90	3	2
Pittsfield	4,119	9	0	1	1	7	110	35	73	2	0
Plaistow	7,651	1	0	1	0	0	212	22	185	5	0
Plymouth	6,992	11	0	5	2	4	227	18	209	0	16
Portsmouth	20,888	34	0	5	11	18	588	60	512	16	1
Raymond	10,190	23	1	8	1	13	185	38	142	5	2
Rindge	6,011	6	0	2	1	3	59	12	44	3	0
Rochester	29,992	75	0	7	19	49	1,094	131	934	29	7
Rollinsford	2,548	5	0	1	1	3	43	6	36	1	0
Rye	5,326	3	0	2	0	1	91	2	85	4	0
Salem	28,926	38	2	6	12	18	902	88	771	43	10
Sanbornton	2,978	3	0	1	0	2	64	14	45	5	0
Sandown	6,019	5	1	0	0	4	50	15	33	2	0
Sandwich	1,324	1	0	0	0	1	59	23	36	0	1
Seabrook	8,738	23	0	3	4	16	217	36	175	6	0
Somersworth	11,862	53	0	12	12	29	573	62	501	10	4
South Hampton	819	0	0	0	0	0	1	0	1	0	0
Strafford	4,024	1	0	0	0	1	24	3	20	1	0
Stratham	7,293	4	0	1	0	3	81	8	71	2	2
Sugar Hill	563	0	0	0	0	0	6	4	2	0	0
Sunapee	3,349	1	0	0	0	1	44	16	28	0	1
Thornton	2,489	4	0	1	0	3	32	9	23	0	0
Tilton	3,581	13	0	3	2	8	199	17	177	5	0
Troy	2,142	3	0	0	0	3	23	1	22	0	0
Wakefield	5,068	5	0	1	1	3	118	41	65	12	1
Washington	1,117	2	0	1	0	1	21	11	10	0	0
Waterville Valley	246	1	0	0	0	1	25	4	20	1	1
Weare	8,824	10	0	2	1	7	122	35	82	5	1
Webster	1,877	1	0	0	0	1	38	5	32	1	0
Wilton	3,692	10	0	4	0	6	73	20	50	3	3
Winchester	4,337	14	0	4	2	8	114	27	86	1	3
Windham	13,664	15	0	7	1	7	141	28	108	5	2
Wolfeboro	6,258	8	0	4	0	4	101	23	73	5	1
Woodstock	1,374	5	0	0	1	4	59	12	45	2	0
New Jersey											
Aberdeen Township	18,319	24	0	3	13	8	299	79	216	4	2
Absecon	8,447	22	0	1	8	13	224	70	148	6	1
Allendale	6,580	2	0	0	1	1	59	22	35	2	0
Allenhurst	499	1	0	0	0	1	11	2	9	0	0
Allentown	1,840	2	0	0	1	1	8	1	7	0	0
Alpha	2,374	1	0	0	1	0	18	2	15	1	0
Alpine	1,870	0	0	0	0	0	16	2	12	2	0
Andover Township	6,321	2	0	0	0	2	31	7	24	0	0
Asbury Park	16,211	247	3	10	84	150	1,005	225	747	33	4
Atlantic City	39,722	699	19	35	322	323	2,453	481	1,884	88	4
Atlantic Highlands	4,410	5	0	2	0	3	63	13	50	0	1
Audubon	8,856	12	0	1	9	2	359	29	317	13	0
Audubon Park	1,027	0	0	0	0	0	21	2	18	1	0
Avalon	1,332	3	0	0	0	3	203	38	164	1	0
Avon-by-the-Sea	1,912	1	0	0	0	1	54	15	38	1	1
Barnegat Light	580	0	0	0	0	0	9	4	5	0	0
Barnegat Township	21,141	26	0	0	5	21	252	51	197	4	3
Barrington	7,012	9	0	0	0	9	60	29	24	7	0
Bay Head	978	1	0	1	0	0	45	4	41	0	0

Table 8. Offenses Known to Law Enforcement, by Selected State and City, 2012— continued

(Number)

State/city	Population	Violent crime	Murder and nonnegligent manslaughter	Forcible rape	Robbery	Aggravated assault	Property crime	Burglary	Larceny-theft	Motor vehicle theft	Arson[1]
Bayonne	64,036	132	0	6	41	85	817	205	560	52	1
Beach Haven	1,185	3	0	1	0	2	125	19	106	0	0
Beachwood	11,154	9	0	1	1	7	193	40	151	2	0
Bedminster Township	8,242	2	0	1	1	0	46	14	29	3	0
Belleville	36,158	71	0	1	41	29	860	204	481	175	1
Bellmawr	11,629	21	0	0	7	14	291	70	202	19	0
Belmar	5,829	12	0	2	5	5	258	39	209	10	0
Belvidere	2,686	1	0	0	0	1	35	12	23	0	0
Bergenfield	27,072	19	0	0	3	16	148	18	125	5	5
Berkeley Heights Township	13,319	2	0	0	1	1	103	16	84	3	0
Berlin	7,620	7	0	0	3	4	202	48	151	3	2
Berlin Township	5,379	12	0	1	3	8	270	31	235	4	5
Bernards Township	26,903	5	0	3	1	1	98	37	56	5	0
Bernardsville	7,779	0	0	0	0	0	29	9	19	1	0
Beverly	2,595	13	0	0	4	9	54	20	31	3	2
Blairstown Township	5,976	1	0	0	0	1	56	28	28	0	0
Bloomfield	47,620	126	1	1	73	51	1,089	263	654	172	2
Bloomingdale	7,705	3	0	0	0	3	62	13	49	0	0
Bogota	8,282	3	0	0	0	3	59	12	39	8	0
Boonton	8,435	7	0	0	2	5	110	14	94	2	0
Boonton Township	4,307	4	0	2	0	2	37	15	22	0	0
Bordentown	3,949	2	0	0	1	1	42	9	30	3	0
Bordentown Township	11,444	11	0	1	1	9	178	26	142	10	2
Bound Brook	10,500	12	0	0	6	6	244	71	168	5	0
Bradley Beach	4,323	4	0	0	3	1	152	23	125	4	0
Branchburg Township	14,597	7	0	0	1	6	128	17	109	2	0
Brick Township	75,809	81	0	6	16	59	1,245	265	964	16	3
Bridgeton	25,378	322	2	4	140	176	1,108	484	582	42	3
Bridgewater Township	44,884	13	0	4	5	4	655	85	555	15	2
Brielle	4,802	3	0	0	0	3	48	16	32	0	0
Brooklawn	1,964	15	0	1	7	7	184	30	141	13	0
Buena	4,623	14	0	1	2	11	122	49	70	3	0
Burlington	9,989	45	0	2	17	26	228	59	153	16	2
Burlington Township	22,746	34	0	5	12	17	328	39	272	17	0
Butler	7,619	10	0	3	1	6	90	43	45	2	0
Byram Township	8,349	6	0	3	3	0	51	9	42	0	0
Caldwell	7,872	12	0	0	4	8	97	28	64	5	0
Califon	1,078	0	0	0	0	0	7	0	6	1	0
Camden	77,665	1,993	67	74	755	1,097	4,007	1,089	2,214	704	109
Cape May	3,605	3	0	0	2	1	184	21	161	2	0
Cape May Point	290	0	0	0	0	0	7	0	7	0	0
Carlstadt	6,198	6	0	0	2	4	172	31	116	25	0
Carney's Point Township	8,068	30	0	1	6	23	172	61	102	9	2
Carteret	23,083	49	0	6	14	29	375	99	245	31	0
Cedar Grove Township	12,490	2	0	0	0	2	95	19	69	7	0
Chatham	9,056	3	0	1	1	1	44	8	34	2	0
Chatham Township	10,560	1	0	0	0	1	25	2	21	2	0
Cherry Hill Township	71,337	112	1	0	55	56	2,249	271	1,887	91	2
Chesilhurst	1,641	5	0	0	0	5	48	21	25	2	0
Chester	1,667	0	0	0	0	0	23	7	16	0	0
Chesterfield Township	7,745	1	0	0	0	1	25	5	19	1	0
Chester Township	7,922	1	0	0	0	1	25	13	11	1	0
Cinnaminson Township	15,676	23	0	2	9	12	359	78	271	10	0
Clark Township	14,913	5	1	0	1	3	153	15	132	6	0
Clayton	8,242	11	1	1	3	6	145	27	113	5	2
Clementon	5,021	22	0	0	12	10	263	85	170	8	6
Cliffside Park	23,867	29	1	2	8	18	171	66	102	3	0
Clifton	84,684	184	0	13	80	91	1,579	358	1,080	141	3
Clinton	2,724	3	0	0	1	2	28	10	17	1	0

Table 8. Offenses Known to Law Enforcement, by Selected State and City, 2012— continued

(Number)

State/city	Population	Violent crime	Murder and nonnegligent manslaughter	Forcible rape	Robbery	Aggravated assault	Property crime	Burglary	Larceny-theft	Motor vehicle theft	Arson[1]
Clinton Township	13,514	5	1	1	1	2	81	20	58	3	0
Closter	8,469	1	0	0	1	0	46	12	32	2	0
Collingswood	13,983	25	0	3	17	5	531	123	364	44	3
Colts Neck Township	10,201	7	0	0	2	5	92	29	60	3	1
Cranbury Township	3,897	1	0	0	0	1	61	16	42	3	1
Cranford Township	22,864	13	0	2	7	4	206	50	151	5	1
Cresskill	8,672	1	0	0	0	1	27	10	15	2	1
Deal	755	1	0	0	0	1	48	22	20	6	0
Delanco Township	4,312	3	0	0	2	1	97	26	68	3	0
Delaware Township	4,573	0	0	0	0	0	23	12	11	0	0
Delran Township	17,012	15	0	1	7	7	256	47	200	9	2
Demarest	4,936	0	0	0	0	0	19	6	12	1	0
Denville Township	16,809	2	0	0	1	1	160	42	118	0	0
Deptford Township	30,800	104	2	3	43	56	1,570	277	1,255	38	1
Dover	18,347	47	0	1	24	22	331	82	236	13	0
Dumont	17,682	17	0	3	5	9	133	22	111	0	1
Dunellen	7,304	16	0	0	1	15	245	75	166	4	0
Eastampton Township	6,109	3	0	2	1	0	114	55	55	4	0
East Brunswick Township	48,009	25	0	0	11	14	859	124	716	19	5
East Greenwich Township	9,630	7	0	0	3	4	116	35	78	3	1
East Hanover Township	11,274	13	0	0	1	12	188	17	164	7	0
East Newark	2,444	7	0	0	4	3	27	2	18	7	0
East Orange	64,682	364	5	22	142	195	1,165	349	478	338	17
East Rutherford	9,016	8	1	0	3	4	169	24	122	23	2
East Windsor Township	27,389	30	0	3	7	20	273	54	205	14	5
Eatontown	12,785	32	0	5	8	19	489	71	412	6	0
Edgewater	11,647	9	0	0	5	4	193	26	157	10	0
Edgewater Park Township	8,943	22	0	0	15	7	155	29	116	10	0
Edison Township	101,007	122	0	9	59	54	1,481	341	1,029	111	11
Egg Harbor City	4,261	20	0	3	5	12	141	46	91	4	1
Egg Harbor Township	43,501	99	0	3	24	72	854	194	628	32	7
Elizabeth	126,281	1,007	14	37	535	421	4,351	987	2,197	1,167	6
Elk Township	4,250	12	0	0	2	10	136	51	80	5	1
Elmer	1,398	0	0	0	0	0	14	5	9	0	0
Elmwood Park	19,627	22	0	0	10	12	352	75	255	22	1
Elsinboro Township	1,038	1	0	0	0	1	14	6	8	0	1
Emerson	7,486	1	0	0	0	1	46	8	38	0	0
Englewood	27,460	81	0	2	29	50	439	144	269	26	0
Englewood Cliffs	5,340	0	0	0	0	0	73	15	49	9	0
Englishtown	1,857	1	0	0	0	1	18	2	16	0	0
Essex Fells	2,126	0	0	0	0	0	21	9	9	3	0
Evesham Township	45,849	30	0	2	8	20	684	114	561	9	4
Ewing Township	36,388	76	2	6	35	33	680	218	418	44	4
Fairfield Township, Essex County	7,515	10	0	1	2	7	246	38	177	31	0
Fair Haven	6,158	2	0	0	1	1	43	11	32	0	0
Fair Lawn	32,830	24	0	3	8	13	386	68	307	11	2
Fairview	13,994	24	0	0	13	11	195	69	121	5	2
Fanwood	7,396	2	0	0	1	1	85	17	67	1	0
Far Hills	928	0	0	0	0	0	9	0	9	0	0
Flemington	4,591	8	0	0	1	7	83	12	70	1	0
Florence Township	12,192	14	1	1	5	7	108	41	63	4	1
Florham Park	11,809	5	0	2	1	2	71	9	57	5	1
Fort Lee	35,754	30	1	0	11	18	275	57	203	15	0
Franklin	5,044	9	0	0	2	7	155	16	136	3	0
Franklin Lakes	10,712	4	0	0	1	3	90	23	63	4	0
Franklin Township, Gloucester County	16,952	27	0	2	5	20	365	120	224	21	1
Franklin Township, Hunterdon County	3,204	0	0	0	0	0	40	11	29	0	0

Table 8. Offenses Known to Law Enforcement, by Selected State and City, 2012— continued

(Number)

State/city	Population	Violent crime	Murder and nonnegligent manslaughter	Forcible rape	Robbery	Aggravated assault	Property crime	Burglary	Larceny-theft	Motor vehicle theft	Arson[1]
Franklin Township, Somerset County	62,885	72	1	2	47	22	1,150	354	706	90	5
Freehold	12,122	39	1	4	26	8	179	46	121	12	1
Freehold Township	36,397	36	0	8	13	15	854	87	748	19	1
Frenchtown	1,376	0	0	0	0	0	22	2	20	0	0
Galloway Township[7]	37,506		0	5	17		674	183	461	30	1
Garfield	30,838	65	0	5	26	34	641	123	476	42	1
Garwood	4,271	0	0	0	0	0	81	5	73	3	0
Gibbsboro	2,283	4	0	0	1	3	66	23	41	2	0
Glassboro	18,718	39	1	6	18	14	483	138	329	16	1
Glen Ridge	7,576	11	0	1	3	7	183	62	115	6	0
Glen Rock	11,734	6	0	0	2	4	88	12	75	1	0
Gloucester City	11,501	29	0	2	11	16	359	98	255	6	0
Gloucester Township	64,898	208	0	7	41	160	1,540	394	1,084	62	9
Green Brook Township	7,270	6	0	1	0	5	140	31	105	4	1
Greenwich Township, Gloucester County	4,937	3	0	2	1	0	138	36	99	3	1
Greenwich Township, Warren County	5,720	0	0	0	0	0	70	3	65	2	0
Guttenberg	11,355	36	1	0	11	24	128	43	78	7	0
Hackensack[7]	43,499		0	4	34		879	107	703	69	0
Haddonfield	11,639	6	0	1	4	1	236	72	159	5	4
Haddon Heights	7,505	8	0	2	4	2	136	40	95	1	1
Haddon Township	14,766	21	0	0	13	8	420	91	305	24	0
Haledon	8,372	15	0	0	10	5	202	59	118	25	0
Hamburg	3,277	1	0	0	1	0	36	14	22	0	0
Hamilton Township, Atlantic County	26,613	61	0	2	21	38	925	195	699	31	10
Hamilton Township, Mercer County	89,111	188	0	10	98	80	1,978	489	1,357	132	4
Hammonton	14,852	15	0	0	1	14	186	60	118	8	1
Hanover Township	13,857	9	0	1	3	5	175	40	129	6	0
Harding Township	3,881	3	0	1	0	2	38	15	19	4	1
Hardyston Township	8,212	4	0	0	1	3	169	24	143	2	0
Harrington Park	4,717	0	0	0	0	0	9	1	8	0	0
Harrison	13,841	61	0	1	23	37	412	70	281	61	1
Harrison Township	12,514	10	0	3	1	6	177	63	113	1	0
Harvey Cedars	341	0	0	0	0	0	29	12	13	4	0
Hasbrouck Heights	11,978	4	0	0	2	2	69	17	50	2	0
Haworth	3,420	1	0	1	0	0	10	4	6	0	0
Hawthorne	18,914	8	0	0	0	8	249	61	167	21	0
Hazlet Township	20,456	10	0	0	5	5	242	28	208	6	2
Helmetta	2,201	3	0	1	0	2	11	3	8	0	0
High Bridge	3,657	2	0	0	1	1	33	10	23	0	0
Highland Park	14,129	7	0	0	3	4	247	57	174	16	0
Highlands	5,035	12	0	1	2	9	71	17	50	4	0
Hillsborough Township	38,665	7	0	1	0	6	282	76	200	6	4
Hillsdale	10,337	2	0	1	0	1	76	11	65	0	0
Hillside Township	21,630	78	0	5	47	26	608	144	346	118	2
Hi-Nella	873	4	0	0	0	4	36	17	19	0	0
Hoboken	50,794	150	0	11	43	96	995	151	743	101	1
Ho-Ho-Kus	4,124	1	0	0	0	1	18	5	13	0	0
Holland Township	5,304	1	0	1	0	0	28	8	20	0	0
Holmdel Township	16,873	8	0	2	2	4	208	24	181	3	0
Hopatcong	15,144	7	0	0	1	6	110	26	83	1	0
Hopewell	1,935	2	0	0	0	2	16	5	11	0	0
Hopewell Township	17,430	8	0	0	2	6	163	42	119	2	1
Howell Township	51,379	41	0	1	9	31	638	171	455	12	3
Independence Township	5,671	5	0	0	0	5	54	11	40	3	0
Interlaken	825	1	0	1	0	0	16	9	7	0	0
Irvington	54,274	708	9	20	324	355	1,967	563	797	607	22
Island Heights	1,689	0	0	0	0	0	21	3	18	0	0
Jackson Township[7]	55,400		0	6	9		751	285	453	13	12
Jamesburg	5,977	10	0	4	2	4	63	15	46	2	0

Table 8. Offenses Known to Law Enforcement, by Selected State and City, 2012— continued

(Number)

State/city	Population	Violent crime	Murder and nonnegligent manslaughter	Forcible rape	Robbery	Aggravated assault	Property crime	Burglary	Larceny-theft	Motor vehicle theft	Arson[1]
Jefferson Township	21,539	5	0	0	0	5	229	83	142	4	0
Jersey City	251,554	1,847	11	45	880	911	5,479	1,426	3,291	762	24
Keansburg	10,166	31	2	0	8	21	314	56	251	7	3
Kearny	41,310	100	0	3	53	44	887	123	633	131	3
Kenilworth	7,998	9	0	2	3	4	172	16	148	8	0
Keyport	7,283	24	0	2	8	14	173	40	129	4	6
Kinnelon	10,355	7	0	0	0	7	53	14	36	3	0
Lacey Township	27,918	18	0	1	4	13	665	119	539	7	1
Lake Como	1,769	1	0	0	0	1	28	0	26	2	0
Lakehurst	2,681	2	0	0	0	2	52	5	45	2	0
Lakewood Township	93,742	110	2	1	46	61	1,103	274	785	44	4
Lambertville	3,915	1	0	0	0	1	78	17	59	2	0
Laurel Springs	1,916	2	0	0	1	1	75	29	44	2	0
Lavallette	1,893	3	0	0	0	3	64	21	42	1	0
Lawrence Township, Mercer County	33,483	37	0	5	19	13	786	95	668	23	3
Lebanon Township	6,605	2	0	0	0	2	38	12	22	4	0
Leonia	9,040	5	0	0	2	3	83	31	47	5	0
Lincoln Park	10,628	6	0	1	4	1	99	34	63	2	1
Linden	40,926	131	1	5	56	69	971	162	689	120	1
Lindenwold	17,685	133	1	5	58	69	705	269	379	57	7
Linwood	7,122	5	1	0	1	3	92	35	55	2	2
Little Egg Harbor Township	20,261	34	0	2	2	30	480	143	326	11	11
Little Falls Township	14,520	17	0	1	4	12	232	63	145	24	0
Little Ferry	10,749	11	0	0	2	9	120	20	86	14	0
Little Silver	5,985	5	0	0	0	5	83	22	60	1	0
Livingston Township	29,556	15	0	2	7	6	423	41	342	40	1
Loch Arbour	195	0	0	0	0	0	10	3	4	3	0
Lodi	24,415	43	0	0	23	20	420	102	271	47	0
Logan Township	6,089	7	0	0	1	6	115	31	72	12	0
Long Beach Township	3,081	8	0	2	0	6	181	79	100	2	0
Long Branch	30,902	124	0	6	39	79	803	204	567	32	0
Long Hill Township	8,794	1	0	1	0	0	66	16	49	1	0
Longport	898	1	0	1	0	0	4	1	3	0	0
Lopatcong Township	8,028	2	0	0	1	1	80	13	64	3	0
Lower Alloways Creek Township	1,773	1	0	0	0	1	28	6	19	3	0
Lower Township	22,819	28	2	1	7	18	615	163	441	11	0
Lumberton Township	12,645	14	0	1	4	9	326	45	269	12	2
Lyndhurst Township	20,791	13	1	0	6	6	281	51	213	17	0
Madison	16,002	7	0	0	1	6	106	18	85	3	1
Magnolia	4,359	15	0	0	4	11	120	38	74	8	0
Mahwah Township	26,170	3	1	0	0	2	120	13	99	8	0
Manalapan Township	39,105	23	0	0	9	14	353	98	235	20	3
Manasquan	5,932	13	0	4	1	8	190	28	160	2	1
Manchester Township	43,491	20	0	0	1	19	457	199	255	3	5
Mansfield Township, Burlington County	8,603	2	0	0	1	1	108	12	92	4	0
Mansfield Township, Warren County	7,739	6	0	0	0	6	242	30	211	1	0
Mantoloking	299	1	0	0	0	1	23	1	22	0	0
Mantua Township	15,334	12	0	1	2	9	252	53	192	7	0
Manville	10,443	5	0	0	3	2	208	31	164	13	0
Maple Shade Township	19,261	35	0	4	12	19	467	177	243	47	1
Maplewood Township	24,022	45	2	0	30	13	519	112	361	46	1
Margate City	6,380	1	0	0	0	1	187	21	165	1	0
Marlboro Township	40,430	17	0	1	5	11	321	84	227	10	2
Matawan	8,862	9	0	0	5	4	95	36	56	3	0
Maywood	9,665	5	0	1	2	2	114	43	66	5	0
Medford Lakes	4,173	0	0	0	0	0	30	12	18	0	0
Medford Township	23,191	17	0	7	1	9	267	59	201	7	2
Mendham	5,033	1	0	1	0	0	27	3	21	3	0

Table 8. Offenses Known to Law Enforcement, by Selected State and City, 2012— continued

(Number)

State/city	Population	Violent crime	Murder and nonnegligent manslaughter	Forcible rape	Robbery	Aggravated assault	Property crime	Burglary	Larceny-theft	Motor vehicle theft	Arson[1]
Mendham Township	5,931	1	0	0	0	1	19	12	6	1	0
Merchantville	3,837	6	0	0	2	4	101	29	66	6	0
Metuchen	13,715	11	0	0	5	6	197	38	149	10	1
Middlesex	13,778	4	0	0	3	1	131	29	99	3	0
Middle Township	18,875	47	0	4	12	31	898	184	677	37	1
Middletown Township	66,919	45	1	6	8	30	731	161	555	15	1
Midland Park	7,211	4	0	1	0	3	56	5	51	0	0
Millburn Township	20,279	8	0	0	2	6	566	66	485	15	1
Milltown	6,966	10	0	0	3	7	80	10	70	0	0
Millville	28,651	248	2	14	94	138	2,083	506	1,533	44	11
Mine Hill Township	3,690	1	0	1	0	0	46	12	31	3	0
Monmouth Beach	3,298	1	0	1	0	0	42	7	30	5	0
Monroe Township, Gloucester County	36,410	34	0	1	11	22	881	281	569	31	3
Monroe Township, Middlesex County	39,539	22	0	1	3	18	245	67	169	9	7
Montclair	37,912	49	2	4	26	17	680	220	419	41	3
Montgomery Township	22,464	3	0	1	0	2	132	29	99	4	0
Montvale	7,935	4	0	0	1	3	25	5	19	1	0
Montville Township	21,755	5	0	1	0	4	174	22	149	3	0
Moonachie	2,738	2	0	0	0	2	70	21	46	3	2
Morris Plains	5,588	1	0	0	0	1	70	9	59	2	0
Morristown	18,601	85	0	4	24	57	353	82	255	16	0
Morris Township	22,534	11	0	1	0	10	133	40	85	8	0
Mountain Lakes	4,205	0	0	0	0	0	35	6	26	3	0
Mountainside	6,754	1	0	0	0	1	65	16	42	7	0
Mount Arlington	5,103	1	0	0	0	1	35	2	32	1	0
Mount Ephraim	4,696	9	0	2	3	4	136	20	110	6	0
Mount Holly Township	9,602	34	0	0	11	23	300	54	228	18	2
Mount Laurel Township	42,150	33	0	3	18	12	711	135	552	24	3
Mount Olive Township	28,412	11	0	2	3	6	261	83	165	13	0
Mullica Township	6,174	5	1	0	0	4	129	65	59	5	0
National Park	3,060	13	0	1	4	8	84	23	57	4	2
Neptune City	4,897	8	1	0	2	5	157	22	132	3	0
Neptune Township	28,101	152	0	16	55	81	1,372	298	1,026	48	4
Netcong	3,266	4	0	0	0	4	79	14	61	4	0
Newark	278,906	3,220	96	55	1,976	1,093	10,199	2,144	4,093	3,962	62
New Brunswick	55,717	382	8	24	216	134	1,511	557	871	83	8
Newfield	1,566	1	0	0	0	1	22	7	14	1	2
New Hanover Township	7,432	0	0	0	0	0	9	4	5	0	0
New Milford	16,529	3	0	0	1	2	98	23	74	1	0
New Providence	12,298	2	0	0	1	1	85	17	64	4	0
Newton	7,999	8	1	0	5	2	154	33	120	1	0
North Arlington	15,570	9	0	0	2	7	194	26	146	22	0
North Bergen Township	61,747	89	2	7	36	44	731	124	496	111	3
North Brunswick Township	41,163	51	0	2	26	23	729	219	478	32	0
North Caldwell	6,223	1	0	0	0	1	17	4	10	3	0
Northfield	8,658	1	0	0	1	0	92	19	71	2	0
North Haledon	8,474	2	0	0	1	1	74	32	39	3	2
North Hanover Township	7,730	1	0	0	0	1	55	15	37	3	0
North Plainfield	22,143	49	1	2	20	26	409	114	282	13	1
Northvale	4,692	3	0	0	1	2	24	1	23	0	0
North Wildwood	4,033	23	0	1	3	19	351	80	271	0	1
Norwood	5,776	1	0	0	0	1	27	4	22	1	0
Nutley Township	28,554	22	0	1	6	15	301	82	196	23	1
Oakland	12,899	8	0	0	0	8	109	16	88	5	0
Oaklyn	4,055	4	0	0	3	1	128	34	89	5	1
Ocean City	11,676	15	0	1	1	13	478	88	388	2	0
Ocean Gate	2,032	0	0	0	0	0	72	19	52	1	0

Table 8. Offenses Known to Law Enforcement, by Selected State and City, 2012— continued

(Number)

State/city	Population	Violent crime	Murder and nonnegligent manslaughter	Forcible rape	Robbery	Aggravated assault	Property crime	Burglary	Larceny-theft	Motor vehicle theft	Arson[1]
Oceanport	5,866	11	0	1	2	8	61	15	45	1	1
Ocean Township, Monmouth County	27,454	39	0	3	14	22	547	105	419	23	2
Ocean Township, Ocean County	8,413	4	0	0	0	4	184	18	162	4	0
Ogdensburg	2,410	0	0	0	0	0	28	5	23	0	0
Old Bridge Township	66,057	56	2	2	15	37	912	143	710	59	2
Old Tappan	5,814	0	0	0	0	0	25	6	19	0	0
Oradell	8,071	2	0	0	1	1	50	14	36	0	0
Orange	30,329	262	3	17	138	104	806	264	336	206	6
Oxford Township	2,519	0	0	0	0	0	9	1	8	0	0
Palmyra	7,447	16	0	2	5	9	191	41	137	13	1
Paramus	26,638	29	0	2	19	8	1,373	54	1,291	28	2
Park Ridge	8,744	2	0	0	0	2	39	10	29	0	0
Parsippany-Troy Hills Township	53,793	39	2	5	14	18	496	137	329	30	0
Passaic	70,237	513	6	2	232	273	1,459	439	863	157	6
Paterson	147,148	1,552	21	22	854	655	4,640	1,619	2,114	907	3
Paulsboro	6,143	15	1	0	9	5	242	74	157	11	1
Peapack and Gladstone	2,606	1	0	0	0	1	13	3	10	0	0
Pemberton	1,419	5	0	1	2	2	38	6	30	2	0
Pemberton Township	28,104	102	1	29	27	45	696	259	406	31	18
Pennington	2,605	0	0	0	0	0	11	3	8	0	1
Pennsauken Township	36,033	111	0	5	62	44	1,247	255	826	166	0
Penns Grove	5,157	36	1	1	15	19	170	46	112	12	4
Pennsville Township	13,437	26	0	5	4	17	376	80	289	7	1
Pequannock Township	15,703	6	0	0	4	2	132	34	86	12	1
Perth Amboy	51,345	233	1	9	95	128	1,220	383	711	126	8
Phillipsburg	14,973	34	1	7	11	15	435	83	336	16	1
Pine Beach	2,149	2	0	0	0	2	25	3	22	0	0
Pine Hill	10,273	42	0	3	13	26	266	98	158	10	6
Pine Valley	12	0	0	0	0	0	4	4	0	0	0
Piscataway Township	56,593	64	0	1	21	42	526	133	366	27	6
Pitman	9,079	2	0	0	1	1	174	20	145	9	1
Plainfield	50,332	358	6	14	165	173	1,445	526	818	101	13
Plainsboro Township	23,240	5	0	0	0	5	171	33	131	7	0
Pleasantville	20,334	145	8	20	43	74	582	70	464	48	1
Plumsted Township	8,505	7	0	1	0	6	75	28	46	1	3
Pohatcong Township	3,343	0	0	0	0	0	139	5	132	2	0
Point Pleasant	18,572	13	0	1	4	8	320	64	252	4	1
Point Pleasant Beach	4,711	8	0	1	2	5	256	31	215	10	0
Pompton Lakes	11,169	13	0	1	1	11	88	18	67	3	1
Princeton Township	16,384	6	0	0	1	5	148	41	105	2	1
Prospect Park	5,903	8	0	0	3	5	110	31	67	12	0
Rahway	27,635	77	1	1	43	32	470	110	303	57	2
Ramsey	14,639	14	0	1	2	11	144	7	131	6	1
Randolph Township	26,004	4	0	0	1	3	211	46	152	13	0
Raritan	6,945	9	0	0	5	4	131	28	101	2	0
Raritan Township	22,239	3	0	0	0	3	199	31	163	5	2
Readington Township	16,165	6	0	0	0	6	157	28	127	2	0
Red Bank	12,278	36	1	3	22	10	237	32	198	7	0
Ridgefield	11,159	7	0	0	3	4	67	21	40	6	0
Ridgefield Park	12,875	12	0	0	5	7	136	32	90	14	0
Ridgewood	25,244	11	0	1	3	7	258	40	210	8	0
Ringwood	12,306	4	0	0	1	3	93	21	69	3	0
Riverdale	3,597	0	0	0	0	0	153	6	146	1	0
River Edge	11,470	3	2	0	1	0	97	25	67	5	0
Riverside Township	8,135	21	0	0	9	12	108	49	57	2	0
Riverton	2,798	2	0	0	0	2	55	8	46	1	0
River Vale Township	9,771	0	0	0	0	0	27	6	19	2	0
Robbinsville Township	13,741	7	0	0	1	6	150	30	112	8	0
Rochelle Park Township	5,593	6	0	0	3	3	69	20	47	2	0

Table 8. Offenses Known to Law Enforcement, by Selected State and City, 2012— continued

(Number)

State/city	Population	Violent crime	Murder and nonnegligent manslaughter	Forcible rape	Robbery	Aggravated assault	Property crime	Burglary	Larceny-theft	Motor vehicle theft	Arson[1]
Rockaway	6,506	4	0	0	2	2	70	15	52	3	0
Rockaway Township	24,410	12	0	0	9	3	448	58	384	6	0
Rockleigh	535	0	0	0	0	0	4	1	3	0	0
Roseland	5,857	5	0	0	0	5	46	16	24	6	0
Roselle	21,309	72	4	1	39	28	414	129	229	56	2
Roselle Park	13,438	8	0	0	4	4	127	52	67	8	0
Roxbury Township	23,569	10	0	2	4	4	334	46	278	10	0
Rumson	7,165	1	0	0	0	1	88	18	67	3	0
Runnemede	8,504	16	0	0	6	10	275	86	177	12	1
Rutherford	18,268	8	0	0	3	5	304	76	214	14	5
Saddle Brook Township	13,816	1	0	0	0	1	315	36	273	6	0
Saddle River	3,188	0	0	0	0	0	27	8	14	5	1
Salem	5,158	49	0	4	17	28	264	78	180	6	1
Sayreville	43,151	38	1	1	12	24	579	128	423	28	0
Scotch Plains Township	23,759	12	1	0	4	7	271	58	205	8	1
Sea Bright	1,421	5	0	0	0	5	61	12	43	6	0
Sea Girt	1,839	3	0	1	0	2	36	4	30	2	0
Sea Isle City	2,109	5	0	0	4	1	207	71	136	0	0
Seaside Heights	2,915	30	0	1	6	23	260	40	213	7	0
Seaside Park	1,595	6	0	3	1	2	76	10	64	2	0
Secaucus	16,517	16	0	0	16	0	462	36	377	49	0
Ship Bottom	1,165	1	1	0	0	0	66	9	57	0	0
Shrewsbury	3,832	5	0	1	2	2	74	13	60	1	0
Somerdale	5,172	17	0	1	11	5	330	46	276	8	0
Somers Point	10,840	28	0	0	9	19	351	66	275	10	4
Somerville	12,210	18	0	0	16	2	262	42	211	9	0
South Amboy	8,721	13	0	1	1	11	161	44	109	8	1
South Bound Brook	4,606	2	0	0	2	0	40	15	21	4	0
South Brunswick Township	43,875	34	0	2	7	25	518	108	372	38	2
South Hackensack Township	2,405	6	0	2	2	2	58	10	41	7	0
South Harrison Township	3,188	1	0	0	0	1	36	25	11	0	0
South Orange	16,301	40	0	0	31	9	365	95	227	43	0
South Plainfield	23,629	26	1	0	10	15	425	52	354	19	3
South River	16,176	22	0	2	2	18	206	46	151	9	0
South Toms River	3,719	9	0	0	4	5	92	35	54	3	0
Sparta Township	19,720	2	0	1	1	0	186	30	152	4	0
Spotswood	8,342	5	0	0	3	2	97	15	81	1	3
Springfield	15,985	4	0	1	3	0	201	29	162	10	0
Springfield Township	3,437	4	0	0	1	3	47	16	22	9	0
Spring Lake	3,012	0	0	0	0	0	75	10	65	0	0
Spring Lake Heights	4,741	2	0	0	0	2	15	4	11	0	0
Stafford Township	26,796	16	0	0	2	14	471	60	400	11	0
Stanhope	3,610	1	0	1	0	0	47	20	26	1	0
Stone Harbor	864	1	0	0	0	1	111	17	94	0	0
Stratford	7,070	16	0	0	5	11	158	36	121	1	1
Summit	21,684	12	0	0	3	9	193	29	163	1	0
Surf City	1,217	2	0	0	0	2	36	10	26	0	0
Swedesboro	2,604	3	0	1	0	2	27	7	20	0	0
Tavistock	5	0	0	0	0	0	1	1	0	0	0
Teaneck Township	40,230	56	0	0	29	27	586	120	442	24	3
Tenafly	14,654	3	0	0	0	3	109	35	68	6	0
Teterboro	67	0	0	0	0	0	21	2	17	2	0
Tewksbury Township	6,007	0	0	0	0	0	26	16	10	0	0
Tinton Falls	17,999	13	1	0	2	10	457	66	384	7	0
Toms River Township	92,131	81	1	3	40	37	2,893	640	2,215	38	6
Totowa	10,874	35	0	0	2	33	373	57	285	31	0
Trenton	85,317	1,251	24	23	577	627	2,746	1,291	986	469	19
Union Beach	6,282	12	0	1	0	11	100	52	43	5	0
Union City	67,518	250	1	2	106	141	1,265	241	891	133	1
Union Township	57,234	79	0	5	44	30	1,067	171	768	128	6
Upper Saddle River	8,304	5	0	1	0	4	42	9	28	5	0

Table 8. Offenses Known to Law Enforcement, by Selected State and City, 2012— continued

(Number)

State/city	Population	Violent crime	Murder and nonnegligent manslaughter	Forcible rape	Robbery	Aggravated assault	Property crime	Burglary	Larceny-theft	Motor vehicle theft	Arson[1]
Ventnor City	10,693	12	1	2	8	1	347	99	245	3	2
Vernon Township	23,939	14	1	1	1	11	341	117	220	4	0
Verona	13,418	5	0	2	1	2	154	33	117	4	1
Vineland	61,252	225	1	7	66	151	2,541	694	1,804	43	13
Voorhees Township	29,251	51	2	4	14	31	617	134	466	17	6
Waldwick	9,737	4	0	0	0	4	59	4	54	1	0
Wallington	11,465	8	0	0	4	4	211	60	141	10	0
Wall Township	26,319	22	0	0	2	20	361	83	269	9	0
Wanaque	11,188	2	0	0	0	2	103	6	97	0	0
Warren Township	15,455	1	0	1	0	0	132	47	79	6	0
Washington	6,472	3	0	0	1	2	56	3	53	0	2
Washington Township, Bergen County	9,207	4	0	0	1	3	29	11	17	1	1
Washington Township, Gloucester County	48,940	67	0	3	29	35	1,139	178	920	41	4
Washington Township, Morris County	18,728	4	0	0	1	3	85	15	67	3	0
Washington Township, Warren County	6,662	3	0	0	0	3	37	4	32	1	0
Watchung	5,857	2	0	0	2	0	337	21	306	10	0
Waterford Township	10,693	18	0	2	1	15	168	40	113	15	0
Wayne Township	55,071	40	0	0	13	27	1,227	189	993	45	2
Weehawken Township	12,758	20	0	0	10	10	280	48	196	36	0
Wenonah	2,296	0	0	0	0	0	37	12	24	1	1
Westampton Township	8,873	14	0	1	6	7	184	28	142	14	0
West Amwell Township	3,851	2	0	0	0	2	25	7	18	0	1
West Caldwell Township	10,828	4	0	0	3	1	97	12	73	12	0
West Cape May	1,022	0	0	0	0	0	32	5	27	0	0
West Deptford Township	21,847	15	0	0	7	8	441	104	316	21	1
Westfield	30,637	6	0	1	2	3	298	50	243	5	0
West Long Branch	8,145	8	0	0	4	4	176	48	126	2	0
West Milford Township	26,019	18	1	3	1	13	305	78	216	11	2
West New York	50,507	196	0	8	93	95	733	195	487	51	3
West Orange	46,505	68	2	0	31	35	654	148	436	70	1
Westville	4,322	23	0	0	10	13	149	46	92	11	1
West Wildwood	602	0	0	0	0	0	39	19	19	1	0
West Windsor Township	27,363	5	0	0	3	2	503	68	422	13	0
Westwood	11,033	5	0	0	1	4	68	10	53	5	0
Wharton	6,589	13	0	0	3	10	102	23	78	1	0
Wildwood	5,315	93	0	4	20	69	704	221	469	14	0
Wildwood Crest	3,263	15	0	0	0	15	148	41	106	1	0
Willingboro Township	31,844	111	0	16	53	42	676	200	446	30	6
Winfield Township	1,487	0	0	0	0	0	6	0	6	0	0
Winslow Township	39,660	122	0	3	35	84	704	224	458	22	8
Woodbridge Township	100,612	122	0	3	55	64	1,967	338	1,514	115	11
Woodbury	10,251	43	2	2	18	21	560	98	438	24	0
Woodbury Heights	3,078	3	0	0	2	1	110	18	87	5	0
Woodcliff Lake	5,794	0	0	0	0	0	33	6	27	0	0
Woodland Park	11,895	13	2	0	9	2	168	48	117	3	0
Woodlynne	2,991	29	0	0	15	14	143	44	75	24	1
Wood-Ridge	7,715	5	0	0	0	5	47	8	28	11	0
Woodstown	3,513	2	0	0	0	2	44	16	28	0	0
Woolwich Township	10,278	1	0	0	0	1	68	27	40	1	0
Wyckoff Township	16,885	6	0	0	3	3	135	29	100	6	0
Woodbridge Township	99,915	127	1	8	52	66	2,538	371	2,030	137	6
Woodbury	10,208	29	0	1	16	12	423	77	332	14	3
Woodbury Heights	3,065	6	0	1	4	1	109	16	90	3	0
Woodcliff Lake	5,749	2	0	1	0	1	46	9	37	0	0
Woodland Park	11,858	7	0	0	2	5	255	58	184	13	0

Table 8. Offenses Known to Law Enforcement, by Selected State and City, 2012— continued

(Number)

State/city	Population	Violent crime	Murder and nonnegligent manslaughter	Forcible rape	Robbery	Aggravated assault	Property crime	Burglary	Larceny-theft	Motor vehicle theft	Arson[1]
Woodlynne	2,988	21	1	1	5	14	180	74	87	19	1
Wood-Ridge	7,651	4	1	1	0	2	63	16	37	10	0
Woodstown	3,517	10	0	1	2	7	41	11	29	1	0
Woolwich Township	10,234	7	0	1	1	5	95	32	59	4	0
Wyckoff Township	16,752	4	0	0	1	3	124	47	75	2	0
New Mexico											
Alamogordo	31,377	90	0	4	8	78	816	154	630	32	8
Albuquerque	553,684	4,151	41	278	1,092	2,740	29,718	6,677	20,298	2,743	86
Angel Fire	1,206	4	0	1	0	3	27	11	15	1	0
Artesia	11,389	121	3	3	5	110	580	257	293	30	0
Aztec	6,678	24	0	5	2	17	198	43	144	11	3
Bayard	2,321	4	0	0	0	4	48	10	36	2	0
Capitan	1,487	1	0	0	0	1	12	6	6	0	0
Carlsbad	26,338	141	4	18	12	107	1,247	215	960	72	3
Carrizozo	996	0	0	0	0	0	20	10	10	0	0
Cimarron	1,014	4	0	1	0	3	14	5	9	0	0
Clayton[7]	2,916	16	0	1	2	13			28	10	0
Corrales	8,515	5	0	0	0	5	54	17	36	1	1
Deming	14,987	85	0	9	4	72	648	184	449	15	4
Dexter	1,272	7	0	1	2	4	8	2	4	2	0
Edgewood	3,778	8	0	1	3	4	74	23	44	7	0
Espanola	10,329	270	0	8	51	211	869	356	482	31	1
Eunice	2,959	9	0	0	0	9	73	35	36	2	1
Farmington	45,328	481	4	81	39	357	1,866	332	1,430	104	12
Gallup	22,365	419	7	36	57	319	1,945	380	1,466	99	12
Grants[7]	9,347		1	7	5		290	159	98	33	1
Hobbs	34,543	231	3	20	22	186	1,548	389	1,045	114	3
Jal	2,073	15	0	0	1	14	30	19	10	1	1
Las Cruces	99,824	394	5	56	70	263	4,419	991	3,214	214	9
Las Vegas	13,678	125	0	5	6	114	399	121	257	21	6
Logan	1,043	1	0	0	0	1	21	10	11	0	0
Lordsburg	2,782	16	0	0	1	15	12	1	11	0	2
Los Alamos[7]	18,251	59	0	10	0	49		32		4	3
Lovington	11,146	45	0	5	4	36	225	98	107	20	0
Magdalena	940	12	0	1	0	11	35	17	16	2	0
Milan	3,284	12	0	1	1	10	78	15	55	8	0
Questa	1,772	2	0	0	1	1	16	5	11	0	0
Raton	6,840	9	0	1	3	5	281	144	124	13	4
Red River	480	3	0	0	0	3	24	8	15	1	0
Rio Rancho	89,462	202	2	23	21	156	1,904	364	1,385	155	14
Roswell	48,623	306	8	28	42	228	2,615	552	1,988	75	14
Ruidoso Downs	2,791	23	0	0	1	22	99	14	81	4	0
Santa Clara	1,682	3	0	0	0	3	21	11	8	2	0
Santa Fe	68,751	331	2	15	109	205	3,897	1,907	1,816	174	25
Santa Rosa	2,815	27	0	0	5	22	71	26	43	2	1
Silver City	10,285	86	0	16	14	56	667	168	469	30	3
Socorro	9,069	78	0	1	2	75	387	93	281	13	0
Sunland Park	14,430	6	1	1	2	2	195	58	115	22	2
Taos	5,722	56	2	6	6	42	460	150	306	4	1
Taos Ski Valley	69	0	0	0	0	0	10	5	5	0	0
Texico	1,162	3	0	0	0	3	4	1	3	0	0
Truth or Consequences	6,461	38	1	3	1	33	227	61	151	15	0
Tularosa	2,935	9	0	0	0	9	63	21	42	0	0
Silver City	10,430	82	1	9	4	68	547	134	388	25	4
Socorro	9,152	65	0	0	0	65	377	108	254	15	0
Sunland Park	14,264	12	0	3	2	7	176	43	116	17	1
Taos	5,780	49	1	5	7	36	472	178	277	17	1
Taos Ski Valley	70	1	0	0	0	1	7	0	7	0	0
Tatum	807	1	0	0	1	0	29	0	28	1	1
Texico	1,143	1	0	0	0	1	3	0	3	0	0
Truth or Consequences	6,547	33	0	3	1	29	167	44	114	9	1
Tucumcari	5,423	35	2	0	2	31	289	159	125	5	0

Table 8. Offenses Known to Law Enforcement, by Selected State and City, 2012— continued

(Number)

State/city	Population	Violent crime	Murder and nonnegligent manslaughter	Forcible rape	Robbery	Aggravated assault	Property crime	Burglary	Larceny-theft	Motor vehicle theft	Arson[1]
Tularosa	2,874	24	0	0	1	23	99	28	69	2	0
New York[3]											
Adams Village	1,811	1	0	0	1	0	8	2	6	0	0
Addison Town and Village	2,611	0	0	0	0	0	43	8	34	1	0
Akron Village	2,880	3	0	0	1	2	25	4	20	1	0
Albany	98,187	802	4	43	249	506	4,340	887	3,299	154	
Albion Village	5,993	15	0	1	3	11	282	56	217	9	
Alfred Village	4,193	4	0	1	0	3	45	9	35	1	
Allegany Village	1,814	5	0	0	1	4	32	5	27	0	0
Altamont Village	1,725	1	0	0	0	1	19	2	16	1	
Amherst Town	117,591	88	0	7	28	53	2,261	214	2,010	37	4
Amityville Village	9,608	10	0	0	7	3	200	22	170	8	3
Amsterdam	18,607	18	2	2	7	7	432	124	296	12	1
Arcade Village	2,071	1	0	0	0	1	32	6	25	1	1
Ardsley Village	4,508	2	0	0	1	1	43	8	34	1	0
Asharoken Village	661	0	0	0	0	0	5	0	4	1	0
Attica Village	2,548	3	0	0	0	3	8	5	3	0	0
Auburn	27,739	90	0	3	19	68	984	155	797	32	
Baldwinsville Village	7,415	3	0	0	0	3	102	21	80	1	2
Ballston Spa Village	5,469	20	0	1	2	17	86	13	71	2	0
Batavia	15,527	46	0	5	3	38	562	104	454	4	
Bath Village	5,820	35	0	6	7	22	236	54	181	1	1
Beacon	15,649	66	0	1	17	48	342	80	247	15	2
Bedford Town	17,547	11	0	3	3	5	175	22	149	4	
Bethlehem Town	33,764	16	0	2	2	12	469	64	402	3	
Binghamton	47,250	315	3	15	81	216	2,336	558	1,732	46	
Black River	1,374	0	0	0	0	0	4	2	2	0	0
Blooming Grove Town	12,264	6	0	1	1	4	121	31	82	8	
Bolivar Village	1,050	0	0	0	0	0	1	0	1	0	0
Bolton Town	2,344	2	0	0	0	2	8	2	6	0	0
Brant Town	2,074	2	0	0	0	2	20	4	14	2	0
Brewster	2,408	0	0	0	0	0	11	2	9	0	0
Briarcliff Manor Village	7,962	0	0	0	0	0	14	4	10	0	0
Brighton Town	36,856	28	1	6	10	11	933	173	734	26	
Brockport Village	8,419	17	0	1	3	13	139	31	104	4	
Bronxville Village	6,402	1	0	0	0	1	49	3	43	3	0
Brownville Village	1,142	0	0	0	0	0	7	0	7	0	0
Buffalo	262,434	3,382	48	138	1,388	1,808	13,454	3,976	8,371	1,107	294
Cairo Town	6,667	2	0	0	0	2	33	5	28	0	
Cambridge Village	1,879	1	0	0	0	1	37	13	23	1	
Camillus Town and Village	24,293	20	0	1	3	16	314	39	262	13	0
Canandaigua	10,661	36	0	5	2	29	302	49	244	9	
Canastota Village	4,825	1	0	0	0	1	63	11	48	4	
Canisteo Village	2,283	7	0	0	0	7	41	10	29	2	0
Canton Village	6,339	0	0	0	0	0	59	5	54	0	
Cape Vincent Village	741	0	0	0	0	0	8	0	8	0	0
Carmel Town	34,567	12	0	1	4	7	284	57	211	16	0
Carroll Town	3,528	0	0	0	0	0	7	3	4	0	0
Carthage Village	3,823	1	0	0	0	1	57	10	45	2	
Catskill Village	4,079	17	0	0	3	14	122	15	106	1	
Cattaraugus Village	1,000	0	0	0	0	0	2	0	2	0	0
Cayuga Heights Village	3,755	1	0	0	1	0	37	6	31	0	
Cazenovia Village	2,848	3	0	1	1	1	64	8	55	1	
Central Square Village	1,860	2	0	0	1	1	71	10	60	1	0
Chatham Village	1,763	11	0	1	0	10	91	18	72	1	0
Cheektowaga Town	79,178	175	0	19	66	90	2,821	338	2,396	87	7
Chester Town	8,099	1	0	0	0	1	22	5	14	3	
Chester Village	4,014	6	0	0	3	3	120	7	112	1	0
Chittenango Village	5,103	3	0	0	1	2	85	7	77	1	
Clarkstown Town	80,186	76	0	4	27	45	1,511	107	1,379	25	

Table 8. Offenses Known to Law Enforcement, by Selected State and City, 2012— continued

(Number)

State/city	Population	Violent crime	Murder and nonnegligent manslaughter	Forcible rape	Robbery	Aggravated assault	Property crime	Burglary	Larceny-theft	Motor vehicle theft	Arson[1]
Clayton Village	2,019	0	0	0	0	0	20	4	15	1	
Clyde Village	2,096	7	0	0	1	6	49	9	40	0	
Cobleskill Village	4,683	5	0	1	1	3	169	24	142	3	0
Coeymans Town	7,443	21	0	0	0	21	105	22	71	12	0
Cohocton Town	2,574	0	0	0	0	0	11	3	8	0	0
Cohoes	16,220	43	0	4	8	31	297	91	196	10	
Colchester Town	2,069	0	0	0	0	0	23	7	15	1	0
Colonie Town	77,853	46	0	0	29	17	2,117	214	1,847	56	
Cooperstown Village	1,850	4	0	0	1	3	31	4	27	0	
Corning	11,247	30	0	8	3	19	318	40	275	3	1
Cornwall-on-Hudson Village	3,051	0	0	0	0	0	42	9	33	0	
Cornwall Town	9,736	2	0	1	0	1	88	14	74	0	
Cortland	19,316	35	0	7	13	15	380	120	251	9	2
Crawford Town	9,419	7	0	0	1	6	156	43	109	4	
Croton-on-Hudson Village	8,171	1	0	0	0	1	69	8	58	3	
Cuba Town	3,249	19	1	3	2	13	123	23	97	3	0
Dansville Village	4,718	9	0	1	1	7	142	23	117	2	0
Deerpark Town	7,989	6	0	0	2	4	161	63	94	4	
Delhi Village	3,089	2	0	0	1	1	32	12	19	1	
Depew Village	15,368	24	0	0	10	14	313	57	250	6	0
Deposit Village	1,657	1	0	0	0	1	28	6	22	0	0
Dewitt Town	22,872	30	0	2	10	18	616	92	502	22	3
Dolgeville Village	2,204	12	0	0	0	12	72	10	59	3	
Dryden Village	1,902	2	0	0	0	2	67	3	64	0	
Dunkirk	12,579	47	0	1	10	36	351	97	244	10	
East Aurora-Aurora Town	13,841	2	0	0	1	1	158	19	134	5	1
Eastchester Town	19,805	4	0	0	2	2	223	13	204	6	0
East Fishkill Town	29,239	15	0	3	4	8	223	29	182	12	
East Greenbush Town	16,558	14	0	1	6	7	391	44	342	5	2
East Hampton Town	19,569	14	0	1	0	13	417	62	348	7	
East Hampton Village	1,093	1	0	0	1	0	80	1	78	1	0
Eden Town	7,721	4	0	0	1	3	38	7	30	1	0
Ellicott Town	5,189	11	0	0	5	6	276	18	255	3	
Ellicottville	1,598	2	0	0	0	2	18	5	13	0	
Elmira	29,362	104	2	1	40	61	1,192	250	923	19	1
Elmira Heights Village	4,120	3	0	0	2	1	60	17	42	1	0
Elmira Town	5,991	0	0	0	0	0	0	0	0	0	0
Elmsford Village	4,724	5	0	0	1	4	50	12	31	7	
Endicott Village	13,357	53	0	4	19	30	635	128	497	10	
Evans Town	16,426	26	0	4	6	16	351	72	273	6	0
Fairport Village	5,389	2	0	0	0	2	40	10	29	1	
Fallsburg Town	11,996	13	0	0	2	11	214	82	126	6	
Fishkill Town	20,077	6	0	0	0	6	291	28	259	4	0
Fishkill Village	2,188	2	0	0	0	2	50	2	48	0	
Floral Park Village	16,010	3	0	0	1	2	64	13	48	3	0
Fort Plain Village	2,320	14	0	2	1	11	67	17	49	1	0
Frankfort Town	5,015	2	0	1	0	1	30	9	19	2	
Frankfort Village	2,598	3	0	1	0	2	35	4	31	0	
Franklinville Village	1,738	0	0	0	0	0	32	0	32	0	0
Fredonia Village	11,254	15	1	2	4	8	301	37	264	0	
Freeport Village	43,248	209	5	4	108	92	875	212	604	59	4
Friendship Town	2,008	0	0	0	0	0	33	21	12	0	0
Fulton City	11,970	26	0	5	8	13	567	120	433	14	1
Garden City Village	22,571	5	0	0	2	3	337	48	272	17	0
Gates Town	28,594	66	1	2	29	34	1,234	140	1,049	45	
Geddes Town	10,588	6	0	0	1	5	220	25	195	0	1
Geneseo Village	8,062	1	0	1	0	0	168	2	165	1	0
Geneva	13,396	31	1	6	10	14	307	74	226	7	0
Germantown Town	1,946	0	0	0	0	0	2	0	2	0	0
Glen Park Village	513	1	0	0	0	1	4	1	3	0	0
Glens Falls	14,807	43	1	3	2	37	372	51	315	6	

Table 8. Offenses Known to Law Enforcement, by Selected State and City, 2012— continued

(Number)

State/city	Population	Violent crime	Murder and nonnegligent manslaughter	Forcible rape	Robbery	Aggravated assault	Property crime	Burglary	Larceny-theft	Motor vehicle theft	Arson[1]
Glenville Town	21,916	17	0	2	3	12	402	45	353	4	
Gloversville	15,705	42	0	5	8	29	684	111	545	28	1
Goshen Town	8,312	4	0	0	0	4	110	19	88	3	
Goshen Village	5,514	3	0	0	0	3	78	8	69	1	0
Gowanda Village	2,711	6	0	0	1	5	15	5	10	0	
Granville Village	2,556	1	0	0	1	0	40	8	32	0	0
Great Neck Estates Village	2,788	0	0	0	0	0	15	5	10	0	0
Greece Town	96,752	129	0	18	46	65	2,556	410	2,069	77	
Greenburgh Town	43,409	49	0	0	16	33	590	66	490	34	
Greene Village	1,577	0	0	0	0	0	0	0	0	0	0
Greenport Town	4,150	7	0	0	0	7	164	11	152	1	
Greenwich Village	1,784	2	0	0	0	2	49	9	40	0	
Groton Village	2,380	0	0	0	0	0	60	12	47	1	
Guilderland Town	33,693	23	0	5	10	8	661	52	607	2	
Hamburg Town	45,166	35	0	3	6	26	1,286	189	1,062	35	7
Hamburg Village	9,449	3	0	0	0	3	214	31	178	5	1
Hammondsport Village	666	0	0	0	0	0	17	1	16	0	0
Hancock Village	1,028	1	0	0	1	0	9	5	3	1	0
Harrison Town	27,794	11	0	1	4	6	210	25	181	4	
Hastings-on-Hudson Village	7,947	7	0	0	6	1	64	10	53	1	1
Haverstraw Town	37,244	59	1	9	19	30	419	119	289	11	2
Hempstead Village	54,380	464	9	9	207	239	992	217	636	139	4
Herkimer Village	7,745	60	0	4	2	54	388	52	336	0	2
Homer Village	3,311	1	0	0	0	1	28	8	18	2	0
Hornell	8,612	10	0	0	2	8	158	22	133	3	0
Horseheads Village	6,496	0	0	0	0	0	149	10	139	0	0
Hudson	6,693	37	0	7	8	22	332	47	282	3	
Hudson Falls Village	7,314	10	0	0	3	7	111	26	80	5	
Huntington Bay Village	1,438	0	0	0	0	0	4	1	3	0	0
Hyde Park Town	21,723	24	0	1	8	15	183	47	132	4	0
Ilion Village	8,052	13	0	2	0	11	149	21	124	4	
Interlaken Village	604	0	0	0	0	0	8	1	7	0	0
Irondequoit Town	52,045	79	1	4	37	37	1,633	332	1,248	53	
Irvington Village	6,503	0	0	0	0	0	23	3	20	0	0
Ithaca	30,216	65	0	4	30	31	1,238	177	1,033	28	
Jamestown	31,187	182	0	14	39	129	1,180	359	784	37	
Johnson City Village	15,134	87	1	7	22	57	1,000	138	854	8	
Johnstown	8,765	6	0	0	4	2	302	37	258	7	0
Kenmore Village	15,488	23	0	1	5	17	335	71	256	8	1
Kensington Village	1,171	0	0	0	0	0	2	1	1	0	0
Kent Town	13,608	0	0	0	0	0	91	20	71	0	0
Kingston	24,016	70	0	4	20	46	772	114	648	10	1
Kirkland Town	8,406	2	0	0	1	1	100	19	77	4	
Lackawanna	18,219	77	0	6	17	54	564	125	407	32	1
Lake Placid Village	2,523	1	0	0	0	1	56	11	43	2	1
Lake Success Village	2,958	2	0	0	1	1	39	9	30	0	
Lakewood-Busti	7,360	3	0	0	1	2	293	25	260	8	
Lancaster Town	35,821	15	0	1	7	7	516	60	446	10	0
Larchmont Village	5,940	2	0	0	0	2	107	17	89	1	
Le Roy Village	4,408	12	0	1	1	10	89	24	62	3	
Lewisboro Town	12,569	0	0	0	0	0	32	0	32	0	
Lewiston Town and Village	16,319	6	0	1	1	4	157	36	112	9	
Liberty Village	4,380	26	0	8	6	12	225	54	167	4	
Little Falls	4,945	23	0	1	1	21	140	26	111	3	
Lloyd Harbor Village	3,694	0	0	0	0	0	16	4	12	0	0
Lloyd Town	10,918	3	0	2	0	1	136	20	112	4	2
Lockport	21,233	60	0	2	15	43	730	127	584	19	
Long Beach	33,575	45	0	0	14	31	315	66	236	13	
Lowville Village	3,486	4	0	0	0	4	87	11	75	1	
Lynbrook Village	19,604	12	0	3	4	5	160	24	126	10	
Lyons Village	3,625	14	0	1	0	13	154	30	122	2	

Table 8. Offenses Known to Law Enforcement, by Selected State and City, 2012— continued

(Number)

State/city	Population	Violent crime	Murder and nonnegligent manslaughter	Forcible rape	Robbery	Aggravated assault	Property crime	Burglary	Larceny-theft	Motor vehicle theft	Arson[1]
Macedon Town and Village	9,164	2	0	0	2	0	31	2	27	2	
Malone Village	5,936	3	0	2	1	0	334	48	284	2	
Malverne Village	8,593	1	0	0	1	0	27	10	17	0	0
Mamaroneck Town	12,131	3	0	0	1	2	152	25	123	4	0
Mamaroneck Village	19,170	16	1	1	6	8	151	20	122	9	
Manchester Village	1,727	0	0	0	0	0	0	0	0	0	0
Manlius Town	24,678	25	0	0	4	21	474	61	400	13	0
Marcellus Village	1,823	1	0	0	0	1	15	1	14	0	0
Marlborough Town	8,853	3	0	0	1	2	155	40	108	7	0
Massena Village	10,969	34	0	2	4	28	419	56	357	6	
Mechanicville	5,255	12	0	1	1	10	94	23	67	4	
Medina Village	6,069	11	0	1	3	7	201	40	155	6	
Menands Village	4,002	8	0	1	4	3	163	37	121	5	
Middleport Village	1,846	1	0	0	0	1	36	1	33	2	0
Middletown	28,395	228	2	14	95	117	948	206	723	19	6
Monroe Village	8,458	24	0	3	6	15	163	21	140	2	1
Montgomery Town	8,992	7	0	2	0	5	83	17	63	3	
Montgomery Village	3,856	0	0	0	0	0	19	0	19	0	0
Monticello Village	6,706	52	0	10	8	34	264	79	182	3	
Moravia Village	1,285	1	0	0	0	1	14	1	13	0	0
Moriah Town	3,606	2	0	0	0	2	11	1	10	0	0
Mount Hope Town	7,086	0	0	0	0	0	29	4	24	1	
Mount Kisco Village	11,016	27	0	0	5	22	123	9	110	4	1
Mount Morris Village	2,985	5	0	1	0	4	72	15	53	4	
Mount Pleasant Town	26,504	14	0	3	3	8	240	52	182	6	2
Mount Vernon	68,146	613	10	14	225	364	1,345	324	886	135	
Newark Village	9,162	27	0	3	1	23	324	72	248	4	
New Berlin Town	1,650	0	0	0	0	0	2	0	2	0	0
Newburgh	29,183	544	5	19	214	306	1,217	341	814	62	9
Newburgh Town	30,132	31	0	2	13	16	1,508	131	1,338	39	1
New Hartford Town and Village	20,557	19	0	1	6	12	892	57	821	14	
New Paltz Town and Village	14,077	32	1	1	5	25	269	51	215	3	
New Rochelle	78,025	181	0	3	91	87	1,396	180	1,151	65	
New Windsor Town	25,523	37	0	1	6	30	637	93	531	13	2
New York	8,289,415	52,993	419	1,162	20,201	31,211	142,760	18,635	115,935	8,190	
New York Mills Village	3,339	1	0	0	0	1	60	6	52	2	0
Niagara Falls	50,356	619	3	26	171	419	2,963	750	2,083	130	34
Niagara Town	8,406	16	0	1	2	13	416	57	350	9	
Niskayuna Town	21,946	15	0	0	10	5	357	47	301	9	
Nissequogue Village	1,763	0	0	0	0	0	36	0	36	0	0
Norfolk Town	4,600	4	0	4	0	0	32	6	26	0	0
North Castle Town	11,994	3	0	0	1	2	94	10	84	0	
North Greenbush Town	12,138	11	0	1	1	9	204	31	170	3	
Northport Village	7,468	2	0	0	1	1	81	13	63	5	0
North Tonawanda	31,671	54	1	6	11	36	517	133	369	15	
Northville Village	1,102	1	0	0	0	1	4	1	3	0	0
Norwich	7,178	18	0	10	7	1	314	48	260	6	0
Ogdensburg	11,164	27	0	4	3	20	453	80	369	4	1
Ogden Town	19,990	10	0	0	2	8	231	46	173	12	
Old Brookville Village	2,153	2	1	0	0	1	68	17	45	6	0
Old Westbury Village	4,709	3	0	0	1	2	45	13	27	5	0
Olean	14,441	49	0	6	6	37	711	92	610	9	
Oneida	11,448	22	0	1	2	19	500	88	404	8	
Orangetown Town	37,425	46	0	2	14	30	379	50	298	31	
Orchard Park Town	29,179	12	0	5	3	4	430	67	347	16	1
Ossining Village	25,366	41	0	0	18	23	314	74	227	13	2
Oswego City	18,256	56	0	6	7	43	683	145	523	15	
Owego Village	3,911	5	0	0	4	1	157	34	119	4	
Painted Post Village	1,821	0	0	0	0	0	33	4	29	0	0
Palmyra Village	3,543	2	0	0	1	1	53	12	40	1	
Peekskill	23,883	37	2	4	9	22	221	31	182	8	

Table 8. Offenses Known to Law Enforcement, by Selected State and City, 2012— continued

(Number)

State/city	Population	Violent crime	Murder and nonnegligent manslaughter	Forcible rape	Robbery	Aggravated assault	Property crime	Burglary	Larceny-theft	Motor vehicle theft	Arson[1]
Pelham Manor Village	5,556	1	0	0	1	0	140	20	116	4	
Pelham Village	6,998	7	0	0	5	2	110	15	92	3	
Penn Yan Village	5,208	4	0	1	0	3	109	21	88	0	1
Perry Village	3,674	11	0	2	2	7	99	14	82	3	
Piermont Village	2,552	1	0	0	0	1	40	7	30	3	
Pine Plains Town	2,491	0	0	0	0	0	11	4	7	0	0
Plattekill Town	10,553	11	0	0	0	11	122	43	76	3	
Pleasantville Village	7,093	0	0	0	0	0	34	2	31	1	0
Port Byron Village	1,291	0	0	0	0	0	0	0	0	0	0
Port Chester Village	29,335	67	2	1	44	20	685	61	606	18	0
Port Dickinson Village	1,637	0	0	0	0	0	7	2	5	0	0
Port Jervis	8,926	35	1	4	8	22	271	66	194	11	3
Portville Village	1,012	0	0	0	0	0	2	0	2	0	0
Port Washington	18,978	2	0	0	2	0	115	8	103	4	0
Potsdam Village	9,467	8	0	0	2	6	258	42	209	7	
Poughkeepsie	32,967	342	3	12	87	240	986	247	690	49	
Poughkeepsie Town	42,698	54	0	2	26	26	1,387	85	1,291	11	
Pound Ridge Town	5,169	3	0	0	0	3	19	3	16	0	
Pulaski Village	2,380	2	0	0	0	2	72	10	60	2	0
Quogue Village	976	0	0	0	0	0	26	10	15	1	0
Ramapo Town	85,448	80	0	5	13	62	716	137	563	16	
Red Hook Village	1,975	0	0	0	0	0	40	7	33	0	0
Rensselaer City	9,442	11	0	3	3	5	185	39	141	5	2
Rhinebeck Village	2,673	0	0	0	0	0	54	8	46	0	1
Riverhead Town	33,809	76	0	4	30	42	980	122	835	23	1
Rochester	211,993	2,069	36	112	817	1,104	11,283	2,978	7,683	622	194
Rockville Centre Village	24,241	32	0	0	17	15	328	45	273	10	1
Rome	33,842	46	0	8	21	17	468	133	310	25	4
Rosendale Town	6,112	2	0	0	0	2	72	18	54	0	
Rotterdam Town	29,315	23	0	1	12	10	974	112	836	26	6
Rye Brook Village	9,465	1	0	0	0	1	67	6	59	2	0
Sag Harbor Village	2,189	0	0	0	0	0	47	7	38	2	0
Salamanca	5,811	25	0	0	3	22	232	54	169	9	
Sands Point Village	2,700	0	0	0	0	0	8	1	3	4	0
Saranac Lake Village	5,420	16	0	1	4	11	145	30	113	2	
Saratoga Springs	26,871	26	0	5	3	18	698	104	584	10	3
Saugerties Town	19,581	14	0	6	2	6	349	72	265	12	2
Scarsdale Village	17,386	2	0	0	1	1	144	24	116	4	
Schenectady	66,631	626	7	32	199	388	2,828	810	1,876	142	64
Schodack Town	11,316	8	0	0	4	4	113	30	81	2	
Schoharie Village	922	0	0	0	0	0	16	8	8	0	0
Scotia Village	7,788	6	0	1	1	4	164	21	137	6	1
Shandaken Town	3,103	2	0	0	0	2	92	24	67	1	
Shawangunk Town	14,406	3	0	0	0	3	116	29	86	1	
Shelter Island Town	2,414	0	0	0	0	0	53	17	36	0	0
Sherburne Village	1,365	0	0	0	0	0	13	4	9	0	0
Sherrill	3,082	4	0	0	0	4	35	9	26	0	
Shortsville Village	1,456	0	0	0	0	0	1	0	0	1	0
Sidney Village	3,886	16	0	2	4	10	169	29	139	1	
Silver Creek Village	2,660	1	0	0	0	1	49	2	46	1	0
Skaneateles Village	2,463	1	0	0	0	1	7	3	4	0	0
Sleepy Hollow Village	9,998	9	0	0	2	7	80	14	64	2	1
Sodus Village	1,823	0	0	0	0	0	25	3	22	0	
Solvay Village	6,620	20	0	1	3	16	213	38	166	9	0
Southampton Town	50,256	64	0	3	15	46	1,005	219	724	62	2
Southampton Village	3,137	1	0	0	0	1	120	11	107	2	0
South Glens Falls Village	3,558	9	0	1	3	5	89	22	64	3	
South Nyack Village	3,561	2	0	0	2	0	44	6	37	1	
Southold Town	19,951	21	0	1	5	15	441	93	342	6	
Spring Valley Village	31,872	209	0	7	65	137	497	91	376	30	
Stillwater Town	6,624	0	0	0	0	0	36	5	30	1	0
Stockport Town	2,805	1	0	0	1	0	9	7	2	0	1

Table 8. Offenses Known to Law Enforcement, by Selected State and City, 2012— continued

(Number)

State/city	Population	Violent crime	Murder and nonnegligent manslaughter	Forcible rape	Robbery	Aggravated assault	Property crime	Burglary	Larceny-theft	Motor vehicle theft	Arson[1]
Stony Point Town	15,312	4	0	0	0	4	87	16	66	5	
Suffern Village	10,902	3	0	0	3	0	59	6	53	0	0
Syracuse	145,934	1,372	14	75	454	829	5,976	1,896	3,698	382	45
Tarrytown Village	11,415	2	0	0	0	2	93	11	78	4	1
Ticonderoga Town	5,045	16	0	3	1	12	107	28	75	4	
Tonawanda	15,194	22	0	2	4	16	386	38	338	10	6
Tonawanda Town	58,393	118	1	12	32	73	1,071	198	848	25	3
Troy	50,391	335	7	15	111	202	2,372	593	1,677	102	
Tuckahoe Village	6,567	1	0	1	0	0	23	3	20	0	0
Tupper Lake Village	3,684	8	0	2	1	5	108	25	79	4	
Ulster Town	12,391	10	0	0	2	8	497	30	463	4	
Utica	62,445	411	1	23	126	261	2,704	591	2,014	99	25
Vernon Village	1,175	3	0	0	0	3	25	5	19	1	
Vestal Town	28,018	16	2	2	1	11	625	64	554	7	
Walden Village	7,056	15	0	2	2	11	136	17	117	2	
Wallkill Town	27,730	24	0	1	9	14	719	57	650	12	1
Walton Village	3,077	6	0	1	0	5	62	14	48	0	
Wappingers Falls Village	5,563	4	0	0	1	3	168	11	153	4	0
Warsaw Village	3,473	0	0	0	0	0	69	4	64	1	0
Warwick Town	19,563	18	0	3	1	14	230	34	190	6	
Waterford Town and Village	8,519	1	0	0	1	0	77	22	55	0	0
Waterloo Village	5,192	6	0	1	0	5	172	19	151	2	
Watertown	27,571	154	0	12	20	122	1,576	269	1,183	124	
Watervliet	10,285	26	0	3	14	9	237	53	173	11	
Watkins Glen Village	1,872	2	0	0	1	1	75	8	66	1	
Waverly Village	4,461	6	0	0	2	4	119	23	93	3	
Wayland Village	1,875	0	0	0	0	0	12	1	11	0	
Webster Town and Village	42,936	26	0	2	8	16	464	87	359	18	
Weedsport Village	1,819	0	0	0	0	0	16	3	12	1	0
Westhampton Beach Village	1,737	2	0	0	0	2	57	12	44	1	0
West Seneca Town	44,902	52	0	2	13	37	842	149	663	30	6
Whitehall Village	2,626	8	0	2	1	5	73	23	49	1	
White Plains	57,567	92	1	3	31	57	1,386	82	1,279	25	
Whitesboro Village	3,784	7	0	0	0	7	31	9	20	2	0
Whitestown Town	9,189	1	0	0	1	0	128	16	103	9	0
Woodbury Town	10,805	6	0	1	4	1	422	18	398	6	
Woodstock Town	5,915	2	0	0	1	1	46	15	31	0	
Yonkers	198,464	1,133	4	28	422	679	2,565	535	1,799	231	14
Yorktown Town	36,539	13	0	0	3	10	387	37	349	1	0
North Carolina											
Aberdeen	6,492	24	0	3	6	15	356	57	280	19	0
Ahoskie	5,039	44	2	1	7	34	259	64	186	9	6
Albemarle	16,071	86	0	8	19	59	946	297	615	34	13
Apex	39,085	33	0	3	10	20	557	88	454	15	6
Archdale	11,580	13	0	1	1	11	288	62	212	14	4
Asheboro	25,535	77	1	13	27	36	1,798	404	1,342	52	7
Asheville	85,295	423	6	33	141	243	4,910	742	3,832	336	11
Atlantic Beach	1,531	15	0	2	0	13	135	59	71	5	0
Aulander	886	2	0	0	1	1	44	31	12	1	0
Ayden	5,072	26	0	1	3	22	220	80	131	9	0
Bailey	576	2	0	0	0	2	19	10	9	0	0
Banner Elk	1,029	2	0	0	0	2	42	4	38	0	0
Beaufort	4,135	24	0	2	4	18	159	48	104	7	0
Beech Mountain	324	0	0	0	0	0	18	1	17	0	0
Belhaven	1,702	7	0	0	0	7	62	21	41	0	0
Belmont	10,219	32	2	3	6	21	428	52	365	11	0
Benson	3,416	29	0	0	7	22	275	95	163	17	0
Bethel	1,623	13	0	1	2	10	51	5	44	2	0
Beulaville	1,329	3	0	0	0	3	52	2	48	2	1
Biltmore Forest	1,374	0	0	0	0	0	14	2	12	0	0
Biscoe	1,710	2	0	1	1	0	210	9	198	3	0

Table 8. Offenses Known to Law Enforcement, by Selected State and City, 2012— continued

(Number)

State/city	Population	Violent crime	Murder and nonnegligent manslaughter	Forcible rape	Robbery	Aggravated assault	Property crime	Burglary	Larceny-theft	Motor vehicle theft	Arson[1]
Black Mountain	8,029	9	0	1	3	5	167	24	129	14	0
Bladenboro	1,754	4	0	0	2	2	95	38	57	0	0
Blowing Rock	1,258	0	0	0	0	0	42	13	28	1	0
Boiling Spring Lakes	5,561	6	0	2	0	4	95	31	57	7	1
Boiling Springs	4,668	2	0	1	1	0	46	7	38	1	0
Boone	17,359	34	0	3	5	26	401	98	293	10	0
Brevard	7,626	20	0	2	7	11	259	33	221	5	0
Bryson City	1,444	6	0	0	0	6	83	0	83	0	0
Bunn	349	2	0	1	1	0	34	3	30	1	0
Burgaw	3,979	10	0	0	4	6	102	19	78	5	0
Burlington	51,430	406	2	17	105	282	2,792	671	1,998	123	5
Burnsville	1,702	7	0	1	1	5	87	20	65	2	0
Butner	7,673	25	0	1	2	22	232	82	139	11	6
Canton	4,256	27	0	2	3	22	207	46	149	12	0
Cape Carteret	1,962	2	0	1	0	1	42	12	30	0	0
Carolina Beach	5,867	25	0	2	5	18	308	89	197	22	2
Carrboro	20,087	62	0	3	12	47	595	173	387	35	1
Carthage	2,255	4	0	0	1	3	94	25	65	4	2
Cary	141,016	115	0	11	29	75	1,909	370	1,476	63	8
Catawba	608	1	0	0	0	1	11	6	5	0	0
Chadbourn	1,862	18	0	1	2	15	211	76	126	9	1
Chapel Hill	58,586	87	2	10	30	45	1,493	452	969	72	6
Charlotte-Mecklen-burg	808,504	5,238	52	223	1,798	3,165	32,587	7,761	22,688	2,138	197
Cherryville	5,842	13	0	1	1	11	259	36	220	3	0
China Grove	3,588	15	0	2	6	7	93	9	80	4	0
Claremont	1,365	1	0	0	0	1	41	16	24	1	0
Clayton	16,635	25	0	4	5	16	392	104	280	8	0
Cleveland	877	3	0	0	0	3	21	7	14	0	0
Clinton	8,762	39	2	1	11	25	471	111	348	12	0
Coats	2,219	7	0	1	3	3	79	18	59	2	0
Columbus	996	2	0	0	0	2	15	3	12	0	0
Conover	8,237	25	0	0	4	21	564	70	476	18	1
Cornelius	25,800	59	2	3	10	44	616	94	501	21	2
Cramerton	4,224	5	0	0	0	5	106	27	78	1	0
Creedmoor	4,170	12	0	2	3	7	83	25	54	4	0
Dallas	4,554	29	0	1	2	26	212	47	156	9	0
Dobson	1,602	2	0	0	0	2	44	2	42	0	0
Drexel	1,875	0	0	0	0	0	27	10	15	2	0
Durham	235,563	1,710	21	63	615	1,011	10,279	3,284	6,291	704	59
Eden	15,628	94	1	4	24	65	641	185	410	46	6
Edenton	5,073	35	0	0	12	23	244	77	158	9	2
Elkin	4,042	11	0	1	2	8	296	40	253	3	1
Elon	9,610	4	0	0	1	3	97	22	75	0	0
Emerald Isle	3,742	5	0	1	1	3	294	108	181	5	0
Enfield	2,534	33	1	2	7	23	114	35	74	5	0
Erwin	4,631	18	1	1	8	8	137	8	129	0	2
Fairmont	2,718	28	1	0	5	22	211	52	150	9	1
Farmville	4,785	31	0	0	8	23	193	57	132	4	1
Fayetteville	205,966	1,186	22	70	560	534	13,163	4,109	8,298	756	47
Fletcher	7,338	8	0	4	1	3	187	47	138	2	0
Forest City	7,520	23	0	0	6	17	593	127	450	16	3
Four Oaks	1,982	6	0	1	1	4	63	21	39	3	0
Franklin	3,907	22	0	1	5	16	282	59	213	10	1
Franklinton	2,061	22	0	1	3	18	65	18	43	4	0
Fuquay-Varina	18,712	82	0	5	8	69	564	141	404	19	3
Garner	26,852	65	0	4	31	30	1,225	164	1,007	54	3
Garysburg	1,057	12	0	2	4	6	43	16	26	1	0
Gastonia	72,782	450	1	29	157	263	4,252	978	3,075	199	25
Gibsonville	6,580	9	0	0	3	6	146	93	49	4	1
Goldsboro	37,107	312	13	3	73	223	2,357	584	1,648	125	0
Graham	14,499	75	1	9	17	48	576	160	379	37	8
Granite Falls	4,732	14	0	1	3	10	286	40	242	4	0
Greensboro	276,134	1,555	21	70	556	908	12,064	3,345	8,153	566	129

Table 8. Offenses Known to Law Enforcement, by Selected State and City, 2012— continued

(Number)

State/city	Population	Violent crime	Murder and nonnegligent manslaughter	Forcible rape	Robbery	Aggravated assault	Property crime	Burglary	Larceny-theft	Motor vehicle theft	Arson[1]
Greenville	86,869	455	7	23	169	256	3,845	1,130	2,596	119	11
Hamlet	6,558	41	0	4	14	23	433	172	235	26	2
Haw River	2,356	11	0	0	2	9	67	19	46	2	0
Henderson	15,482	181	8	4	75	94	1,700	416	1,199	85	11
Hendersonville	13,409	79	1	9	19	50	811	193	566	52	1
Hertford	2,168	15	1	1	7	6	63	23	38	2	0
Hickory	40,361	265	3	22	81	159	2,640	475	2,003	162	13
Highlands	937	0	0	0	0	0	58	10	48	0	0
High Point	106,801	556	5	19	185	347	4,417	1,188	2,943	286	39
Hillsborough	6,236	18	0	0	8	10	467	73	390	4	1
Holden Beach	595	4	0	0	0	4	176	118	57	1	0
Holly Ridge	1,297	5	0	0	0	5	27	8	19	0	0
Holly Springs	25,720	14	1	3	4	6	293	50	231	12	0
Hope Mills	15,594	56	0	3	22	31	1,069	223	821	25	12
Hudson	3,783	5	0	0	2	3	118	18	97	3	0
Huntersville	48,524	85	0	6	20	59	1,051	182	844	25	13
Indian Beach	117	1	0	0	0	1	12	4	8	0	0
Jonesville	2,301	14	1	0	0	13	112	44	62	6	1
Kenansville	878	1	0	1	0	0	23	3	19	1	1
Kernersville	23,643	109	0	9	10	90	1,135	149	942	44	3
Kill Devil Hills	6,827	47	1	3	6	37	418	144	260	14	0
King	6,958	23	0	0	5	18	291	53	230	8	1
Kings Mountain	10,348	32	1	4	9	18	443	149	274	20	5
Kinston	21,836	280	1	13	54	212	1,361	378	945	38	6
Kitty Hawk	3,342	1	0	1	0	0	171	28	142	1	1
Knightdale	11,893	25	0	0	4	21	454	85	360	9	5
Lake Lure	1,201	0	0	0	0	0	49	15	33	1	0
Lake Royale	2,563	5	0	0	0	5	80	39	39	2	1
Landis	3,131	4	0	1	0	3	84	27	57	0	0
Laurel Park	2,226	0	0	0	0	0	22	2	20	0	0
Laurinburg	15,988	155	4	5	27	119	1,137	503	604	30	11
Leland	14,145	22	0	2	4	16	436	160	264	12	3
Lenoir	18,270	51	0	1	17	33	935	231	662	42	3
Lexington	19,099	63	0	4	25	34	609	190	399	20	3
Liberty	2,694	4	0	0	0	4	31	10	21	0	0
Lillington	3,312	14	0	0	4	10	162	33	120	9	0
Lincolnton	10,675	38	3	1	11	23	558	105	435	18	6
Long View	4,913	29	1	1	8	19	323	121	185	17	4
Louisburg	3,416	14	0	0	6	8	133	49	81	3	0
Lumberton	21,969	448	6	9	141	292	3,254	854	2,229	171	8
Madison	2,260	12	0	2	4	6	137	33	103	1	0
Maggie Valley	1,157	6	0	1	1	4	118	12	99	7	1
Magnolia	964	0	0	0	0	0	31	15	15	1	1
Maiden	3,340	6	0	0	1	5	121	23	97	1	0
Manteo	1,465	8	0	0	3	5	80	13	62	5	0
Marion	7,932	24	0	0	4	20	560	184	362	14	0
Mars Hill	1,891	11	0	2	1	8	61	17	42	2	2
Marshville	2,474	15	2	0	7	6	102	37	61	4	0
Matthews	28,213	47	0	2	16	29	877	106	730	41	7
Maxton	2,472	17	0	2	10	5	138	84	49	5	2
Mayodan	2,493	7	0	1	0	6	179	19	160	0	0
Maysville	1,015	3	0	0	1	2	13	4	9	0	0
Mebane	11,677	74	0	1	6	67	642	104	526	12	0
Middlesex	833	2	0	0	0	2	19	4	14	1	0
Mint Hill	23,572	39	0	0	21	18	408	100	287	21	11
Mocksville	5,140	6	0	2	3	1	233	40	188	5	1
Monroe	33,807	222	2	5	73	142	2,148	493	1,566	89	13
Mooresville	33,401	97	1	5	23	68	1,445	213	1,167	65	6
Morehead City	8,867	58	1	3	6	48	508	94	404	10	4
Morganton	17,085	52	1	3	17	31	562	156	389	17	1
Morrisville	19,374	11	0	2	4	5	367	54	303	10	0
Mount Airy	10,501	57	1	3	9	44	531	117	385	29	8
Mount Holly	13,855	48	1	2	8	37	314	66	228	20	0
Mount Olive	4,670	57	0	0	15	42	366	117	242	7	3

Table 8. Offenses Known to Law Enforcement, by Selected State and City, 2012— continued

(Number)

State/city	Population	Violent crime	Murder and nonnegligent manslaughter	Forcible rape	Robbery	Aggravated assault	Property crime	Burglary	Larceny-theft	Motor vehicle theft	Arson[1]
Murfreesboro	2,842	4	0	0	1	3	72	22	48	2	0
Murphy	1,629	9	0	0	1	8	124	20	98	6	2
Nags Head	2,816	10	0	3	4	3	309	146	158	5	0
Nashville	5,420	9	0	2	1	6	186	45	133	8	1
New Bern	30,195	163	3	10	36	114	1,861	745	1,066	50	3
Newland	696	2	0	0	0	2	20	1	17	2	0
Newton	13,081	27	0	4	4	19	456	127	308	21	6
North Topsail Beach	759	3	0	0	0	3	50	22	27	1	0
North Wilkesboro	4,267	28	0	2	4	22	241	32	200	9	0
Oak Island	7,030	16	0	0	0	16	321	152	164	5	1
Ocean Isle Beach	575	2	0	0	0	2	84	47	35	2	0
Oxford	8,553	90	0	1	31	58	595	184	403	8	2
Pinebluff	1,367	0	0	0	0	0	16	10	6	0	0
Pinehurst	15,008	12	0	0	1	11	120	6	111	3	0
Pine Knoll Shores	1,370	1	0	1	0	0	43	15	28	0	0
Pine Level	1,756	2	0	0	1	1	32	11	21	0	0
Pinetops	1,374	6	0	2	2	2	47	17	30	0	0
Pineville	7,754	49	0	5	20	24	965	81	840	44	2
Pittsboro	3,818	9	0	1	0	8	139	64	71	4	1
Plymouth	3,843	23	0	0	7	16	148	48	98	2	1
Raeford	4,874	38	0	0	10	28	258	64	184	10	1
Raleigh	420,594	1,780	17	113	665	985	13,779	3,036	9,812	931	59
Ramseur	1,716	2	0	0	1	1	71	21	50	0	1
Randleman	4,171	8	0	0	4	4	350	37	305	8	0
Red Springs	3,496	29	1	0	9	19	253	92	150	11	7
Reidsville	14,616	53	1	1	15	36	813	173	620	20	8
Richlands	1,554	2	0	0	0	2	32	8	22	2	0
River Bend	3,189	2	0	0	0	2	60	26	34	0	0
Roanoke Rapids	15,756	107	1	14	24	68	902	251	626	25	0
Robbins	1,123	0	0	0	0	0	36	14	22	0	0
Robersonville	1,484	10	0	1	3	6	85	39	46	0	0
Rockingham	9,648	37	1	4	14	18	1,071	237	820	14	7
Rockwell	2,122	2	0	0	0	2	72	19	52	1	0
Rocky Mount	58,002	749	8	13	128	600	3,383	1,046	2,192	145	15
Rolesville	3,950	9	0	0	2	7	116	55	60	1	0
Rose Hill	1,671	6	1	2	1	2	54	28	26	0	2
Rowland	1,057	3	0	0	3	0	52	33	16	3	0
Roxboro	8,480	57	0	3	11	43	413	106	298	9	2
Rutherfordton	4,240	2	0	1	1	0	111	0	110	1	0
Salisbury	33,919	212	1	9	95	107	1,935	488	1,346	101	10
Sanford	28,801	88	3	1	38	46	814	207	578	29	5
Scotland Neck	2,060	26	0	0	10	16	93	36	55	2	1
Selma	6,271	46	0	0	12	34	420	187	225	8	1
Shallotte	3,801	7	0	0	2	5	186	62	117	7	1
Shelby	20,402	156	4	14	36	102	887	304	546	37	2
Siler City	8,051	26	0	1	11	14	344	69	270	5	0
Smithfield	11,305	85	0	1	16	68	779	162	596	21	3
Southern Pines	12,611	86	1	4	26	55	510	148	342	20	1
Southern Shores	2,772	2	0	1	0	1	78	39	39	0	2
Southport	2,928	4	0	0	2	2	113	8	103	2	0
Spencer	3,290	20	0	2	0	18	179	54	112	13	2
Spring Hope	1,337	10	0	1	5	4	32	9	22	1	0
Spruce Pine	2,179	2	0	0	2	0	71	8	57	6	0
Stallings	14,263	10	0	1	1	8	205	39	157	9	1
Stanley	3,608	5	0	1	2	2	149	38	106	5	1
St. Pauls	2,077	11	0	0	6	5	87	32	55	0	1
Surf City	1,923	9	0	1	1	7	115	19	94	2	0
Swansboro	2,722	7	1	0	2	4	119	35	83	1	2
Sylva	2,614	18	0	0	2	16	188	64	117	7	1
Tabor City	2,520	24	0	1	4	19	159	23	133	3	0
Tarboro	11,427	51	0	2	8	41	434	101	331	2	1
Taylorsville	2,114	5	1	1	1	2	173	36	135	2	0
Thomasville	26,994	141	0	6	37	98	1,338	291	1,027	20	8
Trent Woods	4,250	1	0	0	1	0	93	35	55	3	0

Table 8. Offenses Known to Law Enforcement, by Selected State and City, 2012— continued

(Number)

State/city	Population	Violent crime	Murder and nonnegligent manslaughter	Forcible rape	Robbery	Aggravated assault	Property crime	Burglary	Larceny-theft	Motor vehicle theft	Arson[1]
Troutman	2,433	11	0	2	2	7	89	31	55	3	1
Troy	3,208	9	1	0	2	6	117	15	95	7	0
Tryon	1,641	4	0	2	1	1	69	30	35	4	0
Valdese	4,537	5	0	1	0	4	68	16	49	3	0
Vass	736	0	0	0	0	0	34	13	20	1	0
Wadesboro	5,797	74	1	2	16	55	439	138	287	14	0
Wake Forest	31,381	49	1	1	14	33	681	113	546	22	1
Wallace	3,988	24	1	2	4	17	180	37	130	13	0
Warrenton	864	7	0	3	0	4	27	2	24	1	0
Warsaw	3,136	12	0	0	3	9	169	71	97	1	0
Washington	9,826	86	1	3	25	57	718	158	553	7	2
Waxhaw	10,167	14	0	1	2	11	293	68	222	3	1
Waynesville	9,939	34	0	5	8	21	413	130	258	25	0
Weaverville	3,752	8	0	0	1	7	223	12	210	1	0
Weldon	1,651	8	0	0	3	5	71	14	55	2	0
West Jefferson	1,306	2	0	0	0	2	97	18	72	7	0
Whispering Pines	2,993	0	0	0	0	0	29	2	26	1	0
Whitakers	748	7	2	0	1	4	27	11	12	4	0
Whiteville	5,413	37	1	1	17	18	532	135	376	21	1
Wilkesboro	3,431	12	0	3	3	6	413	24	387	2	1
Williamston	5,494	81	2	2	22	55	534	178	343	13	2
Wilmington	109,370	618	8	23	261	326	5,910	1,694	3,843	373	9
Wilson	49,785	262	5	3	69	185	2,321	666	1,543	112	13
Wilson's Mills	2,349	5	0	1	1	3	54	33	20	1	0
Wingate	3,578	9	1	0	1	7	121	27	89	5	2
Winston-Salem	234,687	1,556	6	74	428	1,048	13,701	4,529	8,490	682	94
Winterville	9,533	11	0	1	3	7	114	19	90	5	0
Woodfin	6,257	7	0	1	2	4	120	67	49	4	0
Wrightsville Beach	2,546	18	0	2	1	15	199	49	147	3	2
Yadkinville	2,982	23	0	1	3	19	119	32	85	2	1
Youngsville	1,180	2	0	0	2	0	33	8	25	0	0
North Dakota											
Beulah	3,202	7	1	2	0	4	68	18	44	6	1
Bismarck	64,103	218	1	31	16	170	1,945	320	1,522	103	9
Burlington	1,127	1	0	0	0	1	9	1	4	4	1
Carrington	2,111	0	0	0	0	0	6	0	4	2	0
Cavalier	1,319	2	0	1	0	1	16	3	13	0	0
Devils Lake	7,305	15	0	5	2	8	333	64	255	14	1
Dickinson	18,924	41	0	0	3	38	389	27	339	23	0
Ellendale	1,432	0	0	0	0	0	11	4	7	0	0
Fargo	109,813	394	2	69	46	277	2,835	451	2,229	155	16
Fessenden	493	0	0	0	0	0	2	1	1	0	0
Grafton	4,349	21	0	5	0	16	131	8	114	9	1
Grand Forks	53,839	146	0	24	23	99	1,409	228	1,091	90	2
Harvey	1,836	5	0	2	1	2	39	10	29	0	1
Hillsboro	1,647	1	0	0	0	1	13	2	10	1	0
Jamestown	15,753	32	0	12	0	20	419	77	319	23	4
Kenmare	1,165	0	0	0	0	0	3	1	1	1	0
Killdeer	806	2	0	2	0	0	16	2	11	3	0
Lamoure	901	1	0	0	0	1	8	2	4	2	0
Lincoln	2,519	2	0	0	0	2	9	0	8	1	0
Lisbon	2,182	1	0	0	0	1	44	12	27	5	0
Mandan	18,932	50	2	9	5	34	515	51	420	44	5
Medora	119	0	0	0	0	0	2	1	1	0	0
Minot	43,460	101	0	20	6	75	763	78	605	80	6
Napoleon	808	0	0	0	0	0	8	1	7	0	0
Northwood	963	1	0	0	0	1	8	2	6	0	0
Rolla	1,335	1	0	0	0	1	21	5	12	4	0
Rugby	2,952	1	0	0	0	1	61	10	47	4	0
Sherwood	249	0	0	0	0	0	1	0	1	0	0
Stanley	1,575	1	0	0	0	1	5	0	4	1	0
Steele	725	0	0	0	0	0	15	4	10	1	1
Surrey	994	1	0	0	0	1	1	1	0	0	0

Table 8. Offenses Known to Law Enforcement, by Selected State and City, 2012— continued

(Number)

State/city	Population	Violent crime	Murder and nonnegligent manslaughter	Forcible rape	Robbery	Aggravated assault	Property crime	Burglary	Larceny-theft	Motor vehicle theft	Arson[1]
Thompson	1,006	0	0	0	0	0	1	0	1	0	0
Valley City	6,730	10	0	1	0	9	127	26	98	3	1
Wahpeton	7,908	8	0	2	1	5	152	21	122	9	0
Watford City	1,967	15	1	1	0	13	63	5	58	0	1
West Fargo	26,894	62	0	2	5	55	482	77	370	35	6
Williston	16,373	64	1	12	2	49	760	44	603	113	3
Ohio											
Ada	5,947	6	0	3	1	2	64	18	44	2	0
Akron	198,390	1,759	24	167	577	991	10,034	3,429	5,884	721	103
Alliance	22,293	96	2	17	31	46	1,080	279	777	24	13
Amberley Village	3,576	2	0	0	2	0	53	9	41	3	0
Amherst	12,030	4	0	0	3	1	200	31	159	10	2
Arlington Heights	742	2	0	1	0	1	31	4	26	1	0
Ashland	20,366	19	0	9	3	7	599	95	497	7	3
Ashville	4,120	1	0	0	0	1	67	15	50	2	1
Athens	23,834	15	0	1	8	6	454	89	359	6	0
Aurora	15,567	7	0	2	2	3	174	26	146	2	2
Austintown	36,478	63	0	6	19	38	1,304	344	903	57	1
Barberton	26,453	55	0	14	23	18	1,114	190	867	57	12
Barnesville	4,178	0	0	0	0	0	21	7	12	2	0
Batavia	1,524	2	0	2	0	0	81	11	69	1	0
Bath Township, Summit County	9,667	6	0	3	2	1	84	9	73	2	0
Bazetta Township	5,844	8	0	0	2	6	245	46	194	5	0
Beachwood	11,866	32	0	1	2	29	566	13	547	6	0
Beavercreek	45,563	25	0	6	13	6	1,073	114	945	14	3
Beaver Township	6,667	1	0	0	1	0	137	48	82	7	0
Bedford	12,971	29	0	1	14	14	567	42	490	35	0
Bedford Heights	10,665	41	0	4	18	19	244	49	132	63	0
Bellbrook	7,001	3	0	1	1	1	99	6	93	0	0
Bellefontaine	13,321	33	0	12	6	15	700	131	562	7	0
Bellville	1,903	0	0	0	0	0	47	1	46	0	0
Belpre	6,439	2	0	1	0	1	89	32	53	4	0
Berea	18,959	7	0	0	1	6	328	57	259	12	4
Bethel	2,735	3	0	1	0	2	119	15	101	3	5
Beverly	1,312	1	0	1	0	0	49	11	38	0	0
Bexley	13,220	14	0	1	11	2	381	121	253	7	1
Blanchester	4,231	1	0	0	0	1	62	7	52	3	1
Blue Ash	12,082	7	0	0	3	4	365	47	310	8	1
Bluffton	4,120	5	0	1	1	3	66	16	46	4	0
Boardman	40,608	43	1	6	31	5	1,698	273	1,371	54	10
Bowling Green	30,219	70	1	16	14	39	840	109	716	15	0
Brecksville	13,554	4	0	0	0	4	84	8	75	1	0
Brewster	2,108	1	0	0	0	1	6	3	2	1	0
Bridgeport	1,824	0	0	0	0	0	20	4	16	0	0
Brimfield Township	10,390	14	0	5	4	5	262	31	225	6	0
Broadview Heights	19,246	4	0	0	0	4	16	5	9	2	0
Brookfield Township	8,809	14	0	2	3	9	214	76	130	8	5
Brooklyn	11,081	35	2	5	15	13	628	77	483	68	2
Brook Park	19,062	10	0	3	2	5	133	33	66	34	0
Brookville	5,910	11	0	3	2	6	71	14	55	2	1
Brunswick Hills Township	9,950	1	0	1	0	0	51	14	35	2	0
Burton	1,453	0	0	0	0	0	1	0	0	1	0
Butler Township	7,904	14	0	1	11	2	301	23	269	9	0
Cadiz	3,349	6	0	2	0	4	77	17	57	3	0
Cambridge	10,592	62	1	8	13	40	673	213	436	24	1
Campbell	8,178	10	1	1	3	5	165	79	79	7	1
Canal Fulton	5,472	3	0	0	0	3	105	20	84	1	0
Canfield	7,464	2	1	1	0	0	60	15	43	2	1
Canton	72,914	729	10	64	414	241	4,722	1,590	2,671	461	39
Cardington	2,047	4	1	2	0	1	39	3	35	1	0
Carlisle	4,967	1	0	0	0	1	39	17	22	0	0
Carrollton	3,242	10	0	0	0	10	4	2	0	2	0

Table 8. Offenses Known to Law Enforcement, by Selected State and City, 2012— continued

(Number)

State/city	Population	Violent crime	Murder and nonnegligent manslaughter	Forcible rape	Robbery	Aggravated assault	Property crime	Burglary	Larceny-theft	Motor vehicle theft	Arson[1]
Centerville	24,107	19	0	2	5	12	437	40	388	9	2
Chagrin Falls	4,081	3	0	0	2	1	31	7	23	1	1
Chardon	5,139	12	3	0	1	8	78	6	72	0	1
Cheviot	8,352	9	0	1	7	1	208	49	151	8	0
Chillicothe	21,954	101	0	11	26	64	2,120	465	1,608	47	2
Cincinnati	296,204	2,887	46	188	1,725	928	18,173	5,483	11,590	1,100	386
Circleville	13,388	31	1	6	14	10	920	196	712	12	2
Clayton	13,268	9	0	2	5	2	214	52	144	18	0
Clearcreek Township	14,224	1	0	0	0	1	110	26	84	0	1
Cleveland	393,781	5,449	84	363	3,252	1,750	24,309	9,740	10,808	3,761	302
Cleveland Heights	45,761	168	0	10	110	48	1,648	305	1,267	76	6
Cleves	3,225	1	0	0	0	1	76	11	63	2	0
Clyde	6,303	3	0	1	1	1	202	64	136	2	0
Coitsville Township	1,382	0	0	0	0	0	39	19	19	1	0
Coldwater	4,430	0	0	0	0	0	40	8	31	1	0
Colerain Township	58,345	16	0	0	0	16	1,557	158	1,398	1	0
Commercial Point	1,590	2	0	0	0	2	16	8	8	0	0
Conneaut	12,823	21	0	0	6	15	340	121	216	3	2
Covington	2,593	0	0	0	0	0	26	3	23	0	0
Cuyahoga Falls	49,470	65	0	17	13	35	1,274	230	984	60	12
Danville	1,051	2	0	1	0	1	26	4	22	0	0
Dayton	142,139	1,384	24	112	633	615	8,385	3,043	4,649	693	129
Deer Park	5,723	11	0	1	2	8	112	22	82	8	3
Defiance	16,621	26	0	12	4	10	616	102	508	6	3
Delaware	35,539	53	0	17	23	13	1,062	189	834	39	10
Delhi Township	29,433	13	0	3	6	4	636	94	524	18	1
Delphos	7,075	5	0	4	1	0	184	36	146	2	0
Delta	3,088	0	0	0	0	0	51	11	39	1	0
Dublin	42,343	15	1	1	8	5	544	96	439	9	0
East Cleveland	17,704	88	0	4	0	84	14	1	4	9	0
Eastlake	18,564	23	0	1	13	9	495	48	428	19	2
East Palestine	4,708	3	0	0	1	2	157	29	122	6	0
Eaton	8,369	17	0	3	1	13	486	102	379	5	0
Englewood	13,526	9	0	2	5	2	384	37	336	11	0
Fairfield	42,727	146	4	7	28	107	1,338	194	1,102	42	11
Fairfield Township	21,484	19	0	2	4	13	935	155	768	12	4
Fairport Harbor	3,107	7	0	2	2	3	152	42	108	2	0
Forest	1,458	1	0	0	1	0	38	15	23	0	0
Forest Park	18,672	28	1	4	23	0	476	110	343	23	2
Fort Recovery	1,429	1	0	0	0	1	33	4	29	0	0
Fremont	16,676	27	0	1	12	14	1,096	177	901	18	1
Gahanna	33,692	22	1	8	5	8	822	124	677	21	2
Galion	10,415	11	0	2	3	6	621	150	464	7	0
Gallipolis	3,644	8	0	1	3	4	371	60	307	4	1
Garfield Heights	28,623	78	6	9	33	30	1,040	303	666	71	0
Gates Mills	2,251	1	0	1	0	0	20	8	12	0	0
Geneva-on-the-Lake	1,286	5	0	2	0	3	15	6	7	2	0
Genoa Township	23,643	2	0	0	0	2	198	35	158	5	1
Georgetown	4,470	4	0	0	1	3	181	47	132	2	1
Germantown	5,574	5	0	2	0	3	41	11	30	0	1
German Township, Clark County	7,079	2	0	0	2	0	121	25	94	2	0
German Township, Montgomery County	2,895	1	0	1	0	0	69	25	42	2	0
Gibsonburg	2,572	8	0	1	1	6	50	11	39	0	0
Girard	9,906	19	0	3	6	10	387	133	232	22	0
Glendale	2,150	1	0	0	1	0	25	7	17	1	0
Goshen Township, Clermont County	15,644	6	0	5	0	1	318	70	241	7	2
Goshen Township, Mahoning County	3,221	11	0	1	0	10	128	24	100	4	0
Grandview Heights	6,625	1	0	0	1	0	76	15	60	1	0
Granville	5,662	2	0	1	0	1	49	9	40	0	0
Greenfield	4,623	7	0	1	4	2	189	49	133	7	0
Greenhills	3,605	1	0	0	0	1	49	16	32	1	1

Table 8. Offenses Known to Law Enforcement, by Selected State and City, 2012— continued

(Number)

State/city	Population	Violent crime	Murder and nonnegligent manslaughter	Forcible rape	Robbery	Aggravated assault	Property crime	Burglary	Larceny-theft	Motor vehicle theft	Arson[1]
Greenville	13,188	54	0	3	9	42	580	171	393	16	0
Grove City	36,050	37	1	12	20	4	1,354	188	1,127	39	11
Groveport	5,435	2	0	0	1	1	119	16	101	2	0
Hamilton	62,791	372	3	89	157	123	4,713	1,295	3,218	200	45
Hamilton Township, Warren County	21,033	12	0	2	1	9	242	37	200	5	0
Harrison	9,870	8	0	1	4	3	313	35	273	5	0
Hartville	2,941	1	0	0	0	1	55	16	37	2	0
Haskins	1,196	0	0	0	0	0	21	3	18	0	0
Hebron	2,347	2	0	2	0	0	61	3	58	0	0
Hicksville	3,568	1	0	0	0	1	12	0	12	0	0
Highland Heights	8,279	2	0	0	2	0	115	10	103	2	0
Hilliard	28,814	20	0	1	15	4	763	148	584	31	4
Hillsboro	6,585	4	0	3	1	0	280	37	243	0	2
Hinckley Township	7,688	1	0	0	1	0	64	26	36	2	0
Hiram	1,407	0	0	0	0	0	20	1	19	0	0
Holland	1,758	6	0	0	4	2	211	9	202	0	0
Howland Township	17,239	12	0	2	5	5	423	88	322	13	0
Hubbard	7,834	17	0	1	7	9	179	52	126	1	2
Hubbard Township	5,624	1	0	0	1	0	175	82	90	3	0
Hudson	22,181	2	0	0	2	0	142	23	119	0	2
Hunting Valley	700	0	0	0	0	0	4	1	3	0	0
Huron	7,118	15	0	1	0	14	182	49	132	1	0
Independence	7,070	10	0	2	0	8	181	30	151	0	0
Indian Hill	5,771	0	0	0	0	0	63	19	42	2	0
Jackson	6,390	1	0	0	0	1	330	44	280	6	0
Jackson Center	1,460	0	0	0	0	0	23	13	9	1	2
Jackson Township, Montgomery County	3,713	2	0	1	1	0	35	10	21	4	0
Johnstown	4,653	3	0	0	1	2	46	6	38	2	0
Kent	28,933	62	0	7	18	37	636	168	450	18	10
Kenton	8,251	5	0	0	4	1	439	101	333	5	3
Kettering	56,423	50	0	22	20	8	1,291	317	935	39	11
Kirtland	6,860	0	0	0	0	0	46	5	39	2	0
Kirtland Hills	646	0	0	0	0	0	7	1	6	0	0
Lake Township	8,011	0	0	0	0	0	95	24	70	1	0
Lakewood	51,721	64	3	3	34	24	1,025	244	680	101	5
Lawrence Township	8,210	8	0	2	0	6	69	26	42	1	1
Lebanon	20,241	19	0	12	3	4	451	51	389	11	5
Lexington	4,784	5	0	4	1	0	93	24	64	5	0
Liberty Township	12,002	24	0	2	9	13	212	58	135	19	0
Lima	38,691	466	6	51	101	308	2,080	618	1,382	80	22
Lincoln Heights	3,279	24	1	4	12	7	69	22	39	8	0
Linndale	178	2	0	0	1	1	13	0	13	0	0
Liverpool Township	4,005	2	1	1	0	0	62	18	41	3	0
Lockland	3,441	25	2	0	16	7	175	69	101	5	2
Logan	7,155	10	0	3	6	1	331	61	264	6	1
London	9,895	15	0	1	6	8	260	61	187	12	2
Lorain	64,148	325	4	34	136	151	3,233	1,246	1,869	118	32
Lordstown	3,400	1	0	0	0	1	104	25	71	8	0
Loudonville	2,641	3	0	0	1	2	84	26	56	2	0
Louisville	9,173	5	0	0	1	4	194	47	145	2	1
Loveland	12,081	2	0	1	0	1	126	23	101	2	1
Madeira	8,704	0	0	0	0	0	43	8	31	4	0
Madison	3,182	0	0	0	0	0	40	14	25	1	1
Madison Township, Franklin County	18,270	15	0	0	7	8	283	118	158	7	0
Mansfield	47,480	178	1	27	93	57	3,205	1,016	2,104	85	51
Mariemont	3,393	0	0	0	0	0	49	2	47	0	0
Marietta	14,079	9	0	0	4	5	208	22	177	9	0
Marion	36,687	97	2	14	48	33	1,893	851	997	45	10
Martins Ferry	6,890	3	0	0	0	3	76	15	58	3	0
Mason	31,037	11	0	2	6	3	604	82	512	10	1
Massillon	32,104	66	0	14	31	21	1,097	353	713	31	14
Mayfield Heights	19,004	12	0	0	4	8	353	36	300	17	2

Table 8. Offenses Known to Law Enforcement, by Selected State and City, 2012— continued

(Number)

State/city	Population	Violent crime	Murder and nonnegligent manslaughter	Forcible rape	Robbery	Aggravated assault	Property crime	Burglary	Larceny-theft	Motor vehicle theft	Arson[1]
Mayfield Village	3,434	2	0	0	0	2	66	10	56	0	0
McArthur	1,691	0	0	0	0	0	45	7	35	3	0
Mentor	47,123	53	0	15	27	11	1,225	103	1,088	34	4
Mentor-on-the-Lake	7,439	4	0	0	0	4	86	21	59	6	0
Miamisburg	20,273	31	0	6	11	14	641	182	437	22	5
Miami Township, Clermont County	41,213	14	1	3	4	6	790	127	655	8	5
Miami Township, Montgomery County	29,265	39	1	9	21	8	1,157	152	963	42	0
Middlefield	2,690	0	0	0	0	0	44	0	44	0	0
Middleport	2,519	2	0	0	0	2	28	15	13	0	0
Middletown	48,959	359	1	31	82	245	4,027	1,135	2,792	100	12
Milan	1,363	0	0	0	0	0	22	4	18	0	0
Milford	6,768	16	0	0	3	13	347	24	322	1	0
Millersburg	3,052	3	0	2	0	1	117	9	107	1	0
Milton Township	2,562	1	0	0	1	0	84	48	35	1	0
Minerva	3,715	3	0	1	0	2	43	12	28	3	0
Minerva Park	1,288	1	0	0	1	0	37	9	28	0	0
Mingo Junction	3,409	11	0	1	0	10	60	27	33	0	0
Monroe	14,837	52	1	5	4	42	667	99	554	14	0
Montgomery	10,224	1	0	0	1	0	165	23	131	11	3
Montpelier	4,067	10	0	1	1	8	194	20	171	3	0
Montville Township	11,244	5	1	2	1	1	85	15	70	0	0
Moraine	6,336	29	0	5	16	8	725	76	634	15	2
Moreland Hills	3,294	0	0	0	0	0	14	3	11	0	0
Mount Gilead	3,662	1	0	0	1	0	197	21	172	4	0
Munroe Falls	4,994	0	0	0	0	0	35	10	25	0	0
Napoleon	8,701	14	1	6	3	4	410	68	334	8	0
Navarre	1,954	1	0	1	0	0	37	8	27	2	0
New Albany	7,834	2	0	0	0	2	110	21	88	1	0
Newark	47,787	69	0	20	32	17	2,292	501	1,705	86	38
New Boston	2,266	2	0	0	2	0	215	25	187	3	1
Newcomerstown	3,820	13	0	4	1	8	86	22	60	4	2
New Franklin	14,174	3	1	0	0	2	85	27	56	2	2
New Lebanon	4,013	6	0	4	0	2	124	27	83	14	0
New Lexington	4,791	5	0	0	0	5	114	17	95	2	2
New London	2,455	3	0	1	0	2	29	5	24	0	0
New Middletown	1,610	0	0	0	0	0	4	1	3	0	0
New Philadelphia	17,272	4	0	0	1	3	234	6	227	1	0
New Richmond	2,605	1	0	1	0	0	50	10	39	1	0
Newtown	2,665	0	0	0	0	0	38	7	28	3	1
Niles	19,167	46	0	4	25	17	992	217	739	36	1
North Canton	17,464	16	0	1	7	8	318	78	230	10	3
North Ridgeville	29,490	16	0	3	4	9	329	112	206	11	0
Northwood	5,304	8	0	3	2	3	266	55	203	8	1
Norwood	19,158	64	1	9	43	11	1,331	282	1,023	26	2
Oak Hill	1,551	4	1	0	1	2	29	2	23	4	0
Oberlin	8,291	13	0	4	7	2	269	73	194	2	2
Olmsted Falls	8,953	11	0	0	3	8	93	13	78	2	2
Olmsted Township	13,407	2	0	1	0	1	35	10	25	0	0
Ontario	6,175	12	0	0	6	6	582	41	533	8	0
Orange Village	3,297	2	0	0	1	1	13	3	9	1	1
Oregon	20,205	34	1	1	11	21	959	173	759	27	6
Orrville	8,386	12	0	6	6	0	143	41	98	4	2
Ottawa	4,438	1	0	1	0	0	14	0	13	1	0
Ottawa Hills	4,499	5	0	0	0	5	37	21	16	0	1
Oxford	21,443	63	0	11	2	50	626	161	457	8	13
Painesville	19,548	53	0	12	29	12	441	126	303	12	5
Parma	80,963	56	0	4	14	38	451	47	398	6	1
Parma Heights	20,557	33	0	13	8	12	428	81	323	24	0
Pataskala	15,030	3	0	3	0	0	240	50	184	6	1
Paulding	3,568	2	0	1	1	0	18	3	15	0	0
Payne	1,181	0	0	0	0	0	17	7	10	0	0
Peebles	1,776	1	0	0	0	1	45	11	31	3	1

Table 8. Offenses Known to Law Enforcement, by Selected State and City, 2012— continued

(Number)

State/city	Population	Violent crime	Murder and nonnegligent manslaughter	Forcible rape	Robbery	Aggravated assault	Property crime	Burglary	Larceny-theft	Motor vehicle theft	Arson[1]
Pemberville	1,382	0	0	0	0	0	7	1	6	0	0
Perkins Township	12,150	2	0	0	1	1	297	4	292	1	0
Perrysburg	20,771	16	0	3	2	11	419	53	349	17	0
Perry Township, Allen County	3,522	0	0	0	0	0	43	4	36	3	0
Perry Township, Franklin County	3,684	0	0	0	0	0	47	9	38	0	0
Perry Township, Montgomery County	3,372	0	0	0	0	0	49	20	23	6	0
Perry Township, Stark County	28,262	45	1	5	16	23	591	206	374	11	8
Pierce Township	11,313	7	0	1	4	2	165	30	130	5	2
Pioneer	1,379	1	0	1	0	0	47	6	39	2	1
Piqua	20,591	22	1	7	12	2	1,249	217	1,011	21	4
Plain City	4,229	0	0	0	0	0	15	2	13	0	0
Poland Township	12,327	4	0	0	1	3	112	33	77	2	1
Poland Village	2,537	0	0	0	0	0	30	2	28	0	0
Port Clinton	6,050	5	0	0	2	3	221	57	161	3	1
Powell	11,776	0	0	0	0	0	82	14	65	3	0
Powhatan Point	1,586	2	0	0	0	2	34	14	20	0	0
Reminderville	3,391	1	0	0	0	1	18	6	12	0	0
Reynoldsburg	36,291	89	2	7	58	22	1,051	178	838	35	11
Richfield	3,634	0	0	0	0	0	29	5	20	4	0
Richmond Heights	10,464	15	0	2	10	3	304	66	213	25	2
Richwood	2,252	0	0	0	0	0	39	12	24	3	0
Rio Grande	835	2	0	0	0	2	25	14	11	0	0
Rittman	6,497	4	0	0	0	4	139	50	83	6	0
Riverside	25,317	45	1	4	14	26	742	200	503	39	4
Rossford	6,338	1	0	1	0	0	141	25	114	2	1
Russell Township	5,180	0	0	0	0	0	15	6	9	0	0
Sabina	2,557	2	0	0	1	1	70	19	47	4	0
Sagamore Hills	10,906	2	0	0	1	1	44	13	28	3	1
Salem	12,269	4	0	1	1	2	260	23	228	9	1
Sebring	4,391	2	0	1	0	1	148	35	110	3	0
Seven Hills	11,718	1	0	0	0	1	38	15	21	2	0
Seville	2,307	4	0	1	1	2	20	6	14	0	0
Shawnee Township	8,686	4	0	0	2	2	131	32	97	2	0
Sheffield Lake	9,144	1	0	0	1	0	139	40	96	3	2
Shelby	9,241	11	0	5	3	3	410	101	298	11	0
Sidney	21,177	66	0	8	17	41	1,306	302	970	34	12
Silverton	4,769	6	0	0	5	1	89	27	60	2	0
Smith Township	4,441	6	0	1	1	4	72	16	51	5	1
Smithville	1,252	0	0	0	0	0	7	2	5	0	0
Solon	23,165	7	0	0	1	6	193	31	158	4	1
South Bloomfield	1,754	0	0	0	0	0	39	10	26	3	1
South Charleston	1,685	0	0	0	0	0	31	13	16	2	1
South Euclid	22,125	34	2	4	24	4	422	123	288	11	1
South Point	3,961	7	0	2	1	4	19	0	19	0	0
South Russell	3,803	1	0	0	0	1	13	0	13	0	0
South Vienna	381	0	0	0	0	0	16	2	14	0	0
Springboro	17,587	5	0	2	0	3	181	27	154	0	4
Springdale	11,194	41	0	4	26	11	735	58	667	10	2
Springfield	60,329	373	5	38	178	152	4,337	1,420	2,746	171	80
Springfield Township, Hamilton County	36,225	46	1	3	27	15	851	267	545	39	6
Springfield Township, Mahoning County	6,660	2	0	0	0	2	108	41	62	5	1
Springfield Township, Summit County	17,646	24	1	3	10	10	878	118	741	19	4
St. Clair Township	7,936	0	0	0	0	0	34	2	32	0	0
Stow	34,709	26	0	15	8	3	648	85	561	2	3
St. Paris	2,074	1	0	0	0	1	39	6	32	1	0
Strasburg	2,607	0	0	0	0	0	45	7	38	0	0
Streetsboro	16,049	5	0	0	0	5	91	2	89	0	0
Strongsville	44,397	13	0	6	5	2	796	83	700	13	4
Sugarcreek Township	8,104	5	0	1	0	4	322	22	299	1	0

Table 8. Offenses Known to Law Enforcement, by Selected State and City, 2012— continued

(Number)

State/city	Population	Violent crime	Murder and nonnegligent manslaughter	Forcible rape	Robbery	Aggravated assault	Property crime	Burglary	Larceny-theft	Motor vehicle theft	Arson[1]
Swanton	3,675	0	0	0	0	0	79	14	64	1	0
Sycamore	863	0	0	0	0	0	18	4	14	0	0
Sylvania Township	29,397	27	0	0	19	8	770	143	589	38	0
Tallmadge	17,472	18	0	13	0	5	401	72	312	17	0
Tipp City	9,720	6	0	1	4	1	221	34	180	7	1
Toledo[4]	286,020	3,352	39	172	1,126	2,015		6,729		1,334	529
Toronto	5,024	3	0	0	0	3	29	13	16	0	0
Trotwood	24,540	75	1	16	48	10	1,374	511	754	109	11
Troy	25,141	14	0	1	12	1	859	131	709	19	6
Twinsburg	18,726	10	0	4	2	4	139	12	117	10	0
Uhrichsville	5,408	7	0	0	4	3	164	41	111	12	0
Union	6,448	2	0	2	0	0	106	31	73	2	0
Uniontown	3,311	0	0	0	0	0	109	29	78	2	0
Union Township, Clermont County	46,833	36	1	9	17	9	1,653	231	1,387	35	6
University Heights	13,444	16	0	2	10	4	235	36	192	7	0
Upper Arlington	34,221	9	0	0	8	1	471	66	388	17	2
Urbana	11,706	17	1	3	3	10	464	73	379	12	2
Utica	2,142	3	0	0	1	2	75	8	65	2	0
Vandalia	15,316	21	0	4	5	12	405	94	294	17	7
Van Wert	10,792	18	0	2	1	15	433	90	343	0	2
Vermilion	10,568	10	0	0	6	4	204	104	88	12	0
Village of Leesburg	1,313	0	0	0	0	0	36	13	23	0	0
Wadsworth	21,682	11	0	6	0	5	453	66	384	3	1
Waite Hill	471	0	0	0	0	0	1	0	1	0	0
Walbridge	3,040	0	0	0	0	0	26	5	20	1	0
Walton Hills	2,263	0	0	0	0	0	17	2	15	0	0
Wapakoneta	9,842	7	0	0	1	6	224	28	193	3	0
Warren	41,355	279	4	16	102	157	2,010	812	1,086	112	12
Warrensville Heights	13,436	47	0	5	32	10	446	174	188	84	3
Washington Court House	14,168	20	0	4	5	11	544	146	386	12	1
Waterville	5,500	0	0	0	0	0	27	5	22	0	0
Wauseon	7,301	6	0	2	1	3	205	16	188	1	0
Waverly	4,395	2	0	0	2	0	103	10	93	0	0
Weathersfield	8,357	17	0	4	4	9	270	97	158	15	3
Wells Township	2,799	1	0	1	0	0	48	18	28	2	0
West Alexandria	1,352	3	0	1	0	2	48	10	36	2	0
West Carrollton	13,203	25	0	7	10	8	415	133	262	20	2
West Chester Township	58,897	54	0	28	12	14	1,316	215	1,078	23	4
Westerville	36,663	13	0	3	9	1	890	105	768	17	14
West Jefferson	4,217	7	1	0	2	4	106	19	82	5	0
West Liberty	1,798	3	0	2	1	0	16	5	11	0	1
West Salem	1,468	1	0	1	0	0	16	1	15	0	0
Whitehall	18,305	164	1	13	107	43	1,695	316	1,306	73	13
Wickliffe	12,741	5	0	0	0	5	207	23	178	6	0
Williamsburg	2,512	0	0	0	0	0	92	13	77	2	0
Willoughby	22,251	20	0	3	14	3	507	62	427	18	4
Willoughby Hills	9,477	5	1	0	1	3	178	41	126	11	0
Wilmington	12,487	8	0	3	3	2	690	79	608	3	1
Wintersville	3,875	6	0	0	1	5	68	7	58	3	0
Woodlawn	3,286	10	0	0	4	6	125	24	96	5	1
Woodmere Village	876	3	0	0	0	3	35	2	32	1	1
Wooster	26,137	42	1	15	10	16	851	143	679	29	8
Worthington	13,754	4	0	0	2	2	389	116	265	8	9
Wyoming	8,407	7	0	0	0	7	139	33	103	3	0
Xenia	25,923	59	0	14	20	25	1,163	224	911	28	4
Yellow Springs	3,516	3	0	0	1	2	37	4	32	1	0
Youngstown	66,567	684	22	39	244	379	3,636	1,739	1,621	276	263
Zanesville	25,529	85	1	7	31	46	1,677	267	1,361	49	10
Oklahoma											
Achille	502	1	0	0	0	1	8	0	7	1	0
Ada	17,046	167	2	18	9	138	886	206	630	50	0

Table 8. Offenses Known to Law Enforcement, by Selected State and City, 2012— continued

(Number)

State/city	Population	Violent crime	Murder and nonnegligent manslaughter	Forcible rape	Robbery	Aggravated assault	Property crime	Burglary	Larceny-theft	Motor vehicle theft	Arson[1]
Allen	941	1	0	1	0	0	7	0	4	3	0
Altus	19,936	63	1	8	10	44	679	209	445	25	3
Alva	4,914	3	0	0	0	3	88	16	70	2	1
Anadarko	6,788	32	0	2	2	28	241	78	149	14	6
Antlers	2,443	10	0	3	0	7	101	38	58	5	3
Apache	1,454	0	0	0	0	0	6	0	6	0	0
Ardmore	24,704	347	2	32	34	279	1,458	313	1,083	62	13
Arkoma	2,010	2	0	0	0	2	17	5	9	3	0
Atoka	3,133	7	1	1	0	5	137	62	69	6	2
Bartlesville	36,321	99	1	8	16	74	1,066	274	735	57	5
Beaver	1,520	4	0	0	0	4	21	7	14	0	0
Beggs	1,325	1	0	0	1	0	33	8	23	2	1
Bethany	19,525	71	0	6	21	44	719	187	479	53	4
Blackwell	7,074	19	0	8	1	10	153	54	91	8	2
Blanchard	7,848	8	0	2	0	6	94	27	61	6	0
Boise City	1,278	0	0	0	0	0	3	1	2	0	0
Boley	1,194	1	0	0	0	1	12	6	6	0	0
Bristow	4,279	14	0	0	0	14	153	36	104	13	1
Broken Arrow	100,688	155	1	33	39	82	2,187	374	1,698	115	16
Broken Bow	4,148	75	0	2	2	71	153	40	104	9	0
Caddo	1,025	1	0	0	0	1	10	2	8	0	0
Calera	2,213	0	0	0	0	0	25	7	15	3	0
Caney	206	0	0	0	0	0	9	3	6	0	0
Carnegie	1,725	3	0	1	0	2	10	5	5	0	0
Carney	648	3	0	0	0	3	6	2	3	1	1
Catoosa	7,270	51	0	2	1	48	149	39	81	29	1
Chandler	3,109	6	0	1	0	5	116	38	74	4	2
Checotah	3,373	1	0	1	0	0	100	15	79	6	0
Chelsea	1,994	3	0	0	0	3	24	9	14	1	3
Cherokee	1,513	2	0	0	0	2	12	6	5	1	0
Chickasha	16,310	116	0	16	12	88	923	264	601	58	4
Choctaw	11,434	14	1	2	0	11	211	61	135	15	1
Chouteau	2,125	5	0	3	0	2	41	8	28	5	3
Claremore	18,860	50	0	10	9	31	500	99	378	23	1
Clayton	819	2	0	0	0	2	10	4	6	0	0
Cleveland	3,302	11	0	0	3	8	88	22	60	6	0
Coalgate	1,981	1	0	0	0	1	16	8	8	0	0
Colbert	1,165	1	0	0	0	1	2	2	0	0	0
Collinsville	5,707	9	0	0	1	8	117	36	79	2	0
Comanche	1,677	4	0	0	0	4	57	21	36	0	0
Cordell	2,920	3	0	0	0	3	47	18	24	5	0
Coweta	9,563	13	0	2	1	10	112	17	86	9	0
Crescent	1,442	4	0	0	1	3	21	8	12	1	1
Cushing	7,939	17	1	2	0	14	211	35	165	11	0
Davenport	816	3	0	0	0	3	8	4	3	1	0
Davis	2,718	13	0	4	1	8	81	24	47	10	2
Del City	21,880	142	3	14	29	96	1,158	346	718	94	10
Dewar	890	1	0	0	0	1	7	3	4	0	0
Dewey	3,486	19	1	4	0	14	130	32	94	4	1
Dibble	847	0	0	0	0	0	4	1	3	0	0
Drumright	2,946	6	0	0	1	5	58	19	33	6	2
Duncan	23,652	100	2	13	17	68	1,054	285	724	45	3
Durant	16,196	163	0	11	9	143	863	194	635	34	1
Edmond	83,473	85	2	12	20	51	1,680	303	1,330	47	5
Elk City	11,861	22	0	2	0	20	331	73	233	25	2
El Reno	17,374	47	0	11	5	31	521	151	341	29	3
Enid	49,755	164	2	28	21	113	1,978	486	1,402	90	8
Eufaula	2,845	7	0	1	1	5	92	34	52	6	0
Fairfax	1,387	3	0	0	0	3	16	5	10	1	0
Fairview	2,639	6	0	1	0	5	123	35	86	2	0
Fletcher	1,203	0	0	0	0	0	8	3	4	1	0
Forest Park	1,023	2	0	1	0	1	14	6	8	0	0
Fort Gibson	4,181	3	0	0	0	3	91	31	58	2	0
Frederick	3,998	18	0	1	1	16	82	24	53	5	1

Table 8. Offenses Known to Law Enforcement, by Selected State and City, 2012— continued

(Number)

State/city	Population	Violent crime	Murder and nonnegligent manslaughter	Forcible rape	Robbery	Aggravated assault	Property crime	Burglary	Larceny-theft	Motor vehicle theft	Arson[1]
Geary	1,288	0	0	0	0	0	34	16	13	5	0
Glenpool	11,005	86	1	10	6	69	247	54	188	5	2
Goodwell	1,330	1	0	0	0	1	28	3	25	0	0
Grove	6,688	21	0	0	0	21	217	21	194	2	1
Guthrie	10,409	16	0	3	2	11	314	59	237	18	0
Guymon	11,896	29	0	4	6	19	319	61	242	16	6
Haileyville	815	0	0	0	0	0	9	4	5	0	0
Harrah	5,225	14	0	0	1	13	100	32	59	9	0
Hartshorne	2,128	3	0	1	1	1	51	29	21	1	1
Haskell	2,020	1	0	0	0	1	2	0	2	0	0
Healdton	2,836	2	0	0	0	2	26	4	17	5	1
Heavener	3,453	11	0	1	1	9	85	35	43	7	0
Hennessey	2,169	4	0	0	0	4	23	4	17	2	1
Henryetta	5,943	8	0	0	1	7	197	65	123	9	0
Hinton	3,213	0	0	0	0	0	11	2	6	3	0
Hobart	3,768	14	0	1	4	9	154	60	86	8	1
Holdenville	5,749	7	0	0	2	5	67	18	37	12	0
Hollis	2,071	8	0	0	2	6	67	29	36	2	0
Hominy	3,585	4	0	1	0	3	53	21	28	4	0
Hooker	1,994	1	0	0	0	1	16	3	12	1	0
Howe	811	0	0	0	0	0	0	0	0	0	0
Hugo	5,359	22	0	4	3	15	82	31	48	3	2
Hulbert	605	1	0	0	0	1	2	0	1	1	0
Hydro	972	2	0	0	0	2	16	3	13	0	0
Idabel	7,061	30	0	3	5	22	379	85	277	17	2
Jay	2,473	0	0	0	0	0	57	7	50	0	0
Jenks	17,235	31	1	1	4	25	276	52	213	11	0
Jones	2,761	6	0	0	1	5	34	8	22	4	1
Kiefer	1,710	4	0	0	0	4	11	5	3	3	0
Kingfisher	4,716	2	0	1	0	1	84	9	72	3	0
Kingston	1,631	0	0	0	0	0	11	2	9	0	0
Krebs	2,057	9	0	2	1	6	90	25	60	5	0
Lahoma	617	0	0	0	0	0	1	1	0	0	0
Lawton	98,781	920	13	38	173	696	5,208	1,560	3,349	299	41
Lexington	2,211	4	1	0	0	3	69	7	56	6	0
Lindsay	2,844	9	0	0	0	9	51	24	23	4	0
Locust Grove	1,436	2	0	0	0	2	23	7	13	3	0
Lone Grove	5,142	11	0	1	1	9	99	31	62	6	3
Luther	1,252	1	0	0	0	1	9	5	2	2	0
Madill	3,841	0	0	0	0	0	37	4	31	2	0
Mangum	2,963	1	0	0	0	1	35	9	24	2	0
Mannford	3,116	6	1	1	0	4	42	13	27	2	0
Marietta	2,632	9	0	1	1	7	55	13	40	2	0
Marlow	4,707	15	0	2	0	13	164	50	108	6	0
Maysville	1,234	1	0	0	1	0	18	4	8	6	2
McAlester	18,419	57	0	12	12	33	949	252	647	50	3
McCurtain	520	0	0	0	0	0	5	3	1	1	0
McLoud	4,106	8	0	0	1	7	61	11	42	8	1
Medicine Park	390	0	0	0	0	0	0	0	0	0	0
Meeker	1,147	5	0	0	0	5	33	8	22	3	0
Midwest City	55,768	295	6	36	46	207	2,982	786	1,956	240	22
Minco	1,660	3	0	0	0	3	16	5	9	2	0
Moore	56,661	77	1	5	20	51	2,383	496	1,701	186	9
Mooreland	1,193	1	0	0	1	0	29	7	20	2	0
Morris	1,483	0	0	0	0	0	9	1	7	1	0
Mountain View	798	0	0	0	0	0	3	1	0	2	0
Muldrow	3,477	5	0	0	1	4	39	13	22	4	0
Muskogee	39,472	579	1	23	36	519	1,862	690	1,078	94	9
Mustang	18,113	29	0	3	4	22	449	92	340	17	4
Newcastle	7,895	11	0	0	2	9	299	80	186	33	1
Newkirk	2,310	6	0	0	1	5	50	10	37	3	0
Nichols Hills	3,805	1	0	0	0	1	68	18	49	1	0
Nicoma Park	2,456	8	0	1	0	7	62	14	44	4	0
Ninnekah	1,020	0	0	0	0	0	7	1	5	1	0

Table 8. Offenses Known to Law Enforcement, by Selected State and City, 2012— continued

(Number)

State/city	Population	Violent crime	Murder and nonnegligent manslaughter	Forcible rape	Robbery	Aggravated assault	Property crime	Burglary	Larceny-theft	Motor vehicle theft	Arson[1]
Noble	6,665	8	0	4	0	4	171	31	131	9	1
Norman	113,969	173	1	52	54	66	3,050	629	2,252	169	7
North Enid	007	0	0	0	0	0	6	1	5	0	0
Nowata	3,786	13	0	1	0	12	77	22	53	2	0
Oilton	1,026	1	0	0	0	1	24	7	15	2	0
Okemah	3,288	3	1	0	0	2	176	54	117	5	0
Oklahoma City	595,607	5,474	85	389	1,209	3,791	35,390	9,854	21,162	4,374	119
Okmulgee	12,359	52	1	0	5	46	468	94	338	36	4
Oologah	1,166	0	0	0	0	0	15	4	11	0	0
Owasso	30,038	56	0	9	5	42	768	166	575	27	1
Pauls Valley	6,198	32	0	5	3	24	307	83	215	9	2
Pawhuska	3,599	13	0	2	0	11	89	50	34	5	1
Pawnee	2,229	3	0	1	0	2	11	6	0	5	0
Perkins	2,874	6	0	1	0	5	67	21	44	2	1
Perry	5,165	17	0	4	0	13	123	31	79	13	0
Piedmont	5,957	5	0	0	1	4	65	21	36	8	1
Pocola	4,098	3	0	1	0	2	78	27	49	2	1
Ponca City	25,323	116	0	20	22	74	1,151	189	915	47	14
Porum	730	5	0	0	0	5	11	7	4	0	0
Poteau	8,609	39	0	7	1	31	307	69	215	23	0
Prague	2,393	15	0	0	1	14	94	30	62	2	0
Pryor	9,624	82	0	4	1	77	312	119	162	31	2
Purcell	6,043	18	0	1	2	15	389	90	264	35	1
Ramona	544	0	0	0	0	0	4	3	1	0	0
Ringling	1,049	1	0	0	0	1	17	7	5	5	0
Roland	3,175	3	0	1	0	2	52	8	38	6	0
Rush Springs	1,254	1	0	1	0	0	14	7	6	1	1
Sand Springs	19,258	35	0	5	11	19	784	107	623	54	1
Sapulpa	20,818	49	0	10	7	32	496	113	344	39	8
Sawyer	324	2	0	0	0	2	7	1	6	0	0
Sayre	4,424	10	1	0	1	8	60	15	36	9	0
Seiling	875	3	0	0	0	3	24	4	18	2	0
Seminole	7,480	18	1	3	3	11	413	111	271	31	4
Shawnee	30,398	287	2	24	21	240	1,720	381	1,196	143	0
Snyder	1,399	3	0	3	0	0	34	6	28	0	0
South Coffeyville	796	3	0	0	0	3	9	3	3	3	0
Sparks	170	0	0	0	0	0	8	0	7	1	0
Spencer	4,011	6	0	1	1	4	84	26	46	12	0
Spiro	2,187	2	0	1	1	0	23	14	9	0	0
Stigler	2,711	5	0	0	0	5	55	7	45	3	0
Stillwater	46,331	121	1	24	21	75	1,471	260	1,154	57	4
Stilwell	3,961	9	0	0	1	8	83	34	46	3	1
Stonewall	478	0	0	0	0	0	9	6	3	0	0
Stratford	1,527	2	0	0	1	1	6	2	3	1	0
Stringtown	415	0	0	0	0	0	6	4	2	0	0
Stroud	2,696	11	0	0	1	10	59	25	31	3	1
Sulphur	4,986	7	0	0	0	7	70	23	46	1	0
Tahlequah	16,120	47	0	4	4	39	690	182	483	25	2
Talihina	1,127	3	0	0	0	3	29	10	18	1	0
Tecumseh	6,577	12	0	6	0	6	143	34	99	10	0
Texhoma	962	0	0	0	0	0	3	1	1	1	0
The Village	9,159	18	0	2	5	11	326	78	235	13	1
Tishomingo	3,100	5	0	1	0	4	62	16	43	3	0
Tonkawa	3,209	3	0	0	2	1	80	21	52	7	0
Tryon	493	1	0	0	0	1	11	4	6	1	2
Tulsa	398,904	3,949	42	316	1,062	2,529	20,807	6,235	12,162	2,410	238
Tushka	315	1	0	0	0	1	4	2	2	0	0
Tuttle	6,124	6	0	0	0	6	164	49	98	17	2
Valliant	761	1	0	0	0	1	10	2	8	0	0
Verdigris	4,055	2	0	1	0	1	32	20	11	1	4
Vian	1,474	4	0	0	0	4	28	7	21	0	1
Vinita	5,796	6	0	0	0	6	94	22	63	9	3
Wagoner	8,488	78	0	2	13	63	398	93	296	9	6
Walters	2,561	0	0	0	0	0	13	2	11	0	0

Table 8. Offenses Known to Law Enforcement, by Selected State and City, 2012— continued

(Number)

State/city	Population	Violent crime	Murder and nonnegligent manslaughter	Forcible rape	Robbery	Aggravated assault	Property crime	Burglary	Larceny-theft	Motor vehicle theft	Arson[1]
Warner	1,651	4	0	1	1	2	40	15	21	4	0
Warr Acres	10,301	71	1	4	23	43	507	122	322	63	2
Washington	635	3	0	0	0	3	5	2	2	1	0
Watonga	3,022	16	0	1	1	14	82	41	38	3	2
Waukomis	1,295	0	0	0	0	0	7	4	3	0	0
Waurika	2,088	0	0	0	0	0	0	0	0	0	0
Waynoka	921	1	0	0	0	1	3	1	1	1	0
Weatherford	11,006	44	0	7	2	35	256	65	170	21	1
Weleetka	1,017	6	0	0	0	6	51	19	30	2	2
Westville	1,645	4	0	0	0	4	32	15	14	3	1
Wetumka	1,274	2	0	0	1	1	18	12	6	0	0
Wewoka	3,427	9	0	2	1	6	95	32	55	8	1
Wilburton	2,860	2	0	0	0	2	1	0	1	0	0
Wilson	1,756	24	0	1	0	23	33	5	24	4	3
Wright City	769	0	0	0	0	0	5	3	2	0	0
Wyandotte	334	0	0	0	0	0	10	9	1	0	0
Wynnewood	2,217	4	0	0	0	4	23	8	10	5	1
Yale	1,245	2	0	0	0	2	13	2	11	0	1
Yukon	23,635	33	0	3	0	30	590	103	458	29	2
Oregon											
Adair Village	849	0	0	0	0	0	4	1	3	0	0
Albany	51,084	44	0	10	23	11	1,580	224	1,262	94	10
Ashland	20,376	35	0	10	5	20	619	62	543	14	4
Astoria	9,575	22	0	1	10	11	469	92	346	31	2
Athena	1,153	3	0	1	0	2	13	0	12	1	0
Aumsville	3,652	16	0	0	0	16	74	9	58	7	3
Baker City	9,807	1	0	0	1	0	61	11	47	3	0
Banks	1,826	0	0	0	0	0	34	14	17	3	0
Beaverton	92,276	141	0	21	36	84	1,471	196	1,165	110	22
Boardman	3,241	4	0	0	0	4	81	33	45	3	0
Burns	2,809	1	1	0	0	0	132	35	93	4	1
Canby	16,121	17	0	6	3	8	284	51	222	11	1
Cannon Beach	1,707	0	0	0	0	0	27	5	22	0	0
Central Point	17,431	26	0	4	1	21	609	61	523	25	0
Clatskanie	1,750	4	0	1	1	2	51	8	39	4	1
Columbia City	1,963	0	0	0	0	0	23	7	16	0	0
Condon	711	0	0	0	0	0	1	0	1	0	0
Cornelius	12,193	28	0	3	8	17	357	68	267	22	0
Corvallis	55,062	67	1	11	15	40	1,418	235	1,153	30	16
Cottage Grove	9,803	37	0	0	3	34	432	31	385	16	3
Creswell	5,090	23	0	4	4	15	168	60	89	19	1
Dallas	14,802	29	0	4	1	24	375	56	308	11	5
Eagle Point	8,598	8	0	3	1	4	346	43	294	9	2
Estacada	2,744	2	0	1	1	0	84	16	66	2	0
Eugene	158,043	430	0	72	196	162	8,004	1,515	6,054	435	82
Fairview	9,141	13	0	2	2	9	310	38	230	42	1
Florence	8,567	7	0	3	2	2	333	70	246	17	1
Forest Grove	21,641	83	0	10	8	65	711	104	561	46	4
Gaston	656	3	0	0	1	2	29	3	26	0	1
Gearhart	1,477	0	0	0	0	0	13	4	9	0	0
Gervais	2,509	7	0	0	0	7	48	9	34	5	0
Gladstone	11,709	28	0	3	5	20	364	40	292	32	4
Gold Beach	2,276	4	0	1	0	3	82	16	63	3	0
Gresham	108,202	487	4	33	207	243	4,858	886	3,230	742	32
Hermiston	17,059	24	0	4	9	11	551	118	378	55	3
Hillsboro	94,119	180	2	34	52	92	2,154	323	1,716	115	6
Hines	1,563	0	0	0	0	0	32	8	23	1	1
Hubbard	3,233	3	0	0	0	3	40	12	26	2	0
Independence	8,720	17	0	4	3	10	225	30	182	13	1
Jacksonville	2,827	0	0	0	0	0	39	7	30	2	0
John Day	1,751	1	0	0	0	1	15	5	10	0	1
Junction City	5,456	1	0	0	0	1	126	18	101	7	0
Keizer	37,160	65	0	11	9	45	854	121	680	53	3

Table 8. Offenses Known to Law Enforcement, by Selected State and City, 2012— continued

(Number)

State/city	Population	Violent crime	Murder and nonnegligent manslaughter	Forcible rape	Robbery	Aggravated assault	Property crime	Burglary	Larceny-theft	Motor vehicle theft	Arson[1]
King City	3,196	5	0	1	0	4	55	6	48	1	1
Klamath Falls	20,968	79	0	10	27	42	1,017	185	762	70	15
La Grande	13,195	22	0	6	2	14	502	122	368	12	5
Lake Oswego	37,309	35	0	6	10	19	652	145	478	29	12
Lakeview	2,313	23	0	4	0	19	24	7	14	3	0
Lebanon	15,823	38	0	3	8	27	728	105	607	16	2
Lincoln City	7,969	48	0	3	3	42	366	89	260	17	2
Madras	6,102	15	0	4	6	5	322	55	246	21	10
Malin	809	0	0	0	0	0	1	1	0	0	0
Manzanita	605	0	0	0	0	0	7	2	5	0	0
McMinnville	32,681	64	0	9	17	38	928	178	707	43	10
Medford	76,037	425	2	39	64	320	4,418	477	3,764	177	49
Milton-Freewater	7,182	11	0	0	0	11	413	80	297	36	4
Milwaukie	20,664	25	0	3	6	16	533	115	377	41	3
Molalla	8,256	14	0	2	4	8	267	37	216	14	3
Monmouth	9,667	6	0	1	2	3	180	37	139	4	2
Mount Angel	3,345	11	0	0	1	10	71	13	56	2	1
Myrtle Creek	3,458	6	0	2	2	2	97	5	89	3	1
Newberg-Dundee	25,613	23	3	4	2	14	421	119	285	17	6
Newport	10,039	46	0	9	6	31	489	93	382	14	6
North Bend	9,726	11	1	2	7	1	579	115	443	21	2
North Plains	2,000	1	0	0	1	0	38	7	29	2	0
Ontario	11,348	82	0	12	5	65	856	138	698	20	0
Oregon City	32,440	46	1	14	12	19	891	117	695	79	1
Pendleton	16,903	38	1	2	7	28	845	149	646	50	3
Philomath	4,637	3	0	1	0	2	59	15	43	1	1
Phoenix	4,607	5	0	1	1	3	133	8	118	7	3
Pilot Rock	1,530	1	0	0	0	1	14	0	14	0	1
Portland	598,037	3,093	20	231	950	1,892	30,454	4,471	22,398	3,585	254
Prineville	9,257	34	0	3	0	31	307	46	256	5	8
Redmond	26,835	92	0	11	14	67	1,266	195	1,019	52	19
Reedsport	4,175	6	0	3	0	3	152	33	114	5	1
Rockaway Beach	1,329	1	0	0	0	1	53	20	32	1	0
Rogue River	2,163	0	0	0	0	0	80	12	66	2	0
Salem	157,353	564	7	40	138	379	6,731	1,043	4,958	730	51
Scappoose	6,646	30	0	2	1	27	113	8	98	7	0
Sherwood	18,699	11	0	6	2	3	244	26	214	4	5
Silverton	9,394	9	0	3	0	6	143	24	108	11	3
Springfield	60,119	104	0	17	30	57	3,052	413	2,412	227	18
Stanfield	2,082	2	0	0	0	2	26	4	17	5	0
Stayton	7,788	28	0	2	4	22	393	74	286	33	0
St. Helens	12,997	12	0	6	2	4	389	54	318	17	5
Sutherlin	7,852	16	0	3	2	11	252	47	164	41	3
Sweet Home	9,099	27	0	3	5	19	499	99	378	22	3
Talent	6,158	7	0	3	1	3	228	31	194	3	2
The Dalles	13,728	23	2	3	11	7	680	109	537	34	2
Tigard	49,359	67	1	9	36	21	1,717	218	1,448	51	4
Tillamook	5,037	7	0	3	1	3	205	25	176	4	1
Toledo	3,483	29	0	3	3	23	141	35	101	5	1
Troutdale	16,359	30	0	9	11	10	562	87	424	51	4
Tualatin	26,747	29	1	3	10	15	886	128	722	36	14
Turner	1,889	5	3	0	0	2	37	6	23	8	0
Umatilla	7,014	9	1	3	0	5	113	23	78	12	0
Veneta	4,616	28	0	5	3	20	205	60	126	19	2
Vernonia	2,168	6	0	2	0	4	55	15	39	1	1
Warrenton	5,039	1	0	0	1	0	134	12	117	5	0
West Linn	25,572	5	0	2	2	1	249	34	211	4	3
Wilsonville	19,855	8	0	3	4	1	282	37	220	25	1
Winston	5,408	12	0	5	3	4	190	42	138	10	1
Woodburn	24,531	73	1	6	24	42	833	142	618	73	5
Yamhill	1,039	3	0	0	0	3	17	3	12	2	0
Pennsylvania											
Abington Township, Lackawanna County	1,744	0	0	0	0	0	24	9	14	1	0

Table 8. Offenses Known to Law Enforcement, by Selected State and City, 2012— continued

(Number)

State/city	Population	Violent crime	Murder and nonnegligent manslaughter	Forcible rape	Robbery	Aggravated assault	Property crime	Burglary	Larceny-theft	Motor vehicle theft	Arson[1]
Abington Township, Montgomery County	55,731	110	1	8	39	62	1,103	165	920	18	2
Adamstown	1,808	0	0	0	0	0	33	7	24	2	0
Adams Township, Butler County	11,735	7	0	0	1	6	45	13	31	1	2
Adams Township, Cambria County	5,933	2	0	0	1	1	26	8	17	1	0
Akron	3,914	8	0	0	2	6	36	3	31	2	0
Albion	1,519	5	0	2	0	3	12	2	8	2	0
Alburtis	2,389	0	0	0	0	0	20	1	19	0	0
Aldan	4,162	16	0	4	3	9	161	25	133	3	0
Aleppo Township	1,923	0	0	0	0	0	15	0	14	1	0
Aliquippa	9,437	46	2	0	9	35	157	48	95	14	0
Allegheny Township, Blair County	6,747	38	0	1	1	36	120	9	108	3	0
Allegheny Township, Westmoreland County	8,161	5	0	0	1	4	125	18	106	1	0
Allentown3	119,334	653	15	54	374	210	4,603	1,248	2,987	368	11
Altoona	46,404	163	2	31	32	98	903	226	641	36	18
Ambler	6,465	7	0	1	5	1	179	24	151	4	1
Ambridge	7,051	133	2	3	17	111	291	83	202	6	2
Amity Township	12,625	3	0	2	1	0	122	27	88	7	0
Annville Township	4,794	1	0	0	0	1	115	8	106	1	0
Archbald	6,986	16	0	0	3	13	68	22	45	1	0
Arnold	5,155	28	2	1	9	16	101	32	53	16	2
Ashland	2,807	4	0	0	0	4	75	17	53	5	0
Ashville	226	0	0	0	0	0	0	0	0	0	0
Aspinwall	2,811	0	0	0	0	0	28	4	24	0	0
Aston Township	16,629	24	0	4	2	18	258	38	212	8	3
Atglen	1,422	2	0	0	0	2	7	1	4	2	0
Athens	3,386	6	0	1	0	5	87	14	73	0	0
Austin	562	0	0	0	0	0	3	2	1	0	0
Avalon	4,723	32	0	0	2	30	86	13	72	1	0
Avis	1,496	0	0	0	0	0	16	2	13	1	0
Avoca	2,663	2	0	0	0	2	42	9	31	2	0
Avondale	1,280	0	0	0	0	0	1	0	1	0	0
Avonmore Boro	1,012	0	0	0	0	0	0	0	0	0	0
Baden	4,136	3	0	0	1	2	62	6	56	0	0
Baldwin Borough	19,841	22	1	1	8	12	160	36	104	20	0
Baldwin Township	1,999	11	0	0	0	11	19	3	16	0	0
Bally	1,093	1	0	0	0	1	0	0	0	0	0
Barrett Township	4,231	4	0	0	0	4	78	30	46	2	1
Beallsville	469	0	0	0	0	0	0	0	0	0	0
Beaver	4,531	13	0	2	2	9	99	14	80	5	0
Beaver Falls	9,137	67	1	0	10	56	345	39	297	9	3
Beaver Meadows	869	1	0	1	0	0	8	3	5	0	0
Bedford	2,843	4	0	0	0	4	29	6	22	1	0
Bedminster Township	6,601	3	0	1	0	2	67	7	60	0	0
Bellefonte	6,211	3	0	0	1	2	108	13	95	0	1
Bellevue	8,402	35	0	1	13	21	241	44	192	5	1
Bellwood	1,827	1	0	0	0	1	29	2	25	2	1
Ben Avon	1,787	0	0	0	0	0	16	1	15	0	0
Ben Avon Heights	373	0	0	0	0	0	1	0	1	0	0
Bendersville	642	0	0	0	0	0	0	0	0	0	0
Bensalem Township	60,665	80	1	7	39	33	2,205	336	1,780	89	14
Berks-Lehigh Regional	31,206	13	1	1	3	8	356	66	274	16	8
Berlin	2,098	0	0	0	0	0	0	0	0	0	0
Bern Township	6,818	9	0	0	2	7	67	11	51	5	0
Bernville	959	0	0	0	0	0	1	0	1	0	0
Berwick	10,480	25	0	9	6	10	490	148	335	7	4
Bethel Park	32,433	31	0	0	7	24	329	45	276	8	1
Bethel Township, Armstrong County	1,183	0	0	0	0	0	0	0	0	0	0
Bethel Township, Berks County	4,126	2	0	0	0	2	26	4	16	6	0

Table 8. Offenses Known to Law Enforcement, by Selected State and City, 2012— continued

(Number)

State/city	Population	Violent crime	Murder and nonnegligent manslaughter	Forcible rape	Robbery	Aggravated assault	Property crime	Burglary	Larceny-theft	Motor vehicle theft	Arson[1]
Bethel Township, Delaware County	8,811	6	0	0	0	6	88	31	53	4	1
Bethlehem	75,388	238	2	19	121	96	1,948	377	1,488	83	5
Bethlehem Township	23,817	20	0	2	6	12	334	56	271	7	1
Biglerville	1,201	1	0	1	0	0	21	1	20	0	0
Birdsboro	5,179	7	0	1	2	4	93	16	74	3	1
Birmingham Township	4,253	2	0	0	0	2	35	5	25	5	0
Blacklick Township	2,000	0	0	0	0	0	0	0	0	0	0
Blairsville	3,406	16	0	0	1	15	87	15	72	0	0
Blakely	6,567	3	0	0	1	2	97	21	76	0	0
Blawnox	1,437	4	0	0	0	4	2	0	2	0	0
Bloomsburg Town	15,135	20	0	1	2	17	266	51	211	4	1
Boswell	1,273	0	0	0	0	0	0	0	0	0	0
Brackenridge	3,271	1	0	0	1	0	62	7	52	3	0
Bradford	8,736	67	0	3	3	61	353	56	292	5	7
Bradford Township	4,791	11	0	2	0	9	28	1	26	1	1
Branch Township	1,833	1	0	0	0	1	14	1	12	1	0
Brecknock Township, Berks County	4,601	1	0	0	0	1	29	15	14	0	0
Brentwood	9,680	30	0	0	9	21	189	39	135	15	0
Briar Creek Township	3,018	6	0	1	0	5	70	16	53	1	0
Bridgeport	4,588	9	0	0	1	8	170	31	131	8	0
Bridgeville	5,166	16	0	1	1	14	94	16	76	2	0
Bridgewater	704	4	0	0	0	4	20	3	14	3	0
Brighton Township	8,228	14	0	1	0	13	46	3	41	2	0
Bristol	9,764	16	0	2	6	8	293	26	249	18	1
Bristol Township	54,796	112	0	9	73	30	1,724	363	1,256	105	11
Brockway	2,066	5	0	1	0	4	38	6	31	1	1
Brookhaven	8,023	13	0	0	8	5	172	27	139	6	0
Brookville	3,911	2	0	1	0	1	51	3	46	2	0
Brownsville	2,327	7	0	0	2	5	57	15	37	5	0
Bryn Athyn	1,384	0	0	0	0	0	11	0	11	0	0
Buckingham Township	20,154	1	0	0	1	0	141	31	106	4	0
Buffalo Township	7,358	4	0	1	0	3	42	15	25	2	0
Buffalo Valley Region	12,233	7	0	0	1	6	112	31	81	0	0
Burgettstown	1,393	2	0	0	0	2	15	5	10	0	0
Bushkill Township	8,209	23	0	0	0	23	94	25	66	3	0
Butler	13,853	87	2	0	30	55	612	101	497	14	5
Butler Township, Butler County	17,369	30	0	3	4	23	362	30	331	1	0
Butler Township, Luzerne County	9,226	35	1	1	0	33	149	34	110	5	0
Butler Township, Schuylkill County	5,972	0	0	0	0	0	23	11	10	2	1
Caernarvon Township, Berks County	4,020	9	0	1	0	8	103	15	85	3	1
California	6,816	21	0	3	1	17	112	27	84	1	0
Caln Township	13,957	60	1	5	6	48	370	43	321	6	0
Cambria Township	6,068	0	0	0	0	0	87	19	65	3	0
Cambridge Springs	2,594	1	0	0	0	1	4	2	2	0	0
Camp Hill	7,956	6	0	1	4	1	109	8	100	1	0
Canton	1,986	3	0	1	0	2	36	10	24	2	0
Carbondale	8,892	16	0	0	3	13	119	24	84	11	0
Carlisle	19,103	48	0	15	19	14	610	60	547	3	3
Carmichaels	480	0	0	0	0	0	0	0	0	0	0
Carnegie	8,003	12	1	0	9	2	225	22	192	11	0
Carrolltown	848	1	0	0	0	1	18	2	16	0	0
Carroll Township, Washington County	5,661	12	0	2	0	10	64	13	49	2	0
Carroll Township, York County	5,972	5	0	0	0	5	106	30	72	4	0
Carroll Valley	3,882	2	0	0	0	2	49	5	44	0	0
Castle Shannon	8,348	11	0	0	3	8	94	26	64	4	0
Catasauqua	6,509	3	0	0	0	3	119	18	99	2	0
Catawissa	1,554	6	0	2	0	4	32	4	27	1	0

Table 8. Offenses Known to Law Enforcement, by Selected State and City, 2012— continued

(Number)

State/city	Population	Violent crime	Murder and nonnegligent manslaughter	Forcible rape	Robbery	Aggravated assault	Property crime	Burglary	Larceny-theft	Motor vehicle theft	Arson[1]
Cecil Township	11,315	4	0	0	0	4	18	5	13	0	1
Centerville	3,275	2	0	0	2	0	18	5	13	0	0
Chalfont	4,024	0	0	0	0	0	13	5	8	0	0
Chambersburg	20,458	82	2	8	31	41	804	120	661	23	1
Chartiers Township	7,849	3	0	1	2	0	59	11	46	2	0
Cheltenham Township	37,067	90	0	4	53	33	959	168	761	30	3
Cherry Tree	364	0	0	0	0	0	0	0	0	0	0
Chester[3]	34,239	720	22	17	217	464	1,203	465	636	102	26
Chester Township	3,947	41	0	3	10	28	125	47	65	13	0
Cheswick	1,752	1	0	0	0	1	12	3	9	0	0
Chippewa Township	7,998	6	0	0	1	5	248	16	232	0	1
Christiana	1,180	2	0	0	0	2	19	3	16	0	1
Churchill	3,023	15	0	0	1	14	32	5	26	1	0
Clairton	6,822	39	0	1	18	20	186	63	108	15	0
Clarion	5,288	3	0	0	1	2	98	17	78	3	0
Clarks Summit	6,594	1	0	0	0	1	42	10	31	1	0
Claysville	832	0	0	0	0	0	0	0	0	0	0
Clearfield	6,199	42	0	2	1	39	289	21	263	5	2
Cleona	2,094	0	0	0	0	0	14	1	13	0	1
Coal Township	10,404	12	0	1	0	11	250	36	208	6	2
Coatesville	13,237	126	6	9	57	54	429	121	271	37	3
Cochranton	1,135	1	0	0	0	1	7	3	4	0	0
Colebrookdale District	6,042	5	0	1	0	4	103	9	93	1	0
Collegeville	5,118	2	0	1	1	0	75	11	63	1	1
Collier Township	7,107	6	0	0	1	5	191	25	164	2	0
Collingdale	8,805	91	0	1	19	71	305	62	213	30	0
Colonial Regional	19,503	10	0	1	6	3	581	50	522	9	2
Columbia	10,501	21	1	4	6	10	296	79	208	9	0
Colwyn	2,552	29	0	1	4	24	65	26	31	8	1
Conemaugh Township, Cambria County	1,999	1	0	0	0	1	4	1	3	0	0
Conemaugh Township, Somerset County	7,256	9	0	0	1	8	50	17	29	4	0
Conewago Township, Adams County	7,097	8	0	1	0	7	84	3	79	2	0
Conewango Township	3,569	20	0	1	1	18	132	4	122	6	0
Conneaut Lake Regional	3,580	2	0	0	1	1	45	7	38	0	0
Connellsville	7,620	35	0	5	14	16	333	57	266	10	0
Conoy Township	3,225	4	0	2	0	2	40	9	29	2	0
Conshohocken	7,893	31	0	0	3	28	181	26	149	6	1
Conway	2,177	3	0	0	2	1	32	6	26	0	1
Conyngham	1,916	0	0	0	0	0	11	9	2	0	0
Coopersburg	2,411	6	0	0	2	4	15	1	14	0	0
Coplay	3,228	2	0	0	1	1	64	11	52	1	0
Coraopolis	5,698	39	0	0	5	34	93	11	81	1	0
Cornwall	4,141	2	0	0	0	2	2	1	1	0	0
Corry	6,617	48	0	1	0	47	318	29	282	7	1
Coudersport	2,550	0	0	0	0	0	6	1	5	0	0
Covington Township	2,291	2	0	1	0	1	52	8	41	3	2
Crafton	6,431	23	0	1	5	17	162	27	133	2	0
Cranberry Township	28,297	8	0	0	2	6	383	27	351	5	0
Crescent Township	2,650	5	0	0	0	5	40	6	32	2	0
Cresson	1,700	1	0	0	0	1	35	7	28	0	0
Cresson Township	4,473	5	0	0	0	5	35	11	24	0	0
Croyle Township	2,324	0	0	0	0	0	18	4	14	0	0
Cumberland Township, Adams County	6,175	3	0	0	0	3	66	13	52	1	0
Cumberland Township, Greene County	6,590	16	0	2	1	13	153	18	130	5	1
Cumru Township	15,199	20	1	4	8	7	306	54	238	14	2
Curwensville	2,535	9	0	0	1	8	62	6	54	2	4
Dale	1,226	2	0	0	2	0	24	10	14	0	0

Table 8. Offenses Known to Law Enforcement, by Selected State and City, 2012— continued

(Number)

State/city	Population	Violent crime	Murder and nonnegligent manslaughter	Forcible rape	Robbery	Aggravated assault	Property crime	Burglary	Larceny-theft	Motor vehicle theft	Arson[1]
Dallas	2,807	3	0	0	0	3	19	2	17	0	1
Dallas Township	9,002	5	0	0	3	2	110	27	80	3	0
Dalton	1,235	1	0	0	0	1	21	7	14	0	0
Danville	4,715	25	0	5	0	20	116	9	104	3	1
Darby[4]	10,711		0	11	78		498	169	282	47	2
Darby Township	9,286	92	0	1	19	72	231	45	186	0	1
Darlington Township	1,961	0	0	0	0	0	14	3	10	1	0
Decatur Township	4,542	21	0	0	1	20	52	11	41	0	0
Delano Township	443	0	0	0	0	0	0	0	0	0	0
Delmont	2,684	4	0	1	1	2	19	8	11	0	0
Denver	3,898	8	0	1	0	7	51	4	44	3	0
Derry Township, Dauphin County	24,786	44	0	1	5	38	520	72	433	15	1
Donegal Township	2,475	2	0	0	0	2	7	1	4	2	0
Donora	4,800	18	0	2	1	15	88	14	72	2	0
Dormont	8,626	21	0	1	4	16	115	22	88	5	1
Douglass Township, Berks County	3,317	4	0	1	0	3	55	16	36	3	0
Douglass Township, Montgomery County	10,274	14	0	4	1	9	135	19	112	4	0
Downingtown	7,973	14	0	1	4	9	245	18	217	10	0
Doylestown	8,412	12	0	0	2	10	151	16	133	2	1
Doylestown Township	17,630	28	1	4	1	22	252	33	210	9	1
Dublin Borough	2,167	3	0	0	0	3	13	5	8	0	0
Du Bois	7,776	17	0	2	2	13	255	37	212	6	3
Duboistown	1,215	0	0	0	0	0	0	0	0	0	0
Duncansville	1,235	0	0	0	0	0	37	1	34	2	0
Dunnstable Township	1,017	0	0	0	0	0	4	0	4	0	0
Duquesne	5,586	61	4	4	27	26	235	95	119	21	10
Duryea	4,920	9	0	0	1	8	133	34	93	6	0
Earl Township	7,092	0	0	0	0	0	43	4	38	1	0
East Berlin	1,523	0	0	0	0	0	0	0	0	0	0
East Bethlehem Township	2,363	6	0	0	0	6	35	8	26	1	0
East Brandywine Township	6,814	7	0	1	0	6	83	7	74	2	0
East Cocalico Township	10,411	6	0	1	0	5	117	22	84	11	1
East Coventry Township	6,705	5	0	1	0	4	69	13	54	2	0
East Earl Township	6,572	2	0	1	0	1	68	13	52	3	0
Eastern Adams Regional	10,721	5	0	0	2	3	69	14	52	3	0
Eastern Pike Regional	4,759	20	0	4	10	6	268	23	241	4	0
East Fallowfield Township	7,528	2	0	0	0	2	70	25	42	3	0
East Hempfield Township	23,755	15	0	3	10	2	539	87	428	24	0
East Lampeter Township	16,588	23	1	0	14	8	704	68	627	9	0
East Marlborough Township	7,098	0	0	0	0	0	14	2	11	1	0
East McKeesport	2,717	8	0	0	0	8	27	6	20	1	0
East Norriton Township	13,693	8	0	1	3	4	325	20	293	12	0
East Norwegian Township	859	0	0	0	0	0	0	0	0	0	0
Easton	27,039	112	6	6	48	52	709	136	526	47	5
East Pennsboro Township	20,796	13	0	6	4	3	292	55	235	2	0
East Penn Township	2,882	0	0	0	0	0	44	7	34	3	0
East Petersburg	4,551	2	0	0	0	2	39	6	33	0	0
East Pikeland Township	7,153	3	0	0	2	1	59	9	50	0	0
East Pittsburgh	1,829	45	0	1	2	42	59	15	43	1	1
East Rochester	567	0	0	0	0	0	34	0	34	0	0
Easttown Township	10,587	8	0	1	2	5	122	23	99	0	0
East Union Township	1,600	0	0	0	0	0	0	0	0	0	0
East Vincent Township	6,892	5	0	0	1	4	50	15	34	1	0

Table 8. Offenses Known to Law Enforcement, by Selected State and City, 2012— continued

(Number)

State/city	Population	Violent crime	Murder and nonnegligent manslaughter	Forcible rape	Robbery	Aggravated assault	Property crime	Burglary	Larceny-theft	Motor vehicle theft	Arson[1]
East Washington	2,242	7	0	0	0	7	33	4	24	5	1
East Whiteland Township	10,756	5	0	0	0	5	143	8	128	7	0
Ebensburg	3,330	10	0	1	1	8	51	7	42	2	1
Economy	8,971	3	0	1	1	1	51	7	44	0	0
Eddystone	2,416	10	0	1	6	3	312	10	297	5	1
Edgewood	3,129	8	0	0	5	3	200	13	179	8	1
Edgeworth	1,686	2	0	0	0	2	1	0	1	0	0
Edinboro	6,811	4	0	0	1	3	110	19	89	2	0
Edwardsville	4,819	48	0	3	1	44	247	32	212	3	1
Elizabethtown	11,647	14	0	5	7	2	180	21	157	2	1
Elizabeth Township	13,322	14	0	3	3	8	112	31	80	1	1
Elkland	1,845	0	0	0	0	0	25	8	17	0	1
Ellwood City	7,885	19	1	1	8	9	169	29	138	2	0
Emlenton Borough	623	0	0	0	0	0	1	0	1	0	0
Emmaus	11,339	11	0	0	7	4	253	23	220	10	4
Emsworth	2,459	2	0	0	0	2	21	2	18	1	0
Ephrata	13,527	28	0	3	10	15	286	37	243	6	3
Ephrata Township	9,491	3	0	0	1	2	196	18	174	4	1
Erie	101,972	458	8	64	172	214	3,510	1,095	2,311	104	27
Etna	3,464	17	0	0	6	11	107	20	84	3	0
Evans City	1,845	0	0	0	0	0	15	1	14	0	0
Everett	1,835	2	0	0	1	1	47	3	41	3	0
Exeter	5,657	20	0	0	5	15	104	18	82	4	0
Exeter Township, Berks County	25,637	19	0	3	5	11	410	42	357	11	3
Fairview Township, Luzerne County	4,524	0	0	0	0	0	34	4	28	2	1
Fairview Township, York County	16,761	22	0	3	4	15	257	40	217	0	0
Falls Township, Bucks County	34,434	36	0	6	17	13	912	180	692	40	2
Fawn Township	2,385	4	0	1	0	3	34	14	20	0	0
Fayette City	595	0	0	0	0	0	12	3	9	0	0
Ferguson Township	17,763	10	0	4	2	4	131	23	103	5	3
Ferndale	1,625	7	0	0	0	7	1	1	0	0	0
Findlay Township	5,080	2	0	0	0	2	45	5	39	1	0
Fleetwood	4,100	17	0	0	2	15	92	21	70	1	0
Folcroft	6,620	30	0	3	2	25	236	55	173	8	1
Ford City	2,979	6	0	0	0	6	48	6	39	3	0
Forest City	1,907	1	0	1	0	0	44	26	15	3	0
Forest Hills	6,544	6	0	0	1	5	80	16	62	2	0
Forks Township	14,775	11	0	4	3	4	109	7	102	0	0
Forty Fort	4,216	6	0	0	2	4	78	10	67	1	1
Forward Township	3,387	1	0	0	0	1	49	13	36	0	0
Foster Township, McKean County	4,298	2	0	1	0	1	57	6	50	1	0
Foster Township, Schuylkill County	250	0	0	0	0	0	0	0	0	0	0
Fountain Hill	4,649	15	0	2	6	7	149	29	115	5	1
Fox Chapel	5,409	2	0	0	0	2	13	4	9	0	0
Frackville	3,790	1	0	0	1	0	3	3	0	0	1
Franconia Township	13,162	11	0	0	0	11	111	8	98	5	1
Franklin	6,520	7	0	2	0	5	136	19	112	5	0
Franklin Park	13,521	6	0	1	0	5	52	12	39	1	0
Franklin Township, Carbon County	4,262	12	0	0	1	11	90	14	75	1	0
Frazer Township	1,161	0	0	0	0	0	38	0	38	0	0
Freedom Township	3,465	1	0	0	0	1	38	4	33	1	0
Freeland	3,535	24	0	0	2	22	138	39	97	2	0
Freeport	1,806	1	0	1	0	0	5	1	4	0	0
Gaines Township	549	0	0	0	0	0	7	3	4	0	0
Galeton	1,151	1	0	0	0	1	13	2	11	0	0
Gallitzin	1,904	2	0	0	0	2	26	9	17	0	0
Gallitzin Township	1,315	1	0	0	0	1	1	0	1	0	0
Garrett	455	0	0	0	0	0	1	0	1	0	0
Geistown	2,451	2	0	0	0	2	25	10	14	1	0

Table 8. Offenses Known to Law Enforcement, by Selected State and City, 2012— continued

(Number)

State/city	Population	Violent crime	Murder and nonnegligent manslaughter	Forcible rape	Robbery	Aggravated assault	Property crime	Burglary	Larceny-theft	Motor vehicle theft	Arson[1]
Gettysburg	7,634	27	1	5	1	20	182	24	155	3	4
Girard	3,110	2	0	0	1	1	25	3	21	1	0
Girardville	1,513	0	0	0	0	0	6	1	5	0	2
Glassport	4,500	14	0	1	5	8	137	35	102	0	2
Glenolden	7,170	33	0	0	10	23	206	22	173	11	0
Granville Township	5,132	1	0	0	0	1	138	5	131	2	0
Greencastle	4,036	7	0	0	1	6	61	12	45	4	0
Greenfield Township, Blair County	4,167	4	0	0	0	4	64	12	48	4	0
Greensburg	14,889	26	0	1	8	17	357	41	309	7	1
Green Tree	4,449	3	0	0	1	2	85	15	70	0	0
Greenville	6,062	16	0	5	3	8	218	57	154	7	2
Greenwood Township	1,952	0	0	0	0	0	0	0	0	0	0
Halifax	845	2	0	0	0	2	9	3	5	1	0
Hamburg	4,303	12	0	0	0	12	100	18	76	6	2
Hamiltonban Township	2,376	1	0	0	0	1	2	0	2	0	0
Hampden Township	27,898	7	0	0	6	1	306	29	271	6	0
Hampton Township	18,432	22	0	2	1	19	147	23	123	1	0
Hanover	15,373	31	0	6	13	12	609	30	573	6	12
Hanover Township, Luzerne County	11,085	12	0	3	4	5	265	47	209	9	1
Harmar Township	2,931	7	0	1	0	6	90	13	73	4	0
Harmony Township	3,196	0	0	0	0	0	87	16	68	3	0
Harrisburg	49,753	727	11	56	388	272	2,426	613	1,655	158	20
Harrisville	902	0	0	0	0	0	0	0	0	0	0
Hartleton	285	2	0	0	0	2	1	0	1	0	0
Harveys Lake	2,794	2	0	0	0	2	31	3	28	0	0
Hatboro	7,416	5	0	0	3	2	82	10	69	3	0
Hatfield Township	20,699	22	0	4	5	13	257	45	201	11	3
Haverford Township	48,599	25	0	0	8	17	578	72	492	14	1
Hawley	1,223	2	0	0	0	2	7	1	6	0	0
Hazleton	25,358	114	3	19	46	46	600	210	344	46	10
Heidelberg	1,248	3	0	0	0	3	5	3	2	0	0
Heidelberg Township, Berks County	1,731	2	0	0	0	2	12	3	9	0	0
Hellam Township	8,764	25	0	2	0	23	111	23	78	10	0
Hellertown	5,920	26	0	0	0	26	55	11	44	0	0
Hemlock Township	2,249	4	0	1	1	2	187	4	183	0	0
Hempfield Township, Mercer County	3,729	8	0	1	2	5	201	28	166	7	1
Hermitage	16,159	29	0	1	8	20	543	81	455	7	0
Hickory Township	2,457	0	0	0	0	0	34	12	22	0	2
Highland Township	1,286	0	0	0	0	0	1	0	1	0	0
Highspire	2,410	11	1	1	2	7	73	10	61	2	0
Hilltown Township	15,087	17	0	4	2	11	269	27	228	14	0
Hollidaysburg	5,800	8	0	1	0	7	62	6	55	1	0
Homer City	1,701	1	0	0	0	1	13	1	12	0	0
Homestead	3,177	46	1	4	16	25	274	71	188	15	0
Honesdale	4,520	7	0	0	1	6	137	26	110	1	3
Honey Brook	1,731	0	0	0	0	0	4	1	3	0	0
Hooversville	643	0	0	0	0	0	2	0	2	0	0
Hopewell Township	12,594	9	1	3	1	4	209	24	166	19	0
Horsham Township	26,345	21	0	1	5	15	281	57	215	9	5
Houston	1,301	0	0	0	0	0	2	0	2	0	0
Hughestown	1,393	3	0	0	0	3	18	3	14	1	0
Hughesville	2,142	6	0	1	1	4	56	5	49	2	0
Hulmeville	1,008	1	0	0	0	1	0	0	0	0	0
Hummelstown	4,558	15	0	1	3	11	58	22	35	1	1
Huntingdon	7,077	12	0	0	0	12	69	9	60	0	0
Independence Township, Beaver County	2,504	0	0	0	0	0	11	0	7	4	0
Indiana	14,644	201	0	1	5	195	243	36	201	6	2
Indiana Township	7,280	1	0	0	0	1	56	17	38	1	1
Ingram	3,341	2	0	0	0	2	24	3	21	0	0

Table 8. Offenses Known to Law Enforcement, by Selected State and City, 2012— continued

(Number)

State/city	Population	Violent crime	Murder and nonnegligent manslaughter	Forcible rape	Robbery	Aggravated assault	Property crime	Burglary	Larceny-theft	Motor vehicle theft	Arson[1]
Irwin	3,971	12	0	0	0	12	101	19	77	5	0
Ivyland	1,046	0	0	0	0	0	11	4	7	0	0
Jackson Township, Butler County	3,682	8	0	0	0	8	28	8	19	1	0
Jackson Township, Cambria County	4,364	2	0	0	0	2	16	3	13	0	0
Jackson Township, Luzerne County	4,652	3	0	0	0	3	14	9	4	1	0
Jamestown	614	1	0	0	0	1	7	0	7	0	0
Jefferson Hills Borough	10,658	14	0	0	1	13	81	21	53	7	1
Jefferson Township, Mercer County	1,872	0	0	0	0	0	10	2	8	0	0
Jenkins Township	4,444	6	0	0	2	4	114	25	88	1	0
Jenkintown	4,456	5	0	0	1	4	42	4	38	0	0
Jennerstown	693	0	0	0	0	0	1	1	0	0	0
Jermyn	2,171	20	0	1	2	17	65	24	35	6	0
Jim Thorpe	4,782	16	0	2	3	11	130	12	113	5	0
Johnsonburg	2,472	1	0	0	0	1	67	13	54	0	3
Johnstown	22,360	131	1	6	31	93	822	285	499	38	3
Juniata Valley Regional	2,786	0	0	0	0	0	0	0	0	0	0
Kane	3,715	4	0	0	0	4	111	31	77	3	0
Kennett Square	6,137	19	0	1	6	12	82	30	51	1	1
Kidder Township	1,935	12	0	2	1	9	113	38	72	3	0
Kilbuck Township	700	0	0	0	0	0	10	4	5	1	0
Kingston	13,191	22	0	3	13	6	352	67	271	14	1
Kingston Township	7,003	7	0	0	1	6	70	12	57	1	0
Kiskiminetas Township	4,781	4	0	0	1	3	36	6	27	3	0
Kittanning	4,029	5	0	0	1	4	35	6	27	2	0
Kline Township	1,431	3	0	2	0	1	30	2	28	0	0
Koppel	762	6	0	0	1	5	29	6	21	2	0
Kutztown	5,029	19	0	1	7	11	160	38	119	3	3
Laceyville	380	0	0	0	0	0	1	0	0	1	0
Laflin Borough	1,488	4	0	0	0	4	16	3	12	1	0
Lake City	3,035	2	0	0	1	1	59	7	52	0	0
Lamar Township	2,536	0	0	0	0	0	17	4	13	0	0
Lancaster	60,155	465	7	37	208	213	2,900	439	2,351	110	20
Lancaster Township, Butler County	1,249	4	0	1	0	3	8	1	7	0	0
Lancaster Township, Lancaster County	16,302	20	0	2	11	7	429	84	330	15	1
Langhorne Borough	1,629	1	0	0	1	0	10	0	10	0	0
Langhorne Manor	1,447	0	0	0	0	0	12	3	9	0	0
Lansdale	16,393	35	1	6	17	11	286	45	230	11	3
Lansdowne	10,644	30	2	0	18	10	221	66	147	8	0
Lansford	3,941	7	0	0	2	5	28	7	21	0	1
Larksville	4,482	4	0	2	2	0	79	17	59	3	0
Latimore Township	2,585	0	0	0	0	0	23	7	16	0	0
Latrobe	8,336	22	0	0	2	20	177	32	144	1	2
Lawrence Park Township	3,988	6	0	0	0	6	36	1	35	0	0
Lawrence Township, Clearfield County	7,663	60	0	5	2	53	289	43	239	7	5
Lawrence Township, Tioga County	1,742	7	0	0	0	7	1	1	0	0	0
Lawrenceville	585	0	0	0	0	0	10	1	8	1	0
Lebanon	25,662	99	2	6	48	43	696	123	544	29	5
Leetsdale	1,222	12	0	1	1	10	42	7	34	1	0
Leet Township	1,640	0	0	0	0	0	0	0	0	0	0
Lehighton	5,500	13	0	2	1	10	133	28	95	10	0
Lehigh Township, Northampton County	10,565	13	0	1	0	12	139	23	111	5	2
Lehigh Township, Wayne County	1,897	0	0	0	0	0	11	5	5	1	0
Lehman Township	3,511	10	0	0	0	10	19	9	9	1	0
Lewistown	8,383	50	0	3	4	43	428	63	357	8	1
Liberty	2,561	3	0	0	0	3	26	10	14	2	1

Table 8. Offenses Known to Law Enforcement, by Selected State and City, 2012— continued

(Number)

State/city	Population	Violent crime	Murder and nonnegligent manslaughter	Forcible rape	Robbery	Aggravated assault	Property crime	Burglary	Larceny-theft	Motor vehicle theft	Arson[1]
Liberty Township, Adams County	1,240	0	0	0	0	0	20	2	18	0	0
Ligonier	1,573	4	0	0	0	4	14	1	10	3	0
Ligonier Township	6,602	12	0	1	0	11	26	3	23	0	1
Limerick Township	18,213	8	0	1	2	5	462	53	404	5	2
Lincoln	1,077	1	0	0	0	1	16	3	13	0	0
Linesville	1,039	1	0	0	0	1	7	2	5	0	0
Lititz	9,458	3	1	0	2	0	119	10	104	5	0
Little Beaver Township	1,407	0	0	0	0	0	0	0	0	0	0
Littlestown	4,443	17	1	0	1	15	75	9	66	0	1
Lock Haven	9,570	22	0	7	1	14	214	29	180	5	4
Locust Township	2,546	2	0	0	0	2	46	9	37	0	0
Logan Township	12,325	57	1	3	2	51	300	32	260	8	2
Loretto	1,646	0	0	0	0	0	0	0	0	0	0
Lower Allen Township	18,222	15	0	4	2	9	268	34	232	2	1
Lower Burrell	11,758	12	0	2	2	8	176	43	129	4	0
Lower Chichester Township	3,476	43	0	1	5	37	97	11	79	7	0
Lower Frederick Township	4,877	2	0	0	0	2	39	10	29	0	1
Lower Gwynedd Township	11,491	9	0	0	0	9	198	37	154	7	0
Lower Heidelberg Township	5,533	7	0	0	0	7	43	12	29	2	0
Lower Mahanoy Township	1,704	0	0	0	0	0	1	0	1	0	0
Lower Makefield Township	32,686	16	0	0	2	14	429	90	330	9	0
Lower Merion Township	58,252	47	0	2	32	13	1,034	192	818	24	0
Lower Milford Township	3,817	2	0	0	0	2	18	4	14	0	1
Lower Moreland Township	13,082	8	0	1	3	4	157	30	124	3	8
Lower Paxton Township	47,578	114	0	12	45	57	1,044	165	862	17	8
Lower Pottsgrove Township	12,151	26	0	3	3	20	275	54	214	7	6
Lower Providence Township	25,620	45	0	0	3	42	309	47	253	9	4
Lower Salford Township	15,073	4	0	0	1	3	69	13	55	1	2
Lower Saucon Township	10,812	11	0	0	1	10	95	25	64	6	0
Lower Southampton Township	18,984	25	0	1	4	20	408	67	321	20	3
Lower Swatara Township	8,407	10	1	0	0	9	142	31	110	1	0
Lower Windsor Township	7,422	9	0	0	0	9	92	14	73	5	0
Luzerne	2,848	5	0	2	0	3	81	15	64	2	1
Luzerne Township	5,960	3	0	0	0	3	33	11	20	2	1
Lykens	1,787	3	0	0	1	2	12	2	10	0	0
Macungie	3,109	1	0	0	0	1	16	4	12	0	0
Madison Township	1,605	0	0	0	0	0	0	0	0	0	0
Mahanoy City	4,146	9	0	1	3	5	138	20	106	12	0
Mahanoy Township	3,152	0	0	0	0	0	6	3	3	0	0
Mahoning Township, Carbon County	4,304	30	0	0	2	28	142	29	112	1	2
Mahoning Township, Lawrence County	3,069	4	0	0	0	4	38	7	31	0	0
Mahoning Township, Montour County	4,184	3	0	0	1	2	28	1	27	0	0
Main Township	1,235	0	0	0	0	0	0	0	0	0	0
Malvern	3,030	5	0	2	0	3	36	13	23	0	0
Manheim	4,907	12	1	0	4	7	166	41	117	8	2
Manheim Township	38,507	29	0	3	11	15	882	97	770	15	2
Manor	3,239	0	0	0	0	0	8	4	2	2	0
Manor Township, Armstrong County	4,208	0	0	0	0	0	0	0	0	0	0

Table 8. Offenses Known to Law Enforcement, by Selected State and City, 2012— continued

(Number)

State/city	Population	Violent crime	Murder and nonnegligent manslaughter	Forcible rape	Robbery	Aggravated assault	Property crime	Burglary	Larceny-theft	Motor vehicle theft	Arson[1]
Manor Township, Lancaster County	19,805	5	0	2	1	2	266	47	208	11	0
Mansfield	3,655	2	0	0	0	2	5	0	5	0	0
Marcus Hook	2,403	26	0	0	1	25	79	6	72	1	0
Marietta	2,613	8	0	0	0	8	74	21	51	2	2
Marion Township, Beaver County	913	0	0	0	0	0	4	1	3	0	0
Marion Township, Berks County	1,694	0	0	0	0	0	12	5	6	1	0
Marlborough Township	3,203	0	0	0	0	0	38	18	19	1	1
Marple Township	23,479	9	0	0	1	8	362	43	314	5	1
Martinsburg	1,962	1	0	0	0	1	34	3	30	1	0
Marysville	2,542	4	0	0	0	4	38	4	33	1	0
Masontown	3,443	5	0	2	2	1	62	12	46	4	0
Mayfield	1,808	0	0	0	0	0	0	0	0	0	0
McAdoo	2,291	6	0	0	1	5	35	3	32	0	0
McCandless	28,561	9	0	0	5	4	268	39	223	6	0
McDonald Borough	2,156	7	0	1	0	6	44	9	34	1	0
McKeesport[4]	21,603		10	13	69		721	279	409	33	16
McKees Rocks	6,128	92	5	0	40	47	328	100	204	24	1
McSherrystown	3,045	6	0	0	1	5	42	6	36	0	0
Meadville	13,638	32	0	1	6	25	357	100	257	0	6
Mechanicsburg	9,060	5	0	0	4	1	245	37	206	2	1
Media	5,340	20	0	0	2	18	89	8	80	1	2
Mercer	1,994	1	0	0	0	1	20	5	14	1	0
Mercersburg	1,577	2	0	0	0	2	30	7	22	1	0
Meshoppen	1,464	8	0	0	0	8	31	10	17	4	0
Meyersdale	2,178	0	0	0	0	0	12	0	12	0	0
Middleburg	1,310	4	0	2	2	0	79	15	64	0	0
Middlesex Township, Butler County	5,428	2	0	0	0	2	35	8	25	2	0
Middlesex Township, Cumberland County	7,099	7	0	0	4	3	180	17	156	7	0
Middletown	8,942	26	1	7	4	14	159	31	123	5	1
Middletown Township	45,614	39	0	2	19	18	1,594	233	1,312	49	9
Midland	2,634	19	0	1	2	16	86	16	69	1	0
Midway	916	2	0	0	0	2	11	3	8	0	0
Mifflinburg	3,549	0	0	0	0	0	59	5	54	0	0
Mifflin County Regional	20,833	10	0	3	0	7	299	32	257	10	2
Milford	1,016	1	0	0	1	0	39	6	33	0	0
Millbourne	1,161	11	0	0	4	7	41	5	36	0	0
Millcreek Township, Erie County	53,615	50	2	6	22	20	1,093	292	771	30	1
Millcreek Township, Lebanon County	5,450	1	0	0	0	1	37	7	29	1	0
Millersburg	2,569	7	0	0	0	7	46	15	31	0	1
Millersville	7,900	12	0	3	5	4	140	54	84	2	0
Mill Hall	1,625	0	0	0	0	0	0	0	0	0	0
Millvale	3,758	10	0	2	0	8	84	24	59	1	0
Millville	949	0	0	0	0	0	0	0	0	0	0
Minersville	4,381	9	0	0	0	9	33	4	26	3	0
Mohnton	3,055	5	0	0	0	5	21	9	10	2	0
Monaca	5,737	8	0	1	1	6	129	22	97	10	0
Monessen	7,718	61	1	3	5	52	234	47	175	12	1
Monongahela	4,316	24	0	1	3	20	138	39	93	6	0
Monroeville	28,491	70	0	0	11	59	420	98	298	24	3
Montgomery Township	24,981	12	0	0	9	3	423	20	394	9	0
Montoursville	4,649	3	0	0	0	3	76	5	70	1	0
Montrose	1,613	1	0	0	0	1	13	2	11	0	0
Moon Township	24,272	21	0	2	3	16	285	52	230	3	0
Moore Township	9,232	4	0	0	0	4	86	13	71	2	0
Moosic	5,720	39	0	2	7	30	248	36	205	7	0
Morris-Cooper Regional	5,631	3	0	1	0	2	37	7	29	1	0

Table 8. Offenses Known to Law Enforcement, by Selected State and City, 2012— continued

(Number)

State/city	Population	Violent crime	Murder and nonnegligent manslaughter	Forcible rape	Robbery	Aggravated assault	Property crime	Burglary	Larceny-theft	Motor vehicle theft	Arson[1]
Morrisville	8,761	14	1	2	3	8	321	76	223	22	0
Morton	2,674	9	0	0	3	6	143	6	136	1	1
Moscow	2,027	1	0	0	0	1	18	3	14	1	0
Mount Carmel	5,906	10	0	2	0	8	115	21	84	10	1
Mount Carmel Township	3,146	13	0	0	2	11	20	1	18	1	1
Mount Gretna Borough	200	0	0	0	0	0	0	0	0	0	0
Mount Holly Springs	2,049	6	0	0	4	2	53	11	41	1	0
Mount Jewett	915	1	0	1	0	0	0	0	0	0	0
Mount Joy	7,484	17	0	3	3	11	168	19	145	4	1
Mount Lebanon	33,260	15	0	2	4	9	207	44	154	9	1
Mount Oliver	3,416	68	1	3	19	45	149	44	100	5	1
Mount Pleasant	4,454	7	0	0	1	6	80	4	75	1	0
Mount Pleasant Township	3,528	4	0	0	0	4	35	9	24	2	1
Mount Union	2,439	2	0	0	0	2	30	4	23	3	2
Mountville	2,829	5	0	0	2	3	35	4	30	1	0
Muhlenberg Township	19,696	34	0	2	14	18	744	83	632	29	0
Muncy	2,495	0	0	0	0	0	0	0	0	0	0
Munhall	11,449	26	1	0	10	15	277	84	166	27	3
Murrysville	20,072	8	0	2	4	2	93	25	68	0	1
Myerstown	3,084	14	0	0	3	11	76	1	70	5	1
Nanticoke	10,473	27	0	3	12	12	366	99	252	15	6
Nanty Glo	2,716	9	0	1	1	7	90	32	55	3	1
Narberth	4,316	1	0	0	1	0	33	8	24	1	0
Nazareth	5,767	22	0	2	2	18	91	5	85	1	1
Nescopeck	1,585	1	0	1	0	0	10	5	5	0	0
Neshannock Township	9,561	12	0	0	3	9	89	26	60	3	0
Nesquehoning	3,348	5	0	1	2	2	71	3	67	1	0
Nether Providence Towship	13,736	21	1	0	4	16	200	44	154	2	1
Neville Township	1,088	0	0	0	0	0	45	2	43	0	0
New Beaver	1,493	0	0	0	0	0	2	0	2	0	0
New Berlin	874	0	0	0	0	0	6	0	6	0	0
Newberry Township	15,368	18	0	2	2	14	327	78	239	10	2
New Brighton	9,213	64	0	6	11	47	363	64	299	0	0
New Britain	3,162	8	0	1	0	7	31	6	25	0	0
New Britain Township	11,113	1	0	0	1	0	95	20	74	1	1
New Castle	23,165	356	3	7	76	270	1,074	392	643	39	8
New Castle Township	414	1	0	0	0	1	15	2	13	0	0
New Cumberland	7,341	5	0	1	3	1	134	38	92	4	0
New Florence	686	0	0	0	0	0	2	0	2	0	0
New Garden Township	12,109	17	0	1	6	10	162	41	112	9	1
New Hanover Township	11,024	1	0	1	0	0	73	23	48	2	1
New Holland	5,432	4	0	0	2	2	92	15	76	1	1
New Hope	2,538	6	0	0	0	6	86	10	76	0	0
New Kensington	13,112	59	0	8	28	23	464	106	324	34	8
New Philadelphia	1,082	3	0	0	0	3	3	2	1	0	0
New Sewickley Township	7,359	16	0	2	3	11	139	36	93	10	1
Newton Township	2,848	2	0	0	0	2	5	2	3	0	1
Newtown	2,257	1	0	0	1	0	29	7	22	0	0
Newtown Township, Bucks County	22,382	9	0	0	2	7	205	43	161	1	0
Newtown Township, Delaware County	12,244	13	0	0	2	11	132	27	100	5	0
Newville	1,337	2	0	0	1	1	46	5	41	0	0
New Wilmington	2,463	5	0	0	1	4	40	6	34	0	0
Norristown	34,584	317	4	10	173	130	1,002	293	613	96	11
Northampton	9,962	5	0	0	1	4	142	34	104	4	0
Northampton Township	39,883	16	0	3	4	9	311	58	247	6	3
North Beaver	4,101	1	0	0	0	1	8	4	4	0	0

Table 8. Offenses Known to Law Enforcement, by Selected State and City, 2012— continued

(Number)

State/city	Population	Violent crime	Murder and nonnegligent manslaughter	Forcible rape	Robbery	Aggravated assault	Property crime	Burglary	Larceny-theft	Motor vehicle theft	Arson[1]
North Belle Vernon	1,970	10	0	0	4	6	81	16	63	2	2
North Catasauqua	2,859	1	0	0	0	1	25	4	20	1	0
North Cornwall Township	7,634	18	0	1	3	14	176	12	162	2	0
North Coventry Township	7,949	12	0	2	1	9	222	31	184	7	0
North East, Erie County	4,302	5	0	0	0	5	136	13	123	0	1
Northeastern Regional	11,485	16	0	7	2	7	160	25	127	8	0
Northern Berks Regional	12,734	5	0	0	1	4	148	26	116	6	1
Northern Cambria Borough	3,810	7	0	1	1	5	59	13	44	2	0
Northern Lancaster County Regional	33,197	32	0	6	2	24	378	53	310	15	2
Northern Regional	30,795	11	0	2	1	8	297	45	246	6	0
Northern York Regional	66,974	66	2	3	14	47	1,163	101	1,020	42	7
North Fayette Township	13,988	7	0	0	3	4	250	26	223	1	1
North Franklin Township	4,601	14	0	1	3	10	102	8	89	5	0
North Huntingdon Township	30,599	21	0	8	3	10	464	51	402	11	0
North Lebanon Township	11,512	18	0	1	0	17	276	30	243	3	0
North Londonderry Township	8,126	8	0	1	1	6	151	11	136	4	2
North Middleton Township	11,243	4	0	1	1	2	141	20	115	6	1
North Sewickley Township	5,489	8	0	0	0	8	60	13	42	5	0
North Strabane Township	13,460	6	0	2	0	4	140	26	109	5	0
Northumberland	3,813	2	1	0	0	1	67	8	58	1	0
North Union Township	1,470	0	0	0	0	0	0	0	0	0	0
North Versailles Township	10,269	54	1	0	12	41	195	32	153	10	1
North Wales	3,254	3	0	0	0	3	44	6	37	1	1
Northwest Lancaster County Regional	18,306	5	0	2	1	2	172	0	166	6	1
North Woodbury	2,650	0	0	0	0	0	14	0	13	1	0
Norwood	5,903	9	0	1	1	7	97	19	77	1	0
Oakland	615	1	0	0	0	1	6	3	2	1	0
Oakmont	6,327	14	0	0	1	13	115	25	89	1	0
O'Hara Township	8,438	1	0	0	0	1	60	8	49	3	0
Ohio Township	4,775	2	0	0	0	2	83	3	80	0	0
Ohioville	3,533	6	0	1	0	5	32	9	21	2	0
Oil City	10,516	26	1	6	2	17	219	20	196	3	0
Old Forge	8,314	9	0	0	6	3	114	19	88	7	3
Old Lycoming Township	4,974	7	0	1	3	3	116	16	92	8	4
Oley Township	3,632	4	0	0	0	4	2	0	2	0	0
Orangeville Area	1,767	0	0	0	0	0	0	0	0	0	0
Orwigsburg	3,089	1	0	0	0	1	60	6	52	2	0
Osceola Township	667	0	0	0	0	0	0	0	0	0	0
Otto Eldred Regional	2,372	0	0	0	0	0	1	0	1	0	0
Overfield Township	2,937	0	0	0	0	0	7	2	5	0	0
Oxford	5,129	21	0	1	3	17	114	18	90	6	0
Paint Township	5,282	29	0	0	0	29	60	19	40	1	0
Palmerton	5,415	15	0	0	3	12	161	29	130	2	0
Palmer Township	20,767	19	0	2	6	11	358	48	303	7	1
Palmyra	7,374	18	0	0	2	16	157	27	125	5	1
Palo Alto	1,029	0	0	0	0	0	9	1	8	0	0
Parker	835	0	0	0	0	0	0	0	0	0	0
Parkesburg	3,630	8	0	0	1	7	45	9	31	5	0
Parkside	2,334	10	0	0	1	9	56	8	43	5	0
Patterson Township	3,029	6	0	1	1	4	82	11	66	5	1
Patton	1,758	1	0	1	0	0	12	6	6	0	0

Table 8. Offenses Known to Law Enforcement, by Selected State and City, 2012— continued

(Number)

State/city	Population	Violent crime	Murder and nonnegligent manslaughter	Forcible rape	Robbery	Aggravated assault	Property crime	Burglary	Larceny-theft	Motor vehicle theft	Arson[1]
Patton Township	15,375	3	0	1	1	1	173	20	151	2	0
Paxtang	1,570	14	0	0	11	3	98	8	90	0	0
Pen Argyl	[illegible]	7	0	0	0	7	81	8	71	2	1
Penbrook	3,022	14	0	3	4	7	71	18	49	4	2
Penndel	2,513	7	0	0	3	4	57	14	37	6	0
Penn Hills	42,488	131	5	6	40	80	841	309	480	52	12
Pennridge Regional	11,006	16	0	1	0	15	128	44	79	5	0
Penn Township, Butler County	5,107	2	0	0	0	2	48	11	35	2	0
Penn Township, Perry County	3,235	6	0	0	1	5	75	6	68	1	3
Penn Township, Westmoreland County	19,999	14	0	0	0	14	76	19	56	1	0
Penn Township, York County	15,697	19	0	0	1	18	264	28	226	10	3
Pequea Township	4,650	6	0	3	0	3	44	13	31	0	0
Perkasie	8,544	7	0	1	3	3	184	19	164	1	0
Perryopolis	1,781	1	0	0	0	1	28	7	20	1	0
Peters Township	21,296	6	0	0	2	4	141	45	94	2	0
Philadelphia	1,538,957	17,853	331	880	7,984	8,658	56,997	12,004	38,592	6,401	
Phoenixville	16,612	43	0	0	3	40	435	44	385	6	1
Pine Creek Township	3,240	4	0	0	0	4	31	2	29	0	0
Pitcairn	3,306	43	0	1	8	34	148	36	109	3	1
Pittsburgh	312,112	2,347	41	47	1,134	1,125	10,691	2,537	7,610	544	248
Pittston	7,745	17	0	2	3	12	209	29	178	2	0
Plainfield Township	6,161	0	0	0	0	0	57	9	45	3	0
Plains Township	9,969	26	0	1	4	21	237	38	191	8	0
Pleasant Hills	8,298	2	0	0	2	0	87	10	75	2	0
Plum	27,227	100	0	0	5	95	193	48	138	7	0
Plumstead Township	12,492	5	0	1	0	4	148	30	110	8	1
Plymouth Township, Montgomery County	16,651	24	1	1	17	5	560	61	471	28	3
Pocono Mountain Regional	39,122	58	2	11	12	33	888	320	542	26	12
Pocono Township	11,078	17	0	0	7	10	260	55	202	3	1
Point Marion	1,156	15	0	1	0	14	12	2	10	0	0
Point Township	3,692	14	0	0	0	14	51	15	35	1	0
Polk	814	4	0	0	0	4	0	0	0	0	0
Portage	2,621	12	0	3	0	9	40	7	33	0	0
Port Allegany	2,148	2	0	0	0	2	28	6	22	0	0
Port Carbon	1,882	0	0	0	0	0	1	0	1	0	0
Portland	521	0	0	0	0	0	5	0	5	0	0
Port Vue	3,812	11	1	1	0	9	43	12	29	2	0
Pottstown	22,546	161	1	20	61	79	962	158	768	36	13
Pottsville	14,272	54	1	11	3	39	253	33	211	9	2
Pringle	980	2	0	0	1	1	126	13	107	6	0
Prospect Park	6,467	19	0	1	5	13	113	13	93	7	0
Pulaski Township, Lawrence County	3,437	6	0	0	0	6	35	11	24	0	0
Punxsutawney	5,945	8	0	0	1	7	101	14	87	0	2
Pymatuning Township	3,270	1	0	0	1	0	176	43	126	7	1
Quakertown	9,013	38	0	0	5	33	240	26	209	5	3
Quarryville	2,600	10	0	0	0	10	70	4	63	3	0
Raccoon Township	3,064	0	0	0	0	0	24	3	20	1	0
Radnor Township	31,598	35	0	2	10	23	393	48	343	2	0
Rankin	2,130	15	0	1	1	13	26	12	13	1	0
Reading	88,557	828	15	44	382	387	3,612	1,447	1,629	536	17
Redstone Township	5,553	7	0	0	2	5	14	5	9	0	0
Reilly Township	723	0	0	0	0	0	5	1	4	0	0
Reserve Township	3,344	2	0	0	1	1	50	9	38	3	0
Reynoldsville	2,750	16	0	2	1	13	13	11	1	1	1
Rice Township	3,338	2	0	1	1	0	32	13	18	1	0
Richland Township, Bucks County	13,104	9	0	5	2	2	268	17	246	5	0
Richland Township, Cambria County	12,919	4	0	1	1	2	576	14	556	6	0

Table 8. Offenses Known to Law Enforcement, by Selected State and City, 2012— continued

(Number)

State/city	Population	Violent crime	Murder and nonnegligent manslaughter	Forcible rape	Robbery	Aggravated assault	Property crime	Burglary	Larceny-theft	Motor vehicle theft	Arson[1]
Ridgway	4,060	9	0	3	0	6	125	25	98	2	2
Ridley Park	7,017	12	0	0	2	10	89	11	71	7	1
Ridley Township	30,837	50	0	4	17	29	507	74	404	29	1
Ringtown	814	1	0	0	0	1	1	0	1	0	0
Riverside	1,937	1	0	0	0	1	10	0	9	1	0
Roaring Brook Township	1,908	1	0	0	0	1	25	6	19	0	1
Roaring Spring	2,589	0	0	0	0	0	22	0	22	0	0
Robeson Township	7,240	11	0	0	0	11	90	37	41	12	1
Robinson Township, Allegheny County	13,405	27	0	0	2	25	340	25	307	8	0
Robinson Township, Washington County	1,937	2	0	1	0	1	29	8	20	1	0
Rochester	3,657	18	0	2	7	9	245	33	207	5	0
Rochester Township	2,803	9	0	0	0	9	37	5	28	4	0
Rockledge	2,563	3	0	0	0	3	67	5	60	2	0
Roseto	1,574	0	0	0	0	0	18	2	16	0	0
Rosslyn Farms	429	0	0	0	0	0	2	0	2	0	0
Ross Township	31,222	38	0	2	11	25	729	78	641	10	0
Rostraver Township	11,358	25	0	2	9	14	392	32	346	14	1
Royalton	911	0	0	0	0	0	0	0	0	0	0
Royersford	4,789	8	0	0	1	7	98	15	80	3	0
Rural Valley	878	0	0	0	0	0	2	0	2	0	0
Rush Township	3,400	2	0	0	1	1	85	11	73	1	0
Ryan Township	2,457	0	0	0	0	0	1	0	1	0	0
Sadsbury Township, Chester County	3,607	0	0	0	0	0	17	2	15	0	0
Salem Township, Luzerne County	4,257	11	0	0	0	11	84	20	63	1	0
Salisbury Township	13,657	8	2	1	1	4	277	37	218	22	1
Saltsburg	872	0	0	0	0	0	23	5	17	1	0
Sandy Lake	656	1	0	0	1	0	8	0	8	0	0
Sandy Township	10,600	35	0	1	0	34	344	59	280	5	1
Sankertown	671	0	0	0	0	0	5	2	3	0	0
Saxton	735	0	0	0	0	0	0	0	0	0	0
Sayre	6,656	37	0	5	2	30	244	42	198	4	1
Schuylkill Haven	5,416	7	0	2	0	5	102	12	85	5	0
Scottdale	4,382	25	0	0	6	19	196	12	180	4	1
Scott Township, Allegheny County	17,087	10	0	0	5	5	205	47	157	1	0
Scott Township, Columbia County	5,113	2	0	0	0	2	139	14	123	2	0
Scott Township, Lackawanna County	4,906	6	0	0	0	6	17	4	12	1	0
Scranton	76,118	252	0	23	129	100	2,553	641	1,796	116	27
Selinsgrove	5,781	77	0	4	3	70	190	37	149	4	1
Seward	495	0	0	0	0	0	1	1	0	0	0
Sewickley	4,391	9	0	0	0	9	42	7	32	3	0
Sewickley Heights	814	0	0	0	0	0	5	2	3	0	0
Shaler Township	28,865	12	0	0	6	6	367	77	288	2	2
Shamokin	7,390	5	0	0	1	4	54	6	45	3	0
Shamokin Dam	1,687	1	0	0	0	1	36	4	32	0	1
Sharon	13,986	87	1	13	42	31	603	212	372	19	2
Sharon Hill	5,709	36	0	0	7	29	212	44	153	15	0
Sharpsburg	3,459	24	0	0	1	23	93	21	65	7	1
Sharpsville	4,399	32	0	0	0	32	92	7	85	0	0
Shenandoah	5,053	27	0	3	2	22	147	49	96	2	1
Shillington	5,291	5	0	0	4	1	91	22	61	8	0
Shinglehouse	1,129	1	0	0	0	1	2	0	2	0	0
Shippensburg	5,540	10	0	4	2	4	99	17	79	3	0
Shippingport	214	0	0	0	0	0	6	2	4	0	0
Shiremanstown	1,582	2	0	0	0	2	2	1	1	0	0
Shohola Township	2,457	0	0	0	0	0	20	11	8	1	0
Silver Lake Township	1,712	1	0	0	0	1	24	8	13	3	0
Silver Spring Township	13,777	2	0	0	1	1	230	18	201	11	1
Sinking Spring	4,023	6	0	4	1	1	57	11	41	5	0

Table 8. Offenses Known to Law Enforcement, by Selected State and City, 2012— continued

(Number)

State/city	Population	Violent crime	Murder and nonnegligent manslaughter	Forcible rape	Robbery	Aggravated assault	Property crime	Burglary	Larceny-theft	Motor vehicle theft	Arson[1]
Slatington	4,280	4	0	0	0	4	84	15	66	3	0
Slippery Rock	3,645	3	0	0	2	1	38	3	35	0	0
Smithfield	873	0	0	0	0	0	0	0	0	0	0
Smith Township	4,493	0	0	0	0	0	0	0	0	0	0
Solebury Township	8,726	1	0	1	0	0	76	13	61	2	1
Somerset	6,258	20	0	3	2	15	170	32	137	1	0
Souderton	6,669	20	0	4	3	13	92	5	77	10	0
South Abington Township	9,078	10	0	1	1	8	79	18	60	1	0
South Beaver Township	2,716	1	0	0	0	1	32	9	23	0	0
South Buffalo Township	2,627	0	0	0	0	0	19	4	15	0	0
South Centre Township	4,260	0	0	0	0	0	16	4	11	1	0
South Coatesville	1,316	5	0	0	2	3	15	7	6	2	0
South Connellsville Borough	1,966	6	0	2	2	2	29	3	25	1	0
Southern Regional Lancaster County	3,812	2	0	1	1	0	22	2	19	1	0
Southern Regional York County	10,649	11	0	0	7	4	150	22	126	2	0
South Fayette Township	14,470	3	0	0	2	1	97	20	76	1	1
South Fork	923	0	0	0	0	0	1	1	0	0	0
South Greensburg	2,115	1	0	1	0	0	43	14	29	0	1
South Heidelberg Township	7,295	19	0	0	1	18	62	11	50	1	1
South Heights	475	0	0	0	0	0	0	0	0	0	0
South Lebanon Township	9,525	5	0	0	2	3	107	15	92	0	1
South Londonderry Township	7,044	1	0	0	1	0	39	8	31	0	0
South Park Township	13,466	4	0	0	1	3	50	14	32	4	0
South Pymatuning Township	2,686	2	0	1	0	1	27	10	15	2	0
South Strabane Township	9,382	9	0	2	6	1	508	28	476	4	0
Southwestern Regional	17,625	12	1	0	2	9	107	17	88	2	1
Southwest Greensburg	2,153	12	0	2	0	10	47	12	33	2	0
Southwest Mercer County Regional	10,496	44	0	2	11	31	227	59	160	8	1
Southwest Regional	13,870	29	0	0	3	26	120	39	81	0	2
South Whitehall Township	19,394	31	1	7	4	19	736	73	653	10	7
South Williamsport	6,426	5	0	1	1	3	133	11	118	4	0
Springdale	3,418	3	0	0	1	2	37	13	22	2	0
Springdale Township	1,642	8	0	0	0	8	8	2	6	0	0
Springettsbury Township	26,801	34	1	5	18	10	1,005	50	938	17	0
Springfield Township, Bucks County	5,056	4	0	2	0	2	70	23	45	2	0
Springfield Township, Delaware County	24,264	11	0	1	6	4	681	58	610	13	0
Springfield Township, Montgomery County	19,563	25	1	2	7	15	229	52	175	2	0
Spring Garden Township	12,785	26	0	3	7	16	411	42	360	9	0
Spring Township, Berks County	27,212	15	0	1	5	9	338	36	291	11	2
Spring Township, Centre County	7,500	4	0	0	1	3	48	4	44	0	1
State College	57,020	53	1	11	12	29	787	115	658	14	11
Steelton	6,018	35	0	4	14	17	207	61	133	13	2
Stewartstown	2,099	8	0	1	2	5	51	6	45	0	0
Stoneboro	1,047	1	0	0	0	1	5	2	3	0	0
Stowe Township	6,385	26	0	0	11	15	228	46	173	9	0
Stroud Area Regional	34,775	95	0	16	45	34	1,536	184	1,338	14	1
Sugarcreek	5,273	3	0	2	0	1	92	8	84	0	2
Sugarloaf Township, Luzerne County	4,225	0	0	0	0	0	0	0	0	0	0

Table 8. Offenses Known to Law Enforcement, by Selected State and City, 2012— continued

(Number)

State/city	Population	Violent crime	Murder and nonnegligent manslaughter	Forcible rape	Robbery	Aggravated assault	Property crime	Burglary	Larceny-theft	Motor vehicle theft	Arson[1]
Sugar Notch	990	0	0	0	0	0	5	3	2	0	0
Summerhill Township	2,452	4	1	1	0	2	42	10	32	0	1
Summit Township	2,265	1	0	0	0	1	8	2	6	0	0
Sunbury	9,926	86	0	10	1	75	286	45	233	8	1
Susquehanna	1,640	4	0	1	1	2	16	5	11	0	0
Susquehanna Regional	7,833	4	0	1	2	1	108	24	82	2	2
Susquehanna Township, Dauphin County	24,145	54	3	8	17	26	388	87	286	15	1
Swarthmore	6,207	4	0	0	0	4	78	20	56	2	0
Swatara Township	23,464	112	0	0	17	95	754	107	637	10	4
Swoyersville	5,065	6	0	1	0	5	119	25	92	2	1
Sykesville	1,153	0	0	0	0	0	0	0	0	0	0
Tamaqua	7,080	17	0	0	3	14	290	18	268	4	0
Tatamy	1,208	1	0	0	0	1	9	1	8	0	0
Taylor	6,265	43	0	1	5	37	308	27	279	2	1
Telford	4,901	10	0	0	5	5	35	8	26	1	0
Terre Hill	1,307	2	0	1	0	1	15	7	8	0	2
Throop	4,089	16	0	0	0	16	54	15	37	2	1
Tiadaghton Valley Regional	6,722	5	0	2	2	1	140	11	129	0	0
Tidioute	684	0	0	0	0	0	8	6	2	0	0
Tilden Township	3,610	3	0	0	0	3	145	8	133	4	0
Tinicum Township, Bucks County	4,010	1	0	0	0	1	26	6	20	0	0
Tinicum Township, Delaware County	4,101	31	1	0	10	20	172	26	131	15	0
Tioga	674	0	0	0	0	0	6	3	2	1	0
Titusville	5,592	6	0	1	2	3	171	16	152	3	0
Towamencin Township	17,715	21	0	3	1	17	158	15	138	5	0
Towanda	2,937	7	0	2	0	5	114	15	95	4	0
Tower City	1,340	2	0	0	2	0	2	2	0	0	0
Trafford	3,173	6	0	0	0	6	41	14	27	0	0
Tredyffrin Township	29,643	8	0	1	0	7	280	46	228	6	0
Troy	1,329	2	0	0	0	2	46	8	37	1	0
Tullytown	1,880	0	0	0	0	0	1	1	0	0	0
Tulpehocken Township	3,285	0	0	0	0	0	25	9	16	0	0
Tunkhannock	1,839	2	0	1	0	1	46	11	32	3	1
Tunkhannock Township, Wyoming County	6,282	1	0	0	0	1	97	20	76	1	0
Turtle Creek	5,369	15	0	0	0	15	17	4	11	2	0
Tyrone	5,488	20	0	1	2	17	111	8	101	2	0
Union City	3,326	2	0	1	0	1	129	19	109	1	0
Union Dale	264	0	0	0	0	0	0	0	0	0	0
Uniontown	10,351	56	1	1	26	28	453	74	366	13	0
Union Township, Lawerence County	5,165	9	0	0	0	9	217	0	213	4	1
Union Township, Schuylkill County	1,268	0	0	0	0	0	0	0	0	0	0
Upland	3,245	67	0	3	6	58	137	34	93	10	0
Upper Allen Township	18,547	0	0	0	0	0	179	28	147	4	1
Upper Burrell Township	2,325	1	0	0	0	1	20	5	15	0	0
Upper Chichester Township	16,774	36	0	4	15	17	483	96	363	24	2
Upper Darby Township	82,978	517	3	16	270	228	1,975	223	1,639	113	8
Upper Dublin Township	25,766	25	0	0	4	21	301	54	236	11	2
Upper Gwynedd Township	15,670	12	0	0	1	11	87	20	67	0	0
Upper Leacock Township	8,794	4	2	0	1	1	122	23	92	7	0
Upper Makefield Township	8,223	8	0	0	0	8	102	28	69	5	0
Upper Merion Township	28,613	21	2	1	11	7	1,366	65	1,276	25	6

Table 8. Offenses Known to Law Enforcement, by Selected State and City, 2012— continued

(Number)

State/city	Population	Violent crime	Murder and nonnegligent manslaughter	Forcible rape	Robbery	Aggravated assault	Property crime	Burglary	Larceny-theft	Motor vehicle theft	Arson[1]
Upper Moreland Township	24,199	9	0	3	5	1	485	57	418	10	3
Upper Perkiomen	6,845	12	0	1	3	8	148	30	116	2	1
Upper Pottsgrove Township	5,355	13	0	0	2	11	77	21	53	3	1
Upper Providence Town, Delaware County	10,164	5	0	0	0	5	59	28	28	3	0
Upper Providence Township, Montgomery County	21,382	13	0	3	2	8	344	58	277	9	0
Upper Saucon Township	15,076	13	0	4	3	6	174	32	141	1	1
Upper Southampton Township	15,211	4	0	3	0	1	168	35	126	7	0
Upper St. Clair Township	19,300	7	0	0	1	6	102	13	88	1	0
Upper Uwchlan Township	11,346	2	1	1	0	0	90	8	79	3	0
Upper Yoder Township	5,420	4	0	0	0	4	16	5	11	0	0
Uwchlan Township	18,281	15	0	1	4	10	227	31	191	5	4
Valley Township	6,865	49	0	1	2	46	122	34	86	2	0
Vandergrift	5,203	13	0	1	0	12	30	6	24	0	0
Vandling	751	1	0	0	0	1	8	3	5	0	0
Vernon Township	5,620	1	0	0	1	0	74	1	73	0	1
Verona	2,484	11	0	0	1	10	83	13	67	3	0
Vintondale	411	0	0	0	0	0	0	0	0	0	0
Walker Township	1,050	0	0	0	0	0	1	0	1	0	0
Walnutport	2,078	1	0	0	1	0	14	2	11	1	0
Wampum	712	0	0	0	0	0	9	3	6	0	0
Warminster Township	32,810	27	1	6	14	6	482	70	406	6	3
Warrington Township	23,509	16	0	3	2	11	240	41	192	7	1
Warwick Township, Bucks County	14,493	14	0	3	0	11	91	15	76	0	0
Washington, Washington County	13,713	89	3	9	40	37	608	98	468	42	11
Washington Township, Fayette County	3,894	5	0	0	1	4	45	7	37	1	0
Washington Township, Franklin County	14,146	7	0	1	2	4	259	40	215	4	2
Washington Township, Northampton County	5,141	1	0	0	0	1	71	19	51	1	0
Washington Township, Westmoreland County	7,421	8	0	3	1	4	42	5	35	2	0
Watsontown	2,355	4	0	1	0	3	57	3	50	4	0
Waymart	1,352	0	0	0	0	0	5	0	5	0	0
Waynesboro	10,670	18	0	1	4	13	220	33	179	8	3
Waynesburg	4,333	14	0	0	2	12	94	11	80	3	0
Weatherly	2,526	15	0	0	0	15	71	25	45	1	0
Wellsboro	3,302	0	0	0	0	0	42	4	36	2	0
Wesleyville	3,347	14	0	0	7	7	162	22	137	3	0
West Brandywine Township	7,473	17	0	2	0	15	91	20	67	4	2
West Caln Township	9,109	10	0	2	1	7	72	20	44	8	0
West Carroll Township	1,287	1	0	0	0	1	9	3	6	0	0
West Chester	19,279	75	1	12	25	37	571	122	425	24	0
West Cocalico Township	7,354	3	0	2	0	1	37	10	22	5	0
West Conshohocken	1,330	5	0	0	4	1	31	7	22	2	0
West Cornwall Township	1,958	2	0	0	0	2	3	1	2	0	0
West Deer Township	11,816	1	0	0	1	0	116	36	66	14	0
West Earl Township	7,946	2	0	1	1	0	71	14	49	8	0
Western Berks Regional	4,570	4	0	0	1	3	66	15	50	1	0
West Fallowfield Township	2,594	0	0	0	0	0	28	7	21	0	0
Westfield	1,077	0	0	0	0	0	5	1	4	0	0
West Goshen Township	22,096	17	0	1	1	15	405	38	351	16	1

Table 8. Offenses Known to Law Enforcement, by Selected State and City, 2012— continued

(Number)

State/city	Population	Violent crime	Murder and nonnegligent manslaughter	Forcible rape	Robbery	Aggravated assault	Property crime	Burglary	Larceny-theft	Motor vehicle theft	Arson[1]
West Grove Borough	2,884	3	0	1	0	2	19	8	10	1	0
West Hazleton	4,596	20	0	2	4	14	173	51	115	7	1
West Hempfield Township	16,313	13	0	0	6	7	250	24	214	12	0
West Hills Regional	10,839	8	1	3	4	0	83	27	53	3	0
West Homestead	1,936	17	0	0	1	16	29	1	28	0	0
West Lampeter Township	15,357	6	0	0	2	4	180	24	153	3	0
West Lebanon Township	787	9	0	1	2	6	148	12	134	2	0
West Mahanoy Township	2,861	0	0	0	0	0	8	1	7	0	0
West Manchester Township	18,996	32	0	2	11	19	714	47	653	14	3
West Manheim Township	7,786	6	0	0	1	5	59	10	47	2	1
West Mead Township	5,238	0	0	0	0	0	10	1	9	0	0
West Mifflin	20,389	38	4	2	19	13	447	76	355	16	0
West Newton	2,633	3	0	1	0	2	61	8	53	0	1
West Norriton Township	15,784	29	0	10	3	16	361	38	313	10	1
West Nottingham Township	2,751	0	0	0	0	0	9	0	9	0	0
West Penn Township	4,424	3	0	0	1	2	29	3	26	0	3
West Pikeland Township	4,067	1	0	0	0	1	74	7	65	2	0
West Pike Run	1,593	0	0	0	0	0	0	0	0	0	0
West Pittston	4,871	4	0	0	1	3	118	29	87	2	0
West Pottsgrove Township	3,904	9	0	4	3	2	269	34	219	16	1
West Reading	4,227	22	1	1	8	12	181	23	149	9	0
West Sadsbury Township	2,469	0	0	0	0	0	97	0	97	0	0
West Salem Township	3,527	2	0	0	0	2	38	17	20	1	0
West Shore Regional	7,689	6	0	1	3	2	88	24	56	8	0
Westtown-East Goshen Regional	32,207	30	0	1	6	23	325	50	265	10	0
West View	6,797	12	0	0	0	12	183	9	171	3	0
West Vincent Township	4,613	3	0	0	0	3	94	20	73	1	1
West Whiteland Township	18,464	10	0	3	4	3	472	39	428	5	10
West Wyoming	2,727	2	0	0	0	2	57	17	38	2	1
Whitaker Borough	1,275	1	0	0	0	1	23	5	15	3	0
Whitehall	13,996	16	1	0	3	12	57	15	40	2	0
Whitehall Township	27,042	30	1	2	22	5	1,365	102	1,232	31	2
White Haven Borough	1,098	2	0	0	1	1	2	1	1	0	0
Whitemarsh Township	17,481	23	0	3	5	15	219	38	166	15	0
White Oak	7,891	7	0	0	4	3	75	14	58	3	2
Whitpain Township	19,020	23	0	2	4	17	244	37	202	5	1
Wiconisco Township	1,216	0	0	0	0	0	4	0	4	0	0
Wilkes-Barre	41,532	172	3	30	76	63	1,243	271	869	103	3
Wilkes-Barre Township	2,970	17	0	0	13	4	726	18	702	6	1
Wilkins Township	6,380	10	0	0	4	6	160	18	141	1	1
Williamsburg	1,256	0	0	0	0	0	16	0	15	1	0
Williamsport	29,582	111	2	5	62	42	1,235	266	926	43	19
Willistown Township	10,606	5	0	0	1	4	144	15	125	4	0
Wilson	7,924	51	0	4	19	28	340	65	262	13	2
Wind Gap	2,730	3	0	0	1	2	48	3	44	1	0
Womelsdorf	2,819	14	0	0	4	10	25	4	20	1	0
Woodward Township	2,391	0	0	0	0	0	26	4	22	0	0
Worthington	636	0	0	0	0	0	1	0	1	0	0
Wright Township	5,654	0	0	0	0	0	48	4	42	2	0
Wyoming	3,076	5	0	0	0	5	110	5	105	0	0
Wyomissing	10,496	16	0	0	11	5	525	24	493	8	0
Yardley	2,444	3	0	0	0	3	23	2	19	2	0
Yeadon	11,468	58	0	0	43	15	275	47	203	25	1

Table 8. Offenses Known to Law Enforcement, by Selected State and City, 2012— continued

(Number)

State/city	Population	Violent crime	Murder and nonnegligent manslaughter	Forcible rape	Robbery	Aggravated assault	Property crime	Burglary	Larceny-theft	Motor vehicle theft	Arson[1]
York	43,955	587	11	44	189	343	1,582	433	1,050	99	36
York Area Regional	60,732	73	1	14	16	42	639	158	461	20	0
Youngsville	1,717	5	0	1	0	4	8	2	6	0	0
Zelienople	3,840	8	0	1	0	7	55	6	45	4	0
Rhode Island											
Barrington	16,268	6	0	2	3	1	179	30	146	3	1
Bristol	22,900	15	0	2	1	12	259	45	211	3	1
Burrillville	15,941	8	0	2	2	4	231	71	146	14	1
Central Falls	19,360	142	1	14	47	80	590	133	337	120	5
Charlestown	7,793	5	0	0	0	5	127	26	99	2	0
Coventry	34,850	25	1	5	1	18	677	150	490	37	12
Cranston	80,315	130	2	16	34	78	1,908	392	1,362	154	17
Cumberland	33,475	18	0	3	5	10	541	112	404	25	3
East Greenwich	13,085	1	0	0	1	0	162	30	128	4	1
East Providence	46,994	71	2	13	14	42	834	144	631	59	9
Foster	4,603	4	0	0	0	4	48	17	28	3	0
Glocester	9,738	6	0	0	0	6	42	12	24	6	0
Hopkinton	8,151	4	0	2	0	2	129	19	106	4	2
Jamestown	5,386	2	0	0	0	2	93	8	83	2	0
Johnston	28,743	38	1	3	7	27	531	109	363	59	7
Lincoln	21,088	18	0	4	5	9	506	98	376	32	1
Little Compton	3,480	0	0	0	0	0	46	11	35	0	0
Middletown	16,096	6	0	0	3	3	271	34	230	7	2
Narragansett	15,799	6	0	0	0	6	280	50	219	11	0
Newport	24,595	104	1	11	15	77	987	223	742	22	12
New Shoreham	1,046	2	0	0	0	2	38	2	35	1	0
North Kingstown	26,371	9	0	3	1	5	434	90	330	14	1
North Providence	32,048	53	0	8	10	35	534	148	315	71	1
North Smithfield	11,957	10	0	2	3	5	326	32	274	20	1
Pawtucket	71,085	288	4	35	81	168	2,449	679	1,393	377	23
Portsmouth	17,331	5	0	0	0	5	251	53	188	10	5
Providence	177,882	1,133	17	84	362	670	7,977	1,929	4,884	1,164	24
Richmond	7,674	0	0	0	0	0	83	12	71	0	0
Scituate	10,320	4	0	0	0	4	87	27	53	7	0
Smithfield	21,411	13	0	1	0	12	293	37	237	19	2
South Kingstown	30,524	26	0	4	6	16	273	67	197	9	5
Tiverton	15,728	22	0	2	2	18	402	122	258	22	2
Warren	10,584	19	0	2	7	10	281	71	202	8	4
Warwick	82,282	102	1	15	29	57	2,117	334	1,688	95	8
Westerly	22,686	17	1	3	5	8	424	57	358	9	1
West Warwick	29,053	67	1	12	6	48	584	158	386	40	8
Woonsocket	41,147	220	0	23	59	138	1,259	346	840	73	20
South Carolina											
Abbeville	5,232	59	0	1	5	53	204	59	143	2	1
Aiken	29,909	112	7	7	40	58	1,614	246	1,290	78	1
Allendale	3,424	25	0	0	3	22	148	85	58	5	2
Anderson	27,127	250	7	10	38	195	1,970	386	1,458	126	7
Andrews	2,879	20	1	0	3	16	207	46	155	6	0
Bamberg	3,638	26	0	0	5	21	139	34	102	3	0
Barnwell	4,739	79	2	1	22	54	392	150	229	13	4
Batesburg-Leesville	5,503	58	1	4	3	50	301	51	236	14	1
Beaufort	12,653	139	2	4	29	104	824	147	656	21	2
Belton	4,204	7	0	0	0	7	187	29	146	12	1
Bennettsville	9,034	143	1	2	14	126	543	97	431	15	3
Bishopville	3,457	54	0	2	10	42	339	74	248	17	1
Blacksburg	1,873	18	0	2	1	15	114	41	65	8	0
Blackville	2,401	30	3	0	6	21	107	30	72	5	0
Bluffton	12,855	39	0	5	15	19	461	72	372	17	4
Branchville	1,028	1	0	0	0	1	18	2	15	1	0
Burnettown	2,713	6	0	0	0	6	61	17	42	2	0
Calhoun Falls	2,001	6	0	0	1	5	52	14	35	3	1
Camden	6,968	87	0	2	6	79	489	164	313	12	1
Cayce	12,864	103	3	4	13	83	688	120	497	71	1

Table 8. Offenses Known to Law Enforcement, by Selected State and City, 2012— continued

(Number)

State/city	Population	Violent crime	Murder and nonnegligent manslaughter	Forcible rape	Robbery	Aggravated assault	Property crime	Burglary	Larceny-theft	Motor vehicle theft	Arson[1]
Central	5,224	19	1	1	5	12	269	29	236	4	0
Chapin	1,485	7	0	1	2	4	62	7	55	0	0
Charleston	123,856	296	12	19	104	161	3,373	374	2,764	235	6
Cheraw	5,885	32	0	5	6	21	386	65	304	17	1
Chesnee	883	2	0	0	0	2	62	5	54	3	1
Chester	5,623	70	0	4	7	59	322	85	231	6	0
Chesterfield	1,473	9	0	0	1	8	72	5	66	1	0
Clemson	14,079	42	1	4	3	34	465	86	343	36	1
Clinton	8,570	67	1	7	5	54	456	109	334	13	1
Clio	722	5	0	0	2	3	44	8	35	1	0
Clover	5,245	129	0	3	5	121	177	38	131	8	1
Cottageville	766	1	0	0	1	0	22	9	10	3	2
Coward	764	1	0	0	0	1	11	1	8	2	0
Cowpens	2,202	5	0	0	1	4	45	12	32	1	0
Darlington	6,313	58	1	2	12	43	523	59	453	11	1
Denmark	3,562	39	0	1	13	25	192	88	98	6	1
Duncan	3,240	7	0	1	3	3	78	12	61	5	1
Easley	20,249	106	3	10	12	81	1,329	224	1,048	57	1
Edgefield	4,763	17	1	3	0	13	76	20	56	0	0
Edisto Beach	415	2	0	0	0	2	71	13	47	11	0
Ehrhardt	550	3	0	0	0	3	17	2	15	0	0
Elgin	1,336	11	0	0	6	5	72	14	56	2	2
Elloree	704	1	0	0	0	1	12	1	10	1	0
Estill	2,033	31	0	1	4	26	103	39	62	2	0
Fairfax	1,992	10	0	1	1	8	113	43	67	3	0
Florence	37,681	328	3	25	83	217	2,897	566	2,190	141	6
Folly Beach	2,700	8	0	0	1	7	101	37	64	0	0
Forest Acres	10,596	74	0	5	24	45	839	181	625	33	0
Fort Lawn	897	2	0	0	0	2	45	10	32	3	0
Fort Mill	11,132	25	1	0	1	23	224	33	182	9	0
Fountain Inn	8,012	36	1	0	1	34	167	32	126	9	0
Gaffney	12,574	77	2	11	7	57	453	105	322	26	0
Gaston	1,690	6	0	0	2	4	68	10	57	1	0
Georgetown	9,225	108	1	2	17	88	734	156	555	23	2
Goose Creek	37,387	117	2	15	21	79	927	161	704	62	5
Great Falls	1,984	13	0	0	1	12	84	23	60	1	0
Greeleyville	431	0	0	0	0	0	22	14	7	1	0
Greenville	60,953	509	1	21	104	383	3,223	603	2,411	209	12
Greenwood	23,564	344	3	16	48	277	1,715	486	1,182	47	7
Greer	26,249	121	1	16	20	84	826	181	587	58	4
Hampton	2,796	16	0	1	7	8	129	43	84	2	1
Hardeeville	3,047	31	2	2	5	22	204	36	146	22	1
Harleyville	706	7	0	0	1	6	42	19	20	3	1
Hartsville	7,796	95	5	5	24	61	942	168	724	50	1
Hemingway	459	5	0	0	2	3	47	9	35	3	1
Holly Hill	1,280	14	0	0	0	14	100	11	82	7	0
Honea Path	3,655	37	1	0	1	35	272	80	183	9	1
Inman	2,375	15	0	2	2	11	74	5	65	4	0
Isle of Palms	4,265	8	0	0	1	7	162	32	124	6	1
Jackson	1,722	5	0	0	1	4	30	10	18	2	0
Jamestown	75	0	0	0	0	0	3	3	0	0	0
Johnsonville	1,505	9	0	0	1	8	48	21	27	0	0
Johnston	2,354	14	0	0	3	11	49	17	30	2	0
Jonesville	910	1	0	0	0	1	20	3	16	1	0
Kingstree	3,325	51	0	2	14	35	321	83	214	24	1
Lake City	6,789	62	1	3	12	46	546	115	399	32	3
Lake View	808	11	0	0	2	9	47	14	33	0	0
Lamar	988	8	0	0	1	7	39	10	26	3	1
Lancaster	8,749	160	3	8	23	126	631	117	495	19	9
Landrum	2,423	11	0	0	3	8	40	10	27	3	0
Latta	1,378	34	1	0	4	29	142	32	107	3	4
Laurens	9,221	100	2	2	25	71	663	130	516	17	2
Lexington	18,352	57	0	5	7	45	757	44	677	36	0
Liberty	3,309	12	0	0	3	9	110	8	91	11	0

Table 8. Offenses Known to Law Enforcement, by Selected State and City, 2012— continued

(Number)

State/city	Population	Violent crime	Murder and nonnegligent manslaughter	Forcible rape	Robbery	Aggravated assault	Property crime	Burglary	Larceny-theft	Motor vehicle theft	Arson[1]
Lyman	3,305	3	0	0	1	2	116	16	99	1	0
Lynchburg	371	2	0	0	0	2	22	8	14	0	0
Manning	4,118	61	0	3	12	46	367	54	297	16	1
Marion	6,960	106	2	6	28	70	634	252	363	19	3
Mauldin	23,631	48	0	5	6	37	461	84	345	32	1
Mayesville	738	0	0	0	0	0	11	1	7	3	0
McColl	2,157	29	0	3	4	22	89	33	52	4	0
McCormick	2,774	16	0	1	4	11	71	20	49	2	0
Moncks Corner	8,229	46	1	3	8	34	520	54	444	22	6
Mount Pleasant	70,016	153	0	5	6	142	1,230	172	1,000	58	3
Mullins	4,680	89	2	3	12	72	443	150	284	9	1
Myrtle Beach	28,085	472	7	43	195	227	4,313	670	3,300	343	13
Newberry	10,430	85	0	3	15	67	501	111	383	7	1
New Ellenton	2,079	15	0	0	3	12	59	18	39	2	0
Nichols	369	4	0	0	0	4	5	0	5	0	0
Ninety Six	2,023	6	0	1	0	5	35	19	14	2	0
North Augusta	21,639	46	2	3	17	24	883	127	691	65	1
North Charleston	100,675	737	13	61	212	451	5,757	854	4,363	540	17
Orangeburg	14,017	59	0	5	26	28	906	244	611	51	5
Pacolet	2,277	27	0	1	20	6	96	20	66	10	1
Pageland	2,733	33	0	2	1	30	200	36	154	10	1
Pelion	692	4	0	0	0	4	15	4	11	0	0
Pickens	3,165	15	0	1	2	12	170	30	125	15	0
Port Royal	10,893	36	1	4	13	18	243	61	170	12	3
Prosperity	1,198	2	0	0	0	2	29	9	20	0	0
Ridgeland	4,123	11	2	1	7	1	141	30	108	3	0
Rock Hill	68,064	447	8	36	112	291	2,575	403	2,008	164	9
Salem	136	0	0	0	0	0	0	0	0	0	0
Salley	404	0	0	0	0	0	7	2	5	0	0
Saluda	3,600	47	0	0	3	44	106	40	63	3	0
Santee	964	4	0	0	2	2	76	10	54	12	0
Scranton	946	1	0	0	1	0	13	2	11	0	0
Seneca	8,194	63	0	1	8	54	297	63	212	22	1
Simpsonville	18,829	57	0	11	7	39	647	82	533	32	1
Society Hill	565	0	0	0	0	0	21	3	17	1	0
Spartanburg	37,689	537	2	20	120	395	2,694	479	2,120	95	14
Springdale	2,709	7	0	0	3	4	76	12	57	7	0
St. George	2,161	28	0	1	3	24	115	21	85	9	0
St. Matthews	2,038	18	0	0	3	15	60	15	36	9	0
St. Stephen	1,767	10	0	0	3	7	134	65	66	3	0
Sullivans Island	1,847	1	0	0	0	1	25	5	20	0	0
Summerton	1,002	9	0	1	3	5	44	8	34	2	0
Summerville	45,209	83	2	2	32	47	1,319	192	1,022	105	0
Sumter	40,911	403	7	8	65	323	2,147	599	1,409	139	15
Surfside Beach	3,976	19	0	3	5	11	396	89	294	13	0
Swansea	852	7	0	0	2	5	32	4	25	3	0
Tega Cay	7,847	6	0	0	0	6	90	15	73	2	0
Travelers Rest	4,725	8	0	0	2	6	346	29	306	11	0
Turbeville	767	5	0	0	1	4	21	6	13	2	0
Union	8,390	64	0	6	11	47	449	118	323	8	2
Wagener	808	8	0	0	1	7	31	8	21	2	0
Walhalla	4,313	12	0	1	1	10	130	27	95	8	1
Walterboro	5,411	78	0	2	16	60	486	69	392	25	2
Ware Shoals	2,189	30	0	2	7	21	169	54	109	6	0
Wellford	2,423	1	0	0	0	1	55	18	29	8	0
West Columbia	15,610	146	1	5	37	103	831	143	621	67	2
Westminster	2,445	34	0	0	1	33	115	23	90	2	0
West Pelzer	895	7	0	1	0	6	152	9	138	5	0
West Union	295	5	0	1	0	4	41	8	32	1	0
Whitmire	1,464	4	0	1	0	3	51	17	34	0	1
Williamston	4,002	34	0	2	9	23	185	28	151	6	0
Williston	3,133	12	0	0	3	9	119	37	78	4	0
Winnsboro	3,527	32	1	3	6	22	214	32	181	1	1
York	7,963	56	0	6	13	37	447	66	368	13	2

Table 8. Offenses Known to Law Enforcement, by Selected State and City, 2012— continued

(Number)

State/city	Population	Violent crime	Murder and nonnegligent manslaughter	Forcible rape	Robbery	Aggravated assault	Property crime	Burglary	Larceny-theft	Motor vehicle theft	Arson[1]
South Dakota											
Aberdeen	26,593	69	0	23	1	45	507	88	392	27	3
Armour	700	0	0	0	0	0	0	0	0	0	0
Avon	587	0	0	0	0	0	0	0	0	0	0
Belle Fourche	5,739	24	0	9	0	15	126	31	95	0	0
Beresford	2,072	2	0	0	0	2	20	5	13	2	0
Box Elder	7,997	23	0	8	0	15	202	5	188	9	0
Brandon	9,008	1	0	0	0	1	32	2	29	1	0
Brookings	22,478	8	0	0	0	8	40	0	40	0	0
Burke	603	0	0	0	0	0	0	0	0	0	0
Canton	3,224	11	0	1	0	10	59	14	42	3	0
Centerville	890	0	0	0	0	0	2	0	2	0	0
Chamberlain	2,427	11	0	3	0	8	99	18	73	8	0
Deadwood	1,298	2	0	0	0	2	29	1	25	3	0
Eagle Butte	1,350	1	0	0	0	1	8	5	3	0	4
Estelline	786	1	0	0	0	1	8	3	5	0	0
Faith	429	0	0	0	0	0	1	0	1	0	0
Flandreau	2,363	9	0	3	0	6	53	5	47	1	1
Freeman	1,305	1	0	0	0	1	5	2	2	1	0
Gettysburg	1,192	1	0	0	0	1	1	0	0	1	0
Hermosa	408	0	0	0	0	0	0	0	0	0	0
Hot Springs	3,694	6	0	0	0	6	25	8	12	5	0
Hoven	418	0	0	0	0	0	0	0	0	0	0
Huron	12,849	41	0	9	0	32	429	64	347	18	0
Irene	428	0	0	0	0	0	1	0	1	0	0
Jefferson	562	0	0	0	0	0	1	0	1	0	0
Kadoka	690	3	0	0	0	3	8	5	2	1	0
Kimball	715	0	0	0	0	0	1	0	1	0	0
Lead	3,189	4	0	0	0	4	37	5	28	4	0
Lemmon	1,247	0	0	0	0	0	1	0	1	0	0
Lennox	2,225	1	0	0	0	1	10	1	8	1	0
Leola	461	0	0	0	0	0	0	0	0	0	0
Madison	6,723	5	1	2	0	2	92	15	72	5	0
Martin	1,086	8	0	0	0	8	14	2	9	3	1
McIntosh	173	0	0	0	0	0	0	0	0	0	0
Menno	608	0	0	0	0	0	0	0	0	0	0
Miller	1,502	0	0	0	0	0	6	3	3	0	0
Mitchell	15,541	51	0	17	3	31	433	61	350	22	3
Mobridge	3,593	6	0	2	0	4	74	9	61	4	0
North Sioux City	2,604	0	0	0	0	0	29	0	28	1	0
Parkston	1,505	0	0	0	0	0	12	4	6	2	0
Philip	776	0	0	0	0	0	0	0	0	0	0
Pierre	14,016	44	1	14	2	27	507	58	423	26	2
Rapid City	69,979	425	4	111	55	255	3,555	591	2,734	230	15
Rosholt	433	0	0	0	0	0	1	1	0	0	0
Scotland	837	0	0	0	0	0	0	0	0	0	0
Selby	664	3	0	0	1	2	3	0	3	0	0
Sioux Falls	158,354	631	2	139	70	420	5,041	899	3,843	299	56
Sisseton	2,530	8	0	0	0	8	67	10	52	5	0
Spearfish	10,704	18	0	8	0	10	375	47	320	8	0
Springfield	1,999	0	0	0	0	0	0	0	0	0	0
Sturgis	6,731	4	0	1	0	3	145	25	115	5	0
Summerset	1,841	0	0	0	0	0	8	1	6	1	0
Tea	4,021	8	0	0	0	8	90	25	57	8	1
Tripp	646	0	0	0	0	0	1	1	0	0	0
Tyndall	1,064	0	0	0	0	0	0	0	0	0	0
Vermillion	10,826	30	0	4	1	25	248	37	201	10	0
Viborg	791	0	0	0	0	0	0	0	0	0	0
Wagner	1,599	0	0	0	0	0	23	0	23	0	0
Watertown	21,902	62	0	13	2	47	523	112	387	24	2
Whitewood	949	0	0	0	0	0	2	0	2	0	0
Winner	2,914	4	0	0	0	4	14	1	10	3	0
Worthing	926	0	0	0	0	0	0	0	0	0	0

Table 8. Offenses Known to Law Enforcement, by Selected State and City, 2012— continued

(Number)

State/city	Population	Violent crime	Murder and nonnegligent manslaughter	Forcible rape	Robbery	Aggravated assault	Property crime	Burglary	Larceny-theft	Motor vehicle theft	Arson[1]
Yankton	14,728	42	0	19	2	21	453	57	378	18	1
Tennessee											
Adamsville	[illegible]	0	0	0	0	0	[illegible]	10	[illegible]	1	1
Alamo	2,476	19	0	4	1	14	57	12	42	3	0
Alcoa	8,587	71	0	7	14	50	565	86	452	27	1
Alexandria	981	3	0	0	1	2	12	3	9	0	0
Algood	3,555	17	0	1	1	15	153	20	133	0	0
Ardmore	1,219	4	0	0	2	2	31	13	18	0	0
Ashland City	4,575	28	0	1	3	24	228	41	181	6	1
Athens	13,632	170	0	9	31	130	1,178	232	895	51	3
Atoka	8,488	10	0	3	1	6	132	33	89	10	2
Baileyton	438	3	0	0	0	3	13	2	11	0	0
Baneberry	488	0	0	0	0	0	0	0	0	0	0
Bartlett	55,510	132	0	7	19	106	778	125	624	29	4
Baxter	1,388	10	0	1	2	7	58	16	38	4	1
Bean Station	2,865	17	0	2	0	15	120	23	86	11	0
Belle Meade	2,978	0	0	0	0	0	43	10	33	0	0
Bells	2,452	30	0	1	1	28	39	11	27	1	0
Benton	1,393	6	0	0	0	6	28	4	24	0	0
Berry Hill	550	7	0	0	4	3	55	6	49	0	1
Big Sandy	561	1	0	0	0	1	4	2	1	1	0
Blaine	1,881	2	0	1	0	1	24	9	14	1	1
Bluff City	1,753	6	0	0	0	6	44	8	36	0	0
Bolivar	5,371	53	1	0	9	43	222	59	156	7	1
Bradford	1,062	0	0	0	0	0	8	2	6	0	0
Brighton	2,769	2	0	0	1	1	51	11	39	1	0
Bristol	27,024	143	0	12	9	122	1,102	184	850	68	5
Brownsville	10,201	111	0	3	7	101	423	141	269	13	2
Bruceton	1,486	3	0	0	0	3	22	6	16	0	0
Burns	1,492	2	0	0	0	2	25	6	19	0	0
Calhoun	497	0	0	0	0	0	5	0	5	0	0
Camden	3,598	11	0	2	0	9	159	33	120	6	0
Carthage	2,324	4	0	0	2	2	68	17	47	4	0
Caryville	2,304	8	0	2	0	6	94	22	65	7	1
Celina	1,489	4	0	0	0	4	27	8	19	0	0
Centerville	3,630	4	0	0	0	4	93	22	69	2	0
Chapel Hill	1,470	4	0	0	0	4	14	3	10	1	0
Charleston	663	0	0	0	0	0	18	6	10	2	0
Church Hill	6,773	15	0	1	1	13	137	25	105	7	0
Clarksburg	394	0	0	0	0	0	2	1	1	0	0
Clarksville	137,356	875	10	46	99	720	3,741	976	2,598	167	25
Cleveland	42,068	371	0	29	39	303	2,225	398	1,751	76	5
Clifton	2,712	3	0	0	0	3	4	2	1	1	0
Clinton	9,936	66	0	3	5	58	403	70	304	29	2
Collegedale	8,353	10	0	1	1	8	143	17	121	5	1
Collierville	44,690	77	0	5	7	65	887	81	787	19	1
Collinwood	985	1	0	0	0	1	8	1	7	0	1
Columbia	35,203	282	4	11	37	230	1,362	284	1,048	30	8
Cookeville	30,946	146	0	12	26	108	1,522	370	1,097	55	1
Coopertown	4,368	4	0	0	1	3	19	8	7	4	0
Cornersville	1,215	6	0	0	0	6	14	2	12	0	2
Cowan	1,744	4	0	0	0	4	22	5	16	1	0
Cross Plains	1,749	1	0	0	0	1	17	4	13	0	1
Crossville	10,993	163	0	11	17	135	1,119	243	833	43	1
Crump	1,432	5	0	1	0	4	43	15	28	0	0
Cumberland City	310	1	1	0	0	0	7	5	2	0	0
Cumberland Gap	498	3	0	0	0	3	8	2	6	0	0
Dandridge	2,848	16	0	1	4	11	87	15	66	6	0
Dayton	7,308	26	0	2	4	20	312	69	217	26	0
Decatur	1,609	10	0	0	1	9	51	10	38	3	0
Decaturville	870	3	0	0	0	3	16	7	7	2	0
Decherd	2,373	11	0	2	1	8	56	24	26	6	0
Dickson	14,780	59	1	7	1	50	756	100	636	20	1

Table 8. Offenses Known to Law Enforcement, by Selected State and City, 2012— continued

(Number)

State/city	Population	Violent crime	Murder and nonnegligent manslaughter	Forcible rape	Robbery	Aggravated assault	Property crime	Burglary	Larceny-theft	Motor vehicle theft	Arson[1]
Dover	1,416	6	0	0	1	5	29	5	23	1	1
Dresden	3,027	4	0	0	0	4	74	18	54	2	1
Dunlap	4,933	23	0	1	2	20	259	54	190	15	1
Dyer	2,372	4	0	0	0	4	43	13	28	2	0
Dyersburg	17,223	184	0	7	20	157	1,150	278	848	24	3
Eagleville	623	0	0	0	0	0	1	0	1	0	0
East Ridge	21,435	151	0	6	33	112	1,057	230	741	86	4
Elizabethton	14,240	36	0	2	5	29	774	127	621	26	1
Elkton	581	1	0	0	0	1	2	1	1	0	0
Englewood	1,552	2	0	0	0	2	29	7	21	1	0
Erin	1,322	5	0	0	0	5	25	4	15	6	0
Erwin	6,136	15	0	0	1	14	131	20	99	12	1
Estill Springs	2,065	6	0	0	0	6	24	5	15	4	0
Ethridge	472	3	0	2	0	1	26	8	18	0	0
Etowah	3,535	26	0	6	1	19	139	41	91	7	3
Fairview	8,013	23	0	0	1	22	125	24	97	4	1
Fayetteville	6,896	71	1	3	5	62	424	46	366	12	1
Franklin	64,848	93	1	11	11	70	1,033	90	902	41	3
Friendship	672	1	0	0	0	1	7	0	7	0	0
Gadsden	472	6	0	0	0	6	11	2	9	0	0
Gainesboro	952	10	0	0	1	9	26	3	21	2	0
Gallatin	31,093	133	0	5	12	116	556	99	434	23	1
Gallaway	688	4	0	0	0	4	8	2	5	1	0
Gates	650	1	0	0	0	1	17	8	8	1	0
Gatlinburg	4,047	30	0	2	11	17	467	172	275	20	0
Germantown	39,484	31	0	2	5	24	623	134	478	11	6
Gibson	401	0	0	0	0	0	8	1	6	1	0
Gleason	1,455	3	0	0	0	3	15	2	13	0	0
Goodlettsville	16,310	90	3	4	24	59	896	128	749	19	1
Gordonsville	1,222	3	0	0	0	3	15	5	10	0	0
Grand Junction	322	0	0	0	0	0	23	4	17	2	1
Graysville	1,530	3	0	0	0	3	13	3	8	2	0
Greenbrier	6,568	10	0	0	1	9	107	32	69	6	0
Greeneville	15,295	116	1	5	18	92	1,012	191	781	40	3
Greenfield	2,198	5	0	0	1	4	25	9	15	1	0
Halls	2,268	11	0	0	1	10	39	19	20	0	1
Harriman	6,363	27	0	2	3	22	283	85	183	15	3
Henderson	6,363	27	0	1	0	26	150	73	74	3	1
Hendersonville	52,781	127	0	6	13	108	941	141	772	28	10
Henning	950	0	0	0	0	0	17	8	9	0	0
Henry	469	0	0	0	0	0	14	3	10	1	0
Hohenwald	3,782	23	0	0	4	19	127	19	103	5	1
Hollow Rock	723	4	0	0	0	4	10	2	8	0	0
Hornbeak	426	0	0	0	0	0	3	2	1	0	0
Humboldt	8,563	108	0	3	11	94	342	86	245	11	7
Huntingdon	4,009	14	0	0	1	13	153	25	125	3	0
Huntland	877	2	0	0	0	2	10	4	6	0	0
Jacksboro	2,027	7	0	0	0	7	141	9	132	0	0
Jackson	65,725	972	11	22	191	748	3,246	972	2,139	135	21
Jamestown	1,982	9	0	0	0	9	177	21	150	6	0
Jasper	3,304	13	0	0	1	12	68	11	53	4	0
Jefferson City	8,149	23	0	2	10	11	373	61	300	12	0
Jellico	2,366	8	0	0	3	5	87	19	65	3	0
Johnson City	64,342	319	1	14	51	253	2,875	540	2,238	97	14
Jonesborough	5,146	11	0	0	0	11	106	15	89	2	2
Kenton	1,295	4	0	1	0	3	26	8	17	1	0
Kimball	1,407	5	0	0	0	5	111	8	98	5	0
Kingsport	49,639	367	2	31	50	284	2,950	431	2,387	132	14
Kingston	5,946	12	1	1	6	4	107	24	78	5	4
Kingston Springs	2,777	0	0	0	0	0	11	0	10	1	0
Knoxville	182,254	1,774	18	119	528	1,109	12,169	2,882	8,373	914	23
Lafayette	4,557	12	0	1	0	11	61	17	34	10	1
La Follette	7,481	69	0	5	14	50	643	202	424	17	5
Lake City	1,798	3	0	0	1	2	113	34	75	4	2

Table 8. Offenses Known to Law Enforcement, by Selected State and City, 2012— continued

(Number)

State/city	Population	Violent crime	Murder and nonnegligent manslaughter	Forcible rape	Robbery	Aggravated assault	Property crime	Burglary	Larceny-theft	Motor vehicle theft	Arson[1]
La Vergne	33,665	157	0	11	18	128	555	168	345	42	3
Lawrenceburg	10,576	70	0	4	6	60	594	125	457	12	5
Lebanon	26,991	197	2	10	24	161	1,137	188	896	53	1
Lenoir City	8,836	52	0	3	14	35	518	113	385	20	1
Lewisburg	11,287	64	1	7	1	55	287	89	189	9	4
Lexington	7,755	116	0	4	6	106	427	69	341	17	1
Livingston	4,106	19	0	0	1	18	90	6	80	4	2
Lookout Mountain	1,871	2	0	0	0	2	21	2	17	2	0
Loretto	1,737	1	0	0	0	1	25	4	21	0	0
Loudon	5,499	4	0	0	1	3	44	9	34	1	0
Madisonville	4,651	17	1	0	5	11	304	49	242	13	0
Manchester	10,226	82	0	5	7	70	608	103	489	16	1
Martin	11,556	34	0	0	1	33	346	55	287	4	3
Maryville	27,874	59	0	4	13	42	853	198	631	24	1
Mason	1,626	22	1	1	2	18	45	10	26	9	0
Maury City	678	5	0	0	0	5	15	4	10	1	0
Maynardville	2,443	8	0	1	1	6	129	25	96	8	1
McEwen	1,757	4	0	0	0	4	11	1	10	0	0
McKenzie	5,344	18	0	2	1	15	167	52	111	4	1
McMinnville	13,746	111	1	14	8	88	644	133	472	39	6
Medina	3,527	1	0	0	0	1	25	8	17	0	0
Memphis	657,436	11,507	133	420	3,382	7,572	41,503	12,575	25,959	2,969	407
Middleton	698	0	0	0	0	0	9	1	8	0	0
Milan	7,955	64	0	2	6	56	282	76	199	7	2
Millersville	6,609	25	0	1	1	23	92	28	61	3	1
Millington	10,342	69	0	4	14	51	417	68	331	18	2
Minor Hill	539	0	0	0	0	0	0	0	0	0	0
Monteagle	1,192	9	0	0	0	9	9	1	8	0	0
Monterey	2,898	2	0	0	0	2	74	4	67	3	0
Morristown	29,617	203	0	13	45	145	1,798	191	1,522	85	4
Moscow	562	4	0	0	1	3	13	5	7	1	0
Mountain City	2,550	12	0	1	0	11	54	8	44	2	0
Mount Carmel	5,458	12	0	1	0	11	74	18	51	5	0
Mount Juliet	24,419	55	1	3	5	46	449	68	367	14	2
Mount Pleasant	4,629	32	0	2	1	29	149	22	123	4	0
Munford	6,002	25	0	0	4	21	110	23	82	5	0
Murfreesboro	112,247	701	3	55	134	509	4,006	923	2,899	184	4
Nashville	620,886	7,550	62	311	1,724	5,453	26,052	5,736	18,885	1,431	93
Newbern	3,329	18	0	1	1	16	92	38	53	1	0
New Hope	1,092	0	0	0	0	0	0	0	0	0	0
New Johnsonville	1,959	3	0	0	0	3	13	1	12	0	0
New Market	1,352	0	0	0	0	0	7	2	5	0	0
Newport	6,979	62	0	2	12	48	706	86	595	25	0
New Tazewell	3,059	7	0	0	1	6	43	8	35	0	0
Niota	728	0	0	0	0	0	37	8	27	2	0
Nolensville	6,086	3	0	0	0	3	38	3	34	1	0
Norris	1,505	0	0	0	0	0	25	4	21	0	0
Oakland	6,695	6	1	0	2	3	75	8	66	1	0
Oak Ridge	29,593	81	1	8	21	51	1,026	212	752	62	5
Obion	1,127	4	0	0	0	4	14	1	13	0	0
Oliver Springs	3,255	8	0	0	0	8	115	20	85	10	0
Oneida	3,765	22	0	2	1	19	197	34	160	3	1
Paris	10,246	59	0	1	11	47	538	153	374	11	0
Parsons	2,378	5	0	0	0	5	45	11	31	3	0
Petersburg	550	0	0	0	0	0	7	2	5	0	0
Pigeon Forge	6,024	59	0	8	9	42	725	200	487	38	4
Pikeville	1,619	1	0	0	0	1	28	2	25	1	0
Piperton	1,460	1	0	0	0	1	20	7	12	1	0
Pittman Center	515	0	0	0	0	0	8	5	2	1	0
Plainview	2,154	2	0	1	0	1	42	11	28	3	0
Pleasant View	4,180	4	0	0	1	3	69	19	50	0	0
Portland	11,801	60	0	5	2	53	307	96	201	10	5
Powells Crossroads	1,332	0	0	0	0	0	0	0	0	0	0
Pulaski	7,910	58	0	6	7	45	394	87	296	11	3

Table 8. Offenses Known to Law Enforcement, by Selected State and City, 2012— continued

(Number)

State/city	Population	Violent crime	Murder and nonnegligent manslaughter	Forcible rape	Robbery	Aggravated assault	Property crime	Burglary	Larceny-theft	Motor vehicle theft	Arson[1]
Puryear	678	4	0	0	0	4	17	3	14	0	0
Red Boiling Springs	1,133	1	0	0	0	1	32	12	19	1	0
Ridgely	1,792	11	0	0	2	9	19	11	8	0	0
Ridgetop	1,914	2	0	0	1	1	13	3	9	1	1
Ripley	8,494	116	3	4	13	96	477	209	257	11	1
Rockwood	5,573	31	0	1	2	28	356	80	268	8	0
Rogersville	4,464	19	0	0	3	16	287	56	220	11	1
Rossville	672	0	0	0	0	0	7	0	7	0	0
Rutherford	1,168	1	0	0	0	1	16	8	8	0	0
Rutledge	1,138	2	0	0	0	2	46	9	34	3	0
Saltillo	519	0	0	0	0	0	5	0	5	0	0
Samburg	220	1	0	0	0	1	8	2	6	0	0
Savannah	7,000	58	1	5	8	44	493	110	362	21	3
Scotts Hill	992	1	0	0	0	1	10	5	4	1	0
Selmer	4,436	42	0	1	4	37	195	46	141	8	0
Sevierville	15,161	80	0	6	11	63	840	124	667	49	0
Sewanee	2,351	0	0	0	0	0	48	20	28	0	2
Sharon	950	1	0	0	0	1	42	11	31	0	0
Shelbyville	20,706	129	0	15	16	98	640	134	485	21	0
Signal Mountain	7,718	3	0	0	0	3	67	10	55	2	0
Smithville	4,599	39	2	0	8	29	290	72	203	15	5
Smyrna	41,284	106	2	12	21	71	987	135	802	50	2
Sneedville	1,386	3	0	2	0	1	78	8	69	1	1
Soddy-Daisy	12,989	56	0	3	5	48	419	61	340	18	2
South Carthage	1,332	7	0	0	1	6	48	16	31	1	0
South Fulton	2,371	18	0	0	1	17	53	20	31	2	1
Sparta	5,022	22	0	1	5	16	334	75	245	14	3
Spencer	1,597	1	0	0	0	1	21	4	15	2	0
Spring City	2,013	10	0	0	0	10	45	5	34	6	0
Springfield	16,776	176	2	14	46	114	783	122	635	26	3
Spring Hill	29,981	59	0	6	7	46	382	70	307	5	1
St. Joseph	794	7	0	1	0	6	12	6	5	1	1
Surgoinsville	1,811	0	0	0	0	0	23	1	20	2	0
Sweetwater	5,884	32	0	0	2	30	207	52	136	19	1
Tazewell	2,237	27	1	1	1	24	114	17	89	8	1
Tellico Plains	894	3	0	0	0	3	36	7	28	1	1
Tiptonville	4,482	9	0	0	0	9	48	14	33	1	4
Toone	361	3	0	0	0	3	4	2	2	0	0
Townsend	455	0	0	0	0	0	19	4	14	1	0
Trenton	4,319	17	0	0	2	15	127	27	97	3	0
Trezevant	865	1	0	0	0	1	19	9	10	0	0
Trimble	639	1	0	0	0	1	5	1	4	0	0
Troy	1,381	2	0	0	1	1	35	4	30	1	0
Tullahoma	18,880	101	1	2	7	91	653	151	475	27	3
Tusculum	2,700	0	0	0	0	0	17	3	13	1	0
Union City	10,978	62	0	10	11	41	710	122	575	13	5
Vonore	1,499	9	0	0	0	9	67	10	54	3	2
Wartburg	921	3	0	0	0	3	30	4	26	0	0
Wartrace	662	0	0	0	0	0	3	1	2	0	0
Watauga	459	0	0	0	0	0	1	0	1	0	0
Watertown	1,524	1	0	0	1	0	36	16	19	1	1
Waverly	4,125	6	0	0	0	6	103	18	82	3	0
Waynesboro	2,459	6	0	0	0	6	39	2	37	0	0
Westmoreland	2,265	2	0	0	0	2	38	11	27	0	0
White Bluff	3,261	5	0	1	0	4	49	10	38	1	0
White House	10,505	25	0	2	5	18	204	19	182	3	1
White Pine	2,225	8	1	0	3	4	88	5	79	4	2
Whiteville	4,655	10	0	0	1	9	53	18	31	4	2
Whitwell	1,710	2	0	0	0	2	40	7	30	3	0
Winchester	8,272	56	1	5	4	46	324	60	261	3	0
Winfield	972	2	1	0	0	1	13	2	9	2	0
Woodbury	2,694	22	0	0	0	22	96	13	73	10	0
Texas											

Table 8. Offenses Known to Law Enforcement, by Selected State and City, 2012— continued

(Number)

State/city	Population	Violent crime	Murder and nonnegligent manslaughter	Forcible rape	Robbery	Aggravated assault	Property crime	Burglary	Larceny-theft	Motor vehicle theft	Arson[1]
Abernathy	2,877	3	1	1	0	1	31	14	15	2	0
Abilene	119,886	472	3	38	127	304	4,393	1,037	3,185	171	18
Alamo	19,178	182	0	11	10	161	1,492	264	1,147	81	1
Alamo Heights	7,305	14	0	6	4	4	240	34	198	8	0
Alice	19,627	172	10	8	6	148	1,216	278	884	54	13
Allen	88,783	55	0	11	13	31	1,432	215	1,173	44	0
Alpine	6,091	7	0	1	0	6	74	18	49	7	1
Alton	14,178	9	0	3	4	2	335	85	222	28	1
Alvarado	3,888	24	0	1	7	16	136	39	89	8	0
Alvin	25,145	62	0	11	13	38	675	149	502	24	2
Amarillo	196,576	1,278	10	110	278	880	8,900	2,087	6,184	629	54
Andrews	11,751	89	0	18	0	71	261	50	199	12	0
Angleton	19,569	59	2	9	1	47	601	101	487	13	7
Anna	8,724	7	0	0	2	5	133	41	86	6	1
Anson	2,458	3	0	0	0	3	41	9	32	0	0
Anthony	5,166	9	0	0	4	5	181	16	153	12	1
Aransas Pass[7]	8,325	48	2	7	4	35			371	18	2
Archer City	1,819	3	0	0	0	3	9	4	5	0	0
Arcola	1,724	4	0	1	2	1	30	10	17	3	0
Argyle	3,454	2	0	2	0	0	32	9	23	0	0
Arlington	379,295	1,909	17	135	532	1,225	15,109	3,543	10,616	950	51
Arp	1,003	0	0	0	0	0	2	0	2	0	0
Athens	12,946	55	0	14	6	35	445	104	320	21	0
Atlanta	5,717	44	0	7	7	30	220	58	153	9	1
Aubrey	2,731	7	0	2	0	5	61	11	49	1	1
Austin	832,901	3,405	31	209	978	2,187	43,472	7,244	33,913	2,315	121
Azle	11,337	25	0	2	4	19	384	90	279	15	7
Baird	1,515	0	0	0	0	0	10	8	2	0	0
Balch Springs	24,574	177	0	23	27	127	1,382	215	1,030	137	0
Balcones Heights	2,859	27	0	0	17	10	578	54	487	37	2
Ballinger	3,831	7	0	2	0	5	81	25	54	2	0
Bangs	1,630	4	0	0	0	4	5	2	2	1	0
Bastrop	7,415	22	0	3	5	14	468	46	412	10	3
Bay City	17,928	54	1	8	10	35	678	143	528	7	4
Bayou Vista	1,584	9	0	0	0	9	34	11	20	3	0
Baytown	74,420	247	5	15	97	130	3,684	939	2,438	307	23
Beaumont	120,323	1,242	13	76	408	745	5,824	1,828	3,717	279	49
Bedford	48,763	143	1	10	29	103	1,331	282	972	77	2
Bee Cave	4,137	12	0	2	0	10	145	17	121	7	0
Beeville	13,179	30	1	0	4	25	257	43	203	11	2
Bellaire	17,481	23	0	2	15	6	332	56	261	15	0
Bellmead	10,212	182	0	8	14	160	1,152	137	972	43	2
Bellville	4,193	9	0	3	0	6	107	21	85	1	0
Belton	18,763	64	1	1	13	49	725	145	578	2	0
Benbrook	22,040	31	1	3	9	18	440	78	343	19	0
Bertram	1,384	1	0	0	0	1	30	15	15	0	2
Beverly Hills	2,056	15	0	2	5	8	90	25	63	2	1
Big Sandy	1,380	1	0	0	0	1	9	4	5	0	0
Big Spring	27,774	160	2	15	11	132	1,099	271	785	43	6
Bishop	3,211	4	0	2	0	2	73	20	50	3	0
Blanco	1,781	4	0	0	0	4	42	9	32	1	0
Bloomburg	406	0	0	0	0	0	0	0	0	0	0
Blue Mound	2,484	0	0	0	0	0	24	3	21	0	0
Boerne	11,047	17	0	2	4	11	352	34	309	9	0
Bogata	1,157	5	0	0	1	4	34	14	19	1	0
Bonham	10,288	21	1	5	2	13	287	78	207	2	2
Borger	13,438	131	0	18	4	109	573	152	407	14	5
Bovina	1,906	6	0	1	0	5	6	1	5	0	0
Bowie	5,293	12	0	2	1	9	272	47	212	13	0
Brady	5,616	10	0	0	0	10	124	46	72	6	1
Brazoria	3,133	7	0	1	0	6	47	3	38	6	0
Breckenridge	5,815	9	0	4	0	5	84	28	53	3	1
Bremond	950	3	0	0	0	3	26	9	17	0	0
Brenham	15,988	34	1	0	7	26	444	86	339	19	1

Table 8. Offenses Known to Law Enforcement, by Selected State and City, 2012— continued

(Number)

State/city	Population	Violent crime	Murder and nonnegligent manslaughter	Forcible rape	Robbery	Aggravated assault	Property crime	Burglary	Larceny-theft	Motor vehicle theft	Arson[1]
Bridge City	8,020	22	0	4	3	15	165	32	127	6	0
Bridgeport	6,138	14	0	4	0	10	102	19	82	1	0
Brookshire	4,865	17	1	2	3	11	107	34	64	9	4
Brookside Village	1,581	0	0	0	0	0	12	7	5	0	0
Brownfield	9,820	35	0	3	7	25	175	65	105	5	2
Brownsville	181,102	473	3	38	125	307	8,337	1,145	6,986	206	20
Brownwood	19,618	103	0	16	9	78	926	137	765	24	3
Bruceville-Eddy	1,521	2	1	0	0	1	8	2	6	0	0
Bryan	78,479	312	1	31	69	211	2,473	496	1,889	88	21
Buda	7,797	10	0	2	3	5	225	21	197	7	0
Bullard	2,546	12	0	5	0	7	44	6	35	3	0
Bulverde	4,852	3	0	0	0	3	69	14	54	1	0
Burkburnett	10,901	34	1	6	1	26	311	65	230	16	1
Burleson	37,774	67	1	7	21	38	1,032	195	803	34	2
Burnet	6,128	14	0	1	3	10	154	35	112	7	1
Cactus	3,234	14	0	4	1	9	18	9	7	2	0
Caddo Mills	1,364	1	0	0	0	1	11	6	5	0	0
Caldwell	4,180	5	1	0	0	4	41	2	36	3	0
Calvert	1,218	7	0	0	0	7	36	15	20	1	4
Cameron	5,621	21	0	1	5	15	238	44	193	1	1
Canton	3,637	4	0	0	1	3	105	12	90	3	0
Canyon	13,773	17	1	2	0	14	103	23	74	6	2
Carrollton	124,477	180	2	7	75	96	3,414	771	2,358	285	10
Carthage	6,954	34	0	4	4	26	309	58	243	8	2
Castle Hills	4,280	3	0	0	3	0	311	30	271	10	0
Castroville	2,740	8	0	2	2	4	51	20	26	5	1
Cedar Hill	46,633	106	0	11	38	57	1,646	367	1,194	85	2
Cedar Park	52,051	109	0	11	9	89	765	93	653	19	1
Celina	6,350	3	0	1	0	2	71	17	52	2	0
Center	5,307	45	0	3	13	29	253	48	195	10	2
Childress	6,149	29	0	0	1	28	84	33	47	4	0
Chillicothe	723	0	0	0	0	0	17	1	16	0	0
Cibolo	16,090	23	1	4	1	17	242	52	184	6	0
Cisco	3,972	9	0	0	0	9	183	95	86	2	0
Clarksville	3,285	3	0	0	2	1	47	27	20	0	0
Cleburne	30,126	147	1	27	21	98	1,330	267	1,005	58	4
Cleveland	7,847	84	0	5	15	64	693	114	529	50	5
Clifton	3,509	0	0	0	0	0	20	6	14	0	1
Clint	964	0	0	0	0	0	12	2	8	2	0
Clute	11,631	25	0	3	4	18	268	53	207	8	1
Clyde	3,759	2	0	0	0	2	54	12	37	5	0
Cockrell Hill	4,343	44	0	2	7	35	124	38	72	14	3
Coleman	4,709	12	0	0	2	10	188	92	90	6	1
College Station	96,567	491	3	34	38	416	2,398	576	1,762	60	0
Colleyville	23,677	5	0	1	1	3	181	32	146	3	0
Collinsville	1,655	3	0	1	0	2	20	9	11	0	0
Colorado City	4,221	33	0	0	0	33	172	72	100	0	1
Columbus	3,699	25	0	6	1	18	130	16	112	2	0
Comanche	4,373	11	0	1	1	9	167	36	130	1	1
Combes	2,996	7	1	1	0	5	36	11	22	3	2
Commerce	8,229	40	1	7	9	23	285	83	194	8	0
Conroe	59,856	221	2	13	74	132	2,061	447	1,501	113	1
Converse	18,922	71	0	9	11	51	524	97	402	25	1
Coppell	40,053	27	0	3	4	20	663	129	519	15	1
Copperas Cove	33,009	118	1	10	23	84	955	312	636	7	20
Corinth	20,971	34	0	0	3	31	297	73	213	11	1
Corpus Christi	312,565	2,057	16	184	375	1,482	14,061	2,452	11,166	443	39
Corrigan	1,633	7	0	0	3	4	41	13	24	4	0
Corsicana	24,284	157	0	25	33	99	1,258	342	875	41	1
Crandall	2,957	2	0	1	0	1	18	9	6	3	0
Crane	3,410	8	0	1	0	7	18	7	11	0	0
Crockett	6,975	20	0	0	1	19	180	41	132	7	0
Crosbyton	1,776	2	0	1	1	0	26	15	9	2	0
Crowell	965	0	0	0	0	0	0	0	0	0	0

Table 8. Offenses Known to Law Enforcement, by Selected State and City, 2012— continued

(Number)

State/city	Population	Violent crime	Murder and nonnegligent manslaughter	Forcible rape	Robbery	Aggravated assault	Property crime	Burglary	Larceny-theft	Motor vehicle theft	Arson[1]
Crowley	13,328	17	0	5	4	8	297	49	237	11	0
Crystal City	7,355	30	1	0	1	28	91	26	60	5	0
Cuero	7,001	77	0	6	4	67	234	52	173	9	0
Cumby	794	0	0	0	0	0	25	10	13	2	0
Daingerfield	2,579	16	0	1	2	13	87	30	55	2	1
Dalhart	8,124	43	1	6	1	35	238	71	157	10	1
Dallas	1,241,549	8,380	154	486	4,093	3,647	54,300	16,090	31,148	7,062	581
Dalworthington Gar-den	2,345	0	0	0	0	0	19	3	16	0	0
Danbury	1,780	2	0	2	0	0	6	0	6	0	0
Dayton	7,416	20	0	7	5	8	173	45	116	12	0
Decatur	6,206	10	0	1	1	8	214	19	186	9	0
Deer Park	33,196	46	0	13	14	19	874	117	720	37	2
De Kalb	1,708	10	0	0	3	7	54	12	39	3	0
De Leon	2,266	6	0	1	0	5	27	6	19	2	0
Del Rio	36,302	61	1	0	10	50	731	157	561	13	8
Denison	23,125	94	1	10	15	68	1,081	251	767	63	1
Denton	118,942	369	1	86	82	200	3,262	632	2,473	157	27
Denver City	4,617	4	0	2	2	0	95	37	56	2	0
Desoto	50,795	132	1	11	43	77	1,782	622	1,042	118	3
Devine	4,452	7	1	0	0	6	71	10	59	2	0
Diboll	4,896	11	0	4	4	3	110	30	75	5	1
Dickinson	19,251	49	0	6	15	28	600	131	430	39	0
Dilley	3,988	4	0	0	3	1	106	54	51	1	2
Dimmitt	4,489	6	0	0	1	5	159	48	106	5	0
Donna	16,518	139	0	4	18	117	975	240	690	45	5
Double Oak	3,014	0	0	0	0	0	13	0	12	1	0
Dublin	3,746	11	0	1	0	10	141	52	87	2	1
Dumas	14,946	33	0	4	1	28	391	67	310	14	4
Duncanville	39,899	119	0	7	63	49	1,363	344	863	156	4
Eagle Lake	3,684	4	0	1	0	3	44	27	17	0	0
Eagle Pass	27,208	53	0	0	3	50	924	238	665	21	0
Early	2,810	13	1	2	1	9	87	16	71	0	0
Eastland	4,029	13	0	0	4	9	134	38	86	10	0
East Mountain	815	3	1	1	0	1	22	14	6	2	0
Edcouch	3,305	22	0	0	1	21	73	28	41	4	4
Edgewood	1,467	1	0	0	0	1	2	1	1	0	0
Edinburg	80,332	357	1	29	50	277	4,732	857	3,666	209	10
Edna	5,561	10	0	0	0	10	141	25	111	5	0
El Campo	11,786	37	1	2	5	29	319	73	235	11	2
Electra	2,814	3	0	0	0	3	52	23	25	4	0
Elgin	8,386	21	0	4	3	14	232	51	177	4	1
El Paso	675,536	2,859	23	184	471	2,181	16,411	1,826	13,425	1,160	94
Elsa	5,918	23	0	1	2	20	372	130	233	9	2
Ennis	19,184	62	2	2	23	35	865	136	696	33	3
Euless	53,228	95	0	10	38	47	1,588	324	1,123	141	2
Everman	6,342	34	0	2	12	20	196	63	119	14	1
Fairfield	2,974	5	0	0	3	2	35	12	23	0	0
Fair Oaks Ranch	6,254	1	0	0	0	1	44	30	13	1	0
Falfurrias	5,055	11	1	2	0	8	103	31	72	0	4
Farmers Branch	29,637	35	1	2	13	19	1,124	169	864	91	6
Farmersville	3,478	20	0	5	1	14	87	17	65	5	1
Farwell	1,393	1	0	0	0	1	7	2	4	1	0
Ferris	2,524	10	0	1	0	9	54	13	40	1	0
Flatonia	1,415	1	0	0	0	1	16	9	7	0	0
Florence	1,209	0	0	0	0	0	8	4	4	0	0
Floresville	6,672	9	0	2	2	5	240	30	202	8	0
Flower Mound	68,023	21	0	0	5	16	563	107	439	17	2
Floydada	3,058	13	0	2	1	10	55	15	37	3	2
Forest Hill	12,825	64	2	3	20	39	507	156	311	40	0
Forney[7]	15,174	21	0	5	5	11			237	21	1
Fort Stockton	8,530	47	1	4	2	40	278	60	216	2	1
Fort Worth	770,101	4,524	44	391	1,280	2,809	32,514	8,442	21,648	2,424	118
Frankston	1,243	3	0	1	0	2	45	17	27	1	0

Table 8. Offenses Known to Law Enforcement, by Selected State and City, 2012— continued

(Number)

State/city	Population	Violent crime	Murder and nonnegligent manslaughter	Forcible rape	Robbery	Aggravated assault	Property crime	Burglary	Larceny-theft	Motor vehicle theft	Arson[1]
Fredericksburg	10,802	7	0	0	2	5	224	19	192	13	0
Freeport	12,501	36	1	6	7	22	408	127	262	19	0
Freer	2,832	36	1	0	3	32	74	17	49	8	1
Friendswood	36,965	15	0	4	4	7	353	66	274	13	0
Friona	4,211	4	0	1	1	2	19	8	9	2	0
Frisco	123,205	98	0	8	24	66	2,527	440	2,033	54	4
Gainesville	16,223	89	1	7	13	68	971	256	675	40	5
Galveston	49,170	296	2	37	118	139	2,469	517	1,792	160	12
Ganado	2,028	0	0	0	0	0	0	0	0	0	0
Garden Ridge	3,413	0	0	0	0	0	38	12	25	1	0
Garland	234,984	540	7	47	236	250	8,675	2,218	5,866	591	51
Gatesville	16,224	17	0	3	2	12	183	46	132	5	0
Georgetown	50,304	66	0	14	5	47	920	147	755	18	8
Gilmer	5,030	30	0	2	7	21	198	27	164	7	0
Gladewater	6,612	39	0	7	7	25	280	68	201	11	1
Glenn Heights	11,683	49	0	4	5	40	292	97	176	19	1
Godley	1,036	2	0	0	0	2	37	10	25	2	0
Gonzales	7,381	77	2	9	3	63	300	72	219	9	1
Gorman	1,102	2	0	0	1	1	7	4	3	0	1
Graham	9,005	21	0	7	1	13	315	73	235	7	0
Granbury	8,170	19	0	3	1	15	572	48	514	10	2
Grand Prairie	181,782	499	1	50	160	288	5,246	1,298	3,316	632	33
Grand Saline	3,195	1	0	0	0	1	82	19	61	2	0
Granger	1,501	0	0	0	0	0	20	5	15	0	0
Granite Shoals	5,027	10	0	0	1	9	47	13	27	7	0
Grapeland	1,494	4	0	0	0	4	28	17	11	0	0
Grapevine	48,095	71	1	13	13	44	1,338	164	1,100	74	4
Greenville	26,061	166	0	11	40	115	1,208	249	885	74	8
Gregory	1,934	8	0	0	1	7	37	13	22	2	0
Groesbeck	4,431	8	0	4	1	3	42	21	18	3	1
Groves	16,423	73	1	7	8	57	538	124	399	15	0
Gruver	1,207	2	0	0	0	2	19	8	11	0	0
Gun Barrel City	5,777	21	0	0	2	19	299	81	201	17	0
Hale Center	2,301	5	1	1	0	3	22	8	12	2	0
Hallettsville	2,610	12	0	0	0	12	86	12	71	3	0
Hallsville	3,656	6	0	1	1	4	43	24	18	1	0
Haltom City	44,024	106	0	7	27	72	1,454	446	881	127	5
Hamlin	2,148	7	0	0	1	6	47	8	39	0	0
Harker Heights	27,542	123	0	13	20	90	887	293	569	25	2
Harlingen	67,112	271	4	23	62	182	3,272	606	2,555	111	20
Haskell	3,419	8	0	0	0	8	60	21	37	2	0
Hawk Cove	493	1	0	0	0	1	11	6	5	0	0
Hawkins	1,303	5	0	0	0	5	48	14	32	2	0
Hawley	639	1	0	1	0	0	9	6	2	1	0
Hearne	4,558	36	0	0	4	32	95	39	53	3	1
Hedwig Village	2,652	7	0	0	6	1	189	15	161	13	1
Helotes	7,636	4	1	1	1	1	122	15	104	3	0
Hemphill	1,206	0	0	0	0	0	42	7	33	2	0
Hempstead	5,968	18	0	0	4	14	171	48	112	11	2
Hereford	15,779	32	0	1	6	25	290	62	212	16	5
Hewitt	13,973	11	0	0	1	10	146	38	97	11	0
Hickory Creek	3,414	5	0	1	4	0	82	4	74	4	0
Hidalgo	11,706	12	0	0	3	9	194	38	139	17	3
Highland Park	8,871	3	0	0	2	1	248	17	224	7	2
Highland Village	15,836	6	0	0	3	3	178	7	169	2	0
Hill Country Village	1,024	2	0	1	1	0	52	7	41	4	0
Hillsboro	8,653	28	0	3	8	17	297	55	237	5	1
Hitchcock	7,174	22	1	1	6	14	215	71	133	11	1
Holliday	1,743	4	0	0	0	4	15	5	9	1	0
Hollywood Park	3,185	1	0	0	1	0	156	26	123	7	0
Hondo	8,992	34	0	5	0	29	238	28	200	10	1
Hooks	2,819	1	0	0	0	1	29	11	18	0	0
Horizon City	17,418	28	0	0	3	25	198	53	132	13	6
Horseshoe Bay	3,459	3	0	0	0	3	54	10	38	6	0

Table 8. Offenses Known to Law Enforcement, by Selected State and City, 2012— continued

(Number)

State/city	Population	Violent crime	Murder and nonnegligent manslaughter	Forcible rape	Robbery	Aggravated assault	Property crime	Burglary	Larceny-theft	Motor vehicle theft	Arson[1]
Houston	2,177,273	21,610	217	665	9,385	11,343	107,678	26,630	67,978	13,070	754
Howe	2,652	4	0	0	0	4	16	4	12	0	0
Hubbard	1,455	0	0	1	1	1	22	10	11	1	0
Hudson	4,849	18	0	1	0	17	84	27	55	2	0
Hudson Oaks	1,702	2	0	0	0	2	101	8	91	2	0
Hughes Springs	1,774	10	0	0	0	10	9	2	7	0	0
Humble[7]	15,684	106	1	25	51	29			1,301	104	1
Huntington	2,168	11	1	7	0	3	37	14	19	4	0
Huntsville	39,243	202	1	28	13	160	1,038	263	740	35	2
Hurst	38,756	217	0	12	33	172	1,899	266	1,581	52	5
Hutchins	5,484	6	0	0	1	5	202	36	125	41	0
Hutto	15,635	21	0	4	1	16	196	47	145	4	0
Idalou	2,326	4	0	0	0	4	36	9	25	2	0
Ingleside	9,516	34	1	14	2	17	208	60	142	6	6
Ingram	1,836	5	0	2	1	2	54	15	37	2	1
Iowa Park	6,407	19	0	2	0	17	93	18	68	7	2
Irving	224,007	507	3	27	135	342	6,307	1,277	4,466	564	18
Italy	1,930	10	0	1	0	9	34	5	28	1	1
Itasca	1,684	8	0	1	1	6	33	17	16	0	0
Jacinto City	10,941	29	0	1	15	13	436	126	255	55	0
Jacksboro	4,574	23	0	6	0	17	67	17	47	3	1
Jacksonville	14,856	159	1	19	22	117	707	200	480	27	4
Jamaica Beach	1,013	0	0	0	0	0	23	11	10	2	0
Jarrell	1,048	2	0	0	0	2	16	0	15	1	0
Jasper	7,830	65	0	10	4	51	411	54	350	7	1
Jefferson	2,132	16	0	2	2	12	53	19	33	1	0
Jersey Village	7,903	26	0	0	11	15	262	58	168	36	0
Johnson City	1,698	0	0	0	0	0	12	2	10	0	0
Jones Creek	2,095	0	0	0	0	0	7	2	4	1	0
Jonestown	1,935	7	0	0	2	5	51	18	33	0	0
Joshua	6,072	9	0	3	0	6	123	51	66	6	2
Jourdanton	3,988	4	0	0	1	3	18	11	7	0	0
Junction	2,627	3	0	0	0	3	49	9	39	1	0
Karnes City	3,114	9	1	1	1	6	65	6	54	5	1
Katy	14,642	30	0	1	8	21	663	67	562	34	2
Kaufman	6,934	17	0	0	4	13	109	28	73	8	0
Keene	6,259	6	0	0	0	6	134	38	91	5	0
Keller	41,137	15	0	2	4	9	388	72	303	13	0
Kemah	1,827	7	0	1	3	3	197	38	157	2	0
Kenedy	3,380	15	1	0	0	14	121	21	99	1	0
Kennedale	7,020	17	0	1	6	10	222	67	140	15	0
Kerens	1,608	7	0	1	1	5	25	9	16	0	0
Kermit	5,849	29	0	0	1	28	38	12	22	4	0
Kerrville	22,759	39	1	2	3	33	596	81	496	19	0
Kilgore	13,306	63	0	6	9	48	692	102	547	43	13
Killeen	131,965	851	12	82	236	521	4,986	1,498	3,296	192	36
Kingsville	26,716	142	0	5	17	120	1,018	312	690	16	3
Kirby	8,322	25	0	0	4	21	203	65	110	28	1
Kountze	2,179	8	0	0	1	7	42	6	34	2	0
Kress	720	0	0	0	0	0	11	7	4	0	0
Krugerville	1,745	1	0	1	0	0	19	5	13	1	0
Kyle	29,732	107	1	15	6	85	484	103	352	29	1
Lacy-Lakeview	6,692	43	0	11	4	28	233	72	149	12	2
La Feria	7,516	11	0	2	2	7	318	54	263	1	2
Lago Vista	6,369	11	0	4	1	6	63	9	53	1	1
La Grange	4,745	5	0	0	1	4	51	12	37	2	0
La Grulla	1,667	5	0	0	0	5	10	6	3	1	0
Laguna Vista	3,222	3	0	0	0	3	75	35	39	1	0
La Joya	4,166	5	0	0	1	4	24	5	19	0	1
Lake Dallas	7,473	9	0	0	1	8	164	21	137	6	1
Lake Jackson	27,862	24	0	4	9	11	575	88	474	13	4
Lakeside	1,357	1	0	0	0	1	17	5	12	0	0
Lakeview, Harris County	6,481	14	0	1	2	11	72	14	51	7	1

Table 8. Offenses Known to Law Enforcement, by Selected State and City, 2012— continued

(Number)

State/city	Population	Violent crime	Murder and nonnegligent manslaughter	Forcible rape	Robbery	Aggravated assault	Property crime	Burglary	Larceny-theft	Motor vehicle theft	Arson[1]
Lakeway	12,007	23	0	0	0	23	181	24	151	6	0
Lake Worth	4,755	21	0	0	7	14	588	140	430	18	0
La Marque	14,953	75	1	11	23	40	721	188	491	42	9
Lamesa	9,497	25	0	11	1	13	266	72	174	20	0
Lampasas	6,850	30	0	11	0	19	253	50	201	2	5
La Porte	35,054	61	1	25	8	27	604	127	439	38	8
Laredo	245,558	1,036	8	81	183	764	10,685	1,718	8,586	381	86
La Vernia	1,071	3	0	0	0	3	50	5	44	1	0
La Villa	2,023	2	0	0	2	0	10	5	4	1	0
Lavon	2,337	5	0	0	0	5	12	3	9	0	0
League City	86,127	79	0	16	28	35	1,734	299	1,366	69	0
Leander	28,244	41	0	2	3	36	352	53	291	8	2
Leon Valley	10,558	28	0	1	9	18	810	94	664	52	0
Levelland	13,719	86	1	11	8	66	579	186	385	8	2
Lexington	1,200	12	0	0	0	12	59	23	31	5	0
Liberty	8,282	90	0	4	8	78	572	88	451	33	0
Linden	2,004	3	0	0	0	3	41	11	30	0	0
Little Elm	27,246	25	0	2	8	15	267	55	205	7	1
Littlefield	6,560	27	1	0	3	23	255	84	165	6	2
Live Oak	13,657	27	0	1	6	20	686	77	568	41	0
Llano	3,261	0	0	0	0	0	82	25	57	0	0
Lockhart	13,013	61	0	9	8	44	402	101	281	20	0
Lockney	1,854	6	0	0	0	6	33	16	15	2	2
Lometa	879	1	0	0	0	1	14	5	9	0	0
Lone Star	1,594	5	0	0	1	4	58	23	35	0	0
Longview	82,554	463	7	28	131	297	4,212	950	2,946	316	5
Lorena	1,743	7	0	1	0	6	44	9	34	1	0
Lorenzo	1,171	0	0	0	0	0	13	6	6	1	0
Los Fresnos	5,737	13	0	2	1	10	158	21	134	3	1
Lubbock	237,241	1,962	11	104	325	1,522	12,273	3,099	8,429	745	46
Lufkin	35,956	221	2	12	43	164	2,231	456	1,711	64	9
Luling	5,549	40	0	4	4	32	142	32	106	4	2
Lumberton	12,258	14	0	3	2	9	227	41	176	10	1
Lyford	2,643	6	0	0	0	6	26	13	10	3	0
Lytle	2,562	12	0	0	2	10	126	12	112	2	0
Madisonville	4,494	15	0	1	4	10	129	33	87	9	0
Magnolia	1,464	12	0	0	3	9	34	16	18	0	0
Malakoff	2,367	4	0	3	0	1	30	8	22	0	0
Manor	5,313	22	0	2	4	16	145	40	103	2	1
Mansfield	58,490	74	2	23	22	27	916	169	700	47	0
Manvel	5,375	4	0	0	1	3	105	51	47	7	3
Marble Falls	6,222	25	0	8	3	14	273	35	228	10	0
Marlin	6,082	16	0	4	3	9	83	31	50	2	0
Marshall	24,109	146	2	10	13	121	934	299	587	48	7
Martindale	1,143	2	0	0	0	2	10	3	6	1	0
Mathis	5,010	34	0	3	0	31	80	25	49	6	0
McAllen	135,745	166	1	3	56	106	5,465	503	4,751	211	13
McGregor	5,142	12	1	0	4	7	82	29	53	0	0
McKinney	138,105	229	0	54	58	117	2,786	492	2,190	104	26
Meadows Place	4,904	4	0	0	4	0	145	43	94	8	0
Melissa	4,936	1	0	0	1	0	44	12	32	0	0
Memorial Villages	11,540	3	0	0	2	1	94	16	75	3	0
Memphis	2,341	5	0	0	0	5	46	16	25	5	0
Mercedes	16,417	108	0	10	17	81	879	168	672	39	7
Meridian	1,523	0	0	0	0	0	5	3	2	0	0
Merkel	2,653	7	0	1	0	6	44	17	26	1	1
Mesquite	144,811	442	2	14	183	243	6,285	1,568	4,030	687	19
Mexia	7,652	43	2	1	6	34	309	84	206	19	2
Midland	115,637	398	4	21	52	321	3,008	559	2,313	136	6
Midlothian	18,693	17	0	3	1	13	307	54	246	7	2
Milford	753	1	0	0	0	1	4	1	3	0	0
Mineola	4,590	8	0	0	1	7	121	19	100	2	3
Mineral Wells	17,045	60	1	5	11	43	978	173	770	35	4
Mission	80,557	104	3	6	46	49	2,370	423	1,788	159	18

Table 8. Offenses Known to Law Enforcement, by Selected State and City, 2012— continued

(Number)

State/city	Population	Violent crime	Murder and nonnegligent manslaughter	Forcible rape	Robbery	Aggravated assault	Property crime	Burglary	Larceny-theft	Motor vehicle theft	Arson[1]
Missouri City	70,819	86	0	8	34	44	879	219	613	47	2
Monahans	7,095	21	0	1	1	19	190	40	146	4	0
Mont Belvieu	3,942	16	0	5	3	8	179	21	131	27	0
Montgomery	653	1	0	1	0	0	22	2	20	0	0
Morgans Point Resort	4,302	6	0	2	0	4	55	10	45	0	0
Moulton	902	5	0	0	0	5	20	2	18	0	0
Mount Pleasant	15,941	32	0	0	3	29	637	149	458	30	3
Muleshoe	5,295	8	1	1	1	5	128	43	80	5	0
Munday	1,333	3	0	0	0	3	18	3	14	1	0
Murphy	18,662	5	0	1	0	4	127	16	110	1	0
Mustang Ridge	900	0	0	0	0	0	27	16	9	2	0
Nacogdoches	33,905	133	1	10	27	95	1,204	280	886	38	2
Naples	1,394	10	0	0	0	10	36	10	26	0	1
Nash	3,012	15	0	1	1	13	79	29	50	0	0
Nassau Bay	4,151	6	0	2	1	3	119	23	89	7	0
Navasota	7,312	70	0	4	6	60	241	60	166	15	0
Nederland	17,850	61	2	2	4	53	529	115	372	42	0
Needville	2,970	8	0	3	0	5	27	6	20	1	0
New Boston	4,630	29	0	1	2	26	229	42	173	14	0
New Braunfels	60,482	115	1	19	27	68	2,110	300	1,718	92	4
New Deal	821	0	0	0	0	0	0	0	0	0	0
Nixon	2,433	5	0	0	0	5	44	10	31	3	0
Nocona	3,077	3	0	2	0	1	39	12	20	7	0
Nolanville	4,394	22	0	2	0	20	78	18	60	0	0
Northlake	1,815	1	0	0	0	1	25	8	17	0	0
North Richland Hills	65,750	170	1	18	23	128	1,572	301	1,195	76	2
Oak Ridge	142	0	0	0	0	0	1	1	0	0	0
Oak Ridge North	3,203	8	0	0	5	3	99	13	76	10	0
Odessa	103,635	1,103	5	43	141	914	3,717	770	2,565	382	23
O'Donnell	838	0	0	0	0	0	1	1	0	0	1
Olmos Park	2,327	0	0	0	0	0	104	18	86	0	0
Olney	3,322	2	0	1	0	1	67	28	34	5	1
Olton	2,279	5	0	0	0	5	15	7	5	3	0
Omaha	1,039	0	0	0	0	0	18	9	9	0	0
Onalaska	1,784	1	0	0	0	1	38	10	27	1	0
Orange	19,025	112	0	2	31	79	587	256	290	41	3
Orange Grove	1,356	0	0	0	0	0	10	5	3	2	0
Overton	2,616	12	0	4	0	8	43	13	28	2	1
Ovilla	3,620	10	0	1	0	9	30	6	23	1	1
Oyster Creek	1,153	11	0	0	1	10	49	14	31	4	0
Paducah	1,199	0	0	0	0	0	4	3	1	0	0
Palacios	4,804	9	0	1	5	3	159	51	99	9	0
Palestine	18,936	162	2	18	21	121	878	211	616	51	4
Palmer	2,074	1	0	0	0	1	34	14	20	0	1
Palmhurst	2,725	3	0	0	0	3	227	11	214	2	1
Palm Valley	1,350	1	0	0	0	1	68	24	44	0	0
Palmview	5,716	6	0	0	4	2	215	38	167	10	0
Pampa	18,452	110	0	1	6	103	794	226	541	27	4
Panhandle	2,520	1	0	1	0	0	10	5	1	4	0
Pantego	2,486	6	0	1	2	3	136	15	112	9	0
Paris	25,693	155	3	7	35	110	1,328	295	1,001	32	0
Parker	4,017	1	0	0	0	1	39	9	30	0	0
Pasadena	154,562	622	8	52	147	415	5,610	999	4,087	524	39
Pearland	94,702	123	1	18	28	76	1,753	277	1,393	83	8
Pearsall	9,378	13	0	1	1	11	203	70	132	1	1
Pecos	8,891	15	2	0	3	10	198	26	160	12	3
Penitas	4,605	23	0	0	0	23	115	7	93	15	0
Perryton	9,201	25	0	0	0	25	104	24	72	8	1
Pflugerville	49,483	61	1	9	6	45	802	140	637	25	3
Pharr	73,599	270	0	14	44	212	2,324	552	1,628	144	5
Pilot Point	4,053	6	0	0	1	5	52	14	37	1	0
Pinehurst	2,142	13	0	1	3	9	53	11	41	1	0
Pittsburg	4,567	26	0	3	2	21	187	46	138	3	1
Plainview	22,678	61	0	5	10	46	906	181	709	16	5

Table 8. Offenses Known to Law Enforcement, by Selected State and City, 2012— continued

(Number)

State/city	Population	Violent crime	Murder and nonnegligent manslaughter	Forcible rape	Robbery	Aggravated assault	Property crime	Burglary	Larceny-theft	Motor vehicle theft	Arson[1]
Plano	273,816	358	1	55	110	192	6,453	1,095	5,043	315	7
Pleasanton	9,206	22	0	3	2	17	528	108	393	27	1
Ponder	1,468	0	0	0	0	0	16	1	14	1	0
Port Aransas	3,565	26	1	1	3	21	356	45	289	22	1
Port Arthur	54,745	344	4	19	121	200	2,406	854	1,428	124	45
Port Isabel	5,187	17	0	1	4	12	380	96	280	4	0
Portland	15,306	15	1	4	6	4	494	56	424	14	1
Port Neches	13,266	33	0	2	2	29	267	81	176	10	3
Poteet	3,359	13	1	0	3	9	119	35	78	6	0
Poth	1,976	6	0	0	0	6	26	3	21	2	0
Pottsboro	2,202	1	0	0	0	1	29	11	17	1	0
Premont	2,725	8	0	0	1	7	39	19	19	1	1
Presidio	4,460	1	0	0	0	1	17	2	13	2	0
Primera	4,189	12	0	1	0	11	72	30	37	5	0
Princeton	7,175	19	0	4	2	13	103	21	79	3	0
Progreso	5,756	9	0	0	2	7	53	13	36	4	3
Prosper	10,037	10	0	0	1	9	196	95	98	3	0
Queen City	1,494	6	0	0	0	6	53	23	25	5	0
Quitman	1,845	1	0	1	0	0	26	18	7	1	0
Ralls	1,984	2	0	0	0	2	5	4	1	0	0
Rancho Viejo	2,523	0	0	0	0	0	23	13	10	0	0
Ranger	2,510	14	0	2	1	11	50	18	30	2	0
Ransom Canyon	1,134	0	0	0	0	0	7	5	2	0	0
Raymondville	11,428	78	0	5	3	70	398	113	281	4	7
Red Oak	11,160	11	0	0	3	8	283	61	205	17	3
Refugio	2,900	8	0	1	2	5	62	15	45	2	0
Reno	3,236	2	1	0	1	0	51	12	38	1	0
Richardson	103,266	171	2	27	80	62	3,004	698	2,175	131	4
Richland Hills	8,095	11	0	0	4	7	255	58	173	24	0
Richmond	12,248	45	1	5	7	32	214	71	129	14	1
Richwood	3,642	4	0	1	0	3	56	22	27	7	0
Riesel	1,039	0	0	0	0	0	5	0	3	2	0
Rio Grande City	14,175	24	0	0	6	18	451	129	294	28	2
Rio Hondo	2,480	2	0	0	0	2	46	6	38	2	0
River Oaks	7,711	7	0	0	2	5	150	45	101	4	0
Roanoke	6,272	7	0	0	2	5	162	23	131	8	0
Robinson	10,840	9	1	1	2	5	191	24	159	8	1
Robstown	11,764	21	0	1	8	12	425	119	289	17	1
Rockdale	5,655	8	1	0	1	6	165	40	121	4	0
Rockport	8,978	33	0	6	3	24	515	125	375	15	1
Rockwall	39,613	42	1	2	4	35	858	127	686	45	0
Rollingwood	1,489	0	0	0	0	0	16	8	6	2	0
Roma	10,034	17	0	4	0	13	151	55	82	14	2
Roman Forest	1,617	3	0	1	0	2	26	1	23	2	1
Roscoe	1,348	0	0	0	0	0	7	3	4	0	0
Rosebud	1,440	8	0	0	1	7	16	5	11	0	0
Rose City	515	3	0	0	0	3	22	7	12	3	0
Rosenberg	32,230	81	0	15	19	47	638	143	468	27	3
Round Rock	106,232	141	0	32	45	64	2,636	336	2,222	78	6
Rowlett	58,324	71	0	17	9	45	1,007	221	742	44	2
Royse City	9,834	6	0	2	0	4	138	32	101	5	2
Runaway Bay	1,321	1	0	0	0	1	14	4	10	0	0
Rusk	5,661	20	0	4	0	16	92	26	64	2	0
Sabinal	1,729	0	0	0	0	0	44	6	38	0	0
Sachse	21,172	23	1	8	2	12	198	36	152	10	1
Saginaw	20,561	35	0	3	8	24	510	80	399	31	1
Salado	2,193	2	0	0	1	1	35	6	29	0	1
San Antonio	1,380,123	6,943	89	549	1,864	4,441	82,668	15,668	60,633	6,367	245
San Augustine	2,138	5	0	0	1	4	13	1	11	1	0
San Benito	25,099	71	1	0	19	51	1,328	363	935	30	8
San Diego	4,528	11	0	0	1	10	78	35	40	3	2
Sanger	7,275	12	0	2	0	10	183	52	118	13	0
San Juan	35,394	201	2	31	16	152	1,224	219	938	67	2
San Marcos	47,384	164	1	27	28	108	1,557	253	1,197	107	4

Table 8. Offenses Known to Law Enforcement, by Selected State and City, 2012— continued

(Number)

State/city	Population	Violent crime	Murder and nonnegligent manslaughter	Forcible rape	Robbery	Aggravated assault	Property crime	Burglary	Larceny-theft	Motor vehicle theft	Arson[1]
San Saba	3,173	6	0	0	0	6	47	9	38	0	1
Sansom Park Village	4,861	5	0	1	0	4	116	59	43	14	0
Santa Anna	1,098	3	0	0	0	3	17	7	10	0	0
Santa Fe	12,597	22	1	3	3	15	243	84	148	11	0
Santa Rosa	2,972	3	0	0	1	2	70	12	56	2	1
Schertz	32,964	64	0	8	4	52	642	100	504	38	4
Schulenburg	2,915	14	0	1	1	12	52	11	39	2	0
Seabrook	12,395	8	0	0	5	3	207	41	150	16	1
Seagoville	15,320	15	2	0	6	7	635	114	435	86	1
Seagraves	2,519	4	0	1	1	2	29	15	14	0	0
Sealy	6,161	17	1	0	3	13	211	53	149	9	1
Seguin	26,332	60	1	7	12	40	1,146	205	916	25	0
Selma	5,774	13	0	4	2	7	253	28	207	18	1
Seminole	6,703	9	0	2	0	7	87	14	69	4	0
Seven Points	1,493	7	0	0	3	4	101	18	79	4	0
Seymour	2,792	6	0	0	0	6	47	10	35	2	1
Shallowater	2,568	0	0	0	0	0	14	3	9	2	0
Shamrock	1,958	0	0	0	0	0	14	4	10	0	1
Shavano Park	3,156	0	0	0	0	0	94	19	72	3	0
Shenandoah	2,242	8	0	0	6	2	182	16	161	5	0
Sherman	39,269	139	2	3	28	106	1,542	372	1,077	93	4
Silsbee	6,783	12	0	0	6	6	199	33	163	3	0
Sinton	5,742	36	0	1	0	35	182	51	124	7	0
Slaton	6,328	14	1	6	1	6	110	51	54	5	0
Smithville	3,924	4	0	1	1	2	50	9	36	5	0
Snyder	11,368	51	1	7	4	39	313	90	213	10	1
Socorro	33,326	55	0	4	6	45	445	79	336	30	2
Somerset	1,696	2	0	0	0	2	36	11	24	1	0
Somerville	1,403	5	0	2	0	3	35	13	20	2	0
Sonora	2,982	3	0	0	1	2	27	2	21	4	0
Sour Lake	1,860	3	0	0	0	3	25	8	15	2	1
South Houston	17,614	90	1	9	30	50	848	222	488	138	0
Southlake	27,596	10	1	0	5	4	485	73	409	3	5
South Padre Island	2,914	51	0	14	4	33	658	52	591	15	0
Southside Place	1,780	1	0	0	1	0	14	5	9	0	0
Spearman	3,396	17	0	0	3	14	50	10	36	4	1
Splendora	1,696	9	0	1	2	6	52	10	39	3	0
Springtown	2,735	22	0	1	2	19	86	25	57	4	0
Spring Valley	3,853	6	0	1	0	5	128	16	105	7	0
Spur	1,316	2	0	0	0	2	8	6	2	0	0
Stafford	18,623	78	2	3	29	44	697	135	492	70	3
Stagecoach	564	0	0	0	0	0	4	1	3	0	0
Stamford	3,160	14	0	0	1	13	100	33	59	8	1
Stanton	2,599	4	0	1	0	3	14	6	8	0	1
Stephenville	17,511	33	0	7	3	23	620	114	485	21	2
Stratford	2,050	0	0	0	0	0	11	4	6	1	0
Sugar Land	82,924	109	0	4	37	68	1,541	289	1,217	35	3
Sullivan City	4,184	1	0	0	0	1	11	3	8	0	0
Sulphur Springs	15,774	39	0	0	3	36	211	47	149	15	0
Sunray	1,959	0	0	0	0	0	15	7	6	2	0
Sunrise Beach Village	719	0	0	0	0	0	12	2	10	0	0
Sunset Valley	789	8	0	0	6	2	105	3	95	7	0
Surfside Beach	500	3	1	0	0	2	35	18	16	1	0
Sweeny	3,866	8	0	0	1	7	102	21	80	1	2
Sweetwater	11,107	121	0	27	9	85	445	118	309	18	1
Taft	3,090	17	0	6	1	10	74	12	59	3	0
Tahoka	2,702	3	0	1	0	2	46	9	37	0	0
Tatum	1,420	5	0	0	0	5	52	15	37	0	1
Taylor	16,240	23	0	2	10	11	447	91	348	8	1
Teague	3,587	19	0	1	2	16	149	67	77	5	1
Temple7	68,194	202	1	22	74	105			1,433	89	0
Terrell	16,353	64	1	7	15	41	685	168	483	34	4
Terrell Hills	5,073	8	0	0	0	8	93	66	27	0	1
Texarkana	37,048	392	5	16	71	300	2,506	616	1,761	129	10

Table 8. Offenses Known to Law Enforcement, by Selected State and City, 2012— continued

(Number)

State/city	Population	Violent crime	Murder and nonnegligent manslaughter	Forcible rape	Robbery	Aggravated assault	Property crime	Burglary	Larceny-theft	Motor vehicle theft	Arson[1]
Texas City	46,448	148	2	11	51	84	1,700	355	1,278	67	3
The Colony	38,217	38	0	6	9	23	554	115	394	45	10
Thorndale	1,353	1	0	0	0	1	6	3	3	0	0
Thrall	892	4	0	0	0	4	13	6	7	0	0
Three Rivers	1,861	9	0	0	0	9	52	22	22	8	11
Timpson	1,189	9	0	2	2	5	20	6	13	1	0
Tioga	815	0	0	0	0	0	9	5	4	0	0
Tolar	698	0	0	0	0	0	3	3	0	0	0
Tomball	11,143	36	0	10	5	21	463	84	360	19	1
Tom Bean	1,067	2	0	0	0	2	21	11	8	2	0
Tool	2,277	3	0	0	0	3	64	28	35	1	0
Trenton	647	3	0	1	0	2	23	8	12	3	0
Trinity	2,753	6	0	0	1	5	64	20	42	2	0
Trophy Club	8,435	1	0	1	0	0	82	11	71	0	0
Troup	1,930	4	0	1	0	3	63	21	38	4	0
Troy	1,696	7	0	0	0	7	38	11	25	2	0
Tulia	5,010	14	0	0	2	12	61	23	38	0	0
Tye	1,272	3	0	0	1	2	24	7	16	1	0
Tyler	100,040	536	3	45	92	396	4,506	1,025	3,350	131	7
Universal City	19,271	70	0	1	13	56	458	90	326	42	4
University Park	23,842	11	0	2	5	4	433	61	359	13	0
Uvalde	16,065	75	1	7	3	64	648	130	501	17	4
Valley Mills	1,228	2	0	0	0	2	40	11	27	2	1
Valley View	768	0	0	0	0	0	0	0	0	0	0
Van Alstyne	3,104	5	0	0	1	4	71	32	35	4	0
Venus	3,027	2	0	0	0	2	36	19	15	2	0
Vernon	11,060	55	1	14	1	39	324	72	237	15	6
Victoria	64,076	405	5	31	47	322	2,584	594	1,887	103	15
Vidor	10,974	38	1	1	3	33	484	97	340	47	0
Waco	128,595	635	6	63	182	384	5,844	1,550	4,139	155	53
Waelder	1,087	3	0	2	0	1	21	12	9	0	0
Wake Village	5,587	4	2	0	2	0	110	32	75	3	0
Waller	2,410	23	3	1	5	14	132	72	49	11	0
Wallis	1,281	2	0	0	1	1	13	3	9	1	0
Watauga	24,390	46	0	6	11	29	518	110	385	23	0
Waxahachie	30,676	45	0	0	14	31	1,176	173	972	31	6
Weatherford	25,940	35	0	0	8	27	751	126	610	15	4
Webster	10,780	43	0	10	21	12	669	77	553	39	0
Weimar	2,177	2	0	1	0	1	28	5	20	3	0
Weslaco	37,271	410	1	25	60	324	2,814	433	2,288	93	2
West	2,849	0	0	0	0	0	28	6	19	3	0
West Columbia	4,052	16	0	4	1	11	85	27	55	3	0
West Lake Hills	3,230	1	0	1	0	0	93	21	71	1	0
West Orange	3,523	14	0	1	4	9	308	26	277	5	1
Westover Hills	709	0	0	0	0	0	9	4	5	0	0
West Tawakoni	1,608	0	0	0	0	0	21	12	6	3	0
West University Place	15,335	13	0	0	11	2	209	127	73	9	0
Westworth	2,567	5	0	0	1	4	73	27	45	1	0
Wharton	8,971	67	0	6	12	49	490	85	391	14	5
Whitehouse	7,913	8	0	2	1	5	78	22	53	3	0
White Oak	6,642	11	0	8	0	3	126	36	71	19	1
Whitesboro	3,868	6	0	3	1	2	81	14	61	6	1
White Settlement	16,716	30	0	0	16	14	434	123	277	34	0
Whitewright	1,634	6	0	0	0	6	36	15	17	4	0
Whitney	2,137	1	0	0	0	1	94	13	80	1	1
Wichita Falls	105,488	475	5	36	150	284	5,021	1,259	3,532	230	6
Willis	6,079	20	0	1	6	13	182	53	123	6	1
Willow Park	4,093	1	0	1	0	0	33	7	26	0	0
Wills Point	3,588	9	0	0	0	9	46	17	29	0	0
Wilmer	3,805	5	0	0	1	4	102	42	56	4	1
Windcrest	5,575	6	1	0	3	2	392	38	332	22	1
Wink	962	0	0	0	0	0	2	0	2	0	0
Winnsboro	3,494	12	0	1	0	11	50	19	27	4	0
Winters	2,605	15	0	3	0	12	31	19	10	2	0

Table 8. Offenses Known to Law Enforcement, by Selected State and City, 2012— continued

(Number)

State/city	Population	Violent crime	Murder and nonnegligent manslaughter	Forcible rape	Robbery	Aggravated assault	Property crime	Burglary	Larceny-theft	Motor vehicle theft	Arson[1]
Wolfe City	1,440	7	0	1	2	4	28	10	15	3	0
Wolfforth	3,795	4	0	0	0	4	32	11	19	2	0
Woodbranch	1,348	1	0	1	0	0	15	2	12	1	0
Woodville	2,613	0	0	0	0	0	28	7	21	0	0
Woodway	8,587	11	0	5	1	5	134	13	119	2	0
Wortham	1,083	5	0	0	1	4	24	5	16	3	0
Wylie	43,645	28	2	1	3	22	613	100	485	28	1
Yoakum	5,935	9	0	0	1	8	189	74	108	7	2
Yorktown	2,142	7	0	3	0	4	30	11	19	0	0
Utah											
American Fork/Cedar Hills	37,549	34	0	5	6	23	819	117	672	30	2
Big Water	491	2	0	2	0	0	1	0	1	0	0
Blanding	3,440	7	0	0	0	7	52	17	35	0	0
Bluffdale	7,848	5	0	0	1	4	107	30	70	7	1
Bountiful	43,888	37	1	17	2	17	940	143	748	49	0
Brian Head	85	0	0	0	0	0	23	8	14	1	0
Brigham City	18,255	56	0	7	4	45	668	95	554	19	3
Cedar City	29,608	76	1	17	3	55	745	117	600	28	1
Centerfield	1,395	1	0	0	1	0	5	3	2	0	0
Centerville	15,807	5	0	2	0	3	488	58	411	19	1
Clearfield	31,032	51	0	9	6	36	735	92	626	17	1
Clinton	21,064	12	0	3	0	9	320	38	273	9	0
Cottonwood Heights	34,528	42	1	12	12	17	864	159	646	59	3
Draper	43,600	43	1	6	4	32	866	153	677	36	4
East Carbon	1,312	18	0	3	0	15	139	49	83	7	0
Enoch	5,958	23	0	1	0	22	73	27	38	8	0
Fairview	1,273	0	0	0	0	0	12	3	8	1	0
Farmington	18,836	6	0	3	0	3	283	7	257	19	5
Grantsville	9,185	11	0	0	1	10	88	40	31	17	2
Harrisville	5,722	5	0	0	4	1	291	36	248	7	0
Heber	11,954	1	0	1	0	0	75	15	59	1	0
Helper	2,219	8	7	0	1	0	52	11	41	0	1
Hurricane	14,284	21	0	5	1	15	282	29	241	12	2
Kamas	1,899	1	0	0	0	1	23	3	19	1	0
Kanab	4,450	5	0	0	0	5	53	4	44	5	1
Kaysville	28,153	12	0	3	0	9	290	55	222	13	0
La Verkin	4,222	8	0	2	0	6	75	13	62	0	1
Layton	69,420	84	0	33	7	44	1,908	326	1,513	69	9
Lehi	49,375	18	0	4	3	11	653	126	498	29	0
Lindon	10,488	14	0	2	0	12	273	28	236	9	0
Logan	49,672	32	0	1	3	28	1,047	206	805	36	3
Lone Peak	26,123	7	0	2	1	4	201	64	130	7	0
Mapleton	8,309	2	0	1	0	1	93	12	80	1	0
Moab	5,170	12	0	2	0	10	212	25	170	17	1
Monticello	2,008	5	0	1	0	4	31	3	26	2	0
Moroni	1,451	0	0	0	0	0	10	0	10	0	0
Mount Pleasant	3,323	7	0	0	4	3	64	14	48	2	0
Naples	1,811	1	0	1	0	0	52	8	39	5	0
Nephi	5,509	5	0	2	0	3	118	17	97	4	0
North Ogden	17,838	7	0	4	1	2	286	64	211	11	2
North Park	12,496	11	0	8	0	3	275	66	203	6	3
North Salt Lake	16,831	24	0	9	4	11	477	58	383	36	1
Ogden	85,083	353	2	25	96	230	4,001	734	3,051	216	13
Orem	91,953	41	2	11	21	7	2,168	203	1,887	78	0
Park City	7,928	25	0	3	5	17	444	21	409	14	0
Parowan	2,864	4	0	0	1	3	73	21	50	2	0
Payson	19,052	16	2	3	1	10	574	82	477	15	1
Perry	4,600	12	0	5	1	6	102	24	77	1	3
Pleasant Grove	34,900	10	0	1	2	7	516	68	427	21	1
Pleasant View	8,198	7	0	1	0	6	94	17	72	5	0
Price	8,799	23	1	4	0	18	405	70	325	10	3
Provo	116,879	149	0	36	19	94	2,465	301	2,051	113	5
Richfield	7,714	15	0	4	1	10	244	28	208	8	1

Table 8. Offenses Known to Law Enforcement, by Selected State and City, 2012— continued

(Number)

State/city	Population	Violent crime	Murder and nonnegligent manslaughter	Forcible rape	Robbery	Aggravated assault	Property crime	Burglary	Larceny-theft	Motor vehicle theft	Arson[1]
Riverdale	8,658	14	0	4	3	7	458	51	389	18	0
Roosevelt	6,189	9	0	3	0	6	233	37	186	10	1
Roy	37,900	43	1	24	7	11	772	113	636	23	4
Salem	6,692	3	0	0	0	3	96	14	79	3	0
Salina	2,543	3	0	2	0	1	106	16	87	3	1
Salt Lake City	192,465	1,300	8	122	316	854	14,357	1,824	10,827	1,706	39
Sandy	90,405	147	2	24	35	86	2,663	453	2,068	142	2
Santa Clara/Ivins	13,266	3	0	1	0	2	87	38	49	0	0
Santaquin/Genola	10,934	0	0	0	0	0	145	33	110	2	0
Saratoga Springs	18,546	14	0	2	4	8	184	25	156	3	0
Smithfield	9,805	3	0	1	1	1	98	22	70	6	1
South Jordan	52,071	23	0	4	10	9	1,029	173	797	59	0
South Ogden	16,986	13	0	5	2	6	319	99	208	12	1
South Salt Lake	24,340	208	3	51	30	124	1,574	241	1,127	206	2
Spanish Fork	36,141	14	0	7	3	4	485	82	393	10	4
Springdale	550	0	0	0	0	0	29	7	22	0	0
Springville	30,690	35	0	4	7	24	680	66	598	16	1
St. George	75,780	155	0	27	23	105	1,561	307	1,167	87	5
Stockton	636	0	0	0	0	0	2	2	0	0	0
Sunset	5,283	0	0	0	0	0	138	14	119	5	0
Syracuse	25,090	10	0	5	0	5	226	27	195	4	0
Tooele	32,641	96	0	15	17	64	1,396	214	1,112	70	18
Tremonton	7,799	17	0	4	1	12	180	28	144	8	3
Vernal	9,373	43	0	7	3	33	394	62	317	15	3
Washington	19,509	38	1	6	4	27	609	73	513	23	0
West Bountiful	5,429	7	0	1	1	5	163	19	133	11	0
West Jordan	107,103	199	2	24	33	140	2,966	474	2,264	228	9
West Valley	133,725	599	1	90	120	388	5,569	940	3,972	657	19
Willard	1,806	1	0	0	1	0	14	2	12	0	0
Woods Cross	10,066	13	0	7	1	5	242	68	155	19	0
Vermont											
Barre	9,060	22	0	8	2	12	463	83	374	6	1
Barre Town	7,932	7	0	1	1	5	190	33	151	6	0
Bellows Falls	3,129	14	0	1	2	11	91	20	68	3	0
Bennington	15,691	27	0	2	3	22	574	145	405	24	2
Berlin	2,884	9	0	1	1	7	89	0	89	0	0
Bradford	2,802	0	0	0	0	0	17	2	14	1	0
Brandon	3,940	1	0	0	0	1	100	40	58	2	0
Brattleboro	11,970	39	0	2	13	24	421	62	347	12	1
Brighton	1,217	0	0	0	0	0	3	1	2	0	0
Bristol	3,882	2	0	0	0	2	24	7	17	0	0
Canaan	969	0	0	0	0	0	9	3	6	0	0
Castleton	4,692	12	0	0	0	12	77	16	55	6	0
Chester	3,151	3	0	0	0	3	36	18	18	0	1
Colchester	17,153	21	0	2	3	16	609	182	418	9	0
Dover	1,116	1	0	0	0	1	98	23	75	0	0
Essex	19,700	11	0	2	2	7	481	80	389	12	2
Fair Haven	2,716	6	0	1	1	4	108	32	75	1	0
Hardwick	3,001	5	0	0	0	5	76	18	55	3	0
Hartford	9,945	20	2	7	0	11	194	47	140	7	4
Hinesburg	4,422	2	0	0	0	2	38	16	19	3	0
Ludlow	1,962	0	0	0	0	0	36	12	24	0	0
Lyndonville	1,204	0	0	0	0	0	17	10	7	0	0
Manchester	4,368	9	0	1	1	7	81	18	60	3	0
Middlebury	8,477	7	0	2	1	4	99	8	90	1	3
Milton	10,411	11	0	4	1	6	207	75	125	7	1
Morristown	5,273	10	0	0	0	10	83	9	70	4	0
Newport	4,576	20	0	7	0	13	80	20	58	2	1
Northfield	6,217	7	0	3	0	4	91	29	57	5	1
Norwich	3,412	0	0	0	0	0	59	20	37	2	2
Randolph	4,785	2	0	0	0	2	66	21	43	2	1
Richmond	4,105	9	0	0	1	8	44	13	30	1	0
Rutland	16,388	61	0	3	12	46	1,070	208	842	20	2

Table 8. Offenses Known to Law Enforcement, by Selected State and City, 2012— continued

(Number)

State/city	Population	Violent crime	Murder and nonnegligent manslaughter	Forcible rape	Robbery	Aggravated assault	Property crime	Burglary	Larceny-theft	Motor vehicle theft	Arson[1]
Shelburne	7,183	5	0	1	0	4	103	29	72	2	1
South Burlington	18,005	22	1	2	5	14	771	89	679	3	0
Springfield	9,367	32	0	3	4	25	286	62	213	11	2
St. Albans	6,966	31	0	2	8	21	458	65	373	20	0
St. Johnsbury	7,589	8	0	1	2	5	135	36	94	5	0
Stowe	4,353	2	0	1	0	1	131	10	117	4	0
Swanton	6,473	11	0	0	2	9	68	15	49	4	0
Vergennes	2,580	6	0	0	1	5	40	10	28	2	0
Vernon	2,191	5	0	0	0	5	16	2	12	2	0
Williston	8,749	11	0	0	2	9	230	41	179	10	0
Wilmington	1,864	2	0	0	0	2	37	9	25	3	0
Windsor	3,551	1	0	0	1	0	79	28	47	4	1
Winhall	764	0	0	0	0	0	62	4	57	1	0
Winooski	7,307	22	0	2	2	18	153	35	115	3	3
Woodstock	3,045	4	0	1	0	3	55	24	31	0	0
Virginia											
Abingdon	8,273	14	2	1	3	8	270	36	227	7	2
Alexandria	145,892	243	0	9	138	96	2,990	281	2,383	326	8
Altavista	3,500	5	0	0	0	5	79	11	65	3	0
Amherst	2,242	0	0	0	0	0	27	5	21	1	0
Appalachia	1,778	5	0	0	1	4	71	27	44	0	4
Ashland	7,336	26	0	2	4	20	234	12	214	8	1
Bedford	6,249	12	0	3	3	6	205	20	176	9	0
Berryville	4,299	1	0	0	0	1	39	2	35	2	1
Big Stone Gap	5,684	7	0	1	2	4	187	37	145	5	0
Blacksburg	43,070	39	0	12	11	16	475	80	377	18	7
Blackstone	3,656	14	2	0	3	9	97	14	76	7	0
Bloxom	394	0	0	0	0	0	0	0	0	0	0
Bluefield	5,462	12	0	1	0	11	240	22	211	7	0
Bowling Green	1,127	0	0	0	0	0	0	0	0	0	0
Boykins	565	0	0	0	0	0	14	2	12	0	0
Bridgewater	5,722	3	0	1	0	2	87	59	27	1	0
Bristol	17,946	60	2	5	17	36	653	117	505	31	3
Broadway	3,745	1	0	0	0	1	4	0	2	2	0
Brookneal	1,127	0	0	0	0	0	17	1	16	0	0
Burkeville	437	0	0	0	0	0	8	0	8	0	0
Cape Charles	1,019	2	0	2	0	0	7	1	5	1	0
Charlottesville	43,991	198	2	17	50	129	1,502	162	1,246	94	9
Chase City	2,368	4	0	0	2	2	75	10	62	3	0
Chatham	1,272	0	0	0	0	0	14	2	12	0	0
Chesapeake	227,531	839	12	36	202	589	6,292	1,034	4,979	279	27
Chilhowie	1,792	0	0	0	0	0	57	5	50	2	0
Chincoteague	2,989	5	0	1	1	3	61	5	50	6	0
Christiansburg	21,262	30	0	7	4	19	675	87	576	12	3
Clarksville	1,149	2	0	0	0	2	25	7	18	0	0
Clifton Forge	3,909	6	0	1	0	5	94	19	73	2	0
Clintwood	1,414	1	0	0	0	1	35	7	28	0	1
Coeburn	2,168	11	0	3	2	6	78	15	60	3	0
Colonial Beach	3,609	8	1	2	0	5	31	1	28	2	0
Colonial Heights	17,632	40	0	2	9	29	976	57	878	41	7
Covington	6,004	13	1	0	1	11	147	26	118	3	4
Crewe	2,351	7	0	3	2	2	76	20	51	5	0
Culpeper	16,846	45	0	8	13	24	573	34	516	23	0
Damascus	822	7	0	1	0	6	23	1	19	3	0
Danville	43,324	135	3	15	54	63	1,944	422	1,477	45	15
Dayton	1,552	0	0	0	0	0	8	1	7	0	0
Dublin	2,647	2	0	0	0	2	60	8	50	2	0
Dumfries	5,227	4	0	0	1	3	73	9	58	6	0
Edinburg	1,059	0	0	0	0	0	8	4	3	1	0
Elkton	2,767	0	0	0	0	0	43	7	31	5	0
Emporia	5,936	32	0	3	5	24	299	71	213	15	2
Exmore	1,474	6	0	0	3	3	76	18	52	6	0
Fairfax City	22,798	19	0	4	6	9	440	22	396	22	1

Table 8. Offenses Known to Law Enforcement, by Selected State and City, 2012— continued

(Number)

State/city	Population	Violent crime	Murder and nonnegligent manslaughter	Forcible rape	Robbery	Aggravated assault	Property crime	Burglary	Larceny-theft	Motor vehicle theft	Arson[1]
Falls Church	12,892	11	1	1	7	2	211	14	194	3	0
Farmville	8,297	11	0	3	2	6	376	34	332	10	1
Franklin	8,683	35	2	4	11	18	362	40	304	18	1
Fredericksburg	25,974	108	2	1	19	86	1,022	87	914	21	5
Front Royal	14,718	19	0	6	5	8	496	51	425	20	1
Galax	7,060	36	0	10	1	25	285	17	262	6	0
Gate City	2,066	4	0	2	0	2	46	14	31	1	0
Glen Lyn	115	0	0	0	0	0	7	3	3	1	0
Gordonsville	1,534	4	0	0	1	3	15	2	11	2	0
Gretna	1,268	0	0	0	0	0	20	1	16	3	0
Grottoes	2,708	2	0	0	0	2	34	2	30	2	0
Grundy	1,007	0	0	0	0	0	16	0	15	1	0
Halifax	1,317	0	0	0	0	0	9	0	9	0	0
Hampton	137,905	314	9	16	146	143	4,657	758	3,637	262	27
Harrisonburg	50,524	110	1	14	25	70	1,067	152	888	27	6
Haymarket	1,877	1	0	0	0	1	27	1	26	0	0
Haysi	495	0	0	0	0	0	16	7	8	1	1
Herndon	23,966	28	0	5	5	18	367	27	332	8	0
Hillsville	2,704	7	0	1	2	4	88	8	79	1	0
Honaker	1,457	0	0	0	0	0	7	4	3	0	0
Hopewell	22,829	91	2	3	32	54	878	209	615	54	5
Hurt	1,304	1	1	0	0	0	6	1	2	3	0
Independence	946	2	0	0	0	2	12	0	11	1	0
Jonesville	1,026	4	0	0	1	3	21	3	18	0	0
Kenbridge	1,267	1	0	0	0	1	4	0	4	0	0
Kilmarnock	1,491	2	1	0	0	1	37	7	30	0	0
La Crosse	609	0	0	0	0	0	3	0	2	1	0
Lawrenceville	1,439	1	0	0	0	1	30	7	22	1	0
Lebanon	3,465	10	0	1	2	7	147	5	140	2	0
Leesburg	44,889	72	1	11	18	42	974	46	907	21	7
Lexington	7,072	1	0	0	0	1	88	37	51	0	0
Louisa	1,583	2	0	0	1	1	54	9	44	1	1
Luray	4,932	5	0	1	3	1	140	25	114	1	0
Lynchburg	77,347	267	3	34	46	184	2,093	365	1,659	69	13
Manassas	39,733	135	2	8	51	74	900	111	741	48	7
Manassas Park	15,501	21	0	1	1	19	233	20	200	13	0
Marion	6,001	24	0	0	5	19	194	31	156	7	4
Martinsville	13,708	39	1	6	7	25	412	77	315	20	5
Middleburg	709	1	0	0	0	1	9	0	9	0	0
Middletown	1,302	1	0	0	0	1	26	4	22	0	0
Mount Jackson	2,031	1	0	0	0	1	22	7	14	1	0
Narrows	2,033	5	0	1	0	4	20	3	17	0	0
New Market	2,185	1	0	0	0	1	24	5	19	0	0
Newport News	181,591	754	20	50	271	413	5,722	1,029	4,431	262	71
Norfolk	245,303	1,332	34	75	491	732	11,391	2,261	8,403	727	58
Norton	4,099	4	0	0	0	4	215	10	202	3	0
Occoquan	986	0	0	0	0	0	1	0	1	0	0
Onancock	1,284	2	0	2	0	0	16	3	13	0	0
Onley	524	0	0	0	0	0	4	0	4	0	0
Orange	4,831	3	0	1	1	1	131	12	118	1	0
Parksley	854	2	0	1	1	0	13	1	11	1	0
Pearisburg	2,791	2	0	1	0	1	94	4	90	0	1
Pembroke	1,128	1	0	0	0	1	36	6	30	0	0
Pennington Gap	1,857	1	0	0	1	0	73	17	56	0	2
Petersburg	32,682	172	5	7	56	104	1,311	391	820	100	5
Pocahontas	389	3	2	0	0	1	1	1	0	0	0
Poquoson	12,132	10	0	0	0	10	34	3	30	1	4
Portsmouth	96,739	461	11	41	182	227	4,821	1,218	3,392	211	14
Pound	1,051	1	0	0	0	1	16	5	10	1	0
Pulaski	9,116	35	0	3	7	25	347	56	281	10	2
Purcellville	8,132	4	0	1	0	3	59	3	54	2	0
Radford	16,595	78	1	9	9	59	457	102	336	19	2
Rich Creek	776	1	0	1	0	0	1	0	1	0	0
Richlands	5,839	9	0	0	4	5	265	49	212	4	3

Table 8. Offenses Known to Law Enforcement, by Selected State and City, 2012— continued

(Number)

State/city	Population	Violent crime	Murder and nonnegligent manslaughter	Forcible rape	Robbery	Aggravated assault	Property crime	Burglary	Larceny-theft	Motor vehicle theft	Arson[1]
Richmond	207,799	1,348	42	38	633	635	9,103	2,030	6,138	935	50
Roanoke	97,780	542	9	40	141	352	4,771	940	3,583	248	42
Rocky Mount	4,873	14	0	2	0	12	213	17	192	4	0
Rural Retreat	1,498	0	0	0	0	0	8	1	7	0	0
Salem	25,236	8	0	0	5	3	578	75	476	27	0
Saltville	2,089	2	0	0	0	2	66	18	46	2	0
Shenandoah	2,392	3	0	0	0	3	55	17	36	2	0
Smithfield	8,197	14	1	0	4	9	102	8	90	4	1
South Boston	8,191	29	0	1	8	20	432	91	327	14	1
South Hill	4,686	20	0	2	6	12	189	18	158	13	0
Stanley	1,702	1	0	1	0	0	30	5	24	1	0
Staunton	24,031	42	0	8	11	23	527	62	456	9	5
Stephens City	1,881	1	0	1	0	0	38	2	35	1	0
St. Paul	985	4	0	1	0	3	32	3	29	0	0
Strasburg	6,514	8	0	0	1	7	85	5	80	0	1
Tappahannock	2,411	11	0	3	2	6	146	25	120	1	0
Tazewell	4,640	7	0	1	0	6	144	56	86	2	1
Timberville	2,560	0	0	0	0	0	8	1	7	0	0
Victoria	1,739	7	0	0	1	6	16	4	11	1	2
Vienna	16,140	6	0	1	3	2	184	30	149	5	0
Vinton	8,220	36	0	1	2	33	240	23	212	5	0
Virginia Beach	447,588	758	21	58	326	353	11,717	1,573	9,662	482	123
Warrenton	9,842	22	0	3	4	15	190	16	172	2	0
Warsaw	1,524	0	0	0	0	0	17	2	14	1	0
Waverly	2,174	6	0	1	0	5	22	3	18	1	1
Waynesboro	21,546	70	0	11	9	50	744	88	617	39	1
Weber City	1,329	1	0	0	1	0	16	0	16	0	0
West Point	3,352	2	0	1	0	1	53	18	31	4	0
White Stone	352	0	0	0	0	0	3	0	3	0	0
Williamsburg	14,603	20	0	2	8	10	259	26	222	11	0
Winchester	26,880	59	0	9	17	33	1,194	161	1,004	29	5
Windsor	2,662	3	0	0	0	3	61	17	44	0	0
Wise	3,332	9	0	0	1	8	79	8	67	4	0
Woodstock	5,189	9	0	3	1	5	179	19	153	7	1
Wytheville	8,293	15	0	0	5	10	160	7	147	6	0
Washington											
Aberdeen	17,000	59	1	13	18	27	907	221	605	81	2
Airway Heights	6,198	10	0	1	9	0	328	67	236	25	1
Algona	3,104	2	0	0	1	1	75	13	56	6	1
Anacortes	16,097	16	0	1	2	13	577	157	386	34	6
Arlington	18,332	32	2	3	9	18	900	173	653	74	4
Asotin	1,282	2	0	0	0	2	14	3	10	1	0
Auburn	72,218	248	6	23	110	109	3,985	984	2,415	586	18
Bainbridge Island	23,490	12	0	4	0	8	288	54	225	9	2
Battle Ground	18,068	28	0	5	4	19	361	53	277	31	2
Bellevue	126,022	161	2	26	67	66	3,503	685	2,649	169	24
Bellingham	82,665	220	0	29	53	138	3,975	614	3,223	138	5
Bingen	731	0	0	0	0	0	27	5	20	2	0
Black Diamond	4,279	1	0	0	1	0	71	13	47	11	0
Blaine	4,791	7	0	0	1	6	140	23	116	1	1
Bonney Lake	17,751	19	0	1	6	12	529	122	370	37	5
Bothell	34,389	35	1	7	8	19	893	179	654	60	8
Bremerton	39,434	230	1	38	44	147	2,123	444	1,487	192	22
Brewster	2,409	4	0	2	0	2	34	18	14	2	0
Brier	6,225	1	0	0	0	1	97	33	58	6	0
Buckley	4,933	3	0	1	1	1	130	41	81	8	1
Burien	34,310	267	2	44	95	126	2,560	584	1,388	588	4
Burlington	8,557	26	0	7	11	8	919	108	775	36	1
Camas	19,905	12	0	2	1	9	401	90	293	18	6
Carnation	1,841	0	0	0	0	0	40	12	23	5	0
Castle Rock	2,002	4	0	1	1	2	66	12	49	5	1
Centralia	16,593	80	2	12	18	48	796	183	559	54	8
Chehalis	7,371	20	0	4	4	12	433	46	376	11	1

Table 8. Offenses Known to Law Enforcement, by Selected State and City, 2012— continued

(Number)

State/city	Population	Violent crime	Murder and nonnegligent manslaughter	Forcible rape	Robbery	Aggravated assault	Property crime	Burglary	Larceny-theft	Motor vehicle theft	Arson[1]
Cheney	10,747	28	0	4	7	17	340	80	242	18	1
Chewelah	2,632	6	0	0	0	6	89	18	68	3	0
Cle Elum	2,845	3	0	0	1	2	128	30	94	4	2
Clyde Hill	3,077	2	0	0	0	2	27	7	20	0	1
Colfax	2,867	2	0	1	0	1	45	13	30	2	2
College Place	8,975	10	0	3	1	6	212	31	166	15	1
Colville	4,715	1	0	0	0	1	136	11	122	3	0
Connell	5,328	6	0	1	2	3	34	13	19	2	0
Coulee Dam	1,118	4	0	1	1	2	16	6	8	2	0
Coupeville	1,860	2	0	2	0	0	36	18	17	1	0
Covington	18,105	45	1	11	8	25	644	134	469	41	0
Des Moines	30,555	93	0	2	34	57	1,206	244	740	222	6
Dupont	8,379	12	0	0	1	11	66	19	45	2	0
Duvall	6,895	1	0	0	0	1	51	11	38	2	2
East Wenatchee	13,506	18	1	7	4	6	372	74	289	9	1
Eatonville	2,818	5	0	1	0	4	75	20	53	2	0
Edgewood	9,592	13	0	1	1	11	345	144	179	22	0
Edmonds	40,609	57	1	4	20	32	1,004	260	694	50	7
Ellensburg	18,649	30	0	9	4	17	810	121	647	42	4
Elma	3,125	7	0	2	2	3	181	47	126	8	1
Enumclaw	11,195	5	0	3	0	2	307	48	224	35	6
Ephrata	7,919	17	1	3	5	8	386	93	284	9	1
Everett	105,318	481	1	46	182	252	6,416	1,165	4,281	970	29
Everson	2,538	3	0	2	0	1	31	4	26	1	0
Federal Way	91,978	296	3	43	106	144	5,106	944	3,364	798	9
Ferndale	11,677	16	0	3	2	11	409	109	282	18	3
Fife	9,372	54	0	5	11	38	580	135	360	85	0
Fircrest	6,637	7	0	0	2	5	139	48	77	14	1
Forks	3,587	5	1	1	0	3	111	35	68	8	1
Gig Harbor	7,279	18	0	2	1	15	433	83	326	24	6
Goldendale	3,505	12	0	2	1	9	172	37	124	11	0
Grand Coulee	1,054	8	0	1	0	7	80	30	39	11	0
Grandview	11,147	33	1	1	3	28	277	104	137	36	3
Granger	3,330	5	0	0	1	4	85	22	48	15	0
Granite Falls	3,449	19	0	2	0	17	90	18	63	9	0
Hoquiam	8,781	21	2	2	7	10	439	86	330	23	1
Issaquah	31,341	18	0	2	6	10	752	102	612	38	4
Kalama	2,369	4	0	0	0	4	46	10	31	5	1
Kelso	12,051	42	0	6	7	29	707	134	551	22	3
Kenmore	21,075	17	0	3	4	10	357	117	211	29	1
Kennewick	76,971	229	1	33	35	160	2,372	450	1,795	127	19
Kent	122,102	543	2	68	194	279	5,468	1,239	3,365	864	15
Kettle Falls	1,609	3	0	0	0	3	57	8	47	2	0
Kirkland	50,243	92	0	14	24	54	1,654	330	1,237	87	8
La Center	2,880	0	0	0	0	0	44	7	33	4	0
Lacey	43,540	77	4	6	9	58	1,464	236	1,154	74	1
Lake Forest Park	12,975	8	0	2	2	4	292	93	190	9	0
Lake Stevens	28,710	47	0	4	18	25	665	176	418	71	1
Lakewood	59,416	465	1	39	108	317	2,893	715	1,960	218	13
Liberty Lake	7,709	4	0	1	1	2	96	23	68	5	0
Long Beach	1,407	1	0	0	0	1	59	23	34	2	0
Longview	37,032	156	1	26	55	74	2,211	468	1,604	139	37
Lynden	12,223	8	1	1	1	5	177	30	145	2	1
Lynnwood	36,647	74	0	5	36	33	2,180	290	1,703	187	5
Maple Valley	23,366	25	0	9	8	8	358	108	219	31	7
Marysville	61,381	116	2	16	36	62	1,769	398	1,170	201	17
Medina	3,059	0	0	0	0	0	48	12	33	3	0
Mercer Island	23,381	11	0	2	2	7	335	84	245	6	5
Mill Creek	18,661	34	2	2	7	23	341	62	253	26	5
Milton	7,127	11	0	0	4	7	312	74	206	32	2
Monroe	17,665	55	1	2	5	47	471	98	339	34	2
Montesano	4,001	2	0	0	1	1	74	8	64	2	0
Morton	1,143	4	0	0	0	4	11	0	10	1	0
Mountlake Terrace	20,363	43	0	8	11	24	558	136	371	51	7

Table 8. Offenses Known to Law Enforcement, by Selected State and City, 2012— continued

(Number)

State/city	Population	Violent crime	Murder and nonnegligent manslaughter	Forcible rape	Robbery	Aggravated assault	Property crime	Burglary	Larceny-theft	Motor vehicle theft	Arson[1]
Mount Vernon	32,384	79	1	13	21	44	1,552	315	1,155	82	9
Moxee	3,394	3	1	1	0	1	16	1	13	2	0
Mukilteo	20,715	17	0	4	5	8	[illegible]	110	[illegible]	28	3
Newcastle	10,692	8	0	3	2	3	301	108	175	18	2
Normandy Park	6,524	9	0	0	2	7	205	47	147	11	0
North Bend	6,005	14	0	3	1	10	225	52	162	11	3
Oak Harbor	22,457	38	0	7	3	28	676	173	472	31	5
Ocean Shores	5,603	7	0	1	1	5	203	100	101	2	1
Olympia	47,729	150	5	45	37	63	2,085	468	1,504	113	2
Omak	4,929	29	0	2	4	23	201	46	139	16	2
Oroville	1,715	2	0	1	0	1	78	20	57	1	0
Orting	6,890	5	0	0	2	3	248	79	160	9	2
Othello	7,554	20	0	0	5	15	412	75	308	29	8
Pacific	6,803	5	1	0	0	4	194	39	123	32	0
Palouse	1,021	0	0	0	0	0	4	0	4	0	0
Pasco	63,806	194	1	13	41	139	1,663	419	1,076	168	11
Port Angeles	19,342	80	0	13	11	56	906	255	596	55	4
Port Orchard	11,444	69	0	5	10	54	834	159	605	70	0
Port Townsend	9,219	18	0	6	1	11	288	55	222	11	8
Poulsbo	9,428	24	2	2	8	12	366	81	272	13	0
Prosser	5,952	13	0	1	2	10	155	26	108	21	1
Pullman	30,206	29	0	5	3	21	230	60	166	4	0
Puyallup[5]	37,821	96	0	18	36	42			2,320	264	14
Quincy	6,985	32	0	9	1	22	234	103	112	19	1
Rainier	1,844	0	0	0	0	0	48	20	24	4	0
Raymond	2,911	4	0	0	0	4	69	23	43	3	0
Reardan	573	0	0	0	0	0	9	2	7	0	0
Redmond	55,770	36	0	8	11	17	1,192	172	971	49	8
Renton	93,722	283	2	27	115	139	4,562	897	3,048	617	11
Richland	50,057	82	0	20	11	51	1,270	187	1,019	64	10
Ridgefield	4,899	2	0	1	0	1	58	8	49	1	1
Ritzville	1,716	4	0	1	1	2	65	22	43	0	0
Royal City	2,215	2	0	0	1	1	35	11	20	4	0
Ruston	766	1	0	0	1	0	27	6	19	2	0
Sammamish	47,158	16	0	7	1	8	343	109	221	13	4
Seatac	27,699	155	1	30	69	55	1,753	350	974	429	0
Seattle	626,865	3,746	23	119	1,421	2,183	31,931	6,523	21,852	3,556	77
Sequim	6,710	37	0	11	2	24	378	52	312	14	0
Shelton	9,963	59	2	15	11	31	870	183	621	66	6
Shoreline	54,574	99	3	23	41	32	1,654	442	1,103	109	18
Snoqualmie	10,991	2	0	0	0	2	141	28	110	3	1
Spokane	212,163	1,369	13	81	537	738	18,522	3,827	12,600	2,095	44
Spokane Valley	91,164	196	1	31	67	97	4,805	889	3,484	432	33
Springdale	288	1	0	0	0	1	4	3	1	0	
Stanwood	6,373	9	0	1	4	4	166	31	129	6	1
Steilacoom	6,115	8	0	1	0	7	75	31	38	6	1
Sultan	4,756	15	0	1	3	11	138	64	63	11	0
Sumas	1,338	1	0	0	0	1	32	6	26	0	0
Sumner	9,656	31	1	2	10	18	469	132	300	37	2
Sunnyside	16,271	23	0	3	5	15	544	107	358	79	1
Tacoma	202,646	1,615	12	93	486	1,024	12,866	2,965	7,995	1,906	72
Tenino	1,741	2	0	0	1	1	30	9	18	3	0
Tonasket	1,048	3	0	0	1	2	36	5	26	5	0
Toppenish	9,184	43	1	1	9	32	473	92	310	71	2
Tukwila	19,677	200	2	20	98	80	3,161	282	2,493	386	6
Tumwater	17,844	46	0	11	9	26	627	158	440	29	2
University Place	31,820	86	0	10	19	57	895	242	588	65	2
Vader	632	0	0	0	0	0	17	5	12	0	0
Vancouver	166,375	592	5	72	172	343	6,478	1,044	4,343	1,091	47
Walla Walla	32,463	113	0	16	18	79	1,446	274	1,101	71	11
Wapato	5,123	30	0	2	5	23	254	85	119	50	2
Warden	2,785	0	0	0	0	0	36	9	21	6	0
Washougal	14,498	17	0	8	2	7	306	62	225	19	6
Westport	2,113	0	0	0	0	0	90	29	57	4	2

Table 8. Offenses Known to Law Enforcement, by Selected State and City, 2012— continued

(Number)

State/city	Population	Violent crime	Murder and nonnegligent manslaughter	Forcible rape	Robbery	Aggravated assault	Property crime	Burglary	Larceny-theft	Motor vehicle theft	Arson[1]
West Richland	12,303	14	0	0	1	13	140	41	97	2	1
White Salmon	2,288	3	0	2	0	1	46	8	38	0	0
Winlock	1,359	2	0	2	0	0	36	15	21	0	0
Woodland	5,566	14	0	5	2	7	221	44	159	18	1
Woodway	1,337	0	0	0	0	0	12	3	9	0	0
Yakima	93,419	566	11	52	152	351	5,774	1,573	3,106	1,095	11
Yarrow Point	1,032	0	0	0	0	0	9	3	6	0	0
Yelm	7,033	18	0	5	9	4	379	55	309	15	0
Zillah	3,041	4	0	0	1	3	82	26	46	10	0
West Virginia											
Alderson	1,193	0	0	0	0	0	30	5	25	0	0
Barboursville	3,976	2	0	0	1	1	370	32	338	0	1
Beckley	17,675	189	6	21	55	107	1,588	335	1,221	32	6
Belington	1,914	4	0	0	0	4	11	2	9	0	0
Benwood	1,406	0	0	0	0	0	1	0	1	0	0
Bridgeport	8,200	7	0	1	2	4	221	20	200	1	1
Capon Bridge	351	0	0	0	0	0	0	0	0	0	0
Chapmanville	1,222	3	0	0	0	3	50	5	44	1	0
Clarksburg	16,649	112	1	10	10	91	665	110	532	23	3
Clearview	562	0	0	0	0	0	0	0	0	0	0
Dunbar	7,876	38	0	5	7	26	238	70	155	13	1
East Bank	955	0	0	0	0	0	6	3	3	0	0
Eleanor	1,533	1	0	0	0	1	0	0	0	0	0
Elkins	7,108	64	0	5	3	56	283	70	210	3	4
Glasgow	901	1	0	0	0	1	6	1	5	0	0
Glen Dale	1,511	8	0	1	0	7	26	8	17	1	1
Glenville	1,538	0	0	0	0	0	18	3	15	0	0
Hamlin	1,134	16	0	0	0	16	26	1	24	1	0
Harpers Ferry/Bolivar	1,350	1	0	0	1	0	4	2	2	0	0
Harrisville	1,850	1	0	1	0	0	5	0	5	0	0
Hinton	2,664	13	0	0	4	9	165	50	115	0	0
Hurricane[5]	6,333	11	1	2	1	7		31		5	0
Kenova	3,188	10	0	0	1	9	171	38	127	6	1
Keyser	5,421	8	0	0	1	7	113	26	87	0	0
Kingwood	2,958	0	0	0	0	0	0	0	0	0	0
Lewisburg	3,859	8	0	2	0	6	160	6	147	7	0
Lumberport	884	0	0	0	0	0	1	0	1	0	0
Martinsburg	17,487	89	0	3	33	53	886	127	732	27	7
Mason	966	2	0	0	1	1	10	3	7	0	0
Matoaka	224	0	0	0	0	0	0	0	0	0	0
Milton	2,422	1	0	0	1	0	35	2	32	1	0
Monongah	1,050	0	0	0	0	0	0	0	0	0	0
Moorefield	2,523	21	0	0	0	21	21	4	16	1	1
Morgantown	30,294	107	1	4	26	76	823	175	632	16	9
Mount Hope	1,400	2	0	0	1	1	29	11	17	1	0
New Cumberland	1,100	0	0	0	0	0	1	1	0	0	0
Nitro	7,163	10	0	1	4	5	269	42	215	12	0
Nutter Fort	1,602	1	0	0	0	1	12	3	7	2	0
Oak Hill	7,672	9	0	1	0	8	196	53	137	6	0
Oceana	1,372	40	0	1	2	37	106	16	88	2	0
Paden City	2,601	0	0	0	0	0	1	1	0	0	0
Parkersburg	31,558	146	1	17	22	106	1,698	433	1,199	66	25
Parsons	1,452	0	0	0	0	0	0	0	0	0	0
Pennsboro	1,161	1	0	0	0	1	1	0	1	0	0
Philippi	2,955	33	0	0	0	33	22	12	10	0	0
Point Pleasant	4,343	7	1	1	0	5	143	32	104	7	0
Princeton	6,453	74	3	1	16	54	452	114	334	4	1
Ravenswood	3,876	9	0	0	2	7	70	9	59	2	0
Reedsville	597	0	0	0	0	0	0	0	0	0	0
Ridgeley	675	0	0	0	0	0	0	0	0	0	0
Ripley	3,255	0	0	0	0	0	11	1	10	0	0
Romney	1,837	1	0	0	0	1	2	2	0	0	0
Ronceverte	1,781	0	0	0	0	0	14	5	8	1	0

Table 8. Offenses Known to Law Enforcement, by Selected State and City, 2012— continued

(Number)

State/city	Population	Violent crime	Murder and nonnegligent manslaughter	Forcible rape	Robbery	Aggravated assault	Property crime	Burglary	Larceny-theft	Motor vehicle theft	Arson[1]
Shepherdstown	1,749	1	0	0	1	0	15	2	13	0	0
Shinnston	2,213	7	0	0	0	7	44	10	34	0	1
Sistersville	1,000	0	0	0	0	0	20	1	10	0	0
Sophia	1,348	6	0	1	1	4	71	22	46	3	0
South Charleston	13,396	74	0	3	15	56	492	66	411	15	1
Spencer	2,311	1	0	0	0	1	71	13	58	0	0
St. Albans	11,001	24	0	0	9	15	459	81	354	24	1
Stonewood	1,814	0	0	0	0	0	0	0	0	0	0
Summersville	3,576	42	0	0	0	42	122	9	108	5	2
Terra Alta	1,487	1	0	0	0	1	3	0	3	0	0
Triadelphia	804	0	0	0	0	0	1	1	0	0	0
Vienna	10,770	13	0	1	3	9	294	19	271	4	0
Wayne	1,425	0	0	0	0	0	10	2	8	0	0
Weirton	19,652	17	0	2	2	13	308	61	231	16	1
Welch	2,366	20	0	0	1	19	21	0	21	0	0
Wellsburg	2,778	1	0	0	0	1	37	7	28	2	0
Weston	4,107	0	0	0	0	0	8	1	7	0	0
West Union	821	0	0	0	0	0	6	4	2	0	0
Wheeling	28,356	245	0	17	42	186	767	265	455	47	1
White Sulphur Springs	2,464	0	0	0	0	0	1	1	0	0	0
Williamson	3,164	9	0	0	2	7	49	17	30	2	0
Winfield	2,322	1	0	0	1	0	10	0	10	0	0
Wisconsin											
Adams	1,957	3	0	0	0	3	97	25	72	0	0
Albany	1,022	5	0	0	0	5	24	3	20	1	0
Algoma	3,177	4	0	2	0	2	99	2	95	2	0
Altoona	6,806	36	0	5	2	29	106	15	87	4	0
Amery	2,898	4	0	0	0	4	51	16	35	0	0
Antigo	8,177	24	0	0	0	24	551	83	448	20	0
Appleton	73,431	213	0	28	22	163	1,392	254	1,111	27	3
Arcadia	2,952	3	0	0	0	3	24	3	21	0	0
Ashland	8,230	31	0	1	2	28	455	56	386	13	1
Ashwaubenon	17,204	41	1	6	2	32	662	55	594	13	0
Athens	1,110	2	0	0	0	2	6	0	5	1	0
Bangor	1,477	0	0	0	0	0	25	3	22	0	0
Baraboo	12,138	25	0	4	2	19	446	52	388	6	5
Barneveld	1,229	0	0	0	0	0	15	0	15	0	0
Bayfield	491	0	0	0	0	0	11	2	8	1	0
Beaver Dam	16,235	8	0	0	3	5	490	83	402	5	0
Belleville	2,425	0	0	0	0	0	11	0	11	0	0
Beloit	37,008	119	1	8	38	72	1,294	299	946	49	13
Beloit Town	7,672	23	0	1	9	13	154	32	116	6	0
Berlin	5,551	3	0	1	0	2	168	24	141	3	2
Big Bend	1,296	1	0	0	0	1	50	15	32	3	0
Black River Falls	3,652	12	0	1	0	11	195	8	187	0	0
Blair	1,379	1	0	1	0	0	10	4	6	0	0
Blanchardville	826	0	0	0	0	0	4	0	3	1	0
Bloomer	3,569	2	0	1	0	1	30	8	21	1	6
Bloomfield	6,317	11	0	1	0	10	95	13	76	6	0
Boscobel	3,240	31	0	0	0	31	63	15	48	0	0
Brandon-Fairwater	1,260	0	0	0	0	0	5	0	5	0	0
Brillion	3,190	2	0	0	0	2	35	7	28	0	0
Brodhead	3,304	4	0	2	1	1	93	7	79	7	0
Brookfield	38,098	19	3	1	4	11	1,108	85	1,012	11	0
Brookfield Township	6,145	16	0	0	1	15	139	14	123	2	0
Brown Deer	12,092	14	0	0	2	12	331	55	265	11	1
Burlington	10,490	16	0	2	2	12	292	24	266	2	0
Butler	1,851	6	0	1	0	5	44	15	26	3	0
Caledonia	24,764	55	0	2	5	48	348	85	256	7	0
Campbellsport	2,030	0	0	0	0	0	16	5	11	0	0
Campbell Township	4,362	5	0	1	1	3	98	21	76	1	0
Cashton	1,114	0	0	0	0	0	2	2	0	0	0
Cedarburg	11,465	2	0	0	0	2	127	14	111	2	0

Table 8. Offenses Known to Law Enforcement, by Selected State and City, 2012— continued

(Number)

State/city	Population	Violent crime	Murder and nonnegligent manslaughter	Forcible rape	Robbery	Aggravated assault	Property crime	Burglary	Larceny-theft	Motor vehicle theft	Arson[1]
Chenequa	593	0	0	0	0	0	1	0	1	0	0
Chetek	2,228	3	0	0	1	2	24	6	18	0	0
Chilton	3,984	5	0	0	1	4	49	4	44	1	0
Chippewa Falls	13,773	28	0	3	4	21	219	55	154	10	0
Cleveland	1,481	0	0	0	0	0	14	2	10	2	0
Clinton	2,158	1	0	0	1	0	27	5	21	1	0
Clintonville	4,594	5	0	3	1	1	237	24	210	3	1
Colby-Abbotsford	4,181	2	0	0	0	2	52	12	39	1	0
Columbus	5,010	7	0	1	0	6	115	16	99	0	0
Cornell	1,479	0	0	0	0	0	44	4	38	2	0
Cottage Grove	6,311	4	0	0	0	4	158	21	132	5	3
Crandon	1,911	1	0	0	0	1	42	3	36	3	0
Cross Plains	3,612	1	0	1	0	0	41	1	38	2	0
Cuba City	2,090	0	0	0	0	0	33	4	29	0	0
Cumberland	2,176	3	1	0	0	2	56	7	49	0	0
Dane	1,014	0	0	0	0	0	0	0	0	0	0
Darien	1,589	3	0	0	0	3	21	1	20	0	0
Darlington	2,455	3	0	0	2	1	38	6	32	0	0
Deforest	9,108	8	0	2	1	5	115	12	102	1	0
Delafield	7,118	2	0	1	1	0	171	15	155	1	0
Delavan	8,514	11	0	1	3	7	283	23	250	10	0
Delavan Town	5,319	2	0	1	0	1	120	25	87	8	0
Denmark	2,154	0	0	0	0	0	7	1	6	0	0
De Pere	24,122	20	3	5	1	11	285	49	231	5	0
Dodgeville	4,689	5	0	0	0	5	51	8	41	2	0
Durand	1,923	2	0	0	0	2	13	2	8	3	1
Eagle River	1,403	3	0	1	0	2	78	9	67	2	0
Edgar	1,485	0	0	0	0	0	3	0	3	0	0
Edgerton	5,468	5	0	0	3	2	132	20	110	2	0
Eleva	677	0	0	0	0	0	11	5	5	1	0
Elkhart Lake	966	0	0	0	0	0	25	1	23	1	0
Elkhorn	10,144	6	0	0	1	5	216	29	184	3	0
Elk Mound	882	0	0	0	0	0	10	1	9	0	0
Ellsworth	3,289	2	0	0	1	1	78	11	62	5	1
Elm Grove	5,962	1	0	0	0	1	46	12	34	0	0
Evansville	5,019	7	0	0	0	7	121	21	98	2	0
Everest	17,123	16	1	1	1	13	352	67	275	10	5
Fall Creek	1,333	0	0	0	0	0	28	19	9	0	0
Fall River	1,718	0	0	0	0	0	24	6	16	2	2
Fennimore	2,502	0	0	0	0	0	121	22	99	0	0
Fitchburg	25,731	52	3	5	11	33	491	80	395	16	0
Fond du Lac	43,319	183	0	35	11	137	1,210	118	1,057	35	6
Fontana	1,682	5	0	0	0	5	25	4	21	0	0
Fort Atkinson	12,439	16	0	0	0	16	267	34	226	7	2
Fountain City	859	2	0	1	0	1	4	2	2	0	0
Fox Lake	1,521	0	0	0	0	0	6	2	4	0	0
Fox Point	6,751	0	0	0	0	0	82	14	66	2	0
Fox Valley Metro	20,425	17	0	1	2	14	276	48	223	5	1
Franklin	35,711	16	0	4	3	9	766	90	669	7	1
Frederic	1,135	1	0	0	0	1	11	1	10	0	0
Freedom	5,892	1	0	0	0	1	12	2	9	1	0
Geneva Town	5,024	0	0	0	0	0	108	25	82	1	0
Genoa City	3,060	0	0	0	0	0	37	7	29	1	0
Germantown	19,874	11	0	1	4	6	387	29	351	7	0
Gillett	1,384	0	0	0	0	0	19	6	13	0	0
Glendale	12,968	23	0	0	19	4	938	34	867	37	0
Grafton	11,510	5	0	0	1	4	164	12	151	1	1
Grand Chute	21,102	29	1	0	7	21	843	54	766	23	3
Grand Rapids	7,670	0	0	0	0	0	46	11	34	1	0
Green Bay	106,080	514	1	44	87	382	2,978	659	2,210	109	15
Greendale	14,153	11	0	0	1	10	522	27	489	6	0
Greenfield	36,998	53	1	4	24	24	1,269	163	1,074	32	6
Green Lake	965	2	0	0	1	1	17	1	15	1	0
Hales Corners	7,750	7	0	3	2	2	147	17	125	5	0

Table 8. Offenses Known to Law Enforcement, by Selected State and City, 2012— continued

(Number)

State/city	Population	Violent crime	Murder and nonnegligent manslaughter	Forcible rape	Robbery	Aggravated assault	Property crime	Burglary	Larceny-theft	Motor vehicle theft	Arson[1]
Hartford	14,314	8	0	0	2	6	317	43	269	5	0
Hartland	9,159	8	0	4	0	4	110	13	97	0	0
Hazel Green	1,260	1	0	0	0	1	9	2	7	0	0
Highland	841	0	0	0	0	0	20	15	5	0	0
Hobart-Lawrence	10,615	6	0	0	0	6	69	16	49	4	0
Holmen	9,104	10	0	0	1	9	240	90	146	4	0
Horicon	3,660	0	0	0	0	0	60	3	57	0	0
Hortonville	2,735	0	0	0	0	0	82	6	76	0	0
Hudson	12,848	6	0	2	0	4	500	29	457	14	1
Independence	1,348	0	0	0	0	0	13	6	5	2	0
Iron Ridge	930	0	0	0	0	0	11	4	7	0	0
Iron River	1,133	2	0	0	0	2	16	10	6	0	0
Jackson	6,796	3	0	1	0	2	49	7	42	0	0
Janesville	63,642	179	2	21	35	121	2,463	339	2,059	65	6
Jefferson	8,017	15	1	5	0	9	256	23	229	4	1
Juneau	2,819	1	1	0	0	0	47	7	40	0	1
Kaukauna	15,601	17	0	3	2	12	186	14	170	2	0
Kenosha	99,993	274	1	36	105	132	2,999	707	2,194	98	15
Kewaskum	4,030	1	0	0	1	0	39	7	32	0	0
Kewaunee	2,963	3	1	0	0	2	56	8	48	0	0
Kiel	3,730	6	0	0	1	5	65	6	58	1	0
Kronenwetter	7,248	6	0	3	0	3	59	15	41	3	0
La Crosse	51,851	154	4	21	38	91	1,954	404	1,501	49	2
Ladysmith	3,392	8	0	0	1	7	8	1	6	1	0
Lake Delton	2,946	19	0	4	2	13	625	27	591	7	1
Lake Geneva	7,699	14	0	0	3	11	266	35	225	6	0
Lake Hallie	6,503	18	0	1	2	15	259	21	231	7	0
Lake Mills	5,741	3	0	2	0	1	43	8	35	0	0
Lancaster	3,878	3	0	0	0	3	46	4	41	1	0
Lodi	3,062	2	0	0	0	2	72	11	60	1	0
Lomira	2,433	3	0	2	0	1	49	3	45	1	0
Luxemburg	2,524	0	0	0	0	0	23	0	19	4	0
Madison	237,508	897	3	114	241	539	7,753	1,601	5,898	254	45
Manawa	1,381	1	0	0	0	1	11	5	5	1	0
Manitowoc	33,631	62	0	4	12	46	991	128	844	19	3
Marathon City	1,533	5	0	0	0	5	12	2	10	0	0
Marinette	10,971	11	0	2	9	0	443	67	360	16	1
Marion	1,270	2	0	1	0	1	29	4	24	1	0
Markesan	1,483	0	0	0	0	0	37	4	33	0	0
Marshall Village	3,937	1	0	1	0	0	58	11	47	0	1
Marshfield	19,178	13	1	1	4	7	558	68	476	14	0
Mauston	4,444	18	0	4	1	13	151	21	125	5	0
Mayville	5,159	1	0	0	0	1	96	12	83	1	0
McFarland	7,957	3	0	0	0	3	151	14	136	1	0
Medford	4,332	1	0	1	0	0	69	4	63	2	0
Menasha	17,487	34	0	10	2	22	429	68	354	7	1
Menomonee Falls	35,795	14	0	1	6	7	408	51	346	11	0
Mequon	23,237	16	0	0	3	13	198	66	129	3	0
Merrill	9,639	32	0	3	0	29	272	62	204	6	3
Middleton	17,774	17	0	4	8	5	423	86	329	8	0
Milton	5,552	16	0	0	7	9	126	16	107	3	0
Milwaukee	599,395	7,759	91	230	3,027	4,411	30,228	6,977	18,448	4,803	306
Mineral Point	2,485	1	0	0	0	1	53	6	46	1	0
Minocqua	4,372	17	0	2	0	15	132	12	118	2	0
Mishicot	1,439	0	0	0	0	0	1	0	1	0	0
Monona	7,678	6	0	0	3	3	516	28	480	8	0
Monroe	10,869	12	0	0	0	12	309	30	272	7	1
Montello	1,502	4	0	0	0	4	31	5	26	0	0
Mosinee	4,007	1	0	0	0	1	115	16	96	3	0
Mount Horeb	7,142	3	1	1	1	0	125	17	107	1	0
Mount Pleasant	26,262	19	1	2	7	9	890	105	770	15	1
Mukwonago	7,389	6	0	0	0	6	155	18	134	3	0
Mukwonago Town	7,996	0	0	0	0	0	50	5	45	0	0
Muskego	24,249	4	0	1	1	2	243	52	181	10	1

Table 8. Offenses Known to Law Enforcement, by Selected State and City, 2012— continued

(Number)

State/city	Population	Violent crime	Murder and nonnegligent manslaughter	Forcible rape	Robbery	Aggravated assault	Property crime	Burglary	Larceny-theft	Motor vehicle theft	Arson[1]
Neenah	25,681	35	0	2	2	31	495	76	404	15	0
Neillsville	2,473	1	0	0	0	1	42	5	37	0	0
Neshkoro	436	0	0	0	0	0	8	3	5	0	0
New Glarus	2,180	0	0	0	0	0	56	7	48	1	2
New Holstein	3,277	4	0	0	0	4	71	4	66	1	0
New Lisbon	2,565	5	0	0	0	5	20	2	17	1	0
New London	7,354	6	0	1	0	5	144	25	118	1	1
New Richmond[7]	8,454	13	0	2	1	10			206	1	3
Niagara	1,625	0	0	0	0	0	29	6	17	6	0
North Fond du Lac	5,051	10	0	1	0	9	60	8	49	3	0
North Hudson	3,803	0	0	0	0	0	17	1	16	0	0
North Prairie	2,150	1	0	0	0	1	23	3	20	0	0
Oak Creek	34,715	57	6	5	13	33	1,048	115	917	16	3
Oconomowoc	15,832	5	0	0	3	2	291	24	265	2	0
Oconomowoc Town	8,449	1	0	0	1	0	36	7	27	2	0
Oconto	4,502	4	0	0	1	3	187	34	146	7	0
Oconto Falls	2,883	2	0	0	0	2	91	12	74	5	0
Omro	3,540	5	0	0	0	5	66	10	55	1	0
Onalaska	17,945	10	0	1	2	7	504	61	439	4	0
Oregon	9,406	3	0	2	0	1	122	20	101	1	0
Osceola	2,564	10	0	0	1	9	51	6	44	1	0
Oshkosh	66,514	191	0	13	18	160	1,722	340	1,345	37	0
Osseo	1,715	1	0	0	0	1	70	5	65	0	0
Oxford	610	1	0	1	0	0	12	2	7	3	0
Park Falls	2,441	0	0	0	0	0	44	3	39	2	0
Pepin	833	0	0	0	0	0	37	2	35	0	0
Peshtigo	3,504	1	0	0	0	1	58	23	33	2	0
Pewaukee Village	8,204	10	0	1	2	7	174	14	156	4	0
Phillips	1,465	3	0	0	0	3	39	6	31	2	0
Plainfield	867	1	0	1	0	0	8	2	4	2	0
Platteville	11,255	6	0	4	0	2	340	25	313	2	0
Pleasant Prairie	19,873	11	0	0	3	8	505	40	453	12	0
Plymouth	8,441	3	0	0	0	3	226	29	192	5	3
Portage	10,362	21	0	2	3	16	79	26	48	5	0
Port Washington	11,301	10	0	0	2	8	149	17	131	1	0
Poynette	2,538	1	0	0	0	1	33	2	31	0	0
Prescott	4,266	16	0	0	0	16	107	12	93	2	2
Pulaski	3,585	5	0	0	0	5	32	5	27	0	0
Racine	79,055	374	4	31	211	128	3,181	1,101	1,950	130	24
Reedsburg	9,270	14	1	4	0	9	116	6	110	0	0
Rhinelander	7,776	15	0	2	0	13	268	28	235	5	1
Richland Center	5,195	5	0	0	0	5	78	12	66	0	0
Ripon	7,783	7	0	0	1	6	127	12	112	3	0
River Falls	14,927	47	3	4	4	36	389	41	336	12	5
River Hills	1,608	1	0	0	0	1	6	1	4	1	0
Rome Town	2,707	1	0	0	0	1	31	14	17	0	0
Rothschild	5,297	2	0	0	0	2	110	4	104	2	0
Sauk Prairie	4,583	6	0	2	1	3	166	12	153	1	0
Saukville	4,470	4	0	0	0	4	123	13	106	4	0
Seymour	3,481	8	0	0	0	8	8	0	8	0	0
Sheboygan	49,261	170	4	19	21	126	1,517	262	1,212	43	5
Sheboygan Falls	7,770	9	1	4	1	3	129	14	107	8	0
Shiocton	929	0	0	0	0	0	14	1	13	0	0
Shorewood	13,262	22	0	0	14	8	376	24	340	12	0
Shorewood Hills	1,595	0	0	0	0	0	39	1	38	0	0
Silver Lake	2,430	3	0	1	0	2	9	0	9	0	1
Siren	811	2	0	0	0	2	66	3	63	0	0
Slinger	5,101	5	0	0	4	1	71	1	70	0	0
South Milwaukee	21,316	37	0	4	12	21	431	76	344	11	8
Sparta	9,627	10	0	1	1	8	343	60	268	15	3
Spooner	2,688	10	0	1	0	9	53	4	48	1	0
Stanley	3,629	9	0	0	1	8	61	8	53	0	0
St. Croix Falls	2,131	1	0	0	1	0	79	6	70	3	0
Stevens Point	26,809	48	0	8	3	37	717	131	571	15	2

Table 8. Offenses Known to Law Enforcement, by Selected State and City, 2012— continued

(Number)

State/city	Population	Violent crime	Murder and nonnegligent manslaughter	Forcible rape	Robbery	Aggravated assault	Property crime	Burglary	Larceny-theft	Motor vehicle theft	Arson[1]
St. Francis	9,435	15	0	2	5	8	224	21	200	3	0
Stoughton	12,850	14	1	0	4	9	291	23	262	6	0
Strum	1,123	0	0	0	0	0	3	0	3	0	0
Sturgeon Bay	9,179	9	0	1	0	8	158	13	141	4	2
Sturtevant	6,988	2	0	0	0	2	70	20	44	6	1
Summit	4,696	2	0	1	0	1	15	4	8	3	0
Sun Prairie	29,925	41	0	2	8	31	737	72	656	9	2
Superior	27,281	83	1	9	22	51	1,309	221	1,016	72	21
Theresa	1,264	3	0	0	0	3	29	6	22	1	0
Thiensville	3,250	4	0	0	0	4	12	2	10	0	0
Three Lakes	2,125	2	0	0	0	2	27	5	20	2	0
Tomah	9,192	21	0	1	2	18	523	68	449	6	0
Tomahawk	3,390	3	0	0	0	3	55	14	36	5	1
Town of East Troy	4,046	6	0	0	1	5	40	6	32	2	0
Town of Madison	6,398	23	0	4	7	12	231	51	162	18	2
Town of Menasha	18,628	28	0	2	2	24	264	52	202	10	2
Trempealeau	1,542	1	0	0	1	0	15	0	14	1	0
Twin Lakes	6,036	7	0	2	1	4	97	21	74	2	0
Two Rivers	11,674	15	0	2	0	13	271	56	203	12	0
Valders	958	2	0	0	0	2	15	1	14	0	0
Verona	10,824	5	0	0	1	4	271	19	250	2	0
Viroqua	4,397	2	0	1	0	1	79	3	73	3	0
Walworth	2,833	4	0	0	0	4	17	3	14	0	0
Washburn	2,134	4	0	0	0	4	39	4	31	4	0
Waterloo	3,354	0	0	0	0	0	49	9	39	1	0
Waukesha	71,049	107	1	26	24	56	1,304	233	1,039	32	1
Waunakee	12,326	3	0	0	0	3	114	18	94	2	0
Waupaca	6,115	27	0	2	2	23	213	23	190	0	0
Waupun	11,379	9	0	3	0	6	163	24	137	2	1
Wausau	39,313	120	1	21	21	77	1,079	241	806	32	29
Wautoma	2,227	4	0	0	0	4	79	9	70	0	0
Wauwatosa	46,748	78	1	0	56	21	1,926	266	1,623	37	0
West Allis	60,870	191	0	11	97	83	2,918	552	2,234	132	19
West Bend	31,275	29	1	3	9	16	794	55	726	13	1
Westfield	1,259	1	0	0	1	0	21	3	18	0	0
West Milwaukee	4,239	24	0	1	11	12	430	61	343	26	1
West Salem	4,849	4	0	1	0	3	81	5	70	6	1
Whitefish Bay	14,218	11	0	1	5	5	191	14	170	7	0
Whitewater	14,807	17	0	5	1	11	265	44	219	2	0
Williams Bay	2,580	0	0	0	0	0	43	7	32	4	0
Winneconne	2,400	2	0	0	0	2	22	7	15	0	0
Wisconsin Dells	2,697	20	0	1	0	19	253	28	220	5	0
Wisconsin Rapids	18,424	15	0	6	6	3	845	136	697	12	0
Woodruff	2,049	2	0	0	0	2	15	2	12	1	0
Wyoming											
Afton	1,934	0	0	0	0	0	17	4	13	0	0
Basin	1,314	4	0	1	1	2	19	5	14	0	1
Buffalo	4,691	14	1	1	0	12	109	7	100	2	2
Casper	56,801	86	3	2	12	69	1,968	363	1,501	104	18
Cheyenne	60,969	140	0	21	21	98	2,081	255	1,730	96	9
Cody	9,793	17	1	1	1	14	186	32	148	6	2
Douglas	6,172	15	0	2	0	13	255	17	228	10	1
Evanston	12,460	5	0	3	0	2	295	30	259	6	0
Evansville	2,614	14	0	0	0	14	35	8	25	2	0
Gillette	29,816	38	0	0	1	37	1,194	138	1,018	38	11
Glenrock	2,599	9	0	1	0	8	30	3	25	2	0
Green River	12,805	74	0	1	1	72	198	39	151	8	3
Greybull	1,889	6	0	0	0	6	12	4	8	0	0
Hanna	847	4	0	0	0	4	0	0	0	0	0
Hulett	390	2	0	1	0	1	7	5	1	1	0
Jackson	9,851	40	0	4	1	35	237	28	203	6	0
Kemmerer	2,690	0	0	0	0	0	36	2	32	2	0
Lander	7,681	9	1	3	0	5	261	30	225	6	2

Table 8. Offenses Known to Law Enforcement, by Selected State and City, 2012— continued

(Number)

State/city	Population	Violent crime	Murder and nonnegligent manslaughter	Forcible rape	Robbery	Aggravated assault	Property crime	Burglary	Larceny-theft	Motor vehicle theft	Arson[1]
Laramie	31,767	34	1	14	2	17	710	102	585	23	8
Lusk	1,594	2	0	0	0	2	4	1	2	1	0
Mills	3,555	13	0	0	0	13	97	25	68	4	1
Moorcroft	1,028	0	0	0	0	0	76	7	69	0	0
Newcastle	3,536	4	0	1	0	3	89	10	75	4	0
Pine Bluffs	1,157	10	0	1	0	9	20	6	13	1	0
Powell	6,486	24	0	13	1	10	211	50	160	1	2
Rawlins	9,337	25	0	9	0	16	258	39	204	15	3
Riverton	11,025	42	1	15	3	23	554	30	500	24	1
Rock Springs	23,566	89	2	15	1	71	623	61	546	16	2
Saratoga	1,702	1	0	0	0	1	15	1	14	0	0
Sheridan	17,771	26	1	4	0	21	461	95	350	16	3
Sundance	1,204	0	0	0	0	0	12	4	8	0	0
Thermopolis	3,045	6	0	0	0	6	45	6	37	2	1
Torrington	6,787	26	0	0	0	26	142	33	108	1	0
Wheatland	3,733	4	0	1	0	3	67	15	48	4	0
Worland	5,537	4	0	0	0	4	37	0	36	1	0

1 A blank cell in the arson column indicates that the FBI did not receive 12 complete months of arson data for that agency. 2 The population for the city of Mobile, Alabama, includes 55,819 inhabitants from the jurisdiction of the Mobile County Sheriff's Department. 3 Because of changes in the state/local agency's reporting practices, figures are not comparable to previous years' data. 4 The FBI determined that the agency did not follow national Uniform Crime Reporting (UCR) Program guidelines for reporting an offense. Consequently, this figure is not included in this table. 5 The FBI determined that the agency's data were underreported. Consequently, those data are not included in this table. 6 The data collection methodology for the offense of forcible rape used by Chicago, Illinois, and the Minnesota state UCR Program (with the exception of Minneapolis and St. Paul, Minnesota) does not comply with national UCR Program guidelines. Consequently, its figures for forcible rape and violent crime (of which forcible rape is a part) are not published in this table. 7 The FBI determined that the agency's data were overreported. Consequently, those data are not included in this table.

Table 9. Offenses Known to Law Enforcement, by Selected State and University and College, 2012

(Number)

State and university/college	Student enrollment[1]	Violent crime	Murder and nonnegligent manslaughter	Forcible rape	Robbery	Aggravated assault	Property crime	Burglary	Larceny-theft	Motor vehicle theft	Arson[2]
Alabama											
Alabama A&M University	4,922	15	0	2	7	6	186	17	166	3	
Jacksonville State University	9,490	4	0	2	0	2	81	12	67	2	
Samford University	4,758	2	0	0	1	1	95	13	81	1	
Troy University	26,172	3	0	1	2	0	89	12	75	2	
University of Alabama, Tuscaloosa	31,647	10	0	3	3	4	436	37	395	4	
University of Montevallo	3,066	1	0	0	0	1	32	4	28	0	
University of North Alabama	7,233	7	0	2	3	2	55	13	42	0	
University of South Alabama	14,769	12	0	1	2	9	146	16	128	2	
Alaska											
University of Alaska											
Anchorage	18,128	3	0	0	0	3	89	1	87	1	0
Fairbanks	9,712	6	0	0	2	4	82	3	79	0	0
Arizona											
Arizona State University	72,254	38	0	15	11	12	1,241	119	1,110	12	1
Central Arizona College	7,442	0	0	0	0	0	27	3	23	1	0
Northern Arizona University	25,359	22	0	9	1	12	275	39	236	0	3
Pima Community College	36,969	0	0	0	0	0	120	6	106	8	0
University of Arizona	39,236	20	0	6	2	12	948	72	847	29	4
Yavapai College	7,837	0	0	0	0	0	8	2	6	0	0
Arkansas											
Arkansas State University, Jonesboro	13,900	5	0	0	1	4	124	19	104	1	0
Arkansas Tech University	10,464	3	0	1	1	1	123	37	86	0	0
Henderson State University	3,774	4	0	2	0	2	70	13	56	1	0
Southern Arkansas University	3,382	2	0	0	1	1	53	20	33	0	0
University of Arkansas											
Fayetteville	23,199	12	0	4	3	5	220	43	165	12	1
Little Rock	13,068	11	0	0	4	7	156	39	114	3	0
Medical Sciences	2,819	7	0	0	1	6	177	3	170	4	0
Monticello	3,920	0	0	0	0	0	41	6	34	1	0
University of Central Arkansas	11,163	7	0	4	1	2	157	67	88	2	0
California											
Allan Hancock College	10,955	0	0	0	0	0	58	5	51	2	0
California State Polytechnic University											
Pomona	21,107	7	0	0	5	2	172	22	133	17	1
San Luis Obispo	18,762	1	0	0	1	0	162	3	155	4	2
California State University											
Bakersfield	8,002	2	0	0	0	2	57	13	43	1	1
Channel Islands	4,179	0	0	0	0	0	62	3	58	1	0
Chico	15,920	5	0	1	2	2	227	15	211	1	0
Dominguez Hills	14,364	6	0	0	0	6	102	25	74	3	0
East Bay	13,160	4	0	0	4	0	101	15	85	1	0
Fresno	21,981	18	0	1	5	12	531	62	458	11	0
Fullerton	36,156	11	0	2	3	6	313	38	255	20	0
Long Beach	34,870	1	0	1	0	0	232	23	203	6	1
Los Angeles	21,284	1	0	0	0	1	189	9	170	10	2
Monterey Bay	5,173	2	0	2	0	0	59	10	46	3	0
Northridge	36,911	12	0	3	6	3	388	19	357	12	2
Sacramento	28,016	0	0	0	0	0	257	35	217	5	0
San Bernardino	17,250	7	0	4	0	3	148	21	115	12	1
San Jose	30,236	18	0	3	9	6	468	37	418	13	0
San Marcos	10,276	2	0	1	0	1	37	8	28	1	0
Stanislaus	9,246	2	0	0	2	0	66	4	60	2	0
College of the Sequoias	11,625	1	0	0	1	0	88	10	75	3	0
Contra Costa Community College	7,671	8	0	0	5	3	269	20	226	23	0
Cuesta College	10,759	0	0	0	0	0	21	2	18	1	0
El Camino College	24,463	2	0	0	1	1	140	17	120	3	1
Foothill-De Anza College	39,952	0	0	0	0	0	85	17	67	1	0
Humboldt State University	8,046	4	0	2	0	2	156	10	141	5	1

Table 9. Offenses Known to Law Enforcement, by Selected State and University and College, 2012— continued

(Number)

State and university/college	Student enrollment[1]	Violent crime	Murder and nonnegligent manslaughter	Forcible rape	Robbery	Aggravated assault	Property crime	Burglary	Larceny-theft	Motor vehicle theft	Arson[2]
Marin Community College	7,075	4	0	0	1	3	34	3	30	1	0
Pasadena Community College	26,057	4	0	0	2	2	141	4	134	3	0
Riverside Community College	18,395	3	0	0	2	1	109	9	94	6	0
San Bernardino Community College	18,015	1	0	0	0	1	117	24	74	19	0
San Diego State University	30,541	35	0	11	14	10	620	61	548	11	0
San Francisco State University	29,541	9	0	1	7	1	274	48	203	23	4
San Jose/Evergreen Community College	20,671	1	0	0	0	1	63	1	54	8	0
Santa Rosa Junior College	24,199	6	0	1	1	4	97	4	91	2	0
Solano Community College	11,029	0	0	0	0	0	35	0	33	2	0
Sonoma State University	8,668	4	0	1	0	3	110	7	98	5	0
State Center Community College District	34,192	7	0	0	6	1	280	20	244	16	1
University of California:											
Berkeley	36,137	33	0	2	21	10	1,129	77	1,037	15	5
Davis	31,732	14	0	6	1	7	696	33	659	4	7
Hastings College of Law	1,289	12	0	0	9	3	28	9	19	0	0
Irvine	27,189	12	0	5	2	5	490	48	429	13	3
Los Angeles	39,271	62	0	14	21	27	923	173	736	14	1
Medical Center, Sacramento[3]	n.a.	6	0	0	2	4	153	13	128	12	0
Merced	5,198	0	0	0	0	0	53	2	51	0	0
Riverside	20,900	10	0	1	4	5	409	40	355	14	0
San Diego	28,593	8	0	1	1	6	464	20	425	19	0
San Francisco	3,054	13	0	1	9	3	457	24	422	11	0
Santa Barbara	21,685	9	0	4	4	1	375	40	334	1	3
Santa Cruz	17,454	6	0	1	1	4	276	20	253	3	4
Ventura County Community College District	13,758	0	0	0	0	0	98	0	98	0	8
West Valley-Mission College	20,985	2	0	0	1	1	66	14	44	8	0
Colorado											
Aims Community College	5,290	0	0	0	0	0	4	0	4	0	0
Arapahoe Community College	11,148	0	0	0	0	0	11	0	11	0	0
Auraria Higher Education Center[3]	n.a.	5	0	0	2	3	335	7	310	18	0
Colorado State University: Fort Collins	30,467	9	0	5	1	3	441	29	410	2	9
Fort Lewis College	3,841	1	0	0	1	0	62	10	52	0	0
Pikes Peak Community College	14,725	0	0	0	0	0	22	0	22	0	0
Red Rocks Community College	9,544	0	0	0	0	0	16	0	16	0	0
University of Colorado:											
Boulder	32,558	18	0	3	1	14	503	32	464	7	8
Colorado Springs	10,183	1	0	1	0	0	73	2	69	2	0
Denver	22,495	1	0	0	1	0	86	25	54	7	0
Health Sciences Center[3]	n.a.	0	0	0	0	0	14	14	0	0	0
University of Northern Colorado	13,038	2	0	0	2	0	169	10	159	0	0
Connecticut											
Central Connecticut State University	12,521	1	0	0	0	1	48	16	32	0	0
Eastern Connecticut State University	5,586	2	0	1	0	1	75	3	71	1	0
Southern Connecticut State University	11,533	2	0	0	1	1	70	3	67	0	0
University of Connecticut:											
Health Center[3]	n.a.	0	0	0	0	0	4	0	3	1	0
Storrs, Avery Point, and Hartford[3]	n.a.	4	0	4	0	0	288	32	217	39	4
Western Connecticut State University	6,407	2	0	2	0	0	38	7	31	0	1
Yale University	11,875	6	0	2	3	1	295	41	248	6	0
Delaware											
Delaware State University	4,154	12	0	3	3	6	62	24	38	0	0
University of Delaware	21,489	7	0	1	1	5	222	9	212	1	0
Florida											
Edison State College	17,107	4	0	1	0	3	23	0	23	0	0
Florida A&M University	13,204	14	0	3	3	8	183	20	158	5	0
Florida Atlantic University	29,246	4	0	0	1	3	284	32	244	8	0
Florida Gulf Coast University	12,651	3	0	0	0	3	81	2	79	0	0
Florida International University	44,616	9	0	2	3	4	426	37	368	21	1
Florida State University:											
Panama City[3]	n.a.	0	0	0	0	0	10	0	10	0	0

Table 9. Offenses Known to Law Enforcement, by Selected State and University and College, 2012— continued

(Number)

State and university/college	Student enrollment[1]	Violent crime	Murder and nonnegligent manslaughter	Forcible rape	Robbery	Aggravated assault	Property crime	Burglary	Larceny-theft	Motor vehicle theft	Arson[2]
Tallahassee	41,087	31	0	6	17	8	527	84	430	13	1
New College of Florida	845	1	0	1	0	0	27	1	25	1	0
Pensacola State College	11,531	3	0	0	0	3	64	20	42	2	0
Santa Fe College	15,493	1	0	0	1	0	45	4	39	2	0
Tallahassee Community College	15,090	2	0	0	0	2	97	1	96	0	0
University of Central Florida	58,465	26	0	5	5	16	402	34	356	12	1
University of Florida	49,589	18	0	1	3	14	507	28	467	12	1
University of North Florida	16,198	2	0	1	1	0	160	10	150	0	2
University of South Florida:											
St. Petersburg	4,310	2	0	0	0	2	52	5	44	3	0
Tampa	39,596	10	0	4	1	5	400	57	329	14	0
University of West Florida	11,982	2	0	0	1	1	110	12	92	6	1
Georgia											
Abraham Baldwin Agricultural College	3,250	2	0	0	0	2	36	1	35	0	0
Agnes Scott College	871	0	0	0	0	0	19	1	14	4	0
Albany State University	4,663	4	0	0	3	1	65	7	55	3	0
Armstrong Atlantic State University	7,493	0	0	0	0	0	59	5	54	0	0
Atlanta Metropolitan College	2,782	1	0	0	0	1	14	0	7	7	0
Augusta State University	6,741	1	0	0	1	0	77	6	71	0	0
Berry College	2,093	0	0	0	0	0	47	3	44	0	0
Clark Atlanta University	3,843	14	0	1	11	2	79	42	34	3	0
College of Coastal Georgia	3,474	0	0	0	0	0	15	4	11	0	0
Columbus State University	8,307	1	0	0	1	0	57	3	54	0	0
Dalton State College	5,485	0	0	0	0	0	3	0	3	0	0
Darton State College	6,097	2	0	0	2	0	44	2	42	0	0
Emory University	13,893	17	0	14	1	2	548	15	525	8	1
Fort Valley State University	3,896	1	0	0	1	0	38	6	31	1	0
Gainesville State College	8,569	0	0	0	0	0	20	0	19	1	0
Georgia College and State University	6,636	1	0	0	0	1	69	12	55	2	0
Georgia Gwinnett College	7,742	5	0	0	1	4	154	3	151	0	0
Georgia Institute of Technology	20,941	10	0	1	4	5	387	19	359	9	1
Georgia Military College	1,701	0	0	0	0	0	7	0	6	1	0
Georgia Perimeter College	26,996	4	0	0	4	0	88	0	87	1	0
Georgia Southern University	20,212	4	0	2	2	0	254	18	234	2	0
Georgia Southwestern State University	3,046	2	0	0	0	2	49	0	46	3	0
Georgia State University	32,022	33	0	4	26	3	257	5	246	6	0
Gordon College	4,664	0	0	0	0	0	35	5	30	0	0
Kennesaw State University	24,175	5	0	1	2	2	159	27	131	1	0
Macon State College	5,702	0	0	0	0	0	27	1	26	0	0
Medical College of Georgia	2,442	1	0	0	1	0	107	3	92	12	0
Mercer University	8,329	3	0	0	2	1	124	13	108	3	0
Middle Georgia College	3,424	1	0	1	0	0	41	2	39	0	0
Morehouse College	2,438	6	0	0	5	1	130	28	99	3	0
North Georgia College and State University	6,067	2	0	2	0	0	28	0	28	0	0
Piedmont College	2,818	0	0	0	0	0	0	0	0	0	0
Savannah State University	4,552	16	0	4	7	5	187	10	176	1	0
Southern Crescent Technical College	5,155	1	0	0	0	1	19	2	17	0	0
Southern Polytechnic State University	5,784	2	0	0	1	1	75	3	71	1	0
South Georgia College	2,270	0	0	0	0	0	27	11	16	0	0
Spelman College	2,170	8	0	0	6	2	36	7	29	0	0
University of Georgia	34,816	15	0	6	4	5	303	44	249	10	5
University of West Georgia	11,646	3	0	0	0	3	255	20	233	2	0
Valdosta State University	13,089	5	1	1	2	1	302	29	273	0	1
Wesleyan College	681	1	0	1	0	0	11	0	11	0	0
West Georgia Technical College	7,331	0	0	0	0	0	21	3	17	1	0
Young Harris College	886	1	0	0	0	1	17	0	16	1	0
Illinois											
Benedictine University: Lisle	7,013	0	0	0	0	0	27	4	22	1	0
Black Hawk College											
Kewannee[3]	n.a.	0	0	0	0	0	10	2	8	0	0
Moline	6,403	0	0	0	0	0	9	0	9	0	0
Chicago State University	6,882	6	0	0	6	0	47	3	44	0	0

Table 9. Offenses Known to Law Enforcement, by Selected State and University and College, 2012— continued

(Number)

State and university/college	Student enrollment[1]	Violent crime	Murder and nonnegligent manslaughter	Forcible rape	Robbery	Aggravated assault	Property crime	Burglary	Larceny-theft	Motor vehicle theft	Arson[2]
Eastern Illinois University	11,178	16	0	5	2	9	77	7	70	0	0
Elgin Community College	11,811	1	0	0	0	1	28	0	28	0	0
Harper College	16,007	0	0	0	0	0	42	5	37	0	0
Illinois State University	12,283	1	0	0	0	1	34	2	32	0	0
Illinois State University	21,310	18	0	3	2	13	223	38	183	2	2
John A. Logan College	7,294	0	0	0	0	0	8	0	8	0	0
Joliet Junior College	15,322	0	0	0	0	0	45	0	45	0	0
Lake Land College	8,867	4	0	1	0	3	20	0	20	0	0
Lewis University	6,394	2	0	1	0	1	34	3	31	0	0
Lincoln Land Community College	7,337	0	0	0	0	0	15	0	15	0	0
Loyola University	16,040	14	0	0	14	0	198	14	179	5	0
McHenry County College	7,104	0	0	0	0	0	17	0	17	0	0
Moraine Valley Community College	18,169	1	0	0	0	1	86	1	85	0	0
Morton College	5,321	0	0	0	0	0	21	2	19	0	0
Northeastern Illinois University	11,580	2	0	0	1	1	74	0	74	0	0
Northern Illinois University	22,990	14	0	5	2	7	207	30	175	2	0
Northwestern University:											
Chicago[3]	n.a.	0	0	0	0	0	40	4	36	0	0
Evanston	20,959	2	0	1	0	1	270	44	226	0	0
Oakton Community College	11,175	2	0	0	0	2	21	0	20	1	0
Rock Valley College	8,628	0	0	0	0	0	31	1	30	0	0
Southern Illinois University:											
Carbondale	19,817	26	0	6	12	8	372	65	302	5	1
Edwardsville	14,235	3	0	2	1	0	155	22	131	2	1
School of Medicine[3]	n.a.	0	0	0	0	0	14	0	14	0	0
South Suburban College	7,524	0	0	0	0	0	27	0	26	1	0
Southwestern Illinois College	12,779	5	0	0	0	5	38	2	35	1	0
University of Illinois:											
Chicago	28,091	15	0	2	9	4	498	6	488	4	0
Springfield	5,137	2	0	1	0	1	19	2	17	0	0
Urbana	44,407	12	0	3	6	3	378	15	362	1	2
Western Illinois University	12,554	12	0	9	0	3	187	57	129	1	3
Indiana											
Ball State University	22,147	9	0	1	4	4	333	37	291	5	4
Butler University	4,626	4	0	2	0	2	137	17	115	5	1
Indiana State University	11,528	10	0	0	0	10	246	5	239	2	0
Indiana University:											
Gary	6,035	2	0	1	1	0	27	0	25	2	0
Indianapolis	30,530	7	0	1	0	6	345	65	274	6	1
Southeast	7,256	1	0	0	0	1	22	0	22	0	0
Marian University	2,550	1	0	0	1	0	32	2	30	0	0
Purdue University	40,849	12	0	1	5	6	482	34	439	9	0
Iowa											
Iowa State University	29,611	8	0	7	0	1	257	32	225	0	4
University of Iowa	29,810	10	0	4	3	3	192	25	166	1	1
University of Northern Iowa	13,168	2	0	1	0	1	103	11	91	1	0
Kansas											
Emporia State University	5,976	1	0	0	0	1	20	1	18	1	0
Fort Hays State University	12,802	3	0	0	1	2	30	6	24	0	1
Kansas City Kansas Community College	7,555	1	0	0	1	0	53	2	50	1	0
Kansas State University	23,863	5	0	0	2	3	135	23	108	4	0
Pittsburg State University	7,275	5	0	2	0	3	93	2	90	1	0
University of Kansas: Main Campus	27,939	2	0	0	2	0	212	34	175	3	0
Washburn University	7,303	2	0	0	1	1	65	9	51	5	1
Wichita State University	14,909	2	0	1	1	0	128	3	110	15	3
Kentucky											
Eastern Kentucky University	16,062	5	0	4	1	0	236	48	183	5	1
Kentucky State University	2,746	0	0	0	0	0	97	4	93	0	0
Morehead State University	10,968	2	0	1	1	0	79	23	56	0	0
Murray State University	10,623	4	0	1	2	1	108	9	97	2	0

Table 9. Offenses Known to Law Enforcement, by Selected State and University and College, 2012— continued

(Number)

State and university/college	Student enrollment[1]	Violent crime	Murder and nonnegligent manslaughter	Forcible rape	Robbery	Aggravated assault	Property crime	Burglary	Larceny-theft	Motor vehicle theft	Arson[2]
Northern Kentucky University	15,724	0	0	0	0	0	106	4	102	0	0
University of Kentucky	27,226	5	0	0	3	2	570	40	509	21	1
University of Louisville	21,152	17	0	2	14	1	296	21	268	7	0
Western Kentucky University	21,036	2	0	0	1	1	215	66	148	1	1
Louisiana											
Delgado Community College	20,436	0	0	0	0	0	13	3	9	1	0
Louisiana State University:											
Baton Rouge	29,718	25	0	0	10	15	444	49	390	5	0
Eunice	2,982	0	0	0	0	0	0	0	0	0	0
Health Sciences Center, New Orleans	2,777	0	0	0	0	0	0	0	0	0	0
Health Sciences Center, Shreveport	867	9	1	0	0	8	47	1	45	1	0
Shreveport	4,562	4	0	0	0	4	27	0	27	0	0
Louisiana Tech University	11,518	2	0	1	1	0	84	10	71	3	0
Nicholls State University	6,767	1	0	0	1	0	31	9	22	0	0
Northwestern State University	9,191	1	0	0	0	1	88	25	63	0	0
Southern University and A&M College:											
Baton Rouge	6,866	19	0	2	11	6	186	22	160	4	0
New Orleans	3,245	0	0	0	0	0	0	0	0	0	
Shreveport	2,831	0	0	0	0	0	24	1	23	0	0
Tulane University	12,845	2	0	1	0	1	145	2	142	1	0
University of Louisiana											
Lafayette	16,885	12	1	2	6	3	198	36	160	2	0
Monroe	8,583	2	0	0	1	1	38	5	31	2	0
University of New Orleans	10,903	2	0	0	1	1	60	3	56	1	0
Maine											
University of Maine:											
Farmington	2,310	1	0	1	0	0	18	5	13	0	0
Orono	11,168	8	0	4	0	4	172	5	167	0	5
University of Southern Maine	9,301	4	0	3	0	1	45	3	41	1	6
Maryland											
Bowie State University	5,608	12	0	4	1	7	94	52	41	1	0
Coppin State University	3,813	5	0	0	4	1	90	4	84	2	5
Frostburg State University	5,429	0	0	0	0	0	67	11	56	0	0
Hagerstown Community College	4,714	0	0	0	0	0	10	0	10	0	0
Morgan State University	8,018	18	0	0	16	2	156	12	143	1	0
Salisbury University	8,606	3	0	3	0	0	121	5	116	0	0
St. Mary's College	1,992	0	0	0	0	0	51	3	48	0	0
Towson University	21,464	4	0	0	0	4	130	8	120	2	0
University of Baltimore	6,406	1	0	0	1	0	58	8	50	0	0
University of Maryland											
Baltimore City	6,395	11	0	0	10	1	142	2	139	1	0
Baltimore County	13,199	6	0	2	1	3	133	5	126	2	0
College Park	37,631	8	0	0	6	2	435	46	361	28	2
Eastern Shore	4,509	12	0	1	2	9	86	30	56	0	0
Massachusetts											
Bentley College	5,574	6	0	1	0	5	77	15	62	0	
Boston College	14,754	5	0	3	0	2	147	3	144	0	
Boston University	32,439	20	0	4	7	9	349	43	305	1	1
Brandeis University	5,828	0	0	0	0	0	62	3	59	0	
Bridgewater State College	11,294	4	0	0	0	4	59	5	54	0	0
Bristol Community College	9,000	0	0	0	0	0	13	0	13	0	
Bunker Hill Community College	12,934	2	0	0	0	2	81	0	80	1	
Clark University	3,462	7	0	2	3	2	62	7	54	1	
Dean College	1,398	1	0	1	0	0	32	7	25	0	
Emerson College	4,469	3	0	1	1	1	55	7	48	0	
Fitchburg State College	6,891	11	0	1	3	7	31	6	25	0	
Framingham State College	6,415	6	0	4	0	2	26	14	12	0	0
Harvard University	27,392	4	0	1	1	2	550	37	510	3	0
Holyoke Community College	7,144	3	0	0	0	3	22	0	21	1	
Lasell College	1,741	7	0	1	1	5	40	6	34	0	

Table 9. Offenses Known to Law Enforcement, by Selected State and University and College, 2012— continued

(Number)

State and university/college	Student enrollment[1]	Violent crime	Murder and nonnegligent manslaughter	Forcible rape	Robbery	Aggravated assault	Property crime	Burglary	Larceny-theft	Motor vehicle theft	Arson[2]
Massachusetts College of Art	2,442	0	0	0	0	0	55	3	52	0	
Massachusetts College of Liberal Arts	1,886	4	0	0	0	4	35	12	23	0	0
Massachusetts Institute of Technology	10,894	6	0	1	0	5	373	10	362	1	0
Merrimack College	2,447	6	0	0	0	6	46	10	36	0	
Mount Holyoke College	2,362	0	0	0	0	0	121	19	102	0	0
Northeastern University	26,959	12	0	0	6	6	401	17	382	2	
North Shore Community College	7,974	1	0	0	0	1	25	0	25	0	
Salem State University	9,646	4	0	3	0	1	84	25	59	0	
Smith College	3,162	0	0	0	0	0	76	7	69	0	0
Springfield College	3,377	3	0	0	3	0	56	7	49	0	
Tufts University: Worcester	10,777	1	0	0	1	0	21	4	17	0	0
University of Massachusetts											
Amherst	28,084	15	0	8	0	7	322	48	272	2	0
Dartmouth	9,225	17	0	1	4	12	248	32	215	1	
Wellesley College	2,502	0	0	0	0	0	43	8	35	0	
Western New England College	3,729	0	0	0	0	0	25	2	23	0	
Westfield State University	6,092	8	0	7	0	1	41	8	33	0	2
Worcester Polytechnic Institute	5,778	2	0	0	1	1	42	2	40	0	0
Michigan											
Central Michigan University	28,194	5	0	3	0	2	185	15	166	4	0
Delta College	11,478	1	0	0	0	1	41	0	41	0	0
Eastern Michigan University	23,419	8	0	0	1	7	235	11	215	9	8
Ferris State University	14,560	1	0	1	0	0	71	3	67	1	0
Grand Rapids Community College	17,575	0	0	0	0	0	94	0	94	0	0
Grand Valley State University	24,662	6	0	4	0	2	145	3	142	0	0
Kalamazoo Valley Community College	11,395	0	0	0	0	0	36	0	36	0	2
Kellogg Community College	6,071	0	0	0	0	0	3	0	3	0	0
Lansing Community College	20,640	3	0	0	3	0	109	1	107	1	0
Macomb Community College	23,969	0	0	0	0	0	48	1	45	2	0
Michigan State University	47,825	14	0	8	1	5	641	47	583	11	1
Michigan Technological University	7,022	1	0	1	0	0	61	2	58	1	0
Mott Community College	11,760	11	0	1	3	7	88	1	85	2	1
Northern Michigan University	9,405	3	0	2	0	1	109	4	105	0	0
Oakland Community College	29,158	3	0	1	1	1	54	0	49	5	0
Oakland University	19,379	4	0	0	0	4	79	8	69	2	0
Saginaw Valley State University	10,790	3	0	0	0	3	86	5	79	2	0
University of Michigan											
Ann Arbor	42,716	14	0	2	3	9	786	36	740	10	6
Flint	8,262	3	0	0	3	0	104	1	100	3	0
Western Michigan University	25,086	4	0	0	1	3	127	8	117	2	2
Minnesota [4]											
University of Minnesota											
Duluth	11,806		0		1	1	55	4	51	0	1
Morris	1,932		0		0	0	6	0	6	0	0
Twin Cities	52,557		0		3	1	529	36	480	13	0
Mississippi											
Coahoma Community College	2,999	0	0	0	0	0	6	6	0	0	0
Jackson State University	8,903	30	0	0	28	2	220	53	162	5	0
Mississippi State University	20,424	1	1	0	0	0	246	15	229	2	1
Northeast Mississippi Community College	3,633	0	0	0	0	0	60	3	57	0	0
University of Mississippi											
Medical Center	2,016	1	0	0	0	1	153	2	149	2	0
Oxford	18,224	5	0	1	2	2	279	31	247	1	0
Missouri											
Lincoln University	3,388	3	0	1	0	2	51	6	44	1	0
Metropolitan Community College	21,285	1	0	1	0	0	93	5	87	1	0
Mineral Area College	4,035	1	0	0	0	1	4	1	3	0	0
Missouri Southern State University	5,591	1	0	1	0	0	36	7	27	2	1
Missouri University of Science and Technology	7,521	1	0	1	0	0	71	6	65	0	3
Missouri Western State University	6,260	0	0	0	0	0	64	1	63	0	0

Table 9. Offenses Known to Law Enforcement, by Selected State and University and College, 2012— continued

(Number)

State and university/college	Student enrollment[1]	Violent crime	Murder and nonnegligent manslaughter	Forcible rape	Robbery	Aggravated assault	Property crime	Burglary	Larceny-theft	Motor vehicle theft	Arson[2]
Northwest Missouri State University	7,225	3	0	0	1	2	65	6	59	0	0
Southeast Missouri State University	11,378	1	0	0	1	0	35	6	29	0	0
St. Charles Community College	8,174	1	0	0	0	1	22	0	22	0	0
St. Louis Community College											
Florissant Valley[3]	n.a.	0	0	0	0	0	58	0	57	1	0
Meramec	29,200	0	0	0	0	0	40	0	40	0	0
Three Rivers Community College	4,234	1	0	0	0	1	7	1	6	0	0
Truman State University	6,101	2	0	0	0	2	50	0	50	0	0
University of Central Missouri	11,637	6	0	1	1	4	139	25	112	2	0
University of Missouri											
Columbia	33,762	15	0	1	2	12	373	11	358	4	2
Kansas City	15,473	1	0	0	0	1	157	59	92	6	1
St. Louis	16,809	3	0	1	1	1	109	13	95	1	1
Washington University	13,908	2	0	0	1	1	96	1	93	2	0
Montana											
Montana State University	13,671	5	0	1	0	4	229	20	207	2	18
University of Montana	15,669	0	0	0	0	0	96	3	93	0	0
Nebraska											
Metropolitan Community College											
Douglas County	18,518	0	0	0	0	0	45	1	43	1	0
Sarpy County[3]	n.a.	0	0	0	0	0	0	0	0	0	0
University of Nebraska											
Kearney	7,100	0	0	0	0	0	66	12	54	0	0
Lincoln	24,593	7	0	1	2	4	248	9	238	1	1
Nevada											
Truckee Meadows Community College	11,131	1	0	0	1	0	12	0	11	1	0
University of Nevada											
Las Vegas	27,364	11	0	0	5	6	274	27	222	25	0
Reno	18,004	5	0	0	1	4	167	19	141	7	3
New Hampshire											
University of New Hampshire	15,128	16	0	9	1	6	175	6	165	4	4
New Jersey											
Brookdale Community College	14,952	0	0	0	0	0	30	6	24	0	0
Essex County College	12,532	7	0	0	5	2	89	0	89	0	0
Kean University	16,187	3	0	0	1	2	126	14	112	0	0
Middlesex County College	12,732	1	0	0	0	1	52	1	50	1	0
Monmouth University	6,570	0	0	0	0	0	51	7	43	1	2
Montclair State University	18,498	7	0	1	1	5	176	5	168	3	0
New Jersey Institute of Technology	9,558	8	0	0	6	2	137	6	117	14	0
Richard Stockton College of New Jersey	8,108	1	0	0	0	1	44	2	42	0	1
Rowan University	11,786	4	0	1	1	2	111	15	94	2	0
Rutgers University											
Camden	6,428	2	0	0	1	1	72	9	62	1	0
Newark	11,804	22	0	0	21	1	231	48	163	20	0
New Brunswick	39,950	36	0	7	12	17	655	81	567	7	0
Stevens Institute of Technology	5,541	1	0	0	1	0	34	0	33	1	0
The College of New Jersey	7,152	0	0	0	0	0	71	6	65	0	0
University of Medicine and Dentistry	7,115	1	0	0	0	1	95	6	83	6	0
Camden[3]		0	0	0	0	0	6	0	6	0	0
Newark	7,212	17	0	0	6	11	148	2	132	14	0
New Brunswick[3]	n.a.	1	0	0	1	0	13	0	13	0	0
William Paterson University	11,518	3	0	0	0	3	75	1	74	0	0
New Mexico											
Eastern New Mexico University	5,566	1	0	0	0	1	63	11	52	0	0
New Mexico Institute of Mining and Technology	1,859	3	0	1	0	2	27	4	22	1	0
New York [5]											
Cornell University	21,131	4	0	2	1	1	271	19	250	2	

Table 9. Offenses Known to Law Enforcement, by Selected State and University and College, 2012— continued

(Number)

State and university/college	Student enrollment[1]	Violent crime	Murder and nonnegligent manslaughter	Forcible rape	Robbery	Aggravated assault	Property crime	Burglary	Larceny-theft	Motor vehicle theft	Arson[2]
Ithaca College	6,760	0	0	0	0	0	103	18	85	0	1
Rensselaer Polytechnic Institute	6,538	0	0	0	0	0	93	1	92	0	0
State University of New York:											
Binghamton	14,746	5	0	2	0	3	192	19	172	1	
Buffalo	28,849	4	0	0	3	1	328	53	273	2	0
Downstate Medical Center	1,751	4	0	0	4	0	72	1	69	2	
Maritime College	1,823	0	0	0	0	0	27	13	14	0	
Stony Brook	23,920	18	0	1	2	15	371	47	320	4	1
Upstate Medical Center	1,589	2	0	0	1	1	105	0	105	0	0
State University of New York Agricultural and Technical College											
Alfred	3,616	2	0	1	0	1	79	8	71	0	
Canton	3,825	0	0	0	0	0	66	2	64	0	
Cobleskill	2,516	3	0	2	0	1	53	18	35	0	
Farmingdale	7,633	1	0	0	1	0	36	1	35	0	
Morrisville	3,230	1	0	1	0	0	58	4	54	0	
State University of New York College											
Brockport	8,413	3	0	0	0	3	67	4	62	1	
Buffalo	12,204	4	0	3	1	0	127	20	105	2	4
Cortland	7,331	0	0	0	0	0	42	14	28	0	
Fredonia	5,720	1	0	1	0	0	45	10	35	0	
Geneseo	5,683	0	0	0	0	0	124	9	114	1	
New Paltz	7,857	4	0	1	0	3	63	9	54	0	
Old Westbury	4,459	2	0	0	2	0	31	4	26	1	
Oswego	8,216	5	0	4	1	0	171	35	136	0	
Plattsburgh	6,350	0	0	0	0	0	87	6	81	0	
Potsdam	4,395	2	0	0	0	2	125	26	99	0	
Purchase	4,267	2	0	0	1	1	48	13	35	0	
Technology	3,249	0	0	0	0	0	56	9	47	0	0
United States Merchant Marine Academy	1,034	0	0	0	0	0	8	5	3	0	0
North Carolina											
Appalachian State University	17,344	1	0	0	1	0	81	12	69	0	1
Duke University	15,427	4	0	1	1	2	639	39	586	14	0
East Carolina University	27,386	5	0	3	1	1	196	9	187	0	0
Elizabeth City State University	2,930	1	0	0	0	1	52	15	32	5	0
Elon University	5,916	1	0	1	0	0	77	12	65	0	0
Fayetteville State University	5,930	5	0	2	1	2	85	26	56	3	0
North Carolina Agricultural and Technical State University	10,881	12	0	1	4	7	132	11	119	2	1
North Carolina Central University	8,359	0	0	0	0	0	165	22	142	1	1
North Carolina School of the Arts	893	0	0	0	0	0	28	1	27	0	1
North Carolina State University, Raleigh	34,767	17	0	1	7	9	446	28	409	9	0
University of North Carolina											
Asheville	3,863	1	0	1	0	0	42	2	40	0	0
Chapel Hill	29,137	1	0	1	0	0	372	24	344	4	0
Greensboro	18,627	1	0	0	1	0	188	0	186	2	0
Pembroke	6,251	0	0	0	0	0	94	6	88	0	0
Wilmington	13,145	3	0	2	1	0	387	12	372	3	0
Wake Forest University	7,351	6	0	2	1	3	188	47	132	9	0
Western Carolina University	9,352	1	0	1	0	0	93	10	83	0	0
Winston-Salem State University	6,163	5	0	1	3	1	63	3	55	5	0
North Dakota											
North Dakota State College of Science	3,127	1	0	1	0	0	29	10	17	2	0
North Dakota State University	14,399	3	0	2	1	0	79	6	72	1	0
University of North Dakota	14,697	5	0	1	1	3	162	12	150	0	1
Ohio											
Bowling Green State University	17,577	2	0	1	0	1	190	35	153	2	7
Capital University	3,550	1	0	1	0	0	40	6	34	0	0
Central State University	2,503	1	0	0	0	1	70	9	61	0	0
Cleveland State University	17,229	0	0	0	0	0	41	1	39	1	0
Columbus State Community College	30,921	1	0	0	1	0	102	0	101	1	0

Table 9. Offenses Known to Law Enforcement, by Selected State and University and College, 2012— continued

(Number)

State and university/college	Student enrollment[1]	Violent crime	Murder and nonnegligent manslaughter	Forcible rape	Robbery	Aggravated assault	Property crime	Burglary	Larceny-theft	Motor vehicle theft	Arson[2]
Cuyahoga Community College	30,853	3	0	0	3	0	150	11	138	1	0
Kent State University	27,855	3	0	0	3	0	192	8	183	1	3
Lakeland Community College	9,521	0	0	0	0	0	43	0	42	1	0
Miami University	17,395	13	0	11	0	2	190	14	175	1	0
Ohio State University, Columbus	56,867	14	0	9	4	1	972	21	947	4	7
Ohio University	26,201	12	0	6	2	4	213	30	183	0	2
Otterbein University	2,997	0	0	0	0	0	35	4	31	0	0
Shawnee State University	4,711	2	0	0	0	2	33	3	30	0	0
Sinclair Community College	21,106	0	0	0	0	0	23	0	23	0	0
University of Akron	27,470	4	0	0	4	0	270	9	252	9	0
University of Cincinnati	33,329	13	0	1	4	8	453	19	434	0	2
University of Toledo	22,610	4	0	0	4	0	364	46	315	3	0
Wright State University	18,304	6	0	5	0	1	155	15	136	4	0
Youngstown State University	14,483	1	0	0	1	0	143	5	135	3	0
Oklahoma											
Cameron University	6,463	0	0	0	0	0	19	0	19	0	0
East Central University	4,851	0	0	0	0	0	12	0	12	0	0
Northeastern Oklahoma A&M College	2,542	5	0	0	0	5	60	23	35	2	0
Northeastern State University											
Broken Arrow[3]	n.a.	0	0	0	0	0	4	0	4	0	0
Tahlequah	9,316	2	0	0	1	1	46	11	35	0	0
Oklahoma City University	3,575	4	0	0	2	2	52	11	39	2	0
Oklahoma State University											
Main Campus	24,390	9	0	5	3	1	190	34	154	2	0
Okmulgee	3,995	0	0	0	0	0	22	4	18	0	0
Tulsa	427	1	0	0	0	1	10	0	9	1	0
Rogers State University	4,803	0	0	0	0	0	7	2	5	0	0
Seminole State College	2,282	0	0	0	0	0	7	3	4	0	0
Southeastern Oklahoma State University	4,140	0	0	0	0	0	24	13	10	1	0
Southwestern Oklahoma State University	5,263	0	0	0	0	0	32	11	20	1	0
Tulsa Community College	20,154	1	0	0	1	0	35	1	34	0	0
University of Central Oklahoma	17,239	2	0	1	1	0	124	19	104	1	0
University of Oklahoma											
Health Sciences Center	3,590	13	0	1	2	10	205	7	196	2	0
Norman	27,138	4	0	3	0	1	271	10	249	12	0
Oregon											
Portland State University	28,035	4	0	1	2	1	321	40	280	1	1
Pennsylvania											
Bloomsburg University	10,159	5	0	4	0	1	82	2	80	0	1
California University	9,483	2	0	0	0	2	24	0	24	0	0
Cheyney University	1,200	6	0	2	1	3	72	26	46	0	0
Clarion University	6,991	1	0	1	0	0	29	3	26	0	2
Dickinson College	2,397	0	0	0	0	0	71	15	55	1	0
East Stroudsburg University	7,353	8	0	1	1	6	68	12	56	0	0
Edinboro University	8,262	3	0	1	0	2	53	4	49	0	0
Elizabethtown College	2,389	0	0	0	0	0	44	0	44	0	0
Indiana University	15,340	6	0	2	0	4	80	6	72	2	0
Kutztown University	10,283	4	0	3	1	0	134	13	120	1	0
Lehigh University	7,055	3	0	3	0	0	70	2	68	0	0
Lock Haven University	5,366	0	0	0	0	0	38	6	31	1	0
Mansfield University	3,275	0	0	0	0	0	21	2	19	0	0
Millersville University	8,725	3	0	2	0	1	33	2	31	0	0
Moravian College	2,002	3	0	0	0	3	41	1	40	0	0
Pennsylvania State University											
Altoona	4,105	1	0	0	0	1	40	7	33	0	0
Beaver	870	0	0	0	0	0	9	0	9	0	0
Behrend	4,226	0	0	0	0	0	23	4	19	0	0
Berks	2,873	0	0	0	0	0	38	10	28	0	0
Harrisburg	4,269	0	0	0	0	0	33	2	31	0	0
Hazelton	1,172	1	0	0	0	1	13	2	11	0	0
McKeesport	701	5	0	0	0	5	5	0	5	0	0

Table 9. Offenses Known to Law Enforcement, by Selected State and University and College, 2012— continued

(Number)

State and university/college	Student enrollment[1]	Violent crime	Murder and nonnegligent manslaughter	Forcible rape	Robbery	Aggravated assault	Property crime	Burglary	Larceny-theft	Motor vehicle theft	Arson[2]
Mont Alto	1,217	0	0	0	0	0	10	3	7	0	0
Schuykill	1,012	0	0	0	0	0	12	3	9	0	0
University Park	45,628	20	0	5	2	13	463	48	411	4	3
Shippensburg University	8,183	3	0	3	0	0	35	9	26	0	0
Slippery Rock University	8,712	0	0	0	0	0	41	2	39	0	0
University of Pittsburgh											
Bradford	1,564	0	0	0	0	0	38	23	15	0	0
Johnstown	2,957	2	0	0	2	0	42	2	40	0	0
Pittsburgh	28,766	15	0	0	4	11	237	19	218	0	4
Titusville	448	0	0	0	0	0	9	0	9	0	1
West Chester University	15,100	2	0	0	0	2	117	12	104	1	4
Rhode Island											
Brown University	8,768	0	0	0	0	0	140	21	119	0	0
University of Rhode Island	16,317	3	0	0	1	2	176	14	160	2	0
South Carolina											
Benedict College	3,213	3	0	1	2	0	247	113	130	4	1
Bob Jones University	3,631	0	0	0	0	0	39	23	16	0	0
Clemson University	19,914	3	0	1	0	2	248	29	211	8	0
Coastal Carolina University	9,084	8	0	1	3	4	214	33	179	2	0
College of Charleston	11,649	3	0	2	0	1	84	1	81	2	1
Columbia College	1,266	1	0	1	0	0	8	0	6	2	0
Denmark Technical College	1,607	7	0	0	1	6	50	4	46	0	0
Erskine College	773	2	0	2	0	0	8	0	8	0	1
Francis Marion University	4,187	0	0	0	0	0	47	1	46	0	0
Greenville Technical College	14,453	4	0	0	0	4	81	13	62	6	0
Lander University	3,069	3	0	2	1	0	39	8	31	0	0
Medical University of South Carolina	2,678	4	0	0	0	4	155	0	155	0	0
Midlands Technical College	12,224	1	0	0	0	1	19	0	18	1	0
South Carolina State University	4,326	12	0	0	4	8	105	28	71	6	1
Spartanburg Methodist College	803	1	0	0	0	1	10	2	7	1	0
The Citadel	3,390	5	0	0	4	1	66	33	33	0	0
Trident Technical College	16,781	2	0	0	1	1	48	2	41	5	0
University of South Carolina											
Aiken	3,277	0	0	0	0	0	24	0	22	2	0
Columbia	30,721	5	0	1	3	1	365	32	293	40	3
Upstate	5,493	1	0	1	0	0	32	3	29	0	0
Winthrop University	5,913	3	0	2	0	1	57	0	56	1	0
South Dakota											
South Dakota State University	12,725	0	0	0	0	0	46	0	46	0	0
Tennessee											
Austin Peay State University	10,873	2	0	1	1	0	130	14	113	3	0
Christian Brothers University	1,694	3	0	0	1	2	31	10	20	1	0
East Tennessee State University	15,250	7	0	1	1	5	111	16	93	2	0
Middle Tennessee State University	26,442	12	0	1	3	8	218	28	187	3	1
Northeast State Community College	6,478	1	0	0	0	1	12	0	12	0	0
Southwest Tennessee Community College	12,958	1	0	0	0	1	54	0	54	0	0
Tennessee State University	9,165	14	0	0	7	7	154	16	136	2	0
Tennessee Technological University	11,768	6	0	0	0	6	115	27	87	1	2
University of Memphis	22,725	7	0	1	2	4	229	43	181	5	0
University of Tennessee											
Chattanooga	11,438	8	0	1	1	6	174	28	146	0	1
Health Science Center[3]	n.a.	0	0	0	0	0	38	6	31	1	0
Knoxville	30,194	8	0	1	2	5	501	29	459	13	0
Martin	7,910	3	0	0	1	2	57	17	40	0	0
Vanderbilt University	12,836	25	0	6	4	15	535	12	522	1	1
Volunteer State Community College	8,666	0	0	0	0	0	6	0	6	0	0
Walters State Community College	6,733	1	0	0	0	1	11	1	10	0	0
Texas											
Abilene Christian University	4,558	2	0	0	2	0	75	0	74	1	0

Table 9. Offenses Known to Law Enforcement, by Selected State and University and College, 2012— continued

(Number)

State and university/college	Student enrollment[1]	Violent crime	Murder and nonnegligent manslaughter	Forcible rape	Robbery	Aggravated assault	Property crime	Burglary	Larceny-theft	Motor vehicle theft	Arson[2]
Alamo Community College District	61,507	2	0	0	1	1	363	19	314	30	0
Alvin Community College	5,129	0	0	0	0	0	11	0	10	1	0
Amarillo College	11,616	0	0	0	0	0	32	2	30	0	0
Angelo State University	7,084	2	0	1	0	1	81	5	76	0	0
Austin College	1,353	0	0	0	0	0	42	10	32	0	2
Baylor Health Care System[3]	n.a.	2	0	2	0	0	415	4	400	11	0
Baylor University, Waco	15,029	4	0	2	0	2	125	12	110	3	0
Blinn College	18,106	10	0	4	0	6	70	11	59	0	0
Central Texas College	26,995	1	0	0	0	1	33	0	33	0	0
College of the Mainland	4,168	0	0	0	0	0	20	0	19	1	0
El Paso Community College	30,723	2	0	0	0	2	86	4	76	6	0
Grayson County College	5,207	1	0	0	0	1	12	1	10	1	0
Hardin-Simmons University	2,358	0	0	0	0	0	26	3	23	0	0
Houston Baptist University	2,432	0	0	0	0	0	21	15	6	0	0
Houston Community College	63,015	20	0	0	6	14	348	17	316	15	0
Lamar University, Beaumont	14,020	3	0	2	0	1	37	4	32	1	0
Laredo Community College	10,076	0	0	0	0	0	18	0	18	0	0
McLennan Community College	10,185	0	0	0	0	0	19	0	19	0	0
Midwestern State University	6,181	0	0	0	0	0	52	17	35	0	0
Mountain View College	9,431	3	0	0	2	1	41	6	32	3	0
North Lake College	11,865	1	0	0	0	1	31	4	27	0	0
Paris Junior College	5,936	2	0	1	0	1	20	8	12	0	0
Prairie View A&M University	8,425	16	0	5	5	6	139	43	89	7	0
Rice University	6,224	10	0	3	5	2	189	2	187	0	0
Richland College	20,000	1	0	0	1	0	71	0	70	1	0
Southern Methodist University	10,982	6	0	3	1	2	158	5	146	7	0
South Plains College	10,482	1	0	0	1	0	6	2	4	0	0
Southwestern University	1,347	0	0	0	0	0	35	2	33	0	0
Stephen F. Austin State University	12,903	8	0	7	0	1	201	17	183	1	0
St. Mary's University	4,188	2	0	0	0	2	60	6	49	5	0
Sul Ross State University	2,940	0	0	0	0	0	39	5	32	2	0
Tarleton State University	11,693	1	0	1	0	0	60	14	46	0	0
Texas A&M International University	7,037	1	0	0	0	1	41	5	35	1	0
Texas A&M University											
College Station	50,230	7	0	2	2	3	487	57	427	3	0
Commerce	11,417	2	0	0	0	2	78	17	61	0	1
Corpus Christi	10,162	0	0	0	0	0	55	6	49	0	0
Galveston	2,035	0	0	0	0	0	19	1	18	0	0
Kingsville	10,290	7	0	0	1	6	134	40	92	2	1
San Antonio[3]	n.a.	0	0	0	0	0	23	0	23	0	0
Texas Christian University	9,518	2	0	2	0	0	187	16	169	2	0
Texas Southern University	9,730	21	0	3	10	8	252	44	204	4	1
Texas State Technical College											
Harlingen	5,807	1	0	0	0	1	52	1	50	1	0
Waco	4,730	7	0	1	1	5	85	33	51	1	0
West Texas	856	0	0	0	0	0	2	1	1	0	0
Texas State University, San Marcos	34,087	7	0	0	0	7	308	41	264	3	1
Texas Tech University, Lubbock	32,327	9	0	4	1	4	327	16	309	2	1
Texas Woman's University	14,718	3	0	2	0	1	34	1	33	0	0
Tyler Junior College	11,540	3	0	0	0	3	97	0	96	1	0
University of Houston											
Central Campus	39,820	15	0	1	12	2	496	58	419	19	0
Clearlake	8,185	0	0	0	0	0	14	0	14	0	0
Downtown Campus	12,918	2	0	0	2	0	78	0	78	0	0
University of Mary Hardin-Baylor	3,137	1	0	0	0	1	40	5	35	0	0
University of North Texas											
Denton	37,818	6	0	1	0	5	193	19	170	4	0
Health Science Center	1,760	1	0	0	1	0	10	0	10	0	0
University of Texas											
Arlington	33,439	13	0	6	5	2	323	31	283	9	0
Austin	51,112	8	0	3	4	1	485	36	441	8	2
Brownsville	14,918	1	0	1	0	0	96	0	92	4	0
Dallas	18,864	3	0	1	0	2	117	8	106	3	0
El Paso	22,640	5	0	1	0	4	202	26	174	2	0

Table 9. Offenses Known to Law Enforcement, by Selected State and University and College, 2012— continued

(Number)

State and university/college	Student enrollment[1]	Violent crime	Murder and nonnegligent manslaughter	Forcible rape	Robbery	Aggravated assault	Property crime	Burglary	Larceny-theft	Motor vehicle theft	Arson[2]
Health Science Center, San Antonio	3,234	0	0	0	0	0	103	1	101	1	0
Health Science Center, Tyler[3]	n.a.	1	0	0	0	1	6	2	4	0	0
Houston	4,916	5	0	1	3	1	276	23	247	6	0
Medical Branch	2,825	0	0	0	0	0	77	0	77	0	0
Pan American	19,034	2	0	0	0	2	150	4	146	0	1
Permian Basin	3,831	0	0	0	0	0	21	1	20	0	0
San Antonio	30,968	2	0	1	0	1	173	5	167	1	0
Southwestern Medical School	2,487	1	0	0	1	0	146	2	131	13	0
Tyler	6,696	0	0	0	0	0	35	4	31	0	0
West Texas A&M University	7,886	1	0	1	0	0	65	13	52	0	0
Utah											
Brigham Young University	34,101	3	0	0	0	3	236	4	230	2	1
College of Eastern Utah	2,323	1	0	0	0	1	7	0	7	0	0
Snow College	4,465	0	0	0	0	0	25	0	25	0	0
Southern Utah University	7,750	0	0	0	0	0	31	2	29	0	0
University of Utah	31,660	10	0	3	2	5	478	58	399	21	2
Utah State University	26,757	0	0	0	0	0	97	6	91	0	0
Utah Valley University	33,395	1	0	0	0	1	89	3	81	5	0
Weber State University	25,301	2	0	2	0	0	50	5	45	0	0
Vermont											
University of Vermont	13,478	2	0	0	0	2	97	8	89	0	0
Virginia											
Christopher Newport University	4,990	1	0	0	0	1	161	6	154	1	0
College of William and Mary	8,200	0	0	0	0	0	211	11	199	1	1
Emory and Henry College	982	0	0	0	0	0	1	0	1	0	0
Ferrum College	1,512	5	0	3	2	0	42	19	22	1	0
George Mason University	33,320	1	0	0	1	0	244	37	204	3	2
Hampton University	5,221	4	0	0	1	3	78	18	59	1	1
James Madison University	19,722	1	0	1	0	0	131	3	127	1	0
J. Sargeant Reynolds Community College	13,367	1	0	0	0	1	18	0	18	0	0
Longwood University	4,860	1	0	0	1	0	49	2	45	2	0
Lord Fairfax Community College	7,270	0	0	0	0	0	1	0	1	0	0
Norfolk State University	7,091	8	0	2	3	3	134	20	112	2	3
Northern Virginia Community College	50,044	1	0	0	1	0	30	0	30	0	0
Old Dominion University	24,753	23	0	5	8	10	330	39	282	9	1
Radford University	9,370	5	0	2	0	3	64	2	60	2	1
Richard Bland College	1,629	0	0	0	0	0	14	8	6	0	0
Thomas Nelson Community College	10,999	1	0	0	0	1	9	0	9	0	0
University of Mary Washington	5,170	4	0	0	2	2	77	1	76	0	4
University of Richmond	4,348	0	0	0	0	0	100	18	77	5	1
University of Virginia	24,297	4	0	1	1	2	299	61	228	10	2
University of Virginia's College at Wise	2,067	0	0	0	0	0	2	0	2	0	0
Virginia Commonwealth University	31,627	21	0	0	7	14	566	16	540	10	1
Virginia Military Institute	1,605	0	0	0	0	0	45	30	15	0	1
Virginia Polytechnic Institute and State University	30,936	11	0	4	0	7	191	27	162	2	1
Virginia State University	5,890	8	0	0	2	6	116	3	107	6	1
Virginia Western Community College	8,557	0	0	0	0	0	6	0	6	0	0
Washington											
Central Washington University	11,320	5	0	2	1	2	158	18	135	5	4
Eastern Washington University	12,126	3	0	2	1	0	112	11	98	3	0
Evergreen State College	4,794	1	0	1	0	0	99	13	85	1	1
University of Washington	42,444	5	0	1	4	0	590	74	509	7	3
Washington State University											
Pullman	27,329	6	0	4	1	1	206	33	172	1	3
Vancouver[3]	n.a.	1	0	1	0	0	8	1	7	0	0
Western Washington University	14,842	9	0	4	0	5	126	11	114	1	1
West Virginia											
Concord University	2,797	0	0	0	0	0	8	3	5	0	0
Marshall University	13,966	13	0	0	1	12	85	2	83	0	0

Table 9. Offenses Known to Law Enforcement, by Selected State and University and College, 2012— continued

(Number)

State and university/college	Student enrollment[1]	Violent crime	Murder and nonnegligent manslaughter	Forcible rape	Robbery	Aggravated assault	Property crime	Burglary	Larceny-theft	Motor vehicle theft	Arson[2]
Potomac State College	1,802	4	0	0	0	4	10	2	8	0	0
Shepherd University	4,393	2	0	1	1	0	25	4	21	0	0
West Liberty State College	2,790	1	0	1	0	0	4	0	4	0	0
West Virginia State University	2,827	0	0	0	0	0	28	5	21	2	0
West Virginia University	29,617	24	0	2	3	19	195	21	174	0	1
Wisconsin											
University of Wisconsin											
Eau Claire	11,300	0	0	0	0	0	74	0	72	2	0
Green Bay	6,671	0	0	0	0	0	22	1	19	2	0
La Crosse	10,284	0	0	0	0	0	0	0	0	0	0
Madison	41,946	8	0	1	2	5	408	54	352	2	1
Milwaukee	29,350	3	0	2	1	0	415	21	393	1	3
Oshkosh	13,513	1	0	1	0	0	97	14	82	1	0
Parkside	4,829	0	0	0	0	0	51	0	50	1	0
Platteville	8,262	5	0	2	1	2	92	0	92	0	0
River Falls	6,803	0	0	0	0	0	38	0	37	1	0
Stevens Point	9,484	0	0	0	0	0	89	1	88	0	0
Stout	9,350	1	0	0	0	1	121	10	110	1	0
Superior	2,814	0	0	0	0	0	25	0	25	0	1
Whitewater	11,629	0	0	0	0	0	57	3	53	1	0
Wyoming											
Sheridan College	4,296	0	0	0	0	0	1	0	1	0	0
University of Wyoming	12,925	1	0	0	0	1	166	5	160	1	0

Note: Caution should be exercised in making any intercampus comparisons or ranking schools because university/college crime statistics are affected by a variety of factors. These include demographic characteristics of the surrounding community, ratio of male to female students, number of on-campus residents, accessibility of the campus to outside visitors, size of enrollment, etc. 1 The student enrollment figures provided by the United States Department of Education are for the 2011 school year, the most recent available. The enrollment figures include full-time and part-time students. 2 A blank cell in the arson column indicates that the FBI did not receive 12 complete months of arson data for that agency. 3 Student enrollment figures were not available. 4 The data collection methodology for the offense of forcible rape used by the Minnesota state Uniform Crime Reporting (UCR) Program does not comply with national UCR Program guidelines. Consequently, its figures for forcible rape and violent crime (of which forcible rape is a part) are not published in this table. 5 Because of changes in the state/local agency's reporting practices, figures are not comparable to previous years' data. n.a. = not available

Table 10. Offenses Known to Law Enforcement, by Selected State Metropolitan and Nonmetropolitan Counties, 2012

(Number)

State/county	Violent crime	Murder and nonnegligent manslaughter	Forcible rape	Robbery	Aggravated assault	Property crime	Burglary	Larceny-theft	Motor vehicle theft	Arson[1]
Alabama—Metropolitan Counties										
Autauga	81	0	9	5	67	512	186	291	35	
Baldwin	130	3	9	27	91	870	317	496	57	
Bibb	18	0	4	0	14	155	73	65	17	
Blount	79	1	8	6	64	959	329	573	57	
Calhoun	22	0	8	3	11	791	322	468	1	
Chilton	78	0	6	5	67	599	234	315	50	
Colbert	36	1	5	1	29	339	141	171	27	
Elmore	52	3	13	10	26	812	339	428	45	
Etowah	109	1	9	2	97	598	226	324	48	
Geneva	25	0	4	1	20	196	61	124	11	
Hale	16	0	2	1	13	97	50	34	13	
Henry	28	2	3	1	22	130	66	55	9	
Houston	92	2	12	9	69	625	177	403	45	
Jefferson	676	4	49	196	427	3,670	2,035	1,550	85	
Lawrence	83	0	4	3	76	479	169	273	37	
Limestone	79	3	0	4	72	544	185	331	28	
Lowndes	37	1	3	6	27	198	92	88	18	
Madison	286	4	30	45	207	2,185	795	1,232	158	
Mobile	231	6	23	30	172	2,356	801	1,386	169	
Montgomery	67	0	4	6	57	552	226	260	66	
Pickens	10	0	0	0	10	47	21	24	2	
Shelby	133	4	21	19	89	1,270	297	888	85	
Tuscaloosa	228	4	12	32	180	1,541	449	981	111	
Walker	99	0	5	7	87	935	370	495	70	
Alabama—Nonmetropolitan Counties										
Barbour	21	0	1	2	18	87	33	48	6	
Butler	46	3	4	3	36	252	117	119	16	
Chambers	6	0	0	1	5	89	33	54	2	
Cherokee	63	0	2	1	60	501	196	255	50	
Choctaw	5	0	0	0	5	42	25	15	2	
Clarke	36	0	9	3	24	119	47	63	9	
Clay	20	0	0	0	20	43	14	24	5	
Coffee	24	0	1	0	23	161	79	70	12	
Conecuh	34	1	1	4	28	153	48	87	18	
Coosa	21	0	2	2	17	224	74	138	12	
Covington	40	1	8	1	30	328	134	173	21	
Crenshaw	45	1	1	2	41	151	66	68	17	
Cullman	146	1	9	3	133	1,165	359	739	67	
Dale	61	0	4	5	52	162	42	110	10	
Dallas	74	4	3	9	58	538	204	298	36	
De Kalb	211	0	13	4	194	937	390	471	76	
Escambia	55	2	3	1	49	354	117	216	21	
Fayette	26	1	8	1	16	82	27	42	13	
Franklin	71	0	5	3	63	286	98	180	8	
Jackson	107	0	9	1	97	707	306	337	64	
Macon	39	1	1	2	35	323	167	119	37	
Marengo	42	3	2	0	37	170	80	76	14	
Marion	33	1	4	2	26	207	86	103	18	
Marshall	62	1	10	5	46	708	315	357	36	
Monroe	23	0	0	1	22	120	59	55	6	
Pike	18	1	0	1	16	144	50	82	12	
Randolph	35	0	2	0	33	425	181	212	32	
Sumter	20	1	0	0	19	74	37	32	5	
Talladega	71	1	3	10	57	839	286	484	69	
Tallapoosa	24	1	2	1	20	171	82	82	7	
Washington	45	2	3	2	38	154	51	88	15	
Wilcox	10	0	0	1	9	45	19	21	5	
Winston	57	1	4	2	50	317	110	178	29	

Table 10. Offenses Known to Law Enforcement, by Selected State Metropolitan and Nonmetropolitan Counties, 2012— continued

(Number)

State/county	Violent crime	Murder and nonnegligent manslaughter	Forcible rape	Robbery	Aggravated assault	Property crime	Burglary	Larceny-theft	Motor vehicle theft	Arson[1]
Arizona— Metropolitan Counties										
Cochise	338	2	8	16	312	847	298	492	57	17
Coconino	75	2	7	2	64	501	177	306	18	24
Mohave	125	5	12	16	92	2,288	790	1,343	155	10
Pima	661	13	94	160	394	11,662	2,771	8,054	837	88
Pinal[2]	173	5	29	15	124		687	2,440		12
Yavapai	252	3	23	9	217	1,315	456	749	110	11
Yuma	138	2	8	10	118	837	362	404	71	10
Arizona— Nonmetropolitan Counties										
Apache	55	0	2	3	50	204	99	99	6	41
Gila	65	0	4	4	57	383	77	275	31	8
Graham[3]		1	0	0		218	80	120	18	7
Greenlee	50	1	3	1	45	96	25	68	3	0
La Paz	52	0	0	0	52	418	100	279	39	0
Navajo	72	0	5	2	65	582	325	217	40	4
Santa Cruz	8	0	0	3	5	255	116	114	25	0
Arkansas— Metropolitan Counties										
Benton	169	0	30	3	136	576	265	282	29	5
Cleveland	5	0	0	0	5	94	48	38	8	0
Craighead	9	0	3	0	6	293	135	154	4	3
Crawford	100	0	5	0	95	396	122	247	27	0
Crittenden	142	2	2	17	121	470	184	258	28	2
Grant	38	0	2	2	34	219	81	118	20	4
Jefferson	71	0	10	4	57	485	220	200	65	4
Lincoln	11	0	2	2	7	112	63	45	4	0
Madison	47	0	9	0	38	131	47	77	7	3
Miller	21	0	6	0	15	220	51	140	29	4
Poinsett	14	0	10	0	4	15	9	3	3	1
Pulaski	311	5	8	19	279	2,068	809	1,057	202	23
Sebastian	56	1	6	2	47	340	148	178	14	2
Washington	187	4	14	0	169	610	220	344	46	6
Arkansas— Nonmetropolitan Counties										
Arkansas	9	0	0	0	9	98	19	70	9	0
Ashley	16	1	2	1	12	198	67	115	16	4
Baxter	35	3	5	3	24	626	172	421	33	1
Boone	73	0	10	2	61	420	135	242	43	3
Carroll	18	1	1	0	16	247	51	161	35	1
Chicot	2	0	0	0	2	87	24	63	0	0
Clark	16	0	2	0	14	139	44	89	6	0
Clay	7	0	2	0	5	69	30	38	1	2
Cleburne	43	0	7	3	33	532	200	294	38	8
Columbia	17	0	0	0	17	101	34	58	9	0
Conway	26	0	3	0	23	274	72	173	29	10
Cross	37	0	3	0	34	50	20	28	2	3
Dallas	2	0	1	0	1	26	8	18	0	0
Drew	30	1	5	1	23	126	33	78	15	2
Franklin	34	2	1	0	31	208	44	144	20	3
Fulton	15	0	2	1	12	125	7	108	10	1
Greene	19	0	5	1	13	236	87	142	7	1
Hempstead	49	1	5	0	43	316	101	193	22	2
Howard	15	0	3	0	12	79	28	51	0	0
Independence	207	0	21	16	170	1,537	598	818	121	25
Izard	24	0	7	1	16	324	132	179	13	5
Jackson	33	0	5	1	27	198	55	118	25	4
Johnson	33	2	5	1	25	182	136	38	8	3
Logan	29	0	9	0	20	230	90	117	23	1
Marion	44	0	4	0	40	209	91	112	6	1
Mississippi	18	0	1	2	15	397	96	252	49	0

Table 10. Offenses Known to Law Enforcement, by Selected State Metropolitan and Nonmetropolitan Counties, 2012— continued

(Number)

State/county	Violent crime	Murder and nonnegligent manslaughter	Forcible rape	Robbery	Aggravated assault	Property crime	Burglary	Larceny-theft	Motor vehicle theft	Arson[1]
Monroe	1	0	1	0	0	54	5	49	0	0
Nevada	2	0	0	0	2	50	19	27	4	1
Ouachita	15	1	0	1	13	90	47	43	0	2
Pike	6	0	1	1	4	31	12	12	7	0
Polk	42	0	4	1	37	223	105	114	4	5
Pope	51	1	7	0	43	457	149	270	38	0
Prairie	0	0	0	0	0	118	9	109	0	0
Randolph	1	0	0	0	1	47	37	10	0	2
Searcy	12	0	1	0	11	34	18	13	3	1
Sevier	11	0	1	0	10	210	66	131	13	0
St. Francis	18	0	1	7	10	330	96	232	2	3
Stone	16	0	1	0	15	94	34	53	7	2
Union	49	0	2	7	40	374	91	255	28	0
Van Buren	38	1	3	0	34	225	30	174	21	4
White	46	1	7	3	35	1,087	451	511	125	2
Yell	27	1	1	0	25	221	74	126	21	3
California—Metropolitan Counties										
Alameda	651	5	23	206	417	2,662	730	1,182	750	8
Butte	126	8	8	16	94	1,165	481	676	8	1
Contra Costa	472	10	25	120	317	2,307	993	1,298	16	13
El Dorado	241	3	14	22	202	2,024	766	1,240	18	9
Fresno	825	15	20	136	654	5,248	1,934	2,366	948	191
Imperial	139	0	6	12	121	791	352	419	20	10
Kern	2,179	22	85	490	1,582	11,713	4,015	5,592	2,106	285
Kings	183	1	13	19	150	515	207	263	45	8
Los Angeles	5,458	75	161	1,490	3,732	16,981	4,816	8,223	3,942	207
Madera	353	0	14	19	320	1,660	794	840	26	8
Marin	107	0	3	25	79	733	218	511	4	4
Merced	544	8	15	45	476	2,036	741	1,267	28	5
Monterey	199	7	17	63	112	1,336	523	792	21	11
Napa	53	0	4	3	46	342	115	226	1	0
Orange	258	0	9	33	216	1,405	338	954	113	3
Placer	278	0	24	27	227	1,670	568	1,069	33	11
Riverside	831	18	22	183	608	8,197	2,633	4,354	1,210	19
Sacramento	3,047	32	186	999	1,830	12,936	4,645	8,190	101	55
San Benito	55	0	3	7	45	273	76	182	15	0
San Bernardino	988	13	61	164	750	6,460	2,317	2,919	1,224	62
San Diego	1,630	17	82	239	1,292	6,438	1,939	3,457	1,042	22
San Joaquin	810	12	27	155	616	4,550	1,771	2,625	154	20
San Luis Obispo	219	4	11	25	179	1,309	494	806	9	8
San Mateo	300	0	19	45	236	2,526	471	1,767	288	6
Santa Barbara	273	3	43	28	199	1,826	568	1,243	15	14
Santa Clara	232	2	25	20	185	1,709	350	1,164	195	2
Santa Cruz	285	5	20	32	228	1,910	721	1,182	7	7
Shasta	506	4	25	23	454	996	522	430	44	29
Sonoma	605	0	35	38	532	1,406	539	856	11	16
Stanislaus	418	13	14	115	276	2,337	1,021	1,252	64	12
Sutter	71	1	4	2	64	786	257	487	42	1
Tulare[4]	638	17	40	90	491		1,177	1,848		0
Ventura	157	5	14	20	118	1,211	331	794	86	19
Yolo	73	0	9	10	54	451	122	317	12	4
Yuba	193	6	17	20	150	1,307	429	873	5	14
California—Nonmetropolitan Counties										
Alpine	8	0	3	0	5	39	18	20	1	0
Amador	75	0	3	10	62	468	155	310	3	1
Calaveras	87	0	17	6	64	973	348	618	7	0
Colusa	26	0	4	2	20	283	78	200	5	1
Del Norte	104	1	22	15	66	375	234	138	3	5
Glenn	25	0	1	1	23	239	99	137	3	0
Humboldt	115	2	10	31	72	1,130	509	604	17	10

Table 10. Offenses Known to Law Enforcement, by Selected State Metropolitan and Nonmetropolitan Counties, 2012— continued

(Number)

State/county	Violent crime	Murder and nonnegligent manslaughter	Forcible rape	Robbery	Aggravated assault	Property crime	Burglary	Larceny-theft	Motor vehicle theft	Arson[1]
Inyo	67	0	4	4	59	177	72	104	1	0
Lake	190	1	12	31	146	812	430	374	8	7
Lassen	36	0	3	2	31	189	62	125	2	5
Mariposa	71	3	2	2	64	313	93	218	2	0
Mendocino	183	5	18	25	135	669	276	382	11	30
Modoc	33	0	8	0	25	85	36	49	0	2
Mono	6	0	1	0	5	62	32	30	0	0
Nevada	144	1	8	8	127	703	355	338	10	4
Plumas	107	0	15	1	91	404	141	256	7	0
Sierra	17	0	0	0	17	52	16	36	0	1
Siskiyou	29	3	3	1	22	184	85	98	1	0
Tehama	189	3	5	7	174	303	133	169	1	0
Trinity	21	4	3	1	13	157	81	76	0	0
Tuolumne	85	0	12	11	62	776	386	386	4	20
Colorado—Metropolitan Counties										
Adams	419	7	70	55	287	2,346	521	1,404	421	24
Arapahoe	218	1	38	31	148	1,293	358	818	117	16
Boulder	54	0	13	5	36	521	147	339	35	8
Clear Creek	14	0	1	0	13	72	17	49	6	7
Douglas[5]	139	0	28	5	106	1,343	300	1,007	36	17
Elbert	4	0	0	0	4	66	29	34	3	1
El Paso[3]	424	2	68	30	324			1,416	205	38
Gilpin	14	0	3	0	11	33	19	11	3	0
Jefferson	148	1	22	11	114	2,666	471	2,083	112	17
Larimer	150	1	14	9	126	1,005	208	740	57	6
Mesa	194	3	54	13	124	1,303	224	960	119	15
Park	20	0	3	0	17	59	27	30	2	4
Teller	21	0	3	0	18	78	28	47	3	2
Weld	151	4	9	5	133	804	248	492	64	11
Colorado—Nonmetropolitan Counties										
Alamosa	7	0	0	0	7	35	14	19	2	1
Archuleta	14	0	2	0	12	104	43	54	7	3
Baca	3	0	0	0	3	4	2	2	0	0
Bent	14	0	0	1	13	89	37	50	2	0
Chaffee	3	0	2	0	1	78	24	51	3	1
Cheyenne	2	0	0	0	2	20	3	15	2	1
Conejos	3	0	0	0	3	50	23	20	7	3
Costilla	6	0	0	0	6	13	8	1	4	0
Crowley	11	0	0	0	11	2	1	1	0	0
Custer	5	0	1	0	4	51	13	35	3	1
Delta	9	0	0	0	9	153	21	117	15	0
Dolores	1	0	0	0	1	26	15	11	0	0
Eagle	26	1	6	1	18	344	73	267	4	10
Fremont	34	0	6	1	27	249	111	128	10	0
Garfield	14	1	4	0	9	165	39	116	10	1
Gunnison	11	0	0	0	11	40	9	28	3	0
Hinsdale	0	0	0	0	0	10	5	5	0	0
Huerfano	1	0	0	0	1	16	3	4	9	0
Kiowa	2	0	0	0	2	1	0	0	1	0
Kit Carson	2	0	1	0	1	25	4	18	3	0
Lake	5	0	0	0	5	29	8	20	1	0
Lincoln	1	0	0	0	1	28	9	18	1	0
Logan	15	1	1	1	12	98	40	54	4	0
Mineral	0	0	0	0	0	1	0	0	1	0
Moffat	3	0	0	0	3	23	10	13	0	0
Montezuma	32	1	1	2	28	112	41	60	11	1
Montrose	30	1	4	0	25	232	91	123	18	2
Morgan	8	0	0	0	8	101	23	74	4	1
Otero	12	0	3	0	9	76	33	42	1	0
Ouray	0	0	0	0	0	3	2	1	0	0

Table 10. Offenses Known to Law Enforcement, by Selected State Metropolitan and Nonmetropolitan Counties, 2012— continued

(Number)

State/county	Violent crime	Murder and nonnegligent manslaughter	Forcible rape	Robbery	Aggravated assault	Property crime	Burglary	Larceny-theft	Motor vehicle theft	Arson[1]
Pitkin	11	0	1	0	10	34	0	34	0	0
Prowers	10	0	0	0	10	26	6	18	2	0
Rio Blanco	2	0	0	0	2	43	3	40	0	0
Rio Grande	3	0	0	0	3	3	2	1	0	0
Routt	6	0	0	0	6	32	5	20	7	0
Saguache	9	0	0	0	9	44	17	23	4	0
San Juan	1	0	0	0	1	16	4	11	1	0
San Miguel	0	0	0	0	0	0	0	0	0	0
Sedgwick	5	0	0	0	5	18	6	11	1	0
Summit	17	1	10	0	6	227	28	194	5	2
Washington	16	0	3	0	13	76	15	56	5	1
Yuma	2	2	0	0	0	23	1	20	2	0
Delaware—Metropolitan Counties										
New Castle County Police Department	1,076	14	66	284	712	6,304	2,213	3,690	401	3
Florida—Metropolitan Counties										
Alachua	583	4	56	69	454	2,403	740	1,576	87	13
Baker	63	0	4	9	50	293	51	228	14	0
Bay	336	3	41	52	240	2,694	702	1,871	121	6
Brevard	876	13	67	101	695	5,233	1,254	3,788	191	12
Broward	335	2	23	76	234	1,113	289	770	54	7
Charlotte	387	1	24	33	329	3,229	861	2,252	116	6
Citrus	451	5	26	57	363	2,837	737	1,971	129	16
Clay	684	5	33	71	575	3,806	732	2,959	115	20
Collier	785	6	39	146	594	4,776	1,224	3,322	230	15
Escambia	1,960	15	132	412	1,401	11,285	3,156	7,579	550	42
Flagler	204	0	5	34	165	1,680	362	1,255	63	5
Gadsden	101	3	7	11	80	522	224	270	28	3
Gilchrist	28	0	0	0	28	208	79	116	13	0
Gulf	51	1	3	3	44	226	110	109	7	0
Hernando	437	2	40	49	346	4,168	1,184	2,830	154	6
Highlands	203	3	19	40	141	1,908	689	1,123	96	7
Hillsborough	2,152	28	116	495	1,513	17,903	4,143	12,707	1,053	21
Indian River	319	1	15	38	265	2,461	552	1,838	71	1
Jefferson	70	0	3	4	63	140	76	58	6	2
Lake	452	3	29	38	382	3,096	991	1,908	197	12
Lee	1,241	17	66	340	818	8,854	2,771	5,482	601	31
Leon	240	5	13	31	191	1,577	641	837	99	15
Manatee	1,512	18	109	271	1,114	8,125	2,010	5,812	303	7
Marion	1,215	14	122	62	1,017	3,986	1,293	2,527	166	9
Martin	339	4	31	78	226	2,557	623	1,825	109	10
Miami-Dade	6,046	81	267	1,686	4,012	41,270	7,851	29,989	3,430	53
Nassau	80	1	0	13	66	1,077	338	678	61	12
Okaloosa	643	0	52	60	531	3,062	577	2,359	126	0
Orange	4,918	49	305	1,208	3,356	27,195	8,728	16,095	2,372	0
Osceola	752	5	33	65	649	5,031	1,740	3,089	202	0
Palm Beach	2,158	19	164	524	1,451	14,626	3,767	9,722	1,137	67
Pasco	1,256	11	97	238	910	10,945	3,015	7,334	596	85
Pinellas	926	12	94	143	677	6,040	1,535	4,239	266	35
Polk	1,140	19	59	154	908	8,754	3,186	5,098	470	74
Santa Rosa	215	0	24	23	168	1,772	491	1,193	88	6
Sarasota	638	11	22	132	473	6,510	1,647	4,627	236	4
Seminole	583	5	37	86	455	3,255	900	2,183	172	5
St. Johns	485	7	7	43	428	3,539	766	2,637	136	3
St. Lucie	261	0	26	31	204	1,583	480	1,016	87	4
Sumter	117	0	13	12	92	788	269	483	36	0
Volusia	780	8	52	111	609	5,210	1,687	3,199	324	17
Wakulla	91	0	13	4	74	683	149	513	21	7
Walton	163	0	11	7	145	1,140	305	773	62	5

Table 10. Offenses Known to Law Enforcement, by Selected State Metropolitan and Nonmetropolitan Counties, 2012— continued

(Number)

State/county	Violent crime	Murder and nonnegligent manslaughter	Forcible rape	Robbery	Aggravated assault	Property crime	Burglary	Larceny-theft	Motor vehicle theft	Arson[1]
Florida—Nonmetropolitan Counties										
Bradford	86	0	11	2	73	330	163	154	13	2
Calhoun	15	0	1	0	14	69	34	30	5	0
Columbia	261	0	14	20	227	1,178	559	583	36	0
DeSoto	84	0	2	14	68	635	234	381	20	2
Dixie	51	0	5	5	41	397	203	167	27	4
Franklin	87	1	15	1	70	182	62	110	10	1
Glades	39	0	3	1	35	192	72	111	9	0
Hamilton	38	0	0	2	36	245	107	128	10	0
Hardee	54	1	8	9	36	505	148	326	31	0
Hendry	201	0	15	24	162	988	489	452	47	7
Holmes	42	1	4	3	34	208	74	120	14	1
Jackson	137	0	13	12	112	590	162	406	22	0
Lafayette	27	1	1	1	24	67	28	38	1	1
Levy	87	0	18	3	66	540	183	324	33	0
Liberty	13	1	1	0	11	53	22	31	0	0
Madison	115	1	5	6	103	290	99	177	14	2
Monroe	183	2	12	15	154	1,770	344	1,378	48	3
Okeechobee	184	0	18	23	143	1,081	518	525	38	0
Putnam	360	5	28	29	298	2,205	823	1,318	64	4
Suwannee	94	1	2	5	86	448	171	258	19	1
Taylor	54	1	3	1	49	122	54	62	6	1
Union	39	1	1	7	30	153	64	80	9	2
Washington	47	0	2	1	44	253	73	166	14	0
Georgia—Metropolitan Counties										
Augusta-Richmond	879	28	85	542	224	11,592	3,146	7,276	1,170	51
Barrow	269	0	9	9	251	866	231	572	63	6
Bartow	329	0	13	24	292	2,726	821	1,703	202	0
Bibb	207	3	13	40	151	2,370	542	1,649	179	10
Brantley	37	1	9	5	22	326	215	111	0	0
Brooks	21	0	11	1	9	228	84	119	25	0
Bryan	41	0	2	4	35	284	56	217	11	0
Butts	40	0	9	9	22	406	96	268	42	0
Catoosa	84	1	6	14	63	1,033	246	682	105	5
Chatham	0	0	0	0	0	0	0	0	0	0
Chattahoochee	0	0	0	0	0	23	19	3	1	1
Cherokee	117	3	24	17	73	1,854	604	1,126	124	1
Clarke	4	0	0	0	4	1	0	1	0	0
Clayton	7	0	0	1	6	5	0	3	2	0
Clayton County Police Department	1,157	24	57	535	541	9,580	3,777	4,478	1,325	30
Cobb	0	0	0	0	0	0	0	0	0	0
Cobb County Police Department	974	11	86	397	480	10,658	3,055	6,856	747	34
Columbia	68	1	10	20	37	2,297	396	1,804	97	11
Coweta	86	0	9	17	60	1,419	339	1,000	80	7
Crawford	42	1	1	4	36	404	152	233	19	0
Dawson	11	0	0	2	9	374	69	281	24	3
DeKalb	0	0	0	0	0	0	0	0	0	0
DeKalb County Police Department	3,420	76	122	1,787	1,435	30,285	9,468	15,995	4,822	176
Dougherty	2	0	2	0	0	122	9	112	1	0
Dougherty County Police Department	40	0	3	9	28	443	171	235	37	0
Douglas	174	1	15	34	124	1,915	530	1,265	120	2
Echols	0	0	0	0	0	46	20	25	1	0
Effingham	38	1	14	4	19	242	159	61	22	1
Fayette	43	3	4	7	29	579	182	353	44	0
Floyd	26	2	1	0	23	70	18	50	2	
Fulton	4	0	0	0	4	4	1	3	0	1
Fulton County Police Department	805	18	34	379	374	5,855	1,627	3,458	770	9
Glynn	0	0	0	0	0	0	0	0	0	0
Glynn County Police Department	230	2	10	64	154	2,680	652	1,947	81	2
Gwinnett County Police Department	1,578	34	161	662	721	14,179	4,100	8,984	1,095	54
Hall	187	4	20	37	126	2,357	626	1,506	225	21

Table 10. Offenses Known to Law Enforcement, by Selected State Metropolitan and Nonmetropolitan Counties, 2012— continued

(Number)

State/county	Violent crime	Murder and nonnegligent manslaughter	Forcible rape	Robbery	Aggravated assault	Property crime	Burglary	Larceny-theft	Motor vehicle theft	Arson[1]
Haralson	123	1	1	1	120	466	237	171	58	1
Harris	19	0	0	0	19	209	51	151	7	2
Heard	21	0	1	0	20	127	38	76	13	0
Henry	18	0	0	0	18	148	9	138	1	
Henry County Police Department	286	5	26	94	161	4,655	1,378	2,888	389	15
Houston	59	2	6	9	42	996	233	730	33	0
Jasper	38	0	4	0	34	195	75	110	10	0
Jones	19	1	2	2	14	489	138	318	33	4
Lamar	24	0	1	1	22	220	44	158	18	4
Lanier	14	0	2	0	12	124	45	75	4	0
Lee	92	1	1	5	85	630	150	453	27	2
Liberty	62	1	3	4	54	367	107	241	19	0
Long	21	1	10	2	8	275	147	110	18	0
Lowndes	102	1	1	6	94	640	191	416	33	
Madison	42	0	3	7	32	741	191	505	45	6
McDuffie	13	1	1	1	10	283	107	161	15	0
McIntosh	25	1	0	4	20	400	146	231	23	0
Meriwether	28	0	1	0	27	356	119	211	26	1
Monroe	25	0	2	1	22	392	113	244	35	4
Morgan	16	0	2	1	13	196	55	122	19	3
Murray	84	1	5	2	76	752	150	560	42	0
Newton	279	4	13	33	229	1,868	774	897	197	11
Oconee	37	0	0	4	33	436	52	355	29	1
Oglethorpe	60	1	12	4	43	444	112	320	12	1
Paulding	188	1	17	23	147	2,374	622	1,513	239	9
Peach	20	0	0	2	18	276	83	174	19	0
Pickens	47	2	0	0	45	456	109	329	18	0
Pike	5	0	3	0	2	84	40	43	1	0
Pulaski	39	0	2	2	35	255	80	171	4	0
Rockdale	246	1	13	29	203	2,302	643	1,474	185	1
Spalding	146	1	17	29	99	1,549	492	935	122	0
Terrell	16	2	1	1	12	88	21	61	6	2
Twiggs	13	0	0	4	9	166	59	101	6	1
Walton	85	0	6	12	67	1,071	301	674	96	2
Whitfield	183	1	12	11	159	1,736	548	1,106	82	7
Worth	5	1	0	2	2	162	57	92	13	1
Georgia— Nonmetropolitan Counties										
Appling	19	0	2	1	16	329	70	250	9	0
Baldwin	177	2	11	5	159	628	151	451	26	0
Banks	49	0	2	1	46	523	94	401	28	0
Ben Hill	26	0	11	3	12	151	35	103	13	0
Berrien	9	0	3	1	5	167	42	118	7	0
Bleckley	9	0	2	1	6	131	50	76	5	0
Bulloch	29	2	5	10	12	734	192	503	39	0
Camden	50	0	0	6	44	387	87	289	11	1
Charlton	15	0	2	0	13	106	28	73	5	2
Chattooga	38	0	1	0	37	391	130	250	11	0
Clay	2	0	0	0	2	2	2	0	0	0
Clinch	5	0	0	2	3	67	20	47	0	1
Coffee	65	3	4	11	47	840	221	588	31	7
Cook	8	0	1	2	5	116	56	55	5	0
Crisp	20	0	0	8	12	371	76	284	11	0
Decatur	38	1	0	2	35	336	102	219	15	0
Dodge	31	0	4	0	27	376	114	250	12	0
Dooly	11	0	0	5	6	71	11	56	4	0
Early	16	1	1	2	12	133	40	91	2	0
Elbert	31	2	2	7	20	455	127	301	27	0
Emanuel	3	0	0	0	3	366	90	242	34	0
Evans	9	0	0	2	7	36	18	11	7	0
Fannin	69	0	3	0	66	364	134	203	27	4
Franklin	9	0	1	6	2	352	115	216	21	0
Gilmer	54	0	5	0	49	407	117	279	11	0

Table 10. Offenses Known to Law Enforcement, by Selected State Metropolitan and Nonmetropolitan Counties, 2012— continued

(Number)

State/county	Violent crime	Murder and nonnegligent manslaughter	Forcible rape	Robbery	Aggravated assault	Property crime	Burglary	Larceny-theft	Motor vehicle theft	Arson[1]
Gordon	149	4	8	5	132	732	208	479	45	0
Grady	20	0	0	2	18	168	45	112	11	0
Greene	19	1	0	0	18	205	39	164	2	0
Habersham	33	0	3	0	30	495	203	267	25	0
Hancock	0	0	0	0	0	72	18	48	6	0
Hart	65	0	3	4	58	477	141	328	8	0
Irwin	13	0	3	0	10	114	48	62	4	0
Jackson	69	0	9	7	53	892	175	672	45	2
Jeff Davis	76	1	0	3	72	257	65	183	9	2
Jefferson	17	0	0	3	14	170	74	90	6	0
Johnson	15	0	0	0	15	90	33	52	5	0
Laurens	34	3	2	7	22	766	235	492	39	1
Lumpkin	79	0	9	2	68	428	117	283	28	2
Macon	0	0	0	0	0	85	33	43	9	0
Miller	5	0	0	0	5	34	9	19	6	1
Mitchell	34	0	2	2	30	204	63	132	9	0
Pierce	32	0	1	0	31	236	97	128	11	0
Polk	0	0	0	0	0	0	0	0	0	0
Polk County Police Department	52	1	6	5	40	671	277	340	54	5
Putnam	71	0	2	3	66	346	127	213	6	1
Rabun	9	1	0	0	8	235	71	154	10	0
Schley	2	0	0	0	2	24	8	15	1	0
Screven	14	1	1	0	12	225	74	132	19	0
Seminole	22	1	1	2	18	92	26	65	1	0
Stephens	32	3	3	3	23	413	122	275	16	0
Stewart	1	0	0	1	0	20	16	4	0	0
Sumter	15	0	4	2	9	341	111	218	12	0
Talbot	5	1	0	3	1	87	22	61	4	0
Taliaferro	3	0	0	0	3	58	24	28	6	0
Taylor	8	0	0	1	7	91	44	45	2	1
Thomas	46	1	3	9	33	513	156	310	47	6
Tift	97	5	9	12	71	703	152	517	34	8
Toombs	21	1	5	1	14	178	71	91	16	1
Towns	13	0	0	0	13	124	24	97	3	0
Treutlen	4	0	0	0	4	76	26	50	0	0
Troup	30	2	4	4	20	712	172	503	37	1
Turner	9	0	1	0	8	96	27	65	4	2
Union	18	0	0	1	17	275	93	169	13	5
Upson	20	0	4	7	9	430	163	250	17	
Ware	85	1	4	12	68	731	194	499	38	0
Warren	18	0	0	0	18	36	12	21	3	0
Washington	24	1	0	2	21	172	52	117	3	2
Wayne	129	5	6	7	111	840	207	618	15	0
Webster	1	0	0	0	1	42	23	16	3	0
White	26	1	5	1	19	411	177	214	20	0
Wilcox	17	0	3	1	13	97	45	46	6	0
Wilkes	5	1	1	0	3	20	6	14	0	
Wilkinson	8	0	0	0	8	86	41	39	6	0
Hawaii - Metropolitan Counties										
Maui Police Department	411	5	44	115	247	6,003	1,067	4,419	517	73
Idaho— Metropolitan Counties										
Ada	128	0	17	6	105	1,036	248	758	30	10
Bannock	15	2	2	0	11	85	27	56	2	0
Boise	15	0	2	2	11	154	32	109	13	1
Bonneville	61	0	15	2	44	688	147	514	27	2
Butte	5	0	0	0	5	1	0	1	0	0
Canyon	92	1	14	5	72	583	247	294	42	5
Franklin	2	0	1	0	1	26	1	25	0	0
Gem	8	0	0	0	8	34	18	14	2	0
Jefferson	13	0	2	0	11	81	19	53	9	0
Kootenai	88	1	18	3	66	1,409	472	871	66	13

Table 10. Offenses Known to Law Enforcement, by Selected State Metropolitan and Nonmetropolitan Counties, 2012— continued

(Number)

State/county	Violent crime	Murder and nonnegligent manslaughter	Forcible rape	Robbery	Aggravated assault	Property crime	Burglary	Larceny-theft	Motor vehicle theft	Arson[1]
Nez Perce	7	0	2	0	5	113	32	77	4	1
Owyhee	13	1	4	0	8	93	26	58	9	2
Idaho— Nonmetropolitan Counties										
Adams	1	0	0	0	1	16	3	13	0	0
Bear Lake	2	0	0	0	2	28	6	21	1	1
Benewah	12	0	0	0	12	55	28	22	5	2
Bingham	38	0	8	1	29	283	82	182	19	3
Blaine	8	0	0	0	8	33	14	14	5	1
Bonner	30	1	2	1	26	451	183	224	44	0
Boundary	7	0	0	0	7	106	67	32	7	0
Camas	1	0	0	0	1	9	3	6	0	0
Caribou	2	0	1	0	1	23	9	13	1	0
Cassia	34	2	9	1	22	354	70	268	16	0
Clark	0	0	0	0	0	8	3	5	0	0
Clearwater	7	0	0	0	7	99	12	86	1	0
Custer	1	0	1	0	0	14	2	12	0	0
Elmore	10	0	0	0	10	92	22	66	4	1
Fremont	7	0	2	0	5	79	20	56	3	0
Gooding	13	0	4	0	9	55	24	27	4	1
Idaho	21	0	0	0	21	85	29	51	5	1
Jerome	19	0	6	1	12	145	71	65	9	1
Latah	25	0	6	0	19	170	72	90	8	1
Lemhi	4	0	1	0	3	19	5	14	0	0
Lewis	0	0	0	0	0	21	8	10	3	0
Lincoln	5	0	1	0	4	8	5	2	1	0
Madison	21	1	7	0	13	91	24	66	1	0
Minidoka	14	0	5	1	8	198	59	118	21	2
Oneida	1	0	0	0	1	26	6	19	1	0
Payette	17	0	1	0	16	127	45	74	8	0
Power	4	0	0	0	4	41	6	35	0	0
Shoshone	23	0	1	0	22	150	50	86	14	0
Teton	6	0	2	0	4	52	22	29	1	0
Twin Falls	33	4	2	1	26	183	87	82	14	5
Valley	9	0	3	0	6	72	21	49	2	1
Washington	2	0	0	0	2	29	14	13	2	0
Illinois— Metropolitan Counties										
Alexander	19	0	1	1	17	64	12	46	6	1
Bond	3	0	0	1	2	110	34	71	5	0
Champaign	100	1	27	5	67	715	238	460	17	9
Clinton	3	0	1	0	2	106	14	88	4	0
Cook	267	1	27	40	199	1,166	384	684	98	16
De Kalb	24	0	2	1	21	255	40	208	7	0
De Witt	10	0	1	1	8	55	13	42	0	1
Du Page	73	0	3	16	54	1,120	288	773	59	1
Ford	35	0	9	1	25	93	35	57	1	0
Grundy	4	0	3	0	1	194	59	130	5	7
Henry	4	0	0	0	4	115	27	87	1	1
Jackson	28	1	3	0	24	312	97	196	19	1
Kane	58	0	15	2	41	526	189	319	18	15
Kankakee	47	1	8	4	34	474	169	278	27	12
Kendall	58	0	16	0	42	295	86	202	7	1
Lake	68	2	9	10	47	1,760	451	1,236	73	4
Macon	54	0	13	2	39	382	122	250	10	1
Macoupin	4	0	0	0	4	228	72	151	5	1
Madison	58	0	5	9	44	718	256	437	25	4
Marshall	10	0	0	1	9	54	34	18	2	2
McHenry	85	0	28	5	52	613	190	422	1	12
McLean	36	0	6	1	29	192	73	104	15	2
Mercer	29	1	4	3	21	141	59	79	3	1
Monroe	5	0	3	0	2	92	26	64	2	0

Table 10. Offenses Known to Law Enforcement, by Selected State Metropolitan and Nonmetropolitan Counties, 2012— continued

(Number)

State/county	Violent crime	Murder and nonnegligent manslaughter	Forcible rape	Robbery	Aggravated assault	Property crime	Burglary	Larceny-theft	Motor vehicle theft	Arson[1]
Peoria	125	3	20	11	91	966	263	670	33	6
Piatt	18	0	7	1	10	109	48	57	4	2
Rock Island	27	0	1	3	23	336	99	236	1	1
Sangamon	173	2	27	23	121	867	286	543	38	8
Stark	5	0	0	0	5	69	24	41	4	1
St. Clair	90	1	30	20	39	831	341	429	61	16
Tazewell	6	0	0	2	4	250	71	169	10	1
Vermilion	49	1	10	0	38	600	178	390	32	2
Will	154	6	24	26	98	1,426	521	827	78	18
Williamson	18	0	6	3	9	334	103	205	26	1
Winnebago	139	1	35	19	84	1,026	340	625	61	7
Woodford	11	0	3	0	8	198	50	140	8	1
Illinois—Nonmetropolitan Counties										
Adams	19	0	4	0	15	262	63	195	4	1
Brown	10	0	0	0	10	16	8	7	1	1
Bureau	23	0	7	1	15	211	77	126	8	5
Carroll	0	0	0	0	0	87	20	67	0	0
Cass	7	0	1	0	6	7	1	6	0	0
Clark	5	0	2	0	3	52	25	27	0	2
Clay	1	0	1	0	0	83	32	49	2	1
Coles	12	0	1	0	11	83	14	65	4	1
Cumberland	3	0	0	0	3	33	13	19	1	1
Douglas	14	0	1	0	13	72	39	31	2	1
Edgar	22	0	0	0	22	93	52	39	2	1
Edwards	10	0	0	0	10	41	14	26	1	0
Effingham	8	0	0	0	8	154	27	120	7	1
Fayette	4	0	4	0	0	119	34	83	2	1
Franklin	8	0	0	0	8	302	96	185	21	1
Fulton	8	0	2	0	6	189	58	125	6	0
Greene	2	0	0	0	2	46	19	26	1	0
Henderson	32	0	0	1	31	141	56	85	0	1
Iroquois	12	1	4	0	7	203	61	134	8	1
Jefferson	55	0	1	1	53	292	108	171	13	7
Jo Daviess	7	0	7	0	0	112	37	71	4	0
Johnson	26	0	0	1	25	91	14	72	5	0
Knox	21	0	2	0	19	207	79	124	4	0
La Salle	30	0	11	3	16	416	147	253	16	4
Lawrence	6	0	1	0	5	24	10	14	0	0
Livingston	25	0	9	3	13	275	59	211	5	89
Logan	17	0	3	0	14	138	61	72	5	1
Marion	15	0	3	0	12	282	89	168	25	1
Mason	24	0	3	2	19	118	30	79	9	0
Massac	5	1	0	0	4	81	23	54	4	0
McDonough	4	0	0	0	4	86	17	69	0	0
Montgomery	65	0	3	1	61	124	39	83	2	1
Morgan	18	0	7	1	10	111	58	52	1	1
Moultrie	6	0	2	0	4	70	20	49	1	0
Ogle	13	1	0	1	11	189	59	126	4	2
Perry	16	0	1	0	15	61	24	35	2	3
Pike	2	0	2	0	0	39	9	29	1	0
Pulaski	20	0	3	2	15	65	27	37	1	0
Putnam	2	0	2	0	0	50	10	36	4	0
Saline	15	0	0	0	15	126	29	86	11	1
Schuyler	6	0	0	0	6	7	2	5	0	0
Scott	0	0	0	0	0	34	9	25	0	1
Shelby	7	0	0	0	7	116	35	73	8	1
Stephenson	9	0	4	1	4	180	58	119	3	1
Union	12	0	0	0	12	94	17	73	4	0
Wabash	2	0	0	0	2	40	11	27	2	0
Warren	4	0	0	0	4	94	38	55	1	1
Wayne	17	0	0	0	17	122	39	81	2	2
White	15	2	1	0	12	132	35	87	10	0

Table 10. Offenses Known to Law Enforcement, by Selected State Metropolitan and Nonmetropolitan Counties, 2012— continued

(Number)

State/county	Violent crime	Murder and nonnegligent manslaughter	Forcible rape	Robbery	Aggravated assault	Property crime	Burglary	Larceny-theft	Motor vehicle theft	Arson[1]
Whiteside	18	0	1	0	17	251	65	178	8	0
Indiana—Metropolitan Counties										
Allen	70	2	8	14	46	1,022	203	760	59	1
Bartholomew	51	0	6	3	42	534	120	362	52	0
Boone	1	0	0	0	1	127	47	80	0	1
Brown	2	1	1	0	0	84	38	41	5	1
Delaware	38	0	1	1	36	489	181	286	22	2
Elkhart	46	3	13	19	11	1,411	428	895	88	11
Floyd	5	0	1	1	3	627	136	450	41	0
Hancock	14	0	5	2	7	273	113	143	17	1
Harrison	24	0	2	4	18	400	100	267	33	0
Howard	39	0	2	1	36	453	208	239	6	0
Johnson	68	0	1	10	57	735	163	553	19	3
Lake	59	2	5	10	42	1,106	278	739	89	0
Monroe	53	1	18	5	29	911	239	592	80	3
Newton	11	0	0	0	11	204	74	121	9	1
Porter	46	2	4	4	36	893	184	659	50	2
Shelby	14	0	1	1	12	296	109	171	16	2
St. Joseph	122	0	13	17	92	1,309	368	871	70	6
Sullivan	8	0	1	0	7	316	59	240	17	0
Tippecanoe	38	0	13	2	23	725	203	485	37	5
Vermillion	13	0	1	0	12	65	23	40	2	0
Vigo	33	2	7	5	19	1,144	276	816	52	7
Warrick	117	0	8	5	104	692	97	564	31	2
Wells	1	0	0	0	1	168	53	112	3	0
Indiana—Nonmetropolitan Counties										
Blackford	1	0	1	0	0	61	26	32	3	0
Cass	7	0	0	2	5	275	74	197	4	0
Clinton	24	0	5	5	14	303	78	201	24	1
Crawford	2	0	0	0	2	112	103	5	4	0
Daviess	5	0	0	0	5	114	44	51	19	0
Franklin	1	0	0	0	1	179	88	84	7	0
Fulton	12	0	1	3	8	121	40	68	13	0
Gibson	14	0	4	0	10	188	42	136	10	3
Grant	15	0	5	1	9	289	100	183	6	0
Greene	2	0	2	0	0	189	37	137	15	0
Henry	6	0	3	2	1	600	227	347	26	0
Huntington	13	0	4	2	7	124	32	84	8	13
Jackson	12	0	3	0	9	502	128	357	17	0
Jay	17	0	0	4	13	112	18	91	3	0
Knox	0	0	0	0	0	0	0	0	0	0
LaGrange	14	1	0	3	10	251	75	164	12	1
Lawrence	65	0	1	1	63	385	154	210	21	6
Martin	6	0	0	0	6	90	22	59	9	5
Miami	3	0	1	1	1	174	56	113	5	2
Montgomery	13	0	2	2	9	387	128	242	17	0
Parke	8	0	2	1	5	37	17	19	1	1
Pike	17	1	0	0	16	280	37	234	9	0
Pulaski	26	0	1	1	24	180	42	123	15	4
Randolph	2	0	0	0	2	222	95	117	10	1
Steuben	8	1	4	2	1	505	134	353	18	3
Tipton	14	0	1	0	13	65	47	14	4	0
Wayne	0	0	0	0	0	117	24	92	1	0
White	11	1	0	2	8	111	14	83	14	2
Iowa—Metropolitan Counties										
Benton	5	0	1	0	4	169	107	57	5	2
Black Hawk	24	0	5	0	19	207	78	117	12	0
Bremer	15	2	1	1	11	51	17	34	0	0
Dallas	24	0	0	1	23	105	17	75	13	0

Table 10. Offenses Known to Law Enforcement, by Selected State Metropolitan and Nonmetropolitan Counties, 2012— continued

(Number)

State/county	Violent crime	Murder and nonnegligent manslaughter	Forcible rape	Robbery	Aggravated assault	Property crime	Burglary	Larceny-theft	Motor vehicle theft	Arson[1]
Dubuque	18	0	3	1	14	223	89	107	27	2
Grundy	7	0	0	0	7	64	12	50	2	1
Johnson	60	0	8	2	51	231	66	151	14	4
Linn	28	1	9	0	18	275	121	129	25	6
Mills	20	0	4	4	12	241	98	109	34	4
Plymouth	7	2	2	0	3	57	11	42	4	1
Polk	75	0	10	7	58	767	238	466	63	5
Pottawattamie	41	0	7	1	33	509	141	305	63	9
Scott	37	0	1	0	36	191	72	107	12	1
Story	14	0	4	1	9	175	83	81	11	1
Warren	31	0	7	0	24	207	72	112	23	4
Washington	26	0	8	0	18	89	34	49	6	1
Woodbury	14	0	0	0	14	137	60	66	11	1
Iowa— Nonmetropolitan Counties										
Adair	5	0	0	0	5	71	27	39	5	1
Adams	15	0	1	0	14	48	11	35	2	0
Allamakee	0	0	0	0	0	0	0	0	0	1
Appanoose	13	0	2	0	11	133	56	63	14	6
Boone	3	0	0	1	2	18	7	9	2	0
Butler	0	0	0	0	0	14	8	3	3	0
Calhoun	3	0	0	0	3	18	6	11	1	0
Cass	9	0	0	0	9	74	25	44	5	0
Cedar	16	0	2	0	14	136	5	122	9	1
Cerro Gordo	2	0	0	0	2	119	47	64	8	0
Cherokee	4	0	0	0	4	47	8	37	2	0
Clarke	7	0	0	0	7	45	16	26	3	0
Clay	4	0	1	0	3	18	11	6	1	0
Clayton	14	0	1	0	13	58	18	37	3	2
Clinton	23	0	1	0	22	110	53	56	1	3
Crawford	0	0	0	0	0	4	2	2	0	0
Davis	6	0	0	0	6	10	5	5	0	0
Delaware	9	0	1	0	8	15	10	4	1	1
Des Moines	18	0	0	0	18	155	57	87	11	0
Emmet	1	0	0	0	1	25	7	16	2	0
Fayette	13	0	2	0	11	54	15	29	10	8
Floyd	4	0	0	1	3	22	9	12	1	0
Hancock	6	0	0	0	6	28	16	12	0	0
Hardin	13	0	0	0	13	125	47	75	3	2
Henry	30	0	1	0	29	106	27	62	17	0
Howard	3	0	1	0	2	57	29	25	3	3
Humboldt	1	0	0	0	1	52	22	23	7	0
Ida	9	0	2	0	7	90	39	50	1	1
Iowa	10	0	0	0	10	75	18	54	3	0
Jasper	23	0	2	0	21	186	94	78	14	1
Kossuth	3	0	0	0	3	59	35	22	2	0
Lee	7	0	0	0	7	133	40	78	15	1
Louisa	16	0	0	0	16	91	35	53	3	1
Lucas	3	0	2	0	1	84	27	46	11	3
Lyon	28	0	3	0	25	80	22	48	10	0
Marshall	6	0	1	0	5	78	30	37	11	0
Mitchell	0	0	0	0	0	26	7	17	2	0
Monona	1	0	1	0	0	26	5	17	4	0
Monroe	3	0	1	0	2	57	12	42	3	1
Muscatine	29	0	5	2	22	129	66	52	11	1
O'Brien	6	0	0	0	6	83	38	42	3	1
Osceola	0	0	0	0	0	12	3	7	2	0
Page	13	0	0	0	13	53	18	34	1	0
Palo Alto	9	0	1	0	8	83	43	35	5	1
Pocahontas	12	0	4	0	8	72	23	48	1	0
Sac	11	0	3	2	6	52	22	23	7	0
Shelby	1	0	0	0	1	4	1	1	2	0
Sioux	23	0	2	0	21	83	36	42	5	0

Table 10. Offenses Known to Law Enforcement, by Selected State Metropolitan and Nonmetropolitan Counties, 2012— continued

(Number)

State/county	Violent crime	Murder and nonnegligent manslaughter	Forcible rape	Robbery	Aggravated assault	Property crime	Burglary	Larceny-theft	Motor vehicle theft	Arson[1]
Tama	33	0	1	0	32	85	41	36	8	17
Taylor	1	0	0	0	1	18	3	15	0	0
Union	3	0	0	0	3	35	18	15	2	0
Van Buren	15	0	0	0	15	60	22	32	6	1
Wapello	10	1	0	0	9	138	59	59	20	2
Wayne	1	0	0	0	1	16	6	10	0	0
Webster	24	0	0	0	24	168	47	111	10	0
Winnebago	0	0	0	0	0	3	2	1	0	0
Winneshiek	0	0	0	0	0	18	6	12	0	0
Worth	9	0	1	0	8	99	42	48	9	1
Wright	0	0	0	0	0	36	9	25	2	0
Kansas—Metropolitan Counties										
Butler	48	0	7	1	40	605	183	377	45	4
Doniphan	5	0	1	0	4	31	13	14	4	2
Douglas	25	0	2	2	21	172	64	99	9	9
Harvey	8	0	1	0	7	103	49	50	4	0
Jackson	12	0	0	0	12	129	48	72	9	1
Jefferson	35	0	2	0	33	349	101	213	35	3
Johnson	49	1	6	1	41	282	86	174	22	5
Kingman	7	0	2	1	4	68	29	35	4	1
Leavenworth	64	0	4	1	59	323	137	158	28	22
Linn	19	0	3	0	16	133	50	70	13	5
Miami	23	0	9	0	14	227	91	116	20	12
Osage	23	0	1	0	22	113	36	70	7	2
Pottawatomie	36	0	2	1	33	237	54	168	15	13
Riley County Police Department	174	1	27	22	124	1,355	225	1,090	40	14
Shawnee	78	3	4	4	67	1,006	287	663	56	14
Sumner	22	0	1	1	20	147	58	82	7	1
Wabaunsee	9	0	1	0	8	57	13	33	11	1
Wyandotte	19	0	0	2	17	43	2	39	2	2
Kansas—Nonmetropolitan Counties										
Allen	4	0	1	0	3	78	17	57	4	3
Anderson	8	0	0	0	8	82	44	32	6	1
Barber	5	0	0	0	5	46	4	36	6	1
Barton	11	0	1	1	9	151	57	87	7	1
Bourbon	17	0	3	0	14	134	57	68	9	3
Brown	10	1	3	0	6	60	20	36	4	2
Chase	7	0	0	0	7	45	37	7	1	1
Chautauqua	3	0	0	0	3	23	9	13	1	1
Cherokee	23	2	3	1	17	268	124	122	22	13
Cheyenne	3	0	0	0	3	24	4	19	1	0
Clark	3	0	0	0	3	23	7	15	1	0
Clay	7	0	1	0	6	23	5	14	4	1
Cloud	15	0	2	0	13	66	29	33	4	5
Coffey	9	0	0	0	9	58	14	42	2	0
Cowley	37	0	2	0	35	153	49	93	11	2
Crawford	16	0	1	0	15	222	89	116	17	13
Dickinson	11	0	0	0	11	179	100	68	11	1
Edwards	1	0	0	0	1	29	10	19	0	0
Elk	0	0	0	0	0	34	5	25	4	1
Ellis	8	0	1	0	7	89	32	51	6	0
Ellsworth	6	0	0	0	6	38	9	29	0	0
Finney	37	0	8	3	26	200	57	137	6	2
Ford	25	0	0	1	24	124	57	62	5	4
Franklin	29	0	3	1	25	224	87	122	15	5
Geary	16	0	1	0	15	40	9	29	2	1
Graham	2	0	0	0	2	16	4	10	2	0
Grant	2	0	0	0	2	19	5	11	3	0
Gray	5	0	0	0	5	51	25	23	3	0
Greeley	1	0	1	0	0	4	1	3	0	0

Table 10. Offenses Known to Law Enforcement, by Selected State Metropolitan and Nonmetropolitan Counties, 2012— continued

(Number)

State/county	Violent crime	Murder and nonnegligent manslaughter	Forcible rape	Robbery	Aggravated assault	Property crime	Burglary	Larceny-theft	Motor vehicle theft	Arson[1]
Greenwood	10	1	1	0	8	72	31	40	1	0
Harper	3	0	0	0	3	35	4	26	5	2
Haskell	10	0	0	0	10	50	11	[illegible]	5	0
Hodgeman	2	0	1	0	1	24	18	6	0	0
Kearny	12	0	2	0	10	61	16	43	2	0
Kiowa	1	0	0	0	1	33	14	15	4	0
Labette	4	0	0	0	4	97	43	43	11	4
Lane	4	1	0	0	3	14	3	7	4	1
Lyon	13	0	0	0	13	88	18	66	4	12
McPherson	6	0	2	0	4	62	26	32	4	1
Marion	2	0	0	0	2	15	5	6	4	0
Marshall	2	0	0	0	2	46	20	20	6	1
Mitchell	7	0	2	0	5	14	2	11	1	0
Montgomery	25	0	1	0	24	170	57	102	11	2
Morris	4	0	0	0	4	81	44	34	3	0
Morton	7	0	1	0	6	29	5	22	2	0
Nemaha	8	0	0	0	8	54	11	38	5	0
Neosho	10	0	2	1	7	91	45	42	4	1
Ness	6	0	1	0	5	27	5	17	5	0
Norton	1	0	0	0	1	11	5	6	0	0
Osborne	0	0	0	0	0	42	11	28	3	0
Pawnee	0	0	0	0	0	34	17	15	2	0
Phillips	8	0	0	0	8	17	5	12	0	0
Pratt	3	0	1	0	2	42	18	20	4	1
Rawlins	2	0	1	0	1	14	3	9	2	0
Republic	4	0	0	0	4	28	5	21	2	0
Rice	2	0	0	0	2	61	24	33	4	0
Rooks	4	1	1	0	2	32	9	19	4	0
Rush	4	0	0	0	4	49	22	25	2	0
Russell	5	0	0	0	5	52	14	34	4	0
Saline	23	1	2	3	17	141	47	83	11	2
Scott	2	0	0	0	2	20	6	12	2	0
Seward	9	0	3	0	6	26	9	14	3	0
Sherman	1	0	1	0	0	9	3	6	0	1
Thomas	6	0	3	0	3	40	10	28	2	0
Trego	1	0	1	0	0	20	6	12	2	0
Washington	2	0	1	0	1	8	3	4	1	0
Wichita	5	0	0	0	5	30	7	23	0	0
Wilson	4	0	0	0	4	92	37	51	4	0
Woodson	4	0	1	0	3	43	18	25	0	1
Kentucky— Metropolitan Counties										
Allen	3	0	1	1	1	110	44	56	10	0
Boone	55	1	22	13	19	1,399	359	952	88	5
Bourbon	0	0	0	0	0	73	30	42	1	0
Boyd	11	0	1	2	8	180	53	104	23	0
Bracken	1	0	0	0	1	110	45	62	3	0
Bullitt	28	0	4	6	18	518	214	272	32	2
Butler	6	0	1	1	4	56	25	28	3	1
Campbell County Police Department	17	0	6	2	9	268	94	163	11	1
Christian	19	2	7	3	7	403	153	233	17	2
Clark	7	0	2	4	1	263	125	123	15	0
Daviess	16	0	4	2	10	545	143	379	23	4
Edmonson	6	0	1	1	4	68	46	19	3	0
Gallatin	5	0	0	0	5	77	41	30	6	2
Grant	6	0	0	3	3	136	54	72	10	0
Greenup	2	0	0	1	1	41	17	22	2	0
Hancock	0	0	0	0	0	13	5	7	1	0
Hardin	6	0	2	2	2	121	44	72	5	1
Henderson	11	0	3	3	5	153	59	88	6	0
Henry	0	0	0	0	0	11	6	5	0	0
Jessamine	7	1	0	1	5	269	113	148	8	0
Kenton	0	0	0	0	0	10	0	9	1	0

Table 10. Offenses Known to Law Enforcement, by Selected State Metropolitan and Nonmetropolitan Counties, 2012— continued

(Number)

State/county	Violent crime	Murder and nonnegligent manslaughter	Forcible rape	Robbery	Aggravated assault	Property crime	Burglary	Larceny-theft	Motor vehicle theft	Arson[1]
Kenton County Police Department	13	0	6	4	3	218	89	121	8	1
Larue	2	0	0	0	2	43	23	17	3	0
McLean	2	0	0	0	2	31	16	14	1	0
Meade	6	0	0	1	5	142	81	52	9	0
Oldham	1	0	0	0	1	6	2	4	0	0
Oldham County Police Department	11	0	2	1	8	424	166	247	11	3
Pendleton	7	0	1	0	6	133	49	75	9	0
Scott	6	0	1	3	2	266	109	139	18	2
Shelby	11	0	1	3	7	455	150	283	22	3
Spencer	4	0	0	2	2	64	27	34	3	0
Trigg	7	0	2	0	5	81	24	55	2	0
Warren	20	0	6	2	12	452	150	272	30	1
Woodford	0	0	0	0	0	15	2	12	1	0
Kentucky— Nonmetropolitan Counties										
Adair	9	0	0	2	7	29	14	14	1	0
Anderson	3	0	1	1	1	43	18	21	4	0
Ballard	8	0	1	0	7	148	41	100	7	3
Barren	4	0	1	0	3	79	36	36	7	0
Bell	9	0	2	4	3	106	53	43	10	0
Boyle	9	0	1	3	5	49	24	23	2	0
Breckinridge	6	0	2	0	4	30	16	10	4	0
Caldwell	2	0	0	0	2	97	50	40	7	2
Calloway	6	0	0	2	4	289	133	140	16	2
Carlisle	1	0	0	0	1	38	15	22	1	0
Carroll	2	0	0	0	2	74	18	49	7	1
Carter	1	0	0	0	1	46	23	19	4	0
Casey	2	0	0	1	1	46	25	21	0	0
Clay	11	0	0	1	10	68	24	38	6	4
Crittenden	1	0	0	0	1	17	7	7	3	0
Cumberland	1	0	0	0	1	31	23	6	2	0
Elliott	1	0	0	0	1	5	3	2	0	0
Estill	1	0	0	1	0	44	18	19	7	0
Fleming	1	0	0	0	1	19	10	6	3	2
Floyd	1	0	0	0	1	71	20	45	6	0
Franklin	18	1	2	4	11	311	95	196	20	1
Fulton	1	0	0	0	1	31	11	19	1	0
Garrard	1	0	0	0	1	39	16	20	3	0
Graves	24	4	4	3	13	275	134	115	26	0
Grayson	11	0	5	0	6	162	91	58	13	0
Harlan	4	0	1	0	3	65	22	43	0	0
Harrison	6	0	0	3	3	186	87	89	10	0
Hart	3	0	0	0	3	20	9	7	4	0
Hickman	2	0	0	0	2	20	7	10	3	0
Hopkins	18	1	4	3	10	263	116	123	24	1
Jackson	0	0	0	0	0	47	21	21	5	0
Johnson	7	2	1	1	3	95	51	38	6	0
Knox	9	0	0	4	5	238	165	55	18	2
Laurel	25	1	3	9	12	473	236	196	41	0
Lawrence	4	0	0	0	4	69	32	27	10	0
Lee	1	0	0	1	0	11	1	9	1	0
Letcher	4	1	1	0	2	92	46	42	4	0
Lewis	2	0	1	0	1	48	26	21	1	1
Lincoln	5	1	0	2	2	63	27	22	14	0
Livingston	6	0	3	0	3	86	27	49	10	1
Logan	12	1	1	4	6	136	70	56	10	3
Lyon	1	0	0	0	1	25	8	16	1	0
Madison	14	0	5	2	7	480	201	263	16	1
Magoffin	3	1	0	0	2	20	8	11	1	0
Marion	2	0	1	0	1	64	31	24	9	0
Marshall	21	0	3	3	15	318	129	165	24	2
Martin	10	0	0	1	9	91	28	45	18	0
Mason	5	0	1	0	4	113	56	55	2	0

Table 10. Offenses Known to Law Enforcement, by Selected State Metropolitan and Nonmetropolitan Counties, 2012— continued

(Number)

State/county	Violent crime	Murder and nonnegligent manslaughter	Forcible rape	Robbery	Aggravated assault	Property crime	Burglary	Larceny-theft	Motor vehicle theft	Arson[1]
McCracken	35	0	14	8	13	505	176	304	25	0
McCreary	9	0	1	7	1	89	54	30	5	2
Menifee	0	0	0	0	0	32	7	21	4	0
Mercer	3	0	1	1	1	63	35	21	7	0
Metcalfe	0	0	0	0	0	56	22	27	7	0
Monroe	2	0	0	0	2	0	0	0	0	0
Montgomery	21	0	2	7	12	539	275	238	26	0
Muhlenberg	5	0	2	0	3	40	22	8	10	1
Nelson	18	0	4	4	10	196	95	85	16	2
Nicholas	1	0	0	0	1	19	10	6	3	0
Ohio	19	1	3	0	15	190	104	67	19	4
Owen	0	0	0	0	0	54	38	15	1	0
Owsley	0	0	0	0	0	20	4	15	1	0
Perry	2	0	0	0	2	26	15	9	2	0
Perry County Police Department	0	0	0	0	0	4	1	2	1	0
Pike	0	0	0	0	0	16	6	9	1	0
Powell	1	0	0	0	1	99	51	43	5	0
Pulaski	17	1	4	4	8	664	328	315	21	2
Rockcastle	1	0	0	1	0	78	52	23	3	0
Rowan	4	0	1	1	2	54	8	45	1	0
Russell	2	0	0	1	1	47	23	18	6	0
Simpson	12	0	4	2	6	115	52	56	7	0
Taylor	13	0	4	2	7	204	106	92	6	1
Todd	4	0	0	2	2	79	42	31	6	0
Union	9	0	3	0	6	43	19	21	3	2
Washington	0	0	0	0	0	23	17	5	1	0
Wayne	1	0	0	0	1	15	9	4	2	0
Webster	0	0	0	0	0	10	4	4	2	0
Whitley	17	1	1	4	11	152	94	45	13	1
Wolfe	0	0	0	0	0	33	16	15	2	0
Louisiana— Metropolitan Counties										
Ascension[2]		0	21	42			656	2,069		
Bossier[2]		0	1	2			65	431		
Caddo[2]		0	7	8			223	621		
Calcasieu[2]		0	56	31			1,275	2,544		
Cameron[2]		0	1	0			26	90		
De Soto	309	2	0	7	300	376	67	256	53	
East Baton Rouge	371	18	6	237	110	8,193	1,802	6,225	166	
East Feliciana	1	0	0	0	1	38	10	24	4	
Iberia[2]		0	14	69			562	1,165		
Iberville	292	5	6	18	263	657	170	468	19	0
Jefferson	1,651	33	64	412	1,142	12,479	2,568	9,128	783	87
Lafayette	388	3	21	44	320	1,630	507	1,009	114	14
Lafourche	112	3	0	17	92	1,848	616	1,164	68	1
Livingston	370	1	9	23	337	2,324	729	1,504	91	0
Ouachita	183	6	8	28	141	2,688	817	1,784	87	5
Pointe Coupee	105	0	3	4	98	313	109	183	21	
Rapides[2]		0	23	14			605	1,095		
St. Bernard	94	0	7	33	54	667	133	499	35	5
St. Charles	265	2	8	32	223	1,605	409	1,118	78	18
St. Helena	54	0	1	2	51	247	87	140	20	0
St. John the Baptist	61	8	3	26	24	1,308	423	812	73	1
St. Martin	127	2	6	14	105	675	120	548	7	
St. Tammany	261	7	15	15	224	2,564	651	1,755	158	13
Tangipahoa	732	7	44	53	628	3,724	1,384	2,151	189	1
Terrebonne	221	3	19	41	158	2,625	483	1,963	179	3
Union	35	0	0	0	35	28	11	17	0	0
Vermilion	86	1	12	7	66	772	248	495	29	
Webster	69	0	11	2	56	195	97	80	18	0
West Baton Rouge	75	3	2	6	64	610	65	512	33	0
West Feliciana[2]		0	6	2		135	24	111	0	

Table 10. Offenses Known to Law Enforcement, by Selected State Metropolitan and Nonmetropolitan Counties, 2012— continued

(Number)

State/county	Violent crime	Murder and nonnegligent manslaughter	Forcible rape	Robbery	Aggravated assault	Property crime	Burglary	Larceny-theft	Motor vehicle theft	Arson[1]
Louisiana— Nonmetropolitan Counties										
Allen	18	0	1	2	15	201	57	144	0	0
Assumption	87	2	13	7	65	407	96	290	21	3
Avoyelles	152	1	28	4	119	531	176	342	13	2
Bienville	54	0	4	5	45	188	60	118	10	0
Caldwell	24	0	0	1	23	269	86	175	8	3
Catahoula	24	3	1	7	13	91	30	58	3	
Claiborne	55	0	9	2	44	294	87	175	32	3
Concordia	59	2	2	2	53	236	62	158	16	0
Evangeline[2]		0	3	2			75	287		
Franklin	50	0	3	0	47	164	39	111	14	0
La Salle	53	0	1	0	52	90	20	63	7	0
Lincoln	28	1	6	1	20	251	85	162	4	0
Madison[2]		0	0	2			19	65		
Morehouse[2]		0	0	1			11		0	
Natchitoches	65	3	1	5	56	595	109	447	39	0
Red River	52	0	0	1	51	101	14	75	12	0
Richland	10	0	1	0	9	214	35	169	10	0
St. Landry	68	0	6	12	50	747	297	415	35	0
St. Mary	160	0	11	20	129	925	223	644	58	1
Vernon	84	1	11	4	68	713	53	586	74	9
Washington	89	2	10	3	74	838	263	536	39	0
West Carroll	65	0	0	0	65	344	49	285	10	3
Winn	5	0	0	0	5	88	31	45	12	
Maine— Metropolitan Counties										
Androscoggin	11	0	8	2	1	239	106	129	4	2
Cumberland	29	0	2	7	20	775	312	425	38	7
Penobscot	11	0	2	6	3	616	219	365	32	0
Sagadahoc	3	0	1	1	1	180	71	103	6	0
York	30	0	4	3	23	383	129	231	23	1
Maine— Nonmetropolitan Counties										
Aroostook	1	0	0	0	1	68	26	38	4	1
Franklin	8	0	5	1	2	96	32	61	3	0
Hancock	2	0	0	1	1	246	47	196	3	0
Kennebec	20	0	11	2	7	425	162	242	21	1
Knox	13	0	0	1	12	282	79	188	15	0
Lincoln	31	0	6	2	23	305	117	181	7	2
Oxford	19	0	9	4	6	355	125	220	10	1
Piscataquis	4	0	0	2	2	105	59	43	3	0
Somerset	21	0	10	3	8	376	156	209	11	0
Waldo	13	0	2	1	10	242	104	130	8	1
Washington	25	0	0	0	25	159	63	88	8	0
Maryland— Metropolitan Counties										
Allegany	49	0	2	6	41	311	96	204	11	0
Anne Arundel	0	0	0	0	0	0	0	0	0	0
Baltimore County	0	0	0	0	0	0	0	0	0	0
Baltimore County Police Department	4,145	24	145	1,367	2,609	23,327	4,061	17,704	1,562	252
Calvert	100	2	7	20	71	1,492	351	1,101	40	0
Carroll	97	0	18	10	69	1,097	405	659	33	0
Cecil	166	0	21	25	120	885	319	510	56	0
Charles	536	6	32	145	353	3,062	581	2,302	179	0
Frederick	182	0	22	13	147	1,450	278	1,121	51	15
Harford	487	2	43	100	342	2,451	779	1,542	130	4
Howard	0	0	0	0	0	0	0	0	0	0
Howard County Police Department	574	4	34	177	359	6,410	1,185	4,913	312	62
Montgomery	0	0	0	0	0	0	0	0	0	0
Montgomery County Police Department	1,795	14	102	829	850	16,695	2,600	13,083	1,012	224
Prince George's	73	0	0	0	73	0	0	0	0	0

Table 10. Offenses Known to Law Enforcement, by Selected State Metropolitan and Nonmetropolitan Counties, 2012— continued

(Number)

State/county	Violent crime	Murder and nonnegligent manslaughter	Forcible rape	Robbery	Aggravated assault	Property crime	Burglary	Larceny-theft	Motor vehicle theft	Arson[1]
Prince George's County Police Department	3,955	49	145	1,996	1,765	24,192	4,758	15,115	4,319	142
Queen Anne's	57	1	2	3	51	618	131	472	15	4
Somerset	6	1	0	0	5	39	6	32	1	0
St. Mary's	210	0	11	48	151	2,433	691	1,665	77	3
Washington	155	0	7	21	127	1,332	423	835	74	0
Wicomico	81	2	4	18	57	794	254	505	35	5
Worcester	30	1	2	3	24	165	42	122	1	0
Maryland— Nonmetropolitan Counties										
Caroline	25	1	2	8	14	389	156	218	15	0
Dorchester	22	0	3	0	19	251	78	161	12	0
Garrett	30	1	0	2	27	321	74	231	16	0
Kent	31	0	3	5	23	144	60	82	2	0
Talbot	13	0	1	3	9	235	92	139	4	1
Michigan— Metropolitan Counties										
Bay	44	0	8	5	31	704	123	549	32	3
Berrien	91	2	14	6	69	640	195	416	29	2
Clinton	10	0	4	1	5	182	68	100	14	1
Ingham	93	1	13	5	74	670	199	441	30	6
Jackson	103	4	9	5	85	589	161	406	22	2
Kent	357	1	58	57	241	3,031	886	2,039	106	13
Lapeer	51	0	15	2	34	388	125	244	19	1
Livingston	42	0	18	4	20	792	189	553	50	3
Macomb	308	0	48	38	222	2,259	441	1,668	150	20
Midland	52	1	25	0	26	415	132	275	8	3
Monroe	209	4	41	58	106	2,614	708	1,738	168	23
Montcalm	43	1	11	1	30	459	141	301	17	4
Muskegon	46	0	8	1	37	821	217	575	29	5
Oakland	1,025	19	66	204	736	5,412	1,697	3,379	336	82
Ottawa	319	2	118	21	178	3,427	919	2,439	69	24
Saginaw	91	0	11	15	65	621	167	416	38	1
St. Clair	134	2	21	8	103	1,380	348	958	74	17
Washtenaw	446	1	66	67	312	2,217	878	1,172	167	29
Wayne	0	0	0	0	0	1	0	1	0	0
Michigan— Nonmetropolitan Counties										
Alcona	13	0	2	0	11	198	69	127	2	0
Alger	1	0	0	0	1	5	1	4	0	1
Allegan	93	0	18	2	73	900	264	606	30	3
Alpena	1	0	0	0	1	75	21	54	0	0
Antrim	22	0	7	0	15	264	81	161	22	0
Arenac	17	0	3	1	13	188	66	110	12	3
Baraga	2	0	0	0	2	17	2	15	0	0
Branch	21	0	6	0	15	242	102	134	6	0
Charlevoix	10	0	6	0	4	140	25	107	8	2
Cheboygan	15	0	9	0	6	122	60	59	3	1
Chippewa	10	0	1	0	9	114	48	62	4	3
Crawford	25	0	5	0	20	153	71	76	6	0
Emmet	22	0	8	0	14	228	43	182	3	1
Gladwin	24	1	6	1	16	222	108	108	6	2
Gogebic	4	1	0	0	3	99	11	84	4	3
Grand Traverse	107	0	36	8	63	848	194	621	33	5
Gratiot	9	0	6	0	3	207	50	149	8	1
Houghton	2	0	0	0	2	96	16	78	2	0
Huron	15	0	6	0	9	207	77	123	7	0
Ionia	29	1	12	1	15	376	122	231	23	4
Iosco	1	0	0	0	1	15	4	10	1	1
Iron	9	0	1	0	8	56	25	29	2	0
Isabella	45	1	10	1	33	415	122	277	16	2
Kalkaska	23	0	11	1	11	383	131	237	15	1

Table 10. Offenses Known to Law Enforcement, by Selected State Metropolitan and Nonmetropolitan Counties, 2012— continued

(Number)

State/county	Violent crime	Murder and nonnegligent manslaughter	Forcible rape	Robbery	Aggravated assault	Property crime	Burglary	Larceny-theft	Motor vehicle theft	Arson[1]
Keweenaw	0	0	0	0	0	26	10	14	2	1
Luce	4	0	2	0	2	25	4	21	0	0
Mackinac	3	0	0	0	3	89	30	56	3	0
Manistee	23	1	4	2	16	136	31	101	4	1
Marquette	7	1	4	0	2	188	29	151	8	1
Mason	38	2	19	1	16	501	93	391	17	3
Mecosta	193	0	6	0	187	464	119	329	16	3
Menominee	15	0	6	0	9	162	69	91	2	0
Montmorency	3	0	1	0	2	24	21	3	0	0
Oceana	20	2	6	2	10	278	102	168	8	1
Ogemaw	21	0	1	1	19	247	93	139	15	2
Ontonagon	2	0	0	0	2	18	8	10	0	1
Osceola	16	0	2	2	12	184	48	126	10	1
Oscoda	13	0	1	0	12	232	83	139	10	1
Otsego	8	0	5	0	3	38	10	26	2	1
Presque Isle	5	0	0	0	5	61	35	26	0	1
Roscommon	21	0	7	2	12	224	62	158	4	2
Sanilac	30	0	5	1	24	245	92	142	11	5
Shiawassee	55	1	13	5	36	441	110	318	13	2
Tuscola	39	0	14	1	24	353	133	203	17	1
Minnesota—Metropolitan Counties [6]										
Anoka	n.a.	0	n.a.	2	44	1,448	320	1,068	60	5
Benton	n.a.	0	n.a.	0	3	204	48	143	13	2
Blue Earth	n.a.	0	n.a.	0	7	156	42	102	12	1
Carlton	n.a.	0	n.a.	0	7	250	65	176	9	5
Carver	n.a.	1	n.a.	4	21	749	126	601	22	3
Clay	n.a.	0	n.a.	0	3	93	33	55	5	1
Dakota	n.a.	0	n.a.	0	28	184	57	87	40	1
Dodge	n.a.	0	n.a.	1	29	236	43	181	12	0
Fillmore	n.a.	0	n.a.	1	7	121	42	72	7	1
Hennepin	n.a.	0	n.a.	2	13	100	5	92	3	0
Houston	n.a.	0	n.a.	0	11	70	25	39	6	0
Isanti	n.a.	0	n.a.	0	9	273	63	187	23	0
Le Sueur	n.a.	0	n.a.	0	2	121	25	89	7	0
Mille Lacs	n.a.	0	n.a.	6	45	672	178	448	46	3
Nicollet	n.a.	0	n.a.	0	4	97	23	65	9	0
Olmsted	n.a.	1	n.a.	0	16	386	149	207	30	6
Polk	n.a.	0	n.a.	1	20	222	69	146	7	11
Ramsey	n.a.	0	n.a.	0	5	35	5	27	3	0
Scott	n.a.	0	n.a.	0	5	20	6	13	1	0
Sherburne	n.a.	0	n.a.	1	18	509	109	365	35	0
Sibley	n.a.	0	n.a.	0	0	0	0	0	0	0
Stearns	n.a.	3	n.a.	3	17	442	90	332	20	3
St. Louis	n.a.	0	n.a.	2	36	711	273	385	53	10
Wabasha	n.a.	0	n.a.	0	3	53	12	38	3	1
Washington	n.a.	0	n.a.	0	20	960	222	695	43	5
Wright	n.a.	0	n.a.	7	44	1828	169	1587	72	7
Minnesota—Nonmetropolitan Counties [6]										
Aitkin	n.a.	0	n.a.	2	12	456	181	246	29	0
Becker	n.a.	0	n.a.	0	13	123	35	60	28	0
Beltrami	n.a.	0	n.a.	6	30	422	138	270	14	5
Big Stone	n.a.	0	n.a.	0	0	53	13	37	3	0
Brown	n.a.	0	n.a.	0	0	11	4	7	0	0
Cass	n.a.	3	n.a.	1	18	1,059	216	785	58	2
Chippewa	n.a.	0	n.a.	0	5	30	4	25	1	0
Clearwater	n.a.	0	n.a.	1	0	97	43	47	7	0
Cook	n.a.	0	n.a.	0	2	173	17	152	4	0
Cottonwood	n.a.	0	n.a.	0	0	55	14	41	0	0
Crow Wing	n.a.	1	n.a.	2	20	523	194	307	22	2
Douglas	n.a.	1	n.a.	0	8	185	66	107	12	3

Table 10. Offenses Known to Law Enforcement, by Selected State Metropolitan and Nonmetropolitan Counties, 2012— continued

(Number)

State/county	Violent crime	Murder and nonnegligent manslaughter	Forcible rape	Robbery	Aggravated assault	Property crime	Burglary	Larceny-theft	Motor vehicle theft	Arson[1]
Faribault	n.a.	0	n.a.	0	1	60	28	28	4	0
Freeborn	n.a.	0	n.a.	0	7	146	31	106	9	0
Goodhue	n.a.	0	n.a.	0	14	257	70	164	23	1
Grant	n.a.	0	n.a.	0	2	96	37	52	7	0
Hubbard	n.a.	0	n.a.	0	5	229	83	135	11	0
Itasca	n.a.	0	n.a.	0	24	359	72	283	4	0
Jackson	n.a.	0	n.a.	1	5	85	11	72	2	0
Kanabec	n.a.	0	n.a.	1	36	357	104	226	27	3
Kandiyohi	n.a.	0	n.a.	0	7	344	83	240	21	2
Kittson	n.a.	0	n.a.	0	1	22	6	15	1	0
Koochiching	n.a.	0	n.a.	0	7	102	34	55	13	0
Lac Qui Parle	n.a.	0	n.a.	0	0	38	9	26	3	0
Lake	n.a.	0	n.a.	0	3	33	14	17	2	0
Lake of the Woods	n.a.	0	n.a.	0	1	15	7	8	0	1
Lincoln	n.a.	0	n.a.	0	6	20	4	16	0	0
Lyon	n.a.	0	n.a.	0	3	37	14	20	3	1
Mahnomen	n.a.	0	n.a.	0	14	114	36	74	4	0
Martin	n.a.	0	n.a.	0	1	31	13	14	4	0
McLeod	n.a.	0	n.a.	0	7	115	43	63	9	0
Meeker	n.a.	0	n.a.	0	8	286	63	207	16	0
Morrison	n.a.	2	n.a.	0	2	211	38	161	12	0
Mower	n.a.	0	n.a.	0	12	197	75	99	23	0
Murray	n.a.	0	n.a.	0	4	32	15	15	2	0
Nobles	n.a.	0	n.a.	1	2	23	11	9	3	0
Norman	n.a.	0	n.a.	0	0	0	0	0	0	0
Otter Tail	n.a.	1	n.a.	0	17	460	161	272	27	1
Pennington	n.a.	1	n.a.	0	0	51	10	36	5	1
Pine	n.a.	0	n.a.	2	46	1,049	198	774	77	1
Pipestone	n.a.	0	n.a.	0	2	66	17	48	1	0
Pope	n.a.	0	n.a.	0	3	60	19	40	1	1
Red Lake	n.a.	0	n.a.	0	0	2	0	2	0	0
Redwood	n.a.	0	n.a.	0	2	44	9	32	3	0
Renville	n.a.	0	n.a.	0	2	100	27	71	2	1
Rice	n.a.	0	n.a.	2	7	160	60	92	8	2
Rock[7]	n.a.	0	n.a.	0		64	9	52	3	0
Roseau	n.a.	1	n.a.	0	3	50	4	45	1	0
Steele	n.a.	0	n.a.	0	4	118	36	77	5	1
Stevens	n.a.	0	n.a.	0	3	30	10	20	0	0
Swift	n.a.	0	n.a.	0	0	24	9	10	5	0
Todd	n.a.	0	n.a.	0	17	215	70	136	9	1
Traverse	n.a.	0	n.a.	0	2	22	6	15	1	0
Wadena	n.a.	0	n.a.	0	6	72	24	43	5	0
Waseca	n.a.	0	n.a.	0	1	93	51	39	3	1
Watonwan	n.a.	0	n.a.	0	4	34	9	20	5	0
Wilkin	n.a.	0	n.a.	0	2	35	8	27	0	0
Winona	n.a.	0	n.a.	1	3	95	12	76	7	4
Yellow Medicine	n.a.	0	n.a.	0	3	19	7	11	1	1
Mississippi— Metropolitan Counties										
Harrison	43	5	5	11	22	1,155	410	682	63	7
Hinds	34	3	1	5	25	469	230	183	56	5
Jackson	132	1	24	20	87	1,618	519	976	123	3
Madison	34	1	6	3	24	405	150	228	27	0
Rankin	38	3	2	6	27	638	134	456	48	8
Simpson	30	0	1	3	26	265	101	149	15	2
Tunica	36	4	10	13	9	504	77	379	48	1
Mississippi— Nonmetropolitan Counties										
Adams	21	1	0	4	16	372	143	228	1	1
Choctaw	12	0	2	0	10	57	16	40	1	0
Claiborne	24	2	5	3	14	227	126	80	21	4
Franklin	20	1	1	3	15	63	49	7	7	0

Table 10. Offenses Known to Law Enforcement, by Selected State Metropolitan and Nonmetropolitan Counties, 2012— continued

(Number)

State/county	Violent crime	Murder and nonnegligent manslaughter	Forcible rape	Robbery	Aggravated assault	Property crime	Burglary	Larceny-theft	Motor vehicle theft	Arson[1]
George	8	2	1	0	5	82	32	48	2	0
Greene	3	0	0	0	3	27	10	11	6	0
Grenada	20	0	0	0	20	128	67	50	11	0
Itawamba	28	1	2	0	25	226	69	143	14	0
Jefferson	22	0	1	0	21	42	12	30	0	1
Kemper	4	0	1	0	3	45	28	13	4	0
Lauderdale	41	2	9	10	20	612	330	242	40	3
Lee	46	0	3	7	36	652	243	383	26	20
Leflore	89	0	0	6	83	433	156	252	25	2
Lincoln	22	1	5	1	15	337	96	230	11	7
Marion	26	1	5	5	15	361	179	161	21	5
Panola	115	2	1	4	108	739	398	319	22	0
Pike	23	2	1	2	18	321	154	155	12	0
Tippah	9	0	0	0	9	6	1	5	0	0
Tishomingo	1	1	0	0	0	6	5	0	1	1
Union	5	0	0	1	4	203	78	112	13	4
Warren	15	0	5	2	8	277	75	173	29	0
Washington	19	2	2	4	11	463	126	274	63	0
Winston	8	1	2	0	5	26	8	17	1	0
Missouri— Metropolitan Counties										
Andrew	5	1	0	0	4	92	32	57	3	0
Bates	33	0	0	0	33	195	58	115	22	1
Bollinger	12	1	0	0	11	79	33	44	2	0
Boone	114	0	3	14	97	779	200	530	49	6
Buchanan	20	0	0	2	18	247	71	163	13	4
Caldwell	29	0	1	0	28	125	55	68	2	0
Callaway	53	0	1	3	49	737	209	497	31	1
Cape Girardeau	9	0	1	1	7	320	116	187	17	6
Cass	46	1	6	1	38	367	94	244	29	1
Christian	55	0	0	2	53	350	124	180	46	0
Clay	36	2	7	2	25	235	96	112	27	6
Clinton	22	1	0	0	21	117	31	79	7	3
Cole	55	0	3	2	50	262	91	151	20	0
De Kalb	7	0	0	0	7	70	22	37	11	0
Franklin	50	2	1	2	45	561	147	371	43	0
Greene	88	1	20	6	61	1,737	524	1,050	163	22
Jackson	56	1	2	5	48	605	203	351	51	0
Jasper	172	0	9	3	160	753	271	415	67	6
Jefferson	303	5	23	12	263	2,498	456	1,844	198	17
Lafayette	12	1	1	0	10	184	57	111	16	0
Lincoln	57	0	0	0	57	297	123	151	23	0
McDonald	122	1	1	3	117	274	83	171	20	5
Moniteau	10	0	0	0	10	97	45	49	3	1
Newton	74	3	17	4	50	909	254	575	80	16
Osage	5	0	1	0	4	115	50	46	19	0
Platte	55	2	3	1	49	353	87	240	26	4
Polk	78	1	6	1	70	402	141	240	21	0
Ray	37	0	4	0	33	198	71	113	14	3
St. Charles	142	0	6	12	124	1,039	280	726	33	9
St. Louis County Police Department	1,003	8	50	250	695	8,465	1,829	5,929	707	47
Warren	43	0	4	0	39	266	97	153	16	4
Webster	14	3	0	0	11	304	156	111	37	8
Missouri— Nonmetropolitan Counties										
Adair	3	0	0	0	3	144	27	110	7	0
Atchison	1	0	1	0	0	13	7	5	1	1
Audrain	4	0	0	0	4	125	43	76	6	0
Barry	54	0	5	1	48	488	186	266	36	5
Benton	63	1	12	3	47	336	155	170	11	1
Butler	100	0	11	7	82	672	177	460	35	0
Camden	38	0	1	0	37	409	117	273	19	0

Table 10. Offenses Known to Law Enforcement, by Selected State Metropolitan and Nonmetropolitan Counties, 2012— continued

(Number)

State/county	Violent crime	Murder and nonnegligent manslaughter	Forcible rape	Robbery	Aggravated assault	Property crime	Burglary	Larceny-theft	Motor vehicle theft	Arson[1]
Carroll	9	2	0	0	7	59	19	35	5	0
Carter	2	0	0	0	2	32	10	18	4	1
Cedar	26	0	4	0	22	125	51	69	5	0
Chariton	23	0	1	0	22	62	18	41	3	0
Clark	5	0	0	0	5	26	16	6	4	0
Cooper	6	1	0	2	3	162	67	84	11	0
Crawford	25	3	4	0	18	270	116	146	8	0
Dade	6	0	0	0	6	47	39	3	5	1
Daviess	4	0	0	0	4	84	35	40	9	1
Dent	19	0	4	0	15	109	49	50	10	0
Douglas	18	0	1	0	17	74	25	43	6	5
Dunklin	33	0	2	1	30	265	79	166	20	4
Gasconade	16	0	0	1	15	159	59	83	17	3
Gentry	0	0	0	0	0	37	12	24	1	0
Grundy	5	1	0	0	4	71	26	43	2	0
Harrison	8	2	0	0	6	49	8	37	4	1
Henry	40	0	3	1	36	362	130	213	19	2
Hickory	1	0	1	0	0	137	55	77	5	0
Holt	3	0	0	0	3	72	29	38	5	0
Howard	6	0	1	0	5	38	11	24	3	2
Howell	33	1	0	1	31	377	123	222	32	4
Iron	45	1	1	3	40	62	29	25	8	0
Johnson	17	1	1	0	15	393	124	246	23	0
Knox	0	0	0	0	0	38	15	23	0	2
Laclede	85	1	4	0	80	274	71	182	21	4
Lawrence	64	1	1	1	61	477	211	237	29	1
Lewis	2	0	1	1	0	57	26	24	7	1
Linn	6	0	0	0	6	73	35	35	3	0
Livingston	3	0	0	0	3	51	21	29	1	1
Macon	18	0	1	0	17	126	59	65	2	1
Madison	8	0	0	0	8	52	12	34	6	0
Maries	15	0	2	1	12	84	33	46	5	1
Marion	8	1	0	0	7	199	27	161	11	0
Mercer	1	0	0	0	1	20	7	12	1	0
Miller	18	0	4	0	14	289	113	168	8	1
Mississippi	10	0	0	1	9	52	19	30	3	2
Monroe	4	0	1	0	3	45	15	25	5	1
Montgomery	3	0	0	0	3	61	20	37	4	0
Morgan	97	3	0	1	93	280	126	133	21	0
New Madrid	22	2	1	1	18	53	17	31	5	3
Nodaway	13	0	3	1	9	101	34	58	9	0
Oregon	22	1	0	1	20	55	23	32	0	2
Ozark	30	1	2	2	25	139	82	55	2	1
Pemiscot	15	0	1	3	11	122	47	68	7	0
Perry	12	0	0	0	12	75	28	41	6	1
Pettis	16	0	1	1	14	349	117	207	25	1
Phelps	49	0	6	1	42	433	104	305	24	0
Pike	9	0	0	0	9	133	53	69	11	0
Pulaski	154	3	12	9	130	512	221	265	26	2
Putnam	0	0	0	0	0	11	5	6	0	0
Ralls	6	0	0	0	6	143	36	99	8	0
Randolph	9	0	2	1	6	92	28	62	2	3
Reynolds	22	3	0	0	19	78	32	41	5	6
Ripley	27	0	0	0	27	263	59	192	12	0
Saline	4	0	0	0	4	92	36	45	11	0
Schuyler	3	0	0	0	3	26	6	19	1	1
Scotland	3	0	0	0	3	55	17	36	2	0
Scott	17	0	0	1	16	83	29	48	6	0
Shannon	10	0	2	0	8	59	11	42	6	0
Shelby	5	0	0	0	5	34	9	23	2	0
St. Clair	9	0	0	1	8	179	65	112	2	0
Ste. Genevieve	49	0	3	0	46	109	26	77	6	1
St. Francois	76	0	6	2	68	552	189	301	62	2
Stoddard	21	1	2	1	17	255	95	133	27	3

Table 10. Offenses Known to Law Enforcement, by Selected State Metropolitan and Nonmetropolitan Counties, 2012— continued

(Number)

State/county	Violent crime	Murder and nonnegligent manslaughter	Forcible rape	Robbery	Aggravated assault	Property crime	Burglary	Larceny-theft	Motor vehicle theft	Arson[1]
Stone	121	1	4	1	115	456	130	292	34	3
Sullivan	8	0	1	0	7	73	28	38	7	0
Taney	83	0	5	3	75	494	146	302	46	1
Texas	13	1	2	0	10	290	120	152	18	1
Vernon	37	0	1	0	36	315	102	185	28	3
Washington	39	1	2	1	35	377	114	225	38	6
Wayne	9	0	1	0	8	85	39	40	6	1
Worth	2	0	1	0	1	40	15	22	3	0
Wright	5	0	0	0	5	135	56	70	9	4
Montana—Metropolitan Counties										
Carbon	13	0	1	0	12	47	12	30	5	0
Cascade	39	0	6	1	32	327	71	229	27	2
Golden Valley	2	0	0	0	2	2	2	0	0	0
Missoula	100	0	16	5	79	479	80	358	41	7
Yellowstone	52	0	1	1	50	634	164	412	58	8
Montana—Nonmetropolitan Counties										
Beaverhead	2	0	0	1	1	29	7	21	1	4
Blaine	19	0	1	0	18	27	3	22	2	0
Broadwater	16	0	2	0	14	44	3	40	1	2
Carter	0	0	0	0	0	2	1	1	0	0
Chouteau	1	0	0	0	1	11	1	9	1	0
Custer	2	0	0	0	2	35	3	28	4	0
Daniels	2	0	0	0	2	5	0	5	0	0
Dawson	7	0	0	0	7	100	14	78	8	0
Deer Lodge	27	1	5	0	21	178	13	157	8	0
Fallon	0	0	0	0	0	4	0	4	0	0
Fergus	12	0	1	0	11	58	12	42	4	1
Flathead	150	0	12	5	133	1,258	318	878	62	8
Gallatin	52	0	16	1	35	380	54	309	17	8
Garfield	0	0	0	0	0	1	1	0	0	0
Glacier	33	1	0	0	32	65	9	48	8	0
Granite	0	0	0	0	0	50	3	45	2	0
Hill	22	0	1	0	21	158	12	135	11	3
Jefferson	11	0	0	0	11	90	13	71	6	5
Judith Basin	3	0	1	0	2	4	0	1	3	0
Lake	61	1	7	0	53	343	93	201	49	2
Lewis and Clark	59	3	12	2	42	366	79	258	29	0
Lincoln	36	3	1	0	32	123	30	88	5	2
Madison	4	0	0	0	4	48	4	42	2	3
McCone	1	1	0	0	0	5	0	5	0	1
Meagher	3	0	0	0	3	22	2	19	1	0
Mineral	1	0	0	0	1	5	1	4	0	0
Musselshell	17	0	6	0	11	91	11	74	6	1
Park	15	0	2	0	13	61	8	44	9	4
Phillips	7	0	0	0	7	77	3	68	6	0
Pondera	0	0	0	0	0	6	0	5	1	0
Powell	15	1	2	0	12	60	6	52	2	0
Prairie	2	0	0	0	2	6	0	4	2	0
Ravalli	43	0	3	1	39	357	37	304	16	2
Richland	6	0	0	0	6	84	18	53	13	1
Roosevelt	14	0	0	0	14	36	7	24	5	0
Rosebud	7	0	1	1	5	33	5	23	5	0
Sanders	10	2	1	0	7	75	8	59	8	1
Sheridan	17	0	3	0	14	64	7	51	6	0
Silver Bow	88	0	3	6	79	1,274	197	973	104	4
Stillwater	22	0	4	0	18	83	50	29	4	1
Sweet Grass	6	0	1	0	5	51	6	36	9	0
Teton	5	1	1	0	3	49	6	40	3	0
Toole	0	0	0	0	0	99	14	75	10	1
Valley	6	0	1	0	5	23	5	13	5	0

Table 10. Offenses Known to Law Enforcement, by Selected State Metropolitan and Nonmetropolitan Counties, 2012— continued

(Number)

State/county	Violent crime	Murder and nonnegligent manslaughter	Forcible rape	Robbery	Aggravated assault	Property crime	Burglary	Larceny-theft	Motor vehicle theft	Arson[1]
Wheatland	4	0	0	0	4	4	1	2	1	1
Wibaux	0	0	0	0	0	3	2	1	0	0
Nebraska—Metropolitan Counties										
Cass	20	0	12	0	8	309	53	233	23	1
Dakota	4	0	0	0	4	27	7	16	4	0
Dixon	9	0	3	0	6	84	25	57	2	3
Douglas	100	0	8	5	87	1,207	331	777	99	0
Hall	6	0	2	0	4	228	49	168	11	0
Hamilton	0	0	0	0	0	88	44	43	1	1
Lancaster	24	1	9	2	12	370	130	232	8	5
Sarpy	18	0	8	5	5	695	101	544	50	0
Saunders	4	0	0	1	3	141	27	110	4	1
Seward	3	0	1	0	2	20	7	8	5	0
Nebraska—Nonmetropolitan Counties										
Adams	1	0	0	0	1	138	47	83	8	0
Antelope	4	2	0	0	2	14	4	10	0	0
Arthur	0	0	0	0	0	0	0	0	0	0
Box Butte	0	0	0	0	0	5	0	5	0	0
Brown	0	0	0	0	0	39	11	25	3	0
Buffalo	12	0	3	1	8	138	35	100	3	1
Cedar	4	0	0	0	4	34	1	33	0	0
Chase	2	0	0	0	2	24	5	18	1	0
Cherry	2	0	0	0	2	17	4	12	1	0
Cuming	0	0	0	0	0	22	7	15	0	0
Custer	6	0	0	0	6	48	11	36	1	1
Dawes	3	0	0	0	3	14	2	11	1	0
Dawson	8	0	3	0	5	73	12	55	6	0
Deuel	1	0	0	0	1	26	5	21	0	0
Dodge	4	0	2	0	2	168	29	125	14	0
Franklin	0	0	0	0	0	15	4	11	0	0
Gage	5	0	0	0	5	124	32	83	9	0
Gosper	1	0	1	0	0	31	5	25	1	1
Hitchcock	2	0	1	0	1	23	18	4	1	0
Holt	2	0	0	0	2	21	6	15	0	0
Hooker	0	0	0	0	0	0	0	0	0	0
Jefferson	0	0	0	0	0	48	15	31	2	0
Kearney	4	0	0	0	4	83	12	68	3	1
Keith	2	0	1	1	0	24	5	17	2	0
Keya Paha	0	0	0	0	0	0	0	0	0	0
Kimball	3	0	0	0	3	26	1	24	1	0
Knox	1	0	0	0	1	30	6	23	1	0
Lincoln	4	0	3	1	0	133	29	100	4	0
Madison	1	0	0	0	1	53	17	34	2	0
Morrill	2	0	0	0	2	13	0	10	3	0
Nemaha	4	0	2	0	2	18	7	10	1	0
Otoe	2	0	0	0	2	62	5	53	4	0
Pawnee	0	0	0	0	0	24	3	19	2	0
Perkins	2	0	2	0	0	11	4	7	0	0
Phelps	7	0	4	0	3	42	6	35	1	0
Pierce	1	0	0	0	1	31	5	26	0	1
Platte	3	0	0	0	3	152	19	123	10	1
Polk	0	0	0	0	0	40	11	28	1	2
Red Willow	3	0	1	0	2	36	10	25	1	1
Rock	2	0	0	0	2	5	2	3	0	0
Saline	5	0	1	0	4	50	25	20	5	0
Scotts Bluff	4	0	1	0	3	92	23	56	13	0
Sheridan	4	0	0	1	3	57	14	40	3	4
Sherman	0	0	0	0	0	23	5	18	0	0
Stanton	1	0	0	0	1	65	7	57	1	0
Thayer	4	0	0	0	4	78	26	51	1	0

Table 10. Offenses Known to Law Enforcement, by Selected State Metropolitan and Nonmetropolitan Counties, 2012— continued

(Number)

State/county	Violent crime	Murder and nonnegligent manslaughter	Forcible rape	Robbery	Aggravated assault	Property crime	Burglary	Larceny-theft	Motor vehicle theft	Arson[1]
Wayne	3	0	0	0	3	23	5	16	2	1
Webster	1	0	0	0	1	34	9	22	3	0
Wheeler	0	0	0	0	0	2	0	2	0	0
York	3	0	2	1	0	57	20	33	4	0
Nevada—Metropolitan Counties										
Carson City	132	0	0	14	118	1,107	298	731	78	4
Storey	48	0	7	2	39	86	23	55	8	2
Washoe	188	4	8	10	166	956	335	523	98	14
Nevada—Nonmetropolitan Counties										
Churchill	22	1	1	0	20	215	93	107	15	1
Douglas	53	1	6	6	40	829	144	656	29	6
Elko	39	1	7	2	29	219	82	107	30	3
Esmeralda	2	0	1	0	1	8	2	3	3	0
Eureka	6	0	2	0	4	29	14	13	2	0
Humboldt	39	1	0	0	38	64	20	32	12	0
Lander	40	0	9	0	31	104	38	55	11	3
Lincoln	2	0	0	0	2	71	17	49	5	0
Lyon	141	1	17	12	111	1,028	294	662	72	9
Mineral	9	0	0	0	9	58	20	32	6	0
Nye	258	0	11	26	221	1,147	334	687	126	10
Pershing	47	0	3	0	44	30	11	16	3	0
White Pine	46	0	11	1	34	123	61	58	4	1
New Hampshire—Metropolitan Counties										
Rockingham	5	0	0	0	5	9	0	9	0	0
New Hampshire—Nonmetropolitan Counties										
Carroll	9	0	0	0	9	71	31	36	4	2
Cheshire	5	0	0	0	5	9	4	5	0	0
Merrimack	6	0	2	0	4	9	1	8	0	0
New Jersey—Metropolitan Counties										
Atlantic	0	0	0	0	0	0	0	0	0	0
Bergen	0	0	0	0	0	0	0	0	0	0
Bergen County Police Department	7	0	1	0	6	122	5	112	5	1
Burlington	0	0	0	0	0	0	0	0	0	0
Camden	1	0	0	0	1	2	2	0	0	0
Cape May	0	0	0	0	0	0	0	0	0	0
Cumberland	0	0	0	0	0	2	0	2	0	0
Essex	81	0	4	49	28	84	14	67	3	0
Gloucester	0	0	0	0	0	0	0	0	0	0
Hudson	0	0	0	0	0	0	0	0	0	0
Hunterdon	0	0	0	0	0	0	0	0	0	0
Mercer	0	0	0	0	0	0	0	0	0	0
Middlesex	0	0	0	0	0	0	0	0	0	0
Monmouth	0	0	0	0	0	0	0	0	0	0
Morris	0	0	0	0	0	0	0	0	0	0
Ocean	0	0	0	0	0	0	0	0	0	0
Passaic	3	0	0	0	3	0	0	0	0	0
Salem	5	0	0	0	5	0	0	0	0	0
Somerset	0	0	0	0	0	0	0	0	0	0
Sussex	0	0	0	0	0	0	0	0	0	0
Union	0	0	0	0	0	0	0	0	0	0
New Mexico—Metropolitan Counties										
Bernalillo	756	7	41	87	621	2,424	908	1,307	209	51
Dona Ana	289	1	38	8	242	1,436	549	758	129	8
Sandoval	15	1	0	1	13	102	51	49	2	1

Table 10. Offenses Known to Law Enforcement, by Selected State Metropolitan and Nonmetropolitan Counties, 2012— continued

(Number)

State/county	Violent crime	Murder and nonnegligent manslaughter	Forcible rape	Robbery	Aggravated assault	Property crime	Burglary	Larceny-theft	Motor vehicle theft	Arson[1]
San Juan	285	2	34	14	235	942	272	605	65	10
Santa Fe	94	4	4	7	79	1,078	636	388	54	6
Valencia[2]	170	1	3	7	159				110	3
New Mexico—Nonmetropolitan Counties										
Cibola[3]		0	7	1		101	48	44	9	1
Colfax	2	0	0	0	2	7	3	4	0	0
Eddy	48	0	5	0	43	467	130	309	28	4
Guadalupe	4	0	0	1	3	22	6	10	6	0
Hidalgo	3	0	0	3	0	17	6	8	3	0
Lea	39	1	3	1	34	585	151	392	42	1
Lincoln	6	0	0	0	6	105	38	62	5	0
Luna	59	0	0	2	57	194	50	132	12	0
McKinley	87	0	6	9	72	300	132	143	25	6
Quay	2	0	0	0	2	39	17	18	4	0
Rio Arriba	41	1	0	3	37	225	144	65	16	2
Roosevelt	9	0	2	0	7	85	36	39	10	0
Sierra	7	0	0	0	7	58	21	32	5	0
New York—Metropolitan Counties [5]										
Albany	5	1	0	0	4	162	35	124	3	
Broome	72	1	9	7	55	855	208	626	21	
Chemung	63	1	1	2	59	546	87	441	18	2
Dutchess	53	0	3	9	41	764	182	558	24	
Erie	119	1	3	9	106	1,233	284	906	43	5
Herkimer	0	0	0	0	0	16	0	16	0	0
Jefferson	26	0	1	1	24	287	11	274	2	
Livingston	24	0	6	0	18	508	100	402	6	
Madison	14	0	2	1	11	257	85	165	7	
Monroe	230	2	27	57	144	3,912	734	3,067	111	14
Nassau	1,654	12	56	723	863	13,303	2,026	10,562	715	
Niagara	52	0	10	5	37	1,056	306	711	39	
Oneida	34	0	3	7	24	484	141	334	9	7
Onondaga	194	1	16	39	138	2,481	550	1,836	95	11
Ontario	68	1	15	10	42	1,148	264	869	15	0
Orleans	23	0	1	3	19	285	76	200	9	
Oswego	44	0	7	6	31	628	172	430	26	
Putnam	20	0	5	4	11	321	74	238	9	0
Rensselaer	37	0	3	2	32	200	70	126	4	1
Rockland	10	0	0	0	10	39	0	38	1	
Saratoga	43	1	1	3	38	1,302	245	1,041	16	8
Schenectady	1	0	0	1	0	6	0	6	0	0
Schoharie	0	0	0	0	0	49	15	32	2	0
Suffolk	102	0	0	0	102	16	0	12	4	0
Suffolk County Police Department	1,790	23	42	681	1,044	22,431	3,699	17,686	1,046	148
Tioga	15	0	0	0	15	195	60	131	4	
Ulster	32	0	1	2	29	331	81	245	5	
Warren	66	0	8	7	51	730	102	616	12	
Washington	26	0	6	2	18	388	101	275	12	
Wayne	42	1	5	8	28	452	132	310	10	
Westchester Public Safety	9	0	1	0	8	204	7	194	3	1
Yates	13	0	3	0	10	284	88	193	3	2
New York—Nonmetropolitan Counties [5]										
Cattaraugus	44	1	7	3	33	572	201	362	9	
Cayuga	26	1	4	2	19	373	81	286	6	
Chautauqua	25	1	4	0	20	698	201	486	11	
Chenango	20	0	1	1	18	454	76	371	7	
Clinton	2	0	0	0	2	20	3	17	0	
Columbia	21	0	0	3	18	429	92	333	4	
Cortland	20	0	1	6	13	464	93	367	4	
Delaware	11	1	4	1	5	106	35	66	5	

Table 10. Offenses Known to Law Enforcement, by Selected State Metropolitan and Nonmetropolitan Counties, 2012— continued

(Number)

State/county	Violent crime	Murder and nonnegligent manslaughter	Forcible rape	Robbery	Aggravated assault	Property crime	Burglary	Larceny-theft	Motor vehicle theft	Arson[1]
Essex	3	0	0	0	3	6	3	3	0	
Franklin	0	0	0	0	0	0	0	0	0	0
Fulton	3	0	0	0	3	391	115	270	6	1
Genesee	26	0	5	3	18	624	130	472	22	
Hamilton	1	0	0	0	1	10	6	4	0	0
Lewis	11	0	0	2	9	198	73	119	6	
Montgomery	19	0	4	3	12	402	46	351	5	
Otsego	27	0	1	0	26	116	41	67	8	
Schuyler	13	1	0	0	12	57	23	27	7	
Seneca	12	0	0	0	12	116	32	82	2	
Steuben	18	0	7	0	11	270	51	211	8	0
St. Lawrence	13	0	0	0	13	68	7	57	4	
Sullivan	27	0	2	5	20	564	165	392	7	
Wyoming	20	0	3	4	13	259	42	207	10	1
North Carolina—Metropolitan Counties										
Alamance	116	1	7	8	100	1,033	429	526	78	1
Alexander	36	1	6	6	23	803	335	425	43	16
Brunswick	108	1	20	17	70	1,825	684	1,052	89	13
Buncombe	144	4	18	34	88	1,954	812	960	182	11
Burke	100	2	3	22	73	1,644	741	833	70	3
Cabarrus	39	3	7	9	20	910	343	536	31	3
Caldwell	61	2	7	10	42	1,553	541	929	83	21
Catawba	132	9	7	22	94	1,803	737	991	75	13
Chatham	68	1	8	7	52	781	367	383	31	7
Craven	116	0	8	19	89	1,540	832	630	78	6
Cumberland	505	7	15	123	360	4,197	1,714	2,283	200	43
Currituck	37	0	2	2	33	544	114	419	11	6
Davidson	83	0	4	13	66	1,830	824	887	119	14
Davie	67	1	6	8	52	728	268	432	28	2
Durham	66	0	5	13	48	799	358	395	46	1
Edgecombe	55	0	6	11	38	602	295	272	35	7
Forsyth	258	2	13	27	216	2,334	679	1,565	90	14
Franklin	110	0	8	10	92	957	348	542	67	7
Gaston	7	0	0	0	7	2	0	1	1	0
Gaston County Police Department	193	2	13	17	161	1,308	567	615	126	22
Guilford	131	2	4	13	112	1,580	608	885	87	15
Haywood	89	1	6	7	75	969	428	490	51	3
Henderson	106	5	15	10	76	1,530	546	877	107	2
Iredell	164	0	8	14	142	1,965	771	1,083	111	10
Johnston	121	0	21	11	89	2,228	895	1,238	95	3
Lincoln	67	0	6	5	56	1,462	544	883	35	3
Nash	49	4	5	5	35	642	322	267	53	1
New Hanover	171	1	17	32	121	2,181	603	1,479	99	7
Onslow	219	2	29	37	151	2,911	848	1,943	120	13
Orange	38	3	3	11	21	586	341	218	27	3
Pamlico	27	0	1	3	23	296	57	234	5	1
Pender	106	1	10	9	86	763	171	556	36	5
Person	50	0	11	3	36	587	272	291	24	3
Pitt	153	4	6	21	122	1,238	461	729	48	3
Randolph	131	8	16	19	88	2,221	675	1,457	89	12
Rockingham	82	5	6	7	64	1,345	630	653	62	4
Rowan	140	2	9	14	115	1,537	592	882	63	4
Stokes	135	2	5	1	127	1,009	401	554	54	4
Union	234	6	14	32	182	2,226	667	1,456	103	20
Wake	170	2	23	27	118	2,462	1,000	1,276	186	23
Wayne	155	7	5	20	123	2,101	876	1,094	131	3
Yadkin	87	1	5	3	78	732	300	405	27	4
North Carolina—Nonmetropolitan Counties										
Anson	50	0	12	10	28	716	331	367	18	2
Ashe	26	0	4	1	21	431	196	210	25	2

Table 10. Offenses Known to Law Enforcement, by Selected State Metropolitan and Nonmetropolitan Counties, 2012— continued

(Number)

State/county	Violent crime	Murder and nonnegligent manslaughter	Forcible rape	Robbery	Aggravated assault	Property crime	Burglary	Larceny-theft	Motor vehicle theft	Arson[1]
Avery	20	0	0	1	19	180	55	120	5	5
Beaufort	73	0	4	10	59	745	323	396	26	10
Bertie	22	0	1	6	15	[illegible]	81	102	10	0
Bladen	100	2	1	14	83	1,102	362	707	33	12
Camden	12	0	1	2	9	113	40	70	3	0
Carteret	87	3	20	6	58	774	246	480	48	2
Caswell	62	2	8	4	48	519	214	288	17	7
Cherokee	32	3	3	1	25	599	246	327	26	5
Chowan	11	0	0	3	8	136	61	68	7	2
Clay	26	0	2	0	24	238	100	128	10	0
Cleveland	45	1	8	14	22	1,283	512	735	36	1
Columbus	131	3	14	32	82	1,498	723	685	90	12
Dare	25	1	7	3	14	721	215	487	19	5
Duplin	150	7	10	16	117	990	476	468	46	9
Granville	77	0	1	10	66	896	421	436	39	2
Halifax	115	5	12	11	87	859	396	416	47	12
Harnett	259	3	16	42	198	2,654	1,099	1,419	136	16
Hertford	26	2	4	7	13	279	139	116	24	0
Jackson	78	0	7	10	61	728	420	283	25	8
Lee	23	1	4	1	17	648	211	383	54	2
Lenoir	103	0	5	22	76	970	418	523	29	5
Macon	16	1	2	1	12	398	146	234	18	0
Martin	32	1	1	7	23	465	208	230	27	4
McDowell	45	0	6	4	35	768	293	428	47	5
Montgomery	39	3	4	2	30	466	212	233	21	3
Moore	56	5	4	7	40	815	411	353	51	2
Pasquotank	45	0	0	12	33	355	160	187	8	5
Perquimans	10	1	1	0	8	165	96	63	6	1
Richmond	135	7	16	21	91	1,280	565	659	56	13
Robeson	530	5	18	98	409	3,580	1,786	1,616	178	48
Rutherford	79	1	4	7	67	1,329	716	531	82	11
Sampson	82	4	5	16	57	1,393	772	544	77	5
Stanly	22	0	3	3	16	522	224	281	17	4
Surry	143	6	11	16	110	1,294	505	706	83	10
Swain	39	1	4	1	33	242	120	112	10	0
Transylvania	28	0	4	1	23	301	143	141	17	2
Tyrrell	5	0	1	2	2	60	10	45	5	0
Vance	53	3	4	22	24	1,292	613	597	82	1
Warren	47	2	3	6	36	479	203	232	44	5
Washington	20	0	1	4	15	167	50	109	8	2
Watauga	32	1	0	0	31	364	77	272	15	3
Wilkes	122	2	3	15	102	1,360	565	734	61	4
Wilson	65	4	3	9	49	650	229	395	26	4
North Dakota— Metropolitan Counties										
Burleigh	20	0	4	1	15	188	64	111	13	3
Cass	22	0	6	2	14	188	74	107	7	1
Grand Forks	6	0	0	0	6	68	23	38	7	0
Morton	10	0	4	0	6	88	15	67	6	0
Oliver	1	0	0	0	1	2	0	1	1	0
Sioux	0	0	0	0	0	0	0	0	0	0
North Dakota— Nonmetropolitan Counties										
Adams	0	0	0	0	0	9	6	3	0	0
Barnes	2	0	2	0	0	38	11	25	2	0
Benson	3	0	3	0	0	20	4	12	4	0
Billings	0	0	0	0	0	16	5	10	1	0
Bottineau	5	2	0	0	3	59	15	40	4	0
Burke	1	0	0	0	1	25	6	14	5	0
Cavalier	0	0	0	0	0	26	7	18	1	1
Dickey	1	0	0	0	1	9	0	9	0	0
Divide	0	0	0	0	0	17	5	9	3	0

Table 10. Offenses Known to Law Enforcement, by Selected State Metropolitan and Nonmetropolitan Counties, 2012— continued

(Number)

State/county	Violent crime	Murder and nonnegligent manslaughter	Forcible rape	Robbery	Aggravated assault	Property crime	Burglary	Larceny-theft	Motor vehicle theft	Arson[1]
Dunn	7	0	0	0	7	29	8	18	3	1
Eddy	1	0	0	0	1	18	3	15	0	0
Emmons	0	0	0	0	0	27	7	15	5	0
Foster	0	0	0	0	0	0	0	0	0	0
Golden Valley	0	0	0	0	0	7	3	4	0	0
Grant	5	0	1	1	3	22	11	8	3	0
Griggs	3	0	0	0	3	5	2	3	0	0
Hettinger	5	0	0	1	4	14	3	7	4	1
Kidder	0	0	0	0	0	8	3	4	1	1
Lamoure	1	0	0	1	0	2	0	1	1	0
Logan	0	0	0	0	0	14	1	12	1	0
McHenry	2	0	0	0	2	44	11	27	6	0
McIntosh	0	0	0	0	0	5	2	3	0	0
McKenzie	8	0	0	1	7	86	7	74	5	0
McLean	8	0	1	1	6	127	37	77	13	0
Mercer	1	0	0	0	1	26	6	17	3	0
Mountrail	14	4	0	0	10	114	17	72	25	4
Nelson	4	0	0	0	4	30	11	11	8	0
Pembina	5	0	0	0	5	35	11	21	3	1
Ramsey	0	0	0	0	0	11	0	10	1	0
Ransom	2	1	0	0	1	16	8	7	1	0
Renville	1	0	0	0	1	19	2	17	0	0
Richland	5	0	1	0	4	103	23	69	11	0
Rolette	1	0	0	0	1	16	8	4	4	0
Sargent	0	0	0	0	0	21	8	13	0	0
Sheridan	0	0	0	0	0	33	6	24	3	0
Slope	0	0	0	0	0	2	1	1	0	0
Stark	4	0	0	0	4	84	2	74	8	1
Steele	1	0	1	0	0	6	4	1	1	0
Stutsman	4	0	3	0	1	52	13	29	10	0
Towner	0	0	0	0	0	6	4	2	0	0
Traill	1	0	0	0	1	48	14	32	2	1
Walsh	1	0	0	0	1	85	22	56	7	0
Ward	22	0	6	0	16	184	46	108	30	0
Wells	4	0	1	0	3	16	9	6	1	2
Williams	46	1	5	0	40	272	48	172	52	2
Ohio—Metropolitan Counties										
Allen	69	2	18	12	37	1,160	310	816	34	2
Belmont	21	0	4	3	14	642	188	418	36	2
Brown	2	0	0	1	1	198	72	122	4	0
Butler	314	1	6	11	296	990	308	679	3	5
Carroll	45	0	1	0	44	225	71	141	13	4
Clark	28	0	7	2	19	1,118	280	803	35	12
Clermont	64	0	11	3	50	1,773	686	1,041	46	12
Delaware	25	1	8	3	13	1,184	375	796	13	5
Fairfield	26	0	9	10	7	928	222	684	22	1
Franklin	120	2	6	61	51	1,419	410	925	84	7
Fulton	24	1	3	0	20	376	113	249	14	3
Geauga	18	0	5	4	9	325	105	209	11	1
Greene	25	1	12	4	8	477	181	267	29	3
Hamilton[5]	275	4	54	136	81	5,771	1,168	4,342	261	20
Hocking	9	3	2	0	4	378	142	230	6	1
Jefferson	9	0	1	4	4	92	25	64	3	0
Lake	208	0	21	5	182	350	111	228	11	3
Lawrence	86	1	8	11	66	1,080	309	708	63	3
Licking	407	0	51	13	343	1,242	389	817	36	7
Lorain	33	1	8	17	7	1,169	596	539	34	11
Lucas	82	0	4	22	56	1,331	394	855	82	11
Madison	13	0	3	2	8	472	180	271	21	4
Mahoning	7	0	2	2	3	165	72	90	3	1
Miami	16	0	5	5	6	542	156	357	29	9
Montgomery	296	2	35	109	150	1,736	702	883	151	15

Table 10. Offenses Known to Law Enforcement, by Selected State Metropolitan and Nonmetropolitan Counties, 2012— continued

(Number)

State/county	Violent crime	Murder and nonnegligent manslaughter	Forcible rape	Robbery	Aggravated assault	Property crime	Burglary	Larceny-theft	Motor vehicle theft	Arson[1]
Morrow	16	0	3	3	10	481	231	237	13	3
Pickaway	27	0	4	5	18	1,094	493	580	21	5
Portage	41	0	2	21	18	1,804	634	1,151	19	0
Richland	34	2	8	12	12	1,433	630	762	41	5
Stark	90	0	11	53	26	1,859	758	977	124	10
Summit	29	0	11	8	10	1,063	239	762	62	3
Trumbull	26	1	5	1	19	534	263	259	12	1
Wood	6	0	2	0	4	503	126	359	18	0
Trumbull	18	1	2	6	9	653	246	369	38	2
Warren	58	1	16	9	32	1,115	309	790	16	3
Washington	19	0	3	2	14	422	140	263	19	3
Wood	12	0	2	4	6	471	127	330	14	3
Ohio—Nonmetropolitan Counties										
Adams	13	0	2	1	10	414	195	208	11	1
Ashland	12	0	6	0	6	434	195	230	9	1
Ashtabula	65	2	10	10	43	1,346	369	921	56	4
Athens	19	0	5	6	8	641	206	419	16	2
Auglaize	4	0	1	0	3	149	53	90	6	0
Champaign	14	0	0	1	13	396	139	243	14	4
Clinton	9	0	3	0	6	75	24	46	5	0
Columbiana	14	1	1	1	11	79	61	15	3	0
Coshocton	19	0	0	5	14	895	294	590	11	3
Crawford	8	0	1	0	7	351	172	168	11	1
Darke	13	0	2	3	8	461	151	293	17	3
Defiance	6	0	5	0	1	173	40	130	3	1
Fayette	23	0	2	11	10	684	218	448	18	4
Gallia	17	2	3	7	5	610	248	345	17	1
Guernsey	6	2	1	3	0	189	73	107	9	3
Hancock	4	0	1	0	3	248	90	151	7	0
Hardin	4	0	0	0	4	281	132	145	4	2
Harrison	4	0	3	1	0	96	39	47	10	0
Highland	44	0	3	0	41	614	227	354	33	3
Holmes	4	0	2	2	0	230	61	156	13	1
Logan	10	0	4	0	6	555	238	301	16	0
Marion	34	0	6	20	8	1,427	409	1,009	9	4
Meigs	16	1	5	5	5	331	156	159	16	1
Mercer	10	1	3	1	5	213	55	154	4	0
Monroe	4	0	2	0	2	97	40	57	0	1
Muskingum	53	1	22	12	18	1,304	350	887	67	7
Ottawa	3	0	1	2	0	327	66	252	9	0
Paulding	8	0	2	0	6	136	47	89	0	1
Pike	15	3	3	3	6	312	78	216	18	6
Ross	47	0	13	9	25	1,797	539	1,196	62	8
Scioto	12	0	4	7	1	874	307	536	31	16
Seneca	1	0	1	0	0	320	128	189	3	0
Tuscarawas	7	1	2	1	3	322	170	127	25	2
Van Wert	1	0	0	0	1	176	72	100	4	1
Vinton	14	2	3	2	7	298	133	156	9	1
Washington	26	0	9	0	17	477	210	252	15	3
Wayne	21	0	8	2	11	678	299	347	32	8
Wyandot	5	0	1	1	3	16	8	7	1	0
Oklahoma—Metropolitan Counties										
Canadian	16	0	1	1	14	175	54	95	26	1
Cleveland	42	1	9	3	29	355	124	189	42	9
Comanche	38	0	4	1	33	410	139	242	29	1
Cotton	1	0	0	0	1	17	6	10	1	0
Creek	56	3	5	5	43	375	133	203	39	5
Grady	53	1	4	1	47	239	108	118	13	2
Le Flore	49	1	1	0	47	367	163	179	25	5
Lincoln	26	0	3	0	23	347	153	154	40	1

Table 10. Offenses Known to Law Enforcement, by Selected State Metropolitan and Nonmetropolitan Counties, 2012— continued

(Number)

State/county	Violent crime	Murder and nonnegligent manslaughter	Forcible rape	Robbery	Aggravated assault	Property crime	Burglary	Larceny-theft	Motor vehicle theft	Arson[1]
Logan	23	0	1	1	21	403	157	218	28	6
McClain	21	0	2	6	13	349	126	195	28	3
Oklahoma	32	0	1	1	30	318	68	215	35	0
Okmulgee	11	0	4	0	7	222	88	112	22	9
Osage	31	0	5	3	23	400	141	221	38	12
Pawnee	23	1	2	0	20	87	29	54	4	1
Sequoyah	42	0	4	0	38	335	128	192	15	7
Tulsa	171	1	9	11	150	662	272	328	62	10
Wagoner	47	2	5	2	38	444	170	244	30	3
Oklahoma—Nonmetropolitan Counties										
Adair	54	1	5	0	48	211	103	96	12	5
Alfalfa	3	0	0	0	3	29	7	22	0	0
Atoka	4	0	2	0	2	93	45	41	7	1
Beaver	4	0	0	0	4	44	13	29	2	0
Beckham	4	0	0	0	4	73	27	45	1	1
Blaine	3	0	1	0	2	45	6	36	3	0
Bryan	64	1	5	0	58	367	147	184	36	1
Caddo	78	1	5	1	71	210	86	106	18	2
Carter	67	2	8	2	55	268	95	141	32	3
Cherokee	42	0	2	1	39	230	67	134	29	2
Choctaw	17	0	1	1	15	148	55	77	16	7
Cimarron	0	0	0	0	0	0	0	0	0	0
Coal	7	0	2	0	5	58	14	40	4	1
Craig	8	1	3	0	4	106	23	65	18	3
Custer	5	0	1	0	4	52	18	29	5	0
Delaware	52	1	5	0	46	380	137	197	46	3
Dewey	1	0	0	0	1	27	10	13	4	0
Ellis	5	0	0	0	5	40	10	26	4	0
Garfield	4	0	2	0	2	76	23	44	9	5
Garvin	23	0	3	5	15	255	97	142	16	12
Grant	2	0	0	0	2	54	22	28	4	0
Greer	6	0	1	1	4	4	1	1	2	1
Harmon	1	1	0	0	0	22	3	18	1	0
Harper	0	0	0	0	0	25	15	7	3	0
Haskell	24	0	2	0	22	68	25	33	10	3
Hughes	3	0	2	0	1	89	20	56	13	1
Jackson	6	0	2	0	4	60	25	33	2	0
Jefferson	2	0	0	0	2	32	10	18	4	0
Johnston	12	1	0	0	11	5	1	3	1	1
Kay	22	0	0	7	15	78	40	37	1	0
Kingfisher	1	0	0	0	1	50	17	31	2	0
Kiowa	1	0	0	0	1	47	25	20	2	1
Latimer	6	0	0	0	6	19	6	13	0	0
Love	4	0	0	0	4	66	14	49	3	0
Major	3	0	0	0	3	35	8	24	3	0
Marshall	42	2	4	0	36	83	29	41	13	1
McCurtain	46	0	4	3	39	514	181	297	36	12
McIntosh	20	0	4	0	16	225	65	139	21	2
Murray	8	1	2	1	4	74	31	38	5	1
Muskogee	79	2	10	4	63	336	134	160	42	14
Noble	3	0	0	0	3	41	14	27	0	2
Nowata	6	0	0	1	5	85	28	47	10	0
Okfuskee	10	0	0	0	10	116	44	58	14	4
Ottawa	14	0	2	1	11	126	49	60	17	1
Payne	15	0	2	2	11	253	88	147	18	3
Pittsburg	31	0	13	2	16	349	121	211	17	6
Pontotoc	27	1	6	2	18	196	80	92	24	0
Pottawatomie	30	2	2	0	26	619	233	307	79	2
Pushmataha	10	0	2	0	8	83	37	30	16	3
Roger Mills	5	0	0	1	4	40	3	35	2	0
Seminole	2	0	1	0	1	286	122	150	14	3
Stephens	14	1	4	2	7	229	82	132	15	1

Table 10. Offenses Known to Law Enforcement, by Selected State Metropolitan and Nonmetropolitan Counties, 2012— continued

(Number)

State/county	Violent crime	Murder and nonnegligent manslaughter	Forcible rape	Robbery	Aggravated assault	Property crime	Burglary	Larceny-theft	Motor vehicle theft	Arson[1]
Texas	5	0	2	0	3	37	6	29	2	1
Tillman	9	0	0	1	8	90	40	50	0	3
Washington	24	0	3	0	21	197	66	119	12	1
Washita	15	0	2	0	13	99	31	53	15	1
Woods	2	0	0	0	2	13	3	9	1	0
Woodward	6	0	1	0	5	108	42	55	11	1
Oregon—Metropolitan Counties										
Benton	21	0	6	0	15	157	42	99	16	1
Clackamas	218	8	55	85	70	5,610	1,000	4,108	502	12
Columbia	20	0	3	2	15	187	75	85	27	1
Deschutes	118	0	9	5	104	897	252	601	44	13
Jackson	167	2	14	9	142	1,304	313	917	74	10
Josephine	71	0	1	6	64	825	322	411	92	4
Lane	203	7	22	21	153	1,105	436	558	111	12
Linn	35	0	10	9	16	1,135	308	736	91	4
Marion	70	2	17	18	33	2,448	511	1,636	301	9
Multnomah	43	0	12	3	28	997	134	809	54	1
Polk	39	0	1	0	38	300	91	190	19	0
Washington	317	6	75	63	173	2,669	556	1,946	167	26
Yamhill	32	1	9	3	19	679	236	406	37	6
Oregon—Nonmetropolitan Counties										
Baker	0	0	0	0	0	15	9	6	0	0
Clatsop	3	0	0	0	3	155	37	107	11	2
Coos	28	0	1	1	26	473	123	321	29	0
Crook	24	0	1	1	22	127	49	76	2	1
Curry	14	0	1	3	10	272	71	179	22	5
Douglas	51	0	14	7	30	1,360	389	893	78	11
Gilliam	1	0	0	0	1	15	5	8	2	1
Grant	0	0	0	0	0	37	5	30	2	2
Harney	3	0	0	0	3	15	5	10	0	0
Hood River	27	0	2	3	22	182	37	129	16	1
Jefferson	4	1	2	0	1	194	58	122	14	1
Klamath	71	2	12	11	46	386	133	183	70	7
Lincoln	44	0	4	4	36	341	99	218	24	8
Malheur	1	0	0	0	1	185	57	118	10	0
Morrow	12	1	2	1	8	177	46	120	11	2
Sherman	2	0	1	0	1	42	6	34	2	0
Tillamook	6	0	0	1	5	263	88	163	12	4
Umatilla	22	2	4	2	14	566	149	299	118	4
Union	17	0	8	0	9	234	65	151	18	2
Wallowa	0	0	0	0	0	29	9	20	0	1
Wasco	13	0	1	0	12	153	52	92	9	1
Pennsylvania—Metropolitan Counties										
Allegheny	8	0	0	1	7	6	1	5	0	0
Allegheny County Police Department	59	0	3	0	56	107	6	91	10	78
Beaver	0	0	0	0	0	0	0	0	0	0
Blair	2	0	0	0	2	0	0	0	0	0
Butler	0	0	0	0	0	0	0	0	0	0
Cumberland	0	0	0	0	0	0	0	0	0	0
Lancaster	0	0	0	0	0	0	0	0	0	0
Lycoming	0	0	0	0	0	0	0	0	0	0
Mercer	0	0	0	0	0	0	0	0	0	0
Monroe	0	0	0	0	0	0	0	0	0	0
Northampton	0	0	0	0	0	0	0	0	0	0
Washington	4	0	0	0	4	3	0	3	0	0
Westmoreland	0	0	0	0	0	1	0	1	0	0
York	1	0	0	0	1	0	0	0	0	0

Table 10. Offenses Known to Law Enforcement, by Selected State Metropolitan and Nonmetropolitan Counties, 2012— continued

(Number)

State/county	Violent crime	Murder and nonnegligent manslaughter	Forcible rape	Robbery	Aggravated assault	Property crime	Burglary	Larceny-theft	Motor vehicle theft	Arson[1]
Pennsylvania—Nonmetropolitan Counties										
Bedford	0	0	0	0	0	0	0	0	0	0
Clarion	0	0	0	0	0	0	0	0	0	0
Elk	0	0	0	0	0	0	0	0	0	0
Greene	0	0	0	0	0	0	0	0	0	0
Indiana	0	0	0	0	0	0	0	0	0	0
Lawrence	0	0	0	0	0	0	0	0	0	0
Schuylkill	0	0	0	0	0	1	0	1	0	0
Snyder	0	0	0	0	0	0	0	0	0	0
Tioga	0	0	0	0	0	0	0	0	0	0
Union	0	0	0	0	0	0	0	0	0	0
Warren	0	0	0	0	0	0	0	0	0	0
Wayne	0	0	0	0	0	0	0	0	0	0
South Carolina—Metropolitan Counties										
Aiken	351	4	41	47	259	3,776	1,187	2,173	416	3
Anderson	809	10	40	110	649	6,816	1,890	4,251	675	27
Beaufort	706	9	34	89	574	3,489	1,015	2,306	168	15
Berkeley	487	10	37	82	358	3,558	1,010	2,173	375	10
Calhoun	53	0	6	6	41	468	200	227	41	2
Chester	110	2	8	17	83	891	276	561	54	2
Darlington	345	4	10	33	298	2,332	938	1,243	151	8
Dorchester	345	3	25	53	264	2,074	582	1,292	200	3
Edgefield	20	1	3	4	12	389	109	246	34	3
Fairfield	125	3	5	9	108	665	177	422	66	4
Florence	225	2	8	38	177	2,451	755	1,514	182	1
Greenville	1,994	17	142	319	1,516	10,827	3,000	6,912	915	50
Jasper	34	5	10	13	6	461	135	290	36	1
Kershaw	256	2	27	14	213	1,557	485	962	110	1
Lancaster	245	10	18	45	172	2,497	764	1,637	96	13
Laurens	306	4	21	20	261	1,252	477	689	86	8
Lexington	534	7	59	81	387	4,549	1,068	3,061	420	13
Pickens	254	4	14	16	220	2,096	608	1,285	203	10
Richland	2,266	15	105	388	1,758	9,747	2,657	5,891	1,199	27
Saluda	37	0	4	3	30	292	113	156	23	1
Spartanburg	596	8	61	95	432	5,874	1,783	3,619	472	33
Sumter	424	5	20	39	360	2,487	1,004	1,280	203	34
Union	93	2	2	9	80	599	147	430	22	6
York	499	1	20	37	441	2,300	531	1,641	128	19
South Carolina—Nonmetropolitan Counties										
Abbeville	49	0	2	3	44	412	126	269	17	2
Allendale	2	0	0	0	2	80	23	51	6	0
Bamberg	32	0	1	2	29	291	103	157	31	0
Barnwell	88	0	3	2	83	474	110	314	50	5
Cherokee	79	1	0	12	66	440	190	187	63	3
Chesterfield	138	2	7	11	118	977	244	677	56	6
Clarendon	113	1	6	15	91	896	284	551	61	4
Colleton	204	2	11	8	183	1,180	326	699	155	9
Dillon	192	4	13	20	155	1,054	370	608	76	6
Greenwood	428	4	17	19	388	1,725	409	1,248	68	5
Hampton	75	0	5	7	63	308	114	172	22	1
Lee	76	0	2	8	66	429	137	244	48	7
Marion	99	4	3	10	82	837	370	403	64	6
Marlboro	172	2	14	11	145	863	269	551	43	2
McCormick	18	0	1	0	17	108	36	55	17	0
Newberry	79	1	0	7	71	481	127	322	32	3
Oconee	268	5	26	7	230	1,677	535	1,018	124	11
Orangeburg	256	12	26	69	149	3,266	1,035	1,830	401	17
South Dakota—Metropolitan Counties										

Table 10. Offenses Known to Law Enforcement, by Selected State Metropolitan and Nonmetropolitan Counties, 2012— continued

(Number)

State/county	Violent crime	Murder and nonnegligent manslaughter	Forcible rape	Robbery	Aggravated assault	Property crime	Burglary	Larceny-theft	Motor vehicle theft	Arson[1]
Custer	5	0	1	0	4	31	7	20	4	0
Lincoln	10	0	3	0	7	180	74	94	12	2
McCook	3	0	1	0	2	30	11	[illegible]	0	0
Meade	9	0	1	0	8	21	8	12	1	0
Minnehaha	41	0	14	0	27	317	82	224	11	6
Pennington	63	0	20	0	43	408	116	271	21	6
Turner	7	0	0	0	7	42	21	15	6	0
Union	4	0	0	0	4	63	14	47	2	0
South Dakota—Nonmetropolitan Counties										
Aurora	0	0	0	0	0	17	6	10	1	0
Beadle	2	0	0	0	2	29	3	23	3	0
Bennett	1	0	1	0	0	7	0	6	1	0
Bon Homme	0	0	0	0	0	1	1	0	0	0
Brookings	2	0	0	0	2	61	11	47	3	2
Brown	3	0	0	0	3	32	11	18	3	0
Butte	3	0	3	0	0	43	13	28	2	1
Campbell	0	0	0	0	0	7	1	4	2	1
Charles Mix	12	1	2	0	9	51	29	20	2	1
Clark	0	0	0	0	0	4	3	1	0	0
Clay	6	0	2	1	3	52	8	40	4	0
Codington	7	0	1	0	6	65	20	40	5	0
Corson	1	0	0	0	1	24	14	6	4	0
Davison	6	0	1	0	5	16	1	13	2	0
Deuel	3	2	1	0	0	33	15	14	4	0
Dewey	2	0	0	0	2	2	2	0	0	0
Douglas	0	0	0	0	0	0	0	0	0	0
Edmunds	0	0	0	0	0	1	0	0	1	0
Faulk	1	0	0	0	1	2	0	2	0	0
Hamlin	3	0	1	0	2	39	13	24	2	0
Hand	4	0	0	0	4	9	0	9	0	0
Hanson	2	0	1	0	1	3	1	2	0	0
Harding	1	0	0	0	1	0	0	0	0	0
Hughes	4	0	1	0	3	20	6	11	3	0
Hutchinson	2	0	0	0	2	1	1	0	0	0
Jerauld	0	0	0	0	0	5	1	3	1	0
Lawrence	8	0	1	0	7	177	12	165	0	0
Marshall	15	0	6	0	9	40	11	24	5	0
McPherson	0	0	0	0	0	1	0	1	0	0
Mellette	2	0	0	0	2	16	6	8	2	0
Miner	1	0	0	1	0	8	6	2	0	0
Moody	3	0	1	0	2	34	5	26	3	0
Perkins	0	0	0	0	0	10	2	7	1	0
Potter	1	0	0	0	1	0	0	0	0	0
Roberts	13	0	0	0	13	25	5	15	5	0
Spink	10	0	4	0	6	41	7	30	4	3
Stanley	5	0	2	0	3	32	17	15	0	0
Tripp	2	0	0	0	2	10	6	4	0	0
Walworth	1	0	0	0	1	6	1	3	2	0
Yankton	12	0	1	1	10	107	27	70	10	1
Ziebach	0	0	0	0	0	1	0	0	1	0
Tennessee—Metropolitan Counties										
Anderson	107	1	17	10	79	805	333	391	81	9
Blount	301	3	28	16	254	1,782	704	968	110	3
Bradley	220	1	6	14	199	965	272	612	81	2
Campbell	57	0	12	8	37	669	336	301	32	14
Cannon	8	0	0	0	8	95	47	33	15	1
Carter	53	4	2	1	46	666	295	315	56	4
Chester	16	0	1	0	15	131	36	86	9	0
Crockett	33	1	5	0	27	134	50	74	10	0
Dickson	105	1	9	2	93	548	212	306	30	7

Table 10. Offenses Known to Law Enforcement, by Selected State Metropolitan and Nonmetropolitan Counties, 2012— continued

(Number)

State/county	Violent crime	Murder and nonnegligent manslaughter	Forcible rape	Robbery	Aggravated assault	Property crime	Burglary	Larceny-theft	Motor vehicle theft	Arson[1]
Fayette	62	0	4	8	50	320	104	194	22	2
Grainger	17	0	2	2	13	279	63	203	13	0
Hamblen	87	0	4	13	70	607	182	398	27	8
Hamilton	252	2	20	18	212	1,826	625	1,088	113	4
Hickman	63	0	4	3	56	330	148	157	25	0
Knox	539	7	30	81	421	5,589	1,285	3,863	441	21
Loudon	60	0	4	1	55	565	168	360	37	1
Macon	54	0	1	0	53	135	27	96	12	0
Madison	146	1	11	6	128	799	320	440	39	6
Marion	56	0	1	3	52	283	88	165	30	1
Maury	131	1	12	5	113	636	197	396	43	3
Montgomery	105	2	9	4	90	770	178	534	58	3
Morgan	77	2	5	4	66	429	157	242	30	1
Polk	45	4	1	2	38	326	108	179	39	0
Roane	51	0	7	0	44	553	248	268	37	5
Robertson	53	0	4	2	47	348	121	199	28	0
Rutherford	241	0	12	13	216	1,299	397	799	103	3
Sequatchie	35	0	2	1	32	175	60	92	23	6
Shelby	601	1	37	79	484	3,073	945	1,966	162	11
Smith	35	0	6	1	28	258	96	140	22	2
Sullivan	407	1	17	15	374	1,526	470	949	107	17
Sumner	119	1	10	3	105	736	263	439	34	10
Tipton	152	0	12	7	133	621	201	364	56	3
Unicoi	17	0	0	0	17	273	39	224	10	2
Union	51	1	5	8	37	512	198	278	36	9
Washington	174	0	5	9	160	1,076	445	575	56	7
Williamson	74	0	7	8	59	488	154	308	26	6
Wilson	142	1	3	14	124	949	296	564	89	0
Tennessee—Nonmetropolitan Counties										
Bedford	45	1	3	0	41	278	103	164	11	2
Benton	29	0	1	1	27	164	58	90	16	1
Bledsoe	10	0	0	1	9	73	20	45	8	1
Carroll	27	0	1	0	26	192	82	93	17	2
Claiborne	139	0	3	11	125	670	339	288	43	8
Clay	10	0	0	0	10	71	34	27	10	0
Cocke	160	3	2	12	143	895	397	434	64	15
Coffee	67	1	0	3	63	380	112	241	27	0
Decatur	49	0	1	3	45	218	77	121	20	1
DeKalb	24	0	1	0	23	235	84	138	13	0
Dyer	56	0	1	2	53	273	70	178	25	0
Fentress	36	1	4	4	27	293	95	186	12	3
Franklin	35	3	6	0	26	294	93	178	23	3
Gibson	52	0	1	2	49	315	129	164	22	0
Giles	45	1	3	4	37	247	109	130	8	1
Greene	154	4	10	23	117	1,094	429	579	86	11
Grundy	110	3	4	1	102	348	142	144	62	11
Hancock	16	0	0	0	16	108	39	62	7	0
Hardeman	82	3	3	1	75	330	140	154	36	3
Haywood	36	0	4	2	30	224	84	126	14	3
Henderson	60	1	3	4	52	354	132	197	25	2
Henry	39	1	7	0	31	428	131	280	17	0
Houston	28	0	0	1	27	89	31	50	8	1
Humphreys	23	0	0	0	23	188	54	129	5	1
Jackson	25	0	0	1	24	202	79	108	15	3
Johnson	76	2	3	2	69	248	88	124	36	2
Lake	5	0	0	0	5	21	3	15	3	0
Lauderdale	63	0	5	4	54	382	173	179	30	2
Lawrence	98	0	2	2	94	565	218	310	37	6
Lewis	17	0	3	0	14	162	33	116	13	2
Lincoln	89	4	3	1	81	369	149	204	16	3
Marshall	31	0	0	0	31	163	55	95	13	0
McMinn	69	0	2	5	62	656	194	387	75	7

Table 10. Offenses Known to Law Enforcement, by Selected State Metropolitan and Nonmetropolitan Counties, 2012— continued

(Number)

State/county	Violent crime	Murder and nonnegligent manslaughter	Forcible rape	Robbery	Aggravated assault	Property crime	Burglary	Larceny-theft	Motor vehicle theft	Arson[1]
McNairy	82	0	3	1	78	326	95	200	31	1
Monroe	135	4	3	3	125	685	214	411	60	9
Moore	4	0	0	0	4	89	20	65	4	0
Obion	23	0	1	1	21	242	64	161	17	3
Overton	47	1	3	1	42	213	114	90	9	3
Perry	24	0	1	1	22	104	32	64	8	1
Putnam	142	0	7	3	132	982	270	652	60	2
Rhea	80	0	2	4	74	385	123	223	39	1
Scott	23	1	1	0	21	336	132	179	25	2
Sevier	142	2	13	13	114	2,047	859	1,092	96	4
Stewart	34	0	1	2	31	133	50	70	13	3
Van Buren	12	0	1	0	11	86	11	72	3	0
Warren	39	0	1	1	37	402	129	238	35	1
Wayne	41	1	2	0	38	94	40	46	8	2
Weakley	65	2	3	1	59	203	77	107	19	0
White	88	1	5	1	81	404	94	272	38	2
Texas— Metropolitan Counties										
Aransas	23	1	4	1	17	291	89	187	15	4
Archer	5	0	0	0	5	72	18	40	14	0
Armstrong	1	0	0	0	1	28	14	11	3	0
Atascosa	27	2	0	0	25	492	208	269	15	0
Austin	25	0	2	1	22	146	63	69	14	0
Bastrop	210	0	43	11	156	1,084	405	600	79	4
Bell	36	3	17	4	12	706	270	411	25	9
Bexar	487	10	70	99	308	6,398	2,081	3,865	452	80
Bowie	131	0	15	9	107	848	331	425	92	17
Brazoria	92	3	5	26	58	1,523	587	836	100	0
Brazos	41	1	0	0	40	415	158	244	13	3
Burleson	14	0	5	2	7	124	46	69	9	0
Caldwell	40	0	8	3	29	219	79	126	14	0
Callahan	14	0	0	2	12	41	22	16	3	0
Cameron	143	4	15	19	105	1,732	619	1,027	86	19
Carson	4	0	1	0	3	44	11	31	2	1
Chambers	67	0	4	9	54	579	191	339	49	3
Clay	4	1	0	2	1	83	61	17	5	0
Collin	74	1	16	2	55	624	247	323	54	2
Comal	219	2	25	7	185	926	280	594	52	6
Coryell	8	2	1	0	5	116	45	62	9	1
Crosby	1	0	0	0	1	3	2	1	0	0
Dallas	51	0	2	6	43	296	91	181	24	0
Denton	61	1	4	4	52	901	255	584	62	6
Ector	57	0	1	23	33	1,417	321	956	140	3
Ellis	44	4	2	2	36	615	233	327	55	1
El Paso	250	5	28	23	194	1,260	303	829	128	13
Falls	7	1	0	0	6	45	30	15	0	2
Fort Bend	804	1	38	116	649	4,398	1,672	2,452	274	15
Galveston	106	0	16	22	68	794	302	441	51	14
Goliad	10	0	3	2	5	116	39	74	3	0
Grayson	50	0	15	3	32	800	278	459	63	6
Gregg	71	0	28	6	37	524	157	340	27	2
Guadalupe	109	0	44	8	57	576	191	346	39	5
Hardin	48	3	4	3	38	413	104	236	73	3
Harris	7,416	77	295	2,744	4,300	52,551	13,848	32,259	6,444	331
Hays	67	2	3	0	62	869	381	457	31	1
Hidalgo	526	22	65	138	301	6,273	2,435	3,556	282	89
Hood	49	1	0	2	46	507	120	343	44	3
Hudspeth	2	0	0	0	2	30	11	18	1	0
Hunt	176	0	2	14	160	1,217	485	651	81	1
Irion	2	0	0	0	2	34	16	18	0	0
Jefferson	38	0	6	11	21	519	141	330	48	2
Johnson	144	3	25	3	113	1,078	354	637	87	14
Jones	0	0	0	0	0	68	18	49	1	0

Table 10. Offenses Known to Law Enforcement, by Selected State Metropolitan and Nonmetropolitan Counties, 2012— continued

(Number)

State/county	Violent crime	Murder and nonnegligent manslaughter	Forcible rape	Robbery	Aggravated assault	Property crime	Burglary	Larceny-theft	Motor vehicle theft	Arson[1]
Kaufman	143	1	19	11	112	1,114	443	557	114	2
Kendall	24	1	16	0	7	245	76	157	12	0
Lampasas	4	0	0	2	2	111	26	82	3	0
Liberty	152	1	2	8	141	890	297	492	101	8
Lynn	3	0	0	0	3	48	19	27	2	0
Martin	5	0	0	0	5	47	8	37	2	0
McLennan	80	0	21	4	55	717	287	387	43	4
Medina	28	0	10	2	16	202	74	120	8	0
Midland	37	1	0	0	36	560	127	359	74	3
Montgomery	521	10	30	106	375	6,076	1,732	3,830	514	12
Newton	1	0	0	0	1	66	23	37	6	0
Nueces	63	1	6	6	50	210	79	125	6	0
Oldham	2	0	0	0	2	26	4	22	0	0
Orange	93	0	7	3	83	641	246	314	81	1
Parker	67	3	9	3	52	1,174	419	684	71	0
Potter	19	0	0	1	18	182	68	97	17	0
Randall	43	0	3	1	39	325	119	182	24	3
Robertson	13	0	3	1	9	174	63	104	7	1
Rusk	102	0	6	8	88	689	254	388	47	0
San Patricio	39	0	1	2	36	351	144	196	11	0
Smith	264	2	37	18	207	1,936	772	996	168	13
Somervell	5	0	0	0	5	108	48	58	2	1
Tarrant	126	1	17	12	96	1,246	411	746	89	15
Taylor	30	0	5	2	23	149	65	72	12	1
Tom Green	26	1	19	1	5	279	103	172	4	2
Travis	448	1	15	36	396	3,182	966	2,073	143	24
Upshur	65	0	5	1	59	682	274	365	43	3
Waller	30	2	5	2	21	255	98	148	9	0
Webb	87	0	5	4	78	268	99	141	28	0
Wichita	37	0	2	3	32	146	57	82	7	2
Williamson	114	2	23	9	80	1,147	292	819	36	9
Wilson	28	3	4	1	20	284	105	151	28	0
Wise	64	1	3	6	54	542	193	304	45	1
Texas— Nonmetropolitan Counties										
Anderson	52	1	3	2	46	444	199	204	41	3
Andrews	3	1	2	0	0	93	28	59	6	0
Angelina	73	2	5	6	60	658	262	363	33	1
Bailey	2	0	0	0	2	61	34	26	1	0
Baylor	0	0	0	0	0	4	1	3	0	0
Bee	30	1	3	1	25	120	39	68	13	0
Blanco	16	0	1	0	15	75	37	34	4	0
Borden	1	0	0	0	1	6	3	2	1	0
Bosque	12	0	3	0	9	128	48	75	5	1
Brewster	3	0	0	0	3	17	11	6	0	0
Briscoe	0	0	0	0	0	3	0	2	1	0
Brown	19	2	0	0	17	161	59	97	5	2
Burnet	20	0	6	0	14	290	105	167	18	0
Camp	10	0	2	1	7	152	60	88	4	3
Cass	29	2	4	1	22	392	204	161	27	0
Castro	2	0	0	0	2	66	24	37	5	0
Cherokee	76	1	10	3	62	639	209	357	73	4
Childress	0	0	0	0	0	15	3	9	3	0
Cochran	6	0	3	0	3	122	49	63	10	0
Coke	0	0	0	0	0	23	7	16	0	0
Coleman	0	0	0	0	0	68	36	29	3	0
Collingsworth	0	0	0	0	0	0	0	0	0	0
Comanche	7	0	0	0	7	96	33	56	7	0
Concho	6	0	0	0	6	5	4	1	0	0
Cottle	0	0	0	0	0	1	0	1	0	0
Crane	1	0	0	0	1	29	6	22	1	0
Culberson	1	0	0	1	0	7	4	3	0	0
Dallam	0	0	0	0	0	22	4	16	2	0

Table 10. Offenses Known to Law Enforcement, by Selected State Metropolitan and Nonmetropolitan Counties, 2012— continued

(Number)

State/county	Violent crime	Murder and nonnegligent manslaughter	Forcible rape	Robbery	Aggravated assault	Property crime	Burglary	Larceny-theft	Motor vehicle theft	Arson[1]
Dawson	1	0	0	1	0	50	14	31	5	0
Deaf Smith	1	0	0	0	1	93	36	48	9	1
Delta	8	0	0	1	7	128	66	52	10	2
DeWitt	15	0	1	1	13	101	34	58	9	0
Dickens	0	0	0	0	0	5	3	2	0	0
Dimmit	51	0	4	2	45	438	167	249	22	4
Donley	10	0	0	0	10	34	12	18	4	0
Duval	41	0	0	1	40	205	60	90	55	2
Edwards	1	0	0	0	1	26	6	18	2	0
Erath	12	0	2	0	10	88	37	43	8	0
Fannin	37	3	12	1	21	183	70	97	16	0
Fayette	5	1	1	1	2	161	58	93	10	1
Fisher	6	0	0	0	6	66	34	30	2	0
Floyd	3	1	0	0	2	28	10	15	3	1
Foard	2	0	0	0	2	1	1	0	0	0
Franklin	8	0	2	1	5	95	41	44	10	0
Freestone	18	1	0	0	17	150	81	56	13	2
Frio	6	0	1	0	5	60	22	34	4	0
Gaines	8	2	0	1	5	89	30	53	6	0
Garza	0	0	0	0	0	56	19	35	2	0
Gillespie	13	0	5	2	6	119	41	78	0	0
Glasscock	1	0	0	0	1	13	3	9	1	0
Gonzales	19	0	4	1	14	177	72	92	13	0
Gray	1	0	1	0	0	119	43	68	8	0
Grimes	31	1	3	2	25	327	127	173	27	0
Hale	7	0	0	0	7	111	44	62	5	0
Hall	0	0	0	0	0	1	1	0	0	0
Hamilton	15	0	2	2	11	123	59	59	5	1
Hansford	0	0	0	0	0	18	2	9	7	0
Hardeman	0	0	0	0	0	96	47	48	1	0
Harrison	70	1	0	3	66	556	251	289	16	1
Hartley	2	0	0	0	2	16	8	6	2	1
Haskell	3	0	0	0	3	19	9	8	2	0
Hemphill	18	0	0	0	18	66	16	44	6	0
Henderson	204	2	31	7	164	1,157	419	609	129	7
Hill	54	1	5	2	46	420	170	237	13	3
Hockley	13	0	5	0	8	67	35	29	3	1
Hopkins	23	0	4	0	19	121	47	69	5	1
Houston	11	1	0	0	10	186	73	94	19	2
Howard	33	1	5	1	26	166	32	123	11	1
Hutchinson	10	0	2	1	7	121	32	82	7	0
Jack[3]	4	0	0	0	4		22	43		0
Jackson	8	0	0	0	8	59	22	34	3	0
Jasper	70	2	22	3	43	365	147	204	14	0
Jeff Davis	2	0	0	1	1	8	4	4	0	0
Jim Hogg	2	1	0	0	1	6	2	4	0	0
Jim Wells	108	3	9	0	96	368	158	175	35	0
Karnes	1	0	0	0	1	214	71	128	15	1
Kenedy	6	0	3	1	2	13	5	4	4	0
Kent	3	0	0	0	3	13	5	7	1	0
Kerr	31	1	8	4	18	362	125	221	16	5
Kimble	5	0	0	1	4	20	14	5	1	0
King	0	0	0	0	0	0	0	0	0	0
Kinney	0	0	0	0	0	3	2	1	0	0
Kleberg	9	1	0	0	8	198	18	178	2	0
Knox	2	0	0	0	2	15	4	11	0	0
Lamar	20	1	2	1	16	351	126	216	9	0
Lamb	7	0	1	2	4	113	28	76	9	2
La Salle	13	0	0	1	12	43	13	29	1	3
Lee	13	0	2	0	11	117	41	71	5	0
Leon	15	1	4	1	9	228	94	112	22	0
Limestone	31	0	5	0	26	321	141	156	24	3
Lipscomb	0	0	0	0	0	12	3	9	0	0
Live Oak	17	0	4	1	12	162	62	88	12	0

Table 10. Offenses Known to Law Enforcement, by Selected State Metropolitan and Nonmetropolitan Counties, 2012—continued

(Number)

State/county	Violent crime	Murder and nonnegligent manslaughter	Forcible rape	Robbery	Aggravated assault	Property crime	Burglary	Larceny-theft	Motor vehicle theft	Arson[1]
Llano	7	0	1	0	6	261	99	156	6	11
Loving	0	0	0	0	0	2	0	2	0	0
Madison	5	0	1	1	3	71	25	32	14	0
Marion	59	1	7	3	48	219	96	111	12	4
Mason	1	0	0	0	1	31	7	24	0	0
Matagorda	58	0	2	4	52	246	96	143	7	1
Maverick	114	3	4	1	106	623	274	328	21	1
McCulloch	1	0	0	0	1	34	11	23	0	0
McMullen	3	0	0	0	3	43	9	27	7	0
Menard	4	0	0	0	4	2	2	0	0	1
Milam	23	1	0	0	22	177	58	104	15	1
Mills	1	0	0	0	1	43	14	28	1	1
Mitchell	0	0	0	0	0	28	11	14	3	1
Montague	11	0	0	1	10	180	50	124	6	0
Moore	7	1	0	0	6	79	20	50	9	0
Morris	27	0	0	1	26	98	42	54	2	0
Motley	0	0	0	0	0	26	10	15	1	0
Nacogdoches	73	0	7	3	63	450	133	289	28	3
Navarro	19	0	4	3	12	582	228	339	15	0
Nolan	10	0	0	1	9	53	21	31	1	0
Ochiltree	7	0	0	0	7	53	11	38	4	3
Palo Pinto	15	1	0	0	14	158	68	80	10	1
Panola	38	0	3	4	31	370	147	187	36	2
Parmer	0	0	0	0	0	51	18	31	2	0
Pecos	1	0	0	0	1	53	14	39	0	0
Polk[3]	66	0	20	7	39			406	49	7
Presidio	0	0	0	0	0	6	3	3	0	0
Rains	21	0	7	0	14	185	53	122	10	0
Reagan	1	0	0	0	1	19	9	9	1	0
Real	3	2	0	0	1	17	3	12	2	0
Red River	9	0	1	0	8	136	64	62	10	0
Reeves	4	0	0	0	4	108	18	89	1	0
Refugio	6	0	0	0	6	38	7	30	1	1
Roberts	5	0	1	0	4	17	1	13	3	0
Runnels	0	0	0	0	0	22	1	20	1	0
Sabine	15	0	2	5	8	82	33	48	1	2
San Augustine	23	0	1	2	20	115	35	68	12	1
San Jacinto	66	0	1	8	57	718	274	355	89	3
San Saba	7	1	0	0	6	6	0	3	3	0
Schleicher	1	0	0	0	1	15	9	6	0	0
Scurry	12	0	2	0	10	75	18	47	10	0
Shackelford	1	1	0	0	0	31	8	19	4	1
Shelby	29	5	5	3	16	303	115	165	23	1
Sherman	0	0	0	0	0	1	0	1	0	0
Starr	101	2	5	4	90	341	157	155	29	1
Stephens	4	0	0	0	4	30	13	16	1	0
Sterling	1	0	0	0	1	2	1	0	1	0
Stonewall	6	0	0	0	6	5	2	2	1	0
Sutton	0	0	0	0	0	2	2	0	0	0
Swisher	13	0	1	0	12	51	24	24	3	0
Terrell	2	0	0	0	2	3	3	0	0	0
Terry	2	0	0	0	2	50	15	33	2	0
Throckmorton	1	0	0	0	1	5	1	4	0	0
Titus	34	0	0	1	33	265	123	129	13	3
Trinity	13	1	1	0	11	129	51	70	8	1
Tyler	65	1	9	1	54	255	123	113	19	3
Upton	1	0	0	0	1	17	6	10	1	0
Uvalde	31	2	0	0	29	106	45	56	5	0
Val Verde	6	0	0	0	6	118	50	63	5	0
Van Zandt	75	4	0	5	66	706	267	352	87	1
Walker	68	0	17	2	49	389	171	197	21	2
Ward	37	2	4	1	30	113	30	80	3	0
Washington	27	0	1	2	24	197	78	107	12	0
Wharton	61	0	0	7	54	323	138	170	15	2

Table 10. Offenses Known to Law Enforcement, by Selected State Metropolitan and Nonmetropolitan Counties, 2012— continued

(Number)

State/county	Violent crime	Murder and nonnegligent manslaughter	Forcible rape	Robbery	Aggravated assault	Property crime	Burglary	Larceny-theft	Motor vehicle theft	Arson[1]
Wheeler[3]	10	0	1	0	9		10		1	1
Wilbarger	2	0	0	0	2	39	17	21	1	0
Willacy	47	0	9	1	37	260	97	160	0	0
Winkler	3	0	0	0	3	24	5	17	2	0
Wood	28	1	2	2	23	565	202	334	29	4
Yoakum	6	1	3	2	0	61	18	37	6	0
Young	4	0	0	0	4	77	29	46	2	4
Zapata	30	0	1	1	28	167	73	80	14	1
Zavala	20	0	0	1	19	69	32	33	4	0
Utah—Metropolitan Counties										
Box Elder	7	0	1	0	6	192	37	146	9	0
Cache	13	0	9	0	4	409	74	316	19	0
Davis	16	0	5	0	11	208	48	154	6	0
Juab	1	0	0	0	1	63	14	43	6	0
Morgan	2	0	1	0	1	44	7	35	2	1
Salt Lake County Unified Police Department	694	5	112	169	408	10,118	1,667	7,617	834	35
Tooele	25	0	6	2	17	132	43	62	27	4
Utah	19	0	3	0	16	288	48	230	10	2
Washington	19	2	2	2	13	122	31	83	8	1
Weber	40	0	6	5	29	923	179	698	46	7
Utah—Nonmetropolitan Counties										
Beaver	11	0	0	0	11	37	12	22	3	0
Carbon	7	0	2	0	5	181	43	129	9	0
Daggett	0	0	0	0	0	28	13	15	0	0
Duchesne	24	0	2	0	22	309	58	237	14	3
Emery	8	0	2	0	6	184	52	121	11	2
Grand	14	0	3	0	11	89	27	57	5	0
Iron	38	0	5	1	32	154	43	97	14	3
Millard	22	0	4	0	18	250	52	189	9	0
Piute	0	0	0	0	0	26	4	18	4	0
Rich	5	0	0	0	5	35	8	26	1	0
San Juan	7	0	1	1	5	69	21	46	2	0
Sanpete	15	0	10	0	5	253	36	202	15	0
Sevier	20	0	3	0	17	214	37	154	23	1
Summit	34	0	5	3	26	483	65	399	19	1
Uintah	45	0	10	1	34	211	53	141	17	3
Wasatch	10	0	0	0	10	141	21	114	6	0
Wayne	1	0	0	0	1	15	3	12	0	1
Vermont—Metropolitan Counties										
Franklin	11	0	0	4	7	98	36	51	11	0
Grand Isle	4	0	0	0	4	76	32	41	3	0
Vermont—Nonmetropolitan Counties										
Addison	0	0	0	0	0	0	0	0	0	0
Bennington	1	0	0	0	1	1	0	1	0	0
Essex	0	0	0	0	0	32	15	17	0	0
Lamoille	9	0	1	0	8	171	27	113	31	1
Orange	7	0	6	0	1	53	15	34	4	0
Orleans	0	0	0	0	0	41	23	18	0	0
Washington	0	0	0	0	0	0	0	0	0	0
Windham	1	0	0	0	1	13	4	9	0	0
Virginia—Metropolitan Counties										
Albemarle County Police Department	99	4	22	17	56	1,469	232	1,187	50	12
Amelia	24	0	1	0	23	145	34	99	12	1
Amherst	15	0	7	1	7	504	125	365	14	2
Appomattox	5	0	0	1	4	134	34	95	5	0

Table 10. Offenses Known to Law Enforcement, by Selected State Metropolitan and Nonmetropolitan Counties, 2012— continued

(Number)

State/county	Violent crime	Murder and nonnegligent manslaughter	Forcible rape	Robbery	Aggravated assault	Property crime	Burglary	Larceny-theft	Motor vehicle theft	Arson[1]
Arlington County Police Department	305	5	31	117	152	3,855	286	3,383	186	4
Augusta	86	2	7	2	75	847	131	676	40	3
Bedford	36	1	5	2	28	754	227	491	36	2
Botetourt	25	0	3	1	21	285	74	202	9	2
Buckingham	28	0	4	4	20	397	208	165	24	1
Campbell	60	2	13	8	37	768	163	568	37	2
Caroline	33	1	8	7	17	382	87	284	11	9
Charles City	4	0	0	0	4	8	1	7	0	0
Chesterfield County Police Department	394	10	52	149	183	6,869	1,669	4,914	286	73
Clarke	16	0	1	0	15	139	40	94	5	3
Craig	5	0	0	0	5	7	1	6	0	0
Culpeper	25	0	5	1	19	308	67	216	25	1
Dinwiddie	49	2	7	6	34	421	111	278	32	3
Fairfax County Police Department	848	15	107	343	383	14,501	1,059	12,643	799	70
Fauquier	30	2	8	4	16	558	100	420	38	10
Floyd	10	0	3	0	7	142	29	107	6	2
Fluvanna	16	0	3	0	13	205	56	142	7	4
Franklin	37	0	6	3	28	598	131	428	39	1
Frederick	82	2	26	11	43	1,563	293	1,180	90	2
Giles	7	0	3	0	4	128	29	93	6	0
Gloucester	32	2	8	6	16	664	103	550	11	3
Goochland	16	2	0	0	14	207	49	151	7	0
Greene	19	0	8	0	11	250	30	211	9	2
Hanover	83	5	6	17	55	975	99	827	49	3
Henrico County Police Department	545	14	20	225	286	7,730	1,173	6,180	377	56
Isle of Wight	31	3	3	6	19	428	80	329	19	5
James City County Police Department	71	1	14	14	42	952	150	786	16	9
King William	12	0	0	0	12	95	21	67	7	0
Loudoun	216	1	48	34	133	2,906	297	2,483	126	29
Mathews	8	0	3	0	5	117	17	95	5	1
Montgomery	35	0	6	1	28	479	146	311	22	7
Nelson	15	0	1	1	13	250	74	164	12	1
New Kent	18	0	3	1	14	327	102	216	9	1
Powhatan	8	0	1	2	5	236	67	161	8	1
Prince George County Police Department	32	0	5	8	19	459	83	324	52	1
Prince William County Police Department	627	2	44	214	367	6,809	927	5,520	362	56
Pulaski	35	1	5	4	25	727	152	548	27	3
Rappahannock	6	0	3	0	3	18	3	15	0	0
Roanoke County Police Department	107	2	17	12	76	1,267	292	927	48	1
Rockingham	52	0	11	4	37	384	131	235	18	0
Scott	16	0	6	2	8	323	89	220	14	3
Spotsylvania	265	2	36	61	166	2,326	236	1,934	156	11
Stafford	195	2	23	40	130	2,264	228	1,931	105	19
Sussex	14	1	1	5	7	132	36	84	12	3
Warren	18	0	7	1	10	378	49	314	15	0
Washington	40	0	12	1	27	929	203	670	56	4
York	83	0	2	16	65	1,337	127	1,184	26	12
Virginia—Nonmetropolitan Counties										
Accomack	43	2	5	11	25	489	159	318	12	2
Alleghany	11	1	1	1	8	150	46	102	2	3
Bath	1	0	0	1	0	25	7	18	0	0
Bland	1	0	0	1	0	63	17	46	0	0
Brunswick	9	0	1	2	6	113	49	52	12	1
Buchanan	33	1	2	3	27	429	113	295	21	2
Carroll	19	0	4	1	14	383	82	279	22	3
Charlotte	21	1	4	3	13	132	46	85	1	2
Cumberland	19	0	0	0	19	71	20	38	13	1
Dickenson	7	1	0	0	6	140	9	119	12	0
Essex	17	0	1	0	16	88	38	45	5	0
Grayson	14	1	2	1	10	167	35	116	16	6

Table 10. Offenses Known to Law Enforcement, by Selected State Metropolitan and Nonmetropolitan Counties, 2012— continued

(Number)

State/county	Violent crime	Murder and nonnegligent manslaughter	Forcible rape	Robbery	Aggravated assault	Property crime	Burglary	Larceny-theft	Motor vehicle theft	Arson[1]
Greensville	14	0	1	0	13	119	35	78	6	1
Halifax	30	0	3	3	24	470	147	301	22	3
Henry	187	5	8	27	147	1,259	378	809	72	6
Highland	1	0	0	0	1	5	3	2	0	0
King and Queen	7	0	1	0	6	25	13	9	3	1
King George	23	0	5	3	15	348	57	278	13	2
Lancaster	6	0	4	1	1	102	18	79	5	2
Lee	30	1	1	9	19	329	95	233	1	1
Louisa	39	1	7	1	30	423	71	325	27	5
Lunenburg	17	0	1	0	16	91	40	42	9	1
Madison	11	1	4	1	5	150	17	131	2	3
Mecklenburg	33	0	8	4	21	414	188	211	15	13
Middlesex	7	0	4	0	3	62	22	37	3	0
Northampton	12	0	2	4	6	165	57	97	11	0
Northumberland	11	1	2	0	8	56	7	47	2	1
Nottoway	4	0	0	0	4	111	20	88	3	1
Orange	23	1	5	2	15	227	41	179	7	0
Page	20	2	3	4	11	221	62	153	6	11
Patrick	23	0	3	5	15	310	66	216	28	1
Pittsylvania	30	1	6	8	15	574	205	339	30	6
Prince Edward	15	0	5	3	7	88	47	37	4	0
Richmond	1	0	0	0	1	46	7	26	13	1
Rockbridge	20	0	1	3	16	308	97	199	12	4
Russell	49	0	6	1	42	308	113	186	9	4
Shenandoah	29	0	2	4	23	396	146	243	7	2
Smyth	18	2	1	2	13	372	77	283	12	14
Southampton	27	0	3	4	20	337	91	213	33	2
Surry	21	1	0	3	17	70	30	34	6	1
Tazewell	39	0	10	3	26	589	158	405	26	2
Westmoreland	11	0	1	0	10	179	37	136	6	5
Wise	34	4	6	6	18	409	140	246	23	2
Wythe	15	0	2	1	12	92	15	74	3	0
Washington—Metropolitan Counties										
Asotin	27	0	4	1	22	208	52	141	15	0
Benton	67	0	8	5	54	527	159	332	36	4
Chelan	37	1	6	6	24	620	194	397	29	0
Clark	283	2	46	51	184	3,987	1,155	2,297	535	31
Columbia	7	1	2	0	4	165	47	116	2	0
Cowlitz	84	3	35	1	45	537	186	309	42	8
Douglas	20	0	4	3	13	464	184	257	23	3
Franklin	19	0	5	2	12	239	84	137	18	0
King	405	7	64	127	207	5,555	2,436	2,525	594	59
Kitsap	338	2	54	47	235	4,317	1,287	2,711	319	17
Pend Oreille	19	3	3	1	12	477	161	282	34	0
Pierce	1,000	17	102	198	683	9,990	3,663	5,233	1,094	46
Skagit	95	1	12	8	74	1,382	538	774	70	11
Skamania	13	0	6	0	7	114	37	71	6	0
Spokane	147	4	19	36	88	3,985	1,248	2,407	330	19
Stevens	26	0	4	0	22	610	268	292	50	1
Thurston	258	1	30	24	203	2,832	1,174	1,457	201	21
Walla Walla	17	0	1	3	13	443	144	281	18	3
Whatcom	158	1	35	7	115	1,130	412	648	70	11
Yakima	125	4	11	25	85	1,992	876	854	262	33
Washington—Nonmetropolitan Counties										
Adams	19	0	7	2	10	261	84	147	30	2
Clallam	72	4	9	11	48	880	302	543	35	2
Ferry	10	0	1	0	9	29	9	19	1	1
Garfield	7	0	1	0	6	53	16	35	2	1
Grant	109	3	19	13	74	1,266	357	787	122	10
Island	72	1	15	2	54	778	326	421	31	4

Table 10. Offenses Known to Law Enforcement, by Selected State Metropolitan and Nonmetropolitan Counties, 2012— continued

(Number)

State/county	Violent crime	Murder and nonnegligent manslaughter	Forcible rape	Robbery	Aggravated assault	Property crime	Burglary	Larceny-theft	Motor vehicle theft	Arson[1]
Jefferson	43	0	8	1	34	429	143	257	29	4
Kittitas	8	0	2	0	6	258	92	142	24	2
Lewis	47	1	5	1	40	696	296	354	46	3
Lincoln	9	0	0	0	9	153	45	97	11	2
Mason	102	4	10	11	77	1,687	718	782	187	6
Okanogan	43	0	6	3	34	418	173	207	38	3
San Juan	13	0	4	0	9	216	73	132	11	0
Wahkiakum	3	0	0	0	3	2	1	0	1	0
Whitman	6	1	2	0	3	102	30	64	8	2
West Virginia—Metropolitan Counties										
Berkeley	81	1	10	23	47	1,322	363	905	54	8
Boone	19	0	1	0	18	92	34	53	5	1
Brooke	5	0	2	0	3	88	42	34	12	0
Fayette	71	5	2	13	51	472	201	237	34	4
Hampshire	87	0	2	1	84	102	50	49	3	1
Hancock	2	0	0	0	2	7	2	5	0	0
Jefferson	28	0	0	5	23	390	22	361	7	1
Marshall	27	0	1	0	26	177	53	115	9	1
Mineral	27	0	1	4	22	53	11	41	1	0
Preston	53	0	3	1	49	161	48	100	13	1
Raleigh	144	3	15	42	84	1,215	573	569	73	5
Wirt	23	0	1	0	22	48	14	26	8	2
West Virginia—Nonmetropolitan Counties										
Braxton	9	0	0	1	8	46	8	38	0	0
Grant	5	0	1	0	4	13	8	5	0	0
Greenbrier	6	0	2	0	4	94	23	63	8	2
Hardy	3	0	0	0	3	22	11	10	1	1
Harrison	46	0	0	2	44	313	94	197	22	5
Jackson	1	0	0	0	1	42	4	30	8	1
Lewis	3	0	0	0	3	30	5	25	0	0
Logan	43	3	1	0	39	39	10	23	6	1
Mason	9	1	1	1	6	137	0	123	14	0
McDowell	13	0	0	3	10	74	24	46	4	1
Mercer	60	1	2	9	48	488	241	204	43	3
Mingo	3	0	0	0	3	2	1	1	0	0
Monroe	15	0	1	2	12	88	19	66	3	0
Morgan	9	0	1	0	8	100	37	55	8	0
Nicholas	154	0	5	2	147	200	58	131	11	7
Pleasants	0	0	0	0	0	2	0	2	0	0
Randolph	30	1	0	1	28	59	10	48	1	0
Ritchie	7	0	0	1	6	39	10	28	1	2
Roane	15	0	2	0	13	55	0	48	7	0
Summers	3	0	0	0	3	25	11	14	0	0
Taylor	2	0	0	0	2	11	4	6	1	0
Tucker	7	0	0	0	7	10	2	7	1	0
Tyler	5	0	0	0	5	77	23	54	0	1
Upshur	3	0	0	1	2	78	22	54	2	0
Wyoming	38	1	2	5	30	275	106	151	18	2
Wisconsin—Metropolitan Counties										
Brown	115	1	11	7	96	765	202	539	24	0
Calumet	15	0	3	2	10	150	38	101	11	0
Chippewa	21	0	9	0	12	381	132	237	12	3
Columbia	33	0	11	0	22	377	137	226	14	2
Dane	33	3	11	3	16	843	220	592	31	3
Douglas	12	0	2	0	10	316	138	158	20	1
Eau Claire	19	0	5	3	11	275	114	159	2	0
Fond du Lac	22	0	4	1	17	316	101	203	12	0
Green	6	0	1	0	5	197	53	121	23	0
Iowa	32	4	8	2	18	115	32	72	11	1

Table 10. Offenses Known to Law Enforcement, by Selected State Metropolitan and Nonmetropolitan Counties, 2012— continued

(Number)

State/county	Violent crime	Murder and nonnegligent manslaughter	Forcible rape	Robbery	Aggravated assault	Property crime	Burglary	Larceny-theft	Motor vehicle theft	Arson[1]
Kenosha	39	1	8	8	22	685	142	508	35	5
Kewaunee	1	0	0	0	1	76	18	55	3	1
La Crosse	14	0	1	1	12	228	59	160	9	0
Milwaukee	104	0	1	47	136	421	67	312	42	0
Oconto	2	0	0	2	0	488	197	269	22	10
Outagamie	39	0	5	1	33	336	73	251	12	1
Ozaukee	6	0	1	0	5	133	41	89	3	0
Pierce	24	0	1	0	23	205	82	116	7	0
Racine	18	1	3	1	13	509	95	387	27	
Rock	34	0	14	3	17	454	152	281	21	3
Sheboygan	13	0	2	1	10	495	101	373	21	1
St. Croix	30	2	3	1	24	400	101	270	29	2
Washington	62	1	5	1	55	611	167	432	12	4
Waukesha	41	0	1	5	35	637	166	443	28	0
Winnebago	25	0	0	0	25	318	112	187	19	0
Wisconsin—Nonmetropolitan Counties										
Adams	19	0	6	6	7	450	185	249	16	0
Ashland	22	0	0	0	22	48	22	25	1	0
Barron	2	0	0	1	1	213	100	101	12	0
Bayfield	13	0	1	0	12	229	126	100	3	1
Buffalo	0	0	0	0	0	29	9	18	2	0
Burnett	32	0	2	2	28	344	134	172	38	2
Clark	98	0	0	1	97	195	66	112	17	4
Dodge	27	0	6	2	19	299	80	204	15	4
Door	11	1	1	0	9	166	28	134	4	0
Dunn	51	0	6	1	44	202	55	133	14	1
Florence	11	0	0	0	11	107	43	61	3	0
Forest	6	0	3	1	2	169	41	120	8	0
Grant	28	0	5	0	23	290	97	173	20	3
Green Lake	6	0	2	0	4	111	21	83	7	0
Iron	3	0	0	0	3	60	18	42	0	0
Jackson	10	0	5	3	2	175	51	114	10	0
Jefferson	31	0	2	1	28	436	116	306	14	5
Juneau	29	0	5	0	24	283	82	193	8	0
Lafayette	3	0	1	0	2	159	27	119	13	1
Lincoln	10	0	3	0	7	192	91	94	7	1
Manitowoc	24	0	2	1	21	204	60	131	13	1
Marinette	10	1	6	1	2	549	366	158	25	7
Marquette	3	0	0	0	3	145	40	90	15	5
Menominee	2	0	0	0	2	59	31	25	3	0
Monroe	14	0	2	0	12	253	40	202	11	3
Oneida	25	0	2	0	23	243	87	147	9	0
Pepin	4	0	3	0	1	35	24	10	1	0
Polk	78	1	10	2	65	349	122	200	27	0
Portage	19	0	4	0	15	223	77	139	7	1
Price	8	0	0	0	8	133	31	96	6	1
Sauk	23	0	7	2	14	533	118	389	26	1
Sawyer	25	0	3	1	21	336	152	172	12	1
Shawano	22	1	8	0	13	524	201	291	32	1
Taylor	6	0	4	0	2	154	51	96	7	0
Trempealeau	14	0	10	1	3	152	45	102	5	0
Vernon	13	0	4	0	9	154	45	103	6	1
Vilas	4	0	0	1	3	158	52	100	6	0
Walworth	40	1	1	2	36	268	67	184	17	1
Waupaca	16	0	2	2	12	526	161	344	21	1
Waushara	22	0	7	2	13	354	74	264	16	4
Wood	2	0	0	0	2	225	57	150	18	0
Wyoming—Metropolitan Counties										
Laramie	77	2	11	6	58	615	164	404	47	7
Natrona	39	0	5	0	34	246	78	145	23	4

Table 10. Offenses Known to Law Enforcement, by Selected State Metropolitan and Nonmetropolitan Counties, 2012— continued

(Number)

State/county	Violent crime	Murder and nonnegligent manslaughter	Forcible rape	Robbery	Aggravated assault	Property crime	Burglary	Larceny-theft	Motor vehicle theft	Arson[1]
Wyoming—Nonmetropolitan Counties										
Albany	9	0	1	0	8	53	11	37	5	1
Big Horn	5	0	2	0	3	16	7	9	0	0
Campbell	24	0	1	3	20	229	64	153	12	2
Carbon	9	0	1	0	8	58	9	46	3	1
Converse	10	0	2	0	8	86	11	74	1	2
Crook	4	0	2	0	2	48	4	37	7	0
Fremont	16	0	3	0	13	210	67	134	9	0
Goshen	11	0	0	1	10	72	33	38	1	0
Hot Springs	1	0	0	0	1	39	8	31	0	0
Johnson	0	0	0	0	0	48	6	41	1	0
Lincoln	9	0	0	0	9	62	18	42	2	1
Niobrara	1	0	0	0	1	4	0	4	0	0
Park	31	0	2	0	29	84	27	51	6	0
Platte	0	0	0	0	0	22	8	13	1	0
Sheridan	2	0	0	2	0	50	13	35	2	0
Sublette	12	0	1	0	11	83	22	57	4	1
Sweetwater	33	1	2	3	27	131	20	97	14	2
Uinta	2	0	0	0	2	87	7	74	6	0
Washakie	1	0	0	0	1	10	2	8	0	0
Weston	1	0	0	0	1	2	0	1	1	0

Note: The data shown in this table do not reflect county totals but are the number of offenses reported by the sheriff's office or county police department. 1 A blank cell in the arson column indicates that the FBI did not receive 12 complete months of arson data for that agency. 2 The FBI determined that the agency's data were underreported. Consequently, those data are not included in this table. 3 The FBI determined that the agency's data were overreported. Consequently, affected data are not included in this table. 4 The Tulare County Highway Patrol collects the motor vehicle thefts for this county. These data can be found in Table 11. 5 Because of changes in the state/local agency's reporting practices, figures are not comparable to previous years' data. 6 The data collection methodology for the offense of forcible rape used by the Minnesota state UCR Program does not comply with national UCR Program guidelines. Consequently, its figures for forcible rape and violent crime (of which forcible rape is a part) are not published in this table. 7 The FBI determined that the agency did not follow national Uniform Crime Reporting (UCR) Program guidelines for reporting an offense. Consequently, this figure is not included in this table. n.a. = not available

Table 11. Offenses Known to Law Enforcement, by Selected State, Tribal, and Other Agencies, 2012

(Number)

State/Other Agency Unit/Office	Violent crime	Murder and nonnegligent manslaughter	Forcible rape	Robbery	Aggravated assault	Property crime	Burglary	Larceny-theft	Motor vehicle theft	Arson[1]
Alabama										
State Agency										
State Fire Marshal	2	1	0	0	1	17	14	3	0	
Tribal Agency										
Poarch Creek Tribal	4	0	0	3	1	296	77	207	12	
Alaska										
State Agency										
Alaska State Troopers[2]	928	8	137	37	746	3,366	1,129	1,960	277	51
Tribal Agency										
Metlakatla Tribal	1	1	0	0	0	0	0	0	0	0
Other Agencies										
Anchorage International Airport	0	0	0	0	0	96	0	83	13	1
Fairbanks International Airport	0	0	0	0	0	15	0	14	1	1
Arizona										
State Agency										
Arizona Department of Public Safety	46	0	0	5	41	94	1	93	0	0
Tribal Agencies										
Ak-Chin Tribal	8	0	1	0	7	3	0	2	1	0
Cocopah Tribal	14	0	0	1	13	30	4	22	4	0
Colorado River Agency	9	1	2	0	6	1	1	0	0	9
Colorado River Tribal	21	3	0	1	17	75	50	1	24	19
Fort Apache Agency	10	5	0	0	5	0	0	0	0	5
Fort Mojave Tribal	34	1	3	0	30	90	7	77	6	5
Hopi Tribal	199	0	0	1	198	138	0	136	2	0
Hualapai Tribal	80	0	0	1	79	38	32	5	1	
Kaibab Paiute Tribal	1	0	0	0	1	0	0	0	0	0
Navajo Nation	623	3	357	45	218	2,668	936	1,008	724	378
Pascua Yaqui Tribal	15	0	0	1	14	211	39	158	14	1
Quechan Tribal	5	0	0	0	5	34	9	24	1	0
Salt River Tribal	71	2	8	11	50	542	87	409	46	0
San Carlos Agency	26	1	1	0	24	0	0	0	0	3
	280	1	5	4	270	169	64	100	5	28
Tohono O'odham Nation	64	2	11	2	49	99	41	22	36	2
Tonto Apache Tribal	2	0	0	0	2	3	2	1	0	0
Truxton Canon Agency	11	0	0	0	11	3	3	0	0	0
White Mountain Apache Tribal	71	2	30	4	35	630	368	239	23	80
Yavapai-Apache Nation	13	0	0	0	13	30	3	24	3	2
Yavapai-Prescott Tribal	1	0	1	0	0	65	2	61	2	0
Other Agencies										
Tucson Airport Authority	1	0	0	0	1	89	4	33	52	0
Arkansas										
State Agency										
Camp Robinson	0	0	0	0	0	15	1	14	0	0
California										
State Agencies										
Atascadero State Hospital	125	0	0	0	125	10	0	10	0	0
California State Fair	0	0	0	0	0	55	0	51	4	0
Coalinga State Hospital	47	0	0	1	46	32	1	31	0	0
Department of Parks and Recreation										
Angeles	0	0	0	0	0	0	0	0	0	0
Bay Area	1	0	0	0	1	13	2	11	0	0
Calaveras County	0	0	0	0	0	0	0	0	0	1
Capital	2	0	0	0	2	14	4	10	0	0
Channel Coast	1	0	1	0	0	82	0	82	0	0
Colorado	0	0	0	0	0	0	0	0	0	0
Four Rivers District	0	0	0	0	0	7	3	4	0	0
Gold Fields District	0	0	0	0	0	76	0	76	0	0
Hollister Hills	0	0	0	0	0	0	0	0	0	0
Hungry Valley	0	0	0	0	0	2	0	0	2	0

Table 11. Offenses Known to Law Enforcement, by Selected State, Tribal, and Other Agencies, 2012— continued

(Number)

State/Other Agency Unit/Office	Violent crime	Murder and nonnegligent manslaughter	Forcible rape	Robbery	Aggravated assault	Property crime	Burglary	Larceny-theft	Motor vehicle theft	Arson[1]
Inland Empire	3	0	0	0	3	8	4	4	0	0
Marin County	1	0	0	0	1	3	1	2	0	0
Mendocino Headquarters	1	0	0	0	1	12	2	10	0	0
Monterey County	0	0	0	0	0	30	21	9	0	0
North Coast Redwoods	0	0	0	0	0	17	1	15	1	0
Northern Buttes	1	0	0	0	1	27	0	26	1	0
Oceano Dunes	7	0	0	0	7	50	4	41	5	0
Ocotillo Wells	0	0	0	0	0	2	0	2	0	0
Orange Coast	0	0	0	0	0	72	13	58	1	0
Russian River	1	0	0	0	1	15	0	15	0	0
San Diego Coast	0	0	0	0	0	100	11	88	1	2
San Joaquin	2	0	0	0	2	7	2	5	0	0
San Luis Obispo Coast	1	0	0	0	1	13	1	12	0	0
Santa Cruz Mountains	0	0	0	0	0	52	0	52	0	0
Sierra	0	0	0	0	0	13	1	12	0	2
Silverado	0	0	0	0	0	0	0	0	0	0
Tehachapi District	2	0	0	0	2	4	1	3	0	0
Twin Cities	0	0	0	0	0	1	0	1	0	0
Fairview Developmental Center	188	0	0	1	187	7	1	6	0	1
Highway Patrol										
Alameda County	2	0	0	0	2	202	0	33	169	0
Alpine County	0	0	0	0	0	4	0	0	4	0
Amador County	0	0	0	0	0	22	0	0	22	0
Butte County	0	0	0	0	0	213	0	40	173	0
Calaveras County	0	0	0	0	0	90	0	7	83	0
Colusa County	0	0	0	0	0	26	0	0	26	0
Contra Costa County	2	1	0	0	1	1,239	1	2	1,236	0
Del Norte County	0	0	0	0	0	97	0	2	95	0
El Dorado County	0	0	0	0	0	189	0	50	139	0
Fresno County	2	0	0	1	1	212	0	25	187	0
Glenn County	0	0	0	0	0	49	0	4	45	0
Humboldt County	0	0	0	0	0	283	0	83	200	0
Imperial County	0	0	0	0	0	93	1	11	81	0
Inyo County	0	0	0	0	0	11	0	5	6	0
Kern County	3	0	0	0	3	244	1	16	227	0
Kings County	0	0	0	0	0	38	0	1	37	0
Lake County	0	0	0	0	0	114	0	14	100	0
Lassen County	0	0	0	0	0	19	0	3	16	0
Los Angeles County	38	0	0	0	38	432	9	46	377	0
Madera County	0	0	0	0	0	288	0	43	245	0
Marin County	0	0	0	0	0	96	0	12	84	0
Mariposa County	0	0	0	0	0	24	0	4	20	0
Mendocino County	0	0	0	0	0	134	0	8	126	0
Merced County	0	0	0	0	0	670	2	129	539	0
Modoc County	0	0	0	0	0	5	0	3	2	0
Mono County	0	0	0	0	0	0	0	0	0	0
Monterey County	2	0	0	0	2	456	0	43	413	0
Napa County	0	0	0	0	0	45	0	14	31	0
Nevada County	0	0	0	0	0	96	0	33	63	0
Orange County	2	0	0	0	2	45	0	16	29	0
Placer County	1	0	0	0	1	204	0	36	168	0
Plumas County	1	0	0	0	1	31	2	13	16	0
Riverside County	15	0	0	0	15	97	29	4	64	0
Sacramento County	8	0	0	0	8	4,579	16	766	3,797	0
San Benito County	0	0	0	0	0	26	0	1	25	0
San Bernardino County	5	0	0	0	5	60	0	17	43	0
San Diego County	9	0	0	0	9	111	7	53	51	0
San Francisco County	1	0	0	0	1	14	0	7	7	0
San Joaquin County	2	0	0	0	2	1,006	0	307	699	0
San Luis Obispo County	2	0	0	0	2	171	0	11	160	0
San Mateo County	0	0	0	0	0	11	0	6	5	0
Santa Barbara County	1	0	0	0	1	152	0	41	111	0
Santa Clara County	0	0	0	0	0	136	0	28	108	0
Santa Cruz County	2	0	0	0	2	434	0	63	371	0

Table 11. Offenses Known to Law Enforcement, by Selected State, Tribal, and Other Agencies, 2012— continued

(Number)

State/Other Agency Unit/Office	Violent crime	Murder and nonnegligent manslaughter	Forcible rape	Robbery	Aggravated assault	Property crime	Burglary	Larceny-theft	Motor vehicle theft	Arson[1]
Shasta County	0	0	0	0	0	297	0	34	263	0
Sierra County	0	0	0	0	0	3	0	1	2	0
Siskiyou County	0	0	0	0	0	46	3	4	39	0
Solano County	2	0	0	0	2	87	0	3	84	0
Sonoma County	0	0	0	0	0	277	0	73	204	0
Stanislaus County	3	0	0	1	2	960	1	66	893	0
Sutter County	0	0	0	0	0	62	0	0	62	0
Tehama County	2	0	0	1	1	112	1	12	99	0
Trinity County	0	0	0	0	0	30	0	6	24	0
Tulare County	1	0	0	0	1	557	0	73	484	0
Tuolumne County	0	0	0	0	0	103	0	27	76	0
Ventura County	0	0	0	0	0	53	0	0	53	0
Yolo County	0	0	0	0	0	49	0	6	43	0
Yuba County	0	0	0	0	0	167	0	10	157	0
Lanterman State Hospital	0	0	0	0	0	0	0	0	0	0
Napa State Hospital	138	0	0	1	137	11	3	8	0	0
Patton State Hospital	154	0	4	3	147	15	0	15	0	1
Porterville Developmental Center	2	0	1	0	1	18	5	13	0	0
Sonoma Developmental Center	1	0	0	0	1	5	0	5	0	0
Tribal Agencies										
Tule River Tribal	64	4	2	3	55	95	11	71	13	0
Yurok Tribal	29	0	5	2	22	68	21	44	3	4
Other Agencies										
East Bay Municipal Utility	0	0	0	0	0	3	0	3	0	0
East Bay Regional Parks										
Alameda County	7	0	4	1	2	128	0	121	7	2
Contra Costa County	8	0	1	7	0	174	0	164	10	5
Fontana Unified School District	18	0	1	8	9	133	38	91	4	0
Los Angeles County Metropolitan Transportation Authority	11	0	0	1	10	53	1	52	0	0
Los Angeles Transportation Services Bureau	665	1	4	379	281	899	20	791	88	1
Monterey Peninsula Airport	0	0	0	0	0	11	2	5	4	0
Port of San Diego Harbor	31	0	4	7	20	493	18	475	0	0
San Bernardino Unified School District	82	0	1	76	5	502	237	238	27	5
San Francisco Bay Area Rapid Transit										
Alameda County	172	0	2	116	54	1,577	9	1,309	259	0
Contra Costa County	49	0	0	33	16	746	12	557	177	1
San Francisco County	62	0	0	45	17	367	3	363	1	0
San Mateo County	13	0	0	7	6	101	0	90	11	1
Santa Clara Transit District	44	0	1	25	18	108	7	79	22	0
Shasta County Marshal	0	0	0	0	0	0	0	0	0	0
Stockton Unified School District	79	0	1	43	35	402	150	247	5	13
Twin Rivers Unified School District	41	0	2	10	29	158	91	59	8	0
Union Pacific Railroad										
Alameda County[3]	4	0	0	0	4		125		0	0
Amador County	0	0	0	0	0	0	0	0	0	0
Butte County	0	0	0	0	0	12	2	10	0	0
Calaveras County	0	0	0	0	0	0	0	0	0	0
Colusa County	0	0	0	0	0	0	0	0	0	0
Contra Costa County	3	0	0	1	2	4	1	3	0	1
El Dorado County	0	0	0	0	0	0	0	0	0	0
Fresno County	0	0	0	0	0	6	0	6	0	0
Glenn County	0	0	0	0	0	0	0	0	0	0
Humboldt County	0	0	0	0	0	0	0	0	0	0
Imperial County	0	0	0	0	0	8	1	7	0	0
Inyo County	0	0	0	0	0	0	0	0	0	0
Kern County	0	0	0	0	0	34	0	34	0	0
Kings County	0	0	0	0	0	0	0	0	0	0
Lassen County	0	0	0	0	0	3	0	3	0	0
Los Angeles County	2	0	0	0	2	247	201	46	0	2
Madera County	0	0	0	0	0	2	0	2	0	0
Marin County	0	0	0	0	0	0	0	0	0	0
Mendocino County	0	0	0	0	0	0	0	0	0	0

Table 11. Offenses Known to Law Enforcement, by Selected State, Tribal, and Other Agencies, 2012— continued

(Number)

State/Other Agency Unit/Office	Violent crime	Murder and nonnegligent manslaughter	Forcible rape	Robbery	Aggravated assault	Property crime	Burglary	Larceny-theft	Motor vehicle theft	Arson[1]
Merced County	0	0	0	0	0	16	0	16	0	0
Modoc County	0	0	0	0	0	0	0	0	0	0
Monterey County	0	0	0	0	0	2	0	2	0	0
Napa County	0	0	0	0	0	0	0	0	0	0
Nevada County	0	0	0	0	0	1	0	1	0	0
Orange County	0	0	0	0	0	3	0	3	0	0
Placer County	1	0	0	0	1	28	6	22	0	1
Plumas County	0	0	0	0	0	2	0	2	0	0
Riverside County	1	0	0	0	1	38	4	34	0	0
Sacramento County	6	0	0	0	6	19	2	17	0	0
San Benito County	0	0	0	0	0	0	0	0	0	0
San Bernardino County	1	0	0	0	1	37	13	24	0	0
San Francisco County	0	0	0	0	0	0	0	0	0	0
San Joaquin County	8	0	0	0	8	86	69	17	0	0
San Luis Obispo County	0	0	0	0	0	1	1	0	0	0
San Mateo County	0	0	0	0	0	2	0	2	0	0
Santa Barbara County	0	0	0	0	0	1	0	1	0	0
Santa Clara County	0	0	0	0	0	14	5	9	0	0
Santa Cruz County	0	0	0	0	0	1	0	1	0	0
Shasta County	0	0	0	0	0	1	0	1	0	0
Sierra County	0	0	0	0	0	0	0	0	0	0
Siskiyou County	0	0	0	0	0	1	0	1	0	0
Solano County	2	0	0	0	2	4	0	4	0	0
Sonoma County	0	0	0	0	0	0	0	0	0	0
Stanislaus County	0	0	0	0	0	24	7	17	0	0
Sutter County	0	0	0	0	0	2	0	2	0	0
Tehama County	0	0	0	0	0	0	0	0	0	0
Trinity County	0	0	0	0	0	0	0	0	0	0
Tulare County	0	0	0	0	0	1	0	1	0	0
Ventura County	0	0	0	0	0	1	0	1	0	0
Yolo County	1	0	0	0	1	7	0	7	0	1
Yuba County	2	0	0	0	2	1	1	0	0	0
Colorado										
State Agencies										
Colorado Bureau of Investigation	0	0	0	0	0	0	0	0	0	0
Colorado Mental Health Institute	6	0	0	0	6	8	0	8	0	0
Colorado State Patrol	12	0	0	0	12	15	2	8	5	0
Tribal Agencies										
Southern Ute Tribal	1	0	0	0	1	8	5	0	3	0
Ute Mountain Tribal	15	0	4	1	10	2	0	0	2	2
Other Agencies										
22nd Judicial District Drug Task Force	0	0	0	0	0	0	0	0	0	0
Delta Montrose Drug Task Force	0	0	0	0	0	0	0	0	0	0
Southwest Drug Task Force	0	0	0	0	0	0	0	0	0	0
Connecticut										
State Agencies										
Connecticut State Police	356	36	54	59	207	4,612	1,312	2,986	314	61
State Capitol Police	0	0	0	0	0	7	0	7	0	0
Tribal Agencies										
Mashantucket Pequot Tribal	0	0	0	0	0	21	1	18	2	0
Mohegan Tribal	8	0	1	1	6	87	8	74	5	0
Other Agency										
Metropolitan Transportation Authority	3	0	0	3	0	89	0	88	1	0
Delaware										
State Agencies										
Attorney General										
Kent County	0	0	0	0	0	1	0	1	0	0
New Castle County	0	0	0	0	0	3	0	3	0	0
Division of Alcohol and Tobacco Enforcement	0	0	0	0	0	0	0	0	0	0
Environmental Control	0	0	0	0	0	3	0	3	0	0

Table 11. Offenses Known to Law Enforcement, by Selected State, Tribal, and Other Agencies, 2012— continued

(Number)

State/Other Agency Unit/Office	Violent crime	Murder and nonnegligent manslaughter	Forcible rape	Robbery	Aggravated assault	Property crime	Burglary	Larceny-theft	Motor vehicle theft	Arson[1]
Fish and Wildlife	6	0	0	0	6	13	1	12	0	0
Park Rangers	0	0	0	0	0	57	18	38	1	0
River and Bay Authority	2	0	0	0	2	13	1	11	1	0
State Capitol Police	4	0	0	1	3	33	0	33	0	0
State Fire Marshal	18	0	0	0	18	16	16	0	0	182
State Police										
Kent County	425	3	24	59	339	2,570	827	1,617	126	1
New Castle County	586	7	12	311	256	5,532	527	4,836	169	3
Sussex County	569	4	47	75	443	3,832	1,279	2,398	155	2
District of Columbia										
Other Agency: Metro Transit Police	416	0	0	311	105	1,472	0	1,360	112	1
Florida										
State Agencies										
Capitol Police	0	0	0	0	0	14	1	13	0	0
Department of Corrections, Office of the Inspector General										
Calhoun County	0	0	0	0	0	0	0	0	0	0
Hamilton County	0	0	0	0	0	0	0	0	0	0
Jackson County	0	0	0	0	0	0	0	0	0	0
Lake County	0	0	0	0	0	0	0	0	0	0
Marion County	0	0	0	0	0	0	0	0	0	0
Polk County	0	0	0	0	0	0	0	0	0	0
Santa Rosa County	0	0	0	0	0	0	0	0	0	0
Taylor County	0	0	0	0	0	0	0	0	0	0
Washington County	0	0	0	0	0	0	0	0	0	0
Department of Environmental Protection, Division of Law Enforcement										
Okeechobee County	0	0	0	0	0	0	0	0	0	0
Department of Insurance										
Broward County	0	0	0	0	0	0	0	0	0	0
Duval County	0	0	0	0	0	0	0	0	0	0
Escambia County	0	0	0	0	0	0	0	0	0	0
Hillsborough County	0	0	0	0	0	0	0	0	0	0
Lee County	0	0	0	0	0	0	0	0	0	0
Miami-Dade County	0	0	0	0	0	0	0	0	0	0
Orange County	0	0	0	0	0	0	0	0	0	0
Palm Beach County	0	0	0	0	0	0	0	0	0	0
Pinellas County	0	0	0	0	0	0	0	0	0	0
Department of Law Enforcement										
Duval County, Jacksonville	0	0	0	0	0	0	0	0	0	0
Escambia County, Pensacola	0	0	0	0	0	0	0	0	0	0
Hillsborough County, Tampa	0	0	0	0	0	0	0	0	0	0
Lee County, Fort Myers	0	0	0	0	0	0	0	0	0	0
Leon County, Tallahassee	0	0	0	0	0	0	0	0	0	0
Miami-Dade County, Miami	0	0	0	0	0	0	0	0	0	0
Orange County, Orlando	1	0	0	0	1	1	0	1	0	0
Division of Alcoholic Beverages and Tobacco										
Alachua County	0	0	0	0	0	0	0	0	0	0
Baker County	0	0	0	0	0	0	0	0	0	0
Bay County	0	0	0	0	0	0	0	0	0	0
Bradford County	0	0	0	0	0	0	0	0	0	0
Brevard County	0	0	0	0	0	0	0	0	0	0
Broward County	0	0	0	0	0	0	0	0	0	0
Calhoun County	0	0	0	0	0	0	0	0	0	0
Charlotte County	0	0	0	0	0	0	0	0	0	0
Citrus County	0	0	0	0	0	0	0	0	0	0
Clay County	0	0	0	0	0	0	0	0	0	0
Collier County	0	0	0	0	0	0	0	0	0	0
Columbia County	0	0	0	0	0	0	0	0	0	0
DeSoto County	0	0	0	0	0	0	0	0	0	0
Dixie County	0	0	0	0	0	0	0	0	0	0
Duval County	0	0	0	0	0	0	0	0	0	0

Table 11. Offenses Known to Law Enforcement, by Selected State, Tribal, and Other Agencies, 2012— continued

(Number)

State/Other Agency Unit/Office	Violent crime	Murder and nonnegligent manslaughter	Forcible rape	Robbery	Aggravated assault	Property crime	Burglary	Larceny-theft	Motor vehicle theft	Arson[1]
Escambia County	0	0	0	0	0	0	0	0	0	0
Franklin County	0	0	0	0	0	0	0	0	0	0
Gadsden County	0	0	0	0	0	0	0	0	0	0
Gilchrist County	0	0	0	0	0	0	0	0	0	0
Glades County	0	0	0	0	0	0	0	0	0	0
Gulf County	0	0	0	0	0	0	0	0	0	0
Hamilton County	0	0	0	0	0	0	0	0	0	0
Hardee County	0	0	0	0	0	0	0	0	0	0
Hendry County	0	0	0	0	0	0	0	0	0	0
Hernando County	0	0	0	0	0	0	0	0	0	0
Highlands County	0	0	0	0	0	0	0	0	0	0
Hillsborough County	0	0	0	0	0	0	0	0	0	0
Holmes County	0	0	0	0	0	0	0	0	0	0
Indian River County	0	0	0	0	0	0	0	0	0	0
Jackson County	0	0	0	0	0	0	0	0	0	0
Jefferson County	0	0	0	0	0	0	0	0	0	0
Lafayette County	0	0	0	0	0	0	0	0	0	0
Lake County	0	0	0	0	0	0	0	0	0	0
Lee County	0	0	0	0	0	0	0	0	0	0
Leon County	0	0	0	0	0	0	0	0	0	0
Levy County	0	0	0	0	0	0	0	0	0	0
Liberty County	0	0	0	0	0	0	0	0	0	0
Madison County	0	0	0	0	0	0	0	0	0	0
Manatee County	0	0	0	0	0	0	0	0	0	0
Marion County	0	0	0	0	0	0	0	0	0	0
Martin County	0	0	0	0	0	0	0	0	0	0
Miami-Dade County	0	0	0	0	0	0	0	0	0	0
Monroe County	0	0	0	0	0	0	0	0	0	0
Nassau County	0	0	0	0	0	0	0	0	0	0
Okaloosa County	0	0	0	0	0	0	0	0	0	0
Okeechobee County	0	0	0	0	0	0	0	0	0	0
Orange County	0	0	0	0	0	0	0	0	0	0
Osceola County	0	0	0	0	0	0	0	0	0	0
Palm Beach County	0	0	0	0	0	0	0	0	0	0
Pasco County	0	0	0	0	0	0	0	0	0	0
Pinellas County	0	0	0	0	0	0	0	0	0	0
Polk County	0	0	0	0	0	0	0	0	0	0
Putnam County	0	0	0	0	0	0	0	0	0	0
Santa Rosa County	0	0	0	0	0	0	0	0	0	0
Sarasota County	0	0	0	0	0	0	0	0	0	0
Seminole County	0	0	0	0	0	0	0	0	0	0
St. Johns County	0	0	0	0	0	0	0	0	0	0
St. Lucie County	0	0	0	0	0	0	0	0	0	0
Sumter County	0	0	0	0	0	0	0	0	0	0
Suwannee County	0	0	0	0	0	0	0	0	0	0
Taylor County	0	0	0	0	0	0	0	0	0	0
Union County	0	0	0	0	0	0	0	0	0	0
Volusia County	0	0	0	0	0	0	0	0	0	0
Wakulla County	0	0	0	0	0	0	0	0	0	0
Walton County	0	0	0	0	0	0	0	0	0	0
Washington County	0	0	0	0	0	0	0	0	0	0
Florida Game Commission										
Alachua County	0	0	0	0	0	0	0	0	0	0
Baker County	0	0	0	0	0	0	0	0	0	0
Bay County	0	0	0	0	0	0	0	0	0	0
Bradford County	0	0	0	0	0	0	0	0	0	0
Brevard County	0	0	0	0	0	0	0	0	0	0
Broward County	0	0	0	0	0	0	0	0	0	0
Calhoun County	0	0	0	0	0	0	0	0	0	0
Charlotte County	0	0	0	0	0	0	0	0	0	0
Citrus County	0	0	0	0	0	0	0	0	0	0
Clay County	0	0	0	0	0	0	0	0	0	0
Collier County	0	0	0	0	0	0	0	0	0	0
Columbia County	0	0	0	0	0	0	0	0	0	0

Table 11. Offenses Known to Law Enforcement, by Selected State, Tribal, and Other Agencies, 2012— continued

(Number)

State/Other Agency Unit/Office	Violent crime	Murder and nonnegligent manslaughter	Forcible rape	Robbery	Aggravated assault	Property crime	Burglary	Larceny-theft	Motor vehicle theft	Arson[1]
DeSoto County	0	0	0	0	0	0	0	0	0	0
Dixie County	0	0	0	0	0	0	0	0	0	0
Duval County	0	0	0	0	0	0	0	0	0	0
Escambia County	0	0	0	0	0	0	0	0	0	0
Flagler County	0	0	0	0	0	0	0	0	0	0
Franklin County	0	0	0	0	0	0	0	0	0	0
Gadsden County	0	0	0	0	0	0	0	0	0	0
Gilchrist County	0	0	0	0	0	0	0	0	0	0
Glades County	0	0	0	0	0	0	0	0	0	0
Gulf County	0	0	0	0	0	0	0	0	0	0
Hamilton County	0	0	0	0	0	0	0	0	0	0
Hardee County	0	0	0	0	0	0	0	0	0	0
Hendry County	0	0	0	0	0	0	0	0	0	0
Hernando County	0	0	0	0	0	0	0	0	0	0
Highlands County	0	0	0	0	0	0	0	0	0	0
Hillsborough County	0	0	0	0	0	0	0	0	0	0
Holmes County	0	0	0	0	0	0	0	0	0	0
Indian River County	0	0	0	0	0	0	0	0	0	0
Jackson County	0	0	0	0	0	0	0	0	0	0
Jefferson County	0	0	0	0	0	0	0	0	0	0
Lafayette County	0	0	0	0	0	0	0	0	0	0
Lake County	0	0	0	0	0	0	0	0	0	0
Lee County	0	0	0	0	0	0	0	0	0	0
Leon County	0	0	0	0	0	0	0	0	0	0
Levy County	0	0	0	0	0	0	0	0	0	0
Liberty County	0	0	0	0	0	0	0	0	0	0
Madison County	0	0	0	0	0	0	0	0	0	0
Manatee County	0	0	0	0	0	0	0	0	0	0
Marion County	0	0	0	0	0	0	0	0	0	0
Martin County	0	0	0	0	0	0	0	0	0	0
Miami-Dade County	0	0	0	0	0	0	0	0	0	0
Monroe County	0	0	0	0	0	0	0	0	0	0
Nassau County	0	0	0	0	0	0	0	0	0	0
Okaloosa County	0	0	0	0	0	0	0	0	0	0
Okeechobee County	0	0	0	0	0	0	0	0	0	0
Orange County	0	0	0	0	0	0	0	0	0	0
Osceola County	0	0	0	0	0	0	0	0	0	0
Palm Beach County	0	0	0	0	0	0	0	0	0	0
Pasco County	0	0	0	0	0	0	0	0	0	0
Pinellas County	0	0	0	0	0	0	0	0	0	0
Polk County	0	0	0	0	0	0	0	0	0	0
Putnam County	0	0	0	0	0	0	0	0	0	0
Santa Rosa County	0	0	0	0	0	0	0	0	0	0
Sarasota County	0	0	0	0	0	0	0	0	0	0
Seminole County	0	0	0	0	0	0	0	0	0	0
St. Johns County	0	0	0	0	0	0	0	0	0	0
St. Lucie County	0	0	0	0	0	0	0	0	0	0
Sumter County	0	0	0	0	0	0	0	0	0	0
Suwannee County	0	0	0	0	0	0	0	0	0	0
Taylor County	0	0	0	0	0	0	0	0	0	0
Union County	0	0	0	0	0	0	0	0	0	0
Volusia County	0	0	0	0	0	0	0	0	0	0
Wakulla County	0	0	0	0	0	0	0	0	0	0
Walton County	0	0	0	0	0	0	0	0	0	0
Washington County	0	0	0	0	0	0	0	0	0	0
Highway Patrol										
Alachua County	0	0	0	0	0	3	0	2	1	0
Baker County	1	0	0	0	1	4	0	2	2	0
Bay County	5	0	0	0	5	6	0	6	0	0
Bradford County	3	0	0	0	3	1	0	1	0	0
Broward County	6	0	0	0	6	30	0	28	2	0
Calhoun County	2	0	0	0	2	0	0	0	0	0
Charlotte County	1	0	0	0	1	0	0	0	0	0
Citrus County	0	0	0	0	0	0	0	0	0	0

Table 11. Offenses Known to Law Enforcement, by Selected State, Tribal, and Other Agencies, 2012— continued

(Number)

State/Other Agency Unit/Office	Violent crime	Murder and nonnegligent manslaughter	Forcible rape	Robbery	Aggravated assault	Property crime	Burglary	Larceny-theft	Motor vehicle theft	Arson[1]
Clay County	0	0	0	0	0	0	0	0	0	0
Collier County	0	0	0	0	0	2	0	1	1	0
Columbia County	2	0	0	0	2	0	0	0	0	0
DeSoto County	0	0	0	0	0	0	0	0	0	0
Dixie County	0	0	0	0	0	1	0	1	0	0
Duval County	2	0	0	0	2	10	0	9	1	0
Escambia County	4	0	0	0	4	8	0	6	2	0
Flagler County	0	0	0	0	0	1	0	1	0	0
Franklin County	0	0	0	0	0	1	0	1	0	0
Gadsden County	0	0	0	0	0	0	0	0	0	0
Gilchrist County	0	0	0	0	0	0	0	0	0	0
Glades County	0	0	0	0	0	2	0	0	2	0
Gulf County	0	0	0	0	0	0	0	0	0	0
Hamilton County	0	0	0	0	0	1	0	1	0	0
Hardee County	0	0	0	0	0	0	0	0	0	0
Hendry County	0	0	0	0	0	0	0	0	0	0
Hernando County	0	0	0	0	0	1	0	1	0	0
Highlands County	0	0	0	0	0	0	0	0	0	0
Hillsborough County	10	0	0	0	10	11	0	7	4	0
Holmes County	1	0	0	0	1	0	0	0	0	0
Indian River County	3	0	0	0	3	5	0	4	1	0
Jackson County	2	0	0	0	2	0	0	0	0	0
Jefferson County	2	0	0	0	2	0	0	0	0	0
Lafayette County	0	0	0	0	0	0	0	0	0	0
Lake County	4	0	0	0	4	2	0	0	2	0
Lee County	0	0	0	0	0	0	0	0	0	0
Leon County	3	0	0	0	3	6	1	5	0	0
Levy County	0	0	0	0	0	0	0	0	0	0
Liberty County	0	0	0	0	0	0	0	0	0	0
Madison County	0	0	0	0	0	0	0	0	0	0
Manatee County	2	0	0	0	2	2	0	1	1	0
Marion County	0	0	0	0	0	0	0	0	0	0
Martin County	3	0	0	0	3	5	0	4	1	0
Miami-Dade County	16	0	0	0	16	38	0	27	11	0
Monroe County	0	0	0	0	0	1	0	0	1	0
Nassau County	0	0	0	0	0	0	0	0	0	0
Okaloosa County	1	0	0	0	1	1	0	0	1	0
Okeechobee County	1	0	0	0	1	2	0	2	0	0
Orange County	15	0	0	0	15	19	1	9	9	0
Osceola County	0	0	0	0	0	6	0	3	3	0
Palm Beach County	15	0	0	0	15	24	0	18	6	0
Pasco County	8	0	0	0	8	3	0	3	0	0
Pinellas County	4	0	0	0	4	2	0	0	2	0
Polk County	3	0	0	0	3	4	0	2	2	0
Putnam County	1	0	0	0	1	0	0	0	0	0
Santa Rosa County	0	0	0	0	0	0	0	0	0	0
Sarasota County	0	0	0	0	0	5	0	2	3	0
Seminole County	0	0	0	0	0	0	0	0	0	0
St. Johns County	2	0	0	0	2	1	0	1	0	0
St. Lucie County	2	0	0	0	2	8	0	5	3	0
Sumter County	0	0	0	0	0	0	0	0	0	0
Suwannee County	0	0	0	0	0	0	0	0	0	0
Taylor County	1	0	0	0	1	0	0	0	0	0
Union County	0	0	0	0	0	0	0	0	0	0
Volusia County	12	0	0	0	12	3	0	3	0	0
Wakulla County	1	0	0	0	1	1	0	0	1	0
Walton County	0	0	0	0	0	1	0	0	1	0
Washington County	0	0	0	0	0	2	0	0	2	0
State Treasurer's Office, Division of Insurance Fraud	0	0	0	0	0	0	0	0	0	0
Tribal Agencies										
Miccosukee Tribal	4	0	0	0	4	144	4	132	8	0
Seminole Tribal	60	0	3	17	40	933	69	800	64	0
Other Agencies										

Table 11. Offenses Known to Law Enforcement, by Selected State, Tribal, and Other Agencies, 2012— continued

(Number)

State/Other Agency Unit/Office	Violent crime	Murder and nonnegligent manslaughter	Forcible rape	Robbery	Aggravated assault	Property crime	Burglary	Larceny-theft	Motor vehicle theft	Arson[1]
Duval County Schools	50	0	0	7	43	636	141	486	9	8
Florida School for the Deaf and Blind	0	0	0	0	0	1	0	1	0	0
Fort Lauderdale Airport	2	0	1	1	0	295	2	280	13	0
Jacksonville Aviation Authority	1	0	0	0	1	37	2	24	11	0
Lee County Port Authority	0	0	0	0	0	85	2	81	2	0
Melbourne International Airport	0	0	0	0	0	3	0	0	3	0
Miami-Dade County Public Schools	188	0	7	80	101	1,438	403	1,014	21	4
Northwest Florida Beaches International Airport	0	0	0	0	0	4	0	4	0	0
Palm Beach County School District	110	0	2	16	92	932	51	880	1	6
Port Everglades	8	0	2	0	6	55	1	53	1	0
Sarasota-Manatee Airport Authority	1	0	0	1	0	9	0	7	2	0
St. Petersburg-Clearwater International Airport	0	0	0	0	0	11	0	7	4	0
Tampa International Airport	2	0	0	0	2	170	2	154	14	0
Volusia County Beach Management	11	0	2	1	8	190	2	186	2	0
Georgia										
State Agencies										
Atlanta State Farmers Market	0	0	0	0	0	42	1	39	2	0
Central State Hospital	0	0	0	0	0	3	1	2	0	0
Georgia Department of Public Safety	0	0	0	0	0	79	1	78	0	0
Georgia Department of Transportation, Office of Investigations	0	0	0	0	0	0	0	0	0	0
Georgia Forestry Commission	0	0	0	0	0	0	0	0	0	145
Georgia Public Safety Training Center	0	0	0	0	0	0	0	0	0	0
Georgia World Congress	16	0	0	13	3	246	5	239	2	1
Ports Authority, Savannah	1	0	0	0	1	10	0	9	1	0
State Board of Workers Compensation, Fraud Investigation Division	0	0	0	0	0	0	0	0	0	0
Other Agencies										
Atlanta Public Schools	86	1	2	25	58	372	53	268	51	2
Augusta Board of Education	11	0	0	2	9	8	1	6	1	0
Chatham County Board of Education	11	0	1	4	6	190	17	172	1	0
Cherokee County Board of Education	22	0	0	0	22	137	2	135	0	0
Cherokee County Marshal	0	0	0	0	0	0	0	0	0	0
Cobb County Board of Education	104	0	5	11	88	450	18	432	0	2
Decatur County Schools	2	0	0	0	2	0	0	0	0	0
Dougherty County Board of Education	4	0	0	2	2	34	3	30	1	0
Fayette County Marshal	0	0	0	0	0	0	0	0	0	0
Fulton County Marshal	1	0	0	0	1	2	1	1	0	0
Fulton County School System	11	0	2	2	7	121	15	90	16	3
Glynn County School System	6	0	0	0	6	74	7	67	0	0
Gwinnett County Public Schools	11	0	2	3	6	262	7	253	2	6
Habersham County Public Schools	5	0	0	0	5	9	1	8	0	0
Hartsfield-Jackson Atlanta International Airport	7	0	0	2	5	374	3	323	48	0
Metropolitan Atlanta Rapid Transit Authority	123	0	0	54	69	379	4	295	80	3
Muscogee City Marshal	0	0	0	0	0	0	0	0	0	0
Richmond County Marshal	0	0	0	0	0	0	0	0	0	0
Savannah Fire and Emergency Services, Arson Unit	0	0	0	0	0	0	0	0	0	23
Stone Mountain Park	0	0	0	0	0	40	0	40	0	0
Washington County Board of Education	0	0	0	0	0	0	0	0	0	0
Idaho										
State Agency										
Idaho State Police	20	4	4	1	11	15	1	5	9	1
Tribal Agencies										
Coeur d'Alene Tribal	35	1	0	1	33	44	21	22	1	2
Fort Hall Tribal	49	2	18	3	26	31	2	26	3	11
Nez Perce Tribal	23	1	2	1	19	116	26	87	3	2
Illinois										

Table 11. Offenses Known to Law Enforcement, by Selected State, Tribal, and Other Agencies, 2012— continued

(Number)

State/Other Agency Unit/Office	Violent crime	Murder and nonnegligent manslaughter	Forcible rape	Robbery	Aggravated assault	Property crime	Burglary	Larceny-theft	Motor vehicle theft	Arson[1]
State Agencies										
Illinois Department of Natural Resources	6	0	0	0	6	45	11	34	0	2
Secretary of State Police	2	0	0	0	2	24	0	23	1	0
State Fire Marshal	0	0	0	0	0	0	0	0	0	1,077
Other Agencies										
Belt Railway	0	0	0	0	0	5	1	4	0	0
Canton Park District	0	0	0	0	0	0	0	0	0	0
Capitol Airport Authority	0	0	0	0	0	0	0	0	0	0
Chicago Fire Department, Arson Investigations	0	0	0	0	0	0	0	0	0	586
Cook County Forest Preserve	9	0	2	6	1	105	12	90	3	1
Decatur Park District	4	0	0	3	1	28	14	13	1	2
Du Page County Forest Preserve	0	0	0	0	0	34	0	34	0	0
Fon du Lac Park District	0	0	0	0	0	11	2	9	0	0
Fox Valley Park District	11	0	0	5	6	81	0	81	0	0
Indiana Harbor Belt Railroad	0	0	0	0	0	14	6	8	0	0
Kane County Forest Preserve	1	0	0	0	1	8	0	8	0	0
Lake County Forest Preserve	0	0	0	0	0	13	0	13	0	0
McHenry County Conservation District	0	0	0	0	0	0	0	0	0	0
Naperville Park District	0	0	0	0	0	36	0	36	0	5
Norfolk Southern Railway:										
Macon County	0	0	0	0	0	9	0	9	0	0
Madison County	0	0	0	0	0	11	2	9	0	0
Rockford Metro Centre	0	0	0	0	0	2	0	2	0	0
Rockford Park District	61	0	0	14	47	91	46	40	5	4
Terminal Railroad Association	0	0	0	0	0	10	2	8	0	0
Union Pacific Railroad, St Clair County	1	0	0	0	1	29	17	12	0	0
Indiana										
State Agencies										
Indiana State Excise Police	5	0	0	0	5	37	0	37	0	0
Northern Indiana Commuter Transportation District	1	0	0	1	0	54	1	47	6	0
State Police										
Clinton County	0	0	0	0	0	7	3	3	1	0
De Kalb County	2	1	1	0	0	5	2	3	0	0
Delaware County	3	0	0	0	3	20	6	12	2	0
Elkhart County	0	0	0	0	0	14	0	12	2	0
Fayette County	1	0	0	0	1	8	1	7	0	
Fountain County	0	0	0	0	0	6	0	6	0	0
Franklin County	2	0	1	0	1	9	4	5	0	0
Fulton County	3	0	0	0	3	2	1	1	0	0
Hendricks County	3	0	1	0	2	7	1	6	0	
Henry County	4	2	0	0	2	2	0	2	0	
Huntington County	3	0	1	1	1	12	1	11	0	
Jefferson County	3	0	0	0	3	19	1	18	0	0
Kosciusko County	4	0	0	0	4	5	1	3	1	0
Lake County	15	2	1	2	10	91	1	39	51	0
La Porte County	6	0	0	1	5	24	3	17	4	0
Madison County	9	0	1	0	8	21	5	15	1	0
Marion County	25	1	5	0	19	144	2	105	37	0
Marshall County	5	0	0	1	4	16	3	12	1	
Newton County	0	0	0	0	0	2	0	2	0	0
Noble County	1	0	0	0	1	22	4	18	0	0
Porter County	8	0	0	0	8	35	1	22	12	0
Scott County	7	1	2	0	4	21	4	16	1	0
Starke County	0	0	0	0	0	2	0	2	0	
Steuben County	3	1	0	2	0	15	0	14	1	0
St. Joseph County	2	0	1	0	1	35	4	29	2	0
Switzerland County	3	0	1	0	2	6	2	4	0	0
Tippecanoe County	10	0	5	0	5	26	0	24	2	0
Warren County	4	0	0	0	4	1	0	1	0	0
Wayne County	0	0	0	0	0	6	0	6	0	

Table 11. Offenses Known to Law Enforcement, by Selected State, Tribal, and Other Agencies, 2012— continued

(Number)

State/Other Agency Unit/Office	Violent crime	Murder and nonnegligent manslaughter	Forcible rape	Robbery	Aggravated assault	Property crime	Burglary	Larceny-theft	Motor vehicle theft	Arson[1]
Other Agencies										
Indianapolis International Airport	2	0	0	0	2	66	1	59	6	0
St. Joseph County Airport Authority	0	0	0	0	0	14	0	6	8	0
Kansas										
State Agencies										
Kansas Alcoholic Beverage Control	1	0	0	0	1	0	0	0	0	0
Kansas Department of Wildlife and Parks	5	0	0	0	5	30	3	27	0	0
Kansas Highway Patrol	28	0	1	0	27	50	5	34	11	0
Tribal Agencies										
Kickapoo Tribal	0	0	0	0	0	22	7	13	2	0
Potawatomi Tribal	5	0	1	1	3	39	5	31	3	0
Sac and Fox Tribal	0	0	0	0	0	14	1	13	0	0
Other Agencies										
Shawnee Mission Public Schools	0	0	0	0	0	11	0	11	0	0
Unified School District										
Auburn-Washburn	0	0	0	0	0	1	0	1	0	0
Goddard	1	0	0	0	1	24	0	24	0	0
Shawnee Heights	0	0	0	0	0	1	0	1	0	0
Kentucky										
State Agencies										
Fish and Wildlife Enforcement	0	0	0	0	0	1	0	1	0	0
Kentucky Fairgrounds Security	0	0	0	0	0	4	0	3	1	0
Kentucky Horse Park	0	0	0	0	0	59	2	57	0	0
Motor Vehicle Enforcement	2	0	0	0	2	13	0	11	2	0
Park Security	0	0	0	0	0	17	5	12	0	0
State Police										
Ashland	39	0	16	1	22	344	152	165	27	9
Bowling Green	49	5	24	2	18	213	100	88	25	7
Campbellsburg	48	2	24	0	22	266	168	82	16	2
Cannabis Suppression Section	0	0	0	0	0	0	0	0	0	0
Columbia	81	8	45	4	24	159	87	59	13	17
Drug Enforcement Area[2]	0	0	0	0	0	7	0	7	0	1
Dry Ridge	35	0	11	4	20	388	175	195	18	25
Electronic Crimes	0	0	0	0	0	1	0	1	0	0
Elizabethtown	58	3	29	7	19	291	125	131	35	7
Frankfort	39	2	25	0	12	190	70	95	25	7
Harlan	61	4	15	15	27	428	198	205	25	4
Hazard	83	7	16	18	42	462	221	193	48	9
Henderson	25	2	6	3	14	119	50	60	9	2
London	62	6	28	6	22	336	150	154	32	8
Madisonville	26	6	12	2	6	162	80	62	20	5
Mayfield	63	0	27	2	34	282	87	164	31	6
Morehead	65	7	30	5	23	376	194	135	47	3
Pikeville	129	3	25	36	65	941	456	375	110	10
Richmond	60	3	26	9	22	479	239	203	37	18
Special Investigations	0	0	0	0	0	3	0	3	0	0
West Drug Enforcement Branch	0	0	0	0	0	1	0	1	0	0
Unlawful Narcotics Investigation, Treatment and Education	0	0	0	0	0	1	0	1	0	0
Other Agencies										
Barren County Drug Task Force	0	0	0	0	0	0	0	0	0	0
Buffalo Trace-Gateway Narcotics Task Force	0	0	0	0	0	2	0	2	0	0
Cincinnati-Northern Kentucky International Airport	0	0	0	0	0	57	0	54	3	0
Fayette County Schools	2	0	0	0	2	178	5	173	0	1
FIVCO Area Drug Task Force	0	0	0	0	0	1	0	1	0	0
Graves County Schools	0	0	0	0	0	1	0	1	0	0
Greater Hardin County Narcotics Task Force	0	0	0	0	0	1	0	1	0	0
Jefferson County Board of Education	13	0	0	1	12	78	37	41	0	1
Lee County Constable, District[3]	0	0	0	0	0	27	7	18	2	0
Lexington Bluegrass Airport	0	0	0	0	0	11	1	9	1	0

Table 11. Offenses Known to Law Enforcement, by Selected State, Tribal, and Other Agencies, 2012— continued

(Number)

State/Other Agency Unit/Office	Violent crime	Murder and nonnegligent manslaughter	Forcible rape	Robbery	Aggravated assault	Property crime	Burglary	Larceny-theft	Motor vehicle theft	Arson[1]
Louisville Regional Airport Authority	0	0	0	0	0	41	1	21	19	0
McCracken County Public Schools	1	0	0	0	1	14	0	14	0	0
Montgomery County School District	0	0	0	0	0	6	0	6	0	0
Northern Kentucky Narcotics Enforcement Unit	0	0	0	0	0	2	0	2	0	0
Ohio County School System	1	0	0	0	1	2	0	2	0	0
Pennyrile Narcotics Task Force	0	0	0	0	0	6	0	6	0	0
South Central Kentucky Drug Task Force	1	0	0	1	0	3	0	3	0	0
Louisiana										
State Agency										
Tensas Basin Levee District	0	0	0	0	0	0	0	0	0	0
Tribal Agencies										
Chitimacha Tribal	1	0	1	0	0	64	4	60	0	0
Coushatta Tribal	7	0	0	1	6	163	6	156	1	0
Maine										
State Agencies										
Drug Enforcement Agency										
Androscoggin County	0	0	0	0	0	0	0	0	0	0
Aroostook County	0	0	0	0	0	0	0	0	0	0
Cumberland County	0	0	0	0	0	0	0	0	0	0
Franklin County	0	0	0	0	0	0	0	0	0	0
Hancock County	0	0	0	0	0	0	0	0	0	0
Kennebec County	0	0	0	0	0	0	0	0	0	0
Knox County	0	0	0	0	0	0	0	0	0	0
Lincoln County	0	0	0	0	0	0	0	0	0	0
Oxford County	0	0	0	0	0	0	0	0	0	0
Penobscot County	0	0	0	0	0	0	0	0	0	0
Piscataquis County	0	0	0	0	0	0	0	0	0	0
Sagadahoc County	0	0	0	0	0	0	0	0	0	0
Somerset County	0	0	0	0	0	0	0	0	0	0
Waldo County	0	0	0	0	0	0	0	0	0	0
Washington County	0	0	0	0	0	0	0	0	0	0
York County	1	0	0	1	0	0	0	0	0	0
State Police Computer Crimes Task Force										
Androscoggin County	0	0	0	0	0	0	0	0	0	0
Aroostook County	0	0	0	0	0	0	0	0	0	0
Cumberland County	0	0	0	0	0	0	0	0	0	0
Franklin County	0	0	0	0	0	0	0	0	0	0
Hancock County	0	0	0	0	0	0	0	0	0	0
Kennebec County	1	0	1	0	0	0	0	0	0	0
Knox County	0	0	0	0	0	0	0	0	0	0
Lincoln County	0	0	0	0	0	0	0	0	0	0
Oxford County	0	0	0	0	0	0	0	0	0	0
Penobscot County	0	0	0	0	0	0	0	0	0	0
Piscataquis County	0	0	0	0	0	0	0	0	0	0
Sagadahoc County	0	0	0	0	0	0	0	0	0	0
Somerset County	0	0	0	0	0	0	0	0	0	0
Waldo County	0	0	0	0	0	0	0	0	0	0
Washington County	0	0	0	0	0	0	0	0	0	0
York County	0	0	0	0	0	0	0	0	0	0
State Police										
Androscoggin County	4	0	0	1	3	140	51	77	12	4
Aroostook County	16	1	4	2	9	295	105	174	16	5
Cumberland County	1	0	0	0	1	71	27	36	8	2
Franklin County	5	0	1	0	4	74	18	52	4	1
Hancock County	15	3	2	0	10	211	77	118	16	1
Kennebec County	23	0	0	3	20	432	135	284	13	7
Knox County	2	1	1	0	0	27	8	18	1	0
Lincoln County	0	0	0	0	0	5	2	2	1	1
Oxford County	9	0	4	1	4	192	87	96	9	9
Penobscot County	12	1	1	3	7	430	140	269	21	7

Table 11. Offenses Known to Law Enforcement, by Selected State, Tribal, and Other Agencies, 2012— continued

(Number)

State/Other Agency Unit/Office	Violent crime	Murder and nonnegligent manslaughter	Forcible rape	Robbery	Aggravated assault	Property crime	Burglary	Larceny-theft	Motor vehicle theft	Arson[1]
Piscataquis County	1	0	0	0	1	12	6	6	0	0
Sagadahoc County	1	0	0	0	1	5	2	3	0	3
Somerset County	6	0	0	1	5	230	53	171	6	10
Waldo County	7	1	2	0	4	164	49	110	5	5
Washington County	5	0	0	0	5	171	87	77	7	2
York County	13	1	0	0	12	205	94	104	7	6
Tribal Agencies										
Passamaquoddy Pleasant Point Tribal	4	0	0	0	4	6	5	0	1	3
Penobscot Nation	1	0	0	0	1	40	6	34	0	2
Maryland										
State Agencies										
Comptroller of the Treasury, Field Enforcement Division	0	0	0	0	0	0	0	0	0	0
Department of Public Safety and Correctional Services, Internal Investigations Unit	176	0	0	0	176	2	0	2	0	0
General Services										
Annapolis, Anne Arundel County	0	0	0	0	0	20	0	20	0	0
Baltimore City	0	0	0	0	0	35	0	34	1	0
Maryland State Police Statewide	2	0	0	0	2	0	0	0	0	0
Natural Resources Police	1	0	0	0	1	244	27	217	0	39
Springfield Hospital	0	0	0	0	0	12	1	11	0	0
State Fire Marshal	0	0	0	0	0	0	0	0	0	0
State Police										
Allegany County	39	4	4	4	27	505	80	399	26	5
Anne Arundel County	6	1	0	0	5	45	1	37	7	0
Baltimore City	1	0	0	0	1	2	0	2	0	0
Baltimore County	26	0	0	0	26	39	5	28	6	0
Calvert County	15	0	1	2	12	208	49	154	5	11
Caroline County	17	1	1	3	12	152	64	76	12	9
Carroll County	71	3	0	11	57	564	139	391	34	5
Cecil County	169	0	4	35	130	849	269	547	33	31
Charles County	2	0	0	0	2	27	0	25	2	28
Dorchester County	6	0	2	0	4	74	39	26	9	4
Frederick County	45	0	2	10	33	474	121	335	18	7
Garrett County	36	0	1	3	32	188	89	90	9	3
Harford County	63	0	0	10	53	383	48	314	21	25
Howard County	6	1	0	1	4	9	0	8	1	0
Kent County	18	0	3	2	13	50	17	30	3	1
Montgomery County	0	0	0	0	0	12	0	9	3	0
Prince George's County	17	0	0	0	17	44	0	13	31	2
Queen Anne's County	34	0	0	4	30	147	27	108	12	2
Somerset County	22	0	4	3	15	163	57	101	5	4
St. Mary's County	47	0	1	3	43	294	59	225	10	12
Talbot County	5	0	0	1	4	104	45	53	6	5
Washington County	31	0	2	7	22	194	59	122	13	16
Wicomico County	74	1	2	9	62	270	114	142	14	18
Worcester County	18	0	0	3	15	205	63	132	10	2
Transit Administration	0	0	0	0	0	0	0	0	0	0
Transportation Authority	6	0	0	2	4	241	5	213	23	0
Other Agencies										
Maryland-National Capital Park Police										
Montgomery County	18	0	3	7	8	143	8	133	2	3
Prince George's County	68	1	5	41	21	216	21	186	9	0
Massachusetts										
State Agencies										
Division of Law Enforcement, Environmental Police	7	0	0	0	7	14	2	9	3	1
State Police										
Barnstable County	8	0	0	0	8	1	0	1	0	
Dukes County	1	0	0	0	1	0	0	0	0	
Hampshire County	3	0	0	1	2	3	2	1	0	0
Plymouth County	6	0	0	0	6	1	1	0	0	

Table 11. Offenses Known to Law Enforcement, by Selected State, Tribal, and Other Agencies, 2012— continued

(Number)

State/Other Agency Unit/Office	Violent crime	Murder and nonnegligent manslaughter	Forcible rape	Robbery	Aggravated assault	Property crime	Burglary	Larceny-theft	Motor vehicle theft	Arson[1]
Tribal Agency										
Wampanoag Tribe of Gay Head	0	0	0	0	0	3	1	1	1	0
Michigan										
State Agencies										
State Police										
Alcona County	0	0	0	0	0	0	0	0	0	0
Alger County	11	1	1	1	8	56	26	28	2	0
Allegan County	57	0	18	1	38	272	82	183	7	2
Alpena County	12	0	3	1	8	112	35	75	2	1
Antrim County	9	0	4	0	5	21	6	12	3	2
Arenac County	4	0	4	0	0	12	2	10	0	1
Baraga County	12	0	0	0	12	29	14	14	1	0
Barry County	28	0	10	0	18	120	39	74	7	3
Bay County	42	0	16	5	21	206	63	133	10	1
Benzie County	1	0	0	0	1	11	3	8	0	0
Berrien County	30	0	11	1	18	245	55	173	17	0
Branch County	31	0	17	1	13	95	38	54	3	4
Calhoun County	19	0	12	0	7	109	39	61	9	5
Cass County	12	0	6	1	5	42	13	28	1	1
Charlevoix County	12	0	12	0	0	17	5	12	0	0
Cheboygan County	4	0	3	0	1	40	16	23	1	0
Chippewa County	32	1	6	1	24	81	27	48	6	1
Clare County	11	0	6	0	5	49	21	25	3	0
Clinton County	4	0	4	0	0	12	4	8	0	0
Crawford County	2	0	2	0	0	12	6	6	0	0
Delta County	12	0	7	0	5	51	23	27	1	1
Dickinson County	8	0	6	0	2	27	8	17	2	0
Eaton County	13	0	6	1	6	47	15	31	1	1
Emmet County	16	0	11	0	5	139	24	113	2	0
Genesee County	38	0	13	3	22	162	75	79	8	2
Gladwin County	12	0	8	0	4	45	19	24	2	2
Gogebic County	6	0	3	0	3	20	4	15	1	0
Grand Traverse County	18	0	16	0	2	50	8	40	2	0
Gratiot County	20	0	6	0	14	69	22	46	1	1
Hillsdale County	39	0	10	1	28	116	52	57	7	5
Houghton County	10	0	7	0	3	72	28	41	3	2
Huron County	5	0	2	0	3	27	11	15	1	0
Ingham County	18	0	9	0	9	69	37	25	7	1
Ionia County	24	0	9	0	15	234	63	158	13	1
Iosco County	27	0	11	0	16	170	65	95	10	13
Iron County	5	0	3	0	2	10	5	3	2	0
Isabella County	43	0	20	0	23	160	51	104	5	0
Jackson County	85	0	25	4	56	186	59	110	17	6
Kalamazoo County	11	0	7	0	4	58	14	26	18	1
Kalkaska County	20	0	16	0	4	58	28	28	2	0
Kent County	14	0	9	0	5	20	0	20	0	0
Lake County	16	0	10	0	6	37	16	21	0	0
Lapeer County	23	0	8	1	14	85	40	39	6	2
Lenawee County	35	3	3	1	28	99	29	63	7	4
Livingston County	37	0	10	1	26	306	74	208	24	3
Luce County	13	0	0	1	12	46	20	24	2	0
Mackinac County	15	0	5	0	10	49	12	35	2	0
Macomb County	10	0	7	0	3	64	21	34	9	1
Manistee County	20	0	5	1	14	86	52	29	5	0
Marquette County	51	0	11	1	39	254	56	187	11	3
Mason County	5	0	2	0	3	79	12	64	3	1
Mecosta County	15	0	6	0	9	65	13	49	3	0
Menominee County	3	0	0	0	3	29	15	13	1	0
Midland County	7	0	6	0	1	35	17	14	4	0
Monroe County	58	0	13	7	38	236	68	151	17	2
Montcalm County	31	0	18	0	13	280	114	154	12	4
Montmorency County	4	0	1	0	3	19	13	6	0	0
Muskegon County	61	0	25	0	36	277	83	183	11	2

Table 11. Offenses Known to Law Enforcement, by Selected State, Tribal, and Other Agencies, 2012— continued

(Number)

State/Other Agency Unit/Office	Violent crime	Murder and nonnegligent manslaughter	Forcible rape	Robbery	Aggravated assault	Property crime	Burglary	Larceny-theft	Motor vehicle theft	Arson[1]
Newaygo County	52	0	26	2	24	254	80	156	18	2
Oakland County	36	2	6	3	25	211	85	110	16	1
Oceana County	9	0	5	0	4	84	24	56	4	0
Ogemaw County	25	0	12	2	11	111	44	64	3	4
Ontonagon County	8	0	4	0	4	45	14	28	3	0
Osceola County	23	0	6	2	15	89	34	51	4	1
Oscoda County	0	0	0	0	0	5	3	2	0	0
Otsego County	22	0	11	0	11	112	32	71	9	1
Ottawa County	4	0	1	0	3	3	0	2	1	1
Presque Isle County	5	0	1	0	4	5	3	2	0	0
Roscommon County	10	0	4	0	6	123	42	77	4	1
Saginaw County	57	1	16	2	38	149	50	88	11	13
Sanilac County	25	1	17	0	7	71	40	27	4	0
Schoolcraft County	16	0	6	0	10	51	30	21	0	0
Shiawassee County	14	0	11	0	3	129	41	81	7	1
St. Clair County	20	0	5	0	15	157	57	94	6	0
St. Joseph County	33	0	9	1	23	124	42	70	12	4
Tuscola County	31	0	7	1	23	112	43	58	11	2
Van Buren County	43	0	9	2	32	262	104	140	18	4
Washtenaw County	46	0	10	2	34	152	64	72	16	0
Wayne County	63	1	10	8	44	92	3	70	19	0
Wexford County	13	0	5	2	6	113	29	83	1	1
Tribal Agencies										
Grand Traverse Tribal	2	0	0	1	1	15	1	11	3	0
Little Traverse Bay Bands of Odawa Indians	11	0	0	0	11	43	0	43	0	0
Nottawaseppi Huron Band of Potawatomi	3	0	0	0	3	47	8	38	1	0
Saulte Ste. Marie Tribal	16	0	8	0	8	75	17	57	1	0
Other Agencies										
Genesee County Parks and Recreation	2	0	1	0	1	26	5	21	0	0
Gerald R. Ford International Airport	0	0	0	0	0	19	0	13	6	0
Huron-Clinton Metropolitan Authority										
Kensington Metropark	0	0	0	0	0	12	0	12	0	1
Lower Huron Metropark	0	0	0	0	0	15	0	14	1	0
Stony Creek Metropark	5	0	0	1	4	30	0	29	1	0
Wayne County Airport	6	0	0	1	5	175	2	107	66	0
Minnesota										
State Agencies[4]										
Capitol Security, St. Paul		0		0	0	12	1	11	0	0
Minnesota State Patrol		0		0	0	0	0	0	0	0
State Patrol										
Brainerd		0		0	1	0	0	0	0	0
Detroit Lakes		0		0	0	0	0	0	0	0
Duluth		0		0	0	0	0	0	0	0
Golden Valley		0		0	0	0	0	0	0	0
Mankato		0		0	0	0	0	0	0	0
Marshall		0		0	0	0	0	0	0	0
Oakdale		0		0	0	0	0	0	0	0
Rochester		0		0	0	0	0	0	0	0
St. Cloud		0		0	0	0	0	0	0	0
Thief River Falls		0		0	0	0	0	0	0	0
Virginia		0		0	0	0	0	0	0	0
Tribal Agencies										
Leech Lake Band of Ojibwe	64	1	6	3	54	316	55	231	30	4
Nett Lake Tribal	1	0	0	0	1	3	1	0	2	2
White Earth Tribal	30	0	2	0	28	358	90	238	30	90
Other Agencies[4]										
Minneapolis-St. Paul International Airport		0		0	1	233	0	218	15	0
Three Rivers Park District		0		1	3	83	1	82	0	2
Mississippi										

Table 11. Offenses Known to Law Enforcement, by Selected State, Tribal, and Other Agencies, 2012— continued

(Number)

State/Other Agency Unit/Office	Violent crime	Murder and nonnegligent manslaughter	Forcible rape	Robbery	Aggravated assault	Property crime	Burglary	Larceny-theft	Motor vehicle theft	Arson[1]
State Agency										
State Capitol Police	0	0	0	0	0	21	6	14	1	0
Tribal Agency										
Choctaw Tribal	111	1	12	8	90	295	150	40	105	10
Missouri										
State Agencies										
Capitol Police	0	0	0	0	0	20	0	20	0	0
Department of Conservation	0	0	0	0	0	1	0	1	0	0
Department of Social Services, State Technical Assistance	1	0	0	0	1	0	0	0	0	0
Division of Alcohol and Tobacco Control	0	0	0	0	0	0	0	0	0	0
Gaming Commission, Enforcement Division	9	0	0	1	8	203	0	201	2	0
State Fire Marshal	0	0	0	0	0	0	0	0	0	261
State Highway Patrol										
Jefferson City	4	0	0	0	4	83	2	75	6	3
Kirkwood	3	1	0	0	2	7	0	6	1	0
Lee's Summit	5	1	0	0	4	25	0	10	15	2
Macon	7	3	1	0	3	13	0	12	1	0
Poplar Bluff	3	0	0	0	3	11	0	9	2	0
Rolla	1	0	0	0	1	3	0	0	3	0
Springfield	2	1	0	0	1	61	1	51	9	0
St. Joseph	16	0	0	0	16	29	0	15	14	0
Willow Springs	2	0	0	0	2	2	0	1	1	0
State Park Rangers	1	0	0	0	1	88	6	80	2	2
Other Agencies										
Bootheel Drug Task Force	0	0	0	0	0	0	0	0	0	0
Clay County Drug Task Force	0	0	0	0	0	0	0	0	0	0
Clay County Park Authority	1	0	0	0	1	8	0	8	0	0
Jackson County Drug Task Force	0	0	0	0	0	0	0	0	0	0
Jackson County Park Rangers	0	0	0	0	0	13	0	13	0	1
Lambert-St. Louis International Airport	0	0	0	0	0	161	3	158	0	0
Platte County Multi-Jurisdictional Enforcement Group	0	0	0	0	0	0	0	0	0	0
Springfield-Branson Airport	0	0	0	0	0	7	0	7	0	0
St. Charles County Park Rangers	0	0	0	0	0	0	0	0	0	1
St. Peters Ranger Division	0	0	0	0	0	48	0	48	0	0
Western Missouri Cyber Crimes Task Force	0	0	0	0	0	0	0	0	0	0
Montana										
Tribal Agencies										
Blackfeet Agency	20	0	6	1	13	90	35	7	48	57
Crow Agency	38	1	6	0	31	154	42	89	23	13
Flathead Tribal	68	2	9	2	55	105	65	7	33	3
Fort Belknap Tribal	17	1	2	0	14	30	4	24	2	1
Fort Peck Assiniboine and Sioux Tribes	42	1	5	0	36	190	53	109	28	19
Northern Cheyenne Agency	20	2	9	0	9	9	9	0	0	0
Rocky Boys Tribal	18	0	13	0	5	19	15	3	1	1
Nebraska										
State Agencies										
Nebraska State Patrol	4	0	0	0	4	13	0	13	0	0
State Patrol										
Adams County	0	0	0	0	0	1	0	1	0	0
Antelope County	0	0	0	0	0	0	0	0	0	0
Arthur County	0	0	0	0	0	0	0	0	0	0
Banner County	0	0	0	0	0	1	0	1	0	0
Blaine County	0	0	0	0	0	0	0	0	0	0
Boone County	0	0	0	0	0	0	0	0	0	0
Box Butte County	0	0	0	0	0	0	0	0	0	0
Boyd County	0	0	0	0	0	0	0	0	0	0

Table 11. Offenses Known to Law Enforcement, by Selected State, Tribal, and Other Agencies, 2012— continued

(Number)

State/Other Agency Unit/Office	Violent crime	Murder and nonnegligent manslaughter	Forcible rape	Robbery	Aggravated assault	Property crime	Burglary	Larceny-theft	Motor vehicle theft	Arson[1]
Brown County	0	0	0	0	0	0	0	0	0	0
Buffalo County	2	0	0	0	2	0	0	0	0	0
Burt County	0	0	0	0	0	0	0	0	0	0
Butler County	0	0	0	0	0	1	0	0	1	0
Cass County	0	0	0	0	0	3	0	2	1	0
Cedar County	0	0	0	0	0	0	0	0	0	0
Chase County	0	0	0	0	0	0	0	0	0	0
Cherry County	0	0	0	0	0	0	0	0	0	0
Cheyenne County	0	0	0	0	0	2	0	2	0	0
Clay County	0	0	0	0	0	0	0	0	0	0
Colfax County	0	0	0	0	0	0	0	0	0	0
Cuming County	0	0	0	0	0	1	1	0	0	0
Custer County	0	0	0	0	0	0	0	0	0	0
Dakota County	0	0	0	0	0	0	0	0	0	0
Dawes County	0	0	0	0	0	0	0	0	0	0
Dawson County	0	0	0	0	0	1	0	0	1	0
Deuel County	0	0	0	0	0	0	0	0	0	0
Dixon County	0	0	0	0	0	0	0	0	0	0
Dodge County	0	0	0	0	0	1	0	1	0	0
Douglas County	0	0	0	0	0	2	0	2	0	0
Dundy County	0	0	0	0	0	0	0	0	0	0
Fillmore County	0	0	0	0	0	1	0	1	0	0
Franklin County	1	1	0	0	0	2	2	0	0	0
Frontier County	0	0	0	0	0	0	0	0	0	0
Furnas County	0	0	0	0	0	3	1	2	0	0
Gage County	0	0	0	0	0	1	0	1	0	0
Garden County	0	0	0	0	0	1	0	1	0	0
Garfield County	0	0	0	0	0	0	0	0	0	0
Gosper County	0	0	0	0	0	0	0	0	0	0
Grant County	0	0	0	0	0	0	0	0	0	0
Greeley County	0	0	0	0	0	0	0	0	0	0
Hall County	0	0	0	0	0	6	0	6	0	0
Hamilton County	1	0	0	0	1	1	0	1	0	0
Harlan County	0	0	0	0	0	0	0	0	0	0
Hayes County	0	0	0	0	0	0	0	0	0	0
Hitchcock County	0	0	0	0	0	0	0	0	0	0
Holt County	0	0	0	0	0	0	0	0	0	0
Hooker County	0	0	0	0	0	0	0	0	0	0
Howard County	0	0	0	0	0	0	0	0	0	0
Jefferson County	0	0	0	0	0	0	0	0	0	0
Johnson County	0	0	0	0	0	0	0	0	0	0
Kearney County	0	0	0	0	0	0	0	0	0	0
Keith County	0	0	0	0	0	2	0	1	1	0
Keya Paha County	0	0	0	0	0	0	0	0	0	0
Kimball County	0	0	0	0	0	0	0	0	0	0
Knox County	0	0	0	0	0	1	0	1	0	0
Lancaster County	1	0	0	0	1	5	0	2	3	0
Lincoln County	0	0	0	0	0	0	0	0	0	0
Logan County	0	0	0	0	0	0	0	0	0	0
Loup County	0	0	0	0	0	0	0	0	0	0
Madison County	0	0	0	0	0	3	0	1	2	0
McPherson County	0	0	0	0	0	0	0	0	0	0
Merrick County	0	0	0	0	0	0	0	0	0	0
Morrill County	0	0	0	0	0	0	0	0	0	0
Nance County	0	0	0	0	0	0	0	0	0	0
Nemaha County	0	0	0	0	0	0	0	0	0	0
Nuckolls County	0	0	0	0	0	0	0	0	0	0
Otoe County	0	0	0	0	0	0	0	0	0	0
Pawnee County	0	0	0	0	0	0	0	0	0	0
Perkins County	0	0	0	0	0	0	0	0	0	0
Phelps County	0	0	0	0	0	0	0	0	0	0
Pierce County	0	0	0	0	0	2	1	1	0	0
Platte County	0	0	0	0	0	0	0	0	0	0
Polk County	0	0	0	0	0	0	0	0	0	0

Table 11. Offenses Known to Law Enforcement, by Selected State, Tribal, and Other Agencies, 2012— continued

(Number)

State/Other Agency Unit/Office	Violent crime	Murder and nonnegligent manslaughter	Forcible rape	Robbery	Aggravated assault	Property crime	Burglary	Larceny-theft	Motor vehicle theft	Arson[1]
Red Willow County	0	0	0	0	0	0	0	0	0	0
Richardson County	0	0	0	0	0	0	0	0	0	0
Rock County	0	0	0	0	0	2	0	2	0	0
Saline County	0	0	0	0	0	1	0	1	0	0
Sarpy County	1	0	0	0	1	0	0	0	0	0
Saunders County	0	0	0	0	0	0	0	0	0	0
Scotts Bluff County	0	0	0	0	0	0	0	0	0	0
Seward County	0	0	0	0	0	1	0	1	0	0
Sheridan County	0	0	0	0	0	0	0	0	0	0
Sherman County	0	0	0	0	0	1	1	0	0	0
Sioux County	0	0	0	0	0	1	1	0	0	0
Stanton County	0	0	0	0	0	0	0	0	0	0
Thayer County	0	0	0	0	0	2	1	1	0	0
Thomas County	0	0	0	0	0	0	0	0	0	0
Thurston County	0	0	0	0	0	0	0	0	0	0
Valley County	0	0	0	0	0	0	0	0	0	0
Washington County	0	0	0	0	0	0	0	0	0	0
Wayne County	0	0	0	0	0	0	0	0	0	0
Webster County	0	0	0	0	0	0	0	0	0	0
Wheeler County	0	0	0	0	0	0	0	0	0	0
York County	0	0	0	0	0	0	0	0	0	0
Tribal Agencies										
Omaha Tribal	42	0	15	0	27	20	14	0	6	8
Santee Tribal	35	0	0	0	35	37	33	2	2	2
Winnebago Tribal	30	0	1	1	28	7	0	4	3	0
Nevada										
Tribal Agencies										
Duckwater Tribal	1	0	0	0	1	0	0	0	0	0
Eastern Nevada Agency	0	0	0	0	0	5	4	0	1	0
Ely Shoshone Tribal	1	0	0	0	1	4	4	0	0	1
Fallon Tribal	2	2	0	0	0	28	2	25	1	0
Las Vegas Paiute Tribal	4	0	0	0	4	63	1	60	2	0
Pyramid Lake Tribal	26	0	2	2	22	38	16	15	7	3
Reno-Sparks Indian Colony	17	0	1	1	15	26	19	6	1	0
South Fork Band Tribal	0	0	0	0	0	0	0	0	0	0
Walker River Tribal	11	2	0	0	9	18	15	3	0	1
Washoe Tribal	39	1	2	1	35	39	18	14	7	30
Western Nevada Agency	11	0	2	0	9	15	8	6	1	16
Western Shoshone Tribal	4	1	0	0	3	14	2	11	1	2
Yomba Shoshone Tribal	7	0	0	0	7	3	1	2	0	1
Other Agencies										
Clark County School District	116	0	5	26	85	1065	160	879	26	31
Washoe County School District	10	0	2	4	4	203	30	172	1	6
New Hampshire										
State Agency: Liquor Commission	0	0	0	0	0	13	0	13	0	0
New Jersey										
State Agencies										
New Jersey Transit Police	61	0	0	43	18	479	6	459	14	0
Palisades Interstate Parkway	2	0	0	0	2	3	0	3	0	0
Port Authority of New York and New Jersey	47	0	0	18	29	488	6	446	36	0
State Police										
Atlantic County	22	0	0	7	15	819	95	708	16	1
Bergen County	12	0	0	4	8	112	3	98	11	0
Burlington County	31	0	1	5	25	646	200	418	28	7
Cape May County	21	0	1	4	16	434	106	313	15	1
Cumberland County	71	2	7	15	47	1,022	349	638	35	6
Essex County	16	1	0	6	9	32	1	19	12	0
Gloucester County	1	0	0	0	1	28	2	11	15	0
Hunterdon County	12	2	0	0	10	225	69	144	12	2
Mercer County	7	0	0	4	3	115	6	105	4	0

Table 11. Offenses Known to Law Enforcement, by Selected State, Tribal, and Other Agencies, 2012— continued

(Number)

State/Other Agency Unit/Office	Violent crime	Murder and nonnegligent manslaughter	Forcible rape	Robbery	Aggravated assault	Property crime	Burglary	Larceny-theft	Motor vehicle theft	Arson[1]
Middlesex County	4	0	0	1	3	41	0	38	3	1
Monmouth County	8	0	1	1	6	239	92	141	6	0
Morris County	4	0	1	0	3	37	6	20	11	0
Ocean County	6	0	0	2	4	64	8	53	3	0
Salem County	26	0	2	5	19	440	190	237	13	4
Sussex County	29	3	3	6	17	491	115	357	19	3
Union County	7	0	0	3	4	17	0	2	15	0
Warren County	9	0	0	2	7	262	94	157	11	0
Other Agencies										
Park Police										
Camden County	1	0	0	0	1	10	2	7	1	0
Morris County	0	0	0	0	0	2	1	1	0	0
Prosecutor										
Atlantic County	0	0	0	0	0	0	0	0	0	0
Bergen County	0	0	0	0	0	0	0	0	0	0
Burlington County	0	0	0	0	0	0	0	0	0	0
Camden County	0	0	0	0	0	0	0	0	0	0
Cape May County	0	0	0	0	0	0	0	0	0	0
Cumberland County	0	0	0	0	0	0	0	0	0	0
Essex County	0	0	0	0	0	0	0	0	0	0
Gloucester County	0	0	0	0	0	0	0	0	0	0
Hudson County	0	0	0	0	0	0	0	0	0	0
Hunterdon County	0	0	0	0	0	0	0	0	0	0
Mercer County	0	0	0	0	0	0	0	0	0	0
Middlesex County	0	0	0	0	0	0	0	0	0	0
Monmouth County	1	1	0	0	0	0	0	0	0	0
Morris County	0	0	0	0	0	0	0	0	0	0
Ocean County	0	0	0	0	0	0	0	0	0	0
Passaic County	0	0	0	0	0	0	0	0	0	0
Salem County	0	0	0	0	0	0	0	0	0	0
Somerset County	0	0	0	0	0	0	0	0	0	0
Sussex County	0	0	0	0	0	0	0	0	0	0
Union County	0	0	0	0	0	0	0	0	0	0
Warren County	0	0	0	0	0	0	0	0	0	0
New Mexico										
State Agencies										
Motor Transportation Police	0	0	0	0	0	7	0	7	0	0
New Mexico State Police	75	5	13	15	42	1,025	764	166	95	5
Tribal Agencies										
Acoma Tribal	17	0	1	1	15	10	1	6	3	1
Isleta Tribal	75	0	0	0	75	141	25	98	18	0
Jemez Pueblo	0	0	0	0	0	20	13	7	0	1
Jicarilla Apache Tribal	3	0	2	0	1	1	0	0	1	0
Mescalero Tribal	36	1	7	1	27	26	12	13	1	65
Northern Pueblos Agency	32	3	7	2	20	21	12	8	1	2
Ohkay Owingeh Tribal	20	0	0	1	19	37	9	22	6	3
Ramah Navajo Tribal	4	0	0	0	4	1	0	1	0	0
Santa Ana Tribal	1	0	0	0	1	49	9	36	4	6
Santa Clara Pueblo	12	0	2	2	8	24	15	5	4	0
Southern Pueblos Agency	3	0	0	0	3	10	8	1	1	0
Taos Pueblo	5	0	0	0	5	12	10	2	0	0
Tesuque Pueblo	0	0	0	0	0	5	0	5	0	0
Zuni Tribal	34	0	7	1	26	6	2	4	0	0
New York										
State Agencies[2]										
State Police										
Albany County	13	0	6	0	7	134	8	119	7	0
Allegany County	13	1	3	0	9	342	124	205	13	
Broome County	51	0	20	5	26	601	131	437	33	
Cattaraugus County	21	0	5	3	13	306	72	227	7	1
Cayuga County	25	0	6	1	18	269	65	197	7	3
Chautauqua County	10	0	5	1	13	314	60	240	14	1

Table 11. Offenses Known to Law Enforcement, by Selected State, Tribal, and Other Agencies, 2012— continued

(Number)

State/Other Agency Unit/Office	Violent crime	Murder and nonnegligent manslaughter	Forcible rape	Robbery	Aggravated assault	Property crime	Burglary	Larceny-theft	Motor vehicle theft	Arson[1]
Chemung County	52	1	0	2	49	265	34	223	8	
Chenango County	19	0	6	1	12	171	51	108	12	
Clinton County	57	0	14	5	38	955	191	735	29	
Columbia County	28	0	7	6	15	285	87	195	3	
Cortland County	8	1	3	0	4	126	14	107	5	0
Delaware County	27	0	4	0	23	239	61	169	9	
Dutchess County	110	2	8	9	91	671	167	482	22	2
Erie County	32	0	5	1	26	434	40	383	11	0
Essex County	21	1	4	2	14	294	87	200	7	
Franklin County	28	1	9	0	18	388	106	264	18	
Fulton County	0	0	0	0	0	126	37	86	3	0
Genesee County	8	0	1	1	6	81	8	70	3	0
Greene County	53	0	7	3	43	402	147	239	16	
Hamilton County	0	0	0	0	0	47	16	28	3	0
Herkimer County	13	2	1	0	10	354	147	189	18	
Jefferson County	25	1	1	2	21	689	159	506	24	
Lewis County	4	0	0	0	4	112	40	69	3	1
Livingston County	10	0	4	0	6	50	11	38	1	0
Madison County	15	0	6	0	9	203	58	136	9	
Monroe County	6	0	3	1	2	86	4	76	6	0
Montgomery County	4	2	1	1	0	103	29	70	4	0
Nassau County	1	0	0	0	1	13	0	12	1	0
New York County	3	0	1	0	2	70	0	70	0	0
Niagara County	10	0	1	2	7	199	24	170	5	1
Oneida County	63	1	8	1	53	691	203	463	25	
Onondaga County	47	0	14	15	18	728	162	540	26	
Ontario County	15	0	10	0	5	242	43	192	7	0
Orange County	48	1	12	6	29	905	114	760	31	
Orleans County	11	0	2	0	9	57	13	43	1	0
Oswego County	62	0	10	3	49	844	282	519	43	
Otsego County	23	0	3	4	16	372	58	299	15	0
Putnam County	9	0	1	0	8	115	34	73	8	0
Rensselaer County	29	2	5	3	19	558	150	394	14	
Rockland County	8	1	1	1	5	16	1	11	4	0
Saratoga County	42	1	9	7	25	690	108	563	19	2
Schenectady County	11	0	1	1	9	142	24	114	4	0
Schoharie County	11	0	3	0	8	190	68	115	7	
Schuyler County	6	0	4	0	2	28	9	18	1	
Seneca County	26	0	4	0	22	131	23	105	3	0
Steuben County	56	0	19	3	34	533	154	343	36	
St. Lawrence County	36	0	4	2	30	567	170	378	19	
Suffolk County	9	0	0	2	7	51	5	42	4	0
Sullivan County	61	1	14	8	38	472	183	268	21	
Tioga County	7	0	0	1	6	114	31	79	4	0
Tompkins County	12	0	4	0	8	237	54	176	7	1
Ulster County	71	0	13	4	54	514	150	337	27	
Warren County	12	0	7	0	5	184	15	162	7	
Washington County	22	6	3	0	13	176	49	116	11	
Wayne County	34	0	11	4	19	514	169	325	20	
Westchester County	56	0	10	7	39	436	98	323	15	
Wyoming County	15	0	0	0	15	29	5	22	2	0
Yates County	3	0	2	0	1	13	2	10	1	0
Tribal Agencies										
Oneida Indian Nation	9	0	0	4	5	306	7	297	2	3
St. Regis Tribal	4	0	2	1	1	115	20	80	15	34
Other Agencies[2]										
Board of Water										
Delaware County	0	0	0	0	0	0	0	0	0	0
Sullivan County	0	0	0	0	0	0	0	0	0	0
Ulster County	0	0	0	0	0	6	0	6	0	0
Westchester County	0	0	0	0	0	8	0	8	0	0
Onondaga County Parks	0	0	0	0	0	35	3	32	0	0
North Carolina										

Table 11. Offenses Known to Law Enforcement, by Selected State, Tribal, and Other Agencies, 2012— continued

(Number)

State/Other Agency Unit/Office	Violent crime	Murder and nonnegligent manslaughter	Forcible rape	Robbery	Aggravated assault	Property crime	Burglary	Larceny-theft	Motor vehicle theft	Arson[1]
State Agencies										
Division of Alcohol Law Enforcement	0	0	0	0	0	0	0	0	0	0
North Carolina Highway Patrol	0	0	0	0	0	0	0	0	0	0
State Park Rangers										
Crowders Mountain	0	0	0	0	0	1	0	1	0	0
Elk Knob	0	0	0	0	0	0	0	0	0	0
Kerr Lake	0	0	0	0	0	4	0	4	0	0
Morrow Mountain	0	0	0	0	0	3	0	3	0	0
New River-Mount Jefferson	0	0	0	0	0	0	0	0	0	0
Pettigrew	0	0	0	0	0	0	0	0	0	0
Stone Mountain	0	0	0	0	0	3	0	3	0	0
Weymouth Woods/Sandhills Nature Preserve	0	0	0	0	0	0	0	0	0	0
Tribal Agency										
Cherokee Tribal	86	2	5	9	70	667	150	500	17	6
Other Agencies										
Beaufort County Alcohol Beverage Control Enforcement	0	0	0	0	0	9	1	8	0	0
Pitt County Memorial Hospital	2	0	1	0	1	76	2	73	1	0
Raleigh-Durham International Airport	0	0	0	0	0	66	1	59	6	0
WakeMed Campus Police	2	0	0	0	2	65	0	62	3	0
North Dakota										
Tribal Agencies										
Fort Totten Agency	26	0	4	0	22	84	24	45	15	0
Standing Rock Agency	123	1	12	5	105	150	65	51	34	8
Turtle Mountain Agency	56	4	9	4	39	230	59	131	40	14
Ohio										
State Agencies										
Ohio Department of Natural Resources	1	0	0	0	1	90	3	87	0	1
Ohio Investigative Unit	0	0	0	0	0	0	0	0	0	0
Ohio State Highway Patrol	277	5	14	8	250	362	15	270	77	4
Other Agencies										
Hamilton County Park District	1	0	1	0	0	43	7	34	2	1
Holden Arboretum	0	0	0	0	0	1	0	1	0	0
Lake Metroparks	1	0	0	1	0	17	0	17	0	0
Lorain County Metropolitan Park District	0	0	0	0	0	3	0	3	0	0
Mill Creek MetroPark	1	0	0	1	0	10	0	10	0	0
Port Columbus International Airport	1	0	0	0	1	145	3	99	43	0
Robinson Memorial Hospital	0	0	0	0	0	3	1	2	0	0
Oklahoma										
State Agencies										
Capitol Park Police	0	0	0	0	0	15	1	14	0	0
Grand River Dam Authority, Lake Patrol	0	0	0	0	0	30	1	28	1	0
Tribal Agencies										
Absentee Shawnee Tribal	8	1	1	2	4	58	35	16	7	1
Anadarko Agency	11	0	1	0	10	36	4	28	4	2
Cherokee Nation	13	1	3	2	7	28	8	16	4	0
Chickasaw Nation	84	0	0	19	65	748	98	570	80	8
Choctaw Nation	4	0	0	0	4	352	36	306	10	0
Citizen Potawatomi Nation	10	0	1	0	9	136	24	99	13	0
Concho Agency	1	0	0	0	1	16	1	12	3	1
Eastern Shawnee Tribal	0	0	0	0	0	12	0	11	1	0
Iowa Tribal	1	0	0	0	1	3	0	3	0	2
Kaw Tribal	1	0	0	0	1	18	11	7	0	0
Kickapoo Tribal	11	1	1	3	6	33	5	19	9	0
Miami Agency	4	0	0	0	4	23	3	14	6	0
Miami Tribal	0	0	0	0	0	0	0	0	0	0
Muscogee Nation Tribal	15	0	1	5	9	89	18	59	12	2
Osage Nation	10	0	0	3	7	80	17	45	18	12
Otoe-Missouria Tribal	5	0	0	0	5	16	4	10	2	0

Table 11. Offenses Known to Law Enforcement, by Selected State, Tribal, and Other Agencies, 2012— continued

(Number)

State/Other Agency Unit/Office	Violent crime	Murder and nonnegligent manslaughter	Forcible rape	Robbery	Aggravated assault	Property crime	Burglary	Larceny-theft	Motor vehicle theft	Arson[1]
Pawnee Agency	3	1	0	0	2	5	2	3	0	0
Pawnee Tribal	1	0	0	0	1	6	2	3	1	2
Ponca Tribal	2	0	0	0	2	17	5	11	1	2
Quapaw Tribal	4	0	0	1	3	65	6	59	0	0
Sac and Fox Tribal	4	0	1	1	2	22	15	5	2	6
Seminole Nation Lighthorse	4	0	1	1	2	30	10	16	4	1
Wyandotte Nation	0	0	0	0	0	18	0	18	0	0
Other Agencies										
Jenks Public Schools	3	0	0	0	3	9	0	9	0	0
McAlester Public Schools	0	0	0	0	0	5	4	1	0	0
Norman Public Schools	0	0	0	0	0	44	2	39	3	1
Putnam City Campus	4	0	0	0	4	30	1	29	0	2
Oregon										
State Agency: State Police	0	0	0	0	0	0	0	0	0	0
Tribal Agencies										
Burns Paiute Tribal	0	0	0	0	0	3	1	2	0	0
Columbia River Inter-Tribal Fisheries Enforcement	11	0	0	0	11	37	7	26	4	3
Coquille Tribal	4	1	0	0	3	13	1	11	1	6
Siletz Tribal	3	0	1	1	1	65	16	43	6	0
Umatilla Tribal	11	0	1	0	10	130	37	78	15	0
Warm Springs Tribal	87	3	9	1	74	142	59	60	23	10
Other Agencies										
Blue Mountain Enforcement Narcotics Team, Morrow County	0	0	0	0	0	0	0	0	0	0
Port of Portland	2	0	0	0	2	289	2	266	21	0
Pennsylvania										
State Agencies										
Bureau of Narcotics										
Adams County	0	0	0	0	0	0	0	0	0	0
Allegheny County	0	0	0	0	0	0	0	0	0	0
Armstrong County	0	0	0	0	0	0	0	0	0	0
Beaver County	0	0	0	0	0	0	0	0	0	0
Bedford County	0	0	0	0	0	0	0	0	0	0
Berks County	0	0	0	0	0	0	0	0	0	0
Blair County	0	0	0	0	0	0	0	0	0	0
Bradford County	0	0	0	0	0	0	0	0	0	0
Bucks County	0	0	0	0	0	0	0	0	0	0
Butler County	0	0	0	0	0	0	0	0	0	0
Cambria County	0	0	0	0	0	0	0	0	0	0
Cameron County	0	0	0	0	0	0	0	0	0	0
Carbon County	0	0	0	0	0	0	0	0	0	0
Centre County	0	0	0	0	0	0	0	0	0	0
Chester County	0	0	0	0	0	0	0	0	0	0
Clarion County	0	0	0	0	0	0	0	0	0	0
Clearfield County	0	0	0	0	0	0	0	0	0	0
Clinton County	0	0	0	0	0	0	0	0	0	0
Columbia County	0	0	0	0	0	0	0	0	0	0
Cumberland County	0	0	0	0	0	0	0	0	0	0
Dauphin County	0	0	0	0	0	0	0	0	0	0
Delaware County	0	0	0	0	0	0	0	0	0	0
Elk County	0	0	0	0	0	0	0	0	0	0
Erie County	0	0	0	0	0	0	0	0	0	0
Fayette County	0	0	0	0	0	0	0	0	0	0
Forest County	0	0	0	0	0	0	0	0	0	0
Franklin County	0	0	0	0	0	0	0	0	0	0
Fulton County	0	0	0	0	0	0	0	0	0	0
Greene County	0	0	0	0	0	0	0	0	0	0
Huntingdon County	0	0	0	0	0	0	0	0	0	0
Indiana County	0	0	0	0	0	0	0	0	0	0
Jefferson County	0	0	0	0	0	0	0	0	0	0
Juniata County	0	0	0	0	0	0	0	0	0	0

Table 11. Offenses Known to Law Enforcement, by Selected State, Tribal, and Other Agencies, 2012— continued

(Number)

State/Other Agency Unit/Office	Violent crime	Murder and nonnegligent manslaughter	Forcible rape	Robbery	Aggravated assault	Property crime	Burglary	Larceny-theft	Motor vehicle theft	Arson[1]
Lackawanna County	0	0	0	0	0	0	0	0	0	0
Lancaster County	0	0	0	0	0	0	0	0	0	0
Lawrence County	0	0	0	0	0	0	0	0	0	0
Lebanon County	0	0	0	0	0	0	0	0	0	0
Lehigh County	0	0	0	0	0	0	0	0	0	0
Luzerne County	0	0	0	0	0	0	0	0	0	0
Lycoming County	0	0	0	0	0	0	0	0	0	0
McKean County	0	0	0	0	0	0	0	0	0	0
Mercer County	0	0	0	0	0	0	0	0	0	0
Mifflin County	0	0	0	0	0	0	0	0	0	0
Monroe County	0	0	0	0	0	0	0	0	0	0
Montgomery County	0	0	0	0	0	0	0	0	0	0
Montour County	0	0	0	0	0	0	0	0	0	0
Northampton County	0	0	0	0	0	0	0	0	0	0
Northumberland County	0	0	0	0	0	0	0	0	0	0
Perry County	0	0	0	0	0	0	0	0	0	0
Philadelphia County	0	0	0	0	0	0	0	0	0	0
Pike County	0	0	0	0	0	0	0	0	0	0
Potter County	0	0	0	0	0	0	0	0	0	0
Schuylkill County	0	0	0	0	0	0	0	0	0	0
Snyder County	0	0	0	0	0	0	0	0	0	0
Somerset County	0	0	0	0	0	0	0	0	0	0
Sullivan County	0	0	0	0	0	0	0	0	0	0
Susquehanna County	0	0	0	0	0	0	0	0	0	0
Tioga County	0	0	0	0	0	0	0	0	0	0
Union County	0	0	0	0	0	0	0	0	0	0
Venango County	0	0	0	0	0	0	0	0	0	0
Warren County	0	0	0	0	0	0	0	0	0	0
Washington County	0	0	0	0	0	0	0	0	0	0
Wayne County	0	0	0	0	0	0	0	0	0	0
Westmoreland County	0	0	0	0	0	0	0	0	0	0
Wyoming County	0	0	0	0	0	0	0	0	0	0
York County	0	0	0	0	0	0	0	0	0	0
Pennsylvania Fish and Boat Commission	0	0	0	0	0	1	0	1	0	0
State Capitol Police	0	0	0	0	0	37	5	32	0	0
State Park Police										
Ohiopyle	0	0	0	0	0	10	0	10	0	0
Pine Grove Furnace	0	0	0	0	0	3	0	3	0	0
Presque Isle	0	0	0	0	0	42	0	42	0	0
Prince Gallitzin	0	0	0	0	0	0	0	0	0	0
Pymatuning	1	0	0	0	1	25	1	24	0	0
State Police, Bureau of Criminal Investigation										
Adams County	0	0	0	0	0	0	0	0	0	0
Allegheny County	0	0	0	0	0	17	0	14	3	0
Armstrong County	0	0	0	0	0	0	0	0	0	0
Beaver County	0	0	0	0	0	0	0	0	0	0
Bedford County	0	0	0	0	0	0	0	0	0	0
Berks County	0	0	0	0	0	0	0	0	0	0
Blair County	0	0	0	0	0	0	0	0	0	0
Bradford County	0	0	0	0	0	0	0	0	0	0
Bucks County	0	0	0	0	0	0	0	0	0	0
Butler County	0	0	0	0	0	4	1	3	0	0
Cambria County	0	0	0	0	0	0	0	0	0	0
Cameron County	0	0	0	0	0	0	0	0	0	0
Carbon County	0	0	0	0	0	0	0	0	0	0
Centre County	0	0	0	0	0	0	0	0	0	0
Chester County	0	0	0	0	0	0	0	0	0	0
Clarion County	0	0	0	0	0	0	0	0	0	0
Clearfield County	0	0	0	0	0	0	0	0	0	0
Clinton County	0	0	0	0	0	0	0	0	0	0
Columbia County	0	0	0	0	0	0	0	0	0	0
Crawford County	0	0	0	0	0	0	0	0	0	0

Table 11. Offenses Known to Law Enforcement, by Selected State, Tribal, and Other Agencies, 2012— continued

(Number)

State/Other Agency Unit/Office	Violent crime	Murder and nonnegligent manslaughter	Forcible rape	Robbery	Aggravated assault	Property crime	Burglary	Larceny-theft	Motor vehicle theft	Arson[1]
Cumberland County	0	0	0	0	0	0	0	0	0	0
Dauphin County	0	0	0	0	0	0	0	0	0	0
Delaware County	0	0	0	0	0	0	0	0	0	0
Elk County	0	0	0	0	0	0	0	0	0	0
Erie County	0	0	0	0	0	0	0	0	0	0
Fayette County	0	0	0	0	0	2	0	2	0	0
Forest County	0	0	0	0	0	0	0	0	0	0
Franklin County	0	0	0	0	0	0	0	0	0	0
Fulton County	0	0	0	0	0	0	0	0	0	0
Greene County	0	0	0	0	0	0	0	0	0	0
Huntingdon County	0	0	0	0	0	0	0	0	0	0
Indiana County	0	0	0	0	0	0	0	0	0	0
Jefferson County	0	0	0	0	0	0	0	0	0	0
Juniata County	0	0	0	0	0	0	0	0	0	0
Lackawanna County	0	0	0	0	0	1	0	0	1	0
Lancaster County	0	0	0	0	0	0	0	0	0	0
Lawrence County	0	0	0	0	0	0	0	0	0	0
Lebanon County	0	0	0	0	0	0	0	0	0	0
Lehigh County	0	0	0	0	0	0	0	0	0	0
Luzerne County	0	0	0	0	0	0	0	0	0	0
Lycoming County	0	0	0	0	0	0	0	0	0	0
McKean County	0	0	0	0	0	0	0	0	0	0
Mercer County	0	0	0	0	0	2	0	1	1	0
Mifflin County	0	0	0	0	0	0	0	0	0	0
Monroe County	0	0	0	0	0	0	0	0	0	0
Montgomery County	0	0	0	0	0	0	0	0	0	0
Montour County	0	0	0	0	0	0	0	0	0	0
Northampton County	0	0	0	0	0	0	0	0	0	0
Northumberland County	0	0	0	0	0	0	0	0	0	0
Perry County	0	0	0	0	0	0	0	0	0	0
Philadelphia County	0	0	0	0	0	1	0	1	0	0
Pike County	0	0	0	0	0	0	0	0	0	0
Potter County	0	0	0	0	0	0	0	0	0	0
Schuylkill County	0	0	0	0	0	0	0	0	0	0
Snyder County	0	0	0	0	0	0	0	0	0	0
Somerset County	0	0	0	0	0	0	0	0	0	0
Sullivan County	0	0	0	0	0	0	0	0	0	0
Susquehanna County	0	0	0	0	0	0	0	0	0	0
Tioga County	0	0	0	0	0	0	0	0	0	0
Union County	0	0	0	0	0	0	0	0	0	0
Venango County	0	0	0	0	0	0	0	0	0	0
Warren County	0	0	0	0	0	0	0	0	0	0
Washington County	0	0	0	0	0	7	0	0	7	0
Wayne County	0	0	0	0	0	0	0	0	0	0
Westmoreland County	0	0	0	0	0	0	0	0	0	0
Wyoming County	0	0	0	0	0	0	0	0	0	0
York County	0	0	0	0	0	1	0	1	0	0
State Police										
Adams County	42	3	7	1	31	574	179	354	41	6
Allegheny County	59	0	2	1	56	495	1	492	2	0
Armstrong County	45	0	12	7	26	450	147	283	20	3
Beaver County	34	0	8	2	24	194	93	86	15	5
Bedford County	117	1	79	1	36	541	173	338	30	7
Berks County	101	2	17	11	71	725	262	412	51	5
Blair County	25	3	7	1	14	265	68	181	16	2
Bradford County	33	0	15	2	16	558	178	340	40	14
Bucks County	30	2	5	7	16	419	87	316	16	3
Butler County	47	1	6	9	31	613	208	373	32	6
Cambria County	71	3	10	3	55	285	125	131	29	3
Cameron County	5	0	3	2	0	55	34	20	1	1
Carbon County	45	3	5	2	35	334	154	171	9	1
Centre County	58	0	11	8	39	489	132	338	19	7
Chester County	172	0	55	33	84	1,356	426	880	50	9
Clarion County	51	2	26	2	21	507	116	370	21	4

Table 11. Offenses Known to Law Enforcement, by Selected State, Tribal, and Other Agencies, 2012— continued

(Number)

State/Other Agency Unit/Office	Violent crime	Murder and nonnegligent manslaughter	Forcible rape	Robbery	Aggravated assault	Property crime	Burglary	Larceny-theft	Motor vehicle theft	Arson[1]
Clearfield County	60	0	26	5	29	495	142	336	17	4
Clinton County	22	0	6	1	15	376	96	270	10	0
Columbia County	13	2	5	0	6	152	47	97	8	0
Crawford County	36	1	10	6	19	710	280	399	31	0
Cumberland County	41	0	7	12	22	775	191	565	19	10
Delaware County	52	0	2	12	38	940	152	761	27	1
Elizabethville	185	1	32	16	136	1,129	281	805	43	13
Elk County	5	0	0	0	5	233	62	165	6	6
Erie County	92	0	17	19	56	1,635	298	1,276	61	6
Fayette County	169	2	34	50	83	2,085	629	1,340	116	62
Franklin County	94	3	23	9	59	1,105	279	787	39	9
Fulton County	18	0	1	1	16	190	54	131	5	4
Greene County	40	2	7	11	20	506	149	327	30	8
Huntingdon County	63	0	27	2	34	444	136	294	14	2
Indiana County	66	5	26	10	25	907	247	616	44	8
Jefferson County	35	1	11	4	19	272	106	154	12	3
Juniata County	17	0	6	2	9	216	78	127	11	1
Lackawanna County	29	0	4	3	22	207	83	109	15	11
Lancaster County	71	2	24	16	29	816	306	477	33	8
Lawrence County	36	0	5	4	27	309	119	168	22	3
Lebanon County	83	1	12	2	68	504	118	360	26	1
Lehigh County	61	0	16	15	30	888	175	685	28	7
Luzerne County	148	6	8	27	107	1,048	263	730	55	20
Lycoming County	74	0	17	12	45	738	201	518	19	2
McKean County	11	0	9	0	2	133	53	71	9	0
Mercer County	33	1	9	2	21	364	103	255	6	2
Mifflin County	12	0	4	0	8	130	38	90	2	0
Monroe County	484	2	22	30	430	1,656	601	1,001	54	4
Montour County	23	0	3	0	20	114	56	54	4	5
Northampton County	25	2	3	5	15	412	86	314	12	2
Northumberland County	35	2	5	1	27	324	132	175	17	3
Perry County	65	0	8	8	49	586	164	399	23	11
Philadelphia County	13	1	1	0	11	2	0	2	0	0
Pike County	50	1	13	6	30	747	389	333	25	8
Potter County	23	1	10	0	12	166	84	70	12	0
Schuylkill County	131	3	18	16	94	731	208	480	43	15
Skippack	74	0	3	3	68	440	114	315	11	10
Snyder County	19	0	4	6	9	347	78	258	11	1
Somerset County	42	2	8	5	27	494	138	334	22	14
Sullivan County	19	0	1	0	18	98	44	50	4	0
Susquehanna County	46	2	19	15	10	402	166	219	17	9
Tioga County	37	0	8	1	28	481	196	251	34	4
Tionesta	33	2	4	0	27	158	83	71	4	3
Union County	23	1	10	4	8	313	102	202	9	1
Venango County	29	2	12	3	12	361	78	271	12	0
Warren County	35	1	8	1	25	325	114	194	17	3
Washington County	100	2	23	20	55	892	281	565	46	21
Wayne County	51	1	21	5	24	680	231	423	26	14
Westmoreland County	141	2	35	29	75	1,613	396	1,147	70	39
Wyoming County	16	0	6	1	9	213	55	142	16	1
York County	80	0	10	14	56	672	134	513	25	5
Other Agencies										
Allegheny County District Attorney, Criminal Investigation Division	0	0	0	0	0	47	0	47	0	0
Allegheny County Port Authority	109	0	0	23	86	82	0	78	4	0
County Detective										
Bucks County	3	0	2	0	1	13	0	13	0	0
Butler County	0	0	0	0	0	0	0	0	0	0
Clarion County	2	0	1	0	1	0	0	0	0	0
Cumberland County	2	0	0	0	2	4	0	4	0	0
Dauphin County	19	0	0	0	19	6	0	6	0	2
Erie County	2	1	1	0	0	2	0	2	0	0
Lackawanna County	4	0	1	0	3	0	0	0	0	0
Lebanon County	0	0	0	0	0	3	0	3	0	0

Table 11. Offenses Known to Law Enforcement, by Selected State, Tribal, and Other Agencies, 2012— continued

(Number)

State/Other Agency Unit/Office	Violent crime	Murder and nonnegligent manslaughter	Forcible rape	Robbery	Aggravated assault	Property crime	Burglary	Larceny-theft	Motor vehicle theft	Arson[1]
Lehigh County	11	0	0	10	1	85	2	5	78	0
Luzerne County	4	0	0	0	4	3	0	3	0	0
Montour County	0	0	0	0	0	0	0	0	0	0
Pike County	0	0	0	0	0	1	0	1	0	0
Westmoreland County	6	0	0	0	6	107	0	107	0	0
Wyoming County	1	0	0	0	1	2	0	2	0	0
Delaware County District Attorney, Criminal Investigation Division	24	0	4	0	20	5	0	5	0	0
Delaware County Park	6	0	0	0	6	109	0	109	0	0
Fort Cherry School District	0	0	0	0	0	0	0	0	0	0
Fort Indiantown Gap	2	0	2	0	0	11	2	9	0	0
Harrisburg International Airport	2	0	0	0	2	5	0	1	4	0
Lehigh Valley International Airport	0	0	0	0	0	10	0	3	7	0
Westmoreland County Park	0	0	0	0	0	14	0	14	0	0
Wyoming Area School District	0	0	0	0	0	1	0	0	1	0
Rhode Island										
State Agencies										
Department of Environmental Management	2	0	0	0	2	45	2	43	0	0
Rhode Island State Airport	0	0	0	0	0	24	0	23	1	0
Rhode Island State Police Headquarters	23	2	7	0	14	89	2	21	66	0
State Police										
Chepachet	3	0	1	0	2	36	1	26	9	0
Hope Valley	3	0	2	0	1	49	9	33	7	0
Lincoln	14	0	5	1	8	89	2	61	26	0
Portsmouth	0	0	0	0	0	3	1	2	0	0
Wickford	2	0	1	1	0	57	9	40	8	1
Tribal Agency										
Narragansett Tribal	0	0	0	0	0	4	0	2	2	0
South Carolina										
State Agencies										
Bureau of Protective Services	0	0	0	0	0	23	7	16	0	0
Department of Mental Health	1	0	0	0	1	17	0	17	0	0
Employment Security Commission	0	0	0	0	0	0	0	0	0	0
Highway Patrol										
Abbeville County	1	0	0	0	1	1	0	0	1	0
Aiken County	0	0	0	0	0	1	0	0	1	0
Allendale County	0	0	0	0	0	0	0	0	0	0
Anderson County	0	0	0	0	0	1	0	1	0	0
Bamberg County	1	0	0	0	1	0	0	0	0	0
Barnwell County	0	0	0	0	0	1	0	0	1	0
Beaufort County	0	0	0	0	0	0	0	0	0	0
Berkeley County	0	0	0	0	0	1	0	0	1	0
Calhoun County	0	0	0	0	0	0	0	0	0	0
Charleston County	0	0	0	0	0	0	0	0	0	0
Cherokee County	0	0	0	0	0	0	0	0	0	0
Chester County	0	0	0	0	0	0	0	0	0	0
Chesterfield County	0	0	0	0	0	0	0	0	0	0
Clarendon County	0	0	0	0	0	1	0	0	1	0
Colleton County	0	0	0	0	0	0	0	0	0	0
Darlington County	0	0	0	0	0	0	0	0	0	0
Dillon County	0	0	0	0	0	0	0	0	0	0
Dorchester County	0	0	0	0	0	1	0	0	1	0
Edgefield County	0	0	0	0	0	0	0	0	0	0
Fairfield County	0	0	0	0	0	1	0	0	1	0
Florence County	0	0	0	0	0	0	0	0	0	0
Georgetown County	0	0	0	0	0	0	0	0	0	0
Greenville County	1	0	0	0	1	0	0	0	0	0
Greenwood County	0	0	0	0	0	0	0	0	0	0
Hampton County	0	0	0	0	0	0	0	0	0	0
Horry County	0	0	0	0	0	1	0	0	1	0
Jasper County	0	0	0	0	0	0	0	0	0	0

Table 11. Offenses Known to Law Enforcement, by Selected State, Tribal, and Other Agencies, 2012— continued

(Number)

State/Other Agency Unit/Office	Violent crime	Murder and nonnegligent manslaughter	Forcible rape	Robbery	Aggravated assault	Property crime	Burglary	Larceny-theft	Motor vehicle theft	Arson[1]
Kershaw County	0	0	0	0	0	0	0	0	0	0
Laurens County	0	0	0	0	0	0	0	0	0	0
Lee County	0	0	0	0	0	0	0	0	0	0
Lexington County	0	0	0	0	0	0	0	0	0	0
Marion County	0	0	0	0	0	0	0	0	0	0
Newberry County	0	0	0	0	0	0	0	0	0	0
Oconee County	0	0	0	0	0	0	0	0	0	0
Orangeburg County	0	0	0	0	0	0	0	0	0	0
Pickens County	0	0	0	0	0	0	0	0	0	0
Richland County	2	0	0	0	2	0	0	0	0	0
Saluda County	0	0	0	0	0	0	0	0	0	0
Spartanburg County	0	0	0	0	0	0	0	0	0	0
Sumter County	0	0	0	0	0	0	0	0	0	0
Union County	0	0	0	0	0	0	0	0	0	0
Williamsburg County	0	0	0	0	0	0	0	0	0	0
York County	1	0	0	0	1	0	0	0	0	0
State Museum	0	0	0	0	0	0	0	0	0	0
State Ports Authority	0	0	0	0	0	11	0	11	0	0
State Transport Police										
Abbeville County	0	0	0	0	0	0	0	0	0	0
Aiken County	0	0	0	0	0	0	0	0	0	0
Bamberg County	0	0	0	0	0	0	0	0	0	0
Barnwell County	0	0	0	0	0	0	0	0	0	0
Beaufort County	0	0	0	0	0	0	0	0	0	0
Berkeley County	0	0	0	0	0	0	0	0	0	0
Calhoun County	0	0	0	0	0	0	0	0	0	0
Charleston County	0	0	0	0	0	0	0	0	0	0
Cherokee County	0	0	0	0	0	0	0	0	0	0
Chester County	0	0	0	0	0	0	0	0	0	0
Chesterfield County	0	0	0	0	0	0	0	0	0	0
Clarendon County	0	0	0	0	0	0	0	0	0	0
Colleton County	0	0	0	0	0	0	0	0	0	0
Darlington County	0	0	0	0	0	0	0	0	0	0
Dillon County	0	0	0	0	0	0	0	0	0	0
Dorchester County	0	0	0	0	0	0	0	0	0	0
Edgefield County	0	0	0	0	0	0	0	0	0	0
Fairfield County	0	0	0	0	0	0	0	0	0	0
Georgetown County	0	0	0	0	0	0	0	0	0	0
Greenville County	0	0	0	0	0	0	0	0	0	0
Greenwood County	0	0	0	0	0	1	0	1	0	0
Hampton County	0	0	0	0	0	0	0	0	0	0
Horry County	0	0	0	0	0	0	0	0	0	0
Jasper County	0	0	0	0	0	0	0	0	0	0
Kershaw County	0	0	0	0	0	0	0	0	0	0
Lancaster County	0	0	0	0	0	0	0	0	0	0
Lee County	0	0	0	0	0	0	0	0	0	0
Lexington County	0	0	0	0	0	0	0	0	0	0
Marion County	0	0	0	0	0	0	0	0	0	0
Marlboro County	0	0	0	0	0	0	0	0	0	0
McCormick County	0	0	0	0	0	0	0	0	0	0
Newberry County	0	0	0	0	0	0	0	0	0	0
Oconee County	0	0	0	0	0	0	0	0	0	0
Orangeburg County	0	0	0	0	0	0	0	0	0	0
Pickens County	0	0	0	0	0	0	0	0	0	0
Richland County	0	0	0	0	0	0	0	0	0	0
Saluda County	0	0	0	0	0	0	0	0	0	0
Sumter County	0	0	0	0	0	0	0	0	0	0
Union County	0	0	0	0	0	0	0	0	0	0
Williamsburg County	0	0	0	0	0	0	0	0	0	0
York County	0	0	0	0	0	0	0	0	0	0
United States Department of Energy, Savannah River Plant	0	0	0	0	0	37	0	37	0	0
Other Agencies										
Charleston County Aviation Authority	0	0	0	0	0	44	0	38	6	0

Table 11. Offenses Known to Law Enforcement, by Selected State, Tribal, and Other Agencies, 2012— continued

(Number)

State/Other Agency Unit/Office	Violent crime	Murder and nonnegligent manslaughter	Forcible rape	Robbery	Aggravated assault	Property crime	Burglary	Larceny-theft	Motor vehicle theft	Arson[1]
Columbia Metropolitan Airport	0	0	0	0	0	4	0	4	0	0
Greenville-Spartanburg International Airport	0	0	0	0	0	29	0	28	1	0
Lexington County Medical Center	2	0	0	0	2	40	3	31	6	0
South Dakota										
State Agency										
Division of Criminal Investigation	11	3	2	0	6	8	5	1	2	1
Tribal Agencies										
Crow Creek Tribal	42	0	5	0	37	76	21	40	15	3
Flandreau Tribal	3	0	1	0	2	13	3	10	0	2
Lower Brule Tribal	88	0	12	2	74	110	47	49	14	40
Oglala Sioux Tribal	59	4	19	2	34	177	25	127	25	8
Rosebud Tribal	385	1	27	6	351	332	150	144	38	43
Sisseton-Wahpeton Tribal	21	0	0	0	21	200	34	136	30	10
Yankton Tribal	32	1	3	2	26	10	5	2	3	1
Tennessee										
State Agencies										
Alcoholic Beverage Commission	0	0	0	0	0	0	0	0	0	0
Department of Correction, Internal Affairs	18	0	0	0	18	1	1	0	0	0
Department of Safety	52	1	0	0	51	53	0	15	38	2
State Fire Marshal	0	0	0	0	0	0	0	0	0	27
State Park Rangers										
Bicentennial Capitol Mall	0	0	0	0	0	2	0	2	0	0
Big Hill Pond	0	0	0	0	0	0	0	0	0	0
Big Ridge	0	0	0	0	0	0	0	0	0	0
Bledsoe Creek	0	0	0	0	0	1	0	1	0	0
Booker T. Washington	0	0	0	0	0	0	0	0	0	0
Burgess Falls Natural Area	0	0	0	0	0	1	0	1	0	0
Cedars of Lebanon	0	0	0	0	0	2	0	2	0	0
Chickasaw	0	0	0	0	0	2	0	2	0	0
Cove Lake	0	0	0	0	0	5	0	5	0	0
Cumberland Mountain	0	0	0	0	0	0	0	0	0	0
Cumberland Trail	2	0	0	1	1	10	0	9	1	0
Cummins Falls	0	0	0	0	0	0	0	0	0	0
David Crockett	0	0	0	0	0	0	0	0	0	0
Davy Crockett Birthplace	0	0	0	0	0	3	0	3	0	0
Dunbar Cave Natural Area	0	0	0	0	0	4	0	4	0	0
Edgar Evins	0	0	0	0	0	7	0	7	0	0
Fall Creek Falls	0	0	0	0	0	2	0	2	0	0
Fort Loudon State Historic Park	0	0	0	0	0	0	0	0	0	0
Fort Pillow State Historic Park	0	0	0	0	0	0	0	0	0	0
Frozen Head Natural Area	0	0	0	0	0	0	0	0	0	0
Harpeth Scenic Rivers	0	0	0	0	0	2	0	2	0	0
Harrison Bay	0	0	0	0	0	0	0	0	0	0
Henry Horton	0	0	0	0	0	6	1	5	0	0
Hiwassee/Ocoee State Scenic Rivers	0	0	0	0	0	4	0	3	1	0
Indian Mountain	0	0	0	0	0	0	0	0	0	0
Johnsonville State Historic Park	0	0	0	0	0	0	0	0	0	0
Long Hunter	0	0	0	0	0	3	0	3	0	0
Meeman-Shelby Forest	0	0	0	0	0	2	0	2	0	0
Montgomery Bell	0	0	0	0	0	3	0	3	0	0
Mousetail Landing	0	0	0	0	0	0	0	0	0	0
Natchez Trace	0	0	0	0	0	0	0	0	0	0
Nathan Bedford Forrest	0	0	0	0	0	0	0	0	0	0
Norris Dam	0	0	0	0	0	1	0	1	0	0
Old Stone Fort State Archaeological Park	0	0	0	0	0	6	0	6	0	0
Panther Creek	0	0	0	0	0	10	0	10	0	0
Paris Landing	0	0	0	0	0	2	0	2	0	0
Pickett	0	0	0	0	0	2	0	2	0	0
Pickwick Landing	2	0	0	0	2	2	0	2	0	0

Table 11. Offenses Known to Law Enforcement, by Selected State, Tribal, and Other Agencies, 2012— continued

(Number)

State/Other Agency Unit/Office	Violent crime	Murder and nonnegligent manslaughter	Forcible rape	Robbery	Aggravated assault	Property crime	Burglary	Larceny-theft	Motor vehicle theft	Arson[1]
Pinson Mounds State Archaeological Park	0	0	0	0	0	0	0	0	0	0
Radnor Lake Natural Area	0	0	0	0	0	1	0	1	0	0
Red Clay State Historic Park	0	0	0	0	0	0	0	0	0	0
Reelfoot Lake	0	0	0	0	0	0	0	0	0	0
Roan Mountain	0	0	0	0	0	0	0	0	0	0
Rock Island	0	0	0	0	0	3	0	3	0	0
Sgt. Alvin C. York	0	0	0	0	0	0	0	0	0	0
South Cumberland Recreation Area	0	0	0	0	0	0	0	0	0	0
Standing Stone	0	0	0	0	0	0	0	0	0	0
Sycamore Shoals State Historic Park	0	0	0	0	0	1	0	1	0	0
Tim's Ford	0	0	0	0	0	1	0	1	0	0
T.O. Fuller	0	0	0	0	0	4	1	3	0	0
Warrior's Path	0	0	0	0	0	0	0	0	0	0
TennCare Office of Inspector General	0	0	0	0	0	0	0	0	0	0
Tennessee Bureau of Investigation	4	0	0	0	4	6	1	5	0	0
Tennessee Department of Revenue, Special Investigations Unit	0	0	0	0	0	0	0	0	0	0
Wildlife Resources Agency										
Region 1	0	0	0	0	0	0	0	0	0	0
Region 2	0	0	0	0	0	0	0	0	0	0
Region 3	0	0	0	0	0	0	0	0	0	0
Region 4	0	0	0	0	0	0	0	0	0	0
Other Agencies										
Chattanooga Housing Authority	2	0	0	0	2	2	0	2	0	0
Chattanooga Metropolitan Airport	0	0	0	0	0	2	0	2	0	0
Dickson Parks and Recreation	0	0	0	0	0	0	0	0	0	0
Drug Task Force										
1st Judicial District	0	0	0	0	0	0	0	0	0	0
2nd Judicial District	0	0	0	0	0	0	0	0	0	0
3rd Judicial District	0	0	0	0	0	0	0	0	0	0
4th Judicial District	0	0	0	0	0	2	0	2	0	0
5th Judicial District	0	0	0	0	0	2	1	1	0	0
8th Judicial District	0	0	0	0	0	0	0	0	0	0
9th Judicial District	0	0	0	0	0	0	0	0	0	0
10th Judicial District	0	0	0	0	0	1	0	1	0	0
12th Judicial District	0	0	0	0	0	0	0	0	0	0
13th Judicial District	0	0	0	0	0	0	0	0	0	0
14th Judicial District	0	0	0	0	0	0	0	0	0	0
15th Judicial District	0	0	0	0	0	0	0	0	0	0
17th Judicial District	0	0	0	0	0	0	0	0	0	0
18th Judicial District	0	0	0	0	0	0	0	0	0	0
19th Judicial District	0	0	0	0	0	3	0	3	0	0
21st Judicial District	0	0	0	0	0	0	0	0	0	0
22nd Judicial District	0	0	0	0	0	0	0	0	0	0
23rd Judicial District	0	0	0	0	0	0	0	0	0	0
24th Judicial District	1	0	0	1	0	2	0	2	0	0
25th Judicial District	0	0	0	0	0	0	0	0	0	0
27th Judicial District	0	0	0	0	0	0	0	0	0	0
31st Judicial District	0	0	0	0	0	0	0	0	0	0
Knoxville Metropolitan Airport	0	0	0	0	0	21	0	21	0	0
Memphis International Airport	2	0	0	1	1	131	0	124	7	0
Metropolitan Nashville Park Police	9	0	0	6	3	141	3	135	3	0
Nashville International Airport	1	0	0	0	1	33	0	24	9	0
Smyrna/Rutherford County Airport Authority	0	0	0	0	0	1	0	1	0	0
Tri-Cities Regional Airport	0	0	0	0	0	0	0	0	0	0
West Tennessee Violent Crime Task Force	0	0	0	0	0	0	0	0	0	0
Texas										
Tribal Agency										
Ysleta Del Sur Pueblo Tribal	77	0	0	1	76	53	8	42	3	0
Other Agencies										
Amarillo International Airport	0	0	0	0	0	1	0	1	0	0

Table 11. Offenses Known to Law Enforcement, by Selected State, Tribal, and Other Agencies, 2012— continued

(Number)

State/Other Agency Unit/Office	Violent crime	Murder and nonnegligent manslaughter	Forcible rape	Robbery	Aggravated assault	Property crime	Burglary	Larceny-theft	Motor vehicle theft	Arson[1]
Dallas-Fort Worth International Airport	10	0	1	1	8	623	10	583	30	2
Hospital District										
Dallas County	6	0	0	1	5	429	6	419	4	0
Tarrant County	2	0	1	0	1	143	3	136	4	0
Houston Metropolitan Transit Authority	4	0	0	4	0	32	0	27	5	0
Independent School District										
Aldine	3	0	0	2	1	131	28	99	4	1
Alvin	11	0	2	0	9	50	12	37	1	1
Angleton	6	0	1	0	5	22	6	15	1	0
Austin	12	0	1	4	7	668	27	640	1	4
Barbers Hill	0	0	0	0	0	15	1	13	1	0
Cedar Hill	15	0	0	0	15	31	0	31	0	0
Columbia-Barzoria	1	0	0	0	1	21	0	21	0	0
Conroe	4	0	0	0	4	274	1	272	1	0
East Central	1	0	0	0	1	0	0	0	0	0
Ector County	27	0	1	1	25	85	11	74	0	0
Edinburg	5	0	0	0	5	190	4	185	1	3
El Paso	29	0	3	0	26	390	48	341	1	2
Floresville	0	0	0	0	0	19	0	19	0	0
Fort Bend	11	0	0	2	9	446	13	433	0	0
Hallsville	0	0	0	0	0	8	1	7	0	0
Humble	14	0	3	1	10	177	3	172	2	1
Judson	0	0	0	0	0	8	0	8	0	0
Katy	8	0	3	2	3	377	6	368	3	0
Killeen	2	0	1	0	1	77	2	75	0	3
Klein	2	0	0	0	2	36	2	34	0	0
Lyford	0	0	0	0	0	10	2	8	0	0
Midland	1	0	0	0	1	13	1	12	0	0
North East	97	0	5	0	92	372	7	365	0	0
Pasadena	4	0	1	3	0	196	12	176	8	0
Pflugerville	5	0	0	0	5	73	3	65	5	2
Raymondville	0	0	0	0	0	9	1	8	0	0
Rio Grande City	15	0	0	0	15	60	2	58	0	0
Sealy	1	0	0	0	1	10	0	10	0	0
Socorro	3	0	0	0	3	93	4	89	0	0
Spring	14	0	4	1	9	134	4	128	2	2
Spring Branch	3	0	0	3	0	122	11	108	3	0
Taft	0	0	0	0	0	1	0	1	0	0
United	3	0	0	0	3	68	3	65	0	1
Port of Brownsville	0	0	0	0	0	33	4	27	2	0
Port of Houston Authority	0	0	0	0	0	35	1	33	1	0
Utah										
State Agencies										
Parks and Recreation	2	0	1	0	1	21	1	14	6	2
Utah Highway Patrol	45	3	2	1	39	196	8	166	22	1
Wildlife Resources	2	1	0	0	1	3	1	2	0	0
Tribal Agency										
Uintah and Ouray Tribal	5	0	0	0	5	13	8	0	5	1
Other Agencies										
Cache-Rich Drug Task Force	0	0	0	0	0	4	2	2	0	0
Davis Metropolitan Narcotics Strike Force	0	0	0	0	0	1	0	1	0	0
Granite School District	9	0	1	0	8	162	10	151	1	11
Utah County Attorney, Investigations Division	0	0	0	0	0	0	0	0	0	0
Utah County Major Crime Task Force	1	0	0	1	0	7	2	3	2	1
Utah Transit Authority	12	0	0	2	10	2,263	1	2,233	29	0
Vermont										
State Agencies										
Attorney General	1	1	0	0	0	1	0	1	0	0
Department of Motor Vehicles	0	0	0	0	0	2	0	0	2	0

Table 11. Offenses Known to Law Enforcement, by Selected State, Tribal, and Other Agencies, 2012— continued

(Number)

State/Other Agency Unit/Office	Violent crime	Murder and nonnegligent manslaughter	Forcible rape	Robbery	Aggravated assault	Property crime	Burglary	Larceny-theft	Motor vehicle theft	Arson[1]
Fish and Wildlife Department, Law Enforcement Division	0	0	0	0	0	1	0	1	0	0
Secretary of State, Investigations Unit	0	0	0	0	0	2	0	2	0	0
State Police										
Bradford	9	1	0	1	7	290	143	136	11	8
Brattleboro	15	0	3	1	11	132	71	57	4	0
Derby	18	0	6	0	12	335	123	190	22	2
Middlesex	9	0	0	2	7	310	118	191	1	2
New Haven	7	0	0	0	7	356	151	193	12	0
Rockingham	24	0	0	1	23	227	107	106	14	0
Royalton	13	0	0	0	13	211	103	96	12	2
Rutland	32	2	5	5	20	657	246	392	19	11
Shaftsbury	20	0	2	0	18	240	109	124	7	1
St. Albans	45	0	6	4	35	512	199	272	41	1
St. Johnsbury	17	1	2	3	11	419	187	222	10	2
Williston	6	0	1	0	5	308	91	209	8	7
Vermont State Police	0	0	0	0	0	0	0	0	0	0
Vermont State Police Headquarters, Bureau of Criminal Investigations	2	0	0	0	2	2	0	2	0	0
Virginia										
State Agencies										
Alcoholic Beverage Control Commission	0	0	0	0	0	28	0	28	0	0
Department of Conservation and Recreation	0	0	0	0	0	61	1	60	0	0
Department of Game and Inland Fisheries, Enforcement Division	4	0	0	0	4	18	0	18	0	0
Department of Motor Vehicles	0	0	0	0	0	11	0	3	8	0
Southside Virginia Training Center	1	0	0	0	1	12	0	12	0	1
State Police										
Accomack County	11	0	0	1	10	18	1	16	1	39
Albemarle County	1	0	0	0	1	3	0	3	0	0
Alexandria	1	0	0	0	1	0	0	0	0	0
Alleghany County	0	0	0	0	0	2	0	2	0	1
Amelia County	2	0	0	0	2	2	0	2	0	1
Amherst County	0	0	0	0	0	1	0	0	1	0
Appomattox County	0	0	0	0	0	0	0	0	0	0
Arlington County	0	0	0	0	0	0	0	0	0	0
Augusta County	0	0	0	0	0	0	0	0	0	0
Bath County	1	1	0	0	0	1	0	1	0	1
Bedford	0	0	0	0	0	0	0	0	0	0
Bedford County	0	0	0	0	0	8	0	4	4	0
Bland County	0	0	0	0	0	5	0	5	0	0
Botetourt County	4	0	0	0	4	1	1	0	0	0
Bristol	0	0	0	0	0	0	0	0	0	0
Brunswick County	0	0	0	0	0	3	0	3	0	0
Buchanan County	3	0	0	1	2	19	4	13	2	4
Buckingham County	0	0	0	0	0	2	0	2	0	0
Buena Vista	0	0	0	0	0	0	0	0	0	0
Campbell County	0	0	0	0	0	0	0	0	0	0
Caroline County	3	0	1	0	2	16	2	9	5	1
Carroll County	0	0	0	0	0	3	0	2	1	0
Charles City County	0	0	0	0	0	0	0	0	0	0
Charlotte County	0	0	0	0	0	0	0	0	0	0
Charlottesville	0	0	0	0	0	2	0	2	0	0
Chesapeake	1	0	0	0	1	12	1	3	8	0
Chesterfield County	12	0	0	0	12	7	0	4	3	0
Clarke County	0	0	0	0	0	3	0	2	1	0
Clifton Forge	0	0	0	0	0	0	0	0	0	0
Colonial Heights	1	0	0	0	1	0	0	0	0	0
Covington	0	0	0	0	0	1	0	1	0	0
Craig County	1	0	0	0	1	5	1	4	0	0
Culpeper County	2	1	0	0	1	1	0	1	0	0
Cumberland County	0	0	0	0	0	0	0	0	0	0
Danville	0	0	0	0	0	3	0	2	1	0

Table 11. Offenses Known to Law Enforcement, by Selected State, Tribal, and Other Agencies, 2012— continued

(Number)

State/Other Agency Unit/Office	Violent crime	Murder and nonnegligent manslaughter	Forcible rape	Robbery	Aggravated assault	Property crime	Burglary	Larceny-theft	Motor vehicle theft	Arson[1]
Dickenson County	3	0	1	0	2	10	0	8	2	4
Dinwiddie County	9	0	1	0	8	1	0	1	0	0
Emporia	0	0	0	0	0	0	0	0	0	0
Essex County	2	0	0	0	2	3	0	2	1	0
Fairfax City	0	0	0	0	0	0	0	0	0	0
Fairfax County	7	0	2	0	5	24	0	17	7	0
Falls Church	0	0	0	0	0	0	0	0	0	0
Fauquier County	0	0	0	0	0	1	0	1	0	0
Floyd County	0	0	0	0	0	1	0	0	1	0
Fluvanna County	1	0	0	0	1	1	0	1	0	0
Franklin	0	0	0	0	0	0	0	0	0	0
Franklin County	5	0	1	0	4	7	1	4	2	0
Frederick County	1	0	0	0	1	3	0	3	0	0
Fredericksburg	0	0	0	0	0	0	0	0	0	2
Galax	0	0	0	0	0	1	0	1	0	0
Giles County	0	0	0	0	0	2	0	2	0	0
Gloucester County	1	0	0	0	1	5	0	4	1	0
Goochland County	0	0	0	0	0	3	1	2	0	0
Grayson County	0	0	0	0	0	1	0	1	0	0
Greene County	0	0	0	0	0	0	0	0	0	0
Greensville County	3	0	0	0	3	0	0	0	0	0
Halifax County	0	0	0	0	0	11	1	9	1	0
Hampton	4	0	0	0	4	2	0	1	1	0
Hanover County	0	0	0	0	0	3	0	2	1	0
Harrisonburg	0	0	0	0	0	2	0	2	0	0
Henrico County	6	0	0	0	6	14	0	11	3	0
Henry County	1	0	0	1	0	5	0	4	1	0
Highland County	0	0	0	0	0	0	0	0	0	0
Hopewell	0	0	0	0	0	0	0	0	0	0
Isle of Wight County	0	0	0	0	0	0	0	0	0	0
James City County	0	0	0	0	0	0	0	0	0	1
King and Queen County	0	0	0	0	0	0	0	0	0	1
King George County	0	0	0	0	0	2	0	1	1	0
King William County	1	0	0	1	0	0	0	0	0	0
Lancaster County	1	0	0	0	1	0	0	0	0	0
Lee County	0	0	0	0	0	3	0	2	1	3
Lexington	0	0	0	0	0	0	0	0	0	0
Loudoun County	0	0	0	0	0	1	0	1	0	0
Louisa County	0	0	0	0	0	4	3	1	0	0
Lunenburg County	0	0	0	0	0	1	0	0	1	0
Lynchburg	0	0	0	0	0	1	0	1	0	0
Madison County	0	0	0	0	0	2	0	0	2	2
Manassas	0	0	0	0	0	0	0	0	0	0
Manassas Park	0	0	0	0	0	0	0	0	0	0
Martinsville	0	0	0	0	0	0	0	0	0	0
Mathews County	0	0	0	0	0	0	0	0	0	0
Mecklenburg County	0	0	0	0	0	3	0	1	2	0
Middlesex County	0	0	0	0	0	1	0	1	0	0
Montgomery County	1	0	0	0	1	1	0	1	0	2
Nelson County	0	0	0	0	0	0	0	0	0	0
New Kent County	0	0	0	0	0	0	0	0	0	0
Newport News	1	0	0	0	1	1	0	0	1	0
Norfolk	0	0	0	0	0	10	0	1	9	0
Northampton County	0	0	0	0	0	1	0	1	0	0
Northumberland County	0	0	0	0	0	1	0	1	0	0
Norton	0	0	0	0	0	0	0	0	0	0
Nottoway County	0	0	0	0	0	1	0	1	0	1
Orange County	1	0	1	0	0	1	0	0	1	0
Page County	0	0	0	0	0	2	0	1	1	0
Patrick County	0	0	0	0	0	1	0	1	0	1
Petersburg	0	0	0	0	0	0	0	0	0	0
Pittsylvania County	0	0	0	0	0	27	0	12	15	0
Poquoson	0	0	0	0	0	0	0	0	0	0
Portsmouth	0	0	0	0	0	4	0	0	4	0

Table 11. Offenses Known to Law Enforcement, by Selected State, Tribal, and Other Agencies, 2012— continued

(Number)

State/Other Agency Unit/Office	Violent crime	Murder and nonnegligent manslaughter	Forcible rape	Robbery	Aggravated assault	Property crime	Burglary	Larceny-theft	Motor vehicle theft	Arson[1]
Powhatan County	7	0	0	0	7	0	0	0	0	0
Prince Edward County	1	1	0	0	0	0	0	0	0	0
Prince George County	0	0	0	0	0	0	0	0	0	0
Prince William County	8	0	1	0	7	12	0	8	4	1
Pulaski County	0	0	0	0	0	7	0	7	0	0
Radford	0	0	0	0	0	0	0	0	0	0
Rappahannock County	0	0	0	0	0	0	0	0	0	0
Richmond	3	0	0	1	2	3	0	1	2	1
Richmond County	0	0	0	0	0	0	0	0	0	0
Roanoke	0	0	0	0	0	2	0	2	0	1
Roanoke County	5	0	2	0	3	3	0	3	0	0
Rockbridge County	0	0	0	0	0	2	0	1	1	1
Rockingham County	0	0	0	0	0	31	0	11	20	0
Russell County	1	1	0	0	0	0	0	0	0	1
Salem	0	0	0	0	0	2	0	2	0	0
Scott County	1	0	0	0	1	3	0	2	1	2
Shenandoah County	1	0	0	0	1	5	0	2	3	1
Smyth County	2	0	1	0	1	4	0	2	2	0
Southampton County	0	0	0	0	0	1	0	0	1	0
South Boston	0	0	0	0	0	0	0	0	0	0
Spotsylvania County	0	0	0	0	0	0	0	0	0	0
Stafford County	0	0	0	0	0	3	0	2	1	0
Staunton	0	0	0	0	0	0	0	0	0	0
Suffolk	0	0	0	0	0	2	0	1	1	0
Surry County	2	0	0	0	2	0	0	0	0	0
Sussex County	4	0	0	0	4	1	0	1	0	0
Tazewell County	2	0	1	0	1	2	0	2	0	5
Virginia Beach	0	0	0	0	0	10	0	7	3	0
Warren County	0	0	0	0	0	1	0	1	0	0
Washington County	3	0	0	0	3	3	0	2	1	0
Waynesboro	0	0	0	0	0	1	0	1	0	0
Westmoreland County	0	0	0	0	0	0	0	0	0	1
Williamsburg	0	0	0	0	0	0	0	0	0	0
Winchester	0	0	0	0	0	2	0	2	0	0
Wise County	1	0	0	0	1	3	0	3	0	1
Wythe County	0	0	0	0	0	21	0	17	4	0
York County	0	0	0	0	0	0	0	0	0	0
Virginia State Capitol	0	0	0	0	0	31	0	31	0	0
Other Agencies										
Norfolk Airport Authority	0	0	0	0	0	70	0	66	4	0
Port Authority, Norfolk	0	0	0	0	0	1	0	1	0	0
Reagan National Airport	1	0	0	1	0	495	1	420	74	0
Richmond International Airport	0	0	0	0	0	4	0	3	1	0
Washington										
State Agency										
State Patrol[2]	0	0	0	0	0	0	0	0	0	0
Tribal Agencies										
Chehalis Tribal	5	0	2	3	0	90	13	68	9	4
Colville Tribal	59	0	6	3	50	267	64	154	49	24
Hoh Tribal	2	0	0	0	2	2	0	2	0	0
Jamestown S'Klallam Tribal	1	0	0	0	1	12	0	9	3	0
Kalispel Tribal	46	0	3	3	40	92	20	62	10	0
La Push Tribal	7	0	1	2	4	24	19	4	1	0
Lower Elwha Tribal	6	0	1	1	4	15	13	0	2	0
Lummi Tribal	66	2	27	1	36	298	123	171	4	2
Port Gamble S'Klallam Tribal	5	0	1	1	3	46	14	27	5	0
Puyallup Tribal	34	0	8	16	10	583	102	304	177	2
Quinault Indian Nation	2	0	2	0	0	25	18	0	7	0
Sauk-Suiattle Tribal	1	0	1	0	0	10	5	5	0	0
Shoalwater Bay Tribal	0	0	0	0	0	2	0	2	0	0
Skokomish Tribal	3	0	0	0	3	21	11	5	5	0
Spokane Agency	24	0	0	0	24	49	35	0	14	6
Stillaguamish Tribal	0	0	0	0	0	51	1	46	4	0

Table 11. Offenses Known to Law Enforcement, by Selected State, Tribal, and Other Agencies, 2012— continued

(Number)

State/Other Agency Unit/Office	Violent crime	Murder and nonnegligent manslaughter	Forcible rape	Robbery	Aggravated assault	Property crime	Burglary	Larceny-theft	Motor vehicle theft	Arson[1]
Suquamish Tribal	18	0	1	0	17	153	41	94	18	0
Swinomish Tribal	1	0	1	0	0	81	32	49	0	0
Upper Skagit Tribal	2	0	1	1	0	13	3	6	4	0
Yakama Nation	24	1	7	0	16	623	242	278	103	8
Other Agency										
Port of Seattle	18	0	0	0	18	708	12	631	65	0
West Virginia										
State Agencies										
Division of Natural Resources	0	0	0	0	0	0	0	0	0	0
Barbour County	0	0	0	0	0	0	0	0	0	0
Berkeley County	0	0	0	0	0	0	0	0	0	0
Boone County	0	0	0	0	0	0	0	0	0	0
Brooke County	0	0	0	0	0	0	0	0	0	0
Cabell County	0	0	0	0	0	0	0	0	0	0
Calhoun County	0	0	0	0	0	0	0	0	0	0
Clay County	0	0	0	0	0	0	0	0	0	0
Doddridge County	0	0	0	0	0	0	0	0	0	0
Fayette County	0	0	0	0	0	0	0	0	0	0
Gilmer County	0	0	0	0	0	0	0	0	0	0
Grant County	0	0	0	0	0	0	0	0	0	0
Greenbrier County	0	0	0	0	0	0	0	0	0	0
Hampshire County	0	0	0	0	0	0	0	0	0	0
Hancock County	0	0	0	0	0	0	0	0	0	0
Hardy County	0	0	0	0	0	0	0	0	0	0
Harrison County	0	0	0	0	0	0	0	0	0	0
Jackson County	0	0	0	0	0	0	0	0	0	0
Jefferson County	0	0	0	0	0	0	0	0	0	0
Kanawha County	0	0	0	0	0	0	0	0	0	0
Lincoln County	0	0	0	0	0	0	0	0	0	0
Logan County	0	0	0	0	0	0	0	0	0	0
Marion County	0	0	0	0	0	0	0	0	0	0
Marshall County	0	0	0	0	0	0	0	0	0	0
Mason County	0	0	0	0	0	0	0	0	0	0
McDowell County	0	0	0	0	0	0	0	0	0	0
Mercer County	0	0	0	0	0	0	0	0	0	0
Mineral County	0	0	0	0	0	0	0	0	0	0
Mingo County	0	0	0	0	0	0	0	0	0	0
Monongalia County	0	0	0	0	0	0	0	0	0	0
Monroe County	0	0	0	0	0	0	0	0	0	0
Morgan County	0	0	0	0	0	0	0	0	0	0
Ohio County	0	0	0	0	0	0	0	0	0	0
Pendleton County	0	0	0	0	0	0	0	0	0	0
Pleasants County	0	0	0	0	0	0	0	0	0	0
Preston County	0	0	0	0	0	0	0	0	0	0
Putnam County	0	0	0	0	0	0	0	0	0	0
Raleigh County	0	0	0	0	0	0	0	0	0	0
Ritchie County	0	0	0	0	0	0	0	0	0	0
Roane County	0	0	0	0	0	0	0	0	0	0
Summers County	0	0	0	0	0	0	0	0	0	0
Taylor County	0	0	0	0	0	0	0	0	0	0
Tucker County	0	0	0	0	0	0	0	0	0	0
Tyler County	0	0	0	0	0	0	0	0	0	0
Wayne County	0	0	0	0	0	0	0	0	0	0
Wetzel County	0	0	0	0	0	0	0	0	0	0
Wirt County	0	0	0	0	0	0	0	0	0	0
Wood County	0	0	0	0	0	0	0	0	0	0
Wyoming County	0	0	0	0	0	0	0	0	0	0
State Fire Marshall										
Kanawha County	0	0	0	0	0	0	0	0	0	27
Preston County	0	0	0	0	0	0	0	0	0	0
State Police										
Beckley	32	0	2	4	26	317	83	213	21	1
Berkeley Springs	12	0	1	1	10	122	54	55	13	0

Table 11. Offenses Known to Law Enforcement, by Selected State, Tribal, and Other Agencies, 2012— continued

(Number)

State/Other Agency Unit/Office	Violent crime	Murder and nonnegligent manslaughter	Forcible rape	Robbery	Aggravated assault	Property crime	Burglary	Larceny-theft	Motor vehicle theft	Arson[1]
Bridgeport	4	0	2	0	2	189	53	119	17	0
Buckhannon	4	1	0	0	3	88	24	63	1	0
Clay	11	1	0	1	9	66	22	34	10	0
Elizabeth	6	0	0	0	6	51	26	23	2	0
Elkins	32	1	9	1	21	328	74	233	21	3
Fairmont	7	0	0	0	7	70	22	43	5	0
Franklin	5	0	0	0	5	52	36	13	3	1
Gauley Bridge	8	0	0	1	7	47	8	36	3	0
Gilbert	13	0	1	1	11	57	18	34	5	0
Glenville	8	0	0	0	8	29	4	22	3	0
Grafton	1	0	0	0	1	20	4	14	2	0
Grantsville	14	1	2	1	10	42	13	27	2	8
Hamlin	43	1	1	3	38	349	96	226	27	2
Harrisville	7	0	2	0	5	56	19	24	13	0
Hinton	4	0	0	0	4	67	38	25	4	0
Hundred	8	0	0	0	8	54	19	26	9	2
Huntington	27	0	0	5	22	635	83	524	28	1
Internet Crimes Against Children Unit	0	0	0	0	0	0	0	0	0	0
Jesse	6	0	1	0	5	37	6	26	5	1
Kearneysville	22	0	1	1	20	293	98	180	15	1
Keyser	36	0	6	1	29	231	87	129	15	1
Kingwood	34	1	4	2	27	135	45	75	15	3
Logan	94	0	7	8	79	444	94	298	52	0
Madison	25	0	0	1	24	217	48	151	18	1
Marlinton	17	0	2	0	15	59	20	37	2	1
Martinsburg	71	3	6	10	52	621	189	375	57	1
Moorefield	18	0	3	0	15	44	15	23	6	0
Morgantown	41	1	9	6	25	630	128	458	44	0
Moundsville	2	0	0	0	2	35	5	30	0	0
New Cumberland	6	0	2	1	3	16	1	15	0	0
Oak Hill	13	0	0	3	10	141	30	104	7	0
Paden City	10	0	1	0	9	33	16	14	3	2
Parkersburg	4	0	1	0	3	94	18	67	9	0
Parsons	2	0	1	0	1	30	9	20	1	0
Petersburg	9	0	1	0	8	44	17	22	5	0
Philippi	6	0	0	0	6	68	30	29	9	0
Point Pleasant	11	1	2	2	6	98	41	48	9	1
Princeton	35	1	3	5	26	491	130	312	49	1
Quincy	14	0	2	1	11	203	33	155	15	0
Rainelle	4	0	0	0	4	90	29	54	7	2
Richwood	4	0	0	0	4	33	5	27	1	1
Ripley	6	0	1	0	5	113	35	72	6	0
Romney	15	0	2	1	12	104	36	59	9	0
South Charleston	29	0	4	0	25	525	67	427	31	2
Spencer	10	0	2	0	8	57	24	29	4	2
St. Marys[3]	3	0	0	0	3			12	1	0
Summersville	5	0	1	0	4	41	10	28	3	5
Sutton	14	0	1	0	13	93	22	61	10	1
Union	7	0	1	1	5	39	15	20	4	0
Upperglade	29	3	0	1	25	58	25	29	4	0
Wayne	30	2	6	1	21	361	106	222	33	2
Welch[3]	34	0	6	1	27		57	99		2
Wellsburg	2	0	0	0	2	18	7	10	1	0
Weston	17	0	0	0	17	91	16	72	3	0
West Union	8	0	0	0	8	29	8	20	1	1
Wheeling	4	0	3	0	1	30	4	25	1	0
Whitesville	8	0	1	1	6	93	29	56	8	1
Williamson	45	2	1	2	40	165	43	100	22	1
Winfield	10	0	1	2	7	156	19	129	8	0
State Police, Bureau of Criminal Investigation										
Beckley	0	0	0	0	0	1	1	0	0	0
Bluefield	0	0	0	0	0	0	0	0	0	0
Buckhannon	0	0	0	0	0	0	0	0	0	0

Table 11. Offenses Known to Law Enforcement, by Selected State, Tribal, and Other Agencies, 2012— continued

(Number)

State/Other Agency Unit/Office	Violent crime	Murder and nonnegligent manslaughter	Forcible rape	Robbery	Aggravated assault	Property crime	Burglary	Larceny-theft	Motor vehicle theft	Arson[1]
Charleston	0	0	0	0	0	3	0	3	0	0
Fairmont	0	0	0	0	0	0	0	0	0	0
State Police, Parkway Authority										
Fayette County	0	0	0	0	0	0	0	0	0	0
Kanawha County	0	0	0	0	0	2	0	2	0	0
Mercer County	0	0	0	0	0	3	0	3	0	0
Raleigh County	0	0	0	0	0	8	0	8	0	0
Other Agencies										
Central West Virginia Drug Task Force	1	1	0	0	0	0	0	0	0	0
Eastern Panhandle Drug and Violent Crime Task Force	0	0	0	0	0	0	0	0	0	0
Hancock/Brooke/Weirton Drug Task Force	0	0	0	0	0	0	0	0	0	0
Harrison County Drug and Violent Crime Task Force	0	0	0	0	0	0	0	0	0	0
Huntington Drug and Violent Crime Task Force	1	0	0	0	1	1	0	1	0	0
Kanawha County Parks and Recreation	0	0	0	0	0	2	1	1	0	0
Logan County Drug and Violent Crime Task Force	0	0	0	0	0	1	0	1	0	0
Metropolitan Drug Enforcement Network Team	0	0	0	0	0	0	0	0	0	0
Ohio Valley Drug and Violent Crime Task Force	0	0	0	0	0	0	0	0	0	0
Parkersburg Narcotics and Violent Crime Task Force	0	0	0	0	0	0	0	0	0	0
Potomac Highlands Drug and Violent Crime Task Force	0	0	0	0	0	0	0	0	0	0
Three Rivers Drug and Violent Crime Task Force	0	0	0	0	0	0	0	0	0	0
Wisconsin										
State Agencies										
Capitol Police	0	0	0	0	0	100	2	98	0	0
Department of Natural Resources	0	0	0	0	0	0	0	0	0	0
Wisconsin State Patrol	0	0	0	0	0	0	0	0	0	0
Tribal Agencies										
Lac du Flambeau Tribal	39	0	4	1	34	355	72	272	11	0
Menominee Tribal	44	0	5	2	37	115	27	69	19	2
Oneida Tribal	15	0	1	0	14	99	26	68	5	1
St. Croix Tribal	1	0	0	0	1	45	9	31	5	0
Stockbridge Munsee Tribal	4	0	1	0	3	133	34	91	8	1
Wyoming										
Tribal Agency										
Wind River Agency	40	0	3	0	37	79	13	45	21	8

1 A blank cell in the arson column indicates that the FBI did not receive 12 complete months of arson data for that agency. 2 Because of changes in the state/local agency's reporting practices, figures are not comparable to previous years' data. 3 The FBI determined that the agency's data were overreported. Consequently, those data are not included in this table. 4 The data collection methodology for the offense of forcible rape used by the Minnesota state Uniform Crime Reporting (UCR) Program does not comply with national UCR Program guidelines. Consequently, its figures for forcible rape and violent crime (of which forcible rape is a part) are not published in this table.

Table 12. Crime Trends, by Population Group, 2011–2012

(Number, percent change)

Population group	Violent crime	Murder and nonnegligent manslaughter	Forcible rape	Robbery	Aggravated assault	Property crime	Burglary	Larceny-theft	Motor vehicle theft	Arson	Number of agencies	Estimated population, 2012
Total, All Agencies												
2011	1,144,896	13,993	76,332	341,608	712,963	8,497,732	2,045,019	5,760,018	[illegible]	51,400		
2012	1,153,016	14,168	76,233	341,680	720,935	8,412,497	1,965,533	5,757,766	689,198	51,500	15,091	296,448,440
Percent change	0.7	1.3	-0.1	*	1.1	-1.0	-3.9	-0.2	0.8	*		
Total, Cities												
2011	917,848	10,866	57,117	299,629	550,236	6,612,306	1,492,393	4,575,350	544,563	38,921		
2012	927,974	11,123	57,086	300,458	559,307	6,585,512	1,437,602	4,597,894	550,016	39,472	10,999	200,116,329
Percent change	1.1	2.4	-0.1	0.3	1.6	-0.4	-3.7	0.5	1.0	1.4		
Group I (250,000 and over)												
2011	416,837	5,591	18,364	162,554	230,328	2,113,634	505,616	1,353,301	254,717	13,686		
2012	427,038	5,830	18,716	164,631	237,861	2,105,693	480,366	1,370,050	255,277	13,150	75	56,306,634
Percent change	2.4	4.3	1.9	1.3	3.3	-0.4	-5.0	1.2	0.2	-3.9		
1,000,000 and over (Group I subset)												
2011	176,602	2,223	5,947	74,249	94,183	791,320	172,588	520,049	98,683	3,604		
2012	179,159	2,255	6,134	74,843	95,927	783,251	166,197	523,397	93,657	3,547	10	25,494,200
Percent change	1.4	1.4	3.1	0.8	1.9	-1.0	-3.7	0.6	-5.1	-1.6		
500,000 to 999,999 (Group I subset)												
2011	131,848	1,719	6,407	46,787	76,935	721,725	177,004	460,101	84,620	4,940		
2012	137,075	1,886	6,493	47,226	81,470	720,829	169,023	465,025	86,781	4,520	24	16,540,300
Percent change	4.0	9.7	1.3	0.9	5.9	-0.1	-4.5	1.1	2.6	-8.5		
250,000 to 499,999 (Group I subset)												
2011	108,387	1,649	6,010	41,518	59,210	600,589	156,024	373,151	71,414	5,142		
2012	110,804	1,689	6,089	42,562	60,464	601,613	145,146	381,628	74,839	5,083	41	14,272,134
Percent change	2.2	2.4	1.3	2.5	2.1	0.2	-7.0	2.3	4.8	-1.1		
Group II (100,000 to 249,999)												
2011	155,680	1,871	9,872	50,811	93,126	1,184,388	283,947	797,286	103,155	6,546		
2012	158,138	1,875	9,752	51,430	95,081	1,181,869	274,186	800,207	107,476	6,733	215	32,127,222
Percent change	1.6	0.2	-1.2	1.2	2.1	-0.2	-3.4	0.4	4.2	2.9		
Group III (50,000 to 99,999)												
2011	112,153	1,079	8,023	34,515	68,536	955,972	213,573	670,821	71,578	5,070		
2012	112,484	1,100	8,036	33,776	69,572	952,709	207,854	671,567	73,288	5,247	454	31,358,005
Percent change	0.3	1.9	0.2	-2.1	1.5	-0.3	-2.7	0.1	2.4	3.5		
Group IV (25,000 to 49,999)												
2011	87,164	872	7,732	23,530	55,030	839,653	177,620	614,572	47,461	4,122		
2012	85,801	936	7,484	23,041	54,340	832,839	171,529	614,582	46,728	4,538	828	28,600,336
Percent change	-1.6	7.3	-3.2	-2.1	-1.3	-0.8	-3.4	*	-1.5	10.1		
Group V (10,000 to 24,999)												
2011	77,877	787	6,874	17,543	52,673	801,201	169,020	593,921	38,260	3,585		
2012	76,658	766	6,834	16,926	52,132	799,108	164,116	597,089	37,903	3,574	1,786	28,412,426
Percent change	-1.6	-2.7	-0.6	-3.5	-1.0	-0.3	-2.9	0.5	-0.9	-0.3		
Group VI (under 10,000)												
2011	68,137	666	6,252	10,676	50,543	717,458	142,617	545,449	29,392	5,912		
2012	67,855	616	6,264	10,654	50,321	713,294	139,551	544,399	29,344	6,230	7,641	23,311,706
Percent change	-0.4	-7.5	0.2	-0.2	-0.4	-0.6	-2.1	-0.2	-0.2	5.4		
Metropolitan Counties												
2011	181,571	2,318	14,069	38,772	126,412	1,486,329	414,593	956,707	115,029	9,508		
2012	180,410	2,198	13,911	38,030	126,271	1,440,722	395,115	929,984	115,623	8,953	1,778	71,061,093
Percent change	-0.6	-5.2	-1.1	-1.9	-0.1	-3.1	-4.7	-2.8	0.5	-5.8		
Nonmetropolitan Counties [1]												
2011	45,477	809	5,146	3,207	36,315	399,097	138,033	236,991	24,073	3,059		
2012	44,632	847	5,236	3,192	35,357	386,263	132,816	229,888	23,559	3,075	2,314	25,271,018
Percent change	-1.9	4.7	1.7	-0.5	-2.6	-3.2	-3.8	-3.0	-2.1	0.5		
Suburban Areas [2]												
2011	327,061	3,677	26,272	75,042	222,070	3,042,697	723,602	2,121,293	197,802	17,076		
2012	323,450	3,590	25,963	73,694	220,203	2,988,958	695,245	2,096,435	197,278	16,669	8,267	129,683,417
Percent change	-1.1	-2.4	-1.2	-1.8	-0.8	-1.8	-3.9	-1.2	-0.3	-2.4		

1 Includes state police agencies that report aggregately for the entire state. 2 Suburban areas include law enforcement agencies in cities with less than 50,000 inhabitants and county law enforcement agencies that are within a Metropolitan Statistical Area. Suburban areas exclude all metropolitan agencies associated with a principal city. The agencies associated with suburban areas also appear in other groups within this table.
* = Less than one-tenth of 1 percent.

Table 13. Crime Trends, by Suburban and Nonsuburban Cities, by Population Group, 2011–2012[1]

(Number, percent change)

Population group	Violent crime	Murder and nonnegligent manslaughter	Forcible rape	Robbery	Aggravated assault	Property crime	Burglary	Larceny-theft	Motor vehicle theft	Arson	Number of agencies	Estimated population, 2012
Suburban Cities												
2011	145,459	1,359	12,172	36,270	95,658	1,556,368	309,009	1,164,586	82,773	7,532		
2012	143,019	1,392	12,031	35,664	93,932	1,548,236	300,130	1,166,451	81,655	7,652	6,489	58,622,324
Percent change	-1.7	2.4	-1.2	-1.7	-1.8	-0.5	-2.9	0.2	-1.4	1.6		
Group IV (25,000 to 49,999)												
2011	56,621	557	4,638	15,893	35,533	568,483	116,991	416,283	35,209	2,503		
2012	55,909	572	4,510	15,821	35,006	565,929	113,421	418,020	34,488	2,677	647	22,202,159
Percent change	-1.3	2.7	-2.8	-0.5	-1.5	-0.4	-3.1	0.4	-2.0	7.0		
Group V (10,000 to 24,999)												
2011	49,605	483	4,160	12,787	32,175	534,053	109,176	396,221	28,656	2,316		
2012	48,304	509	4,154	12,318	31,323	532,139	105,749	397,905	28,485	2,325	1,354	21,737,741
Percent change	-2.6	5.4	-0.1	-3.7	-2.6	-0.4	-3.1	0.4	-0.6	0.4		
Group VI (under 10,000)												
2011	39,233	319	3,374	7,590	27,950	453,832	82,842	352,082	18,908	2,713		
2012	38,806	311	3,367	7,525	27,603	450,168	80,960	350,526	18,682	2,650	4,488	14,682,424
Percent change	-1.1	-2.5	-0.2	-0.9	-1.2	-0.8	-2.3	-0.4	-1.2	-2.3		
Nonsuburban Cities												
2011	88,021	967	8,708	15,530	62,816	804,542	180,680	591,344	32,518	6,101		
2012	87,819	933	8,585	15,035	63,266	801,216	175,876	592,828	32,512	6,717	3,769	21,797,062
Percent change	-0.2	-3.5	-1.4	-3.2	0.7	-0.4	-2.7	0.3	*	10.1		
Group IV (25,000 to 49,999)												
2011	30,711	316	3,105	7,652	19,638	272,704	60,846	199,479	12,379	1,629		
2012	30,227	365	2,987	7,243	19,632	269,533	58,583	198,550	12,400	1,882	183	6,475,420
Percent change	-1.6	15.5	-3.8	-5.3	*	-1.2	-3.7	-0.5	0.2	15.5		
Group V (10,000 to 24,999)												
2011	28,406	304	2,725	4,792	20,585	268,212	60,059	198,498	9,655	1,273		
2012	28,543	263	2,701	4,663	20,916	268,557	58,702	200,405	9,450	1,255	433	6,692,360
Percent change	0.5	-13.5	-0.9	-2.7	1.6	0.1	-2.3	1.0	-2.1	-1.4		
Group VI (under 10,000)												
2011	28,904	347	2,878	3,086	22,593	263,626	59,775	193,367	10,484	3,199		
2012	29,049	305	2,897	3,129	22,718	263,126	58,591	193,873	10,662	3,580	3,153	8,629,282
Percent change	1	-12	1	1	1	0	-2	0	2	12		

1 Suburban cities include law enforcement agencies in cities with less than 50,000 inhabitants that are within a Metropolitan Statistical Area. Suburban cities exclude all metropolitan agencies associated with a principal city. Nonsuburban cities include law enforcement agencies in cities with less than 50,000 inhabitants that are not associated with a Metropolitan Statistical Area. * = Less than one-tenth of 1 percent.

Table 14. Crime Trends, by Metropolitan and Nonmetropolitan Counties, by Population Group, 2011–2012[1]

(Number, percent change)

Population group and range	Violent crime	Murder and nonnegligent manslaughter	Forcible rape	Robbery	Aggravated assault	Property crime	Burglary	Larceny-theft	Motor vehicle theft	Arson	Number of agencies	Estimated population, 2012
Metropolitan Counties												
100,000 and over												
2011	124,890	1,541	8,157	32,474	82,718	968,280	257,404	634,619	76,257	5,855		
2012	124,960	1,500	8,143	31,958	83,359	938,926	245,668	616,917	76,341	5,425	164	42,951,469
Percent change	0.1	-2.7	-0.2	-1.6	0.8	-3.0	-4.6	-2.8	0.1	-7.3		
25,000 to 99,999												
2011	41,849	592	4,315	4,598	32,344	390,780	125,050	243,683	22,047	2,246		
2012	40,621	530	4,236	4,306	31,549	376,928	119,087	236,809	21,032	2,261	444	23,204,448
Percent change	-2.9	-10.5	-1.8	-6.4	-2.5	-3.5	-4.8	-2.8	-4.6	0.7		
Under 25,000												
2011	14,560	183	1,512	1,673	11,192	123,542	30,921	76,049	16,572	1,392		
2012	14,960	165	1,474	1,754	11,567	121,502	29,397	73,969	18,136	1,247	1,155	4,624,728
Percent change	2.7	-9.8	-2.5	4.8	3.4	-1.7	-4.9	-2.7	9.4	-10.4		
Nonmetropolitan Counties												
25,000 and over												
2011	18,840	289	1,896	1,714	14,941	176,760	63,158	103,709	9,893	1,105		
2012	18,327	298	2,010	1,678	14,341	170,830	60,352	101,210	9,268	1,085	277	10,537,737
Percent change	-2.7	3.1	6.0	-2.1	-4.0	-3.4	-4.4	-2.4	-6.3	-1.8		
10,000 to 24,999												
2011	14,853	275	1,465	870	12,243	133,557	45,304	80,621	7,632	991		
2012	14,981	271	1,493	870	12,347	128,370	43,817	77,001	7,552	987	580	9,403,854
Percent change	0.9	-1.5	1.9	0.0	0.8	-3.9	-3.3	-4.5	-1.0	-0.4		
Under 10,000												
2011	8,350	150	1,163	315	6,722	64,059	20,505	38,991	4,563	629		
2012	8,109	148	1,135	328	6,498	62,019	19,385	37,860	4,774	674	1,294	4,199,830
Percent change	-2.9	-1.3	-2.4	4.1	-3.3	-3.2	-5.5	-2.9	4.6	7.2		

1 Metropolitan counties include sheriffs and county law enforcement agencies associated with a Metropolitan Statistical Area. Nonmetropolitan counties include sheriffs and county law enforcement agencies that are not associated with a Metropolitan Statistical Area. The offenses from state police agencies are not included in this table.

Table 15. Crime Trends, Additional Information About Selected Offenses, by Population Group, 2011–2012

(Number, percent change)

Population group	Forcible rape		Robbery				Aggravated assault				Burglary		
	Rape by force	Assault to rape-attempts	Firearm	Knife or cutting instrument	Other weapon	Strong-arm	Firearm	Knife or cutting instrument	Other weapon	Hands, fists, feet, etc.	Forcible entry	Unlawful entry	Attempted forcible entry
Total, All Agencies													
2011	67,019	5,039	123,834	23,339	25,956	126,459	136,754	123,489	213,429	176,153	1,170,654	641,052	122,700
2012	66,582	4,732	122,974	23,338	26,255	127,537	142,568	123,344	214,626	177,782	1,109,117	634,636	119,819
Percent change	-0.7	-6.1	-0.7	*	1.2	0.9	4.3	-0.1	0.6	0.9	-5.3	-1.0	-2.3
Total, Cities													
2011	49,417	4,002	105,470	20,250	21,951	110,392	106,729	97,645	159,490	126,697	841,697	458,477	93,771
2012	49,603	3,926	104,859	20,239	22,283	111,924	112,066	97,638	161,507	127,577	799,013	455,698	92,166
Percent change	0.4	-1.9	-0.6	-0.1	1.5	1.4	5.0	*	1.3	0.7	-5.1	-0.6	-1.7
Group I (250,000 and over)													
2011	15,519	1,620	56,584	9,252	9,372	52,338	53,224	37,867	63,742	31,678	308,962	118,018	28,071
2012	15,801	1,644	57,045	9,407	9,653	53,865	56,449	38,288	65,601	32,455	291,015	116,231	27,036
Percent change	1.8	1.5	0.8	1.7	3.0	2.9	6.1	1.1	2.9	2.5	-5.8	-1.5	-3.7
1,000,000 and over (Group I subset)													
2011	4,249	606	16,910	3,400	3,166	17,025	13,823	11,603	18,298	8,222	87,994	33,100	6,915
2012	4,380	592	17,072	3,471	3,225	17,398	14,265	11,624	18,405	8,150	86,764	31,529	6,521
Percent change	3.1	-2.3	1.0	2.1	1.9	2.2	3.2	0.2	0.6	-0.9	-1.4	-4.7	-5.7
500,000 to 999,999 (Group I subset)													
2011	5,878	529	21,381	3,449	3,618	18,339	21,092	15,995	27,613	12,235	122,496	42,551	11,957
2012	5,934	559	21,237	3,495	3,632	18,862	22,900	16,063	29,018	13,489	113,105	44,092	11,826
Percent change	1.0	5.7	-0.7	1.3	0.4	2.9	8.6	0.4	5.1	10.2	-7.7	3.6	-1.1
250,000 to 499,999 (Group I subset)													
2011	5,392	485	18,293	2,403	2,588	16,974	18,309	10,269	17,831	11,221	98,472	42,367	9,199
2012	5,487	493	18,736	2,441	2,796	17,605	19,284	10,601	18,178	10,816	91,146	40,610	8,689
Percent change	1.8	1.6	2.4	1.6	8.0	3.7	5.3	3.2	1.9	-3.6	-7.4	-4.1	-5.5
Group II (100,000 to 249,999)													
2011	8,752	580	20,104	3,865	4,445	20,124	20,133	19,182	30,088	19,116	161,439	88,024	19,394
2012	8,707	582	20,002	3,889	4,499	20,683	21,469	19,071	30,538	19,379	152,016	89,031	19,369
Percent change	-0.5	0.3	-0.5	0.6	1.2	2.8	6.6	-0.6	1.5	1.4	-5.8	1.1	-0.1
Group III (50,000 to 99,999)													
2011	7,236	440	11,505	3,049	3,243	15,648	11,726	13,720	21,976	18,927	118,405	74,309	14,211
2012	7,306	408	10,926	3,005	3,393	15,371	12,147	13,624	22,122	19,515	112,846	73,995	14,661
Percent change	1.0	-7.3	-5.0	-1.4	4.6	-1.8	3.6	-0.7	0.7	3.1	-4.7	-0.4	3.2
Group IV (25,000 to 49,999)													
2011	6,600	445	7,743	1,844	2,236	10,113	8,355	10,053	16,235	16,308	93,881	61,356	11,914
2012	6,450	398	7,534	1,815	2,188	10,072	8,583	9,929	15,811	16,167	89,799	60,418	11,558
Percent change	-2.3	-10.6	-2.7	-1.6	-2.1	-0.4	2.7	-1.2	-2.6	-0.9	-4.3	-1.5	-3.0
Group V (10,000 to 24,999)													
2011	5,910	359	6,033	1,405	1,713	7,170	7,481	8,992	15,262	18,169	86,927	61,220	10,433
2012	5,923	360	5,790	1,226	1,638	7,006	7,660	8,846	14,989	18,040	83,318	60,946	10,082
Percent change	0.2	0.3	-4.0	-12.7	-4.4	-2.3	2.4	-1.6	-1.8	-0.7	-4.2	-0.4	-3.4
Group VI (under 10,000)													
2011	5,400	558	3,501	835	942	4,999	5,810	7,831	12,187	22,499	72,083	55,550	9,748
2012	5,416	534	3,562	897	912	4,927	5,758	7,880	12,446	22,021	70,019	55,077	9,460
Percent change	0.3	-4.3	1.7	7.4	-3.2	-1.4	-0.9	0.6	2.1	-2.1	-2.9	-0.9	-3.0
Metropolitan Counties													
2011	12,819	780	17,057	2,814	3,610	14,872	23,826	20,846	43,535	35,424	246,044	135,206	23,518
2012	12,109	538	16,831	2,783	3,578	14,438	24,151	20,898	43,161	36,574	230,315	133,212	22,534
Percent change	-5.5	-31.0	-1.3	-1.1	-0.9	-2.9	1.4	0.2	-0.9	3.2	-6.4	-1.5	-4.2
Nonmetropolitan Counties													
2011	4,783	257	1,307	275	395	1,195	6,199	4,998	10,404	14,032	82,913	47,369	5,411
2012	4,870	268	1,284	316	394	1,175	6,351	4,808	9,958	13,631	79,789	45,726	5,119
Percent change	1.8	4.3	-1.8	14.9	-0.3	-1.7	2.5	-3.8	-4.3	-2.9	-3.8	-3.5	-5.4
Suburban Areas [1]													
2011	23,215	1,530	29,006	5,613	6,849	30,534	36,157	36,408	70,647	69,840	403,483	246,537	44,862
2012	22,947	1,303	28,531	5,468	6,752	30,052	36,895	36,295	69,763	69,937	382,012	242,833	43,432
Percent change	-1.2	-14.8	-1.6	-2.6	-1.4	-1.6	2.0	-0.3	-1.3	0.1	-5.3	-1.5	-3.2

Table 15. Crime Trends, Additional Information About Selected Offenses, by Population Group, 2011–2012

(Number, percent change)

Population group	Motor vehicle theft			Arson			Number of agencies	Estimated population, 2012
	Autos	Trucks and buses	Other vehicles	Structure	Mobile	Other		
Total, All Agencies								
2011	471,638	102,557	67,001	21,237	11,131	13,796		
2012	481,512	99,604	71,088	21,919	10,760	14,513	14,398	274,808,793
Percent change	2.1	-2.9	6.1	3.2	-3.3	5.2		
Total, Cities								
2011	381,590	78,501	43,840	16,058	8,055	10,487		
2012	389,613	76,554	48,050	16,632	7,838	11,184	10,419	180,921,466
Percent change	2.1	-2.5	9.6	3.6	-2.7	6.6		
Group I (250,000 and over)								
2011	165,128	43,724	14,868	6,017	3,653	3,337		
2012	170,284	41,991	16,215	6,007	3,498	3,411	72	45,057,321
Percent change	3.1	-4.0	9.1	-0.2	-4.2	2.2		
1,000,000 and over (Group I subset)								
2011	44,702	19,204	5,897	1,289	1,131	1,146		
2012	43,313	19,048	6,105	1,274	1,077	1,196	8	14,496,403
Percent change	-3.1	-0.8	3.5	-1.2	-4.8	4.4		
500,000 to 999,999 (Group I subset)								
2011	66,051	13,614	4,955	2,318	1,365	945		
2012	67,321	13,752	5,708	2,212	1,230	940	24	16,540,300
Percent change	1.9	1.0	15.2	-4.6	-9.9	-0.5		
250,000 to 499,999 (Group I subset)								
2011	54,375	10,906	4,016	2,410	1,157	1,246		
2012	59,650	9,191	4,402	2,521	1,191	1,275	40	14,020,618
Percent change	9.7	-15.7	9.6	4.6	2.9	2.3		
Group II (100,000 to 249,999)								
2011	76,989	14,397	8,520	2,615	1,396	1,737		
2012	79,544	14,626	10,279	2,864	1,402	1,958	207	30,872,288
Percent change	3.3	1.6	20.6	9.5	0.4	12.7		
Group III (50,000 to 99,999)								
2011	54,988	8,473	6,846	2,103	1,140	1,551		
2012	56,224	8,431	7,442	2,318	1,081	1,535	433	29,965,640
Percent change	2.2	-0.5	8.7	10.2	-5.2	-1.0		
Group IV (25,000 to 49,999)								
2011	35,249	4,688	5,297	1,619	674	1,382		
2012	34,372	4,541	5,790	1,767	721	1,568	769	26,628,962
Percent change	-2.5	-3.1	9.3	9.1	7.0	13.5		
Group V (10,000 to 24,999)								
2011	27,920	4,166	4,175	1,519	655	1,089		
2012	27,582	4,046	4,374	1,593	598	1,050	1658	26,274,300
Percent change	-1.2	-2.9	4.8	4.9	-8.7	-3.6		
Group VI (under 10,000)								
2011	21,316	3,053	4,134	2,185	537	1,391		
2012	21,607	2,919	3,950	2,083	538	1,662	7280	22,122,955
Percent change	1.4	-4.4	-4.5	-4.7	0.2	19.5		
Metropolitan Counties								
2011	75,268	20,225	17,944	3,610	2,496	2,626		
2012	77,182	19,320	18,151	3,713	2,326	2,630	1,723	69,304,933
Percent change	2.5	-4.5	1.2	2.9	-6.8	0.2		
Nonmetropolitan Counties								
2011	14,780	3,831	5,217	1,569	580	683		
2012	14,717	3,720	4,887	1,574	596	699	2,256	24,582,394
Percent change	-0.4	-2.9	-6.3	0.3	2.8	2.3		
Suburban Areas [1]								
2011	135,958	28,903	27,044	6,547	3,584	4,875		
2012	137,279	27,702	27,347	6,633	3,402	5,022	7,818	123,622,613
Percent change	1.0	-4.2	1.1	1.3	-5.1	3.0		

1 Suburban areas include law enforcement agencies in cities with less than 50,000 inhabitants and county law enforcement agencies that are within a Metropolitan Statistical Area. Suburban areas exclude all metropolitan agencies associated with a principal city. The agencies associated with suburban areas also appear in other groups within this table.

Table 16. Number and Rate of Violent Crimes Per 100,000 Population, by Population Group, 2012

(Number, rate)

Population group	Violent crime		Murder and nonnegligent manslaughter		Forcible rape		Robbery		Aggravated assault	
	Number of offenses known	Rate	Number of offenses known	Rate	Number of offenses known	Rate	Number of offenses known	Rate	Number of offenses known	Rate
Total, All Agencies	1,152,921	394.4	14,173	4.8	78,174	26.7	339,997	116.3	720,577	246.5
Total, Cities	929,366	468.5	11,096	5.6	58,894	29.7	298,817	150.6	560,559	282.6
Group I (250,000 and over)	422,469	769.4	5,777	10.5	18,963	34.5	162,260	295.5	235,469	428.8
1,000,000 and over (Group I subset)	179,888	705.6	2,255	8.8	6,863	26.9	74,843	293.6	95,927	376.3
500,000 to 999,999 (Group I subset)	131,639	869.2	1,831	12.1	6,007	39.7	44,804	295.8	78,997	521.6
250,000 to 499,999 (Group I subset)	110,942	777.3	1,691	11.8	6,093	42.7	42,613	298.6	60,545	424.2
Group II (100,000 to 249,999)	157,242	494.1	1,857	5.8	9,794	30.8	51,036	160.4	94,555	297.1
Group III (50,000 to 99,999)	114,810	364.5	1,122	3.6	8,434	26.8	34,060	108.1	71,194	226.0
Group IV (25,000 to 49,999)	89,589	306.4	956	3.3	7,862	26.9	23,748	81.2	57,023	195.0
Group V (10,000 to 24,999)	77,627	273.5	785	2.8	7,137	25.1	17,107	60.3	52,598	185.3
Group VI (under 10,000)	67,629	300.2	599	2.7	6,704	29.8	10,606	47.1	49,720	220.7
Metropolitan Counties	179,920	258.6	2,249	3.2	13,917	20.0	38,081	54.7	125,673	180.6
Nonmetropolitan Counties [1]	43,635	179.2	828	3.4	5,363	22.0	3,099	12.7	34,345	141.0
Suburban Areas [2]	323,732	252.6	3,647	2.8	26,320	20.5	74,103	57.8	219,662	171.4

1 Includes state police agencies that report aggregately for the entire state. 2 Suburban areas include law enforcement agencies in cities with less than 50,000 inhabitants and county law enforcement agencies that are within a Metropolitan Statistical Area. Suburban areas exclude all metropolitan agencies associated with a principal city. The agencies associated with suburban areas also appear in other groups within this table.

Table 16A. Number and Rate of Property Crimes Per 100,000 Population, by Population Group, 2012

(Number, rate)

Population group	Property crime		Burglary		Larceny-theft		Motor vehicle theft		Number of agencies	Estimated population, 2012
	Number of offenses known	Rate	Number of offenses known	Rate	Number of offenses known	Rate	Number of offenses known	Rate		
Total, All Agencies	8,400,371	2,873.8	1,959,909	670.5	5,754,377	1,968.6	686,085	234.7	14,651	292,313,576
Total, Cities	6,591,485	3,322.7	1,434,809	723.3	4,609,737	2,323.7	546,939	275.7	10,659	198,379,015
Group I (250,000 and over)	2,081,272	3,790.2	469,380	854.8	1,361,784	2,480.0	250,108	455.5	73	54,911,213
1,000,000 and over (Group I subset)	783,251	3,072.3	166,197	651.9	523,397	2,053.0	93,657	367.4	10	25,494,200
500,000 to 999,999 (Group I subset)	687,391	4,538.8	157,706	1,041.3	448,124	2,958.9	81,561	538.5	22	15,144,879
250,000 to 499,999 (Group I subset)	610,630	4,278.5	145,477	1,019.3	390,263	2,734.4	74,890	524.7	41	14,272,134
Group II (100,000 to 249,999)	1,171,472	3,681.1	271,985	854.7	792,744	2,491.0	106,743	335.4	213	31,823,848
Group III (50,000 to 99,999)	962,685	3,056.5	210,344	667.8	678,456	2,154.0	73,885	234.6	455	31,496,825
Group IV (25,000 to 49,999)	861,266	2,945.3	177,838	608.2	634,836	2,171.0	48,592	166.2	846	29,242,075
Group V (10,000 to 24,999)	808,147	2,847.8	167,107	588.9	602,448	2,122.9	38,592	136.0	1,779	28,378,392
Group VI (under 10,000)	706,643	3,136.9	138,155	613.3	539,469	2,394.8	29,019	128.8	7,293	22,526,662
Metropolitan Counties	1,430,919	2,056.4	395,026	567.7	920,152	1,322.4	115,741	166.3	1,741	69,583,617
Nonmetropolitan Counties [1]	377,967	1,552.2	130,074	534.2	224,488	921.9	23,405	96.1	2,251	24,350,944
Suburban Areas [2]	2,994,269	2,336.5	699,364	545.7	2,095,865	1,635.5	199,040	155.3	8,054	128,150,344

1 Includes state police agencies that report aggregately for the entire state. 2 Suburban areas include law enforcement agencies in cities with less than 50,000 inhabitants and county law enforcement agencies that are within a Metropolitan Statistical Area. Suburban areas exclude all metropolitan agencies associated with a principal city. The agencies associated with suburban areas also appear in other groups within this table.

Table 17. Number and Rate of Violent Crimes Per 100,000 Inhabitants, by Suburban and Nonsuburban Cities, by Population Group, 2012[1]

(Number, rate)

Population group	Violent crime		Murder and nonnegligent manslaughter		Forcible rape		Robbery		Aggravated assault	
	Number of offenses known	Rate	Number of offenses known	Rate	Number of offenses known	Rate	Number of offenses known	Rate	Number of offenses known	Rate
Total, Suburban Cities	143,829	245.6	1,398	2.4	12,420	21.2	36,022	61.5	93,989	160.5
Group IV (25,000 to 49,999)	57,375	253.7	583	2.6	4,768	21.1	16,213	71.7	35,811	158.4
Group V (10,000 to 24,999)	48,499	222.8	512	2.4	4,300	19.8	12,349	56.7	31,338	144.0
Group VI (under 10,000)	37,955	267.5	303	2.1	3,352	23.6	7,460	52.6	26,840	189.2
Total, Nonsuburban Cities	91,016	421.8	942	4.4	9,283	43.0	15,439	71.5	65,352	302.8
Group IV (25,000 to 49,999)	32,214	485.8	373	5.6	3,094	46.7	7,535	113.6	21,212	319.9
Group V (10,000 to 24,999)	29,128	440.7	273	4.1	2,837	42.9	4,758	72.0	21,260	321.7
Group VI (under 10,000)	29,674	355.8	296	3.5	3,352	40.2	3,146	37.7	22,880	274.3

1 Suburban cities include law enforcement agencies in cities with less than 50,000 inhabitants that are within a Metropolitan Statistical Area. Suburban cities exclude all metropolitan agencies associated with a principal city. Nonsuburban cities include law enforcement agencies in cities with less than 50,000 inhabitants that are not associated with a Metropolitan Statistical Area.

Table 17A. Number and Rate of Property Crimes Per 100,000 Inhabitants, by Suburban and Nonsuburban Cities, by Population Group, 2012[1]

(Number, rate)

Population group	Property crime		Burglary		Larceny-theft		Motor vehicle theft		Number of agencies	Estimated population, 2012
	Number of offenses known	Rate	Number of offenses known	Rate	Number of offenses known	Rate	Number of offenses known	Rate		
Total, Suburban Cities	1,563,350	[illegible]	[illegible]	[illegible]	1,175,713	[illegible]	[illegible]	[illegible]	[illegible]	[illegible]
Group IV (25,000 to 49,999)	580,427	2,567.0	116,828	516.7	427,845	1,892.2	35,754	158.1	659	22,611,079
Group V (10,000 to 24,999)	537,597	2,469.5	107,788	495.1	400,671	1,840.6	29,138	133.9	1,353	21,769,084
Group VI (under 10,000)	445,326	3,139.1	79,722	562.0	347,197	2,447.4	18,407	129.7	4,301	14,186,564
Total, Nonsuburban Cities	812,706	3,765.9	178,762	828.4	601,040	2,785.1	32,904	152.5	3,605	21,580,402
Group IV (25,000 to 49,999)	280,839	4,235.2	61,010	920.1	206,991	3,121.6	12,838	193.6	187	6,630,996
Group V (10,000 to 24,999)	270,550	4,093.5	59,319	897.5	201,777	3,052.9	9,454	143.0	426	6,609,308
Group VI (under 10,000)	261,317	3,133.3	58,433	700.6	192,272	2,305.4	10,612	127.2	2,992	8,340,098

1 Suburban cities include law enforcement agencies in cities with less than 50,000 inhabitants that are within a Metropolitan Statistical Area. Suburban cities exclude all metropolitan agencies associated with a principal city. Nonsuburban cities include law enforcement agencies in cities with less than 50,000 inhabitants that are not associated with a Metropolitan Statistical Area.

Table 18. Number and Rate of Violent Crimes Per 100,000 Inhabitants, by Metropolitan and Nonmetropolitan Counties, by Population Group, 2012[1]

(Number, rate)

Population group	Violent crime		Murder and nonnegligent manslaughter		Forcible rape		Robbery		Aggravated assault	
	Number of offenses known	Rate	Number of offenses known	Rate	Number of offenses known	Rate	Number of offenses known	Rate	Number of offenses known	Rate
Metropolitan Counties										
100,000 and over	121,642	293.2	1,489	3.6	7,927	19.1	31,488	75.9	80,738	194.6
25,000 to 99,999	42,675	183.7	578	2.5	4,357	18.8	4,749	20.4	32,991	142.0
Under 25,000	15,603	320.6	182	3.7	1,633	33.6	1,844	37.9	11,944	245.4
Nonmetropolitan Counties										
25,000 and over	17,912	175.3	292	2.9	1,987	19.4	1,649	16.1	13,984	136.8
10,000 to 24,999	14,835	163.1	266	2.9	1,572	17.3	866	9.5	12,131	133.4
Under 10,000	7,902	195.1	142	3.5	1,167	28.8	322	7.9	6,271	154.8

1 Metropolitan counties include sheriffs and county law enforcement agencies associated with a Metropolitan Statistical Area. Nonmetropolitan counties include sheriffs and county law enforcement agencies that are not associated with a Metropolitan Statistical Area. The offenses from state police agencies are not included in this table.

Table 18A. Number and Rate of Property Crimes Per 100,000 Inhabitants, by Metropolitan and Nonmetropolitan Counties, by Population Group, 2012[1]

(Number, rate)

Population group	Property crime		Burglary		Larceny-theft		Motor vehicle theft		Number of agencies	Estimated population, 2012
	Number of offenses known	Rate	Number of offenses known	Rate	Number of offenses known	Rate	Number of offenses known	Rate		
Metropolitan Counties										
100,000 and over	916,667	2,209.3	241,374	581.7	600,670	1,447.7	74,613	179.8	159	41,491,299
25,000 to 99,999	386,882	1,665.8	122,260	526.4	241,967	1,041.8	22,655	97.5	442	23,225,322
Under 25,000	127,370	2,617.0	31,392	645.0	77,505	1,592.5	18,473	379.6	1,140	4,866,996
Nonmetropolitan Counties										
25,000 and over	168,264	1,646.3	59,522	582.4	99,513	973.7	9,229	90.3	268	10,220,449
10,000 to 24,999	127,290	1,399.4	43,442	477.6	76,308	838.9	7,540	82.9	562	9,096,220
Under 10,000	61,206	1,511.0	18,993	468.9	37,282	920.4	4,931	121.7	1,259	4,050,755

1 Metropolitan counties include sheriffs and county law enforcement agencies associated with a Metropolitan Statistical Area. Nonmetropolitan counties include sheriffs and county law enforcement agencies that are not associated with a Metropolitan Statistical Area. The offenses from state police agencies are not included in this table.

Table 19. Number and Rate of Crimes Per 100,000 Inhabitants, Additional Information About Selected Offenses, by Population Group, 2012

(Number, rate)

Population group	Forcible rape		Robbery				Aggravated assault				Burglary		
	Rape by force	Assault to rape-attempts	Firearm	Knife or cutting instrument	Other weapon	Strong-arm	Firearm	Knife or cutting instrument	Other weapon	Hands, fists, feet, etc.	Forcible entry	Unlawful entry	Attempted forcible entry
Total, All Agencies													
Number of offenses known	68,655	4,942	122,174	23,167	26,270	126,600	143,119	123,701	214,484	176,241	1,111,849	631,788	118,044
Rate	25.3	1.8	45.1	8.5	9.7	46.7	52.8	45.6	79.1	65.0	410.2	233.1	43.5
Total, Cities													
Number of offenses known	50,801	3,958	103,849	20,101	22,223	111,093	112,325	98,148	161,642	127,301	799,024	454,124	90,723
Rate	28.4	2.2	58.0	11.2	12.4	62.1	62.7	54.8	90.3	71.1	446.3	253.7	50.7
Group I (250,000 and over)													
Number of offenses known	15,294	1,597	55,845	9,203	9,408	52,602	55,751	37,715	64,405	31,774	282,866	113,248	25,664
Rate	35.3	3.7	129.0	21.3	21.7	121.5	128.8	87.1	148.7	73.4	653.3	261.5	59.3
1,000,000 and over (Group I subset)													
Number of offenses known	4,380	592	17,072	3,471	3,225	17,398	14,265	11,624	18,405	8,150	86,764	31,529	6,521
Rate	30.2	4.1	117.8	23.9	22.2	120.0	98.4	80.2	127.0	56.2	598.5	217.5	45.0
500,000 to 999,999 (Group I subset)													
Number of offenses known	5,486	521	20,316	3,307	3,431	17,750	22,363	15,603	28,152	12,879	106,093	41,115	10,498
Rate	36.2	3.4	134.1	21.8	22.7	117.2	147.7	103.0	185.9	85.0	700.5	271.5	69.3
250,000 to 499,999 (Group I subset)													
Number of offenses known	5,428	484	18,457	2,425	2,752	17,454	19,123	10,488	17,848	10,745	90,009	40,604	8,645
Rate	39.7	3.5	135.1	17.8	20.1	127.8	140.0	76.8	130.7	78.7	659.0	297.3	63.3
Group II (100,000 to 249,999)													
Number of offenses known	8,742	589	19,683	3,877	4,522	20,599	21,111	19,046	30,383	19,414	150,867	88,076	19,329
Rate	28.6	1.9	64.4	12.7	14.8	67.4	69.1	62.3	99.4	63.5	493.5	288.1	63.2
Group III (50,000 to 99,999)													
Number of offenses known	7,685	410	11,041	3,025	3,427	15,514	12,605	13,973	22,572	19,742	115,483	73,641	14,817
Rate	25.5	1.4	36.7	10.1	11.4	51.6	41.9	46.4	75.0	65.6	383.7	244.7	49.2
Group IV (25,000 to 49,999)													
Number of offenses known	6,813	424	7,827	1,860	2,270	10,402	9,126	10,455	16,709	17,031	94,379	62,890	11,243
Rate	25.0	1.6	28.7	6.8	8.3	38.1	33.4	38.3	61.2	62.4	345.7	230.4	41.2
Group V (10,000 to 24,999)													
Number of offenses known	6,237	377	5,910	1,244	1,686	7,057	8,000	9,121	15,290	17,761	85,685	61,938	10,292
Rate	24	1	22	5	6	27	30	35	58	67	325	235	39
Group VI (under 10,000)													
Number of offenses known	6,030	561	3,543	892	910	4,919	5,732	7,838	12,283	21,579	69,744	54,331	9,378
Rate	28.2	2.6	16.5	4.2	4.2	23.0	26.8	36.6	57.4	100.8	325.7	253.7	43.8
Metropolitan Counties													
Number of offenses known	12,865	703	17,065	2,761	3,658	14,380	24,535	20,815	43,021	35,979	234,481	132,837	22,385
Rate	18.8	1.0	25.0	4.0	5.4	21.1	35.9	30.5	63.0	52.7	343.4	194.5	32.8
Nonmetropolitan Counties													
Number of offenses known	4,989	281	1,260	305	389	1,127	6,259	4,738	9,821	12,961	78,344	44,827	4,936
Rate	21.0	1.2	5.3	1.3	1.6	4.7	26.3	19.9	41.3	54.5	329.7	188.7	20.8
Suburban Areas [1]													
Number of offenses known	23,453	1,470	28,944	5,485	6,897	30,107	37,517	36,374	69,777	68,824	389,601	243,195	43,510
Rate	19.1	1.2	23.6	4.5	5.6	24.5	30.6	29.7	56.9	56.1	317.7	198.3	35.5

Table 19. Number and Rate of Crimes Per 100,000 Inhabitants, Additional Information About Selected Offenses, by Population Group, 2012

(Number, rate)

Population group	Motor vehicle theft			Number of agencies	Estimated population, 2012
	Autos	Trucks and buses	Other vehicles		
Total, All Agencies					
Number of offenses known	479,084	98,458	70,705	13,985	271,070,610
Rate	176.7	36.3	26.1		
Total, Cities					
Number of offenses known	386,411	75,644	48,041	10,088	179,023,674
Rate	215.8	42.3	26.8		
Group I (250,000 and over)					
Number of offenses known	165,461	40,875	15,814	69	43,299,026
Rate	382.1	94.4	36.5		
1,000,000 and over (Group I subset)					
Number of offenses known	43,313	19,048	6,105	8	14,496,403
Rate	298.8	131.4	42.1		
500,000 to 999,999 (Group I subset)					
Number of offenses known	63,628	12,634	5,299	22	15,144,879
Rate	420.1	83.4	35.0		
250,000 to 499,999 (Group I subset)					
Number of offenses known	58,520	9,193	4,410	39	13,657,744
Rate	428.5	67.3	32.3		
Group II (100,000 to 249,999)					
Number of offenses known	78,879	14,585	10,258	205	30,568,914
Rate	258.0	47.7	33.6		
Group III (50,000 to 99,999)					
Number of offenses known	56,562	8,495	7,614	434	30,093,472
Rate	188.0	28.2	25.3		
Group IV (25,000 to 49,999)					
Number of offenses known	35,918	4,679	6,019	788	27,297,902
Rate	131.6	17.1	22.0		
Group V (10,000 to 24,999)					
Number of offenses known	28,331	4,110	4,335	1,659	26,351,834
Rate	108	16	17		
Group VI (under 10,000)					
Number of offenses known	21,260	2,900	4,001	6,933	21,412,526
Rate	99.3	13.5	18.7		
Metropolitan Counties					
Number of offenses known	77,931	19,139	17,901	1,696	68,285,432
Rate	114.1	28.0	26.2		
Nonmetropolitan Counties					
Number of offenses known	14,742	3,675	4,763	2,201	23,761,504
Rate	62.0	15.5	20.0		
Suburban Areas [1]					
Number of offenses known	139,284	27,675	27,352	7,615	122,643,637
Rate	113.6	22.6	22.3		

1 Suburban areas include law enforcement agencies in cities with less than 50,000 inhabitants and county law enforcement agencies that are within a Metropolitan Statistical Area. Suburban areas exclude all metropolitan agencies associated with a principal city. The agencies associated with suburban areas also appear in other groups within this table.

Table 20. Murder, by Selected State, Territory, and Type of Weapon, 2012

(Number)

State/territory	Total murders[1]	Total firearms	Handguns	Rifles	Shotguns	Firearms (type unknown)	Knives or cutting instruments	Other weapons	Hands, fists, feet, etc.[2]
Alabama[3]	2	1	1	0	0	0	0	1	0
Alaska	29	11	1	0	0	10	9	7	2
Arizona	321	211	157	12	9	33	40	58	12
Arkansas	166	108	55	4	6	43	28	25	5
California	1,879	1,304	899	38	52	315	261	227	87
Colorado	160	92	61	3	5	23	29	22	17
Connecticut	146	112	50	27	1	34	17	14	3
Delaware	57	41	25	1	2	13	5	8	3
Georgia	541	390	344	10	12	24	57	85	9
Hawaii	13	3	3	0	0	0	2	4	4
Idaho	26	17	12	1	2	2	3	4	2
Illinois[3]	509	439	429	4	2	4	39	19	12
Indiana	275	205	128	9	7	61	20	37	13
Iowa	44	25	13	3	1	8	1	12	6
Kansas	84	50	36	1	1	12	12	13	9
Kentucky	192	122	101	4	8	9	28	29	13
Louisiana	455	370	341	9	8	12	35	27	23
Maine	25	14	6	1	0	7	7	1	3
Maryland	365	277	265	5	2	5	45	28	15
Massachusetts	121	70	32	0	1	37	33	12	6
Michigan	682	536	309	36	19	172	48	61	37
Minnesota	89	41	37	2	2	0	21	16	11
Mississippi	174	132	99	7	5	21	13	21	8
Missouri	389	283	153	8	8	114	29	64	13
Montana	22	11	8	2	0	1	6	3	2
Nebraska	52	42	37	2	1	2	5	4	1
Nevada	116	70	41	1	2	26	17	23	6
New Hampshire	14	9	4	0	0	5	3	2	0
New Jersey	385	273	237	6	3	27	63	32	17
New Mexico	109	67	42	5	5	15	14	21	7
New York	682	407	358	11	6	32	126	126	23
North Carolina	470	309	208	12	30	59	43	77	41
North Dakota	16	4	1	0	1	2	2	8	2
Ohio	410	278	176	5	8	89	34	74	24
Oklahoma	212	149	121	10	10	8	24	18	21
Oregon	81	42	11	2	3	26	17	20	2
Pennsylvania	684	522	412	9	10	91	68	74	20
Rhode Island	34	19	7	0	0	12	5	6	4
South Carolina	324	237	134	9	13	81	31	45	11
South Dakota	14	4	2	1	1	0	1	4	5
Tennessee	387	254	183	7	6	58	37	73	23
Texas	1,141	745	493	28	41	183	173	122	101
Utah	49	29	22	2	1	4	10	6	4
Vermont	8	2	2	0	0	0	2	3	1
Virginia	314	220	103	9	2	106	37	38	19
Washington	194	106	71	4	3	28	43	33	12
West Virginia	66	47	26	5	2	14	7	7	5
Wisconsin	169	108	85	5	1	17	30	21	10
Wyoming	14	5	2	0	0	3	3	2	4

1 Total number of murders for which supplemental homicide data were received. 2 Pushed is included in hands, fists, feet, etc. 3 Limited supplemental homicide data were received.

Table 21. Robbery, by State and Type of Weapon, 2012

(Number)

State	Total robberies[1]	Firearms	Knives or cutting instruments	Other weapons	Strong-arm	Agency count	Population
Alabama	2,971	1,630	154	354	833	267	3,747,888
Alaska	628	125	69	56	378	33	726,997
Arizona	7,247	3,055	759	750	2,683	105	5,923,115
Arkansas	2,183	1,072	117	184	810	200	2,071,400
California	55,901	16,940	4,879	5,223	28,859	724	37,664,003
Colorado	3,307	1,344	294	367	1,302	206	4,786,721
Connecticut	3,687	1,261	359	285	1,782	104	3,590,347
Delaware	1,492	678	110	122	582	52	916,825
District of Columbia	4,036	1,658	336	176	1,866	2	632,323
Florida	23,853	9,909	1,454	2,064	10,426	618	19,290,951
Georgia	11,773	6,795	468	1,108	3,402	506	8,825,893
Hawaii	115	20	11	15	69	1	158,760
Idaho	240	72	35	36	97	103	1,568,760
Illinois[2]	499	211	45	40	203	1	152,293
Indiana	6,211	2,976	348	546	2,341	216	5,058,554
Iowa	921	277	100	114	430	187	2,634,244
Kansas	1,456	682	121	117	536	240	2,639,179
Kentucky	3,341	1,507	301	314	1,219	365	4,213,291
Louisiana	3,736	1,728	147	316	1,545	153	3,122,133
Maine	423	92	53	52	226	183	1,329,192
Maryland	9,689	4,206	898	567	4,018	153	5,374,159
Massachusetts	6,404	1,673	1,200	723	2,808	308	6,252,640
Michigan	10,197	5,068	483	804	3,842	539	9,240,757
Minnesota	3,382	987	224	510	1,661	317	5,225,091
Mississippi	1,731	1,065	70	185	411	102	1,669,496
Missouri	5,770	2,731	336	419	2,284	601	5,946,698
Montana	189	59	18	26	86	104	981,401
Nebraska	1,122	540	82	85	415	216	1,698,322
Nevada	4,915	1,690	431	486	2,308	46	2,750,068
New Hampshire	454	104	65	50	235	148	1,167,974
New Jersey	10,850	3,873	897	658	5,422	553	8,473,818
New Mexico	1,761	727	256	134	644	84	1,806,790
New York	8,292	2,450	908	963	3,971	488	10,783,597
North Carolina	9,177	4,718	661	740	3,058	373	9,433,770
North Dakota	124	27	17	17	63	93	685,149
Ohio	11,451	4,597	526	1,036	5,292	459	8,690,062
Oklahoma	3,216	1,407	275	241	1,293	334	3,659,108
Oregon	1,368	275	141	148	804	146	3,083,727
Pennsylvania	15,395	6,416	1,069	970	6,940	1,216	12,324,409
Rhode Island	712	230	101	82	299	48	1,044,186
South Carolina	3,635	1,924	231	296	1,184	306	4,112,716
South Dakota	152	36	15	26	75	121	753,107
Tennessee	7,594	4,095	437	687	2,375	446	6,030,333
Texas	30,092	14,697	2,428	2,528	10,439	995	25,503,316
Utah	1,064	273	139	128	524	129	2,829,066
Vermont	92	27	15	11	39	76	557,989
Virginia	4,653	2,532	317	416	1,388	410	8,076,619
Washington	5,631	1,273	474	643	3,241	237	6,491,889
West Virginia	460	168	66	65	161	248	1,142,404
Wisconsin	4,559	2,258	220	382	1,699	364	5,378,896
Wyoming	60	16	7	5	32	59	550,101

1 The number of robberies from agencies that submitted 12 months of data in 2012 for which breakdowns by type of weapon were included. 2 Limited data were received.

Table 22. Aggravated Assault, by State and Type of Weapon, 2012

(Number)

State	Total aggravated assaults[1]	Firearms	Knives or cutting instruments	Other weapons	Personal weapons	Agency count	Population
Alabama	11,142	1,610	1,679	5,509	2,344	267	3,747,888
Alaska	3,119	549	597	774	1,199	33	726,997
Arizona	16,532	4,010	2,883	4,834	4,805	105	5,923,115
Arkansas	8,886	2,541	1,238	1,746	3,361	200	2,371,483
California	93,356	17,680	15,011	31,294	29,371	724	37,664,003
Colorado	9,731	2,428	2,431	2,445	2,427	206	4,786,721
Connecticut	5,408	711	1,169	1,979	1,549	104	3,590,347
Delaware	3,226	859	775	1,266	326	52	916,825
District of Columbia	3,504	659	1,072	1,110	663	2	632,323
Florida	63,845	13,486	11,360	23,167	15,832	618	19,290,951
Georgia	20,425	5,856	3,624	5,667	5,278	506	8,825,893
Hawaii	247	0	18	117	112	1	158,760
Idaho	2,490	398	457	829	806	103	1,568,760
Illinois[2]	1,451	728	171	260	292	1	152,293
Indiana	11,913	2,103	1,557	3,353	4,900	216	5,058,554
Iowa	5,554	649	887	1,209	2,809	187	2,634,244
Kansas	7,195	2,046	1,595	2,152	1,402	240	2,639,179
Kentucky	4,625	1,021	781	1,614	1,209	365	4,213,291
Louisiana	12,078	2,737	1,781	3,978	3,582	153	3,122,133
Maine	811	73	166	227	345	183	1,329,192
Maryland	14,795	2,135	3,995	5,508	3,157	153	5,374,159
Massachusetts	18,001	2,010	4,433	8,580	2,978	308	6,252,640
Michigan	27,944	8,407	5,601	9,890	4,046	539	9,240,757
Minnesota	6,549	1,161	1,199	1,677	2,512	317	5,225,091
Mississippi	2,842	764	382	742	954	102	1,669,496
Missouri	19,322	5,346	2,537	5,229	6,210	601	5,946,698
Montana	2,089	280	268	706	835	104	981,401
Nebraska	2,836	632	514	929	761	216	1,698,322
Nevada	10,699	1,600	2,114	4,714	2,271	46	2,750,068
New Hampshire	1,386	177	406	313	490	148	1,167,974
New Jersey	12,215	2,329	2,663	3,660	3,563	553	8,473,818
New Mexico	7,652	1,582	1,323	2,308	2,439	84	1,806,790
New York	15,804	2,257	5,091	4,358	4,098	488	10,783,597
North Carolina	21,980	7,186	4,209	5,540	5,045	373	9,433,770
North Dakota	1,123	20	123	221	759	93	685,149
Ohio	12,565	3,101	2,164	4,585	2,715	459	8,690,062
Oklahoma	12,595	2,202	2,025	4,418	3,950	334	3,659,108
Oregon	3,750	431	690	1,134	1,495	146	3,083,727
Pennsylvania	24,012	4,817	3,664	5,759	9,772	1,216	12,324,409
Rhode Island	1,616	378	426	539	273	48	1,044,186
South Carolina	16,939	5,069	3,025	4,455	4,390	306	4,112,716
South Dakota	1,793	252	459	482	600	121	753,107
Tennessee	29,160	8,635	5,531	10,941	4,053	446	6,030,333
Texas	66,032	15,227	14,761	22,317	13,727	995	25,503,316
Utah	3,681	556	1,047	1,250	828	129	2,829,066
Vermont	561	61	110	109	281	76	557,989
Virginia	8,877	1,887	1,910	2,957	2,123	410	8,076,619
Washington	11,792	1,850	1,903	4,145	3,894	237	6,491,889
West Virginia	2,808	578	422	828	980	248	1,142,404
Wisconsin	9,696	1,953	1,304	2,393	4,046	364	5,378,896
Wyoming	893	92	150	267	384	59	550,101

1 The number of aggravated assaults from agencies that submitted 12 months of data in 2012 for which breakdowns by type of weapon were included. 2 Limited data were received.

Table 23. Offense Analysis, Number and Percent Change, 2011–2012

(Number, percent, dollars; 14,232 agencies; 2012 estimated population 276,061,506)

Classification	Number of offenses, 2012	Percent change from 2011	Percent distribution[1]	Average value (dollars)
Murder	12,417	2.7	. . .	n.a.
Forcible Rape	71,301	0.7	. . .	n.a.
Robbery	292,074	*	100.0	1,167
By location				
Street/highway	126,922	-0.5	43.5	798
Commercial house	38,788	1.9	13.3	1,754
Gas or service station	7,124	1.4	2.4	943
Convenience store	14,955	-0.4	5.1	706
Residence	49,340	-1.0	16.9	1,631
Bank	5,484	-5.5	1.9	3,810
Miscellaneous	49,461	1.6	16.9	1,071
Burglary	1,854,167	-3.4	100.0	2,230
By location				
Residence (dwelling)	1,381,122	-3.5	74.5	2,188
Residence, night	377,579	-2.1	20.4	1,755
Residence, day	731,975	-3.2	39.5	2,403
Residence, unknown	271,568	-6.2	14.6	2,498
Nonresidence (store, office, etc.)	473,045	-3.2	25.5	2,179
Nonresidence, night	194,021	-2.3	10.5	1,820
Nonresidence, day	169,572	-1.7	9.1	2,076
Nonresidence, unknown	109,452	-6.7	5.9	3,019
Larceny-theft (except motor vehicle theft)	5,362,935	-0.4	100.0	987
By type				
Pocket-picking	25,689	10.2	0.5	627
Purse-snatching	22,957	-2.6	0.4	468
Shoplifting	997,739	6.3	18.6	202
From motor vehicles (except accessories)	1,287,331	-3.6	24.0	751
Motor vehicle accessories	406,309	-7.2	7.6	573
Bicycles	194,549	3.0	3.6	384
From buildings	647,876	2.3	12.1	1,479
From coin-operated machines	14,988	-9.9	0.3	412
All others	1,765,497	-1.3	32.9	1,473
By value				
Over $200	2,497,171	-0.1	46.6	1,955
$50 to $200	1,216,113	-1.0	22.7	106
Under $50	1,649,651	-0.5	30.8	36
Motor Vehicle Theft	638,964	1.9	*	6,019

1 Because of rounding, the percentages may not add to 100.0. * = Less than one-tenth of 1 percent.

Table 24. Property Stolen and Recovered, by Type and Value, 2012

(Dollars, percent; 13,658 agencies; 2012 estimated population 267,206,950)

Type of property	Value of property (dollars)		Percent recovered
	Stolen	Recovered	
Total	13,018,440,484	2,672,518,711	20.5
Currency, notes, etc.	1,114,798,222	29,970,580	2.7
Jewelry and precious metals	1,884,197,755	76,079,980	4.0
Clothing and furs	283,544,521	35,231,828	12.4
Locally stolen motor vehicles	3,837,736,642	2,068,239,691	53.9
Office equipment	687,150,488	38,934,127	5.7
Televisions, radios, stereos, etc.	756,448,834	35,320,311	4.7
Firearms	139,015,479	12,939,361	9.3
Household goods	341,701,901	12,220,451	3.6
Consumable goods	126,411,259	15,010,704	11.9
Livestock	15,628,200	1,245,493	8.0
Miscellaneous	3,831,807,183	347,326,185	9.1

SECTION III

OFFENSES CLEARED

OFFENSES CLEARED

Figure III-1. Percentage of Crimes Cleared by Arrest or Exceptional Means, 2012

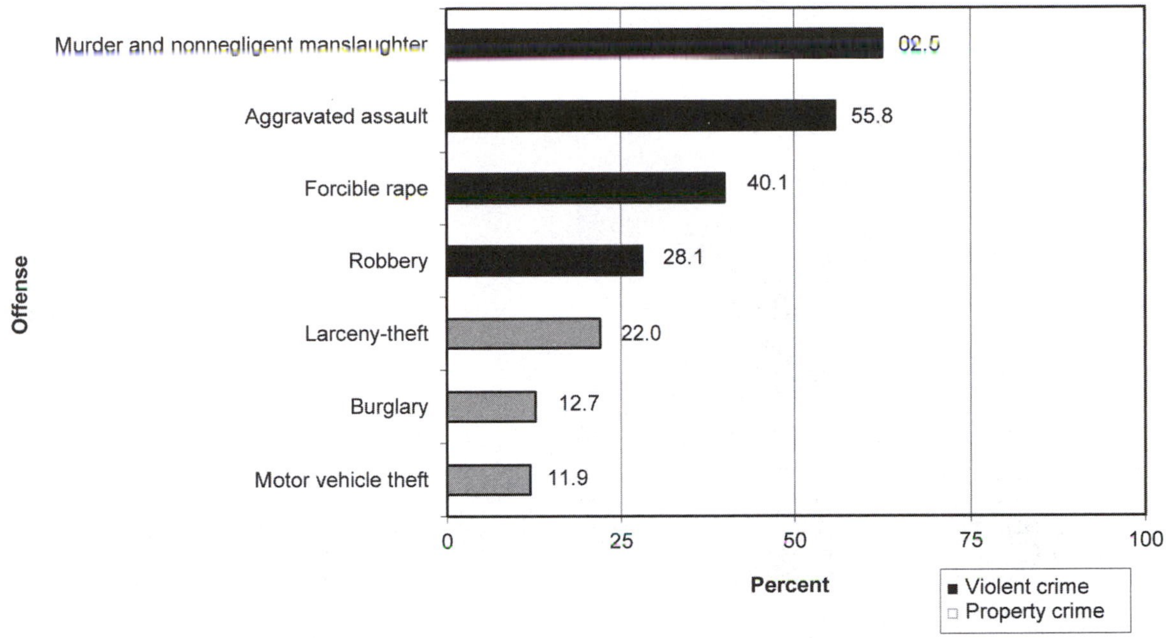

Source: Table 25

Law enforcement agencies that report crime to the Federal Bureau of Investigation (FBI) can clear, or "close," offenses in one of two ways: by arrest or by exceptional means. However, the administrative closing of a case by a local law enforcement agency does not necessarily mean that the agency can clear an offense for UCR purposes. To clear an offense within the program's guidelines, the reporting agency must adhere to certain criteria, which are outlined in this section. **(Note: The UCR program does not distinguish between offenses cleared by arrest and those cleared by exceptional means in its data presentations. The distinction is made solely for the purpose of a definition and not for data collection and publication.) See Appendix II for information on the UCR program's statistical methodology.**

Cleared by Arrest

In the UCR program, a law enforcement agency reports that an offense is cleared by arrest, or solved for crime reporting purposes, when at least one person is arrested, charged with the commission of the offense, and turned over to the court for prosecution (whether following arrest, court summons, or police notice). To qualify as a clearance, all of these conditions must be met.

In its calculations, the UCR program counts the number of offenses that are cleared, not the number of arrestees. Therefore, the arrest of one person may clear several crimes, and the arrest of many persons may clear only one offense. In addition, some clearances recorded by an agency during a particular calendar year, such as 2012, may pertain to offenses that occurred in previous years.

Cleared by Exceptional Means

In certain situations, elements beyond law enforcement's control prevent the agency from arresting and formally charging the offender. When this occurs, the agency can clear the offense exceptionally. There are four UCR program requirements that law enforcement must meet in order to clear an offense by exceptional means. The agency must have:

- Identified the offender
- Gathered enough evidence to support an arrest, make a charge, and turn over the offender to the court for prosecution
- Identified the offender's exact location so that the suspect could be taken into custody immediately

- Encountered a circumstance outside the control of law enforcement that prohibits the agency from arresting, charging, and prosecuting the offender

Examples of exceptional clearances include, but are not limited to, the death of the offender (e.g., suicide or justifiably killed by a law enforcement officer or a citizen), the victim's refusal to cooperate with the prosecution after the offender has been identified, or the denial of extradition because the offender committed a crime in another jurisdiction and is being prosecuted for that offense. In the UCR program, the recovery of property does not clear an offense.

Figure III-2. Violent Crime Clearance Rates by Region and Offense, 2012

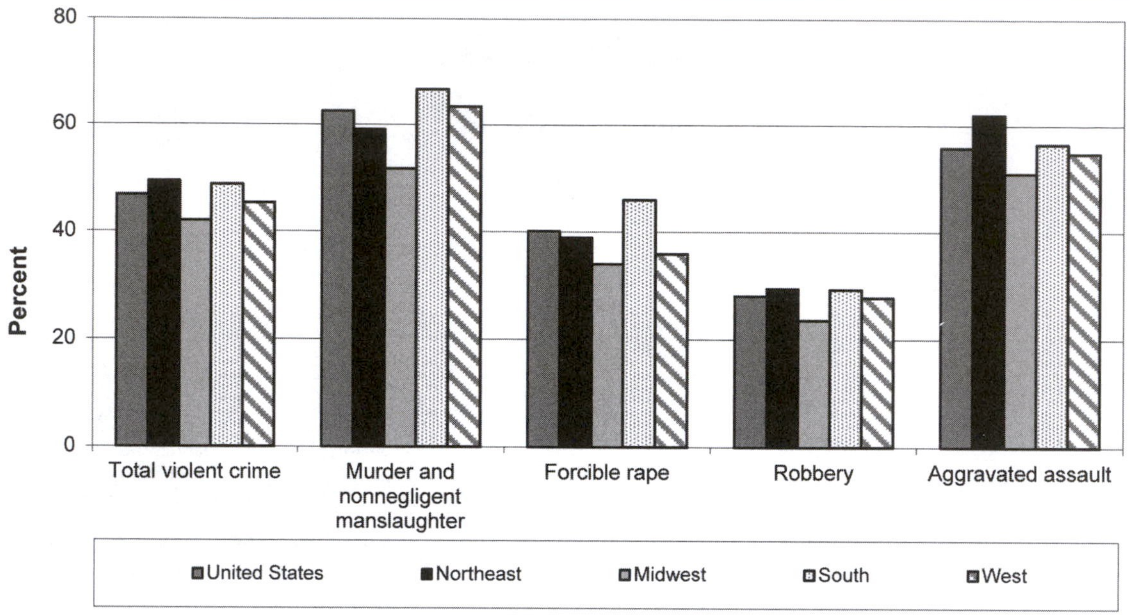

Source: Table 26

National Clearances

A review of the data for 2012 revealed law enforcement agencies in the United States cleared 46.8 percent of violent crimes (murder, forcible rape, robbery, and aggravated assault) and 19.0 percent of property crimes (burglary, larceny-theft, and motor vehicle theft) brought to their attention. In addition, law enforcement cleared 20.4 percent of arson offenses, which are reported in a slightly different manner than the other property crimes. (Table 25) More details concerning this offense are furnished in the arson text in this section.

As in most years, law enforcement agencies cleared a higher percentage of violent crimes than property crimes in 2012, although only the clearance rates for property crime was increased from 2011. The decrease in the clearance rate for violent crime is a departure from previous years; as a rule, clearance rates generally rise due to the more vigorous investigative efforts put forth for violent crimes. In addition, violent crimes more often involve victims and/or witnesses who are able to identify the perpetrators. Clearance rates for arson crimes, however, rose from 2011.

A breakdown of the clearances for violent crimes for 2012 revealed that the nation's law enforcement agencies cleared 62.5 percent of murder offenses (a decrease from 2011), 55.8 percent of aggravated assault offenses, 40.1 percent of forcible rape offenses (down more than a percentage point from 2011), and 28.1 percent of robbery offenses. (Table 25)

For property crime offenses in 2012, law enforcement agencies throughout the nation collectively 12.7 percent of burglary offenses (unchanged from 2011), 22.0 percent of larceny-theft offenses, and 11.9 percent of motor vehicle theft offenses (also unchanged from 2011). (Table 25)

Regional Clearances

The UCR program divides the nation into four regions: the Northeast, the Midwest, the South, and the West. (See Appendix IV for further details.) A review of clearance data for 2012 by region showed that agencies in the Northeast cleared the greatest proportion of their violent crime offenses (49.4 percent). Law enforcement agencies in the South cleared 48.7 percent of their violent crimes (a decrease from 2011), while agencies in the West and Midwest cleared 45.3 percent and 42.0 percent of their violent crimes, respectively. (Table 26)

For murder and nonnegligent manslaughter in 2012, the South cleared 66.7 percent of offenses, followed by the West (63.4 percent), the Northeast (59.1 percent), and the Midwest (51.7 percent). Forcible rape offenses were cleared 46.0 percent of the time in the South, 38.9 percent of the time in the Northeast, 35.9 percent of the time in the West, and 34.0 percent of the time in the Midwest. For robbery, the Northeast had the highest clearance rate, at 29.5 percent. The Northeast also had the highest proportion of clearances for aggravated assault (62.0 percent). (Table 26)

Clearance data for 2012 showed that, among the regions, law enforcement agencies in the Northeast cleared the highest percentage of their property crimes (21.7 percent). Agencies in the South and Midwest cleared 20.0 percent and 19.3 percent, respectively. Agencies in the West cleared 15.7 percent of their property crimes. (Table 26)

Agencies in the Northeast cleared the highest percentage of burglary offenses at 15.3 percent, followed by the South at 13.6 percent, the West at 11.3 percent, and the Midwest at 10.8 percent. For larceny-theft, the Northeast (24.1 percent) was followed by the Midwest at 23.0 percent, the South at 22.9 percent, and the West at 16.8 percent. The South cleared the highest proportion of motor vehicle thefts at 15.0 percent, followed by the Northeast at 14.4 percent. The Northeast cleared the greatest percentage of arson offenses (24.3 percent), followed by the South (22.5 percent). (Table 26)

Clearances by Population Groups

The UCR program uses the following population group designations in its data presentations: cities (grouped according to population size) and counties (classified as either metropolitan or nonmetropolitan counties). A breakdown of these classifications is furnished in Appendix IV.

CITIES

In 2012, the clearance data collected showed that law enforcement agencies in the nation's cities cleared 44.6 percent of their violent crime offenses. Among the city population groups, agencies in the smallest cities, those with fewer than 10,000 inhabitants, cleared the greatest proportion of their violent crime offenses (56.7 percent), and law enforcement in cities with 500,000 to 999,999 inhabitants cleared the smallest proportion of their violent crime offenses (38.2 percent). (Table 25)

The clearance data for murder showed that among the city population groups, cities with populations of less than 10,000 inhabitants cleared the greatest percentage of their murders (71.5 percent). Law enforcement agencies in cities with 500,000 to 999,999 inhabitants cleared the lowest percentage of their murders (50.9 percent). For forcible rape, cities with 1,000,000 or more inhabitants cleared the largest percentage of offenses at 47.9 percent, while cities with 25,000 to 49,999 inhabitants cleared the lowest percentage of offenses at 35.2 percent. Cities with under 10,000 inhabitants cleared the greatest percentage of their robbery offenses at 36.3 percent, and cities with 250,000 to 499,999 inhabitants cleared the lowest proportion of their robbery offenses at 22.9 percent. For aggravated assault, cities with fewer than 10,000 inhabitants cleared the highest proportion of offenses (63.3 percent); cities with 500,000 to 999,999 inhabitants cleared the lowest percentage of offenses (46.7 percent). (Table 25)

In 2012, agencies in the nation's cities collectively cleared 19.1 percent of their property crime offenses. Law enforcement in cities with 10,000 to 24,999 inhabitants cleared the highest proportion of the property crimes (25.1 percent) brought to their attention; cities with 1,000,000 or more inhabitants cleared the smallest proportion of their property crimes (12.8 percent). (Table 25)

Law enforcement agencies in cities cleared 12.1 percent of burglaries, 22.4 percent of larceny-thefts, 10.7 percent of motor vehicle thefts, and 19.6 percent of arsons in 2012. For burglaries, cities with fewer than 10,000 inhabitants cleared the largest percentage of their offenses, at 16.6 percent, while cities with 1,000,000 or more inhabitants cleared the smallest percentage of their offenses, at 8.1 percent. Cities with 10,000 to 24,999 inhabitants cleared the greatest percentage of their larceny-theft offenses (28.2 percent), and cities with 500,000 to 999,999 inhabitants cleared the lowest proportion of larceny-theft offenses (15.6 percent). For motor vehicle theft, cities with fewer than 10,000 inhabitants cleared the highest percentages of their offenses, at 23.0 percent. Cities with 10,000 to 24,999 inhabitants cleared the greatest percentage of their arson offenses, at 25.7 percent. (Table 25)

METROPOLITAN AND NONMETROPOLITAN COUNTIES

In 2012, law enforcement agencies in metropolitan counties cleared 54.2 percent of their violent crime offenses. Of the violent crimes made known to law enforcement agencies in metropolitan counties, murder offenses had the highest proportion of clearance (67.7 percent), followed by aggravated assaults (61.5 percent), forcible rapes (45.8 percent), and robberies (32.1 percent). Law enforcement agencies in metropolitan counties cleared 18.5 percent of their total property crimes, 14.1 percent of burglaries, 20.9 percent of larceny-thefts, 14.6 percent of motor vehicle thefts, and 21.2 percent of their arsons. (Table 25)

Like their counterparts in metropolitan counties, nonmetropolitan counties collectively cleared a greater proportion of their violent crimes than did the nation as a whole in 2012. Nonmetropolitan counties cleared 58.4 percent of their violent crime offenses and 18.6 percent of property crimes. Of the violent crimes known to them, law enforcement in nonmetropolitan counties had the highest number of clearances for murder (74.0 percent), with 44.9 percent of forcible rapes, 41.4 percent of robberies, and 61.6 percent of aggravated assaults being cleared. Agencies in nonmetropolitan counties reported clearing 15.3 percent of their burglaries, 19.9 percent of their larceny-thefts, 24.4 percent of their motor vehicle thefts, and 27.6 percent of their arsons. (Table 25)

Figure III-3. Percent of Clearances Involving Only Persons Under 18 Years Old, 2012

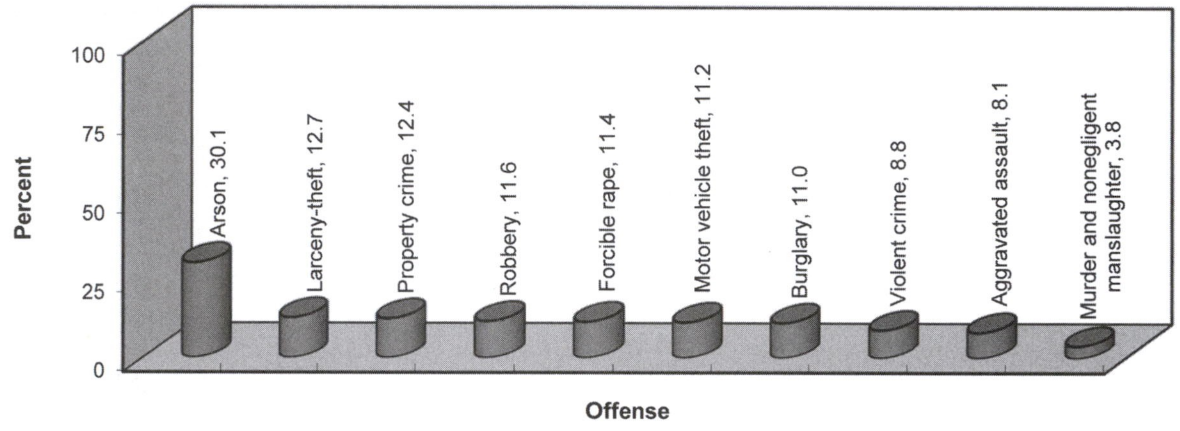

Source: Table 28

Clearances by Classification Group and Type

For forcible rape, by classification group and type, law enforcement agencies cleared 41.7 percent of assault to rape attempts and 39.0 percent of rapes by force in 2012. Cleared robbery offenses included 31.5 percent of offenses involving strong-arm tactics, 31.2 percent of offenses involving knives or other cutting instruments, 31.0 percent of offenses involving other weapons, and 22.7 percent of offenses involving firearms. For aggravated assaults, agencies cleared 63.9 percent of offenses involving knives or other cutting instruments; 61.1 percent of offenses involving hands, feet, fists, etc.; 55.8 percent of offenses involving other weapons; and 41.5 percent of offenses involving firearms. (Table 27)

For property crime clearances grouped by classification and type, data showed that the highest percentage of burglary clearances in the nation in 2012 (14.2 percent) were of offenses that involved unlawful entry of structures. Law enforcement agencies cleared 11.7 percent of burglaries involving forcible entry and 11.0 percent of attempted forcible entry offenses. For motor vehicle theft, agencies cleared 12.1 percent of motor vehicle theft offenses involving automobiles and 9.7 percent of motor vehicle theft offenses involving trucks and buses. (Table 27)

In 2012, 23.4 percent of structural arson offenses were cleared by arrest or exceptional means, while 11.0 percent of mobile arson offenses and 19.7 percent of other arson crimes were cleared. (Table 27)

CLEARANCES AND JUVENILES

When an offender under 18 years of age is cited to appear in juvenile court or before other juvenile authorities, the UCR program considers the incident for which the juvenile is being held responsible to be cleared by arrest, although a physical arrest may not have occurred. In addition, according to program definitions, clearances that include both adult and juvenile offenders are classified as clearances for crimes committed by adults. Therefore, the juvenile clearance data are limited to those clearances involving juveniles only, and the figures in this publication should not be used to present a definitive picture of juvenile involvement in crime.

Of the clearances for violent crimes that were reported in the nation in 2012, 8.8 percent involved only juveniles, down from 9.5 percent in 2011. In the nation's cities, collectively, 8.9 percent of violent crime clearances involved only juveniles, with juveniles in cities exclusively involved in 4.0 percent of murder clearances, 11.0 percent of forcible rape clearances, 11.8 percent of robbery clearances, and 8.1 percent of aggravated assault clearances. Of the nation's city population groups, cities with fewer than 10,000 inhabitants had the highest percentage of overall clearances for violent crime only involving juveniles (10.0 percent); cities with 1,000,000 or more inhabitants had the lowest percentage (7.2 percent). (Table 28)

Law enforcement agencies in metropolitan counties reported that 9.2 percent of their violent crime clearances—including 3.4 percent of their murder clearances, 12.4 percent of their forcible rape clearances, 11.5 percent of their robbery clearances, and 8.7 percent of their aggravated assault clearances—involved only juveniles. Agencies in nonmetropolitan counties reported that 6.5 percent of their clearances for violent crime involved only juveniles, including 2.8 percent of their murder clearances, 13.8 percent of their forcible rape clearances, 4.1 percent of their robbery clearances, and 5.9 percent of their aggravated assault clearances. The murder and robbery numbers each represent a decrease of a percentage point since 2011. (Table 28)

In 2012, 12.4 percent of clearances for property crime involved only juveniles, a decrease of nearly two percent since 2011. In cities collectively, 12.8 percent of the clearances for property crime, 11.7 percent of clearances for burglary, 13.1 percent of clearances for larceny-theft, 11.3 percent of clearances for motor vehicle theft, and 31.9 percent of clearances for arson involved juveniles only. Among the population groups labeled city, the percentages of clearances involving only juveniles for overall property crime ranged from a low of 10.2 percent in cities with more than 1,000,000 inhabitants to a high of 14.6 percent in cities with populations of 100,000 to 249,999. (Table 28)

Metropolitan counties reported that 11.2 percent of all property crime clearances, 10.0 percent of burglary clearances, 11.6 percent of larceny-theft clearances, 10.9 percent of motor vehicle theft clearances, and 28.5 percent of arson clearances involved persons under 18 years of age. In nonmetropolitan counties, 8.5 percent of property crime clearances, 7.8 percent of burglary clearances, 8.6 percent of larceny-theft clearances, 10.6 percent of motor vehicle theft clearances, and 17.1 percent of arson clearances involved juveniles exclusively. In suburban areas, 32.4 percent of arson clearances involved only juveniles. Arson offenses had the highest percentage of clearances involving only juveniles—30.1 percent—nationally in 2012. (Table 28)

Table 25. Number and Percent of Offenses Cleared by Arrest or Exceptional Means, by Population Group, 2012

(Number, percent)

Population group	Violent crime	Murder and nonnegligent manslaughter	Forcible rape	Robbery	Aggravated assault	Property crime	Burglary	Larceny-theft	Motor vehicle theft	Arson[1]	Number of agencies	Estimated population, 2012
Total, All Agencies												
Offenses known	1,060,028	13,092	73,574	304,905	668,457	8,015,405	1,897,748	5,459,213	658,444	48,196	14,601	278,152,589
Percent cleared by arrest	46.8	62.5	40.1	28.1	55.8	19.0	12.7	22.0	11.9	20.4		
Total Cities												
Offenses known	834,273	9,998	54,669	263,305	506,301	6,199,142	1,372,439	4,308,727	517,976	36,349	10,582	183,453,318
Percent cleared by arrest	44.6	60.3	38.2	27.3	54.0	19.1	12.1	22.4	10.7	19.6		
Group I (250,000 and over)												
Offenses known	346,619	4,878	17,513	130,546	193,682	1,839,561	436,518	1,173,458	229,585	13,340	72	45,057,321
Percent cleared by arrest	38.4	57.0	40.7	23.7	47.7	13.8	9.2	16.8	7.5	15.5		
1,000,000 and over (Group I subset)												
Offenses known	99,918	1,336	4,972	41,166	52,444	528,025	124,814	334,745	68,466	3,547	8	14,496,403
Percent cleared by arrest	39.7	68.3	47.9	25.3	49.4	12.8	8.1	15.8	6.6	15.0		
500,000 to 999,999 (Group I subset)												
Offenses known	137,073	1,883	6,493	47,227	81,470	720,830	169,023	465,026	86,781	4,768	24	16,540,300
Percent cleared by arrest	38.2	50.9	39.1	23.0	46.7	13.2	9.2	15.6	7.8	15.7		
250,000 to 499,999 (Group I subset)												
Offenses known	109,628	1,659	6,048	42,153	59,768	590,706	142,681	373,687	74,338	5,025	40	14,020,618
Percent cleared by arrest	37.4	54.7	36.6	22.9	47.3	15.5	10.2	19.0	8.1	15.6		
Group II (100,000 to 249,999)												
Offenses known	154,057	1,780	9,818	49,841	92,618	1,131,898	262,866	764,418	104,614	6,437	206	30,723,714
Percent cleared by arrest	43.6	59.5	36.1	27.8	52.7	17.6	11.2	20.8	10.0	19.9		
Group III (50,000 to 99,999)												
Offenses known	113,210	1,158	8,072	33,584	70,396	950,446	209,189	667,524	73,733	5,289	444	30,723,376
Percent cleared by arrest	47.9	58.5	36.9	29.8	57.6	20.2	12.6	23.6	11.0	19.9		
Group IV (25,000 to 49,999)												
Offenses known	84,484	903	7,123	22,802	53,656	827,833	171,739	609,897	46,197	4,357	801	27,807,739
Percent cleared by arrest	50.3	67.6	35.2	33.2	59.3	23.3	13.6	26.8	14.2	22.3		
Group V (10,000 to 24,999)												
Offenses known	74,008	753	6,445	16,233	50,577	773,096	160,445	575,330	37,321	3,434	1,685	26,712,732
Percent cleared by arrest	54.5	70.1	39.0	36.2	62.0	25.1	15.4	28.2	18.2	25.7		
Group VI (under 10,000)												
Offenses known	61,895	526	5,698	10,299	45,372	676,308	131,682	518,100	26,526	3,492	7,374	22,428,436
Percent cleared by arrest	56.7	71.5	39.1	36.3	63.3	22.7	16.6	24.2	23.0	25.1		
Metropolitan Counties												
Offenses known	182,017	2,236	13,685	38,395	127,701	1,437,003	394,157	926,088	116,758	8,903	1,802	70,247,102
Percent cleared by arrest	54.2	67.7	45.8	32.1	61.5	18.5	14.1	20.9	14.6	21.2		
Nonmetropolitan Counties												
Offenses known	43,738	858	5,220	3,205	34,455	379,260	131,152	224,398	23,710	2,944	2,217	24,452,169
Percent cleared by arrest	58.4	74.0	44.9	41.4	61.6	18.6	15.3	19.9	24.4	27.6		
Suburban Areas[2]												
Offenses known	317,116	3,530	24,832	72,372	216,382	2,918,223	682,887	2,039,621	195,715	15,665	8,014	125,678,423
Percent cleared by arrest	54.1	67.4	42.9	33.1	62.1	20.9	14.5	23.5	15.1	22.8		

1 Not all agencies submit data reports for arson to the FBI. Therefore, the agency counts and estimated population presented in this table do not represent participation for the reporting of arson. 2 Suburban areas include law enforcement agencies in cities with less than 50,000 inhabitants and county law enforcement agencies that are within a Metropolitan Statistical Area. Suburban areas exclude all metropolitan agencies associated with a principal city. The agencies associated with suburban areas also appear in other groups within this table.

Table 26. Number and Percent of Offenses Cleared by Arrest or Exceptional Means, by Region and Geographic Division, 2012

(Number, percent)

Geographic region/division	Violent crime	Murder and nonnegligent manslaughter	Forcible rape	Robbery	Aggravated assault	Property crime	Burglary	Larceny-theft	Motor vehicle theft	Arson[1]	Number of agencies	Estimated population, 2012
Total, All Agencies												
Offenses known	1,060,028	13,092	73,574	304,905	668,457	8,015,405	1,897,748	5,459,213	658,444	48,196	14,601	278,152,589
Percent cleared by arrest	46.8	62.5	40.1	28.1	55.8	19.0	12.7	22.0	11.9	20.4		
Northeast												
Offenses known	137,059	1,671	9,513	46,357	79,518	981,920	210,530	711,890	59,500	5,750	3,261	46,037,892
Percent cleared by arrest	49.4	59.1	38.9	29.5	62.0	21.7	15.3	24.1	14.4	24.3		
New England												
Offenses known	43,093	346	3,670	11,588	27,489	315,814	69,611	226,477	19,726	1,772	898	14,155,466
Percent cleared by arrest	47.7	61.8	27.4	26.4	59.3	17.4	12.6	19.3	11.4	21.8		
Middle Atlantic												
Offenses known	93,966	1,325	5,843	34,769	52,029	666,106	140,919	485,413	39,774	3,978	2,363	31,882,426
Percent cleared by arrest	50.2	58.3	46.1	30.6	63.5	23.7	16.6	26.4	15.9	25.5		
Midwest												
Offenses known	170,412	2,209	14,857	46,858	106,488	1,367,084	323,722	943,337	100,025	11,591	3,609	48,691,992
Percent cleared by arrest	42.0	51.7	34.0	23.6	51.0	19.3	10.8	23.0	12.0	16.7		
East North Central												
Offenses known	108,129	1,528	9,635	34,078	62,888	809,761	211,201	538,818	59,742	7,534	1,706	28,699,354
Percent cleared by arrest	36.9	44.0	32.6	21.6	45.7	17.7	10.0	21.6	10.7	14.7		
West North Central												
Offenses known	62,283	681	5,222	12,780	43,600	557,323	112,521	404,519	40,283	4,057	1,903	19,992,638
Percent cleared by arrest	50.9	68.9	36.7	29.1	58.7	21.5	12.2	24.9	14.1	20.5		
South												
Offenses known	480,032	6,226	30,383	128,527	314,896	3,625,960	901,334	2,481,739	242,887	17,417	5,774	112,574,365
Percent cleared by arrest	48.7	66.7	46.0	29.3	56.5	20.0	13.6	22.9	15.0	22.5		
South Atlantic												
Offenses known	249,028	3,248	14,174	70,426	161,180	1,878,854	458,216	1,296,498	124,140	8,702	2,809	60,073,083
Percent cleared by arrest	52.2	69.4	51.8	32.2	60.6	22.0	15.8	24.7	16.2	25.3		
East South Central												
Offenses known	75,659	1,008	5,049	17,517	52,085	526,947	144,072	352,093	30,782	2,359	1,275	17,045,971
Percent cleared by arrest	45.5	59.9	40.6	27.0	51.9	20.8	13.2	23.9	20.8	19.0		
West South Central												
Offenses known	155,345	1,970	11,160	40,584	101,631	1,220,159	299,046	833,148	87,965	6,356	1,690	35,455,311
Percent cleared by arrest	44.7	65.8	41.1	25.4	52.3	16.7	10.4	19.6	11.2	19.9		
West												
Offenses known	272,525	2,986	18,821	83,163	167,555	2,040,441	462,162	1,322,247	256,032	13,438	1,957	70,848,340
Percent cleared by arrest	45.3	63.4	35.9	27.8	54.8	15.7	11.3	18.6	8.3	19.2		
Mountain												
Offenses known	79,486	804	7,356	18,413	52,913	614,659	138,726	423,586	52,347	3,743	809	21,950,778
Percent cleared by arrest	46.5	72.6	31.4	26.9	55.0	19.2	10.2	23.2	10.9	25.3		
Pacific												
Offenses known	193,039	2,182	11,465	64,750	114,642	1,425,782	323,436	898,661	203,685	9,695	1,148	48,897,562
Percent cleared by arrest	44.8	60.0	38.8	28.1	54.6	14.1	11.8	16.5	7.6	16.8		

1 Not all agencies submit data reports for arson to the FBI. Therefore, the agency counts and estimated population presented in this table do not represent participation for the reporting of arson.

Table 27. Number and Percent of Offenses Cleared by Arrest or Exceptional Means, Additional Information About Selected Offenses, by Population Group, 2012

(Number, percent)

Population group	Forcible rape		Robbery				Aggravated assault				Burglary		
	Rape by force	Assault to rape-attempts	Firearm	Knife or cutting instrument	Other weapon	Strong-arm	Firearm	Knife or cutting instrument	Other weapon	Hands, fists, feet, etc.	Forcible entry	Unlawful entry	Attempted forcible entry
Total, All Agencies													
Offenses known	63,560	4,657	114,463	22,064	24,629	118,429	132,015	113,648	194,459	162,615	1,038,273	592,276	108,262
Percent cleared by arrest	39.0	41.7	22.7	31.2	31.0	31.5	41.5	63.9	55.8	61.1	11.7	14.2	11.0
Total Cities													
Offenses known	47,939	3,752	99,028	19,425	21,144	105,696	106,098	92,058	150,624	119,668	761,276	434,494	84,927
Percent cleared by arrest	37.6	41.6	22.4	30.5	30.5	30.8	37.3	63.0	54.7	61.0	11.0	13.9	10.8
Group I (250,000 and over)													
Offenses known	15,391	1,609	54,862	9,160	9,381	52,579	54,137	36,851	63,420	30,933	281,025	112,919	26,306
Percent cleared by arrest	40.1	42.9	19.8	25.8	26.3	27.2	32.9	60.0	49.7	53.6	8.4	10.7	9.0
1,000,000 and over (Group I subset)													
Offenses known	4,380	592	17,072	3,471	3,225	17,398	14,265	11,624	18,405	8,150	86,764	31,529	6,521
Percent cleared by arrest	47.6	50.5	20.5	25.9	28.0	29.4	36.1	61.6	50.2	53.7	7.6	9.4	9.0
500,000 to 999,999 (Group I subset)													
Offenses known	5,618	534	20,395	3,401	3,483	18,577	21,642	15,429	27,843	13,172	107,278	42,554	11,559
Percent cleared by arrest	38.4	37.1	18.9	25.2	26.0	26.1	33.3	57.4	47.4	53.2	8.4	10.8	8.3
250,000 to 499,999 (Group I subset)													
Offenses known	5,393	483	17,395	2,288	2,673	16,604	18,230	9,798	17,172	9,611	86,983	38,836	8,226
Percent cleared by arrest	35.8	40.2	20.1	26.5	24.8	26.0	30.1	62.2	53.0	54.1	9.4	11.8	10.0
Group II (100,000 to 249,999)													
Offenses known	8,324	550	17,863	3,571	4,120	18,221	19,146	17,017	26,879	17,668	136,521	79,652	16,226
Percent cleared by arrest	35.0	43.1	23.9	32.2	32.5	31.7	35.8	62.6	54.7	60.9	10.4	12.9	10.7
Group III (50,000 to 99,999)													
Offenses known	7,042	375	9,976	2,824	3,059	14,066	11,682	12,743	19,774	18,850	107,578	69,827	13,005
Percent cleared by arrest	36.7	37.6	24.5	30.8	31.5	32.5	39.1	62.6	59.6	63.8	11.1	14.6	12.4
Group IV (25,000 to 49,999)													
Offenses known	6,321	372	7,272	1,814	2,149	9,543	8,287	9,739	15,165	15,986	88,122	60,199	10,899
Percent cleared by arrest	34.4	34.4	26.7	38.0	35.4	36.1	45.4	65.5	58.8	62.5	12.6	15.0	10.8
Group V (10,000 to 24,999)													
Offenses known	5,813	355	5,645	1,195	1,585	6,584	7,463	8,398	14,057	16,702	81,925	59,779	9,704
Percent cleared by arrest	38.3	46.2	29.3	41.4	37.6	41.5	49.3	69.3	61.5	65.2	14.9	16.4	12.6
Group VI (under 10,000)													
Offenses known	5,048	491	3,410	861	850	4,703	5,383	7,310	11,329	19,529	66,105	52,118	8,787
Percent cleared by arrest	38.5	40.7	31.4	41.6	38.4	38.3	53.9	69.0	59.5	65.2	16.2	17.4	12.4
Metropolitan Counties													
Offenses known	10,859	629	14,217	2,341	3,104	11,609	19,791	17,018	34,312	30,642	198,756	114,613	18,269
Percent cleared by arrest	43.1	42.4	23.1	35.7	33.1	36.6	58.4	67.9	59.5	62.3	13.1	14.8	11.4
Nonmetropolitan Counties													
Offenses known	4,762	276	1,218	298	381	1,124	6,126	4,572	9,523	12,305	78,241	43,169	5,066
Percent cleared by arrest	44.3	40.9	36.5	42.6	41.2	43.8	59.7	66.7	60.3	59.0	14.6	15.6	11.9
Suburban Areas[1]													
Offenses known	20,578	1,332	25,159	4,918	6,099	25,868	31,347	31,266	58,431	60,956	342,428	218,557	37,494
Percent cleared by arrest	40.9	42.2	24.8	37.2	35.4	37.7	55.2	68.6	60.4	64.5	13.6	15.6	11.8

Table 27. Number and Percent of Offenses Cleared by Arrest or Exceptional Means, Additional Information About Selected Offenses, by Population Group, 2012

(Number, percent)

Population group	Motor vehicle theft			Arson[2]			Number of agencies	Estimated population, 2012
	Autos	Trucks and buses	Other vehicles	Structure	Mobile	Other		
Total, All Agencies								
Offenses known	462,368	91,547	65,273	20,968	10,623	13,869	13,988	258,921,815
Percent cleared by arrest	12.1	9.7	10.6	23.4	11.0	19.7		
Total Cities								
Offenses known	377,050	71,761	44,789	16,043	7,798	10,656	10,260	173,955,369
Percent cleared by arrest	11.1	8.5	9.7	22.3	10.6	19.2		
Group I (250,000 and over)								
Offenses known	167,043	40,934	15,607	6,005	3,510	3,404	69	43,451,576
Percent cleared by arrest	7.9	6.0	7.3	18.4	7.4	18.2		
1,000,000 and over (Group I subset)								
Offenses known	43,313	19,048	6,105	1,274	1,077	1,196	8	14,496,403
Percent cleared by arrest	7.9	4.2	4.9	23.9	8.4	11.5		
500,000 to 999,999 (Group I subset)								
Offenses known	66,469	13,183	5,490	2,307	1,295	948	23	15,699,640
Percent cleared by arrest	7.5	7.2	10.2	16.9	6.7	23.8		
250,000 to 499,999 (Group I subset)								
Offenses known	57,261	8,703	4,012	2,424	1,138	1,260	38	13,255,533
Percent cleared by arrest	8.3	8.1	7.0	16.8	7.3	20.2		
Group II (100,000 to 249,999)								
Offenses known	75,033	12,450	8,923	2,645	1,347	1,895	188	27,884,555
Percent cleared by arrest	10.1	9.6	9.3	22.2	11.3	24.0		
Group III (50,000 to 99,999)								
Offenses known	54,635	7,884	6,798	2,277	1,116	1,603	414	28,690,740
Percent cleared by arrest	11.2	9.9	8.2	22.3	10.9	22.6		
Group IV (25,000 to 49,999)								
Offenses known	33,513	4,031	5,556	1,783	742	1,615	762	26,379,365
Percent cleared by arrest	14.7	13.5	10.8	25.4	14.4	21.3		
Group V (10,000 to 24,999)								
Offenses known	27,629	3,715	4,179	1,568	611	1,060	1,618	25,640,853
Percent cleared by arrest	19.2	15.0	13.8	30.4	14.6	25.1		
Group VI (under 10,000)								
Offenses known	19,197	2,747	3,726	1,765	472	1,079	7,209	21,908,280
Percent cleared by arrest	24.5	20.5	17.2	25.9	19.9	25.7		
Metropolitan Counties								
Offenses known	70,604	16,124	15,645	3,370	2,239	2,513	1,604	61,084,315
Percent cleared by arrest	14.6	12.4	11.0	25.2	10.4	20.1		
Nonmetropolitan Counties								
Offenses known	14,714	3,662	4,839	1,555	586	700	2,124	23,882,131
Percent cleared by arrest	26.6	22.7	17.0	30.2	18.8	26.3		
Suburban Areas[1]								
Offenses known	128,463	23,616	24,339	6,207	3,351	4,918	7,592	113,975,426
Percent cleared by arrest	15.4	12.8	12.0	27.1	12.2	21.8		

1 Suburban areas include law enforcement agencies in cities with less than 50,000 inhabitants and county law enforcement agencies that are within a Metropolitan Statistical Area. Suburban areas exclude all metropolitan agencies associated with a principal city. The agencies associated with suburban areas also appear in other groups within this table. 2 Not all agencies submit data reports for arson to the FBI. Therefore, the agency counts and estimated population presented in this table do not represent participation for the reporting of arson. Agencies must report arson clearances by detailed property classification as specified on the Monthly Return of Arson Offenses Known to Law Enforcement to be included in this table; therefore, clearances in this table may differ from other clearance tables.

Table 28. Number of Offenses Cleared by Arrest or Exceptional Means and Percent Involving Persons Under 18 Years of Age, by Population Group, 2012

(Number, percent)

Population group	Violent crime	Murder and nonnegligent manslaughter	Forcible rape	Robbery	Aggravated assault	Property crime	Burglary	Larceny-theft	Motor vehicle theft	Arson[1]	Number of agencies	2012 estimated population
Total, All Agencies												
Offenses known	442,506	7,384	26,474	76,985	331,663	1,383,878	215,979	1,096,464	71,435	9,253	13,873	257,144,425
Percent under 18 years	8.8	3.8	11.4	11.6	8.1	12.4	11.0	12.7	11.2	30.1		
Total Cities												
Offenses known	341,447	5,540	19,351	66,412	250,144	1,102,821	152,552	898,297	51,972	6,835	10,233	172,837,062
Percent under 18 years	8.9	4.0	11.0	11.8	8.1	12.8	11.7	13.1	11.3	31.9		
Group I (250,000 and over)												
Offenses known	124,675	2,594	6,674	29,315	86,092	241,194	37,957	186,572	16,665	1,998	68	42,819,253
Percent under 18 years	8.3	4.2	8.7	12.0	7.1	12.5	12.1	12.7	11.2	29.3		
1,000,000 and over (Group I subset)												
Offenses known	39,640	913	2,384	10,417	25,926	67,606	10,104	52,988	4,514	533	8	14,496,403
Percent under 18 years	7.2	1.8	7.3	10.0	6.3	10.2	10.1	10.4	8.1	31.0		
500,000 to 999,999 (Group I subset)												
Offenses known	47,089	824	2,165	9,827	34,273	86,755	14,250	66,091	6,414	709	22	15,067,317
Percent under 18 years	9.1	5.7	9.8	13.8	7.7	13.5	13.6	13.4	13.5	29.1		
250,000 to 499,999 (Group I subset)												
Offenses known	37,946	857	2,125	9,071	25,893	86,833	13,603	67,493	5,737	756	38	13,255,533
Percent under 18 years	8.4	5.4	9.1	12.3	7.1	13.2	12.0	13.7	10.9	28.3		
Group II (100,000 to 249,999)												
Offenses known	59,198	950	3,149	12,473	42,626	178,384	25,851	142,974	9,559	1,205	187	27,761,703
Percent under 18 years	8.8	4.5	11.5	12.3	7.7	14.6	13.4	15.0	11.3	31.1		
Group III (50,000 to 99,999)												
Offenses known	48,463	605	2,717	8,835	36,306	174,748	23,755	143,547	7,446	1,006	412	28,566,757
Percent under 18 years	9.3	3.0	10.9	12.7	8.5	14.3	11.4	15.0	11.7	31.2		
Group IV (25,000 to 49,999)												
Offenses known	38,430	531	2,287	6,768	28,844	177,978	21,045	150,933	6,000	924	758	26,232,274
Percent under 18 years	9.4	2.6	13.3	11.2	8.8	13.0	11.0	13.3	12.6	35.5		
Group V (10,000 to 24,999)												
Offenses known	37,317	502	2,386	5,470	28,959	182,979	23,212	153,354	6,413	849	1,616	25,611,040
Percent under 18 years	9.3	3.2	12.6	10.0	9.0	11.6	10.9	11.8	10.9	32.9		
Group VI (under 10,000)												
Offenses known	33,364	358	2,138	3,551	27,317	147,538	20,732	120,917	5,889	853	7,192	21,846,035
Percent under 18 years	10.0	6.7	12.8	10.1	9.8	10.8	11.2	10.8	10.6	35.4		
Metropolitan Counties												
Offenses known	77,576	1,236	4,923	9,365	62,052	214,856	44,807	156,105	13,944	1,627	1,561	60,664,315
Percent under 18 years	9.2	3.4	12.4	11.5	8.7	11.2	10.0	11.6	10.9	28.5		
Nonmetropolitan Counties												
Offenses known	23,483	608	2,200	1,208	19,467	66,201	18,620	42,062	5,519	791	2,079	23,643,048
Percent under 18 years	6.5	2.8	13.8	4.1	5.9	8.6	7.8	8.6	10.6	17.1		
Suburban Areas[2]												
Offenses known	143,481	2,001	8,936	19,935	112,609	532,979	84,654	422,696	25,629	3,235	7,534	113,428,377
Percent under 18 years	9.7	3.5	12.5	11.4	9.3	11.5	10.4	11.8	10.7	32.4		

1 Not all agencies submit data reports for arson to the FBI. Therefore, the agency counts and estimated population presented in this table do not represent participation for the reporting of arson. 2 Suburban areas include law enforcement agencies in cities with less than 50,000 inhabitants and county law enforcement agencies that are within a Metropolitan Statistical Area. Suburban areas exclude all metropolitan agencies associated with a principal city. The agencies associated with suburban areas also appear in other groups within this table.

SECTION IV

PERSONS ARRESTED

PERSONS ARRESTED

Figure IV-1. Percent Change in the Number of Persons Arrested by Offense, 2003–2012

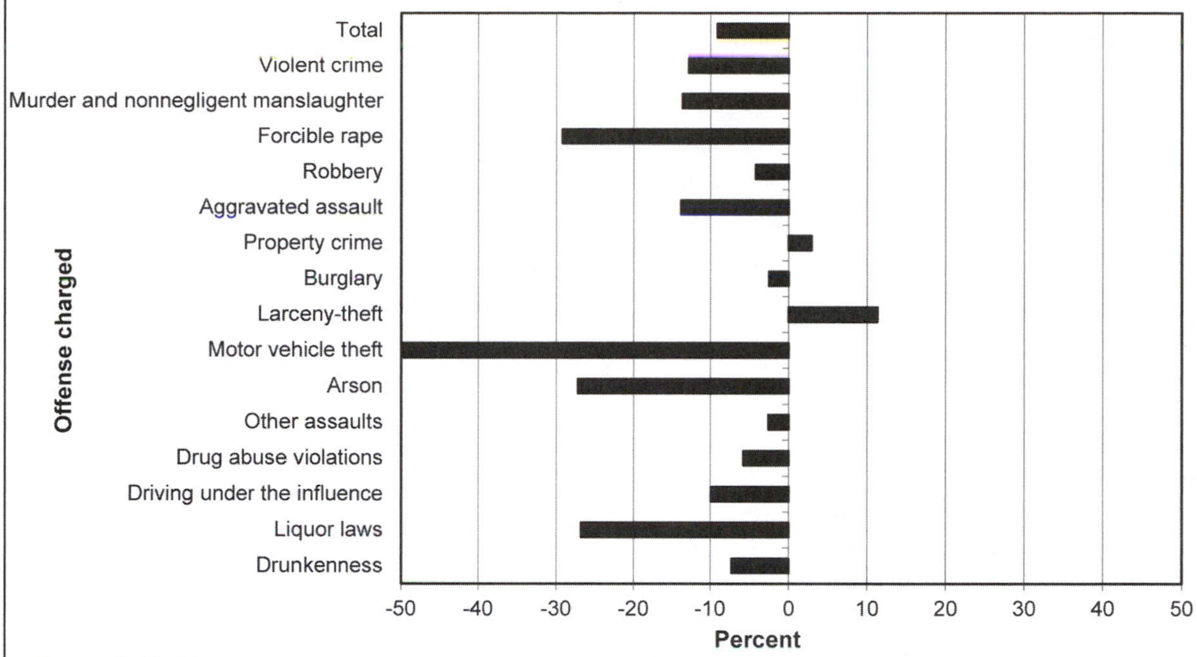

Source: Table 32

In the Uniform Crime Reporting (UCR) program, one arrest is counted for each separate instance in which an individual is arrested, cited, or summoned for criminal acts in Part I and Part II crimes. (See Appendix II for additional information concerning Part I and Part II crimes.) One person may be arrested multiple times during the year; as a result, the arrest figures in this section should not be taken as the total number of individuals arrested. Instead, it provides the number of *arrest occurrences* reported by law enforcement. Information regarding the UCR program's statistical methodology and table construction can be found in Appendix II.

National Volume, Trends, and Rates

VOLUME

The FBI estimated that 12,196,959 arrests occurred in 2012 for all offenses (except traffic violations). Of these arrests, 521,196 were for violent crimes and 1,646,212 were for property crimes. Of the total violent crimes in 2012, aggravated assaults accounted for 74.5 percent of the violent crime total, or 388,362 incidents. Robbery had the next highest proportion with just under 20.0 percent, or 103,661 incidents; followed by forcible rape, at 3.5 percent (or 18,098 incidents); and murder and non-negligent manslaughter, at 2.1 percent (or 11,075 incidents). Of the estimated arrests for property crimes in 2012, 1,282,352 (77.9 percent) were for larceny-theft, 283,582 (17.2 percent) were for burglary, 68,845 (4.2 percent) were for motor vehicle theft, and 11,433 (0.7 percent) were for arson. The most frequent identifiable arrests made in 2012 were for drug abuse violations (estimated at 1,552,432 arrests). These arrests composed 12.7 percent of the total number of all arrests. (Table 29)

A comparison of arrest figures from 2011 to 2012 revealed a 2.0 percent decrease. Arrests for violent crimes decreased 1.8 percent and arrests for property crimes increased 0.3 percent over this time period. An examination of the 5-year and 10-year arrest trends showed that the total number of arrests in 2012 fell 12.3 percent from the 2008 total. Arrests for violent crimes showed an 12.2 percent decrease from 2008 to 2012 and property crimes showed a 2.4 percent decrease. In the 10-year trend data (2003 to 2012), the number of arrests decreased 9.1 percent. For violent crimes, the number of arrests fell 12.8 percent, while arrests for property crimes increased 2.9 percent. (Tables 32, 34, and 36)

The number of adults arrested for violent crime (arrestees age 18 years and over) decreased 0.6 percent from 2011 to 2012, decreased 7.5 percent from 2008 to 2012, and decreased 8.6 percent from 2003 to 2012. The number of juveniles arrested for violent crime (arrestees under 18 years of age) decreased 10.3 percent from 2011 to 2012, decreased 36.4 percent from 2008 to 2012, and decreased 36.0 percent from 2003 to 2012. (Tables 32, 34, and 36)

TRENDS

The trend data for murder and nonnegligent manslaughter showed that the number of arrests for this offense decreased 0.6 percent from 2011 to 2012, decreased 14.1 percent from 2008 to 2012, and decreased 13.6 percent from 2003 to 2012. The number of adults arrested for murder increased 0.5 percent from 2011 to 2012, decreased 10.8 percent from 2008 to 2012, and fell 11.4 percent from 2003 to 2012. The number of juveniles arrested for murder fell 14.4 percent from 2011 to 2012, decreased 44.1 percent from 2008 to 2012, and fell 37.0 percent from 2003 to 2012. (Tables 32, 34, and 36)

For forcible rape, the trend data showed that arrests decreased 5.6 percent from 2011 to 2012, with adult arrests decreasing 5.5 percent and juvenile arrests dropping 6.0 percent. The 5-year trend data showed that arrests decreased 17.3 percent from 2008 to 2012; adult arrests decreased 16.4 percent and juvenile arrests declined 22.0 percent during this period. The 10-year trend data showed that forcible rape arrests dropped 29.2 percent from 2003 to 2012, with adult arrests falling 27.9 percent and juvenile arrests falling 36.2 percent. (Tables 32, 34, and 36)

For robbery, the data showed that arrests decreased 3.4 percent from 2011 to 2012, with adult arrests decreasing 1.4 percent and juvenile arrests falling 10.9 percent. The 5-year trend data showed that total robbery arrests fell 19.6 percent from 2008 to 2012; adult arrests decreased 12.1 percent and juvenile arrests dropped 39.4 percent during this period. The 10-year trend data showed that arrests fell 4.2 percent from 2003 to 2012, with adult arrests increasing 0.4 percent and juvenile arrests falling by 19.5 percent. (Tables 32, 34, and 36)

The aggravated assault trend data showed that the number of arrests for this offense fell 1.2 percent from 2011 to 2012, dropped 9.7 percent from 2008 to 2012, and fell 13.8 percent from 2003 to 2012. The number of adults arrested for aggravated assault decreased 0.2 percent from 2011 to 2012, declined 5.9 percent from 2008 to 2012, and declined 9.4 percent from 2003 to 2012. The number of juveniles arrested for aggravated assault dropped 10.2 percent from 2011 to 2012, fell 39.2 percent from 2008 to 2012, and dropped 42.7 percent from 2003 to 2012. (Tables 32, 34, and 36)

The 2-year, 5-year, and 10-year trend data showed that the number of arrests for property crime increased 0.3 percent from 2011 to 2012, decreased 2.4 percent from 2008 to 2012, and increased 2.9 percent from 2003 to 2012. The number of adults arrested for property crime offenses (arrestees age 18 years and over) increased 3.4 percent from 2011 to 2012, increased 8.2 percent from 2008 to 2012, and increased 18.9 percent from 2003 to 2012. The number of juveniles arrested for property crime (arrestees under 18 years of age) decreased 11.6 percent from 2011 to 2012, decreased 32.4 percent from 2008 to 2012, and decreased 36.0 percent from 2003 to 2012. (Tables 32, 34, and 36)

The trend data for burglary showed that the number of arrests for this offense decreased 3.0 percent from 2011 to 2012, decreased 8.4 percent from 2008 to 2012, and decreased 2.5 percent from 2003 to 2012. The number of adults arrested for burglary fell 0.6 percent from 2011 to 2012, rose 1.9 percent from 2008 to 2012, and rose 11.3 percent from 2003 to 2012. The number of juveniles arrested for burglary decreased 12.3 percent from 2011 to 2012, decreased 35.9 percent from 2008 to 2012, and fell 36.5 percent from 2003 to 2012. (Tables 32, 34, and 36)

For larceny-theft, the 2-year trend data showed that arrests rose 1.0 percent from 2011 to 2012, with adult arrests increasing 4.2 percent and juvenile arrests decreasing 11.8 percent. The 5-year trend data showed that total larceny-theft arrests increased 1.2 percent from 2008 to 2012; adult arrests increased 12.1 percent, while juvenile arrests dropped by 30.4 percent during this period. The 10-year trend data showed that larceny-theft arrests rose 11.3 percent from 2003 to 2012, with adult arrests increasing 28.7 percent and juvenile arrests falling 31.7 percent. (Tables 32, 34, and 36)

For motor vehicle theft, the 2-year trend data showed that arrests rose 2.9 percent from 2011 to 2012, with adult arrests increasing 5.2 percent and juvenile arrests decreasing 5.9 percent. The 5-year trend data showed that total motor vehicle theft arrests dropped 28.2 percent from 2008 to 2012; juvenile arrests fell by 46.4 percent and adult arrests dropped 22.0 percent during this period. The 10-year trend data showed that arrests dropped 51.1 percent from 2003 to 2012, with adult arrests falling 43.8 percent and juvenile arrests dropping by more than two-thirds (69.0 percent). (Tables 32, 34, and 36)

The arson trend data showed that the number of arrests for this offense increased 0.7 percent from 2011 to 2012, fell 18.4 percent from 2008 to 2012, and fell 27.2 percent from 2003 to 2012. The number of adults arrested for arson rose 6.4 percent from 2011 to 2012, fell 5.8 percent from 2008 to 2012, and fell 7.1 percent from 2003 to 2012. The number of juveniles arrested for arson dropped 7.4 from 2011 to 2012, dropped 32.9 percent from 2008 to 2012, and dropped 46.1 percent from 2003 to 2012. (Tables 32, 34, and 36)

RATES

The rate of arrests was estimated at 3,888.2 arrests per 100,000 inhabitants in 2012. The arrest rate for violent crime was 166.3 arrests per 100,000 inhabitants, and the arrest rate for property crime was 467.9 arrests per 100,000 inhabitants. Law enforcement agencies throughout the nation reported 3.5 murder arrests, 5.8 forcible rape arrests, 33.1 robbery arrests, and 123.9 aggravated assault arrests per 100,000 inhabitants in 2012. Rates for all violent crimes were down from the 2011 rates, except for murder, which remained unchanged. Law enforcement agencies throughout the nation reported 528.1 property crime arrests, 90.7 burglary arrests, 411.9 larceny-theft arrests, 21.9 motor vehicle theft arrests, and 3.7 arson arrests per 100,000 inhabitants in 2012. Rates for property crimes were also down from the 2011 rates, except for larceny-theft and motor vehicle theft. (Table 30)

Figure IV-2. Arrest Distribution by Age, 2011, Violent Crime

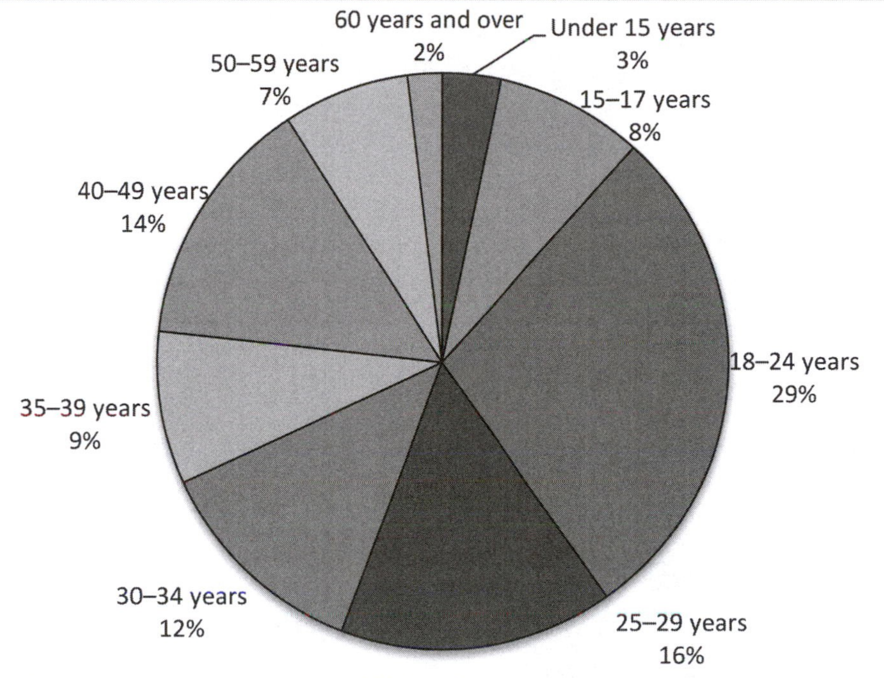

Source: Table 38

By Age, Sex, and Race

Law enforcement agencies that contributed arrest data to the UCR program reported information on the age, sex, and race of the persons they arrested. According to the data for 2012, adults accounted for 89.2 percent of arrestees nationally. (Table 38)

A review of arrest data by age from 2011 to 2012 showed that arrests of adults decreased 2.0 percent during this period. Arrests of adults for property crimes, however, increased 0.3 percent, while arrests of adults for violent crimes decreased 1.8 percent over the same time span. The arrest total for juveniles (those under 18 years of age) decreased 10.4 percent from 2011 to 2012. Over the 2-year period, arrests of juveniles for violent crimes fell 10.3 percent; juvenile arrests for property crimes decreased 11.6 percent. (Table 36)

By sex, males accounted for 73.8 percent of all persons arrested in 2012. Males represented 80.1 percent of arrestees for violent crime, 88.7 percent of arrestees for murder, 99.1 percent of arrestees for forcible rape, 87.0 percent for robbery, and 77.1 percent for aggravated assault. Females accounted for 19.9 percent of violent crime arrestees, 11.3 percent of murder arrestees, 0.9 percent of forcible rape arrestees, 13.0 percent of robbery arrestees, and 22.9 percent of aggravated assault arrestees. (Table 42)

Most arrestees for property crime in 2012 (82.0 percent) were over 18 years of age. By sex, males accounted for 62.6 percent of arrestees for property crime, 83.6 percent of arrestees for burglary, 56.9 percent of arrestees for larceny-theft, 81.1 percent of arrestees for motor vehicle theft, and 82.0 percent of arrestees for arson. Females accounted for 37.4 percent of property crime arrestees. Of the four property crimes, larceny-theft had the highest proportion of female arrestees at 43.1 percent. (Tables 38 and 42)

In 2012, 69.3 percent of all persons arrested were White, 28.1 percent were Black, and the remaining 2.6 percent were of other races (American Indian or Alaskan Native and Asian or Pacific Islander). Of all arrestees for violent crimes, 58.7 percent were White, 38.5 percent were Black, and 2.7 percent were of other races. For murder, 48.2 percent of arrestees were White, 49.4 percent were Black, and 2.4 percent were of other races. For forcible rape, 65.0 percent of arrestees were White, 32.5 percent were Black, and 2.5 percent of arrestees were of other races. For robbery, 43.4 percent of arrestees were White, 54.9 percent of arrestees were Black, and 1.7 percent of arrestees were of other races. For aggravated assault, 62.8 percent of arrestees were White, 34.1 percent of arrestees were Black, and 3.0 percent were of other races. (Table 43)

Of all arrestees for property crimes in 2012, 68.0 percent were White, 29.3 percent were Black, and 2.7 percent were of other races. For burglary, 67,1 percent of arrestees were White, 30.8 percent were Black, and 2.1 percent were of other races. For larceny-theft, 68.2 percent of arrestees were White, 29.0 percent were Black, and 2.8 percent were of other races. For motor vehicle theft, 66.6 percent of arrestees were White, 30.8 percent of arrestees were Black, and 2.6 percent were of other races. For arson, 73.6 percent of arrestees were White, 23.6 percent of arrestees were Black, and 2.8 percent were of other races. (Table 43)

White adults were most commonly arrested for driving under the influence (830,498 arrests) and drug abuse violations (801,198 arrests). Black adults were most frequently arrested for property crime (373,963 arrests) and drug abuse violations (372,914 arrests). (Table 43)

Figure IV-3. Arrest Distribution by Age, Property Crime

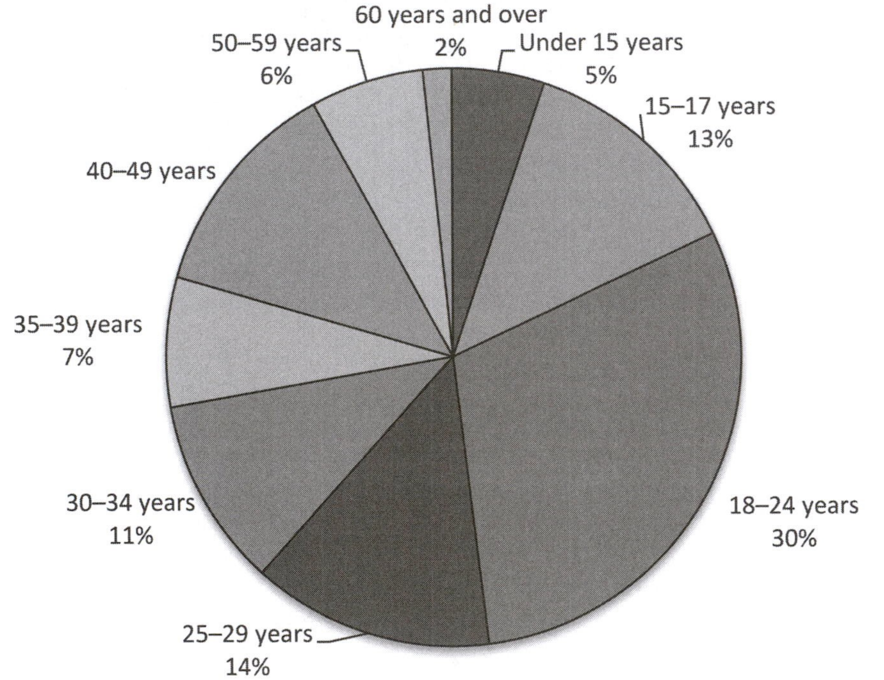

Source: Table 38

Regional Arrest Rates

The UCR program divides the United States into four regions: the Northeast, the Midwest, the South, and the West. (Appendix IV provides more information about the regions.) Law enforcement agencies in the Northeast had an overall arrest rate of 3,292.3 arrests per 100,000 inhabitants, below the national rate (3,888.2 arrests per 100,000 inhabitants). In this region, the arrest rate for violent crimes was 148.6 arrests per 100,000 inhabitants, and for property crime, the arrest rate was 467.9 arrests per 100,000 inhabitants. In the Midwest, law enforcement agencies reported an arrest rate of 3,889.3 arrests per 100,000 inhabitants. The arrest rate for violent crimes was 131.9 and the arrest rate for property crime was 543.1. Law enforcement agencies in the South, the nation's most populous region, reported an arrest rate of 4,352.4 per 100,000 inhabitants. Arrests for violent crime occurred at a rate of 156.3 arrests per 100,000 residents, and for property crime, the arrest rate was 587.1 arrests per 100,000 inhabitants. In the West, law enforcement agencies reported an overall arrest rate of 3.718.7 arrests per 100,000 inhabitants. The region's violent crime arrest rate was 214.3, the highest of the regions, while its property crime arrest rate was 485.9. (Table 30)

The regional murder arrest rates were 2.7 in the Northeast, 3.0 in the Midwest, 4.1 in the South, and 3.6 in the West. For forcible rape, the regional arrest rates were 5.3 in the Northeast, 6.2 in the Midwest, 6.1 in the South, and 5.3 in the West. Regional arrest rates for robbery were 38.0 in the Northeast, 26.9 in the Midwest, 31.1 in the South, and 36.7 in the West. For aggravated assault, the regional arrest rates were 102.6 in the Northeast, 95.7 in the Midwest, 115.0 in the South, and 168.7 in the West. (Table 30)

The regional burglary arrest rates were 76.8 in the Northeast, 69.5 in the Midwest, 96.3 in the South, and 107.8 in the West. For larceny-theft, the regional arrest rates were 372.0 in the Northeast, 447.4 in the Midwest, 469.3 in the South, and 343.7 in the West. Regional arrest rates for motor vehicle theft were 15.6 in the Northeast, 22.9 in the Midwest, 18.2 in the South, and 30.0 in the West (up from 25.5 in 2011). For arson, the regional arrest rates were 3.5 in the Northeast, 3.3 in the Midwest, 3.3 in the South, and 4.4 in the West. (Table 30)

Population Groups: Trends and Rates

The national UCR program aggregates data by various population groups, which include cities, metropolitan counties, and nonmetropolitan counties. Definitions of these groups can be found in Appendix IV. The total number of arrests in U.S. cities fell 1.7 percent from 2011 to 2012. The number of arrests for violent crimes declined 1.9 percent and arrests for property crimes decreased 1.1 percent during the 2-year time frame. (Table 44)

In 2012, law enforcement agencies in cities collectively recorded an arrest rate of 4,222.1 arrests per 100,000 inhabitants. The nation's smallest cities, those with fewer than 10,000 inhabitants, had the highest arrest rate among the city population groups with 5,274.4 arrests per 100,000 inhabitants. Law enforcement agencies in cities with 50,000 to 99,999 inhabitants recorded the lowest rate, 3,798.9. In the nation's metropolitan counties, law enforcement agencies reported an arrest rate of 3,081.9 per 100,000 inhabitants. Agencies in nonmetropolitan counties reported an arrest rate of 3,414.7. (Table 31)

By population group, law enforcement agencies in the nation's cities collectively reported 189.4 violent crime arrests per 100,000 inhabitants in 2012. In the city population groups, cities with 250,000 or more inhabitants reported the highest violent crime arrest rate (269.7) and cities with less than 10,000 inhabitants reported the lowest violent crime arrest rate (132.9). Cities reported an overall murder arrest rate of 3.8 per 100,000 inhabitants; cities with 250,000 or more inhabitants had the highest murder arrest rate (6.7) and cities with under 10,000 inhabitants had the lowest murder arrest rate (1.9). The collective city forcible rape arrest rate was 6.2 per 100,000 inhabitants, with the highest rate in cities with 250,000 or more inhabitants (8.5) and the lowest rate in cities with 25,000 to 49,999 inhabitants (5.1). The overall robbery arrest rate for cities was 41.2 per 100,000 inhabitants; cities with 250,000 or more inhabitants had the highest robbery arrest rate (69.2) and cities with fewer than 10,000 inhabitants had the lowest robbery arrest rate (17.9). For aggravated assault, the collective city arrest rate was 138.1 per 100,000 inhabitants, with the greatest arrest rate in cities with 250,000 or more inhabitants (185.3) and the lowest arrest rate in cities with 10,000 to 24,999 inhabitants (106.2). (Table 31)

Agencies in metropolitan counties reported a violent crime arrest rate of 125.1 per 100,000 inhabitants, with arrest rates of 2.8 for murder, 4.4 for forcible rape, 19.2 for robbery, and 98.6 for aggravated assault. Agencies in nonmetropolitan counties reported arrest rates of 96.2 for violent crime, 3.0 for murder, 5.6 for forcible rape, 7.2 for robbery, and 80.5 for aggravated assault. (Table 31)

By population group, law enforcement agencies in the nation's cities collectively reported 626.4 property crime arrests per 100,000 inhabitants in 2012. In the city population groups, cities with 10,000 to 24,999 inhabitants reported the highest property crime arrest rate (675.3) and cities with 250,000 or more inhabitants reported the lowest property crime arrest rate (587.1). Cities reported an overall burglary arrest rate of 97.4 per 100,000 inhabitants; cities with 100,000 to 249,999 inhabitants had the highest burglary arrest rate (113.7) and cities with 25,000 to 49,999 inhabitants had the lowest burglary arrest rate (84.7). The collective city larceny-theft arrest rate was 501.2 per 100,000 inhabitants, with the highest rate in cities with 10,000 to 24,999 inhabitants (566.6) and the lowest rate in cities with 250,000 or more inhabitants (448.4). The overall motor vehicle theft arrest rate for cities was 23.7 per 100,000 inhabitants; cities with 250,000 or more inhabitants had the highest motor vehicle theft arrest rate (33.5), and cities with 25,000 to 49,999 inhabitants had the lowest motor vehicle theft arrest rate (16.7). For arson, the collective city arrest rate was 4.1 per 100,000 inhabitants, with the greatest arrest rate in cities with fewer than 10,000 inhabitants (4.9) and the lowest arrest rate in cities with 100,000 to 249,999 inhabitants (3.5). (Table 31)

Agencies in metropolitan counties reported a property crime arrest rate of 337.0 per 100,000 inhabitants, with arrest rates of 73.7 for burglary, 242.4 for larceny-theft, 18.3 for motor vehicle theft, and 2.5 for arson. Agencies in nonmetropolitan counties reported arrest rates of 268.3 for property crime, 82.8 for burglary, 164.6 for larceny-theft, 17.6 for motor vehicle theft, and 3.4 for arson. (Table 31)

In suburban areas, the rates per 100,000 inhabitants for violent crime and property crime were 127.8 and 473.3, respectively. The rate for murder was 2.4; for forcible rape, 4.6; for robbery, 22.0; and for aggravated assault, 98.8. Specific property crime rates included 77.6 for burglary, 375.2 for larceny-theft, 17.4 for motor vehicle theft, and 3.1 for arson. (Table 31)

Community Types

In 2012, law enforcement agencies in the nation's cities reported that 88.1 percent of arrests in their jurisdictions were of adults and 11.9 percent of arrests were of juveniles. Adults accounted for 87.7 percent of arrestees for violent crimes, while juveniles accounted for 12.3 percent of these arrests. Adults made up 81.3 percent of the arrestees for property crimes, and juveniles accounted for the remaining 18,7 percent. Of all arrests in the nation's cities in 2012, 41.2 percent were of individuals under 25 years of age. In metropolitan counties, 36.2 percent of arrests were of individuals under 25 years of age. In nonmetropolitan counties, 31.8 percent of persons arrested were of individuals under 25 years of age. (Tables 46, 47, 53, and 59)

Males accounted for 73.5 percent and females accounted for 26.5 percent of arrestees in the nation's cities in 2012. In metropolitan counties, males comprised 74.4 percent of arrestees, and in nonmetropolitan counties, males represented 75.1 percent of all arrestees. (Tables 48, 54, and 60)

By race, 67.0 percent of arrestees in the nation's cities in 2012 were White, 30.3 percent were Black, and 2.7 percent were of other races (American Indian or Alaska Native and Asian or Pacific Islander). Whites accounted for 72.4 percent of arrestees in metropolitan counties in 2012, Blacks made up 25.4 percent of arrestees, and persons of other races made up 2.2 percent of the total. In nonmetropolitan counties, Whites made up 83.3 percent of arrestees, Blacks accounted for 13.5 percent of arrestees, and other races made up 3.2 percent of the total. (Tables 49, 55, and 61)

Table 29. Estimated Number of Arrests, 2012

(Number)

Offense	Arrests
Total [1]	12,196,959
Violent crime [2]	521,196
Murder and nonnegligent manslaughter	11,075
Forcible rape	18,098
Robbery	103,661
Aggravated assault	388,362
Property crime [2]	1,646,212
Burglary	283,582
Larceny-theft	1,282,352
Motor vehicle theft	68,845
Arson	11,433
Other assaults	1,199,476
Forgery and counterfeiting	67,046
Fraud	153,535
Embezzlement	16,023
Stolen property; buying, receiving, possessing	97,670
Vandalism	228,463
Weapons; carrying, possessing, etc.	149,286
Prostitution and commercialized vice	56,575
Sex offenses (except forcible rape and prostitution)	68,355
Drug abuse violations	1,552,432
Gambling	7,868
Offenses against the family and children	107,018
Driving under the influence	1,282,957
Liquor laws	441,532
Drunkenness	511,271
Disorderly conduct	543,995
Vagrancy	27,003
All other offenses	3,448,856
Suspicion	1,532
Curfew and loitering law violations	70,190

1 Does not include suspicion. 2 Violent crimes are offenses of murder and nonnegligent manslaughter, forcible rape, robbery, and aggravated assault. Property crimes are offenses of burglary, larceny-theft, motor vehicle theft, and arson.

Table 30. Number and Rate of Arrests, by Geographic Region, 2012

(Number, rate per 100,000)

Offense charged	United States total (12,196 agencies; population 242,925,157)		Northeast (2,971 agencies; population 45,295,024)		Midwest (3,004 agencies; population 46,969,870)		South (4,428 agencies; population 82,826,596)		West (1,793 agencies; population 67,833,667)	
	Total	Rate	Total	Rate	Total	Rate	Total	Rate	Total	Rate
Total [1]	9,445,500	3,888.2	1,491,232	3,292.3	1,826,800	3,889.3	3,604,931	4,352.4	2,522,537	3,718.7
Violent crime [2]	404,037	166.3	67,297	148.6	61,941	131.9	129,446	156.3	145,353	214.3
Murder and nonnegligent manslaughter	8,514	3.5	1,205	2.7	1,428	3.0	3,435	4.1	2,446	3.6
Forcible rape	13,971	5.8	2,409	5.3	2,918	6.2	5,037	6.1	3,607	5.3
Robbery	80,487	33.1	17,203	38.0	12,647	26.9	25,749	31.1	24,888	36.7
Aggravated assault	301,065	123.9	46,480	102.6	44,948	95.7	95,225	115.0	114,412	168.7
Property crime [2]	1,282,906	528.1	211,930	467.9	255,097	543.1	486,248	587.1	329,631	485.9
Burglary	220,284	90.7	34,784	76.8	32,666	69.5	79,732	96.3	73,102	107.8
Larceny-theft	1,000,496	411.9	168,504	372.0	210,144	447.4	388,703	469.3	233,145	343.7
Motor vehicle theft	53,244	21.9	7,056	15.6	10,749	22.9	15,059	18.2	20,380	30.0
Arson	8,882	3.7	1,586	3.5	1,538	3.3	2,754	3.3	3,004	4.4
Other assaults	930,210	382.9	167,336	369.4	183,609	390.9	375,164	453.0	204,101	300.9
Forgery and counterfeiting	51,987	21.4	9,673	21.4	7,461	15.9	22,944	27.7	11,909	17.6
Fraud	118,374	48.7	20,812	45.9	20,251	43.1	60,462	73.0	16,849	24.8
Embezzlement	12,429	5.1	1,309	2.9	1,894	4.0	6,891	8.3	2,335	3.4
Stolen property; buying, receiving, possessing	75,989	31.3	15,146	33.4	13,276	28.3	20,261	24.5	27,306	40.3
Vandalism	177,325	73.0	41,276	91.1	37,007	78.8	46,022	55.6	53,020	78.2
Weapons; carrying, possessing, etc.	115,464	47.5	15,564	34.4	22,206	47.3	39,940	48.2	37,754	55.7
Prostitution and commercialized vice	43,395	17.9	5,381	11.9	5,847	12.4	15,719	19.0	16,448	24.2
Sex offenses (except forcible rape and prostitution)	52,768	21.7	8,953	19.8	10,245	21.8	15,460	18.7	18,110	26.7
Drug abuse violations	1,200,538	494.2	208,351	460.0	222,495	473.7	450,386	543.8	319,306	470.7
Gambling	5,976	2.5	525	1.2	2,774	5.9	2,112	2.5	565	0.8
Offenses against the family and children	82,121	33.8	16,862	37.2	17,664	37.6	35,068	42.3	12,527	18.5
Driving under the influence	987,224	406.4	140,014	309.1	205,543	437.6	318,531	384.6	323,136	476.4
Liquor laws	341,328	140.5	43,337	95.7	111,281	236.9	92,827	112.1	93,883	138.4
Drunkenness	399,920	164.6	35,089	77.5	27,876	59.3	233,492	281.9	103,463	152.5
Disorderly conduct	422,382	173.9	104,887	231.6	123,407	262.7	131,900	159.2	62,188	91.7
Vagrancy	20,900	8.6	1,889	4.2	3,570	7.6	5,968	7.2	9,473	14.0
All other offenses (except traffic)	2,666,096	1,097.5	356,840	787.8	484,204	1,030.9	1,104,223	1,333.2	720,829	1,062.6
Suspicion	1,160	0.5	52	0.1	257	0.5	822	1.0	29	0.0
Curfew and loitering law violations	54,131	22.3	18,761	41.4	9,152	19.5	11,867	14.3	14,351	21.2

1 Does not include suspicion. 2 Violent crimes are offenses of murder and nonnegligent manslaughter, forcible rape, robbery, and aggravated assault. Property crimes are offenses of burglary, larceny-theft, motor vehicle theft, and arson.

Table 31. Number and Rate of Arrests, by Population Group, 2012

(Number, rate per 100,000 population)

Offense charged	Total (12,196 agencies; population 242,925,157)		Cities											
			Total cities (8,871 cities; population 165,509,499)		Group I (63 cities, 250,000 and over; population 43,104,213)		Group II (179 cities, 100,000 to 249,999; population 26,589,685)		Group III (394 cities, 50,000 to 99,999; population 27,345,457)		Group IV (717 cities, 25,000 to 49,999; population 24,749,466)		Group V (1,510 cities, 10,000 to 24,999; population 24,038,826)	
	Total	Rate	Total	Rate	Total	Rate	Total	Rate	Total	Rate	Total	Rate	Total	Rate
Total [1]	9,445,500	3,888.2	6,988,016	4,222.1	1,842,000	4,275.4	1,079,000	4,059.2	1,038,825	3,798.9	977,023	3,947.7	1,011,849	4,209.2
Violent crime [2]	404,037	166.3	313,440	189.4	116,235	269.7	55,773	209.8	46,472	169.9	35,822	144.7	32,989	137.2
Murder and nonnegligent manslaughter	8,514	3.5	6,308	3.8	2,887	6.7	1,136	4.3	729	2.7	662	2.7	521	2.2
Forcible rape	13,971	5.8	10,304	6.2	3,669	8.5	1,531	5.8	1,411	5.2	1,271	5.1	1,240	5.2
Robbery	80,487	33.1	68,207	41.2	29,816	69.2	12,284	46.2	9,646	35.3	7,249	29.3	5,687	23.7
Aggravated assault	301,065	123.9	228,621	138.1	79,863	185.3	40,822	153.5	34,686	126.8	26,640	107.6	25,541	106.2
Property crime [2]	1,282,906	528.1	1,036,807	626.4	253,079	587.1	166,275	625.3	167,891	614.0	164,861	666.1	162,337	675.3
Burglary	220,284	90.7	161,277	97.4	43,382	100.6	30,243	113.7	27,398	100.2	20,962	84.7	21,110	87.8
Larceny-theft	1,000,496	411.9	829,563	501.2	193,259	448.4	127,934	481.1	133,883	489.6	138,878	561.1	136,202	566.6
Motor vehicle theft	53,244	21.9	39,234	23.7	14,447	33.5	7,081	26.6	5,568	20.4	4,138	16.7	4,195	17.5
Arson	8,882	3.7	6,733	4.1	1,991	4.6	1,017	3.8	1,042	3.8	883	3.6	830	3.5
Other assaults	930,210	382.9	699,670	422.7	194,812	452.0	114,989	432.5	107,589	393.4	97,009	392.0	95,623	397.8
Forgery and counterfeiting	51,987	21.4	38,298	23.1	8,876	20.6	5,435	20.4	5,994	21.9	5,913	23.9	6,443	26.8
Fraud	118,374	48.7	77,873	47.1	15,975	37.1	10,741	40.4	11,149	40.8	12,307	49.7	12,254	51.0
Embezzlement	12,429	5.1	9,436	5.7	2,179	5.1	1,534	5.8	1,536	5.6	1,588	6.4	1,511	6.3
Stolen property; buying, receiving, possessing	75,989	31.3	56,619	34.2	13,809	32.0	9,518	35.8	10,546	38.6	8,612	34.8	8,194	34.1
Vandalism	177,325	73.0	137,216	82.9	35,219	81.7	20,496	77.1	21,891	80.1	20,463	82.7	19,961	83.0
Weapons; carrying, possessing, etc.	115,464	47.5	90,466	54.7	35,029	81.3	14,729	55.4	13,013	47.6	9,702	39.2	8,651	36.0
Prostitution and commercialized vice	43,395	17.9	40,536	24.5	29,495	68.4	5,251	19.7	2,345	8.6	1,946	7.9	1,065	4.4
Sex offenses (except forcible rape and prostitution)	52,768	21.7	37,482	22.6	12,749	29.6	5,322	20.0	5,458	20.0	4,735	19.1	4,828	20.1
Drug abuse violations	1,200,538	494.2	888,894	537.1	280,244	650.2	137,259	516.2	131,786	481.9	112,055	452.8	109,619	456.0
Gambling	5,976	2.5	5,018	3.0	3,726	8.6	462	1.7	129	0.5	220	0.9	189	0.8
Offenses against the family and children	82,121	33.8	39,871	24.1	5,580	12.9	7,597	28.6	5,334	19.5	7,448	30.1	6,799	28.3
Driving under the influence	987,224	406.4	580,534	350.8	124,929	289.8	81,800	307.6	82,966	303.4	83,886	338.9	97,514	405.7
Liquor laws	341,328	140.5	274,760	166.0	48,647	112.9	35,299	132.8	33,302	121.8	37,971	153.4	45,795	190.5
Drunkenness	399,920	164.6	345,951	209.0	75,046	174.1	62,560	235.3	57,521	210.3	49,954	201.8	49,241	204.8
Disorderly conduct	422,382	173.9	357,193	215.8	78,074	181.1	46,933	176.5	49,365	180.5	50,788	205.2	60,109	250.0
Vagrancy	20,900	8.6	18,204	11.0	8,955	20.8	2,064	7.8	3,608	13.2	1,588	6.4	825	3.4
All other offenses (except traffic)	2,666,096	1,097.5	1,889,294	1,141.5	474,128	1,100.0	290,868	1,093.9	274,753	1,004.7	265,116	1,071.2	283,622	1,179.8
Suspicion	1,160	0.5	777	0.5	4	0.0	0	0.0	157	0.6	311	1.3	54	0.2
Curfew and loitering law violations	54,131	22.3	50,454	30.5	26,100	60.6	4,428	16.7	6,181	22.6	5,039	20.4	4,280	17.8

Table 31. Number and Rate of Arrests, by Population Group, 2012

(Number, rate per 100,000 population)

Offense charged	Cities		Counties					
	Group VI (6,006 cities, under 10,000; population 19,681,852)		Metropolitan counties (1,363 agencies; population 55,902,687)		Nonmetropolitan counties (1,962 agencies; population 21,512,971)		Suburban areas[3] (6,766 agencies; population 110,031,559)	
	Total	Rate	Total	Rate	Total	Rate	Total	Rate
Total [1]	1,038,096	5,274.4	1,722,871	3,081.9	734,613	3,414.7	3,914,513	3,557.6
Violent crime [2]	26,149	132.9	69,908	125.1	20,689	96.2	140,613	127.8
Murder and nonnegligent manslaughter	373	1.9	1,565	2.8	641	3.0	2,662	2.4
Forcible rape	1,182	6.0	2,470	4.4	1,197	5.6	5,038	4.6
Robbery	3,525	17.9	10,738	19.2	1,542	7.2	24,196	22.0
Aggravated assault	21,069	107.0	55,135	98.6	17,309	80.5	108,717	98.8
Property crime [2]	122,364	621.7	188,370	337.0	57,729	268.3	520,748	473.3
Burglary	18,182	92.4	41,203	73.7	17,804	82.8	85,407	77.6
Larceny-theft	99,407	505.1	135,521	242.4	35,412	164.6	412,871	375.2
Motor vehicle theft	3,805	19.3	10,229	18.3	3,781	17.6	19,093	17.4
Arson	970	4.9	1,417	2.5	732	3.4	3,377	3.1
Other assaults	89,648	455.5	165,969	296.9	64,571	300.1	365,535	332.2
Forgery and counterfeiting	5,637	28.6	10,586	18.9	3,103	14.4	23,633	21.5
Fraud	15,447	78.5	27,251	48.7	13,250	61.6	55,519	50.5
Embezzlement	1,088	5.5	2,394	4.3	599	2.8	5,227	4.8
Stolen property; buying, receiving, possessing	5,940	30.2	14,945	26.7	4,425	20.6	33,073	30.1
Vandalism	19,186	97.5	29,665	53.1	10,444	48.5	71,949	65.4
Weapons; carrying, possessing, etc.	9,342	47.5	18,757	33.6	6,241	29.0	39,839	36.2
Prostitution and commercialized vice	434	2.2	2,720	4.9	139	0.6	5,819	5.3
Sex offenses (except forcible rape and prostitution)	4,390	22.3	10,924	19.5	4,362	20.3	21,003	19.1
Drug abuse violations	117,931	599.2	226,123	404.5	85,521	397.5	484,599	440.4
Gambling	292	1.5	762	1.4	196	0.9	1,290	1.2
Offenses against the family and children	7,113	36.1	30,601	54.7	11,649	54.1	44,450	40.4
Driving under the influence	109,439	556.0	240,955	431.0	165,735	770.4	455,803	414.2
Liquor laws	73,746	374.7	42,191	75.5	24,377	113.3	148,963	135.4
Drunkenness	51,629	262.3	36,185	64.7	17,784	82.7	139,655	126.9
Disorderly conduct	71,924	365.4	45,761	81.9	19,428	90.3	174,435	158.5
Vagrancy	1,164	5.9	2,494	4.5	202	0.9	5,414	4.9
All other offenses (except traffic)	300,807	1,528.3	552,957	989.1	223,845	1,040.5	1,163,506	1,057.4
Suspicion	251	1.3	218	0.4	165	0.8	765	0.7
Curfew and loitering law violations	4,426	22.5	3,353	6.0	324	1.5	13,440	12.2

1 Does not include suspicion. 2 Violent crimes are offenses of murder and nonnegligent manslaughter, forcible rape, robbery, and aggravated assault. Property crimes are offenses of burglary, larceny-theft, motor vehicle theft, and arson. 3 Suburban areas include law enforcement agencies in cities with less than 50,000 inhabitants and county law enforcement agencies that are within a Metropolitan Statistical Area. Suburban areas exclude all metropolitan agencies associated with a principal city. The agencies associated with suburban areas also appear in other groups within this table.

Table 32. Ten-Year Arrest Trends, 2003 and 2012

(Number, percent change; 9,529 agencies; 2012 estimated population 208,644,788; 2003 estimated population 193,680,679)

Offense charged	Number of persons arrested								
	Total, all ages			Under 18 years of age			18 years of age and over		
	2003	2012	Percent change	2003	2012	Percent change	2003	2012	Percent change
Total [1]	8,985,000	8,169,312	-9.1	1,403,497	881,528	-37.2	7,581,503	7,287,784	-3.9
Violent crime [2]	398,052	347,241	-12.8	60,065	38,444	-36.0	337,987	308,797	-8.6
Murder and nonnegligent manslaughter	8,258	7,133	-13.6	703	443	-37.0	7,555	6,690	-11.4
Forcible rape	16,788	11,891	-29.2	2,629	1,682	-36.0	14,159	10,209	-27.9
Robbery	71,067	68,065	-4.2	16,401	13,200	-19.5	54,666	54,865	.4
Aggravated assault	301,939	260,152	-13.8	40,332	23,119	-42.7	261,607	237,033	-9.4
Property crime [2]	1,079,664	1,111,084	2.9	313,968	200,824	-36.0	765,696	910,260	18.9
Burglary	198,856	193,882	-2.5	57,322	36,424	-36.5	141,534	157,458	11.3
Larceny-theft	775,764	863,220	11.3	223,900	152,983	-31.7	551,864	710,237	28.7
Motor vehicle theft	94,173	46,070	-51.1	27,149	8,403	-69.0	67,024	37,667	-43.8
Arson	10,871	7,912	-27.2	5,597	3,014	-46.1	5,274	4,898	-7.1
Other assaults	821,515	800,534	-2.6	158,286	113,619	-28.2	663,229	686,915	3.6
Forgery and counterfeiting	77,002	45,048	-41.5	3,246	955	-70.6	73,756	44,093	-40.2
Fraud	221,652	105,482	-52.4	5,544	3,215	-42.0	216,108	102,267	-52.7
Embezzlement	12,727	10,981	-13.7	873	309	-64.6	11,854	10,672	-10.0
Stolen property; buying, receiving, possessing	87,625	67,517	-22.9	16,843	8,903	-47.1	70,782	58,614	-17.2
Vandalism	183,465	153,004	-16.6	73,330	40,689	-44.5	110,135	112,315	2.0
Weapons; carrying, possessing, etc.	111,093	98,855	-11.0	26,016	16,137	-38.0	85,077	82,718	-2.8
Prostitution and commercialized vice	48,513	36,931	-23.9	955	564	-40.9	47,558	36,367	-23.5
Sex offenses (except forcible rape and prostitution)	60,155	47,369	-21.3	12,389	8,576	-30.8	47,766	38,793	-18.8
Drug abuse violations	1,090,948	1,028,218	-5.8	126,782	91,552	-27.8	964,166	936,666	-2.9
Gambling	4,391	2,809	-36.0	427	175	-59.0	3,964	2,634	-33.6
Offenses against the family and children	88,778	71,429	-19.5	4,370	2,144	-50.9	84,408	69,285	-17.9
Driving under the influence	955,224	860,683	-9.9	13,871	6,295	-54.6	941,353	854,388	-9.2
Liquor laws	421,176	308,191	-26.8	94,437	56,973	-39.7	326,739	251,218	-23.1
Drunkenness	378,366	350,835	-7.3	11,657	6,873	-41.0	366,709	343,962	-6.2
Disorderly conduct	420,798	349,368	-17.0	129,108	77,685	-39.8	291,690	271,683	-6.9
Vagrancy	19,787	16,704	-15.6	1,383	580	-58.1	18,404	16,124	-12.4
All other offenses (except traffic)	2,409,364	2,308,003	-4.2	255,242	157,990	-38.1	2,154,122	2,150,013	-.2
Suspicion	1,716	1,109	-35.4	373	242	-35.1	1,343	867	-35.4
Curfew and loitering law violations	94,705	49,026	-48.2	94,705	49,026	-48.2	n.a.	n.a.	n.a.

1 Does not include suspicion. 2 Violent crimes are offenses of murder and nonnegligent manslaughter, forcible rape, robbery, and aggravated assault. Property crimes are offenses of burglary, larceny-theft, motor vehicle theft, and arson. n.a. = not available

Table 33. Ten-Year Arrest Trends, by Age and Sex, 2003 and 2012

(Number, percent change; 9,529 agencies; 2012 estimated population 208,644,788; 2003 estimated population 193,680,679)

Offense charged	Male						Female					
	Total			Under 18			Total			Under 18		
	2003	2012	Percent change	2003	2012	Percent change	2003	2012	Percent change	2003	2012	Percent change
Total [1]	6,904,010	6,028,378	-12.7	1,017,933	622,485	-38.8	2,080,990	2,140,934	2.9	385,564	259,043	-32.8
Violent crime [2]	326,975	278,167	-14.9	49,002	31,170	-36.4	71,077	69,074	-2.8	11,063	7,274	-34.2
Murder and nonnegligent manslaughter	7,353	6,303	-14.3	637	403	-36.7	905	830	-8.3	66	40	-39.4
Forcible rape	16,578	11,782	-28.9	2,585	1,657	-35.9	210	109	-48.1	44	25	-43.2
Robbery	63,555	59,033	-7.1	14,904	11,831	-20.6	7,512	9,032	20.2	1,497	1,369	-8.6
Aggravated assault	239,489	201,049	-16.1	30,876	17,279	-44.0	62,450	59,103	-5.4	9,456	5,840	-38.2
Property crime [2]	745,246	694,051	-6.9	213,708	130,291	-39.0	334,418	417,033	24.7	100,260	70,533	-29.6
Burglary	170,581	161,450	-5.4	50,456	31,926	-36.7	28,275	32,432	14.7	6,866	4,498	-34.5
Larceny-theft	486,870	488,888	.4	135,857	88,715	-34.7	288,894	374,332	29.6	88,043	64,268	-27.0
Motor vehicle theft	78,642	37,237	-52.6	22,493	7,083	-68.5	15,531	8,833	-43.1	4,656	1,320	-71.6
Arson	9,153	6,476	-29.2	4,902	2,567	-47.6	1,718	1,436	-16.4	695	447	-35.7
Other assaults	622,089	577,611	-7.1	107,045	71,954	-32.8	199,426	222,923	11.8	51,241	41,665	-18.7
Forgery and counterfeiting	45,818	28,225	-38.4	2,076	685	-67.0	31,184	16,823	-46.1	1,170	270	-76.9
Fraud	120,139	62,673	-47.8	3,648	2,156	-40.9	101,513	42,809	-57.8	1,896	1,059	-44.1
Embezzlement	6,301	5,605	-11.0	522	185	-64.6	6,426	5,376	-16.3	351	124	-64.7
Stolen property; buying, receiving, possessing	71,587	53,781	-24.9	14,304	7,442	-48.0	16,038	13,736	-14.4	2,539	1,461	-42.5
Vandalism	153,555	122,544	-20.2	63,188	34,251	-45.8	29,910	30,460	1.8	10,142	6,438	-36.5
Weapons; carrying, possessing, etc.	102,092	90,790	-11.1	23,275	14,607	-37.2	9,001	8,065	-10.4	2,741	1,530	-44.2
Prostitution and commercialized vice	16,382	11,977	-26.9	248	139	-44.0	32,131	24,954	-22.3	707	425	-39.9
Sex offenses (except forcible rape and prostitution)	54,794	43,629	-20.4	11,207	7,711	-31.2	5,361	3,740	-30.2	1,182	865	-26.8
Drug abuse violations	887,736	817,198	-7.9	104,941	75,510	-28.0	203,212	211,020	3.8	21,841	16,042	-26.6
Gambling	3,694	2,284	-38.2	402	160	-60.2	697	525	-24.7	25	15	-40.0
Offenses against the family and children	68,432	52,719	-23.0	2,689	1,310	-51.3	20,346	18,710	-8.0	1,681	834	-50.4
Driving under the influence	780,679	649,664	-16.8	11,044	4,676	-57.7	174,545	211,019	20.9	2,827	1,619	-42.7
Liquor laws	311,799	217,530	-30.2	61,238	34,194	-44.2	109,377	90,661	-17.1	33,199	22,779	-31.4
Drunkenness	324,213	286,633	-11.6	8,988	5,006	-44.3	54,153	64,202	18.6	2,669	1,867	-30.0
Disorderly conduct	312,480	249,828	-20.0	88,951	49,943	-43.9	108,318	99,540	-8.1	40,157	27,742	-30.9
Vagrancy	15,521	13,647	-12.1	1,041	463	-55.5	4,266	3,057	-28.3	342	117	-65.8
All other offenses (except traffic)	1,868,452	1,734,857	-7.2	184,390	115,667	-37.3	540,912	573,146	6.0	70,852	42,323	-40.3
Suspicion	1,447	828	-42.8	282	174	-38.3	269	281	4.5	91	68	-25.3
Curfew and loitering law violations	66,026	34,965	-47.0	66,026	34,965	-47.0	28,679	14,061	-51.0	28,679	14,061	-51.0

1 Does not include suspicion. 2 Violent crimes are offenses of murder and nonnegligent manslaughter, forcible rape, robbery, and aggravated assault. Property crimes are offenses of burglary, larceny-theft, motor vehicle theft, and arson.

Table 34. Five-Year Arrest Trends, by Age, 2008 and 2012

(Number, percent change; 10,469 agencies; 2012 estimated population 226,864,503; 2008 estimated population 219,913,275)

Offense charged	Number of persons arrested								
	Total, all ages			Under 18 years of age			18 years of age and over		
	2008	2012	Percent change	2008	2012	Percent change	2008	2012	Percent change
Total [1]	10,092,276	8,853,229	-12.3	1,470,147	975,346	-33.7	8,622,129	7,877,884	-8.6
Violent crime [2]	435,413	382,183	-12.2	70,525	44,842	-36.4	364,888	337,341	-7.5
Murder and nonnegligent manslaughter	9,239	7,932	-14.1	921	515	-44.1	8,318	7,417	-10.8
Forcible rape	16,196	13,399	-17.3	2,423	1,891	-22.0	13,773	11,508	-16.4
Robbery	95,529	76,796	-19.6	26,387	15,999	-39.4	69,142	60,797	-12.1
Aggravated assault	314,449	284,056	-9.7	40,794	26,437	-35.2	273,655	257,619	-5.9
Property crime [2]	1,235,117	1,205,016	-2.4	323,622	218,896	-32.4	911,495	986,120	8.2
Burglary	226,149	207,179	-8.4	61,744	39,579	-35.9	164,405	167,600	1.9
Larceny-theft	927,243	938,154	1.2	238,923	166,357	-30.4	688,320	771,797	12.1
Motor vehicle theft	71,273	51,150	-28.2	18,100	9,701	-46.4	53,173	41,449	-22.0
Arson	10,452	8,533	-18.4	4,855	3,259	-32.9	5,597	5,274	-5.8
Other assaults	934,759	870,225	-6.9	168,213	123,725	-26.4	766,546	746,500	-2.6
Forgery and counterfeiting	66,387	47,943	-27.8	1,966	1,045	-46.8	64,421	46,898	-27.2
Fraud	170,204	112,074	-34.2	5,583	3,535	-36.7	164,621	108,539	-34.1
Embezzlement	16,113	11,318	-29.8	966	328	-66.0	15,147	10,990	-27.4
Stolen property; buying, receiving, possessing	75,968	72,094	-5.1	14,037	9,569	-31.8	61,931	62,525	1.0
Vandalism	212,069	168,648	-20.5	80,637	44,708	-44.6	131,432	123,940	-5.7
Weapons; carrying, possessing, etc.	132,213	110,262	-16.6	29,613	18,284	-38.3	102,600	91,978	-10.4
Prostitution and commercialized vice	55,856	41,494	-25.7	1,141	602	-47.2	54,715	40,892	-25.3
Sex offenses (except forcible rape and prostitution)	57,842	50,225	-13.2	10,558	9,056	-14.2	47,284	41,169	-12.9
Drug abuse violations	1,254,579	1,133,076	-9.7	133,021	101,968	-23.3	1,121,558	1,031,108	-8.1
Gambling	7,331	5,277	-28.0	1,259	669	-46.9	6,072	4,608	-24.1
Offenses against the family and children	83,374	73,598	-11.7	3,958	2,428	-38.7	79,416	71,170	-10.4
Driving under the influence	1,073,811	921,399	-14.2	11,638	6,868	-41.0	1,062,173	914,531	-13.9
Liquor laws	457,513	334,210	-27.0	96,936	61,516	-36.5	360,577	272,694	-24.4
Drunkenness	446,907	368,806	-17.5	11,362	7,303	-35.7	435,545	361,503	-17.0
Disorderly conduct	502,365	402,639	-19.9	137,513	87,654	-36.3	364,852	314,985	-13.7
Vagrancy	23,857	20,943	-12.2	1,248	577	-53.8	22,609	20,366	-9.9
All other offenses (except traffic)	2,749,630	2,464,587	-10.4	265,383	174,560	-34.2	2,484,247	2,290,027	-7.8
Suspicion	1,149	1,148	-.1	190	249	31.1	959	899	-6.3
Curfew and loitering law violations	100,968	57,212	-43.3	100,968	57,212	-43.3	n.a.	n.a.	n.a.

1 Does not include suspicion. 2 Violent crimes are offenses of murder and nonnegligent manslaughter, forcible rape, robbery, and aggravated assault. Property crimes are offenses of burglary, larceny-theft, motor vehicle theft, and arson. n.a. = not available

Table 35. Five-Year Arrest Trends, by Age and Sex, 2008 and 2012

(Number, percent change; 10,469 agencies; 2012 estimated population 226,864,503; 2008 estimated population 219,913,275)

Offense charged	Male						Female					
	Total			Under 18			Total			Under 18		
	2008	2012	Percent change	2008	2012	Percent change	2008	2012	Percent change	2008	2012	Percent change
Total [1]	7,647,153	6,551,018	-14.3	1,054,437	691,630	-34.4	2,445,123	2,302,211	-5.8	415,710	283,715	-31.8
Violent crime [2]	355,888	306,856	-13.8	58,494	36,463	-37.7	79,525	75,327	-5.3	12,031	8,379	-30.4
Murder and nonnegligent manslaughter	8,257	7,040	-14.7	860	467	-45.7	982	892	-9.2	61	48	-21.3
Forcible rape	16,005	13,277	-17.0	2,386	1,862	-22.0	191	122	-36.1	37	29	-21.6
Robbery	84,411	66,808	-20.9	23,907	14,357	-39.9	11,118	9,988	-10.2	2,480	1,642	-33.8
Aggravated assault	247,215	219,731	-11.1	31,341	19,777	-36.9	67,234	64,325	-4.3	9,453	6,660	-29.5
Property crime [2]	806,231	754,826	-6.4	207,520	142,424	-31.4	428,886	450,190	5.0	116,102	76,472	-34.1
Burglary	192,726	172,944	-10.3	54,137	34,817	-35.7	33,423	34,235	2.4	7,607	4,762	-37.4
Larceny-theft	545,625	533,419	-2.2	133,844	96,647	-27.8	381,618	404,735	6.1	105,079	69,710	-33.7
Motor vehicle theft	59,101	41,477	-29.8	15,282	8,185	-46.4	12,172	9,673	-20.5	2,818	1,516	-46.2
Arson	8,779	6,986	-20.4	4,257	2,775	-34.8	1,673	1,547	-7.5	598	484	-19.1
Other assaults	695,514	629,577	-9.5	110,878	78,232	-29.4	239,245	240,648	.6	57,335	45,493	-20.7
Forgery and counterfeiting	41,216	30,102	-27.0	1,316	743	-43.5	25,171	17,841	-29.1	650	302	-53.5
Fraud	95,302	66,664	-30.0	3,638	2,375	-34.7	74,902	45,410	-39.4	1,945	1,160	-40.4
Embezzlement	7,801	5,821	-25.4	553	199	-64.0	8,312	5,497	-33.9	413	129	-68.8
Stolen property; buying, receiving, possessing	61,585	57,529	-6.6	11,778	8,084	-31.4	14,383	14,565	1.3	2,259	1,485	-34.3
Vandalism	176,055	135,272	-23.2	69,928	37,758	-46.0	36,014	33,376	-7.3	10,709	6,950	-35.1
Weapons; carrying, possessing, etc.	122,328	101,436	-17.1	26,792	16,582	-38.1	9,885	8,826	-10.7	2,821	1,702	-39.7
Prostitution and commercialized vice	17,069	13,434	-21.3	277	140	-49.5	38,787	28,060	-27.7	864	462	-46.5
Sex offenses (except forcible rape and prostitution)	52,875	46,296	-12.4	9,528	8,124	-14.7	4,967	3,929	-20.9	1,030	932	-9.5
Drug abuse violations	1,022,705	905,751	-11.4	112,499	84,619	-24.8	231,874	227,325	-2.0	20,522	17,349	-15.5
Gambling	6,810	4,724	-30.6	1,235	646	-47.7	521	553	6.1	24	23	-4.2
Offenses against the family and children	62,248	53,992	-13.3	2,552	1,499	-41.3	21,126	19,606	-7.2	1,406	929	-33.9
Driving under the influence	842,366	695,861	-17.4	8,740	5,105	-41.6	231,445	225,538	-2.6	2,898	1,763	-39.2
Liquor laws	329,520	236,823	-28.1	60,255	37,037	-38.5	127,993	97,387	-23.9	36,681	24,479	-33.3
Drunkenness	374,745	301,008	-19.7	8,669	5,302	-38.8	72,162	67,798	-6.0	2,693	2,001	-25.7
Disorderly conduct	371,206	290,139	-21.8	92,809	56,733	-38.9	131,159	112,500	-14.2	44,704	30,921	-30.8
Vagrancy	18,716	16,775	-10.4	996	478	-52.0	5,141	4,168	-18.9	252	99	-60.7
All other offenses (except traffic)	2,117,469	1,857,381	-12.3	196,476	128,336	-34.7	632,161	607,206	-3.9	68,907	46,224	-32.9
Suspicion	901	868	-3.7	149	181	21.5	248	280	12.9	41	68	65.9
Curfew and loitering law violations	69,504	40,751	-41.4	69,504	40,751	-41.4	31,464	16,461	-47.7	31,464	16,461	-47.7

1 Does not include suspicion. 2 Violent crimes are offenses of murder and nonnegligent manslaughter, forcible rape, robbery, and aggravated assault. Property crimes are offenses of burglary, larceny-theft, motor vehicle theft, and arson.

Table 36. Current Year over Previous Year Arrest Trends, 2011–2012

(Number, percent change; 11,407 agencies; 2012 estimated population 234,487,402; 2011 estimated population 232,627,938)

Offense charged	Number of persons arrested											
	Total, all ages			Under 15 years of age			Under 18 years of age			18 years of age and over		
	2011	2012	Percent change	2011	2012	Percent change	2011	2012	Percent change	2011	2012	Percent change
Total [1]	9,179,091	8,996,418	-2.0	297,647	270,470	-9.1	1,081,197	968,534	-10.4	8,097,894	8,027,884	.0
Violent crime[2]	386,599	379,773	-1.8	12,790	11,929	-6.7	47,265	42,378	-10.3	339,334	337,395	-.6
Murder and nonnegligent manslaughter	7,759	7,714	-.6	66	60	-9.1	583	499	-14.4	7,176	7,215	.5
Forcible rape	13,795	13,028	-5.6	690	697	1.0	1,955	1,837	-6.0	11,840	11,191	-5.5
Robbery	75,364	72,785	-3.4	2,921	2,719	-6.9	16,068	14,315	-10.9	59,296	58,470	-1.4
Aggravated assault	289,681	286,246	-1.2	9,113	8,453	-7.2	28,659	25,727	-10.2	261,022	260,519	-.2
Property crime[2]	1227334	1231286	.3	71071	64321	-9.5	251833	222658	-11.6	975501	1008628	3.4
Burglary	220,518	213,878	-3.0	12,538	11,294	-9.9	46,006	40,351	-12.3	174,512	173,527	-.6
Larceny-theft	951,377	960,552	1.0	54,559	49,126	-10.0	192,683	169,992	-11.8	758,694	790,560	4.2
Motor vehicle theft	46,790	48,148	2.9	1,923	1,940	.9	9,553	8,991	-5.9	37,237	39,157	5.2
Arson	8,649	8,708	.7	2,051	1,961	-4.4	3,591	3,324	-7.4	5,058	5,384	6.4
Other assaults	914,757	886,249	-3.1	54,051	49,605	-8.2	140,131	127,132	-9.3	774,626	759,117	-2.0
Forgery and counterfeiting	53,321	50,577	-5.1	154	152	-1.3	1,186	1,070	-9.8	52,135	49,507	-5.0
Fraud	125,565	117,574	-6.4	595	653	9.7	3,873	3,599	-7.1	121,692	113,975	-6.3
Embezzlement	12,360	12,235	-1.0	31	23	-25.8	321	341	6.2	12,039	11,894	-1.2
Stolen property; buying, receiving, possessing	71,702	75,547	5.4	2,252	2,247	-.2	10,321	10,037	-2.8	61,381	65,510	6.7
Vandalism	178,084	169,038	-5.1	19,885	17,573	-11.6	51,238	44,578	-13.0	126,846	124,460	-1.9
Weapons; carrying, possessing, etc.	110,193	107,747	-2.2	6,792	6,097	-10.2	20,170	17,647	-12.5	90,023	90,100	.1
Prostitution and commercialized vice	38,123	37,667	-1.2	67	44	-34.3	718	579	-19.4	37,405	37,088	-.8
Sex offenses (except forcible rape and prostitution)	51,129	50,945	-.4	4,582	4,701	2.6	9,452	9,417	-.4	41,677	41,528	-.4
Drug abuse violations	1,095,101	1,116,307	1.9	18,636	17,484	-6.2	106,561	100,498	-5.7	988,540	1,015,809	2.8
Gambling	3,495	3,187	-8.8	47	31	-34.0	307	287	-6.5	3,188	2,900	-9.0
Offenses against the family and children	86,381	83,136	-3.8	798	819	2.6	2,604	2,571	-1.3	83,777	80,565	-3.8
Driving under the influence	902,425	864,815	-4.2	121	128	5.8	7,637	6,844	-10.4	894,788	857,971	-4.1
Liquor laws	363,576	337,237	-7.2	6,551	6,001	-8.4	68,282	62,380	-8.6	295,294	274,857	-6.9
Drunkenness	411,893	397,507	-3.5	1,076	914	-15.1	8,902	7,637	-14.2	402,991	389,870	-3.3
Disorderly conduct	428,986	404,195	-5.8	39,178	34,030	-13.1	102,400	87,983	-14.1	326,586	316,212	-3.2
Vagrancy	21,864	20,622	-5.7	390	255	-34.6	1,366	981	-28.2	20,498	19,641	-4.2
All other offenses (except traffic)	2,649,306	2,610,649	-1.5	46,578	42,917	-7.9	199,733	179,792	-10.0	2,449,573	2,430,857	-.8
Suspicion	987	1,175	19.0	34	88	158.8	114	247	116.7	873	928	6.3
Curfew and loitering law violations	46,897	40,125	-14.4	12,002	10,546	-12.1	46,897	40,125	-14.4	n.a.	n.a.	n.a.

1 Does not include suspicion. 2 Violent crimes are offenses of murder and nonnegligent manslaughter, forcible rape, robbery, and aggravated assault. Property crimes are offenses of burglary, larceny-theft, motor vehicle theft, and arson. n.a. = not available

Table 37. Current Year over Previous Year Arrest Trends, by Age and Sex, 2011–2012

(Number, percent change; 11,407 agencies; 2012 estimated population 234,487,402; 2011 estimated population 232,627,938)

Offense charged	Male						Female					
	Total			Under 18			Total			Under 18		
	2011	2012	Percent change	2011	2012	Percent change	2011	2012	Percent change	2011	2012	Percent change
Total [1]	6,784,643	6,619,871	-2.4	761,351	682,409	-10.4	2,394,448	2,376,547	-.7	319,846	286,125	-10.5
Violent crime [2]	311,164	304,438	-2.2	38,743	34,347	-11.3	75,435	75,335	-.1	8,522	8,031	-5.8
Murder and nonnegligent manslaughter	6,827	6,822	-.1	533	448	-15.9	932	892	-4.3	50	51	2.0
Forcible rape	13,641	12,900	-5.4	1,913	1,810	-5.4	154	128	-16.9	42	27	-35.7
Robbery	66,172	63,239	-4.4	14,640	12,873	-12.1	9,192	9,546	3.9	1,428	1,442	1.0
Aggravated assault	224,524	221,477	-1.4	21,657	19,216	-11.3	65,157	64,769	-.6	7,002	6,511	-7.0
Property crime [2]	768,202	767,677	-.1	159,850	144,438	-9.6	459,132	463,609	1.0	91,983	78,220	-15.0
Burglary	185,517	178,258	-3.9	40,478	35,472	-12.4	35,001	35,620	1.8	5,528	4,879	-11.7
Larceny-theft	537,318	543,384	1.1	108,263	98,565	-9.0	414,059	417,168	.8	84,420	71,427	-15.4
Motor vehicle theft	38,233	38,894	1.7	8,016	7,570	-5.6	8,557	9,254	8.1	1,537	1,421	-7.5
Arson	7,134	7,141	.1	3,093	2,831	-8.5	1,515	1,567	3.4	498	493	-1.0
Other assaults	662,274	638,691	-3.6	90,224	80,552	-10.7	252,483	247,558	-2.0	49,907	46,580	-6.7
Forgery and counterfeiting	33,293	31,607	-5.1	842	756	-10.2	20,028	18,970	-5.3	344	314	-8.7
Fraud	74,154	69,618	-6.1	2,531	2,428	-4.1	51,411	47,956	-6.7	1,342	1,171	-12.7
Embezzlement	6,217	6,307	1.4	198	209	5.6	6,143	5,928	-3.5	123	132	7.3
Stolen property; buying, receiving, possessing	57,200	60,143	5.1	8,581	8,388	-2.2	14,502	15,404	6.2	1,740	1,649	-5.2
Vandalism	143,936	134,879	-6.3	43,582	37,456	-14.1	34,148	34,159	*	7,656	7,122	-7.0
Weapons; carrying, possessing, etc.	101,224	98,871	-2.3	18,154	16,008	-11.8	8,969	8,876	-1.0	2,016	1,639	-18.7
Prostitution and commercialized vice	11,734	12,343	5.2	154	136	-11.7	26,389	25,324	-4.0	564	443	-21.5
Sex offenses (except forcible rape and prostitution)	47,315	47,067	-.5	8,429	8,463	.4	3,814	3,878	1.7	1,023	954	-6.7
Drug abuse violations	872,927	884,037	1.3	88,091	82,656	-6.2	222,174	232,270	4.5	18,470	17,842	-3.4
Gambling	2,916	2,565	-12.0	268	247	-7.8	579	622	7.4	39	40	2.6
Offenses against the family and children	64,799	61,473	-5.1	1,607	1,593	-.9	21,582	21,663	.4	997	978	-1.9
Driving under the influence	679,679	650,223	-4.3	5,688	5,067	-10.9	222,746	214,592	-3.7	1,949	1,777	-8.8
Liquor laws	255,986	238,705	-6.8	40,987	37,587	-8.3	107,590	98,532	-8.4	27,295	24,793	-9.2
Drunkenness	336,831	324,122	-3.8	6,588	5,567	-15.5	75,062	73,385	-2.2	2,314	2,070	-10.5
Disorderly conduct	307,112	288,390	-6.1	66,669	56,656	-15.0	121,874	115,805	-5.0	35,731	31,327	-12.3
Vagrancy	17,526	16,428	-6.3	1,058	782	-26.1	4,338	4,194	-3.3	308	199	-35.4
All other offenses (except traffic)	1,997,772	1,954,773	-2.2	146,725	131,559	-10.3	651,534	655,876	.7	53,008	48,233	-9.0
Suspicion	752	891	18.5	82	178	117.1	235	284	20.9	32	69	115.6
Curfew and loitering law violations	32,382	27,514	-15.0	32,382	27,514	-15.0	14,515	12,611	-13.1	14,515	12,611	-13.1

1 Does not include suspicion. 2 Violent crimes are offenses of murder and nonnegligent manslaughter, forcible rape, robbery, and aggravated assault. Property crimes are offenses of burglary, larceny-theft, motor vehicle theft, and arson. * = Less than one-tenth of 1 percent.

Table 38. Arrests, Distribution by Age, 2012

(Number, percent; 12,196 agencies; 2012 estimated population 242,925,157)

Offense charged	Total, all ages	Ages under 15	Ages under 18	Ages 18 and over	Under 10	10–12	13–14	15	16	17	18	19	20
Total	9,446,660	283,565	1,020,334	8,426,326	7,099	60,624	215,842	190,906	247,028	298,835	384,488	419,201	419,158
Total percent distribution[1]	100.0	3.0	10.8	89.2	0.1	0.6	2.3	2.0	2.6	3.2	4.1	4.4	4.4
Violent crime [2]	404,037	13,218	47,237	356,800	307	2,960	9,951	9,084	11,578	13,357	16,121	17,116	17,059
Violent crime percent distribution[1]	100.0	3.3	11.7	88.3	0.1	0.7	2.5	2.2	2.9	3.3	4.0	4.2	4.2
Murder and nonnegligent manslaughter	8,514	63	560	7,954	1	10	52	78	157	262	418	544	558
Forcible rape	13,971	740	1,954	12,017	7	177	556	336	393	485	685	579	577
Robbery	80,487	3,212	16,563	63,924	28	401	2,783	3,327	4,524	5,500	6,338	5,933	5,089
Aggravated assault	301,065	9,203	28,160	272,905	271	2,372	6,560	5,343	6,504	7,110	8,680	10,060	10,835
Property crime [2]	1,282,906	66,402	230,803	1,052,103	1,320	14,479	50,603	44,066	56,382	63,953	73,024	66,771	59,488
Property crime percent distribution[1]	100.0	5.2	18.0	82.0	0.1	1.1	3.9	3.4	4.4	5.0	5.7	5.2	4.6
Burglary	220,284	11,743	42,075	178,209	331	2,428	8,984	8,192	10,286	11,854	14,474	13,197	11,529
Larceny-theft	1,000,496	50,581	175,261	825,235	805	11,149	38,627	33,039	42,781	48,860	55,207	50,632	45,407
Motor vehicle theft	53,244	2,138	10,185	43,059	9	229	1,900	2,318	2,878	2,851	2,963	2,644	2,318
Arson	8,882	1,940	3,282	5,600	175	673	1,092	517	437	388	380	298	234
Other assaults	930,210	51,196	132,198	798,012	1,549	13,213	36,434	25,252	27,873	27,877	26,298	28,257	30,865
Forgery and counterfeiting	51,987	158	1,106	50,881	4	21	133	103	254	591	1,378	2,025	2,214
Fraud	118,374	638	3,610	114,764	15	104	519	561	959	1,452	2,749	3,707	4,302
Embezzlement	12,429	23	341	12,088	0	4	19	27	95	196	511	698	732
Stolen property; buying, receiving, possessing	75,989	2,285	10,176	65,813	29	362	1,894	2,061	2,642	3,188	4,143	4,011	3,662
Vandalism	177,325	18,213	46,468	130,857	865	5,033	12,315	8,487	9,829	9,939	9,791	8,805	8,098
Weapons; carrying, possessing, etc.	115,464	6,350	18,856	96,608	384	1,713	4,253	3,284	4,180	5,042	6,071	6,028	5,698
Prostitution and commercialized vice	43,395	46	616	42,779	0	5	41	84	183	303	1,251	1,724	1,922
Sex offenses (except forcible rape and prostitution)	52,768	4,794	9,570	43,198	177	1,403	3,214	1,625	1,543	1,608	1,935	1,827	1,758
Drug abuse violations	1,200,538	18,038	107,095	1,093,443	118	2,306	15,614	17,705	28,251	43,101	66,085	69,921	66,941
Gambling	5,976	75	732	5,244	1	10	64	127	228	302	397	397	377
Offenses against the family and children	82,121	855	2,663	79,458	54	193	608	525	622	661	1,159	1,394	1,663
Driving under the influence	987,224	140	7,236	979,988	17	12	111	280	1,644	5,172	15,606	23,557	29,091
Liquor laws	341,328	6,027	62,611	278,717	36	408	5,583	9,238	17,737	29,609	55,101	60,807	52,581
Drunkenness	399,920	928	7,618	392,302	27	67	834	1,221	1,769	3,700	9,181	10,855	11,552
Disorderly conduct	422,382	35,051	92,017	330,365	642	7,936	26,473	18,704	19,567	18,695	16,517	15,696	15,620
Vagrancy	20,900	251	984	19,916	1	37	213	222	251	260	854	832	809
All other offenses (except traffic)	2,666,096	43,846	184,073	2,482,023	1,268	7,714	34,864	35,964	46,959	57,304	76,265	94,709	104,670
Suspicion	1,160	78	193	967	5	24	49	34	44	37	51	64	56
Curfew and loitering law violations	54,131	14,953	54,131	n.a.	280	2,620	12,053	12,252	14,438	12,488	n.a.	n.a.	n.a.

Table 38. Arrests, Distribution by Age, 2012

(Number, percent; 12,196 agencies; 2012 estimated population 242,925,157)

Offense charged	21	22	23	24	25–29	30–34	35–39	40–44	45–49	50–54	55–59	60–64	65 and over
Total	405,847	387,024	359,529	337,233	1,444,699	1,137,938	803,258	729,886	641,864	491,121	264,550	118,772	81,758
Total percent distribution[1]	4.3	4.1	3.8	3.6	15.3	12.0	8.5	7.7	6.8	5.2	2.8	1.3	0.9
Violent crime [2]	17,613	16,735	15,601	14,763	63,112	49,961	34,790	30,624	26,173	18,830	10,102	4,609	3,591
Violent crime percent distribution[1]	4.4	4.1	3.9	3.7	15.6	12.4	8.6	7.6	6.5	4.7	2.5	1.1	0.9
Murder and nonnegligent manslaughter	540	465	423	393	1,455	983	635	472	408	289	178	100	93
Forcible rape	539	498	483	408	1,815	1,672	1,276	1,165	960	634	359	200	167
Robbery	4,409	3,881	3,351	3,051	11,017	7,262	4,289	3,661	2,883	1,704	698	250	108
Aggravated assault	12,125	11,891	11,344	10,911	48,825	40,044	28,590	25,326	21,922	16,203	8,867	4,059	3,223
Property crime [2]	53,267	48,740	44,254	41,000	174,791	135,686	93,299	86,209	73,933	53,582	27,672	11,832	8,555
Property crime percent distribution[1]	4.2	3.8	3.4	3.2	13.6	10.6	7.3	6.7	5.8	4.2	2.2	0.9	0.7
Burglary	10,231	9,161	8,319	7,597	30,863	22,800	14,650	13,163	10,646	6,945	3,016	1,011	607
Larceny-theft	40,651	37,210	33,917	31,422	135,078	105,642	73,740	69,119	60,342	44,819	23,810	10,482	7,757
Motor vehicle theft	2,144	2,133	1,814	1,808	8,003	6,518	4,345	3,479	2,471	1,451	625	225	118
Arson	241	236	204	173	847	726	564	448	474	367	221	114	73
Other assaults	34,663	34,555	32,951	31,986	141,436	117,488	85,890	77,612	65,620	47,163	23,845	10,631	8,752
Forgery and counterfeiting	2,157	2,162	2,172	2,064	9,899	8,511	5,858	4,779	3,582	2,339	1,074	428	239
Fraud	3,880	4,128	4,136	4,098	19,766	18,097	14,005	12,775	9,783	6,524	3,736	1,755	1,323
Embezzlement	802	652	559	486	1,992	1,590	1,186	1,070	774	518	299	141	78
Stolen property; buying, receiving, possessing	3,462	3,363	3,019	2,813	12,281	9,586	6,208	5,256	3,869	2,439	1,060	430	211
Vandalism	8,213	7,262	6,330	5,727	23,215	16,338	10,707	9,021	7,375	5,268	2,554	1,177	976
Weapons; carrying, possessing, etc.	5,699	5,454	4,939	4,601	18,087	13,096	7,785	6,191	4,954	3,841	2,117	1,094	953
Prostitution and commercialized vice	1,992	1,950	1,930	1,817	7,497	5,826	4,475	4,492	3,711	2,263	1,077	481	371
Sex offenses (except forcible rape and prostitution)	1,649	1,458	1,278	1,216	5,576	5,155	4,364	4,350	4,061	3,401	2,208	1,340	1,622
Drug abuse violations	63,460	58,784	53,087	48,313	199,360	147,310	93,564	78,938	65,481	46,942	23,002	8,604	3,651
Gambling	306	264	272	207	718	442	363	373	302	286	217	167	156
Offenses against the family and children	2,094	2,317	2,421	2,631	14,519	14,779	11,926	9,874	7,030	4,401	2,007	733	510
Driving under the influence	45,378	46,724	45,057	42,900	179,559	134,935	98,046	91,049	82,193	68,106	40,922	21,462	15,403
Liquor laws	8,724	6,132	4,626	3,882	15,228	12,221	9,927	11,483	13,295	12,309	7,141	3,409	1,851
Drunkenness	18,341	16,527	14,991	13,740	58,991	47,945	37,300	39,727	42,167	37,500	20,662	8,497	4,326
Disorderly conduct	19,643	17,418	15,163	13,918	53,588	40,150	28,738	26,642	25,657	21,233	11,467	5,290	3,625
Vagrancy	650	598	614	499	2,247	2,059	1,662	2,078	2,366	2,323	1,417	617	291
All other offenses (except traffic)	113,807	111,752	106,089	100,530	442,680	356,636	253,080	227,278	199,467	151,803	81,934	36,062	25,261
Suspicion	47	49	40	42	157	127	85	65	71	50	37	13	13
Curfew and loitering law violations	n.a.	n.a.	n.a.	n.a.	n.a.	n.a.	n.a.	n.a.	n.a.	n.a.	n.a.	n.a.	n.a.

1 Because of rounding, the percentages may not sum to 100 percent. 2 Violent crimes are offenses of murder and nonnegligent manslaughter, forcible rape, robbery, and aggravated assault. Property crimes are offenses of burglary, larceny-theft, motor vehicle theft, and arson. n.a. = not available

Table 39. Male Arrests, Distribution by Age, 2012

(Number, percent; 12,196 agencies; 2012 estimated population 242,925,157)

Offense charged	Total, all ages	Ages under 15	Ages under 18	Ages 18 and over	Under 10	10–12	13–14	15	16	17	18	19	20
Total	6,972,023	196,357	722,855	6,249,168	5,747	43,745	146,865	131,331	175,582	219,585	286,423	311,000	309,671
Total percent distribution[1]	100.0	2.8	10.4	89.6	0.1	0.6	2.1	1.9	2.5	3.1	4.1	4.5	4.4
Violent crime [2]	323,489	10,270	38,161	285,328	267	2,351	7,652	7,178	9,436	11,277	13,641	14,207	13,849
Violent crime percent distribution[1]	100.0	3.2	11.8	88.2	0.1	0.7	2.4	2.2	2.9	3.5	4.2	4.4	4.3
Murder and nonnegligent manslaughter	7,549	55	506	7,043	0	10	45	70	144	237	384	505	518
Forcible rape	13,840	727	1,926	11,914	6	175	546	333	388	478	681	575	572
Robbery	70,059	2,825	14,897	55,162	28	347	2,450	2,981	4,075	5,016	5,748	5,323	4,468
Aggravated assault	232,041	6,663	20,832	211,209	233	1,819	4,611	3,794	4,829	5,546	6,828	7,804	8,291
Property crime [2]	803,567	44,048	150,368	653,199	1,021	9,831	33,196	28,911	36,351	41,058	47,286	42,769	37,577
Property crime percent distribution[1]	100.0	5.5	18.7	81.3	0.1	1.2	4.1	3.6	4.5	5.1	5.9	5.3	4.7
Burglary	184,249	10,199	37,089	147,160	277	2,117	7,805	7,221	9,138	10,531	12,800	11,498	9,817
Larceny-theft	568,859	30,451	101,848	467,011	577	6,945	22,929	19,304	24,352	27,741	31,588	28,805	25,651
Motor vehicle theft	43,176	1,748	8,610	34,566	9	192	1,547	1,936	2,474	2,452	2,575	2,208	1,916
Arson	7,283	1,650	2,821	4,462	158	577	915	450	387	334	323	258	193
Other assaults	672,170	32,438	83,673	588,497	1,273	9,018	22,147	15,175	17,568	18,492	18,062	19,319	21,294
Forgery and counterfeiting	32,627	123	779	31,848	4	16	103	74	179	403	933	1,312	1,391
Fraud	70,486	434	2,424	68,062	11	73	350	377	639	974	1,803	2,381	2,666
Embezzlement	6,414	18	209	6,205	0	4	14	21	54	116	273	374	424
Stolen property; buying, receiving, possessing	60,538	1,849	8,512	52,026	23	287	1,539	1,709	2,210	2,744	3,524	3,324	2,998
Vandalism	141,568	15,243	39,038	102,530	758	4,183	10,302	7,113	8,289	8,393	8,190	7,192	6,492
Weapons; carrying, possessing, etc.	105,923	5,654	17,056	88,867	347	1,518	3,789	2,940	3,816	4,646	5,694	5,673	5,300
Prostitution and commercialized vice	14,024	20	146	13,878	0	2	18	18	46	62	168	238	297
Sex offenses (except forcible rape and prostitution)	48,647	4,305	8,608	40,039	153	1,266	2,886	1,422	1,401	1,480	1,760	1,676	1,605
Drug abuse violations	956,962	14,044	88,819	868,143	99	1,815	12,130	14,431	23,729	36,615	55,585	57,915	55,133
Gambling	5,258	67	689	4,569	0	10	57	123	218	281	383	376	337
Offenses against the family and children	60,251	504	1,661	58,590	41	112	351	319	404	434	775	955	1,089
Driving under the influence	743,029	102	5,371	737,658	11	8	83	197	1,195	3,877	11,802	17,735	21,790
Liquor laws	241,175	3,025	37,722	203,453	20	224	2,781	4,890	10,740	19,067	36,618	41,761	36,768
Drunkenness	326,264	588	5,571	320,693	22	44	522	817	1,253	2,913	7,201	8,670	9,200
Disorderly conduct	303,198	22,223	59,502	243,696	520	5,446	16,257	11,580	12,695	13,004	11,887	11,423	11,285
Vagrancy	16,667	181	774	15,893	1	22	158	175	202	216	624	594	577
All other offenses (except traffic)	2,000,269	30,749	135,018	1,865,251	948	5,575	24,226	25,307	34,699	44,263	60,170	73,056	79,553
Suspicion	883	52	140	743	4	16	32	28	34	26	44	50	46
Curfew and loitering law violations	38,614	10,420	38,614	n.a.	224	1,924	8,272	8,526	10,424	9,244	n.a.	n.a.	n.a.

Table 39. Male Arrests, Distribution by Age, 2012

(Number, percent; 12,196 agencies; 2012 estimated population 242,925,157)

Offense charged	21	22	23	24	25–29	30–34	35–39	40–44	45–49	50–54	55–59	60–64	65 and over
Total	301,057	285,599	264,316	246,910	1,056,515	832,564	584,878	534,503	481,044	381,053	211,593	96,269	65,773
Total percent distribution[1]	4.3	4.1	3.8	3.5	15.2	11.9	8.4	7.7	6.9	5.5	3.0	1.4	0.9
Violent crime [2]	14,107	13,421	12,248	11,741	50,045	39,436	27,378	24,103	20,596	15,173	8,332	3,944	3,107
Violent crime percent distribution[1]	4.4	4.1	3.8	3.6	15.5	12.2	8.5	7.5	6.4	4.7	2.6	1.2	1.0
Murder and nonnegligent manslaughter	489	430	376	346	1,281	860	548	401	333	248	145	93	86
Forcible rape	533	494	478	406	1,792	1,655	1,263	1,155	956	630	359	199	166
Robbery	3,864	3,365	2,869	2,641	9,294	6,076	3,534	3,109	2,454	1,481	623	223	90
Aggravated assault	9,221	9,132	8,525	8,348	37,678	30,845	22,033	19,438	16,853	12,814	7,205	3,429	2,765
Property crime [2]	33,494	29,955	26,963	24,947	104,999	81,902	56,284	53,919	47,941	35,380	17,711	7,114	4,958
Property crime percent distribution[1]	4.2	3.7	3.4	3.1	13.1	10.2	7.0	6.7	6.0	4.4	2.2	0.9	0.6
Burglary	8,634	7,661	6,826	6,304	24,854	18,117	11,743	10,546	8,748	5,787	2,499	843	483
Larceny-theft	22,945	20,406	18,555	17,108	73,297	58,111	40,610	40,214	36,843	28,084	14,510	5,981	4,303
Motor vehicle theft	1,718	1,681	1,412	1,401	6,177	5,091	3,494	2,829	2,007	1,227	527	196	107
Arson	197	207	170	134	671	583	437	330	343	282	175	94	65
Other assaults	24,190	24,396	23,591	22,895	103,959	87,897	63,670	58,336	49,713	36,569	18,947	8,544	7,115
Forgery and counterfeiting	1,340	1,333	1,346	1,258	6,021	5,180	3,501	2,973	2,327	1,631	807	327	168
Fraud	2,406	2,517	2,480	2,500	11,463	10,138	7,689	7,343	6,081	4,150	2,421	1,151	873
Embezzlement	436	303	299	261	1,062	781	570	492	388	259	166	77	40
Stolen property; buying, receiving, possessing	2,762	2,624	2,331	2,139	9,376	7,324	4,820	4,178	3,156	2,030	890	371	179
Vandalism	6,527	5,712	4,911	4,421	17,860	12,670	8,230	6,875	5,619	4,050	2,037	961	783
Weapons; carrying, possessing, etc.	5,326	5,064	4,545	4,228	16,630	11,982	7,083	5,546	4,452	3,485	1,948	1,023	888
Prostitution and commercialized vice	421	397	466	455	2,354	2,043	1,706	1,569	1,346	995	694	388	341
Sex offenses (except forcible rape and prostitution)	1,490	1,312	1,159	1,092	5,100	4,701	4,037	4,001	3,820	3,255	2,129	1,311	1,591
Drug abuse violations	51,530	47,368	42,452	38,327	156,795	115,001	72,036	59,648	49,887	36,929	18,940	7,414	3,183
Gambling	294	247	252	194	651	380	307	307	234	207	159	124	117
Offenses against the family and children	1,358	1,488	1,603	1,780	9,866	10,752	9,071	7,867	5,674	3,632	1,681	594	405
Driving under the influence	32,763	34,135	33,386	31,846	135,268	102,581	74,345	67,442	60,583	51,612	32,235	17,406	12,729
Liquor laws	6,683	4,727	3,631	3,004	11,906	9,521	7,640	9,028	10,716	10,461	6,258	3,094	1,637
Drunkenness	14,833	13,499	12,292	11,041	47,900	38,708	29,894	31,501	34,320	31,768	18,207	7,708	3,951
Disorderly conduct	14,607	12,983	11,159	10,377	39,284	29,114	20,522	19,150	18,893	16,476	9,234	4,325	2,977
Vagrancy	507	478	491	396	1,741	1,549	1,254	1,652	1,982	1,974	1,284	527	263
All other offenses (except traffic)	85,948	83,600	78,683	73,978	324,127	260,809	184,777	168,521	153,260	120,973	67,486	29,854	20,456
Suspicion	35	40	28	30	108	95	64	52	56	44	27	12	12
Curfew and loitering law violations	n.a.	n.a.	n.a.	n.a.	n.a.	n.a.	n.a.	n.a.	n.a.	n.a.	n.a.	n.a.	n.a.

1 Because of rounding, the percentages may not sum to 100 percent. 2 Violent crimes are offenses of murder and nonnegligent manslaughter, forcible rape, robbery, and aggravated assault. Property crimes are offenses of burglary, larceny-theft, motor vehicle theft, and arson. n.a. = not available

Table 40. Female Arrests, Distribution by Age, 2012

(Number, percent; 12,196 agencies; 2012 estimated population 242,925,157)

Offense charged	Total, all ages	Ages under 15	Ages under 18	Ages 18 and over	Under 10	10–12	13–14	15	16	17	18	19	20
Total	2,474,637	87,208	297,479	2,177,158	1,352	16,879	68,977	59,575	71,446	79,250	98,065	108,201	109,487
Total percent distribution[1]	100.0	3.5	12.0	88.0	0.1	0.7	2.8	2.4	2.9	3.2	4.0	4.4	4.4
Violent crime [2]	80,548	2,948	9,076	71,472	40	609	2,299	1,906	2,142	2,080	2,480	2,909	3,210
Violent crime percent distribution[1]	100.0	3.7	11.3	88.7	*	0.8	2.9	2.4	2.7	2.6	3.1	3.6	4.0
Murder and nonnegligent manslaughter	965	8	54	911	1	0	7	8	13	25	34	39	40
Forcible rape	131	13	28	103	1	2	10	3	5	7	4	4	5
Robbery	10,428	387	1,666	8,762	0	54	333	346	449	484	590	610	621
Aggravated assault	69,024	2,540	7,328	61,696	38	553	1,949	1,549	1,675	1,564	1,852	2,256	2,544
Property crime [2]	479,339	22,354	80,435	398,904	299	4,648	17,407	15,155	20,031	22,895	25,738	24,002	21,911
Property crime percent distribution[1]	100.0	4.7	16.8	83.2	0.1	1.0	3.6	3.2	4.2	4.8	5.4	5.0	4.6
Burglary	36,035	1,544	4,986	31,049	54	311	1,179	971	1,148	1,323	1,674	1,699	1,712
Larceny-theft	431,637	20,130	73,413	358,224	228	4,204	15,698	13,735	18,429	21,119	23,619	21,827	19,756
Motor vehicle theft	10,068	390	1,575	8,493	0	37	353	382	404	399	388	436	402
Arson	1,599	290	461	1,138	17	96	177	67	50	54	57	40	41
Other assaults	258,040	18,758	48,525	209,515	276	4,195	14,287	10,077	10,305	9,385	8,236	8,938	9,571
Forgery and counterfeiting	19,360	35	327	19,033	0	5	30	29	75	188	445	713	823
Fraud	47,888	204	1,186	46,702	4	31	169	184	320	478	946	1,326	1,636
Embezzlement	6,015	5	132	5,883	0	0	5	6	41	80	238	324	308
Stolen property; buying, receiving, possessing	15,451	436	1,664	13,787	6	75	355	352	432	444	619	687	664
Vandalism	35,757	2,970	7,430	28,327	107	850	2,013	1,374	1,540	1,546	1,601	1,613	1,606
Weapons; carrying, possessing, etc.	9,541	696	1,800	7,741	37	195	464	344	364	396	377	355	398
Prostitution and commercialized vice	29,371	26	470	28,901	0	3	23	66	137	241	1,083	1,486	1,625
Sex offenses (except forcible rape and prostitution)	4,121	489	962	3,159	24	137	328	203	142	128	175	151	153
Drug abuse violations	243,576	3,994	18,276	225,300	19	491	3,484	3,274	4,522	6,486	10,500	12,006	11,808
Gambling	718	8	43	675	1	0	7	4	10	21	14	21	40
Offenses against the family and children	21,870	351	1,002	20,868	13	81	257	206	218	227	384	439	574
Driving under the influence	244,195	38	1,865	242,330	6	4	28	83	449	1,295	3,804	5,822	7,301
Liquor laws	100,153	3,002	24,889	75,264	16	184	2,802	4,348	6,997	10,542	18,483	19,046	15,813
Drunkenness	73,656	340	2,047	71,609	5	23	312	404	516	787	1,980	2,185	2,352
Disorderly conduct	119,184	12,828	32,515	86,669	122	2,490	10,216	7,124	6,872	5,691	4,630	4,273	4,335
Vagrancy	4,233	70	210	4,023	0	15	55	47	49	44	230	238	232
All other offenses (except traffic)	665,827	13,097	49,055	616,772	320	2,139	10,638	10,657	12,260	13,041	16,095	21,653	25,117
Suspicion	277	26	53	224	1	8	17	6	10	11	7	14	10
Curfew and loitering law violations	15,517	4,533	15,517	n.a.	56	696	3,781	3,726	4,014	3,244	n.a.	n.a.	n.a.

Table 40. Female Arrests, Distribution by Age, 2012

(Number, percent; 12,196 agencies; 2012 estimated population 242,925,157)

Offense charged	21	22	23	24	25–29	30–34	35–39	40–44	45–49	50–54	55–59	60–64	65 and over
Total	104,790	101,425	95,213	90,323	388,184	305,374	218,380	195,383	160,820	110,068	52,957	22,503	15,985
Total percent distribution[1]	4.2	4.1	3.8	3.6	15.7	12.3	8.8	7.9	6.5	4.4	2.1	0.9	0.6
Violent crime [2]	3,506	3,314	3,353	3,022	13,067	10,525	7,412	6,521	5,577	3,657	1,770	665	484
Violent crime percent distribution[1]	4.4	4.1	4.2	3.8	16.2	13.1	9.2	8.1	6.9	4.5	2.2	0.8	0.6
Murder and nonnegligent manslaughter	51	35	47	47	174	123	87	71	75	41	33	7	7
Forcible rape	6	4	5	2	23	17	13	10	4	4	0	1	1
Robbery	545	516	482	410	1,723	1,186	755	552	429	223	75	27	18
Aggravated assault	2,904	2,759	2,819	2,563	11,147	9,199	6,557	5,888	5,069	3,389	1,662	630	458
Property crime [2]	19,773	18,785	17,291	16,053	69,792	53,784	37,015	32,290	25,992	18,202	9,961	4,718	3,597
Property crime percent distribution[1]	4.1	3.9	3.6	3.3	14.6	11.2	7.7	6.7	5.4	3.8	2.1	1.0	0.8
Burglary	1,597	1,500	1,493	1,293	6,009	4,683	2,907	2,617	1,898	1,158	517	168	124
Larceny-theft	17,706	16,804	15,362	14,314	61,781	47,531	33,130	28,905	23,499	16,735	9,300	4,501	3,454
Motor vehicle theft	426	452	402	407	1,826	1,427	851	650	464	224	98	29	11
Arson	44	29	34	39	176	143	127	118	131	85	46	20	8
Other assaults	10,473	10,159	9,360	9,091	37,477	29,591	22,220	19,276	15,907	10,594	4,898	2,087	1,637
Forgery and counterfeiting	817	829	826	806	3,878	3,331	2,357	1,806	1,255	708	267	101	71
Fraud	1,474	1,611	1,656	1,598	8,303	7,959	6,316	5,432	3,702	2,374	1,315	604	450
Embezzlement	366	349	260	225	930	809	616	578	386	259	133	64	38
Stolen property; buying, receiving, possessing	700	739	688	674	2,905	2,262	1,388	1,078	713	409	170	59	32
Vandalism	1,686	1,550	1,419	1,306	5,355	3,668	2,477	2,146	1,756	1,218	517	216	193
Weapons; carrying, possessing, etc.	373	390	394	373	1,457	1,114	702	645	502	356	169	71	65
Prostitution and commercialized vice	1,571	1,553	1,464	1,362	5,143	3,783	2,769	2,923	2,365	1,268	383	93	30
Sex offenses (except forcible rape and prostitution)	159	146	119	124	476	454	327	349	241	146	79	29	31
Drug abuse violations	11,930	11,416	10,635	9,986	42,565	32,309	21,528	19,290	15,594	10,013	4,062	1,190	468
Gambling	12	17	20	13	67	62	56	66	68	79	58	43	39
Offenses against the family and children	736	829	818	851	4,653	4,027	2,855	2,007	1,356	769	326	139	105
Driving under the influence	12,615	12,589	11,671	11,054	44,291	32,354	23,701	23,607	21,610	16,494	8,687	4,056	2,674
Liquor laws	2,041	1,405	995	878	3,322	2,700	2,287	2,455	2,579	1,848	883	315	214
Drunkenness	3,508	3,028	2,699	2,699	11,091	9,237	7,406	8,226	7,847	5,732	2,455	789	375
Disorderly conduct	5,036	4,435	4,004	3,541	14,304	11,036	8,216	7,492	6,764	4,757	2,233	965	648
Vagrancy	143	120	123	103	506	510	408	426	384	349	133	90	28
All other offenses (except traffic)	27,859	28,152	27,406	26,552	118,553	95,827	68,303	58,757	46,207	30,830	14,448	6,208	4,805
Suspicion	12	9	12	12	49	32	21	13	15	6	10	1	1
Curfew and loitering law violations	n.a.	n.a.	n.a.	n.a.	n.a.	n.a.	n.a.	n.a.	n.a.	n.a.	n.a.	n.a.	n.a.

1 Because of rounding, the percentages may not sim to 100. 2 Violent crimes are offenses of murder and nonnegligent manslaughter, forcible rape, robbery, and aggravated assault. Property crimes are offenses of burglary, larceny-theft, motor vehicle theft, and arson. * Less than one-tenth of 1 percent n.a = not available

Table 41. Arrests of Persons under 15, 18, 21, and 25 Years of Age, 2012

(Number, percent; 12,196 agencies; 2012 estimated population 242,925,157)

Offense charged	Total, all ages	Number of persons arrested				Percent of total all ages			
		Under 15	Under 18	Under 21	Under 25	Under 15	Under 18	Under 21	Under 25
Total	9,446,660	283,565	1,020,334	2,243,181	3,732,814	3.0	10.8	23.7	39.5
Violent crime [1]	404,037	13,218	47,237	97,533	162,245	3.3	11.7	24.1	40.2
Murder and nonnegligent manslaughter	8,514	63	560	2,080	3,901	0.7	6.6	24.4	45.8
Forcible rape	13,971	740	1,954	3,795	5,723	5.3	14.0	27.2	41.0
Robbery	80,487	3,212	16,563	33,923	48,615	4.0	20.6	42.1	60.4
Aggravated assault	301,065	9,203	28,160	57,735	104,006	3.1	9.4	19.2	34.5
Property crime [1]	1,282,906	66,402	230,803	430,086	617,347	5.2	18.0	33.5	48.1
Burglary	220,284	11,743	42,075	81,275	116,583	5.3	19.1	36.9	52.9
Larceny-theft	1,000,496	50,581	175,261	326,507	469,707	5.1	17.5	32.6	46.9
Motor vehicle theft	53,244	2,138	10,185	18,110	26,009	4.0	19.1	34.0	48.8
Arson	8,882	1,940	3,282	4,194	5,048	21.8	37.0	47.2	56.8
Other assaults	930,210	51,196	132,198	217,618	351,773	5.5	14.2	23.4	37.8
Forgery and counterfeiting	51,987	158	1,106	6,723	15,278	0.3	2.1	12.9	29.4
Fraud	118,374	638	3,610	14,368	30,610	0.5	3.0	12.1	25.9
Embezzlement	12,429	23	341	2,282	4,781	0.2	2.7	18.4	38.5
Stolen property; buying, receiving, possessing	75,989	2,285	10,176	21,992	34,649	3.0	13.4	28.9	45.6
Vandalism	177,325	18,213	46,468	73,162	100,694	10.3	26.2	41.3	56.8
Weapons; carrying, possessing, etc.	115,464	6,350	18,856	36,653	57,346	5.5	16.3	31.7	49.7
Prostitution and commercialized vice	43,395	46	616	5,513	13,202	0.1	1.4	12.7	30.4
Sex offenses (except forcible rape and prostitution)	52,768	4,794	9,570	15,090	20,691	9.1	18.1	28.6	39.2
Drug abuse violations	1,200,538	18,038	107,095	310,042	533,686	1.5	8.9	25.8	44.5
Gambling	5,976	75	732	1,903	2,952	1.3	12.2	31.8	49.4
Offenses against the family and children	82,121	855	2,663	6,879	16,342	1.0	3.2	8.4	19.9
Driving under the influence	987,224	140	7,236	75,490	255,549	*	0.7	7.6	25.9
Liquor laws	341,328	6,027	62,611	231,100	254,464	1.8	18.3	67.7	74.6
Drunkenness	399,920	928	7,618	39,206	102,805	0.2	1.9	9.8	25.7
Disorderly conduct	422,382	35,051	92,017	139,850	205,992	8.3	21.8	33.1	48.8
Vagrancy	20,900	251	984	3,479	5,840	1.2	4.7	16.6	27.9
All other offenses (except traffic)	2,666,096	43,846	184,073	459,717	891,895	1.6	6.9	17.2	33.5
Suspicion	1,160	78	193	364	542	6.7	16.6	31.4	46.7
Curfew and loitering law violations	54,131	14,953	54,131	54,131	54,131	27.6	100.0	100.0	100.0

1 Violent crimes are offenses of murder and nonnegligent manslaughter, forcible rape, robbery, and aggravated assault. Property crimes are offenses of burglary, larceny-theft, motor vehicle theft, and arson.
* = Less than one-tenth of one percent

Table 42. Arrests, Distribution by Sex, 2012

(Number, percent; 12,196 agencies; 2012 estimated population 242,925,157)

Offense charged	Number of persons arrested			Percent male	Percent female	Percent distribution[1]		
	Total	Male	Female			Total	Male	Female
Total	9,446,660	6,972,023	2,474,637	73.8	26.2	100.0	100.0	100.0
Violent crime [2]	404,037	323,489	80,548	80.1	19.9	4.3	4.6	3.3
Murder and nonnegligent manslaughter	8,514	7,549	965	88.7	11.3	0.1	0.1	*
Forcible rape	13,971	13,840	131	99.1	0.9	0.1	0.2	*
Robbery	80,487	70,059	10,428	87.0	13.0	0.9	1.0	0.4
Aggravated assault	301,065	232,041	69,024	77.1	22.9	3.2	3.3	2.8
Property crime [2]	1,282,906	803,567	479,339	62.6	37.4	13.6	11.5	19.4
Burglary	220,284	184,249	36,035	83.6	16.4	2.3	2.6	1.5
Larceny-theft	1,000,496	568,859	431,637	56.9	43.1	10.6	8.2	17.4
Motor vehicle theft	53,244	43,176	10,068	81.1	18.9	0.6	0.6	0.4
Arson	8,882	7,283	1,599	82.0	18.0	0.1	0.1	0.1
Other assaults	930,210	672,170	258,040	72.3	27.7	9.8	9.6	10.4
Forgery and counterfeiting	51,987	32,627	19,360	62.8	37.2	0.6	0.5	0.8
Fraud	118,374	70,486	47,888	59.5	40.5	1.3	1.0	1.9
Embezzlement	12,429	6,414	6,015	51.6	48.4	0.1	0.1	0.2
Stolen property; buying, receiving, possessing	75,989	60,538	15,451	79.7	20.3	0.8	0.9	0.6
Vandalism	177,325	141,568	35,757	79.8	20.2	1.9	2.0	1.4
Weapons; carrying, possessing, etc.	115,464	105,923	9,541	91.7	8.3	1.2	1.5	0.4
Prostitution and commercialized vice	43,395	14,024	29,371	32.3	67.7	0.5	0.2	1.2
Sex offenses (except forcible rape and prostitution)	52,768	48,647	4,121	92.2	7.8	0.6	0.7	0.2
Drug abuse violations	1,200,538	956,962	243,576	79.7	20.3	12.7	13.7	9.8
Gambling	5,976	5,258	718	88.0	12.0	0.1	0.1	*
Offenses against the family and children	82,121	60,251	21,870	73.4	26.6	0.9	0.9	0.9
Driving under the influence	987,224	743,029	244,195	75.3	24.7	10.5	10.7	9.9
Liquor laws	341,328	241,175	100,153	70.7	29.3	3.6	3.5	4.0
Drunkenness	399,920	326,264	73,656	81.6	18.4	4.2	4.7	3.0
Disorderly conduct	422,382	303,198	119,184	71.8	28.2	4.5	4.3	4.8
Vagrancy	20,900	16,667	4,233	79.7	20.3	0.2	0.2	0.2
All other offenses (except traffic)	2,666,096	2,000,269	665,827	75.0	25.0	28.2	28.7	26.9
Suspicion	1,160	883	277	76.1	23.9	*	*	*
Curfew and loitering law violations	54,131	38,614	15,517	71.3	28.7	0.6	0.6	0.6

1 Because of rounding, the percentages may not sum to 100. 2 Violent crimes are offenses of murder and nonnegligent manslaughter, forcible rape, robbery, and aggravated assault. Property crimes are offenses of burglary, larceny-theft, motor vehicle theft, and arson.
* = Less than one-tenth of 1 percent

Table 43. Arrests, Distribution by Race, 2012

(Number, percent; 12,196 agencies; 2012 estimated population 242,925,157)

Offense charged	Total arrests					Percent distribution[1]				
	Total	White	Black	American Indian or Alaskan Native	Asian or Pacific Islander	Total	White	Black	American Indian or Alaskan Native	Asian or Pacific Islander
Total	9,390,473	6,502,919	2,640,067	135,165	112,322	100.0	69.3	28.1	1.4	1.2
Violent crime [2]	402,470	236,394	155,088	5,198	5,790	100.0	58.7	38.5	1.3	1.4
Murder and nonnegligent manslaughter	8,506	4,101	4,203	102	100	100.0	48.2	49.4	1.2	1.2
Forcible rape	13,886	9,027	4,512	183	164	100.0	65.0	32.5	1.3	1.2
Robbery	80,135	34,761	44,002	601	771	100.0	43.4	54.9	0.7	1.0
Aggravated assault	299,943	188,505	102,371	4,312	4,755	100.0	62.8	34.1	1.4	1.6
Property crime [2]	1,275,315	866,802	373,963	17,804	16,746	100.0	68.0	29.3	1.4	1.3
Burglary	219,232	147,156	67,554	1,966	2,556	100.0	67.1	30.8	0.9	1.2
Larceny-theft	994,304	677,895	288,025	15,052	13,332	100.0	68.2	29.0	1.5	1.3
Motor vehicle theft	52,952	35,251	16,301	645	755	100.0	66.6	30.8	1.2	1.4
Arson	8,827	6,500	2,083	141	103	100.0	73.6	23.6	1.6	1.2
Other assaults	924,839	606,048	294,678	13,898	10,215	100.0	65.5	31.9	1.5	1.1
Forgery and counterfeiting	51,759	33,950	16,900	239	670	100.0	65.6	32.7	0.5	1.3
Fraud	117,706	78,331	37,171	1,143	1,061	100.0	66.5	31.6	1.0	0.9
Embezzlement	12,371	7,994	4,103	74	200	100.0	64.6	33.2	0.6	1.6
Stolen property; buying, receiving, possessing	75,516	50,144	23,787	615	970	100.0	66.4	31.5	0.8	1.3
Vandalism	175,243	125,987	44,650	2,845	1,761	100.0	71.9	25.5	1.6	1.0
Weapons; carrying, possessing, etc.	114,979	66,909	45,842	764	1,464	100.0	58.2	39.9	0.7	1.3
Prostitution and commercialized vice	43,216	23,172	18,486	175	1,383	100.0	53.6	42.8	0.4	3.2
Sex offenses (except forcible rape and prostitution)	52,354	38,063	12,850	628	813	100.0	72.7	24.5	1.2	1.6
Drug abuse violations	1,194,956	801,198	372,914	8,299	12,545	100.0	67.0	31.2	0.7	1.0
Gambling	5,951	1,707	4,008	22	214	100.0	28.7	67.4	0.4	3.6
Offenses against the family and children	81,762	53,760	25,698	1,740	564	100.0	65.8	31.4	2.1	0.7
Driving under the influence	981,110	830,498	118,557	13,313	18,742	100.0	84.6	12.1	1.4	1.9
Liquor laws	337,687	275,457	46,355	11,314	4,561	100.0	81.6	13.7	3.4	1.4
Drunkenness	398,600	324,209	62,944	7,218	4,229	100.0	81.3	15.8	1.8	1.1
Disorderly conduct	418,960	262,810	145,183	7,751	3,216	100.0	62.7	34.7	1.9	0.8
Vagrancy	20,698	13,034	7,080	389	195	100.0	63.0	34.2	1.9	0.9
All other offenses (except traffic)	2,649,909	1,773,792	808,609	41,206	26,302	100.0	66.9	30.5	1.6	1.0
Suspicion	1,160	610	535	4	11	100.0	52.6	46.1	0.3	0.9
Curfew and loitering law violations	53,912	32,050	20,666	526	670	100.0	59.4	38.3	1.0	1.2

Table 43. Arrests, Distribution by Race, 2012

(Number, percent; 12,196 agencies; 2012 estimated population 242,925,157)

Offense charged	Arrests under 18					Percent distribution[1]				
	Total	White	Black	American Indian or Alaskan Native	Asian or Pacific Islander	Total	White	Black	American Indian or Alaskan Native	Asian or Pacific Islander
Total	1,002,285	653,949	322,602	13,428	12,306	100.0	65.2	32.2	1.3	1.2
Violent crime [2]	46,544	21,682	23,982	393	487	100.0	46.6	51.5	0.8	1.0
Murder and nonnegligent manslaughter	559	264	284	10	1	100.0	47.2	50.8	1.8	0.2
Forcible rape	1,931	1,237	655	22	17	100.0	64.1	33.9	1.1	0.9
Robbery	16,312	4,880	11,190	67	175	100.0	29.9	68.6	0.4	1.1
Aggravated assault	27,742	15,301	11,853	294	294	100.0	55.2	42.7	1.1	1.1
Property crime [2]	226,973	139,749	80,467	3,002	3,755	100.0	61.6	35.5	1.3	1.7
Burglary	41,422	24,464	16,091	353	514	100.0	59.1	38.8	0.9	1.2
Larceny-theft	172,307	107,108	59,637	2,486	3,076	100.0	62.2	34.6	1.4	1.8
Motor vehicle theft	10,007	5,799	3,937	142	129	100.0	57.9	39.3	1.4	1.3
Arson	3,237	2,378	802	21	36	100.0	73.5	24.8	0.6	1.1
Other assaults	130,024	76,806	50,626	1,503	1,089	100.0	59.1	38.9	1.2	0.8
Forgery and counterfeiting	1,063	737	310	8	8	100.0	69.3	29.2	0.8	0.8
Fraud	3,485	2,022	1,363	56	44	100.0	58.0	39.1	1.6	1.3
Embezzlement	340	215	113	5	7	100.0	63.2	33.2	1.5	2.1
Stolen property; buying, receiving, possessing	9,868	5,204	4,459	90	115	100.0	52.7	45.2	0.9	1.2
Vandalism	45,016	33,860	10,184	573	399	100.0	75.2	22.6	1.3	0.9
Weapons; carrying, possessing, etc.	18,633	11,449	6,775	121	288	100.0	61.4	36.4	0.6	1.5
Prostitution and commercialized vice	609	242	362	0	5	100.0	39.7	59.4	0.0	0.8
Sex offenses (except forcible rape and prostitution)	9,331	6,675	2,462	90	104	100.0	71.5	26.4	1.0	1.1
Drug abuse violations	104,830	77,608	24,684	1,178	1,360	100.0	74.0	23.5	1.1	1.3
Gambling	727	77	643	1	6	100.0	10.6	88.4	0.1	0.8
Offenses against the family and children	2,631	1,796	713	106	16	100.0	68.3	27.1	4.0	0.6
Driving under the influence	7,114	6,546	361	123	84	100.0	92.0	5.1	1.7	1.2
Liquor laws	61,611	54,522	4,294	1,882	913	100.0	88.5	7.0	3.1	1.5
Drunkenness	7,587	6,617	694	168	108	100.0	87.2	9.1	2.2	1.4
Disorderly conduct	90,497	50,695	38,043	1,088	671	100.0	56.0	42.0	1.2	0.7
Vagrancy	975	698	269	4	4	100.0	71.6	27.6	0.4	0.4
All other offenses (except traffic)	180,322	124,553	51,086	2,511	2,172	100.0	69.1	28.3	1.4	1.2
Suspicion	193	146	46	0	1	100.0	75.6	23.8	0.0	0.5
Curfew and loitering law violations	53,912	32,050	20,666	526	670	100.0	59.4	38.3	1.0	1.2

Table 43. Arrests, Distribution by Race, 2012

(Number, percent; 12,196 agencies; 2012 estimated population 242,925,157)

Offense charged	Arrests 18 and over					Percent distribution[1]				
	Total	White	Black	American Indian or Alaskan Native	Asian or Pacific Islander	Total	White	Black	American Indian or Alaskan Native	Asian or Pacific Islander
Total	8,388,188	5,848,970	2,317,465	121,737	100,016	100.0	69.7	27.6	1.5	1.2
Violent crime [2]	355,926	214,712	131,106	4,805	5,303	100.0	60.3	36.8	1.3	1.5
Murder and nonnegligent manslaughter	7,947	3,837	3,919	92	99	100.0	48.3	49.3	1.2	1.2
Forcible rape	11,955	7,790	3,857	161	147	100.0	65.2	32.3	1.3	1.2
Robbery	63,823	29,881	32,812	534	596	100.0	46.8	51.4	0.8	0.9
Aggravated assault	272,201	173,204	90,518	4,018	4,461	100.0	63.6	33.3	1.5	1.6
Property crime [2]	1,048,342	727,053	293,496	14,802	12,991	100.0	69.4	28.0	1.4	1.2
Burglary	177,810	122,692	51,463	1,613	2,042	100.0	69.0	28.9	0.9	1.1
Larceny-theft	821,997	570,787	228,388	12,566	10,256	100.0	69.4	27.8	1.5	1.2
Motor vehicle theft	42,945	29,452	12,364	503	626	100.0	68.6	28.8	1.2	1.5
Arson	5,590	4,122	1,281	120	67	100.0	73.7	22.9	2.1	1.2
Other assaults	794,815	529,242	244,052	12,395	9,126	100.0	66.6	30.7	1.6	1.1
Forgery and counterfeiting	50,696	33,213	16,590	231	662	100.0	65.5	32.7	0.5	1.3
Fraud	114,221	76,309	35,808	1,087	1,017	100.0	66.8	31.3	1.0	0.9
Embezzlement	12,031	7,779	3,990	69	193	100.0	64.7	33.2	0.6	1.6
Stolen property; buying, receiving, possessing	65,648	44,940	19,328	525	855	100.0	68.5	29.4	0.8	1.3
Vandalism	130,227	92,127	34,466	2,272	1,362	100.0	70.7	26.5	1.7	1.0
Weapons; carrying, possessing, etc.	96,346	55,460	39,067	643	1,176	100.0	57.6	40.5	0.7	1.2
Prostitution and commercialized vice	42,607	22,930	18,124	175	1,378	100.0	53.8	42.5	0.4	3.2
Sex offenses (except forcible rape and prostitution)	43,023	31,388	10,388	538	709	100.0	73.0	24.1	1.3	1.6
Drug abuse violations	1,090,126	723,590	348,230	7,121	11,185	100.0	66.4	31.9	0.7	1.0
Gambling	5,224	1,630	3,365	21	208	100.0	31.2	64.4	0.4	4.0
Offenses against the family and children	79,131	51,964	24,985	1,634	548	100.0	65.7	31.6	2.1	0.7
Driving under the influence	973,996	823,952	118,196	13,190	18,658	100.0	84.6	12.1	1.4	1.9
Liquor laws	276,076	220,935	42,061	9,432	3,648	100.0	80.0	15.2	3.4	1.3
Drunkenness	391,013	317,592	62,250	7,050	4,121	100.0	81.2	15.9	1.8	1.1
Disorderly conduct	328,463	212,115	107,140	6,663	2,545	100.0	64.6	32.6	2.0	0.8
Vagrancy	19,723	12,336	6,811	385	191	100.0	62.5	34.5	2.0	1.0
All other offenses (except traffic)	2,469,587	1,649,239	757,523	38,695	24,130	100.0	66.8	30.7	1.6	1.0
Suspicion	967	464	489	4	10	100.0	48.0	50.6	0.4	1.0
Curfew and loitering law violations	n.a.	n.a.	n.a.	n.a.	n.a.	n.a.	n.a.	n.a.	n.a.	n.a.

1 Because of rounding, the percentages may not sum to 100. 2 Violent crimes are offenses of murder and nonnegligent manslaughter, forcible rape, robbery, and aggravated assault. Property crimes are offenses of burglary, larceny-theft, motor vehicle theft, and arson. n.a. = not available

Table 44. Arrest Trends, Cities, 2011–2012

(Number, percent change; 8,348 agencies; 2012 estimated population 157,742,885; 2011 estimated population 156,392,975)

Offense charged	Number of persons arrested								
	Total, all ages			Under 18 years of age			18 years of age and over		
	2011	2012	Percent change	2011	2012	Percent change	2011	2012	Percent change
Total [1]	6,760,296	6,644,359	-1.7	876,607	783,029	-10.7	5,883,689	5,861,330	-.4
Violent crime [2]	294,501	288,943	-1.9	37,897	34,046	-10.2	256,604	254,897	-.7
Murder and nonnegligent manslaughter	5,449	5,584	2.5	433	387	-10.6	5,016	5,197	3.6
Forcible rape	9,925	9,379	-5.5	1,437	1,346	-6.3	8,488	8,033	-5.4
Robbery	63,368	61,001	-3.7	13,955	12,425	-11.0	49,413	48,576	-1.7
Aggravated assault	215,759	212,979	-1.3	22,072	19,888	-9.9	193,687	193,091	-.3
Property crime [2]	982,361	992,743	1.1	211,631	187,477	-11.4	770,730	805,266	4.5
Burglary	158,886	154,476	-2.8	35,500	31,465	-11.4	123,386	123,011	-.3
Larceny-theft	783,330	796,086	1.6	165,859	146,431	-11.7	617,471	649,655	5.2
Motor vehicle theft	33,993	35,569	4.6	7,403	6,845	-7.5	26,590	28,724	8.0
Arson	6,152	6,612	7.5	2,869	2,736	-4.6	3,283	3,876	18.1
Other assaults	677,420	656,800	-3.0	105,709	95,979	-9.2	571,711	560,821	-1.9
Forgery and counterfeiting	39,565	37,398	-5.5	929	803	-13.6	38,636	36,595	-5.3
Fraud	79,241	76,621	-3.3	3,010	2,842	-5.6	76,231	73,779	-3.2
Embezzlement	9,214	9,237	.2	256	272	6.3	8,958	8,965	.1
Stolen property; buying, receiving, possessing	53,014	56,094	5.8	8,522	8,306	-2.5	44,492	47,788	7.4
Vandalism	137,180	129,668	-5.5	40,652	34,925	-14.1	96,528	94,743	-1.8
Weapons; carrying, possessing, etc.	84,832	83,141	-2.0	16,180	14,374	-11.2	68,652	68,767	.2
Prostitution and commercialized vice	35,535	34,867	-1.9	653	514	-21.3	34,882	34,353	-1.5
Sex offenses (except forcible rape and prostitution)	35,801	35,740	-.2	6,600	6,540	-.9	29,201	29,200	*
Drug abuse violations	789,519	809,470	2.5	83,392	78,659	-5.7	706,127	730,811	3.5
Gambling	2,615	2,238	-14.4	248	232	-6.5	2,367	2,006	-15.3
Offenses against the family and children	39,578	39,350	-.6	2,005	1,958	-2.3	37,573	37,392	-.5
Driving under the influence	579,805	556,738	-4.0	5,195	4,644	-10.6	574,610	552,094	-3.9
Liquor laws	293,249	270,614	-7.7	52,147	47,124	-9.6	241,102	223,490	-7.3
Drunkenness	354,411	342,619	-3.3	7,774	6,560	-15.6	346,637	336,059	-3.1
Disorderly conduct	361,962	340,330	-6.0	88,313	75,594	-14.4	273,649	264,736	-3.3
Vagrancy	19,345	17,999	-7.0	1,266	836	-34.0	18,079	17,163	-5.1
All other offenses (except traffic)	1,848,667	1,827,365	-1.2	161,747	144,960	-10.4	1,686,920	1,682,405	-.3
Suspicion	798	820	2.8	55	130	136.4	743	690	-7.1
Curfew and loitering law violations	42,481	36,384	-14.4	42,481	36,384	-14.4	n.a.	n.a.	n.a.

1 Does not include suspicion. 2 Violent crimes are offenses of murder and nonnegligent manslaughter, forcible rape, robbery, and aggravated assault. Property crimes are offenses of burglary, larceny-theft, motor vehicle theft, and arson. *Less than one-tenth of 1 percent. n.a. = not available

Table 45. Arrest Trends, Cities, by Age and Sex, 2011–2012

(Number, percent change; 8,348 agencies; 2012 estimated population 157,742,885; 2011 estimated population 156,392,975)

Offense charged	Male						Female					
	Total			Under 18			Total			Under 18		
	2011	2012	Percent change	2011	2012	Percent change	2011	2012	Percent change	2011	2012	Percent change
Total [1]	4,967,758	4,865,123	-2.1	613,404	548,232	-10.6	1,792,538	1,779,236	-0.7	[illegible]	201,707	10.0
Violent crime [2]	236,413	230,937	-2.3	31,209	27,647	-11.4	58,088	58,006	-0.1	6,688	6,399	-4.3
Murder and nonnegligent manslaughter	4,828	4,957	2.7	409	347	-15.2	621	627	1.0	24	40	66.7
Forcible rape	9,815	9,297	-5.3	1,402	1,323	-5.6	110	82	-25.5	35	23	-34.3
Robbery	55,571	52,977	-4.7	12,711	11,159	-12.2	7,797	8,024	2.9	1,244	1,266	1.8
Aggravated assault	166,199	163,706	-1.5	16,687	14,818	-11.2	49,560	49,273	-0.6	5,385	5,070	-5.8
Property crime [2]	597,724	603,579	1.0	131,032	118,840	-9.3	384,637	389,164	1.2	80,599	68,637	-14.8
Burglary	133,044	128,465	-3.4	30,969	27,399	-11.5	25,842	26,011	0.7	4,531	4,066	-10.3
Larceny-theft	431,899	441,023	2.1	91,348	83,352	-8.8	351,431	355,063	1.0	74,511	63,079	-15.3
Motor vehicle theft	27,710	28,708	3.6	6,234	5,765	-7.5	6,283	6,861	9.2	1,169	1,080	-7.6
Arson	5,071	5,383	6.2	2,481	2,324	-6.3	1,081	1,229	13.7	388	412	6.2
Other assaults	489,821	472,531	-3.5	67,832	60,455	-10.9	187,599	184,269	-1.8	37,877	35,524	-6.2
Forgery and counterfeiting	24,700	23,363	-5.4	649	582	-10.3	14,865	14,035	-5.6	280	221	-21.1
Fraud	48,108	46,474	-3.4	1,971	1,927	-2.2	31,133	30,147	-3.2	1,039	915	-11.9
Embezzlement	4,562	4,721	3.5	159	156	-1.9	4,652	4,516	-2.9	97	116	19.6
Stolen property; buying, receiving, possessing	42,097	44,618	6.0	7,075	6,992	-1.2	10,917	11,476	5.1	1,447	1,314	-9.2
Vandalism	110,577	103,378	-6.5	34,653	29,438	-15.0	26,603	26,290	-1.2	5,999	5,487	-8.5
Weapons; carrying, possessing, etc.	78,049	76,546	-1.9	14,657	13,115	-10.5	6,783	6,595	-2.8	1,523	1,259	-17.3
Prostitution and commercialized vice	10,617	11,162	5.1	132	117	-11.4	24,918	23,705	-4.9	521	397	-23.8
Sex offenses (except forcible rape and prostitution)	32,951	32,868	-0.3	5,858	5,829	-0.5	2,850	2,872	0.8	742	711	-4.2
Drug abuse violations	633,586	646,275	2.0	69,185	64,786	-6.4	155,933	163,195	4.7	14,207	13,873	-2.4
Gambling	2,252	1,889	-16.1	235	217	-7.7	363	349	-3.9	13	15	15.4
Offenses against the family and children	25,936	25,772	-0.6	1,210	1,223	1.1	13,642	13,578	-0.5	795	735	-7.5
Driving under the influence	434,102	416,477	-4.1	3,911	3,451	-11.8	145,703	140,261	-3.7	1,284	1,193	-7.1
Liquor laws	207,325	192,567	-7.1	31,405	28,500	-9.3	85,924	78,047	-9.2	20,742	18,624	-10.2
Drunkenness	290,586	280,154	-3.6	5,737	4,781	-16.7	63,825	62,465	-2.1	2,037	1,779	-12.7
Disorderly conduct	258,763	242,443	-6.3	57,140	48,507	-15.1	103,199	97,887	-5.1	31,173	27,087	-13.1
Vagrancy	15,640	14,459	-7.6	971	672	-30.8	3,705	3,540	-4.5	295	164	-44.4
All other offenses (except traffic)	1,394,549	1,369,886	-1.8	118,983	105,973	-10.9	454,118	457,479	0.7	42,764	38,987	-8.8
Suspicion	608	640	5.3	44	102	131.8	190	180	-5.3	11	28	154.5
Curfew and loitering law violations	29,400	25,024	-14.9	29,400	25,024	-14.9	13,081	11,360	-13.2	13,081	11,360	-13.2

1 Does not include suspicion. 2 Violent crimes are offenses of murder and nonnegligent manslaughter, forcible rape, robbery, and aggravated assault. Property crimes are offenses of burglary, larceny-theft, motor vehicle theft, and arson.

Table 46. Arrests, Cities, Distribution by Age, 2012

(Number, percent; 8,871 agencies; 2012 estimated population 165,509,499)

Offense charged	Total, all ages	Ages under 15	Ages under 18	Ages 18 and over	Under 10	10–12	13–14	15	16	17	18	19	20
Total	6,988,793	234,528	831,162	6,157,631	5,459	49,737	179,332	158,674	201,075	236,885	299,610	322,716	318,275
Total percent distribution[1]	100.0	3.4	11.9	88.1	0.1	0.7	2.6	2.3	2.9	3.4	4.3	4.6	4.6
Violent crime [2]	313,440	10,753	38,701	274,739	238	2,360	8,155	7,515	9,554	10,879	12,920	13,691	13,525
Violent crime percent distribution[1]	100.0	3.4	12.3	87.7	0.1	0.8	2.6	2.4	3.0	3.5	4.1	4.4	4.3
Murder and nonnegligent manslaughter	6,308	46	438	5,870	1	3	42	63	121	208	316	441	446
Forcible rape	10,304	544	1,450	8,854	3	121	420	266	296	344	497	405	393
Robbery	68,207	2,872	14,531	53,676	23	365	2,484	2,946	3,959	4,754	5,371	5,027	4,263
Aggravated assault	228,621	7,291	22,282	206,339	211	1,871	5,209	4,240	5,178	5,573	6,736	7,818	8,423
Property crime [2]	1,036,807	56,712	194,146	842,661	1,094	12,348	43,270	37,553	47,355	52,526	59,286	53,816	47,908
Property crime percent distribution[1]	100.0	5.5	18.7	81.3	0.1	1.2	4.2	3.6	4.6	5.1	5.7	5.2	4.6
Burglary	161,277	9,487	32,946	128,331	274	1,915	7,298	6,546	8,018	8,895	10,542	9,533	8,273
Larceny-theft	829,563	43,928	150,611	678,952	661	9,691	33,576	28,733	36,791	41,159	46,202	42,062	37,707
Motor vehicle theft	39,234	1,666	7,916	31,318	6	184	1,476	1,846	2,213	2,191	2,272	2,017	1,752
Arson	6,733	1,631	2,673	4,060	153	558	920	428	333	281	270	204	176
Other assaults	699,670	39,274	100,614	599,056	1,075	10,071	28,128	19,438	20,951	20,951	20,154	22,012	23,930
Forgery and counterfeiting	38,298	128	823	37,475	2	16	110	75	200	420	1,050	1,519	1,603
Fraud	77,873	492	2,855	75,018	8	81	403	449	776	1,138	2,102	2,853	3,263
Embezzlement	9,436	20	272	9,164	0	3	17	19	75	158	409	573	577
Stolen property; buying, receiving, possessing	56,619	1,968	8,389	48,230	22	306	1,640	1,741	2,138	2,542	3,198	3,097	2,782
Vandalism	137,216	14,658	36,614	100,602	676	4,115	9,867	6,772	7,562	7,622	7,575	6,763	6,316
Weapons; carrying, possessing, etc.	90,466	5,106	15,570	74,896	240	1,351	3,515	2,783	3,473	4,208	5,124	5,074	4,676
Prostitution and commercialized vice	40,536	34	542	39,994	0	3	31	67	168	273	1,164	1,623	1,814
Sex offenses (except forcible rape and prostitution)	37,482	3,379	6,750	30,732	115	970	2,294	1,172	1,100	1,099	1,271	1,230	1,205
Drug abuse violations	888,894	14,691	85,101	803,793	81	1,881	12,729	14,563	22,663	33,184	50,608	52,703	49,658
Gambling	5,018	67	677	4,341	0	10	57	118	216	276	380	361	333
Offenses against the family and children	39,871	634	1,973	37,898	35	144	455	393	487	459	790	954	1,078
Driving under the influence	580,534	81	4,775	575,759	15	3	63	181	1,113	3,400	9,565	14,437	17,512
Liquor laws	274,760	4,911	47,668	227,092	33	324	4,554	7,199	13,382	22,176	43,953	49,017	42,352
Drunkenness	345,951	830	6,573	339,378	20	60	750	1,071	1,502	3,170	7,820	9,310	9,950
Disorderly conduct	357,193	30,304	78,870	278,323	490	6,843	22,971	16,162	16,663	15,741	14,109	13,591	13,557
Vagrancy	18,204	198	836	17,368	0	26	172	190	226	222	762	736	721
All other offenses (except traffic)	1,889,294	36,175	148,889	1,740,405	1,037	6,285	28,853	29,820	38,168	44,726	57,325	69,300	75,473
Suspicion	777	14	70	707	1	6	7	12	18	26	45	56	42
Curfew and loitering law violations	50,454	14,099	50,454	n.a.	277	2,531	11,291	11,381	13,285	11,689	n.a.	n.a.	n.a.

Table 46. Arrests, Cities, Distribution by Age, 2012

(Number, percent; 8,871 agencies; 2012 estimated population 165,509,499)

Offense charged	21	22	23	24	25–29	30–34	35–39	40–44	45–49	50–54	55–59	60–64	65 and over
Total	305,018	287,476	264,759	247,268	1,044,652	812,544	568,591	520,437	465,054	361,773	195,282	86,579	57,597
Total percent distribution[1]	4.4	4.1	3.8	3.5	14.9	11.6	8.1	7.4	6.7	5.2	2.8	1.2	0.8
Violent crime [2]	13,907	13,177	12,327	11,555	49,036	38,445	26,558	23,018	19,505	14,016	7,327	3,311	2,421
Violent crime percent distribution[1]	4.4	4.2	3.9	3.7	15.6	12.3	8.5	7.3	6.2	4.5	2.3	1.1	0.8
Murder and nonnegligent manslaughter	425	367	337	286	1,101	711	448	316	271	188	113	58	46
Forcible rape	398	358	347	304	1,374	1,277	952	880	715	460	246	130	118
Robbery	3,679	3,209	2,819	2,517	9,140	6,070	3,661	3,105	2,443	1,466	603	220	83
Aggravated assault	9,405	9,243	8,824	8,448	37,421	30,387	21,497	18,717	16,076	11,902	6,365	2,903	2,174
Property crime [2]	42,498	38,825	35,285	32,514	137,951	107,344	73,999	69,104	60,083	44,205	23,067	9,778	6,998
Property crime percent distribution[1]	4.1	3.7	3.4	3.1	13.3	10.4	7.1	6.7	5.8	4.3	2.2	0.9	0.7
Burglary	7,202	6,445	5,898	5,359	21,672	16,107	10,433	9,785	8,111	5,384	2,384	775	428
Larceny-theft	33,531	30,646	27,864	25,691	109,797	86,060	60,099	56,552	49,899	37,530	20,097	8,763	6,452
Motor vehicle theft	1,582	1,577	1,376	1,331	5,864	4,632	3,066	2,432	1,737	1,028	424	154	74
Arson	183	157	147	133	618	545	401	335	336	263	162	86	44
Other assaults	27,172	27,031	25,677	24,949	108,686	88,104	63,034	56,164	47,519	34,192	17,100	7,452	5,880
Forgery and counterfeiting	1,611	1,613	1,607	1,545	7,357	6,294	4,256	3,490	2,589	1,683	782	316	160
Fraud	2,849	2,946	2,829	2,792	13,254	11,646	8,585	7,780	6,031	4,053	2,241	1,053	741
Embezzlement	656	520	434	379	1,553	1,191	857	749	550	364	203	97	52
Stolen property; buying, receiving, possessing	2,620	2,523	2,212	2,068	9,035	6,876	4,392	3,759	2,732	1,754	735	319	128
Vandalism	6,495	5,750	5,010	4,481	18,028	12,599	8,170	6,713	5,482	3,878	1,865	826	651
Weapons; carrying, possessing, etc.	4,662	4,395	3,937	3,676	14,068	10,068	5,803	4,460	3,441	2,714	1,436	734	628
Prostitution and commercialized vice	1,870	1,832	1,799	1,687	6,975	5,406	4,226	4,205	3,513	2,112	989	444	335
Sex offenses (except forcible rape and prostitution)	1,192	1,008	905	882	3,963	3,733	3,045	3,107	2,993	2,536	1,637	960	1,065
Drug abuse violations	46,841	43,180	38,983	35,648	145,526	107,088	67,810	57,654	48,080	34,551	16,720	6,188	2,555
Gambling	293	250	257	196	656	376	243	248	209	199	141	106	93
Offenses against the family and children	1,303	1,388	1,407	1,407	7,473	6,661	5,028	3,959	2,914	1,918	932	364	322
Driving under the influence	27,883	28,335	27,146	25,716	106,593	79,321	57,143	52,221	46,746	38,766	23,371	12,205	8,799
Liquor laws	7,203	4,953	3,699	3,090	12,198	9,823	8,086	9,644	11,433	10,837	6,288	2,973	1,543
Drunkenness	16,108	14,454	13,080	11,960	50,834	40,983	31,891	34,236	36,505	32,880	18,180	7,507	3,680
Disorderly conduct	17,190	15,254	13,086	11,918	45,486	33,499	23,666	21,945	20,966	17,404	9,414	4,342	2,896
Vagrancy	534	487	509	411	1,812	1,724	1,420	1,839	2,142	2,129	1,311	565	266
All other offenses (except traffic)	82,095	79,515	74,542	70,361	304,062	241,270	170,323	156,098	141,571	111,546	61,517	27,030	18,377
Suspicion	36	40	28	33	106	93	56	44	50	36	26	9	7
Curfew and loitering law violations	n.a.	n.a.	n.a.	n.a.	n.a.	n.a.	n.a.	n.a.	n.a.	n.a.	n.a.	n.a.	n.a.

1 Because of rounding, the percentages may not sum to 100.

2 Violent crimes are offenses of murder and nonnegligent manslaughter, forcible rape, robbery, and aggravated assault. Property crimes are offenses of burglary, larceny-theft, motor vehicle theft, and arson.

n.a. = Not available

Table 47. Arrests, Cities, Persons under 15, 18, 21, and 25 Years of Age, 2012

(Number, percent; 8,871 agencies; 2012 estimated population 165,509,499)

Offense charged	Total, all ages	Number of persons arrested				Percent of total all ages			
		Under 15	Under 18	Under 21	Under 25	Under 15	Under 18	Under 21	Under 25
Total	6,988,793	234,528	831,162	1,771,763	2,876,284	3.4	11.9	25.4	41.2
Violent crime [1]	313,440	10,753	38,701	78,837	129,803	3.4	12.3	25.2	41.4
Murder and nonnegligent manslaughter	6,308	46	438	1,641	3,056	0.7	6.9	26.0	48.4
Forcible rape	10,304	544	1,450	2,745	4,152	5.3	14.1	26.6	40.3
Robbery	68,207	2,872	14,531	29,192	41,416	4.2	21.3	42.8	60.7
Aggravated assault	228,621	7,291	22,282	45,259	81,179	3.2	9.7	19.8	35.5
Property crime [1]	1,036,807	56,712	194,146	355,156	504,278	5.5	18.7	34.3	48.6
Burglary	161,277	9,487	32,946	61,294	86,198	5.9	20.4	38.0	53.4
Larceny-theft	829,563	43,928	150,611	276,582	394,314	5.3	18.2	33.3	47.5
Motor vehicle theft	39,234	1,666	7,916	13,957	19,823	4.2	20.2	35.6	50.5
Arson	6,733	1,631	2,673	3,323	3,943	24.2	39.7	49.4	58.6
Other assaults	699,670	39,274	100,614	166,710	271,539	5.6	14.4	23.8	38.8
Forgery and counterfeiting	38,298	128	823	4,995	11,371	0.3	2.1	13.0	29.7
Fraud	77,873	492	2,855	11,073	22,489	0.6	3.7	14.2	28.9
Embezzlement	9,436	20	272	1,831	3,820	0.2	2.9	19.4	40.5
Stolen property; buying, receiving, possessing	56,619	1,968	8,389	17,466	26,889	3.5	14.8	30.8	47.5
Vandalism	137,216	14,658	36,614	57,268	79,004	10.7	26.7	41.7	57.6
Weapons; carrying, possessing, etc.	90,466	5,106	15,570	30,444	47,114	5.6	17.2	33.7	52.1
Prostitution and commercialized vice	40,536	34	542	5,143	12,331	0.1	1.3	12.7	30.4
Sex offenses (except forcible rape and prostitution)	37,482	3,379	6,750	10,456	14,443	9.0	18.0	27.9	38.5
Drug abuse violations	888,894	14,691	85,101	238,070	402,722	1.7	9.6	26.8	45.3
Gambling	5,018	67	677	1,751	2,747	1.3	13.5	34.9	54.7
Offenses against the family and children	39,871	634	1,973	4,795	10,300	1.6	4.9	12.0	25.8
Driving under the influence	580,534	81	4,775	46,289	155,369	*	0.8	8.0	26.8
Liquor laws	274,760	4,911	47,668	182,990	201,935	1.8	17.3	66.6	73.5
Drunkenness	345,951	830	6,573	33,653	89,255	0.2	1.9	9.7	25.8
Disorderly conduct	357,193	30,304	78,870	120,127	177,575	8.5	22.1	33.6	49.7
Vagrancy	18,204	198	836	3,055	4,996	1.1	4.6	16.8	27.4
All other offenses (except traffic)	1,889,294	36,175	148,889	350,987	657,500	1.9	7.9	18.6	34.8
Suspicion	777	14	70	213	350	1.8	9.0	27.4	45.0
Curfew and loitering law violations	50,454	14,099	50,454	50,454	50,454	27.9	100.0	100.0	100.0

1 Violent crimes are offenses of murder and nonnegligent manslaughter, forcible rape, robbery, and aggravated assault. Property crimes are offenses of burglary, larceny-theft, motor vehicle theft, and arson.
* = Less than one-tenth of one percent.

Table 48. Arrests, Cities, Distribution by Sex, 2012

(Number, percent; 8,871 agencies; 2012 estimated population 165,509,499)

Offense charged	Number of persons arrested			Percent male	Percent female	Percent distribution[1]		
	Total	Male	Female			Total	Male	Female
Total	6,988,793	5,138,468	1,850,325	73.5	26.5	100.0	100.0	100.0
Violent crime [2]	313,440	250,116	63,324	79.8	20.2	4.5	4.9	3.4
Murder and nonnegligent manslaughter	6,308	5,625	683	89.2	10.8	0.1	0.1	*
Forcible rape	10,304	10,219	85	99.2	0.8	0.1	0.2	*
Robbery	68,207	59,329	8,878	87.0	13.0	1.0	1.2	0.5
Aggravated assault	228,621	174,943	53,678	76.5	23.5	3.3	3.4	2.9
Property crime [2]	1,036,807	635,486	401,321	61.3	38.7	14.8	12.4	21.7
Burglary	161,277	134,589	26,688	83.5	16.5	2.3	2.6	1.4
Larceny-theft	829,563	463,548	366,015	55.9	44.1	11.9	9.0	19.8
Motor vehicle theft	39,234	31,870	7,364	81.2	18.8	0.6	0.6	0.4
Arson	6,733	5,479	1,254	81.4	18.6	0.1	0.1	0.1
Other assaults	699,670	505,254	194,416	72.2	27.8	10.0	9.8	10.5
Forgery and counterfeiting	38,298	23,989	14,309	62.6	37.4	0.5	0.5	0.8
Fraud	77,873	47,382	30,491	60.8	39.2	1.1	0.9	1.6
Embezzlement	9,436	4,825	4,611	51.1	48.9	0.1	0.1	0.2
Stolen property; buying, receiving, possessing	56,619	45,052	11,567	79.6	20.4	0.8	0.9	0.6
Vandalism	137,216	109,497	27,719	79.8	20.2	2.0	2.1	1.5
Weapons; carrying, possessing, etc.	90,466	83,229	7,237	92.0	8.0	1.3	1.6	0.4
Prostitution and commercialized vice	40,536	12,814	27,722	31.6	68.4	0.6	0.2	1.5
Sex offenses (except forcible rape and prostitution)	37,482	34,432	3,050	91.9	8.1	0.5	0.7	0.2
Drug abuse violations	888,894	715,077	173,817	80.4	19.6	12.7	13.9	9.4
Gambling	5,018	4,569	449	91.1	8.9	0.1	0.1	*
Offenses against the family and children	39,871	26,036	13,835	65.3	34.7	0.6	0.5	0.7
Driving under the influence	580,534	435,185	145,349	75.0	25.0	8.3	8.5	7.9
Liquor laws	274,760	194,999	79,761	71.0	29.0	3.9	3.8	4.3
Drunkenness	345,951	283,067	62,884	81.8	18.2	5.0	5.5	3.4
Disorderly conduct	357,193	256,589	100,604	71.8	28.2	5.1	5.0	5.4
Vagrancy	18,204	14,643	3,561	80.4	19.6	0.3	0.3	0.2
All other offenses (except traffic)	1,889,294	1,419,430	469,864	75.1	24.9	27.0	27.6	25.4
Suspicion	777	608	169	78.2	21.8	*	*	*
Curfew and loitering law violations	50,454	36,189	14,265	71.7	28.3	0.7	0.7	0.8

1 Because of rounding, the percentages may not sum to 100. 2 Violent crimes are offenses of murder and nonnegligent manslaughter, forcible rape, robbery, and aggravated assault. Property crimes are offenses of burglary, larceny-theft, motor vehicle theft, and arson. * = Less than one-tenth of one percent

Table 49. Arrests, Cities, Distribution by Race, 2012

(Number, percent; 8,791 agencies; 2011 estimated population 163,760,401)

Offense charged	Total arrests					Percent distribution[1]				
	Total	White	Black	American Indian or Alaskan Native	Asian or Pacific Islander	Total	White	Black	American Indian or Alaskan Native	Asian or Pacific Islander
Total	6,949,486	4,657,288	2,105,421	101,962	84,815	100.0	67.0	30.3	1.5	1.2
Violent crime [2]	312,226	174,615	129,050	3,749	4,812	100.0	55.9	41.3	1.2	1.5
Murder and nonnegligent manslaughter	6,302	2,723	3,439	65	75	100.0	43.2	54.6	1.0	1.2
Forcible rape	10,242	6,184	3,783	148	127	100.0	60.4	36.9	1.4	1.2
Robbery	67,926	28,914	37,875	490	647	100.0	42.6	55.8	0.7	1.0
Aggravated assault	227,756	136,794	83,953	3,046	3,963	100.0	60.1	36.9	1.3	1.7
Property crime [2]	1,031,038	690,018	311,490	15,336	14,194	100.0	66.9	30.2	1.5	1.4
Burglary	160,572	102,253	54,877	1,300	2,142	100.0	63.7	34.2	0.8	1.3
Larceny-theft	824,754	558,570	241,339	13,463	11,382	100.0	67.7	29.3	1.6	1.4
Motor vehicle theft	39,028	24,448	13,528	469	583	100.0	62.6	34.7	1.2	1.5
Arson	6,684	4,747	1,746	104	87	100.0	71.0	26.1	1.6	1.3
Other assaults	695,559	435,182	241,124	10,887	8,366	100.0	62.6	34.7	1.6	1.2
Forgery and counterfeiting	38,150	24,655	12,767	193	535	100.0	64.6	33.5	0.5	1.4
Fraud	77,457	48,978	26,902	766	811	100.0	63.2	34.7	1.0	1.0
Embezzlement	9,389	5,945	3,217	53	174	100.0	63.3	34.3	0.6	1.9
Stolen property; buying, receiving, possessing	56,332	36,189	18,883	437	823	100.0	64.2	33.5	0.8	1.5
Vandalism	135,685	94,970	36,961	2,276	1,478	100.0	70.0	27.2	1.7	1.1
Weapons; carrying, possessing, etc.	90,098	50,047	38,293	559	1,199	100.0	55.5	42.5	0.6	1.3
Prostitution and commercialized vice	40,383	21,473	17,534	166	1,210	100.0	53.2	43.4	0.4	3.0
Sex offenses (except forcible rape and prostitution)	37,206	25,806	10,230	502	668	100.0	69.4	27.5	1.3	1.8
Drug abuse violations	885,321	568,225	301,897	5,787	9,412	100.0	64.2	34.1	0.7	1.1
Gambling	4,997	1,059	3,786	10	142	100.0	21.2	75.8	0.2	2.8
Offenses against the family and children	39,643	26,823	11,270	1,183	367	100.0	67.7	28.4	3.0	0.9
Driving under the influence	577,758	486,356	73,099	7,948	10,355	100.0	84.2	12.7	1.4	1.8
Liquor laws	272,204	217,766	40,608	10,019	3,811	100.0	80.0	14.9	3.7	1.4
Drunkenness	344,752	277,153	57,523	6,305	3,771	100.0	80.4	16.7	1.8	1.1
Disorderly conduct	354,212	218,240	126,687	6,472	2,813	100.0	61.6	35.8	1.8	0.8
Vagrancy	18,012	11,098	6,358	375	181	100.0	61.6	35.3	2.1	1.0
All other offenses (except traffic)	1,878,032	1,212,985	617,500	28,448	19,099	100.0	64.6	32.9	1.5	1.0
Suspicion	777	384	381	4	8	100.0	49.4	49.0	0.5	1.0
Curfew and loitering law violations	50,255	29,321	19,861	487	586	100.0	58.3	39.5	1.0	1.2

Table 49. Arrests, Cities, Distribution by Race, 2012

(Number, percent; 8,791 agencies; 2011 estimated population 163,760,401)

Offense charged	Arrests under 18					Percent distribution[1]				
	Total	White	Black	American Indian or Alaskan Native	Asian or Pacific Islander	Total	White	Black	American Indian or Alaskan Native	Asian or Pacific Islander
Total	818,337	526,491	270,708	10,734	10,404	100.0	64.3	33.1	1.3	1.3
Violent crime [2]	38,186	17,138	20,358	284	406	100.0	44.9	53.3	0.7	1.1
Murder and nonnegligent manslaughter	438	207	226	5	0	100.0	47.3	51.6	1.1	0.0
Forcible rape	1,438	849	561	15	13	100.0	59.0	39.0	1.0	0.9
Robbery	14,341	4,292	9,848	57	144	100.0	29.9	68.7	0.4	1.0
Aggravated assault	21,969	11,790	9,723	207	249	100.0	53.7	44.3	0.9	1.1
Property crime [2]	191,475	117,428	68,112	2,646	3,289	100.0	61.3	35.6	1.4	1.7
Burglary	32,503	18,451	13,352	259	441	100.0	56.8	41.1	0.8	1.4
Larceny-theft	148,546	92,878	50,713	2,253	2,702	100.0	62.5	34.1	1.5	1.8
Motor vehicle theft	7,792	4,186	3,376	117	113	100.0	53.7	43.3	1.5	1.5
Arson	2,634	1,913	671	17	33	100.0	72.6	25.5	0.6	1.3
Other assaults	98,989	57,874	39,097	1,112	906	100.0	58.5	39.5	1.1	0.9
Forgery and counterfeiting	802	549	241	6	6	100.0	68.5	30.0	0.7	0.7
Fraud	2,769	1,549	1,140	44	36	100.0	55.9	41.2	1.6	1.3
Embezzlement	271	167	92	5	7	100.0	61.6	33.9	1.8	2.6
Stolen property; buying, receiving, possessing	8,213	4,269	3,769	74	101	100.0	52.0	45.9	0.9	1.2
Vandalism	35,602	26,542	8,270	446	344	100.0	74.6	23.2	1.3	1.0
Weapons; carrying, possessing, etc.	15,402	9,374	5,686	94	248	100.0	60.9	36.9	0.6	1.6
Prostitution and commercialized vice	539	203	331	0	5	100.0	37.7	61.4	0.0	0.9
Sex offenses (except forcible rape and prostitution)	6,594	4,542	1,894	70	88	100.0	68.9	28.7	1.1	1.3
Drug abuse violations	83,605	60,939	20,681	928	1,057	100.0	72.9	24.7	1.1	1.3
Gambling	672	42	626	0	4	100.0	6.3	93.2	0.0	0.6
Offenses against the family and children	1,944	1,272	571	90	11	100.0	65.4	29.4	4.6	0.6
Driving under the influence	4,718	4,339	247	72	60	100.0	92.0	5.2	1.5	1.3
Liquor laws	47,145	41,190	3,617	1,610	728	100.0	87.4	7.7	3.4	1.5
Drunkenness	6,544	5,688	613	140	103	100.0	86.9	9.4	2.1	1.6
Disorderly conduct	77,545	43,242	32,892	812	599	100.0	55.8	42.4	1.0	0.8
Vagrancy	831	614	210	4	3	100.0	73.9	25.3	0.5	0.4
All other offenses (except traffic)	146,166	100,178	42,362	1,810	1,816	100.0	68.5	29.0	1.2	1.2
Suspicion	70	31	38	0	1	100.0	44.3	54.3	0.0	1.4
Curfew and loitering law violations	50,255	29,321	19,861	487	586	100.0	58.3	39.5	1.0	1.2

Table 49. Arrests, Cities, Distribution by Race, 2012

(Number, percent; 8,791 agencies; 2011 estimated population 163,760,401)

Offense charged	Arrests 18 and over					Percent distribution[1]				
	Total	White	Black	American Indian or Alaskan Native	Asian or Pacific Islander	Total	White	Black	American Indian or Alaskan Native	Asian or Pacific Islander
Total	6,131,149	4,130,797	1,834,713	91,228	74,411	100.0	67.4	29.9	1.5	1.2
Violent crime [2]	274,040	157,477	108,692	3,465	4,406	100.0	57.5	39.7	1.3	1.6
Murder and nonnegligent manslaughter	5,864	2,516	3,213	60	75	100.0	42.9	54.8	1.0	1.3
Forcible rape	8,804	5,335	3,222	133	114	100.0	60.6	36.6	1.5	1.3
Robbery	53,585	24,622	28,027	433	503	100.0	45.9	52.3	0.8	0.9
Aggravated assault	205,787	125,004	74,230	2,839	3,714	100.0	60.7	36.1	1.4	1.8
Property crime [2]	839,563	572,590	243,378	12,690	10,905	100.0	68.2	29.0	1.5	1.3
Burglary	128,069	83,802	41,525	1,041	1,701	100.0	65.4	32.4	0.8	1.3
Larceny-theft	676,208	465,692	190,626	11,210	8,680	100.0	68.9	28.2	1.7	1.3
Motor vehicle theft	31,236	20,262	10,152	352	470	100.0	64.9	32.5	1.1	1.5
Arson	4,050	2,834	1,075	87	54	100.0	70.0	26.5	2.1	1.3
Other assaults	596,570	377,308	202,027	9,775	7,460	100.0	63.2	33.9	1.6	1.3
Forgery and counterfeiting	37,348	24,106	12,526	187	529	100.0	64.5	33.5	0.5	1.4
Fraud	74,688	47,429	25,762	722	775	100.0	63.5	34.5	1.0	1.0
Embezzlement	9,118	5,778	3,125	48	167	100.0	63.4	34.3	0.5	1.8
Stolen property; buying, receiving, possessing	48,119	31,920	15,114	363	722	100.0	66.3	31.4	0.8	1.5
Vandalism	100,083	68,428	28,691	1,830	1,134	100.0	68.4	28.7	1.8	1.1
Weapons; carrying, possessing, etc.	74,696	40,673	32,607	465	951	100.0	54.5	43.7	0.6	1.3
Prostitution and commercialized vice	39,844	21,270	17,203	166	1,205	100.0	53.4	43.2	0.4	3.0
Sex offenses (except forcible rape and prostitution)	30,612	21,264	8,336	432	580	100.0	69.5	27.2	1.4	1.9
Drug abuse violations	801,716	507,286	281,216	4,859	8,355	100.0	63.3	35.1	0.6	1.0
Gambling	4,325	1,017	3,160	10	138	100.0	23.5	73.1	0.2	3.2
Offenses against the family and children	37,699	25,551	10,699	1,093	356	100.0	67.8	28.4	2.9	0.9
Driving under the influence	573,040	482,017	72,852	7,876	10,295	100.0	84.1	12.7	1.4	1.8
Liquor laws	225,059	176,576	36,991	8,409	3,083	100.0	78.5	16.4	3.7	1.4
Drunkenness	338,208	271,465	56,910	6,165	3,668	100.0	80.3	16.8	1.8	1.1
Disorderly conduct	276,667	174,998	93,795	5,660	2,214	100.0	63.3	33.9	2.0	0.8
Vagrancy	17,181	10,484	6,148	371	178	100.0	61.0	35.8	2.2	1.0
All other offenses (except traffic)	1,731,866	1,112,807	575,138	26,638	17,283	100.0	64.3	33.2	1.5	1.0
Suspicion	707	353	343	4	7	100.0	49.9	48.5	0.6	1.0
Curfew and loitering law violations	n.a.	n.a.	n.a.	n.a.	n.a.	n.a.	n.a.	n.a.	n.a.	n.a.

1 Because of rounding, the percentages may not sum to 100. 2 Violent crimes are offenses of murder and nonnegligent manslaughter, forcible rape, robbery, and aggravated assault. Property crimes are offenses of burglary, larceny-theft, motor vehicle theft, and arson. n.a. = not available

Table 50. Arrest Trends, Metropolitan Counties, 2011–2012

(Number, percent change; 1,260 agencies; 2012 estimated population 55,888,792; 2011 estimated population 55,364,450)

Offense charged	Number of persons arrested								
	Total, all ages			Under 18 years of age			18 years of age and over		
	2011	2012	Percent change	2011	2012	Percent change	2011	2012	Percent change
Total [1]	1,714,478	1,662,277	-3.0	163,513	146,958	-10.1	1,550,965	1,515,319	-2.3
Violent crime [2]	71,816	70,962	-1.2	7,982	6,994	-12.4	63,834	63,968	0.2
Murder and nonnegligent manslaughter	1,665	1,503	-9.7	116	83	-28.4	1,549	1,420	-8.3
Forcible rape	2,617	2,480	-5.2	351	337	-4.0	2,266	2,143	-5.4
Robbery	10,416	10,314	-1.0	1,995	1,779	-10.8	8,421	8,535	1.4
Aggravated assault	57,118	56,665	-0.8	5,520	4,795	-13.1	51,598	51,870	0.5
Property crime [2]	188,430	183,390	-2.7	33,486	28,697	-14.3	154,944	154,693	-0.2
Burglary	43,690	42,239	-3.3	8,065	6,693	-17.0	35,625	35,546	-0.2
Larceny-theft	133,637	130,605	-2.3	23,197	20,005	-13.8	110,440	110,600	0.1
Motor vehicle theft	9,292	9,142	-1.6	1,623	1,539	-5.2	7,669	7,603	-0.9
Arson	1,811	1,404	-22.5	601	460	-23.5	1,210	944	-22.0
Other assaults	172,692	166,517	-3.6	27,630	25,285	-8.5	145,062	141,232	-2.6
Forgery and counterfeiting	10,558	10,194	-3.4	208	226	8.7	10,350	9,968	-3.7
Fraud	31,367	28,061	-10.5	671	595	-11.3	30,696	27,466	-10.5
Embezzlement	2,500	2,425	-3.0	56	58	3.6	2,444	2,367	-3.2
Stolen property; buying, receiving, possessing	14,219	15,273	7.4	1,416	1,474	4.1	12,803	13,799	7.8
Vandalism	30,647	29,177	-4.8	8,264	7,377	-10.7	22,383	21,800	-2.6
Weapons; carrying, possessing, etc.	19,323	18,635	-3.6	3,476	2,817	-19.0	15,847	15,818	-0.2
Prostitution and commercialized vice	2,464	2,666	8.2	60	55	-8.3	2,404	2,611	8.6
Sex offenses (except forcible rape and prostitution)	11,086	11,091	*	2,045	2,090	2.2	9,041	9,001	-0.4
Drug abuse violations	224,893	225,925	0.5	18,837	17,990	-4.5	206,056	207,935	0.9
Gambling	669	757	13.2	47	44	-6.4	622	713	14.6
Offenses against the family and children	34,889	32,625	-6.5	397	420	5.8	34,492	32,205	-6.6
Driving under the influence	179,157	166,916	-6.8	1,412	1,231	-12.8	177,745	165,685	-6.8
Liquor laws	46,590	43,800	-6.0	11,209	10,488	-6.4	35,381	33,312	-5.8
Drunkenness	39,611	37,491	-5.4	814	774	-4.9	38,797	36,717	-5.4
Disorderly conduct	48,195	45,197	-6.2	11,100	9,453	-14.8	37,095	35,744	-3.6
Vagrancy	2,248	2,433	8.2	72	125	73.6	2,176	2,308	6.1
All other offenses (except traffic)	579,036	565,286	-2.4	30,243	27,309	-9.7	548,793	537,977	-2.0
Suspicion	83	197	137.3	23	4	-82.6	60	193	221.7
Curfew and loitering law violations	4,088	3,456	-15.5	4,088	3,456	-15.5	n.a.	n.a.	n.a.

1 Does not include suspicion. 2 Violent crimes are offenses of murder and nonnegligent manslaughter, forcible rape, robbery, and aggravated assault. Property crimes are offenses of burglary, larceny-theft, motor vehicle theft, and arson. * = Less than one-tenth of one percent n.a. = not available

Table 51. Arrest Trends, Metropolitan Counties, by Age and Sex, 2011–2012

(Number, percent change; 1,260 agencies; 2012 estimated population 55,888,792; 2011 estimated population 55,364,450)

Offense charged	Male						Female					
	Total			Under 18			Total			Under 18		
	2011	2012	Percent change	2011	2012	Percent change	2011	2012	Percent change	2011	2012	Percent change
Total [1]	1,284,844	1,236,202	-3.8	118,035	106,043	-10.2	429,634	426,075	-0.8	45,478	40,915	-10.0
Violent crime [2]	57,972	57,177	-1.4	6,397	5,580	-12.8	13,844	13,785	-0.4	1,585	1,414	-10.8
Murder and nonnegligent manslaughter	1,453	1,333	-8.3	95	73	-23.2	212	170	-19.8	21	10	-52.4
Forcible rape	2,596	2,454	-5.5	348	333	-4.3	21	26	23.8	3	4	33.3
Robbery	9,195	9,005	-2.1	1,821	1,614	-11.4	1,221	1,309	7.2	174	165	-5.2
Aggravated assault	44,728	44,385	-0.8	4,133	3,560	-13.9	12,390	12,280	-0.9	1,387	1,235	-11.0
Property crime [2]	127,924	123,346	-3.6	23,454	20,421	-12.9	60,506	60,044	-0.8	10,032	8,276	-17.5
Burglary	37,150	35,438	-4.6	7,282	6,086	-16.4	6,540	6,801	4.0	783	607	-22.5
Larceny-theft	81,694	79,386	-2.8	14,309	12,640	-11.7	51,943	51,219	-1.4	8,888	7,365	-17.1
Motor vehicle theft	7,613	7,365	-3.3	1,357	1,305	-3.8	1,679	1,777	5.8	266	234	-12.0
Arson	1,467	1,157	-21.1	506	390	-22.9	344	247	-28.2	95	70	-26.3
Other assaults	125,276	119,955	-4.2	17,969	16,169	-10.0	47,416	46,562	-1.8	9,661	9,116	-5.6
Forgery and counterfeiting	6,738	6,471	-4.0	158	144	-8.9	3,820	3,723	-2.5	50	82	64.0
Fraud	18,162	16,305	-10.2	459	393	-14.4	13,205	11,756	-11.0	212	202	-4.7
Embezzlement	1,320	1,291	-2.2	31	45	45.2	1,180	1,134	-3.9	25	13	-48.0
Stolen property; buying, receiving, possessing	11,472	12,180	6.2	1,194	1,192	-0.2	2,747	3,093	12.6	222	282	27.0
Vandalism	24,970	23,180	-7.2	6,977	6,085	-12.8	5,677	5,997	5.6	1,287	1,292	0.4
Weapons; carrying, possessing, etc.	17,593	16,828	-4.3	3,042	2,485	-18.3	1,730	1,807	4.5	434	332	-23.5
Prostitution and commercialized vice	1,046	1,108	5.9	18	12	-33.3	1,418	1,558	9.9	42	43	2.4
Sex offenses (except forcible rape and prostitution)	10,405	10,391	-0.1	1,856	1,936	4.3	681	700	2.8	189	154	-18.5
Drug abuse violations	177,218	176,003	-0.7	15,445	14,833	-4.0	47,675	49,922	4.7	3,392	3,157	-6.9
Gambling	505	527	4.4	26	24	-7.7	164	230	40.2	21	20	-4.8
Offenses against the family and children	29,391	27,018	-8.1	262	250	-4.6	5,498	5,607	2.0	135	170	25.9
Driving under the influence	134,556	124,898	-7.2	1,010	903	-10.6	44,601	42,018	-5.8	402	328	-18.4
Liquor laws	32,017	30,293	-5.4	6,601	6,270	-5.0	14,573	13,507	-7.3	4,608	4,218	-8.5
Drunkenness	32,249	30,503	-5.4	611	558	-8.7	7,362	6,988	-5.1	203	216	6.4
Disorderly conduct	34,845	32,378	-7.1	7,510	6,187	-17.6	13,350	12,819	-4.0	3,590	3,266	-9.0
Vagrancy	1,658	1,827	10.2	60	100	66.7	590	606	2.7	12	25	108.3
All other offenses (except traffic)	436,744	422,214	-3.3	22,172	20,147	-9.1	142,292	143,072	0.5	8,071	7,162	-11.3
Suspicion	69	140	102.9	19	2	-89.5	14	57	307.1	4	2	-50.0
Curfew and loitering law violations	2,783	2,309	-17.0	2,783	2,309	-17.0	1,305	1,147	-12.1	1,305	1,147	-12.1

1 Does not include suspicion. 2 Violent crimes are offenses of murder and nonnegligent manslaughter, forcible rape, robbery, and aggravated assault. Property crimes are offenses of burglary, larceny-theft, motor vehicle theft, and arson.

Table 52. Arrests, Metropolitan Counties, Distribution by Age, 2012

(Number, percent; 1,363 agencies; 2012 estimated population 55,902,687)

Offense charged	Total, all ages	Ages under 15	Ages under 18	Ages 18 and over	Under 10	10–12	13–14	15	16	17	18	19	20
Total	1,723,089	39,319	148,759	1,574,330	1,249	8,648	29,422	26,063	36,060	47,317	60,815	68,265	71,150
Total percent distribution[1]	100.0	2.3	8.6	91.4	0.1	0.5	1.7	1.5	2.1	2.7	3.5	4.0	4.1
Violent crime[2]	69,908	2,048	7,141	62,767	57	484	1,507	1,336	1,733	2,024	2,590	2,788	2,840
Violent crime percent distribution[1]	100.0	2.9	10.2	89.8	0.1	0.7	2.2	1.9	2.5	2.9	3.7	4.0	4.1
Murder and nonnegligent manslaughter	1,565	12	92	1,473	0	5	7	11	27	42	78	89	91
Forcible rape	2,470	131	344	2,126	1	36	94	50	68	95	119	115	118
Robbery	10,738	329	1,923	8,815	5	33	291	368	534	692	873	810	721
Aggravated assault	55,135	1,576	4,782	50,353	51	410	1,115	907	1,104	1,195	1,520	1,774	1,910
Property crime[2]	188,370	7,971	29,849	158,521	168	1,717	6,086	5,455	7,329	9,094	10,653	9,888	8,915
Property crime percent distribution[1]	100.0	4.2	15.8	84.2	0.1	0.9	3.2	2.9	3.9	4.8	5.7	5.2	4.7
Burglary	41,203	1,738	6,835	34,368	46	392	1,300	1,277	1,674	2,146	2,748	2,602	2,276
Larceny-theft	135,521	5,664	20,916	114,605	102	1,206	4,356	3,753	5,085	6,414	7,322	6,776	6,170
Motor vehicle theft	10,229	319	1,631	8,598	2	29	288	361	482	469	516	458	432
Arson	1,417	250	467	950	18	90	142	64	88	65	67	52	37
Other assaults	165,969	9,897	25,492	140,477	393	2,641	6,863	4,756	5,464	5,375	4,385	4,549	4,983
Forgery and counterfeiting	10,586	27	242	10,344	1	5	21	23	42	150	266	417	505
Fraud	27,251	102	590	26,661	4	15	83	95	147	246	470	599	730
Embezzlement	2,394	2	58	2,336	0	1	1	6	16	34	95	115	143
Stolen property; buying, receiving, possessing	14,945	268	1,515	13,430	4	43	221	280	423	544	752	696	683
Vandalism	29,665	2,676	7,507	22,158	127	676	1,873	1,354	1,776	1,701	1,630	1,460	1,275
Weapons; carrying, possessing, etc.	18,757	1,070	2,814	15,943	128	320	622	437	594	713	776	780	820
Prostitution and commercialized vice	2,720	9	63	2,657	0	1	8	14	11	29	82	98	101
Sex offenses (except forcible rape and prostitution)	10,924	1,034	2,002	8,922	41	317	676	323	300	345	418	409	374
Drug abuse violations	226,123	2,765	17,929	208,194	24	349	2,392	2,602	4,547	8,015	11,639	12,783	12,794
Gambling	762	8	44	718	1	0	7	6	11	19	7	13	10
Offenses against the family and children	30,601	142	485	30,116	11	32	99	86	98	159	259	297	393
Driving under the influence	240,955	35	1,407	239,548	1	6	28	58	293	1,021	3,353	5,227	6,713
Liquor laws	42,191	731	9,932	32,259	2	61	668	1,345	2,908	4,948	7,040	7,319	6,296
Drunkenness	36,185	75	738	35,447	4	4	67	117	188	358	918	1,058	1,059
Disorderly conduct	45,761	3,651	10,087	35,674	112	820	2,719	2,016	2,232	2,188	1,700	1,487	1,466
Vagrancy	2,494	53	127	2,367	1	11	41	28	17	29	82	92	82
All other offenses (except traffic)	552,957	5,976	27,379	525,578	168	1,070	4,738	4,934	6,855	9,614	13,695	18,184	20,956
Suspicion	218	2	5	213	0	0	2	1	1	1	5	6	12
Curfew and loitering law violations	3,353	777	3,353	n.a.	2	75	700	791	1,075	710	n.a.	n.a.	n.a.

Table 52. Arrests, Metropolitan Counties, Distribution by Age, 2012

(Number, percent; 1,363 agencies; 2012 estimated population 55,902,687)

Offense charged	21	22	23	24	25–29	30–34	35–39	40–44	45–49	50–54	55–59	60–64	65 and over
Total	71,733	71,217	67,375	63,893	279,519	224,620	160,672	143,974	121,804	87,745	46,131	20,573	14,844
Total percent distribution[1]	4.2	4.1	3.9	3.7	16.2	13.0	9.3	8.4	7.1	5.1	2.7	1.2	0.9
Violent crime [2]	2,913	2,841	2,583	2,527	10,810	8,719	6,142	5,727	4,950	3,575	2,045	929	788
Violent crime percent distribution[1]	4.2	4.1	3.7	3.6	15.5	12.5	8.8	8.2	7.1	5.1	2.9	1.3	1.1
Murder and nonnegligent manslaughter	90	83	66	74	238	197	127	101	85	58	38	25	33
Forcible rape	91	94	90	68	299	272	221	196	166	127	72	51	27
Robbery	627	585	456	465	1,563	989	523	472	391	208	87	25	20
Aggravated assault	2,105	2,079	1,971	1,920	8,710	7,261	5,271	4,958	4,308	3,182	1,848	828	708
Property crime [2]	8,234	7,504	6,779	6,404	27,347	21,060	14,284	12,917	10,797	7,354	3,612	1,629	1,144
Property crime percent distribution[1]	4.4	4.0	3.6	3.4	14.5	11.2	7.6	6.9	5.7	3.9	1.9	0.9	0.6
Burglary	2,142	1,906	1,659	1,547	6,214	4,510	2,828	2,298	1,772	1,128	457	168	113
Larceny-theft	5,650	5,164	4,792	4,469	19,392	15,057	10,439	9,788	8,388	5,849	2,966	1,402	981
Motor vehicle theft	405	388	302	365	1,588	1,378	920	762	552	313	149	37	33
Arson	37	46	26	23	153	115	97	69	85	64	40	22	17
Other assaults	5,394	5,503	5,264	5,036	23,331	20,760	15,980	15,097	12,719	8,933	4,622	2,068	1,853
Forgery and counterfeiting	435	437	435	410	1,909	1,627	1,209	993	799	525	224	92	61
Fraud	736	830	896	936	4,438	4,253	3,581	3,295	2,490	1,665	977	439	326
Embezzlement	126	114	104	84	348	309	251	253	168	117	63	29	17
Stolen property; buying, receiving, possessing	672	646	627	574	2,466	2,034	1,364	1,154	881	504	242	76	59
Vandalism	1,238	1,090	984	900	3,841	2,689	1,879	1,746	1,413	1,045	512	245	211
Weapons; carrying, possessing, etc.	832	820	769	729	3,007	2,231	1,382	1,223	1,007	743	411	225	188
Prostitution and commercialized vice	115	112	127	126	496	396	235	280	195	144	85	33	32
Sex offenses (except forcible rape and prostitution)	315	319	275	243	1,184	1,032	932	917	792	654	417	273	368
Drug abuse violations	12,231	11,427	10,312	9,310	38,665	28,421	18,113	15,092	12,314	8,647	4,251	1,547	648
Gambling	10	12	13	9	51	48	105	118	81	67	65	53	56
Offenses against the family and children	545	638	702	862	4,960	5,800	4,994	4,423	3,116	1,909	821	265	132
Driving under the influence	10,869	11,669	11,361	10,832	45,478	33,669	24,201	22,333	19,951	16,056	9,487	4,940	3,409
Liquor laws	852	720	558	483	1,909	1,495	1,187	1,196	1,253	961	538	275	177
Drunkenness	1,507	1,422	1,348	1,262	5,547	4,535	3,460	3,556	3,795	3,182	1,732	652	414
Disorderly conduct	1,750	1,553	1,419	1,348	5,459	4,552	3,400	3,171	3,210	2,627	1,411	647	474
Vagrancy	110	104	97	79	407	313	231	225	211	175	92	46	21
All other offenses (except traffic)	22,840	23,450	22,713	21,731	97,830	80,649	57,716	50,241	41,643	28,850	14,513	6,106	4,461
Suspicion	9	6	9	8	36	28	26	17	19	12	11	4	5
Curfew and loitering law violations	n.a.	n.a.	n.a.	n.a.	n.a.	n.a.	n.a.	n.a.	n.a.	n.a.	n.a.	n.a.	n.a.

1 Because of rounding, the percentages may not sum to 100. 2 Violent crimes are offenses of murder and nonnegligent manslaughter, forcible rape, robbery, and aggravated assault. Property crimes are offenses of burglary, larceny-theft, motor vehicle theft, and arson. n.a. = not available

Table 53. Arrests, Metropolitan Counties, Persons under 15, 18, 21, and 25 Years of Age, 2012

(Number, percent; 1,280 agencies; 2011 estimated population 51,699,773)

Offense charged	Total, all ages	Number of persons arrested				Percent of total all ages			
		Under 15	Under 18	Under 21	Under 25	Under 15	Under 18	Under 21	Under 25
Total	1,723,089	39,319	148,759	348,989	623,207	2.3	8.6	20.3	36.2
Violent crime [1]	69,908	2,048	7,141	15,359	26,223	2.9	10.2	22.0	37.5
Murder and nonnegligent manslaughter	1,565	12	92	350	663	0.8	5.9	22.4	42.4
Forcible rape	2,470	131	344	696	1,039	5.3	13.9	28.2	42.1
Robbery	10,738	329	1,923	4,327	6,460	3.1	17.9	40.3	60.2
Aggravated assault	55,135	1,576	4,782	9,986	18,061	2.9	8.7	18.1	32.8
Property crime [1]	188,370	7,971	29,849	59,305	88,226	4.2	15.8	31.5	46.8
Burglary	41,203	1,738	6,835	14,461	21,715	4.2	16.6	35.1	52.7
Larceny-theft	135,521	5,664	20,916	41,184	61,259	4.2	15.4	30.4	45.2
Motor vehicle theft	10,229	319	1,631	3,037	4,497	3.1	15.9	29.7	44.0
Arson	1,417	250	467	623	755	17.6	33.0	44.0	53.3
Other assaults	165,969	9,897	25,492	39,409	60,606	6.0	15.4	23.7	36.5
Forgery and counterfeiting	10,586	27	242	1,430	3,147	0.3	2.3	13.5	29.7
Fraud	27,251	102	590	2,389	5,787	0.4	2.2	8.8	21.2
Embezzlement	2,394	2	58	411	839	0.1	2.4	17.2	35.0
Stolen property; buying, receiving, possessing	14,945	268	1,515	3,646	6,165	1.8	10.1	24.4	41.3
Vandalism	29,665	2,676	7,507	11,872	16,084	9.0	25.3	40.0	54.2
Weapons; carrying, possessing, etc.	18,757	1,070	2,814	5,190	8,340	5.7	15.0	27.7	44.5
Prostitution and commercialized vice	2,720	9	63	344	824	0.3	2.3	12.6	30.3
Sex offenses (except forcible rape and prostitution)	10,924	1,034	2,002	3,203	4,355	9.5	18.3	29.3	39.9
Drug abuse violations	226,123	2,765	17,929	55,145	98,425	1.2	7.9	24.4	43.5
Gambling	762	8	44	74	118	1.0	5.8	9.7	15.5
Offenses against the family and children	30,601	142	485	1,434	4,181	0.5	1.6	4.7	13.7
Driving under the influence	240,955	35	1,407	16,700	61,431	*	0.6	6.9	25.5
Liquor laws	42,191	731	9,932	30,587	33,200	1.7	23.5	72.5	78.7
Drunkenness	36,185	75	738	3,773	9,312	0.2	2.0	10.4	25.7
Disorderly conduct	45,761	3,651	10,087	14,740	20,810	8.0	22.0	32.2	45.5
Vagrancy	2,494	53	127	383	773	2.1	5.1	15.4	31.0
All other offenses (except traffic)	552,957	5,976	27,379	80,214	170,948	1.1	5.0	14.5	30.9
Suspicion	218	2	5	28	60	0.9	2.3	12.8	27.5
Curfew and loitering law violations	3,353	777	3,353	3,353	3,353	23.2	100.0	100.0	100.0

1 Violent crimes are offenses of murder and nonnegligent manslaughter, forcible rape, robbery, and aggravated assault. Property crimes are offenses of burglary, larceny-theft, motor vehicle theft, and arson.
* – Less than one-tenth of one percent

Table 54. Arrests, Metropolitan Counties, Distribution by Sex, 2012

(Number, percent; 1,363 agencies; 2012 estimated population 55,902,687)

Offense charged	Number of persons arrested			Percent male	Percent female	Percent distribution[1]		
	Total	Male	Female			Total	Male	Female
Total	1,723,089	1,281,657	441,432	74.4	25.6	100.0	100.0	100.0
Violent crime [2]	69,908	56,372	13,536	80.6	19.4	4.1	4.4	3.1
Murder and nonnegligent manslaughter	1,565	1,382	183	88.3	11.7	0.1	0.1	*
Forcible rape	2,470	2,445	25	99.0	1.0	0.1	0.2	*
Robbery	10,738	9,416	1,322	87.7	12.3	0.6	0.7	0.3
Aggravated assault	55,135	43,129	12,006	78.2	21.8	3.2	3.4	2.7
Property crime [2]	188,370	125,491	62,879	66.6	33.4	10.9	9.8	14.2
Burglary	41,203	34,770	6,433	84.4	15.6	2.4	2.7	1.5
Larceny-theft	135,521	81,309	54,212	60.0	40.0	7.9	6.3	12.3
Motor vehicle theft	10,229	8,241	1,988	80.6	19.4	0.6	0.6	0.5
Arson	1,417	1,171	246	82.6	17.4	0.1	0.1	0.1
Other assaults	165,969	119,554	46,415	72.0	28.0	9.6	9.3	10.5
Forgery and counterfeiting	10,586	6,788	3,798	64.1	35.9	0.6	0.5	0.9
Fraud	27,251	16,033	11,218	58.8	41.2	1.6	1.3	2.5
Embezzlement	2,394	1,279	1,115	53.4	46.6	0.1	0.1	0.3
Stolen property; buying, receiving, possessing	14,945	11,955	2,990	80.0	20.0	0.9	0.9	0.7
Vandalism	29,665	23,538	6,127	79.3	20.7	1.7	1.8	1.4
Weapons; carrying, possessing, etc.	18,757	16,951	1,806	90.4	9.6	1.1	1.3	0.4
Prostitution and commercialized vice	2,720	1,133	1,587	41.7	58.3	0.2	0.1	0.4
Sex offenses (except forcible rape and prostitution)	10,924	10,181	743	93.2	6.8	0.6	0.8	0.2
Drug abuse violations	226,123	176,632	49,491	78.1	21.9	13.1	13.8	11.2
Gambling	762	535	227	70.2	29.8	*	*	0.1
Offenses against the family and children	30,601	25,202	5,399	82.4	17.6	1.8	2.0	1.2
Driving under the influence	240,955	180,790	60,165	75.0	25.0	14.0	14.1	13.6
Liquor laws	42,191	29,313	12,878	69.5	30.5	2.4	2.3	2.9
Drunkenness	36,185	29,453	6,732	81.4	18.6	2.1	2.3	1.5
Disorderly conduct	45,761	32,542	13,219	71.1	28.9	2.7	2.5	3.0
Vagrancy	2,494	1,877	617	75.3	24.7	0.1	0.1	0.1
All other offenses (except traffic)	552,957	413,657	139,300	74.8	25.2	32.1	32.3	31.6
Suspicion	218	157	61	72.0	28.0	*	*	*
Curfew and loitering law violations	3,353	2,224	1,129	66.3	33.7	0.2	0.2	0.3

1 Because of rounding, the percentages may not sum to 100. 2 Violent crimes are offenses of murder and nonnegligent manslaughter, forcible rape, robbery, and aggravated assault. Property crimes are offenses of burglary, larceny-theft, motor vehicle theft, and arson. * = Less than one-tenth of one percent

Table 55. Arrests, Metropolitan Counties, Distribution by Race, 2012

(Number, percent; 1,363 agencies; 2012 estimated population 55,902,687)

Offense charged	Total arrests					Percent distribution[1]				
	Total	White	Black	American Indian or Alaskan Native	Asian or Pacific Islander	Total	White	Black	American Indian or Alaskan Native	Asian or Pacific Islander
Total	1,714,020	1,240,340	436,210	14,150	23,320	100.0	72.4	25.4	0.8	1.4
Violent crime [2]	69,644	45,602	22,487	652	903	100.0	65.5	32.3	0.9	1.3
Murder and nonnegligent manslaughter	1,564	902	629	9	24	100.0	57.7	40.2	0.6	1.5
Forcible rape	2,456	1,836	569	20	31	100.0	74.8	23.2	0.8	1.3
Robbery	10,672	4,911	5,589	52	120	100.0	46.0	52.4	0.5	1.1
Aggravated assault	54,952	37,953	15,700	571	728	100.0	69.1	28.6	1.0	1.3
Property crime [2]	186,948	128,635	54,869	1,005	2,439	100.0	68.8	29.3	0.5	1.3
Burglary	40,953	30,097	10,287	176	393	100.0	73.5	25.1	0.4	1.0
Larceny-theft	134,416	89,866	41,940	741	1,869	100.0	66.9	31.2	0.6	1.4
Motor vehicle theft	10,165	7,557	2,364	80	164	100.0	74.3	23.3	0.8	1.6
Arson	1,414	1,115	278	8	13	100.0	78.9	19.7	0.6	0.9
Other assaults	165,216	117,620	44,687	1,221	1,688	100.0	71.2	27.0	0.7	1.0
Forgery and counterfeiting	10,544	6,777	3,613	31	123	100.0	64.3	34.3	0.3	1.2
Fraud	27,124	18,817	7,937	144	226	100.0	69.4	29.3	0.5	0.8
Embezzlement	2,389	1,531	822	10	26	100.0	64.1	34.4	0.4	1.1
Stolen property; buying, receiving, possessing	14,796	10,394	4,174	98	130	100.0	70.2	28.2	0.7	0.9
Vandalism	29,207	22,087	6,609	248	263	100.0	75.6	22.6	0.8	0.9
Weapons; carrying, possessing, etc.	18,666	12,034	6,299	84	249	100.0	64.5	33.7	0.5	1.3
Prostitution and commercialized vice	2,695	1,592	928	3	172	100.0	59.1	34.4	0.1	6.4
Sex offenses (except forcible rape and prostitution)	10,823	8,416	2,211	68	128	100.0	77.8	20.4	0.6	1.2
Drug abuse violations	224,927	162,248	58,855	1,163	2,661	100.0	72.1	26.2	0.5	1.2
Gambling	760	515	180	6	59	100.0	67.8	23.7	0.8	7.8
Offenses against the family and children	30,514	18,315	11,874	160	165	100.0	60.0	38.9	0.5	0.5
Driving under the influence	240,061	203,428	29,003	1,525	6,105	100.0	84.7	12.1	0.6	2.5
Liquor laws	41,707	35,774	4,742	546	645	100.0	85.8	11.4	1.3	1.5
Drunkenness	36,138	31,156	4,223	350	409	100.0	86.2	11.7	1.0	1.1
Disorderly conduct	45,493	29,336	15,443	364	350	100.0	64.5	33.9	0.8	0.8
Vagrancy	2,488	1,806	664	4	14	100.0	72.6	26.7	0.2	0.6
All other offenses (except traffic)	550,321	381,729	155,657	6,457	6,478	100.0	69.4	28.3	1.2	1.2
Suspicion	218	76	139	0	3	100.0	34.9	63.8	0.0	1.4
Curfew and loitering law violations	3,341	2,452	794	11	84	100.0	73.4	23.8	0.3	2.5

Table 55. Arrests, Metropolitan Counties, Distribution by Race, 2012

(Number, percent; 1,363 agencies; 2012 estimated population 55,902,687)

Offense charged	Arrests under 18					Percent distribution[1]				
	Total	White	Black	American Indian or Alaskan Native	Asian or Pacific Islander	Total	White	Black	American Indian or Alaskan Native	Asian or Pacific Islander
Total	144,535	94,531	47,065	1,157	1,782	100.0	65.4	32.6	0.8	1.2
Violent crime [2]	6,967	3,486	3,362	43	76	100.0	50.0	48.3	0.6	1.1
Murder and nonnegligent manslaughter	91	42	47	1	1	100.0	46.2	51.6	1.1	1.1
Forcible rape	335	246	81	5	3	100.0	73.4	24.2	1.5	0.9
Robbery	1,862	532	1,297	3	30	100.0	28.6	69.7	0.2	1.6
Aggravated assault	4,679	2,666	1,937	34	42	100.0	57.0	41.4	0.7	0.9
Property crime [2]	28,839	16,786	11,438	164	451	100.0	58.2	39.7	0.6	1.6
Burglary	6,660	4,181	2,382	26	71	100.0	62.8	35.8	0.4	1.1
Larceny-theft	20,132	11,193	8,450	128	361	100.0	55.6	42.0	0.6	1.8
Motor vehicle theft	1,583	1,068	491	8	16	100.0	67.5	31.0	0.5	1.0
Arson	464	344	115	2	3	100.0	74.1	24.8	0.4	0.6
Other assaults	25,073	14,281	10,449	180	163	100.0	57.0	41.7	0.7	0.7
Forgery and counterfeiting	220	153	63	2	2	100.0	69.5	28.6	0.9	0.9
Fraud	555	342	201	4	8	100.0	61.6	36.2	0.7	1.4
Embezzlement	58	37	21	0	0	100.0	63.8	36.2	0.0	0.0
Stolen property; buying, receiving, possessing	1,386	729	631	12	14	100.0	52.6	45.5	0.9	1.0
Vandalism	7,109	5,257	1,737	66	49	100.0	73.9	24.4	0.9	0.7
Weapons; carrying, possessing, etc.	2,761	1,716	994	12	39	100.0	62.2	36.0	0.4	1.4
Prostitution and commercialized vice	59	28	31	0	0	100.0	47.5	52.5	0.0	0.0
Sex offenses (except forcible rape and prostitution)	1,936	1,403	511	10	12	100.0	72.5	26.4	0.5	0.6
Drug abuse violations	17,306	13,176	3,696	141	293	100.0	76.1	21.4	0.8	1.7
Gambling	44	26	15	1	2	100.0	59.1	34.1	2.3	4.5
Offenses against the family and children	482	351	119	7	5	100.0	72.8	24.7	1.5	1.0
Driving under the influence	1,362	1,257	66	18	21	100.0	92.3	4.8	1.3	1.5
Liquor laws	9,726	8,878	594	85	169	100.0	91.3	6.1	0.9	1.7
Drunkenness	738	658	66	10	4	100.0	89.2	8.9	1.4	0.5
Disorderly conduct	9,933	5,344	4,457	71	61	100.0	53.8	44.9	0.7	0.6
Vagrancy	123	64	58	0	1	100.0	52.0	47.2	0.0	0.8
All other offenses (except traffic)	26,512	18,104	7,760	320	328	100.0	68.3	29.3	1.2	1.2
Suspicion	5	3	2	0	0	100.0	60.0	40.0	0.0	0.0
Curfew and loitering law violations	3,341	2,452	794	11	84	100.0	73.4	23.8	0.3	2.5

Table 55. Arrests, Metropolitan Counties, Distribution by Race, 2012

(Number, percent; 1,363 agencies; 2012 estimated population 55,902,687)

Offense charged	Arrests 18 and over					Percent distribution[1]				
	Total	White	Black	American Indian or Alaskan Native	Asian or Pacific Islander	Total	White	Black	American Indian or Alaskan Native	Asian or Pacific Islander
Total	1,569,485	1,145,809	389,145	12,993	21,538	100.0	73.0	24.8	0.8	1.4
Violent crime [2]	62,677	42,116	19,125	609	827	100.0	67.2	30.5	1.0	1.3
Murder and nonnegligent manslaughter	1,473	860	582	8	23	100.0	58.4	39.5	0.5	1.6
Forcible rape	2,121	1,590	488	15	28	100.0	75.0	23.0	0.7	1.3
Robbery	8,810	4,379	4,292	49	90	100.0	49.7	48.7	0.6	1.0
Aggravated assault	50,273	35,287	13,763	537	686	100.0	70.2	27.4	1.1	1.4
Property crime [2]	158,109	111,849	43,431	841	1,988	100.0	70.7	27.5	0.5	1.3
Burglary	34,293	25,916	7,905	150	322	100.0	75.6	23.1	0.4	0.9
Larceny-theft	114,284	78,673	33,490	613	1,508	100.0	68.8	29.3	0.5	1.3
Motor vehicle theft	8,582	6,489	1,873	72	148	100.0	75.6	21.8	0.8	1.7
Arson	950	771	163	6	10	100.0	81.2	17.2	0.6	1.1
Other assaults	140,143	103,339	34,238	1,041	1,525	100.0	73.7	24.4	0.7	1.1
Forgery and counterfeiting	10,324	6,624	3,550	29	121	100.0	64.2	34.4	0.3	1.2
Fraud	26,569	18,475	7,736	140	218	100.0	69.5	29.1	0.5	0.8
Embezzlement	2,331	1,494	801	10	26	100.0	64.1	34.4	0.4	1.1
Stolen property; buying, receiving, possessing	13,410	9,665	3,543	86	116	100.0	72.1	26.4	0.6	0.9
Vandalism	22,098	16,830	4,872	182	214	100.0	76.2	22.0	0.8	1.0
Weapons; carrying, possessing, etc.	15,905	10,318	5,305	72	210	100.0	64.9	33.4	0.5	1.3
Prostitution and commercialized vice	2,636	1,564	897	3	172	100.0	59.3	34.0	0.1	6.5
Sex offenses (except forcible rape and prostitu-tion)	8,887	7,013	1,700	58	116	100.0	78.9	19.1	0.7	1.3
Drug abuse violations	207,621	149,072	55,159	1,022	2,368	100.0	71.8	26.6	0.5	1.1
Gambling	716	489	165	5	57	100.0	68.3	23.0	0.7	8.0
Offenses against the family and children	30,032	17,964	11,755	153	160	100.0	59.8	39.1	0.5	0.5
Driving under the influence	238,699	202,171	28,937	1,507	6,084	100.0	84.7	12.1	0.6	2.5
Liquor laws	31,981	26,896	4,148	461	476	100.0	84.1	13.0	1.4	1.5
Drunkenness	35,400	30,498	4,157	340	405	100.0	86.2	11.7	1.0	1.1
Disorderly conduct	35,560	23,992	10,986	293	289	100.0	67.5	30.9	0.8	0.8
Vagrancy	2,365	1,742	606	4	13	100.0	73.7	25.6	0.2	0.5
All other offenses (except traffic)	523,809	363,625	147,897	6,137	6,150	100.0	69.4	28.2	1.2	1.2
Suspicion	213	73	137	0	3	100.0	34.3	64.3	0.0	1.4
Curfew and loitering law violations	n.a.	n.a.	n.a.	n.a.	n.a.	n.a.	n.a.	n.a.	n.a.	n.a.

1 Because of rounding, the percentages may not sum to 100. 2 Violent crimes are offenses of murder and nonnegligent manslaughter, forcible rape, robbery, and aggravated assault. Property crimes are offenses of burglary, larceny-theft, motor vehicle theft, and arson. n.a. = not available

Table 56. Arrest Trends, Nonmetropolitan Counties, 2011–2012

(Number, percent change; 1,799 agencies; 2012 estimated population 20,855,725; 2011 estimated population 20,870,513)

Offense charged	Number of persons arrested								
	Total, all ages			Under 18 years of age			18 years of age and over		
	2011	2012	Percent change	2011	2012	Percent change	2011	2012	Percent change
Total [1]	704,317	689,782	-2.1	41,077	38,547	-6.2	663,240	651,235	-1.8
Violent crime [2]	20,282	19,868	-2.0	1,386	1,338	-3.5	18,896	18,530	-1.9
Murder and nonnegligent manslaughter	645	627	-2.8	34	29	-14.7	611	598	-2.1
Forcible rape	1,253	1,169	-6.7	167	154	-7.8	1,086	1,015	-6.5
Robbery	1,580	1,470	-7.0	118	111	-5.9	1,462	1,359	-7.0
Aggravated assault	16,804	16,602	-1.2	1,067	1,044	-2.2	15,737	15,558	-1.1
Property crime [2]	56,543	55,153	-2.5	6,716	6,484	-3.5	49,827	48,669	-2.3
Burglary	17,942	17,163	-4.3	2,441	2,193	-10.2	15,501	14,970	-3.4
Larceny-theft	34,410	33,861	-1.6	3,627	3,556	-2.0	30,783	30,305	-1.6
Motor vehicle theft	3,505	3,437	-1.9	527	607	15.2	2,978	2,830	-5.0
Arson	686	692	0.9	121	128	5.8	565	564	-0.2
Other assaults	64,645	62,932	-2.6	6,792	5,868	-13.6	57,853	57,064	-1.4
Forgery and counterfeiting	3,198	2,985	-6.7	49	41	-16.3	3,149	2,944	-6.5
Fraud	14,957	12,892	-13.8	192	162	-15.6	14,765	12,730	-13.8
Embezzlement	646	573	-11.3	9	11	22.2	637	562	-11.8
Stolen property; buying, receiving, possessing	4,469	4,180	-6.5	383	257	-32.9	4,086	3,923	-4.0
Vandalism	10,257	10,193	-0.6	2,322	2,276	-2.0	7,935	7,917	-0.2
Weapons; carrying, possessing, etc.	6,038	5,971	-1.1	514	456	-11.3	5,524	5,515	-0.2
Prostitution and commercialized vice	124	134	8.1	5	10	100.0	119	124	4.2
Sex offenses (except forcible rape and prostitution)	4,242	4,114	-3.0	807	787	-2.5	3,435	3,327	-3.1
Drug abuse violations	80,689	80,912	0.3	4,332	3,849	-11.1	76,357	77,063	0.9
Gambling	211	192	-9.0	12	11	-8.3	199	181	-9.0
Offenses against the family and children	11,914	11,161	-6.3	202	193	-4.5	11,712	10,968	-6.4
Driving under the influence	143,463	141,161	-1.6	1,030	969	-5.9	142,433	140,192	-1.6
Liquor laws	23,737	22,823	-3.9	4,926	4,768	-3.2	18,811	18,055	-4.0
Drunkenness	17,871	17,397	-2.7	314	303	-3.5	17,557	17,094	-2.6
Disorderly conduct	18,829	18,668	-0.9	2,987	2,936	-1.7	15,842	15,732	-0.7
Vagrancy	271	190	-29.9	28	20	-28.6	243	170	-30.0
All other offenses (except traffic)	221,603	217,998	-1.6	7,743	7,523	-2.8	213,860	210,475	-1.6
Suspicion	106	158	49.1	36	113	213.9	70	45	-35.7
Curfew and loitering law violations	328	285	-13.1	328	285	-13.1	n.a.	n.a.	n.a.

1 Does not include suspicion. 2 Violent crimes are offenses of murder and nonnegligent manslaughter, forcible rape, robbery, and aggravated assault. Property crimes are offenses of burglary, larceny-theft, motor vehicle theft, and arson. n.a. = not available

Table 57. Arrest Trends, Nonmetropolitan Counties, by Age and Sex, 2011–2012

(Number, percent; 1,799 agencies; 2012 estimated population 20,855,725; 2011 estimated population 20,870,513)

Offense charged	Male						Female					
	Total			Under 18			Total			Under 18		
	2011	2012	Percent change	2011	2012	Percent change	2011	2012	Percent change	2011	2012	Percent change
Total [1]	532,041	518,546	-2.5	29,912	28,134	-5.9	172,276	171,236	-0.6	11,165	10,413	-6.7
Violent crime [2]	16,779	16,324	-2.7	1,137	1,120	-1.5	3,503	3,544	1.2	249	218	-12.4
Murder and nonnegligent manslaughter	546	532	-2.6	29	28	-3.4	99	95	-4.0	5	1	-80.0
Forcible rape	1,230	1,149	-6.6	163	154	-5.5	23	20	-13.0	4	0	-100.0
Robbery	1,406	1,257	-10.6	108	100	-7.4	174	213	22.4	10	11	10.0
Aggravated assault	13,597	13,386	-1.6	837	838	0.1	3,207	3,216	0.3	230	206	-10.4
Property crime [2]	42,554	40,752	-4.2	5,364	5,177	-3.5	13,989	14,401	2.9	1,352	1,307	-3.3
Burglary	15,323	14,355	-6.3	2,227	1,987	-10.8	2,619	2,808	7.2	214	206	-3.7
Larceny-theft	23,725	22,975	-3.2	2,606	2,573	-1.3	10,685	10,886	1.9	1,021	983	-3.7
Motor vehicle theft	2,910	2,821	-3.1	425	500	17.6	595	616	3.5	102	107	4.9
Arson	596	601	0.8	106	117	10.4	90	91	1.1	15	11	-26.7
Other assaults	47,177	46,205	-2.1	4,423	3,928	-11.2	17,468	16,727	-4.2	2,369	1,940	-18.1
Forgery and counterfeiting	1,855	1,773	-4.4	35	30	-14.3	1,343	1,212	-9.8	14	11	-21.4
Fraud	7,884	6,839	-13.3	101	108	6.9	7,073	6,053	-14.4	91	54	-40.7
Embezzlement	335	295	-11.9	8	8	0.0	311	278	-10.6	1	3	200.0
Stolen property; buying, receiving, possessing	3,631	3,345	-7.9	312	204	-34.6	838	835	-0.4	71	53	-25.4
Vandalism	8,389	8,321	-0.8	1,952	1,933	-1.0	1,868	1,872	0.2	370	343	-7.3
Weapons; carrying, possessing, etc.	5,582	5,497	-1.5	455	408	-10.3	456	474	3.9	59	48	-18.6
Prostitution and commercialized vice	71	73	2.8	4	7	75.0	53	61	15.1	1	3	200.0
Sex offenses (except forcible rape and prostitution)	3,959	3,808	-3.8	715	698	-2.4	283	306	8.1	92	89	-3.3
Drug abuse violations	62,123	61,759	-0.6	3,461	3,037	-12.3	18,566	19,153	3.2	871	812	-6.8
Gambling	159	149	-6.3	7	6	-14.3	52	43	-17.3	5	5	0.0
Offenses against the family and children	9,472	8,683	-8.3	135	120	-11.1	2,442	2,478	1.5	67	73	9.0
Driving under the influence	111,021	108,848	-2.0	767	713	-7.0	32,442	32,313	-0.4	263	256	-2.7
Liquor laws	16,644	15,845	-4.8	2,981	2,817	-5.5	7,093	6,978	-1.6	1,945	1,951	0.3
Drunkenness	13,996	13,465	-3.8	240	228	-5.0	3,875	3,932	1.5	74	75	1.4
Disorderly conduct	13,504	13,569	0.5	2,019	1,962	-2.8	5,325	5,099	-4.2	968	974	0.6
Vagrancy	228	142	-37.7	27	10	-63.0	43	48	11.6	1	10	900.0
All other offenses (except traffic)	166,479	162,673	-2.3	5,570	5,439	-2.4	55,124	55,325	0.4	2,173	2,084	-4.1
Suspicion	75	111	48.0	19	74	289.5	31	47	51.6	17	39	129.4
Curfew and loitering law violations	199	181	-9.0	199	181	-9.0	129	104	-19.4	129	104	-19.4

1 Does not include suspicion. 2 Violent crimes are offenses of murder and nonnegligent manslaughter, forcible rape, robbery, and aggravated assault. Property crimes are offenses of burglary, larceny-theft, motor vehicle theft, and arson.

Table 58. Arrests, Nonmetropolitan Counties, Distribution by Age, 2012

(Number, percent; 1,962 agencies; 2012 estimated population 21,512,971)

Offense charged	Total, all ages	Ages under 15	Ages under 18	Ages 18 and over	Under 10	10–12	13–14	15	16	17	18
Total	734,778	9,718	40,413	694,365	391	2,239	7,088	6,169	9,893	14,633	24,063
Total percent distribution[1]	100.0	1.3	5.5	94.5	0.1	0.3	1.0	0.8	1.3	2.0	3.3
Violent crime [2]	20,689	417	1,395	19,294	12	116	289	233	291	454	611
Violent crime per-cent distribution[1]	100	2	7	93	0	1	1	1	1	2	3
Murder and non-negligent manslaugh-ter	641	5	30	611	0	2	3	4	9	12	24
Forcible rape	1,197	65	160	1,037	3	20	42	20	29	46	69
Robbery	1,542	11	109	1,433	0	3	8	13	31	54	94
Aggravated assault	17,309	336	1,096	16,213	9	91	236	196	222	342	424
Property crime [2]	57,729	1,719	6,808	50,921	58	414	1,247	1,058	1,698	2,333	3,085
Property crime percent distribution[1]	100	3	12	88	0	1	2	2	3	4	5
Burglary	17,804	518	2,294	15,510	11	121	386	369	594	813	1,184
Larceny-theft	35,412	989	3,734	31,678	42	252	695	553	905	1,287	1,683
Motor vehicle theft	3,781	153	638	3,143	1	16	136	111	183	191	175
Arson	732	59	142	590	4	25	30	25	16	42	43
Other assaults	64,571	2,025	6,092	58,479	81	501	1,443	1,058	1,458	1,551	1,759
Forgery and counterfeiting	3,103	3	41	3,062	1	0	2	5	12	21	62
Fraud	13,250	44	165	13,085	3	8	33	17	36	68	177
Embezzlement	599	1	11	588	0	0	1	2	4	4	7
Stolen property; buying, receiving, possessing	4,425	49	272	4,153	3	13	33	40	81	102	193
Vandalism	10,444	879	2,347	8,097	62	242	575	361	491	616	586
Weapons; carrying, possessing, etc.	6,241	174	472	5,769	16	42	116	64	113	121	171
Prostitution and commercialized vice	139	3	11	128	0	1	2	3	4	1	5
Sex offenses (except forcible rape and prostitution)	4,362	381	818	3,544	21	116	244	130	143	164	246
Drug abuse violations	85,521	582	4,065	81,456	13	76	493	540	1,041	1,902	3,838
Gambling	196	0	11	185	0	0	0	3	1	7	10
Offenses against the family and children	11,649	79	205	11,444	8	17	54	46	37	43	110
Driving under the influence	165,735	24	1,054	164,681	1	3	20	41	238	751	2,688
Liquor laws	24,377	385	5,011	19,366	1	23	361	694	1,447	2,485	4,108
Drunkenness	17,784	23	307	17,477	3	3	17	33	79	172	443
Disorderly conduct	19,428	1,096	3,060	16,368	40	273	783	526	672	766	708
Vagrancy	202	0	21	181	0	0	0	4	8	9	10
All other offenses (except traffic)	223,845	1,695	7,805	216,040	63	359	1,273	1,210	1,936	2,964	5,245
Suspicion	165	62	118	47	4	18	40	21	25	10	1
Curfew and loitering law violations	324	77	324	n.a.	1	14	62	80	78	89	n.a.

Table 58. Arrests, Nonmetropolitan Counties, Distribution by Age, 2012

(Number, percent; 1,962 agencies; 2012 estimated population 21,512,971)

Offense charged	19	20	21	22	23	24	25–29	30–34	35–39	40–44	45–49	50–54	55–59	60–64	65 and over
Total	28,220	29,733	29,096	28,331	27,395	26,072	120,528	100,774	73,995	65,475	55,006	41,603	23,137	11,620	9,317
Total percent distribution[1]	3.8	4.0	4.0	3.9	3.7	3.5	16.4	13.7	10.1	8.9	7.5	5.7	3.1	1.6	1.3
Violent crime [2]	637	694	793	717	691	681	3,266	2,797	2,090	1,879	1,718	1,239	730	369	382
Violent crime percent distribution[1]	3	3	4	4	3	3	16	14	10	9	8	6	4	2	2
Murder and nonnegligent manslaughter	14	21	25	15	20	33	116	75	60	55	52	43	27	17	14
Forcible rape	59	66	50	46	46	36	142	123	103	89	79	47	41	19	22
Robbery	96	105	103	87	76	69	314	203	105	84	49	30	8	5	5
Aggravated assault	468	502	615	569	549	543	2,694	2,396	1,822	1,651	1,538	1,119	654	328	341
Property crime [2]	3,067	2,665	2,535	2,411	2,190	2,082	9,493	7,282	5,016	4,188	3,053	2,023	993	425	413
Property crime percent distribution[1]	5	5	4	4	4	4	16	13	9	7	5	4	2	1	1
Burglary	1,062	980	887	810	762	691	2,977	2,183	1,389	1,080	763	433	175	68	66
Larceny-theft	1,794	1,530	1,470	1,400	1,261	1,262	5,889	4,525	3,202	2,779	2,055	1,440	747	317	324
Motor vehicle theft	169	134	157	168	136	112	551	508	359	285	182	110	52	34	11
Arson	42	21	21	33	31	17	76	66	66	44	53	40	19	6	12
Other assaults	1,696	1,952	2,097	2,021	2,010	2,001	9,419	8,624	6,876	6,351	5,382	4,038	2,123	1,111	1,019
Forgery and counterfeiting	89	106	111	112	130	109	633	590	393	296	194	131	68	20	18
Fraud	255	309	295	352	411	370	2,074	2,198	1,839	1,700	1,262	806	518	263	256
Embezzlement	10	12	20	18	21	23	91	90	78	68	56	37	33	15	9
Stolen property; buying, receiving, possessing	218	197	170	194	180	171	780	676	452	343	256	181	83	35	24
Vandalism	582	507	480	422	336	346	1,346	1,050	658	562	480	345	177	106	114
Weapons; carrying, possessing, etc.	174	202	205	239	233	196	1,012	797	600	508	506	384	270	135	137
Prostitution and commercialized vice	3	7	7	6	4	4	26	24	14	7	3	7	3	4	4
Sex offenses (except forcible rape and prostitution)	188	179	142	131	98	91	429	390	387	326	276	211	154	107	189
Drug abuse violations	4,435	4,489	4,388	4,177	3,792	3,355	15,169	11,801	7,641	6,192	5,087	3,744	2,031	869	448
Gambling	23	34	3	2	2	2	11	18	15	7	12	20	11	8	7
Offenses against the family and children	143	192	246	291	312	362	2,086	2,318	1,904	1,492	1,000	574	254	104	56
Driving under the influence	3,893	4,866	6,626	6,720	6,550	6,352	27,488	21,945	16,702	16,495	15,496	13,284	8,064	4,317	3,195
Liquor laws	4,471	3,933	669	459	369	309	1,121	903	654	643	609	511	315	161	131
Drunkenness	487	543	726	651	563	518	2,610	2,427	1,949	1,935	1,867	1,438	750	338	232
Disorderly conduct	618	597	703	611	658	652	2,643	2,099	1,672	1,526	1,481	1,202	642	301	255
Vagrancy	4	6	6	7	8	9	28	22	11	14	13	19	14	6	4
All other offenses (except traffic)	7,225	8,241	8,872	8,787	8,834	8,438	40,788	34,717	25,041	20,939	16,253	11,407	5,904	2,926	2,423
Suspicion	2	2	2	3	3	1	15	6	3	4	2	2	0	0	1
Curfew and loitering law violations	n.a.	n.a.	n.a.	n.a.	n.a.	n.a.	n.a.	n.a.	n.a.	n.a.	n.a.	n.a.	n.a.	n.a.	n.a.

1 Because of rounding, the percentages may not sum to 100. 2 Violent crimes are offenses of murder and nonnegligent manslaughter, forcible rape, robbery, and aggravated assault. Property crimes are offenses of burglary, larceny-theft, motor vehicle theft, and arson. n.a. = not available

Table 59. Arrests, Nonmetropolitan Counties, Persons under 15, 18, 21, and 25 Years of Age, 2012

(Number, percent; 1,962 agencies; 2012 estimated population 21,512,971)

Offense charged	Total, all ages	Number of persons arrested				Percent of total all ages			
		Under 15	Under 18	Under 21	Under 25	Under 15	Under 18	Under 21	Under 25
Total	734,778	9,718	40,413	122,429	233,323	1.3	5.5	16.7	31.8
Violent crime [1]	20,689	417	1,395	3,337	6,219	2.0	6.7	16.1	30.1
Murder and nonnegligent manslaughter	641	5	30	89	182	0.8	4.7	13.9	28.4
Forcible rape	1,197	65	160	354	532	5.4	13.4	29.6	44.4
Robbery	1,542	11	109	404	739	0.7	7.1	26.2	47.9
Aggravated assault	17,309	336	1,096	2,490	4,766	1.9	6.3	14.4	27.5
Property crime [1]	57,729	1,719	6,808	15,625	24,843	3.0	11.8	27.1	43.0
Burglary	17,804	518	2,294	5,520	8,670	2.9	12.9	31.0	48.7
Larceny-theft	35,412	989	3,734	8,741	14,134	2.8	10.5	24.7	39.9
Motor vehicle theft	3,781	153	638	1,116	1,689	4.0	16.9	29.5	44.7
Arson	732	59	142	248	350	8.1	19.4	33.9	47.8
Other assaults	64,571	2,025	6,092	11,499	19,628	3.1	9.4	17.8	30.4
Forgery and counterfeiting	3,103	3	41	298	760	0.1	1.3	9.6	24.5
Fraud	13,250	44	165	906	2,334	0.3	1.2	6.8	17.6
Embezzlement	599	1	11	40	122	0.2	1.8	6.7	20.4
Stolen property; buying, receiving, possessing	4,425	49	272	880	1,595	1.1	6.1	19.9	36.0
Vandalism	10,444	879	2,347	4,022	5,606	8.4	22.5	38.5	53.7
Weapons; carrying, possessing, etc.	6,241	174	472	1,019	1,892	2.8	7.6	16.3	30.3
Prostitution and commercialized vice	139	3	11	26	47	2.2	7.9	18.7	33.8
Sex offenses (except forcible rape and prostitution)	4,362	381	818	1,431	1,893	8.7	18.8	32.8	43.4
Drug abuse violations	85,521	582	4,065	16,827	32,539	0.7	4.8	19.7	38.0
Gambling	196	0	11	78	87	0.0	5.6	39.8	44.4
Offenses against the family and children	11,649	79	205	650	1,861	0.7	1.8	5.6	16.0
Driving under the influence	165,735	24	1,054	12,501	38,749	*	0.6	7.5	23.4
Liquor laws	24,377	385	5,011	17,523	19,329	1.6	20.6	71.9	79.3
Drunkenness	17,784	23	307	1,780	4,238	0.1	1.7	10.0	23.8
Disorderly conduct	19,428	1,096	3,060	4,983	7,607	5.6	15.8	25.6	39.2
Vagrancy	202	0	21	41	71	0.0	10.4	20.3	35.1
All other offenses (except traffic)	223,845	1,695	7,805	28,516	63,447	0.8	3.5	12.7	28.3
Suspicion	165	62	118	123	132	37.6	71.5	74.5	80.0
Curfew and loitering law violations	324	77	324	324	324	23.8	100.0	100.0	100.0

1 Violent crimes are offenses of murder and nonnegligent manslaughter, forcible rape, robbery, and aggravated assault. Property crimes are offenses of burglary, larceny-theft, motor vehicle theft, and arson.
* = Less than one-tenth of one percent.

Table 60. Arrests, Nonmetropolitan Counties, Distribution by Sex, 2012

(Number, percent; 1,962 agencies; 2012 estimated population 21,512,971)

Offense charged	Number of persons arrested			Percent male	Percent female	Percent distribution[1]		
	Total	Male	Female			Total	Male	Female
Total	734,778	551,898	182,880	75.1	24.9	100.0	100.0	100.0
Violent crime [2]	20,689	17,001	3,688	82.2	17.8	2.8	3.1	2.0
Murder and nonnegligent manslaughter	641	542	99	84.6	15.4	0.1	0.1	0.1
Forcible rape	1,197	1,176	21	98.2	1.8	0.2	0.2	0.1
Robbery	1,542	1,314	228	85.2	14.8	0.2	0.2	0.1
Aggravated assault	17,309	13,969	3,340	80.7	19.3	2.4	2.5	1.8
Property crime [2]	57,729	42,590	15,139	73.8	26.2	7.9	7.7	8.3
Burglary	17,804	14,890	2,914	83.6	16.4	2.4	2.7	1.6
Larceny-theft	35,412	24,002	11,410	67.8	32.2	4.8	4.3	6.2
Motor vehicle theft	3,781	3,065	716	81.1	18.9	0.5	0.6	0.4
Arson	732	633	99	86.5	13.5	0.1	0.1	0.1
Other assaults	64,571	47,362	17,209	73.3	26.7	8.8	8.6	9.4
Forgery and counterfeiting	3,103	1,850	1,253	59.6	40.4	0.4	0.3	0.7
Fraud	13,250	7,071	6,179	53.4	46.6	1.8	1.3	3.4
Embezzlement	599	310	289	51.8	48.2	0.1	0.1	0.2
Stolen property; buying, receiving, possessing	4,425	3,531	894	79.8	20.2	0.6	0.6	0.5
Vandalism	10,444	8,533	1,911	81.7	18.3	1.4	1.5	1.0
Weapons; carrying, possessing, etc.	6,241	5,743	498	92.0	8.0	0.8	1.0	0.3
Prostitution and commercialized vice	139	77	62	55.4	44.6	*	*	*
Sex offenses (except forcible rape and prostitution)	4,362	4,034	328	92.5	7.5	0.6	0.7	0.2
Drug abuse violations	85,521	65,253	20,268	76.3	23.7	11.6	11.8	11.1
Gambling	196	154	42	78.6	21.4	*	*	*
Offenses against the family and children	11,649	9,013	2,636	77.4	22.6	1.6	1.6	1.4
Driving under the influence	165,735	127,054	38,681	76.7	23.3	22.6	23.0	21.2
Liquor laws	24,377	16,863	7,514	69.2	30.8	3.3	3.1	4.1
Drunkenness	17,784	13,744	4,040	77.3	22.7	2.4	2.5	2.2
Disorderly conduct	19,428	14,067	5,361	72.4	27.6	2.6	2.5	2.9
Vagrancy	202	147	55	72.8	27.2	*	*	*
All other offenses (except traffic)	223,845	167,182	56,663	74.7	25.3	30.5	30.3	31.0
Suspicion	165	118	47	71.5	28.5	*	*	*
Curfew and loitering law violations	324	201	123	62.0	38.0	*	*	0.1

1 Because of rounding, the percentages may not sum to 100. 2 Violent crimes are offenses of murder and nonnegligent manslaughter, forcible rape, robbery, and aggravated assault. Property crimes are offenses of burglary, larceny-theft, motor vehicle theft, and arson. * = Less than one-tenth of one percent

Table 61. Arrests, Nonmetropolitan Counties, Distribution by Race, 2012

(Number, percent; 1,962 agencies; 2012 estimated population 21,512,971)

Offense charged	Total arrests					Percent distribution[1]				
	Total	White	Black	American Indian or Alaskan Native	Asian or Pacific Islander	Total	White	Black	American Indian or Alaskan Native	Asian or Pacific Islander
Total	726,967	605,291	98,436	19,053	4,187	100.0	83.3	13.5	2.6	0.6
Violent crime [2]	20,600	16,177	3,551	797	75	100.0	78.5	17.2	3.9	0.4
Murder and nonnegligent manslaughter	640	476	135	28	1	100.0	74.4	21.1	4.4	0.2
Forcible rape	1,188	1,007	160	15	6	100.0	84.8	13.5	1.3	0.5
Robbery	1,537	936	538	59	4	100.0	60.9	35.0	3.8	0.3
Aggravated assault	17,235	13,758	2,718	695	64	100.0	79.8	15.8	4.0	0.4
Property crime [2]	57,329	48,149	7,604	1,463	113	100.0	84.0	13.3	2.6	0.2
Burglary	17,707	14,806	2,390	490	21	100.0	83.6	13.5	2.8	0.1
Larceny-theft	35,134	29,459	4,746	848	81	100.0	83.8	13.5	2.4	0.2
Motor vehicle theft	3,759	3,246	409	96	8	100.0	86.4	10.9	2.6	0.2
Arson	729	638	59	29	3	100.0	87.5	8.1	4.0	0.4
Other assaults	64,064	53,246	8,867	1,790	161	100.0	83.1	13.8	2.8	0.3
Forgery and counterfeiting	3,065	2,518	520	15	12	100.0	82.2	17.0	0.5	0.4
Fraud	13,125	10,536	2,332	233	24	100.0	80.3	17.8	1.8	0.2
Embezzlement	593	518	64	11	0	100.0	87.4	10.8	1.9	0.0
Stolen property; buying, receiving, possessing	4,388	3,561	730	80	17	100.0	81.2	16.6	1.8	0.4
Vandalism	10,351	8,930	1,080	321	20	100.0	86.3	10.4	3.1	0.2
Weapons; carrying, possessing, etc.	6,215	4,828	1,250	121	16	100.0	77.7	20.1	1.9	0.3
Prostitution and commercialized vice	138	107	24	6	1	100.0	77.5	17.4	4.3	0.7
Sex offenses (except forcible rape and prostitution)	4,325	3,841	409	58	17	100.0	88.8	9.5	1.3	0.4
Drug abuse violations	84,708	70,725	12,162	1,349	472	100.0	83.5	14.4	1.6	0.6
Gambling	194	133	42	6	13	100.0	68.6	21.6	3.1	6.7
Offenses against the family and children	11,605	8,622	2,554	397	32	100.0	74.3	22.0	3.4	0.3
Driving under the influence	163,291	140,714	16,455	3,840	2,282	100.0	86.2	10.1	2.4	1.4
Liquor laws	23,776	21,917	1,005	749	105	100.0	92.2	4.2	3.2	0.4
Drunkenness	17,710	15,900	1,198	563	49	100.0	89.8	6.8	3.2	0.3
Disorderly conduct	19,255	15,234	3,053	915	53	100.0	79.1	15.9	4.8	0.3
Vagrancy	198	130	58	10	0	100.0	65.7	29.3	5.1	0.0
All other offenses (except traffic)	221,556	179,078	35,452	6,301	725	100.0	80.8	16.0	2.8	0.3
Suspicion	165	150	15	0	0	100.0	90.9	9.1	0.0	0.0
Curfew and loitering law violations	316	277	11	28	0	100.0	87.7	3.5	8.9	0.0

Table 61. Arrests, Nonmetropolitan Counties, Distribution by Race, 2012

(Number, percent; 1,962 agencies; 2012 estimated population 21,512,971)

Offense charged	Arrests under 18					Percent distribution[1]				
	Total	White	Black	American Indian or Alaskan Native	Asian or Pacific Islander	Total	White	Black	American Indian or Alaskan Native	Asian or Pacific Islander
Total	39,413	32,927	4,829	1,537	120	100.0	83.5	12.3	3.9	0.3
Violent crime [2]	1,391	1,058	262	66	5	100.0	76.1	18.8	4.7	0.4
Murder and nonnegligent manslaughter	30	15	11	4	0	100.0	50.0	36.7	13.3	0.0
Forcible rape	158	142	13	2	1	100.0	89.9	8.2	1.3	0.6
Robbery	109	56	45	7	1	100.0	51.4	41.3	6.4	0.9
Aggravated assault	1,094	845	193	53	3	100.0	77.2	17.6	4.8	0.3
Property crime [2]	6,659	5,535	917	192	15	100.0	83.1	13.8	2.9	0.2
Burglary	2,259	1,832	357	68	2	100.0	81.1	15.8	3.0	0.1
Larceny-theft	3,629	3,037	474	105	13	100.0	83.7	13.1	2.9	0.4
Motor vehicle theft	632	545	70	17	0	100.0	86.2	11.1	2.7	0.0
Arson	139	121	16	2	0	100.0	87.1	11.5	1.4	0.0
Other assaults	5,962	4,651	1,080	211	20	100.0	78.0	18.1	3.5	0.3
Forgery and counterfeiting	41	35	6	0	0	100.0	85.4	14.6	0.0	0.0
Fraud	161	131	22	8	0	100.0	81.4	13.7	5.0	0.0
Embezzlement	11	11	0	0	0	100.0	100.0	0.0	0.0	0.0
Stolen property; buying, receiving, possessing	269	206	59	4	0	100.0	76.6	21.9	1.5	0.0
Vandalism	2,305	2,061	177	61	6	100.0	89.4	7.7	2.6	0.3
Weapons; carrying, possessing, etc.	470	359	95	15	1	100.0	76.4	20.2	3.2	0.2
Prostitution and commercialized vice	11	11	0	0	0	100.0	100.0	0.0	0.0	0.0
Sex offenses (except forcible rape and prostitution)	801	730	57	10	4	100.0	91.1	7.1	1.2	0.5
Drug abuse violations	3,919	3,493	307	109	10	100.0	89.1	7.8	2.8	0.3
Gambling	11	9	2	0	0	100.0	81.8	18.2	0.0	0.0
Offenses against the family and children	205	173	23	9	0	100.0	84.4	11.2	4.4	0.0
Driving under the influence	1,034	950	48	33	3	100.0	91.9	4.6	3.2	0.3
Liquor laws	4,740	4,454	83	187	16	100.0	94.0	1.8	3.9	0.3
Drunkenness	305	271	15	18	1	100.0	88.9	4.9	5.9	0.3
Disorderly conduct	3,019	2,109	694	205	11	100.0	69.9	23.0	6.8	0.4
Vagrancy	21	20	1	0	0	100.0	95.2	4.8	0.0	0.0
All other offenses (except traffic)	7,644	6,271	964	381	28	100.0	82.0	12.6	5.0	0.4
Suspicion	118	112	6	0	0	100.0	94.9	5.1	0.0	0.0
Curfew and loitering law violations	316	277	11	28	0	100.0	87.7	3.5	8.9	0.0

Table 61. Arrests, Nonmetropolitan Counties, Distribution by Race, 2012

(Number, percent; 1,962 agencies; 2012 estimated population 21,512,971)

Offense charged	Arrests 18 and over					Percent distribution[1]				
	Total	White	Black	American Indian or Alaskan Native	Asian or Pacific Islander	Total	White	Black	American Indian or Alaskan Native	Asian or Pacific Islander
Total	687,554	572,364	93,607	17,516	4,067	100.0	83.2	13.6	2.5	0.6
Violent crime [2]	19,209	15,119	3,289	731	70	100.0	78.7	17.1	3.8	0.4
Murder and nonnegligent manslaughter	610	461	124	24	1	100.0	75.6	20.3	3.9	0.2
Forcible rape	1,030	865	147	13	5	100.0	84.0	14.3	1.3	0.5
Robbery	1,428	880	493	52	3	100.0	61.6	34.5	3.6	0.2
Aggravated assault	16,141	12,913	2,525	642	61	100.0	80.0	15.6	4.0	0.4
Property crime [2]	50,670	42,614	6,687	1,271	98	100.0	84.1	13.2	2.5	0.2
Burglary	15,448	12,974	2,033	422	19	100.0	84.0	13.2	2.7	0.1
Larceny-theft	31,505	26,422	4,272	743	68	100.0	83.9	13.6	2.4	0.2
Motor vehicle theft	3,127	2,701	339	79	8	100.0	86.4	10.8	2.5	0.3
Arson	590	517	43	27	3	100.0	87.6	7.3	4.6	0.5
Other assaults	58,102	48,595	7,787	1,579	141	100.0	83.6	13.4	2.7	0.2
Forgery and counterfeiting	3,024	2,483	514	15	12	100.0	82.1	17.0	0.5	0.4
Fraud	12,964	10,405	2,310	225	24	100.0	80.3	17.8	1.7	0.2
Embezzlement	582	507	64	11	0	100.0	87.1	11.0	1.9	0.0
Stolen property; buying, receiving, possessing	4,119	3,355	671	76	17	100.0	81.5	16.3	1.8	0.4
Vandalism	8,046	6,869	903	260	14	100.0	85.4	11.2	3.2	0.2
Weapons; carrying, possessing, etc.	5,745	4,469	1,155	106	15	100.0	77.8	20.1	1.8	0.3
Prostitution and commercialized vice	127	96	24	6	1	100.0	75.6	18.9	4.7	0.8
Sex offenses (except forcible rape and prostitution)	3,524	3,111	352	48	13	100.0	88.3	10.0	1.4	0.4
Drug abuse violations	80,789	67,232	11,855	1,240	462	100.0	83.2	14.7	1.5	0.6
Gambling	183	124	40	6	13	100.0	67.8	21.9	3.3	7.1
Offenses against the family and children	11,400	8,449	2,531	388	32	100.0	74.1	22.2	3.4	0.3
Driving under the influence	162,257	139,764	16,407	3,807	2,279	100.0	86.1	10.1	2.3	1.4
Liquor laws	19,036	17,463	922	562	89	100.0	91.7	4.8	3.0	0.5
Drunkenness	17,405	15,629	1,183	545	48	100.0	89.8	6.8	3.1	0.3
Disorderly conduct	16,236	13,125	2,359	710	42	100.0	80.8	14.5	4.4	0.3
Vagrancy	177	110	57	10	0	100.0	62.1	32.2	5.6	0.0
All other offenses (except traffic)	213,912	172,807	34,488	5,920	697	100.0	80.8	16.1	2.8	0.3
Suspicion	47	38	9	0	0	100.0	80.9	19.1	0.0	0.0
Curfew and loitering law violations	n.a.	n.a.	n.a.	n.a.	n.a.	n.a.	n.a.	n.a.	n.a.	n.a.

1 Because of rounding, the percentages may not sum to 100. 2 Violent crimes are offenses of murder and nonnegligent manslaughter, forcible rape, robbery, and aggravated assault. Property crimes are offenses of burglary, larceny-theft, motor vehicle theft, and arson. n.a. = not available

Table 62. Arrest Trends, Suburban Areas, 2011–2012[1]

(Number, percent change; 6,246 agencies; 2012 estimated population 104,853,965; 2011 estimated population 103,841,553)

Offense charged	Number of persons arrested								
	Total, all ages			Under 18 years of age			18 years of age and over		
	2011	2012	Percent change	2011	2012	Percent change	2011	2012	Percent change
Total [2]	3,632,998	3,549,881	-2.3	431,590	382,995	-11.3	3,201,408	3,166,886	-1.1
Violent crime [3]	133,518	130,975	1.0	16,718	14,665	-12.3	116,800	116,310	-0.4
Murder and nonnegligent manslaughter	2,469	2,343	-5.1	176	142	-19.3	2,293	2,201	-4.0
Forcible rape	4,827	4,566	-5.4	713	683	-4.2	4,114	3,883	-5.6
Robbery	22,101	21,652	-2.0	4,400	3,887	-11.7	17,701	17,765	0.4
Aggravated assault	104,121	102,414	-1.6	11,429	9,953	-12.9	92,692	92,461	-0.2
Property crime [3]	466,913	467,300	0.1	90,872	79,075	-13.0	376,041	388,225	3.2
Burglary	82,891	80,807	-2.5	16,580	14,165	-14.6	66,311	66,642	0.5
Larceny-theft	363,542	366,376	0.8	69,338	60,472	-12.8	294,204	305,904	4.0
Motor vehicle theft	16,659	16,874	1.3	3,264	3,005	-7.9	13,395	13,869	3.5
Arson	3,821	3,243	-15.1	1,690	1,433	-15.2	2,131	1,810	-15.1
Other assaults	346,080	333,014	-3.8	58,437	53,004	-9.3	287,643	280,010	-2.7
Forgery and counterfeiting	22,281	21,246	-4.6	552	491	-11.1	21,729	20,755	-4.5
Fraud	57,417	52,342	-8.8	1,703	1,487	-12.7	55,714	50,855	-8.7
Embezzlement	4,900	4,749	-3.1	131	101	-22.9	4,769	4,648	-2.5
Stolen property; buying, receiving, possessing	29,984	31,271	4.3	4,139	3,873	-6.4	25,845	27,398	6.0
Vandalism	68,918	64,661	-6.2	21,100	18,104	-14.2	47,818	46,557	-2.6
Weapons; carrying, possessing, etc.	37,802	36,878	-2.4	7,552	6,555	-13.2	30,250	30,323	0.2
Prostitution and commercialized vice	4,514	5,085	12.6	108	93	-13.9	4,406	4,992	13.3
Sex offenses (except forcible rape and prostitution)	19,673	19,747	0.4	3,812	3,915	2.7	15,861	15,832	-0.2
Drug abuse violations	444,348	453,615	2.1	48,046	45,812	-4.6	396,302	407,803	2.9
Gambling	1,087	1,146	5.4	90	81	-10.0	997	1,065	6.8
Offenses against the family and children	46,286	44,115	-4.7	1,042	1,010	-3.1	45,244	43,105	-4.7
Driving under the influence	377,348	358,082	-5.1	3,464	3,031	-12.5	373,884	355,051	-5.0
Liquor laws	147,288	134,184	-8.9	32,090	29,116	-9.3	115,198	105,068	-8.8
Drunkenness	128,485	123,637	-3.8	3,379	3,084	-8.7	125,106	120,553	-3.6
Disorderly conduct	166,026	154,827	-6.7	43,863	36,419	-17.0	122,163	118,408	-3.1
Vagrancy	4,582	4,431	-3.3	352	263	-25.3	4,230	4,168	-1.5
All other offenses (except traffic)	1,111,518	1,096,740	-1.3	80,110	70,980	-11.4	1,031,408	1,025,760	-0.5
Suspicion	278	545	96.0	45	103	128.9	233	442	89.7
Curfew and loitering law violations	14,030	11,836	-15.6	14,030	11,836	-15.6	n.a.	n.a.	n.a.

1 Suburban areas include law enforcement agencies in cities with less than 50,000 inhabitants and county law enforcement agencies that are within a Metropolitan Statistical Area. Suburban areas exclude all metropolitan agencies associated with a principal city. 2 Does not include suspicion. 3 Violent crimes are offenses of murder and nonnegligent manslaughter, forcible rape, robbery, and aggravated assault. Property crimes are offenses of burglary, larceny-theft, motor vehicle theft, and arson. n.a. = not available

Table 63. Arrest Trends, Suburban Areas, by Age and Sex, 2011–2012[1]

(Number, percent change; 6,246 agencies; 2012 estimated population 104,853,965; 2011 estimated population 103,841,553)

Offense charged	Male						Female					
	Total			Under 18			Total			Under 18		
	2011	2012	Percent change	2011	2012	Percent change	2011	2012	Percent change	2011	2012	Percent change
Total [2]	2,679,780	2,603,347	-2.9	307,331	272,953	-11.2	953,218	946,534	-0.7	124,259	110,042	-11.4
Violent crime [3]	107,439	105,126	-2.2	13,494	11,696	-13.3	26,079	25,849	-0.9	3,224	2,969	-7.9
Murder and nonnegligent manslaughter	2,158	2,069	-4.1	152	122	-19.7	311	274	-11.9	24	20	-16.7
Forcible rape	4,782	4,511	-5.7	704	671	-4.7	45	55	22.2	9	12	33.3
Robbery	19,451	18,803	-3.3	4,034	3,541	-12.2	2,650	2,849	7.5	366	346	-5.5
Aggravated assault	81,048	79,743	-1.6	8,604	7,362	-14.4	23,073	22,671	-1.7	2,825	2,591	-8.3
Property crime [3]	297,169	295,624	-0.5	60,199	53,094	-11.8	169,744	171,676	1.1	30,673	25,981	-15.3
Burglary	70,330	67,906	-3.4	14,733	12,640	-14.2	12,561	12,901	2.7	1,847	1,525	-17.4
Larceny-theft	210,116	211,596	0.7	41,310	36,726	-11.1	153,426	154,780	0.9	28,028	23,746	-15.3
Motor vehicle theft	13,563	13,454	-0.8	2,727	2,533	-7.1	3,096	3,420	10.5	537	472	-12.1
Arson	3,160	2,668	-15.6	1,429	1,195	-16.4	661	575	-13.0	261	238	-8.8
Other assaults	249,812	238,946	-4.3	38,124	34,000	-10.8	96,268	94,068	-2.3	20,313	19,004	-6.4
Forgery and counterfeiting	13,896	13,303	-4.3	414	329	-20.5	8,385	7,943	-5.3	138	162	17.4
Fraud	33,782	30,737	-9.0	1,130	995	-11.9	23,635	21,605	-8.6	573	492	-14.1
Embezzlement	2,508	2,484	-1.0	77	75	-2.6	2,392	2,265	-5.3	54	26	-51.9
Stolen property; buying, receiving, possessing	23,579	24,629	4.5	3,367	3,146	-6.6	6,405	6,642	3.7	772	727	-5.8
Vandalism	56,433	51,996	-7.9	17,953	15,181	-15.4	12,485	12,665	1.4	3,147	2,923	-7.1
Weapons; carrying, possessing, etc.	34,412	33,477	-2.7	6,722	5,867	-12.7	3,390	3,401	0.3	830	688	-17.1
Prostitution and commercialized vice	1,848	2,072	12.1	36	33	-8.3	2,666	3,013	13.0	72	60	-16.7
Sex offenses (except forcible rape and prostitution)	18,346	18,419	0.4	3,443	3,559	3.4	1,327	1,328	0.1	369	356	-3.5
Drug abuse violations	351,059	355,496	1.3	39,587	37,722	-4.7	93,289	98,119	5.2	8,459	8,090	-4.4
Gambling	854	836	-2.1	67	58	-13.4	233	310	33.0	23	23	0.0
Offenses against the family and children	37,048	34,751	-6.2	627	627	0.0	9,238	9,364	1.4	415	383	-7.7
Driving under the influence	281,048	266,266	-5.3	2,525	2,237	-11.4	96,300	91,816	-4.7	939	794	-15.4
Liquor laws	101,254	92,771	-8.4	19,178	17,653	-8.0	46,034	41,413	-10.0	12,912	11,463	-11.2
Drunkenness	103,304	99,069	-4.1	2,465	2,230	-9.5	25,181	24,568	-2.4	914	854	-6.6
Disorderly conduct	118,502	110,177	-7.0	29,260	23,972	-18.1	47,524	44,650	-6.0	14,603	12,447	-14.8
Vagrancy	3,578	3,478	-2.8	283	219	-22.6	1,004	953	-5.1	69	44	-36.2
All other offenses (except traffic)	834,298	815,679	-2.2	58,769	52,249	-11.1	277,220	281,061	1.4	21,341	18,731	-12.2
Suspicion	216	411	90.3	38	77	102.6	62	134	116.1	7	26	271.4
Curfew and loitering law violations	9,611	8,011	-16.6	9,611	8,011	-16.6	4,419	3,825	-13.4	4,419	3,825	-13.4

1 Suburban areas include law enforcement agencies in cities with less than 50,000 inhabitants and county law enforcement agencies that are within a Metropolitan Statistical Area. Suburban areas exclude all metropolitan agencies associated with a principal city. 2 Does not include suspicion. 3 Violent crimes are offenses of murder and nonnegligent manslaughter, forcible rape, robbery, and aggravated assault. Property crimes are offenses of burglary, larceny-theft, motor vehicle theft, and arson.

Table 64. Suburban Area Arrests, Distribution by Age, 2012[1]

(Number, percent; 6,766 agencies; 2012 estimated population 110,031,559)

Offense charged	Total, all ages	Ages under 15	Ages under 18	Ages 18 and over	Under 10	10–12	13–14	15	16	17	18
Total	3,915,278	114,860	419,136	3,496,142	3,069	24,618	87,173	76,191	100,818	127,267	170,817
Total percent distribution[2]	100.0	2.9	10.7	89.3	0.1	0.6	2.2	1.9	2.6	3.3	4.4
Violent crime [3]	140,613	4,715	16,046	124,567	141	1,135	3,439	2,974	3,844	4,513	5,690
Violent crime percent distribution[2]	100.0	3.4	11.4	88.6	0.1	0.8	2.4	2.1	2.7	3.2	4.0
Murder and nonnegligent manslaughter	2,662	24	176	2,486	0	5	19	19	51	82	133
Forcible rape	5,038	278	763	4,275	1	69	208	111	165	209	285
Robbery	24,196	774	4,403	19,793	10	91	673	848	1,212	1,569	1,964
Aggravated assault	108,717	3,639	10,704	98,013	130	970	2,539	1,996	2,416	2,653	3,308
Property crime [3]	520,748	24,686	88,810	431,938	494	5,314	18,878	16,490	21,649	25,985	29,888
Property crime percent distribution[2]	100.0	4.7	17.1	82.9	0.1	1.0	3.6	3.2	4.2	5.0	5.7
Burglary	85,407	4,229	15,285	70,122	115	911	3,203	2,995	3,674	4,387	5,704
Larceny-theft	412,871	18,939	68,761	344,110	315	4,032	14,592	12,525	16,814	20,483	23,063
Motor vehicle theft	19,093	678	3,341	15,752	4	77	597	743	964	956	979
Arson	3,377	840	1,423	1,954	60	294	486	227	197	159	142
Other assaults	365,535	22,906	57,821	307,714	767	5,950	16,189	10,954	12,046	11,915	10,454
Forgery and counterfeiting	23,633	66	554	23,079	1	10	55	52	121	315	705
Fraud	55,519	259	1,626	53,893	5	38	216	254	423	690	1,260
Embezzlement	5,227	5	111	5,116	0	1	4	8	30	68	214
Stolen property; buying, receiving, possessing	33,073	980	4,255	28,818	16	164	800	860	1,086	1,329	1,840
Vandalism	71,949	7,611	19,691	52,258	331	2,086	5,194	3,423	4,337	4,320	4,368
Weapons; carrying, possessing, etc.	39,839	2,660	6,980	32,859	204	759	1,697	1,137	1,468	1,715	2,016
Prostitution and commercialized vice	5,819	16	104	5,715	0	3	13	17	20	51	141
Sex offenses (except forcible rape and prostitution)	21,003	2,067	4,120	16,883	83	583	1,401	698	664	691	850
Drug abuse violations	484,599	7,912	48,389	436,210	49	1,000	6,863	7,639	12,619	20,219	31,346
Gambling	1,290	13	89	1,201	1	2	10	10	21	45	31
Offenses against the family and children	44,450	362	1,206	43,244	19	81	262	218	282	344	532
Driving under the influence	455,803	53	3,414	452,389	3	6	44	126	734	2,501	7,176
Liquor laws	148,963	2,701	31,078	117,885	9	174	2,518	4,409	8,856	15,112	28,473
Drunkenness	139,655	403	3,218	136,437	10	31	362	507	759	1,549	3,923
Disorderly conduct	174,435	15,093	40,130	134,305	279	3,351	11,463	8,139	8,509	8,389	7,548
Vagrancy	5,414	78	301	5,113	1	14	63	60	71	92	201
All other offenses (except traffic)	1,163,506	18,739	77,709	1,085,797	629	3,436	14,674	14,979	19,351	24,640	34,123
Suspicion	765	11	44	721	1	4	6	5	10	18	38
Curfew and loitering law violations	13,440	3,524	13,440	n.a.	26	476	3,022	3,232	3,918	2,766	n.a.

Table 64. Suburban Area Arrests, Distribution by Age, 2012[1]

(Number, percent; 6,766 agencies; 2012 estimated population 110,031,559)

Offense charged	19	20	21	22	23	24	25–29	30–34	35–39	40–44	45–49	50–54	55–59	60–64	65 and over
Total	183,093	178,799	169,919	163,160	151,006	141,079	601,415	471,833	333,658	299,940	258,644	191,473	101,487	45,854	33,965
Total percent distribution[2]	4.7	4.6	4.3	4.2	3.9	3.6	15.4	12.1	8.5	7.7	6.6	4.9	2.6	1.2	0.9
Violent crime [3]	5,971	5,918	6,013	5,774	5,361	5,055	21,598	17,147	12,081	11,087	9,342	6,661	3,705	1,734	1,430
Violent crime percent distribution[2]	4.2	4.2	4.3	4.1	3.8	3.6	15.4	12.2	8.6	7.9	6.6	4.7	2.6	1.2	1.0
Murder and nonnegligent manslaughter	159	156	172	151	111	121	401	323	213	160	137	98	59	46	46
Forcible rape	251	233	196	188	186	157	600	549	430	399	320	229	122	77	53
Robbery	1,864	1,568	1,355	1,258	1,060	984	3,460	2,295	1,229	1,097	849	499	199	73	39
Aggravated assault	3,697	3,961	4,290	4,177	4,004	3,793	17,137	13,980	10,209	9,431	8,036	5,835	3,325	1,538	1,292
Property crime [3]	27,416	24,641	22,149	20,424	18,561	17,184	73,506	56,484	38,275	34,734	29,198	20,867	10,470	4,661	3,480
Property crime percent distribution[2]	5.3	4.7	4.3	3.9	3.6	3.3	14.1	10.8	7.4	6.7	5.6	4.0	2.0	0.9	0.7
Burglary	5,258	4,507	4,202	3,704	3,385	3,106	12,789	9,138	5,732	4,777	3,757	2,491	1,015	354	203
Larceny-theft	21,122	19,272	17,139	15,878	14,520	13,353	57,453	44,664	30,688	28,490	24,314	17,669	9,105	4,190	3,190
Motor vehicle theft	918	777	724	748	597	670	2,969	2,462	1,642	1,326	958	573	272	81	56
Arson	118	85	84	94	59	55	295	220	213	141	169	134	78	36	31
Other assaults	10,982	11,585	12,768	12,754	11,980	11,486	51,932	44,858	33,927	31,622	26,793	18,791	9,660	4,335	3,787
Forgery and counterfeiting	1,052	1,080	967	963	962	975	4,351	3,718	2,601	2,099	1,691	1,093	489	203	130
Fraud	1,633	1,876	1,785	1,891	1,871	1,912	9,262	8,470	6,694	6,181	4,724	3,092	1,816	814	612
Embezzlement	275	313	320	273	221	198	795	692	543	492	335	220	131	63	31
Stolen property; buying, receiving, possessing	1,740	1,576	1,541	1,471	1,359	1,246	5,321	4,118	2,733	2,311	1,743	1,046	473	194	106
Vandalism	3,779	3,255	3,252	2,767	2,412	2,201	8,917	6,283	4,178	3,715	2,998	2,133	1,053	497	450
Weapons; carrying, possessing, etc.	1,913	1,836	1,826	1,790	1,599	1,511	6,001	4,356	2,695	2,255	1,854	1,504	842	450	411
Prostitution and commercialized vice	225	213	256	254	264	222	1,032	785	552	606	487	302	205	85	86
Sex offenses (except forcible rape and prostitution)	829	744	663	627	520	476	2,236	1,926	1,655	1,666	1,510	1,195	792	512	682
Drug abuse violations	32,156	29,391	27,030	24,629	21,868	19,552	78,630	56,148	35,111	28,487	23,431	16,387	7,918	2,851	1,275
Gambling	32	43	29	30	36	30	109	101	148	167	108	112	85	67	73
Offenses against the family and children	632	769	958	1,113	1,185	1,339	7,417	7,984	6,756	5,851	4,216	2,641	1,192	391	268
Driving under the influence	10,675	13,276	20,923	21,982	21,253	20,090	82,859	61,373	44,717	42,201	38,651	31,659	18,766	9,817	6,971
Liquor laws	29,899	24,026	3,583	2,572	1,861	1,527	5,738	4,186	3,222	3,274	3,548	2,949	1,682	788	557
Drunkenness	4,478	4,290	6,830	6,059	5,337	4,742	20,233	16,405	12,868	13,441	14,293	12,457	6,729	2,778	1,574
Disorderly conduct	6,815	6,624	8,041	7,039	6,084	5,512	21,164	15,916	11,568	10,864	10,528	8,374	4,427	2,133	1,668
Vagrancy	214	195	203	190	189	155	771	657	480	476	541	433	233	118	57
All other offenses (except traffic)	42,332	47,108	50,748	50,525	48,057	45,635	199,439	160,131	112,784	98,363	82,589	59,516	30,789	13,351	10,307
Suspicion	45	40	34	33	26	31	104	95	70	48	64	41	30	12	10
Curfew and loitering law violations	n.a.	n.a.	n.a.	n.a.	n.a.	n.a.	n.a.	n.a.	n.a.	n.a.	n.a.	n.a.	n.a.	n.a.	n.a.

1 Suburban areas include law enforcement agencies in cities with less than 50,000 inhabitants and county law enforcement agencies that are within a Metropolitan Statistical Area. Suburban areas exclude all metropolitan agencies associated with a principal city. 2 Because of rounding, the percentages may not sum to 100.0. 3 Violent crimes are offenses of murder and nonnegligent manslaughter, forcible rape, robbery, and aggravated assault. Property crimes are offenses of burglary, larceny-theft, motor vehicle theft, and arson. n.a. = not available

Table 65. Arrests, Suburban Areas, Persons under 15, 18, 21, and 25 Years of Age, 2012[1]

(Number, percent; 6,766 agencies; 2012 estimated population 110,031,559)

Offense charged	Total, all ages	Number of persons arrested				Percent of total all ages			
		Under 15	Under 18	Under 21	Under 25	Under 15	Under 18	Under 21	Under 25
Total	3,915,278	114,860	419,136	951,845	1,577,009	2.9	10.7	24.3	40.3
Violent crime [2]	140,613	4,715	16,046	33,625	55,828	3.4	11.4	23.9	39.7
Murder and nonnegligent manslaughter	2,662	24	176	624	1,179	0.9	6.6	23.4	44.3
Forcible rape	5,038	278	763	1,532	2,259	5.5	15.1	30.4	44.8
Robbery	24,196	774	4,403	9,799	14,456	3.2	18.2	40.5	59.7
Aggravated assault	108,717	3,639	10,704	21,670	37,934	3.3	9.8	19.9	34.9
Property crime [2]	520,748	24,686	88,810	170,755	249,073	4.7	17.1	32.8	47.8
Burglary	85,407	4,229	15,285	30,754	45,151	5.0	17.9	36.0	52.9
Larceny-theft	412,871	18,939	68,761	132,218	193,108	4.6	16.7	32.0	46.8
Motor vehicle theft	19,093	678	3,341	6,015	8,754	3.6	17.5	31.5	45.8
Arson	3,377	840	1,423	1,768	2,060	24.9	42.1	52.4	61.0
Other assaults	365,535	22,906	57,821	90,842	139,830	6.3	15.8	24.9	38.3
Forgery and counterfeiting	23,633	66	554	3,391	7,258	0.3	2.3	14.3	30.7
Fraud	55,519	259	1,626	6,395	13,854	0.5	2.9	11.5	25.0
Embezzlement	5,227	5	111	913	1,925	0.1	2.1	17.5	36.8
Stolen property; buying, receiving, possessing	33,073	980	4,255	9,411	15,028	3.0	12.9	28.5	45.4
Vandalism	71,949	7,611	19,691	31,093	41,725	10.6	27.4	43.2	58.0
Weapons; carrying, possessing, etc.	39,839	2,660	6,980	12,745	19,471	6.7	17.5	32.0	48.9
Prostitution and commercialized vice	5,819	16	104	683	1,679	0.3	1.8	11.7	28.9
Sex offenses (except forcible rape and prostitution)	21,003	2,067	4,120	6,543	8,829	9.8	19.6	31.2	42.0
Drug abuse violations	484,599	7,912	48,389	141,282	234,361	1.6	10.0	29.2	48.4
Gambling	1,290	13	89	195	320	1.0	6.9	15.1	24.8
Offenses against the family and children	44,450	362	1,206	3,139	7,734	0.8	2.7	7.1	17.4
Driving under the influence	455,803	53	3,414	34,541	118,789	*	0.7	7.6	26.1
Liquor laws	148,963	2,701	31,078	113,476	123,019	1.8	20.9	76.2	82.6
Drunkenness	139,655	403	3,218	15,909	38,877	0.3	2.3	11.4	27.8
Disorderly conduct	174,435	15,093	40,130	61,117	87,793	8.7	23.0	35.0	50.3
Vagrancy	5,414	78	301	911	1,648	1.4	5.6	16.8	30.4
All other offenses (except traffic)	1,163,506	18,739	77,709	201,272	396,237	1.6	6.7	17.3	34.1
Suspicion	765	11	44	167	291	1.4	5.8	21.8	38.0
Curfew and loitering law violations	13,440	3,524	13,440	13,440	13,440	26.2	100.0	100.0	100.0

1 Suburban areas include law enforcement agencies in cities with less than 50,000 inhabitants and county law enforcement agencies that are within a Metropolitan Statistical Area. Suburban areas exclude all metropolitan agencies associated with a principal city. 2 Violent crimes are offenses of murder and nonnegligent manslaughter, forcible rape, robbery, and aggravated assault. Property crimes are offenses of burglary, larceny-theft, motor vehicle theft, and arson. * = Less than one-tenth of one percent

Table 66. Arrests, Suburban Areas, Distribution by Sex, 2012[1]

(Number, percent; 6,766 agencies; 2012 estimated population 110,031,559)

Offense charged	Number of persons arrested			Percent male	Percent female	Percent distribution[2]		
	Total	Male	Female			Total	Male	Female
Total	3,915,278	2,865,218	1,050,060	73.2	26.8	100.0	100.0	100.0
Violent crime [3]	140,613	112,923	27,690	80.3	19.7	3.6	3.9	2.6
Murder and nonnegligent manslaughter	2,662	2,355	307	88.5	11.5	0.1	0.1	*
Forcible rape	5,038	4,979	59	98.8	1.2	0.1	0.2	*
Robbery	24,196	21,071	3,125	87.1	12.9	0.6	0.7	0.3
Aggravated assault	108,717	84,518	24,199	77.7	22.3	2.8	2.9	2.3
Property crime [3]	520,748	325,991	194,757	62.6	37.4	13.3	11.4	18.5
Burglary	85,407	72,045	13,362	84.4	15.6	2.2	2.5	1.3
Larceny-theft	412,871	235,888	176,983	57.1	42.9	10.5	8.2	16.9
Motor vehicle theft	19,093	15,248	3,845	79.9	20.1	0.5	0.5	0.4
Arson	3,377	2,810	567	83.2	16.8	0.1	0.1	0.1
Other assaults	365,535	262,021	103,514	71.7	28.3	9.3	9.1	9.9
Forgery and counterfeiting	23,633	14,755	8,878	62.4	37.6	0.6	0.5	0.8
Fraud	55,519	32,845	22,674	59.2	40.8	1.4	1.1	2.2
Embezzlement	5,227	2,713	2,514	51.9	48.1	0.1	0.1	0.2
Stolen property; buying, receiving, possessing	33,073	26,072	7,001	78.8	21.2	0.8	0.9	0.7
Vandalism	71,949	57,772	14,177	80.3	19.7	1.8	2.0	1.4
Weapons; carrying, possessing, etc.	39,839	36,180	3,659	90.8	9.2	1.0	1.3	0.3
Prostitution and commercialized vice	5,819	2,280	3,539	39.2	60.8	0.1	0.1	0.3
Sex offenses (except forcible rape and prostitution)	21,003	19,522	1,481	92.9	7.1	0.5	0.7	0.1
Drug abuse violations	484,599	380,382	104,217	78.5	21.5	12.4	13.3	9.9
Gambling	1,290	936	354	72.6	27.4	*	*	*
Offenses against the family and children	44,450	34,446	10,004	77.5	22.5	1.1	1.2	1.0
Driving under the influence	455,803	339,777	116,026	74.5	25.5	11.6	11.9	11.0
Liquor laws	148,963	103,033	45,930	69.2	30.8	3.8	3.6	4.4
Drunkenness	139,655	112,114	27,541	80.3	19.7	3.6	3.9	2.6
Disorderly conduct	174,435	123,817	50,618	71.0	29.0	4.5	4.3	4.8
Vagrancy	5,414	4,261	1,153	78.7	21.3	0.1	0.1	0.1
All other offenses (except traffic)	1,163,506	863,752	299,754	74.2	25.8	29.7	30.1	28.5
Suspicion	765	587	178	76.7	23.3	*	*	*
Curfew and loitering law violations	13,440	9,039	4,401	67.3	32.7	0.3	0.3	0.4

1 Suburban areas include law enforcement agencies in cities with less than 50,000 inhabitants and county law enforcement agencies that are within a Metropolitan Statistical Area. Suburban areas exclude all metropolitan agencies associated with a principal city. 2 Because of rounding, the percentages may not sum to 100. 3 Violent crimes are offenses of murder and nonnegligent manslaughter, forcible rape, robbery, and aggravated assault. Property crimes are offenses of burglary, larceny-theft, motor vehicle theft, and arson. * = Less than one-tenth of one percent

Table 67. Arrests, Suburban Areas, Distribution by Race, 2012[1]

(Number, percent; 6,766 agencies; 2012 estimated population 110,031,559)

Offense charged	Total arrests					Percent distribution[2]				
	Total	White	Black	American Indian or Alaskan Native	Asian or Pacific Islander	Total	White	Black	American Indian or Alaskan Native	Asian or Pacific Islander
Total	3,893,728	2,858,792	954,810	34,184	45,942	100.0	73.4	24.5	0.9	1.2
Violent crime[3]	140,091	91,383	45,775	1,249	1,684	100.0	65.2	32.7	0.9	1.2
Murder and nonnegligent manslaughter	2,659	1,458	1,143	17	41	100.0	54.8	43.0	0.6	1.5
Forcible rape	5,005	3,633	1,264	42	66	100.0	72.6	25.3	0.8	1.3
Robbery	24,080	11,682	12,060	132	206	100.0	48.5	50.1	0.5	0.9
Aggravated assault	108,347	74,610	31,308	1,058	1,371	100.0	68.9	28.9	1.0	1.3
Property crime[3]	517,263	365,131	142,122	4,004	6,006	100.0	70.6	27.5	0.8	1.2
Burglary	84,983	62,278	21,518	379	808	100.0	73.3	25.3	0.4	1.0
Larceny-theft	409,913	286,222	115,328	3,457	4,906	100.0	69.8	28.1	0.8	1.2
Motor vehicle theft	19,000	13,965	4,623	151	261	100.0	73.5	24.3	0.8	1.4
Arson	3,367	2,666	653	17	31	100.0	79.2	19.4	0.5	0.9
Other assaults	363,467	259,205	97,735	2,874	3,653	100.0	71.3	26.9	0.8	1.0
Forgery and counterfeiting	23,536	15,576	7,602	79	279	100.0	66.2	32.3	0.3	1.2
Fraud	55,218	37,677	16,792	250	499	100.0	68.2	30.4	0.5	0.9
Embezzlement	5,206	3,429	1,714	16	47	100.0	65.9	32.9	0.3	0.9
Stolen property; buying, receiving, possessing	32,834	22,742	9,571	191	330	100.0	69.3	29.1	0.6	1.0
Vandalism	71,002	54,610	15,187	576	629	100.0	76.9	21.4	0.8	0.9
Weapons; carrying, possessing, etc.	39,635	26,190	12,773	193	479	100.0	66.1	32.2	0.5	1.2
Prostitution and commercialized vice	5,785	3,685	1,715	16	369	100.0	63.7	29.6	0.3	6.4
Sex offenses (except forcible rape and prostitution)	20,811	16,112	4,274	149	276	100.0	77.4	20.5	0.7	1.3
Drug abuse violations	481,998	354,904	119,725	2,350	5,019	100.0	73.6	24.8	0.5	1.0
Gambling	1,281	825	361	8	87	100.0	64.4	28.2	0.6	6.8
Offenses against the family and children	44,271	28,969	14,526	481	295	100.0	65.4	32.8	1.1	0.7
Driving under the influence	453,858	388,434	52,708	3,306	9,410	100.0	85.6	11.6	0.7	2.1
Liquor laws	147,535	126,633	15,703	2,825	2,374	100.0	85.8	10.6	1.9	1.6
Drunkenness	139,264	119,091	17,764	1,197	1,212	100.0	85.5	12.8	0.9	0.9
Disorderly conduct	173,471	119,501	51,177	1,462	1,331	100.0	68.9	29.5	0.8	0.8
Vagrancy	5,399	3,793	1,538	26	42	100.0	70.3	28.5	0.5	0.8
All other offenses (except traffic)	1,157,666	810,397	322,675	12,845	11,749	100.0	70.0	27.9	1.1	1.0
Suspicion	765	338	412	4	11	100.0	44.2	53.9	0.5	1.4
Curfew and loitering law violations	13,372	10,167	2,961	83	161	100.0	76.0	22.1	0.6	1.2

Table 67. Arrests, Suburban Areas, Distribution by Race, 2012[1]

(Number, percent; 6,766 agencies; 2012 estimated population 110,031,559)

Offense charged	Arrests under 18					Percent distribution[2]				
	Total	White	Black	American Indian or Alaskan Native	Asian or Pacific Islander	Total	White	Black	American Indian or Alaskan Native	Asian or Pacific Islander
Total	410,869	286,714	116,320	3,108	4,727	100.0	69.8	28.3	0.8	1.2
Violent crime [3]	15,786	8,339	7,196	96	155	100.0	52.8	45.6	0.6	1.0
Murder and nonnegligent manslaughter	175	89	83	2	1	100.0	50.9	47.4	1.1	0.6
Forcible rape	751	552	182	6	11	100.0	73.5	24.2	0.8	1.5
Robbery	4,315	1,452	2,803	12	48	100.0	33.7	65.0	0.3	1.1
Aggravated assault	10,545	6,246	4,128	76	95	100.0	59.2	39.1	0.7	0.9
Property crime [3]	86,992	54,390	30,723	666	1,213	100.0	62.5	35.3	0.8	1.4
Burglary	15,033	9,749	5,055	65	164	100.0	64.9	33.6	0.4	1.1
Larceny-theft	67,253	41,359	24,315	571	1,008	100.0	61.5	36.2	0.8	1.5
Motor vehicle theft	3,292	2,196	1,039	24	33	100.0	66.7	31.6	0.7	1.0
Arson	1,414	1,086	314	6	8	100.0	76.8	22.2	0.4	0.6
Other assaults	56,804	35,493	20,568	344	399	100.0	62.5	36.2	0.6	0.7
Forgery and counterfeiting	520	380	130	3	7	100.0	73.1	25.0	0.6	1.3
Fraud	1,572	938	603	5	26	100.0	59.7	38.4	0.3	1.7
Embezzlement	110	75	34	0	1	100.0	68.2	30.9	0.0	0.9
Stolen property; buying, receiving, possessing	4,081	2,275	1,739	32	35	100.0	55.7	42.6	0.8	0.9
Vandalism	18,922	14,784	3,876	131	131	100.0	78.1	20.5	0.7	0.7
Weapons; carrying, possessing, etc.	6,892	4,679	2,084	31	98	100.0	67.9	30.2	0.4	1.4
Prostitution and commercialized vice	99	58	41	0	0	100.0	58.6	41.4	0.0	0.0
Sex offenses (except forcible rape and prostitution)	4,001	2,966	979	24	32	100.0	74.1	24.5	0.6	0.8
Drug abuse violations	47,148	37,620	8,518	352	658	100.0	79.8	18.1	0.7	1.4
Gambling	89	46	40	1	2	100.0	51.7	44.9	1.1	2.2
Offenses against the family and children	1,196	914	254	20	8	100.0	76.4	21.2	1.7	0.7
Driving under the influence	3,340	3,113	150	32	45	100.0	93.2	4.5	1.0	1.3
Liquor laws	30,650	27,661	2,136	363	490	100.0	90.2	7.0	1.2	1.6
Drunkenness	3,214	2,880	263	40	31	100.0	89.6	8.2	1.2	1.0
Disorderly conduct	39,693	24,054	15,132	218	289	100.0	60.6	38.1	0.5	0.7
Vagrancy	292	175	115	1	1	100.0	59.9	39.4	0.3	0.3
All other offenses (except traffic)	76,052	55,688	18,754	666	944	100.0	73.2	24.7	0.9	1.2
Suspicion	44	19	24	0	1	100.0	43.2	54.5	0.0	2.3
Curfew and loitering law violations	13,372	10,167	2,961	83	161	100.0	76.0	22.1	0.6	1.2

Table 67. Arrests, Suburban Areas, Distribution by Race, 2012[1]

(Number, percent; 6,766 agencies; 2012 estimated population 110,031,559)

Offense charged	Arrests 18 and over					Percent distribution[2]				
	Total	White	Black	American Indian or Alaskan Native	Asian or Pacific Islander	Total	White	Black	American Indian or Alaskan Native	Asian or Pacific Islander
Total	3,482,859	2,572,078	838,490	31,076	41,215	100.0	73.8	24.1	0.9	1.2
Violent crime [3]	124,305	83,044	38,579	1,153	1,529	100.0	66.8	31.0	0.9	1.2
Murder and nonnegligent manslaughter	2,484	1,369	1,060	15	40	100.0	55.1	42.7	0.6	1.6
Forcible rape	4,254	3,081	1,082	36	55	100.0	72.4	25.4	0.8	1.3
Robbery	19,765	10,230	9,257	120	158	100.0	51.8	46.8	0.6	0.8
Aggravated assault	97,802	68,364	27,180	982	1,276	100.0	69.9	27.8	1.0	1.3
Property crime [3]	430,271	310,741	111,399	3,338	4,793	100.0	72.2	25.9	0.8	1.1
Burglary	69,950	52,529	16,463	314	644	100.0	75.1	23.5	0.4	0.9
Larceny-theft	342,660	244,863	91,013	2,886	3,898	100.0	71.5	26.6	0.8	1.1
Motor vehicle theft	15,708	11,769	3,584	127	228	100.0	74.9	22.8	0.8	1.5
Arson	1,953	1,580	339	11	23	100.0	80.9	17.4	0.6	1.2
Other assaults	306,663	223,712	77,167	2,530	3,254	100.0	73.0	25.2	0.8	1.1
Forgery and counterfeiting	23,016	15,196	7,472	76	272	100.0	66.0	32.5	0.3	1.2
Fraud	53,646	36,739	16,189	245	473	100.0	68.5	30.2	0.5	0.9
Embezzlement	5,096	3,354	1,680	16	46	100.0	65.8	33.0	0.3	0.9
Stolen property; buying, receiving, possessing	28,753	20,467	7,832	159	295	100.0	71.2	27.2	0.6	1.0
Vandalism	52,080	39,826	11,311	445	498	100.0	76.5	21.7	0.9	1.0
Weapons; carrying, possessing, etc.	32,743	21,511	10,689	162	381	100.0	65.7	32.6	0.5	1.2
Prostitution and commercialized vice	5,686	3,627	1,674	16	369	100.0	63.8	29.4	0.3	6.5
Sex offenses (except forcible rape and prostitution)	16,810	13,146	3,295	125	244	100.0	78.2	19.6	0.7	1.5
Drug abuse violations	434,850	317,284	111,207	1,998	4,361	100.0	73.0	25.6	0.5	1.0
Gambling	1,192	779	321	7	85	100.0	65.4	26.9	0.6	7.1
Offenses against the family and children	43,075	28,055	14,272	461	287	100.0	65.1	33.1	1.1	0.7
Driving under the influence	450,518	385,321	52,558	3,274	9,365	100.0	85.5	11.7	0.7	2.1
Liquor laws	116,885	98,972	13,567	2,462	1,884	100.0	84.7	11.6	2.1	1.6
Drunkenness	136,050	116,211	17,501	1,157	1,181	100.0	85.4	12.9	0.9	0.9
Disorderly conduct	133,778	95,447	36,045	1,244	1,042	100.0	71.3	26.9	0.9	0.8
Vagrancy	5,107	3,618	1,423	25	41	100.0	70.8	27.9	0.5	0.8
All other offenses (except traffic)	1,081,614	754,709	303,921	12,179	10,805	100.0	69.8	28.1	1.1	1.0
Suspicion	721	319	388	4	10	100.0	44.2	53.8	0.6	1.4
Curfew and loitering law violations	n.a.	n.a.	n.a.	n.a.	n.a.	n.a.	n.a.	n.a.	n.a.	n.a.

1 Suburban areas include law enforcement agencies in cities with less than 50,000 inhabitants and county law enforcement agencies that are within a Metropolitan Statistical Area. Suburban areas exclude all metropolitan agencies associated with a principal city. 2 Because of rounding, the percentages may not sum to 100. 3 Violent crimes are offenses of murder and nonnegligent manslaughter, forcible rape, robbery, and aggravated assault. Property crimes are offenses of burglary, larceny-theft, motor vehicle theft, and arson. n.a. = not available

Table 68. Police Disposition of Juvenile Offenders Taken into Custody, 2012

(Number, percent)

Population group	Total[1]	Handled within department and released	Referred to juvenile court jurisdiction	Referred to welfare agency	Referred to other police agency	Referred to criminal or adult court	Number of agencies	Estimated population, 2012
Total Agencies								
Number	395,874	85,482	269,771	2,982	6,182	31,457	4,949	119,450,843
Percent[2]	100.0	21.6	68.1	0.8	1.6	7.9		
Total Cities								
Number	315,377	73,881	211,089	2,517	4,392	23,498	3,766	82,987,304
Percent[2]	100.0	23.4	66.9	0.8	1.4	7.5		
Group I (250,000 and over)								
Number	79,964	27,855	49,921	80	510	1,598	32	21,237,640
Percent[2]	100.0	34.8	62.4	0.1	0.6	2.0		
Group II (100,000 to 249,999)								
Number	45,832	9,330	33,471	1,168	231	1,632	87	13,066,244
Percent[2]	100.0	20.4	73.0	2.5	0.5	3.6		
Group III (50,000 to 99,999)								
Number	58,746	12,228	40,673	381	1,365	4,099	229	15,912,636
Percent[2]	100.0	20.8	69.2	0.6	2.3	7.0		
Group IV (25,000 to 49,999)								
Number	42,980	8,040	29,491	211	1,260	3,978	354	12,264,755
Percent[2]	100.0	18.7	68.6	0.5	2.9	9.3		
Group V (10,000 to 24,999)								
Number	47,465	8,099	32,107	363	593	6,303	750	12,033,818
Percent[2]	100.0	17.1	67.6	0.8	1.2	13.3		
Group VI (under 10,000)								
Number	40,390	8,329	25,426	314	433	5,888	2,314	8,472,211
Percent[2]	100.0	20.6	63.0	0.8	1.1	14.6		
Metropolitan Counties								
Number	68,944	9,605	51,119	373	1,656	6,191	655	28,781,270
Percent[2]	100.0	13.9	74.1	0.5	2.4	9.0		
Nonmetropolitan Counties								
Number	11,553	1,996	7,563	92	134	1,768	528	7,682,269
Percent[2]	100.0	17.3	65.5	0.8	1.2	15.3		
Suburban Areas [3]								
Number	190,880	35,513	129,440	1,366	4,274	20,287	3,302	64,482,767
Percent[2]	100.0	18.6	67.8	0.7	2.2	10.6		

1 Includes all offenses except traffic and neglect cases. 2 Because of rounding, the percentages may not sum to 100. 3 Suburban areas include law enforcement agencies in cities with less than 50,000 inhabitants and county law enforcement agencies that are within a Metropolitan Statistical Area. Suburban areas exclude all metropolitan agencies associated with a principal city. The agencies associated with suburban areas also appear in other groups within this table.

Table 69. Arrests, by State, 2012

(Number)

State	Total, all classes[1]	Violent crime[2]	Property crime[2]	Murder and nonnegligent manslaughter	Forcible rape	Robbery	Aggravated assault
Alabama[3]							
Under 18	132	5	61	0	1	3	1
Total, all ages	1,918	23	489	1	1	14	7
Alaska							
Under 18	2,559	127	767	0	3	16	108
Total, all ages	29,690	1,618	3,602	16	86	203	1,313
Arizona							
Under 18	32,428	997	7,267	7	31	289	670
Total, all ages	256,968	8,101	38,802	235	220	1,836	5,810
Arkansas							
Under 18	9,939	385	2,694	9	20	111	245
Total, all ages	137,962	4,137	16,680	119	172	626	3,220
California							
Under 18	115,682	9,178	27,322	100	148	3,464	5,466
Total, all ages	1,228,185	103,122	144,300	1,594	1,642	16,676	83,210
Colorado							
Under 18	26,333	546	5,435	2	49	128	367
Total, all ages	213,769	5,375	23,128	116	333	868	4,058
Connecticut							
Under 18	10,853	583	2,163	4	31	274	274
Total, all ages	110,186	4,438	16,280	134	209	1,299	2,796
Delaware							
Under 18	4,562	356	1,140	1	8	135	212
Total, all ages	39,680	2,387	8,017	26	67	596	1,698
Florida[3, 4]							
Under 18	78,195	4,824	23,188	52	196	1,622	2,954
Total, all ages	960,086	41,610	125,581	707	1,620	8,298	30,985
Georgia							
Under 18	34,441	1,680	9,194	33	31	565	1,051
Total, all ages	330,261	13,663	50,380	408	311	2,829	10,115
Hawaii							
Under 18	617	37	123	0	1	24	12
Total, all ages	8,832	267	972	3	22	76	166
Idaho							
Under 18	9,876	163	2,245	1	8	17	137
Total, all ages	64,164	1,482	7,225	19	90	100	1,273
Illinois[5]							
Under 18	21,693	2,334	4,336	37	55	1,155	1,087
Total, all ages	125,398	6,685	18,344	319	381	2,440	3,545
Indiana							
Under 18	19,005	741	4,532	14	15	226	486
Total, all ages	151,935	5,987	22,874	169	114	1,104	4,600
Iowa							
Under 18							
Total, all ages	14,469	521	3,838	2	27	43	449
	102,554	4,128	13,911	28	89	244	3,767
Kansas							
Under 18	7,105	255	1,849	0	41	36	178
Total, all ages	78,153	2,269	7,934	43	146	221	1,859
Kentucky							
Under 18	7,001	398	2,450	11	26	224	137
Total, all ages	179,435	3,704	21,538	161	248	1,231	2,064
Louisiana							
Under 18	13,492	1,097	3,414	31	30	265	771
Total, all ages	122,931	7,741	21,778	182	222	937	6,400
Maine							
Under 18	5,351	68	1,421	1	5	17	45
Total, all ages	51,052	770	8,260	19	51	233	467
Maryland							
Under 18	23,556	1,633	6,098	13	40	789	791
Total, all ages	214,837	9,665	27,862	218	336	2,989	6,122
Massachusetts							
Under 18	11,018	1,066	1,835	2	14	236	814

Table 69. Arrests, by State, 2012— continued

(Number)

State	Total, all classes[1]	Violent crime[2]	Property crime[2]	Murder and nonnegligent manslaughter	Forcible rape	Robbery	Aggravated assault
Total, all ages	137,532	10,719	18,900	52	243	1,590	8,834
Michigan							
Under 18	24,166	1,339	6,537	14	69	409	847
Total, all ages	252,589	11,537	33,189	157	557	2,003	8,820
Minnesota[6]							
Under 18			6,276	3		174	389
Total, all ages			24,025	44		579	2,598
Mississippi							
Under 18	7,364	108	1,712	8	13	45	42
Total, all ages	94,386	1,724	10,320	83	127	406	1,108
Missouri							
Under 18	28,657	1,105	7,424	21	61	377	646
Total, all ages	289,864	10,020	42,838	289	389	1,968	7,374
Montana							
Under 18	6,715	106	1,437	0	10	6	90
Total, all ages	32,384	907	4,671	10	54	57	786
Nebraska							
Under 18	11,700	210	3,117	1	24	68	117
Total, all ages	77,665	2,080	10,893	30	200	334	1,516
Nevada							
Under 18	13,283	714	2,764	5	24	220	465
Total, all ages	142,459	6,557	15,569	120	199	1,519	4,719
New Hampshire							
Under 18	5,387	64	773	0	4	13	47
Total, all ages	45,492	879	4,602	8	58	208	605
New Jersey							
Under 18							
Total, all ages	26,688	1,822	4,778	20	46	920	836
	328,432	11,341	32,995	220	316	3,528	7,277
New Mexico							
Under 18	9,354	389	2,456	8	19	32	330
Total, all ages	98,410	4,016	12,560	83	122	337	3,474
New York[3]							
Under 18	39,453	2,330	10,957	15	81	954	1,280
Total, all ages	338,463	14,318	62,766	206	455	3,720	9,937
North Carolina							
Under 18	32,868	1,495	8,933	42	58	535	860
Total, all ages	435,932	18,825	66,248	560	530	3,774	13,961
North Dakota							
Under 18	4,730	57	860	0	16	12	29
Total, all ages	29,084	528	3,119	7	40	46	435
Ohio							
Under 18							
Total, all ages	25,052	767	5,405	10	42	358	357
	227,243	6,236	35,439	181	376	2,020	3,659
Oklahoma							
Under 18	12,614	500	3,697	10	37	104	349
Total, all ages	127,825	4,760	17,664	133	228	591	3,808
Oregon							
Under 18	16,616	477	4,371	4	24	167	282
Total, all ages	127,754	4,205	25,279	83	221	1,110	2,791
Pennsylvania							
Under 18	66,833	3,692	9,376	27	152	1,370	2,143
Total, all ages	433,863	23,412	62,665	548	947	6,432	15,485
Rhode Island							
Under 18	3,705	129	743	0	20	44	65
Total, all ages	33,191	901	3,638	10	69	172	650
South Carolina							
Under 18	14,385	611	3,810	12	39	188	372
Total, all ages	169,384	7,257	27,199	261	320	1,320	5,356
South Dakota							
Under 18	5,682	68	1,169	3	10	8	47
Total, all ages	35,365	769	3,865	10	67	49	643

Table 69. Arrests, by State, 2012— continued

(Number)

State	Total, all classes[1]	Violent crime[2]	Property crime[2]	Murder and nonnegligent manslaughter	Forcible rape	Robbery	Aggravated assault
Tennessee							
Under 18	28,273	1,721	5,825	4	93	417	1,207
Total, all ages	356,340	16,800	44,154	261	378	2,171	13,990
Texas							
Under 18	110,740	3,592	23,334	49	263	1,007	2,273
Total, all ages	1,009,136	30,245	129,856	708	1,724	6,365	21,448
Utah							
Under 18	19,053	277	4,850	4	52	46	175
Total, all ages	117,185	2,045	19,502	32	154	373	1,486
Vermont							
Under 18	1,036	37	208	0	7	0	30
Total, all ages	13,073	519	1,824	8	61	21	429
Virginia							
Under 18	25,330	614	5,133	7	31	262	314
Total, all ages	339,362	6,765	37,598	271	312	1,699	4,483
Washington							
Under 18	18,006	859	5,487	8	64	281	506
Total, all ages	172,362	7,200	31,512	122	437	1,704	4,937
West Virginia							
Under 18	1,678	73	413	2	5	18	48
Total, all ages	46,364	1,750	6,465	43	61	201	1,445
Wisconsin							
Under 18	63,281	1,318	10,107	13	104	504	697
Total, all ages	324,207	8,481	38,666	151	559	1,639	6,132
Wyoming							
Under 18	3,973	27	667	2	2	7	16
Total, all ages	30,404	458	2,509	13	27	29	389

Table 69. Arrests, by State, 2012

(Number)

State	Burglary	Larceny-theft	Motor vehicle theft	Arson	Other assaults	Forgery and counterfeiting	Fraud	Embezzlement
Alabama [3]								
Under 18	10	50	1	0	23	0	1	0
Total, all ages	24	462	3	0	243	6	22	20
Alaska								
Under 18	87	622	45	13	297	1	4	14
Total, all ages	309	3,055	203	35	3,864	63	158	104
Arizona								
Under 18	1,077	5,822	295	73	4,117	15	64	9
Total, all ages	4,315	32,314	1,535	638	23,323	1,659	2,037	213
Arkansas								
Under 18	522	2,110	53	9	1,583	10	24	3
Total, all ages	2,743	13,532	352	53	11,635	821	1,824	46
California								
Under 18	9,366	15,831	1,718	407	13,016	113	271	19
Total, all ages	51,443	78,489	13,303	1,065	78,755	5,693	7,054	1,074
Colorado								
Under 18	471	4,635	205	124	1,500	9	59	2
Total, all ages	2,177	19,726	1,002	223	13,604	655	1,491	103
Connecticut								
Under 18	451	1,568	112	32	2,836	15	42	10
Total, all ages	2,694	12,884	584	118	21,308	616	1,182	168
Delaware								
Under 18	223	866	32	19	1,135	3	91	3
Total, all ages	1,233	6,608	142	34	7,990	493	1,911	188
Florida [3, 4]								
Under 18	6,854	14,985	1,230	119	11,892	51	436	6
Total, all ages	26,451	93,335	5,444	351	85,915	3,034	14,988	910
Georgia								
Under 18	1,908	6,804	414	68	5,035	84	230	8
Total, all ages	8,215	40,239	1,721	205	33,107	4,051	5,496	418
Hawaii								
Under 18	17	94	12	0	15	0	0	0
Total, all ages	163	699	106	4	505	18	6	0
Idaho								
Under 18	279	1,835	74	57	928	4	24	1
Total, all ages	1,057	5,894	195	79	5,444	159	419	50
Illinois [5]								
Under 18	843	2,660	813	20	3,195	2	20	0
Total, all ages	2,317	13,579	2,387	61	18,286	170	212	1
Indiana								
Under 18	612	3,546	320	54	3,389	10	33	4
Total, all ages	3,094	18,588	1,063	129	15,110	679	1,421	79
Iowa								
Under 18								
Total, all ages	657	3,004	114	63	1,698	24	46	9
	1,857	11,584	342	128	8,442	548	766	95
Kansas								
Under 18	176	1,553	97	23	1,073	17	16	10
Total, all ages	1,009	6,444	426	55	11,035	391	841	196
Kentucky								
Under 18	531	1,760	96	63	1,049	8	12	12
Total, all ages	3,939	16,744	674	181	10,956	1,104	976	432
Louisiana								
Under 18	808	2,465	107	34	2,170	4	11	0
Total, all ages	3,791	17,310	577	100	14,414	354	1,217	20
Maine								
Under 18	224	1,087	71	39	739	4	13	1
Total, all ages	1,302	6,618	264	76	6,364	284	659	55
Maryland								
Under 18	1,180	4,360	441	117	4,468	47	28	4
Total, all ages	6,083	19,861	1,619	299	24,108	802	1,288	266
Massachusetts								
Under 18	439	1,271	73	52	2,089	6	27	2

Table 69. Arrests, by State, 2012— continued

(Number)

State	Burglary	Larceny-theft	Motor vehicle theft	Arson	Other assaults	Forgery and counterfeiting	Fraud	Embezzlement
Total, all ages	3,486	14,741	563	110	21,656	571	1,329	143
Michigan								
Under 18	1,061	5,059	353	64	3,231	8	265	10
Total, all ages	5,386	25,928	1,612	363	27,750	620	4,282	825
Minnesota [6]								
Under 18	474	5,464	248	90	2,206	23	62	3
Total, all ages	2,331	20,612	928	154	12,600	843	1,748	33
Mississippi								
Under 18	350	1,296	62	4	1,105	0	44	2
Total, all ages	1,894	8,032	347	47	9,605	513	1,355	559
Missouri								
Under 18	1,040	5,999	281	104	4,328	32	57	3
Total, all ages	5,584	35,286	1,684	284	28,617	1,698	2,493	284
Montana								
Under 18	94	1,248	78	17	553	4	8	3
Total, all ages	331	4,098	197	45	3,892	46	139	40
Nebraska								
Under 18	198	2,792	75	52	1,545	8	74	4
Total, all ages	851	9,586	369	87	7,778	332	1,456	77
Nevada								
Under 18	455	2,165	115	29	1,853	3	42	3
Total, all ages	2,917	11,875	664	113	16,166	760	1,531	436
New Hampshire								
Under 18	90	639	20	24	870	8	25	1
Total, all ages	579	3,879	93	51	5,883	209	793	39
New Jersey								
Under 18								
Total, all ages	978	3,544	137	119	2,159	46	78	5
	6,526	25,560	674	235	23,491	1,728	3,106	204
New Mexico								
Under 18	270	2,048	58	80	1,337	5	15	12
Total, all ages	1,717	10,282	307	254	9,389	216	468	194
New York [3]								
Under 18	2,151	8,142	540	124	4,925	115	292	1
Total, all ages	9,180	51,088	2,124	374	37,449	3,571	6,062	97
North Carolina								
Under 18	2,358	6,306	178	91	5,907	46	294	30
Total, all ages	15,218	49,443	1,217	370	54,167	2,039	14,901	1,352
North Dakota								
Under 18	52	744	55	9	432	4	15	8
Total, all ages	219	2,736	145	19	2,249	61	423	43
Ohio								
Under 18								
Total, all ages	922	4,297	117	69	4,656	25	121	0
	5,493	29,238	550	158	29,501	965	2,162	11
Oklahoma								
Under 18	602	2,911	94	90	917	6	42	23
Total, all ages	2,532	14,444	495	193	8,425	624	1,711	408
Oregon								
Under 18	512	3,601	139	119	1,569	16	64	1
Total, all ages	2,488	21,158	1,404	229	12,645	716	1,700	36
Pennsylvania								
Under 18	1,468	7,224	439	245	6,138	60	182	29
Total, all ages	9,959	49,597	2,543	566	45,280	2,509	6,866	440
Rhode Island								
Under 18	178	521	21	23	550	1	10	4
Total, all ages	728	2,757	123	30	4,353	120	549	115
South Carolina								
Under 18	759	2,902	104	45	2,332	16	75	3
Total, all ages	4,665	21,598	776	160	18,126	1,723	4,477	319
South Dakota								
Under 18	108	993	53	15	453	3	35	8
Total, all ages	389	3,294	152	30	3,926	75	674	52

Table 69. Arrests, by State, 2012— continued

(Number)

State	Burglary	Larceny-theft	Motor vehicle theft	Arson	Other assaults	Forgery and counterfeiting	Fraud	Embezzlement
Tennessee								
Under 18	1,056	4,442	252	75	4,840	31	142	11
Total, all ages	6,852	34,996	2,087	219	31,990	2,174	7,908	782
Texas								
Under 18	3,777	18,633	749	175	16,851	137	315	20
Total, all ages	17,029	108,304	3,985	538	105,747	5,558	10,205	429
Utah								
Under 18	310	4,365	138	37	1,752	36	38	1
Total, all ages	1,315	17,697	408	82	10,613	761	817	26
Vermont								
Under 18	45	125	30	8	185	1	1	2
Total, all ages	330	1,380	88	26	1,552	65	266	48
Virginia								
Under 18	821	4,023	151	138	4,201	41	132	27
Total, all ages	4,574	31,879	835	310	39,139	2,294	6,460	1,522
Washington								
Under 18	846	4,361	197	83	3,165	19	35	0
Total, all ages	4,604	25,737	970	201	23,210	1,112	846	56
West Virginia								
Under 18	55	336	18	4	271	4	3	1
Total, all ages	940	5,251	229	45	5,512	388	711	130
Wisconsin								
Under 18	1,111	8,559	370	67	3,087	31	126	13
Total, all ages	4,136	33,269	1,091	170	18,315	1,170	3,773	198
Wyoming								
Under 18	53	579	20	15	425	1	2	0
Total, all ages	266	2,121	86	36	2,691	51	183	3

Table 69. Arrests, by State, 2012

(Number)

State	Stolen property; buying, receiving, possessing	Vandalism	Weapons; carrying, possessing, etc.	Prostitution and commercialized vice	Sex offenses (except forcible rape and prostitution)	Drug abuse violations	Gambling	Offenses against the family and children	Driving under the influence
Alabama [3]									
Under 18	2	0	1	0	0	25	0	0	1
Total, all ages	18	4	10	0	4	306	0	0	286
Alaska									
Under 18	6	125	26	0	29	321	0	0	28
Total, all ages	18	770	225	38	275	1,547	1	240	2,951
Arizona									
Under 18	99	2,250	223	7	265	4,282	0	280	317
Total, all ages	1,209	10,437	2,281	679	1,489	27,273	2	2,580	31,263
Arkansas									
Under 18	91	293	118	3	42	884	1	1	81
Total, all ages	1,057	1,430	1,158	255	184	11,083	21	258	9,226
California									
Under 18	2,102	6,205	5,037	229	1,448	10,326	28	6	736
Total, all ages	19,007	18,488	25,841	10,484	11,139	194,290	460	266	172,345
Colorado									
Under 18	95	1,160	321	6	150	2,996	0	52	326
Total, all ages	770	4,963	1,743	307	619	15,953	0	3,092	26,180
Connecticut									
Under 18	59	484	163	1	128	761	3	37	43
Total, all ages	450	2,199	1,227	371	598	9,651	71	1,514	8,612
Delaware									
Under 18	54	184	67	1	53	500	0	0	0
Total, all ages	384	922	327	39	211	5,463	3	244	292
Florida [3, 4]									
Under 18	211	1,414	1,022	41	227	8,812	27	0	197
Total, all ages	3,133	6,881	6,177	4,753	2,797	127,919	330	0	44,894
Georgia									
Under 18	420	828	605	28	521	2,994	9	235	185
Total, all ages	3,247	4,124	3,500	1,614	3,829	42,889	385	4,059	27,903
Hawaii									
Under 18	0	2	10	0	0	131	0	1	5
Total, all ages	0	56	108	15	32	892	34	6	879
Idaho									
Under 18	45	419	132	0	82	1,030	0	8	113
Total, all ages	218	1,152	525	27	300	6,848	0	710	9,097
Illinois [5]									
Under 18	15	956	903	10	44	4,156	429	10	16
Total, all ages	90	3,504	3,982	2,154	549	35,715	2,467	319	4,192
Indiana									
Under 18	181	663	208	2	239	1,786	10	65	81
Total, all ages	787	1,872	1,462	828	1,327	18,372	18	1,192	14,844
Iowa									
Under 18									
Total, all ages	62	823	139	3	55	1,147	0	3	134
	248	2,197	618	189	191	8,666	6	1,041	10,845
Kansas									
Under 18	27	323	52	1	100	845	0	8	118
Total, all ages	324	1,974	616	154	279	7,629	1	243	10,378
Kentucky									
Under 18	158	234	87	0	77	722	0	6	100
Total, all ages	1,772	1,126	1,122	270	400	21,141	19	4,752	23,157
Louisiana									
Under 18	206	443	222	5	115	1,176	9	43	27
Total, all ages	1,300	2,102	1,519	447	563	15,748	75	863	5,259
Maine									
Under 18	10	399	32	2	52	517	1	1	53
Total, all ages	199	1,472	406	56	277	5,544	3	121	5,834
Maryland									
Under 18	7	1,016	567	15	187	3,421	18	5	93
Total, all ages	162	3,205	3,189	1,116	1,143	39,733	206	1,929	16,769
Massachusetts									

Table 69. Arrests, by State, 2012— continued

(Number)

State	Stolen property; buying, receiving, possessing	Vandalism	Weapons; carrying, possessing, etc.	Prostitution and commercialized vice	Sex offenses (except forcible rape and prostitution)	Drug abuse violations	Gambling	Offenses against the family and children	Driving under the influence
Under 18	181	603	168	5	69	505	0	126	74
Total, all ages	1,450	3,217	1,311	941	547	11,599	19	1,818	8,541
Michigan									
Under 18	268	753	531	10	207	2,722	9	8	325
Total, all ages	1,626	3,088	3,843	386	859	31,823	45	4,029	29,206
Minnesota [6]									
Under 18	296	1,033	231	1	238	2,601	2	9	260
Total, all ages	1,477	3,002	931	297	1,076	15,087	15	338	22,278
Mississippi									
Under 18	79	171	110	3	31	643	8	331	67
Total, all ages	694	887	841	193	246	10,678	172	3,346	10,221
Missouri									
Under 18									
Total, all ages	389	1,346	360	2	461	2,763	7	60	261
	2,666	5,126	3,230	381	1,801	34,943	21	3,420	26,860
Montana									
Under 18	4	387	14	0	27	380	0	64	58
Total, all ages	28	1,072	91	4	96	2,077	0	379	4,418
Nebraska									
Under 18	129	884	103	0	114	1,309	0	27	159
Total, all ages	780	2,571	914	198	570	10,433	8	1,295	10,639
Nevada									
Under 18	145	690	118	56	90	1,189	10	37	76
Total, all ages	1,466	1,782	1,464	3,620	1,257	15,001	52	1,073	11,576
New Hampshire									
Under 18	81	319	0	1	25	646	0	5	50
Total, all ages	741	1,273	74	103	132	3,941	3	176	4,109
New Jersey									
Under 18									
Total, all ages	629	1,220	727	15	195	4,811	39	55	229
	3,322	4,638	3,957	892	1,260	51,111	99	11,123	25,697
New Mexico									
Under 18	57	335	149	0	33	1,238	0	37	116
Total, all ages	683	1,132	609	289	153	8,044	0	1,457	10,126
New York [3]									
Under 18	1,076	4,020	602	20	742	5,186	11	17	196
Total, all ages	5,689	17,728	4,011	802	3,419	65,840	188	389	33,053
North Carolina									
Under 18	466	1,250	1,270	10	146	2,943	4	51	388
Total, all ages	4,436	7,621	6,618	808	1,636	38,240	194	7,534	46,855
North Dakota									
Under 18	39	210	24	1	27	321	0	63	42
Total, all ages	132	504	213	34	84	2,446	0	131	5,730
Ohio									
Under 18									
Total, all ages	463	1,180	327	3	168	1,935	3	266	62
	3,325	3,969	2,518	794	659	26,936	55	2,706	35,629
Oklahoma									
Under 18	273	308	190	8	42	1,366	0	19	134
Total, all ages	2,366	1,302	1,984	364	543	16,688	5	724	13,801
Oregon									
Under 18	69	1,096	163	2	112	2,514	0	5	78
Total, all ages	496	4,049	1,712	431	1,144	18,929	2	544	13,592
Pennsylvania									
Under 18	355	2,555	1,096	13	547	4,720	3	37	467
Total, all ages	2,749	9,279	4,154	2,139	2,584	55,610	136	1,276	49,103
Rhode Island									
Under 18	80	242	131	0	27	411	0	76	12
Total, all ages	415	1,106	404	74	104	3,665	6	129	2,548
South Carolina									
Under 18	135	441	364	13	106	2,159	0	11	99
Total, all ages	1,986	2,731	1,966	528	543	27,174	167	940	17,906
South Dakota									

Table 69. Arrests, by State, 2012— continued

(Number)

State	Stolen property; buying, receiving, possessing	Vandalism	Weapons; carrying, possessing, etc.	Prostitution and commercialized vice	Sex offenses (except forcible rape and prostitution)	Drug abuse violations	Gambling	Offenses against the family and children	Driving under the influence
Under 18	38	175	47	2	26	816	0	207	84
Total, all ages	106	580	164	49	71	4,372	0	436	5,816
Tennessee									
Under 18	53	1,141	521	5	167	2,647	56	33	146
Total, all ages	719	4,414	3,568	2,174	842	43,448	289	2,368	26,858
Texas									
Under 18	127	3,119	868	78	628	14,006	8	64	592
Total, all ages	858	10,796	10,222	7,009	4,087	133,110	527	5,159	85,436
Utah									
Under 18	151	1,130	309	10	322	1,799	4	8	72
Total, all ages	875	3,741	1,291	104	871	12,710	10	1,324	6,061
Vermont									
Under 18									
Total, all ages	10	89	9	1	5	127	0	6	23
	131	364	20	3	32	1,390	0	316	2,517
Virginia									
Under 18	132	871	338	1	184	2,789	6	46	139
Total, all ages	946	4,504	3,556	829	1,079	38,038	46	2,792	28,908
Washington									
Under 18	221	1,133	317	20	153	2,110	0	19	194
Total, all ages	2,482	4,773	1,772	432	615	12,706	3	608	30,501
West Virginia									
Under 18	9	65	13	1	9	177	0	1	19
Total, all ages	316	854	354	73	150	6,647	3	100	5,654
Wisconsin									
Under 18	578	2,729	808	20	1,059	3,650	53	209	315
Total, all ages	1,715	8,620	3,715	383	2,779	26,073	138	2,514	29,126
Wyoming									
Under 18	4	166	35	2	23	592	1	5	42
Total, all ages	54	605	92	18	120	3,036	1	248	4,147

Table 69. Arrests, by State, 2012

(Number)

State	Liquor laws	Drunkenness[7]	Disorderly conduct	Vagrancy	All other offenses (except traffic)	Suspicion	Curfew and loitering law violations	Number of agencies	Estimated population, 2012
Alabama [3]									
Under 18	2	0	7	0	4	0	0	1	82,332
Total, all ages	8	135	17	0	321	0	0		
Alaska									
Under 18	430	10	28	0	335	0	11	30	464,937
Total, all ages	1,837	64	928	1	11,374	1	11		
Arizona									
Under 18	3,581	0	2,087	22	4,112	0	2,434	80	5,945,274
Total, all ages	16,947	1	14,071	1,148	71,019	0	2,434		
Arkansas									
Under 18	316	157	854	0	2,105	0	294	212	2,510,046
Total, all ages	2,414	9,433	3,453	524	62,029	0	294		
California									
Under 18	2,901	2,287	5,373	232	23,371	0	5,482	685	37,416,909
Total, all ages	15,241	94,445	8,831	6,143	305,725	0	5,482		
Colorado									
Under 18	2,752	42	2,192	0	7,256	0	1,434	204	4,700,965
Total, all ages	11,766	1,385	8,970	302	91,929	0	1,434		
Connecticut									
Under 18	121	0	1,938	0	1,458	0	8	97	3,388,202
Total, all ages	608	22	12,796	55	28,012	0	8		
Delaware									
Under 18	222	14	256	0	401	0	82	52	916,825
Total, all ages	1,903	550	1,973	830	5,471	0	82		
Florida [3, 4]									
Under 18	1,202	0	0	0	24,645	0	0	618	19,290,951
Total, all ages	26,954	0	0	0	464,210	0	0		
Georgia									
Under 18	1,010	58	3,140	84	7,372	14	707	422	8,827,198
Total, all ages	9,710	3,202	25,067	938	91,804	168	707		
Hawaii									
Under 18	52	0	3	0	170	0	68	1	158,760
Total, all ages	149	0	122	0	4,703	0	68		
Idaho									
Under 18	1,017	72	404	0	2,812	0	377	102	1,582,856
Total, all ages	3,998	478	2,185	8	23,462	0	377		
Illinois [5]									
Under 18	146	0	2,401	0	2,574	0	146	2	2,860,675
Total, all ages	914	0	10,613	55	17,000	0	146		
Indiana									
Under 18	1,658	189	1,519	12	3,115	125	443	149	4,176,156
Total, all ages	8,661	11,071	5,491	42	39,141	234	443		
Iowa									
Under 18									
Total, all ages	1,239	255	1,865	0	2,067	0	541	191	2,706,862
	6,183	12,060	5,954	44	25,881	0	541		
Kansas									
Under 18	991	1	362	0	1,057	0	0	232	2,066,137
Total, all ages	5,845	346	2,833	0	24,865	0	0		
Kentucky									
Under 18	61	114	344	13	1,128	0	28	362	4,192,532
Total, all ages	517	18,837	4,960	296	62,328	0	28		
Louisiana									
Under 18	207	34	2,217	59	1,892	14	127	102	2,304,044
Total, all ages	4,898	2,751	9,572	180	31,706	297	127		
Maine									
Under 18	894	2	185	0	889	0	68	179	1,325,207
Total, all ages	3,887	27	1,883	14	14,869	0	68		
Maryland									
Under 18									
Total, all ages	820	0	1,050	11	3,831	21	216	150	5,351,617
	5,725	5	6,025	102	71,074	247	216		
Massachusetts									

Table 69. Arrests, by State, 2012— continued

(Number)

State	Liquor laws	Drunkenness[7]	Disorderly conduct	Vagrancy	All other offenses (except traffic)	Suspicion	Curfew and loitering law violations	Number of agencies	Estimated population, 2012
Under 18	816	152	781	0	2,505	6	2	302	6,123,817
Total, all ages	4,111	7,027	6,881	3	36,695	52	2		
Michigan									
Under 18	2,406	1	947	0	4,040	0	547	535	9,159,042
Total, all ages	14,450	317	8,561	216	75,481	0	547		
Minnesota [6]									
Under 18	3,692	0	2,770	0	3,247	0	84	322	4,698,199
Total, all ages	14,549	0	9,381	19	21,996	0	84		
Mississippi									
Under 18	168	62	1,200	7	1,149	7	357	91	1,535,347
Total, all ages	1,486	4,841	6,294	50	29,894	110	357		
Missouri									
Under 18									
Total, all ages	1,728	20	1,918	5	4,793	0	1,595	385	5,612,383
	9,895	665	12,274	312	100,725	0	1,595		
Montana									
Under 18	1,155	0	682	0	1,316	0	517	93	949,729
Total, all ages	3,865	0	3,445	9	6,688	0	517		
Nebraska									
Under 18	1,483	0	636	0	1,659	0	239	211	1,691,152
Total, all ages	8,833	2	3,364	28	15,175	0	239		
Nevada									
Under 18	1,318	41	158	13	2,470	3	1,490	30	2,749,103
Total, all ages	7,189	149	1,905	1,684	51,728	4	1,490		
New Hampshire									
Under 18	799	196	233	0	1,263	0	28	148	1,167,974
Total, all ages	4,383	3,265	1,358	59	13,442	0	28		
New Jersey									
Under 18	1,645	0	2,239	29	4,262	0	1,705	496	8,637,883
Total, all ages	5,070	0	17,853	237	128,603	0	1,705		
New Mexico									
Under 18	680	8	532	3	1,944	1	7	67	1,767,251
Total, all ages	4,432	353	3,352	4	40,915	11	7		
New York [3]									
Under 18	855	0	2,064	42	6,002	0	0	487	10,798,302
Total, all ages	4,746	0	11,942	794	65,599	0	0		
North Carolina									
Under 18	1,554	0	3,028	0	5,052	0	1	333	8,780,316
Total, all ages	13,545	0	12,450	564	137,898	0	1		
North Dakota									
Under 18	821	0	759	0	902	0	145	91	685,149
Total, all ages	4,268	322	1,992	4	6,656	0	145		
Ohio									
Under 18	1,211	31	1,803	3	5,805	2	816	416	7,192,479
Total, all ages	8,254	2,986	14,904	8	49,347	23	816		
Oklahoma									
Under 18	253	501	869	0	2,166	0	1,300	304	3,589,287
Total, all ages	1,849	18,683	2,571	4	32,049	0	1,300		
Oregon									
Under 18	2,065	0	1,113	0	1,777	0	1,124	128	3,610,267
Total, all ages	12,458	0	10,185	11	18,496	0	1,124		
Pennsylvania									
Under 18	4,946	303	10,465	50	4,877	0	16,922	1,139	12,251,464
Total, all ages	19,481	24,734	48,505	726	55,293	0	16,922		
Rhode Island									
Under 18	68	1	662	0	530	0	28	47	1,044,186
Total, all ages	656	5	2,990	1	11,384	0	28		
South Carolina									
Under 18	551	94	1,931	0	1,572	0	62	306	4,112,716
Total, all ages	7,624	9,324	13,064	687	25,581	0	62		
South Dakota									
Under 18	967	16	365	0	1,056	0	147	111	747,870

Table 69. Arrests, by State, 2012— continued

(Number)

State	Liquor laws	Drunkenness[7]	Disorderly conduct	Vagrancy	All other offenses (except traffic)	Suspicion	Curfew and loitering law violations	Number of agencies	Estimated population, 2012
Total, all ages	4,599	106	2,184	292	7,082	0	147		
Tennessee									
Under 18	1,018	270	2,725	0	5,328	0	1,593	438	5,863,606
Total, all ages	7,995	20,224	10,847	13	127,180	0	1,593		
Texas									
Under 18	3,610	2,279	13,730	375	21,616	0	5,391	989	25,224,224
Total, all ages	21,803	111,370	29,385	1,482	300,461	0	5,391		
Utah									
Under 18	1,420	166	1,235	1	4,365	0	1,107	125	2,794,195
Total, all ages	8,009	3,993	3,999	16	39,310	0	1,107		
Vermont									
Under 18									
Total, all ages	110	0	95	0	127	0	0	76	557,989
	395	9	679	0	2,943	0	0		
Virginia									
Under 18	1,657	206	921	0	6,229	0	1,663	410	8,178,905
Total, all ages	11,653	32,070	5,141	286	114,073	0	1,663		
Washington									
Under 18	1,594	15	282	0	2,360	0	23	192	5,173,068
Total, all ages	4,985	38	3,191	131	46,165	1	23		
West Virginia									
Under 18	107	12	39	0	415	0	46	256	1,357,601
Total, all ages	1,697	2,067	1,081	12	12,354	0	46		
Wisconsin									
Under 18	4,838	0	11,483	16	18,392	0	4,449	359	5,373,766
Total, all ages	24,830	1	45,856	2,550	100,855	0	4,449		
Wyoming									
Under 18	656	9	127	7	905	0	277	56	520,353
Total, all ages	3,007	2,557	1,004	16	9,315	12	277		

Note: Because the number of agencies submitting arrest data varies from year to year, users are cautioned about making direct comparisons between 2012 arrest totals and those published in previous years' editions of Crime in the United States. Further, arrest figures may vary widely from state to state because some Part II crimes are not considered crimes in some states. 1 Does not include traffic arrests. 2 Violent crimes are offenses of murder and nonnegligent manslaughter, forcible rape, robbery, and aggravated assault. Property crimes are offenses of burglary, larceny-theft, motor vehicle theft, and arson. 3 See 2012 Arrest Data for details; www.fbi.gov/about-us/cjis/ucr/crime-in-the-u.s/2012/crime-in-the-u.s.-2012/persons-arrested/persons-arrested. 4 The arrest category All other offenses for Florida also includes the arrest counts for offenses against the family and children, drunkenness, disorderly conduct, vagrancy, suspicion, curfew and loitering law violations. 5 Forcible rape figures for Illinois include only those data provided by Rockford. 6 Complete forcible rape figures were not available for the state of Minnesota. 7 Drunkenness is not considered a crime in some states; therefore, the figures vary widely from state to state.

SECTION V

LAW ENFORCEMENT PERSONNEL

LAW ENFORCEMENT PERSONNEL

Figure V-1. Average Number of Officers and Employees by Employees in Cities by Region, 2012

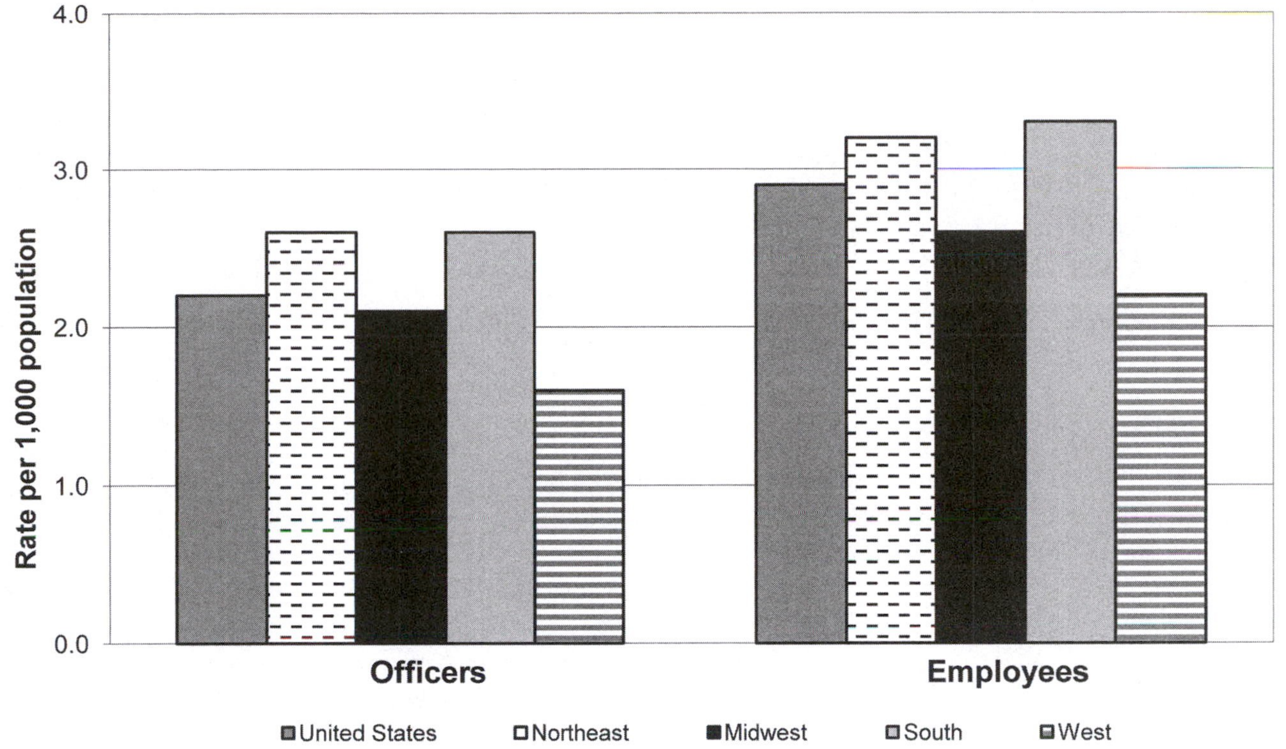

Sources: Tables 70 and 71

The Uniform Crime Reporting (UCR) program defines law enforcement officers as individuals who ordinarily carry a firearm and a badge, have full arrest powers, and are paid from governmental funds set aside specifically for sworn law enforcement representatives. Because of law enforcement's varied service requirements and functions, as well as the distinct demographic traits and characteristics of jurisdictions, readers should use caution when comparing staffing levels between agencies based on police employment data from the UCR program. In addition, the data presented here reflect existing staff levels and should not be interpreted as preferred officer strengths recommended by the Federal Bureau of Investigation (FBI). Also, readers should note that the totals given for sworn officers for any particular agency reflect both patrol officers on the street and officers assigned to various other duties, such as administrative and investigative positions and assignments to special teams.

Each year, law enforcement agencies across the United States report the total number of sworn law enforcement officers and civilians in their agencies as of October 31 to the UCR program. Civilian employees include personnel such as clerks, radio dispatchers, meter attendants, stenographers, jailers, correctional officers, and mechanics, provided that they are full-time employees of the agency.

This section of Crime in the United States presents those data as the number and rate of law enforcement officers and civilian employees throughout the United States. In 2012, 670,439 sworn officers and 285,883 civilians provided law enforcement services to more than 285 million people nationwide. These law enforcement personnel were employed by 14,006 state, city, university/college, metropolitan/nonmetropolitan county, and other designated law enforcement agencies. Of the slightly less than 1 million law enforcement employees, 73.6 percent were male. (Table 74)

The data in this section are broken down by geographic region and division, population group, state, city, university/college, metropolitan/nonmetropolitan county, and other law enforcement agency groups. (Information about geographic regions and divisions and population groups can be found in Appendix IV.) UCR program staff compute the rate of sworn officers and law enforcement employees by taking the number of employees (sworn officers only or in combination with civilians), dividing by the population for which the agency provides law enforcement service, and multiplying by 1,000.

- Tables 70 and 71 present the number and rate of law enforcement personnel per 1,000 inhabitants collectively employed by agencies, broken down by geographic region and division by population group
- Tables 72 and 73 provide a count of law enforcement agencies by population group, based on the employment rate ranges for sworn officer and civilian employees per 1,000 inhabitants
- Table 74 provides the number of total officers, the percentage of male and female sworn officers, and the civilian employees by population group
- Table 75 lists the percentage of full-time civilian law enforcement employees by population group
- Table 76 breaks down by state the number of sworn law enforcement officers and civilians employed by state law enforcement agencies
- Table 77 provides the number of total officers, the percentage of male and female sworn officers, and the civilian employees by state
- Tables 78 to 80 list the number of law enforcement employees for cities, universities and colleges, and metropolitan and nonmetropolitan counties
- Table 81 supplies employee data for those law enforcement agencies that serve the nation's transit systems, parks and forests, schools and school districts, hospitals, etc.

The demographic traits and characteristics of a jurisdiction affect its requirements for law enforcement service. For instance, a village between two large cities may require more law enforcement than a community of the same size with no urban center nearby. A town with legal gambling may have different law enforcement needs than a town near a military base. A city largely made up of college students may have different law enforcement needs than a city whose residents are mainly retirees.

Similarly, the functions of law enforcement agencies are diverse. Employees of these agencies patrol local streets and major highways, protect citizens in the nation's smallest towns and largest cities, and conduct investigations on offenses at the local and state levels. State police in one area may enforce traffic laws on state highways and interstates; in another area, they may be responsible for investigating violent crimes. Sheriff's departments may collect tax monies, serve as the enforcement authority for local and state courts, administer jail facilities, or carry out some combination of these duties. This has an impact on an agency's staffing levels.

Because of the differing service requirements and functions, care should be taken when drawing comparisons between and among the staffing levels of law enforcement agencies. The data in this section are not intended as recommended or preferred officer strength; they should be used merely as guides. Adequate staffing levels can be determined only after careful study of the conditions that affect the service requirements in a particular jurisdiction.

Rate

The UCR program computes these rates by taking the number of employees, dividing by the population of the agency's jurisdiction, and multiplying by 1,000.

An examination of the 2012 law enforcement employee data by population group showed that the nation's cities had a collective rate of 2.9 law enforcement employees per 1,000 inhabitants. Cities with fewer than 10,000 inhabitants had the highest rate of law enforcement employees, with a rate of 4.6 per 1,000 inhabitants. Cities with 50,000 to 99,999 inhabitants had the lowest rate of law enforcement employees (2.1 per 1,000 in population). The nation's largest cities, those with 250,000 or more inhabitants, averaged 3.5 law enforcement employees for every 1,000 inhabitants. (Table 70) These rates are either static or do not significantly differentiate from their 2011 levels.

Sworn Personnel

An analysis of the 2012 data showed that law enforcement agencies in the cities in the Northeast and the South had the highest rate of sworn officers—each at a rate of 2.6 per 1,000 inhabitants, followed by the Midwest (2.1), and the West (1.6). (Table 71) Each of these rates has remained unchanged since 2011.

By population group in 2012, there were 2.2 sworn officers for each 1,000 resident population. This rate dropped by a tenth in 2011 after remaining constant from 2007 through

2010, but remained static from 2011 to 2012. Cities with fewer than 10,000 inhabitants had the highest rate at 3.6 sworn officers per 1,000 inhabitants. The nation's largest cities, those with 250,000 or more inhabitants, averaged 2.7 officers per 1,000 inhabitants, the same as in 2011. (Table 71)

Males accounted for 88.1 percent of all full-time sworn law enforcement officers in 2012, one-tenth of a percentage point less than in 2011. Cities with populations of 1 million and over employed the highest percentage (17.9 percent) of full-time female officers. Of the city population groups, cities with populations of 10,000 to 24,999 inhabitants employed the highest percentage (92.2 percent) of male officers. In metropolitan counties, 86.5 percent of officers were male, and in nonmetropolitan counties, 92.5 percent of officers were male. (Table 74)

Civilian Employees

Civilian employees provide a myriad of services to the nation's law enforcement and criminal justice agencies. Among other duties, they dispatch officers, provide administrative and record-keeping support, and query local, state, and national databases.

In 2012, 29.9 percent of all law enforcement employees in the nation were civilians. Female employees accounted for 60.3 percent of all full-time civilian law enforcement employees in 2012. In cities, civilians made up 22.1 percent of law enforcement agencies employees. Civilians made up 40.6 percent of law enforcement employees in metropolitan counties, 40.1 percent of law enforcement employees in nonmetropolitan counties, and 33.9 percent of law enforcement employees in suburban areas. (Table 74)

Table 70. Full-Time Law Enforcement Employees, by Geographic Region and Division and Population Group, 2012[1]

(Number, rate per 1,000 inhabitants)

Geographic region/division	Total	Group I	Group II	Group III	Group IV	Group V	Group VI	Total city agencies	City population, 2012, estimated	County[2]	Total city and county agencies	Total agency population, 2012, estimated	Suburban Areas[3]
Total													
Number of employees	568,786	199,012	67,506	63,556	62,758	67,544	108,410	11,234	197,246,457	433,198	14,633	293,058,940	465,194
Average number of employees per 1,000 inhabitants	2.9	3.5	2.3	2.1	2.2	2.3	4.5			4.5			3.7
Northeast													
Number of employees	145,007	63,475	8,368	14,802	17,835	18,719	21,808	2,586	44,679,102				
Average number of employees per 1,000 inhabitants	3.2	5.5	2.9	2.3	2.2	2.1	3.3						
New England													
Number of employees	33,529	2,700	4,352	5,919	6,764	7,177	6,617	799	12,948,756				
Average number of employees per 1,000 inhabitants	2.6	4.3	2.9	2.3	2.2	2.2	3.6						
Middle Atlantic													
Number of employees	111,478	60,775	4,016	8,883	11,071	11,542	15,191	1,787	31,730,346				
Average number of employees per 1,000 inhabitants	3.5	5.6	2.9	2.4	2.2	2.0	3.2						
Midwest													
Number of employees	106,774	33,859	8,240	13,023	13,801	16,172	21,679	2,893	41,779,283				
Average number of employees per 1,000 inhabitants	2.6	3.6	2.1	1.9	1.9	2.1	3.4						
East North Central													
Number of employees	74,952	26,171	5,545	9,040	10,471	10,829	12,896	1,710	28,803,901				
Average number of employees per 1,000 inhabitants	2.6	3.8	2.1	1.9	1.9	2.0	3.3						
West North Central													
Number of employees	31,822	7,688	2,695	3,983	3,330	5,343	8,783	1,183	12,975,382				
Average number of employees per 1,000 inhabitants	2.5	3.0	2.1	1.7	1.9	2.1	3.5						
South													
Number of employees	186,573	49,238	29,379	19,164	19,112	21,592	48,088	3,918	55,937,475				
Average number of employees per 1,000 inhabitants	3.3	3.1	2.7	2.6	2.7	2.9	6.3						
South Atlantic													
Number of employees	89,560	21,361	14,946	10,742	9,110	10,041	23,360	1,710	23,582,760				
Average number of employees per 1,000 inhabitants	3.8	4.1	3.0	2.8	2.9	3.1	7.6						
East South Central													
Number of employees	31,882	7,190	4,758	2,227	3,880	4,638	9,189	872	9,318,340				
Average number of employees per 1,000 inhabitants	3.4	2.9	3.4	2.9	2.7	3.1	5.3						
West South Central													
Number of employees	65,131	20,687	9,675	6,195	6,122	6,913	15,539	1,336	23,036,375				
Average number of employees per 1,000 inhabitants	2.8	2.5	2.3	2.3	2.4	2.6	5.6						
West													
Number of employees	113,808	48,423	20,389	15,120	9,105	6,766	14,005	1,429	50,625,885				
Average number of employees per 1,000 inhabitants	2.2	2.5	1.7	1.7	1.8	2.0	5.7						
Mountain													
Number of employees	42,344	16,500	7,313	4,619	3,821	2,570	7,521	657	16,317,532				
Average number of employees per 1,000 inhabitants	2.6	2.7	2.0	2.1	1.9	2.4	6.1						
Pacific													
Number of employees	71,464	31,923	13,076	10,501	5,284	4,196	6,484	772	34,308,353				
Average number of employees per 1,000 inhabitants	2.1	2.5	1.6	1.6	1.7	1.9	5.4						

Note: Demographics Total: 10,826 cities; population, 193,021,745 Group I: 75 cities, 250,000 and over; population, 56,040,960 Group II: 196 cities, 100,000 to 249,999; population 29,282,253 Group III: 426 cities, 50,000 to 99,999; population 29,406,808 Group IV: 798 cities, 25,000 to 49,999; population 27,574,550 Group V: 1,743 cities, 10,000 to 24,999; population 27,664,124 Group VI: 7,588 cities, under 10,000; population 23,053,050 Counties: 3,180 agencies; population 91,998,321 Suburban areas: 7,503 agencies; population 124,099,819 1 Full-time law enforcement employees include civilians. 2 The designation county is a combination of both metropolitan and nonmetropolitan counties. 3 Suburban areas include law enforcement agencies in cities with less than 50,000 inhabitants and county law enforcement agencies that are within a Metropolitan Statistical Area). Suburban areas exclude all metropolitan agencies associated with a principal city. The agencies associated with suburban areas also appear in other groups within this table.

Table 71. Full-Time Law Enforcement Officers, by Geographic Region and Division, and Population Group, 2012

(Number, rate per 1,000 inhabitants)

Geographic region/ division	Total	Group I	Group II	Group III	Group IV	Group V	Group VI	Total city agencies	City population, 2012, estimated	County[1]	Total city and county agencies	Total agency population, 2012, estimated	Suburban Areas[2]
Total													
Number of officers	429,925	150,037	50,669	48,218	47,809	51,253	81,939	10,826	193,021,745	240,514	14,006	285,020,066	303,642
Average number of officers per 1,000 inhabitants	2.2	2.7	1.7	1.6	1.7	1.0	0.0			2.6			2.4
Northeast													
Number of officers	115,267	46,716	7,175	12,347	14,997	15,887	18,145	2,586	44,679,102				
Average number of officers per 1,000 inhabitants	2.6	4.0	2.5	1.9	1.8	1.7	2.7						
New England													
Number of officers	27,745	2,130	3,772	5,048	5,676	5,832	5,287	799	12,948,756				
Average number of officers per 1,000 inhabitants	2.1	3.4	2.6	1.9	1.8	1.8	2.9						
Middle Atlantic													
Number of officers	87,522	44,586	3,403	7,299	9,321	10,055	12,858	1,787	31,730,346				
Average number of officers per 1,000 inhabitants	2.8	4.1	2.5	1.9	1.9	1.7	2.7						
Midwest													
Number of officers	88,523	29,113	6,767	10,585	11,099	13,228	17,731	2,893	41,779,283				
Average number of officers per 1,000 inhabitants	2.1	3.1	1.7	1.5	1.5	1.7	2.8						
East North Central													
Number of officers	63,142	23,314	4,594	7,389	8,448	8,910	10,487	1,710	28,803,901				
Average number of officers per 1,000 inhabitants	2.2	3.4	1.7	1.6	1.6	1.7	2.7						
West North Central													
Number of officers	25,381	5,799	2,173	3,196	2,651	4,318	7,244	1,183	12,975,382				
Average number of officers per 1,000 inhabitants	2.0	2.3	1.7	1.4	1.5	1.7	2.9						
South													
Number of officers	143,964	38,605	22,428	14,670	15,049	17,018	36,194	3,918	55,937,475				
Average number of officers per 1,000 inhabitants	2.6	2.4	2.1	2.0	2.1	2.3	4.8						
South Atlantic													
Number of officers	69,381	16,351	11,463	8,279	7,255	8,104	17,929	1,710	23,582,760				
Average number of officers per 1,000 inhabitants	2.9	3.1	2.3	2.2	2.3	2.5	5.8						
East South Central													
Number of officers	25,359	6,012	3,635	1,757	3,132	3,642	7,181	872	9,318,340				
Average number of officers per 1,000 inhabitants	2.7	2.4	2.6	2.3	2.2	2.4	4.1						
West South Central													
Number of officers	49,224	16,242	7,330	4,634	4,662	5,272	11,084	1,336	23,036,375				
Average number of officers per 1,000 inhabitants	2.1	2.0	1.7	1.7	1.9	2.0	4.0						
West													
Number of officers	82,171	35,603	14,299	10,616	6,664	5,120	9,869	1,429	50,625,885				
Average number of officers per 1,000 inhabitants	1.6	1.9	1.2	1.2	1.3	1.5	4.0						
Mountain													
Number of officers	29,817	11,281	5,219	3,212	2,862	1,944	5,299	657	16,317,532				
Average number of officers per 1,000 inhabitants	1.8	1.8	1.4	1.4	1.4	1.8	4.3						
Pacific													
Number of officers	52,354	24,322	9,080	7,404	3,802	3,176	4,570	772	34,308,353				
Average number of officers per 1,000 inhabitants	1.5	1.9	1.1	1.1	1.2	1.4	3.8						

Note: Demographics Total: 10,826 cities; population, 193,021,745 Group I: 75 cities, 250,000 and over; population, 56,040,960 Group II: 196 cities, 100,000 to 249,999; population 29,282,253 Group III: 426 cities, 50,000 to 99,999; population 29,406,808 Group IV: 798 cities, 25,000 to 49,999; population 27,574,550 Group V: 1,743 cities, 10,000 to 24,999; population 27,664,124 Group VI: 7,588 cities, under 10,000; population 23,053,050 Counties: 3,180 agencies; population 91,998,321 Suburban areas: 7,503 agencies; population 124,099,819 1 The designation county is a combination of both metropolitan and nonmetropolitan counties. 2 Suburban areas include law enforcement agencies in cities with less than 50,000 inhabitants and county law enforcement agencies that are within a Metropolitan Statistical Area (see Data Declaration). Suburban areas exclude all metropolitan agencies associated with a principal city. The agencies associated with suburban areas also appear in other groups within this table.

Table 72. Full-Time Law Enforcement Employees, by Rate Range, 2012[1]

(Number, rate per 1,000 inhabitants)

Rate range	Total[2]	Group I	Group II	Group III	Group IV	Group V	Group VI
Total Cities							
Number	9,610	75	196	426	798	1,743	6,372
Percent[3]	100.0	100.0	100.0	100.0	100.0	100.0	100.0
0.1–0.5							
Number	119	0	0	0	2	5	112
Percent	1.2	0.0	0.0	0.0	0.3	0.3	1.8
0.6–1.0							
Number	537	0	1	8	26	59	443
Percent	5.6	0.0	0.5	1.9	3.3	3.4	7.0
1.1–1.5							
Number	1,274	3	40	88	133	252	758
Percent	13.3	4.0	20.4	20.7	16.7	14.5	11.9
1.6–2.0							
Number	1,954	15	58	135	231	431	1,084
Percent	20.3	20.0	29.6	31.7	28.9	24.7	17.0
2.1–2.5							
Number	1,801	18	39	99	211	428	1,006
Percent	18.7	24.0	19.9	23.2	26.4	24.6	15.8
2.6–3.0							
Number	1,269	13	31	48	99	277	801
Percent	13.2	17.3	15.8	11.3	12.4	15.9	12.6
3.1–3.5							
Number	820	8	16	30	59	140	567
Percent	8.5	10.7	8.2	7.0	7.4	8.0	8.9
3.6–4.0							
Number	525	3	5	10	23	77	407
Percent	5.5	4.0	2.6	2.3	2.9	4.4	6.4
4.1–4.5							
Number	345	7	5	6	5	36	286
Percent	3.6	9.3	2.6	1.4	0.6	2.1	4.5
4.6–5.0							
Number	235	4	0	0	7	19	205
Percent	2.4	5.3	0.0	0.0	0.9	1.1	3.2
5.1 and over							
Number	731	4	1	2	2	19	703
Percent	7.6	5.3	0.5	0.5	0.3	1.1	11.0

Note: Demographics Total: 9,610 cities; population, 193,021,745 Group I: 75 cities, 250,000 and over; population, 56,040,960 Group II: 196 cities, 100,000 to 249,999; population 29,282,253 Group III: 426 cities, 50,000 to 99,999; population 29,406,808 Group IV: 798 cities, 25,000 to 49,999; population 27,574,550 Group V: 1,743 cities, 10,000 to 24,999; population 27,664,124 Group VI: 6,372 cities, under 10,000; population 23,053,050 1 Full-time law enforcement employees include civilians. 2 The number of agencies used to compile these figures differs from other tables that include data about law enforcement employees because agencies with no resident population are excluded from this table. These agencies include those associated with universities and colleges (see Table 79) and other agencies (see Table 81), as well as some state agencies that have concurrent jurisdiction with other local law enforcement. 3 Because of rounding, the percentages may not sum to 100.

Table 73. Full-Time Law Enforcement Officers, by Rate Range, 2012

(Number, rate per 1,000 inhabitants)

Rate range	Total[1]	Group I	Group II	Group III	Group IV	Group V	Group VI
Total Cities							
Number	9,610	75	196	426	798	1,743	6,372
Percent[2]	100.0	100.0	100.0	100.0	100.0	100.0	100.0
0.1–0.5							
Number	132	0	0	0	4	7	121
Percent	1.4	0.0	0.0	0.0	0.5	0.4	1.9
0.6–1.0							
Number	767	3	29	61	72	109	493
Percent	8.0	4.0	14.8	14.3	9.0	6.3	7.7
1.1–1.5							
Number	1,977	13	68	139	257	474	1,026
Percent	20.6	17.3	34.7	32.6	32.2	27.2	16.1
1.6–2.0							
Number	2,450	26	49	139	272	595	1,369
Percent	25.5	34.7	25.0	32.6	34.1	34.1	21.5
2.1–2.5							
Number	1,613	11	28	58	117	326	1,073
Percent	16.8	14.7	14.3	13.6	14.7	18.7	16.8
2.6–3.0							
Number	994	6	13	19	58	135	763
Percent	10.3	8.0	6.6	4.5	7.3	7.7	12.0
3.1–3.5							
Number	541	5	7	8	12	55	454
Percent	5.6	6.7	3.6	1.9	1.5	3.2	7.1
3.6–4.0							
Number	345	4	1	0	4	24	312
Percent	3.6	5.3	0.5	0.0	0.5	1.4	4.9
4.1–4.5							
Number	216	5	1	2	0	12	196
Percent	2.2	6.7	0.5	0.5	0.0	0.7	3.1
4.6–5.0							
Number	124	1	0	0	0	3	120
Percent	1.3	1.3	0.0	0.0	0.0	0.2	1.9
5.1 and over							
Number	451	1	0	0	2	3	445
Percent	4.7	1.3	0.0	0.0	0.3	0.2	7.0

Note: Demographics Total: 10,052 cities; population, 197,246,457 Group I: 75 cities, 250,000 and over; population, 56,398,148 Group II: 196 cities, 100,000 to 249,999; population 29,447,050 Group III: 428 cities, 50,000 to 99,999; population 28,652,012 Group IV: 828 cities, 25,000 to 49,999; population 28,652,012 Group V: 1,834 cities, 10,000 to 24,999; population 29,005,261 Group VI: 6,691 cities, under 10,000; population 24,109,396 1The number of agencies used to compile these figures differs from other tables that include data about law enforcement employees because agencies with no resident population are excluded from this table. These agencies include those associated with universities and colleges (see Table 79) and other agencies (see Table 81), as well as some state agencies that have concurrent jurisdiction with other local law enforcement. 2 Because of rounding, the percentages may not sum to 100.

Table 74. Full-Time Law Enforcement Employees, by Population Group, Percent Male and Female, 2012

(Number, percent)

Population group	Law enforcement employees (number)	Law enforcement employees (percent)		Officers (number)	Officers (percent)		Civilians (number)	Civilians (percent)		Agencies (number)	Population, 2012,estimated
		Male	Female		Male	Female		Male	Female		
Total Agencies	956,322	73.6	26.4	670,439	88.1	11.9	285,883	39.7	60.3	14,006	285,020,066
Total Cities	552,162	75.7	24.3	429,925	88.1	11.9	122,237	32.1	67.9	10,826	193,021,745
Group I (250,000 and over)	194,995	72.3	27.7	150,037	83.5	16.5	44,958	34.8	65.2	75	56,040,960
1,000,000 and over (Group I subset)	103,192	70.6	29.4	78,019	82.1	17.9	25,173	35.0	65.0	9	24,252,651
500,000 to 999,999 (Group I subset)	53,626	75.2	24.8	42,260	85.0	15.0	11,366	39.0	61.0	25	17,516,175
250,000 to 499,999 (Group I subset)	38,177	72.5	27.5	29,758	85.0	15.0	8,419	28.3	71.7	41	14,272,134
Group II (100,000 to 249,999)	66,376	73.4	26.6	50,669	88.1	11.9	15,707	26.0	74.0	196	29,282,253
Group III (50,000 to 99,999)	62,109	76.7	23.3	48,218	90.5	9.5	13,891	28.8	71.2	426	29,406,808
Group IV (25,000 to 49,999)	59,853	78.0	22.0	47,809	90.9	9.1	12,044	26.8	73.2	798	27,574,550
Group V (10,000 to 24,999)	63,249	79.8	20.2	51,253	92.2	7.8	11,996	26.9	73.1	1,743	27,664,124
Group VI (under 10,000)	105,580	79.3	20.7	81,939	91.0	9.0	23,641	38.6	61.4	7,588	23,053,050
Metropolitan Counties	299,358	70.0	30.0	177,730	86.5	13.5	121,628	46.0	54.0	1,268	68,230,997
Nonmetropolitan Counties	104,802	72.9	27.1	62,784	92.5	7.5	42,018	43.5	56.5	1,912	23,767,324
Suburban Areas [1]	459,397	73.2	26.8	303,642	88.4	11.6	155,755	43.6	56.4	7,503	124,099,819

1 Suburban areas include law enforcement agencies in cities with less than 50,000 inhabitants and county law enforcement agencies that are within a Metropolitan Statistical Area. Suburban areas exclude all metropolitan agencies associated with a principal city. The agencies associated with suburban areas also appear in other groups within this table.

Table 75. Full-Time Civilian Law Enforcement Employees, by Population Group, 2012

(Number, percent)

Population group	Civilian employees (percent)	Agencies (number)	Population, 2012, estimated
Total Agencies	29.9	14,006	285,020,066
Total Cities	22.1	10,826	193,021,745
Group I (250,000 and over)	23.1	75	56,040,960
1,000,000 and over (Group I subset)	24.4	9	24,252,651
500,000 to 999,999 (Group I subset)	21.2	25	17,516,175
250,000 to 499,999 (Group I subset)	22.1	41	14,272,134
Group II (100,000 to 249,999)	23.7	196	29,282,253
Group III (50,000 to 99,999)	22.4	426	29,406,808
Group IV (25,000 to 49,999)	20.1	798	27,574,550
Group V (10,000 to 24,999)	19.0	1,743	27,664,124
Group VI (under 10,000)	22.4	7,588	23,053,050
Metropolitan Counties	40.6	1,268	68,230,997
Nonmetropolitan Counties	40.1	1,912	23,767,324
Suburban Areas [1]	33.9	7,503	124,099,819

1 Suburban areas include law enforcement agencies in cities with less than 50,000 inhabitants and county law enforcement agencies that are within a Metropolitan Statistical Area. Suburban areas exclude all metropolitan agencies associated with a principal city. The agencies associated with suburban areas also appear in other groups within this table.

Table 76. Full-Time State Law Enforcement Employees, by Selected State, 2012

(Number)

State/agency	Law enforcement employees	Officers		Civilians	
		Male	Female	Male	Female
Alabama [1]					
Other state agencies	4	3	0	0	1
Alaska					
State Troopers	637	382	17	101	137
Arizona					
Department of Public Safety	1,801	1,011	49	280	461
Arkansas [1]					
Other state agencies	36	29	0	2	5
California					
Highway Patrol	10,885	6,853	565	1,545	1,922
Other state agencies[2]	1,269	924	215	37	93
Colorado					
State Patrol	1,108	699	48	156	205
Other state agencies	309	48	5	110	146
Connecticut					
State Police	1,591	1,004	84	223	280
Other state agencies	37	27	1	7	2
Delaware					
State Police	906	586	73	105	142
Other state agencies	667	283	106	61	217
Florida					
Highway Patrol	2,237	1,514	197	181	345
Other state agencies	2,860	1,194	161	502	1,003
Georgia [1]					
Other state agencies	1,129	336	90	212	491
Idaho					
State Police	451	240	9	52	150
Illinois					
State Police	2,985	1,597	181	484	723
Other state agencies	350	217	18	69	46
Indiana					
State Police	1,785	1,235	67	172	311
Other state agencies	100	76	16	0	8
Iowa					
Department of Public Safety	914	575	40	142	157
Kansas					
Highway Patrol	783	488	18	111	166
Other state agencies	523	294	16	78	135
Kentucky					
State Police	1,797	1,033	35	347	382
Other state agencies	81	48	4	8	21
Louisiana					
State Police	1,630	1,066	58	141	365
Other state agencies	3	2	0	0	1
Maine					
State Police	438	285	25	55	73
Other state agencies[2]	49	21	1	20	7

Table 76. Full-Time State Law Enforcement Employees, by Selected State, 2012— continued

(Number)

State/agency	Law enforcement employees	Officers		Civilians	
		Male	Female	Male	Female
Maryland					
State Police	2,160	1,378	98	366	318
Other state agencies	1,001	885	137	301	308
Massachusetts					
State Police	2,680	2,041	151	188	300
Other state agencies[1]	260	216	33	5	6
Michigan					
State Police	2,395	1,426	174	334	461
Minnesota					
State Patrol	734	473	56	103	102
Other state agencies	57	11	0	38	8
Mississippi [1]					
Other state agencies	73	56	2	2	13
Missouri					
State Highway Patrol	2,223	1,077	57	486	603
Other state agencies	461	405	34	1	21
Montana					
Highway Patrol	278	213	10	15	40
Other state agencies	24	16	0	2	6
Nebraska					
State Patrol	731	444	27	100	160
Nevada					
Highway Patrol	941	476	54	135	276
New Hampshire					
State Police	521	333	31	42	115
Other state agencies	30	13	5	5	7
New Jersey					
State Police	3,875	2,504	106	587	678
Other state agencies[2]	662	498	51	67	46
Port Authority of New York and New Jersey[3]	1,016	865	91	16	44
New Mexico					
State Police	623	461	22	32	108
New York					
State Police	5,463	4,198	384	359	522
Other state agencies	226	189	20	4	13
North Carolina					
Highway Patrol	2,149	1,575	46	296	232
Other state agencies	744	499	102	48	95
North Dakota					
Highway Patrol	190	137	6	16	31
Ohio [1]					
Other state agencies	418	312	22	28	56
Oklahoma					
Department of Public Safety	1,354	744	15	256	339
Other state agencies	120	51	7	47	15

Table 76. Full-Time State Law Enforcement Employees, by Selected State, 2012— continued

(Number)

State/agency	Law enforcement employees	Officers		Civilians	
		Male	Female	Male	Female
Oregon					
State Police	745	563	43	48	91
Other state agencies	56	38	8	0	10
Pennsylvania					
State Police	6,227	4,168	207	928	924
Other state agencies	272	228	10	17	17
Rhode Island					
State Police	273	206	21	28	18
Other state agencies	83	63	4	10	6
South Carolina					
Department of Public Safety	1,382	970	44	127	241
Other state agencies[2]	956	548	127	107	174
South Dakota					
Highway Patrol	238	154	3	53	28
Other state agencies	156	40	4	44	68
Tennessee					
Department of Safety	1,594	764	33	235	562
Other state agencies	1,044	613	131	82	218
Utah					
Highway Patrol	531	394	18	29	90
Other state agencies	132	120	9	1	2
Vermont					
State Police	520	326	53	33	108
Other state agencies	164	84	7	36	37
Virginia					
State Police	2,689	1,860	110	229	490
Other state agencies	739	480	60	78	121
Washington					
State Patrol	2,209	966	83	599	561
West Virginia					
State Police	1,043	652	20	140	231
Other state agencies	212	167	2	16	27
Wisconsin					
State Patrol	612	413	47	68	84
Other state agencies	557	367	58	112	20
Wyoming					
Highway Patrol	358	193	9	61	95

Note: Caution should be used when comparing data from one state to another. The responsibilities of the various state police, highway patrol, and department of public safety agencies range from full law enforcement duties to traffic patrol only, which can affect the data for the level of employment for agencies as well as the ratio of sworn officers to civilians employed. Any valid comparison must take these factors and the other identified variables affecting crime into consideration. 1 Police Employee data were not received from the State Police/Highway Patrol/Department of Public Safety for the state. 2 The total employee count includes employees from agencies that are not represented in other law enforcement employee tables. 3 Data reported are the number of law enforcement employees for the state of New Jersey.

Table 77. Full-Time Law Enforcement Employees, by State, 2012

(Number)

State	Law enforcement employees	Officers		Civilians		Agencies	Population, 2012, estimated
		Male	Female	Male	Female		
Alabama	12,745	7,951	682	1,574	2,538	279	3,793,835
Alaska	1,968	1,177	106	237	448	37	729,244
Arizona	22,999	11,625	1,389	4,556	5,429	124	6,553,255
Arkansas	[illegible]	5,002	504	1,309	2,003	279	2,948,787
California	117,268	66,892	10,181	14,694	25,501	462	32,610,316
Colorado	17,270	10,125	1,441	1,944	3,760	238	5,174,997
Connecticut	10,271	7,667	807	745	1,052	104	3,590,347
Delaware	3,151	1,987	315	315	534	55	916,825
District of Columbia	4,976	3,355	960	282	379	2	632,323
Florida	65,683	34,959	5,960	9,261	15,503	333	16,672,179
Georgia	34,769	21,837	4,230	2,775	5,927	493	9,416,852
Hawaii	3,720	2,657	285	238	540	4	1,392,313
Idaho	4,265	2,579	158	316	1,212	106	1,573,210
Illinois	45,505	26,945	4,948	7,007	6,605	581	11,569,093
Indiana	12,032	8,133	670	1,405	1,824	161	4,502,197
Iowa	7,375	4,353	342	1,086	1,594	229	2,731,249
Kansas	9,675	5,869	586	1,261	1,959	313	2,404,632
Kentucky	9,728	7,111	512	819	1,286	336	4,059,632
Louisiana	19,364	12,197	2,881	1,144	3,142	159	3,792,686
Maine	2,826	2,108	147	219	352	136	1,328,674
Maryland	17,956	12,080	1,937	1,389	2,550	128	5,711,397
Massachusetts	19,282	14,721	1,325	1,311	1,925	329	6,450,418
Michigan	23,165	14,924	2,199	2,816	3,226	588	9,855,046
Minnesota	13,476	7,754	1,047	1,971	2,704	319	5,292,552
Mississippi	5,662	3,224	377	887	1,174	95	1,560,540
Missouri	19,487	12,469	1,381	2,270	3,367	532	5,715,097
Montana	2,405	1,592	113	249	451	99	873,898
Nebraska	4,943	3,155	380	420	988	160	1,812,244
Nevada	9,447	5,139	539	1,345	2,424	53	2,758,931
New Hampshire	3,436	2,413	216	225	582	156	1,204,043
New Jersey	37,881	26,339	2,609	3,372	5,561	541	8,566,377
New Mexico	6,023	3,919	442	576	1,086	106	1,966,211
New York	79,358	51,100	8,105	7,134	13,019	409	18,350,544
North Carolina	33,353	20,524	2,614	4,814	5,401	517	9,749,062
North Dakota	1,968	1,294	150	174	350	104	698,507
Ohio	19,288	13,218	1,631	1,558	2,881	373	7,466,543
Oklahoma	12,445	7,362	591	2,061	2,431	346	3,814,820
Oregon	9,918	5,473	584	1,706	2,155	219	3,862,840
Pennsylvania	30,203	22,824	2,596	1,848	2,935	1,003	9,815,035
Rhode Island	3,045	2,283	175	254	333	49	1,050,292
South Carolina	15,135	9,593	1,241	1,673	2,628	320	4,594,608
South Dakota	2,820	1,490	105	543	682	143	830,046
Tennessee	26,268	14,842	1,552	4,615	5,259	445	6,445,821
Texas	72,877	40,996	5,311	12,260	14,310	984	23,778,955
Utah	7,042	4,576	354	888	1,224	137	2,855,287
Vermont	1,677	1,097	136	144	300	72	379,426
Virginia	23,625	16,405	2,204	1,335	3,681	281	8,183,013
Washington	14,212	9,192	936	1,548	2,536	256	6,880,100
West Virginia	4,475	3,397	131	359	588	355	1,843,496
Wisconsin	18,638	10,949	1,691	2,491	3,507	388	5,687,485
Wyoming	2,074	1,346	114	161	453	68	574,786

Table 78. Full-Time Law Enforcement Employees, by Selected State and City, 2012

(Number)

State/city	Population	Total law enforcement employees	Total officers	Total civilians
ALABAMA				
Abbeville	2,701	17	11	6
Adamsville	4,544	32	19	13
Addison	762	3	3	0
Alabaster	30,498	74	61	13
Albertville	21,262	64	38	26
Alexander City	14,947	66	48	18
Aliceville	2,498	9	8	1
Andalusia	9,058	40	30	10
Anderson	283	1	1	0
Anniston	23,217	128	91	37
Arab	8,089	37	26	11
Ardmore	1,200	11	7	4
Argo	4,091	5	5	0
Ariton	768	1	1	0
Arley	359	3	2	1
Ashford	2,158	9	5	4
Ashland	2,047	14	9	5
Ashville	2,223	5	5	0
Athens	22,002	57	46	11
Atmore	10,243	32	27	5
Auburn	53,637	112	106	6
Baker Hill	280	3	3	0
Bay Minette	8,083	29	21	8
Bayou La Batre	2,570	20	15	5
Bear Creek	1,075	1	1	0
Beatrice	302	1	1	0
Berry	1,154	3	3	0
Bessemer	27,588	133	103	30
Birmingham	213,258	1,163	877	286
Boaz	9,597	32	22	10
Brantley	813	4	4	0
Brent	4,971	5	5	0
Brewton	5,434	32	24	8
Bridgeport	2,430	10	6	4
Brookside	1,370	4	4	0
Brundidge	2,086	13	9	4
Butler	1,903	6	6	0
Calera	11,676	33	27	6
Carrollton	1,024	4	4	0
Centre	3,506	11	10	1
Centreville	2,791	6	6	0
Chatom	1,294	6	6	0
Cherokee	1,053	2	2	0
Chickasaw	6,135	25	21	4
Childersburg	5,200	15	13	2
Citronelle	3,924	10	7	3
Clanton	8,660	28	26	2
Clayhatchee	592	1	1	0
Cleveland	1,309	1	1	0
Clio	1,406	3	3	0
Collinsville	1,993	9	4	5
Columbiana	4,217	12	8	4
Coosada	1,230	3	3	0
Cordova	2,105	7	5	2
Cottonwood	1,295	3	3	0
Courtland	612	6	6	0
Creola	1,935	11	7	4
Crossville	1,871	4	4	0
Cuba	348	1	1	0
Cullman	14,846	67	48	19
Dadeville	3,246	15	14	1

Table 78. Full-Time Law Enforcement Employees, by Selected State and City, 2012— continued

(Number)

State/city	Population	Total law enforcement employees	Total officers	Total civilians
Daleville	5,320	22	16	6
Daphne	21,674	76	46	30
Dauphin Island	1,244	17	10	7
Decatur	55,951	147	126	21
Demopolis	7,319	32	29	3
Dothan	65,811	224	150	74
Double Springs	1,088	6	6	0
Douglas	748	4	4	0
Dozier	331	1	1	0
East Brewton	2,490	7	5	2
Eclectic	1,006	9	5	4
Elberta	1,505	6	5	1
Enterprise	26,690	69	50	19
Eufaula	13,200	50	35	15
Eutaw	2,948	9	8	1
Evergreen	3,963	19	17	2
Fairfield	11,171	44	30	14
Fairhope	15,400	58	34	24
Falkville	1,285	5	5	0
Fayette	4,641	11	11	0
Flomaton	1,447	11	6	5
Florala	1,990	8	8	0
Florence	39,508	134	107	27
Foley	14,688	86	60	26
Fort Deposit	1,350	5	5	0
Fort Payne	14,079	33	28	5
Fultondale	8,420	34	26	8
Gardendale	13,960	38	29	9
Geneva	4,473	12	11	1
Georgiana	1,746	14	8	6
Geraldine	900	3	3	0
Glencoe	5,185	8	6	2
Goodwater	1,482	5	2	3
Gordo	1,758	4	4	0
Greenville	8,174	36	29	7
Grove Hill	1,578	5	5	0
Guin	2,387	5	5	0
Gulf Shores	9,788	53	40	13
Guntersville	8,236	46	33	13
Gurley	805	6	6	0
Haleyville	4,193	17	13	4
Hamilton	6,918	14	13	1
Hammondville	490	1	1	0
Hanceville	2,996	15	11	4
Harpersville	1,645	12	9	3
Hartford	2,637	13	8	5
Hartselle	14,324	37	29	8
Hayneville	936	2	2	0
Headland	4,532	15	11	4
Heflin	3,497	13	12	1
Helena	16,874	24	21	3
Henagar	2,355	8	4	4
Hokes Bluff	4,307	7	7	0
Hollywood	1,005	2	2	0
Hoover	82,012	223	158	65
Hueytown	16,183	43	35	8
Huntsville	180,972	492	395	97
Ider	726	5	4	1
Irondale	12,408	38	31	7
Jackson	5,253	27	21	6
Jacksons Gap	832	1	1	0
Jacksonville	12,608	33	26	7

Table 78. Full-Time Law Enforcement Employees, by Selected State and City, 2012— continued

(Number)

State/city	Population	Total law enforcement employees	Total officers	Total civilians
Jemison	2,597	10	10	0
Killen	1,113	5	5	0
Kimberly	2,724	7	6	1
Kinston	543	1	1	0
Lafayette	3,017	15	14	1
Lake View	1,952	4	3	1
Lanett	6,499	30	27	3
Leeds	11,830	33	27	6
Leighton	733	3	3	0
Level Plains	2,095	5	5	0
Lincoln	6,296	18	17	1
Linden	2,133	7	7	0
Lineville	2,407	12	8	4
Lipscomb	2,221	8	5	3
Littleville	1,016	9	5	4
Livingston	3,502	10	7	3
Louisville	521	4	4	0
Loxley	1,640	19	14	5
Luverne	2,813	14	10	4
Madison	43,145	108	78	30
Maplesville	711	4	4	0
Margaret	4,449	4	4	0
Marion	3,704	6	5	1
Midfield	5,391	16	12	4
Midland City	2,355	7	4	3
Millbrook	14,710	42	32	10
Millport	1,054	1	1	0
Millry	549	4	3	1
Mobile	251,869	723	561	162
Montevallo	6,353	16	12	4
Montgomery	206,754	676	530	146
Moody	11,782	20	19	1
Morris	1,868	8	6	2
Moulton	3,488	11	11	0
Moundville	2,439	8	7	1
Mountain Brook	20,511	62	49	13
Muscle Shoals	13,209	43	34	9
Napier Field	356	2	2	0
New Brockton	1,152	4	2	2
New Hope	2,824	6	6	0
New Site	777	1	1	0
Newton	1,518	4	3	1
Newville	542	1	1	0
Northport	23,442	80	61	19
Notasulga	970	7	4	3
Odenville	3,602	9	8	1
Ohatchee	1,176	5	5	0
Oneonta	6,599	21	20	1
Opelika	26,604	103	82	21
Opp	6,691	27	21	6
Orange Beach	5,467	48	34	14
Owens Crossroads	1,528	6	6	0
Oxford	21,451	56	48	8
Ozark	14,979	36	30	6
Parrish	987	8	4	4
Pelham	21,455	83	67	16
Pell City	12,756	34	31	3
Phenix City	32,980	105	80	25
Phil Campbell	1,154	2	2	0
Pickensville	611	2	1	1
Piedmont	4,901	14	10	4
Pinckard	650	1	1	0

Table 78. Full-Time Law Enforcement Employees, by Selected State and City, 2012— continued

(Number)

State/city	Population	Total law enforcement employees	Total officers	Total civilians
Pine Hill	980	5	5	0
Pleasant Grove	10,159	24	19	5
Powell	960	2	2	0
Prattville	34,123	85	76	9
Priceville	2,671	5	5	0
Ragland	1,647	3	3	0
Rainbow City	9,648	32	21	11
Rainsville	4,972	16	11	5
Ranburne	411	2	2	0
Red Bay	3,173	12	8	4
Reform	1,710	5	5	0
River Falls	529	2	1	1
Riverside	2,219	3	3	0
Roanoke	6,103	28	23	5
Robertsdale	5,301	26	13	13
Rockford	479	2	1	1
Rogersville	1,263	5	5	0
Russellville	9,877	23	19	4
Samson	1,949	6	5	1
Saraland	13,470	45	34	11
Sardis City	1,712	4	4	0
Satsuma	6,198	19	15	4
Scottsboro	14,841	69	46	23
Section	774	2	2	0
Selma	20,856	67	50	17
Sheffield	9,083	35	29	6
Shorter	476	6	3	3
Silverhill	709	4	4	0
Sipsey	439	1	1	0
Skyline	855	4	2	2
Slocomb	1,990	6	6	0
Snead	839	4	4	0
Somerville	727	3	3	0
Southside	8,452	16	10	6
Spanish Fort	6,831	24	20	4
Springville	4,100	10	10	0
Steele	1,048	3	3	0
St. Florian	415	3	2	1
Sulligent	1,936	6	6	0
Sumiton	2,532	14	8	6
Summerdale	866	7	6	1
Sylacauga	12,810	40	38	2
Sylvania	1,846	4	4	0
Talladega	15,751	41	38	3
Tallassee	4,842	26	20	6
Tarrant	6,428	26	22	4
Taylor	2,386	2	2	0
Thomasville	4,229	18	13	5
Thorsby	1,990	5	5	0
Town Creek	1,105	3	3	0
Triana	498	2	2	0
Trinity	2,105	6	6	0
Troy	18,120	68	49	19
Trussville	20,029	59	45	14
Tuscaloosa	90,903	358	284	74
Tuscumbia	8,464	24	17	7
Tuskegee	9,912	32	20	12
Union Springs	3,999	21	13	8
Valley	9,570	34	24	10
Valley Head	561	3	2	1
Vance	1,536	3	3	0
Vernon	2,010	7	7	0

Table 78. Full-Time Law Enforcement Employees, by Selected State and City, 2012— continued

(Number)

State/city	Population	Total law enforcement employees	Total officers	Total civilians
Vestavia Hills	34,197	70	68	2
Weaver	3,053	11	8	3
Webb	1,437	2	2	0
Wedowee	827	7	7	0
West Blocton	1,246	2	2	0
Wetumpka	6,559	37	28	9
Winfield	4,740	11	10	1
Woodstock	1,435	3	3	0
ALASKA				
Anchorage	296,955	535	390	145
Bethel	6,187	21	13	8
Bristol Bay Borough	1,015	9	4	5
Cordova	2,278	11	5	6
Craig	1,222	10	5	5
Dillingham	2,370	21	8	13
Fairbanks	32,089	47	44	3
Haines	1,743	10	5	5
Homer	5,091	20	12	8
Hoonah	773	6	3	3
Juneau	31,825	84	47	37
Kenai	7,225	27	18	9
Ketchikan	8,192	33	23	10
Klawock	768	3	3	0
Kodiak	6,238	39	18	21
Kotzebue	3,257	16	7	9
Nome	3,661	17	11	6
North Pole	2,154	15	14	1
North Slope Borough	9,596	63	36	27
Palmer	6,041	29	16	13
Petersburg	3,000	15	9	6
Sand Point	993	5	4	1
Seldovia	259	1	1	0
Seward	2,740	24	10	14
Sitka	9,037	31	17	14
Skagway	936	8	4	4
Soldotna	4,236	15	13	2
St. Paul	487	6	3	3
Togiak	831	2	2	0
Unalaska	4,453	23	13	10
Valdez	4,046	17	9	8
Wasilla	7,969	45	22	23
Whittier	224	3	3	0
Wrangell	2,411	14	6	8
ARIZONA				
Apache Junction	36,347	85	54	31
Avondale	77,317	157	107	50
Benson	5,177	25	15	10
Bisbee	5,654	19	14	5
Buckeye	51,596	92	68	24
Bullhead City	40,100	115	75	40
Camp Verde	11,027	29	18	11
Casa Grande	49,259	106	78	28
Chandler	239,466	473	319	154
Chino Valley	10,970	28	23	5
Clarkdale	4,155	5	5	0
Clifton	3,358	11	6	5
Colorado City	4,889	12	7	5
Coolidge	11,992	38	29	9
Cottonwood	11,424	46	31	15
Douglas	17,624	44	30	14
Eagar	4,954	10	8	2
El Mirage	32,247	49	41	8

Table 78. Full-Time Law Enforcement Employees, by Selected State and City, 2012— continued

(Number)

State/city	Population	Total law enforcement employees	Total officers	Total civilians
Eloy	16,866	39	27	12
Flagstaff	66,802	158	112	46
Florence	25,897	42	27	15
Fredonia	1,333	4	4	0
Gilbert	211,404	326	220	106
Glendale	229,931	542	401	141
Globe	7,639	31	25	6
Goodyear	66,199	129	95	34
Hayden	1,029	6	5	1
Holbrook	5,125	16	13	3
Huachuca City	1,879	10	5	5
Jerome	450	5	5	0
Kearny	1,978	8	6	2
Kingman	28,465	78	53	25
Lake Havasu City	53,271	115	84	31
Mammoth	1,446	8	5	3
Marana	35,456	104	78	26
Maricopa	44,098	56	49	7
Mesa	445,256	1,136	750	386
Miami	1,863	8	5	3
Nogales	21,132	76	59	17
Oro Valley	41,592	126	97	29
Page	7,350	31	20	11
Paradise Valley	13,001	33	25	8
Parker	3,127	13	11	2
Payson	15,518	40	26	14
Peoria	156,246	273	183	90
Phoenix	1,466,097	4,169	3,079	1,090
Pima	2,421	5	5	0
Pinetop-Lakeside	4,343	25	16	9
Prescott	40,407	85	67	18
Prescott Valley	39,372	73	60	13
Quartzsite	3,729	10	9	1
Safford	9,701	24	20	4
Sahuarita	25,617	47	40	7
San Luis	25,866	47	31	16
Scottsdale	220,462	658	406	252
Sedona	10,173	35	25	10
Show Low	10,811	43	31	12
Sierra Vista	44,509	91	62	29
Snowflake-Taylor	9,839	22	14	8
Somerton	14,489	30	22	8
South Tucson	5,732	18	17	1
Springerville	1,989	9	7	2
St. Johns	3,529	12	9	3
Superior	2,877	12	9	3
Surprise	119,181	177	123	54
Tempe	164,008	475	336	139
Thatcher	4,934	12	11	1
Tolleson	6,638	40	30	10
Tombstone	1,400	10	5	5
Tucson	527,479	1,240	949	291
Wellton	2,923	5	5	0
Wickenburg	6,453	22	15	7
Willcox	3,810	18	10	8
Williams	3,066	16	9	7
Winslow	9,792	35	26	9
Yuma	94,381	236	160	76
ARKANSAS				
Alma	5,460	19	11	8
Altheimer	991	2	2	0
Arkadelphia	10,795	27	22	5

Table 78. Full-Time Law Enforcement Employees, by Selected State and City, 2012— continued

(Number)

State/city	Population	Total law enforcement employees	Total officers	Total civilians
Arkansas City	369	1	1	0
Ashdown	4,759	13	11	2
Ash Flat	1,090	3	3	0
Atkins	3,039	6	5	1
Augusta	2,216	6	6	0
Austin	2,053	3	3	0
Bald Knob	2,919	11	7	4
Barling	4,684	10	10	0
Bay	1,815	4	3	1
Bearden	973	2	2	0
Beebe	7,370	18	12	6
Bella Vista	26,661	34	25	9
Benton	30,913	75	55	20
Bentonville	35,568	83	58	25
Berryville	5,397	13	11	2
Blytheville	15,738	59	38	21
Bono	2,147	4	4	0
Booneville	4,020	12	8	4
Bradford	765	3	3	0
Brinkley	3,212	17	13	4
Bryant	16,814	48	38	10
Bull Shoals	1,965	5	4	1
Cabot	23,956	50	37	13
Caddo Valley	640	4	4	0
Camden	12,275	38	22	16
Cammack Village	774	5	4	1
Caraway	1,289	3	3	0
Carlisle	2,231	9	5	4
Cave City	1,918	3	3	0
Cave Springs	1,742	4	4	0
Centerton	9,587	12	11	1
Charleston	2,513	4	4	0
Cherokee Village	4,706	9	8	1
Clarendon	1,677	4	4	0
Clarksville	9,247	22	18	4
Clinton	2,622	9	8	1
Conway	59,354	142	109	33
Corning	3,403	12	8	4
Cotter	977	3	2	1
Crossett	5,549	23	15	8
Danville	2,427	6	5	1
Dardanelle	4,781	14	10	4
Decatur	1,712	6	6	0
De Queen	6,644	16	13	3
Dermott	2,911	13	7	6
Des Arc	1,730	4	4	0
De Valls Bluff	624	1	1	0
De Witt	3,317	14	8	6
Diamond City	788	1	1	0
Diaz	1,328	2	2	0
Dierks	1,142	3	3	0
Dover	1,388	4	4	0
Dumas	4,742	22	12	10
Earle	2,432	7	5	2
El Dorado	19,027	64	48	16
Elkins	2,668	6	6	0
England	2,846	12	7	5
Etowah	354	1	1	0
Eudora	2,286	8	4	4
Eureka Springs	2,089	16	10	6
Fairfield Bay	2,356	16	7	9
Farmington	6,019	11	10	1

Table 78. Full-Time Law Enforcement Employees, by Selected State and City, 2012— continued

(Number)

State/city	Population	Total law enforcement employees	Total officers	Total civilians
Fayetteville	74,137	162	112	50
Flippin	1,365	6	6	0
Fordyce	4,333	12	8	4
Forrest City	15,487	45	33	12
Fort Smith	86,861	216	166	50
Gassville	2,094	4	4	0
Gentry	3,182	10	8	2
Glenwood	2,245	3	3	0
Gosnell	3,575	8	8	0
Gould	843	1	1	0
Gravette	2,343	9	8	1
Greenbrier	4,742	14	9	5
Green Forest	2,782	10	7	3
Greenland	1,269	4	4	0
Greenwood	9,020	22	20	2
Greers Ferry	898	4	3	1
Gurdon	2,229	4	3	1
Guy	713	3	2	1
Hamburg	2,879	6	5	1
Hampton	1,334	3	3	0
Hardy	778	3	3	0
Harrisburg	2,305	4	4	0
Harrison	13,041	41	29	12
Hazen	1,479	7	5	2
Heber Springs	7,219	24	14	10
Helena-West Helena	12,375	45	32	13
Hermitage	836	2	2	0
Highfill	587	2	2	0
Highland	1,053	3	3	0
Hope	10,171	34	24	10
Horseshoe Bend	2,201	5	5	0
Hot Springs	35,459	133	103	30
Hoxie	2,801	5	4	1
Huntsville	2,364	8	7	1
Jacksonville	28,579	91	76	15
Jonesboro	67,772	155	144	11
Judsonia	2,034	4	3	1
Kensett	1,660	4	4	0
Lake City	2,098	4	4	0
Lakeview	747	2	2	0
Lake Village	2,594	18	9	9
Leachville	2,008	4	4	0
Lepanto	1,907	8	4	4
Lewisville	1,290	2	2	0
Little Flock	2,605	6	5	1
Little Rock	194,988	620	505	115
Lonoke	4,277	16	11	5
Lowell	7,382	23	15	8
Luxora	1,187	2	2	0
Magnolia	11,665	26	18	8
Malvern	10,396	21	18	3
Mansfield	1,148	3	3	0
Marianna	4,146	18	10	8
Marion	12,438	27	24	3
Marked Tree	2,585	12	8	4
Marmaduke	1,119	4	4	0
Marvell	1,195	8	4	4
Maumelle	17,293	38	29	9
Mayflower	2,251	8	6	2
McCrory	1,742	5	5	0
McGehee	4,251	25	7	18
McRae	687	2	2	0

Table 78. Full-Time Law Enforcement Employees, by Selected State and City, 2012— continued

(Number)

State/city	Population	Total law enforcement employees	Total officers	Total civilians
Mena	5,780	14	13	1
Mineral Springs	1,217	3	3	0
Monette	1,512	3	3	0
Monticello	9,539	27	21	6
Morrilton	6,818	33	22	11
Mountain Home	12,542	34	26	8
Mountain View	2,769	9	8	1
Murfreesboro	1,653	3	3	0
Nashville	4,662	17	16	1
Newport	7,939	20	14	6
North Little Rock	62,775	221	186	35
Ola	1,291	3	3	0
Osceola	7,816	38	23	15
Ozark	3,712	11	9	2
Pangburn	606	2	2	0
Paragould	26,311	51	41	10
Paris	3,559	14	9	5
Parkin	1,113	2	2	0
Pea Ridge	4,830	11	11	0
Perryville	1,471	4	4	0
Piggott	3,878	9	8	1
Pine Bluff	49,454	173	149	24
Plainview	613	1	1	0
Plummerville	832	3	3	0
Pocahontas	6,658	14	13	1
Pottsville	2,859	5	5	0
Prescott	3,321	11	10	1
Quitman	768	4	4	0
Ravenden	474	3	2	1
Redfield	1,307	5	4	1
Rison	1,354	3	3	0
Rockport	761	6	4	2
Rogers	56,387	131	93	38
Rose Bud	486	2	2	0
Russellville	28,131	62	56	6
Salem	1,647	2	2	0
Searcy	23,031	64	46	18
Sheridan	4,638	28	14	14
Sherwood	29,746	88	63	25
Siloam Springs	15,153	44	30	14
Smackover	1,879	5	4	1
Springdale	70,325	162	119	43
Stamps	1,706	3	3	0
Star City	2,291	6	5	1
Stuttgart	9,397	26	19	7
Swifton	804	2	2	0
Texarkana	30,145	111	86	25
Trumann	7,298	24	16	8
Tuckerman	1,876	4	3	1
Van Buren	22,963	52	41	11
Vilonia	3,844	8	8	0
Waldron	3,645	9	8	1
Walnut Ridge	4,927	9	8	1
Ward	4,098	9	8	1
Warren	6,048	19	13	6
West Fork	2,335	6	5	1
West Memphis	26,444	94	74	20
White Hall	5,568	16	14	2
Wynne	8,430	19	17	2
CALIFORNIA				
Alameda	74,680	130	84	46
Albany	18,757	34	25	9

Table 78. Full-Time Law Enforcement Employees, by Selected State and City, 2012— continued

(Number)

State/city	Population	Total law enforcement employees	Total officers	Total civilians
Alhambra	84,066	128	84	44
Alturas	2,860	6	5	1
Anaheim	340,218	527	374	153
Anderson	10,049	26	16	10
Antioch	103,575	124	96	28
Arcadia	57,027	93	63	30
Arcata	17,434	37	27	10
Arroyo Grande	17,455	32	24	8
Arvin	19,531	27	18	9
Atascadero	28,643	37	27	10
Atherton	6,995	24	18	6
Atwater	28,499	41	31	10
Auburn	13,487	28	21	7
Avenal	15,687	17	15	2
Azusa	46,906	87	62	25
Bakersfield	351,568	486	347	139
Baldwin Park	76,276	98	70	28
Banning	29,951	42	31	11
Barstow	22,905	50	37	13
Bear Valley	5,233	21	8	13
Beaumont	37,311	75	56	19
Bell	35,894	40	28	12
Bell Gardens	42,567	73	51	22
Belmont	26,139	42	31	11
Belvedere	2,092	9	8	1
Benicia	27,314	51	34	17
Berkeley	113,903	261	165	96
Beverly Hills	34,510	162	112	50
Bishop	3,925	17	12	5
Blythe	21,062	31	22	9
Brawley	25,246	49	36	13
Brea	39,744	131	94	37
Brentwood	52,086	77	60	17
Brisbane	4,332	14	11	3
Broadmoor	4,225	9	9	0
Buena Park	81,477	128	83	45
Burbank	104,555	239	156	83
Burlingame	29,145	49	33	16
Calexico	39,025	57	38	19
California City	14,286	21	14	7
Calipatria	7,796	4	4	0
Calistoga	5,216	14	10	4
Campbell	39,812	62	40	22
Capitola	10,035	28	20	8
Carlsbad	106,566	153	107	46
Carmel	3,766	19	12	7
Cathedral City	51,802	90	53	37
Ceres	45,951	67	51	16
Chico	87,200	149	95	54
Chino	78,900	153	102	51
Chowchilla	18,940	19	14	5
Chula Vista	246,783	309	219	90
Citrus Heights	84,280	130	85	45
City of Angels	3,881	7	6	1
Claremont	35,337	58	35	23
Clayton	11,025	13	11	2
Clearlake	15,429	28	20	8
Cloverdale	8,719	22	14	8
Clovis	96,755	146	99	47
Coalinga	13,537	30	19	11
Colma	1,813	23	17	6
Colton	52,767	69	47	22

Table 78. Full-Time Law Enforcement Employees, by Selected State and City, 2012— continued

(Number)

State/city	Population	Total law enforcement employees	Total officers	Total civilians
Colusa	6,041	9	8	1
Concord	123,502	196	149	47
Corcoran	25,105	31	19	12
Corning	7,753	22	13	9
Corona	154,165	227	159	68
Coronado	24,987	62	43	19
Costa Mesa	111,253	209	134	75
Cotati	7,350	15	10	5
Covina	48,358	83	55	28
Crescent City	7,733	13	12	1
Culver City	39,340	148	105	43
Cypress	48,364	66	53	13
Daly City	102,312	149	109	40
Davis	66,393	90	59	31
Delano	53,665	73	45	28
Del Rey Oaks	1,643	6	6	0
Desert Hot Springs	26,243	36	31	5
Dinuba	21,705	45	35	10
Dixon	18,567	28	23	5
Dos Palos	5,008	7	7	0
Downey	113,086	164	114	50
East Palo Alto	28,486	43	35	8
El Cajon	100,647	183	118	65
El Centro	43,099	68	45	23
El Cerrito	23,826	52	43	9
Elk Grove	154,814	202	128	74
El Monte	114,809	168	121	47
El Segundo	16,850	86	61	25
Emeryville	10,199	51	35	16
Escalon	7,216	12	11	1
Escondido	145,603	208	157	51
Etna	746	1	1	0
Eureka	27,511	77	47	30
Exeter	10,455	16	15	1
Fairfax	7,528	16	11	5
Fairfield	106,559	176	114	62
Farmersville	10,712	16	14	2
Ferndale	1,387	4	4	0
Firebaugh	7,638	15	11	4
Folsom	73,052	104	77	27
Fontana	198,374	268	181	87
Fort Bragg	7,359	19	15	4
Fortuna	12,066	26	17	9
Foster City	30,926	49	36	13
Fountain Valley	55,963	76	56	20
Fowler	5,635	12	10	2
Fremont	216,606	265	166	99
Fresno	500,480	952	751	201
Fullerton	136,750	211	142	69
Galt	23,925	45	34	11
Gardena	59,521	118	93	25
Garden Grove	172,892	221	156	65
Gilroy	49,395	85	58	27
Glendale	193,973	353	237	116
Glendora	50,662	93	51	42
Gonzales	8,283	14	11	3
Grass Valley	13,011	29	22	7
Greenfield	16,522	20	16	4
Gridley	6,661	22	16	6
Grover Beach	13,311	27	17	10
Guadalupe	7,163	14	12	2
Gustine	5,585	10	8	2

Table 78. Full-Time Law Enforcement Employees, by Selected State and City, 2012— continued

(Number)

State/city	Population	Total law enforcement employees	Total officers	Total civilians
Hanford	54,601	76	52	24
Hawthorne	85,284	131	94	37
Hayward	145,881	294	186	108
Healdsburg	11,386	25	16	9
Hemet	79,582	82	60	22
Hercules	24,343	26	23	3
Hermosa Beach	19,735	58	34	24
Hillsborough	10,952	29	22	7
Hollister	35,339	32	24	8
Huntington Beach	192,226	322	204	118
Huntington Park	58,797	110	66	44
Huron	6,833	12	8	4
Imperial	14,931	18	16	2
Indio	76,930	103	65	38
Inglewood	110,962	264	183	81
Ione	8,011	7	6	1
Irvine	214,872	278	198	80
Irwindale	1,439	35	26	9
Isleton	813	3	2	1
Jackson	4,706	10	9	1
Kensington	5,137	10	10	0
Kerman	13,703	21	18	3
King City	13,025	20	17	3
Kingsburg	11,516	20	14	6
Laguna Beach	22,990	85	47	38
La Habra	60,947	105	68	37
Lakeport	4,809	11	9	2
Lake Shastina	2,437	5	4	1
La Mesa	57,736	95	66	29
La Palma	15,751	32	24	8
La Verne	31,428	59	40	19
Lemoore	24,819	36	29	7
Lincoln	43,322	31	22	9
Lindsay	11,906	21	17	4
Livermore	81,920	130	83	47
Livingston	13,212	27	17	10
Lodi	62,864	104	69	35
Lompoc	42,933	70	48	22
Long Beach	467,691	1,193	847	346
Los Alamitos	11,584	26	22	4
Los Altos	29,317	47	30	17
Los Angeles	3,837,207	12,724	9,860	2,864
Los Banos	36,395	57	38	19
Los Gatos	29,759	59	40	19
Madera	62,138	84	59	25
Mammoth Lakes	8,331	21	18	3
Manhattan Beach	35,548	94	60	34
Manteca	67,885	83	59	24
Marina	19,950	38	29	9
Martinez	36,245	49	36	13
Marysville	12,214	31	20	11
McFarland	12,856	19	11	8
Mendota	11,143	12	10	2
Menlo Park	32,402	70	47	23
Merced	79,886	117	85	32
Millbrae	21,785	22	18	4
Mill Valley	14,066	24	20	4
Milpitas	67,575	105	82	23
Modesto	203,530	297	217	80
Monrovia	37,020	73	46	27
Montclair	37,095	71	49	22
Montebello	63,235	105	69	36

Table 78. Full-Time Law Enforcement Employees, by Selected State and City, 2012— continued

(Number)

State/city	Population	Total law enforcement employees	Total officers	Total civilians
Monterey	28,137	59	44	15
Monterey Park	60,978	95	68	27
Moraga	16,204	11	10	1
Morgan Hill	38,327	50	34	16
Morro Bay	10,354	23	18	5
Mountain View	74,937	137	93	44
Mount Shasta	3,434	11	8	3
Murrieta	104,682	127	86	41
Napa	77,819	109	70	39
National City	59,271	108	80	28
Nevada City	3,104	13	12	1
Newark	43,073	74	54	20
Newman	10,344	14	11	3
Newport Beach	86,187	202	131	71
Novato	52,514	69	54	15
Oakdale	20,918	31	21	10
Oakland	395,317	913	647	266
Oceanside	169,050	284	203	81
Ontario	165,851	320	224	96
Orange	138,020	226	158	68
Orland	7,377	12	10	2
Oroville	15,729	37	22	15
Oxnard	200,225	382	235	147
Pacifica	37,672	39	35	4
Pacific Grove	15,218	29	20	9
Palm Springs	45,076	123	85	38
Palo Alto	65,160	141	83	58
Palos Verdes Estates	13,596	36	25	11
Paradise	26,526	36	24	12
Parlier	14,664	20	16	4
Pasadena	138,734	339	231	108
Paso Robles	30,143	39	27	12
Petaluma	58,622	83	62	21
Piedmont	10,792	27	19	8
Pinole	18,606	39	27	12
Pismo Beach	7,745	33	22	11
Pittsburg	64,008	93	71	22
Placentia	51,127	62	44	18
Placerville	10,511	26	17	9
Pleasant Hill	33,542	61	44	17
Pleasanton	71,111	111	80	31
Pomona	150,810	249	148	101
Porterville	54,802	86	59	27
Port Hueneme	21,978	32	24	8
Red Bluff	14,241	31	22	9
Redding	90,917	130	98	32
Redlands	69,555	111	76	35
Redondo Beach	67,533	147	89	58
Redwood City	77,718	114	87	27
Reedley	24,478	46	31	15
Rialto	100,337	134	98	36
Richmond	104,920	285	191	94
Ridgecrest	27,941	47	32	15
Rio Dell	3,408	5	5	0
Rio Vista	7,447	10	9	1
Ripon	14,465	31	22	9
Riverside	307,443	511	367	144
Rocklin	57,644	74	49	25
Rohnert Park	41,453	73	55	18
Roseville	120,184	180	118	62
Ross	2,443	9	9	0
Sacramento	471,972	947	678	269

Table 78. Full-Time Law Enforcement Employees, by Selected State and City, 2012— continued

(Number)

State/city	Population	Total law enforcement employees	Total officers	Total civilians
Salinas	152,210	195	146	49
San Anselmo	12,481	26	19	7
San Bernardino	212,392	465	296	169
San Bruno	41,597	57	42	15
Sand City	338	10	9	1
San Diego	1,316,919	2,455	1,834	621
San Fernando	23,923	50	32	18
San Francisco	814,701	2,650	2,210	440
San Gabriel	40,185	68	54	14
Sanger	24,555	36	33	3
San Jose	957,062	1,456	1,103	353
San Leandro	85,949	126	91	35
San Luis Obispo	45,649	83	57	26
San Marino	13,302	33	27	6
San Mateo	98,350	136	102	34
San Pablo	29,482	71	52	19
San Rafael	58,391	81	61	20
San Ramon	72,996	71	54	17
Santa Ana	328,343	601	336	265
Santa Barbara	89,449	204	134	70
Santa Clara	117,837	197	131	66
Santa Cruz	60,651	108	87	21
Santa Maria	100,723	147	102	45
Santa Monica	90,791	388	204	184
Santa Paula	29,666	38	28	10
Santa Rosa	169,788	235	164	71
Sausalito	7,144	23	18	5
Scotts Valley	11,716	27	19	8
Seal Beach	24,452	49	31	18
Seaside	33,413	48	39	9
Sebastopol	7,466	20	14	6
Selma	23,492	39	31	8
Shafter	17,188	30	21	9
Sierra Madre	11,045	21	16	5
Signal Hill	11,146	49	36	13
Simi Valley	125,698	161	109	52
Soledad	26,041	19	16	3
Sonora	4,961	15	10	5
South Gate	95,506	117	80	37
South Lake Tahoe	21,655	56	39	17
South Pasadena	25,920	45	33	12
South San Francisco	64,380	108	79	29
Stallion Springs	2,517	3	3	0
St. Helena	5,882	15	11	4
Stockton	295,136	494	321	173
Suisun City	28,441	35	24	11
Sunnyvale	141,728	274	203	71
Susanville	18,158	17	16	1
Sutter Creek	2,530	5	5	0
Taft	9,437	27	16	11
Tehachapi	14,583	16	14	2
Tiburon	9,067	16	13	3
Torrance	147,148	336	215	121
Tracy	83,897	124	83	41
Truckee	16,370	30	26	4
Tulare	59,975	97	70	27
Tulelake	1,022	3	3	0
Turlock	69,355	118	77	41
Tustin	76,428	140	92	48
Twin Cities	21,428	37	31	6
Ukiah	16,264	40	26	14
Union City	70,333	102	76	26

Table 78. Full-Time Law Enforcement Employees, by Selected State and City, 2012— continued

(Number)

State/city	Population	Total law enforcement employees	Total officers	Total civilians
Upland	74,599	103	75	28
Vacaville	93,515	146	90	56
Vallejo	117,305	117	91	26
Ventura	107,684	161	122	39
Vernon	113	60	49	11
Visalia	125,905	197	135	62
Walnut Creek	64,927	107	76	31
Watsonville	51,801	82	65	17
Weed	3,002	15	10	5
West Covina	107,345	138	97	41
Westminster	90,756	133	92	41
Westmorland	2,251	5	5	0
West Sacramento	49,317	89	62	27
Wheatland	3,497	7	7	0
Whittier	86,334	166	116	50
Williams	5,183	14	11	3
Willits	4,945	18	12	6
Willows	6,238	10	9	1
Winters	6,702	12	10	2
Woodlake	7,365	13	12	1
Woodland	56,120	78	62	16
Yreka	7,856	20	14	6
Yuba City	65,688	87	62	25
COLORADO				
Alamosa	8,933	28	24	4
Arvada	108,287	216	155	61
Aspen	6,774	36	26	10
Ault	1,545	6	6	0
Aurora	330,740	755	638	117
Avon	6,559	20	18	2
Basalt	3,924	10	8	2
Bayfield	2,374	7	6	1
Berthoud	5,194	9	8	1
Black Hawk	120	33	24	9
Boulder	99,081	257	169	88
Breckenridge	4,619	27	20	7
Brighton	33,933	73	53	20
Broomfield	56,862	189	108	81
Brush	5,558	14	11	3
Buena Vista	2,663	9	7	2
Burlington	4,328	10	9	1
Calhan	794	3	3	0
Campo	111	2	2	0
Canon City	16,686	48	35	13
Carbondale	6,539	17	14	3
Castle Rock	49,071	73	53	20
Cedaredge	2,292	7	6	1
Centennial	102,125	155	119	36
Center	2,269	11	5	6
Central City	675	5	5	0
Cherry Hills Village	6,091	23	18	5
Collbran	720	1	1	0
Colorado Springs	423,680	900	622	278
Columbine Valley	1,278	6	6	0
Commerce City	46,713	120	93	27
Cortez	8,630	51	27	24
Craig	9,629	31	24	7
Crested Butte	1,513	8	7	1
Cripple Creek	1,210	11	9	2
Dacono	4,224	11	9	2
De Beque	513	2	2	0
Del Norte	1,715	6	5	1

Table 78. Full-Time Law Enforcement Employees, by Selected State and City, 2012— continued

(Number)

State/city	Population	Total law enforcement employees	Total officers	Total civilians
Delta	9,070	20	17	3
Denver	610,612	1,646	1,420	226
Dillon	920	10	8	2
Durango	17,181	63	52	11
Eagle	6,621	11	9	2
Eaton	4,441	9	8	1
Edgewater	5,260	17	15	2
Elizabeth	1,382	6	5	1
Empire	287	1	1	0
Englewood	30,782	100	71	29
Erie	18,451	23	21	2
Estes Park	5,960	29	19	10
Evans	18,860	32	30	2
Fairplay	691	3	3	0
Federal Heights	11,667	36	24	12
Firestone	10,324	23	19	4
Florence	3,949	18	9	9
Fort Collins	146,494	263	179	84
Fort Lupton	7,505	14	12	2
Fort Morgan	11,512	29	24	5
Fountain	26,296	44	40	4
Fowler	1,203	3	2	1
Fraser/Winter Park	2,261	9	8	1
Frederick	8,830	17	16	1
Frisco	2,730	16	13	3
Fruita	12,866	18	16	2
Georgetown	1,052	3	3	0
Glendale	4,257	39	27	12
Glenwood Springs	9,781	28	21	7
Golden	19,196	61	43	18
Granby	1,896	7	6	1
Grand Junction	59,586	192	101	91
Greeley	94,507	242	140	102
Green Mountain Falls	651	2	2	0
Greenwood Village	14,168	89	64	25
Gunnison	5,956	26	14	12
Haxtun	962	3	3	0
Hayden	1,842	5	4	1
Holyoke	2,353	2	2	0
Hotchkiss	960	3	3	0
Hugo	743	2	2	0
Idaho Springs	1,747	9	7	2
Ignacio	709	6	6	0
Johnstown	10,059	15	13	2
Kersey	1,479	3	3	0
Kiowa	736	2	2	0
Kremmling	1,469	4	4	0
Lafayette	24,879	44	37	7
La Junta	7,200	20	14	6
Lakeside	8	4	4	0
Lakewood	145,470	410	270	140
Lamar	7,940	35	22	13
La Salle	1,989	6	6	0
Las Animas	2,452	6	5	1
La Veta	814	2	2	0
Leadville	2,647	10	8	2
Limon	1,913	6	5	1
Littleton	42,464	96	70	26
Lochbuie	4,808	6	6	0
Lone Tree	10,396	51	46	5
Longmont	87,773	198	137	61
Louisville	18,696	36	31	5

Table 78. Full-Time Law Enforcement Employees, by Selected State and City, 2012— continued

(Number)

State/city	Population	Total law enforcement employees	Total officers	Total civilians
Loveland	68,024	131	90	41
Mancos	1,359	3	2	1
Manitou Springs	5,079	21	15	6
Manzanola	442	5	4	1
Meeker	2,518	6	6	0
Milliken	5,708	10	9	1
Minturn	1,045	3	2	1
Monte Vista	4,521	14	12	2
Montrose	19,465	55	37	18
Monument	5,626	16	13	3
Morrison	435	5	4	1
Mountain View	516	5	5	0
Mount Crested Butte	815	7	6	1
Nederland	1,470	7	6	1
New Castle	4,597	9	8	1
Northglenn	36,412	71	60	11
Oak Creek	899	2	2	0
Olathe	1,881	6	6	0
Ouray	1,017	4	4	0
Pagosa Springs	1,757	9	8	1
Palisade	2,739	9	8	1
Palmer Lake	2,462	5	5	0
Paonia	1,476	4	4	0
Parachute	1,104	6	5	1
Parker	46,086	82	58	24
Platteville	2,528	6	6	0
Pueblo	108,452	258	209	49
Rangely	2,406	10	5	5
Ridgway	940	2	2	0
Rifle	9,332	23	20	3
Rocky Ford	4,026	10	8	2
Salida	5,327	16	13	3
Sheridan	5,763	33	28	5
Silt	2,981	7	6	1
Silverthorne	3,955	18	15	3
Snowmass Village	2,875	12	9	3
South Fork	393	3	2	1
Springfield	1,476	3	3	0
Steamboat Springs	12,299	34	20	14
Sterling	15,034	24	21	3
Stratton	669	1	1	0
Telluride	2,365	12	9	3
Thornton	120,841	219	158	61
Timnath	636	2	2	0
Trinidad	9,254	34	23	11
Vail	5,397	56	28	28
Victor	404	3	3	0
Walsenburg	3,121	12	10	2
Walsh	556	1	1	0
Westminster	107,962	263	185	78
Wheat Ridge	30,691	103	72	31
Wiggins	909	2	2	0
Windsor	18,969	23	20	3
Woodland Park	7,325	28	20	8
Wray	2,383	8	7	1
Yuma	3,585	8	7	1
CONNECTICUT				
Ansonia	19,285	51	44	7
Avon	18,131	35	29	6
Berlin	19,903	53	41	12
Bethel	18,618	47	35	12
Bloomfield	20,524	57	46	11

Table 78. Full-Time Law Enforcement Employees, by Selected State and City, 2012— continued

(Number)

State/city	Population	Total law enforcement employees	Total officers	Total civilians
Branford	28,078	61	49	12
Bridgeport	144,496	476	421	55
Bristol	60,589	138	112	26
Brookfield	16,482	41	31	10
Canton	10,211	20	15	5
Cheshire	29,315	60	48	12
Clinton	13,285	34	24	10
Coventry	12,458	19	14	5
Cromwell	14,031	35	26	9
Danbury	81,043	152	145	7
Darien	20,770	58	51	7
Derby	12,926	33	31	2
East Hampton	12,983	17	15	2
East Hartford	51,347	158	120	38
East Haven	29,311	52	49	3
Easton	7,504	16	15	1
East Windsor	11,183	30	23	7
Enfield	44,737	112	89	23
Fairfield	59,514	111	105	6
Farmington	25,387	62	45	17
Glastonbury	34,491	73	57	16
Granby	11,303	18	13	5
Greenwich	61,284	176	148	28
Groton	10,408	34	27	7
Groton Long Point	519	7	7	0
Groton Town	29,262	69	65	4
Guilford	22,416	45	37	8
Hamden	61,073	124	106	18
Hartford	125,006	511	440	71
Madison	18,303	38	27	11
Manchester	58,349	151	117	34
Meriden	60,981	133	119	14
Middlebury	7,589	17	11	6
Middletown	47,736	112	97	15
Milford	52,857	123	108	15
Monroe	19,515	48	38	10
Naugatuck	31,921	70	58	12
New Britain	73,341	152	140	12
New Canaan	19,775	49	44	5
New Haven	130,019	527	359	168
Newington	30,619	64	52	12
New London	27,671	112	95	17
New Milford	28,194	63	49	14
Newtown	27,611	50	46	4
North Branford	14,434	27	22	5
North Haven	24,138	58	48	10
Norwalk	85,761	201	164	37
Norwich	40,568	90	74	16
Old Saybrook	10,261	31	25	6
Orange	13,982	51	40	11
Plainfield	15,433	19	16	3
Plainville	17,749	41	34	7
Plymouth	12,266	23	23	0
Portland	9,526	12	11	1
Putnam	9,602	18	15	3
Redding	9,175	21	15	6
Ridgefield	24,684	43	37	6
Rocky Hill	19,745	40	31	9
Seymour	16,571	41	39	2
Shelton	39,632	61	52	9
Simsbury	23,554	45	35	10
Southington	43,149	87	66	21

Table 78. Full-Time Law Enforcement Employees, by Selected State and City, 2012— continued

(Number)

State/city	Population	Total law enforcement employees	Total officers	Total civilians
South Windsor	25,757	55	42	13
Stamford	122,870	291	274	17
Stonington	18,579	47	35	12
Stratford	51,479	101	94	7
Suffield	15,764	23	18	5
Thomaston	7,902	14	11	3
Torrington	36,450	90	83	7
Trumbull	36,085	82	72	10
Vernon	29,233	65	52	13
Wallingford	45,218	94	70	24
Waterbury	110,570	353	290	63
Waterford	19,553	54	47	7
Watertown	22,556	47	38	9
West Hartford	63,385	131	124	7
West Haven	55,667	133	120	13
Weston	10,198	15	14	1
Westport	26,440	84	65	19
Wethersfield	26,717	58	47	11
Willimantic	17,770	44	40	4
Wilton	18,095	47	43	4
Winchester	11,263	23	19	4
Windsor	29,098	59	47	12
Windsor Locks	12,521	29	22	7
Wolcott	16,711	33	24	9
Woodbridge	9,007	34	26	8
DELAWARE				
Bethany Beach	1,071	10	8	2
Blades	1,254	3	3	0
Bridgeville	2,069	8	8	0
Camden	3,499	9	8	1
Cheswold	1,394	2	2	0
Clayton	2,948	8	7	1
Dagsboro	813	3	3	0
Delaware City	1,712	3	3	0
Delmar	1,613	13	12	1
Dewey Beach	344	9	8	1
Dover	36,416	118	90	28
Elsmere	6,194	12	11	1
Felton	1,311	4	3	1
Fenwick Island	383	8	7	1
Frankford	856	2	2	0
Georgetown	6,488	13	12	1
Greenwood	983	3	2	1
Harrington	3,598	11	10	1
Laurel	3,746	14	13	1
Lewes	2,775	14	13	1
Middletown	19,064	33	28	5
Milford	9,657	37	27	10
Millsboro	3,917	12	11	1
Milton	2,602	12	11	1
Newark	31,776	84	68	16
New Castle	5,339	19	17	2
Newport	1,066	8	7	1
Ocean View	1,901	9	8	1
Rehoboth Beach	1,341	26	15	11
Seaford	6,999	37	26	11
Selbyville	2,189	8	7	1
Smyrna	10,126	29	22	7
South Bethany	454	6	6	0
Wilmington	71,577	384	321	63
Wyoming	1,326	3	3	0

Table 78. Full-Time Law Enforcement Employees, by Selected State and City, 2012— continued

(Number)

State/city	Population	Total law enforcement employees	Total officers	Total civilians
DISTRICT OF COLUMBIA				
Washington	617,996	4,299	3,818	481
FLORIDA				
Alachua	9,182	28	20	8
Altamonte Springs	42,062	116	97	19
Altha	543	1	1	0
Apalachicola	2,261	8	7	1
Apopka	42,108	122	87	35
Arcadia	7,741	21	16	5
Astatula	1,835	5	5	0
Atlantic Beach	12,827	37	27	10
Atlantis	2,032	17	12	5
Auburndale	13,691	43	35	8
Aventura	36,249	119	83	36
Avon Park	8,956	26	23	3
Bal Harbour Village	2,547	35	27	8
Bartow	17,534	58	38	20
Bay Harbor Islands	5,705	29	22	7
Belleair	3,922	15	14	1
Belle Isle	6,070	14	13	1
Belleview	4,553	13	11	2
Biscayne Park	3,097	12	11	1
Blountstown	2,548	12	8	4
Boca Raton	85,542	289	191	98
Bonifay	2,831	7	6	1
Bowling Green	2,970	7	7	0
Boynton Beach	69,147	214	163	51
Bradenton	50,221	143	118	25
Bradenton Beach	1,187	10	10	0
Brooksville	7,824	27	24	3
Bushnell	2,451	10	9	1
Cape Coral	156,408	298	214	84
Carrabelle	2,816	5	5	0
Casselberry	26,599	61	51	10
Cedar Key	712	4	4	0
Center Hill	1,001	3	3	0
Chattahoochee	3,702	11	10	1
Chiefland	2,276	13	11	2
Chipley	3,654	11	10	1
Clearwater	109,153	319	229	90
Clermont	29,134	58	54	4
Clewiston	7,253	29	19	10
Cocoa	17,374	88	66	22
Cocoa Beach	11,384	48	32	16
Coconut Creek	53,630	135	91	44
Coral Gables	47,418	239	170	69
Coral Springs	122,746	299	199	100
Cottondale	946	3	3	0
Crescent City	1,598	6	5	1
Crestview	21,264	67	52	15
Cross City	1,752	5	5	0
Dade City	6,525	34	24	10
Davenport	2,927	10	9	1
Davie	93,246	231	168	63
Daytona Beach	61,836	267	228	39
Daytona Beach Shores	4,305	35	27	8
De Funiak Springs	5,248	28	20	8
Deland	27,399	79	61	18
Delray Beach	61,347	210	145	65
Doral	46,327	118	86	32
Dunnellon	1,757	12	9	3
Eatonville	2,188	14	12	2

Table 78. Full-Time Law Enforcement Employees, by Selected State and City, 2012— continued

(Number)

State/city	Population	Total law enforcement employees	Total officers	Total civilians
Edgewater	21,033	32	28	4
Edgewood	2,537	13	11	2
El Portal	2,357	7	7	0
Eustis	18,811	56	43	13
Fellsmere	5,268	10	9	1
Fernandina Beach	11,644	43	32	11
Flagler Beach	4,545	187	130	57
Florida City	11,398	45	34	11
Fort Lauderdale	167,777	657	505	152
Fort Myers	63,147	237	174	63
Fort Pierce	42,157	145	109	36
Fort Walton Beach	19,773	63	49	14
Fruitland Park	4,134	13	13	0
Gainesville	126,049	354	292	62
Golden Beach	932	19	18	1
Graceville	2,309	10	7	3
Greenacres City	38,085	64	47	17
Green Cove Springs	7,002	24	19	5
Gretna	1,480	5	5	0
Groveland	8,848	32	23	9
Gulf Breeze	5,842	31	17	14
Gulfport	12,193	37	29	8
Gulf Stream	797	11	11	0
Haines City	20,815	72	49	23
Hallandale	37,619	129	93	36
Havana	1,778	14	10	4
Hialeah	227,731	390	329	61
Hialeah Gardens	22,040	52	37	15
Highland Beach	3,587	14	13	1
High Springs	5,423	12	10	2
Hillsboro Beach	1,901	18	14	4
Holly Hill	11,818	33	28	5
Hollywood	142,686	465	305	160
Holmes Beach	3,888	21	14	7
Homestead	61,337	142	103	39
Howey-in-the-Hills	1,113	6	6	0
Indialantic	2,757	17	11	6
Indian Creek Village	87	19	13	6
Indian Harbour Beach	8,337	26	19	7
Indian River Shores	3,954	22	19	3
Indian Shores	3,589	13	11	2
Inglis	1,343	6	5	1
Interlachen	1,422	3	3	0
Jacksonville	834,429	3,161	1,645	1,516
Jacksonville Beach	21,653	76	57	19
Jasper	4,608	9	8	1
Jennings	890	2	2	0
Juno Beach	3,219	17	15	2
Jupiter	55,908	123	107	16
Jupiter Inlet Colony	405	4	4	0
Jupiter Island	828	19	15	4
Kenneth City	5,048	15	14	1
Key Biscayne	12,512	42	30	12
Key Colony Beach	808	5	5	0
Key West	24,985	113	87	26
Kissimmee	60,495	194	126	68
Lady Lake	14,116	37	27	10
Lake Alfred	5,083	15	10	5
Lake City	12,210	52	39	13
Lake Clarke Shores	3,422	11	11	0
Lake Hamilton	1,248	7	6	1
Lake Helen	2,660	6	5	1

Table 78. Full-Time Law Enforcement Employees, by Selected State and City, 2012— continued

(Number)

State/city	Population	Total law enforcement employees	Total officers	Total civilians
Lakeland	98,750	324	214	110
Lake Mary	14,010	53	37	16
Lake Placid	2,253	9	7	2
Lake Wales	14,419	50	44	6
Lantana	10,606	35	28	7
Largo	78,706	182	136	46
Lauderhill	67,799	127	112	15
Leesburg	20,391	97	72	25
Lighthouse Point	10,485	43	34	9
Live Oak	6,943	20	16	4
Longboat Key	6,982	24	17	7
Longwood	13,843	45	40	5
Lynn Haven	18,745	36	26	10
Madison	2,882	16	15	1
Maitland	15,966	50	44	6
Manalapan	412	13	9	4
Marco Island	16,637	38	33	5
Margate	54,010	159	103	56
Marianna	6,185	25	18	7
Mascotte	5,171	13	12	1
Medley	849	46	37	9
Melbourne	77,105	226	163	63
Melbourne Beach	3,143	10	9	1
Melbourne Village	671	5	5	0
Mexico Beach	1,087	7	7	0
Miami	404,901	1,404	1,061	343
Miami Beach	88,975	501	361	140
Miami Gardens	108,628	257	200	57
Miami Shores	10,636	44	35	9
Miami Springs	13,997	53	42	11
Milton	8,946	26	19	7
Miramar	123,704	263	199	64
Monticello	2,540	12	8	4
Mount Dora	12,539	45	30	15
Naples	19,803	97	68	29
Neptune Beach	7,133	27	19	8
New Port Richey	15,114	44	35	9
New Smyrna Beach	22,770	51	43	8
Niceville	12,923	29	23	6
North Bay Village	7,234	32	26	6
North Miami	59,587	142	107	35
North Miami Beach	42,089	136	96	40
North Palm Beach	12,179	43	31	12
North Port	58,139	125	100	25
Oakland	2,573	10	9	1
Ocala	57,082	230	154	76
Ocean Ridge	1,810	18	13	5
Ocoee	36,064	88	77	11
Okeechobee	5,698	26	20	6
Orange City	10,743	23	21	2
Orange Park	8,527	28	21	7
Orlando	241,548	913	702	211
Ormond Beach	38,657	92	67	25
Oviedo	33,796	79	61	18
Palatka	10,702	41	34	7
Palm Bay	104,596	241	161	80
Palm Beach	8,462	108	69	39
Palm Beach Gardens	49,112	153	111	42
Palm Beach Shores	1,158	16	11	5
Palmetto	12,778	48	35	13
Palm Springs	19,186	52	40	12
Panama City	36,981	130	94	36

Table 78. Full-Time Law Enforcement Employees, by Selected State and City, 2012— continued

(Number)

State/city	Population	Total law enforcement employees	Total officers	Total civilians
Panama City Beach	12,182	67	51	16
Parker	4,376	10	9	1
Pembroke Pines	156,859	284	227	57
Pensacola	52,631	200	152	48
Perry	7,113	24	22	2
Pinellas Park	49,748	119	99	20
Plantation	86,113	268	173	95
Plant City	35,194	84	66	18
Ponce Inlet	3,073	10	10	0
Port Orange	56,812	90	76	14
Port Richey	2,707	18	12	6
Port St. Joe	3,492	7	7	0
Port St. Lucie	166,846	261	205	56
Punta Gorda	16,868	49	34	15
Riviera Beach	32,931	146	108	38
Rockledge	25,266	68	49	19
Sanford	54,300	137	120	17
Sanibel	6,557	32	22	10
Sarasota	52,625	222	172	50
Satellite Beach	10,247	30	22	8
Sea Ranch Lakes	679	9	5	4
Sebastian	22,228	52	34	18
Sebring	10,634	38	32	6
Sewall's Point	2,023	8	8	0
Shalimar	727	3	3	0
Sneads	1,874	9	5	4
South Daytona	12,419	34	27	7
South Miami	11,816	57	50	7
South Palm Beach	1,187	8	8	0
Springfield	9,024	21	15	6
Starke	5,523	17	16	1
St. Augustine	13,152	61	50	11
St. Augustine Beach	6,260	18	16	2
St. Cloud	35,662	107	72	35
St. Pete Beach	9,473	28	22	6
St. Petersburg	248,105	743	533	210
Stuart	15,806	60	42	18
Sunny Isles Beach	21,116	59	47	12
Sunrise	85,590	260	170	90
Surfside	5,822	33	27	6
Sweetwater	13,683	46	35	11
Tallahassee	183,848	468	346	122
Tampa	340,284	1,219	948	271
Tarpon Springs	23,804	61	47	14
Tavares	14,141	38	27	11
Temple Terrace	24,875	71	51	20
Tequesta	5,706	25	19	6
Titusville	44,357	122	86	36
Treasure Island	6,796	26	19	7
Trenton	2,026	4	3	1
Umatilla	3,503	9	8	1
Valparaiso	5,105	14	10	4
Venice	21,031	62	45	17
Vero Beach	15,427	74	52	22
Village of Pinecrest	18,471	65	48	17
Virginia Gardens	2,407	8	6	2
Waldo	1,029	7	6	1
Wauchula	5,069	20	16	4
Webster	796	3	3	0
Welaka	711	1	1	0
West Melbourne	18,605	44	34	10
West Miami	6,046	22	18	4

Table 78. Full-Time Law Enforcement Employees, by Selected State and City, 2012— continued

(Number)

State/city	Population	Total law enforcement employees	Total officers	Total civilians
West Palm Beach	101,281	359	271	88
White Springs	788	3	3	0
Wildwood	6,800	26	18	8
Williston	2,806	19	11	8
Wilton Manors	11,701	38	28	10
Windermere	2,496	13	12	1
Winter Garden	35,039	83	68	15
Winter Haven	34,336	104	80	24
Winter Park	28,232	105	80	25
Winter Springs	33,736	78	64	14
Zephyrhills	13,469	40	27	13
GEORGIA				
Abbeville	2,946	8	3	5
Acworth	20,694	51	38	13
Adairsville	4,709	15	13	2
Adel	5,404	23	19	4
Alamo	2,834	3	2	1
Albany	78,454	202	169	33
Alma	3,512	13	11	2
Alpharetta	58,309	132	104	28
Alto	1,187	4	3	1
Americus	17,265	45	37	8
Aragon	1,265	5	4	1
Arcade	1,810	4	4	0
Arlington	1,498	4	4	0
Ashburn	4,207	16	16	0
Athens-Clarke County	117,114	295	231	64
Atlanta	425,533	2,069	1,693	376
Auburn	6,978	22	16	6
Austell	6,668	29	23	6
Avondale Estates	2,999	12	12	0
Baldwin	3,322	17	12	5
Ball Ground	1,452	2	2	0
Barnesville	6,844	19	17	2
Barwick	391	1	1	0
Baxley	4,458	12	10	2
Berlin	558	1	1	0
Blairsville	661	8	7	1
Blythe	730	1	1	0
Boston	1,332	4	4	0
Bowdon	2,067	10	7	3
Braselton	7,610	14	13	1
Bremen	6,309	22	20	2
Brooklet	1,413	4	4	0
Brunswick	15,586	71	63	8
Buchanan	1,119	8	7	1
Byron	4,571	22	19	3
Cairo	9,733	26	23	3
Calhoun	15,856	50	42	8
Camilla	5,431	22	19	3
Canon	815	2	2	0
Carrollton	24,709	76	64	12
Cartersville	19,991	64	53	11
Cave Spring	1,216	3	3	0
Cedartown	9,878	35	32	3
Centerville	7,242	18	15	3
Chamblee	10,022	63	44	19
Chatsworth	4,356	16	14	2
Chattahoochee Hills	2,409	10	10	0
Chickamauga	3,142	6	6	0
Clarkesville	1,756	7	6	1
Clarkston	7,653	20	17	3

Table 78. Full-Time Law Enforcement Employees, by Selected State and City, 2012— continued

(Number)

State/city	Population	Total law enforcement employees	Total officers	Total civilians
Claxton	2,782	9	8	1
Cleveland	3,455	14	13	1
Cochran	5,218	15	14	1
College Park	14,126	127	98	29
Collins	592	1	1	0
Colquitt	2,018	10	9	1
Columbus	192,385	569	464	105
Commerce	6,630	26	20	6
Conyers	15,395	79	58	21
Cordele	11,294	32	26	6
Covington	13,291	60	50	10
Crawfordville	541	1	1	0
Dallas	11,696	25	18	7
Dalton	33,564	96	83	13
Danielsville	567	1	1	0
Donalsonville	2,685	9	8	1
Doraville	8,440	57	39	18
Douglasville	31,369	113	86	27
Dublin	16,414	63	55	8
Duluth	26,950	73	56	17
Dunwoody	46,876	55	47	8
East Dublin	2,473	8	8	0
East Point	34,156	163	118	45
Eatonton	6,565	24	23	1
Edison	1,551	5	4	1
Elberton	4,714	25	19	6
Ellaville	1,836	4	4	0
Emerson	1,489	6	6	0
Enigma	1,295	8	6	2
Ephesus	433	1	1	0
Eton	922	3	3	0
Euharlee	4,190	9	8	1
Fairburn	13,121	35	30	5
Fairmount	729	5	4	1
Fayetteville	16,155	44	40	4
Fitzgerald	9,172	33	26	7
Flowery Branch	5,754	15	13	2
Folkston	2,535	6	5	1
Forest Park	18,711	102	80	22
Forsyth	3,838	23	18	5
Fort Oglethorpe	9,385	32	30	2
Fort Valley	9,944	27	24	3
Franklin	1,006	8	7	1
Franklin Springs	965	10	10	0
Gainesville	34,249	108	95	13
Garden City	8,894	45	41	4
Glennville	3,616	17	12	5
Gordon	2,044	11	11	0
Grantville	3,081	14	13	1
Gray	3,319	11	10	1
Greensboro	3,403	22	18	4
Greenville	888	6	5	1
Griffin	23,954	105	92	13
Grovetown	11,364	29	21	8
Guyton	1,706	4	3	1
Hagan	1,009	4	2	2
Hahira	2,773	6	5	1
Hampton	7,079	21	19	2
Hapeville	6,457	38	24	14
Harlem	2,701	10	7	3
Harrison	495	1	1	0
Hartwell	4,528	23	18	5

Table 78. Full-Time Law Enforcement Employees, by Selected State and City, 2012— continued

(Number)

State/city	Population	Total law enforcement employees	Total officers	Total civilians
Hazlehurst	4,282	13	11	2
Helen	517	12	10	2
Hinesville	33,877	99	86	13
Hiram	3,593	24	17	7
Hoboken	606	3	2	1
Hogansville	3,100	20	15	5
Holly Springs	9,310	18	18	0
Homerville	2,488	8	7	1
Jackson	5,111	17	12	5
Jasper	3,733	17	15	2
Jefferson	9,556	24	21	3
Jesup	10,348	28	26	2
Johns Creek	77,738	70	61	9
Jonesboro	4,786	23	19	4
Kennesaw	30,175	66	54	12
Kingsland	16,156	47	44	3
Kingston	645	1	1	0
LaGrange	29,978	97	79	18
Lakeland	3,410	11	8	3
Lavonia	2,184	14	14	0
Lawrenceville	28,922	91	70	21
Lilburn	11,749	35	27	8
Lincolnton	1,587	4	4	0
Locust Grove	5,473	21	19	2
Loganville	10,596	30	25	5
Lookout Mountain	1,623	6	6	0
Louisville	2,526	6	6	0
Ludowici	1,725	11	7	4
Lumber City	1,345	1	1	0
Lumpkin	1,160	5	4	1
Macon	92,554	368	289	79
Madison	4,031	14	12	2
Manchester	4,286	17	12	5
Marietta	57,324	166	132	34
Maysville	1,822	4	4	0
McCaysville	1,070	4	4	0
McDonough	22,375	45	41	4
McIntyre	659	5	5	0
Meigs	1,049	5	4	1
Midville	273	1	1	0
Midway	2,149	7	6	1
Milledgeville	17,948	61	39	22
Millen	3,161	9	9	0
Milton	33,091	29	26	3
Monroe	13,408	44	40	4
Montezuma	3,506	12	10	2
Monticello	2,692	6	5	1
Morrow	6,530	44	32	12
Moultrie	14,456	47	42	5
Mountain City	1,102	3	3	0
Mount Zion	1,718	3	3	0
Nahunta	1,067	4	3	1
Nashville	5,004	17	14	3
Newnan	33,474	82	68	14
Newton	663	2	2	0
Nicholls	2,835	3	2	1
Norcross	9,236	50	38	12
Oakwood	4,022	16	15	1
Ocilla	3,459	13	12	1
Omega	1,237	5	5	0
Oxford	2,162	4	4	0
Palmetto	4,547	16	15	1

Table 78. Full-Time Law Enforcement Employees, by Selected State and City, 2012— continued

(Number)

State/city	Population	Total law enforcement employees	Total officers	Total civilians
Patterson	740	1	1	0
Peachtree City	34,816	68	65	3
Pelham	3,949	14	12	2
Pembroke	2,225	7	5	2
Perry	14,021	40	35	5
Pine Mountain	1,321	8	7	1
Pooler	19,392	34	28	6
Porterdale	1,448	5	5	0
Port Wentworth	5,430	25	21	4
Powder Springs	14,124	31	26	5
Quitman	3,901	18	15	3
Ray City	1,104	2	2	0
Register	177	1	1	0
Remerton	1,138	9	8	1
Reynolds	1,100	6	6	0
Richmond Hill	9,403	38	31	7
Rincon	8,952	17	16	1
Ringgold	3,627	9	9	0
Riverdale	15,333	64	49	15
Roberta	1,020	2	2	0
Rockmart	4,254	18	16	2
Rome	36,781	98	83	15
Rossville	4,159	11	10	1
Royston	2,616	17	14	3
Sandersville	5,990	21	19	2
Sandy Springs	95,089	138	123	15
Savannah-Chatham Metropolitan	226,422	767	563	204
Screven	776	2	2	0
Senoia	3,351	15	13	2
Shiloh	451	2	1	1
Smyrna	51,946	101	90	11
Snellville	18,482	53	43	10
Social Circle	4,318	22	19	3
Sparks	2,079	2	2	0
Sparta	1,418	13	8	5
Springfield	2,890	8	7	1
Statesboro	28,796	74	62	12
Statham	2,440	8	8	0
St. Marys	17,346	36	34	2
Stone Mountain	5,878	19	18	1
Summerville	4,594	16	15	1
Suwanee	15,557	43	35	8
Sylvester	6,269	26	23	3
Tallapoosa	3,212	13	12	1
Tallulah Falls	170	2	2	0
Temple	4,284	13	11	2
Tennille	1,559	10	9	1
Thomaston	9,291	22	18	4
Thomasville	18,655	66	59	7
Thunderbolt	2,703	10	8	2
Tifton	16,565	55	46	9
Tignall	553	2	1	1
Toccoa	8,603	32	30	2
Toomsboro	478	1	1	0
Trion	1,851	10	9	1
Tunnel Hill	867	3	3	0
Tybee Island	3,029	28	19	9
Tyrone	6,970	15	14	1
Union City	19,712	73	55	18
Valdosta	55,236	164	143	21
Vidalia	10,611	37	31	6
Villa Rica	14,140	42	34	8

Table 78. Full-Time Law Enforcement Employees, by Selected State and City, 2012— continued

(Number)

State/city	Population	Total law enforcement employees	Total officers	Total civilians
Warm Springs	431	2	2	0
Warner Robins	67,465	140	103	37
Washington	4,188	14	14	0
Watkinsville	2,869	7	7	0
Waverly Hall	745	3	3	0
Waycross	14,842	67	58	9
Waynesboro	5,842	29	22	7
West Point	3,520	21	16	5
Whigham	477	5	4	1
Willacoochee	1,409	5	4	1
Winder	14,285	48	41	7
Winterville	1,137	3	3	0
Woodstock	24,211	61	52	9
Wrens	2,216	8	8	0
Wrightsville	2,224	5	4	1
Zebulon	1,189	9	6	3
HAWAII				
Honolulu	963,465	2,544	2,063	481
IDAHO				
Aberdeen	2,016	7	4	3
American Falls	4,506	8	7	1
Blackfoot	12,031	29	26	3
Boise	207,945	353	292	61
Bonners Ferry	2,571	7	7	0
Buhl	4,168	9	7	2
Caldwell	46,748	79	64	15
Cascade	949	4	3	1
Chubbuck	14,076	33	20	13
Coeur d'Alene	44,625	88	70	18
Cottonwood	910	1	1	0
Emmett	6,629	14	13	1
Filer	2,536	5	5	0
Fruitland	4,736	11	10	1
Garden City	11,093	35	26	9
Gooding	3,606	8	7	1
Grangeville	3,176	6	6	0
Hagerman	882	1	1	0
Hailey	8,048	20	19	1
Heyburn	3,123	6	5	1
Homedale	2,662	5	5	0
Idaho City	490	1	1	0
Idaho Falls	57,512	128	88	40
Jerome	11,010	21	18	3
Kamiah	1,309	3	3	0
Kellogg	2,143	8	7	1
Ketchum	2,719	14	10	4
Kimberly	3,300	6	6	0
Lewiston	32,247	66	45	21
McCall	3,024	19	15	4
Meridian	75,922	106	84	22
Montpelier	2,626	6	5	1
Moscow	24,063	39	31	8
Mountain Home	14,363	37	28	9
Nampa	82,459	167	116	51
Orofino	3,177	6	5	1
Osburn	1,572	2	2	0
Parma	2,005	4	4	0
Payette	7,515	14	12	2
Pinehurst	1,637	1	1	0
Pocatello	54,855	126	89	37
Ponderay	1,150	7	6	1
Post Falls	27,879	63	37	26

Table 78. Full-Time Law Enforcement Employees, by Selected State and City, 2012— continued

(Number)

State/city	Population	Total law enforcement employees	Total officers	Total civilians
Preston	5,262	7	6	1
Priest River	1,770	6	4	2
Rathdrum	6,901	13	10	3
Rexburg	25,766	37	29	8
Rigby	3,989	9	8	1
Rupert	5,615	12	11	1
Salmon	3,146	7	6	1
Sandpoint	7,446	26	21	5
Shelley	4,458	5	5	0
Soda Springs	3,092	8	7	1
Spirit Lake	1,967	6	5	1
St. Anthony	3,581	4	4	0
St. Maries	2,429	5	5	0
Sun Valley	1,422	11	10	1
Twin Falls	44,613	98	70	28
Weiser	5,568	16	13	3
Wendell	2,813	4	3	1
Wilder	1,550	3	3	0
ILLINOIS				
Abingdon	3,329	5	5	0
Addison	37,053	94	65	29
Albany	894	1	1	0
Albion	1,994	3	3	0
Aledo	3,651	7	6	1
Algonquin	30,136	59	49	10
Alsip	19,335	52	38	14
Altamont	2,326	6	6	0
Alton	27,949	85	60	25
Amboy	2,508	4	4	0
Anna	4,455	7	7	0
Antioch	14,473	37	27	10
Arcola	2,925	6	5	1
Arlington Heights	75,327	138	108	30
Arthur	2,295	4	4	0
Ashland	1,337	1	1	0
Ashton	975	1	1	0
Athens	1,994	3	3	0
Atkinson	975	1	1	0
Atlanta	1,697	1	1	0
Atwood	1,228	2	2	0
Auburn	4,785	10	6	4
Augusta	589	1	1	0
Aurora	198,495	347	285	62
Aviston	1,951	1	1	0
Bannockburn	1,588	7	7	0
Barrington	10,358	27	23	4
Barrington Hills	4,222	29	19	10
Bartlett	41,332	70	53	17
Bartonville	6,490	16	11	5
Batavia	26,123	45	39	6
Beckemeyer	1,043	1	1	0
Bedford Park	582	43	36	7
Beecher	4,372	8	7	1
Belleville	44,612	99	79	20
Bellwood	19,128	43	40	3
Belvidere	25,662	42	39	3
Benld	1,561	4	4	0
Bensenville	18,407	39	32	7
Benton	7,108	11	10	1
Berkeley	5,225	18	14	4
Berwyn	56,828	139	102	37
Bethalto	9,550	18	14	4

Table 78. Full-Time Law Enforcement Employees, by Selected State and City, 2012— continued

(Number)

State/city	Population	Total law enforcement employees	Total officers	Total civilians
Bethany	1,356	1	1	0
Bloomingdale	22,084	60	45	15
Bloomington	76,841	159	125	34
Blue Island	23,777	48	39	9
Bolingbrook	73,987	146	112	34
Bradley	15,943	46	33	13
Braidwood	6,210	13	12	1
Breese	4,455	7	6	1
Bridgeview	16,496	39	37	2
Brighton	2,261	4	4	0
Broadview	7,956	32	25	7
Brookfield	19,035	36	31	5
Buffalo Grove	41,621	77	67	10
Buffalo-Mechanicsburg	1,097	2	2	0
Burbank	29,012	62	46	16
Burnham	4,219	13	9	4
Burr Ridge	10,591	29	26	3
Byron	3,764	8	7	1
Cahokia	15,287	40	30	10
Cairo	2,840	9	4	5
Calumet City	37,154	107	81	26
Calumet Park	7,859	23	21	2
Camp Point	1,135	2	2	0
Campton Hills	11,165	6	6	0
Canton	14,748	35	24	11
Carbondale	25,980	84	65	19
Carlinville	5,935	16	11	5
Carlyle	3,291	8	7	1
Carmi	5,256	10	9	1
Carol Stream	39,831	79	61	18
Carpentersville	37,804	70	60	10
Carrier Mills	1,658	2	2	0
Carrollton	2,491	6	6	0
Carthage	2,613	4	4	0
Cary	18,326	32	28	4
Casey	2,777	8	7	1
Caseyville	4,258	12	10	2
Central City	1,176	4	4	0
Centralia	13,071	34	25	9
Centreville	5,325	16	13	3
Cerro Gordo	1,407	1	1	0
Chadwick	553	1	1	0
Champaign	81,299	143	119	24
Channahon	12,598	27	25	2
Charleston	21,901	34	32	2
Chatham	11,535	21	15	6
Chebanse	1,065	1	1	0
Chenoa	3,226	3	3	0
Cherry Valley	3,172	16	15	1
Chester	8,612	11	8	3
Chicago	2,703,713	12,799	12,092	707
Chicago Heights	30,367	108	80	28
Chicago Ridge	14,348	32	28	4
Chillicothe	6,115	13	9	4
Christopher	2,389	5	5	0
Clinton	7,247	14	13	1
Coal City	5,604	12	11	1
Coal Valley	3,754	7	6	1
Cobden	1,160	3	3	0
Colfax	1,064	1	1	0
Collinsville	25,656	63	44	19
Colona	5,114	10	9	1

Table 78. Full-Time Law Enforcement Employees, by Selected State and City, 2012— continued

(Number)

State/city	Population	Total law enforcement employees	Total officers	Total civilians
Columbia	9,736	22	15	7
Cortland	4,283	3	3	0
Country Club Hills	16,591	52	38	14
Countryside	5,913	31	24	7
Crest Hill	20,900	26	24	2
Crestwood	10,983	4	3	1
Crete	8,284	20	18	2
Creve Coeur	5,467	9	7	2
Crystal Lake	40,866	79	66	13
Danvers	1,157	2	2	0
Darien	22,152	43	36	7
Decatur	76,351	186	158	28
Deer Creek-Goodfield	1,569	1	1	0
Deerfield	18,280	54	39	15
Deer Park	3,210	16	15	1
De Kalb	43,994	75	60	15
De Pue	1,844	3	3	0
De Soto	1,595	3	2	1
Des Plaines	58,540	111	91	20
Divernon	1,176	3	3	0
Dixmoor	3,655	14	10	4
Dixon	15,780	32	28	4
Downers Grove	47,977	102	72	30
Du Quoin	6,127	15	11	4
Durand	1,447	1	1	0
Dwight	4,273	9	8	1
Earlville	1,706	2	2	0
East Alton	6,320	17	11	6
East Dubuque	1,709	6	6	0
East Dundee	2,869	12	11	1
East Hazel Crest	1,548	11	10	1
East Moline	21,366	51	40	11
East Peoria	23,472	55	43	12
East St. Louis	27,087	66	47	19
Edinburg	1,081	1	1	0
Edwardsville	24,366	56	42	14
Effingham	12,365	35	22	13
Elburn	5,619	9	8	1
Eldorado	4,134	11	7	4
Elgin	108,514	233	179	54
Elizabeth	763	1	1	0
Elk Grove Village	33,227	99	84	15
Elmhurst	44,254	85	66	19
Elmwood	2,103	1	1	0
Elmwood Park	24,958	38	32	6
El Paso	2,818	5	5	0
Elwood	2,286	11	10	1
Energy	1,149	4	4	0
Erie	1,607	3	3	0
Essex	804	1	1	0
Eureka	5,311	6	6	0
Evanston	74,710	224	164	60
Evergreen Park	19,912	77	62	15
Fairbury	3,768	8	8	0
Fairfield	5,170	16	12	4
Fairmont City	2,643	8	6	2
Fairview	524	1	1	0
Fairview Heights	17,129	51	42	9
Farmington	2,455	4	4	0
Findlay	685	1	1	0
Fisher	1,887	2	2	0
Flora	5,085	16	11	5

Table 78. Full-Time Law Enforcement Employees, by Selected State and City, 2012— continued

(Number)

State/city	Population	Total law enforcement employees	Total officers	Total civilians
Forest Park	14,210	55	39	16
Forest View	700	12	9	3
Fox Lake	10,611	26	22	4
Fox River Grove	4,869	10	10	0
Frankfort	17,836	34	30	4
Franklin Park	18,388	44	43	1
Freeport	25,715	68	50	18
Fulton	3,491	9	8	1
Galena	3,439	12	10	2
Galesburg	32,292	76	52	24
Galva	2,597	3	3	0
Geneseo	6,606	17	12	5
Geneva	21,560	50	36	14
Genoa	5,209	7	6	1
Georgetown	3,484	4	4	0
Germantown	1,273	1	1	0
Gibson City	3,417	9	7	2
Gifford	978	1	1	0
Gilberts	6,900	9	8	1
Gillespie	3,329	9	6	3
Glasford	1,025	1	1	0
Glen Carbon	12,973	26	19	7
Glencoe	8,749	42	33	9
Glendale Heights	34,311	75	52	23
Glen Ellyn	27,533	47	39	8
Glenview	44,827	78	73	5
Glenwood	8,996	22	21	1
Golf	502	4	4	0
Grafton	676	3	3	0
Grandview	1,445	2	2	0
Granite City	29,939	71	60	11
Grant Park	1,335	4	4	0
Granville	1,431	2	2	0
Grayslake	21,020	37	32	5
Grayville	1,671	2	2	0
Greenfield	1,074	2	2	0
Greenup	1,518	4	4	0
Greenville	7,021	13	9	4
Gurnee	31,389	87	58	29
Hamilton	2,960	4	4	0
Hampshire	5,580	11	11	0
Hampton	1,869	4	4	0
Hanover	847	1	1	0
Hanover Park	38,087	84	61	23
Harrisburg	9,044	15	14	1
Hartford	1,433	5	4	1
Harvard	9,475	23	17	6
Harwood Heights	8,638	33	24	9
Havana	3,311	12	8	4
Hawthorn Woods	7,686	10	9	1
Hazel Crest	14,142	33	29	4
Hebron	1,220	3	3	0
Henry	2,471	4	4	0
Herrin	12,539	24	17	7
Herscher	1,596	3	3	0
Hickory Hills	14,091	36	28	8
Highland	9,949	25	19	6
Highland Park	29,853	73	54	19
Hillsboro	6,226	8	8	0
Hillside	8,182	31	25	6
Hinckley	2,076	3	3	0
Hinsdale	16,867	27	25	2

Table 78. Full-Time Law Enforcement Employees, by Selected State and City, 2012— continued

(Number)

State/city	Population	Total law enforcement employees	Total officers	Total civilians
Hodgkins	1,903	21	19	2
Hoffman Estates	52,051	113	94	19
Homer	1,197	1	1	0
Hometown	4,362	5	1	4
Homewood	19,381	41	36	5
Hoopeston	5,367	14	10	4
Hopedale	868	1	1	0
Indian Head Park	3,820	9	8	1
Inverness	7,421	13	12	1
Irvington	661	1	1	0
Island Lake	8,104	20	14	6
Itasca	8,675	29	23	6
Jacksonville	19,505	50	40	10
Jerseyville	8,490	20	14	6
Johnsburg	6,356	10	9	1
Joliet	147,877	325	251	74
Jonesboro	1,826	2	2	0
Justice	12,965	31	24	7
Kankakee	27,620	80	69	11
Kenilworth	2,521	13	10	3
Kewanee	12,955	30	23	7
Kildeer	3,980	16	15	1
Kincaid	1,510	1	1	0
Kingston	1,168	2	2	0
Knoxville	2,920	5	5	0
Lacon	1,943	3	3	0
La Grange	15,597	42	27	15
La Grange Park	13,620	26	20	6
Lake Forest	19,433	55	39	16
Lakemoor	6,035	8	7	1
Lake Villa	8,767	18	17	1
Lakewood	3,822	9	8	1
Lake Zurich	19,690	51	34	17
La Moille	728	1	1	0
Lansing	28,416	74	55	19
La Salle	9,638	29	23	6
Lawrenceville	4,361	7	7	0
Lebanon	4,431	11	11	0
Leland	980	1	1	0
Leland Grove	1,508	5	5	0
Lemont	16,048	32	27	5
Lenzburg	523	1	1	0
Le Roy	3,571	6	6	0
Lexington	2,066	1	1	0
Libertyville	20,376	50	39	11
Lincoln	14,548	26	25	1
Lincolnshire	7,297	31	23	8
Lincolnwood	12,628	43	32	11
Lisle	22,457	49	38	11
Litchfield	6,960	17	15	2
Lockport	24,914	44	37	7
Lombard	43,526	83	68	15
Loves Park	24,068	36	33	3
Lynwood	9,034	28	19	9
Lyons	10,761	40	30	10
Machesney Park	23,570	26	25	1
Mackinaw	1,956	1	1	0
Macomb	19,346	30	27	3
Madison	3,903	15	11	4
Mahomet	7,280	9	8	1
Manhattan	7,072	11	10	1
Manteno	9,232	18	17	1

Table 78. Full-Time Law Enforcement Employees, by Selected State and City, 2012— continued

(Number)

State/city	Population	Total law enforcement employees	Total officers	Total civilians
Maple Park	1,314	1	1	0
Marengo	7,671	14	14	0
Marion	17,245	40	30	10
Marissa	1,985	4	4	0
Maroa	1,806	3	3	0
Marquette Heights	2,833	5	5	0
Marseilles	5,109	14	9	5
Marshall	3,945	10	9	1
Martinsville	1,171	2	2	0
Maryville	7,510	12	12	0
Mascoutah	7,506	14	13	1
Matteson	19,066	47	39	8
Mattoon	18,611	40	36	4
Maywood	24,163	73	60	13
McCook	229	23	18	5
McHenry	27,073	60	45	15
McLean	832	1	1	0
McLeansboro	2,892	5	5	0
Medora	420	1	1	0
Melrose Park	25,487	79	70	9
Mendota	7,394	20	15	5
Meredosia	1,047	1	1	0
Metropolis	6,557	21	16	5
Midlothian	14,864	29	26	3
Milan	5,114	20	14	6
Milledgeville	1,035	2	2	0
Minier	1,256	2	2	0
Minonk	2,084	3	3	0
Minooka	10,957	22	18	4
Mokena	18,796	33	30	3
Moline	43,614	102	81	21
Momence	3,320	8	8	0
Monee	5,163	13	12	1
Monmouth	9,472	30	20	10
Montgomery	18,494	30	22	8
Monticello	5,565	7	6	1
Morris	13,677	32	23	9
Morrison	4,201	6	6	0
Morton	16,316	26	20	6
Morton Grove	23,340	58	45	13
Mount Carmel	7,306	16	12	4
Mount Carroll	1,722	3	3	0
Mount Morris	3,007	5	4	1
Mount Prospect	54,330	100	82	18
Mount Pulaski	1,571	2	2	0
Mount Sterling	2,031	8	5	3
Mount Vernon	15,323	56	44	12
Mount Zion	5,851	12	10	2
Moweaqua	1,837	2	2	0
Mundelein	31,158	69	52	17
Murphysboro	7,994	22	15	7
Naperville	142,280	263	164	99
Nashville	3,268	7	6	1
New Athens	2,060	4	4	0
New Baden	3,359	5	5	0
New Lenox	24,467	40	36	4
Niles	29,893	67	55	12
Normal	52,655	88	75	13
Norridge	14,616	52	36	16
North Aurora	16,810	30	28	2
Northbrook	33,270	89	63	26
Northfield	5,436	24	18	6

Table 78. Full-Time Law Enforcement Employees, by Selected State and City, 2012— continued

(Number)

State/city	Population	Total law enforcement employees	Total officers	Total civilians
Northlake	12,360	57	40	17
North Pekin	1,578	4	4	0
North Riverside	6,692	33	25	8
Oakbrook Terrace	2,140	22	19	3
Oak Forest	28,046	52	40	12
Oak Lawn	56,861	129	107	22
Oakwood	1,600	1	1	0
Oblong	1,470	1	1	0
O'Fallon	28,366	60	45	15
Oglesby	3,802	12	9	3
Okawville	1,438	3	3	0
Old Shawneetown	194	3	3	0
Olney	9,142	14	13	1
Olympia Fields	5,003	23	20	3
Oregon	3,732	9	8	1
Orion	1,867	3	3	0
Orland Hills	7,171	12	12	0
Orland Park	56,938	123	95	28
Oswego	30,446	56	47	9
Ottawa	18,824	46	35	11
Palatine	68,763	135	110	25
Palestine	1,373	2	2	0
Palmyra	700	2	2	0
Palos Heights	12,553	30	27	3
Palos Hills	17,537	34	31	3
Palos Park	4,862	11	10	1
Pana	5,865	13	9	4
Paris	8,864	21	15	6
Park City	7,593	12	10	2
Park Forest	22,041	53	41	12
Park Ridge	37,593	67	54	13
Pawnee	2,747	5	5	0
Paxton	4,486	6	6	0
Pecatonica	2,202	5	3	2
Pekin	34,197	62	53	9
Peoria	115,353	248	213	35
Peoria Heights	6,175	16	12	4
Peotone	4,154	10	9	1
Peru	10,326	32	25	7
Petersburg	2,267	4	4	0
Phoenix	1,970	2	1	1
Pinckneyville	5,665	8	7	1
Pittsfield	4,590	6	6	0
Plainfield	39,700	67	51	16
Plano	10,889	21	19	2
Pleasant Hill	969	1	1	0
Polo	2,362	4	4	0
Pontiac	11,967	20	19	1
Pontoon Beach	5,854	21	15	6
Posen	6,005	16	14	2
Potomac	752	1	1	0
Princeton	7,683	18	17	1
Prophetstown	2,086	3	3	0
Quincy	40,755	91	76	15
Rantoul	12,980	41	32	9
Richmond	1,880	3	3	0
Richton Park	13,687	32	28	4
Ridge Farm	885	1	1	0
River Forest	11,206	31	28	3
River Grove	10,258	29	23	6
Riverside	8,902	24	19	5
Riverwoods	3,671	7	7	0

Table 78. Full-Time Law Enforcement Employees, by Selected State and City, 2012— continued

(Number)

State/city	Population	Total law enforcement employees	Total officers	Total civilians
Robinson	7,736	14	13	1
Rochester	3,700	8	8	0
Rockdale	1,982	3	3	0
Rock Falls	9,294	26	19	7
Rockford	150,001	294	264	30
Rock Island	39,135	109	82	27
Rolling Meadows	24,172	55	47	8
Romeoville	39,799	85	62	23
Roodhouse	1,819	7	3	4
Roselle	22,832	42	32	10
Round Lake	18,344	25	19	6
Round Lake Beach	28,260	49	42	7
Round Lake Heights	2,684	6	6	0
Roxana	1,547	7	6	1
Rushville	3,202	5	5	0
Salem	7,508	21	13	8
Sandoval	1,278	3	3	0
Sandwich	7,443	20	14	6
Sauget	159	13	12	1
Sauk Village	10,538	30	22	8
Savanna	3,071	8	8	0
Schaumburg	74,450	152	113	39
Schiller Park	11,829	40	33	7
Seneca	2,378	8	4	4
Sesser	1,937	6	5	1
Shannon	759	1	1	0
Shawneetown	1,243	3	3	0
Shelbyville	4,714	8	7	1
Sheridan	2,143	2	2	0
Sherman	4,160	6	6	0
Shiloh	12,689	17	16	1
Shorewood	15,662	28	24	4
Silvis	7,502	20	14	6
Skokie	64,979	139	107	32
Sleepy Hollow	3,314	8	7	1
Somonauk	1,899	5	5	0
South Beloit	7,916	16	15	1
South Chicago Heights	4,151	11	7	4
South Elgin	22,051	40	31	9
Southern View	1,647	4	4	0
South Holland	22,096	46	44	2
South Jacksonville	3,341	6	5	1
South Pekin	1,149	2	2	0
South Roxana	2,059	5	5	0
Sparta	4,315	14	9	5
Springfield	116,600	279	240	39
Spring Grove	5,795	10	8	2
Spring Valley	5,575	14	11	3
St. Anne	1,261	2	2	0
Staunton	5,151	8	5	3
St. Charles	33,073	63	52	11
St. Elmo	1,430	1	1	0
Sterling	15,416	40	28	12
Stickney	6,806	21	15	6
Stockton	1,868	5	4	1
Stone Park	4,961	15	15	0
Stonington	935	2	2	0
Streamwood	39,978	67	57	10
Streator	13,751	30	24	6
Sugar Grove	9,024	14	13	1
Summit	11,087	32	26	6
Sumner	3,184	2	2	0

Table 78. Full-Time Law Enforcement Employees, by Selected State and City, 2012— continued

(Number)

State/city	Population	Total law enforcement employees	Total officers	Total civilians
Swansea	13,470	26	21	5
Sycamore	17,572	32	30	2
Taylorville	11,280	23	18	5
Thornton	2,345	12	11	1
Tinley Park	56,874	94	71	23
Tolono	3,457	3	3	0
Tremont	2,243	3	3	0
Trenton	2,723	5	5	0
Troy	9,918	24	18	6
Tuscola	4,493	8	7	1
University Park	7,150	25	21	4
Urbana	41,374	69	55	14
Valmeyer	1,267	2	2	0
Vandalia	7,063	15	11	4
Venice	1,896	13	9	4
Vernon Hills	25,189	63	43	20
Vienna	1,438	4	4	0
Villa Grove	2,545	5	4	1
Villa Park	21,970	49	37	12
Virginia	1,616	1	1	0
Warren	1,432	4	3	1
Warrensburg	1,214	2	2	0
Warrenville	13,180	38	31	7
Washington	15,180	29	21	8
Washington Park	4,209	8	7	1
Waterloo	9,841	16	15	1
Waterman	1,511	3	3	0
Watseka	5,271	9	9	0
Wauconda	13,644	37	26	11
Waukegan	89,346	174	133	41
Wayne	2,438	5	5	0
Wayne City	1,035	1	1	0
Westchester	16,768	43	32	11
West Chicago	27,168	53	47	6
West City	663	11	6	5
West Dundee	7,353	22	19	3
Western Springs	13,014	27	21	6
West Frankfort	8,207	18	13	5
Westmont	24,759	43	37	6
West Salem	900	1	1	0
Westville	3,212	4	4	0
Wheaton	53,053	79	63	16
Wheeling	37,761	83	61	22
Williamsfield	580	1	1	0
Willowbrook	8,566	24	21	3
Willow Springs	5,541	20	14	6
Wilmette	27,169	56	44	12
Wilmington	5,741	14	13	1
Winfield	9,107	19	17	2
Winnebago	3,110	5	5	0
Winnetka	12,224	34	26	8
Winthrop Harbor	6,762	15	9	6
Wood Dale	13,811	49	32	17
Woodhull	813	1	1	0
Woodridge	33,070	64	49	15
Wood River	10,689	24	18	6
Woodstock	24,845	46	35	11
Worden	1,047	1	1	0
Worth	10,821	25	23	2
Wyoming	1,433	2	2	0
Yates City	695	1	1	0
Yorkville	16,972	27	24	3

Table 78. Full-Time Law Enforcement Employees, by Selected State and City, 2012— continued

(Number)

State/city	Population	Total law enforcement employees	Total officers	Total civilians
Zeigler	1,806	4	4	0
Zion	24,486	60	47	13
INDIANA				
Anderson	56,416	130	117	13
Angola	8,656	19	15	4
Auburn	12,796	27	22	5
Aurora	3,769	13	10	3
Austin	4,317	7	7	0
Avon	12,510	25	23	2
Bargersville	4,033	9	8	1
Batesville	6,553	17	12	5
Bedford	13,482	38	30	8
Berne	4,019	7	6	1
Bicknell	2,930	6	6	0
Bloomington	80,816	131	97	34
Bluffton	9,948	30	20	10
Boonville	6,278	15	14	1
Brazil	7,952	16	13	3
Bremen	4,611	16	12	4
Brownsburg	21,394	49	41	8
Burns Harbor	1,162	5	4	1
Cannelton	1,571	3	3	0
Carmel	79,596	131	110	21
Cedar Lake	11,619	22	17	5
Charlestown	7,624	20	15	5
Chesterton	13,135	26	22	4
Clarks Hill	614	1	1	0
Clarksville	21,835	48	40	8
Clinton	4,918	8	8	0
Columbia City	8,795	20	18	2
Columbus	44,286	83	75	8
Connersville	13,550	28	27	1
Corydon	3,138	7	7	0
Covington	2,659	6	6	0
Crawfordsville	15,996	45	30	15
Crown Point	27,457	54	41	13
Culver	1,360	4	4	0
Cumberland	5,195	15	13	2
Danville	9,047	17	15	2
Decatur	9,453	21	17	4
Delphi	2,908	7	7	0
Dunkirk	2,374	7	5	2
Dyer	16,474	32	25	7
East Chicago	29,850	115	105	10
Edinburgh	4,503	16	11	5
Elkhart	51,209	134	120	14
Ellettsville	6,411	9	9	0
Elwood	8,658	21	16	5
Evansville	118,029	311	282	29
Fairmount	2,969	6	5	1
Fishers	77,186	99	91	8
Fort Wayne	254,987	517	456	61
Fowler	2,329	4	4	0
Frankfort	16,506	31	28	3
Franklin	23,833	55	40	15
Garrett	6,318	17	13	4
Gas City	5,995	14	10	4
Georgetown	2,891	4	4	0
Goshen	31,881	65	59	6
Greencastle	10,379	17	15	2
Greendale	4,543	12	10	2
Greenfield	20,707	42	39	3

Table 78. Full-Time Law Enforcement Employees, by Selected State and City, 2012— continued

(Number)

State/city	Population	Total law enforcement employees	Total officers	Total civilians
Greenwood	50,045	76	56	20
Griffith	16,979	38	30	8
Hagerstown	1,796	5	5	0
Hammond	81,243	252	210	42
Hartford City	6,252	13	12	1
Hebron	3,743	7	7	0
Highland	23,848	44	37	7
Hobart	29,207	70	55	15
Huntingburg	6,088	11	10	1
Huntington	17,480	34	32	2
Indianapolis	833,024	1,857	1,614	243
Jasonville	2,233	5	5	0
Jasper	15,115	28	21	7
Jeffersonville	45,183	88	74	14
Kendallville	9,912	24	17	7
Kingsford Heights	1,442	2	2	0
Knox	3,723	7	7	0
Kokomo	45,700	124	103	21
Lafayette	67,483	168	131	37
Lake Station	12,636	30	25	5
La Porte	22,166	48	43	5
Lawrenceburg	5,068	25	21	4
Lebanon	15,873	30	29	1
Ligonier	4,428	11	10	1
Linton	5,441	15	11	4
Logansport	18,490	41	40	1
Long Beach	1,185	6	5	1
Loogootee	2,765	4	4	0
Lowell	9,323	19	14	5
Madison	12,028	33	27	6
Marion	30,101	86	72	14
Martinsville	11,888	32	23	9
Merrillville	35,426	62	48	14
Michigan City	31,460	100	92	8
Mishawaka	48,498	131	105	26
Mitchell	4,372	11	7	4
Monticello	5,405	17	12	5
Mooresville	9,374	27	21	6
Mount Vernon	6,721	15	14	1
Muncie	70,443	104	99	5
Munster	23,724	42	35	7
Nappanee	6,682	21	15	6
New Albany	36,558	70	65	5
New Castle	18,207	34	32	2
New Chicago	2,045	4	1	3
New Haven	14,870	27	19	8
New Whiteland	5,500	12	7	5
Noblesville	52,234	82	72	10
North Judson	1,781	4	4	0
North Liberty	1,906	3	3	0
North Manchester	6,143	15	11	4
North Vernon	6,762	20	18	2
Peru	11,475	30	28	2
Petersburg	2,395	4	4	0
Plainfield	27,772	49	44	5
Plymouth	10,084	29	24	5
Portage	37,016	67	59	8
Porter	4,883	13	10	3
Portland	6,255	17	13	4
Princeton	8,688	17	16	1
Rensselaer	5,889	15	10	5
Richmond	37,000	80	69	11

Table 78. Full-Time Law Enforcement Employees, by Selected State and City, 2012— continued

(Number)

State/city	Population	Total law enforcement employees	Total officers	Total civilians
Rochester	6,250	16	11	5
Rushville	6,373	17	12	5
Schererville	29,392	61	49	12
Scottsburg	6,781	13	13	0
Seymour	17,502	56	39	17
Shelbyville	19,289	62	50	12
South Bend	101,685	328	258	70
South Whitley	1,760	4	4	0
Speedway	11,872	47	34	13
St. John	14,926	24	18	6
Tell City	7,309	20	12	8
Terre Haute	61,095	144	134	10
Tipton	5,132	14	12	2
Union City	3,602	9	8	1
Valparaiso	31,892	55	49	6
Wabash	10,720	28	27	1
Walkerton	2,155	10	6	4
Warsaw	13,628	42	36	6
Washington	11,568	24	18	6
Waterloo	2,253	5	5	0
Westfield	30,222	44	40	4
West Lafayette	29,747	65	47	18
Westville	5,883	3	3	0
Whitestown	2,882	12	12	0
Whiting	5,023	24	19	5
Winchester	4,960	11	11	0
Zionsville	14,232	27	26	1
IOWA				
Adel	3,701	10	9	1
Albia	3,786	7	6	1
Algona	5,589	14	10	4
Altoona	14,617	25	23	2
Ames	59,274	76	51	25
Anamosa	5,562	7	6	1
Ankeny	45,821	58	50	8
Atlantic	7,149	13	12	1
Audubon	2,187	3	3	0
Belle Plaine	2,547	4	4	0
Belmond	2,388	5	5	0
Bettendorf	33,391	49	45	4
Bloomfield	2,654	5	5	0
Boone	12,727	17	16	1
Burlington	25,797	56	41	15
Camanche	4,471	8	8	0
Carlisle	3,896	7	6	1
Carroll	10,156	15	14	1
Carter Lake	3,805	10	9	1
Cedar Falls	39,466	42	41	1
Cedar Rapids	126,988	265	204	61
Centerville	5,557	18	13	5
Chariton	4,344	6	5	1
Charles City	7,692	19	12	7
Cherokee	5,281	9	8	1
Clarinda	5,601	14	9	5
Clarion	2,865	8	7	1
Clear Lake	7,818	22	16	6
Clinton	27,026	49	41	8
Clive	15,528	26	24	2
Coralville	19,006	37	33	4
Council Bluffs	62,556	132	112	20
Cresco	3,888	7	7	0
Creston	7,875	15	11	4

Table 78. Full-Time Law Enforcement Employees, by Selected State and City, 2012— continued

(Number)

State/city	Population	Total law enforcement employees	Total officers	Total civilians
Davenport	100,207	195	167	28
Decorah	8,170	20	12	8
Denison	8,341	18	13	5
Des Moines	204,498	465	360	105
De Witt	5,350	11	10	1
Dubuque	57,939	103	97	6
Dyersville	4,079	5	5	0
Eagle Grove	3,602	7	7	0
Eldora	2,746	4	4	0
Eldridge	5,681	10	9	1
Emmetsburg	3,924	7	6	1
Estherville	6,393	12	12	0
Evansdale	4,776	7	6	1
Fairfield	9,514	20	14	6
Forest City	4,173	8	8	0
Fort Dodge	25,338	43	40	3
Fort Madison	11,109	20	18	2
Garner	3,145	5	5	0
Glenwood	5,297	10	9	1
Grinnell	9,266	17	15	2
Grundy Center	2,720	4	4	0
Hampton	4,484	11	6	5
Harlan	5,133	9	8	1
Hawarden	2,559	4	4	0
Hiawatha	7,061	12	12	0
Humboldt	4,715	6	6	0
Indianola	14,859	21	19	2
Iowa City	68,217	102	79	23
Iowa Falls	5,265	14	10	4
Jefferson	4,368	6	6	0
Johnston	17,368	23	22	1
Keokuk	10,836	27	24	3
Knoxville	7,351	14	12	2
Le Claire	3,785	8	7	1
Le Mars	9,877	14	13	1
Leon	1,987	3	3	0
Lisbon	2,163	2	2	0
Manchester	5,206	13	9	4
Maquoketa	6,173	17	11	6
Marengo	2,541	4	4	0
Marion	34,950	50	41	9
Marshalltown	27,696	59	42	17
Mason City	28,226	51	46	5
Missouri Valley	2,853	6	6	0
Monticello	3,816	7	6	1
Mount Pleasant	8,713	16	14	2
Mount Vernon	4,530	6	6	0
Muscatine	23,006	43	40	3
Nevada	6,834	8	7	1
New Hampton	3,590	7	7	0
New London	1,907	3	3	0
Newton	15,334	27	22	5
North Liberty	13,444	15	14	1
Norwalk	8,992	16	13	3
Oelwein	6,449	16	11	5
Ogden	2,055	3	3	0
Onawa	3,014	6	6	0
Orange City	6,035	7	7	0
Osage	3,638	6	5	1
Osceola	4,955	11	10	1
Oskaloosa	11,523	18	16	2
Ottumwa	25,154	46	39	7

Table 78. Full-Time Law Enforcement Employees, by Selected State and City, 2012— continued

(Number)

State/city	Population	Total law enforcement employees	Total officers	Total civilians
Pella	10,406	21	14	7
Perry	7,742	20	13	7
Pleasant Hill	8,831	19	17	2
Pleasantville	1,70[illegible]	1	1	0
Polk City	3,436	6	6	0
Prairie City	1,689	3	3	0
Red Oak	5,772	12	10	2
Rock Rapids	2,562	1	1	0
Rock Valley	3,372	5	5	0
Sac City	2,232	4	4	0
Sergeant Bluff	4,249	8	7	1
Sheldon	5,215	7	7	0
Shenandoah	5,177	11	8	3
Sioux Center	7,085	7	7	0
Sioux City	83,117	150	123	27
Spencer	11,292	27	19	8
Spirit Lake	4,865	10	9	1
St. Ansgar	1,113	1	1	0
State Center	1,476	1	1	0
Storm Lake	10,656	23	19	4
Story City	3,449	5	5	0
Tama	2,892	5	5	0
Tipton	3,238	6	6	0
Urbandale	39,670	53	49	4
Vinton	5,285	8	8	0
Washington	7,304	11	10	1
Waterloo	68,764	137	125	12
Waukee	13,862	16	14	2
Waukon	3,917	7	7	0
Waverly	9,926	17	16	1
Webster City	8,112	16	12	4
West Burlington	2,984	10	10	0
West Des Moines	56,905	77	63	14
West Liberty	3,756	8	7	1
West Union	2,499	4	4	0
Williamsburg	3,084	6	6	0
Wilton	2,817	4	4	0
Windsor Heights	4,885	15	13	2
Winterset	5,217	8	8	0
KANSAS				
Abilene	6,887	18	15	3
Altamont	1,087	3	3	0
Andale	934	2	2	0
Andover	11,866	29	22	7
Anthony	2,283	6	5	1
Argonia	504	1	1	0
Arkansas City	12,494	33	26	7
Arma	1,490	5	5	0
Atchison	11,091	23	22	1
Attica	630	1	1	0
Atwood	1,202	2	2	0
Augusta	9,333	31	23	8
Baldwin City	4,544	9	8	1
Basehor	4,642	12	9	3
Baxter Springs	4,265	15	10	5
Bel Aire	6,812	7	7	0
Belle Plaine	1,692	5	5	0
Belleville	2,004	5	5	0
Beloit	3,859	8	7	1
Benton	886	2	2	0
Blue Rapids	1,025	1	1	0
Bonner Springs	7,360	25	23	2

Table 78. Full-Time Law Enforcement Employees, by Selected State and City, 2012— continued

(Number)

State/city	Population	Total law enforcement employees	Total officers	Total civilians
Buhler	1,335	3	3	0
Burden	538	1	1	0
Burlingame	940	2	2	0
Burlington	2,691	9	7	2
Burrton	907	3	2	1
Caldwell	1,075	3	3	0
Caney	2,217	10	6	4
Canton	753	1	1	0
Cedar Vale	583	1	1	0
Chanute	9,177	20	18	2
Chapman	1,402	3	3	0
Chase	480	1	1	0
Cheney	2,107	5	5	0
Cherokee	719	1	1	0
Cherryvale	2,382	5	5	0
Chetopa	1,132	4	4	0
Claflin	649	1	1	0
Clay Center	4,362	8	6	2
Clearwater	2,497	7	6	1
Coffeyville	10,360	33	26	7
Colby	5,421	18	12	6
Columbus	3,333	11	9	2
Colwich	1,335	2	2	0
Concordia	5,429	17	10	7
Conway Springs	1,280	2	2	0
Council Grove	2,196	8	7	1
Derby	22,299	52	42	10
Dodge City	27,514	63	47	16
Eastborough	778	7	7	0
Edwardsville	4,368	17	16	1
El Dorado	13,104	27	24	3
Elkhart	2,219	3	3	0
Ellinwood	2,145	5	5	0
Ellis	2,075	5	5	0
Ellsworth	3,140	7	6	1
Elwood	1,232	5	5	0
Emporia	25,074	63	41	22
Enterprise	860	2	2	0
Erie	1,157	4	3	1
Eudora	6,175	9	8	1
Fairway	3,907	10	8	2
Florence	468	2	2	0
Fort Scott	8,138	28	19	9
Frankfort	731	1	1	0
Fredonia	2,498	7	6	1
Frontenac	3,459	10	7	3
Galena	3,105	11	7	4
Garden City	26,827	87	58	29
Garden Plain	854	2	2	0
Gardner	19,244	29	26	3
Garnett	3,437	8	8	0
Girard	2,807	7	6	1
Goddard	4,372	8	7	1
Goodland	4,518	10	9	1
Grandview Plaza	1,570	6	6	0
Great Bend	16,097	33	28	5
Halstead	2,098	6	6	0
Haven	1,245	3	3	0
Hays	20,640	51	33	18
Haysville	10,895	31	26	5
Herington	2,542	8	7	1
Hesston	3,733	7	6	1

Table 78. Full-Time Law Enforcement Employees, by Selected State and City, 2012— continued

(Number)

State/city	Population	Total law enforcement employees	Total officers	Total civilians
Hiawatha	3,192	7	6	1
Highland	1,018	2	2	0
Hill City	1,483	4	4	0
Hillsboro	3,012	5	5	0
Hoisington	2,723	7	7	0
Holcomb	2,107	4	3	1
Holton	3,350	7	7	0
Holyrood	450	1	1	0
Horton	1,787	9	5	4
Howard	691	1	1	0
Hoxie	1,209	2	2	0
Hugoton	3,929	8	6	2
Humboldt	1,965	5	5	0
Hutchinson	42,347	105	67	38
Independence	9,543	27	19	8
Inman	1,386	3	3	0
Iola	5,740	16	15	1
Junction City	23,501	63	44	19
Kechi	1,921	4	3	1
La Crosse	1,351	3	3	0
La Cygne	1,156	2	2	0
Lansing	11,337	18	17	1
Larned	4,080	11	7	4
Leavenworth	35,475	86	64	22
Leawood	32,069	80	59	21
Lebo	946	1	1	0
Lenexa	48,496	123	84	39
Liberal	20,655	55	40	15
Lindsborg	3,480	7	6	1
Little River	561	1	1	0
Louisburg	4,342	7	7	0
Lyndon	1,059	2	2	0
Lyons	3,763	8	7	1
Macksville	552	1	1	0
Marion	1,939	5	4	1
Marysville	3,315	7	6	1
McLouth	886	2	2	0
McPherson	13,239	33	27	6
Meade	1,732	3	3	0
Medicine Lodge	2,022	7	6	1
Merriam	11,073	33	28	5
Minneapolis	2,045	4	4	0
Mission	9,382	28	26	2
Moran	562	1	1	0
Mound City	698	2	2	0
Moundridge	1,748	3	3	0
Mount Hope	818	1	1	0
Mulberry	523	1	1	0
Mulvane	6,150	17	11	6
Neodesha	2,502	8	7	1
Newton	19,254	37	32	5
Nickerson	1,077	1	1	0
North Newton	1,770	2	2	0
Norton	2,947	3	3	0
Norwich	494	1	1	0
Oakley	2,058	10	6	4
Oberlin	1,799	4	4	0
Olathe	126,671	189	163	26
Osage City	2,962	6	6	0
Osawatomie	4,475	17	11	6
Osborne	1,440	4	4	0
Oswego	1,841	4	4	0

Table 78. Full-Time Law Enforcement Employees, by Selected State and City, 2012— continued

(Number)

State/city	Population	Total law enforcement employees	Total officers	Total civilians
Ottawa	12,729	31	27	4
Overbrook	1,065	2	2	0
Overland Park	174,473	287	240	47
Oxford	1,056	2	2	0
Paola	5,638	21	15	6
Park City	7,343	20	18	2
Parsons	10,567	29	23	6
Peabody	1,218	2	2	0
Pittsburg	20,361	54	38	16
Plainville	1,915	5	5	0
Pleasanton	1,224	2	2	0
Prairie Village	21,583	56	43	13
Pratt	6,878	20	13	7
Protection	517	1	1	0
Roeland Park	6,774	14	12	2
Rolla	445	1	1	0
Rose Hill	3,956	11	9	2
Rossville	1,158	2	2	0
Russell	4,535	19	8	11
Sabetha	2,587	9	5	4
Salina	48,010	109	78	31
Scott City	3,840	12	7	5
Scranton	715	2	2	0
Sedan	1,131	2	2	0
Sedgwick	1,706	2	2	0
Seneca	2,004	5	5	0
Shawnee	62,604	109	87	22
Silver Lake	1,448	2	2	0
South Hutchinson	2,473	10	8	2
Spearville	778	1	1	0
Spring Hill	5,472	12	10	2
Stafford	1,049	3	3	0
Sterling	2,343	5	5	0
St. Francis	1,337	3	2	1
St. John	1,303	4	4	0
St. Marys	2,644	5	5	0
Stockton	1,337	5	5	0
Tonganoxie	5,028	11	10	1
Topeka	128,283	353	290	63
Troy	1,016	1	1	0
Udall	751	1	1	0
Ulysses	6,200	12	11	1
Valley Center	6,865	18	13	5
Victoria	1,222	2	2	0
Wa Keeney	1,874	5	5	0
Wamego	4,400	12	7	5
Waterville	684	1	1	0
Wathena	1,373	2	2	0
Wellington	8,224	20	17	3
Wellsville	1,869	4	4	0
Westwood	2,056	8	7	1
Wichita	384,796	841	646	195
Winfield	12,379	31	22	9
Yates Center	1,426	3	3	0
KENTUCKY				
Adairville	858	3	1	2
Albany	2,047	7	7	0
Alexandria	8,536	15	13	2
Anchorage	2,364	14	10	4
Ashland	21,834	50	46	4
Auburn	1,349	2	2	0
Audubon Park	1,483	8	7	1

Table 78. Full-Time Law Enforcement Employees, by Selected State and City, 2012— continued

(Number)

State/city	Population	Total law enforcement employees	Total officers	Total civilians
Augusta	1,198	3	3	0
Barbourville	3,187	15	14	1
Bardstown	11,781	26	25	1
Beattyville	1,316	5	5	0
Beaver Dam	3,433	5	5	0
Bellevue	5,996	11	10	1
Benham	503	2	2	0
Benton	4,379	7	7	0
Berea	13,655	32	30	2
Bloomfield	844	1	1	0
Brandenburg	2,661	4	4	0
Brooksville	646	1	1	0
Burkesville	1,532	9	5	4
Burnside	615	4	4	0
Butler	616	1	1	0
Cadiz	2,576	9	8	1
Calvert City	2,584	7	6	1
Campbellsville	9,171	24	22	2
Caneyville	612	1	1	0
Carlisle	2,024	9	5	4
Carrollton	3,965	11	10	1
Catlettsburg	1,869	8	8	0
Cave City	2,255	6	6	0
Central City	6,019	12	12	0
Clarkson	881	1	1	0
Clay City	1,084	2	2	0
Clinton	1,398	5	5	0
Cloverport	1,160	2	2	0
Cold Spring	5,953	12	11	1
Corbin	7,354	25	18	7
Covington	40,921	132	108	24
Cynthiana	6,446	17	16	1
Danville	16,330	34	32	2
Dawson Springs	2,783	8	5	3
Dayton	5,375	10	9	1
Earlington	1,423	1	1	0
Eddyville	2,572	6	6	0
Edgewood	8,634	14	14	0
Edmonton	1,606	6	6	0
Elizabethtown	28,728	55	39	16
Elkhorn City	989	4	4	0
Elkton	2,076	7	7	0
Elsmere	8,509	13	12	1
Eminence	2,515	6	6	0
Erlanger	22,034	52	40	12
Eubank	321	2	2	0
Evarts	969	4	4	0
Ferguson	930	1	1	0
Flatwoods	7,474	11	10	1
Florence	30,158	63	59	4
Fort Mitchell	8,264	10	10	0
Fort Thomas	16,438	23	22	1
Fort Wright	5,763	12	12	0
Frankfort	25,703	64	59	5
Franklin	8,466	25	24	1
Fulton	2,462	13	9	4
Georgetown	29,299	46	43	3
Glasgow	14,125	49	37	12
Greensburg	2,178	6	6	0
Greenville	4,342	9	9	0
Hardinsburg	2,359	5	5	0
Harlan	1,757	13	12	1

Table 78. Full-Time Law Enforcement Employees, by Selected State and City, 2012— continued

(Number)

State/city	Population	Total law enforcement employees	Total officers	Total civilians
Harrodsburg	8,398	21	13	8
Hawesville	952	1	1	0
Hazard	4,487	25	18	7
Henderson	28,956	77	57	20
Heritage Creek	1,083	9	9	0
Hillview	8,228	12	12	0
Hindman	782	1	1	0
Hollow Creek	788	1	1	0
Hopkinsville	31,795	98	71	27
Horse Cave	2,327	5	5	0
Hyden	368	4	4	0
Indian Hills	2,888	8	8	0
Inez	722	2	2	0
Irvine	2,734	6	6	0
Irvington	1,189	3	3	0
Jamestown	1,806	5	5	0
Jeffersontown	26,779	60	50	10
Junction City	2,256	3	3	0
La Center	1,016	1	1	0
La Grange	8,138	13	13	0
Lakeside Park-Crestview Hills	5,856	11	10	1
Lancaster	3,466	8	8	0
Lawrenceburg	10,578	23	15	8
Lebanon	5,577	21	15	6
Leitchfield	6,745	15	14	1
Lewisburg	816	1	1	0
Lexington	297,847	595	522	73
London	8,048	37	34	3
Louisville Metro	665,152	1,417	1,233	184
Loyall	1,471	1	1	0
Ludlow	4,437	11	10	1
Madisonville	19,726	56	44	12
Manchester	1,264	11	11	0
Marion	3,060	9	6	3
Mayfield	10,093	24	24	0
Maysville	9,073	29	21	8
Meadow Vale	741	1	1	0
Middlesboro	10,405	26	22	4
Millersburg	797	1	1	0
Monticello	6,231	11	10	1
Morehead	6,892	28	20	8
Morgantown	2,411	6	6	0
Mortons Gap	869	1	1	0
Mount Sterling	6,943	24	22	2
Mount Vernon	2,494	9	9	0
Mount Washington	9,180	14	13	1
Muldraugh	954	4	4	0
Murray	17,864	38	32	6
New Haven	861	1	1	0
Newport	15,379	44	40	4
Nicholasville	28,209	65	58	7
Oak Grove	7,541	22	17	5
Olive Hill	1,610	6	6	0
Owensboro	57,661	130	98	32
Owingsville	1,541	5	5	0
Paducah	25,197	81	71	10
Paintsville	3,483	12	11	1
Paris	8,612	27	25	2
Park Hills	2,991	5	5	0
Pikeville	6,951	29	21	8
Pineville	1,744	9	9	0
Pioneer Village	2,044	5	5	0

Table 78. Full-Time Law Enforcement Employees, by Selected State and City, 2012— continued

(Number)

State/city	Population	Total law enforcement employees	Total officers	Total civilians
Pippa Passes	537	2	2	0
Powderly	750	2	2	0
Prestonsburg	3,277	16	16	0
Princeton	6,373	15	14	1
Prospect	4,730	10	9	1
Richmond	31,581	67	57	10
Russell	3,403	12	12	0
Russell Springs	2,458	9	8	1
Salyersville	1,896	2	2	0
Scottsville	4,255	21	13	8
Sebree	1,614	1	1	0
Shively	15,369	31	26	5
Smiths Grove	719	1	1	0
Somerset	11,273	43	39	4
South Shore	1,130	1	1	0
Springfield	2,536	12	7	5
Stanton	2,752	7	7	0
St. Matthews	17,593	38	33	5
Sturgis	1,911	3	3	0
Taylor Mill	6,650	12	11	1
Uniontown	1,009	2	2	0
Vanceburg	1,528	6	6	0
Versailles	8,627	37	36	1
Villa Hills	7,541	8	7	1
Vine Grove	4,551	7	7	0
Warsaw	1,626	5	5	0
West Liberty	3,459	7	7	0
West Point	803	4	4	0
Wheelwright	785	1	1	0
Wilder	3,056	7	7	0
Williamsburg	5,281	13	12	1
Williamstown	3,952	8	7	1
Wilmore	3,711	12	11	1
Winchester	18,495	44	32	12
Wingo	636	1	1	0
Worthington	1,620	4	4	0
LOUISIANA				
Addis	3,626	12	11	1
Alexandria	48,159	183	149	34
Amite	4,179	26	26	0
Baker	14,022	39	37	2
Baldwin	2,458	8	8	0
Basile	1,838	14	9	5
Bastrop	11,469	29	21	8
Baton Rouge	231,592	823	647	176
Berwick	4,991	12	11	1
Blanchard	2,926	6	5	1
Bogalusa	12,344	54	33	21
Bossier City	61,876	203	162	41
Brusly	2,613	9	8	1
Bunkie	4,209	13	11	2
Carencro	7,595	26	24	2
Cheneyville	631	4	3	1
Church Point	4,602	15	15	0
Clarence	504	1	1	0
Clinton	1,668	8	7	1
Covington	8,845	47	36	11
Crowley	13,386	42	38	4
Denham Springs	10,308	40	35	5
De Quincy	3,265	14	14	0
Dixie Inn	275	3	3	0
Elton	1,138	11	11	0

Table 78. Full-Time Law Enforcement Employees, by Selected State and City, 2012— continued

(Number)

State/city	Population	Total law enforcement employees	Total officers	Total civilians
Erath	2,133	9	6	3
Ferriday	3,543	15	10	5
Florien	639	3	2	1
Folsom	723	5	4	1
Franklin	7,730	23	21	2
Franklinton	3,892	23	17	6
French Settlement	1,126	1	1	0
Georgetown	330	4	3	1
Golden Meadow	2,120	6	5	1
Gonzales	9,870	45	45	0
Grambling	4,994	17	12	5
Gramercy	3,646	7	7	0
Greenwood	3,248	11	10	1
Gretna	17,898	129	97	32
Hammond	20,202	104	78	26
Harahan	9,362	26	20	6
Haughton	3,486	8	8	0
Hodge	474	4	4	0
Homer	3,267	10	9	1
Houma	34,035	93	76	17
Independence	1,680	10	10	0
Iowa	3,023	14	10	4
Jeanerette	5,581	18	13	5
Jena	3,429	6	5	1
Jennings	10,478	37	25	12
Jonesboro	4,747	8	8	0
Kaplan	4,642	23	17	6
Kenner	67,312	232	172	60
Kentwood	2,218	8	7	1
Kinder	2,500	17	17	0
Lafayette	121,726	313	257	56
Lake Charles	72,651	185	183	2
Lake Providence	4,028	14	9	5
Lecompte	1,238	4	4	0
Leesville	6,672	26	23	3
Lutcher	3,592	3	2	1
Mandeville	11,666	49	36	13
Mansfield	5,047	22	18	4
Marion	772	2	2	0
Marksville	5,754	27	22	5
Minden	13,202	35	35	0
Napoleonville	666	1	1	0
New Orleans	346,974	1,609	1,349	260
New Roads	4,875	20	19	1
Oak Grove	1,743	6	6	0
Oil City	1,017	4	4	0
Olla	1,398	4	4	0
Opelousas	16,786	81	64	17
Patterson	6,168	29	29	0
Pearl River	2,529	14	10	4
Pineville	14,688	68	59	9
Pollock	473	4	3	1
Ponchatoula	6,619	28	24	4
Port Allen	5,227	18	17	1
Port Vincent	748	2	2	0
Rayne	8,026	20	20	0
Richwood	3,423	11	9	2
Ruston	22,059	56	42	14
Scott	8,693	25	24	1
Shreveport	201,134	720	616	104
Simmesport	2,181	5	5	0
Slidell	27,316	109	73	36

Table 78. Full-Time Law Enforcement Employees, by Selected State and City, 2012— continued

(Number)

State/city	Population	Total law enforcement employees	Total officers	Total civilians
Sorrento	1,414	8	7	1
Springhill	5,317	19	19	0
Sterlington	1,609	6	6	0
St. Francisville	1,781	9	8	1
St. Gabriel	6,700	20	12	8
Stonewall	1,831	4	4	0
Sulphur	20,597	68	44	24
Sunset	2,923	13	8	5
Tallulah	7,402	17	12	5
Thibodaux	14,699	85	58	27
Tickfaw	700	4	4	0
Vidalia	4,338	34	26	8
Vinton	3,241	12	10	2
Walker	6,194	20	16	4
Washington	973	7	5	2
Westlake	4,610	21	21	0
West Monroe	13,184	76	63	13
Westwego	8,612	39	38	1
Wisner	973	2	2	0
Youngsville	8,179	13	13	0
Zachary	15,097	34	32	2
MAINE				
Ashland	1,302	2	2	0
Auburn	23,052	57	50	7
Augusta	19,134	51	39	12
Baileyville	1,521	3	3	0
Bangor	33,035	99	81	18
Bar Harbor	5,234	17	13	4
Bath	8,513	20	17	3
Belfast	6,667	13	12	1
Berwick	7,245	12	11	1
Biddeford	21,274	66	45	21
Boothbay Harbor	2,165	8	7	1
Brewer	9,481	22	21	1
Bridgton	5,209	8	8	0
Brownville	1,250	2	2	0
Brunswick	20,275	51	36	15
Bucksport	4,923	11	7	4
Buxton	8,033	14	9	5
Calais	3,123	9	8	1
Camden	4,849	12	10	2
Cape Elizabeth	9,014	14	13	1
Caribou	8,188	17	16	1
Carrabassett Valley	781	1	1	0
Clinton	3,486	2	2	0
Cumberland	7,210	10	9	1
Damariscotta	2,218	6	5	1
Dexter	3,894	5	5	0
Dixfield	2,550	4	4	0
Dover-Foxcroft	4,212	6	6	0
East Millinocket	3,072	4	4	0
Eastport	1,331	5	5	0
Eliot	6,203	11	10	1
Ellsworth	7,740	20	16	4
Fairfield	6,734	11	10	1
Falmouth	11,184	25	18	7
Farmington	7,759	14	13	1
Fort Fairfield	3,496	4	4	0
Fort Kent	4,096	8	4	4
Freeport	7,878	14	12	2
Fryeburg	3,449	6	6	0
Gardiner	5,799	14	12	2

Table 78. Full-Time Law Enforcement Employees, by Selected State and City, 2012— continued

(Number)

State/city	Population	Total law enforcement employees	Total officers	Total civilians
Gorham	16,379	25	23	2
Gouldsboro	1,737	2	2	0
Greenville	1,646	3	2	1
Hallowell	2,381	5	5	0
Hampden	7,256	12	11	1
Holden	3,076	3	3	0
Houlton	6,122	20	15	5
Islesboro	566	1	1	0
Jay	4,850	8	7	1
Kennebunk	10,797	21	19	2
Kennebunkport	3,474	17	12	5
Kittery	9,489	25	19	6
Lewiston	36,587	90	79	11
Limestone	2,314	3	3	0
Lincoln	5,084	7	6	1
Lincolnville	2,164	1	1	0
Lisbon	9,008	19	14	5
Livermore Falls	3,187	6	6	0
Machias	2,221	4	4	0
Madawaska	4,034	6	5	1
Madison	4,854	7	6	1
Mechanic Falls	3,031	5	5	0
Mexico	2,681	5	5	0
Milbridge	1,353	2	2	0
Millinocket	4,505	8	8	0
Milo	2,340	2	2	0
Monmouth	4,103	4	4	0
Mount Desert	2,053	11	7	4
Newport	3,275	7	7	0
North Berwick	4,575	9	8	1
Norway	5,013	7	6	1
Oakland	6,239	11	10	1
Ogunquit	892	11	9	2
Old Orchard Beach	8,623	21	18	3
Old Town	7,839	18	16	2
Orono	10,361	15	14	1
Oxford	4,109	6	5	1
Paris	5,182	7	7	0
Phippsburg	2,216	1	1	0
Pittsfield	4,214	6	6	0
Portland	66,185	223	162	61
Presque Isle	9,691	21	17	4
Rangeley	1,168	3	3	0
Richmond	3,411	5	5	0
Rockland	7,296	21	19	2
Rockport	3,330	6	6	0
Rumford	5,840	12	11	1
Sabattus	4,875	6	5	1
Saco	18,480	46	33	13
Sanford	20,795	45	41	4
Scarborough	18,917	53	37	16
Searsport	2,615	4	4	0
Skowhegan	8,588	14	14	0
South Berwick	7,219	12	8	4
South Portland	24,999	56	52	4
Southwest Harbor	1,764	9	5	4
Swan's Island	332	1	1	0
Thomaston	2,781	5	5	0
Topsham	8,783	13	12	1
Van Buren	2,171	3	3	0
Veazie	1,919	4	4	0
Waldoboro	5,074	9	8	1

Table 78. Full-Time Law Enforcement Employees, by Selected State and City, 2012— continued

(Number)

State/city	Population	Total law enforcement employees	Total officers	Total civilians
Washburn	1,687	2	2	0
Waterville	15,720	41	31	10
Wells	9,588	31	23	8
Westbrook	17,492	42	[illegible]	3
Wilton	4,115	6	6	0
Windham	16,999	29	26	3
Winslow	7,793	10	9	1
Winthrop	6,091	12	8	4
Wiscasset	3,732	3	3	0
Yarmouth	8,348	13	12	1
York	12,527	38	27	11
MARYLAND				
Aberdeen	15,101	49	39	10
Annapolis	38,758	148	111	37
Baltimore	626,848	3,470	2,931	539
Baltimore City Sheriff	NA	174	133	41
Bel Air	10,216	42	30	12
Berlin	4,528	18	13	5
Berwyn Heights	3,153	9	8	1
Bladensburg	9,235	23	16	7
Boonsboro	3,368	4	4	0
Bowie	55,246	58	47	11
Brentwood	3,075	3	3	0
Brunswick	5,926	12	10	2
Cambridge	12,443	58	46	12
Capitol Heights	4,378	10	9	1
Centreville	4,326	11	10	1
Chestertown	5,302	14	13	1
Cheverly	6,232	18	16	2
Chevy Chase Village	1,972	15	9	6
Colmar Manor	1,417	5	4	1
Cottage City	1,317	5	4	1
Crisfield	2,752	14	10	4
Cumberland	21,057	54	51	3
Delmar	3,031	13	12	1
Denton	4,460	13	12	1
District Heights	5,892	13	11	2
Easton	16,096	63	46	17
Edmonston	1,459	8	6	2
Elkton	15,589	46	40	6
Fairmount Heights	1,508	2	2	0
Federalsburg	2,765	10	10	0
Forest Heights	2,470	7	5	2
Frederick	65,858	171	131	40
Frostburg	9,087	18	14	4
Fruitland	4,912	21	20	1
Glenarden	6,057	11	10	1
Greenbelt	23,287	65	51	14
Greensboro	1,949	3	3	0
Hagerstown	40,038	108	95	13
Hampstead	6,383	10	9	1
Hancock	1,560	4	3	1
Havre de Grace	13,075	44	35	9
Hurlock	2,112	12	9	3
Hyattsville	17,723	51	39	12
La Plata	8,836	17	16	1
Landover Hills	1,703	5	4	1
Laurel	25,353	83	65	18
Luke	66	1	1	0
Manchester	4,854	7	6	1
Morningside	2,034	7	6	1
Mount Rainier	8,157	21	17	4

Table 78. Full-Time Law Enforcement Employees, by Selected State and City, 2012— continued

(Number)

State/city	Population	Total law enforcement employees	Total officers	Total civilians
New Carrollton	12,250	21	16	5
North East	3,606	10	9	1
Oakland	1,943	2	2	0
Ocean City	7,169	124	101	23
Ocean Pines	11,821	19	15	4
Oxford	657	3	3	0
Perryville	4,402	11	10	1
Pocomoke City	4,224	20	14	6
Port Deposit	659	3	3	0
Preston	726	1	1	0
Princess Anne	3,321	15	13	2
Ridgely	1,655	5	5	0
Rising Sun	2,807	7	6	1
Riverdale Park	7,022	29	20	9
Rock Hall	1,322	5	5	0
Salisbury	30,631	115	90	25
Seat Pleasant	4,585	16	14	2
Smithsburg	3,003	5	4	1
Snow Hill	2,123	9	8	1
St. Michaels	1,039	9	8	1
Sykesville	4,478	7	6	1
Takoma Park	16,873	54	41	13
Taneytown	6,792	15	14	1
Thurmont	6,228	11	9	2
Trappe	1,087	1	1	0
University Park	2,572	8	8	0
Upper Marlboro	637	3	3	0
Westminster	18,766	52	39	13
MASSACHUSETTS				
Abington	16,082	26	22	4
Acton	22,058	45	35	10
Acushnet	10,366	17	15	2
Adams	8,537	19	15	4
Agawam	28,611	61	52	9
Amesbury	16,382	37	30	7
Amherst	38,050	47	45	2
Andover	33,403	67	50	17
Aquinnah	313	4	4	0
Arlington	43,105	80	62	18
Ashburnham	6,118	14	9	5
Ashfield	1,748	1	1	0
Ashland	16,694	33	27	6
Athol	11,655	21	16	5
Attleboro	43,859	86	73	13
Auburn	16,287	45	34	11
Avon	4,383	19	15	4
Ayer	7,472	22	17	5
Barnstable	45,468	127	112	15
Barre	5,431	11	7	4
Becket	1,790	2	2	0
Bedford	13,401	39	28	11
Belchertown	14,738	23	18	5
Bellingham	16,432	34	26	8
Belmont	24,880	56	42	14
Berkley	6,450	6	6	0
Berlin	2,883	11	7	4
Bernardston	2,142	3	3	0
Beverly	39,743	69	65	4
Billerica	40,488	75	63	12
Blackstone	9,081	19	16	3
Bolton	4,927	15	10	5
Boston	621,359	2,719	2,156	563

Table 78. Full-Time Law Enforcement Employees, by Selected State and City, 2012— continued

(Number)

State/city	Population	Total law enforcement employees	Total officers	Total civilians
Bourne	19,874	44	38	6
Boxborough	5,026	16	11	5
Boxford	8,014	13	13	0
Boylston	4,382	13	10	3
Braintree	[illegible]	84	69	15
Brewster	9,880	25	20	5
Bridgewater	26,725	49	21	28
Brockton	94,380	196	177	19
Brookfield	3,411	4	4	0
Brookline	59,090	148	126	22
Buckland	1,914	2	2	0
Burlington	24,647	71	64	7
Cambridge	105,803	310	269	41
Canton	21,692	43	42	1
Carlisle	4,882	10	10	0
Carver	11,579	19	14	5
Charlton	13,060	22	18	4
Chatham	6,162	27	21	6
Chelmsford	34,008	60	46	14
Chelsea	35,391	100	94	6
Chicopee	55,635	129	125	4
Chilmark	871	4	4	0
Clinton	13,689	27	24	3
Cohasset	7,588	20	14	6
Concord	17,776	41	33	8
Dalton	6,797	10	9	1
Danvers	26,654	58	46	12
Dartmouth	34,239	75	61	14
Dedham	24,880	57	54	3
Deerfield	5,156	8	8	0
Dennis	14,294	49	40	9
Dighton	7,129	10	10	0
Douglas	8,523	20	15	5
Dover	5,623	17	16	1
Dracut	29,637	43	38	5
Dudley	11,459	16	13	3
Dunstable	3,198	8	7	1
Duxbury	15,151	35	28	7
East Bridgewater	13,878	23	20	3
East Brookfield	2,196	4	4	0
Eastham	4,986	20	14	6
Easthampton	16,151	32	26	6
East Longmeadow	15,816	26	25	1
Easton	23,253	39	31	8
Edgartown	4,092	18	17	1
Egremont	1,232	7	7	0
Erving	1,811	6	6	0
Essex	3,525	12	8	4
Everett	41,921	100	91	9
Fairhaven	15,970	36	30	6
Fall River	89,399	250	196	54
Falmouth	31,723	60	54	6
Fitchburg	40,564	80	68	12
Foxborough	16,968	37	30	7
Framingham	68,734	126	115	11
Franklin	31,828	52	44	8
Freetown	8,924	18	18	0
Gardner	20,351	40	30	10
Georgetown	8,233	15	11	4
Gill	1,509	2	2	0
Gloucester	28,964	62	57	5
Goshen	1,060	2	2	0

Table 78. Full-Time Law Enforcement Employees, by Selected State and City, 2012— continued

(Number)

State/city	Population	Total law enforcement employees	Total officers	Total civilians
Grafton	17,873	23	18	5
Granby	6,278	12	10	2
Granville	1,576	1	1	0
Great Barrington	7,147	18	17	1
Greenfield	17,562	34	31	3
Groton	10,711	22	17	5
Groveland	6,498	11	9	2
Hadley	5,282	15	11	4
Halifax	7,564	12	11	1
Hamilton	7,811	14	13	1
Hampden	5,170	15	10	5
Hanover	13,964	29	27	2
Hanson	10,271	24	19	5
Hardwick	3,008	3	3	0
Harvard	6,560	13	9	4
Harwich	12,318	33	31	2
Hatfield	3,299	2	2	0
Haverhill	61,250	98	84	14
Hingham	22,292	56	47	9
Hinsdale	2,044	1	1	0
Holbrook	10,857	21	20	1
Holden	17,452	27	24	3
Holland	2,496	2	2	0
Holliston	13,630	24	23	1
Holyoke	40,123	132	120	12
Hopedale	5,947	13	12	1
Hopkinton	15,016	24	19	5
Hubbardston	4,409	7	6	1
Hudson	19,179	37	31	6
Hull	10,356	30	22	8
Ipswich	13,255	30	25	5
Kingston	12,706	29	22	7
Lakeville	10,667	17	13	4
Lancaster	8,104	12	11	1
Lanesboro	3,110	7	7	0
Lawrence	76,843	139	118	21
Lee	5,979	12	11	1
Lenox	5,056	11	11	0
Leominster	41,007	83	66	17
Leverett	1,862	2	2	0
Lexington	31,585	61	46	15
Lincoln	6,401	19	13	6
Littleton	8,978	22	16	6
Longmeadow	15,880	29	24	5
Lowell	107,167	298	226	72
Ludlow	21,232	38	33	5
Lunenburg	10,147	14	14	0
Lynn	90,880	194	175	19
Lynnfield	11,667	22	17	5
Malden	59,812	111	102	9
Manchester-by-the-Sea	5,167	17	14	3
Mansfield	23,325	37	34	3
Marblehead	19,929	36	27	9
Marion	4,937	14	14	0
Marlborough	38,734	77	65	12
Marshfield	25,285	45	42	3
Mashpee	14,091	44	34	10
Mattapoisett	6,082	18	17	1
Maynard	10,168	22	21	1
Medfield	12,097	21	17	4
Medford	56,515	98	96	2
Medway	12,830	24	19	5

Table 78. Full-Time Law Enforcement Employees, by Selected State and City, 2012— continued

(Number)

State/city	Population	Total law enforcement employees	Total officers	Total civilians
Dryden Township	4,764	4	4	0
Dundee	3,954	1	1	0
Durand	3,443	4	4	0
East Grand Rapids	10,686	31	29	2
East Jordan	2,349	4	4	0
East Lansing	48,542	83	57	26
Eastpointe	32,418	48	45	3
Eaton Rapids	5,210	11	10	1
Ecorse	9,505	21	20	1
Elk Rapids	1,641	5	5	0
Elkton	807	2	2	0
Elsie	965	2	2	0
Emmett Township	11,761	22	18	4
Erie Township	4,514	2	2	0
Escanaba	12,606	41	30	11
Essexville	3,475	6	6	0
Evart	1,902	4	4	0
Fair Haven Township	1,106	1	1	0
Farmington	10,364	29	22	7
Farmington Hills	79,680	132	100	32
Fenton	11,747	16	14	2
Ferndale	19,885	49	40	9
Flat Rock	9,871	19	19	0
Flint	102,357	139	120	19
Flint Township	31,905	41	33	8
Flushing	8,383	9	9	0
Flushing Township	10,632	6	6	0
Forsyth Township	6,159	8	7	1
Fowlerville	2,884	7	6	1
Frankenmuth	4,940	7	7	0
Frankfort	1,285	3	3	0
Franklin	3,148	10	10	0
Fraser	14,469	46	37	9
Fremont	4,078	9	8	1
Frost Township	1,046	1	1	0
Fruitport	1,092	9	8	1
Galesburg	2,007	2	2	0
Garden City	27,671	30	28	2
Gaylord	3,642	13	11	2
Genesee Township	21,565	16	14	2
Gerrish Township	2,991	7	7	0
Gibraltar	4,652	9	8	1
Gladstone	4,969	9	9	0
Gladwin	2,931	5	5	0
Grand Beach	272	4	4	0
Grand Blanc	8,270	18	16	2
Grand Blanc Township	37,480	43	40	3
Grand Haven	10,404	36	31	5
Grand Ledge	7,780	15	14	1
Grand Rapids	187,898	382	305	77
Grandville	15,366	26	24	2
Grant	893	1	1	0
Grayling	1,883	5	5	0
Green Oak Township	17,463	16	14	2
Greenville	8,475	21	17	4
Grosse Ile Township	10,363	23	17	6
Grosse Pointe	5,417	25	23	2
Grosse Pointe Farms	9,472	46	33	13
Grosse Pointe Park	11,546	44	38	6
Grosse Pointe Shores	3,006	17	17	0
Grosse Pointe Woods	16,123	38	33	5
Hamburg Township	21,149	15	14	1

Table 78. Full-Time Law Enforcement Employees, by Selected State and City, 2012— continued

(Number)

State/city	Population	Total law enforcement employees	Total officers	Total civilians
Hampton Township	9,645	11	10	1
Hamtramck	22,406	45	45	0
Hancock	4,631	7	7	0
Harbor Beach	1,702	4	4	0
Harbor Springs	1,193	6	5	1
Harper Woods	14,225	36	34	2
Hart	2,124	4	4	0
Hartford	2,686	5	5	0
Hastings	7,344	13	11	2
Hazel Park	16,410	39	34	5
Hesperia	953	1	1	0
Hillsdale	8,299	16	14	2
Holland	33,026	66	57	9
Holly	6,081	16	12	4
Homer	1,667	3	3	0
Home Township	1,340	1	1	0
Hopkins	610	2	2	0
Houghton	7,702	8	7	1
Howard City	1,807	2	2	0
Howell	9,482	20	18	2
Hudson	2,305	3	3	0
Huntington Woods	6,233	18	17	1
Huron Township	15,867	23	18	5
Imlay City	3,594	10	9	1
Inkster	25,350	68	59	9
Ionia	11,385	15	13	2
Iron Mountain	7,618	14	14	0
Iron River	3,027	7	6	1
Ironwood	5,383	10	10	0
Ishpeming	6,465	10	9	1
Ishpeming Township	3,510	1	1	0
Ithaca	2,908	3	3	0
Jackson	33,509	60	47	13
Jonesville	2,256	5	5	0
Kalamazoo	74,206	277	234	43
Kalamazoo Township	21,901	37	30	7
Kalkaska	2,018	3	2	1
Keego Harbor	2,968	4	4	0
Kentwood	48,670	76	63	13
Kingsford	5,129	17	17	0
Kingston	440	1	1	0
Kinross Township	7,555	3	3	0
Laingsburg	1,282	1	1	0
Lake Angelus	290	1	1	0
Lake Linden	1,006	1	1	0
Lake Odessa	2,016	4	4	0
Lake Orion	2,971	8	4	4
Lakeview	1,006	2	2	0
L'Anse	2,009	4	4	0
Lansing	114,211	267	188	79
Lansing Township	8,120	15	14	1
Lapeer	8,834	22	20	2
Lapeer Township	5,052	1	1	0
Lathrup Village	4,072	8	8	0
Laurium	1,976	4	4	0
Lawton	1,899	6	6	0
Leslie	1,850	3	3	0
Lexington	1,177	3	3	0
Lincoln Park	38,115	56	49	7
Lincoln Township	14,680	12	11	1
Linden	3,988	5	5	0
Litchfield	1,368	3	3	0

Table 78. Full-Time Law Enforcement Employees, by Selected State and City, 2012— continued

(Number)

State/city	Population	Total law enforcement employees	Total officers	Total civilians
Livonia	96,869	153	124	29
Lowell	3,780	8	6	2
Ludington	8,070	15	14	1
Luna Pier	1,435	3	3	0
Mackinac Island	492	7	6	1
Mackinaw City	805	6	6	0
Madison Heights	29,672	60	48	12
Madison Township	8,614	3	3	0
Mancelona	1,389	2	2	0
Manistee	6,221	12	12	0
Manistique	3,095	8	8	0
Manton	1,286	1	1	0
Marenisco Township	1,726	1	1	0
Marine City	4,245	3	3	0
Marlette	1,874	3	3	0
Marquette	21,339	38	33	5
Marshall	7,083	14	14	0
Marysville	9,951	16	13	3
Mason	8,246	14	13	1
Mattawan	1,995	5	5	0
Mayville	949	2	2	0
Melvindale	10,707	24	22	2
Memphis	1,182	1	1	0
Menominee	8,593	14	13	1
Meridian Township	39,658	43	38	5
Metamora Township	4,246	5	5	0
Michiana	182	3	3	0
Midland	41,831	47	45	2
Milan	5,832	13	9	4
Milford	15,724	24	18	6
Millington	1,071	1	1	0
Monroe	20,717	41	36	5
Montague	2,359	5	5	0
Montrose Township	7,875	9	8	1
Morenci	2,218	3	3	0
Morrice	926	2	2	0
Mount Morris	3,084	6	6	0
Mount Morris Township	21,485	30	27	3
Mount Pleasant	25,996	36	30	6
Mundy Township	15,071	17	14	3
Munising	2,353	4	4	0
Muskegon	38,372	84	75	9
Muskegon Heights	10,848	16	15	1
Muskegon Township	17,827	15	14	1
Napoleon Township	6,771	2	2	0
Nashville	1,627	2	2	0
Negaunee	4,565	8	7	1
Newaygo	1,975	5	4	1
New Baltimore	12,075	21	16	5
New Buffalo	1,882	8	7	1
New Haven	4,638	10	9	1
Niles	11,591	25	17	8
North Branch	1,032	2	2	0
Northfield Township	8,239	9	9	0
North Muskegon	3,783	7	7	0
Northville	5,965	13	13	0
Northville Township	28,476	46	34	12
Norton Shores	23,976	31	29	2
Norway	2,843	4	4	0
Novi	55,182	83	62	21
Oak Park	29,297	66	58	8
Olivet	1,604	2	2	0

Table 78. Full-Time Law Enforcement Employees, by Selected State and City, 2012— continued

(Number)

State/city	Population	Total law enforcement employees	Total officers	Total civilians
Onaway	879	1	1	0
Ontwa Township-Edwardsburg	6,544	6	6	0
Orchard Lake	2,373	8	7	1
Oscoda Township	6,992	12	11	1
Otisville	863	7	6	1
Otsego	3,953	7	6	1
Ovid	1,602	3	3	0
Owosso	15,183	22	19	3
Oxford	3,433	17	10	7
Paw Paw	3,531	9	8	1
Pentwater	856	3	3	0
Perry	2,186	4	4	0
Petoskey	5,666	20	18	2
Pigeon	1,207	1	1	0
Pinckney	2,425	4	4	0
Pinconning	1,306	2	2	0
Pittsfield Township	34,637	52	40	12
Plainwell	3,801	8	7	1
Pleasant Ridge	2,524	6	6	0
Plymouth	9,125	17	16	1
Plymouth Township	27,503	43	29	14
Portage	46,257	69	53	16
Port Austin	663	1	1	0
Port Huron	30,161	57	48	9
Portland	3,880	5	5	0
Potterville	2,615	2	2	0
Prairieville Township	3,401	2	2	0
Raisin Township	7,553	6	5	1
Redford Township	48,326	65	55	10
Reed City	2,423	4	4	0
Reese	1,453	2	2	0
Richfield Township, Genesee County	8,723	10	8	2
Richfield Township, Roscommon County	3,728	7	6	1
Richland	750	1	1	0
Richland Township, Saginaw County	4,141	4	4	0
Richmond	5,731	12	9	3
River Rouge	7,897	20	19	1
Riverview	12,477	34	26	8
Rochester	12,701	27	21	6
Rockford	5,715	10	9	1
Rockwood	3,287	7	7	0
Rogers City	2,825	6	6	0
Romeo	3,593	11	7	4
Romulus	23,971	51	40	11
Roosevelt Park	3,828	5	5	0
Rose City	653	1	1	0
Roseville	47,263	81	76	5
Royal Oak	57,193	78	66	12
Saginaw	51,469	109	96	13
Saginaw Township	40,809	48	43	5
Saline	8,803	17	13	4
Sandusky	2,677	4	4	0
Saugatuck-Douglas	2,155	9	8	1
Sault Ste. Marie	14,133	26	24	2
Schoolcraft	1,524	3	3	0
Scottville	1,213	2	2	0
Sebewaing	1,758	3	3	0
Shelby	2,063	3	3	0
Shelby Township	73,748	89	69	20
Shepherd	1,514	2	2	0
Somerset Township	4,620	5	4	1
Southfield	71,685	165	134	31

Table 78. Full-Time Law Enforcement Employees, by Selected State and City, 2012— continued

(Number)

State/city	Population	Total law enforcement employees	Total officers	Total civilians
Southgate	30,024	46	40	6
South Haven	4,400	21	19	2
South Lyon	11,318	18	17	1
South Rockwood	1,674	2	2	0
Sparta	4,137	5	5	0
Spaulding Township	2,151	1	1	0
Spring Arbor Township	8,261	2	2	0
Springfield	5,256	14	13	1
Spring Lake-Ferrysburg	5,211	10	9	1
Springport Township	2,157	1	1	0
Standish	1,508	1	1	0
St. Charles	2,052	2	2	0
St. Clair	5,481	9	9	0
St. Clair Shores	59,670	88	83	5
Sterling Heights	129,601	201	157	44
St. Ignace	2,450	7	6	1
St. Johns	7,859	11	10	1
St. Joseph	8,359	23	17	6
St. Joseph Township	10,020	12	11	1
St. Louis	7,476	7	6	1
Stockbridge	1,217	1	1	0
Sturgis	10,986	22	17	5
Sumpter Township	9,542	19	13	6
Suttons Bay	618	1	1	0
Swartz Creek	5,754	7	6	1
Sylvan Lake	1,719	3	3	0
Tawas	4,632	6	5	1
Taylor	63,083	77	60	17
Tecumseh	8,515	14	12	2
Thetford Township	7,044	2	2	0
Thomas Township	11,976	8	7	1
Three Oaks	1,621	1	1	0
Three Rivers	7,805	19	17	2
Tittabawassee Township	9,719	5	4	1
Traverse City	14,663	30	29	1
Trenton	18,839	31	30	1
Troy	80,919	147	102	45
Tuscarora Township	3,036	8	7	1
Ubly	857	2	2	0
Unadilla Township	3,363	2	2	0
Union City	1,598	4	4	0
Utica	4,753	17	13	4
Van Buren Township	28,799	55	41	14
Vassar	2,695	4	4	0
Vernon	782	1	1	0
Vicksburg	2,904	10	9	1
Walker	23,519	36	33	3
Walled Lake	6,994	11	10	1
Warren	133,955	227	190	37
Waterford Township	71,653	64	49	15
Waterloo Township	2,854	3	3	0
Wayland	4,076	6	5	1
Wayne	17,580	39	31	8
West Bloomfield Township	64,641	91	71	20
West Branch	2,137	5	4	1
Westland	84,031	98	77	21
White Cloud	1,407	2	2	0
Whitehall	2,704	8	8	0
White Lake Township	29,996	34	24	10
White Pigeon	1,521	4	4	0
Williamston	3,851	6	5	1
Wixom	13,488	23	20	3

Table 78. Full-Time Law Enforcement Employees, by Selected State and City, 2012— continued

(Number)

State/city	Population	Total law enforcement employees	Total officers	Total civilians
Wolverine Lake	4,309	5	5	0
Woodhaven	12,865	28	27	1
Wyandotte	25,863	46	37	9
Wyoming	72,071	94	82	12
Yale	1,954	3	3	0
Ypsilanti	19,420	35	30	5
Zeeland	5,500	10	9	1
Zilwaukee	1,657	2	2	0
MINNESOTA				
Albany	2,581	3	2	1
Albert Lea	18,155	39	28	11
Alexandria	11,155	25	20	5
Annandale	3,253	4	4	0
Anoka	17,274	33	27	6
Appleton	1,423	3	3	0
Apple Valley	49,463	58	48	10
Aurora	1,695	4	4	0
Austin	24,909	34	31	3
Avon	1,407	3	3	0
Babbitt	1,486	4	4	0
Baxter	7,669	15	14	1
Bayport	3,498	5	5	0
Becker	4,573	6	5	1
Belgrade	746	2	2	0
Belle Plaine	6,712	10	8	2
Bemidji	13,535	30	27	3
Benson	3,265	7	6	1
Big Lake	10,138	14	12	2
Blackduck	791	2	2	0
Blaine	57,627	69	58	11
Blooming Prairie	2,011	3	3	0
Bloomington	83,533	141	112	29
Blue Earth	3,379	3	3	0
Brainerd	13,695	28	22	6
Breckenridge	3,412	7	7	0
Brooklyn Center	30,336	60	48	12
Brooklyn Park	76,366	133	105	28
Brownton	768	2	2	0
Buffalo	15,572	21	17	4
Burnsville	60,771	85	74	11
Caledonia	2,890	4	4	0
Cambridge	8,174	14	13	1
Cannon Falls	4,115	8	7	1
Centennial Lakes	10,842	17	15	2
Champlin	23,267	30	25	5
Chaska	23,953	27	24	3
Chisholm	5,014	11	10	1
Cloquet	12,218	21	19	2
Cold Spring	5,489	8	7	1
Columbia Heights	19,646	33	27	6
Coon Rapids	61,950	67	60	7
Corcoran	5,421	8	7	1
Cottage Grove	34,856	45	39	6
Crookston	7,952	17	15	2
Crosby	2,404	8	7	1
Crystal	22,322	36	30	6
Dawson	1,552	3	3	0
Dayton	4,707	6	5	1
Deephaven-Woodland	4,110	8	7	1
Detroit Lakes	8,635	16	14	2
Dilworth	4,055	7	6	1
Duluth	86,931	174	143	31

Table 78. Full-Time Law Enforcement Employees, by Selected State and City, 2012— continued

(Number)

State/city	Population	Total law enforcement employees	Total officers	Total civilians
Eagan	64,702	80	69	11
Eagle Lake	2,441	2	2	0
East Grand Forks	8,667	23	20	3
Eden Prairie	61,266	90	65	25
Edina	48,311	68	50	18
Elk River	23,151	38	30	8
Elmore	668	1	1	0
Ely	3,487	8	7	1
Eveleth	3,747	10	9	1
Fairmont	10,748	19	16	3
Faribault	23,532	35	30	5
Farmington	21,249	28	25	3
Fergus Falls	13,239	27	22	5
Floodwood	532	3	2	1
Forest Lake	18,517	28	25	3
Fridley	27,418	43	37	6
Gilbert	1,813	6	6	0
Glencoe	5,674	10	9	1
Glenwood	2,584	3	3	0
Golden Valley	20,528	38	30	8
Goodview	4,067	4	4	0
Grand Rapids	10,953	21	18	3
Granite Falls	2,919	4	4	0
Hallock	989	1	1	0
Hastings	22,343	32	28	4
Hermantown	9,487	16	13	3
Hibbing	16,487	33	29	4
Hokah	584	1	1	0
Hopkins	17,727	36	24	12
Houston	987	2	2	0
Hoyt Lakes	2,033	5	5	0
Hutchinson	14,287	31	22	9
International Falls	6,474	12	11	1
Inver Grove Heights	34,141	37	31	6
Janesville	2,273	2	2	0
Jordan	5,512	9	7	2
Kasson	5,977	8	8	0
Kimball	768	2	2	0
La Crescent	4,867	8	7	1
Lake City	5,102	12	10	2
Lake Crystal	2,569	11	4	7
Lakefield	1,707	2	2	0
Lakes Area	9,481	14	12	2
Lakeville	56,386	60	52	8
Lester Prairie	1,743	3	3	0
Le Sueur	4,089	8	7	1
Lewiston	1,633	2	2	0
Lino Lakes	20,372	30	25	5
Litchfield	6,778	10	9	1
Little Falls	8,407	15	13	2
Long Prairie	3,485	5	5	0
Madison	1,563	2	2	0
Mankato	39,612	60	49	11
Maple Grove	62,042	76	62	14
Mapleton	1,770	3	3	0
Maplewood	38,311	56	51	5
Marshall	13,786	22	19	3
Medina	4,930	11	10	1
Melrose	3,626	6	5	1
Mendota Heights	11,156	18	17	1
Milaca	2,969	5	4	1
Minneapolis	385,531	983	852	131

Table 78. Full-Time Law Enforcement Employees, by Selected State and City, 2012— continued

(Number)

State/city	Population	Total law enforcement employees	Total officers	Total civilians
Minnetonka	50,118	72	55	17
Minnetrista	8,734	14	11	3
Montevideo	5,425	11	10	1
Montgomery	2,979	5	4	1
Moorhead	38,359	65	52	13
Moose Lake	2,772	4	4	0
Morris	5,327	10	8	2
Mound	9,122	14	12	2
Mounds View	12,249	21	19	2
Mountain Iron	2,891	5	5	0
Mountain Lake	2,120	3	3	0
New Brighton	21,622	33	28	5
New Hope	20,496	37	30	7
Newport	3,462	7	7	0
New Prague	7,378	11	9	2
New Richland	1,212	2	2	0
New Ulm	13,626	24	21	3
North Branch	10,203	12	10	2
Northfield	20,161	26	21	5
North Mankato	13,497	13	12	1
North St. Paul	11,548	21	19	2
Oakdale	27,589	41	31	10
Oak Park Heights	4,372	10	9	1
Olivia	2,503	5	5	0
Orono	11,501	19	16	3
Ortonville	1,931	3	3	0
Osakis	1,753	4	3	1
Osseo	2,449	6	5	1
Owatonna	25,797	36	33	3
Park Rapids	3,738	11	10	1
Paynesville	2,451	4	4	0
Plainview	3,366	5	5	0
Plymouth	71,121	77	66	11
Princeton	4,734	13	11	2
Prior Lake	22,972	26	23	3
Proctor	3,081	7	6	1
Ramsey	23,851	27	23	4
Red Wing	16,586	31	26	5
Redwood Falls	5,295	13	11	2
Richfield	35,500	55	44	11
Robbinsdale	14,061	26	22	4
Rochester	107,593	186	130	56
Rogers	8,663	15	13	2
Roseau	2,653	6	5	1
Rosemount	22,043	24	22	2
Roseville	33,920	54	48	6
Sartell	15,999	17	16	1
Sauk Centre	4,350	7	6	1
Sauk Rapids	12,872	14	13	1
Savage	27,119	36	32	4
Shakopee	37,362	53	45	8
Silver Bay	1,902	4	4	0
Silver Lake	843	2	2	0
Slayton	2,170	4	4	0
Sleepy Eye	3,627	6	6	0
South Lake Minnetonka	11,747	16	14	2
South St. Paul	20,316	29	27	2
Springfield	2,169	5	5	0
Spring Grove	1,340	2	2	0
Spring Lake Park	6,461	13	11	2
St. Anthony	8,289	26	23	3
Staples	3,004	5	4	1

Table 78. Full-Time Law Enforcement Employees, by Selected State and City, 2012— continued

(Number)

State/city	Population	Total law enforcement employees	Total officers	Total civilians
St. Charles	3,764	4	4	0
St. Cloud	66,350	122	101	21
St. Francis	7,274	12	10	2
Stillwater	18,366	24	21	0
St. James	4,641	8	7	1
St. Joseph	6,584	8	7	1
St. Louis Park	45,599	66	51	15
St. Paul	287,665	793	596	197
St. Paul Park	5,320	9	9	0
St. Peter	11,282	19	14	5
Thief River Falls	8,639	17	15	2
Tracy	2,180	3	3	0
Two Harbors	3,774	9	8	1
Virginia	8,779	19	18	1
Wabasha	2,540	6	5	1
Wadena	4,120	9	8	1
Waite Park	6,767	16	13	3
Warroad	1,795	6	5	1
Waseca	9,483	15	14	1
Wayzata	3,716	13	12	1
Wells	2,361	4	4	0
West Hennepin	5,313	11	9	2
West St. Paul	19,691	30	25	5
Wheaton	1,435	3	3	0
White Bear Lake	23,981	34	27	7
Willmar	19,761	35	31	4
Windom	4,682	9	8	1
Winnebago	1,448	3	3	0
Winona	27,805	41	37	4
Winsted	2,373	3	3	0
Woodbury	62,439	76	64	12
Worthington	12,863	32	22	10
Wyoming	7,851	10	9	1
Zumbrota	3,277	4	4	0
MISSISSIPPI				
Ackerman	1,516	5	5	0
Amory	7,344	23	18	5
Batesville	7,491	47	37	10
Bay St. Louis	9,295	32	25	7
Belzoni	2,243	12	10	2
Biloxi	44,221	175	125	50
Booneville	8,776	24	22	2
Brandon	21,787	55	39	16
Brookhaven	12,560	42	34	8
Byhalia	1,307	14	9	5
Byram	11,532	36	22	14
Carthage	5,094	20	15	5
Charleston	2,201	11	10	1
Cleveland	12,381	52	46	6
Collins	2,596	13	9	4
Columbia	6,607	33	22	11
Columbus	23,729	74	67	7
Como	1,284	3	3	0
Corinth	14,628	42	37	5
Crenshaw	888	5	5	0
D'Iberville	9,522	27	26	1
Durant	2,683	13	9	4
Edwards	1,038	1	1	0
Eupora	2,205	6	5	1
Florence	4,157	18	12	6
Flowood	7,853	62	56	6
Fulton	3,976	10	10	0

Table 78. Full-Time Law Enforcement Employees, by Selected State and City, 2012— continued

(Number)

State/city	Population	Total law enforcement employees	Total officers	Total civilians
Gautier	18,642	55	43	12
Gloster	964	6	4	2
Greenville	34,530	128	99	29
Greenwood	15,262	70	55	15
Grenada	13,141	48	44	4
Heidelberg	721	6	5	1
Hollandale	2,712	12	6	6
Horn Lake	26,165	69	53	16
Indianola	10,723	27	19	8
Itta Bena	2,057	12	7	5
Iuka	3,039	12	9	3
Jackson	174,170	728	439	289
Kosciusko	7,430	19	19	0
Laurel	18,610	77	56	21
Leland	4,498	23	16	7
Long Beach	14,848	51	36	15
Louisville	6,656	27	21	6
Lucedale	2,934	21	15	6
Macon	2,778	9	8	1
Madison	24,240	96	75	21
Magee	4,425	16	12	4
Magnolia	2,429	7	7	0
McComb	12,838	63	32	31
McLain	443	2	1	1
Meridian	41,304	109	98	11
Moss Point	13,756	36	21	15
Natchez	15,852	70	45	25
New Albany	8,064	24	23	1
Newton	3,386	18	12	6
Ocean Springs	17,508	58	41	17
Olive Branch	33,611	90	71	19
Oxford	18,987	68	58	10
Pascagoula	22,477	97	65	32
Pass Christian	4,630	21	19	2
Pearl	25,187	85	66	19
Petal	10,494	30	24	6
Picayune	10,919	44	31	13
Port Gibson	1,573	8	5	3
Purvis	2,183	11	8	3
Ridgeland	24,138	91	70	21
Ripley	5,415	12	11	1
Saltillo	4,770	9	9	0
Senatobia	8,196	24	20	4
Shelby	2,237	4	4	0
Southaven	49,167	129	105	24
Summit	1,711	7	6	1
Tupelo	34,677	113	99	14
Vaiden	737	3	1	2
Vicksburg	23,946	101	78	23
Water Valley	3,405	10	10	0
West Point	11,350	30	26	4
Winona	5,062	11	9	2
Yazoo City	11,446	37	27	10
MISSOURI				
Adrian	1,683	3	3	0
Advance	1,352	2	2	0
Anderson	1,968	5	5	0
Appleton City	1,131	2	2	0
Arbyrd	511	1	1	0
Archie	1,174	3	3	0
Arnold	20,884	56	45	11
Ash Grove	1,477	3	3	0

Table 78. Full-Time Law Enforcement Employees, by Selected State and City, 2012— continued

(Number)

State/city	Population	Total law enforcement employees	Total officers	Total civilians
Ashland	3,720	7	6	1
Aurora	7,535	24	18	6
Ava	3,004	13	7	6
Ballwin	30,514	63	51	12
Bates City	220	1	1	0
Battlefield	5,610	5	5	0
Bella Villa	732	2	2	0
Belle	1,551	4	4	0
Bellefontaine Neighbors	10,899	32	31	1
Bellerive	189	19	18	1
Bellflower	394	1	1	0
Bel-Nor	1,504	7	7	0
Bel-Ridge	2,747	18	15	3
Belton	23,200	61	41	20
Berkeley	9,011	60	47	13
Bernie	1,965	9	5	4
Bethany	3,304	5	5	0
Beverly Hills	576	8	5	3
Billings	1,039	4	4	0
Birch Tree	681	1	1	0
Birmingham	184	4	4	0
Bloomfield	1,940	4	4	0
Blue Springs	52,766	117	85	32
Bolivar	10,363	25	20	5
Bonne Terre	6,889	10	10	0
Boonville	8,349	28	21	7
Bourbon	1,638	6	6	0
Bowling Green	5,353	15	11	4
Branson	10,558	60	44	16
Branson West	480	6	6	0
Braymer	881	1	1	0
Breckenridge Hills	4,763	15	14	1
Brentwood	8,084	34	26	8
Bridgeton	11,592	64	49	15
Brookfield	4,559	18	11	7
Bucklin	469	1	1	0
Buckner	3,087	9	9	0
Buffalo	3,095	8	7	1
Butler	4,234	14	9	5
Butterfield Village	472	2	1	1
Byrnes Mill	2,791	5	5	0
Cabool	2,154	10	6	4
California	4,294	7	6	1
Calverton Park	1,298	7	7	0
Camdenton	3,732	17	13	4
Cameron	9,969	23	17	6
Campbell	1,999	5	5	0
Canton	2,386	3	2	1
Cape Girardeau	38,079	94	75	19
Cardwell	716	2	2	0
Carl Junction	7,472	17	12	5
Carrollton	3,798	8	7	1
Carterville	1,898	7	7	0
Carthage	14,430	35	28	7
Caruthersville	6,190	15	14	1
Cassville	3,278	11	11	0
Center	510	1	1	0
Centralia	4,042	12	7	5
Chaffee	2,966	11	6	5
Charlack	1,368	10	8	2
Charleston	5,969	17	12	5
Chesterfield	47,657	93	83	10

Table 78. Full-Time Law Enforcement Employees, by Selected State and City, 2012— continued

(Number)

State/city	Population	Total law enforcement employees	Total officers	Total civilians
Chillicothe	9,550	22	16	6
Clarkton	1,293	4	4	0
Claycomo	1,435	15	11	4
Clayton	15,997	59	51	8
Clever	2,147	5	5	0
Clinton	9,041	22	21	1
Cole Camp	1,125	3	3	0
Columbia	108,894	186	159	27
Concordia	2,459	6	6	0
Conway	791	1	1	0
Cool Valley	1,200	9	9	0
Cottleville	3,086	10	10	0
Country Club Hills	1,279	9	9	0
Country Club Village	2,458	2	2	0
Crane	1,467	3	3	0
Crestwood	11,955	32	26	6
Creve Coeur	17,898	53	49	4
Crocker	1,114	3	3	0
Crystal City	4,873	21	15	6
Cuba	3,368	13	11	2
Dellwood	5,043	17	15	2
Delta	440	1	1	0
Desloge	5,072	10	10	0
De Soto	6,423	20	15	5
Des Peres	8,403	47	39	8
Dexter	7,893	22	16	6
Diamond	905	2	2	0
Dixon	1,555	10	5	5
Doniphan	2,004	12	8	4
Doolittle	632	1	1	0
Drexel	969	2	2	0
Duenweg	1,125	2	2	0
Duquesne	1,769	6	6	0
East Prairie	3,188	10	7	3
Edmundson	837	11	10	1
Eldon	4,584	12	11	1
El Dorado Springs	3,606	11	7	4
Ellington	991	3	3	0
Ellisville	9,166	20	19	1
Ellsinore	448	1	1	0
Elsberry	1,941	4	4	0
Eureka	10,226	26	22	4
Everton	320	1	1	0
Excelsior Springs	11,124	34	23	11
Exeter	775	2	2	0
Fair Grove	1,398	4	4	0
Fair Play	477	1	1	0
Fairview	384	1	1	0
Farber	323	1	1	0
Farmington	16,299	34	26	8
Fayette	2,698	7	7	0
Ferguson	21,280	63	54	9
Ferrelview	453	1	1	0
Festus	11,644	39	28	11
Flordell Hills	825	9	9	0
Florissant	52,348	110	88	22
Foley	162	2	2	0
Fordland	803	2	2	0
Foristell	507	8	7	1
Forsyth	2,263	6	5	1
Fredericktown	3,999	8	8	0
Freeman	484	1	1	0

Table 78. Full-Time Law Enforcement Employees, by Selected State and City, 2012— continued

(Number)

State/city	Population	Total law enforcement employees	Total officers	Total civilians
Frontenac	3,774	22	21	1
Fulton	12,836	34	27	7
Garden City	1,648	3	3	0
Gerald	1,350	5	5	0
Gideon	1,097	3	3	0
Gladstone	25,502	66	49	17
Glasgow	1,107	4	4	0
Glendale	5,947	14	11	3
Glen Echo Park	161	8	5	3
Gower	1,532	3	3	0
Grain Valley	12,901	25	19	6
Grandview	24,564	65	51	14
Greendale	653	7	7	0
Greenfield	1,376	3	3	0
Greenwood	5,240	7	6	1
Hallsville	1,496	2	2	0
Hamilton	1,816	5	4	1
Hannibal	17,981	45	35	10
Hardin	571	1	1	0
Harrisonville	10,055	33	25	8
Hartville	615	2	2	0
Hayti	2,950	10	9	1
Hazelwood	25,796	84	70	14
Herculaneum	3,481	12	11	1
Hermann	2,440	13	7	6
Higginsville	4,814	15	9	6
Highlandville	914	1	1	0
Hillsboro	2,831	6	6	0
Hillsdale	1,483	14	13	1
Holcomb	637	2	2	0
Holden	2,260	7	6	1
Hollister	4,442	18	12	6
Holt	449	1	1	0
Holts Summit	3,259	11	10	1
Hornersville	665	2	2	0
Houston	2,089	6	6	0
Howardville	384	4	2	2
Humansville	1,052	2	2	0
Huntsville	1,570	3	3	0
Iberia	739	2	2	0
Independence	117,255	280	196	84
Indian Point	530	1	1	0
Ironton	1,465	3	3	0
Jackson	13,808	31	22	9
Jasper	934	1	1	0
Jefferson City	43,236	126	86	40
Jennings	14,765	33	33	0
Jonesburg	771	1	1	0
Joplin	50,332	133	122	11
Kahoka	2,086	3	3	0
Kansas City	461,458	1,961	1,387	574
Kearney	8,411	14	13	1
Kennett	10,972	28	23	5
Kimberling City	2,409	8	7	1
King City	1,017	1	1	0
Kinloch	299	4	4	0
Kirksville	17,569	29	26	3
Kirkwood	27,640	69	58	11
Knob Noster	2,719	13	7	6
Ladue	8,552	32	26	6
Lake Lotawana	1,946	7	6	1
Lake Ozark	1,592	17	11	6

Table 78. Full-Time Law Enforcement Employees, by Selected State and City, 2012— continued

(Number)

State/city	Population	Total law enforcement employees	Total officers	Total civilians
Lakeshire	1,437	4	4	0
Lake St. Louis	14,598	40	30	10
Lake Tapawingo	733	3	3	0
Lake Winnebago	1,135	5	5	0
Lamar	4,548	12	10	2
La Monte	1,144	2	2	0
Lanagan	421	2	2	0
La Plata	1,371	3	3	0
Lathrop	2,094	4	4	0
Laurie	948	5	5	0
Lawson	2,482	6	5	1
Leadington	424	6	5	1
Leadwood	1,287	6	5	1
Leasburg	339	1	1	0
Lebanon	14,527	41	28	13
Lee's Summit	91,696	182	127	55
Lexington	4,743	10	9	1
Liberal	762	1	1	0
Liberty	29,255	54	40	14
Licking	3,135	5	5	0
Lincoln	1,194	3	3	0
Linn	1,464	3	3	0
Linn Creek	245	2	2	0
Lone Jack	1,054	5	5	0
Lowry City	642	2	2	0
Macon	5,491	15	13	2
Malden	4,291	14	13	1
Manchester	18,160	42	37	5
Mansfield	1,301	4	4	0
Maplewood	8,075	33	31	2
Marble Hill	1,482	4	4	0
Marceline	2,241	8	5	3
Marionville	2,233	2	2	0
Marshall	13,112	35	25	10
Marshfield	6,657	10	9	1
Marthasville	1,140	1	1	0
Maryland Heights	27,572	97	79	18
Maryville	12,016	26	20	6
Matthews	630	2	2	0
Maysville	1,118	1	1	0
Mayview	213	1	1	0
Memphis	1,829	3	3	0
Merriam Woods	1,767	2	2	0
Mexico	11,585	35	33	2
Milan	1,967	5	5	0
Miller	702	1	1	0
Mill Spring	190	1	1	0
Miner	988	11	8	3
Moberly	14,025	44	32	12
Moline Acres	2,451	13	12	1
Monett	8,905	30	21	9
Montgomery City	2,844	6	6	0
Morehouse	977	2	2	0
Mosby	191	4	3	1
Moscow Mills	2,518	6	6	0
Mound City	1,163	2	2	0
Mountain View	2,729	8	7	1
Mount Vernon	4,592	12	11	1
Naylor	634	1	1	0
Neosho	11,878	19	18	1
Newburg	472	2	2	0
New Florence	772	2	2	0

Table 78. Full-Time Law Enforcement Employees, by Selected State and City, 2012— continued

(Number)

State/city	Population	Total law enforcement employees	Total officers	Total civilians
New Haven	2,097	6	6	0
New London	978	1	1	0
New Madrid	3,127	6	6	0
New Melle	477	3	3	0
Nixa	19,091	30	25	5
Noel	1,839	4	4	0
Norborne	711	1	1	0
Normandy	5,026	19	18	1
North Kansas City	4,223	47	36	11
Northwoods	4,242	28	18	10
Oak Grove	7,823	15	14	1
Oakland	1,386	69	58	11
Oakview Village	376	6	4	2
Odessa	5,319	11	10	1
O'Fallon	79,617	139	107	32
Old Monroe	266	1	1	0
Olivette	7,765	24	23	1
Oregon	860	1	1	0
Oronogo	2,947	4	4	0
Orrick	840	2	2	0
Osage Beach	4,367	40	26	14
Osceola	950	5	4	1
Overland	16,120	60	47	13
Owensville	2,686	5	5	0
Ozark	17,885	34	30	4
Pacific	7,027	25	18	7
Pagedale	3,316	14	13	1
Palmyra	3,608	7	6	1
Park Hills	8,791	14	13	1
Parkville	5,574	16	15	1
Parma	716	4	3	1
Pasadena Park	472	19	18	1
Peculiar	4,625	9	8	1
Perry	696	1	1	0
Perryville	8,255	29	25	4
Pevely	5,504	20	14	6
Piedmont	1,984	7	7	0
Pierce City	1,297	3	3	0
Pilot Knob	749	1	1	0
Pine Lawn	3,287	24	21	3
Pineville	794	5	5	0
Platte City	4,708	12	11	1
Platte Woods	386	2	2	0
Plattsburg	2,327	5	5	0
Pleasant Hill	8,142	18	12	6
Pleasant Valley	2,972	14	9	5
Polo	577	2	1	1
Poplar Bluff	17,085	55	44	11
Portageville	3,240	14	10	4
Potosi	2,670	13	11	2
Purcell	409	2	2	0
Purdy	1,102	2	2	0
Qulin	460	1	1	0
Randolph	52	2	2	0
Raymore	19,276	39	27	12
Raytown	29,633	74	53	21
Reeds Spring	916	1	1	0
Republic	14,805	34	22	12
Rich Hill	1,401	1	1	0
Richland	1,870	6	5	1
Richmond	5,818	12	10	2
Richmond Heights	8,634	42	41	1

Table 78. Full-Time Law Enforcement Employees, by Selected State and City, 2012— continued

(Number)

State/city	Population	Total law enforcement employees	Total officers	Total civilians
Risco	347	1	1	0
Riverside	2,948	34	23	11
Riverview	2,866	10	10	0
Rockaway Beach	844	2	2	0
Rock Hill	4,652	10	9	1
Rock Port	1,323	3	3	0
Rogersville	3,084	7	7	0
Rolla	19,630	59	40	19
Salem	4,968	16	11	5
Salisbury	1,624	4	3	1
Sarcoxie	1,335	3	3	0
Savannah	5,075	5	5	0
Scott City	4,582	17	12	5
Sedalia	21,465	55	43	12
Senath	1,773	3	3	0
Seneca	2,344	6	6	0
Seymour	1,928	6	6	0
Shelbina	1,710	4	4	0
Shrewsbury	6,277	19	17	2
Sikeston	16,377	77	64	13
Silex	188	2	2	0
Slater	1,863	5	4	1
Smithville	8,456	15	15	0
Southwest City	974	3	3	0
Sparta	1,762	3	3	0
Springfield	160,078	384	312	72
St. Ann	13,067	48	36	12
St. Charles	66,033	152	111	41
St. Clair	4,741	17	15	2
Steele	2,180	5	5	0
Steelville	1,648	6	6	0
Ste. Genevieve	4,426	11	10	1
St. James	4,231	9	8	1
St. John	6,541	25	23	2
St. Joseph	77,059	157	115	42
St. Louis	320,454	1,920	1,363	557
St. Marys	361	1	1	0
Stover	1,098	3	3	0
St. Peters	52,766	111	86	25
Strafford	2,367	8	7	1
St. Robert	4,356	25	19	6
Sturgeon	875	2	2	0
Sugar Creek	3,357	22	17	5
Sullivan	7,107	23	16	7
Summersville	504	2	2	0
Sunset Hills	8,527	32	25	7
Sweet Springs	1,489	4	4	0
Tarkio	1,589	3	3	0
Terre du Lac	2,328	6	6	0
Thayer	2,251	10	6	4
Tipton	3,274	3	3	0
Town and Country	10,854	31	30	1
Tracy	209	1	1	0
Trenton	6,023	18	12	6
Troy	10,578	25	23	2
Union	10,241	23	21	2
Unionville	1,872	4	4	0
University City	35,500	91	74	17
Uplands Park	447	9	7	2
Van Buren	822	3	3	0
Vandalia	3,913	7	5	2
Velda City	1,425	13	11	2

Table 78. Full-Time Law Enforcement Employees, by Selected State and City, 2012— continued

(Number)

State/city	Population	Total law enforcement employees	Total officers	Total civilians
Velda Village Hills	1,059	8	5	3
Verona	621	2	1	1
Versailles	2,491	10	10	0
Viburnum	696	2	2	0
Vienna	612	6	6	0
Vinita Park	1,887	14	13	1
Walnut Grove	667	2	2	0
Wardell	429	2	1	1
Warrensburg	18,906	37	33	4
Warrenton	7,909	24	21	3
Warsaw	2,135	7	7	0
Warson Woods	1,969	8	7	1
Washington	14,033	31	28	3
Waverly	852	1	1	0
Waynesville	4,848	11	10	1
Weatherby Lake	1,729	5	5	0
Webb City	11,036	27	22	5
Webster Groves	23,079	50	47	3
Wellston	2,321	8	7	1
Wellsville	1,221	4	4	0
Wentzville	29,176	74	56	18
Weston	1,647	5	5	0
West Plains	12,030	30	26	4
Wheaton	699	2	2	0
Willard	5,307	11	10	1
Willow Springs	2,192	7	6	1
Winfield	1,409	6	6	0
Winona	1,340	4	4	0
Woodson Terrace	4,078	20	17	3
Wright City	3,130	9	8	1
MONTANA				
Baker	1,756	3	3	0
Belgrade	7,455	18	15	3
Billings	105,095	165	140	25
Boulder	1,194	2	2	0
Bozeman	37,611	67	60	7
Bridger	714	2	2	0
Chinook	1,214	4	4	0
Colstrip	2,234	12	6	6
Columbia Falls	4,730	10	9	1
Columbus	1,910	5	4	1
Conrad	2,593	5	5	0
Cut Bank	2,894	6	6	0
Dillon	4,171	8	7	1
East Helena	2,002	5	5	0
Ennis	845	1	1	0
Eureka	1,046	3	3	0
Fort Benton	1,477	5	4	1
Glasgow	3,279	14	11	3
Glendive	4,979	14	9	5
Great Falls	59,024	125	85	40
Hamilton	4,387	16	15	1
Havre	9,393	23	17	6
Helena	28,440	67	48	19
Hot Springs	549	3	3	0
Joliet	600	1	1	0
Kalispell	20,104	44	35	9
Laurel	6,778	17	13	4
Lewistown	5,953	18	13	5
Libby	2,651	6	6	0
Livingston	7,107	15	14	1
Manhattan	1,533	3	3	0

Table 78. Full-Time Law Enforcement Employees, by Selected State and City, 2012— continued

(Number)

State/city	Population	Total law enforcement employees	Total officers	Total civilians
Miles City	8,485	25	16	9
Missoula	67,381	120	100	20
Plains	1,057	3	3	0
Polson	4,528	14	13	1
Poplar	817	3	3	0
Red Lodge	2,144	7	7	0
Ronan City	1,888	4	4	0
Sidney	5,237	11	10	1
Stevensville	1,825	2	2	0
Thompson Falls	1,325	3	3	0
Three Forks	1,886	1	1	0
Troy	946	3	3	0
West Yellowstone	1,282	12	6	6
Whitefish	6,413	16	15	1
Wolf Point	2,644	9	8	1
NEBRASKA				
Albion	1,665	3	3	0
Alliance	8,567	25	18	7
Ashland	2,475	6	5	1
Auburn	3,491	4	4	0
Aurora	4,519	9	8	1
Bayard	1,220	4	4	0
Beatrice	12,570	31	21	10
Bellevue	50,584	113	98	15
Blair	8,061	20	17	3
Bridgeport	1,559	4	4	0
Broken Bow	3,591	7	6	1
Central City	2,960	6	5	1
Chadron	5,903	20	14	6
Columbus	22,308	51	36	15
Cozad	4,012	6	6	0
Crete	7,022	18	11	7
David City	2,932	4	4	0
Emerson	847	2	2	0
Fairbury	3,977	7	6	1
Falls City	4,364	12	8	4
Fremont	26,633	47	37	10
Gering	8,576	18	15	3
Gordon	1,626	5	4	1
Gothenburg	3,606	7	6	1
Grand Island	48,953	88	77	11
Hastings	25,129	46	35	11
Holdrege	5,544	16	10	6
Imperial	2,089	4	4	0
Kearney	31,062	69	55	14
La Vista	15,899	39	34	5
Lexington	10,321	18	16	2
Lincoln	260,685	421	327	94
Madison	2,460	4	4	0
McCook	7,767	21	16	5
Milford	2,109	4	4	0
Minden	2,949	4	4	0
Mitchell	1,717	4	4	0
Nebraska City	7,354	15	14	1
Norfolk	24,426	58	38	20
North Platte	24,954	62	39	23
Ogallala	4,779	11	10	1
Omaha	412,608	924	778	146
O'Neill	3,738	7	6	1
Ord	2,131	3	3	0
Papillion	19,063	42	38	4
Pierce	1,783	3	3	0

Table 78. Full-Time Law Enforcement Employees, by Selected State and City, 2012— continued

(Number)

State/city	Population	Total law enforcement employees	Total officers	Total civilians
Plainview	1,257	2	2	0
Plattsmouth	6,560	17	14	3
Ralston	5,996	15	13	2
Schuyler	6,266	10	8	2
Scottsbluff	15,173	36	31	5
Scribner	865	1	1	0
Seward	7,026	13	11	2
Sidney	6,817	16	14	2
South Sioux City	13,472	28	27	1
St. Paul	2,310	4	4	0
Superior	1,974	4	4	0
Tekamah	1,751	3	3	0
Valentine	2,761	6	5	1
Valley	1,892	5	4	1
Wahoo	4,548	6	6	0
Wayne	5,711	10	6	4
West Point	3,394	7	6	1
Wilber	1,872	4	4	0
Wymore	1,470	3	3	0
York	7,835	19	13	6
NEVADA				
Fallon	8,679	29	19	10
Henderson	259,902	550	336	214
Las Vegas Metropolitan Police Department	1,458,474	4,962	2,644	2,318
Lovelock	1,910	6	5	1
Reno	227,120	346	288	58
West Wendover	4,447	20	13	7
NEW HAMPSHIRE				
Alexandria	1,615	2	2	0
Alstead	1,940	1	1	0
Alton	5,257	14	12	2
Amherst	11,216	18	17	1
Antrim	2,640	7	5	2
Ashland	2,079	5	5	0
Auburn	4,959	9	7	2
Barnstead	4,599	3	3	0
Barrington	8,587	11	10	1
Bartlett	2,792	4	3	1
Bedford	21,231	47	33	14
Belmont	7,366	18	15	3
Bennington	1,478	2	2	0
Berlin	10,064	30	22	8
Bethlehem	2,529	6	6	0
Boscawen	3,970	7	6	1
Bow	7,529	20	14	6
Bradford	1,652	3	3	0
Brentwood	4,492	5	5	0
Bristol	3,058	10	9	1
Campton	3,337	7	6	1
Candia	3,914	8	7	1
Canterbury	2,355	2	2	0
Carroll	764	4	4	0
Center Harbor	1,097	3	3	0
Charlestown	5,121	8	5	3
Chester	4,774	7	6	1
Claremont	13,372	28	23	5
Colebrook	2,304	5	5	0
Concord	42,751	91	80	11
Conway	10,128	30	20	10
Danville	4,393	5	4	1
Deerfield	4,286	8	7	1

Table 78. Full-Time Law Enforcement Employees, by Selected State and City, 2012— continued

(Number)

State/city	Population	Total law enforcement employees	Total officers	Total civilians
Deering	1,915	2	2	0
Derry	33,152	70	55	15
Dover	30,026	62	44	18
Dublin	1,599	4	3	1
Dunbarton	2,762	4	3	1
Durham	14,657	20	18	2
Effingham	1,467	2	2	0
Enfield	4,588	8	7	1
Epping	6,419	14	13	1
Epsom	4,572	6	5	1
Exeter	14,325	33	23	10
Farmington	6,795	15	13	2
Fitzwilliam	2,399	3	3	0
Franconia	1,105	3	3	0
Franklin	8,488	25	17	8
Freedom	1,491	3	3	0
Fremont	4,289	5	4	1
Gilford	7,135	22	16	6
Gilmanton	3,782	5	4	1
Goffstown	17,674	42	28	14
Gorham	2,852	10	7	3
Grantham	2,989	5	4	1
Greenland	3,554	7	7	0
Hampstead	8,534	8	8	0
Hampton	14,996	43	34	9
Hampton Falls	2,239	4	4	0
Hancock	1,656	3	3	0
Hanover	11,275	30	18	12
Haverhill	4,703	8	7	1
Henniker	4,842	9	8	1
Hillsborough	6,019	19	13	6
Hinsdale	4,051	8	7	1
Hooksett	13,469	33	23	10
Hopkinton	5,596	7	7	0
Hudson	24,499	61	45	16
Jaffrey	5,464	14	13	1
Keene	23,440	57	42	15
Kingston	6,033	10	9	1
Laconia	15,972	46	36	10
Lancaster	3,512	7	6	1
Lebanon	13,168	47	34	13
Lee	4,336	8	7	1
Lincoln	1,664	15	10	5
Lisbon	1,597	4	4	0
Litchfield	8,282	12	10	2
Littleton	5,936	10	9	1
Londonderry	24,161	74	59	15
Loudon	5,324	7	6	1
Madison	2,505	5	4	1
Manchester	109,708	271	207	64
Marlborough	2,066	2	2	0
Meredith	6,249	18	14	4
Merrimack	25,527	52	41	11
Middleton	1,785	3	3	0
Milford	15,135	29	24	5
Milton	4,604	8	7	1
Mont Vernon	2,412	3	3	0
Moultonborough	4,049	12	11	1
Nashua	86,607	226	168	58
New Boston	5,328	4	3	1
Newbury	2,075	4	4	0
New Durham	2,641	6	5	1

Table 78. Full-Time Law Enforcement Employees, by Selected State and City, 2012— continued

(Number)

State/city	Population	Total law enforcement employees	Total officers	Total civilians
Newfields	1,682	4	4	0
New Hampton	2,168	5	5	0
Newington	754	11	10	1
New Ipswich	5,106	5	4	1
New London	4,403	13	8	5
Newmarket	8,948	20	13	7
Newport	6,516	18	13	5
Newton	4,609	8	6	2
Northfield	4,835	10	9	1
North Hampton	4,307	13	12	1
Northumberland	2,291	4	4	0
Northwood	4,247	9	8	1
Nottingham	4,791	7	6	1
Orford	1,239	2	2	0
Ossipee	4,351	10	9	1
Pelham	12,914	27	21	6
Pembroke	7,124	14	12	2
Peterborough	6,292	13	11	2
Pittsfield	4,111	9	8	1
Plaistow	7,619	26	18	8
Plymouth	6,999	15	9	6
Portsmouth	21,261	83	62	21
Raymond	10,151	24	17	7
Rindge	6,022	9	8	1
Rochester	29,791	74	58	16
Rollinsford	2,530	4	4	0
Rye	5,305	10	9	1
Salem	28,814	75	58	17
Sanbornton	2,970	7	6	1
Sandown	5,994	7	7	0
Sandwich	1,328	2	2	0
Seabrook	8,704	32	25	7
Somersworth	11,781	30	24	6
South Hampton	815	2	2	0
Strafford	3,996	4	4	0
Stratham	7,265	11	10	1
Sugar Hill	564	2	2	0
Sunapee	3,369	5	5	0
Thornton	2,493	5	4	1
Tilton	3,572	17	15	2
Troy	2,148	3	3	0
Wakefield	5,798	11	10	1
Walpole	3,739	4	3	1
Warner	2,837	5	4	1
Washington	1,124	1	1	0
Waterville Valley	247	7	6	1
Weare	8,797	12	11	1
Webster	1,874	3	2	1
Wilton	3,682	9	7	2
Winchester	4,347	9	8	1
Windham	13,610	25	19	6
Wolfeboro	6,277	17	12	5
Woodstock	1,376	5	5	0
NEW JERSEY				
Aberdeen Township	18,271	41	34	7
Absecon	8,439	33	26	7
Allendale	6,527	17	12	5
Allenhurst	498	13	9	4
Allentown	1,834	5	5	0
Alpha	2,377	15	14	1
Alpine	1,855	13	13	0
Andover Township	6,340	18	12	6

Table 78. Full-Time Law Enforcement Employees, by Selected State and City, 2012— continued

(Number)

State/city	Population	Total law enforcement employees	Total officers	Total civilians
Asbury Park	16,170	98	87	11
Atlantic City	39,690	440	331	109
Atlantic Highlands	4,400	19	14	5
Audubon	8,848	18	17	1
Avalon	1,338	34	21	13
Avon-by-the-Sea	1,907	11	11	0
Barnegat Township	21,006	55	44	11
Barrington	7,006	15	14	1
Bay Head	971	8	7	1
Bayonne	63,234	219	182	37
Beach Haven	1,174	12	10	2
Beachwood	11,082	19	17	2
Bedminster Township	8,192	17	15	2
Belleville	36,046	105	96	9
Bellmawr	11,622	22	20	2
Belmar	5,813	25	19	6
Belvidere	2,690	6	5	1
Bergenfield	26,853	53	45	8
Berkeley Heights Township	13,227	30	24	6
Berkeley Township	41,392	90	69	21
Berlin	7,613	17	16	1
Berlin Township	5,375	19	18	1
Bernards Township	26,741	50	38	12
Bernardsville	7,733	24	18	6
Beverly	2,586	8	6	2
Blairstown Township	5,987	7	5	2
Bloomfield	47,472	136	122	14
Bloomingdale	7,681	16	15	1
Bogota	8,214	21	16	5
Boonton	8,375	25	20	5
Boonton Township	4,277	12	12	0
Bordentown	3,937	13	11	2
Bordentown Township	11,405	25	23	2
Bound Brook	10,437	28	23	5
Bradley Beach	4,312	20	16	4
Branchburg Township	14,507	25	25	0
Brick Township	75,322	177	127	50
Bridgeton	25,433	77	63	14
Bridgewater Township	44,612	90	74	16
Brielle	4,790	15	15	0
Brigantine	9,481	46	35	11
Brooklawn	1,962	8	8	0
Buena	4,618	12	10	2
Burlington	9,953	35	31	4
Burlington Township	22,669	52	42	10
Butler	7,564	18	17	1
Byram Township	8,378	17	16	1
Caldwell	7,848	21	20	1
Camden	77,604	314	265	49
Cape May	3,619	26	21	5
Carlstadt	6,147	26	23	3
Carney's Point Township	8,076	23	18	5
Carteret	22,920	65	55	10
Cedar Grove Township	12,452	29	28	1
Chatham	8,992	22	19	3
Chatham Township	10,487	23	21	2
Cherry Hill Township	71,281	154	130	24
Chesilhurst	1,639	8	7	1
Chester	1,654	9	8	1
Chesterfield Township	7,725	12	11	1
Chester Township	7,864	18	17	1
Cinnaminson Township	15,621	25	24	1

Table 78. Full-Time Law Enforcement Employees, by Selected State and City, 2012— continued

(Number)

State/city	Population	Total law enforcement employees	Total officers	Total civilians
Clark Township	14,805	48	38	10
Clayton	8,206	18	17	1
Clementon	5,017	13	12	1
Cliffside Park	23,673	43	40	0
Clifton	84,416	170	141	29
Clinton	2,728	10	10	0
Clinton Township	13,523	26	24	2
Closter	8,401	20	19	1
Collingswood	13,972	29	24	5
Colts Neck Township	10,176	20	19	1
Cranbury Township	3,870	18	17	1
Cranford Township	22,700	60	46	14
Cresskill	8,602	24	20	4
Deal	752	21	17	4
Delanco Township	4,297	10	9	1
Delaware Township	4,578	9	8	1
Delran Township	16,952	35	31	4
Demarest	4,897	15	15	0
Denville Township	16,690	43	33	10
Deptford Township	30,663	67	62	5
Dover	18,217	33	30	3
Dumont	17,537	43	34	9
Dunellen	7,251	16	16	0
Eastampton Township	6,089	17	16	1
East Brunswick Township	47,670	105	80	25
East Greenwich Township	9,587	23	21	2
East Hanover Township	11,194	36	32	4
East Newark	2,414	7	7	0
East Orange	64,484	294	237	57
East Rutherford	8,943	40	40	0
East Windsor Township	27,280	57	44	13
Eatontown	12,751	46	35	11
Edgewater	11,551	30	29	1
Edgewater Park Township	8,911	10	10	0
Edison Township	100,300	226	177	49
Egg Harbor City	4,257	15	14	1
Egg Harbor Township	43,467	105	79	26
Elizabeth	125,386	526	312	214
Elk Township	4,230	13	12	1
Elmer	1,400	2	2	0
Elmwood Park	19,468	42	40	2
Emerson	7,426	20	17	3
Englewood	27,237	101	76	25
Englewood Cliffs	5,299	22	21	1
Englishtown	1,853	6	6	0
Essex Fells	2,120	13	13	0
Evesham Township	45,690	78	69	9
Ewing Township	35,909	84	71	13
Fairfield Township, Essex County	7,491	36	35	1
Fair Haven	6,141	13	13	0
Fair Lawn	32,565	65	53	12
Fairview	13,881	36	33	3
Fanwood	7,342	18	17	1
Far Hills	922	6	6	0
Fieldsboro	542	2	2	0
Flemington	4,596	16	16	0
Florence Township	12,149	25	23	2
Florham Park	11,735	40	33	7
Fort Lee	35,463	109	89	20
Franklin	5,062	12	12	0
Franklin Lakes	10,625	28	22	6
Franklin Township, Gloucester County	16,876	22	19	3

Table 78. Full-Time Law Enforcement Employees, by Selected State and City, 2012— continued

(Number)

State/city	Population	Total law enforcement employees	Total officers	Total civilians
Franklin Township, Hunterdon County	3,206	5	5	0
Franklin Township, Somerset County	62,507	119	103	16
Freehold	12,092	34	27	7
Freehold Township	36,304	65	61	4
Frenchtown	1,378	3	3	0
Galloway Township	37,473	74	59	15
Garfield	30,588	68	61	7
Garwood	4,240	20	16	4
Gibbsboro	2,282	8	8	0
Glassboro	18,641	50	46	4
Glen Ridge	7,552	28	24	4
Glen Rock	11,640	22	21	1
Gloucester City	11,494	28	26	2
Gloucester Township	64,849	162	111	51
Green Brook Township	7,227	25	21	4
Greenwich Township, Gloucester County	4,915	20	18	2
Greenwich Township, Warren County	5,731	11	10	1
Guttenberg	11,213	29	22	7
Hackensack	43,157	136	111	25
Hackettstown	9,756	18	18	0
Haddonfield	11,632	23	21	2
Haddon Heights	7,498	17	16	1
Haddon Township	14,756	28	26	2
Haledon	8,346	16	14	2
Hamburg	3,288	8	8	0
Hamilton Township, Atlantic County	26,591	63	46	17
Hamilton Township, Mercer County	88,760	205	170	35
Hammonton	14,840	36	30	6
Hanover Township	13,758	35	28	7
Harding Township	3,851	13	12	1
Hardyston Township	8,240	24	18	6
Harrington Park	4,680	9	9	0
Harrison	13,665	50	39	11
Harrison Township	12,458	17	16	1
Harvey Cedars	338	7	7	0
Hasbrouck Heights	11,881	32	29	3
Haworth	3,393	11	10	1
Hawthorne	18,854	34	30	4
Hazlet Township	20,402	44	38	6
Helmetta	2,185	5	5	0
High Bridge	3,660	7	7	0
Highland Park	14,029	32	25	7
Highlands	5,022	16	13	3
Hillsborough Township	38,430	66	51	15
Hillsdale	10,253	20	19	1
Hillside Township	21,475	79	67	12
Hi-Nella	873	12	12	0
Hoboken	50,171	160	138	22
Ho-Ho-Kus	4,092	19	15	4
Holland Township	5,309	7	6	1
Holmdel Township	16,829	47	39	8
Hopatcong	15,197	32	24	8
Hopewell Township	17,362	39	31	8
Howell Township	51,245	100	83	17
Independence Township	5,681	9	8	1
Irvington	54,105	192	153	39
Island Heights	1,679	4	4	0
Jackson Township	55,039	91	72	19
Jamesburg	5,935	16	12	4
Jefferson Township	21,385	45	38	7
Jersey City	248,423	945	806	139
Keansburg	10,139	36	31	5

Table 78. Full-Time Law Enforcement Employees, by Selected State and City, 2012— continued

(Number)

State/city	Population	Total law enforcement employees	Total officers	Total civilians
Kearny	40,819	121	114	7
Kenilworth	7,940	25	24	1
Keyport	7,264	19	16	3
Kinnelon	10,282	17	16	1
Lacey Township	27,730	52	40	12
Lake Como	1,765	10	10	0
Lakehurst	2,663	8	7	1
Lakewood Township	93,152	143	116	27
Lambertville	3,919	12	10	2
Laurel Springs	1,914	7	7	0
Lavallette	1,881	16	12	4
Lawnside	2,955	9	8	1
Lawrence Township, Mercer County	33,583	77	64	13
Lebanon Township	6,610	10	9	1
Leonia	8,967	18	16	2
Lincoln Park	10,556	27	21	6
Linden	40,634	153	122	31
Lindenwold	17,672	43	40	3
Linwood	7,116	17	16	1
Little Egg Harbor Township	20,132	47	39	8
Little Falls Township	14,480	25	22	3
Little Ferry	10,661	26	22	4
Little Silver	5,970	20	16	4
Livingston Township	29,464	80	68	12
Lodi	24,216	47	39	8
Logan Township	6,062	20	19	1
Long Beach Township	3,061	45	36	9
Long Branch	30,821	100	80	20
Long Hill Township	8,731	26	23	3
Longport	898	17	14	3
Lopatcong Township	8,041	15	14	1
Lower Alloways Creek Township	1,776	13	12	1
Lower Township	22,942	51	40	11
Lumberton Township	12,601	14	12	2
Lyndhurst Township	20,622	52	48	4
Madison	15,898	35	28	7
Magnolia	4,355	14	14	0
Mahwah Township	25,976	61	52	9
Manalapan Township	39,001	66	53	13
Manasquan	5,917	22	16	6
Manchester Township	43,213	80	62	18
Mansfield Township, Burlington County	8,572	13	12	1
Mansfield Township, Warren County	7,751	15	14	1
Mantoloking	297	8	7	1
Mantua Township	15,268	27	25	2
Manville	10,378	28	22	6
Maple Shade Township	19,195	39	34	5
Maplewood Township	23,946	71	60	11
Margate City	6,375	39	29	10
Marlboro Township	40,325	83	67	16
Matawan	8,839	22	21	1
Maywood	9,587	25	21	4
Medford Lakes	4,160	9	8	1
Medford Township	23,110	37	33	4
Mendham	4,998	13	12	1
Mendham Township	5,889	15	13	2
Merchantville	3,834	15	13	2
Metuchen	13,619	31	27	4
Middlesex	13,680	25	25	0
Middle Township	18,974	63	48	15
Middletown Township	66,743	127	100	27
Midland Park	7,152	15	14	1

Table 78. Full-Time Law Enforcement Employees, by Selected State and City, 2012— continued

(Number)

State/city	Population	Total law enforcement employees	Total officers	Total civilians
Millburn Township	20,216	58	48	10
Milltown	6,916	18	15	3
Millville	28,495	86	75	11
Monmouth Beach	3,290	9	9	0
Monroe Township, Gloucester County	36,249	77	59	18
Monroe Township, Middlesex County	39,262	69	51	18
Montclair	37,794	115	101	14
Montgomery Township	22,328	35	30	5
Montvale	7,870	20	19	1
Montville Township	21,600	45	38	7
Moonachie	2,717	19	17	2
Moorestown Township	20,795	39	34	5
Morris Plains	5,550	15	14	1
Morristown	18,472	54	50	4
Morris Township	22,380	44	40	4
Mountain Lakes	4,174	26	13	13
Mountainside	6,707	26	21	5
Mount Arlington	5,067	13	12	1
Mount Ephraim	4,692	14	13	1
Mount Holly Township	9,568	19	18	1
Mount Laurel Township	42,003	64	57	7
Mount Olive Township	28,211	56	47	9
Mullica Township	6,167	13	12	1
Neptune City	4,885	19	17	2
Neptune Township	28,028	87	71	16
Netcong	3,243	8	8	0
Newark	278,064	1,209	1,095	114
New Brunswick	55,365	162	134	28
Newfield	1,558	6	6	0
New Hanover Township	7,410	3	3	0
New Milford	16,395	37	34	3
New Providence	12,212	29	23	6
Newton	8,024	32	23	9
North Arlington	15,443	33	26	7
North Bergen Township	60,975	123	111	12
North Brunswick Township	40,878	93	74	19
North Caldwell	6,204	19	14	5
Northfield	8,653	23	22	1
North Haledon	8,445	21	17	4
North Hanover Township	7,704	11	10	1
North Plainfield	22,009	50	45	5
Northvale	4,655	12	12	0
North Wildwood	4,054	35	25	10
Norwood	5,730	13	12	1
Nutley Township	28,464	86	70	16
Oakland	12,796	31	25	6
Oaklyn	4,051	13	12	1
Ocean City	11,740	72	60	12
Ocean Gate	2,018	8	7	1
Oceanport	5,851	15	14	1
Ocean Township, Monmouth County	27,382	72	60	12
Ocean Township, Ocean County	8,360	23	19	4
Ogdensburg	2,418	6	6	0
Old Bridge Township	65,593	119	93	26
Old Tappan	5,769	13	12	1
Oradell	8,005	20	19	1
Orange	30,234	127	109	18
Palisades Park	19,687	36	28	8
Palmyra	7,423	16	15	1
Paramus	26,430	103	76	27
Park Ridge	8,674	17	17	0
Parsippany-Troy Hills Township	53,415	112	93	19

Table 78. Full-Time Law Enforcement Employees, by Selected State and City, 2012— continued

(Number)

State/city	Population	Total law enforcement employees	Total officers	Total civilians
Passaic	70,013	190	159	31
Paterson	146,685	419	357	62
Paulsboro	6,117	17	16	1
Peapack and Gladstone	2,591	8	7	1
Pemberton	1,414	6	6	0
Pemberton Township	28,005	57	53	4
Pennington	2,594	5	4	1
Pennsauken Township	36,004	107	89	18
Penns Grove	5,164	17	13	4
Pennsville Township	13,454	21	19	2
Pequannock Township	15,592	37	32	5
Perth Amboy	50,983	138	109	29
Phillipsburg	15,000	37	36	1
Pine Beach	2,134	7	6	1
Pine Hill	10,267	22	19	3
Pine Valley	12	4	4	0
Piscataway Township	56,231	100	84	16
Pitman	9,041	15	14	1
Plainfield	49,974	159	137	22
Plainsboro Township	23,076	46	35	11
Pleasantville	20,316	60	47	13
Plumsted Township	8,449	14	12	2
Pohatcong Township	3,350	15	14	1
Point Pleasant	18,453	36	29	7
Point Pleasant Beach	4,681	27	22	5
Pompton Lakes	11,134	26	22	4
Princeton	12,348	39	30	9
Princeton Township	16,319	35	26	9
Prospect Park	5,885	14	14	0
Rahway	27,437	83	74	9
Ramsey	14,521	36	30	6
Randolph Township	25,820	37	33	4
Raritan	6,904	22	18	4
Raritan Township	22,259	34	31	3
Readington Township	16,180	25	23	2
Red Bank	12,247	44	37	7
Ridgefield	11,069	29	27	2
Ridgefield Park	12,771	36	29	7
Ridgewood	25,041	46	41	5
Ringwood	12,269	24	20	4
Riverdale	3,571	18	14	4
River Edge	11,378	26	20	6
Riverside Township	8,106	15	15	0
Riverton	2,788	5	5	0
River Vale Township	9,691	22	20	2
Robbinsville Township	13,687	34	25	9
Rochelle Park Township	5,548	24	20	4
Rockaway	6,459	15	14	1
Rockaway Township	24,236	66	54	12
Roseland	5,838	26	25	1
Roselle	21,155	71	58	13
Roselle Park	13,341	41	34	7
Roxbury Township	23,402	42	39	3
Rumson	7,146	19	15	4
Runnemede	8,496	19	18	1
Rutherford	18,121	39	37	2
Saddle Brook Township	13,704	30	27	3
Saddle River	3,162	22	17	5
Salem	5,163	26	23	3
Sayreville	42,846	98	84	14
Scotch Plains Township	23,588	48	45	3
Sea Bright	1,417	12	12	0

Table 78. Full-Time Law Enforcement Employees, by Selected State and City, 2012— continued

(Number)

State/city	Population	Total law enforcement employees	Total officers	Total civilians
Sea Girt	1,834	13	11	2
Sea Isle City	2,121	34	22	12
Seaside Heights	2,897	31	22	9
Seaside Park	1,584	15	14	1
Secaucus	16,318	60	53	7
Ship Bottom	1,160	12	11	1
Shrewsbury	3,822	19	14	5
Somerdale	5,168	13	13	0
Somers Point	10,831	33	28	5
Somerville	12,138	35	31	4
South Amboy	8,660	28	23	5
South Bound Brook	4,578	13	12	1
South Brunswick Township	43,561	97	70	27
South Hackensack Township	2,386	15	14	1
South Harrison Township	3,173	5	5	0
South Orange	16,252	56	52	4
South Plainfield	23,463	63	49	14
South River	16,061	39	31	8
South Toms River	3,696	12	11	1
Sparta Township	19,788	39	29	10
Spotswood	8,284	23	19	4
Springfield	15,870	48	42	6
Springfield Township	3,425	9	8	1
Spring Lake	3,003	18	13	5
Spring Lake Heights	4,729	12	12	0
Stafford Township	26,623	68	49	19
Stanhope	3,622	10	9	1
Stone Harbor	869	22	16	6
Stratford	7,063	17	16	1
Summit	21,528	54	45	9
Surf City	1,209	10	10	0
Teaneck Township	39,908	108	93	15
Tenafly	14,536	39	33	6
Tewksbury Township	6,013	11	10	1
Tinton Falls	17,952	39	37	2
Toms River Township	91,543	194	150	44
Totowa	10,840	31	27	4
Trenton	85,196	314	238	76
Tuckerton	3,358	8	8	0
Union Beach	6,266	18	14	4
Union City	66,676	184	153	31
Union Township	56,831	186	136	50
Upper Saddle River	8,235	19	15	4
Ventnor City	10,685	49	38	11
Vernon Township	24,023	38	29	9
Verona	13,376	31	27	4
Vineland	60,926	168	142	26
Voorhees Township	29,228	52	45	7
Waldwick	9,657	24	19	5
Wallington	11,373	21	20	1
Wall Township	26,251	75	60	15
Wanaque	11,153	25	21	4
Warren Township	15,362	35	28	7
Washington Township, Bergen County	9,132	21	21	0
Washington Township, Gloucester County	48,720	84	77	7
Washington Township, Morris County	18,595	32	28	4
Washington Township, Warren County	6,673	30	28	2
Watchung	5,820	37	29	8
Waterford Township	10,684	23	21	2
Wayne Township	54,899	146	117	29
Weehawken Township	12,596	52	48	4

Table 78. Full-Time Law Enforcement Employees, by Selected State and City, 2012— continued

(Number)

State/city	Population	Total law enforcement employees	Total officers	Total civilians
Wenonah	2,286	7	7	0
Westampton Township	8,842	23	22	1
West Amwell Township	3,853	6	5	1
West Caldwell Township	10,795	29	23	6
West Deptford Township	21,749	44	41	3
Westfield	30,417	66	54	12
West Long Branch	8,124	27	21	6
West Milford Township	25,936	51	44	7
West New York	49,873	114	104	10
West Orange	46,361	108	95	13
Westville	4,302	16	15	1
West Wildwood	605	2	2	0
West Windsor Township	27,255	58	46	12
Westwood	10,944	29	25	4
Wharton	6,544	21	20	1
Wildwood	5,343	45	37	8
Wildwood Crest	3,281	27	21	6
Willingboro Township	31,734	73	64	9
Winfield Township	1,476	8	8	0
Winslow Township	39,630	86	71	15
Woodbridge Township	99,915	245	192	53
Woodbury	10,208	31	28	3
Woodbury Heights	3,065	7	6	1
Woodcliff Lake	5,749	19	18	1
Woodland Park	11,858	28	25	3
Woodlynne	2,988	6	5	1
Wood-Ridge	7,651	24	20	4
Woodstown	3,517	10	8	2
Woolwich Township	10,234	20	19	1
Wyckoff Township	16,752	29	23	6
NEW MEXICO				
Alamogordo	30,743	107	67	40
Albuquerque	551,961	1,416	1,027	389
Angel Fire	1,230	4	4	0
Artesia	11,427	53	33	20
Aztec	6,839	15	13	2
Bayard	2,354	7	6	1
Belen	7,350	23	20	3
Bernalillo	8,413	23	20	3
Bloomfield	8,203	26	22	4
Bosque Farms	3,948	14	13	1
Capitan	1,506	3	3	0
Carlsbad	26,431	76	49	27
Carrizozo	1,007	4	3	1
Cimarron	1,032	3	3	0
Clayton	3,013	15	8	7
Cloudcroft	682	3	3	0
Clovis	38,198	75	56	19
Corrales	8,422	16	13	3
Cuba	739	5	4	1
Deming	15,021	39	34	5
Dexter	1,280	4	4	0
Edgewood	3,777	8	7	1
Espanola	10,338	36	24	12
Estancia	1,674	6	5	1
Eunice	2,955	15	9	6
Farmington	46,390	153	126	27
Gallup	21,921	73	59	14
Grants	9,285	15	13	2
Hatch	1,666	10	8	2
Hobbs	34,504	89	66	23
Hurley	1,312	7	5	2

Table 78. Full-Time Law Enforcement Employees, by Selected State and City, 2012— continued

(Number)

State/city	Population	Total law enforcement employees	Total officers	Total civilians
Jal	2,070	9	5	4
Las Cruces	98,710	263	183	80
Las Vegas	13,907	51	34	17
Logan	1,054	4	4	0
Lordsburg	2,828	12	10	2
Los Alamos	18,151	72	34	38
Los Lunas	15,001	41	36	5
Lovington	11,132	31	21	10
Magdalena	948	3	3	0
Mesilla	2,221	6	6	0
Milan	3,281	12	7	5
Moriarty	1,931	11	10	1
Portales	12,417	42	23	19
Questa	1,790	2	1	1
Raton	6,962	22	14	8
Red River	482	3	3	0
Rio Rancho	88,500	202	123	79
Roswell	48,907	112	77	35
Ruidoso	8,119	39	24	15
Ruidoso Downs	2,847	17	9	8
Santa Clara	1,705	5	4	1
Santa Fe	68,707	195	152	43
Santa Rosa	2,880	12	7	5
Silver City	10,430	38	34	4
Socorro	9,152	29	20	9
Springer	1,059	1	1	0
Sunland Park	14,264	27	24	3
Taos	5,780	24	17	7
Taos Ski Valley	70	3	3	0
Tatum	807	10	5	5
Texico	1,143	3	3	0
Truth or Consequences	6,547	17	15	2
Tucumcari	5,423	25	15	10
Tularosa	2,874	11	6	5
NEW YORK				
Addison Town and Village	2,607	3	3	0
Akron Village	2,881	1	1	0
Albany	98,296	444	312	132
Albion Village	6,083	11	11	0
Alexandria Bay Village	1,083	2	2	0
Alfred Village	4,193	6	6	0
Allegany Village	1,824	3	2	1
Altamont Village	1,728	1	1	0
Amherst Town	117,610	181	153	28
Amity Town and Belmont Village	2,318	1	1	0
Amityville Village	9,566	28	26	2
Amsterdam	18,704	44	42	2
Arcade Village	2,080	6	6	0
Ardsley Village	4,472	19	19	0
Asharoken Village	657	3	3	0
Attica Village	2,558	5	5	0
Auburn	27,811	74	68	6
Baldwinsville Village	7,411	12	11	1
Ballston Spa Village	5,433	5	5	0
Batavia	15,535	31	29	2
Bath Village	5,812	12	10	2
Beacon	15,611	33	31	2
Bedford Town	17,413	43	38	5
Bethlehem Town	33,807	59	42	17
Binghamton	47,589	138	126	12
Blooming Grove Town	12,183	17	15	2
Bolivar Village	1,052	1	1	0

Table 78. Full-Time Law Enforcement Employees, by Selected State and City, 2012— continued

(Number)

State/city	Population	Total law enforcement employees	Total officers	Total civilians
Boonville Village	2,081	3	3	0
Brant Town	2,074	1	1	0
Briarcliff Manor Village	7,902	19	19	0
Brighton Town	36,774	45	39	6
Brockport Village	8,404	12	11	1
Bronxville Village	6,351	23	21	2
Buffalo	262,484	881	736	145
Cairo Town	6,700	1	1	0
Caledonia Village	2,211	3	3	0
Cambridge Village	1,878	4	4	0
Camden Village	2,241	3	3	0
Camillus Town and Village	24,276	25	23	2
Canajoharie Village	2,239	3	3	0
Canandaigua	10,592	25	23	2
Canastota Village	4,826	6	5	1
Canisteo Village	2,280	2	2	0
Canton Village	6,342	10	8	2
Carmel Town	34,459	41	35	6
Carthage Village	3,764	3	3	0
Catskill Village	4,099	16	15	1
Cayuga Heights Village	3,746	7	6	1
Cazenovia Village	2,848	5	4	1
Centre Island Village	412	7	7	0
Chatham Village	1,778	3	2	1
Cheektowaga Town	79,194	166	125	41
Chester Town	8,048	14	14	0
Chittenango Village	5,104	4	3	1
Cicero Town	29,774	14	13	1
Clarkstown Town	79,221	189	163	26
Clayton Village	1,987	3	3	0
Clifton Springs Village	2,137	2	2	0
Cobleskill Village	4,699	11	11	0
Coeymans Town	7,451	9	6	3
Cohoes	16,241	45	34	11
Colchester Town	2,086	2	2	0
Colonie Town	77,950	148	107	41
Cooperstown Village	1,860	7	6	1
Corning	11,233	25	21	4
Cornwall Town	9,671	15	12	3
Cortland	19,290	45	42	3
Crawford Town	9,358	15	13	2
Croton-on-Hudson Village	8,106	23	21	2
Cuba Town	3,258	4	4	0
Dansville Village	4,740	6	6	0
Deerpark Town	7,937	4	4	0
Delhi Village	3,101	4	4	0
Depew Village	15,372	35	30	5
Deposit Village	1,670	1	1	0
Dewitt Town	22,856	40	36	4
Dobbs Ferry Village	10,924	27	25	2
Dolgeville Village	2,216	2	2	0
Dryden Village	1,898	7	6	1
Dunkirk	12,619	36	35	1
East Aurora-Aurora Town	13,844	21	17	4
Eastchester Town	19,642	53	48	5
East Fishkill Town	29,159	40	32	8
East Greenbush Town	16,547	32	24	8
East Hampton Town	19,479	90	64	26
East Hampton Village	1,088	28	23	5
East Rochester Village	6,617	9	8	1
East Syracuse Village	3,098	8	7	1
Eden Town	7,723	5	4	1

Table 78. Full-Time Law Enforcement Employees, by Selected State and City, 2012— continued

(Number)

State/city	Population	Total law enforcement employees	Total officers	Total civilians
Ellenville Village	4,154	10	9	1
Ellicott Town	5,205	13	12	1
Ellicottville	1,605	2	2	0
Elmira	29,331	90	78	12
Elmira Heights Village	4,115	9	9	0
Elmira Town	5,986	4	4	0
Elmsford Village	4,685	18	18	0
Endicott Village	13,452	38	35	3
Evans Town	16,430	30	24	6
Fairport Village	5,377	11	10	1
Fallsburg Town	12,077	17	17	0
Floral Park Village	15,934	47	34	13
Florida Village	2,846	1	1	0
Fort Edward Village	3,390	5	5	0
Fort Plain Village	2,332	4	4	0
Frankfort Town	5,038	3	3	0
Frankfort Village	2,610	5	5	0
Franklinville Village	1,748	2	2	0
Fredonia Village	11,280	19	15	4
Freeport Village	43,053	105	88	17
Fulton City	11,949	36	34	2
Garden City Village	22,472	65	52	13
Gates Town	28,528	37	30	7
Geddes Town	10,581	16	14	2
Geneseo Village	8,067	8	8	0
Geneva	13,321	40	35	5
Glen Cove	27,085	56	52	4
Glens Falls	14,766	36	30	6
Glenville Town	21,848	35	21	14
Gloversville	15,735	32	30	2
Goshen Town	8,266	11	10	1
Goshen Village	5,479	20	17	3
Gouverneur Village	3,967	7	5	2
Granville Village	2,554	4	4	0
Great Neck Estates Village	2,773	16	13	3
Greece Town	96,527	104	98	6
Greenburgh Town	43,055	135	115	20
Greene Village	1,587	1	1	0
Greenwich Village	1,785	4	4	0
Greenwood Lake Village	3,168	9	7	2
Groton Village	2,374	1	1	0
Guilderland Town	33,734	50	34	16
Hamburg Town	45,177	78	61	17
Hamburg Village	9,451	15	14	1
Hamilton Village	4,258	4	4	0
Harriman Village	2,435	7	7	0
Harrison Town	27,595	66	57	9
Hastings-on-Hudson Village	7,884	21	21	0
Haverstraw Town	36,799	77	71	6
Hempstead Village	54,133	148	119	29
Herkimer Village	7,778	21	21	0
Highland Falls Village	3,918	13	10	3
Holley Village	1,819	2	2	0
Homer Village	3,306	4	4	0
Hoosick Falls Village	3,517	2	2	0
Hornell	8,601	22	21	1
Horseheads Village	6,490	13	13	0
Hudson	6,743	31	25	6
Hudson Falls Village	7,314	16	13	3
Hunter Town	2,744	1	1	0
Huntington Bay Village	1,431	6	6	0
Hyde Park Town	21,668	17	14	3

Table 78. Full-Time Law Enforcement Employees, by Selected State and City, 2012— continued

(Number)

State/city	Population	Total law enforcement employees	Total officers	Total civilians
Ilion Village	8,089	20	18	2
Inlet Town	334	3	2	1
Irondequoit Town	51,924	57	46	11
Irvington Village	6,449	23	22	1
Ithaca	30,149	79	67	12
Jamestown	31,286	70	60	10
Johnson City Village	15,242	33	28	5
Johnstown	8,782	25	24	1
Kenmore Village	15,492	25	25	0
Kensington Village	1,166	6	6	0
Kent Town	13,568	25	20	5
Kings Point Village	5,027	24	22	2
Kingston	24,000	75	69	6
Kirkland Town	8,410	7	7	0
Lackawanna	18,223	53	47	6
Lake Placid Village	2,532	13	10	3
Lake Success Village	2,947	26	23	3
Lakewood-Busti	7,384	10	9	1
Lancaster Town	25,431	62	47	15
Larchmont Village	5,890	27	24	3
Le Roy Village	4,411	8	8	0
Lewisboro Town	12,467	1	1	0
Lewiston Town and Village	16,335	11	10	1
Liberty Village	4,412	20	17	3
Little Falls	4,968	12	11	1
Liverpool Village	2,358	6	5	1
Lloyd Harbor Village	3,676	14	13	1
Lloyd Town	10,912	13	10	3
Lockport	21,260	51	48	3
Long Beach	33,425	92	75	17
Lowville Village	3,486	6	6	0
Lynbrook Village	19,514	54	46	8
Lyons Village	3,635	10	8	2
Macedon Town and Village	9,189	6	5	1
Malone Village	5,938	14	14	0
Malverne Village	8,552	23	23	0
Mamaroneck Town	12,031	40	39	1
Mamaroneck Village	19,014	57	50	7
Manlius Town	24,657	44	36	8
Marlborough Town	8,848	8	6	2
Massena Village	10,985	25	20	5
Maybrook Village	2,971	3	3	0
Mechanicville	5,219	13	12	1
Medina Village	6,092	12	11	1
Menands Village	4,008	14	11	3
Middleport Village	1,848	3	3	0
Middletown	28,212	83	69	14
Mohawk Village	2,743	4	4	0
Monroe Village	8,402	22	18	4
Montgomery Town	8,936	14	13	1
Monticello Village	6,756	25	23	2
Moriah Town	3,621	2	2	0
Mount Hope Town	7,050	4	4	0
Mount Kisco Village	10,926	35	33	2
Mount Morris Village	2,999	5	5	0
Mount Pleasant Town	26,294	51	42	9
Mount Vernon	67,594	229	198	31
Nassau Village	1,138	1	1	0
Newark Village	9,186	18	17	1
Newburgh	28,996	88	76	12
Newburgh Town	29,935	58	48	10
New Castle Town	17,648	41	37	4

Table 78. Full-Time Law Enforcement Employees, by Selected State and City, 2012— continued

(Number)

State/city	Population	Total law enforcement employees	Total officers	Total civilians
New Hartford Town and Village	20,580	22	19	3
New Paltz Town and Village	14,066	27	24	3
New Rochelle	77,408	214	158	56
New Windsor Town	25,357	49	40	9
New York	8,211,875	49,401	34,542	14,859
Niagara Falls	50,419	171	153	18
Niagara Town	8,416	5	4	1
Niskayuna Town	21,879	38	27	11
Nissequogue Village	1,757	3	3	0
North Greenbush Town	12,129	18	16	2
Northport Village	7,434	19	15	4
North Syracuse Village	6,831	11	10	1
North Tonawanda	31,710	56	46	10
Norwich	7,222	19	19	0
Ogdensburg	11,178	32	27	5
Ogden Town	19,945	15	12	3
Old Brookville Village	2,144	34	26	8
Old Westbury Village	4,692	31	26	5
Olean	14,517	41	34	7
Olive Town	4,439	1	1	0
Oneida	11,444	26	22	4
Oneonta City	13,963	32	27	5
Orangetown Town	36,998	96	86	10
Ossining Village	25,173	65	56	9
Oswego City	18,224	48	43	5
Owego Village	3,914	8	7	1
Oxford Village	1,457	1	1	0
Oyster Bay Cove Village	2,207	11	11	0
Painted Post Village	1,817	3	3	0
Palmyra Village	3,552	6	5	1
Peekskill	23,689	71	58	13
Pelham Manor Village	5,511	28	27	1
Pelham Village	6,941	28	25	3
Penn Yan Village	5,182	12	11	1
Perry Village	3,690	3	3	0
Piermont Village	2,521	8	8	0
Plattsburgh City	20,079	55	49	6
Pleasantville Village	7,051	22	20	2
Port Chester Village	29,097	60	58	2
Port Dickinson Village	1,648	5	4	1
Port Jervis	8,868	31	30	1
Port Washington	18,991	70	62	8
Potsdam Village	9,470	17	13	4
Poughkeepsie	32,883	130	96	34
Poughkeepsie Town	38,511	95	83	12
Pulaski Village	2,376	1	1	0
Quogue Village	971	14	13	1
Ramapo Town	84,431	130	108	22
Red Hook Village	1,970	2	2	0
Rensselaer City	9,434	29	24	5
Riverhead Town	33,657	99	85	14
Rochester	211,511	871	738	133
Rockville Centre Village	24,131	63	53	10
Rome	33,877	77	73	4
Rosendale Town	6,102	3	2	1
Rotterdam Town	29,225	58	42	16
Rouses Point Village	2,219	1	1	0
Rye	15,791	40	35	5
Rye Brook Village	9,389	28	27	1
Sag Harbor Village	2,179	15	14	1
Salamanca	5,841	15	15	0
Sands Point Village	2,687	20	20	0

Table 78. Full-Time Law Enforcement Employees, by Selected State and City, 2012— continued

(Number)

State/city	Population	Total law enforcement employees	Total officers	Total civilians
Saranac Lake Village	5,430	11	11	0
Saratoga Springs	26,705	79	67	12
Saugerties Town	19,570	26	21	5
Scarsdale Village	17,243	48	42	6
Schenectady	66,432	145	105	40
Schoharie Village	926	1	1	0
Scotia Village	7,764	14	13	1
Seneca Falls Village	6,711	14	12	2
Shawangunk Town	14,396	7	7	0
Shelter Island Town	2,403	10	9	1
Sherrill	3,085	3	3	0
Sidney Village	3,918	8	8	0
Silver Creek Village	2,668	5	5	0
Skaneateles Village	2,461	4	4	0
Sleepy Hollow Village	9,914	25	25	0
Solvay Village	6,614	16	14	2
Southampton Town	50,030	137	99	38
Southampton Village	3,123	44	29	15
South Glens Falls Village	3,534	6	6	0
South Nyack Village	3,526	6	6	0
Southold Town	19,860	67	52	15
Spring Valley Village	31,488	63	55	8
St. Johnsville Village	1,740	2	2	0
Stony Point Town	15,127	28	27	1
Suffern Village	10,771	25	24	1
Syracuse	145,822	564	494	70
Tarrytown Village	11,328	38	33	5
Ticonderoga Town	5,065	7	7	0
Tonawanda	15,198	33	28	5
Tonawanda Town	58,406	152	104	48
Troy	50,354	138	124	14
Tuckahoe Village	6,515	27	24	3
Tupper Lake Village	3,683	8	8	0
Tuxedo Town	3,014	15	12	3
Ulster Town	12,382	29	25	4
Utica	62,515	198	178	20
Vernon Village	1,177	1	1	0
Vestal Town	28,169	39	35	4
Walden Village	7,009	17	14	3
Wallkill Town	27,549	40	35	5
Walton Village	3,102	6	5	1
Wappingers Falls Village	5,547	7	4	3
Warsaw Village	3,489	5	5	0
Warwick Town	19,438	37	32	5
Washingtonville Village	5,926	15	13	2
Waterford Town and Village	8,461	13	10	3
Waterloo Village	5,194	9	8	1
Watertown	27,144	68	64	4
Watervliet	10,300	29	26	3
Watkins Glen Village	1,867	4	4	0
Waverly Village	4,464	11	10	1
Wayland Village	1,873	1	1	0
Webb Town	1,815	5	5	0
Webster Town and Village	42,833	34	29	5
Wellsville Village	4,700	12	10	2
Westfield Village	3,238	5	5	0
Westhampton Beach Village	1,729	16	14	2
West Seneca Town	44,912	79	67	12
Whitehall Village	2,626	4	4	0
White Plains	57,109	205	194	11
Whitesboro Village	3,789	6	6	0
Whitestown Town	9,199	7	7	0

Table 78. Full-Time Law Enforcement Employees, by Selected State and City, 2012— continued

(Number)

State/city	Population	Total law enforcement employees	Total officers	Total civilians
Windham Town	1,711	2	2	0
Woodbury Town	10,734	21	21	0
Woodridge Village	851	1	1	0
Woodstock Town	5,910	10	10	0
Yonkers	196,857	694	619	75
Yorktown Town	36,243	63	54	9
Yorkville Village	2,701	3	3	0
NORTH CAROLINA				
Aberdeen	6,431	28	26	2
Ahoskie	5,103	22	16	6
Albemarle	16,105	52	46	6
Andrews	1,804	5	5	0
Angier	4,405	12	12	0
Apex	37,951	68	53	15
Archdale	11,560	31	25	6
Asheboro	25,329	85	78	7
Asheville	84,450	238	198	40
Atlantic Beach	1,514	19	18	1
Aurora	527	2	2	0
Ayden	4,995	22	18	4
Badin	1,999	4	4	0
Bailey	576	2	2	0
Bakersville	470	1	1	0
Bald Head Island	160	21	12	9
Banner Elk	1,041	10	9	1
Beaufort	4,090	19	18	1
Beech Mountain	324	14	10	4
Belhaven	1,709	10	6	4
Belmont	10,204	44	33	11
Benson	3,353	15	14	1
Bethel	1,597	5	5	0
Beulaville	1,312	4	4	0
Biltmore Forest	1,360	15	13	2
Biscoe	1,722	9	8	1
Black Creek	779	2	2	0
Black Mountain	7,948	21	17	4
Bladenboro	1,772	5	5	0
Blowing Rock	1,257	13	10	3
Boiling Spring Lakes	5,440	9	8	1
Boiling Springs	4,706	8	8	0
Bolton	700	3	2	1
Boone	17,339	41	34	7
Boonville	1,237	5	5	0
Brevard	7,705	28	22	6
Broadway	1,245	4	4	0
Brookford	387	1	1	0
Bryson City	1,442	8	7	1
Bunn	348	2	2	0
Burgaw	3,921	13	12	1
Burlington	50,597	162	122	40
Burnsville	1,714	8	8	0
Butner	7,687	45	40	5
Cameron	289	1	1	0
Candor	851	5	5	0
Canton	4,281	20	14	6
Cape Carteret	1,941	6	6	0
Carolina Beach	5,778	30	28	2
Carrboro	19,830	42	39	3
Carthage	2,233	11	10	1
Cary	136,949	211	173	38
Caswell Beach	403	4	4	0
Catawba	611	1	1	0

Table 78. Full-Time Law Enforcement Employees, by Selected State and City, 2012— continued

(Number)

State/city	Population	Total law enforcement employees	Total officers	Total civilians
Chadbourn	1,880	10	9	1
Chapel Hill	57,959	129	114	15
Charlotte-Mecklenburg[1]	789,478	2,214	1,726	488
Cherryville	5,833	22	17	5
China Grove	3,608	13	13	0
Chocowinity	830	3	3	0
Claremont	1,369	9	8	1
Clayton	16,320	46	42	4
Cleveland	882	5	5	0
Clinton	8,749	34	30	4
Clyde	1,239	4	4	0
Coats	2,139	5	5	0
Columbus	1,012	6	6	0
Concord	80,069	182	154	28
Conover	8,269	26	25	1
Conway	847	1	1	0
Cooleemee	972	4	4	0
Cornelius	25,181	68	51	17
Cramerton	4,218	13	13	0
Creedmoor	4,176	17	13	4
Dallas	4,545	16	12	4
Davidson	11,083	18	17	1
Denton	1,657	6	6	0
Dobson	1,606	6	6	0
Drexel	1,882	5	5	0
Duck	374	9	8	1
Dunn	9,380	51	35	16
Durham	231,225	618	476	142
East Bend	620	2	2	0
East Spencer	1,553	4	4	0
Eden	15,724	52	43	9
Edenton	5,067	18	15	3
Elizabeth City	18,920	71	58	13
Elizabethtown	3,628	17	16	1
Elkin	4,052	21	17	4
Elon	9,538	16	15	1
Emerald Isle	3,701	16	13	3
Enfield	2,564	17	16	1
Erwin	4,461	11	10	1
Fair Bluff	963	3	3	0
Fairmont	2,697	15	12	3
Farmville	4,713	21	16	5
Fayetteville	203,107	513	366	147
Fletcher	7,278	15	14	1
Forest City	7,571	34	32	2
Four Oaks	1,945	5	5	0
Foxfire Village	913	2	2	0
Franklin	3,894	18	17	1
Franklinton	2,049	9	9	0
Fremont	1,271	4	4	0
Fuquay-Varina	18,164	36	31	5
Garner	26,071	69	64	5
Garysburg	1,070	2	2	0
Gaston	1,167	2	2	0
Gastonia	72,651	204	176	28
Gibsonville	6,491	15	14	1
Glen Alpine	1,536	3	3	0
Goldsboro	36,899	121	110	11
Graham	14,332	37	34	3
Granite Falls	4,782	15	13	2
Granite Quarry	2,967	7	7	0
Greensboro	273,086	773	636	137

Table 78. Full-Time Law Enforcement Employees, by Selected State and City, 2012— continued

(Number)

State/city	Population	Total law enforcement employees	Total officers	Total civilians
Greenville	85,626	236	185	51
Grifton	2,650	7	7	0
Hamlet	6,577	24	20	4
Havelock	20,998	36	29	7
Haw River	2,327	8	8	0
Henderson	15,563	58	50	8
Hendersonville	13,304	49	37	12
Hertford	2,170	9	8	1
Hickory	40,517	147	116	31
Highlands	936	12	11	1
High Point	105,695	247	211	36
Hillsborough	6,164	26	24	2
Holden Beach	582	8	8	0
Holly Ridge	1,284	9	8	1
Holly Springs	24,974	54	44	10
Hope Mills	15,368	40	34	6
Hot Springs	567	1	1	0
Hudson	3,824	12	11	1
Huntersville	47,366	90	81	9
Indian Beach	113	4	4	0
Jackson	520	1	1	0
Jacksonville	71,034	149	120	29
Jefferson	1,631	3	3	0
Jonesville	2,314	11	10	1
Kannapolis	43,166	98	76	22
Kenansville	866	5	5	0
Kenly	1,356	8	8	0
Kernersville	23,416	80	64	16
Kill Devil Hills	6,768	33	29	4
King	6,992	23	20	3
Kings Mountain	10,427	36	30	6
Kinston	21,952	85	75	10
Kitty Hawk	3,313	18	16	2
Knightdale	11,546	29	28	1
Kure Beach	2,038	12	11	1
Lake Lure	1,207	11	10	1
Lake Royale	2,538	6	6	0
Lake Waccamaw	1,499	5	5	0
Landis	3,148	11	10	1
Laurel Park	2,208	7	7	0
Laurinburg	16,164	45	39	6
Leland	13,699	34	31	3
Lenoir	18,459	66	52	14
Lexington	19,171	74	65	9
Liberty	2,690	11	10	1
Lilesville	543	1	1	0
Lillington	3,235	12	11	1
Lincolnton	10,619	36	31	5
Littleton	683	3	3	0
Locust	2,967	13	12	1
Long View	4,933	15	15	0
Louisburg	3,402	14	13	1
Lowell	3,571	9	9	0
Lumberton	21,815	91	81	10
Madison	2,274	14	13	1
Maggie Valley	1,165	11	10	1
Magnolia	951	2	2	0
Maiden	3,352	15	14	1
Manteo	1,452	8	7	1
Marion	7,937	26	25	1
Marshall	883	3	3	0
Mars Hill	1,893	5	5	0

Table 78. Full-Time Law Enforcement Employees, by Selected State and City, 2012— continued

(Number)

State/city	Population	Total law enforcement employees	Total officers	Total civilians
Marshville	2,432	7	7	0
Matthews	27,543	69	57	12
Maxton	2,457	16	12	4
Mayodan	2,509	16	13	3
Maysville	1,032	3	3	0
Mebane	11,537	29	22	7
Middlesex	832	4	4	0
Mint Hill	23,010	30	27	3
Misenheimer	737	4	4	0
Mocksville	5,115	24	22	2
Monroe	33,213	98	86	12
Montreat	732	5	5	0
Mooresville	33,126	79	58	21
Morehead City	8,771	43	37	6
Morganton	17,133	90	59	31
Morrisville	18,812	34	33	1
Morven	517	1	1	0
Mount Airy	10,520	53	41	12
Mount Gilead	1,196	7	7	0
Mount Holly	13,829	36	30	6
Mount Olive	4,647	15	14	1
Murfreesboro	2,871	14	9	5
Murphy	1,648	10	7	3
Nags Head	2,792	23	21	2
Nashville	5,420	16	15	1
Navassa	1,524	4	4	0
New Bern	29,898	111	76	35
Newland	707	5	5	0
Newport	4,203	9	9	0
Newton	13,132	43	35	8
Newton Grove	576	3	3	0
Norlina	1,132	4	4	0
North Topsail Beach	752	12	11	1
Northwest	744	2	2	0
North Wilkesboro	4,299	25	24	1
Norwood	2,409	7	6	1
Oakboro	1,883	6	6	0
Oak Island	6,869	31	25	6
Ocean Isle Beach	557	13	13	0
Old Fort	920	3	3	0
Oxford	8,568	35	29	6
Parkton	442	2	2	0
Pembroke	3,011	17	13	4
Pikeville	687	3	3	0
Pilot Mountain	1,496	9	8	1
Pinebluff	1,354	3	3	0
Pinehurst	13,290	28	23	5
Pine Knoll Shores	1,356	7	7	0
Pine Level	1,722	5	5	0
Pinetops	1,391	9	6	3
Pineville	7,574	45	34	11
Pink Hill	559	2	2	0
Pittsboro	3,790	13	13	0
Plymouth	3,927	13	13	0
Polkton	3,418	1	1	0
Princeton	1,209	4	4	0
Raeford	4,669	16	15	1
Raleigh	409,014	846	746	100
Ramseur	1,713	6	6	0
Randleman	4,165	14	14	0
Ranlo	3,478	7	7	0
Red Springs	3,471	21	17	4

Table 78. Full-Time Law Enforcement Employees, by Selected State and City, 2012— continued

(Number)

State/city	Population	Total law enforcement employees	Total officers	Total civilians
Reidsville	14,704	58	50	8
Richlands	1,539	5	5	0
Rich Square	970	2	2	0
River Bend	3,159	5	5	0
Roanoke Rapids	15,954	41	37	4
Robbins	1,111	5	5	0
Robersonville	1,507	7	7	0
Rockingham	9,679	37	32	5
Rockwell	2,135	5	5	0
Rocky Mount	58,206	207	165	42
Rolesville	3,834	12	11	1
Rose Hill	1,647	4	4	0
Rowland	1,050	7	6	1
Roxboro	8,468	38	33	5
Rutherfordton	4,266	15	14	1
Salisbury	34,089	94	78	16
Saluda	722	4	4	0
Sanford	28,450	100	80	20
Scotland Neck	2,085	9	8	1
Selma	6,150	25	23	2
Seven Devils	194	6	6	0
Shallotte	3,722	14	13	1
Sharpsburg	2,050	8	8	0
Shelby	20,581	82	71	11
Siler City	7,987	26	21	5
Smithfield	11,105	44	42	2
Southern Pines	12,490	40	32	8
Southern Shores	2,748	11	10	1
Southport	2,869	11	10	1
Sparta	1,792	6	6	0
Spencer	3,308	13	12	1
Spindale	4,376	12	12	0
Spring Hope	1,337	6	6	0
Spring Lake	12,116	29	26	3
Spruce Pine	2,203	11	11	0
Stallings	14,006	24	21	3
Stanfield	1,505	3	3	0
Stanley	3,601	10	10	0
Stantonsburg	794	3	3	0
Star	887	4	4	0
Statesville	24,843	96	76	20
Stoneville	1,069	4	4	0
St. Pauls	2,061	18	13	5
Sugar Mountain	201	5	5	0
Sunset Beach	3,617	13	13	0
Surf City	1,876	19	17	2
Swansboro	2,697	9	9	0
Sylva	2,621	14	13	1
Tabor City	2,543	10	9	1
Tarboro	11,560	34	28	6
Taylorsville	2,125	11	11	0
Taylortown	731	1	1	0
Thomasville	27,096	74	68	6
Topsail Beach	373	8	7	1
Trent Woods	4,208	5	5	0
Troutman	2,413	14	14	0
Troy	3,229	12	11	1
Tryon	1,667	10	8	2
Valdese	4,547	12	11	1
Vanceboro	1,018	2	2	0
Vass	729	3	3	0
Wadesboro	5,887	30	25	5

Table 78. Full-Time Law Enforcement Employees, by Selected State and City, 2012— continued

(Number)

State/city	Population	Total law enforcement employees	Total officers	Total civilians
Wagram	851	2	2	0
Wake Forest	30,499	66	55	11
Wallace	3,929	18	15	3
Walnut Cove	1,443	6	6	0
Walnut Creek	846	2	2	0
Warrenton	873	5	4	1
Warsaw	3,093	15	13	2
Washington	9,868	46	38	8
Waxhaw	9,984	21	19	2
Waynesville	9,994	42	34	8
Weaverville	3,160	15	14	1
Weldon	1,676	9	9	0
Wendell	5,919	17	15	2
West Jefferson	1,315	8	8	0
Whispering Pines	2,965	9	8	1
Whitakers	753	2	2	0
White Lake	812	6	6	0
Whiteville	5,462	27	24	3
Wilkesboro	3,456	23	21	2
Williamston	5,581	21	20	1
Wilmington	107,826	310	256	54
Wilson	49,790	133	118	15
Wilson's Mills	2,306	4	4	0
Windsor	3,676	9	9	0
Wingate	3,535	8	8	0
Winston-Salem	232,529	749	585	164
Winterville	9,387	19	18	1
Woodfin	6,201	14	14	0
Woodland	819	2	2	0
Wrightsville Beach	2,508	26	23	3
Yadkinville	2,997	13	12	1
Youngsville	1,172	10	9	1
Zebulon	4,489	23	22	1
NORTH DAKOTA				
Belfield	813	2	2	0
Beulah	3,174	6	5	1
Bismarck	62,305	124	96	28
Bowman	1,678	3	3	0
Burlington	1,078	2	2	0
Cando	1,134	2	2	0
Carrington	2,100	4	4	0
Cavalier	1,324	4	4	0
Devils Lake	7,261	18	16	2
Dickinson	18,087	47	31	16
Ellendale	1,418	2	2	0
Fargo	107,329	162	144	18
Fessenden	487	1	1	0
Grafton	4,356	11	10	1
Grand Forks	53,729	97	82	15
Harvey	1,813	3	3	0
Hazen	2,452	4	4	0
Hillsboro	1,630	2	2	0
Jamestown	15,687	33	29	4
Kenmare	1,114	2	2	0
Killdeer	764	3	3	0
Lamoure	904	1	1	0
Lincoln	2,447	1	1	0
Linton	1,115	1	1	0
Lisbon	2,190	3	3	0
Mandan	18,640	35	27	8
Medora	114	2	2	0
Minot	41,577	84	61	23

Table 78. Full-Time Law Enforcement Employees, by Selected State and City, 2012— continued

(Number)

State/city	Population	Total law enforcement employees	Total officers	Total civilians
Napoleon	805	1	1	0
Northwood	961	2	2	0
Oakes	1,887	3	3	0
Rolla	1,302	4	4	0
Rugby	2,924	4	4	0
Sherwood	246	1	1	0
Stanley	1,483	3	3	0
Steele	727	1	1	0
Surrey	950	1	1	0
Thompson	1,003	1	1	0
Valley City	6,696	18	12	6
Wahpeton	7,897	16	14	2
Watford City	1,773	7	7	0
West Fargo	26,266	46	36	10
Williston	14,964	35	26	9
Wishek	1,019	2	2	0
OHIO				
Ada	5,956	11	8	3
Addyston	939	1	1	0
Akron	199,256	449	410	39
Alliance	22,338	54	41	13
Amberley Village	3,588	21	17	4
Amelia	4,805	5	4	1
American Township	12,486	1	1	0
Amherst	12,030	26	20	6
Andover	1,146	3	3	0
Ansonia	1,175	2	2	0
Arcanum	2,131	3	3	0
Arlington Heights	746	6	4	2
Ashland	20,377	33	26	7
Ashtabula	19,138	32	29	3
Ashville	4,100	10	10	0
Athens	23,849	37	24	13
Aurora	15,559	34	26	8
Austintown	29,699	46	37	9
Avon	21,209	41	32	9
Bainbridge Township	11,403	26	18	8
Barberton	26,569	49	36	13
Barnesville	4,196	7	6	1
Batavia	1,510	3	3	0
Bath Township, Summit County	9,709	27	20	7
Bay Village	15,662	26	24	2
Bazetta Township	5,878	6	6	0
Beachwood	11,962	56	42	14
Beavercreek	45,226	59	43	16
Beaver Township	6,716	15	11	4
Bedford	13,084	41	31	10
Bedford Heights	10,759	53	28	25
Bellaire	4,281	9	9	0
Bellbrook	6,948	17	12	5
Bellefontaine	13,380	29	22	7
Bellville	1,919	4	4	0
Belpre	6,446	14	9	5
Bentleyville Village	865	3	3	0
Berea	19,107	37	31	6
Berlin Heights	715	1	1	0
Bethel	2,713	3	3	0
Bethesda	1,257	1	1	0
Beverly	1,314	3	3	0
Bexley	13,067	33	27	6
Blanchester	4,246	7	7	0
Bluffton	4,128	6	6	0

Table 78. Full-Time Law Enforcement Employees, by Selected State and City, 2012— continued

(Number)

State/city	Population	Total law enforcement employees	Total officers	Total civilians
Boardman	35,402	62	49	13
Bolivar	995	1	1	0
Boston Heights	1,301	5	5	0
Bowling Green	30,050	56	41	15
Brady Lake	464	1	1	0
Bratenahl	1,198	13	10	3
Brecksville	13,666	32	26	6
Brewster	2,114	5	5	0
Bridgeport	1,832	4	4	0
Brimfield Township	10,384	16	13	3
Broadview Heights	19,414	40	28	12
Brookfield Township	8,860	8	8	0
Brooklyn	11,177	37	29	8
Brook Park	19,226	49	40	9
Brookville	5,888	12	11	1
Brunswick	34,280	55	41	14
Brunswick Hills Township	9,905	11	10	1
Bryan	8,551	26	19	7
Bucyrus	12,371	21	17	4
Burton	1,456	3	3	0
Butler Township	7,874	13	12	1
Cadiz	3,355	5	5	0
Caldwell	1,749	2	2	0
Cambridge	10,643	28	23	5
Camden	2,047	1	1	0
Campbell	8,241	14	14	0
Canal Fulton	5,483	10	9	1
Canfield	7,521	20	15	5
Canton	73,060	186	147	39
Carey	3,677	10	7	3
Carlisle	4,919	9	8	1
Carrollton	3,243	7	7	0
Celina	10,408	22	16	6
Centerville	24,017	52	41	11
Chagrin Falls	4,116	19	11	8
Chardon	5,152	17	11	6
Chester Township	10,263	14	13	1
Cheviot	8,381	10	10	0
Chillicothe	21,917	51	46	5
Cincinnati	297,160	1,151	1,038	113
Circleville	13,324	28	21	7
Clayton	13,219	14	14	0
Clay Township, Ottawa County	2,724	5	5	0
Clearcreek Township	14,084	13	13	0
Cleveland	397,106	1,697	1,451	246
Cleveland Heights	46,155	114	102	12
Cleves	3,236	2	2	0
Clinton Township	4,112	8	8	0
Clyde	6,330	16	13	3
Coal Grove	2,167	14	10	4
Coitsville Township	1,393	3	3	0
Coldwater	4,430	8	8	0
Columbiana	6,389	15	11	4
Columbus	787,609	2,114	1,805	309
Commercial Point	1,583	2	2	0
Conneaut	12,850	21	16	5
Copley Township	17,317	31	23	8
Cortland	7,109	9	9	0
Covington	2,586	6	5	1
Crestline	4,633	12	8	4
Cridersville	1,853	3	3	0
Cuyahoga Falls	49,688	75	70	5

Table 78. Full-Time Law Enforcement Employees, by Selected State and City, 2012— continued

(Number)

State/city	Population	Total law enforcement employees	Total officers	Total civilians
Danville	1,045	2	2	0
Dayton	141,631	391	342	49
Deer Park	5,740	14	10	4
Defiance	16,506	29	26	3
Delaware	34,778	58	51	7
Delhi Township	29,532	31	29	2
Delphos	7,106	17	13	4
Delta	3,105	7	6	1
Dennison	2,657	4	4	0
Dover	12,835	22	21	1
Doylestown	3,053	8	7	1
Dublin	41,782	86	64	22
East Canton	1,592	2	2	0
East Cleveland	17,856	75	56	19
Eastlake	18,591	42	29	13
East Liverpool	11,203	24	19	5
East Palestine	4,724	8	6	2
Eaton	8,413	20	15	5
Edgerton	2,013	3	3	0
Edison	437	1	1	0
Elmwood Place	2,190	2	2	0
Englewood	13,475	25	20	5
Enon	2,417	3	3	0
Euclid	48,956	136	93	43
Evendale	2,769	21	19	2
Fairborn	32,376	53	40	13
Fairfax	1,700	10	9	1
Fairfield	42,541	78	59	19
Fairfield Township	21,389	18	17	1
Fairlawn	7,442	30	21	9
Fairport Harbor	3,111	7	6	1
Fairview Park	16,838	25	24	1
Fayette	1,284	3	3	0
Findlay	41,232	82	64	18
Forest	1,462	7	7	0
Forest Park	18,734	43	37	6
Fort Loramie	1,479	2	2	0
Fort Recovery	1,431	2	2	0
Fostoria	13,451	26	22	4
Franklin	11,780	29	23	6
Fredericktown	2,495	4	4	0
Fremont	16,746	37	32	5
Gahanna	33,272	70	55	15
Galion	10,520	20	16	4
Gallipolis	3,644	14	13	1
Garfield Heights	28,870	64	52	12
Gates Mills	2,272	15	11	4
Geneva	6,220	15	11	4
Geneva-on-the-Lake	1,289	5	5	0
Genoa Township	23,107	28	25	3
Germantown	5,551	12	11	1
German Township, Clark County	7,117	3	3	0
German Township, Montgomery County	2,884	6	6	0
Gibsonburg	2,583	5	5	0
Girard	9,965	17	16	1
Glendale	2,157	7	7	0
Glenwillow	924	4	4	0
Gnadenhutten	1,289	2	2	0
Golf Manor	3,614	10	9	1
Goshen Township, Clermont County	15,516	12	11	1
Goshen Township, Mahoning County	3,245	9	8	1
Grandview Heights	6,541	19	15	4

Table 78. Full-Time Law Enforcement Employees, by Selected State and City, 2012— continued

(Number)

State/city	Population	Total law enforcement employees	Total officers	Total civilians
Granville	5,650	13	10	3
Greenfield	4,642	11	9	2
Greenhills	3,618	8	7	1
Green Springs	1,369	2	2	0
Greenville	13,237	28	22	6
Grove City	35,601	78	61	17
Groveport	5,367	21	20	1
Hanging Rock	221	6	3	3
Harrison	9,904	24	22	2
Hartville	2,946	8	8	0
Haskins	1,189	2	2	0
Heath	10,318	25	18	7
Hebron	2,338	8	7	1
Hicksville	3,584	8	7	1
Highland Heights	8,351	28	21	7
Highland Hills	1,131	6	5	1
Hilliard	28,456	63	47	16
Hillsboro	6,610	17	13	4
Hinckley Township	7,652	11	10	1
Hiram	1,407	2	2	0
Holland	1,765	9	9	0
Howland Township	17,340	21	20	1
Hubbard	7,880	16	12	4
Hubbard Township	5,658	9	8	1
Huber Heights	38,129	68	50	18
Hudson	22,278	35	28	7
Huron	7,154	15	12	3
Independence	7,138	43	32	11
Indian Hill	5,789	25	20	5
Ironton	11,137	20	16	4
Jackson Center	1,463	1	1	0
Jackson Township, Mahoning County	2,116	5	5	0
Jackson Township, Montgomery County	3,697	5	5	0
Jackson Township, Stark County	40,403	52	41	11
Jamestown	1,994	3	3	0
Jefferson	3,122	8	7	1
Johnstown	4,635	14	10	4
Junction City	820	1	1	0
Kalida	1,543	1	1	0
Kent	28,925	63	41	22
Kenton	8,268	13	13	0
Kettering	56,204	109	82	27
Kirtland	6,871	14	9	5
Kirtland Hills	646	10	9	1
Lagrange	2,105	6	6	0
Lake Township	7,959	16	15	1
Lakewood	52,169	116	94	22
Lancaster	38,808	82	66	16
Lebanon	20,048	37	28	9
Leipsic	2,095	4	4	0
Lexington	4,826	13	9	4
Liberty Township	12,071	23	17	6
Lima	38,799	97	79	18
Lincoln Heights	3,288	8	8	0
Linndale	179	6	4	2
Lithopolis	1,107	3	3	0
Lockland	3,452	14	13	1
Logan	7,157	20	15	5
London	9,911	21	17	4
Lorain	64,144	117	93	24
Lordstown	3,420	13	9	4
Loudonville	2,643	9	6	3

Table 78. Full-Time Law Enforcement Employees, by Selected State and City, 2012— continued

(Number)

State/city	Population	Total law enforcement employees	Total officers	Total civilians
Louisville	9,183	9	8	1
Loveland	12,090	18	17	1
Lowellville	1,156	3	3	0
Luckey	1,013	1	1	0
Lynchburg	1,500	3	3	0
Lyndhurst	14,011	37	28	9
Macedonia	11,196	24	18	6
Madeira	8,732	13	12	1
Madison	3,186	6	5	1
Madison Township, Franklin County	18,041	15	14	1
Madison Township, Lake County	15,711	19	15	4
Magnolia	979	2	2	0
Manchester	2,024	2	2	0
Mansfield	47,856	109	79	30
Maple Heights	23,155	58	42	16
Marblehead	904	2	2	0
Mariemont	3,405	10	9	1
Marietta	14,095	35	29	6
Marion	36,864	70	56	14
Marlboro Township	4,359	4	3	1
Marysville	22,110	37	31	6
Mason	30,734	48	41	7
Massillon	32,173	52	50	2
Maumee	14,296	57	43	14
Mayfield Heights	19,169	43	34	9
McArthur	1,702	4	4	0
McComb	1,649	3	3	0
McConnelsville	1,785	4	4	0
Mechanicsburg	1,645	4	4	0
Medina Township	8,543	7	6	1
Mentor	47,194	105	76	29
Mentor-on-the-Lake	7,448	13	8	5
Miami Township, Clermont County	40,878	43	40	3
Miami Township, Montgomery County	29,152	45	38	7
Middlefield	2,696	12	9	3
Middletown	48,730	109	76	33
Milan	1,368	3	3	0
Milford	6,714	16	14	2
Millersport	1,045	1	1	0
Milton Township	2,581	4	4	0
Minerva	3,723	14	9	5
Minerva Park	1,273	4	4	0
Mingo Junction	3,457	4	4	0
Minster	2,807	7	6	1
Monroe	14,771	36	28	8
Monroeville	1,401	4	4	0
Montgomery	10,259	24	21	3
Montpelier	4,075	9	8	1
Montville Township	11,193	12	12	0
Moraine	6,312	35	28	7
Moreland Hills	3,322	15	14	1
Mount Orab	3,667	8	7	1
Munroe Falls	5,016	7	6	1
Navarre	1,958	5	5	0
Nelsonville	5,396	8	8	0
New Albany	7,730	22	16	6
Newark	47,608	88	73	15
New Boston	2,274	13	9	4
New Bremen	2,980	6	6	0
Newcomerstown	3,825	10	6	4
New Concord	2,493	4	4	0
New Franklin	14,237	18	13	5

Table 78. Full-Time Law Enforcement Employees, by Selected State and City, 2012— continued

(Number)

State/city	Population	Total law enforcement employees	Total officers	Total civilians
New Lexington	4,734	12	8	4
New London	2,463	4	4	0
New Miami	2,251	1	1	0
New Middletown	1,622	4	4	0
New Philadelphia	17,301	26	22	4
Newton Falls	4,799	10	7	3
Newtown	2,674	8	7	1
Niles	19,280	40	35	5
North Baltimore	3,435	5	5	0
North Canton	17,501	27	20	7
Northfield	3,680	9	9	0
North Kingsville	2,925	4	4	0
North Olmsted	32,742	58	44	14
North Randall	1,028	6	6	0
North Ridgeville	29,487	45	37	8
North Royalton	30,466	58	36	22
Northwood	5,269	21	17	4
Norton	12,094	16	15	1
Norwalk	17,024	28	22	6
Norwood	19,221	51	48	3
Oak Harbor	2,761	6	4	2
Oak Hill	1,552	3	3	0
Oakwood, Montgomery County	9,209	35	30	5
Oakwood, Paulding County	608	1	1	0
Oakwood Village	3,670	11	9	2
Oberlin	8,292	22	16	6
Olmsted Falls	9,031	16	10	6
Olmsted Township	13,523	19	16	3
Ontario	6,230	24	20	4
Orange Village	3,325	15	14	1
Oregon	20,306	58	45	13
Orrville	8,386	18	14	4
Orwell	1,661	5	5	0
Ostrander	643	1	1	0
Ottawa	4,463	8	8	0
Owensville	795	1	1	0
Oxford Township	2,100	12	12	0
Painesville	19,577	42	36	6
Parma	81,661	156	100	56
Parma Heights	20,733	37	31	6
Paulding	3,608	5	4	1
Payne	1,195	1	1	0
Peebles	1,783	2	2	0
Pemberville	1,372	1	1	0
Peninsula	565	3	3	0
Pepper Pike	5,983	21	16	5
Perkins Township	12,211	25	20	5
Perrysburg	20,638	45	33	12
Perrysville	736	1	1	0
Perry Township, Columbiana County	4,554	5	5	0
Perry Township, Montgomery County	3,357	4	4	0
Perry Township, Stark County	28,324	31	24	7
Pickerington	18,304	34	25	9
Pierce Township	11,222	16	16	0
Pioneer	1,381	3	3	0
Piqua	20,537	35	31	4
Plain City	4,228	8	8	0
Plymouth	1,858	3	3	0
Poland Township	12,421	12	11	1
Poland Village	2,557	4	4	0
Port Clinton	6,060	18	12	6
Portsmouth	20,241	43	39	4

Table 78. Full-Time Law Enforcement Employees, by Selected State and City, 2012— continued

(Number)

State/city	Population	Total law enforcement employees	Total officers	Total civilians
Powell	11,508	19	17	2
Powhatan Point	1,593	3	3	0
Ravenna	11,733	32	24	8
Reminderville	3,406	8	7	1
Republic	549	1	1	0
Reynoldsburg	35,919	67	53	14
Richfield	3,651	23	16	7
Richland Township	9,796	4	4	0
Richmond Heights	10,554	23	17	6
Richwood	2,231	6	6	0
Rittman	6,496	10	8	2
Riverside	25,219	29	28	1
Roaming Shores Village	1,509	2	2	0
Rockford	1,121	2	2	0
Roseville	1,853	2	2	0
Rossford	6,298	13	12	1
Ross Township	8,361	2	2	0
Russells Point	1,392	3	3	0
Russell Township	5,194	10	9	1
Russellville	561	6	5	1
Russia	640	1	1	0
Sabina	2,566	5	5	0
Sagamore Hills	10,955	13	9	4
Salem	12,312	19	19	0
Saline Township	1,354	5	5	0
Sandusky	25,812	46	45	1
Seaman	945	1	1	0
Sebring	4,423	10	6	4
Seven Hills	11,813	18	17	1
Seville	2,298	6	6	0
Shadyside	3,788	5	5	0
Shaker Heights	28,469	87	64	23
Sharon Township	2,396	10	10	0
Sharonville	13,570	43	34	9
Shawnee Township	8,713	19	12	7
Sheffield Lake	9,144	12	9	3
Shelby	9,324	19	15	4
Sidney	21,245	48	37	11
Silverton	4,792	13	10	3
Smith Township	4,473	4	4	0
Smithville	1,253	4	4	0
Solon	23,365	69	44	25
Somerset	1,482	3	2	1
South Euclid	22,311	49	39	10
South Point	3,961	5	5	0
South Russell	3,813	9	9	0
South Zanesville	1,990	3	3	0
Spencer	754	1	1	0
Spencerville	2,225	4	4	0
Springboro	17,422	27	24	3
Springdale	11,231	40	33	7
Springfield	60,652	142	126	16
Springfield Township, Hamilton County	36,346	56	50	6
Springfield Township, Mahoning County	6,708	8	8	0
Springfield Township, Summit County	17,725	24	21	3
St. Bernard	4,371	17	16	1
St. Clair Township	7,963	11	10	1
Steubenville	18,673	46	40	6
St. Henry	2,429	2	2	0
St. Marys	8,338	20	15	5
Stow	34,863	57	37	20

Table 78. Full-Time Law Enforcement Employees, by Selected State and City, 2012— continued

(Number)

State/city	Population	Total law enforcement employees	Total officers	Total civilians
St. Paris	2,091	3	3	0
Strasburg	2,610	4	4	0
Streetsboro	16,040	35	27	8
Strongsville	44,783	100	73	27
Struthers	10,721	19	15	4
Sugarcreek	2,222	6	6	0
Sugarcreek Township	8,047	16	15	1
Sycamore	862	1	1	0
Sylvania	18,979	41	34	7
Sylvania Township	29,544	62	45	17
Tallmadge	17,550	26	23	3
Terrace Park	2,253	6	6	0
Thornville	992	1	1	0
Tiffin	17,976	37	27	10
Tipp City	9,696	20	17	3
Toledo	287,418	517	413	104
Toronto	5,095	10	10	0
Tremont City	375	2	2	0
Trotwood	24,449	36	34	2
Twinsburg	18,809	43	32	11
Uhrichsville	5,417	8	8	0
Union City	1,667	3	3	0
Union Township, Clermont County	46,450	66	53	13
University Heights	13,549	31	26	5
Upper Arlington	33,796	60	48	12
Upper Sandusky	6,601	17	13	4
Urbana	11,802	18	18	0
Utica	2,134	7	4	3
Valley View, Cuyahoga County	2,035	18	16	2
Valleyview, Franklin County	620	1	1	0
Vandalia	15,257	38	31	7
Van Wert	10,854	28	20	8
Vermilion	10,602	21	16	5
Vienna Township	3,983	1	1	0
Village of Leesburg	1,315	3	3	0
Wadsworth	21,583	39	30	9
Waite Hill	471	6	6	0
Walbridge	3,021	6	5	1
Walton Hills	2,283	15	12	3
Wapakoneta	9,874	19	14	5
Warren	41,587	82	66	16
Warrensville Heights	13,552	44	34	10
Warren Township	5,555	6	6	0
Washington Court House	14,202	25	20	5
Waterville	5,527	11	10	1
Wauseon	7,337	18	14	4
Waverly	4,411	10	7	3
Weathersfield	8,406	9	8	1
Wellington	4,806	9	6	3
Wellston	5,667	11	8	3
Wells Township	2,837	4	4	0
West Alexandria	1,341	3	3	0
West Carrollton	13,153	28	22	6
West Chester Township	58,638	116	89	27
Westerville	36,146	89	74	15
West Jefferson	4,225	14	11	3
West Lafayette	2,323	5	5	0
Westlake	32,753	67	49	18
West Salem	1,465	2	2	0
West Unity	1,672	8	8	0
Whitehall	18,075	58	46	12
Wickliffe	12,759	40	30	10

Table 78. Full-Time Law Enforcement Employees, by Selected State and City, 2012— continued

(Number)

State/city	Population	Total law enforcement employees	Total officers	Total civilians
Willard	6,241	17	14	3
Willoughby	22,284	57	42	15
Willoughby Hills	9,492	23	17	6
Willowick	14,181	32	23	9
Wilmington	12,529	31	22	9
Winchester	1,052	3	3	0
Windham	2,211	8	8	0
Wintersville	3,927	11	9	2
Woodlawn	3,296	16	15	1
Woodmere Village	885	10	9	1
Woodville	2,137	5	5	0
Wooster	26,138	38	35	3
Worthington	13,585	45	32	13
Wyoming	8,434	21	19	2
Xenia	25,738	66	44	22
Yellow Springs	3,490	9	7	2
Youngstown	67,031	183	144	39
Zanesville	25,506	81	49	32
OKLAHOMA				
Achille	497	3	2	1
Ada	16,990	38	34	4
Allen	942	2	2	0
Altus	20,025	58	42	16
Alva	4,998	11	9	2
Anadarko	6,834	21	16	5
Antlers	2,479	10	5	5
Apache	1,459	7	4	3
Ardmore	24,543	66	47	19
Arkoma	2,010	6	3	3
Atoka	3,140	16	15	1
Bartlesville	36,133	74	53	21
Beaver	1,531	2	2	0
Beggs	1,335	9	3	6
Bethany	19,255	40	30	10
Bixby	21,108	32	24	8
Blackwell	7,168	22	16	6
Blanchard	7,752	18	12	6
Boise City	1,280	3	3	0
Boley	1,197	1	1	0
Bristow	4,267	18	13	5
Broken Arrow	99,908	170	126	44
Broken Bow	4,164	18	14	4
Caddo	1,008	3	3	0
Calera	2,187	8	6	2
Caney	207	4	3	1
Carnegie	1,741	9	6	3
Catoosa	7,228	12	11	1
Chandler	3,133	11	7	4
Checotah	3,371	13	10	3
Chelsea	1,985	8	3	5
Cherokee	1,514	6	2	4
Chickasha	16,208	36	28	8
Choctaw	11,265	13	12	1
Chouteau	2,119	9	8	1
Claremore	18,780	54	38	16
Clayton	830	6	2	4
Cleveland	3,286	5	5	0
Clinton	9,130	26	17	9
Coalgate	1,988	6	6	0
Colbert	1,152	5	4	1
Colcord	824	1	1	0
Collinsville	5,666	15	10	5

Table 78. Full-Time Law Enforcement Employees, by Selected State and City, 2012— continued

(Number)

State/city	Population	Total law enforcement employees	Total officers	Total civilians
Comanche	1,681	4	4	0
Cordell	2,946	9	5	4
Coweta	10,049	21	14	7
Crescent	1,420	5	4	1
Cushing	7,910	22	15	7
Davenport	823	1	1	0
Davis	2,712	11	9	2
Del City	21,560	42	29	13
Dewar	898	1	1	0
Dewey	3,469	11	10	1
Dibble	887	1	1	0
Drumright	2,938	6	6	0
Duncan	23,682	53	46	7
Durant	16,026	41	38	3
Edmond	82,276	132	106	26
Elk City	11,818	35	24	11
El Reno	16,928	42	30	12
Enid	49,908	142	95	47
Eufaula	2,843	16	12	4
Fairfax	1,395	7	4	3
Fairview	2,607	8	5	3
Fletcher	1,190	1	1	0
Forest Park	1,009	3	3	0
Fort Gibson	4,198	10	10	0
Fort Supply	334	2	1	1
Frederick	3,982	14	12	2
Geary	1,294	12	6	6
Glenpool	10,924	28	18	10
Goodwell	1,307	4	4	0
Grove	6,694	28	20	8
Guthrie	10,300	28	21	7
Guymon	11,564	27	18	9
Haileyville	822	3	3	0
Harrah	5,150	9	9	0
Hartshorne	2,148	12	5	7
Haskell	2,028	6	6	0
Healdton	2,818	7	5	2
Heavener	3,451	13	8	5
Hennessey	2,154	8	4	4
Henryetta	5,990	17	12	5
Hinton	3,230	5	5	0
Hobart	3,796	14	8	6
Holdenville	5,833	15	10	5
Hollis	2,082	10	6	4
Hominy	3,603	9	5	4
Hooker	1,939	3	3	0
Howe	811	4	3	1
Hugo	5,367	17	16	1
Hulbert	596	3	3	0
Hydro	979	1	1	0
Idabel	7,085	25	19	6
Jay	2,474	12	9	3
Jenks	17,105	25	19	6
Jones	2,721	5	5	0
Kiefer	1,703	4	4	0
Kingfisher	4,683	12	10	2
Kingston	1,618	7	7	0
Krebs	2,075	6	5	1
Lahoma	618	1	1	0
Lawton	97,904	232	172	60
Lexington	2,175	10	6	4
Lindsay	2,870	11	7	4

Table 78. Full-Time Law Enforcement Employees, by Selected State and City, 2012— continued

(Number)

State/city	Population	Total law enforcement employees	Total officers	Total civilians
Locust Grove	1,438	7	3	4
Lone Grove	5,108	9	6	3
Luther	1,234	6	6	0
Madill	3,810	12	11	1
Mangum	3,042	10	6	4
Mannford	3,109	9	7	2
Marietta	2,654	6	5	1
Marlow	4,712	15	10	5
Maysville	1,245	6	4	2
McAlester	18,580	56	43	13
McCurtain	522	2	1	1
McLoud	4,087	14	9	5
Medicine Park	386	3	2	1
Meeker	1,156	4	4	0
Miami	13,715	42	31	11
Midwest City	54,953	120	94	26
Minco	1,649	4	4	0
Moore	55,671	83	78	5
Mooreland	1,203	2	2	0
Morris	1,495	2	2	0
Mountain View	804	2	2	0
Muldrow	3,503	14	8	6
Muskogee	39,643	102	89	13
Mustang	17,581	27	20	7
Newcastle	7,767	22	16	6
Newkirk	2,342	7	6	1
Nichols Hills	3,750	21	16	5
Nicoma Park	2,419	4	4	0
Ninnekah	1,013	3	3	0
Noble	6,550	15	11	4
Norman	112,112	217	165	52
North Enid	869	3	3	0
Nowata	3,771	12	6	6
Oilton	1,024	3	3	0
Okemah	3,258	11	7	4
Oklahoma City	586,208	1,281	1,020	261
Okmulgee	12,453	29	22	7
Oologah	1,158	3	3	0
Owasso	29,225	60	44	16
Pauls Valley	6,253	19	13	6
Pawhuska	3,622	12	8	4
Pawnee	2,220	5	5	0
Perkins	2,861	7	7	0
Perry	5,181	20	13	7
Piedmont	5,781	13	10	3
Pocola	4,099	8	5	3
Ponca City	25,659	78	48	30
Porum	735	2	2	0
Poteau	8,611	28	23	5
Prague	2,412	13	8	5
Pryor	9,641	29	22	7
Purcell	5,947	22	19	3
Ringling	1,048	2	2	0
Roland	3,203	11	6	5
Rush Springs	1,244	4	4	0
Sallisaw	8,975	31	24	7
Sand Springs	19,108	40	29	11
Sapulpa	20,764	57	46	11
Sawyer	324	2	2	0
Sayre	4,422	12	6	6
Seiling	869	3	3	0
Seminole	7,568	15	12	3

Table 78. Full-Time Law Enforcement Employees, by Selected State and City, 2012— continued

(Number)

State/city	Population	Total law enforcement employees	Total officers	Total civilians
Shawnee	30,177	78	59	19
Skiatook	7,476	26	19	7
Snyder	1,409	3	3	0
South Coffeyville	793	3	3	0
Sparks	171	1	1	0
Spencer	3,954	9	8	1
Spiro	2,187	4	4	0
Stigler	2,714	12	8	4
Stillwater	46,177	114	73	41
Stilwell	3,991	18	13	5
Stonewall	475	2	2	0
Stratford	1,541	3	3	0
Stringtown	414	5	4	1
Stroud	2,719	12	9	3
Sulphur	4,982	11	9	2
Tahlequah	15,922	39	31	8
Talihina	1,126	10	6	4
Tecumseh	6,526	13	12	1
Texhoma	936	2	2	0
The Village	9,025	28	22	6
Tishomingo	3,066	7	6	1
Tonkawa	3,250	10	6	4
Tryon	496	1	1	0
Tulsa	396,101	836	745	91
Tushka	315	3	3	0
Tuttle	6,083	13	10	3
Valliant	762	5	3	2
Verdigris	4,036	3	3	0
Vian	1,482	3	3	0
Vinita	5,804	21	15	6
Wagoner	8,412	19	13	6
Walters	2,578	4	4	0
Warner	1,659	4	4	0
Warr Acres	10,151	29	23	6
Washington	625	2	2	0
Watonga	5,166	9	7	2
Waukomis	1,300	2	2	0
Waurika	2,086	3	3	0
Waynoka	937	3	3	0
Weatherford	10,949	33	22	11
Weleetka	1,009	11	6	5
Westville	1,657	9	5	4
Wetumka	1,296	6	5	1
Wewoka	3,467	10	6	4
Wilburton	2,873	7	6	1
Wilson	1,742	4	4	0
Woodward	12,180	43	28	15
Wright City	770	2	2	0
Wynnewood	2,236	6	5	1
Yale	1,240	6	3	3
Yukon	22,952	60	38	22
OREGON				
Adair Village	849	7	6	1
Albany	50,692	89	58	31
Amity	1,631	2	2	0
Ashland	20,292	33	26	7
Astoria	9,578	25	16	9
Athena	1,138	2	2	0
Aumsville	3,622	7	6	1
Aurora	928	9	8	1
Baker City	9,933	16	15	1
Bandon	3,099	7	6	1

Table 78. Full-Time Law Enforcement Employees, by Selected State and City, 2012— continued

(Number)

State/city	Population	Total law enforcement employees	Total officers	Total civilians
Beaverton	90,759	173	137	36
Bend	77,455	112	88	24
Black Butte	n.a.	7	6	1
Boardman	3,254	7	6	1
Brookings	6,403	20	13	7
Burns	2,836	5	4	1
Canby	15,998	30	25	5
Cannon Beach	1,708	9	8	1
Carlton	2,028	3	3	0
Central Point	17,352	32	26	6
Clatskanie	1,755	6	5	1
Coburg	1,046	4	3	1
Columbia City	1,967	1	1	0
Condon	689	2	1	1
Coos Bay	16,137	37	24	13
Coquille	3,907	8	7	1
Cornelius	11,995	15	14	1
Corvallis	55,042	80	53	27
Cottage Grove	9,789	26	17	9
Dallas	14,738	31	20	11
Eagle Point	8,559	12	11	1
Elgin	1,729	4	3	1
Enterprise	1,961	4	4	0
Eugene	157,848	308	185	123
Fairview	9,015	17	14	3
Florence	8,556	22	14	8
Forest Grove	21,307	33	29	4
Gearhart	1,478	3	3	0
Gervais	2,490	8	7	1
Gladstone	11,619	18	15	3
Gold Beach	2,277	6	5	1
Grants Pass	34,901	79	50	29
Gresham	106,718	141	111	30
Hermiston	16,923	33	24	9
Hillsboro	92,586	164	120	44
Hines	1,580	4	3	1
Hood River	7,243	14	13	1
Hubbard	3,207	7	6	1
Independence	8,681	14	12	2
Jacksonville	2,815	6	5	1
John Day	1,763	4	4	0
Junction City	5,449	16	10	6
Keizer	36,866	46	38	8
King City	3,144	6	5	1
Klamath Falls	21,062	43	38	5
La Grande	13,221	33	18	15
Lake Oswego	37,009	67	42	25
Lakeview	2,318	6	5	1
Lebanon	15,683	37	26	11
Lincoln City	8,014	35	25	10
Madras	6,110	11	10	1
Malin	814	1	1	0
Manzanita	604	3	3	0
McMinnville	32,530	41	34	7
Medford	75,704	134	100	34
Merrill	853	2	1	1
Milton-Freewater	7,125	17	11	6
Milwaukie	20,507	41	37	4
Molalla	8,194	15	12	3
Monmouth	9,635	16	13	3
Mount Angel	3,321	8	4	4
Myrtle Creek	3,476	9	7	2

Table 78. Full-Time Law Enforcement Employees, by Selected State and City, 2012— continued

(Number)

State/city	Population	Total law enforcement employees	Total officers	Total civilians
Myrtle Point	2,541	5	5	0
Newberg-Dundee	25,499	46	33	13
Newport	10,095	24	19	5
North Bend	9,700	23	16	7
North Plains	1,968	2	2	0
Nyssa	3,302	8	8	0
Oakridge	3,239	7	4	3
Ontario	11,487	31	23	8
Oregon City	32,198	47	40	7
Pendleton	16,789	24	21	3
Philomath	4,633	10	9	1
Phoenix	4,586	10	8	2
Pilot Rock	1,518	3	3	0
Portland	589,991	1,201	956	245
Port Orford	1,145	2	2	0
Prineville	9,352	25	15	10
Rainier	1,915	6	5	1
Redmond	26,494	39	30	9
Reedsport	4,198	15	10	5
Rockaway Beach	1,326	3	3	0
Rogue River	2,154	5	4	1
Roseburg	21,406	41	36	5
Salem	156,283	308	191	117
Sandy	9,672	17	14	3
Scappoose	6,662	11	10	1
Seaside	6,526	27	18	9
Sherwood	18,388	26	23	3
Silverton	9,320	15	14	1
Springfield	60,035	118	65	53
Stanfield	2,065	4	4	0
Stayton	7,725	15	13	2
St. Helens	13,020	17	16	1
Sunriver	n.a.	12	11	1
Sutherlin	7,893	17	15	2
Sweet Home	9,020	22	15	7
Talent	6,131	10	8	2
The Dalles	13,765	25	23	2
Tigard	48,546	89	72	17
Tillamook	4,988	11	8	3
Toledo	3,502	16	10	6
Troutdale	16,132	27	23	4
Tualatin	26,331	47	37	10
Turner	1,874	2	2	0
Umatilla	6,980	12	9	3
Vernonia	2,174	3	3	0
Warrenton	5,042	10	9	1
West Linn	25,376	34	31	3
Weston	674	2	2	0
Winston	5,436	8	7	1
Woodburn	24,336	39	31	8
Yamhill	1,035	3	3	0
PENNSYLVANIA				
Abington Township, Lackawanna County	1,749	2	2	0
Abington Township, Montgomery County	55,486	113	89	24
Adams Township, Butler County	11,689	6	6	0
Adams Township, Cambria County	5,991	3	3	0
Akron	3,888	5	5	0
Albion	1,521	6	2	4
Alburtis	2,369	4	4	0
Aldan	4,165	6	6	0
Aleppo Township	1,922	15	12	3

Table 78. Full-Time Law Enforcement Employees, by Selected State and City, 2012— continued

(Number)

State/city	Population	Total law enforcement employees	Total officers	Total civilians
Aliquippa	9,468	18	18	0
Allegheny Township, Blair County	6,759	7	6	1
Allegheny Township, Westmoreland County	8,190	9	8	1
Allentown	118,408	217	197	20
Altoona	46,468	74	66	8
Ambler	6,437	15	13	2
Ambridge	7,072	13	13	0
Amity Township	12,623	13	12	1
Annville Township	4,782	8	5	3
Apollo	1,652	1	1	0
Archbald	7,006	5	5	0
Arnold	5,173	11	10	1
Ashland	2,826	3	3	0
Ashley	2,799	2	2	0
Aspinwall	2,810	7	6	1
Aston Township	16,645	18	16	2
Athens	3,378	5	4	1
Athens Township	5,268	10	9	1
Auburn	743	1	1	0
Austin	564	1	1	0
Avalon	4,720	7	6	1
Avonmore Boro	1,014	1	1	0
Baden	4,148	5	5	0
Baldwin Borough	19,830	27	25	2
Baldwin Township	1,998	5	5	0
Bally	1,093	2	2	0
Bangor	5,290	10	9	1
Barrett Township	4,238	5	5	0
Beaver	4,545	10	9	1
Beaver Falls	9,016	19	18	1
Beaver Meadows	872	1	1	0
Bedford	2,850	5	5	0
Bedminster Township	6,595	7	6	1
Bell Acres	1,392	3	3	0
Bellefonte	6,207	12	10	2
Bellwood	1,834	2	2	0
Ben Avon	1,787	15	12	3
Ben Avon Heights	372	15	12	3
Bensalem Township	60,620	129	100	29
Berks-Lehigh Regional	30,614	31	30	1
Berlin	2,111	2	2	0
Bern Township	6,819	12	12	0
Berwick	10,510	16	15	1
Bethel Park	32,416	44	38	6
Bethel Township, Berks County	4,125	2	2	0
Bethlehem	75,221	184	158	26
Bethlehem Township	23,806	34	32	2
Biglerville	1,204	2	2	0
Birdsboro	5,179	8	7	1
Birmingham Township	4,221	4	4	0
Blairsville	3,423	3	3	0
Blair Township	4,508	4	4	0
Blakely	6,585	5	5	0
Blawnox	1,437	4	4	0
Bloomsburg Town	14,902	21	15	6
Blythe Township	927	2	2	0
Boyertown	4,068	8	7	1
Brackenridge	3,270	4	4	0
Bradford	8,798	22	22	0
Bradford Township	4,820	5	5	0
Branch Township	1,846	1	1	0

Table 78. Full-Time Law Enforcement Employees, by Selected State and City, 2012— continued

(Number)

State/city	Population	Total law enforcement employees	Total officers	Total civilians
Brecknock Township, Berks County	4,600	5	5	0
Brentwood	9,674	17	15	2
Briar Creek Township	3,026	4	4	0
Bridgeport	4,569	9	8	1
Bridgeville	5,164	9	8	1
Bridgewater	706	3	3	0
Brighton Township	8,253	6	6	0
Bristol	9,757	18	16	2
Bristol Township	54,756	82	70	12
Brockway	2,079	2	2	0
Brookhaven	8,032	7	6	1
Brookville	3,937	6	5	1
Brownsville	2,338	2	2	0
Bryn Athyn	1,379	5	5	0
Buckingham Township	20,139	24	22	2
Buffalo Township	7,330	5	5	0
Bushkill Township	8,204	17	16	1
Butler	13,801	24	23	1
Butler Township, Butler County	17,303	23	21	2
Butler Township, Luzerne County	9,250	9	8	1
Butler Township, Schuykill County	6,006	4	4	0
Caernarvon Township, Berks County	4,019	9	8	1
California	6,817	8	7	1
Caln Township	13,861	19	18	1
Cambria Township	6,118	3	3	0
Cambridge Springs	2,603	3	3	0
Camp Hill	7,913	11	10	1
Canonsburg	9,021	17	17	0
Canton	1,982	3	3	0
Carbondale	8,919	12	12	0
Carlisle	18,742	37	32	5
Carnegie	7,997	13	12	1
Carrolltown	856	2	2	0
Carroll Township, Washinton County	5,658	2	2	0
Carroll Township, York County	5,958	11	11	0
Carroll Valley	3,888	4	3	1
Castle Shannon	8,343	13	12	1
Catasauqua	6,457	9	8	1
Catawissa	1,557	2	2	0
Cecil Township	11,307	18	17	1
Center Township	11,833	14	13	1
Centerville	3,273	2	2	0
Central Berks Regional	9,420	15	14	1
Chalfont	4,022	7	6	1
Chambersburg	20,333	35	33	2
Charleroi	5,291	8	6	2
Chartiers Township	7,843	11	11	0
Cheltenham Township	36,910	90	79	11
Chester	34,080	112	102	10
Chester Township	3,953	12	11	1
Cheswick	1,752	2	2	0
Chippewa Township	8,024	9	8	1
Churchill	3,021	10	10	0
Clairton	6,818	8	8	0
Clarion	5,293	9	8	1
Clay Township	6,328	4	4	0
Clearfield	6,235	10	6	4
Cleona	2,087	4	4	0
Clifton Heights	6,673	10	9	1
Coaldale	2,288	4	4	0
Coal Township	10,416	13	12	1
Coatesville	13,142	44	35	9

Table 78. Full-Time Law Enforcement Employees, by Selected State and City, 2012— continued

(Number)

State/city	Population	Total law enforcement employees	Total officers	Total civilians
Cochranton	1,140	2	2	0
Colebrookdale District	6,039	11	9	2
Collegeville	5,105	9	8	1
Collier Township	7,103	15	14	1
Collingdale	8,814	9	8	1
Colonial Regional	19,495	26	24	2
Columbia	10,433	19	16	3
Conemaugh Township, Cambria County	2,018	2	2	0
Conemaugh Township, Somerset County	7,302	7	6	1
Conewago Township, Adams County	7,108	10	9	1
Conewango Township	3,605	4	4	0
Conneaut Lake Regional	3,597	4	3	1
Conoy Township	3,204	16	14	2
Conshohocken	7,858	21	19	2
Conway	2,183	2	2	0
Conyngham	1,920	1	1	0
Coopersburg	2,394	7	7	0
Coplay	3,202	4	4	0
Coraopolis	5,695	13	10	3
Cornwall	4,125	8	7	1
Corry	6,626	11	9	2
Covington Township	2,291	3	3	0
Cranberry Township	28,188	34	28	6
Crescent Township	2,648	4	4	0
Cresson	1,716	10	10	0
Cresson Township	4,350	3	2	1
Croyle Township	2,346	1	1	0
Cumberland Township, Adams County	6,182	6	6	0
Cumberland Township, Greene County	6,644	4	4	0
Cumru Township	15,195	27	25	2
Curwensville	2,550	1	1	0
Dale	1,238	2	2	0
Dallas	2,813	4	4	0
Dallas Township	9,023	8	8	0
Dalton	1,238	2	2	0
Danville	4,714	9	7	2
Darby	10,721	12	11	1
Darby Township	9,294	14	14	0
Decatur Township	4,563	2	2	0
Delmont	2,695	4	4	0
Derry	2,697	3	3	0
Derry Township, Dauphin County	24,758	46	38	8
Dickson City	6,089	8	6	2
Donegal Township	2,473	2	2	0
Donora	4,796	6	6	0
Dormont	8,620	16	15	1
Douglass Township, Berks County	3,317	4	4	0
Douglass Township, Montgomery County	10,228	10	9	1
Downingtown	7,916	19	16	3
Doylestown	8,407	20	15	5
Doylestown Township	17,621	23	21	2
Dublin Borough	2,165	2	2	0
Du Bois	7,819	13	13	0
Duboistown	1,209	1	1	0
Duncannon	1,527	1	1	0
Duncansville	1,237	2	2	0
Dunmore	14,102	19	19	0
Dunnstable Township	1,011	1	1	0
Duquesne	5,583	15	14	1

Table 78. Full-Time Law Enforcement Employees, by Selected State and City, 2012— continued

(Number)

State/city	Population	Total law enforcement employees	Total officers	Total civilians
Duryea	4,933	2	2	0
East Bangor	1,176	1	1	0
East Berlin	1,526	1	1	0
East Bethlehem Township	2,362	1	1	0
East Brandywine Township	6,762	10	9	1
East Buffalo Township	6,434	8	8	0
East Cocalico Township	10,343	24	22	2
East Coventry Township	6,657	8	7	1
East Deer Township	1,505	1	1	0
Eastern Adams Regional	10,735	11	10	1
Eastern Pike Regional	4,807	10	9	1
East Fallowfield Township	7,473	7	7	0
East Hempfield Township	23,597	36	33	3
East Lampeter Township	16,476	42	38	4
East Lansdowne	2,677	5	3	2
East Marlborough Township	7,048	1	1	0
East McKeesport	2,715	3	3	0
East Norriton Township	13,633	30	27	3
East Pennsboro Township	20,293	20	19	1
East Penn Township	2,890	2	2	0
East Pikeland Township	7,102	8	7	1
East Pittsburgh	1,828	1	1	0
East Taylor Township	2,735	1	1	0
Easttown Township	10,510	15	14	1
East Vincent Township	6,843	6	6	0
East Washington	2,241	1	1	0
East Whiteland Township	10,684	21	19	2
Ebensburg	3,362	3	3	0
Economy	8,999	12	11	1
Eddystone	2,418	10	9	1
Edgewood	3,128	12	10	2
Edgeworth	1,685	6	4	2
Edinboro	6,459	8	8	0
Edwardsville	4,831	5	5	0
Elizabethtown	11,582	18	16	2
Elizabeth Township	13,313	11	11	0
Elkland	1,827	2	2	0
Ellwood City	7,946	12	10	2
Emmaus	11,247	20	18	2
Emsworth	2,457	15	12	3
Ephrata	13,437	34	29	5
Erie	102,111	196	172	24
Etna	3,462	7	6	1
Everett	1,840	3	3	0
Exeter	5,670	3	3	0
Exeter Township, Berks County	25,631	33	30	3
Exeter Township, Luzerne County	2,386	7	7	0
Fairview Township, Luzerne County	4,534	5	5	0
Fairview Township, York County	16,721	18	16	2
Falls Township, Bucks County	34,409	60	53	7
Fawn Township	2,384	2	2	0
Ferguson Township	17,746	25	22	3
Ferndale	1,641	1	1	0
Findlay Township	5,076	23	16	7
Fleetwood	4,098	6	6	0
Folcroft	6,627	11	10	1
Ford City	3,001	3	3	0
Forest City	1,917	2	2	0
Forest Hills	6,539	10	10	0
Forks Township	14,768	24	23	1
Forty Fort	4,227	5	5	0
Forward Township	3,387	4	4	0

Table 78. Full-Time Law Enforcement Employees, by Selected State and City, 2012— continued

(Number)

State/city	Population	Total law enforcement employees	Total officers	Total civilians
Foster Township	4,330	4	4	0
Fountain Hill	4,612	11	10	1
Fox Chapel	5,405	12	12	0
Frackville	3,817	4	4	0
Franconia Township	13,106	17	15	2
Franklin	6,566	23	17	6
Franklin Park	13,513	14	13	1
Franklin Township, Carbon County	4,276	4	4	0
Frazer Township	1,161	2	2	0
Freedom Township	3,469	2	2	0
Freeland	3,542	2	2	0
Freemansburg	2,644	2	1	1
Freeport	1,819	2	2	0
Galeton	1,153	1	1	0
Gallitzin	1,919	7	7	0
Geistown	2,475	1	1	0
Gettysburg	7,644	17	13	4
Gilpin Township	2,504	1	1	0
Glassport	4,497	6	6	0
Glenolden	7,176	11	10	1
Granville Township	5,120	9	7	2
Greencastle	4,009	6	5	1
Greenfield Township, Blair County	4,186	4	4	0
Greensburg	14,939	38	28	10
Green Tree	4,446	11	10	1
Greenville	5,938	10	9	1
Greenwood Township	1,958	1	1	0
Grove City	8,349	12	11	1
Hamburg	4,303	7	6	1
Hamiltonban Township	2,380	1	1	0
Hampden Township	28,133	24	23	1
Hanover	15,338	28	25	3
Hanover Township, Luzerne County	11,111	15	14	1
Hanover Township, Washington County	2,682	9	3	6
Harmony Township	3,207	5	5	0
Harrisburg	49,686	230	179	51
Harrison Township	10,494	21	18	3
Harveys Lake	2,800	6	6	0
Hastings	1,282	1	1	0
Hatboro	7,383	17	14	3
Hatfield Township	20,604	32	27	5
Haverford Township	48,646	82	70	12
Hazleton	25,421	44	41	3
Heidelberg	1,248	3	3	0
Heidelberg Township, Berks County	1,729	1	1	0
Hellam Township	8,744	10	8	2
Hellertown	5,917	11	10	1
Hemlock Township	2,256	6	6	0
Hempfield Township, Mercer County	3,753	6	5	1
Hermitage	16,272	32	29	3
Highspire	2,407	6	6	0
Hilltown Township	15,077	20	17	3
Hollidaysburg	5,809	11	8	3
Homer City	1,712	2	2	0
Homestead	3,175	13	12	1
Honesdale	4,494	8	8	0
Honey Brook	1,718	1	1	0
Hooversville	647	1	1	0
Hopewell Township	12,633	16	15	1
Horsham Township	26,230	46	39	7
Hughestown	1,396	1	1	0
Hughesville	2,135	2	2	0

Table 78. Full-Time Law Enforcement Employees, by Selected State and City, 2012— continued

(Number)

State/city	Population	Total law enforcement employees	Total officers	Total civilians
Hummelstown	4,552	7	7	0
Huntingdon	7,116	11	11	0
Independence Township, Beaver County	2,511	3	3	0
Indiana	14,020	24	22	2
Indiana Township	7,276	10	10	0
Industry	1,841	12	12	0
Ingram	3,341	4	4	0
Irwin	3,986	3	3	0
Ivyland	1,044	2	2	0
Jackson Township, Butler County	3,669	10	8	2
Jackson Township, Cambria County	4,406	2	2	0
Jackson Township, Luzerne County	4,661	4	4	0
Jeannette	9,685	17	14	3
Jefferson Hills Borough	10,653	18	17	1
Jefferson Township, Mercer County	1,886	2	2	0
Jenkins Township	4,456	2	2	0
Jenkintown	4,436	13	11	2
Jermyn	2,176	1	1	0
Jim Thorpe	4,796	7	6	1
Johnstown	22,572	41	37	4
Kane	3,742	5	5	0
Kennedy Township	7,696	15	11	4
Kennett Square	6,091	14	12	2
Kidder Township	1,941	6	6	0
Kilbuck Township	699	15	12	3
Kingston	13,224	20	19	1
Kingston Township	7,021	11	11	0
Kiskiminetas Township	4,815	1	1	0
Kittanning	4,057	9	8	1
Knox	1,150	3	3	0
Koppel	764	2	2	0
Kulpmont	2,933	1	1	0
Kutztown	5,028	13	11	2
Laflin Borough	1,492	3	3	0
Lake City	3,041	3	3	0
Lancaster	59,511	165	142	23
Lancaster Township, Butler County	2,540	1	1	0
Langhorne Borough	1,627	8	8	0
Lansdale	16,321	31	23	8
Lansdowne	10,654	19	16	3
Lansford	3,954	10	9	1
Larksville	4,494	4	4	0
Latimore Township	2,588	1	1	0
Latrobe	8,365	12	12	0
Laureldale	3,923	5	5	0
Lawrence Park Township	3,995	8	7	1
Lawrence Township, Clearfield County	7,705	9	8	1
Lebanon	25,558	48	42	6
Leechburg	2,163	3	3	0
Leetsdale	1,222	5	5	0
Leet Township	1,639	4	4	0
Lehighton	5,518	10	9	1
Lehigh Township, Northampton County	10,560	13	12	1
Lehman Township	3,519	2	2	0
Lewisburg	5,810	10	8	2
Lewistown	8,365	13	11	2
Liberty	2,559	1	1	0
Liberty Township, Adams County	1,241	1	1	0
Ligonier	1,578	2	2	0
Ligonier Township	6,624	4	4	0
Limerick Township	18,132	17	16	1

Table 78. Full-Time Law Enforcement Employees, by Selected State and City, 2012— continued

(Number)

State/city	Population	Total law enforcement employees	Total officers	Total civilians
Lincoln	1,075	2	2	0
Lititz	9,399	16	13	3
Littlestown	4,448	8	7	1
Logan Township	12,328	18	16	2
Lower Allen Township	18,037	20	19	1
Lower Burrell	11,799	16	16	0
Lower Chichester Township	3,480	5	5	0
Lower Frederick Township	4,855	2	2	0
Lower Gwynedd Township	11,441	18	17	1
Lower Heidelberg Township	5,531	9	8	1
Lower Makefield Township	32,663	42	38	4
Lower Merion Township	58,009	139	124	15
Lower Milford Township	3,787	2	2	0
Lower Moreland Township	13,023	26	21	5
Lower Paxton Township	47,511	63	56	7
Lower Pottsgrove Township	12,097	19	17	2
Lower Providence Township	25,517	32	32	0
Lower Salford Township	15,007	19	17	2
Lower Saucon Township	10,806	17	15	2
Lower Southampton Township	18,969	33	30	3
Lower Swatara Township	8,294	16	15	1
Lower Windsor Township	7,406	10	9	1
Luzerne Township	5,984	1	1	0
Lykens	1,785	1	1	0
Macungie	3,084	6	6	0
Mahanoy City	4,175	4	4	0
Mahanoy Township	3,162	1	1	0
Mahoning Township, Carbon County	4,319	4	4	0
Mahoning Township, Lawrence County	3,093	2	2	0
Mahoning Township, Montour County	4,184	7	6	1
Malvern	3,008	6	5	1
Manheim	4,873	9	8	1
Manheim Township	38,255	79	63	16
Manor	3,249	2	2	0
Manor Township, Lancaster County	19,675	19	17	2
Mansfield	3,637	5	5	0
Marcus Hook	2,405	7	6	1
Marietta	2,596	16	14	2
Marion Township, Beaver County	916	2	2	0
Marion Township, Berks County	1,693	3	3	0
Marlborough Township	3,188	3	3	0
Marple Township	23,503	32	27	5
Mars	1,704	1	1	0
Martinsburg	1,964	2	2	0
Marysville	2,542	2	2	0
Masontown	3,461	5	5	0
Mayfield	1,813	1	1	0
McAdoo	2,307	3	3	0
McCandless	28,548	29	27	2
McDonald Borough	2,156	3	3	0
McKeesport	19,794	55	52	3
McKees Rocks	6,123	12	11	1
McSherrystown	3,048	4	4	0
Meadville	13,431	25	22	3
Mechanicsburg	9,010	16	15	1
Media	5,344	19	16	3
Mercer	2,008	4	4	0
Mercersburg	1,566	2	2	0
Meshoppen	565	1	1	0
Meyersdale	2,191	2	2	0
Middleburg	1,313	3	2	1
Middlesex Township, Butler County	5,407	3	3	0

Table 78. Full-Time Law Enforcement Employees, by Selected State and City, 2012— continued

(Number)

State/city	Population	Total law enforcement employees	Total officers	Total civilians
Middlesex Township, Cumberland County	7,062	10	9	1
Middletown	8,929	21	16	5
Middletown Township	45,581	57	51	6
Midland	2,643	5	4	1
Mifflin	644	1	1	0
Mifflinburg	3,551	10	9	1
Mifflin County Regional	20,835	16	15	1
Mifflin Township	2,329	4	4	0
Milford	1,024	2	2	0
Millbourne	1,163	1	1	0
Millcreek Township, Erie County	53,686	73	59	14
Millersburg	2,565	5	4	1
Millersville	8,194	14	12	2
Millvale	3,756	4	4	0
Millville	951	1	1	0
Minersville	4,411	5	5	0
Mohnton	3,053	4	4	0
Monaca	5,755	9	9	0
Monessen	7,745	12	12	0
Monongahela	4,314	9	7	2
Monroeville	28,477	56	46	10
Montgomery	1,584	3	3	0
Montgomery Township	24,869	43	36	7
Montrose	1,622	1	1	0
Moon Township	24,262	36	30	6
Moore Township	9,227	9	8	1
Moosic	5,737	10	10	0
Morris-Cooper Regional	5,660	1	1	0
Morrisville	8,756	12	11	1
Morton	2,678	5	4	1
Moscow	2,032	3	3	0
Mount Carmel	5,912	9	9	0
Mount Carmel Township	3,149	6	6	0
Mount Holly Springs	2,036	3	3	0
Mount Joy	7,434	14	13	1
Mount Lebanon	33,243	53	44	9
Mount Oliver	3,414	10	10	0
Mount Pleasant	4,468	3	3	0
Mount Pleasant Township	3,526	3	3	0
Mount Union	2,455	5	5	0
Mountville	2,811	23	20	3
Muhlenberg Township	19,691	34	32	2
Muncy	2,485	3	3	0
Munhall	11,442	25	21	4
Murrysville	20,143	26	21	5
Myerstown	3,072	3	3	0
Nanticoke	10,498	14	13	1
Nanty Glo	2,743	2	2	0
Narberth	4,296	5	5	0
Neshannock Township	9,640	7	7	0
Nesquehoning	3,360	4	4	0
Nether Providence Township	13,750	17	16	1
Neville Township	1,087	15	12	3
Newberry Township	15,334	18	16	2
New Bethlehem	992	4	2	2
New Brighton	9,241	9	7	2
New Britain	3,162	5	4	1
New Britain Township	11,105	14	12	2
New Cumberland	7,300	8	7	1
New Garden Township	12,022	10	9	1
New Hanover Township	10,974	10	9	1
New Holland	5,395	13	12	1

Table 78. Full-Time Law Enforcement Employees, by Selected State and City, 2012— continued

(Number)

State/city	Population	Total law enforcement employees	Total officers	Total civilians
New Hope	2,536	11	9	2
New Kensington	13,158	22	22	0
New Philadelphia	1,088	1	1	0
Newport	1,579	2	2	0
Newport Township	5,391	2	2	0
New Sewickley Township	7,383	7	7	0
Newton Township	2,855	1	1	0
Newtown	2,255	5	5	0
Newtown Township, Bucks County	22,366	32	28	4
Newtown Township, Delaware County	12,255	19	17	2
Norristown	34,433	79	65	14
Northampton	9,958	12	10	2
Northampton Township	39,853	49	43	6
North Belle Vernon	1,977	3	2	1
North Catasauqua	2,858	4	4	0
North Charleroi	1,317	1	1	0
North Cornwall Township	7,577	10	9	1
North Coventry Township	7,891	16	15	1
North East, Erie County	4,308	8	7	1
Northeastern Regional	11,456	13	11	2
Northern Berks Regional	12,730	15	14	1
Northern Cambria Borough	3,847	3	3	0
Northern Regional	30,781	30	28	2
Northern York Regional	66,820	55	50	5
North Fayette Township	13,978	26	20	6
North Franklin Township	4,598	6	6	0
North Huntingdon Township	30,707	35	29	6
North Londonderry Township	8,094	10	9	1
North Middleton Township	11,179	10	9	1
North Strabane Township	13,451	20	19	1
Northumberland	3,816	5	5	0
North Versailles Township	12,459	23	20	3
North Wales	3,239	5	4	1
Northwest Lancaster County Regional	18,190	17	15	2
Norwood	5,909	8	7	1
Oakmont	6,323	7	7	0
O'Hara Township	8,434	16	15	1
Ohio Township	4,772	15	12	3
Ohioville	3,544	2	2	0
Oil City	10,591	23	18	5
Old Forge	8,340	5	5	0
Old Lycoming Township	4,954	11	10	1
Oley Township	3,632	5	5	0
Oliver Township	1,937	1	1	0
Olyphant	5,167	5	5	0
Orangeville Area	1,771	1	1	0
Orwigsburg	3,109	4	4	0
Overfield Township	2,833	3	3	0
Oxford	5,093	12	11	1
Paint Township	3,159	5	4	1
Palmerton	5,431	9	8	1
Palmer Township	20,757	33	30	3
Palmyra	7,343	10	9	1
Palo Alto	1,035	1	1	0
Parkesburg	3,604	10	9	1
Parkside	2,335	3	3	0
Parks Township	2,753	2	2	0
Patterson Township	3,039	4	4	0
Patton	1,775	2	2	0
Patton Township	15,360	19	17	2
Paxtang	1,566	3	3	0

Table 78. Full-Time Law Enforcement Employees, by Selected State and City, 2012— continued

(Number)

State/city	Population	Total law enforcement employees	Total officers	Total civilians
Pen Argyl	3,606	5	5	0
Penbrook	3,018	8	8	0
Penndel	2,335	1	1	0
Penn Hills	42,464	55	51	4
Pennridge Regional	10,997	15	13	2
Penn Township, Butler County	5,087	4	3	1
Penn Township, Lancaster County	8,817	8	7	1
Penn Township, Perry County	3,235	6	5	1
Penn Township, Westmoreland County	20,069	23	21	2
Penn Township, York County	15,662	25	23	2
Pequea Township	4,620	7	7	0
Perkasie	8,538	21	19	2
Perryopolis	1,790	2	2	0
Peters Township	21,281	23	21	2
Philadelphia	1,530,873	7,427	6,625	802
Phoenixville	16,492	28	27	1
Pine Creek Township	3,225	1	1	0
Pine Grove	2,193	1	1	0
Pitcairn	3,305	5	4	1
Pittsburgh	308,609	943	880	63
Pittston	7,764	7	7	0
Plainfield Township	6,158	12	12	0
Plains Township	9,993	20	19	1
Pleasant Hills	8,294	20	18	2
Plum	27,213	30	24	6
Plumstead Township	12,482	18	16	2
Plymouth Township, Montgomery County	16,578	50	43	7
Pocono Mountain Regional	39,202	43	38	5
Pocono Township	11,100	18	17	1
Point Marion	1,163	1	1	0
Point Township	3,697	5	5	0
Polk	819	2	2	0
Portage	2,646	1	1	0
Port Allegany	2,164	3	3	0
Port Carbon	1,895	2	2	0
Port Vue	3,810	3	3	0
Pottstown	22,448	57	45	12
Pottsville	14,370	29	28	1
Pringle	982	20	19	1
Prospect Park	6,475	9	9	0
Pulaski Township, Lawrence County	3,463	2	2	0
Punxsutawney	5,981	10	6	4
Pymatuning Township	3,291	5	5	0
Quakertown	9,008	23	15	8
Quarryville	2,584	4	4	0
Raccoon Township	3,074	3	3	0
Radnor Township	31,632	57	47	10
Ralpho Township	4,335	6	6	0
Rankin	2,129	1	1	0
Reading	88,363	181	156	25
Redstone Township	5,584	2	2	0
Reilly Township	728	1	1	0
Reserve Township	3,344	6	6	0
Reynoldsville	2,768	2	2	0
Rice Township	3,346	5	5	0
Richland Township, Bucks County	13,094	14	12	2
Richland Township, Cambria County	12,855	21	20	1
Ridgway	4,091	6	5	1
Ridley Park	7,024	15	10	5
Ridley Township	30,886	37	32	5
Riverside	1,938	3	3	0

Table 78. Full-Time Law Enforcement Employees, by Selected State and City, 2012— continued

(Number)

State/city	Population	Total law enforcement employees	Total officers	Total civilians
Roaring Brook Township	1,913	1	1	0
Roaring Spring	2,593	3	3	0
Robeson Township	7,239	7	6	1
Robinson Township, Allegheny County	13,397	29	27	2
Rochester	3,669	10	8	2
Rochester Township	2,811	4	4	0
Rockledge	2,551	4	4	0
Rosslyn Farms	428	2	2	0
Ross Township	31,204	48	42	6
Rostraver Township	11,399	15	14	1
Rush Township	3,423	3	3	0
Sadsbury Township, Chester County	3,581	2	2	0
Salem Township, Luzerne County	4,268	4	4	0
Salisbury Township	13,548	19	17	2
Sandy Lake	661	2	1	1
Sandy Township	10,659	8	7	1
Saxton	738	1	1	0
Sayre	5,605	14	14	0
Schuylkill Haven	5,454	8	8	0
Schuylkill Township, Chester County	8,543	13	11	2
Scottdale	4,398	7	7	0
Scott Township, Allegheny County	17,078	21	20	1
Scott Township, Columbia County	5,129	11	11	0
Scott Township, Lackawanna County	4,921	5	5	0
Scranton	76,332	170	150	20
Selinsgrove	5,672	6	5	1
Sewickley	4,388	9	7	2
Sewickley Heights	813	5	3	2
Shaler Township	28,849	25	25	0
Shamokin	7,398	13	12	1
Shamokin Dam	1,691	3	3	0
Sharon Hill	5,715	10	9	1
Sharpsburg	3,457	6	6	0
Sharpsville	4,429	6	5	1
Shenandoah	5,087	4	4	0
Shenango Township, Lawrence County	7,503	6	6	0
Shillington	5,290	9	8	1
Shippensburg	5,510	10	9	1
Shippingport	215	2	2	0
Shiremanstown	1,574	2	2	0
Shohola Township	2,483	1	1	0
Silver Lake Township	1,721	1	1	0
Silver Spring Township	13,701	18	16	2
Sinking Spring	4,021	7	6	1
Slatington	4,245	7	7	0
Slippery Rock	3,637	3	3	0
Smithton Borough	400	1	1	0
Smith Township	4,490	1	1	0
Solebury Township	8,720	16	14	2
Somerset	6,297	8	7	1
Souderton	6,639	7	6	1
South Abington Township	9,102	12	10	2
South Beaver Township	2,726	4	4	0
South Buffalo Township	2,644	2	2	0
South Centre Township	1,943	4	4	0
South Coatesville	1,307	2	2	0
South Connellsville Borough	1,976	2	2	0
Southern Regional Lancaster County	3,788	7	7	0
Southern Regional York County	10,623	12	11	1
South Fayette Township	14,462	18	17	1
South Fork	931	2	2	0

Table 78. Full-Time Law Enforcement Employees, by Selected State and City, 2012— continued

(Number)

State/city	Population	Total law enforcement employees	Total officers	Total civilians
South Greensburg	2,124	2	2	0
South Heidelberg Township	7,294	7	7	0
South Lebanon Township	9,493	8	7	1
South Londonderry Township	7,013	7	6	1
South Park Township	13,459	18	17	1
Southwestern Regional	17,586	14	13	1
Southwest Greensburg	2,162	2	2	0
Southwest Mercer County Regional	10,569	22	21	1
Southwest Regional	8,174	3	2	1
South Whitehall Township	19,241	41	38	3
South Williamsport	6,399	7	7	0
Spring City	3,334	4	3	1
Springdale	3,416	4	4	0
Springdale Township	1,641	4	4	0
Springettsbury Township	26,753	35	32	3
Springfield Township, Bucks County	5,051	4	4	0
Springfield Township, Delaware County	24,288	36	31	5
Springfield Township, Montgomery County	19,480	31	29	2
Spring Garden Township	12,618	22	19	3
Spring Township, Berks County	27,205	30	29	1
Spring Township, Centre County	7,494	8	7	1
State College	56,608	74	61	13
St. Clair Boro	3,014	6	6	0
St. Clair Township	1,523	1	1	0
Steelton	6,009	9	8	1
Stewartstown	2,096	6	5	1
Stoneboro	1,054	1	1	0
Stonycreek Township	2,853	3	3	0
Stowe Township	6,382	8	7	1
Strasburg	2,818	4	4	0
Stroud Area Regional	34,730	62	55	7
Sugarcreek	5,311	5	4	1
Sugarloaf Township, Luzerne County	4,224	2	2	0
Sugar Notch	992	4	1	3
Summerhill Township	2,475	2	2	0
Summit Hill	3,044	6	4	2
Summit Township	2,278	1	1	0
Sunbury	9,937	14	13	1
Susquehanna Regional	7,780	16	14	2
Susquehanna Township, Dauphin County	24,113	41	39	2
Swarthmore	6,214	9	9	0
Swatara Township	23,436	52	49	3
Sweden Township	875	1	1	0
Swissvale	9,012	14	14	0
Swoyersville	5,078	6	6	0
Sykesville	1,161	1	1	0
Tamaqua	7,130	10	9	1
Tarentum	4,544	8	7	1
Tatamy	1,207	1	1	0
Taylor	6,283	6	6	0
Telford	4,888	7	6	1
Throop	4,101	6	6	0
Tiadaghton Valley Regional	6,692	11	10	1
Tidioute	690	1	1	0
Tilden Township	3,608	2	2	0
Tinicum Township, Bucks County	4,008	5	5	0
Tinicum Township, Delaware County	4,104	17	15	2
Titusville	5,619	10	10	0
Towamencin Township	17,634	27	22	5
Towanda	2,928	6	6	0
Trafford	3,184	3	3	0

Table 78. Full-Time Law Enforcement Employees, by Selected State and City, 2012— continued

(Number)

State/city	Population	Total law enforcement employees	Total officers	Total civilians
Tredyffrin Township	29,426	53	47	6
Troy	1,358	3	3	0
Tulpehocken Township	3,284	3	3	0
Tunkhannock	1,842	5	5	0
Tunkhannock Township, Wyoming County	4,287	4	4	0
Turtle Creek	5,366	6	5	1
Tyrone	5,494	14	11	3
Union City	3,331	3	3	0
Uniontown	10,405	23	23	0
Union Township, Lawrence County	5,207	4	4	0
Upland	3,249	6	5	1
Upper Allen Township	18,117	21	20	1
Upper Burrell Township	2,333	2	2	0
Upper Chichester Township	16,791	24	23	1
Upper Darby Township	83,059	145	126	19
Upper Dublin Township	25,651	47	40	7
Upper Gwynedd Township	15,602	24	21	3
Upper Makefield Township	8,216	16	15	1
Upper Merion Township	28,486	79	61	18
Upper Moreland Township	24,092	44	36	8
Upper Nazareth Township	6,251	4	3	1
Upper Perkiomen	6,815	10	9	1
Upper Pottsgrove Township	5,332	9	8	1
Upper Providence Township, Delaware County	10,174	14	13	1
Upper Providence Township, Montgomery County	21,287	26	24	2
Upper Saucon Township	14,855	20	19	1
Upper Southampton Township	15,200	24	21	3
Upper St. Clair Township	19,290	35	28	7
Upper Uwchlan Township	11,263	10	10	0
Upper Yoder Township	5,466	13	13	0
Uwchlan Township	18,146	24	22	2
Valley Township	6,816	5	5	0
Vandergrift	5,222	8	8	0
Vandling	753	2	2	0
Vernon Township	5,648	5	4	1
Verona	2,482	4	3	1
Versailles	1,520	3	3	0
Walker Township	1,057	1	1	0
Walnutport	2,077	3	3	0
Warminster Township	32,786	52	47	5
Warren	9,741	21	15	6
Warrington Township	23,493	32	30	2
Warwick Township, Bucks County	14,483	19	17	2
Warwick Township, Lancaster County	17,840	14	13	1
Washington, Washington County	13,707	33	31	2
Washington Township, Fayette County	3,914	2	2	0
Washington Township, Franklin County	14,054	16	14	2
Washington Township, Northampton County	5,138	5	5	0
Washington Township, Westmoreland County	7,446	6	6	0
Watsontown	2,358	5	5	0
Waynesboro	10,602	20	18	2
Waynesburg	4,189	9	8	1
Weatherly	2,533	4	4	0
Weissport	413	1	1	0
Wellsboro	3,273	6	6	0
Wesleyville	3,352	11	10	1
West Brandywine Township	7,418	4	4	0
West Caln Township	9,043	2	2	0

Table 78. Full-Time Law Enforcement Employees, by Selected State and City, 2012— continued

(Number)

State/city	Population	Total law enforcement employees	Total officers	Total civilians
West Chester	18,520	60	47	13
West Conshohocken	1,324	11	10	1
West Deer Township	11,809	12	11	1
West Earl Township	7,893	6	6	0
Western Berks Regional	4,370	5	5	0
West Fallowfield Township	2,574	2	2	0
Westfield	1,067	2	2	0
West Goshen Township	21,936	32	28	4
West Grove Borough	2,863	2	2	0
West Hazleton	4,609	3	2	1
West Hempfield Township	16,205	23	20	3
West Hills Regional	10,943	12	11	1
West Homestead	1,935	14	6	8
West Lampeter Township	15,258	16	15	1
West Mahanoy Township	2,881	3	3	0
West Manchester Township	18,954	29	26	3
West Manheim Township	7,769	9	8	1
West Mead Township	5,266	2	2	0
West Mifflin	20,378	42	36	6
West Newton	2,641	2	2	0
West Norriton Township	15,713	33	29	4
West Penn Township	4,456	3	3	0
West Pikeland Township	4,037	4	4	0
West Pittston	4,884	3	3	0
West Pottsgrove Township	3,886	10	9	1
West Reading	4,225	17	15	2
West Sadsbury Township	2,452	4	4	0
West Shore Regional	7,648	12	10	2
Westtown-East Goshen Regional	31,972	30	27	3
West View	6,793	12	8	4
West Vincent Township	4,582	6	5	1
West Whiteland Township	18,332	27	25	2
West Wyoming	2,734	1	1	0
West York	4,632	10	10	0
Whitehall	13,988	25	20	5
Whitehall Township	26,823	50	44	6
White Haven Borough	1,100	2	2	0
Whitemarsh Township	17,404	40	34	6
White Oak	7,887	12	11	1
White Township	1,398	4	4	0
Whitpain Township	18,935	38	30	8
Wiconisco Township	1,214	1	1	0
Wilkes-Barre	41,630	87	84	3
Wilkes-Barre Township	2,976	15	14	1
Wilkinsburg	15,981	28	24	4
Wilkins Township	6,377	12	12	0
Williamsburg	1,258	1	1	0
Williamsport	29,475	54	50	4
Willistown Township	10,530	19	17	2
Wilson	7,921	9	8	1
Wrightsville	2,317	3	3	0
Wright Township	5,669	7	7	0
Wyoming	3,083	4	4	0
Wyomissing	10,494	25	23	2
Yardley	2,442	3	3	0
Yeadon	11,479	17	15	2
York	43,857	118	105	13
York Area Regional	60,596	55	50	5
Youngsville	1,735	2	2	0
Zelienople	3,824	10	9	1
RHODE ISLAND				
Barrington	16,290	31	24	7

Table 78. Full-Time Law Enforcement Employees, by Selected State and City, 2012— continued

(Number)

State/city	Population	Total law enforcement employees	Total officers	Total civilians
Bristol	22,927	49	38	11
Burrillville	15,936	27	21	6
Central Falls	19,353	39	33	6
Charlestown	7,818	25	20	5
Coventry	34,972	67	52	15
Cranston	80,290	167	138	29
Cumberland	33,466	56	47	9
East Greenwich	13,130	40	32	8
East Providence	46,980	108	90	18
Foster	4,600	14	8	6
Glocester	9,734	19	14	5
Hopkinton	8,178	20	15	5
Jamestown	5,399	16	12	4
Johnston	28,734	88	71	17
Lincoln	21,080	42	35	7
Little Compton	3,488	13	9	4
Middletown	16,131	43	38	5
Narragansett	15,849	50	38	12
Newport	24,641	92	77	15
New Shoreham	1,050	9	5	4
North Kingstown	26,454	48	40	8
North Providence	32,039	83	62	21
North Smithfield	11,953	26	22	4
Pawtucket	71,062	164	138	26
Portsmouth	17,368	34	33	1
Providence	177,830	561	471	90
Richmond	7,699	15	13	2
Scituate	10,317	22	16	6
Smithfield	21,404	54	40	14
South Kingstown	30,602	68	50	18
Tiverton	15,761	37	27	10
Warren	10,598	27	21	6
Warwick	82,572	209	160	49
Westerly	22,760	60	49	11
West Greenwich	6,128	14	9	5
West Warwick	29,156	69	57	12
Woonsocket	41,137	111	97	14
SOUTH CAROLINA				
Abbeville	5,298	23	19	4
Aiken	29,868	110	83	27
Allendale	3,523	11	10	1
Anderson	26,997	126	86	40
Andrews	2,894	9	8	1
Atlantic Beach	338	4	4	0
Aynor	567	7	6	1
Bamberg	3,649	12	10	2
Barnwell	4,805	17	15	2
Batesburg-Leesville	5,424	26	21	5
Beaufort	12,505	49	45	4
Belton	4,182	12	12	0
Bennettsville	9,175	37	33	4
Bethune	338	1	1	0
Bishopville	3,511	15	13	2
Blacksburg	1,870	11	10	1
Blackville	2,434	11	10	1
Bluffton	12,676	38	35	3
Bonneau	493	3	3	0
Bowman	979	5	5	0
Branchville	1,036	4	3	1
Briarcliffe Acres	462	1	1	0
Brunson	560	1	1	0
Burnettown	2,704	2	2	0

Table 78. Full-Time Law Enforcement Employees, by Selected State and City, 2012— continued

(Number)

State/city	Population	Total law enforcement employees	Total officers	Total civilians
Calhoun Falls	2,027	7	7	0
Camden	6,918	30	27	3
Cameron	429	1	1	0
Campobello	508	5	5	0
Cayce	12,074	67	52	15
Central	5,219	9	8	1
Chapin	1,462	2	2	0
Charleston	121,481	526	396	130
Cheraw	5,919	30	24	6
Chesnee	878	7	7	0
Chester	5,672	28	25	3
Chesterfield	1,489	6	5	1
Clemson	14,067	35	27	8
Clinton	8,589	37	33	4
Clio	734	5	3	2
Clover	5,153	22	18	4
Columbia	130,777	444	382	62
Conway	17,302	58	49	9
Cottageville	771	4	3	1
Coward	761	1	1	0
Cowpens	2,187	5	5	0
Darlington	6,362	29	26	3
Denmark	3,579	11	9	2
Dillon	6,867	27	22	5
Due West	1,262	6	5	1
Duncan	3,218	10	10	0
Easley	20,226	52	42	10
Edgefield	4,805	9	9	0
Edisto Beach	419	6	6	0
Ehrhardt	551	6	3	3
Elgin	1,326	7	7	0
Elloree	700	3	3	0
Estill	2,064	9	7	2
Eutawville	319	1	1	0
Fairfax	2,049	7	6	1
Florence	37,488	136	111	25
Folly Beach	2,647	24	19	5
Forest Acres	10,482	35	26	9
Fort Lawn	905	3	3	0
Fort Mill	10,937	39	34	5
Fountain Inn	7,890	30	24	6
Gaffney	12,559	44	41	3
Gaston	1,664	2	2	0
Georgetown	9,270	35	31	4
Goose Creek	36,357	83	60	23
Great Falls	2,002	5	5	0
Greeleyville	443	3	3	0
Greenville	59,089	235	190	45
Greenwood	23,492	58	51	7
Greer	25,812	68	52	16
Hampton	2,841	11	11	0
Hanahan	18,207	45	34	11
Hardeeville	2,986	19	17	2
Harleyville	685	4	4	0
Hartsville	7,854	35	32	3
Hemingway	464	5	4	1
Holly Hill	1,292	7	7	0
Honea Path	3,639	14	14	0
Inman	2,348	8	8	0
Irmo	11,226	26	24	2
Isle of Palms	4,181	31	20	11
Iva	1,232	7	5	2

Table 78. Full-Time Law Enforcement Employees, by Selected State and City, 2012— continued

(Number)

State/city	Population	Total law enforcement employees	Total officers	Total civilians
Jackson	1,720	4	4	0
Jamestown	73	5	4	1
Johnsonville	1,497	6	5	1
Johnston	2,390	7	7	0
Jonesville	922	5	3	2
Kingstree	3,367	16	14	2
Lake City	6,753	25	21	4
Lake View	816	4	4	0
Lamar	1,001	8	8	0
Lancaster	8,625	44	35	9
Landrum	2,404	11	10	1
Lane	514	4	2	2
Latta	1,395	8	8	0
Laurens	9,245	33	26	7
Lexington	18,078	51	47	4
Liberty	3,307	16	11	5
Lincolnville	1,152	1	1	0
Loris	2,424	13	9	4
Lyman	3,281	9	8	1
Lynchburg	377	3	3	0
Manning	4,156	19	19	0
Marion	7,020	24	21	3
Mauldin	23,156	53	42	11
Mayesville	740	1	1	0
McBee	877	1	1	0
McColl	2,199	7	6	1
McCormick	2,815	7	7	0
Moncks Corner	7,977	27	24	3
Mount Pleasant	68,633	176	138	38
Mullins	4,717	23	21	2
Myrtle Beach	27,425	268	187	81
Newberry	10,397	33	30	3
New Ellenton	2,076	5	5	0
Nichols	372	4	4	0
Ninety Six	2,021	5	5	0
North	763	2	2	0
North Augusta	21,597	76	56	20
North Charleston	98,606	404	337	67
North Myrtle Beach	13,912	123	72	51
Orangeburg	14,127	95	71	24
Pacolet	2,261	6	5	1
Pageland	2,792	17	11	6
Pamplico	1,240	4	4	0
Pawleys Island	104	6	5	1
Pelion	682	3	3	0
Pickens	3,162	15	14	1
Pine Ridge	2,088	1	1	0
Port Royal	10,802	22	21	1
Prosperity	1,194	5	5	0
Ridgeland	4,083	17	17	0
Ridgeville	2,002	2	2	0
Rock Hill	66,924	178	136	42
Salley	403	1	1	0
Saluda	3,607	11	10	1
Santee	972	10	8	2
Scranton	943	1	1	0
Seneca	8,196	46	35	11
Simpsonville	18,450	46	36	10
Society Hill	570	2	1	1
South Congaree	2,333	7	6	1
Spartanburg	37,444	143	121	22
Springdale	2,667	8	8	0

Table 78. Full-Time Law Enforcement Employees, by Selected State and City, 2012— continued

(Number)

State/city	Population	Total law enforcement employees	Total officers	Total civilians
Springfield	530	5	3	2
St. George	2,108	10	10	0
St. Matthews	2,045	6	6	0
St. Stephen	1,717	5	5	0
Sullivans Island	1,812	9	8	1
Summerton	1,012	4	4	0
Summerville	43,897	109	87	22
Sumter	40,996	121	107	14
Surfside Beach	3,882	27	21	6
Swansea	837	5	4	1
Tega Cay	7,709	22	19	3
Timmonsville	2,347	5	4	1
Travelers Rest	4,629	21	15	6
Turbeville	775	3	3	0
Union	8,491	37	33	4
Varnville	2,187	6	6	0
Wagener	806	4	4	0
Walhalla	4,313	16	14	2
Walterboro	5,461	43	30	13
Ware Shoals	2,195	7	7	0
Wellford	2,406	9	7	2
West Columbia	15,163	68	53	15
Westminster	2,446	9	9	0
West Pelzer	890	4	4	0
West Union	294	2	2	0
Whitmire	1,458	5	4	1
Williamston	3,980	15	11	4
Williston	3,176	9	8	1
Winnsboro	3,591	20	20	0
Woodruff	4,138	12	11	1
Yemassee	1,039	5	5	0
York	7,826	32	25	7
SOUTH DAKOTA				
Aberdeen	26,408	51	43	8
Alcester	817	2	2	0
Armour	708	1	1	0
Avon	597	1	1	0
Belle Fourche	5,662	11	10	1
Beresford	2,029	8	4	4
Box Elder	7,895	10	9	1
Brandon	8,892	12	11	1
Brookings	22,324	38	31	7
Burke	611	1	1	0
Canton	3,094	5	5	0
Centerville	893	1	1	0
Chamberlain	2,416	6	6	0
Deadwood	1,285	14	11	3
Eagle Butte	1,334	2	2	0
Elk Point	1,987	4	4	0
Estelline	777	1	1	0
Faith	426	1	1	0
Flandreau	2,369	9	8	1
Freeman	1,322	2	2	0
Gettysburg	1,176	2	2	0
Gregory	1,311	3	3	0
Groton	1,476	4	4	0
Hot Springs	3,756	7	6	1
Hoven	411	1	1	0
Huron	12,745	32	25	7
Jefferson	554	1	1	0
Kadoka	662	1	1	0
Kimball	712	1	1	0

Table 78. Full-Time Law Enforcement Employees, by Selected State and City, 2012— continued

(Number)

State/city	Population	Total law enforcement employees	Total officers	Total civilians
Lead	3,162	6	5	1
Lemmon	1,242	2	2	0
Lennox	2,137	4	4	0
Leola	463	1	1	0
Madison	6,553	11	10	1
McIntosh	175	1	1	0
Menno	615	1	1	0
Milbank	3,394	6	6	0
Miller	1,507	4	4	0
Mitchell	15,440	43	27	16
Mobridge	3,507	14	7	7
North Sioux City	2,561	8	7	1
Parkston	1,526	3	3	0
Philip	788	2	2	0
Pierre	13,812	38	24	14
Platte	1,245	2	2	0
Rapid City	68,782	141	110	31
Rosholt	428	1	1	0
Scotland	851	1	1	0
Selby	650	1	1	0
Sioux Falls	155,760	265	230	35
Sisseton	2,500	7	7	0
Spearfish	10,622	29	20	9
Springfield	2,013	2	2	0
Sturgis	6,708	19	16	3
Summerset	1,836	3	3	0
Tea	3,852	6	6	0
Tripp	655	1	1	0
Tyndall	1,080	1	1	0
Vermillion	10,700	18	17	1
Viborg	792	1	1	0
Wagner	1,585	5	5	0
Watertown	21,743	53	35	18
Webster	1,909	5	5	0
Whitewood	938	3	3	0
Winner	2,932	11	9	2
Worthing	888	1	1	0
Yankton	14,630	35	24	11
TENNESSEE				
Adamsville	2,227	9	6	3
Alamo	2,483	4	4	0
Alcoa	8,525	47	40	7
Alexandria	975	3	3	0
Algood	3,527	13	13	0
Ardmore	1,224	11	7	4
Ashland City	4,582	16	14	2
Athens	13,579	31	30	1
Atoka	8,463	18	17	1
Baileyton	435	2	2	0
Bartlett	55,106	138	107	31
Baxter	1,377	5	5	0
Bean Station	2,851	6	6	0
Belle Meade	2,938	20	16	4
Bells	2,459	5	5	0
Benton	1,397	7	6	1
Berry Hill	542	17	13	4
Bethel Springs	724	3	1	2
Big Sandy	562	1	1	0
Blaine	1,873	1	1	0
Bluff City	1,749	8	8	0
Bolivar	5,466	27	22	5
Bradford	1,057	5	4	1

Table 78. Full-Time Law Enforcement Employees, by Selected State and City, 2012— continued

(Number)

State/city	Population	Total law enforcement employees	Total officers	Total civilians
Brentwood	37,394	72	57	15
Brighton	2,760	6	6	0
Bristol	26,943	89	67	22
Brownsville	10,005	34	30	4
Bruceton	1,491	4	4	0
Burns	1,481	3	3	0
Calhoun	494	2	2	0
Camden	3,614	19	14	5
Carthage	2,327	12	7	5
Caryville	2,318	5	5	0
Celina	1,508	7	5	2
Centerville	3,677	21	13	8
Chapel Hill	1,458	5	5	0
Charleston	657	3	3	0
Chattanooga	169,187	472	370	102
Church Hill	6,798	11	10	1
Clarksville	134,128	316	262	54
Cleveland	41,657	97	87	10
Clifton	2,718	5	5	0
Clinton	9,930	30	28	2
Collegedale	8,357	19	19	0
Collierville	44,362	133	98	35
Collinwood	991	5	5	0
Columbia	34,994	94	84	10
Cookeville	30,710	90	71	19
Coopertown	4,317	3	2	1
Copperhill	357	1	1	0
Cornersville	1,205	4	4	0
Covington	9,120	33	32	1
Cowan	1,753	5	5	0
Cross Plains	1,729	3	3	0
Crossville	10,892	46	43	3
Crump	1,441	4	4	0
Cumberland City	314	3	3	0
Cumberland Gap	498	1	1	0
Dandridge	2,837	12	11	1
Dayton	7,256	20	18	2
Decatur	1,612	5	5	0
Decaturville	875	2	1	1
Decherd	2,382	10	9	1
Dickson	14,669	52	46	6
Dover	1,430	5	5	0
Dresden	3,032	10	9	1
Dunlap	4,858	13	11	2
Dyer	2,362	6	6	0
Dyersburg	17,300	70	61	9
Eagleville	609	1	1	0
East Ridge	21,168	40	36	4
Elizabethton	14,304	44	40	4
Elkton	583	2	2	0
Englewood	1,546	6	5	1
Erin	1,336	6	5	1
Erwin	6,152	12	12	0
Estill Springs	2,074	6	6	0
Etowah	3,521	11	10	1
Fairview	7,790	19	18	1
Fayetteville	6,889	27	25	2
Franklin	63,051	150	124	26
Friendship	674	1	1	0
Gadsden	474	1	1	0
Gainesboro	971	5	4	1
Gallatin	30,551	87	64	23

Table 78. Full-Time Law Enforcement Employees, by Selected State and City, 2012— continued

(Number)

State/city	Population	Total law enforcement employees	Total officers	Total civilians
Gallaway	686	3	3	0
Gates	653	1	1	0
Gatlinburg	3,980	48	40	8
Germantown	39,194	108	87	21
Gibson	400	3	2	1
Gleason	1,458	6	6	0
Goodlettsville	16,065	52	37	15
Gordonsville	1,224	5	5	0
Grand Junction	328	2	2	0
Graysville	1,516	6	5	1
Greenbrier	6,491	14	13	1
Greeneville	15,198	49	46	3
Greenfield	2,202	8	7	1
Halls	2,275	7	7	0
Harriman	6,407	19	18	1
Henderson	6,366	14	13	1
Hendersonville	51,835	121	94	27
Henning	954	4	4	0
Henry	468	2	2	0
Hohenwald	3,791	13	12	1
Hollow Rock	724	2	2	0
Hornbeak	428	1	1	0
Humboldt	8,528	30	25	5
Huntingdon	4,021	16	12	4
Huntland	880	3	3	0
Jacksboro	2,038	6	6	0
Jackson	65,799	255	212	43
Jamestown	1,977	10	10	0
Jasper	3,309	8	8	0
Jefferson City	8,120	21	19	2
Jellico	2,376	9	8	1
Johnson City	63,722	170	143	27
Jonesborough	5,097	22	17	5
Kenton	1,293	4	4	0
Kimball	1,408	9	9	0
Kingsport	48,640	174	115	59
Kingston	5,988	13	12	1
Kingston Springs	2,781	6	5	1
Knoxville	180,488	485	387	98
Lafayette	4,514	20	14	6
La Follette	7,523	30	23	7
Lake City	1,797	9	7	2
La Vergne	32,882	65	49	16
Lawrenceburg	10,522	40	36	4
Lebanon	26,426	88	72	16
Lenoir City	8,720	26	25	1
Lewisburg	11,200	38	27	11
Lexington	7,721	29	25	4
Livingston	4,095	22	17	5
Lookout Mountain	1,849	22	16	6
Loretto	1,729	4	4	0
Loudon	5,430	15	15	0
Madisonville	4,618	17	14	3
Manchester	10,193	40	34	6
Martin	11,576	37	27	10
Maryville	27,713	54	48	6
Mason	1,624	5	5	0
Maury City	680	1	1	0
Maynardville	2,435	3	3	0
McEwen	1,766	7	6	1
McKenzie	5,358	19	16	3
McMinnville	13,728	37	33	4

Table 78. Full-Time Law Enforcement Employees, by Selected State and City, 2012— continued

(Number)

State/city	Population	Total law enforcement employees	Total officers	Total civilians
Medina	3,510	11	11	0
Memphis	652,725	2,855	2,454	401
Middleton	712	4	4	0
Milan	7,922	27	22	5
Millersville	6,498	17	12	5
Millington	10,268	49	36	13
Minor Hill	542	2	2	0
Monteagle	1,203	5	5	0
Monterey	2,876	8	8	0
Morristown	29,400	89	83	6
Moscow	561	2	2	0
Mountain City	2,554	9	9	0
Mount Carmel	5,478	7	7	0
Mount Juliet	23,885	57	45	12
Mount Pleasant	4,602	16	12	4
Munford	5,980	15	14	1
Murfreesboro	109,736	274	225	49
Nashville	612,789	1,618	1,315	303
Newbern	3,343	18	12	6
New Hope	1,092	1	1	0
New Johnsonville	1,969	4	4	0
New Market	1,346	4	4	0
Newport	7,008	31	27	4
New Tazewell	3,064	10	10	0
Niota	725	3	3	0
Nolensville	5,914	7	7	0
Norris	1,504	7	7	0
Oakland	6,683	18	18	0
Oak Ridge	29,595	75	59	16
Obion	1,129	3	3	0
Oliver Springs	3,260	13	9	4
Oneida	3,786	17	12	5
Paris	10,248	34	24	10
Parsons	2,394	6	6	0
Petersburg	549	2	2	0
Pigeon Forge	5,928	63	51	12
Pikeville	1,623	3	3	0
Piperton	1,458	9	9	0
Pittman Center	507	3	3	0
Plainview	2,144	1	1	0
Pleasant View	4,186	5	5	0
Portland	11,584	33	25	8
Powells Crossroads	1,334	1	1	0
Pulaski	7,941	28	25	3
Puryear	677	2	2	0
Red Bank	11,756	25	23	2
Red Boiling Springs	1,122	6	5	1
Ridgely	1,811	5	5	0
Ridgetop	1,891	6	6	0
Ripley	8,521	31	25	6
Rockwood	5,612	16	15	1
Rogersville	4,460	16	12	4
Rossville	670	6	6	0
Rutherford	1,161	3	3	0
Rutledge	1,132	4	4	0
Saltillo	306	2	2	0
Savannah	7,045	21	19	2
Scotts Hill	993	1	1	0
Selmer	4,436	21	19	2
Sevierville	14,941	69	55	14
Sewanee	2,332	13	9	4
Sharon	953	1	1	0

Table 78. Full-Time Law Enforcement Employees, by Selected State and City, 2012— continued

(Number)

State/city	Population	Total law enforcement employees	Total officers	Total civilians
Shelbyville	20,518	45	37	8
Signal Mountain	7,622	16	15	1
Smithville	4,571	13	12	1
Smyrna	40,335	104	76	28
Soddy-Daisy	12,829	30	25	5
Somerville	3,122	11	11	0
South Carthage	1,334	4	4	0
South Fulton	2,375	7	6	1
South Pittsburg	3,019	8	8	0
Sparta	4,969	16	15	1
Spencer	1,615	3	3	0
Spring City	1,999	7	7	0
Springfield	16,588	60	38	22
Spring Hill	29,298	51	42	9
Surgoinsville	1,817	2	2	0
Sweetwater	5,816	19	18	1
Tazewell	2,238	6	6	0
Tellico Plains	888	6	5	1
Tiptonville	4,504	4	4	0
Townsend	452	4	4	0
Tracy City	1,494	5	5	0
Trenton	4,302	25	19	6
Trezevant	867	1	1	0
Trimble	643	1	1	0
Troy	1,383	4	4	0
Tullahoma	18,823	42	37	5
Tusculum	2,687	2	2	0
Union City	10,993	42	34	8
Vonore	1,487	9	9	0
Wartburg	926	5	5	0
Wartrace	657	2	1	1
Watauga	462	1	1	0
Watertown	1,490	4	4	0
Waverly	4,142	13	12	1
Waynesboro	2,471	8	8	0
Westmoreland	2,226	9	6	3
White Bluff	3,235	5	5	0
White House	10,348	22	19	3
White Pine	2,216	9	8	1
Whiteville	4,680	8	8	0
Whitwell	1,714	6	5	1
Winchester	8,607	25	23	2
Winfield	976	1	1	0
Woodbury	2,704	9	8	1
TEXAS				
Abernathy	2,864	4	4	0
Abilene	119,526	241	181	60
Addison	13,331	84	62	22
Alamo	18,739	39	28	11
Alamo Heights	7,179	33	22	11
Alice	19,506	45	37	8
Allen	86,019	155	108	47
Alpine	6,029	18	9	9
Alton	12,601	20	15	5
Alvarado	3,865	23	16	7
Alvin	24,746	78	49	29
Amarillo	194,708	371	320	51
Andrews	11,321	25	16	9
Angleton	19,259	48	36	12
Anna	8,423	13	12	1
Anson	2,481	6	6	0
Anthony	5,116	17	16	1

Table 78. Full-Time Law Enforcement Employees, by Selected State and City, 2012— continued

(Number)

State/city	Population	Total law enforcement employees	Total officers	Total civilians
Aransas Pass	8,377	32	23	9
Archer City	1,873	2	2	0
Arcola	1,677	3	3	0
Argyle	3,351	10	9	1
Arlington	373,128	840	640	200
Arp	990	4	4	0
Athens	12,977	31	24	7
Atlanta	5,794	17	13	4
Aubrey	2,650	6	6	0
Austin	807,022	2,211	1,644	567
Azle	11,177	31	23	8
Baird	1,527	2	2	0
Balch Springs	24,227	55	38	17
Balcones Heights	3,003	24	19	5
Ballinger	3,846	6	6	0
Bangs	1,637	3	3	0
Bastrop	7,370	24	20	4
Bay City	17,985	54	35	19
Bayou Vista	1,569	5	5	0
Baytown	73,313	194	142	52
Beaumont	120,785	295	247	48
Bedford	47,968	129	80	49
Bee Cave	4,008	15	14	1
Beeville	13,134	26	21	5
Bellaire	17,210	55	41	14
Bellmead	10,109	20	14	6
Bellville	4,183	12	11	1
Belton	18,599	40	30	10
Benbrook	21,681	49	40	9
Bertram	1,381	4	4	0
Beverly Hills	2,037	10	7	3
Big Sandy	1,371	6	6	0
Big Spring	27,856	61	48	13
Bishop	3,200	9	5	4
Blanco	1,776	6	5	1
Bloomburg	413	1	1	0
Blue Mound	2,444	10	6	4
Boerne	10,691	45	29	16
Bogata	1,177	4	4	0
Bonham	10,340	27	19	8
Borger	13,530	38	26	12
Bovina	1,907	4	4	0
Bowie	5,328	20	15	5
Brackettville	1,724	1	1	0
Brady	5,644	16	9	7
Brazoria	3,083	12	7	5
Breckenridge	5,902	16	11	5
Bremond	949	2	2	0
Brenham	16,047	38	33	5
Bridge City	8,005	19	15	4
Bridgeport	6,102	22	15	7
Brookshire	4,801	20	16	4
Brookside Village	1,555	4	4	0
Brownfield	9,860	24	18	6
Brownsville	178,706	311	241	70
Brownwood	19,694	59	38	21
Bruceville-Eddy	1,506	3	3	0
Bryan	77,804	169	132	37
Buda	7,449	10	9	1
Bullard	2,515	8	7	1
Bulverde	4,727	15	14	1
Burkburnett	11,038	25	19	6

Table 78. Full-Time Law Enforcement Employees, by Selected State and City, 2012— continued

(Number)

State/city	Population	Total law enforcement employees	Total officers	Total civilians
Burleson	37,462	71	54	17
Burnet	6,113	15	14	1
Cactus	3,246	8	6	2
Caddo Mills	1,366	3	3	0
Caldwell	4,190	13	12	1
Calvert	1,217	4	4	0
Cameron	5,669	13	8	5
Canton	3,656	19	14	5
Canyon	13,583	24	21	3
Carrollton	121,603	198	153	45
Carthage	6,922	22	16	6
Castle Hills	4,203	26	20	6
Castroville	2,736	11	9	2
Cedar Hill	45,975	82	64	18
Cedar Park	49,967	98	76	22
Celina	6,155	6	6	0
Center	5,302	27	19	8
Childress	6,233	12	10	2
Chillicothe	722	3	2	1
Cibolo	15,672	26	24	2
Cisco	3,981	7	5	2
Clarksville	3,354	12	8	4
Cleburne	29,954	70	52	18
Cleveland	7,836	35	21	14
Clifton	3,514	9	8	1
Clint	945	1	1	0
Clute	11,447	40	29	11
Clyde	3,791	10	9	1
Cockrell Hill	4,281	18	12	6
Coleman	4,808	18	10	8
College Station	95,832	171	117	54
Colleyville	23,287	39	35	4
Collinsville	1,658	3	3	0
Colorado City	4,233	12	6	6
Columbus	3,732	11	9	2
Comanche	4,426	10	8	2
Combes	2,956	6	6	0
Commerce	8,248	20	16	4
Conroe	57,390	147	111	36
Converse	18,581	48	33	15
Coppell	39,472	79	62	17
Copperas Cove	32,706	73	55	18
Corinth	20,354	31	28	3
Corpus Christi	311,637	624	428	196
Corrigan	1,629	11	7	4
Corsicana	24,270	53	43	10
Cottonwood Shores	1,147	2	2	0
Crandall	2,918	12	12	0
Crane	3,424	11	7	4
Crockett	7,096	17	16	1
Crosbyton	1,778	3	3	0
Crowell	968	1	1	0
Crowley	13,108	37	28	9
Crystal City	7,288	7	2	5
Cuero	6,985	15	14	1
Cumby	793	6	5	1
Daingerfield	2,614	8	7	1
Dalhart	8,097	18	15	3
Dallas	1,223,021	4,052	3,511	541
Dalworthington Gardens	2,307	18	14	4
Danbury	1,751	4	4	0
Dayton	7,394	27	18	9

Table 78. Full-Time Law Enforcement Employees, by Selected State and City, 2012— continued

(Number)

State/city	Population	Total law enforcement employees	Total officers	Total civilians
Decatur	6,169	27	21	6
Deer Park	32,684	83	59	24
De Kalb	1,735	6	5	1
De Leon	2,293	5	5	0
Del Rio	36,340	92	68	24
Denison	23,159	55	45	10
Denton	115,769	204	150	54
Denver City	4,573	13	8	5
DeSoto	50,079	86	59	27
Devine	4,442	11	9	2
Diboll	4,876	20	14	6
Dickinson	19,073	44	31	13
Dilley	3,976	7	6	1
Dimmitt	4,485	9	7	2
Donna	16,130	37	29	8
Double Oak	2,927	6	6	0
Driscoll	755	7	3	4
Dublin	3,731	11	7	4
Dumas	15,000	31	26	5
Duncanville	39,335	73	60	13
Eagle Lake	3,716	9	8	1
Early	2,820	8	7	1
Eastland	4,043	11	9	2
East Mountain	814	2	2	0
Edcouch	3,228	13	9	4
Edgewood	1,471	2	2	0
Edinburg	78,722	172	124	48
Edna	5,615	11	9	2
El Campo	11,846	40	28	12
Electra	2,850	13	7	6
Elgin	8,306	24	18	6
El Paso	662,780	1,280	1,057	223
Elsa	5,779	18	13	5
Ennis	18,903	40	34	6
Euless	52,356	128	85	43
Everman	6,237	18	13	5
Fairfield	3,013	15	12	3
Fair Oaks Ranch	6,112	16	15	1
Falfurrias	5,086	14	13	1
Farmers Branch	29,218	109	74	35
Farmersville	3,370	11	9	2
Farwell	1,392	2	2	0
Ferris	2,487	13	8	5
Flatonia	1,412	5	5	0
Florence	1,160	2	2	0
Floresville	6,584	16	14	2
Flower Mound	66,030	116	81	35
Floydada	3,102	6	6	0
Forest Hill	12,615	23	17	6
Forney	14,970	33	22	11
Fort Stockton	8,457	30	19	11
Fort Worth	756,803	1,933	1,509	424
Frankston	1,255	6	5	1
Fredericksburg	10,752	34	30	4
Freeport	12,303	49	35	14
Freer	2,877	12	8	4
Friendswood	36,558	77	63	14
Friona	4,210	10	6	4
Frisco	119,451	196	140	56
Gainesville	16,339	53	39	14
Galena Park	11,116	24	18	6
Galveston	48,748	164	129	35

Table 78. Full-Time Law Enforcement Employees, by Selected State and City, 2012— continued

(Number)

State/city	Population	Total law enforcement employees	Total officers	Total civilians
Ganado	2,045	3	3	0
Garden Ridge	3,328	14	14	0
Garland	231,650	442	322	120
Gatesville	16,082	24	16	8
Georgetown	48,397	100	72	28
Giddings	4,984	19	14	5
Gladewater	6,577	21	16	5
Glenn Heights	11,515	25	16	9
Godley	1,030	7	7	0
Gonzales	7,389	22	16	6
Gorman	1,106	2	2	0
Graham	9,090	23	22	1
Granbury	8,146	35	29	6
Grand Prairie	179,087	327	215	112
Grand Saline	3,202	8	8	0
Granger	1,449	4	3	1
Granite Shoals	5,013	8	7	1
Grapeland	1,520	5	5	0
Grapevine	47,309	128	92	36
Greenville	26,095	70	51	19
Gregory	1,947	4	4	0
Groesbeck	4,419	9	8	1
Groves	16,484	23	21	2
Gruver	1,219	2	2	0
Gun Barrel City	5,791	19	14	5
Hale Center	2,299	3	3	0
Hallettsville	2,604	8	7	1
Hallsville	3,652	5	4	1
Haltom City	43,301	89	72	17
Hamlin	2,169	8	4	4
Harker Heights	27,262	57	45	12
Harlingen	66,214	166	128	38
Haskell	3,392	2	2	0
Hawk Cove	493	1	1	0
Hawkins	1,305	5	5	0
Hawley	647	1	1	0
Hearne	4,553	17	12	5
Heath	7,067	18	17	1
Hedwig Village	2,611	21	16	5
Helotes	7,495	22	20	2
Hemphill	1,223	3	3	0
Hempstead	5,891	18	15	3
Henderson	14,001	41	33	8
Hereford	15,693	31	25	6
Hewitt	13,834	30	22	8
Hickory Creek	3,315	11	11	0
Hidalgo	11,434	43	29	14
Highland Park	8,744	69	52	17
Highland Village	15,373	35	29	6
Hill Country Village	1,006	11	11	0
Hillsboro	8,634	36	25	11
Hitchcock	7,107	22	16	6
Holliday	1,795	3	3	0
Hollywood Park	3,126	12	11	1
Hondo	8,988	19	17	2
Hooks	2,827	7	7	0
Horizon City	17,087	24	20	4
Horseshoe Bay	3,490	18	16	2
Houston	2,143,628	6,531	5,294	1,237
Howe	2,655	4	4	0
Hubbard	1,453	4	4	0
Hudson	4,831	5	5	0

Table 78. Full-Time Law Enforcement Employees, by Selected State and City, 2012— continued

(Number)

State/city	Population	Total law enforcement employees	Total officers	Total civilians
Hudson Oaks	1,697	12	11	1
Hughes Springs	1,797	5	5	0
Humble	15,451	78	58	20
Huntington	2,163	5	5	0
Huntsville	39,359	58	51	7
Hurst	38,123	115	74	41
Hutchins	5,450	22	17	5
Hutto	15,007	28	24	4
Idalou	2,297	5	5	0
Ingleside	9,585	22	15	7
Ingram	1,842	7	6	1
Iowa Park	6,489	17	11	6
Irving	220,841	482	336	146
Italy	1,902	4	3	1
Itasca	1,679	7	7	0
Jacinto City	10,775	26	20	6
Jacksboro	4,606	11	9	2
Jacksonville	14,850	38	28	10
Jamaica Beach	1,004	5	5	0
Jarrell	1,005	2	2	0
Jasper	7,750	28	22	6
Jefferson	2,150	4	3	1
Jersey Village	7,780	37	28	9
Johnson City	1,691	4	4	0
Jones Creek	2,063	3	3	0
Jonestown	1,873	9	8	1
Joshua	6,034	15	14	1
Jourdanton	3,952	8	8	0
Junction	2,628	5	5	0
Karnes City	3,106	8	7	1
Katy	14,399	60	44	16
Kaufman	6,844	24	16	8
Keene	6,234	17	11	6
Keller	40,461	79	49	30
Kemah	1,810	22	17	5
Kemp	1,178	5	5	0
Kenedy	3,365	8	7	1
Kennedale	6,905	24	17	7
Kermit	5,828	17	10	7
Kerrville	22,817	67	51	16
Kilgore	13,248	43	33	10
Killeen	130,613	316	227	89
Kingsville	26,765	64	49	15
Kirby	8,168	17	12	5
Kountze	2,168	7	6	1
Kress	730	1	1	0
Kyle	28,606	50	36	14
Lacoste	1,143	2	2	0
Lacy-Lakeview	6,626	22	14	8
La Feria	7,456	17	13	4
Lago Vista	6,168	22	15	7
La Grange	4,739	10	10	0
La Grulla	1,656	6	4	2
Laguna Vista	3,183	7	7	0
La Joya	4,069	16	11	5
Lake Dallas	7,255	23	15	8
Lake Jackson	27,414	60	44	16
Lakeside	1,335	4	4	0
Lakeview, Harris County	6,382	17	13	4
Lakeway	11,631	40	29	11
Lake Worth	4,680	34	27	7
La Marque	14,814	40	28	12

Table 78. Full-Time Law Enforcement Employees, by Selected State and City, 2012— continued

(Number)

State/city	Population	Total law enforcement employees	Total officers	Total civilians
Lamesa	9,620	23	16	7
Lampasas	6,822	28	18	10
Lancaster	37,126	64	50	14
La Porte	34,511	105	75	30
Laredo	241,059	499	425	74
La Vernia	1,056	7	7	0
La Villa	1,998	7	6	1
Lavon	2,266	7	7	0
League City	85,318	138	102	36
Leander	27,079	51	35	16
Leonard	2,032	5	5	0
Leon Valley	10,365	33	24	9
Levelland	13,827	34	23	11
Lewisville	97,295	193	136	57
Liberty	8,574	27	17	10
Lindale	4,919	20	14	6
Linden	2,030	6	5	1
Little Elm	26,443	37	34	3
Littlefield	6,506	19	12	7
Live Oak	13,407	45	31	14
Livingston	5,447	25	18	7
Llano	3,300	10	9	1
Lockhart	12,965	36	25	11
Lockney	1,881	2	2	0
Lometa	874	1	1	0
Lone Star	1,614	5	4	1
Longview	82,148	217	158	59
Lorena	1,727	6	5	1
Lorenzo	1,171	2	2	0
Los Fresnos	5,659	21	15	6
Lott	775	4	4	0
Lubbock	234,404	488	378	110
Lufkin	35,805	95	74	21
Luling	5,525	22	15	7
Lumberton	12,194	18	15	3
Lyford	2,666	2	2	0
Lytle	2,544	7	7	0
Madisonville	4,489	14	12	2
Magnolia	1,422	12	10	2
Malakoff	2,373	6	6	0
Manor	5,143	16	14	2
Mansfield	57,554	205	85	120
Manvel	5,288	14	10	4
Marble Falls	6,205	38	23	15
Marlin	6,093	18	14	4
Marshall	24,018	65	51	14
Mart	2,255	4	4	0
Martindale	1,139	3	3	0
Mathis	5,046	18	12	6
McAllen	132,610	403	270	133
McGregor	5,092	16	9	7
McKinney	133,876	194	153	41
Meadows Place	4,758	16	15	1
Melissa	4,794	9	8	1
Memorial Villages	11,359	39	33	6
Memphis	2,338	4	4	0
Mercedes	15,898	44	36	8
Meridian	1,524	2	2	0
Merkel	2,644	3	3	0
Mesquite	142,766	305	228	77
Mexia	7,616	28	18	10
Midland	113,486	221	172	49

Table 78. Full-Time Law Enforcement Employees, by Selected State and City, 2012— continued

(Number)

State/city	Population	Total law enforcement employees	Total officers	Total civilians
Midlothian	18,417	41	28	13
Milford	743	3	3	0
Mineola	4,610	18	12	6
Mineral Wells	17,141	38	28	10
Mission	78,679	195	140	55
Missouri City	68,775	111	88	23
Monahans	7,099	16	11	5
Mont Belvieu	3,916	15	10	5
Montgomery	634	7	7	0
Morgans Point Resort	4,258	8	7	1
Mount Pleasant	15,892	38	27	11
Muleshoe	5,267	12	8	4
Munday	1,327	3	3	0
Murphy	18,081	32	22	10
Mustang Ridge	879	4	4	0
Nacogdoches	33,690	78	61	17
Naples	1,407	4	4	0
Nash	3,022	10	9	1
Nassau Bay	4,086	13	12	1
Navasota	7,197	26	19	7
Nederland	17,916	36	24	12
Needville	2,882	6	6	0
New Boston	4,646	12	9	3
New Braunfels	58,955	123	100	23
New Deal	811	2	2	0
Nixon	2,435	5	4	1
Nocona	3,097	9	5	4
Nolanville	4,349	5	5	0
Northlake	1,760	9	9	0
North Richland Hills	64,676	155	107	48
Oak Ridge	144	2	2	0
Oak Ridge North	3,113	16	16	0
Odessa	102,043	198	144	54
O'Donnell	848	1	1	0
Olmos Park	2,284	12	12	0
Olney	3,354	7	6	1
Olton	2,262	3	3	0
Onalaska	1,801	6	6	0
Orange	18,986	56	42	14
Orange Grove	1,346	5	5	0
Overton	2,608	9	6	3
Ovilla	3,565	10	9	1
Oyster Creek	1,134	9	5	4
Paducah	1,211	5	1	4
Palacios	4,817	16	11	5
Palestine	19,106	40	34	6
Palmer	2,042	13	9	4
Palmhurst	2,662	14	10	4
Palm Valley	1,331	5	5	0
Palmview	5,575	25	18	7
Pampa	18,373	36	26	10
Panhandle	2,504	4	4	0
Pantego	2,444	17	12	5
Paris	25,701	86	62	24
Parker	3,891	7	7	0
Pasadena	152,179	334	260	74
Pearland	93,172	177	134	43
Pearsall	9,338	15	13	2
Pecos	8,965	41	20	21
Penitas	4,496	12	8	4

Table 78. Full-Time Law Enforcement Employees, by Selected State and City, 2012— continued

(Number)

State/city	Population	Total law enforcement employees	Total officers	Total civilians
Perryton	8,987	18	11	7
Pflugerville	47,924	99	76	23
Pharr	71,881	175	126	49
Pilot Point	3,937	6	6	0
Pinehurst	2,141	8	6	2
Pittsburg	4,592	12	10	2
Plainview	22,661	40	32	8
Plano	265,309	489	336	153
Pleasanton	9,122	24	18	6
Point Comfort	753	1	1	0
Ponder	1,424	1	1	0
Port Aransas	3,553	21	14	7
Port Arthur	54,950	162	125	37
Port Isabel	5,111	25	18	7
Portland	15,417	35	24	11
Port Lavaca	12,506	26	20	6
Port Neches	13,314	21	18	3
Poteet	3,329	8	7	1
Poth	1,948	3	3	0
Pottsboro	2,205	7	7	0
Premont	2,709	6	6	0
Presidio	4,519	5	4	1
Primera	4,156	9	8	1
Princeton	6,950	11	11	0
Progreso	5,623	8	8	0
Prosper	9,621	18	11	7
Queen City	1,507	6	6	0
Quinlan	1,423	4	4	0
Quitman	1,847	6	6	0
Ralls	1,985	3	3	0
Rancho Viejo	2,488	7	7	0
Ranger	2,520	7	6	1
Ransom Canyon	1,119	3	3	0
Raymondville	11,521	22	13	9
Red Oak	10,996	25	23	2
Refugio	2,951	9	8	1
Reno	3,233	4	3	1
Richardson	101,311	240	152	88
Richland Hills	7,965	24	17	7
Richmond	11,925	38	28	10
Richwood	3,584	8	8	0
Riesel	1,028	4	4	0
Rio Grande City	14,125	35	27	8
Rio Hondo	2,406	6	5	1
Rising Star	853	1	1	0
River Oaks	7,583	24	18	6
Roanoke	6,087	38	29	9
Robinson	10,730	29	21	8
Robstown	11,729	35	26	9
Rockdale	5,713	17	11	6
Rockport	8,950	27	25	2
Rockwall	38,279	86	68	18
Rollingwood	1,442	6	6	0
Roma	9,970	34	25	9
Roman Forest	1,570	8	8	0
Roscoe	1,350	1	1	0
Rosebud	1,442	4	4	0
Rose City	513	1	1	0
Rosenberg	31,262	80	63	17
Rowlett	57,382	109	73	36

Table 78. Full-Time Law Enforcement Employees, by Selected State and City, 2012— continued

(Number)

State/city	Population	Total law enforcement employees	Total officers	Total civilians
Royse City	9,546	16	15	1
Runaway Bay	1,313	4	4	0
Rusk	5,668	13	11	2
Sabinal	1,731	4	4	0
Sachse	20,757	41	29	12
Saginaw	20,223	42	35	7
Salado	2,171	4	4	0
San Angelo	95,161	216	163	53
San Antonio	1,355,339	3,002	2,324	678
San Augustine	2,152	7	7	0
San Benito	24,760	47	39	8
San Diego	4,582	6	5	1
Sanger	7,062	15	14	1
San Juan	34,568	56	44	12
San Marcos	45,839	126	95	31
San Saba	3,164	4	4	0
Sansom Park Village	4,785	15	11	4
Santa Anna	1,122	2	2	0
Santa Fe	12,479	27	21	6
Santa Rosa	2,933	6	6	0
Schertz	32,127	67	51	16
Schulenburg	2,912	8	7	1
Seabrook	12,203	41	32	9
Seagoville	15,147	29	22	7
Seagraves	2,468	4	4	0
Sealy	6,146	20	18	2
Seguin	25,705	70	52	18
Selma	5,657	29	26	3
Seminole	6,565	12	11	1
Seven Points	1,486	11	7	4
Seymour	2,798	8	6	2
Shallowater	2,536	5	5	0
Shamrock	1,950	7	3	4
Shavano Park	3,099	17	16	1
Shenandoah	2,179	24	23	1
Sherman	39,332	85	61	24
Silsbee	6,750	21	16	5
Sinton	5,784	12	11	1
Slaton	6,250	16	10	6
Smithville	3,897	13	9	4
Snyder	11,438	22	20	2
Socorro	32,687	39	27	12
Somerset	1,665	3	3	0
Somerville	1,405	5	5	0
Sonora	3,091	6	4	2
Sour Lake	1,851	8	7	1
South Houston	17,340	38	29	9
Southlake	27,134	62	54	8
South Padre Island	2,875	38	28	10
Southside Place	1,751	9	5	4
Spearman	3,439	4	4	0
Springtown	2,714	16	11	5
Spring Valley	3,793	23	18	5
Spur	1,346	2	2	0
Stafford	18,065	60	44	16
Stagecoach	549	3	3	0
Stamford	3,190	9	8	1
Stanton	2,544	3	3	0
Stephenville	17,483	53	36	17
Stratford	2,059	4	4	0
Sugar Land	80,475	173	149	24
Sullivan City	4,086	13	8	5

Table 78. Full-Time Law Enforcement Employees, by Selected State and City, 2012— continued

(Number)

State/city	Population	Total law enforcement employees	Total officers	Total civilians
Sulphur Springs	15,774	40	29	11
Sunray	1,967	8	6	2
Sunrise Beach Village	728	4	4	0
Sunset Valley	765	13	13	0
Surfside Beach	492	6	6	0
Sweeny	3,762	7	7	0
Sweetwater	11,135	27	22	5
Taft	3,112	11	10	1
Tahoka	2,729	4	4	0
Tatum	1,414	5	5	0
Taylor	15,511	35	26	9
Teague	3,635	8	7	1
Temple	67,493	163	134	29
Terrell	16,149	46	36	10
Terrell Hills	4,981	15	14	1
Texarkana	37,177	105	93	12
Texas City	46,048	116	88	28
The Colony	37,092	79	53	26
Thorndale	1,364	2	2	0
Thrall	857	5	5	0
Three Rivers	1,887	8	7	1
Tioga	820	2	2	0
Tolar	695	1	1	0
Tomball	10,979	57	42	15
Tom Bean	1,067	5	4	1
Tool	2,287	12	9	3
Trenton	648	2	2	0
Trinity	2,754	10	6	4
Trophy Club	8,193	15	14	1
Troup	1,908	9	8	1
Troy	1,680	5	5	0
Tulia	5,072	13	8	5
Tye	1,268	4	4	0
Tyler	98,939	240	190	50
Universal City	18,920	39	29	10
University Park	23,553	52	39	13
Uvalde	16,082	48	37	11
Valley Mills	1,228	2	2	0
Valley View	773	3	3	0
Van	2,687	6	6	0
Van Alstyne	3,110	14	9	5
Vernon	11,234	32	21	11
Victoria	63,909	145	110	35
Vidor	10,802	30	22	8
Waco	127,431	322	241	81
Waelder	1,087	4	4	0
Wake Village	5,608	9	8	1
Waller	2,375	10	9	1
Wallis	1,278	3	3	0
Watauga	23,991	50	32	18
Waxahachie	30,244	70	53	17
Weatherford	25,781	74	59	15
Webster	10,619	63	47	16
Weimar	2,196	8	7	1
Weslaco	36,421	76	55	21
West	2,866	7	7	0
West Columbia	3,987	15	9	6
West Lake Hills	3,127	19	13	6
West Orange	3,515	11	9	2
Westover Hills	696	13	10	3
West Tawakoni	1,609	4	4	0
West University Place	15,098	33	22	11

Table 78. Full-Time Law Enforcement Employees, by Selected State and City, 2012— continued

(Number)

State/city	Population	Total law enforcement employees	Total officers	Total civilians
Westworth	2,524	18	13	5
Wharton	9,018	32	22	10
Whitehouse	7,821	19	13	6
White Oak	6,605	19	15	4
Whitesboro	3,873	13	8	5
White Settlement	16,455	50	36	14
Whitewright	1,638	5	5	0
Whitney	2,131	7	6	1
Wichita Falls	106,753	278	189	89
Willis	5,781	14	12	2
Willow Park	4,066	17	12	5
Wills Point	3,598	12	11	1
Wilmer	3,759	16	12	4
Windcrest	5,477	22	15	7
Wink	960	1	1	0
Winnsboro	3,506	13	9	4
Winters	2,616	4	4	0
Wolfe City	1,442	3	3	0
Wolfforth	3,747	10	9	1
Woodbranch	1,309	5	3	2
Woodville	2,640	10	9	1
Woodway	8,630	35	25	10
Wortham	1,096	3	3	0
Wylie	42,299	46	41	5
Yoakum	5,937	17	10	7
Yorktown	2,136	4	4	0
UTAH				
Alta	390	8	4	4
American Fork/Cedar Hills	36,755	38	32	6
Blanding	3,440	6	5	1
Bountiful	43,373	51	36	15
Brian Head	85	5	5	0
Brigham City	18,244	29	25	4
Cedar City	29,414	42	34	8
Centerfield	1,393	1	1	0
Centerville	15,631	20	17	3
Clearfield	30,693	44	31	13
Clinton	20,820	17	16	1
Cottonwood Heights	34,078	42	37	5
Draper	43,090	43	36	7
East Carbon	1,326	4	4	0
Enoch	5,915	6	4	2
Ephraim	6,253	5	5	0
Fairview	1,271	1	1	0
Farmington	18,628	17	14	3
Garland	2,446	4	4	0
Grantsville	9,065	12	10	2
Gunnison	3,348	3	3	0
Harrisville	5,674	9	8	1
Heber	11,581	15	13	2
Helper	2,243	6	6	0
Hildale	2,779	12	7	5
Hurricane	14,013	20	19	1
Ivins	6,883	12	10	2
Kamas	1,846	2	2	0
Kanab	4,395	8	7	1
Kaysville	27,827	22	20	2
La Verkin	4,138	4	4	0
Layton	68,610	106	75	31
Lehi	48,322	44	40	4
Lindon	10,264	15	14	1
Logan	49,104	96	62	34

Table 78. Full-Time Law Enforcement Employees, by Selected State and City, 2012— continued

(Number)

State/city	Population	Total law enforcement employees	Total officers	Total civilians
Lone Peak	25,562	21	19	2
Mantua	700	1	1	0
Mapleton	8,133	9	8	1
Minersville	925	1	1	0
Moab	5,143	20	15	5
Monticello	2,010	3	3	0
Moroni	1,450	1	1	0
Mount Pleasant	3,323	4	4	0
Murray	47,648	82	76	6
Naples	1,789	7	6	1
Nephi	5,493	10	8	2
North Ogden	17,692	21	18	3
North Park	12,336	11	9	2
North Salt Lake	16,637	20	18	2
Ogden	84,423	165	135	30
Orem	90,033	122	88	34
Park City	7,704	41	30	11
Parowan	2,844	3	3	0
Payson	18,647	19	17	2
Perry	4,599	5	4	1
Pleasant Grove	34,156	33	25	8
Pleasant View	8,133	9	8	1
Price	8,883	21	17	4
Provo	114,659	146	99	47
Richfield	7,697	14	13	1
Riverdale	8,589	22	19	3
Roosevelt	6,163	13	11	2
Roy	37,596	45	40	5
Salem	6,547	10	9	1
Salina	2,537	5	4	1
Salt Lake City	190,038	558	414	144
Sandy	89,149	143	107	36
Santa Clara	6,119	10	9	1
Santaquin/Genola	10,700	11	11	0
Saratoga Springs	18,124	27	23	4
Smithfield	9,678	9	8	1
South Jordan	51,391	58	50	8
South Ogden	16,851	27	22	5
South Salt Lake	24,073	69	59	10
Spanish Fork	35,360	31	28	3
Springdale	539	4	3	1
Springville	30,035	31	27	4
St. George	74,304	144	104	40
Stockton	628	1	1	0
Sunset	5,221	8	8	0
Syracuse	24,801	21	19	2
Taylorsville City	59,784	66	61	5
Tooele	32,215	39	33	6
Tremonton	7,795	12	10	2
Vernal	9,264	24	21	3
Washington	19,123	26	21	5
Wellington	1,708	3	3	0
West Bountiful	5,367	10	9	1
West Jordan	105,713	133	94	39
West Valley	131,979	233	189	44
Willard	1,806	2	2	0
Woods Cross	9,949	15	13	2
VERMONT				
Barre	9,062	24	18	6
Barre Town	7,933	7	6	1
Bellows Falls	3,151	12	8	4
Bennington	15,781	32	25	7

Table 78. Full-Time Law Enforcement Employees, by Selected State and City, 2012— continued

(Number)

State/city	Population	Total law enforcement employees	Total officers	Total civilians
Berlin	2,890	7	6	1
Brandon	3,970	7	7	0
Brattleboro	12,059	38	24	14
Bristol	3,898	3	3	0
Burlington	42,464	128	94	34
Castleton	4,722	4	4	0
Chester	3,157	5	4	1
Colchester	17,086	36	28	8
Dover	1,125	6	5	1
Essex	19,609	33	27	6
Fair Haven	2,737	4	4	0
Hardwick	3,013	5	4	1
Hartford	9,963	33	24	9
Hinesburg	4,401	5	5	0
Ludlow	1,965	9	5	4
Lyndonville	1,208	3	3	0
Manchester	4,396	13	9	4
Middlebury	8,505	16	14	2
Milton	10,363	16	15	1
Montpelier	7,864	24	16	8
Morristown	5,233	10	10	0
Newport	4,594	12	10	2
Northfield	6,214	6	5	1
Norwich	3,418	5	4	1
Randolph	4,783	6	6	0
Richmond	4,086	4	4	0
Rutland	16,513	45	37	8
Shelburne	7,152	19	11	8
South Burlington	17,924	41	34	7
Springfield	9,383	15	15	0
St. Albans	6,926	33	23	10
St. Johnsbury	7,611	15	9	6
Stowe	4,319	11	11	0
Swanton	6,434	4	4	0
Thetford	2,591	3	3	0
Vergennes	2,591	6	6	0
Vernon	2,208	5	4	1
Waterbury	5,070	2	2	0
Weathersfield	2,828	1	1	0
Williston	8,708	15	12	3
Wilmington	1,878	7	6	1
Windsor	3,557	8	7	1
Winhall	770	6	5	1
Winooski	7,275	23	16	7
Woodstock	3,051	3	3	0
VIRGINIA				
Abingdon	8,289	28	26	2
Alexandria	141,638	399	300	99
Altavista	3,491	14	13	1
Amherst	2,258	5	5	0
Appalachia	1,775	6	6	0
Ashland	7,311	27	24	3
Bedford	6,296	27	24	3
Berryville	4,235	10	9	1
Big Stone Gap	5,681	16	15	1
Blacksburg	43,129	79	62	17
Blackstone	3,664	18	13	5
Bloxom	392	1	1	0
Bluefield	5,509	22	17	5
Boykins	571	1	1	0
Bridgewater	5,711	9	9	0
Bristol	18,048	70	50	20

Table 78. Full-Time Law Enforcement Employees, by Selected State and City, 2012— continued

(Number)

State/city	Population	Total law enforcement employees	Total officers	Total civilians
Broadway	3,735	4	4	0
Buena Vista	6,729	16	15	1
Burkeville	437	1	1	0
Cape Charles	1,021	5	5	0
Cedar Bluff	1,151	3	3	0
Charlottesville	43,994	144	117	27
Chase City	2,379	10	9	1
Chatham	1,284	3	3	0
Chesapeake	224,864	495	354	141
Chilhowie	1,802	6	6	0
Chincoteague	2,976	14	10	4
Christiansburg	21,292	73	57	16
Clarksville	1,153	8	7	1
Clifton Forge	3,930	12	10	2
Clintwood	1,431	4	4	0
Coeburn	2,165	7	7	0
Colonial Beach	3,584	16	11	5
Colonial Heights	17,619	52	48	4
Covington	6,032	28	17	11
Crewe	2,354	5	4	1
Culpeper	16,575	46	38	8
Damascus	824	5	5	0
Danville	43,569	136	129	7
Dayton	1,548	8	7	1
Dublin	2,564	10	9	1
Dumfries	5,020	8	6	2
Edinburg	1,053	2	2	0
Elkton	2,759	7	6	1
Emporia	5,998	37	26	11
Exmore	1,477	5	5	0
Fairfax City	22,835	82	65	17
Falls Church	12,479	38	30	8
Farmville	8,314	28	27	1
Franklin	8,685	42	29	13
Fredericksburg	24,576	96	71	25
Front Royal	14,612	43	34	9
Galax	7,126	38	24	14
Gate City	2,058	6	6	0
Glade Spring	1,473	3	3	0
Glasgow	1,147	1	1	0
Glen Lyn	116	1	1	0
Gordonsville	1,514	7	6	1
Gretna	1,282	4	4	0
Grottoes	2,700	6	5	1
Grundy	1,033	6	6	0
Halifax	1,325	4	4	0
Hampton	139,078	374	277	97
Harrisonburg	49,498	104	87	17
Haymarket	1,803	6	5	1
Haysi	504	2	2	0
Herndon	23,570	70	54	16
Hillsville	2,713	13	12	1
Honaker	1,466	4	3	1
Hopewell	22,861	73	59	14
Hurt	1,320	2	2	0
Independence	958	2	2	0
Jonesville	1,046	2	2	0
Kenbridge	1,272	6	5	1
Kilmarnock	1,505	5	5	0
La Crosse	611	1	1	0
Lawrenceville	1,455	6	6	0
Lebanon	3,465	12	11	1

Table 78. Full-Time Law Enforcement Employees, by Selected State and City, 2012— continued

(Number)

State/city	Population	Total law enforcement employees	Total officers	Total civilians
Leesburg	43,125	101	85	16
Lexington	7,126	18	16	2
Louisa	1,574	6	6	0
Luray	4,953	13	11	2
Lynchburg	76,471	187	160	27
Manassas	38,273	117	84	33
Manassas Park	14,444	42	30	12
Marion	6,039	21	19	2
Martinsville	13,986	55	50	5
Middleburg	681	5	5	0
Middletown	1,280	2	2	0
Mount Jackson	2,018	4	4	0
Narrows	2,053	4	4	0
New Market	2,172	5	5	0
Newport News	182,878	536	398	138
Norfolk	245,704	808	721	87
Norton	4,005	24	15	9
Onancock	1,278	4	4	0
Onley	522	5	5	0
Orange	4,777	17	15	2
Parksley	852	2	2	0
Pearisburg	2,819	8	7	1
Pembroke	1,141	3	3	0
Pennington Gap	1,802	6	6	0
Petersburg	32,807	163	117	46
Poquoson	12,295	22	21	1
Portsmouth	96,676	335	242	93
Pound	1,049	4	4	0
Pulaski	9,195	36	27	9
Purcellville	7,819	14	13	1
Quantico	486	2	2	0
Radford	16,604	48	37	11
Remington	605	1	1	0
Rich Creek	783	1	1	0
Richlands	5,893	21	15	6
Richmond	206,654	885	727	158
Roanoke	98,191	300	256	44
Rocky Mount	4,856	22	20	2
Rural Retreat	1,501	1	1	0
Salem	25,098	92	64	28
Saltville	2,102	3	3	0
Shenandoah	2,401	5	5	0
Smithfield	8,186	26	22	4
South Boston	8,239	30	27	3
South Hill	4,706	22	20	2
Stanley	1,709	4	4	0
Staunton	24,030	67	51	16
Stephens City	1,851	4	4	0
St. Paul	982	4	4	0
Strasburg	6,474	21	19	2
Suffolk	85,595	245	185	60
Tappahannock	2,403	11	10	1
Tazewell	4,682	15	13	2
Timberville	2,552	4	4	0
Victoria	1,746	6	5	1
Vienna	15,874	50	39	11
Vinton	8,195	24	22	2
Virginia Beach	443,226	945	776	169
Warrenton	9,726	23	21	2
Warsaw	1,530	3	2	1
Waverly	2,175	11	6	5
Waynesboro	21,257	55	43	12

Table 78. Full-Time Law Enforcement Employees, by Selected State and City, 2012— continued

(Number)

State/city	Population	Total law enforcement employees	Total officers	Total civilians
Weber City	1,343	5	5	0
West Point	3,345	10	9	1
White Stone	356	1	1	0
Williamsburg	14,236	39	36	3
Winchester	26,516	100	76	24
Windsor	2,657	6	6	0
Wise	3,325	14	13	1
Woodstock	5,158	16	15	1
Wytheville	8,309	42	28	14
WASHINGTON				
Aberdeen	17,161	48	35	13
Airway Heights	6,210	15	14	1
Algona	3,061	9	8	1
Anacortes	16,026	31	24	7
Arlington	18,207	29	24	5
Asotin	1,271	2	2	0
Auburn	71,281	112	97	15
Bainbridge Island	23,386	28	21	7
Battle Ground	17,847	26	21	5
Bellevue	124,283	209	173	36
Bellingham	82,154	160	109	51
Black Diamond	4,216	11	9	2
Blaine	4,757	13	10	3
Bonney Lake	17,647	35	27	8
Bothell	34,031	84	58	26
Bremerton	38,321	70	57	13
Brewster	2,407	8	6	2
Brier	6,182	9	7	2
Buckley	4,906	14	9	5
Burien	33,836	68	51	17
Burlington	8,520	28	23	5
Camas	19,659	27	23	4
Castle Rock	2,013	6	5	1
Centralia	16,592	40	33	7
Chehalis	7,373	21	16	5
Cheney	10,756	19	13	6
Chewelah	2,648	6	5	1
Clarkston	7,342	15	14	1
Cle Elum	1,901	9	8	1
Clyde Hill	3,031	8	7	1
Colfax	2,849	7	6	1
College Place	8,903	13	10	3
Colville	4,746	12	10	2
Connell	4,275	6	6	0
Cosmopolis	1,675	5	4	1
Coulee City	571	1	1	0
Coulee Dam	1,115	7	7	0
Coupeville	1,860	5	5	0
Covington	17,851	20	17	3
Des Moines	30,139	49	37	12
Dupont	8,328	12	9	3
Duvall	6,800	16	15	1
East Wenatchee	13,397	24	21	3
Eatonville	2,801	6	5	1
Edgewood	9,534	6	6	0
Edmonds	40,332	61	52	9
Ellensburg	18,459	36	27	9
Elma	3,156	8	7	1
Enumclaw	10,836	28	15	13
Ephrata	7,784	19	15	4
Everett	104,635	232	190	42
Everson	2,520	6	6	0

Table 78. Full-Time Law Enforcement Employees, by Selected State and City, 2012— continued

(Number)

State/city	Population	Total law enforcement employees	Total officers	Total civilians
Federal Way	90,707	149	122	27
Ferndale	11,594	18	16	2
Fife	9,317	55	31	24
Fircrest	6,599	9	9	0
Forks	3,387	12	5	7
Gig Harbor	7,238	19	17	2
Goldendale	3,460	10	9	1
Grand Coulee	1,004	8	8	0
Grandview	11,032	24	18	6
Granger	3,297	5	5	0
Granite Falls	3,417	9	7	2
Hoquiam	8,863	20	17	3
Issaquah	30,911	59	31	28
Kalama	2,381	5	5	0
Kelso	12,112	28	25	3
Kenmore	20,781	19	15	4
Kennewick	75,077	104	87	17
Kent	93,861	186	131	55
Kettle Falls	1,620	5	4	1
Kirkland	49,552	122	92	30
Kittitas	1,403	2	2	0
La Center	2,844	10	8	2
Lacey	43,058	65	54	11
Lake Forest Park	12,796	22	18	4
Lake Stevens	28,509	32	27	5
Lakewood	59,075	117	102	15
Langley	1,051	3	3	0
Liberty Lake	7,710	10	9	1
Long Beach	1,414	7	6	1
Longview	37,223	65	54	11
Lynden	12,138	18	14	4
Lynnwood	36,398	102	71	31
Mabton	2,322	2	2	0
Maple Valley	23,040	21	17	4
Marysville	60,962	83	53	30
Mattawa	4,507	3	3	0
McCleary	1,679	3	3	0
Medina	3,016	9	8	1
Mercer Island	23,055	35	31	4
Mill Creek	18,530	26	23	3
Milton	7,077	14	13	1
Monroe	17,575	41	31	10
Montesano	4,038	10	8	2
Morton	1,144	4	3	1
Moses Lake	20,686	42	34	8
Mossyrock	771	2	2	0
Mountlake Terrace	20,221	38	28	10
Mount Vernon	32,241	55	43	12
Moxee	3,360	5	5	0
Mukilteo	20,572	32	28	4
Napavine	1,794	2	2	0
Newcastle	10,543	9	7	2
Normandy Park	6,434	12	11	1
North Bend	5,821	8	6	2
Oak Harbor	22,421	40	27	13
Ocean Shores	5,656	13	11	2
Odessa	924	2	2	0
Olympia	47,207	89	62	27
Omak	4,921	13	11	2
Oroville	1,712	6	5	1
Orting	6,852	10	10	0
Othello	7,480	22	16	6

Table 78. Full-Time Law Enforcement Employees, by Selected State and City, 2012— continued

(Number)

State/city	Population	Total law enforcement employees	Total officers	Total civilians
Pacific	6,710	12	10	2
Palouse	1,014	3	3	0
Pasco	60,719	76	64	12
Port Angeles	19,337	59	32	27
Port Orchard	11,319	24	22	2
Port Townsend	9,256	18	15	3
Poulsbo	9,344	19	16	3
Prosser	5,804	17	11	6
Pullman	30,267	39	28	11
Puyallup	37,603	74	54	20
Quincy	6,856	17	15	2
Raymond	2,927	7	6	1
Reardan	580	1	1	0
Redmond	54,993	124	83	41
Renton	92,354	149	122	27
Republic	1,090	3	2	1
Richland	48,812	70	59	11
Ridgefield	4,838	8	7	1
Ritzville	1,699	4	4	0
Rosalia	559	1	1	0
Roy	805	2	2	0
Royal City	2,174	3	3	0
Ruston	761	3	3	0
Sammamish	46,498	28	22	6
SeaTac	27,331	57	43	14
Seattle	618,209	1,804	1,305	499
Sedro Woolley	10,705	17	14	3
Selah	7,259	15	14	1
Sequim	6,710	21	18	3
Shelton	9,988	21	18	3
Shoreline	53,839	68	51	17
Snohomish	9,241	23	18	5
Snoqualmie	10,837	17	14	3
Soap Lake	1,538	3	3	0
South Bend	1,663	5	4	1
Spokane	212,194	377	275	102
Spokane Valley	91,163	98	97	1
Springdale	289	1	1	0
Stanwood	6,329	13	11	2
Steilacoom	6,079	9	8	1
Sumas	1,328	6	6	0
Sumner	9,599	26	19	7
Sunnyside	16,107	56	31	25
Tacoma	201,510	421	378	43
Tenino	1,722	5	4	1
Tieton	1,210	2	2	0
Toledo	736	2	2	0
Tonasket	1,048	4	3	1
Toppenish	9,089	27	16	11
Tukwila	19,407	83	67	16
Tumwater	17,644	29	24	5
Twisp	933	3	3	0
Union Gap	6,142	19	16	3
University Place	31,633	17	16	1
Vader	631	1	1	0
Vancouver	164,329	205	184	21
Walla Walla	32,229	70	42	28
Wapato	5,075	18	11	7
Warden	2,734	5	4	1
Washougal	14,316	20	18	2
Wenatchee	32,426	50	40	10
Westport	2,132	8	6	2

Table 78. Full-Time Law Enforcement Employees, by Selected State and City, 2012— continued

(Number)

State/city	Population	Total law enforcement employees	Total officers	Total civilians
West Richland	11,996	16	14	2
White Salmon	2,259	7	6	1
Wilbur	898	2	2	0
Winlock	1,360	2	2	0
Winthrop	400	3	3	0
Woodinville	11,110	16	12	4
Woodland	5,595	12	10	2
Yakima	92,496	172	131	41
Yelm	6,955	15	13	2
Zillah	3,011	9	7	2
WEST VIRGINIA				
Albright	299	2	1	1
Alderson	1,186	2	2	0
Anawalt	226	1	1	0
Anmoore	771	5	1	4
Ansted	1,406	2	2	0
Athens	1,049	1	1	0
Barboursville	3,969	20	18	2
Barrackville	1,304	2	2	0
Bayard	290	2	2	0
Beckley	17,637	65	45	20
Belington	1,923	2	2	0
Belle	1,262	4	4	0
Benwood	1,422	10	6	4
Berkeley Springs	625	3	3	0
Bethlehem	2,502	4	4	0
Bluefield	10,460	29	22	7
Bradshaw	337	1	1	0
Bramwell	364	1	1	0
Bridgeport	8,159	32	29	3
Buckhannon	5,646	9	8	1
Burnsville	511	2	2	0
Cameron	947	2	2	0
Capon Bridge	355	2	2	0
Cedar Grove	998	2	2	0
Ceredo	1,452	9	6	3
Chapmanville	1,258	4	4	0
Charleston	51,466	187	161	26
Charles Town	5,266	18	15	3
Chesapeake	1,556	4	4	0
Chester	2,588	7	6	1
Clarksburg	16,599	51	47	4
Clendenin	1,229	4	4	0
Danville	692	1	1	0
Davy	421	1	1	0
Delbarton	580	2	2	0
Dunbar	7,917	13	11	2
East Bank	960	3	3	0
Eleanor	1,520	2	2	0
Elkins	7,103	12	9	3
Fairmont	18,728	40	34	6
Fairview	409	1	1	0
Farmington	375	1	1	0
Fayetteville	2,896	10	9	1
Follansbee	2,990	7	7	0
Fort Gay	706	4	4	0
Gary	969	2	2	0
Gassaway	909	1	1	0
Gauley Bridge	615	3	2	1
Gilbert	451	6	4	2
Glasgow	906	2	2	0
Glen Dale	1,528	9	4	5

Table 78. Full-Time Law Enforcement Employees, by Selected State and City, 2012— continued

(Number)

State/city	Population	Total law enforcement employees	Total officers	Total civilians
Glenville	1,539	3	2	1
Grafton	5,171	7	4	3
Grantsville	562	2	2	0
Grant Town	614	1	1	0
Granville	782	13	12	1
Hamlin	1,143	5	4	1
Handley	349	1	1	0
Harpers Ferry/Bolivar	1,332	5	4	1
Harrisville	1,878	1	1	0
Henderson	271	1	1	0
Hinton	2,679	4	4	0
Huntington	49,201	112	103	9
Hurricane	6,292	17	15	2
Iaeger	302	1	1	0
Kenova	3,220	10	6	4
Kermit	407	1	1	0
Keyser	5,446	15	10	5
Keystone	282	1	1	0
Kimball	194	3	1	2
Kingwood	2,943	2	2	0
Lewisburg	3,835	13	11	2
Logan	1,781	11	8	3
Lumberport	877	2	2	0
Mabscott	1,410	4	4	0
Madison	3,080	5	4	1
Man	760	2	2	0
Mannington	2,066	4	4	0
Marmet	1,505	5	5	0
Martinsburg	17,249	60	48	12
Mason	969	4	4	0
Matewan	500	1	1	0
Matoaka	227	1	1	0
McMechen	1,928	3	3	0
Monongah	1,045	1	1	0
Montgomery	1,640	6	5	1
Moorefield	2,547	9	8	1
Morgantown	29,698	74	64	10
Moundsville	9,330	22	18	4
Mount Hope	1,416	8	5	3
Mullens	1,561	6	6	0
New Cumberland	1,104	3	3	0
New Haven	1,562	2	2	0
New Martinsville	5,373	14	10	4
Nitro	7,187	19	18	1
Nutter Fort	1,595	6	6	0
Oak Hill	7,740	16	14	2
Oceana	1,396	5	5	0
Paden City	2,636	4	3	1
Parkersburg	31,532	74	63	11
Parsons	1,487	1	1	0
Paw Paw	509	1	1	0
Pennsboro	1,172	1	1	0
Petersburg	2,470	5	2	3
Philippi	2,970	6	6	0
Piedmont	877	1	1	0
Pineville	669	3	3	0
Point Pleasant	4,356	10	9	1
Pratt	603	1	1	0
Princeton	6,440	23	19	4
Rainelle	1,507	3	1	2
Ranson	4,446	14	13	1
Ravenswood	3,881	9	8	1

Table 78. Full-Time Law Enforcement Employees, by Selected State and City, 2012— continued

(Number)

State/city	Population	Total law enforcement employees	Total officers	Total civilians
Reedsville	594	1	1	0
Rhodell	173	1	1	0
Richwood	2,054	4	4	0
Ridgeley	676	3	3	0
Ripley	3,256	9	8	1
Rivesville	935	2	2	0
Romney	1,850	4	3	1
Ronceverte	1,767	7	7	0
Rowlesburg	585	1	1	0
Salem	1,588	2	2	0
Shepherdstown	1,736	7	5	2
Shinnston	2,204	8	8	0
Sistersville	1,398	4	4	0
Smithers	814	4	3	1
Sophia	1,346	5	5	0
South Charleston	13,467	41	39	2
Spencer	2,325	6	6	0
St. Albans	11,058	25	23	2
Star City	1,827	6	5	1
St. Marys	1,862	4	4	0
Stonewood	1,808	2	2	0
Summersville	3,577	18	17	1
Sutton	995	2	1	1
Sylvester	160	1	1	0
Terra Alta	1,479	1	1	0
Triadelphia	812	1	1	0
Vienna	10,763	22	17	5
Wardensville	271	1	1	0
Wayne	1,415	2	2	0
Webster Springs	777	2	2	0
Weirton	19,771	38	35	3
Welch	2,409	6	5	1
Wellsburg	2,809	6	6	0
West Logan	425	1	1	0
Weston	4,115	8	6	2
Westover	3,988	9	9	0
West Union	826	1	1	0
Wheeling	28,522	83	80	3
White Sulphur Springs	2,447	7	6	1
Williamson	3,195	10	8	2
Williamstown	2,912	7	6	1
Winfield	2,304	2	2	0
WISCONSIN				
Adams	1,976	4	4	0
Albany	1,022	3	3	0
Algoma	3,181	6	6	0
Altoona	6,735	13	12	1
Amery	2,915	7	6	1
Antigo	8,270	18	15	3
Appleton	72,939	132	107	25
Arcadia	2,938	5	5	0
Ashland	8,252	21	19	2
Ashwaubenon	17,037	54	47	7
Athens	1,110	1	1	0
Avoca	640	1	1	0
Bangor	1,465	2	2	0
Baraboo	12,100	34	28	6
Barron	3,438	6	6	0
Bayfield	489	3	3	0
Bayside	4,408	20	13	7
Beaver Dam	16,285	35	30	5
Belleville	2,395	5	5	0

Table 78. Full-Time Law Enforcement Employees, by Selected State and City, 2012— continued

(Number)

State/city	Population	Total law enforcement employees	Total officers	Total civilians
Beloit	37,127	86	74	12
Beloit Town	7,695	10	9	1
Berlin	5,548	13	12	1
Big Bend	1,296	3	3	0
Black River Falls	3,638	7	6	1
Blair	1,372	2	2	0
Bloomer	3,554	7	6	1
Bloomfield	6,305	7	7	0
Blue Mounds	859	5	4	1
Boscobel	3,245	6	6	0
Brandon-Fairwater	1,256	1	1	0
Brillion	3,162	8	7	1
Brodhead	3,307	12	8	4
Brookfield	38,085	81	64	17
Brookfield Township	6,143	14	13	1
Brown Deer	12,051	34	29	5
Burlington	10,510	27	21	6
Burlington Town	6,530	3	2	1
Butler	1,849	8	7	1
Caledonia	24,813	32	29	3
Campbellsport	2,025	1	1	0
Campbell Township	4,333	4	4	0
Cashton	1,107	2	2	0
Cedarburg	11,462	26	19	7
Chenequa	593	9	8	1
Chetek	2,231	6	5	1
Chilton	3,950	6	6	0
Chippewa Falls	13,721	30	24	6
Cleveland	1,491	2	2	0
Clinton	2,163	6	6	0
Clintonville	4,579	15	11	4
Colby-Abbotsford	4,180	7	6	1
Columbus	5,013	12	11	1
Coon Valley	768	1	1	0
Cornell	1,473	2	2	0
Cottage Grove	6,219	12	11	1
Crandon	1,928	3	2	1
Cross Plains	3,553	6	5	1
Cuba City	2,095	4	3	1
Cudahy	18,347	42	31	11
Cumberland	2,179	4	4	0
Darien	1,587	6	5	1
Darlington	2,462	5	5	0
Deforest	8,975	19	16	3
Delafield	7,116	16	14	2
Delavan	8,500	22	17	5
Delavan Town	5,308	12	11	1
Denmark	2,132	2	2	0
De Pere	23,904	39	34	5
Dodgeville	4,713	10	9	1
Durand	1,939	3	3	0
Eagle River	1,404	5	5	0
Eagle Village	1,958	3	3	0
East Troy	4,300	7	7	0
Eau Claire	66,170	132	95	37
Edgar	1,485	1	1	0
Edgerton	5,485	12	10	2
Eleva	673	1	1	0
Elkhart Lake	971	3	3	0
Elkhorn	10,128	19	16	3
Elk Mound	882	1	1	0
Ellsworth	3,298	6	5	1

Table 78. Full-Time Law Enforcement Employees, by Selected State and City, 2012— continued

(Number)

State/city	Population	Total law enforcement employees	Total officers	Total civilians
Elm Grove	5,960	25	17	8
Elroy	1,448	3	3	0
Evansville	5,034	12	9	3
Everest	17,111	28	25	0
Fall Creek	1,321	2	2	0
Fall River	1,719	2	2	0
Fennimore	2,508	5	5	0
Fitchburg	25,370	56	44	12
Fond du Lac	43,208	79	73	6
Fontana	1,679	7	6	1
Fort Atkinson	12,422	24	18	6
Fountain City	863	1	1	0
Fox Lake	1,526	3	3	0
Fox Point	6,730	18	17	1
Fox Valley Metro	16,991	33	30	3
Franklin	35,605	74	58	16
Frederic	1,142	1	1	0
Freedom	5,867	2	2	0
Geneva Town	5,015	7	6	1
Genoa City	3,055	5	4	1
Germantown	19,835	41	30	11
Gillett	1,392	9	4	5
Glendale	12,928	47	43	4
Grafton	11,509	27	21	6
Grand Chute	21,010	33	29	4
Grand Rapids	7,679	7	5	2
Grantsburg	1,347	3	3	0
Green Bay	104,510	225	186	39
Greendale	14,107	36	28	8
Greenfield	36,880	77	58	19
Green Lake	964	2	2	0
Hales Corners	7,726	19	16	3
Hartford	14,285	29	25	4
Hartland	9,150	18	16	2
Hayward	2,328	10	9	1
Hazel Green	1,261	2	2	0
Highland	846	1	1	0
Hillsboro	1,423	2	2	0
Hobart-Lawrence	10,512	6	4	2
Holmen	9,044	11	10	1
Horicon	3,671	7	6	1
Hortonville	2,723	6	5	1
Hudson	12,774	25	22	3
Hurley	1,554	7	6	1
Independence	1,342	4	4	0
Iron Ridge	933	1	1	0
Iron River	1,128	3	3	0
Jackson	6,782	11	10	1
Janesville	63,852	114	102	12
Jefferson	8,008	17	14	3
Juneau	2,826	5	4	1
Kaukauna	15,529	25	24	1
Kenosha	99,650	208	199	9
Kewaskum	4,021	7	7	0
Kewaunee	2,965	6	6	0
Kiel	3,754	8	7	1
Kohler	2,129	8	7	1
Kronenwetter	7,241	7	6	1
La Crosse	51,544	105	87	18
Ladysmith	3,429	10	9	1
Lake Delton	2,927	21	19	2
Lake Geneva	7,684	31	22	9

Table 78. Full-Time Law Enforcement Employees, by Selected State and City, 2012— continued

(Number)

State/city	Population	Total law enforcement employees	Total officers	Total civilians
Lake Hallie	6,476	7	6	1
Lake Mills	5,733	10	10	0
Lancaster	3,885	6	6	0
Lodi	3,063	6	5	1
Lomira	2,441	3	3	0
Luxemburg	2,526	2	2	0
Madison	234,225	552	447	105
Manawa	1,377	3	3	0
Manitowoc	33,883	71	63	8
Maple Bluff	1,319	6	6	0
Marathon City	1,531	2	2	0
Marinette	11,016	27	23	4
Marion	1,265	3	3	0
Markesan	1,482	3	3	0
Marshall Village	3,879	7	6	1
Marshfield	19,201	46	39	7
Mauston	4,442	9	8	1
Mayville	5,176	9	7	2
McFarland	7,842	16	14	2
Medford	4,345	10	9	1
Menasha	17,429	34	28	6
Menomonee Falls	35,781	78	58	20
Menomonie	16,335	35	27	8
Mequon	23,233	43	35	8
Merrill	9,703	25	22	3
Middleton	17,518	46	36	10
Milton	5,570	13	11	2
Milwaukee	597,426	2,586	1,862	724
Mineral Point	2,498	5	5	0
Minocqua	4,404	15	10	5
Mishicot	1,448	1	1	0
Mondovi	2,789	4	4	0
Monona	7,566	25	20	5
Monroe	10,874	35	26	9
Montello	1,502	3	2	1
Mosinee	4,005	8	7	1
Mount Horeb	7,040	11	10	1
Mount Pleasant	26,311	45	41	4
Mukwonago	7,387	21	14	7
Muskego	24,240	47	37	10
Neenah	25,612	51	41	10
Neillsville	2,474	7	6	1
Neshkoro	436	1	1	0
New Berlin	39,756	84	68	16
New Glarus	2,181	3	3	0
New Holstein	3,250	7	6	1
New Lisbon	2,565	4	4	0
New London	7,327	19	17	2
New Richmond	8,411	15	15	0
Niagara	1,631	4	4	0
North Fond du Lac	5,036	13	11	2
North Hudson	3,784	6	5	1
Oak Creek	34,601	79	58	21
Oconomowoc	15,828	28	22	6
Oconomowoc Town	8,445	12	10	2
Oconto	4,533	8	7	1
Oconto Falls	2,904	5	5	0
Omro	3,532	7	6	1
Onalaska	17,813	28	25	3
Oregon	9,271	17	15	2
Osceola	2,579	7	6	1
Oshkosh	66,371	115	97	18

Table 78. Full-Time Law Enforcement Employees, by Selected State and City, 2012— continued

(Number)

State/city	Population	Total law enforcement employees	Total officers	Total civilians
Osseo	1,708	4	4	0
Palmyra	1,789	3	3	0
Park Falls	2,473	8	7	1
Pepin	841	1	1	0
Peshtigo	3,517	7	6	1
Pewaukee Village	8,202	19	17	2
Phillips	1,484	5	5	0
Plainfield	866	2	2	0
Platteville	11,273	24	18	6
Pleasant Prairie	19,805	32	30	2
Plover	12,176	22	19	3
Plymouth	8,482	16	16	0
Portage	10,369	26	22	4
Port Washington	11,299	24	19	5
Poynette	2,539	5	4	1
Prairie du Chien	5,937	13	12	1
Prescott	4,277	9	8	1
Pulaski	3,554	10	9	1
Racine	79,204	239	202	37
Reedsburg	9,240	28	20	8
Rhinelander	7,832	20	17	3
Rice Lake	8,475	19	18	1
Richland Center	5,207	13	11	2
Ripon	7,767	20	14	6
River Falls	15,065	24	22	2
River Hills	1,604	12	12	0
Rome Town	2,732	8	7	1
Rosendale	1,068	1	1	0
Rothschild	5,292	12	10	2
Sauk Prairie	4,574	16	14	2
Saukville	4,470	13	11	2
Seymour	3,466	6	6	0
Shawano	9,346	21	19	2
Sheboygan	49,503	110	81	29
Sheboygan Falls	7,809	16	14	2
Shiocton	925	2	1	1
Shorewood	13,219	29	24	5
Shorewood Hills	1,572	8	6	2
Silver Lake	2,422	5	4	1
Siren	810	3	3	0
Slinger	5,090	10	9	1
Somerset	2,646	6	5	1
South Milwaukee	21,248	39	33	6
Sparta	9,563	19	17	2
Spencer	1,933	3	3	0
Spooner	2,694	8	7	1
Spring Green	1,635	4	3	1
Stanley	3,624	4	4	0
St. Croix Falls	2,142	5	5	0
Stevens Point	26,833	57	42	15
St. Francis	9,406	26	21	5
Stoughton	12,666	26	20	6
Strum	1,119	2	2	0
Sturgeon Bay	9,184	22	20	2
Sturtevant	7,000	11	10	1
Summit	4,694	8	8	0
Sun Prairie	29,492	71	50	21
Superior	27,363	65	60	5
Theresa	1,267	2	2	0
Thiensville	3,249	8	7	1
Three Lakes	2,140	4	4	0
Tomah	9,133	22	20	2

Table 78. Full-Time Law Enforcement Employees, by Selected State and City, 2012— continued

(Number)

State/city	Population	Total law enforcement employees	Total officers	Total civilians
Tomahawk	3,412	8	7	1
Town of East Troy	4,039	7	6	1
Town of Madison	6,306	18	16	2
Town of Menasha	18,579	31	25	6
Trempealeau	1,536	2	2	0
Twin Lakes	6,015	19	13	6
Two Rivers	11,763	28	24	4
Valders	966	1	1	0
Verona	10,665	22	20	2
Viroqua	4,381	11	9	2
Walworth	2,828	19	12	7
Washburn	2,126	7	7	0
Waterloo	3,348	9	8	1
Watertown	23,965	50	36	14
Waukesha	71,026	149	117	32
Waunakee	12,150	19	17	2
Waupaca	6,095	14	13	1
Waupun	11,389	19	17	2
Wausau	39,276	76	70	6
Wautoma	2,228	7	6	1
Wauwatosa	46,598	115	92	23
West Allis	60,674	155	130	25
West Bend	31,213	72	55	17
Westby	2,210	3	3	0
Westfield	1,259	3	3	0
West Milwaukee	4,224	23	18	5
West Salem	4,820	7	6	1
Whitefish Bay	14,171	26	24	2
Whitehall	1,565	4	4	0
Whitewater	14,453	33	23	10
Williams Bay	2,575	8	7	1
Winneconne	2,360	6	5	1
Wisconsin Dells	2,690	19	13	6
Wisconsin Rapids	18,447	41	36	5
Woodruff	2,064	6	5	1
WYOMING				
Afton	1,926	4	4	0
Alpine	835	1	1	0
Basin	1,295	3	3	0
Buffalo	4,622	20	11	9
Casper	55,761	126	84	42
Cheyenne	59,944	119	97	22
Cody	9,597	24	21	3
Cokeville	539	3	3	0
Diamondville	743	4	3	1
Douglas	6,169	22	14	8
Evanston	12,458	33	27	6
Evansville	2,564	12	10	2
Gillette	29,321	85	54	31
Glenrock	2,597	12	6	6
Green River	12,616	38	28	10
Greybull	1,862	6	5	1
Guernsey	1,156	2	2	0
Hanna	848	1	1	0
Hulett	386	2	2	0
Jackson	9,654	34	26	8
Kemmerer	2,677	8	7	1
La Barge	555	3	3	0
Lander	7,547	19	18	1
Laramie	31,064	77	49	28
Lovell	2,379	10	6	4
Lusk	1,580	4	4	0

Table 78. Full-Time Law Enforcement Employees, by Selected State and City, 2012— continued

(Number)

State/city	Population	Total law enforcement employees	Total officers	Total civilians
Lyman	2,132	5	4	1
Mills	3,489	15	12	3
Moorcroft	1,017	5	4	1
Newcastle	3,560	13	7	6
Pine Bluffs	1,138	6	3	3
Powell	6,365	24	15	9
Rawlins	9,333	29	19	10
Riverton	10,700	39	28	11
Rock Springs	23,221	66	45	21
Saratoga	1,704	10	6	4
Sheridan	17,584	43	28	15
Sundance	1,192	3	3	0
Thermopolis	3,033	13	7	6
Torrington	6,553	21	14	7
Upton	1,109	3	3	0
Wheatland	3,656	9	8	1
Worland	5,531	10	10	0

1 The employee data presented in this table for Charlotte-Mecklenburg represent only Charlotte-Mecklenburg Police Department and exclude Mecklenburg County Sheriff's Office. n.a. = not available

Table 79. Full-Time Law Enforcement Employees, by Selected State and University or College, 2012

(Number)

State and university/college	Student enrollment[1]	Law enforcement employees	Officers	Civilians
ALABAMA				
Alabama A&M University	4,922	31	15	16
Auburn University, Montgomery	5,305	18	10	8
Bishop State Community College	3,982	14	10	4
Jacksonville State University	9,490	19	14	5
Jefferson State Community College	9,460	9	8	1
Northwest-Shoals Community College	3,939	4	4	0
Troy University	26,172	22	12	10
Tuskegee University	3,152	36	18	18
University of Alabama:				
Birmingham	17,575	163	92	71
Huntsville	7,629	22	15	7
University of Montevallo	3,066	18	9	9
University of North Alabama	7,233	14	12	2
University of South Alabama	14,769	36	27	9
University of West Alabama	5,258	11	7	4
Wallace Community College, Dothan	4,949	3	3	0
ALASKA				
University of Alaska:				
Anchorage	18,128	22	14	8
Fairbanks	9,712	15	10	5
ARIZONA				
Arizona State University, Main Campus	72,254	126	66	60
Arizona Western College	8,418	13	8	5
Central Arizona College	7,442	10	7	3
Northern Arizona University	25,359	26	17	9
Pima Community College	36,969	35	26	9
University of Arizona	39,236	111	62	49
Yavapai College	7,837	8	7	1
ARKANSAS				
Arkansas State University:				
Beebe	4,689	5	4	1
Jonesboro	13,900	24	20	4
Arkansas Tech University	10,464	16	14	2
Henderson State University	3,774	9	8	1
Northwest Arkansas Community College	8,528	15	10	5
Southern Arkansas University	3,382	7	6	1
Southern Arkansas University Tech	2,136	4	4	0
University of Arkansas:				
Fayetteville	23,199	40	31	9
Little Rock	13,068	38	26	12
Medical Sciences	2,819	48	34	14
Monticello	3,920	9	8	1
Pine Bluff	3,188	18	13	5
University of Central Arkansas	11,163	32	24	8
CALIFORNIA				
Allan Hancock College	10,955	4	3	1
California State Polytechnic University:				
Pomona	21,107	30	18	12
San Luis Obispo	18,762	34	15	19
California State University:				
Bakersfield	8,002	15	11	4
Channel Islands	4,179	26	15	11
Chico	15,920	26	15	11
Dominguez Hills	14,364	24	17	7
East Bay	13,160	25	14	11
Fresno	21,981	30	21	9
Fullerton	36,156	36	26	10
Long Beach	34,870	45	25	20
Los Angeles	21,284	32	17	15
Monterey Bay	5,173	21	15	6
Northridge	36,911	36	23	13
Sacramento	28,016	34	22	12

Table 79. Full-Time Law Enforcement Employees, by Selected State and University or College, 2012— continued

(Number)

State and university/college	Student enrollment[1]	Law enforcement employees	Officers	Civilians
San Bernardino	17,250	27	15	12
San Jose	30,236	69	28	41
San Marcos	10,276	31	15	16
Stanislaus	9,246	21	12	9
College of the Sequoias	11,625	7	6	1
Contra Costa Community College	7,671	32	22	10
Cuesta College	10,759	12	6	6
El Camino College	24,463	33	25	8
Foothill-De Anza College	39,952	15	9	6
Humboldt State University	8,046	19	11	8
Marin Community College	7,075	9	8	1
Pasadena Community College	26,057	17	9	8
Riverside Community College	18,395	30	23	7
San Bernardino Community College	18,015	14	8	6
San Diego State University	30,541	46	22	24
San Francisco State University	29,541	49	24	25
San Jose/Evergreen Community College	20,671	9	3	6
Santa Rosa Junior College	24,199	25	13	12
Solano Community College	11,029	4	3	1
Sonoma State University	8,668	22	11	11
State Center Community College District	34,192	20	15	5
University of California:				
Berkeley	36,137	115	67	48
Davis	31,732	72	47	25
Hastings College of Law	1,289	12	12	0
Irvine	27,189	43	29	14
Los Angeles	39,271	94	54	40
Merced	5,198	23	12	11
Riverside	20,900	43	30	13
San Diego	28,593	62	31	31
San Francisco	3,054	117	49	68
Santa Barbara	21,685	47	32	15
Santa Cruz	17,454	26	15	11
Ventura County Community College District	13,758	14	13	1
West Valley-Mission College	20,985	15	9	6
COLORADO				
Adams State College	3,302	6	5	1
Arapahoe Community College	11,148	8	5	3
Auraria Higher Education Center[2]	n.a.	38	27	11
Colorado School of Mines	5,524	9	8	1
Colorado State University:				
Fort Collins	30,467	44	33	11
Pueblo	7,174	3	2	1
Fort Lewis College	3,841	9	7	2
Pikes Peak Community College	14,725	20	18	2
Red Rocks Community College	9,544	4	3	1
University of Colorado:				
Boulder	32,558	57	39	18
Colorado Springs	10,183	27	16	11
Denver	22,495	57	25	32
University of Northern Colorado	13,038	20	13	7
CONNECTICUT				
Central Connecticut State University	12,521	27	21	6
Eastern Connecticut State University	5,586	24	17	7
Southern Connecticut State University	11,533	34	27	7
University of Connecticut:				
Health Center[2]	n.a.	34	15	19
Storrs, Avery Point, and Hartford[2]	n.a.	81	66	15
Western Connecticut State University	6,407	23	16	7
Yale University	11,875	99	84	15
DELAWARE				
Delaware State University	4,154	31	14	17

Table 79. Full-Time Law Enforcement Employees, by Selected State and University or College, 2012— continued

(Number)

State and university/college	Student enrollment[1]	Law enforcement employees	Officers	Civilians
University of Delaware	21,489	76	47	29
FLORIDA				
Edison State College	17,107	18	9	9
Florida A&M University	13,204	39	31	8
Florida Atlantic University	29,246	59	37	22
Florida Gulf Coast University	12,651	21	16	5
Florida International University	44,616	76	51	25
New College of Florida	845	18	12	6
Pensacola State College	11,531	14	9	5
Santa Fe College	15,493	24	17	7
Tallahassee Community College	15,090	26	13	13
University of Central Florida	58,465	94	60	34
University of Florida	49,589	134	82	52
University of North Florida	16,198	38	29	9
University of South Florida:				
St. Petersburg	4,310	17	12	5
Tampa	39,596	58	42	16
University of West Florida	11,982	30	20	10
GEORGIA				
Abraham Baldwin Agricultural College	3,250	12	12	0
Albany State University	4,663	31	18	13
Armstrong Atlantic State University	7,493	27	17	10
Atlanta Metropolitan College	2,782	15	8	7
Augusta State University	6,741	22	16	6
Berry College	2,093	16	10	6
Clark Atlanta University	3,843	46	18	28
College of Coastal Georgia	3,474	13	13	0
Columbus State University	8,307	29	24	5
Dalton State College	5,485	17	14	3
Darton State College	6,097	11	10	1
Emory University	13,893	70	51	19
Fort Valley State University	3,896	36	12	24
Gainesville State College	8,569	13	12	1
Georgia College and State University	6,636	27	20	7
Georgia Gwinnett College	7,742	24	20	4
Georgia Institute of Technology	20,941	99	77	22
Georgia Military College	1,701	4	2	2
Georgia Perimeter College	26,996	107	46	61
Georgia Southern University	20,212	47	37	10
Georgia Southwestern State University	3,046	11	10	1
Georgia State University	32,022	139	60	79
Gordon College	4,664	12	11	1
Kennesaw State University	24,175	65	37	28
Macon State College	5,702	8	7	1
Medical College of Georgia	2,442	45	32	13
Mercer University	8,329	33	24	9
Middle Georgia College	3,424	18	17	1
Morehouse College	2,438	49	18	31
Morehouse School of Medicine	344	7	7	0
North Georgia College and State University	6,067	23	17	6
Piedmont College	2,818	1	1	0
Savannah State University	4,552	48	18	30
Southern Crescent Technical College	5,155	4	3	1
Southern Polytechnic State University	5,784	16	13	3
South Georgia College	2,270	12	6	6
Spelman College	2,170	25	16	9
University of Georgia	34,816	105	84	21
University of West Georgia	11,646	29	22	7
Valdosta State University	13,089	30	22	8
Wesleyan College	681	5	5	0
West Georgia Technical College	7,331	6	6	0
Young Harris College	886	5	4	1

Table 79. Full-Time Law Enforcement Employees, by Selected State and University or College, 2012— continued

(Number)

State and university/college	Student enrollment[1]	Law enforcement employees	Officers	Civilians
ILLINOIS				
Benedictine University:				
Lisle	7,013	16	14	2
Springfield[2]	n.a.	3	3	0
Black Hawk College:				
Kewanee[2]	n.a.	2	2	0
Moline	6,403	8	7	1
College of DuPage	26,209	20	15	5
College of Lake County	17,389	23	17	6
Elgin Community College	11,811	15	12	3
Illinois Central College	12,283	20	6	14
Illinois State University	21,310	30	24	6
John A. Logan College	7,294	9	8	1
Joliet Junior College	15,322	21	14	7
Lake Land College	8,867	5	5	0
Lewis University	6,394	16	8	8
Lincoln Land Community College	7,337	14	13	1
Northeastern Illinois University	11,580	26	19	7
Northern Illinois University	22,990	109	70	39
Northwestern University, Evanston	20,959	67	25	42
Oakton Community College	11,175	12	11	1
Southern Illinois University:				
Carbondale	19,817	53	35	18
Edwardsville	14,235	57	39	18
School of Medicine[2]	n.a.	15	6	9
South Suburban College	7,524	15	10	5
Southwestern Illinois College	12,779	21	16	5
University of Illinois:				
Chicago	28,091	141	87	54
Springfield	5,137	22	15	7
Urbana	44,407	84	63	21
Western Illinois University	12,554	30	25	5
INDIANA				
Ball State University	22,147	50	28	22
Butler University	4,626	28	20	8
Indiana State University	11,528	34	24	10
Indiana University:				
Indianapolis	30,530	58	44	14
Southeast	7,256	12	9	3
Purdue University	40,849	55	40	15
IOWA				
Iowa State University	29,611	44	35	9
University of Iowa	29,810	70	41	29
University of Northern Iowa	13,168	25	17	8
KANSAS				
Emporia State University	5,976	10	9	1
Fort Hays State University	12,802	8	7	1
Kansas City Kansas Community College	7,555	15	14	1
Kansas State University	23,863	41	23	18
Pittsburg State University	7,275	16	13	3
University of Kansas, Main Campus	27,939	53	22	31
Washburn University	7,303	20	15	5
Wichita State University	14,909	33	21	12
KENTUCKY				
Eastern Kentucky University	16,062	27	23	4
Kentucky State University	2,746	15	10	5
Morehead State University	10,968	25	15	10
Murray State University	10,623	18	13	5
Northern Kentucky University	15,724	23	17	6
University of Kentucky	27,226	133	48	85
University of Louisville	21,152	73	41	32
Western Kentucky University	21,036	37	28	9

Table 79. Full-Time Law Enforcement Employees, by Selected State and University or College, 2012— continued

(Number)

State and university/college	Student enrollment[1]	Law enforcement employees	Officers	Civilians
LOUISIANA				
Delgado Community College	20,436	37	27	10
Louisiana State University:				
Health Sciences Center, New Orleans	2,777	29	29	0
Shreveport	4,562	47	35	12
McNeese State University	8,784	10	6	4
Nicholls State University	6,767	15	11	4
Northwestern State University	9,191	23	18	5
Southeastern Louisiana University	15,403	29	24	5
Southern University and A&M College:				
Baton Rouge	6,866	42	24	18
New Orleans	3,245	15	15	0
Shreveport	2,831	9	8	1
Tulane University	12,845	125	87	38
University of Louisiana, Monroe	8,583	26	17	9
University of New Orleans	10,903	27	27	0
MAINE				
University of Maine:				
Farmington	2,310	5	4	1
Orono	11,168	26	18	8
University of Southern Maine	9,301	19	11	8
MARYLAND				
Bowie State University	5,608	28	12	16
Coppin State University	3,813	36	22	14
Frostburg State University	5,429	20	16	4
Hagerstown Community College	4,714	2	2	0
Morgan State University	8,018	61	42	19
Salisbury University	8,606	27	15	12
St. Mary's College	1,992	12	1	11
Towson University	21,464	59	37	22
University of Baltimore	6,406	36	15	21
University of Maryland:				
Baltimore City	6,395	144	47	97
Baltimore County	13,199	36	25	11
College Park	37,631	133	85	48
Eastern Shore	4,509	19	15	4
MASSACHUSETTS				
Assumption College	2,795	29	18	11
Bentley University	5,574	35	23	12
Boston College	14,754	70	54	16
Boston University	32,439	67	51	16
Brandeis University	5,828	25	23	2
Bristol Community College	9,000	9	6	3
Bunker Hill Community College	12,934	13	12	1
Clark University	3,462	15	12	3
Dean College	1,398	13	5	8
Emerson College	4,469	16	12	4
Fitchburg State University	6,891	21	17	4
Hampshire College	1,500	12	9	3
Holyoke Community College	7,144	12	12	0
Massachusetts College of Art	2,422	30	9	21
Massachusetts College of Liberal Arts	1,886	12	8	4
Massachusetts Institute of Technology	10,894	59	56	3
Massasoit Community College	8,263	16	14	2
Merrimack College	2,447	19	14	5
Mount Holyoke College	2,362	16	13	3
Northeastern University	26,959	87	56	31
North Shore Community College	7,974	23	21	2
Quinsigamond Community College	9,130	14	13	1
Salem State University	9,646	26	22	4
Smith College	3,162	18	14	4
Springfield College	3,377	39	13	26
Tufts University, Medford	10,777	70	40	30

Table 79. Full-Time Law Enforcement Employees, by Selected State and University or College, 2012— continued

(Number)

State and university/college	Student enrollment[1]	Law enforcement employees	Officers	Civilians
University of Massachusetts:				
Amherst	28,084	78	59	19
Dartmouth	9,225	39	25	14
Harbor Campus, Boston	15,741	37	27	10
Medical Center, Worcester	1,189	30	23	7
Wellesley College	2,502	19	14	5
Wentworth Institute of Technology	3,988	13	11	2
Western New England University	3,729	28	18	10
Westfield State University	6,092	24	18	6
Worcester Polytechnic Institute	5,778	23	17	6
MICHIGAN				
Central Michigan University	28,194	30	23	7
Delta College	11,478	11	8	3
Eastern Michigan University	23,419	42	31	11
Ferris State University	14,560	17	13	4
Grand Rapids Community College	17,575	16	12	4
Grand Valley State University	24,662	19	15	4
Kalamazoo Valley Community College	11,395	9	6	3
Kellogg Community College	6,071	2	2	0
Kirtland Community College	1,815	1	1	0
Lansing Community College	20,640	15	12	3
Macomb Community College	23,969	37	31	6
Michigan State University	47,825	106	71	35
Michigan Technological University	7,022	14	11	3
Mott Community College	11,760	10	5	5
Northern Michigan University	9,405	24	20	4
Oakland Community College	29,158	25	24	1
Oakland University	19,379	27	22	5
Saginaw Valley State University	10,790	13	11	2
University of Michigan:				
Ann Arbor	42,716	82	51	31
Dearborn	8,664	26	9	17
Flint	8,262	27	14	13
Western Michigan University	25,086	61	28	33
MINNESOTA				
University of Minnesota:				
Duluth	11,729	11	9	2
Morris	1,811	5	3	2
Twin Cities	51,721	64	50	14
MISSISSIPPI				
Coahoma Community College	2,999	10	9	1
Jackson State University	8,903	63	41	22
Mississippi State University	20,424	40	32	8
Northeast Mississippi Community College	3,633	7	7	0
University of Mississippi, Oxford	18,224	52	32	20
MISSOURI				
Lincoln University	3,388	15	12	3
Metropolitan Community College	21,285	47	33	14
Mineral Area College	4,035	9	8	1
Missouri Southern State University	5,591	8	7	1
Missouri University of Science and Technology	7,521	19	11	8
Missouri Western State University	6,260	14	11	3
Southeast Missouri State University	11,378	27	18	9
St. Charles Community College	8,174	11	8	3
St. Louis Community College, Florissant Valley[2]	n.a.	11	9	2
Truman State University	6,101	10	9	1
University of Central Missouri	11,637	20	17	3
University of Missouri:				
Columbia	33,762	48	33	15
Kansas City	15,473	42	27	15
St. Louis	16,809	29	23	6
Washington University	13,908	46	26	20

Table 79. Full-Time Law Enforcement Employees, by Selected State and University or College, 2012— continued

(Number)

State and university/college	Student enrollment[1]	Law enforcement employees	Officers	Civilians
MONTANA				
Montana State University	13,671	31	17	14
NEBRASKA				
Metropolitan Community College, Douglas County	18,518	22	16	6
University of Nebraska:				
Kearney	7,100	9	8	1
Lincoln	24,593	58	30	28
NEVADA				
Truckee Meadows Community College	11,131	10	7	3
University Of Nevada:				
Las Vegas	27,364	49	32	17
Reno	18,004	25	19	6
NEW HAMPSHIRE				
University of New Hampshire	15,128	29	17	12
NEW JERSEY				
Brookdale Community College	14,952	20	12	8
Essex County College	12,532	49	12	37
Kean University	16,187	51	28	23
Middlesex County College	12,732	16	11	5
Monmouth University	6,570	45	19	26
Montclair State University	18,498	46	36	10
New Jersey Institute of Technology	9,558	62	30	32
Richard Stockton College of New Jersey	8,108	29	19	10
Rowan University	11,786	71	24	47
Rutgers University:				
Camden	6,428	78	22	56
Newark	11,804	36	31	5
New Brunswick	39,950	84	41	43
Stevens Institute of Technology	5,541	21	17	4
The College of New Jersey	7,152	29	20	9
University of Medicine and Dentistry:				
Camden[2]	n.a.	15	11	4
Newark	7,212	113	39	74
New Brunswick[2]	n.a.	31	19	12
William Paterson University	11,518	46	23	23
NEW MEXICO				
University of New Mexico	28,977	59	35	24
NEW YORK				
Cornell University	21,131	67	46	21
Ithaca College	6,760	38	20	18
Rensselaer Polytechnic Institute	6,538	38	30	8
State University of New York:				
Albany	17,114	63	40	23
Buffalo	28,849	70	61	9
Downstate Medical Center	1,751	116	33	83
Stony Brook	23,920	146	67	79
Upstate Medical Center	1,589	108	15	93
State University of New York Agricultural and Technical College:				
Alfred	3,616	17	12	5
Canton	3,825	11	10	1
Cobleskill	2,516	11	10	1
Farmingdale	7,633	24	15	9
Morrisville	3,230	14	12	2
State University of New York College:				
Brockport	8,413	18	16	2
Buffalo	12,204	34	32	2
Cortland	7,331	24	18	6
Environmental Science and Forestry	2,680	10	9	1
Fredonia	5,720	17	16	1
Geneseo	5,683	17	13	4
New Paltz	7,857	26	23	3
Old Westbury	4,459	21	17	4

Table 79. Full-Time Law Enforcement Employees, by Selected State and University or College, 2012— continued

(Number)

State and university/college	Student enrollment[1]	Law enforcement employees	Officers	Civilians
Oneonta	6,023	27	17	10
Optometry	317	17	6	11
Oswego	8,216	24	21	3
Plattsburgh	6,350	19	14	5
Potsdam	4,395	14	12	2
Purchase	4,267	29	23	6
Technology	3,249	13	11	2
Utica-Rome	2,516	15	11	4
NORTH CAROLINA				
Appalachian State University	17,344	40	26	14
Beaufort County Community College	1,954	3	3	0
Belmont Abbey College	1,711	8	8	0
Davidson College	1,755	9	8	1
Duke University	15,427	151	55	96
East Carolina University	27,386	73	56	17
Elizabeth City State University	2,930	21	12	9
Elon University	5,916	15	14	1
Fayetteville State University	5,930	38	20	18
Methodist University	2,476	12	8	4
North Carolina Agricultural and Technical State University	10,881	55	24	31
North Carolina Central University	8,359	53	27	26
North Carolina School of the Arts	893	16	11	5
North Carolina State University, Raleigh	34,767	48	33	15
Queens University	2,491	7	6	1
Saint Augustine's University	1,506	23	6	17
University of North Carolina:				
Asheville	3,863	21	15	6
Chapel Hill	29,137	92	48	44
Charlotte	25,277	51	41	10
Greensboro	18,627	50	31	19
Pembroke	6,251	22	16	6
Wilmington	13,145	39	27	12
Wake Forest University	7,351	44	23	21
Western Carolina University	9,352	27	19	8
Winston-Salem State University	6,163	30	16	14
NORTH DAKOTA				
North Dakota State College of Science	3,127	4	3	1
North Dakota State University	14,399	25	17	8
University of North Dakota	14,697	17	15	2
OHIO				
Cleveland State University	17,229	42	23	19
Cuyahoga Community College	30,853	36	28	8
Kent State University	27,855	47	32	15
Lakeland Community College	9,521	13	9	4
Miami University	17,395	32	23	9
Muskingum University	2,292	6	6	0
Notre Dame College	2,147	6	5	1
Ohio State University:				
Columbus	56,867	54	47	7
Mansfield	1,388	5	1	4
Marion	1,525	1	1	0
Newark	2,677	6	1	5
Wooster	666	5	5	0
Ohio University	26,201	28	23	5
Shawnee State University	4,711	8	7	1
Sinclair Community College	21,106	23	19	4
University of Cincinnati	33,329	111	51	60
University of Toledo	22,610	45	37	8
Wright State University	18,304	26	17	9
Youngstown State University	14,483	31	25	6
OKLAHOMA				
Cameron University	6,463	12	12	0
East Central University	4,851	6	5	1

Table 79. Full-Time Law Enforcement Employees, by Selected State and University or College, 2012— continued

(Number)

State and university/college	Student enrollment[1]	Law enforcement employees	Officers	Civilians
Northeastern Oklahoma A&M College	2,542	9	8	1
Northeastern State University:				
Broken Arrow[2]	n.a.	5	5	0
Tahlequah	9,316	22	15	7
Oklahoma City University	3,575	19	14	5
Oklahoma State University:				
Main Campus	24,390	41	32	9
Okmulgee	3,995	6	6	0
Tulsa	427	9	8	1
Rogers State University	4,803	5	5	0
Seminole State College	2,282	2	2	0
Southeastern Oklahoma State University	4,140	8	6	2
Southwestern Oklahoma State University	5,263	6	5	1
Tulsa Community College	20,154	17	11	6
University of Central Oklahoma	17,239	21	16	5
University of Oklahoma:				
Health Sciences Center	3,590	59	41	18
Norman	27,138	65	36	29
PENNSYLVANIA				
Bloomsburg University	10,159	22	17	5
California University	9,483	22	18	4
Cheyney University	1,200	21	13	8
Clarion University	6,991	15	10	5
Dickinson College	2,397	20	14	6
East Stroudsburg University	7,353	18	15	3
Edinboro University	8,262	15	14	1
Elizabethtown College	2,389	17	5	12
Indiana University	15,340	28	20	8
Kutztown University	10,283	20	16	4
Lehigh University	7,055	30	21	9
Lock Haven University	5,366	12	10	2
Mansfield University	3,275	12	9	3
Millersville University	8,725	20	16	4
Moravian College	2,002	13	10	3
Pennsylvania State University:				
Altoona	4,105	11	9	2
Beaver	870	6	6	0
Behrend	4,226	11	7	4
Berks	2,873	9	8	1
Harrisburg	4,269	10	7	3
Hazleton	1,172	5	5	0
McKeesport	701	4	4	0
Mont Alto	1,217	5	5	0
Schuylkill	1,012	6	6	0
University Park	45,628	79	47	32
Shippensburg University	8,183	20	17	3
Slippery Rock University	8,712	18	14	4
University of Pittsburgh:				
Bradford	1,564	7	6	1
Greensburg	1,846	7	6	1
Johnstown	2,957	13	12	1
Pittsburgh	28,766	147	78	69
Titusville	448	6	6	0
West Chester University	15,100	19	19	0
RHODE ISLAND				
Brown University	8,768	86	49	37
University of Rhode Island	16,317	28	23	5
SOUTH CAROLINA				
Benedict College	3,213	26	21	5
Bob Jones University	3,631	9	8	1
Clemson University	19,914	39	29	10
College of Charleston	11,649	38	29	9
Columbia College	1,266	13	11	2

Table 79. Full-Time Law Enforcement Employees, by Selected State and University or College, 2012— continued

(Number)

State and university/college	Student enrollment[1]	Law enforcement employees	Officers	Civilians
Denmark Technical College	1,607	8	4	4
Erskine College	773	2	2	0
Francis Marion University	4,187	13	11	2
Greenville Technical College	14,453	2	1	1
Lander University	3,069	15	13	2
Medical University of South Carolina	2,678	77	55	22
Midlands Technical College	12,224	6	6	0
Presbyterian College	1,360	6	5	1
Spartanburg Methodist College	803	4	4	0
The Citadel	3,390	17	16	1
Trident Technical College	16,781	32	28	4
University of South Carolina:				
Aiken	3,277	11	8	3
Columbia	30,721	81	63	18
Upstate	5,493	15	14	1
Winthrop University	5,913	22	15	7
SOUTH DAKOTA				
South Dakota State University	12,725	18	13	5
TENNESSEE				
Austin Peay State University	10,873	23	13	10
Christian Brothers University	1,694	15	9	6
East Tennessee State University	15,250	26	19	7
Middle Tennessee State University	26,442	44	36	8
Northeast State Community College	6,478	6	6	0
Southwest Tennessee Community College	12,958	28	15	13
Tennessee State University	9,165	79	32	47
Tennessee Technological University	11,768	21	14	7
University Of Memphis	22,725	39	33	6
University of Tennessee:				
Chattanooga	11,438	28	17	11
Health Science Center[2]	n.a.	51	24	27
Knoxville	30,194	84	50	34
Martin	7,910	17	13	4
Vanderbilt University	12,836	164	90	74
Volunteer State Community College	8,666	5	4	1
Walters State Community College	6,733	8	8	0
TEXAS				
Abilene Christian University	4,558	15	14	1
Alamo Community College District	61,507	81	63	18
Alvin Community College	5,129	9	7	2
Amarillo College	11,616	12	10	2
Angelo State University	7,084	15	11	4
Austin College	1,353	8	7	1
Baylor Health Care System[2]	n.a.	153	58	95
Baylor University, Waco	15,029	33	26	7
Blinn College	18,106	17	16	1
Brookhaven College	13,705	17	16	1
Central Texas College	26,995	8	7	1
College of the Mainland	4,168	8	7	1
Eastfield College	13,885	18	17	1
El Paso Community College	30,723	42	36	6
Grayson College	5,207	2	1	1
Hardin-Simmons University	2,358	8	7	1
Houston Baptist University	2,432	14	11	3
Houston Community College	63,015	96	64	32
Lamar University, Beaumont	14,020	43	27	16
Laredo Community College	10,076	22	20	2
Midwestern State University	6,181	15	10	5
Mountain View College	9,431	14	14	0
North Lake College	11,865	22	21	1
Paris Junior College	5,936	4	4	0
Prairie View A&M University	8,425	35	20	15

Table 79. Full-Time Law Enforcement Employees, by Selected State and University or College, 2012— continued

(Number)

State and university/college	Student enrollment[1]	Law enforcement employees	Officers	Civilians
Rice University	6,224	41	27	14
Richland College	20,000	19	19	0
Southern Methodist University	10,982	32	24	8
South Plains College	10,482	6	6	0
Southwestern University	1,347	7	6	1
Stephen F. Austin State University	12,903	48	27	21
St. Mary's University	4,188	21	17	4
Sul Ross State University	2,940	9	7	2
Tarleton State University	11,693	18	17	1
Texas A&M International University	7,037	27	18	9
Texas A&M University:				
College Station	50,230	126	63	63
Commerce	11,417	25	18	7
Corpus Christi	10,162	27	16	11
Galveston	2,035	9	8	1
San Antonio[2]	n.a.	13	12	1
Texas Christian University	9,518	43	28	15
Texas Southern University	9,730	63	33	30
Texas State Technical College:				
Harlingen	5,807	13	10	3
West Texas	856	6	6	0
Texas State University, San Marcos	34,087	44	35	9
Texas Tech University, Lubbock	32,327	81	47	34
Texas Woman's University	14,718	35	16	19
Trinity University	2,535	28	16	12
Tyler Junior College	11,540	19	17	2
University of Houston:				
Central Campus	39,820	119	41	78
Clearlake	8,185	27	17	10
Downtown Campus	12,918	32	15	17
University of Mary Hardin-Baylor	3,137	9	6	3
University of North Texas:				
Denton	37,818	77	41	36
Health Science Center	1,760	21	11	10
University of Texas:				
Arlington	33,439	114	36	78
Austin	51,112	136	63	73
Brownsville	14,918	34	12	22
Dallas	18,864	60	22	38
El Paso	22,640	52	22	30
Health Science Center, San Antonio	3,234	104	35	69
Health Science Center, Tyler[2]	n.a.	16	8	8
Houston	4,916	339	90	249
Medical Branch	2,825	93	52	41
Pan American	19,034	41	20	21
Permian Basin	3,831	16	10	6
San Antonio	30,968	111	51	60
Southwestern Medical School	2,487	126	38	88
Tyler	6,696	23	10	13
West Texas A&M University	7,886	18	14	4
UTAH				
Brigham Young University	34,101	45	29	16
College of Eastern Utah	2,323	1	1	0
Snow College	4,465	2	2	0
Southern Utah University	7,750	6	5	1
University of Utah	31,660	102	30	72
Utah State University	26,757	16	11	5
Utah Valley University	33,395	11	9	2
Weber State University	25,301	10	9	1
VERMONT				
University of Vermont	13,478	35	23	12
VIRGINIA				
Christopher Newport University	4,990	19	14	5

Table 79. Full-Time Law Enforcement Employees, by Selected State and University or College, 2012— continued

(Number)

State and university/college	Student enrollment[1]	Law enforcement employees	Officers	Civilians
College of William and Mary	8,200	24	19	5
Eastern Virginia Medical School	1,008	43	15	28
Emory and Henry College	982	4	2	2
Ferrum College	1,512	10	9	1
George Mason University	33,320	72	56	16
Hampton University	5,221	45	27	18
James Madison University	19,722	40	31	9
J. Sargeant Reynolds Community College	13,367	25	16	9
Longwood University	4,860	23	15	8
Lord Fairfax Community College	7,270	2	2	0
Norfolk State University	7,091	37	22	15
Northern Virginia Community College	50,044	60	49	11
Old Dominion University	24,753	50	42	8
Radford University	9,370	30	23	7
Richard Bland College	1,629	5	5	0
Thomas Nelson Community College	10,999	15	10	5
University of Mary Washington	5,170	18	13	5
University of Richmond	4,348	32	19	13
University of Virginia	24,297	121	53	68
University of Virginia's College at Wise	2,067	10	9	1
Virginia Commonwealth University	31,627	142	92	50
Virginia Military Institute	1,605	11	10	1
Virginia Polytechnic Institute and State University	30,936	73	51	22
Virginia State University	5,890	41	25	16
Virginia Western Community College	8,557	8	8	0
WASHINGTON				
Central Washington University	11,320	13	12	1
Eastern Washington University	12,126	13	12	1
Evergreen State College	4,794	15	9	6
University of Washington	42,444	78	43	35
Washington State University				
Pullman	27,329	22	17	5
Vancouver[2]	.a.	4	3	1
Western Washington University	14,842	19	15	4
WEST VIRGINIA				
Bluefield State College	1,929	2	2	0
Concord University	2,797	11	9	2
Fairmont State University	4,629	10	7	3
Glenville State College	1,857	6	3	3
Marshall University	13,966	23	22	1
Potomac State College	1,802	5	4	1
Shepherd University	4,393	10	9	1
West Liberty State College	2,789	5	5	0
West Virginia State University	2,827	6	5	1
West Virginia Tech	1,316	7	6	1
West Virginia University	29,617	61	49	12
Wisconsin				
University of Wisconsin:				
Eau Claire	11,300	11	10	1
Green Bay	6,671	13	9	4
La Crosse	10,284	14	11	3
Madison	41,946	118	66	52
Milwaukee	29,350	55	44	11
Oshkosh	13,513	13	11	2
Parkside	4,829	13	8	5
Platteville	8,262	10	9	1
River Falls	6,803	6	6	0
Stevens Point	9,484	8	3	5
Stout	9,350	9	8	1
Superior	2,814	5	2	3
Whitewater	11,629	15	13	2
Wyoming				

Table 79. Full-Time Law Enforcement Employees, by Selected State and University or College, 2012— continued

(Number)

State and university/college	Student enrollment[1]	Law enforcement employees	Officers	Civilians
Northern Wyoming Community College District	4,296	3	3	0
University of Wyoming	12,925	21	14	7

1 The student enrollment figures provided by the United States Department of Education are for the 2011 school year, the most recent available. The enrollment figures include full-time and part-time students.
2 Student enrollment figures were not available. n.a. = not available

Table 80. Full-Time Law Enforcement Employees, by Selected State Metropolitan and Nonmetropolitan Counties, 2012

(Number)

State/county	Law enforcement employees	Officers	Civilians
ALABAMA			
Metropolitan Counties			
Autauga	63	25	38
Baldwin	282	102	180
Bibb	12	11	1
Elmore	95	48	47
Etowah	155	62	93
Geneva	28	12	16
Hale	12	10	2
Houston	169	66	103
Lauderdale	46	37	9
Lawrence	52	31	21
Lee	151	72	79
Limestone	106	42	64
Lowndes	44	12	32
Madison	346	113	233
Morgan	165	55	110
Pickens	35	10	25
Russell	111	40	71
Shelby	207	118	89
Walker	82	28	54
Nonmetropolitan Counties			
Bullock	12	5	7
Butler	12	10	2
Cherokee	44	23	21
Choctaw	13	7	6
Clarke	31	9	22
Conecuh	34	10	24
Covington	28	25	3
Crenshaw	10	8	2
Cullman	136	78	58
Dale	41	22	19
Dallas	51	25	26
De Kalb	89	38	51
Escambia	90	23	67
Franklin	49	18	31
Greene	33	13	20
Jackson	91	33	58
Jefferson	555	428	127
Marengo	32	16	16
Montgomery	171	124	47
Perry	19	9	10
Pike	28	17	11
Sumter	25	7	18
Talladega	107	38	69
Tallapoosa	55	24	31
Wilcox	29	9	20
Winston	32	15	17
ARIZONA			
Metropolitan Counties			
Cochise	191	83	108
Coconino	236	57	179
Maricopa	3,320	668	2,652
Mohave	264	92	172
Pima	1,505	517	988
Pinal	602	203	399
Yavapai	181	123	58
Yuma	343	86	257

Table 80. Full-Time Law Enforcement Employees, by Selected State Metropolitan and Nonmetropolitan Counties, 2012— continued

(Number)

State/county	Law enforcement employees	Officers	Civilians
Nonmetropolitan Counties			
Apache	73	29	44
Gila	137	49	88
Graham	80	23	57
Greenlee	41	15	26
La Paz	86	28	58
Navajo	157	55	102
Santa Cruz	116	38	78
ARKANSAS			
Metropolitan Counties			
Benton	224	138	86
Cleveland	13	8	5
Craighead	113	31	82
Crawford	63	30	33
Crittenden	150	41	109
Faulkner	158	47	111
Garland	134	47	87
Grant	18	15	3
Jefferson	165	72	93
Lincoln	22	8	14
Little River	17	8	9
Lonoke	56	25	31
Madison	19	10	9
Miller	64	24	40
Perry	19	10	9
Poinsett	44	13	31
Pulaski	496	123	373
Saline	95	41	54
Sebastian	144	106	38
Washington	291	161	130
Nonmetropolitan Counties			
Arkansas	10	10	0
Ashley	45	21	24
Baxter	50	32	18
Boone	52	23	29
Bradley	5	4	1
Calhoun	11	5	6
Carroll	22	19	3
Chicot	12	8	4
Clark	28	12	16
Clay	21	8	13
Cleburne	40	23	17
Columbia	35	17	18
Conway	36	17	19
Cross	38	16	22
Dallas	26	7	19
Desha	7	6	1
Drew	11	10	1
Franklin	24	10	14
Fulton	13	6	7
Greene	51	17	34
Hempstead	53	20	33
Hot Spring	27	15	12
Howard	25	11	14
Independence	77	51	26
Izard	29	15	14
Jackson	24	14	10
Johnson	31	14	17
Lafayette	22	7	15

Table 80. Full-Time Law Enforcement Employees, by Selected State Metropolitan and Nonmetropolitan Counties, 2012— continued

(Number)

State/county	Law enforcement employees	Officers	Civilians
Lawrence	24	13	11
Lee	10	5	5
Logan	25	13	12
Marion	22	20	2
Mississippi	89	33	56
Monroe	14	6	8
Montgomery	20	11	9
Nevada	16	5	11
Newton	12	7	5
Ouachita	38	16	22
Phillips	18	15	3
Pike	21	8	13
Polk	24	12	12
Pope	43	36	7
Prairie	17	7	10
Randolph	11	10	1
Scott	28	8	20
Searcy	14	8	6
Sevier	30	14	16
Sharp	31	13	18
St. Francis	39	17	22
Stone	20	10	10
Union	59	27	32
Van Buren	36	18	18
White	101	48	53
Woodruff	16	6	10
Yell	26	14	12
CALIFORNIA			
Metropolitan Counties			
Alameda	1,599	952	647
Butte	297	106	191
Contra Costa	940	640	300
El Dorado	341	153	188
Fresno	966	779	187
Imperial	270	183	87
Kern	1,163	884	279
Kings	227	74	153
Los Angeles	16,796	9,274	7,522
Madera	104	72	32
Marin	297	192	105
Merced	218	102	116
Monterey	392	291	101
Napa	126	99	27
Orange	3,644	1,885	1,759
Placer	423	229	194
Riverside	3,706	1,916	1,790
Sacramento	1,868	1,186	682
San Benito	44	21	23
San Bernardino	3,186	1,718	1,468
San Diego	3,816	2,270	1,546
San Francisco	1,017	860	157
San Joaquin	682	280	402
San Luis Obispo	378	152	226
San Mateo	601	314	287
Santa Barbara	581	413	168
Santa Clara	1,517	1,131	386
Santa Cruz	286	124	162
Shasta	209	133	76
Solano	409	104	305

Table 80. Full-Time Law Enforcement Employees, by Selected State Metropolitan and Nonmetropolitan Counties, 2012— continued

(Number)

State/county	Law enforcement employees	Officers	Civilians
Sonoma	589	223	366
Stanislaus	518	388	130
Sutter	129	104	25
Tulare	688	501	187
Ventura	1,219	748	471
Yolo	227	83	144
Yuba	172	132	40
Nonmetropolitan Counties			
Alpine	17	14	3
Amador	85	41	44
Calaveras	91	50	41
Colusa	63	30	33
Del Norte	57	26	31
Glenn	60	24	36
Humboldt	210	168	42
Inyo	53	34	19
Lake	138	48	90
Lassen	69	51	18
Mariposa	69	56	13
Mendocino	155	120	35
Modoc	25	13	12
Mono	50	27	23
Nevada	163	64	99
Plumas	54	29	25
Sierra	16	10	6
Siskiyou	101	77	24
Tehama	104	72	32
Trinity	40	18	22
Tuolumne	119	58	61
COLORADO			
Metropolitan Counties			
Adams	500	348	152
Arapahoe	517	250	267
Boulder	346	216	130
Clear Creek	68	26	42
Douglas	436	291	145
Elbert	35	29	6
El Paso	636	411	225
Gilpin	50	31	19
Jefferson	797	544	253
Larimer	367	146	221
Mesa	222	99	123
Park	53	28	25
Pueblo	331	170	161
Teller	52	36	16
Weld	320	243	77
Nonmetropolitan Counties			
Alamosa	43	28	15
Archuleta	35	18	17
Baca	11	4	7
Bent	25	15	10
Chaffee	53	20	33
Cheyenne	5	3	2
Conejos	19	7	12
Costilla	10	7	3
Crowley	10	5	5
Custer	20	10	10
Delta	64	29	35
Dolores	7	5	2

Table 80. Full-Time Law Enforcement Employees, by Selected State Metropolitan and Nonmetropolitan Counties, 2012— continued

(Number)

State/county	Law enforcement employees	Officers	Civilians
Eagle	72	43	29
Fremont	81	30	51
Garfield	132	35	97
Grand	53	23	30
Gunnison	30	13	17
Hinsdale	5	4	1
Huerfano	25	12	13
Jackson	7	4	3
Kiowa	7	6	1
Kit Carson	29	7	22
Lake	18	12	6
La Plata	134	95	39
Las Animas	33	14	19
Lincoln	21	8	13
Logan	49	22	27
Mineral	4	3	1
Moffat	34	19	15
Montezuma	73	31	42
Montrose	108	48	60
Morgan	50	22	28
Otero	22	9	13
Ouray	8	8	0
Phillips	4	4	0
Pitkin	26	22	4
Prowers	31	9	22
Rio Blanco	32	15	17
Rio Grande	33	14	19
Routt	49	19	30
Saguache	18	7	11
San Juan	4	3	1
San Miguel	33	29	4
Sedgwick	9	6	3
Summit	57	50	7
Washington	47	42	5
Yuma	20	10	10
DELAWARE			
Metropolitan Counties			
New Castle County Police Department	461	356	105
FLORIDA			
Metropolitan Counties			
Alachua	502	282	220
Baker	155	47	108
Bay	274	213	61
Brevard	1,182	498	684
Broward	2,871	1,489	1,382
Charlotte	390	274	116
Citrus	337	216	121
Clay	526	255	271
Escambia	1,089	709	380
Flagler	188	131	57
Gadsden	76	51	25
Gilchrist	50	27	23
Gulf	42	28	14
Hernando	487	310	177
Highlands	330	146	184
Hillsborough	3,334	1,240	2,094
Indian River	466	322	144
Jefferson	52	21	31
Lake	453	291	162

Table 80. Full-Time Law Enforcement Employees, by Selected State Metropolitan and Nonmetropolitan Counties, 2012— continued

(Number)

State/county	Law enforcement employees	Officers	Civilians
Lee	902	553	349
Leon	349	237	112
Manatee	1,064	472	592
Marion	760	542	218
Martin	515	252	263
Miami-Dade	4,149	2,978	1,171
Nassau	197	135	62
Okaloosa	334	242	92
Orange	1,999	1,384	615
Osceola	594	382	212
Pasco	1,293	841	452
Pinellas	1,298	737	561
Polk	1,558	601	957
Santa Rosa	294	183	111
Sarasota	925	397	528
Seminole	1,120	402	718
St. Johns	558	259	299
St. Lucie	602	248	354
Sumter	159	112	47
Volusia	758	451	307
Wakulla	88	60	28
Walton	234	163	71
Nonmetropolitan Counties			
Bradford	52	33	19
Calhoun	28	14	14
Columbia	169	91	78
DeSoto	112	54	58
Dixie	72	27	45
Franklin	73	33	40
Glades	148	101	47
Hamilton	60	18	42
Hardee	99	48	51
Hendry	153	73	80
Holmes	47	25	22
Jackson	80	60	20
Lafayette	27	11	16
Levy	138	60	78
Madison	51	35	16
Monroe	491	195	296
Okeechobee	116	82	34
Putnam	234	115	119
Taylor	49	31	18
Union	16	13	3
Washington	77	57	20
GEORGIA			
Metropolitan Counties			
Augusta-Richmond	712	643	69
Barrow	190	129	61
Bartow	234	197	37
Bibb	361	296	65
Brantley	43	19	24
Brooks	51	22	29
Bryan	66	45	21
Butts	75	42	33
Carroll	186	105	81
Catoosa	141	69	72
Chatham	514	450	64
Chattahoochee	13	7	6
Cherokee	388	327	61

Table 80. Full-Time Law Enforcement Employees, by Selected State Metropolitan and Nonmetropolitan Counties, 2012— continued

(Number)

State/county	Law enforcement employees	Officers	Civilians
Clarke	170	147	23
Clayton	473	171	302
Clayton County Police Department	419	363	56
Cobb	717	463	254
Cobb County Police Department	626	570	56
Columbia	369	306	63
Coweta	230	152	78
Crawford	33	15	18
Dade	30	27	3
Dawson	106	61	45
DeKalb	760	579	181
DeKalb County Police Department	1,216	981	235
Dougherty	249	233	16
Dougherty County Police Department	48	41	7
Douglas	311	277	34
Echols	9	8	1
Effingham	125	75	50
Fayette	225	146	79
Floyd	133	81	52
Floyd County Police Department	75	70	5
Forsyth	362	308	54
Fulton	1,290	1,016	274
Fulton County Police Department	180	121	59
Glynn	45	35	10
Glynn County Police Department	127	113	14
Gwinnett County Police Department	961	705	256
Hall	449	386	63
Haralson	61	53	8
Harris	51	49	2
Heard	44	23	21
Henry	300	257	43
Henry County Police Department	253	219	34
Houston	314	112	202
Jones	75	54	21
Lamar	54	28	26
Lanier	13	9	4
Long	21	18	3
Lowndes	236	158	78
Madison	61	39	22
McDuffie	46	31	15
McIntosh	70	45	25
Monroe	94	58	36
Morgan	54	26	28
Murray	69	41	28
Newton	232	143	89
Oconee	88	56	32
Oglethorpe	45	19	26
Paulding	272	236	36
Peach	64	31	33
Pickens	102	93	9
Pulaski	36	24	12
Rockdale	287	263	24
Spalding	179	96	83
Twiggs	42	22	20
Walker	111	73	38
Walton	175	149	26
Whitfield	191	164	27
Worth	31	22	9
Nonmetropolitan Counties			

Table 80. Full-Time Law Enforcement Employees, by Selected State Metropolitan and Nonmetropolitan Counties, 2012— continued

(Number)

State/county	Law enforcement employees	Officers	Civilians
Appling	52	18	34
Baldwin	117	57	60
Banks	52	33	19
Ben Hill	54	50	4
Berrien	57	26	31
Bleckley	39	14	25
Bulloch	119	57	62
Camden	123	62	61
Charlton	30	18	12
Chattooga	45	26	19
Clinch	14	10	4
Coffee	115	52	63
Cook	38	13	25
Crisp	73	54	19
Decatur	36	31	5
Dodge	29	14	15
Dooly	73	31	42
Early	43	20	23
Elbert	57	52	5
Emanuel	28	23	5
Fannin	48	44	4
Franklin	60	30	30
Gilmer	92	72	20
Gordon	87	80	7
Grady	45	21	24
Greene	51	31	20
Habersham	42	39	3
Hancock	42	30	12
Hart	43	27	16
Irwin	21	13	8
Jackson	159	100	59
Jefferson	50	47	3
Johnson	20	9	11
Lumpkin	72	62	10
Macon	23	22	1
Miller	19	9	10
Mitchell	51	25	26
Pierce	33	31	2
Polk	77	77	0
Polk County Police Department	41	38	3
Rabun	53	51	2
Schley	6	3	3
Screven	20	18	2
Seminole	29	15	14
Stephens	59	29	30
Stewart	8	4	4
Sumter	94	48	46
Talbot	14	10	4
Taliaferro	14	8	6
Taylor	24	23	1
Thomas	78	45	33
Tift	109	58	51
Towns	23	20	3
Treutlen	19	9	10
Troup	133	76	57
Union	39	36	3
Upson	74	36	38
Ware	123	44	79
Warren	6	6	0
Washington	38	22	16

Table 80. Full-Time Law Enforcement Employees, by Selected State Metropolitan and Nonmetropolitan Counties, 2012— continued

(Number)

State/county	Law enforcement employees	Officers	Civilians
Wayne	54	29	25
Webster	6	5	1
White	73	40	33
Wilcox	16	10	6
Wilkes	27	14	13
Wilkinson	28	16	12
HAWAII			
Metropolitan Counties			
Maui Police Department	462	343	119
Nonmetropolitan Counties			
Hawaii Police Department	552	421	131
Kauai Police Department	175	121	54
IDAHO			
Metropolitan Counties			
Ada	413	136	277
Bannock	65	41	24
Boise	20	11	9
Bonneville	107	65	42
Butte	13	5	8
Canyon	231	122	109
Franklin	15	12	3
Gem	24	13	11
Jefferson	32	19	13
Kootenai	166	91	75
Nez Perce	41	23	18
Owyhee	21	14	7
Nonmetropolitan Counties			
Adams	26	20	6
Bear Lake	12	6	6
Benewah	16	8	8
Bingham	52	32	20
Blaine	24	19	5
Bonner	56	41	15
Boundary	21	11	10
Camas	6	4	2
Caribou	14	7	7
Cassia	53	34	19
Clark	7	3	4
Clearwater	23	15	8
Custer	15	7	8
Elmore	36	22	14
Fremont	27	18	9
Gooding	17	12	5
Idaho	31	21	10
Jerome	21	17	4
Latah	38	26	12
Lemhi	10	9	1
Lewis	10	5	5
Lincoln	6	5	1
Madison	33	23	10
Minidoka	28	18	10
Oneida	12	8	4
Payette	32	17	15
Power	17	9	8
Twin Falls	67	43	24
Valley	31	16	15
Washington	16	12	4

Table 80. Full-Time Law Enforcement Employees, by Selected State Metropolitan and Nonmetropolitan Counties, 2012— continued

(Number)

State/county	Law enforcement employees	Officers	Civilians
ILLINOIS			
Metropolitan Counties			
Alexander	13	9	4
Bond	20	12	8
Boone	96	33	63
Clinton	36	15	21
Cook	6,587	2,066	4,521
De Witt	30	15	15
Du Page	541	422	119
Ford	25	7	18
Grundy	65	31	34
Henry	64	23	41
Jackson	82	27	55
Kane	260	86	174
Kankakee	198	58	140
Kendall	118	56	62
Lake	501	196	305
Macon	133	61	72
Macoupin	44	31	13
Madison	164	80	84
Marshall	18	8	10
McHenry	387	104	283
McLean	135	54	81
Menard	18	10	8
Mercer	33	12	21
Monroe	35	15	20
Peoria	184	65	119
Piatt	36	11	25
Rock Island	154	64	90
Sangamon	195	64	131
Stark	12	5	7
St. Clair	151	66	85
Tazewell	114	41	73
Vermilion	90	39	51
Will	598	231	367
Williamson	98	35	63
Winnebago	335	100	235
Nonmetropolitan Counties			
Adams	59	59	0
Brown	8	7	1
Bureau	40	20	20
Cass	8	7	1
Clark	10	9	1
Clay	15	10	5
Coles	37	20	17
Cumberland	14	5	9
Edgar	18	8	10
Effingham	46	19	27
Fayette	27	11	16
Franklin	49	18	31
Fulton	44	21	23
Greene	13	6	7
Iroquois	24	13	11
Jefferson	66	21	45
Jo Daviess	37	18	19
Johnson	14	7	7
La Salle	113	45	68
Lee	39	21	18
Livingston	37	30	7

Table 80. Full-Time Law Enforcement Employees, by Selected State Metropolitan and Nonmetropolitan Counties, 2012— continued

(Number)

State/county	Law enforcement employees	Officers	Civilians
Logan	37	20	17
Marion	14	14	0
Mason	22	9	13
Massac	30	14	16
McDonough	25	13	12
Montgomery	38	15	23
Morgan	36	15	21
Ogle	69	28	41
Perry	38	13	25
Pike	26	10	16
Pulaski	15	10	5
Putnam	13	8	5
Randolph	29	12	17
Richland	27	7	20
Saline	44	10	34
Scott	6	2	4
Shelby	27	13	14
Stephenson	56	25	31
Wabash	8	4	4
Wayne	22	11	11
White	26	8	18
Whiteside	49	22	27
INDIANA			
Metropolitan Counties			
Bartholomew	92	40	52
Brown	38	13	25
Delaware	109	42	67
Elkhart	180	66	114
Floyd	98	29	69
Harrison	24	21	3
Johnson	141	115	26
Madison	110	50	60
Newton	43	18	25
Putnam	19	19	0
Shelby	82	28	54
St. Joseph	271	113	158
Sullivan	34	10	24
Tippecanoe	143	46	97
Vigo	115	39	76
Warrick	79	38	41
Washington	32	12	20
Wells	38	15	23
Whitley	48	15	33
Nonmetropolitan Counties			
Blackford	38	8	30
De Kalb	56	20	36
Dubois	38	17	21
Fountain	20	8	12
Franklin	17	13	4
Gibson	41	17	24
Grant	110	45	65
Greene	40	15	25
Henry	55	28	27
Jackson	58	16	42
Jay	47	13	34
Jefferson	40	17	23
LaGrange	56	18	38
Marshall	58	21	37
Martin	19	7	12
Miami	49	16	33

Table 80. Full-Time Law Enforcement Employees, by Selected State Metropolitan and Nonmetropolitan Counties, 2012— continued

(Number)

State/county	Law enforcement employees	Officers	Civilians
Montgomery	63	21	42
Orange	27	9	18
Pike	28	9	19
Pulaski	41	13	28
Ripley	27	11	16
Rush	26	11	15
Steuben	56	21	35
Switzerland	31	12	19
Tipton	30	12	18
Wabash	34	16	18
Warren	7	7	0
IOWA			
Metropolitan Counties			
Benton	28	12	16
Black Hawk	135	102	33
Bremer	30	11	19
Grundy	16	12	4
Guthrie	9	5	4
Harrison	18	10	8
Johnson	88	66	22
Jones	23	10	13
Linn	182	116	66
Madison	16	7	9
Mills	20	11	9
Plymouth	28	10	18
Polk	452	132	320
Pottawattamie	193	50	143
Scott	153	44	109
Story	82	31	51
Warren	33	23	10
Washington	32	17	15
Woodbury	110	34	76
Nonmetropolitan Counties			
Adair	14	5	9
Adams	11	6	5
Allamakee	17	9	8
Appanoose	15	8	7
Audubon	8	5	3
Boone	28	11	17
Buchanan	29	13	16
Buena Vista	30	13	17
Butler	20	11	9
Calhoun	7	6	1
Carroll	15	9	6
Cass	11	8	3
Cedar	40	11	29
Cerro Gordo	74	20	54
Cherokee	19	7	12
Clarke	18	6	12
Clay	21	10	11
Clinton	43	25	18
Crawford	13	10	3
Davis	6	5	1
Decatur	11	6	5
Delaware	17	13	4
Des Moines	48	20	28
Dickinson	23	9	14
Emmet	16	8	8
Fayette	31	10	21

Table 80. Full-Time Law Enforcement Employees, by Selected State Metropolitan and Nonmetropolitan Counties, 2012— continued

(Number)

State/county	Law enforcement employees	Officers	Civilians
Floyd	18	11	7
Franklin	10	7	3
Fremont	17	8	9
Greene	16	7	9
Hamilton	29	10	19
Hancock	17	7	10
Hardin	29	10	19
Henry	28	11	17
Howard	14	7	7
Humboldt	9	8	1
Ida	16	9	7
Iowa	27	12	15
Jasper	43	14	29
Jefferson	29	10	19
Keokuk	10	6	4
Kossuth	25	9	16
Louisa	31	10	21
Lucas	13	5	8
Lyon	25	11	14
Mahaska	25	9	16
Marion	34	12	22
Marshall	55	20	35
Mitchell	15	6	9
Monroe	12	5	7
Montgomery	19	8	11
Muscatine	68	22	46
O'Brien	28	9	19
Osceola	13	9	4
Page	15	8	7
Palo Alto	15	8	7
Pocahontas	16	7	9
Poweshiek	25	11	14
Ringgold	14	7	7
Sac	21	8	13
Shelby	15	9	6
Sioux	38	14	24
Tama	22	13	9
Taylor	8	4	4
Union	12	6	6
Van Buren	11	5	6
Wapello	38	10	28
Wayne	15	6	9
Webster	29	16	13
Winnebago	10	6	4
Winneshiek	23	10	13
Worth	19	7	12
Wright	20	8	12
KANSAS			
Metropolitan Counties			
Butler	113	57	56
Doniphan	14	4	10
Douglas	134	82	52
Harvey	38	36	2
Jackson	39	17	22
Jefferson	41	23	18
Johnson	592	461	131
Kingman	19	7	12
Leavenworth	89	71	18
Linn	23	12	11

Table 80. Full-Time Law Enforcement Employees, by Selected State Metropolitan and Nonmetropolitan Counties, 2012— continued

(Number)

State/county	Law enforcement employees	Officers	Civilians
Miami	44	25	19
Osage	47	26	21
Pottawatomie	43	26	17
Riley County Police Department	195	101	94
Sedgwick	496	171	325
Shawnee	200	108	92
Sumner	45	21	24
Wabaunsee	20	8	12
Nonmetropolitan Counties			
Allen	25	10	15
Anderson	29	9	20
Atchison	37	9	28
Barber	9	4	5
Barton	42	37	5
Bourbon	9	7	2
Brown	26	18	8
Chase	9	5	4
Chautauqua	15	6	9
Cherokee	48	19	29
Cheyenne	4	4	0
Clark	11	6	5
Clay	19	8	11
Cloud	17	7	10
Coffey	32	13	19
Comanche	9	4	5
Cowley	49	23	26
Crawford	67	31	36
Decatur	3	3	0
Dickinson	27	15	12
Edwards	9	5	4
Elk	9	4	5
Ellis	30	17	13
Ellsworth	15	8	7
Ford	64	27	37
Franklin	61	26	35
Gove	5	4	1
Graham	7	3	4
Grant	16	7	9
Gray	17	10	7
Greeley	7	3	4
Greenwood	21	12	9
Harper	11	5	6
Hodgeman	8	3	5
Jewell	10	5	5
Kearny	20	12	8
Kiowa	19	8	11
Labette	31	17	14
Lane	8	3	5
Lincoln	8	8	0
Logan	4	3	1
Lyon	40	26	14
Marion	14	9	5
Marshall	19	8	11
McPherson	19	16	3
Meade	16	5	11
Mitchell	18	6	12
Montgomery	34	23	11
Morris	12	7	5
Nemaha	17	8	9

Table 80. Full-Time Law Enforcement Employees, by Selected State Metropolitan and Nonmetropolitan Counties, 2012— continued

(Number)

State/county	Law enforcement employees	Officers	Civilians
Neosho	37	14	23
Ness	13	7	6
Norton	10	5	5
Osborne	14	7	7
Ottawa	17	5	12
Pawnee	9	8	1
Phillips	12	7	5
Pratt	15	9	6
Rawlins	8	3	5
Republic	13	8	5
Rice	20	5	15
Rooks	9	4	5
Rush	9	4	5
Russell	18	11	7
Saline	105	46	59
Scott	4	4	0
Seward	42	15	27
Sheridan	6	3	3
Smith	5	5	0
Stafford	9	4	5
Stanton	12	4	8
Thomas	11	5	6
Trego	4	3	1
Wallace	8	3	5
Washington	13	6	7
Wichita	8	4	4
Wilson	30	11	19
Woodson	11	7	4
KENTUCKY			
Metropolitan Counties			
Allen	17	15	2
Boone	138	131	7
Bourbon	8	7	1
Boyd	36	28	8
Bracken	5	4	1
Bullitt	52	47	5
Butler	8	6	2
Campbell	15	10	5
Campbell County Police Department	31	30	1
Christian	34	30	4
Clark	17	13	4
Daviess	44	39	5
Edmonson	8	6	2
Fayette	77	47	30
Gallatin	13	12	1
Grant	15	13	2
Greenup	17	15	2
Hardin	41	28	13
Henderson	25	21	4
Henry	9	8	1
Jefferson	267	217	50
Jessamine	34	26	8
Kenton	36	29	7
Kenton County Police Department	33	31	2
Larue	6	5	1
Meade	18	15	3
Oldham	20	18	2
Oldham County Police Department	31	29	2
Pendleton	7	6	1
Scott	31	29	2

Table 80. Full-Time Law Enforcement Employees, by Selected State Metropolitan and Nonmetropolitan Counties, 2012— continued

(Number)

State/county	Law enforcement employees	Officers	Civilians
Spencer	9	8	1
Trigg	10	7	3
Trimble	3	3	0
Warren	83	45	38
Woodford	12	9	3
Nonmetropolitan Counties			
Adair	8	6	2
Anderson	17	15	2
Ballard	14	12	2
Barren	24	20	4
Bath	3	3	0
Bell	24	14	10
Boyle	11	10	1
Breckinridge	12	9	3
Caldwell	10	8	2
Calloway	25	12	13
Carlisle	4	2	2
Carroll	5	4	1
Carter	8	5	3
Casey	9	6	3
Clinton	4	3	1
Crittenden	4	3	1
Cumberland	5	4	1
Estill	6	4	2
Fleming	7	6	1
Franklin	24	20	4
Fulton	4	3	1
Garrard	9	8	1
Graves	16	13	3
Grayson	11	8	3
Green	4	4	0
Harlan	24	21	3
Harrison	10	10	0
Hart	12	8	4
Hopkins	26	19	7
Johnson	14	11	3
Knott	7	6	1
Knox	12	8	4
Laurel	45	32	13
Lawrence	7	4	3
Lee	3	2	1
Letcher	14	12	2
Lewis	6	4	2
Lincoln	9	7	2
Livingston	7	6	1
Lyon	5	5	0
Madison	31	23	8
Magoffin	5	3	2
Marion	9	7	2
Marshall	24	22	2
Mason	13	11	2
McCracken	43	37	6
McCreary	9	7	2
Menifee	6	5	1
Mercer	12	11	1
Metcalfe	5	4	1
Monroe	14	4	10
Montgomery	16	14	2

Table 80. Full-Time Law Enforcement Employees, by Selected State Metropolitan and Nonmetropolitan Counties, 2012— continued

(Number)

State/county	Law enforcement employees	Officers	Civilians
Muhlenberg	13	13	0
Nelson	29	22	7
Nicholas	2	2	0
Ohio	22	18	4
Owen	6	5	1
Owsley	4	3	1
Perry	23	12	11
Perry County Police Department	2	2	0
Pike	26	17	9
Powell	5	3	2
Robertson	1	1	0
Rockcastle	5	4	1
Rowan	15	11	4
Simpson	14	12	2
Taylor	13	11	2
Todd	5	4	1
Union	9	8	1
Washington	5	5	0
Wayne	13	11	2
Webster	8	6	2
Whitley	20	14	6
Wolfe	5	4	1
LOUISIANA			
Metropolitan Counties			
Acadia	103	57	46
Ascension	284	248	36
Bossier	364	304	60
Caddo	668	458	210
Calcasieu	839	604	235
Cameron	71	61	10
East Baton Rouge	840	729	111
Grant	77	69	8
Iberia	312	193	119
Iberville	138	68	70
Jefferson	1,427	1,030	397
Lafayette	648	450	198
Lafourche	316	257	59
Livingston	243	243	0
Plaquemines	177	177	0
Pointe Coupee	90	38	52
Rapides	585	585	0
St. Bernard	238	198	40
St. Charles	369	265	104
St. Helena	48	27	21
St. John the Baptist	238	237	1
St. Martin	204	147	57
St. Tammany	690	526	164
Tangipahoa	258	206	52
Union	51	35	16
West Baton Rouge	178	141	37
West Feliciana	74	74	0
Nonmetropolitan Counties			
Allen	53	36	17
Assumption	81	50	31
Avoyelles	152	152	0
Bienville	57	35	22
Catahoula	114	13	101
East Carroll	138	12	126
Evangeline	62	25	37

Table 80. Full-Time Law Enforcement Employees, by Selected State Metropolitan and Nonmetropolitan Counties, 2012— continued

(Number)

State/county	Law enforcement employees	Officers	Civilians
La Salle	49	32	17
Madison	85	85	0
Morehouse	146	146	0
Richland	132	115	17
St. Mary	189	189	0
Washington	95	39	56
West Carroll	19	19	0
Winn	15	9	6
MAINE			
Metropolitan Counties			
Androscoggin	29	19	10
Cumberland	71	60	11
Penobscot	33	29	4
Sagadahoc	21	19	2
York	38	27	11
Nonmetropolitan Counties			
Aroostook	18	16	2
Franklin	27	15	12
Hancock	18	16	2
Kennebec	21	18	3
Knox	24	23	1
Lincoln	23	21	2
Oxford	22	20	2
Piscataquis	19	7	12
Somerset	17	15	2
Waldo	20	18	2
Washington	11	10	1
MARYLAND			
Metropolitan Counties			
Allegany	29	27	2
Anne Arundel	91	65	26
Anne Arundel County Police Department	871	654	217
Baltimore County	99	84	15
Baltimore County Police Department	2,093	1,838	255
Calvert	157	129	28
Carroll	126	96	30
Cecil	95	84	11
Charles	406	287	119
Frederick	233	171	62
Harford	371	285	86
Howard	67	49	18
Howard County Police Department	632	449	183
Montgomery	161	132	29
Montgomery County Police Department	1,536	1,121	415
Prince George's	314	225	89
Prince George's County Police Department	1,788	1,535	253
Queen Anne's	58	54	4
Somerset	25	19	6
St. Mary's	267	139	128
Washington	242	91	151
Wicomico	105	84	21
Worcester	57	46	11
Nonmetropolitan Counties			
Caroline	33	29	4
Dorchester	36	32	4
Garrett	51	28	23
Kent	27	22	5
Talbot	30	27	3
MICHIGAN			

Table 80. Full-Time Law Enforcement Employees, by Selected State Metropolitan and Nonmetropolitan Counties, 2012— continued

(Number)

State/county	Law enforcement employees	Officers	Civilians
Metropolitan Counties			
Barry	52	30	22
Bay	81	36	45
Berrien	150	64	86
Calhoun	170	76	94
Cass	71	34	37
Clinton	59	25	34
Eaton	133	70	63
Genesee	233	123	110
Ingham	179	102	77
Jackson	128	55	73
Kalamazoo	193	158	35
Kent	502	192	310
Lapeer	77	45	32
Livingston	101	67	34
Macomb	461	232	229
Midland	56	28	28
Monroe	155	70	85
Montcalm	53	26	27
Muskegon	112	45	67
Oakland	974	809	165
Ottawa	222	128	94
Saginaw	129	66	63
St. Clair	177	74	103
Van Buren	93	58	35
Washtenaw	313	139	174
Wayne	852	749	103
Nonmetropolitan Counties			
Alcona	24	14	10
Alger	12	10	2
Allegan	60	53	7
Alpena	26	12	14
Antrim	48	20	28
Arenac	22	12	10
Baraga	13	6	7
Benzie	35	11	24
Branch	49	25	24
Charlevoix	40	19	21
Cheboygan	37	20	17
Chippewa	35	15	20
Clare	80	24	56
Crawford	25	15	10
Delta	25	12	13
Dickinson	28	10	18
Emmet	46	24	22
Gladwin	39	16	23
Gogebic	22	16	6
Grand Traverse	120	63	57
Gratiot	35	19	16
Hillsdale	40	25	15
Houghton	28	19	9
Huron	45	21	24
Ionia	54	22	32
Iosco	23	4	19
Iron	18	9	9
Isabella	48	22	26
Kalkaska	33	16	17
Keweenaw	8	6	2
Lake	71	16	55

Table 80. Full-Time Law Enforcement Employees, by Selected State Metropolitan and Nonmetropolitan Counties, 2012— continued

(Number)

State/county	Law enforcement employees	Officers	Civilians
Leelanau	19	18	1
Lenawee	97	40	57
Luce	4	3	1
Mackinac	24	11	13
Manistee	32	15	17
Marquette	56	23	33
Mason	40	20	20
Mecosta	48	23	25
Menominee	31	14	17
Missaukee	28	13	15
Montmorency	23	9	14
Newaygo	62	25	37
Oceana	36	20	16
Ogemaw	34	16	18
Ontonagon	11	8	3
Osceola	37	18	19
Oscoda	16	10	6
Otsego	23	10	13
Presque Isle	24	13	11
Roscommon	39	25	14
Sanilac	56	24	32
Schoolcraft	10	2	8
Shiawassee	66	31	35
St. Joseph	51	26	25
Tuscola	48	26	22
Wexford	49	23	26
MINNESOTA			
Metropolitan Counties			
Anoka	240	116	124
Benton	71	24	47
Blue Earth	89	24	65
Carlton	45	19	26
Carver	133	69	64
Chisago	72	39	33
Clay	64	29	35
Dakota	176	77	99
Dodge	29	22	7
Fillmore	31	19	12
Hennepin	748	335	413
Houston	26	13	13
Isanti	53	20	33
Le Sueur	31	16	15
Mille Lacs	65	24	41
Nicollet	38	12	26
Olmsted	156	64	92
Polk	27	23	4
Ramsey	389	215	174
Scott	126	41	85
Sherburne	238	80	158
Sibley	22	11	11
St. Louis	240	103	137
Stearns	179	62	117
Wabasha	28	16	12
Washington	230	91	139
Wright	234	143	91
Nonmetropolitan Counties			
Aitkin	48	17	31
Becker	54	19	35
Beltrami	71	30	41

Table 80. Full-Time Law Enforcement Employees, by Selected State Metropolitan and Nonmetropolitan Counties, 2012— continued

(Number)

State/county	Law enforcement employees	Officers	Civilians
Big Stone	8	5	3
Brown	35	10	25
Cass	59	34	25
Chippewa	18	8	10
Clearwater	24	9	15
Cook	21	13	8
Cottonwood	20	9	11
Crow Wing	118	37	81
Douglas	75	26	49
Faribault	25	11	14
Freeborn	64	22	42
Goodhue	101	38	63
Grant	11	6	5
Hubbard	44	16	28
Itasca	71	59	12
Jackson	26	13	13
Kanabec	46	18	28
Kandiyohi	102	33	69
Kittson	10	5	5
Koochiching	18	10	8
Lac Qui Parle	11	7	4
Lake	28	16	12
Lake of the Woods	10	5	5
Lincoln	12	6	6
Lyon	44	13	31
Mahnomen	19	12	7
Marshall	18	12	6
Martin	29	11	18
McLeod	55	22	33
Meeker	42	19	23
Morrison	53	19	34
Mower	64	21	43
Murray	13	9	4
Nobles	34	12	22
Norman	7	4	3
Otter Tail	74	31	43
Pennington	27	7	20
Pine	75	31	44
Pipestone	22	12	10
Pope	15	8	7
Red Lake	11	7	4
Redwood	23	12	11
Renville	26	10	16
Rice	50	24	26
Rock	15	10	5
Roseau	20	9	11
Steele	25	20	5
Stevens	14	6	8
Swift	16	9	7
Todd	29	14	15
Traverse	12	5	7
Wadena	20	8	12
Waseca	26	11	15
Watonwan	21	7	14
Wilkin	17	6	11
Winona	57	20	37
Yellow Medicine	20	9	11
MISSISSIPPI			

Table 80. Full-Time Law Enforcement Employees, by Selected State Metropolitan and Nonmetropolitan Counties, 2012— continued

(Number)

State/county	Law enforcement employees	Officers	Civilians
Metropolitan Counties			
Harrison	339	106	233
Hinds	411	107	304
Jackson	183	143	40
Perry	14	6	8
Tate	47	20	27
Nonmetropolitan Counties			
Adams	63	34	29
Choctaw	11	5	6
Greene	24	4	20
Grenada	15	13	2
Itawamba	23	12	11
Jefferson	54	9	45
Jones	46	41	5
Kemper	16	10	6
Lee	126	44	82
Lincoln	46	20	26
Marion	21	17	4
Monroe	66	29	37
Oktibbeha	52	29	23
Panola	71	31	40
Pearl River	77	37	40
Prentiss	32	14	18
Scott	62	24	38
Tishomingo	24	10	14
Union	33	17	16
Winston	10	9	1
MISSOURI			
Metropolitan Counties			
Andrew	21	16	5
Bates	38	17	21
Bollinger	9	6	3
Boone	71	59	12
Buchanan	102	74	28
Callaway	24	21	3
Cape Girardeau	73	45	28
Cass	89	72	17
Christian	73	42	31
Clay	181	111	70
Clinton	23	15	8
Cole	79	53	26
Dallas	18	15	3
Franklin	137	26	111
Greene	267	140	127
Jackson	128	94	34
Jasper	147	95	52
Jefferson	213	140	73
Lafayette	39	37	2
Lincoln	74	37	37
McDonald	27	25	2
Moniteau	10	6	4
Newton	67	34	33
Osage	13	9	4
Platte	119	83	36
Polk	28	18	10
Ray	38	13	25
St. Charles	228	155	73
St. Louis County Police Department	1,080	821	259
Warren	60	34	26
Webster	31	16	15

Table 80. Full-Time Law Enforcement Employees, by Selected State Metropolitan and Nonmetropolitan Counties, 2012— continued

(Number)

State/county	Law enforcement employees	Officers	Civilians
Nonmetropolitan Counties			
Adair	30	13	17
Atchison	10	5	5
Audrain	38	33	5
Barry	32	18	14
Benton	22	14	8
Butler	40	17	23
Carroll	10	9	1
Carter	10	5	5
Cedar	17	9	8
Chariton	14	10	4
Clark	14	7	7
Cooper	8	7	1
Crawford	37	25	12
Daviess	7	6	1
Dent	19	14	5
Dunklin	19	10	9
Gasconade	13	12	1
Gentry	5	5	0
Grundy	14	4	10
Harrison	6	5	1
Henry	36	23	13
Hickory	14	9	5
Holt	9	4	5
Howard	11	8	3
Howell	31	23	8
Iron	13	8	5
Johnson	57	35	22
Knox	1	1	0
Laclede	23	22	1
Lawrence	37	26	11
Lewis	11	5	6
Linn	7	6	1
Livingston	22	10	12
Macon	15	12	3
Madison	10	8	2
Marion	36	15	21
Mercer	8	3	5
Miller	21	18	3
Mississippi	31	9	22
Monroe	8	7	1
Morgan	47	28	19
New Madrid	27	12	15
Nodaway	12	10	2
Oregon	10	6	4
Ozark	15	8	7
Pemiscot	39	15	24
Perry	31	22	9
Pettis	50	29	21
Phelps	60	27	33
Pike	29	12	17
Putnam	4	3	1
Randolph	36	18	18
Reynolds	9	8	1
Ripley	10	9	1
Saline	34	21	13
Scotland	5	2	3
Shannon	9	5	4
Shelby	9	5	4

Table 80. Full-Time Law Enforcement Employees, by Selected State Metropolitan and Nonmetropolitan Counties, 2012— continued

(Number)

State/county	Law enforcement employees	Officers	Civilians
St. Clair	66	20	46
Ste. Genevieve	21	20	1
St. Francois	69	56	13
Stoddard	24	12	12
Stone	54	44	10
Sullivan	5	4	1
Taney	49	36	13
Texas	37	9	28
Vernon	25	14	11
Washington	29	18	11
Wayne	15	6	9
Worth	4	3	1
Wright	12	5	7
MONTANA			
Metropolitan Counties			
Carbon	14	9	5
Cascade	46	34	12
Golden Valley	2	2	0
Nonmetropolitan Counties			
Beaverhead	18	7	11
Blaine	13	8	5
Broadwater	21	9	12
Carter	4	4	0
Chouteau	18	9	9
Custer	7	6	1
Daniels	3	3	0
Deer Lodge	19	19	0
Fallon	12	4	8
Fergus	21	9	12
Flathead	114	54	60
Gallatin	58	48	10
Garfield	3	2	1
Glacier	20	13	7
Hill	18	12	6
Jefferson	23	12	11
Judith Basin	5	4	1
Lake	39	24	15
Lewis and Clark	78	44	34
Liberty	9	5	4
Lincoln	38	21	17
Madison	16	10	6
McCone	4	4	0
Mineral	6	6	0
Musselshell	9	8	1
Park	16	15	1
Petroleum	1	1	0
Phillips	11	7	4
Pondera	8	7	1
Powder River	7	3	4
Prairie	3	3	0
Ravalli	71	31	40
Richland	10	9	1
Rosebud	22	12	10
Sanders	24	11	13
Sheridan	9	8	1
Silver Bow	96	49	47
Stillwater	15	9	6
Sweet Grass	13	7	6
Teton	14	11	3

Table 80. Full-Time Law Enforcement Employees, by Selected State Metropolitan and Nonmetropolitan Counties, 2012— continued

(Number)

State/county	Law enforcement employees	Officers	Civilians
Toole	21	13	8
Treasure	2	2	0
Valley	15	6	9
Wheatland	9	5	4
Wibaux	2	2	0
NEBRASKA			
Metropolitan Counties			
Dakota	16	15	1
Dixon	12	7	5
Douglas	201	120	81
Hall	38	30	8
Hamilton	19	9	10
Howard	12	5	7
Lancaster	93	77	16
Merrick	11	6	5
Sarpy	197	130	67
Saunders	19	11	8
Seward	21	12	9
Nonmetropolitan Counties			
Adams	19	17	2
Antelope	13	5	8
Arthur	1	1	0
Banner	1	1	0
Boone	12	5	7
Box Butte	18	5	13
Boyd	3	3	0
Brown	8	4	4
Buffalo	42	24	18
Burt	5	5	0
Butler	11	10	1
Cedar	6	6	0
Chase	8	4	4
Cherry	6	5	1
Cheyenne	19	9	10
Colfax	16	8	8
Cuming	6	5	1
Custer	7	6	1
Dawes	12	7	5
Dawson	65	33	32
Deuel	5	4	1
Dodge	26	19	7
Dundy	8	4	4
Fillmore	13	7	6
Franklin	7	3	4
Frontier	8	5	3
Furnas	12	7	5
Gage	16	13	3
Garden	10	4	6
Garfield	2	2	0
Gosper	5	4	1
Greeley	3	2	1
Harlan	8	4	4
Hayes	2	2	0
Hitchcock	7	4	3
Holt	6	5	1
Hooker	2	2	0
Jefferson	15	7	8
Johnson	10	5	5
Kearney	12	7	5

Table 80. Full-Time Law Enforcement Employees, by Selected State Metropolitan and Nonmetropolitan Counties, 2012— continued

(Number)

State/county	Law enforcement employees	Officers	Civilians
Keith	16	8	8
Keya Paha	1	1	0
Kimball	10	4	6
Knox	13	4	9
Lincoln	58	19	39
Logan	2	2	0
Loup	1	1	0
Madison	55	30	25
Morrill	9	4	5
Nance	11	7	4
Nemaha	5	5	0
Nuckolls	7	4	3
Otoe	25	14	11
Pawnee	5	4	1
Perkins	10	5	5
Phelps	23	5	18
Pierce	9	4	5
Platte	67	21	46
Polk	12	7	5
Red Willow	15	6	9
Richardson	10	6	4
Rock	6	2	4
Saline	9	9	0
Scotts Bluff	24	17	7
Sheridan	7	6	1
Sherman	6	5	1
Stanton	8	7	1
Thayer	11	7	4
Thomas	1	1	0
Thurston	10	7	3
Valley	9	4	5
Wayne	6	5	1
Webster	9	6	3
Wheeler	2	2	0
York	23	9	14
NEVADA			
Metropolitan Counties			
Carson City	129	90	39
Storey	21	20	1
Washoe	671	403	268
Nonmetropolitan Counties			
Churchill	44	36	8
Douglas	115	102	13
Elko	66	51	15
Esmeralda	15	9	6
Eureka	21	13	8
Humboldt	49	34	15
Lander	31	19	12
Lincoln	31	25	6
Lyon	104	76	28
Mineral	24	17	7
Nye	135	101	34
Pershing	20	13	7
White Pine	33	27	6
NEW HAMPSHIRE			
Metropolitan County			
Rockingham	45	25	20

Table 80. Full-Time Law Enforcement Employees, by Selected State Metropolitan and Nonmetropolitan Counties, 2012— continued

(Number)

State/county	Law enforcement employees	Officers	Civilians
Nonmetropolitan Counties			
Carroll	26	13	13
Cheshire	20	10	10
Merrimack	32	20	12
NEW JERSEY			
Metropolitan Counties			
Atlantic	140	116	24
Bergen	491	414	77
Bergen County Police Department	183	85	98
Burlington	83	65	18
Camden	176	148	28
Cape May	183	132	51
Cumberland	62	56	6
Essex	440	358	82
Gloucester	93	80	13
Hudson	342	235	107
Hunterdon	25	21	4
Mercer	167	132	35
Middlesex	221	182	39
Monmouth	133	105	28
Morris	118	85	33
Ocean	230	130	100
Passaic	680	549	131
Salem	204	166	38
Somerset	214	175	39
Sussex	147	122	25
Union	208	166	42
Warren	21	17	4
NEW MEXICO			
Metropolitan Counties			
Bernalillo	344	281	63
Dona Ana	213	122	91
Sandoval	56	48	8
Santa Fe	106	81	25
Torrance	17	14	3
Valencia	54	42	12
Nonmetropolitan Counties			
Catron	13	7	6
Chaves	48	38	10
Cibola	23	17	6
Colfax	13	11	2
Curry	28	18	10
Eddy	59	49	10
Grant	43	40	3
Guadalupe	7	5	2
Hidalgo	12	9	3
Lea	60	49	11
Lincoln	28	21	7
Luna	36	32	4
McKinley	43	34	9
Otero	61	42	19
Quay	8	7	1
Rio Arriba	27	24	3
Roosevelt	16	13	3
San Miguel	9	8	1
Sierra	17	15	2
Socorro	14	11	3
Taos	27	20	7
Union	7	7	0

Table 80. Full-Time Law Enforcement Employees, by Selected State Metropolitan and Nonmetropolitan Counties, 2012— continued

(Number)

State/county	Law enforcement employees	Officers	Civilians
NEW YORK			
Metropolitan Counties			
Albany	164	118	46
Broome	73	53	20
Chemung	49	45	4
Dutchess	128	95	33
Erie	181	140	41
Herkimer	14	5	9
Jefferson	53	44	9
Livingston	69	47	22
Madison	40	32	8
Monroe	327	272	55
Nassau	3,022	2,247	775
Niagara	144	106	38
Oneida	101	81	20
Ontario	98	64	34
Orange	110	98	12
Oswego	82	66	16
Rensselaer	35	33	2
Rockland	105	77	28
Saratoga	153	112	41
Schenectady	16	10	6
Schoharie	25	15	10
Suffolk	384	268	116
Suffolk County Police Department	2,960	2,414	546
Tioga	51	32	19
Tompkins	44	41	3
Ulster	76	57	19
Washington	47	33	14
Wayne	61	53	8
Westchester Public Safety	334	262	72
Yates	39	25	14
Nonmetropolitan Counties			
Allegany	45	26	19
Cattaraugus	90	68	22
Cayuga	43	39	4
Chautauqua	100	57	43
Chenango	39	24	15
Cortland	50	33	17
Delaware	24	16	8
Essex	23	21	2
Franklin	50	43	7
Fulton	40	24	16
Genesee	76	48	28
Hamilton	6	5	1
Lewis	29	18	11
Montgomery	97	76	21
Otsego	18	16	2
Schuyler	20	17	3
Seneca	45	32	13
Steuben	52	40	12
St. Lawrence	34	33	1
Sullivan	36	36	0
Wyoming	39	30	9
NORTH CAROLINA			
Metropolitan Counties			
Alamance	277	121	156
Alexander	49	30	19
Brunswick	207	141	66
Buncombe	367	228	139

Table 80. Full-Time Law Enforcement Employees, by Selected State Metropolitan and Nonmetropolitan Counties, 2012— continued

(Number)

State/county	Law enforcement employees	Officers	Civilians
Burke	114	85	29
Cabarrus	320	194	126
Caldwell	103	67	36
Catawba	178	130	48
Chatham	110	85	25
Craven	124	72	52
Cumberland	542	297	245
Currituck	101	64	37
Davidson	192	127	65
Davie	55	48	7
Durham	443	169	274
Edgecombe	135	53	82
Forsyth	487	206	281
Franklin	103	65	38
Gaston	214	124	90
Gaston County Police Department	207	131	76
Gates	12	11	1
Guilford	649	253	396
Haywood	94	52	42
Henderson	184	129	55
Hoke	112	60	52
Iredell	227	160	67
Johnston	179	103	76
Jones	25	15	10
Lincoln	154	101	53
Madison	40	23	17
Mecklenburg[1]	1,179	330	849
Nash	134	77	57
New Hanover	432	325	107
Onslow	253	119	134
Orange	139	105	34
Pamlico	44	15	29
Pender	110	61	49
Person	83	43	40
Pitt	318	124	194
Randolph	225	163	62
Rockingham	141	99	42
Rowan	182	132	50
Stokes	63	43	20
Union	246	183	63
Wake	917	381	536
Wayne	155	90	65
Yadkin	58	32	26
Nonmetropolitan Counties			
Alleghany	26	11	15
Anson	62	32	30
Ashe	56	25	31
Avery	49	26	23
Beaufort	80	46	34
Bertie	36	24	12
Bladen	73	47	26
Camden	20	18	2
Carteret	83	47	36
Caswell	55	34	21
Cherokee	63	26	37
Chowan	33	16	17
Clay	41	15	26
Cleveland	162	90	72
Columbus	116	66	50

Table 80. Full-Time Law Enforcement Employees, by Selected State Metropolitan and Nonmetropolitan Counties, 2012— continued

(Number)

State/county	Law enforcement employees	Officers	Civilians
Dare	121	63	58
Duplin	90	66	24
Graham	23	15	8
Granville	92	54	38
Greene	49	23	26
Halifax	68	63	5
Harnett	215	119	96
Hertford	55	22	33
Hyde	21	16	5
Jackson	74	48	26
Lee	86	52	34
Lenoir	111	63	48
Macon	66	47	19
Martin	36	34	2
McDowell	60	45	15
Mitchell	18	17	1
Montgomery	56	30	26
Moore	116	74	42
Northampton	50	25	25
Pasquotank	48	42	6
Perquimans	14	11	3
Polk	37	28	9
Richmond	82	51	31
Robeson	232	132	100
Rutherford	127	75	52
Sampson	129	92	37
Scotland	65	38	27
Stanly	88	63	25
Surry	99	57	42
Swain	45	23	22
Transylvania	78	59	19
Tyrrell	16	10	6
Vance	75	37	38
Warren	64	36	28
Washington	42	21	21
Watauga	74	44	30
Wilkes	116	69	47
Wilson	135	82	53
Yancey	35	20	15
NORTH DAKOTA			
Metropolitan Counties			
Burleigh	93	47	46
Cass	139	78	61
Grand Forks	39	32	7
Morton	38	21	17
Oliver	5	4	1
Sioux	1	1	0
Nonmetropolitan Counties			
Adams	4	4	0
Barnes	7	6	1
Benson	4	4	0
Billings	5	5	0
Bottineau	14	10	4
Bowman	3	3	0
Burke	7	6	1
Cavalier	10	5	5
Dickey	5	4	1
Divide	7	7	0

Table 80. Full-Time Law Enforcement Employees, by Selected State Metropolitan and Nonmetropolitan Counties, 2012— continued

(Number)

State/county	Law enforcement employees	Officers	Civilians
Dunn	12	11	1
Eddy	5	4	1
Emmons	4	3	1
Foster	3	3	0
Golden Valley	5	4	1
Grant	4	4	0
Griggs	5	4	1
Hettinger	5	5	0
Kidder	4	3	1
Lamoure	5	4	1
Logan	2	2	0
McHenry	7	7	0
McIntosh	3	3	0
McKenzie	24	13	11
McLean	35	19	16
Mercer	23	14	9
Mountrail	22	12	10
Nelson	5	5	0
Pembina	13	7	6
Pierce	7	3	4
Ramsey	7	6	1
Ransom	5	4	1
Renville	5	5	0
Richland	24	13	11
Rolette	18	9	9
Sargent	5	4	1
Sheridan	3	3	0
Slope	1	1	0
Stark	20	17	3
Steele	3	3	0
Stutsman	10	8	2
Towner	3	3	0
Traill	13	8	5
Walsh	15	10	5
Ward	59	25	34
Wells	3	3	0
Williams	51	31	20
OHIO			
Metropolitan Counties			
Allen	149	70	79
Belmont	64	55	9
Brown	46	30	16
Clark	150	120	30
Delaware	209	90	119
Fairfield	137	110	27
Geauga	115	51	64
Hamilton	793	314	479
Hocking	26	21	5
Lake	166	35	131
Mahoning	220	204	16
Medina	138	57	81
Morrow	50	21	29
Portage	133	72	61
Summit	422	328	94
Union	53	33	20
Nonmetropolitan Counties			
Ashland	68	38	30
Ashtabula	68	29	39
Athens	28	23	5
Auglaize	55	23	32

Table 80. Full-Time Law Enforcement Employees, by Selected State Metropolitan and Nonmetropolitan Counties, 2012— continued

(Number)

State/county	Law enforcement employees	Officers	Civilians
Clinton	65	35	30
Columbiana	29	19	10
Coshocton	51	41	10
Crawford	57	23	34
Darke	60	36	24
Defiance	33	20	13
Fayette	36	20	16
Hancock	84	35	49
Highland	46	27	19
Holmes	46	31	15
Logan	78	34	44
Marion	27	22	5
Mercer	52	26	26
Monroe	22	15	7
Morgan	14	9	5
Muskingum	107	71	36
Paulding	16	11	5
Pike	23	16	7
Preble	47	13	34
Putnam	52	28	24
Sandusky	53	31	22
Scioto	74	39	35
Van Wert	34	19	15
Washington	85	46	39
Wayne	60	52	8
Williams	15	12	3
OKLAHOMA			
Metropolitan Counties			
Canadian	69	53	16
Cleveland	177	65	112
Comanche	38	29	9
Cotton	11	4	7
Creek	75	48	27
Grady	16	15	1
Le Flore	18	12	6
Lincoln	44	19	25
Logan	60	33	27
McClain	31	19	12
Oklahoma	750	209	541
Okmulgee	16	15	1
Osage	76	43	33
Pawnee	21	8	13
Rogers	42	36	6
Sequoyah	43	19	24
Tulsa	546	254	292
Wagoner	51	21	30
Nonmetropolitan Counties			
Adair	32	10	22
Alfalfa	9	4	5
Atoka	23	7	16
Beaver	12	7	5
Beckham	32	11	21
Blaine	17	7	10
Bryan	17	15	2
Caddo	36	16	20
Carter	54	21	33
Cherokee	35	25	10
Choctaw	16	5	11
Cimarron	6	4	2

Table 80. Full-Time Law Enforcement Employees, by Selected State Metropolitan and Nonmetropolitan Counties, 2012— continued

(Number)

State/county	Law enforcement employees	Officers	Civilians
Coal	17	5	12
Craig	26	10	16
Custer	53	13	40
Delaware	42	18	24
Dewey	12	5	7
Ellis	16	6	10
Garfield	63	22	41
Garvin	27	17	10
Grant	10	6	4
Greer	8	3	5
Harmon	4	3	1
Harper	8	5	3
Haskell	16	9	7
Hughes	11	5	6
Jackson	36	11	25
Jefferson	27	6	21
Johnston	26	8	18
Kay	20	13	7
Kingfisher	15	7	8
Kiowa	13	7	6
Latimer	13	6	7
Love	19	8	11
Major	11	5	6
Marshall	24	8	16
Mayes	48	20	28
McCurtain	21	17	4
McIntosh	28	13	15
Murray	20	6	14
Muskogee	42	34	8
Noble	22	7	15
Nowata	21	10	11
Okfuskee	17	6	11
Ottawa	47	24	23
Payne	84	32	52
Pittsburg	65	18	47
Pontotoc	41	15	26
Pottawatomie	27	22	5
Pushmataha	13	8	5
Roger Mills	12	7	5
Seminole	37	16	21
Stephens	64	18	46
Texas	40	12	28
Tillman	27	6	21
Washington	57	28	29
Washita	29	9	20
Woods	6	5	1
Woodward	34	9	25
OREGON			
Metropolitan Counties			
Benton	78	64	14
Clackamas	431	219	212
Columbia	14	11	3
Deschutes	210	82	128
Jackson	166	108	58
Josephine	38	8	30
Lane	282	53	229
Linn	163	76	87
Marion	338	96	242
Multnomah	736	102	634
Polk	57	22	35

Table 80. Full-Time Law Enforcement Employees, by Selected State Metropolitan and Nonmetropolitan Counties, 2012— continued

(Number)

State/county	Law enforcement employees	Officers	Civilians
Washington	539	237	302
Yamhill	96	45	51
Nonmetropolitan Counties			
Baker	24	11	13
Clatsop	61	31	30
Coos	86	28	58
Crook	29	17	12
Curry	34	12	22
Douglas	144	112	32
Gilliam	7	6	1
Grant	16	5	11
Harney	21	5	16
Hood River	27	16	11
Jefferson	40	13	27
Klamath	68	27	41
Lake	21	8	13
Lincoln	87	27	60
Malheur	62	19	43
Morrow	27	27	0
Sherman	9	8	1
Tillamook	60	56	4
Umatilla	74	49	25
Union	30	17	13
Wallowa	13	7	6
Wasco	29	16	13
Wheeler	12	3	9
PENNSYLVANIA			
Metropolitan Counties			
Adams	14	12	2
Allegheny	187	155	32
Allegheny County Police Department	262	206	56
Beaver	31	24	7
Berks	110	95	15
Blair	10	6	4
Butler	23	20	3
Cambria	30	24	6
Centre	17	13	4
Cumberland	27	27	0
Erie	43	36	7
Franklin	21	17	4
Lancaster	58	50	8
Lycoming	16	11	5
Mercer	18	15	3
Monroe	44	22	22
Montgomery	121	102	19
Northampton	55	51	4
Pike	22	18	4
Washington	27	27	0
Westmoreland	61	53	8
York	109	99	10
Nonmetropolitan Counties			
Bedford	9	7	2
Bradford	11	9	2
Clarion	10	7	3
Clearfield	12	8	4
Elk	6	5	1
Greene	6	5	1
Huntingdon	11	10	1
Indiana	19	16	3
Jefferson	8	7	1

Table 80. Full-Time Law Enforcement Employees, by Selected State Metropolitan and Nonmetropolitan Counties, 2012— continued

(Number)

State/county	Law enforcement employees	Officers	Civilians
Lawrence	15	11	4
Northumberland	9	7	2
Schuylkill	17	13	4
Snyder	5	5	0
Tioga	8	6	2
Union	9	8	1
Warren	11	9	2
Wayne	18	12	6
SOUTH CAROLINA			
Metropolitan Counties			
Aiken	244	136	108
Anderson	386	226	160
Beaufort	259	233	26
Berkeley	238	150	88
Calhoun	42	26	16
Charleston	765	255	510
Chester	107	43	64
Darlington	134	76	58
Dorchester	233	127	106
Edgefield	64	34	30
Fairfield	52	45	7
Florence	226	118	108
Greenville	503	413	90
Horry	360	67	293
Horry County Police Department	246	228	18
Jasper	39	34	5
Kershaw	71	63	8
Lancaster	163	102	61
Laurens	117	66	51
Lexington	389	256	133
Pickens	133	96	37
Richland	558	515	43
Saluda	53	18	35
Spartanburg	328	299	29
Sumter	145	111	34
Union	35	32	3
York	341	178	163
Nonmetropolitan Counties			
Allendale	15	13	2
Bamberg	18	13	5
Barnwell	14	13	1
Chesterfield	73	41	32
Clarendon	54	45	9
Colleton	121	61	60
Dillon	42	31	11
Georgetown	152	95	57
Greenwood	72	65	7
Hampton	40	35	5
Lee	31	27	4
Marion	37	30	7
Marlboro	30	25	5
McCormick	38	15	23
Newberry	96	47	49
Oconee	120	83	37
Orangeburg	126	92	34
Williamsburg	71	35	36
SOUTH DAKOTA			
Metropolitan Counties			

Table 80. Full-Time Law Enforcement Employees, by Selected State Metropolitan and Nonmetropolitan Counties, 2012— continued

(Number)

State/county	Law enforcement employees	Officers	Civilians
Custer	12	11	1
Lincoln	17	15	2
McCook	7	6	1
Meade	54	17	37
Minnehaha	200	86	114
Pennington	363	77	286
Turner	10	8	2
Union	25	8	17
Nonmetropolitan Counties			
Aurora	4	3	1
Beadle	25	6	19
Bennett	4	4	0
Bon Homme	8	3	5
Brookings	21	13	8
Brown	51	16	35
Brule	9	4	5
Buffalo	1	1	0
Butte	14	4	10
Campbell	2	2	0
Charles Mix	17	6	11
Clark	3	3	0
Clay	11	7	4
Codington	30	9	21
Corson	5	4	1
Davison	8	6	2
Day	6	3	3
Deuel	8	4	4
Dewey	4	3	1
Douglas	3	3	0
Edmunds	7	4	3
Fall River	16	6	10
Faulk	11	4	7
Grant	9	3	6
Gregory	3	2	1
Haakon	1	1	0
Hamlin	4	4	0
Hand	4	3	1
Hanson	2	2	0
Harding	3	2	1
Hughes	45	6	39
Hutchinson	3	3	0
Hyde	2	2	0
Jackson	2	2	0
Jerauld	4	3	1
Jones	2	2	0
Kingsbury	5	4	1
Lake	10	5	5
Lawrence	39	13	26
Lyman	5	4	1
Marshall	11	6	5
McPherson	2	2	0
Mellette	4	4	0
Miner	4	3	1
Moody	8	4	4
Perkins	4	3	1
Potter	3	2	1
Roberts	28	4	24
Sanborn	3	3	0
Shannon	1	1	0

Table 80. Full-Time Law Enforcement Employees, by Selected State Metropolitan and Nonmetropolitan Counties, 2012— continued

(Number)

State/county	Law enforcement employees	Officers	Civilians
Spink	13	8	5
Stanley	6	5	1
Sully	3	3	0
Todd	2	1	1
Tripp	5	4	1
Walworth	11	3	8
Yankton	30	12	18
Ziebach	2	2	0
TENNESSEE			
Metropolitan Counties			
Anderson	176	59	117
Blount	271	129	142
Bradley	201	106	95
Campbell	67	35	32
Cannon	33	14	19
Carter	143	55	88
Cheatham	72	37	35
Chester	46	13	33
Crockett	33	15	18
Dickson	133	61	72
Fayette	91	41	50
Grainger	36	16	20
Hamblen	83	32	51
Hamilton	365	155	210
Hartsville-Trousdale	41	19	22
Hawkins	102	50	52
Hickman	39	20	19
Jefferson	94	44	50
Knox	1,130	459	671
Loudon	69	44	25
Macon	60	25	35
Madison	231	74	157
Marion	45	20	25
Maury	146	80	66
Montgomery	315	75	240
Morgan	50	19	31
Polk	51	19	32
Roane	68	36	32
Robertson	150	43	107
Rutherford	405	213	192
Sequatchie	38	18	20
Shelby	1,827	526	1,301
Smith	55	28	27
Sullivan	255	114	141
Sumner	268	72	196
Tipton	92	51	41
Unicoi	38	26	12
Union	37	24	13
Washington	215	90	125
Williamson	216	110	106
Wilson	219	92	127
Nonmetropolitan Counties			
Bedford	79	36	43
Benton	59	20	39
Bledsoe	38	12	26
Carroll	45	23	22
Claiborne	91	33	58
Clay	22	13	9
Cocke	67	37	30
Coffee	85	46	39

Table 80. Full-Time Law Enforcement Employees, by Selected State Metropolitan and Nonmetropolitan Counties, 2012— continued

(Number)

State/county	Law enforcement employees	Officers	Civilians
Cumberland	104	48	56
Decatur	32	14	18
DeKalb	43	22	21
Dyer	78	32	46
Fentress	35	22	13
Franklin	80	35	45
Gibson	76	30	46
Giles	67	29	38
Greene	148	56	92
Grundy	25	13	12
Hancock	32	12	20
Hardeman	74	27	47
Hardin	44	20	24
Haywood	46	19	27
Henderson	54	24	30
Henry	67	33	34
Houston	24	11	13
Humphreys	37	20	17
Jackson	40	13	27
Johnson	46	16	30
Lake	20	9	11
Lauderdale	62	21	41
Lawrence	90	45	45
Lewis	32	16	16
Lincoln	61	26	35
Marshall	51	22	29
McMinn	69	32	37
McNairy	37	17	20
Meigs	31	14	17
Monroe	68	37	31
Moore	26	12	14
Obion	62	26	36
Overton	56	24	32
Perry	32	16	16
Pickett	15	10	5
Putnam	126	62	64
Rhea	53	53	0
Scott	67	30	37
Sevier	226	98	128
Stewart	41	18	23
Van Buren	17	10	7
Warren	81	42	39
Wayne	47	14	33
Weakley	43	22	21
White	67	32	35
TEXAS			
Metropolitan Counties			
Aransas	71	22	49
Archer	17	8	9
Armstrong	7	3	4
Atascosa	76	31	45
Austin	66	42	24
Bandera	64	27	37
Bastrop	212	70	142
Bell	254	93	161
Bexar	1,627	527	1,100
Bowie	51	43	8
Brazoria	347	166	181

Table 80. Full-Time Law Enforcement Employees, by Selected State Metropolitan and Nonmetropolitan Counties, 2012— continued

(Number)

State/county	Law enforcement employees	Officers	Civilians
Burleson	33	13	20
Caldwell	104	24	80
Callahan	13	5	8
Cameron	502	112	390
Carson	17	6	11
Chambers	80	40	40
Clay	23	11	12
Collin	480	169	311
Comal	246	123	123
Coryell	65	31	34
Crosby	14	5	9
Denton	583	234	349
Ector	203	85	118
Ellis	205	75	130
El Paso	1,126	258	868
Fort Bend	732	568	164
Goliad	27	11	16
Grayson	134	63	71
Gregg	233	104	129
Guadalupe	217	87	130
Hardin	66	31	35
Harris	3,855	2,139	1,716
Hays	294	122	172
Hidalgo	752	240	512
Hood	135	52	83
Hudspeth	29	14	15
Hunt	137	42	95
Irion	8	4	4
Johnson	137	91	46
Jones	23	8	15
Kaufman	233	84	149
Kendall	74	48	26
Lampasas	36	20	16
Liberty	67	48	19
Lubbock	442	188	254
Lynn	21	6	15
Martin	8	4	4
McLennan	338	115	223
Medina	66	30	36
Midland	186	76	110
Montgomery	721	412	309
Newton	20	20	0
Nueces	313	72	241
Oldham	11	6	5
Orange	138	63	75
Parker	117	85	32
Potter	210	100	110
Randall	175	77	98
Robertson	32	13	19
Rockwall	122	39	83
Rusk	78	43	35
San Patricio	100	46	54
Somervell	41	19	22
Tarrant	1,421	410	1,011
Taylor	207	86	121
Tom Green	166	55	111
Travis	1,571	1,173	398
Upshur	73	45	28
Victoria	189	112	77

Table 80. Full-Time Law Enforcement Employees, by Selected State Metropolitan and Nonmetropolitan Counties, 2012— continued

(Number)

State/county	Law enforcement employees	Officers	Civilians
Waller	71	52	19
Webb	357	173	184
Wichita	199	72	127
Williamson	489	221	268
Wilson	72	30	42
Wise	136	53	83
Nonmetropolitan Counties			
Anderson	80	38	42
Andrews	33	13	20
Angelina	111	44	67
Bailey	19	6	13
Baylor	7	2	5
Bee	42	19	23
Blanco	27	10	17
Borden	3	2	1
Bosque	37	17	20
Brewster	23	12	11
Briscoe	2	2	0
Brown	65	26	39
Burnet	60	45	15
Calhoun	63	23	40
Camp	18	7	11
Cass	44	19	25
Castro	19	9	10
Cherokee	74	29	45
Childress	29	5	24
Cochran	14	7	7
Coke	5	4	1
Coleman	6	5	1
Collingsworth	10	5	5
Colorado	50	21	29
Comanche	27	10	17
Concho	14	7	7
Cottle	2	2	0
Crane	11	6	5
Culberson	11	6	5
Dallam	34	5	29
Dawson	19	7	12
Deaf Smith	31	11	20
Delta	19	8	11
Dewitt	45	13	32
Dickens	6	2	4
Dimmit	39	16	23
Donley	9	5	4
Duval	35	21	14
Eastland	27	9	18
Edwards	11	5	6
Erath	58	23	35
Fannin	23	16	7
Fayette	47	23	24
Fisher	9	5	4
Floyd	7	3	4
Foard	4	3	1
Franklin	19	10	9
Freestone	39	24	15
Frio	33	13	20
Gaines	24	14	10
Gillespie	41	28	13
Glasscock	5	4	1

Table 80. Full-Time Law Enforcement Employees, by Selected State Metropolitan and Nonmetropolitan Counties, 2012— continued

(Number)

State/county	Law enforcement employees	Officers	Civilians
Gonzales	43	15	28
Gray	43	13	30
Grimes	52	27	25
Hale	70	20	50
Hall	9	3	6
Hamilton	21	9	12
Hansford	8	3	5
Hardeman	12	7	5
Harrison	103	62	41
Hartley	5	5	0
Haskell	9	3	6
Hemphill	16	8	8
Henderson	149	90	59
Hill	68	29	39
Hockley	27	14	13
Hopkins	52	27	25
Houston	45	20	25
Howard	50	16	34
Hutchinson	35	12	23
Jack	30	10	20
Jackson	33	14	19
Jasper	47	19	28
Jeff Davis	5	3	2
Jim Hogg	43	19	24
Jim Wells	66	29	37
Kenedy	18	11	7
Kent	6	3	3
Kerr	96	45	51
Kimble	14	9	5
King	2	2	0
Kinney	16	7	9
Kleberg	68	19	49
Knox	9	3	6
Lamar	76	25	51
La Salle	19	11	8
Lavaca	30	12	18
Lee	41	13	28
Leon	37	22	15
Limestone	88	22	66
Lipscomb	10	6	4
Live Oak	36	11	25
Llano	53	28	25
Loving	4	3	1
Madison	24	12	12
Marion	15	14	1
Mason	9	5	4
McCulloch	14	6	8
McMullen	8	7	1
Milam	61	19	42
Mills	10	6	4
Mitchell	10	4	6
Montague	28	11	17
Moore	44	17	27
Morris	22	9	13
Motley	2	2	0
Nacogdoches	84	40	44
Navarro	126	65	61
Nolan	28	11	17
Ochiltree	17	8	9

Table 80. Full-Time Law Enforcement Employees, by Selected State Metropolitan and Nonmetropolitan Counties, 2012— continued

(Number)

State/county	Law enforcement employees	Officers	Civilians
Palo Pinto	54	18	36
Panola	52	27	25
Parmer	19	6	13
Pecos	39	24	15
Polk	99	48	51
Presidio	32	14	18
Rains	23	11	12
Reagan	18	10	8
Real	8	4	4
Red River	27	12	15
Reeves	43	18	25
Refugio	45	17	28
Roberts	6	5	1
Sabine	18	8	10
San Augustine	18	8	10
San Jacinto	60	32	28
Schleicher	12	6	6
Scurry	42	9	33
Shackelford	15	5	10
Shelby	35	20	15
Sherman	10	10	0
Stephens	26	8	18
Sterling	5	5	0
Stonewall	10	3	7
Sutton	14	4	10
Swisher	11	4	7
Terrell	12	5	7
Terry	32	10	22
Throckmorton	5	1	4
Titus	63	29	34
Trinity	18	10	8
Tyler	32	17	15
Upton	24	10	14
Uvalde	68	19	49
Val Verde	61	44	17
Van Zandt	72	28	44
Walker	68	33	35
Ward	33	15	18
Washington	52	30	22
Wharton	74	42	32
Wheeler	13	7	6
Wilbarger	18	7	11
Willacy	43	13	30
Winkler	24	10	14
Wood	66	25	41
Yoakum	21	11	10
Young	36	16	20
Zapata	95	43	52
UTAH			
Metropolitan Counties			
Box Elder	83	27	56
Cache	149	112	37
Davis	329	124	205
Juab	24	9	15
Morgan	12	10	2
Salt Lake County Unified Police Department	564	418	146
Tooele	91	72	19
Utah	388	114	274
Washington	155	44	111
Weber	80	79	1

Table 80. Full-Time Law Enforcement Employees, by Selected State Metropolitan and Nonmetropolitan Counties, 2012— continued

(Number)

State/county	Law enforcement employees	Officers	Civilians
Nonmetropolitan Counties			
Beaver	75	19	56
Carbon	49	41	8
Daggett	24	18	6
Duchesne	54	40	14
Emery	41	34	7
Garfield	28	7	21
Grand	35	26	9
Iron	76	69	7
Kane	48	32	16
Millard	48	30	18
Piute	3	3	0
Rich	10	4	6
San Juan	36	26	10
Sanpete	53	39	14
Sevier	68	52	16
Summit	96	54	42
Uintah	68	21	47
Wasatch	45	38	7
Wayne	6	5	1
VERMONT			
Metropolitan Counties			
Chittenden	20	18	2
Franklin	13	12	1
Grand Isle	3	2	1
Nonmetropolitan Counties			
Addison	6	6	0
Bennington	10	7	3
Caledonia	5	5	0
Essex	3	3	0
Lamoille	19	9	10
Orange	14	8	6
Orleans	10	7	3
Rutland	14	11	3
Washington	13	11	2
Windham	15	11	4
Windsor	15	12	3
VIRGINIA			
Metropolitan Counties			
Albemarle County Police Department	142	115	27
Amelia	26	16	10
Amherst	49	44	5
Appomattox	19	18	1
Arlington County Police Department	437	364	73
Augusta	72	62	10
Bedford	89	82	7
Botetourt	115	93	22
Buckingham	25	17	8
Campbell	65	56	9
Caroline	65	45	20
Charles City	14	8	6
Chesterfield County Police Department	592	489	103
Clarke	29	17	12
Craig	14	9	5
Culpeper	92	80	12
Dinwiddie	41	38	3
Fairfax County Police Department	1,650	1,354	296
Fauquier	137	119	18
Floyd	29	19	10

Table 80. Full-Time Law Enforcement Employees, by Selected State Metropolitan and Nonmetropolitan Counties, 2012— continued

(Number)

State/county	Law enforcement employees	Officers	Civilians
Fluvanna	39	26	13
Franklin	90	71	19
Frederick	126	109	17
Giles	38	27	11
Gloucester	56	46	10
Goochland	40	30	10
Greene	37	22	15
Hanover	228	211	17
Henrico County Police Department	772	595	177
Isle of Wight	53	46	7
James City County Police Department	98	93	5
King William	32	20	12
Loudoun	633	527	106
Mathews	18	12	6
Montgomery	121	105	16
Nelson	20	16	4
New Kent	43	30	13
Powhatan	56	40	16
Prince George County Police Department	76	53	23
Prince William County Police Department	710	593	117
Pulaski	52	42	10
Rappahannock	27	26	1
Roanoke County Police Department	141	128	13
Rockingham	63	47	16
Scott	29	29	0
Spotsylvania	216	164	52
Stafford	224	160	64
Sussex	43	38	5
Warren	92	46	46
Washington	73	52	21
York	93	86	7
Nonmetropolitan Counties			
Accomack	70	59	11
Alleghany	60	42	18
Bath	18	18	0
Bland	16	10	6
Brunswick	38	26	12
Buchanan	48	35	13
Carroll	39	33	6
Charlotte	30	28	2
Cumberland	21	15	6
Dickenson	34	21	13
Essex	19	13	6
Grayson	28	22	6
Greensville	35	22	13
Halifax	32	32	0
Henry	127	114	13
Highland	12	7	5
King and Queen	21	13	8
King George	42	28	14
Lancaster	31	25	6
Lee	35	35	0
Louisa	60	48	12
Lunenburg	19	13	6
Madison	32	19	13
Mecklenburg	53	51	2
Middlesex	22	16	6
Northampton	83	66	17
Northumberland	33	20	13

Table 80. Full-Time Law Enforcement Employees, by Selected State Metropolitan and Nonmetropolitan Counties, 2012— continued

(Number)

State/county	Law enforcement employees	Officers	Civilians
Nottoway	25	14	11
Orange	44	36	8
Page	65	49	16
Patrick	65	50	15
Pittsylvania	129	112	17
Prince Edward	35	29	6
Richmond	20	12	8
Rockbridge	39	31	8
Russell	50	33	17
Shenandoah	77	68	9
Smyth	41	41	0
Southampton	75	61	14
Surry	23	13	10
Tazewell	67	45	22
Westmoreland	34	23	11
Wise	64	48	16
Wythe	46	39	7
WASHINGTON			
Metropolitan Counties			
Asotin	13	11	2
Benton	70	58	12
Chelan	69	56	13
Clark	206	130	76
Columbia	8	7	1
Cowlitz	50	40	10
Douglas	34	27	7
Franklin	27	25	2
King	286	190	96
Kitsap	145	115	30
Pend Oreille	19	16	3
Pierce	363	302	61
Skagit	100	49	51
Skamania	23	19	4
Snohomish	337	270	67
Spokane	179	120	59
Stevens	30	26	4
Thurston	106	84	22
Walla Walla	56	27	29
Whatcom	104	84	20
Yakima	108	57	51
Nonmetropolitan Counties			
Adams	28	17	11
Clallam	42	34	8
Ferry	23	7	16
Garfield	14	7	7
Grant	61	48	13
Grays Harbor	76	36	40
Island	57	33	24
Jefferson	47	41	6
Kittitas	64	33	31
Klickitat	39	18	21
Lewis	55	39	16
Lincoln	14	14	0
Mason	95	47	48
Okanogan	34	29	5
Pacific	46	18	28
San Juan	33	20	13
Wahkiakum	16	7	9

Table 80. Full-Time Law Enforcement Employees, by Selected State Metropolitan and Nonmetropolitan Counties, 2012— continued

(Number)

State/county	Law enforcement employees	Officers	Civilians
Whitman	20	16	4
WEST VIRGINIA			
Metropolitan Counties			
Berkeley	88	58	30
Boone	27	22	5
Brooke	30	18	12
Cabell	49	42	7
Clay	6	5	1
Fayette	41	36	5
Hampshire	20	17	3
Hancock	31	26	5
Jefferson	35	28	7
Kanawha	122	97	25
Lincoln	7	7	0
Marshall	31	28	3
Mineral	14	12	2
Monongalia	66	37	29
Ohio	33	31	2
Preston	27	16	11
Putnam	48	37	11
Raleigh	66	44	22
Wayne	23	20	3
Wirt	5	3	2
Wood	54	38	16
Nonmetropolitan Counties			
Barbour	10	8	2
Braxton	10	8	2
Calhoun	3	3	0
Doddridge	6	6	0
Gilmer	5	5	0
Grant	8	8	0
Greenbrier	34	29	5
Hardy	11	9	2
Harrison	46	45	1
Jackson	22	15	7
Lewis	18	14	4
Logan	22	16	6
Marion	47	36	11
Mason	21	15	6
McDowell	15	14	1
Mercer	34	27	7
Mingo	23	20	3
Monroe	8	7	1
Morgan	12	11	1
Nicholas	30	26	4
Pendleton	3	3	0
Pleasants	7	6	1
Pocahontas	16	10	6
Randolph	12	10	2
Ritchie	10	7	3
Roane	10	8	2
Summers	11	6	5
Taylor	15	7	8
Tucker	4	4	0
Tyler	7	7	0
Upshur	15	13	2
Webster	10	5	5
Wetzel	8	8	0
Wyoming	27	21	6

Table 80. Full-Time Law Enforcement Employees, by Selected State Metropolitan and Nonmetropolitan Counties, 2012— continued

(Number)

State/county	Law enforcement employees	Officers	Civilians
WISCONSIN			
Metropolitan Counties			
Brown	315	155	160
Calumet	47	22	25
Chippewa	63	50	13
Columbia	99	39	60
Dane	551	437	114
Douglas	76	28	48
Eau Claire	106	41	65
Fond du Lac	119	57	62
Green	44	31	13
Iowa	36	24	12
Kenosha	325	114	211
Kewaunee	36	34	2
La Crosse	110	40	70
Marathon	167	66	101
Milwaukee	1,056	322	734
Oconto	57	26	31
Outagamie	185	71	114
Ozaukee	95	74	21
Pierce	50	48	2
Racine	207	128	79
Rock	189	91	98
Sheboygan	156	70	86
St. Croix	85	77	8
Washington	171	72	99
Waukesha	335	162	173
Winnebago	183	129	54
Nonmetropolitan Counties			
Adams	58	28	30
Barron	70	31	39
Bayfield	41	20	21
Buffalo	22	12	10
Burnett	31	17	14
Clark	48	30	18
Dodge	173	73	100
Door	59	45	14
Dunn	54	25	29
Florence	16	11	5
Forest	38	18	20
Grant	44	25	19
Green Lake	43	17	26
Iron	19	11	8
Jackson	48	22	26
Jefferson	115	92	23
Juneau	52	44	8
Lafayette	26	15	11
Langlade	40	16	24
Lincoln	62	28	34
Manitowoc	100	59	41
Marinette	61	30	31
Marquette	38	36	2
Menominee	17	9	8
Monroe	37	23	14
Oneida	87	38	49
Pepin	17	7	10
Polk	73	28	45
Portage	93	48	45
Price	24	14	10

Table 80. Full-Time Law Enforcement Employees, by Selected State Metropolitan and Nonmetropolitan Counties, 2012— continued

(Number)

State/county	Law enforcement employees	Officers	Civilians
Richland	31	31	0
Rusk	31	28	3
Sauk	141	48	93
Sawyer	45	30	15
Shawano	108	37	71
Taylor	40	18	22
Trempealeau	52	24	28
Vernon	45	26	19
Vilas	72	33	39
Walworth	198	81	117
Washburn	31	14	17
Waupaca	97	37	60
Waushara	52	24	28
Wood	70	42	28
WYOMING			
Metropolitan Counties			
Laramie	71	54	17
Natrona	59	47	12
Nonmetropolitan Counties			
Albany	21	20	1
Big Horn	12	11	1
Campbell	60	45	15
Carbon	28	18	10
Converse	23	14	9
Crook	20	9	11
Fremont	40	36	4
Goshen	24	16	8
Hot Springs	9	7	2
Johnson	13	12	1
Lincoln	34	20	14
Niobrara	15	4	11
Park	30	20	10
Platte	12	10	2
Sheridan	27	21	6
Sublette	41	36	5
Sweetwater	50	43	7
Teton	36	19	17
Uinta	37	24	13
Washakie	11	10	1
Weston	8	6	2

1 The employee data presented in this table for Mecklenburg represent only the employees of the Mecklenburg County Sheriff's Office and exclude employees of the Charlotte-Mecklenburg Police Department.

Table 81. Full-Time Law Enforcement Employees, by Selected State and Agency, 2012

(Number)

State/agency	Law enforcement employees	Officers	Civilians
ALABAMA			
State Agency			
Alabama Department of Mental Health	4	3	1
Tribal Agency			
Poarch Creek Tribal	54	47	7
Other Agency			
Huntsville International Airport	20	20	0
ALASKA			
Tribal Agency			
Metlakatla Tribal	10	6	4
Other Agencies			
Anchorage International Airport	60	58	2
Fairbanks International Airport	32	25	7
ARIZONA			
Tribal Agencies			
Ak-Chin Tribal	49	16	33
Cocopah Tribal	28	21	7
Colorado River Agency	1	1	0
Colorado River Tribal	36	24	12
Fort Apache Agency	6	5	1
Fort McDowell Tribal	29	22	7
Fort Mojave Tribal	49	32	17
Gila River Indian Community	150	119	31
Hopi Tribal	19	13	6
Hualapai Tribal	17	16	1
Kaibab Paiute Tribal	2	2	0
Navajo Nation	304	236	68
Pascua Yaqui Tribal	84	27	57
Quechan Tribal	14	10	4
Salt River Tribal	140	110	30
San Carlos Agency	3	2	1
San Carlos Apache	49	29	20
Tohono O'odham Nation	115	81	34
Tonto Apache Tribal	8	8	0
Truxton Canon Agency	11	7	4
White Mountain Apache Tribal	50	27	23
Yavapai-Apache Nation	14	12	2
Yavapai-Prescott Tribal	12	9	3
Other Agency			
Tucson Airport Authority	44	22	22
ARKANSAS			
State Agencies			
Camp Robinson	13	9	4
State Capitol Police	23	20	3
CALIFORNIA			
State Agencies			
Atascadero State Hospital	121	107	14
California State Fair	5	1	4
Coalinga State Hospital	243	227	16
Department of Parks and Recreation, Capital	606	562	44
Fairview Developmental Center	12	9	3
Lanterman State Hospital	13	10	3
Napa State Hospital	124	114	10
Patton State Hospital	57	41	16
Porterville Developmental Center	52	48	4

Table 81. Full-Time Law Enforcement Employees, by Selected State and Agency, 2012— continued

(Number)

State/agency	Law enforcement employees	Officers	Civilians
Sonoma Developmental Center	20	9	11
Tribal Agencies			
Hoopa Valley Tribal	15	10	5
Tule River Tribal	21	5	16
Yurok Tribal	8	7	1
Other Agencies			
East Bay Regional Parks, Alameda County	80	56	24
Fontana Unified School District	55	14	41
Monterey Peninsula Airport	6	6	0
Port of San Diego Harbor	150	126	24
San Bernardino Unified School District	76	23	53
San Francisco Bay Area Rapid Transit, Contra Costa County	269	188	81
Shasta County Marshal	23	19	4
Stockton Unified School District	27	22	5
Twin Rivers Unified School District	28	23	5
COLORADO			
State Agencies			
Colorado Bureau of Investigation	232	37	195
Colorado Mental Health Institute	77	16	61
Tribal Agencies			
Southern Ute Tribal	38	19	19
Ute Mountain Tribal	14	8	6
Other Agency			
Two Rivers Drug Enforcement Team	7	6	1
CONNECTICUT			
State Agency			
State Capitol Police	37	28	9
Tribal Agencies			
Mashantucket Pequot Tribal	23	16	7
Mohegan Tribal	29	21	8
Other Agency			
Metropolitan Transportation Authority	734	667	67
DELAWARE			
State Agencies			
Attorney General			
Kent County	66	36	30
New Castle County	290	148	142
Sussex County	47	26	21
Division of Alcohol and Tobacco Enforcement	18	14	4
Environmental Control	11	9	2
Fish and Wildlife	31	26	5
Park Rangers	18	18	0
River and Bay Authority	59	44	15
State Capitol Police	74	48	26
State Fire Marshal	53	20	33
Other Agencies			
Amtrak Police	14	14	0
Drug Enforcement Administration, Wilmington Resident Office	22	18	4
Wilmington Fire Department	12	10	2
DISTRICT OF COLUMBIA			
Other Agency			
Metro Transit Police	644	448	196
FLORIDA			

Table 81. Full-Time Law Enforcement Employees, by Selected State and Agency, 2012— continued

(Number)

State/agency	Law enforcement employees	Officers	Civilians
State Agencies			
Department of Law Enforcement, Leon County, Tallahassee	1,699	425	1,274
Florida Game Commission, Leon county	990	797	193
State Treasurer's Office, Division of Insurance Fraud	171	133	38
Tribal Agencies			
Miccosukee Tribal	41	29	12
Seminole Tribal	231	151	80
Other Agencies			
Duval County Schools	84	74	10
Florida School for the Deaf and Blind	17	9	8
Jacksonville Aviation Authority	52	37	15
Lee County Port Authority	65	39	26
Melbourne International Airport	12	11	1
Miami-Dade County Public Schools	199	158	41
Northwest Florida Beaches International Airport	18	14	4
Palm Beach County School District	194	138	56
Tampa International Airport	157	60	97
Volusia County Beach Management	51	48	3
GEORGIA			
State Agencies			
Atlanta State Farmers Market	13	13	0
Central State Hospital	15	10	5
Georgia Bureau of Investigation, Headquarters	743	250	493
Georgia Department of Transportation, Office of Investigations	3	3	0
Georgia Forestry Commission	4	4	0
Georgia Public Safety Training Center	146	33	113
Georgia World Congress	85	31	54
Ports Authority, Savannah	120	82	38
Other Agencies			
Atlanta Public Schools	19	5	14
Bibb County Board of Education	28	26	2
Chatham County Board of Education	46	38	8
Cherokee County Board of Education	13	11	2
Cherokee County Marshal	14	8	6
Cobb County Board of Education	44	42	2
Fayette County Marshal	11	10	1
Fulton County Marshal	70	59	11
Fulton County School System	65	63	2
Glynn County School System	17	17	0
Gwinnett County Public Schools	28	24	4
Habersham County Public Schools	3	3	0
Hartsfield-Jackson Atlanta International Airport	167	143	24
Metropolitan Atlanta Rapid Transit Authority	364	313	51
Muscogee City Marshal	22	20	2
Stone Mountain Park	25	21	4
Washington County Board of Education	5	5	0
IDAHO			
Tribal Agencies			
Fort Hall Tribal	32	18	14
Nez Perce Tribal	18	13	5
ILLINOIS			
State Agencies			
Illinois Department of Natural Resources	134	119	15
Secretary of State Police	216	116	100
Other Agencies			
Alton & Southern Railway	7	7	0
Belt Railway	6	6	0

Table 81. Full-Time Law Enforcement Employees, by Selected State and Agency, 2012— continued

(Number)

State/agency	Law enforcement employees	Officers	Civilians
Burlington Northern Santa Fe Railway	23	22	1
Canadian National Railway	14	13	1
Canadian Pacific Railway	9	9	0
Capitol Airport Authority	6	6	0
Chicago Fire Department, Arson Investigations	11	3	8
Cook County Forest Preserve	107	101	6
Fon Du Lac Park District	1	1	0
Kane County Forest Preserve	6	6	0
Lake County Forest Preserve	20	18	2
McHenry County Conservation District	13	12	1
Norfolk Southern Railway:			
Macon County	2	2	0
Madison County	6	6	0
Rockford Park District	16	15	1
Springfield Park District	10	9	1
Terminal Railroad Association	8	8	0
Union Pacific Railroad, St. Clair County	6	6	0
Will County Forest Preserve	14	12	2
INDIANA			
State Agencies			
Indiana State Excise Police	92	85	7
Northern Indiana Commuter Transportation District	8	7	1
Other Agencies			
Indianapolis International Airport	47	45	2
KANSAS			
State Agencies			
Kansas Bureau of Investigation	253	72	181
Kansas Department of Wildlife and Parks	180	178	2
Kansas Lottery Security Division	8	5	3
Kansas Racing Commission, Security Division	64	38	26
Securities Office, Investigation Section	4	4	0
State Fire Marshal	14	13	1
Tribal Agencies			
Iowa Tribal	6	6	0
Kickapoo Tribal	20	6	14
Potawatomi Tribal	18	10	8
Sac and Fox Tribal	6	5	1
Other Agencies			
Blue Valley School District	9	7	2
Johnson County Park	18	17	1
Metropolitan Topeka Airport Authority	23	18	5
Shawnee Mission Public Schools	8	8	0
Topeka Fire Department, Arson Investigation	4	3	1
Unified School District:			
Auburn-Washburn	5	2	3
Bluestem	1	1	0
Goddard	6	5	1
Maize	4	4	0
Seaman	3	1	2
Shawnee Heights	1	1	0
KENTUCKY			
State Agencies			
Alcohol Beverage Control	57	30	27
Kentucky Horse Park	7	7	0
Unlawful Narcotics Investigation, Treatment and Education	17	15	2
Other Agencies			
Buffalo Trace-Gateway Narcotics Task Force	4	3	1
Cincinnati-Northern Kentucky International Airport	51	48	3

Table 81. Full-Time Law Enforcement Employees, by Selected State and Agency, 2012— continued

(Number)

State/agency	Law enforcement employees	Officers	Civilians
Clark County School System	2	2	0
Covington Independent Public Schools	1	1	0
Fayette County Schools	31	27	4
FIVCO Area Drug Task Force	7	6	1
Graves County Schools	1	1	0
Greater Hardin County Narcotics Task Force	2	1	1
Jefferson County Board of Education	24	18	6
Lake Cumberland Area Drug Enforcement Task Force	4	3	1
Lexington Bluegrass Airport	28	19	9
Louisville Regional Airport Authority	42	38	4
McCracken County Public Schools	5	5	0
Montgomery County School District	3	3	0
Northern Kentucky Narcotics Enforcement Unit	3	2	1
Pennyrile Narcotics Task Force	7	6	1
South Central Kentucky Drug Task Force	1	1	0
LOUISIANA			
State Agency			
Tensas Basin Levee District	3	2	1
Tribal Agencies			
Chitimacha Tribal	14	14	0
Coushatta Tribal	19	18	1
Tunica-Biloxi Tribal	16	13	3
MAINE			
Tribal Agencies			
Passamaquoddy Indian Township	9	5	4
Passamaquoddy Pleasant Point Tribal	6	6	0
Penobscot Nation	8	4	4
MARYLAND			
State Agencies			
Comptroller of the Treasury, Field Enforcement Division	54	28	26
Department of Public Safety and Correctional Services, Internal Investigations Unit	27	17	10
General Services:			
Annapolis, Anne Arundel County	64	27	37
Baltimore City	100	34	66
Natural Resources Police	492	237	255
Springfield Hospital	38	6	32
State Fire Marshal	74	44	30
Transit Administration	174	159	15
Transportation Authority	608	470	138
Other Agencies			
Maryland-National Capital Park Police:			
Montgomery County	88	72	16
Prince George's County	133	106	27
MASSACHUSETTS			
State Agency			
Massachusetts Bay Transportation Authority	260	249	11
Tribal Agency			
Wampanoag Tribe of Gay Head	2	2	0
MICHIGAN			
Tribal Agencies			
Bay Mills Tribal	10	8	2
Gun Lake Tribal	6	5	1
Keweenaw Bay Tribal	16	14	2
Little River Band of Ottawa Indians	20	19	1
Little Traverse Bay Bands of Odawa Indians	15	11	4
Nottawaseppi Huron Band of Potawatomi	10	9	1

Table 81. Full-Time Law Enforcement Employees, by Selected State and Agency, 2012— continued

(Number)

State/agency	Law enforcement employees	Officers	Civilians
Saginaw Chippewa Tribal	35	27	8
Other Agencies			
Bishop International Airport	8	7	1
Capitol Region Airport Authority	18	10	8
Genesee County Parks and Recreation	3	3	0
Gerald R. Ford International Airport	19	18	1
Huron-Clinton Metropolitan Authority:			
Hudson Mills Metropark	3	3	0
Kensington Metropark	8	8	0
Lower Huron Metropark	9	9	0
Stony Creek Metropark	7	7	0
Wayne County Airport	104	96	8
MINNESOTA			
State Agency			
Capitol Security, St. Paul	57	11	46
Tribal Agencies			
Fond du Lac Tribal	19	16	3
Leech Lake Band of Ojibwe	34	21	13
Mille Lacs Tribal	24	21	3
Nett Lake Tribal	6	5	1
Red Lake Agency	36	25	11
White Earth Tribal	24	23	1
Other Agencies			
Minneapolis-St. Paul International Airport	136	79	57
Three Rivers Park District	37	25	12
MISSISSIPPI			
State Agency			
State Capitol Police	73	58	15
MISSOURI			
State Agencies			
Capitol Police	31	28	3
Department of Conservation	208	200	8
Department of Social Services, State Technical Assistance Team	13	9	4
Division of Alcohol and Tobacco Control	17	16	1
Gaming Commission, Enforcement Division	126	123	3
State Fire Marshal	23	21	2
State Park Rangers	43	42	1
Other Agencies			
Bootheel Drug Task Force	3	3	0
Clay County Drug Task Force	5	5	0
Clay County Park Authority	8	8	0
Jackson County Drug Task Force	17	15	2
Jackson County Park Rangers	18	17	1
Lambert-St. Louis International Airport	97	78	19
Springfield-Branson Airport	10	10	0
St. Charles County Park Rangers	11	11	0
St. Peters Ranger Division	6	6	0
MONTANA			
State Agency			
Gambling Investigations Bureau	24	16	8
Tribal Agencies			
Blackfeet Agency	26	15	11
Crow Agency	29	21	8
Flathead Tribal	31	20	11
Fort Belknap Tribal	18	17	1
Fort Peck Assiniboine and Sioux Tribes	26	23	3

Table 81. Full-Time Law Enforcement Employees, by Selected State and Agency, 2012— continued

(Number)

State/agency	Law enforcement employees	Officers	Civilians
Northern Cheyenne Agency	18	12	6
Rocky Boys Tribal	37	13	24
NEBRASKA			
Tribal Agencies			
Santee Tribal	7	6	1
Winnebago Tribal	16	10	6
NEVADA			
State Agency			
Taxicab Authority	53	27	26
Tribal Agencies			
Duckwater Tribal	2	2	0
Eastern Nevada Agency	11	6	5
Ely Shoshone Tribal	2	2	0
Fallon Tribal	7	6	1
Las Vegas Paiute Tribal	15	9	6
Lovelock Paiute Tribal	3	3	0
Moapa Tribal	14	10	4
Pyramid Lake Tribal	10	9	1
Reno-Sparks Indian Colony	14	13	1
South Fork Band Tribal	2	2	0
Walker River Tribal	8	8	0
Washoe Tribal	10	9	1
Western Nevada Agency	7	6	1
Western Shoshone Tribal	9	7	2
Yerington Paiute Tribal	5	3	2
Yomba Shoshone Tribal	2	2	0
Other Agencies			
Clark County School District	200	160	40
Washoe County School District	42	38	4
NEW HAMPSHIRE			
State Agency			
Liquor Commission	30	18	12
NEW JERSEY			
State Agencies			
Department of Human Services	105	99	6
Division of Fish and Wildlife	57	49	8
New Jersey Transit Police	291	235	56
Palisades Interstate Parkway	25	25	0
State Park Police	85	84	1
Other Agencies			
Park Police:			
Camden County	14	14	0
Morris County	29	28	1
Union County	82	69	13
Prosecutor:			
Atlantic County	171	78	93
Bergen County	202	109	93
Burlington County	131	38	93
Camden County	233	154	79
Cape May County	86	36	50
Cumberland County	106	37	69
Essex County	385	139	246
Gloucester County	90	34	56
Hudson County	286	97	189
Hunterdon County	53	24	29
Mercer County	167	54	113
Middlesex County	336	69	267
Monmouth County	263	77	186

Table 81. Full-Time Law Enforcement Employees, by Selected State and Agency, 2012— continued

(Number)

State/agency	Law enforcement employees	Officers	Civilians
Morris County	142	62	80
Ocean County	171	76	95
Passaic County	186	77	109
Salem County	45	17	28
Somerset County	115	50	65
Sussex County	48	30	18
Union County	239	70	169
Warren County	59	20	39
NEW MEXICO			
Tribal Agencies			
Acoma Tribal	14	10	4
Isleta Tribal	38	25	13
Jemez Pueblo	12	10	2
Jicarilla Apache Tribal	23	20	3
Laguna Tribal	39	27	12
Mescalero Tribal	21	14	7
Northern Pueblos Agency	9	7	2
Ohkay Owingeh Tribal	20	10	10
Pojoaque Tribal	19	12	7
Ramah Navajo Tribal	13	12	1
Santa Ana Tribal	22	21	1
Santa Clara Pueblo	15	8	7
Southern Pueblos Agency	20	14	6
Taos Pueblo	10	9	1
Tesuque Pueblo	18	10	8
Zuni Tribal	33	23	10
NEW YORK			
State Agencies			
State Park:			
Allegany Region	14	12	2
Central Region	19	16	3
Finger Lakes Region	14	12	2
Genesee Region	8	7	1
Long Island Region	52	51	1
New York City Region	21	17	4
Niagara Region	23	22	1
Palisades Region	33	32	1
Saratoga/Capital Region	18	17	1
Taconic Region	9	9	0
Thousand Island Region	15	14	1
Tribal Agencies			
Oneida Indian Nation	45	37	8
St. Regis Tribal	30	25	5
Other Agencies			
Board of Water, Ulster County	206	193	13
New York City Metropolitan Transportation Authority	728	666	62
NORTH CAROLINA			
State Agencies			
Department of Human Resources	7	7	0
Department of Wildlife	218	207	11
Division of Alcohol Law Enforcement	130	112	18
Division of Marine Fisheries	63	55	8
North Carolina Arboretum	4	4	0
State Capitol Police	61	40	21
State Fairgrounds	6	2	4
State Park Rangers:			
Carolina Beach	6	4	2
Chimney Rock	5	3	2
Cliffs of the Neuse	16	5	11
Crowders Mountain	6	5	1

Table 81. Full-Time Law Enforcement Employees, by Selected State and Agency, 2012— continued

(Number)

State/agency	Law enforcement employees	Officers	Civilians
Dismal Swamp	4	3	1
Elk Knob	3	3	0
Eno River	5	5	0
Falls Lake Recreation Area	19	13	6
Fort Fisher	4	4	0
Fort Macon	4	4	0
Goose Creek	8	3	5
Gorges	4	4	0
Grandfather Mountain	4	3	1
Hammocks Beach	9	4	5
Hanging Rock	11	6	5
Haw River	2	2	0
Jockey's Ridge	4	4	0
Jones Lake	3	3	0
Jordan Lake State Recreation Area	16	16	0
Kerr Lake	14	8	6
Lake James	7	4	3
Lake Norman	4	3	1
Lake Waccamaw	4	4	0
Lumber River	8	5	3
Mayo River	3	2	1
Medoc Mountain	5	2	3
Merchants Millpond	4	3	1
Morrow Mountain	9	4	5
Mount Mitchell	5	4	1
New River-Mount Jefferson	8	8	0
Pettigrew	4	3	1
Pilot Mountain	6	3	3
Raven Rock	6	3	3
Singletary Lake	5	2	3
South Mountains	7	6	1
Stone Mountain	12	6	6
Weymouth Woods/Sandhills Nature Preserve	3	3	0
William B. Umstead	8	7	1
Tribal Agency			
Cherokee Tribal	60	56	4
Other Agencies			
Asheville Regional Airport	19	14	5
Beaufort County Alcohol Beverage Control Enforcement	1	1	0
Durham County Alcohol Beverage Control Law Enforcement Office	3	3	0
Nash County Alcohol Beverage Control Enforcement	1	1	0
Piedmont Triad International Airport	25	17	8
Pitt County Memorial Hospital	57	35	22
Raleigh-Durham International Airport	32	30	2
Triad Alcohol Beverage Control Law Enforcement	5	4	1
WakeMed Campus Police	73	43	30
Wilmington International Airport	13	9	4
NORTH DAKOTA			
Tribal Agencies			
Fort Totten Agency	18	11	7
Standing Rock Agency	37	28	9
Turtle Mountain Agency	22	14	8
OHIO			
State Agency			
Ohio Department of Natural Resources	418	334	84
Other Agencies			
Cedar Point	11	11	0

Table 81. Full-Time Law Enforcement Employees, by Selected State and Agency, 2012— continued

(Number)

State/agency	Law enforcement employees	Officers	Civilians
Cleveland Metropolitan Park District	72	62	10
Holden Arboretum	2	2	0
Lake Metroparks	15	13	2
Lake Waynoka Rangers	5	2	3
Preservation Parks of Delaware County	7	7	0
Robinson Memorial Hospital	9	9	0
Wood County Park District	6	6	0
OKLAHOMA			
State Agencies			
Capitol Park Police	84	35	49
Department of Agriculture, Forestry Service Law Enforcement Section	14	11	3
Grand River Dam Authority, Lake Patrol	22	12	10
Tribal Agencies			
Absentee Shawnee Tribal	11	10	1
Anadarko Agency	14	9	5
Cherokee Nation	41	33	8
Chickasaw Nation	38	31	7
Choctaw Nation	32	31	1
Citizen Potawatomi Nation	23	17	6
Comanche Nation	29	20	9
Concho Agency	7	7	0
Eastern Shawnee Tribal	9	8	1
Iowa Tribal	4	4	0
Kaw Tribal	6	6	0
Kickapoo Tribal	13	12	1
Miami Agency	4	4	0
Miami Tribal	6	3	3
Muscogee Nation Tribal	36	28	8
Osage Nation	19	18	1
Otoe-Missouria Tribal	14	8	6
Pawnee Agency	7	7	0
Pawnee Tribal	6	5	1
Quapaw Tribal	13	12	1
Sac and Fox Tribal	9	9	0
Seminole Nation Lighthorse	9	8	1
Tonkawa Tribal	10	5	5
Wyandotte Nation	11	10	1
Other Agencies			
Jenks Public Schools	7	6	1
McAlester Public Schools	1	1	0
Norman Public Schools	5	5	0
Putnam City Campus	13	9	4
OREGON			
State Agency			
Liquor Commission:			
Benton County	1	1	0
Clatsop County	2	1	1
Columbia County	1	1	0
Coos County	2	1	1
Crook County	1	1	0
Douglas County	1	1	0
Harney County	1	1	0
Hood River County	1	1	0
Jackson County	4	3	1
Jefferson County	1	1	0
Josephine County	1	1	0
Klamath County	2	2	0
Lane County	6	5	1
Lincoln County	2	1	1

Table 81. Full-Time Law Enforcement Employees, by Selected State and Agency, 2012— continued

(Number)

State/agency	Law enforcement employees	Officers	Civilians
Linn County	1	1	0
Malheur County	1	1	0
Marion County	4	3	1
Multnomah County	19	15	4
Polk County	1	1	0
Umatilla County	1	1	0
Washington County	2	2	0
Yamhill County	1	1	0
Tribal Agencies			
Burns Paiute Tribal	4	3	1
Columbia River Inter-Tribal Fisheries Enforcement	17	12	5
Siletz Tribal	14	8	6
Umatilla Tribal	21	17	4
Other Agencies			
Blue Mountain Enforcement Narcotics Team			
Morrow County	6	5	1
Umatilla County	9	8	1
Port of Portland	66	49	17
PENNSYLVANIA			
State Agencies			
Pennsylvania Fish and Boat Commission	101	94	7
State Capitol Police	141	132	9
State Park Police:			
Nockamixon	1	1	0
Ohiopyle	12	5	7
Pine Grove Furnace	2	2	0
Presque Isle	5	5	0
Prince Gallitzin	13	3	10
Pymatuning	3	3	0
Other Agencies			
Allegheny County District Attorney, Criminal Investigation Division	39	35	4
Allegheny County Housing Authority	9	8	1
Allegheny County Port Authority	49	38	11
County Detective:			
Beaver County	8	8	0
Berks County	34	31	3
Bucks County	20	16	4
Butler County	4	4	0
Chester County	22	19	3
Cumberland County	7	6	1
Dauphin County	15	12	3
Erie County	9	8	1
Lackawanna County	14	14	0
Lebanon County	7	5	2
Lehigh County	45	19	26
Luzerne County	10	10	0
Montgomery County	65	40	25
Montour County	1	1	0
Pike County	3	3	0
Schuylkill County	6	6	0
Wayne County	2	2	0
Westmoreland County	58	15	43
York County	10	9	1
Delaware County District Attorney, Criminal Investigation Division	47	33	14
Delaware County Park	56	55	1
Erie Municipal Airport Authority	8	7	1
Fort Indiantown Gap	20	8	12
Harrisburg International Airport	16	8	8
Lehigh Valley International Airport	10	8	2

Table 81. Full-Time Law Enforcement Employees, by Selected State and Agency, 2012— continued

(Number)

State/agency	Law enforcement employees	Officers	Civilians
Washington County Alternative Education	1	1	0
Westmoreland County Park	21	20	1
Wyoming Area School District	1	1	0
RHODE ISLAND			
State Agencies			
Department of Environmental Management	39	32	7
Rhode Island State Airport	44	35	9
Tribal Agency			
Narragansett Tribal	5	5	0
SOUTH CAROLINA			
State Agencies			
Bureau of Protective Services	68	62	6
Department of Mental Health	151	102	49
Employment Security Commission	4	4	0
Forestry Commission:			
Aiken County	1	1	0
Anderson County	1	1	0
Barnwell County	1	1	0
Beaufort County	1	1	0
Berkeley County	1	1	0
Charleston County	1	1	0
Chesterfield County	5	5	0
Fairfield County	1	1	0
Florence County	1	1	0
Hampton County	2	2	0
Horry County	1	1	0
Kershaw County	3	3	0
Lexington County	3	3	0
Oconee County	1	1	0
Orangeburg County	1	1	0
Pickens County	1	1	0
Richland County	2	2	0
Spartanburg County	1	1	0
Sumter County	3	3	0
Williamsburg County	3	3	0
York County	1	1	0
South Carolina School for the Deaf and Blind	1	1	0
State Museum	1	1	0
State Ports Authority	68	30	38
State Transport Police:			
Abbeville County	12	12	0
Aiken County	56	31	25
Allendale County	14	14	0
Anderson County	18	16	2
Berkeley County	20	17	3
Cherokee County	7	7	0
Darlington County	10	10	0
United States Department of Energy, Savannah River Plant	53	41	12
Other Agencies			
Charleston County Aviation Authority	43	30	13
Columbia Metropolitan Airport	17	16	1
Greenville-Spartanburg International Airport	16	15	1
Lexington County Medical Center	48	18	30
Whitten Center	1	1	0
SOUTH DAKOTA			
State Agency			
Division of Criminal Investigation	156	44	112
Tribal Agencies			

Table 81. Full-Time Law Enforcement Employees, by Selected State and Agency, 2012— continued

(Number)

State/agency	Law enforcement employees	Officers	Civilians
Crow Creek Tribal	15	9	6
Flandreau Tribal	9	8	1
Lower Brule Tribal	14	9	5
Oglala Sioux Tribal	104	47	57
Pine Ridge Sioux Tribal	8	7	1
Sisseton-Wahpeton Tribal	21	11	10
Yankton Tribal	5	4	1
TENNESSEE			
State Agencies			
Alcoholic Beverage Commission	54	25	29
Department of Correction, Internal Affairs	19	15	4
State Fire Marshal	28	23	5
State Park Rangers:			
Bicentennial Capitol Mall	6	6	0
Big Hill Pond	3	3	0
Big Ridge	4	4	0
Bledsoe Creek	2	2	0
Booker T. Washington	3	3	0
Burgess Falls Natural Area	3	3	0
Cedars of Lebanon	4	4	0
Chickasaw	4	4	0
Cove Lake	4	4	0
Cumberland Mountain	4	4	0
Cumberland Trail	7	7	0
David Crockett	4	4	0
Davy Crockett Birthplace	3	3	0
Dunbar Cave Natural Area	3	3	0
Edgar Evins	4	4	0
Fall Creek Falls	8	8	0
Fort Loudon State Historic Park	4	4	0
Fort Pillow State Historic Park	2	2	0
Frozen Head Natural Area	4	4	0
Harpeth Scenic Rivers	3	3	0
Harrison Bay	4	4	0
Henry Horton	4	4	0
Hiwassee/Ocoee State Scenic Rivers	6	6	0
Indian Mountain	2	2	0
Johnsonville State Historic Park	1	1	0
Long Hunter	4	4	0
Meeman-Shelby Forest	6	6	0
Montgomery Bell	6	6	0
Mousetail Landing	2	2	0
Natchez Trace	5	5	0
Nathan Bedford Forrest	3	3	0
Norris Dam	4	4	0
Old Stone Fort State Archaeological Park	2	2	0
Panther Creek	2	2	0
Paris Landing	5	5	0
Pickett	4	4	0
Pickwick Landing	5	5	0
Pinson Mounds State Archaeological Park	2	2	0
Radnor Lake Natural Area	4	4	0
Red Clay State Historic Park	2	2	0
Reelfoot Lake	4	4	0
Roan Mountain	4	4	0
Rock Island	4	4	0
Sgt. Alvin C. York	2	2	0
South Cumberland Recreation Area	5	5	0
Standing Stone	4	4	0
Sycamore Shoals State Historic Park	2	2	0

Table 81. Full-Time Law Enforcement Employees, by Selected State and Agency, 2012— continued

(Number)

State/agency	Law enforcement employees	Officers	Civilians
Tim's Ford	5	5	0
T.O. Fuller	3	3	0
Warrior's Path	5	5	0
TennCare Office of Inspector General	44	16	28
Tennessee Bureau of Investigation	459	268	191
Tennessee Department of Revenue, Special Investigations Unit	43	21	22
Wildlife Resources Agency			
Region 1	46	42	4
Region 2	64	55	9
Region 3	48	44	4
Region 4	49	45	4
Other Agencies			
Chattanooga Housing Authority	6	5	1
Chattanooga Metropolitan Airport	10	10	0
Dickson Parks and Recreation	11	3	8
Drug Task Force:			
1st Judicial District	5	4	1
3rd Judicial District	5	4	1
4th Judicial District	3	2	1
5th Judicial District	9	8	1
8th Judicial District	4	3	1
9th Judicial District	2	2	0
10th Judicial District	10	9	1
12th Judicial District	2	2	0
14th Judicial District	2	2	0
15th Judicial District	4	3	1
17th Judicial District	3	3	0
18th Judicial District	9	9	0
19th Judicial District	9	8	1
21st Judicial District	9	7	2
22nd Judicial District	2	2	0
23rd Judicial District	8	6	2
24th Judicial District	2	1	1
25th Judicial District	2	2	0
Knoxville Metropolitan Airport	44	26	18
Memphis International Airport	64	50	14
Metropolitan Nashville Park Police	20	20	0
Nashville International Airport	61	45	16
Smyrna/Rutherford County Airport Authority	3	3	0
Tri-Cities Regional Airport	14	14	0
West Tennessee Violent Crime Task Force	7	6	1
TEXAS			
Tribal Agency			
Ysleta Del Sur Pueblo Tribal	11	9	2
Other Agencies			
Amarillo International Airport	15	15	0
Dallas-Fort Worth International Airport	410	237	173
Hospital District:			
Dallas County	98	64	34
Tarrant County	56	40	16
Houston Metropolitan Transit Authority	209	177	32
Independent School District:			
Aldine	50	44	6
Alvin	21	18	3
Angleton	5	4	1
Austin	95	68	27
Barbers Hill	5	4	1
Bay City	6	5	1
Cedar Hill	23	7	16
Columbia-Brazoria	1	1	0

Table 81. Full-Time Law Enforcement Employees, by Selected State and Agency, 2012— continued

(Number)

State/agency	Law enforcement employees	Officers	Civilians
Conroe	65	48	17
Corpus Christi	51	31	20
East Central	9	9	0
Ector County	25	23	2
Edinburg	85	47	38
El Paso	47	39	8
Fort Bend	56	47	9
Hallsville	6	2	4
Humble	37	28	9
Judson	20	19	1
Katy	44	34	10
Killeen	17	17	0
Klein	51	34	17
Laredo	97	25	72
Lyford	2	2	0
Midland	15	9	6
North East	66	60	6
Pasadena	38	30	8
Pflugerville	17	17	0
Raymondville	5	4	1
Rio Grande City	67	14	53
Sealy	3	3	0
Socorro	69	26	43
Spring	44	42	2
Spring Branch	40	32	8
Taft	1	1	0
United	156	55	101
Port of Brownsville	9	8	1
Port of Houston Authority	66	50	16
UTAH			
State Agencies			
Parks and Recreation	55	54	1
Wildlife Resources	77	75	2
Tribal Agencies			
Goshute Tribal	2	2	0
Uintah and Ouray Tribal	13	10	3
Other Agencies			
Granite School District	40	15	25
Utah County Attorney, Investigations Division	7	5	2
Utah Transit Authority	58	55	3
VERMONT			
State Agencies			
Attorney General	20	3	17
Department of Liquor Control, Division of Enforcement and Licensing	50	16	34
Department of Motor Vehicles	42	27	15
Fish and Wildlife Department, Law Enforcement Division	41	39	2
Secretary of State, Investigations Unit	11	6	5
VIRGINIA			
State Agencies			
Alcoholic Beverage Control Commission	149	117	32
Department of Conservation and Recreation	225	98	127
Department of Game and Inland Fisheries, Enforcement Division	180	169	11
Department of Motor Vehicles	89	74	15
Southside Virginia Training Center	17	16	1
Virginia State Capitol	79	66	13
Other Agencies			

Table 81. Full-Time Law Enforcement Employees, by Selected State and Agency, 2012— continued

(Number)

State/agency	Law enforcement employees	Officers	Civilians
Norfolk Airport Authority	44	37	7
Port Authority, Norfolk	38	26	12
Reagan National Airport	306	216	90
Richmond International Airport	27	20	7
WASHINGTON			
Tribal Agencies			
Chehalis Tribal	11	10	1
Colville Tribal	32	23	9
Jamestown S'Klallam Tribal	2	2	0
Kalispel Tribal	13	12	1
La Push Tribal	5	5	0
Lower Elwha Tribal	8	6	2
Lummi Tribal	24	21	3
Makah Tribal	15	8	7
Nisqually Tribal	18	14	4
Nooksack Tribal	10	8	2
Port Gamble S'Klallam Tribal	9	9	0
Puyallup Tribal	43	30	13
Quinault Indian Nation	19	13	6
Sauk-Suiattle Tribal	3	2	1
Shoalwater Bay Tribal	5	5	0
Skokomish Tribal	9	7	2
Spokane Agency	19	13	6
Squaxin Island Tribal	13	11	2
Stillaguamish Tribal	8	8	0
Suquamish Tribal	20	17	3
Swinomish Tribal	17	15	2
Tulalip Tribal	49	32	17
Upper Skagit Tribal	6	5	1
Yakama Nation	22	19	3
Other Agencies			
Port of Seattle	124	97	27
WEST VIRGINIA			
State Agencies			
Capitol Protective Services	38	23	15
Division of Natural Resources:			
Barbour County	1	1	0
Berkeley County	1	1	0
Boone County	1	1	0
Braxton County	2	2	0
Brooke County	1	1	0
Cabell County	3	3	0
Calhoun County	1	1	0
Clay County	2	2	0
Doddridge County	1	1	0
Fayette County	3	3	0
Gilmer County	1	1	0
Grant County	2	2	0
Greenbrier County	3	3	0
Hampshire County	6	5	1
Hancock County	1	1	0
Hardy County	1	1	0
Harrison County	2	2	0
Jackson County	2	2	0
Jefferson County	2	2	0
Kanawha County	12	7	5
Lewis County	3	3	0
Lincoln County	2	2	0
Logan County	2	2	0

Table 81. Full-Time Law Enforcement Employees, by Selected State and Agency, 2012— continued

(Number)

State/agency	Law enforcement employees	Officers	Civilians
Marion County	6	5	1
Marshall County	2	2	0
Mason County	1	1	0
McDowell County	1	1	0
Mercer County	3	3	0
Mineral County	3	3	0
Mingo County	1	1	0
Monongalia County	2	2	0
Monroe County	1	1	0
Nicholas County	1	1	0
Ohio County	1	1	0
Pendleton County	2	2	0
Pleasants County	1	1	0
Pocahontas County	2	2	0
Preston County	2	2	0
Putnam County	7	6	1
Raleigh County	5	4	1
Randolph County	2	2	0
Ritchie County	1	1	0
Roane County	1	1	0
Summers County	3	3	0
Taylor County	2	2	0
Tyler County	1	1	0
Upshur County	4	3	1
Wayne County	1	1	0
Webster County	2	2	0
Wetzel County	2	2	0
Wirt County	1	1	0
Wood County	7	6	1
Wyoming County	2	2	0
State Fire Marshal, Kanawha County	49	32	17
Other Agencies			
Central West Virginia Drug Task Force	2	2	0
Greenbrier County Drug and Violent Crime Task Force	4	3	1
Hancock/Brooke/Weirton Drug Task Force	6	6	0
Harrison County Drug and Violent Crime Task Force	7	7	0
Kanawha County Parks and Recreation	3	3	0
Logan County Drug and Violent Crime Task Force	5	4	1
Metropolitan Drug Enforcement Network Team	19	18	1
Ohio Valley Drug and Violent Crime Task Force	5	5	0
Parkersburg Narcotics and Violent Crime Task Force	6	6	0
Potomac Highlands Drug and Violent Crime Task Force	3	3	0
Southern Regional Drug and Violent Crime Task Force	9	8	1
Three Rivers Drug and Violent Crime Task Force	2	2	0
WISCONSIN			
State Agencies			
Capitol Police	45	34	11
Department of Natural Resources	512	391	121
Tribal Agencies			
Lac du Flambeau Tribal	21	14	7
Menominee Tribal	42	24	18
Oneida Tribal	28	19	9
Red Cliff Tribal	4	3	1
St. Croix Tribal	20	13	7
Stockbridge Munsee Tribal	6	6	0
WYOMING			
Tribal Agency			
Wind River Agency	27	23	4

SECTION VI

HATE CRIMES

HATE CRIMES

Figure VI-1. Percent Distribution of Single-Bias Hate Crime Incidents, 2012

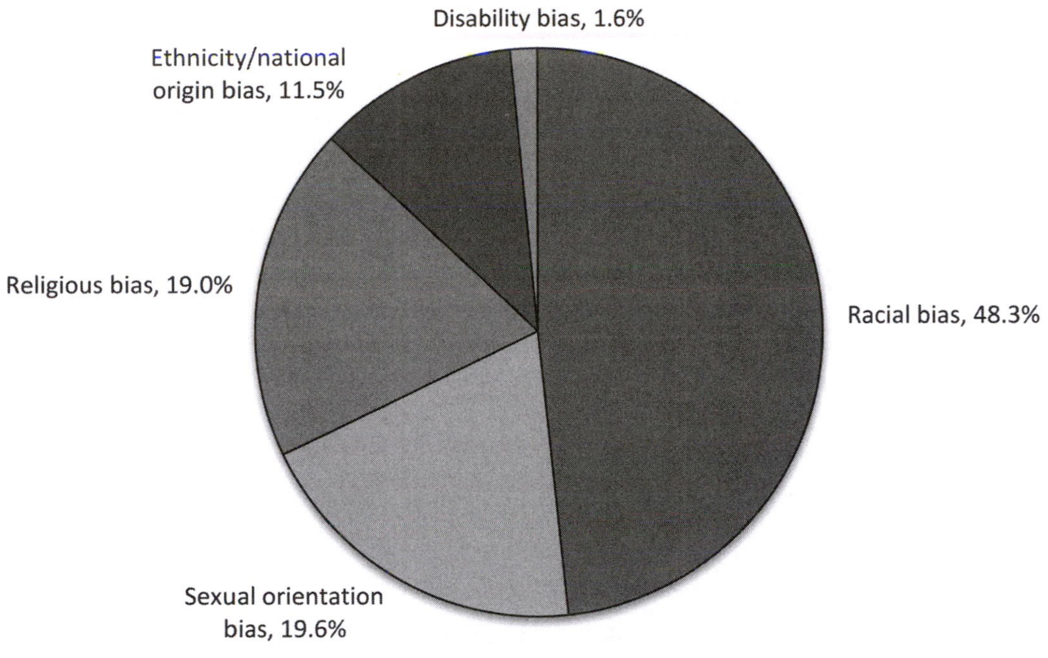

Source: Table 82

The Federal Bureau of Investigation (FBI) began the procedures for implementing, collecting, and managing hate crime data after Congress passed the Hate Crime Statistics Act in 1990 which required the collection of data "about crimes that manifest evidence of prejudice based on race, religion, sexual orientation, or ethnicity." In 1994, the Hate Crime Statistics Act was amended to include bias against persons with disabilities. The Church Arson Prevention Act, which was signed into law in July 1996, removed the sunset clause from the original statute and mandated that the collection of hate crime data become a permanent part of the UCR program. In 2009, Congress further amended the Hate Crime Statistics Act by passing the Matthew Shepard and James Byrd, Jr., Hate Crime Prevention Act. The amendment includes the collection of data for crimes motivated by bias against a particular gender and gender identity, as well as for crimes committed by, and crimes directed against, juveniles.

Definitions

Hate crimes include any crime motivated by bias against race, religion, sexual orientation, ethnicity/national origin, and/or disability. Because motivation is subjective, it is sometimes difficult to know with certainty whether a crime resulted from the offender's bias. Moreover, the presence of bias alone does not necessarily mean that a crime can be considered a hate crime. Only when law enforcement investigation reveals sufficient evidence to lead a reasonable and prudent person to conclude that the offender's actions were motivated, in whole or in part, by his or her bias, should an incident be reported as a hate crime.

Data Collection

The UCR (Uniform Crime Reporting) program collects data about both single-bias and multiple-bias hate crimes. A single-bias incident is defined as an incident in which one or more offense types are motivated by the same bias. A multiple-bias incident is defined as an incident in which more than one offense type occurs and at least two offense types are motivated by different biases.

A table with selected places in the United States that did not report hate crimes in 2012 is available at http://www.fbi.gov/about-us/cjis/ucr/hate-crime/2012/tables-and-data-declarations/14tabledatadecpdf/table_14_hate_crime_zero_data_submitted_per_quarter_by_state_and_agency_2012.xls/view.

CRIMES AGAINST PERSONS, PROPERTY, OR SOCIETY

The UCR program's data collection guidelines stipulate that a hate crime may involve multiple offenses, victims, and offenders within one incident; therefore, the Hate Crime Statistics program is incident-based. According to UCR counting guidelines:

- One offense is counted for each victim in crimes against persons
- One offense is counted for each offense type in crimes against property
- One offense is counted for each offense type in crimes against society

VICTIMS

In the UCR program, the victim of a hate crime may be an individual, a business, an institution, or society as a whole.

OFFENDERS

According to the UCR program, the term known offender does not imply that the suspect's identity is known; rather, the term indicates that some aspect of the suspect was identified, thus distinguishing the suspect from an unknown offender. Law enforcement agencies specify the number of offenders, and when possible, the race of the offender or offenders as a group.

RACE/ETHNICITY

The UCR program uses the following five racial designations in its Hate Crime Statistics program: White; Black; American Indian/Alaskan Native; Asian/Pacific Islander; and Multiple Races, Group. In addition, the UCR program uses the ethnic designations of Hispanic and Other Ethnicity/National Origin.

Agencies that participated in the Hate Crime Statistics program in 2012 represented more than 249 million inhabitants, or 79.3 percent of the nation's population, and their jurisdictions covered 48 states, the District of Columbia, Guam, and the U.S. Virgin Islands. The law enforcement agencies that voluntarily participate in the Hate Crime Statistics program collect details about an offender's bias motivation associated with 11 offense types already being reported to the UCR program: murder and nonnegligent manslaughter, forcible rape, aggravated assault, simple assault, and intimidation (crimes against persons); and robbery, burglary, larceny-theft, motor vehicle theft, arson, and destruction/damage/vandalism (crimes against property). The law enforcement agencies that participate in the UCR program via the National Incident-Based Reporting System (NIBRS) collect data about additional offenses for crimes against persons and crimes against property. These data appear in the category of other. These agencies also collect hate crime data for the category called crimes against society , which includes drug or narcotic offenses, gambling offenses, prostitution offenses, and weapon law violations.

National Volume and Percent Distribution

In 2012, 1,730 law enforcement agencies reported 5,796 hate crime incidents involving 6,718 offenses. Of these, 6,705 were single-bias offenses. An analysis of the single-bias incidents revealed that 48.3 percent were racially motivated, 18.9 percent were motivated by religious bias, 19.6 percent resulted from sexual-orientation bias, 11.5 percent were based on an ethnicity/national origin bias and 1.6 percent were prompted by a disability bias. (Table 82)

The majority of the 2,797 hate crime incidents that were racially motivated resulted from an anti-Black bias (64.5 percent) followed by an anti-White basis (23.5 percent). Bias against people of more than one race accounted for 4.0 percent of incidents, while anti-Asian/Pacific Islander bias accounted for 4.3 percent of racially motivated incidents, and anti-American Indian bias accounted for 3.6 percent of these offenses. (Table 82)

Hate crimes motivated by religious bias accounted for 1,099 incidents reported by law enforcement. A breakdown of these incidents revealed 61.3 percent were motivated by anti-Jewish bias, 11.8 percent by anti-Islamic bias, 8.0 percent were anti-multiple religions or groups, 6.4 percent an anti-Catholic bias, 3.0 percent were anti-Protestant, 1.1 percent were anti-atheism/agnoticism/etc., and the remainder, 8.4 percent, of offenses were based on a bias against other religions—those not specified. (Table 82)

In 2012, slightly more hate crimes (1,135) were committed on the basis of sexual orientation bias than on religious bias. Of the incidents based on sexual orientation, 28.3 percent were classified as having an anti-homosexual bias, 53.3 percent were classified as having an anti-male homosexual bias, 12.9 percent had an anti-female homosexual basis, 3.4 percent had an anti-bisexual bias, and 2.1 percent had an anti-heterosexual bias. (Table 82)

The majority of 822 offenses that were committed on the perceived ethnicity or national origin of the victim had an anti-Hispanic basis (57.6 percent). The remaining 42.4 percent were based on bias against another ethnicity or national origin. (Table 82)

Other hate crime offenses were committed based on disability. The majority (80.4 percent) were classified as anti-mental disability, with the rest (19.6 percent) were classified as anti-physical disability. (Table 82)

Figure VI-2. Hate Crimes by Type of Victim, Property Crime, 2012

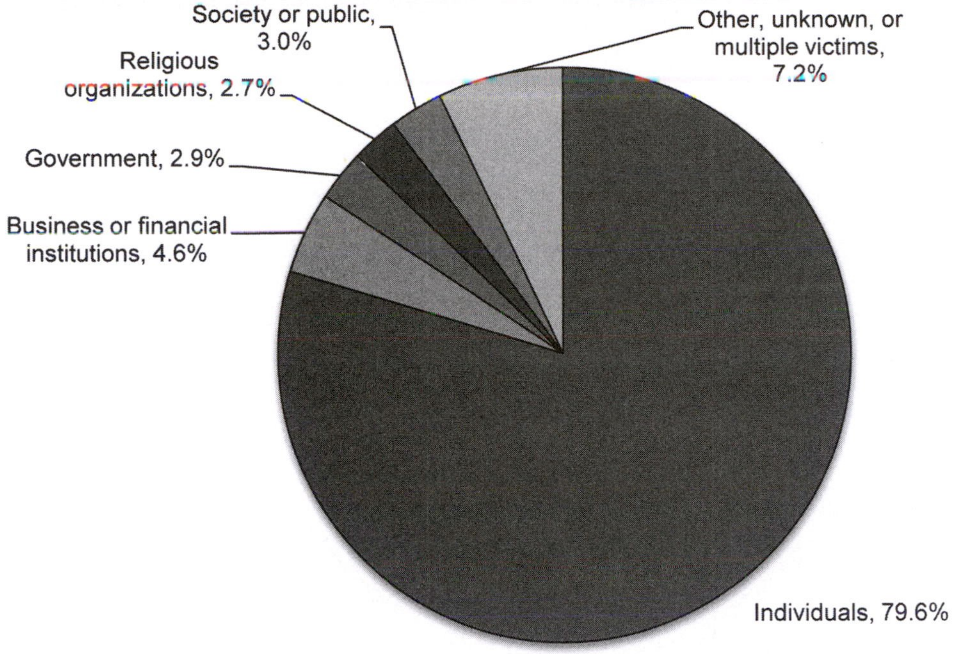

Source: Table 87

Crimes against Persons

Law enforcement agencies reported 3,258 hate crime offenses against persons in 2012, down from 4,623 offenses in 2011. Approximately 37.8 percent involved intimidation, 41.0 percent involved simple assault, and 19.8 percent involved aggravated assault. In addition, there were 5 murders and 15 forcible rapes. (Table 83)

Crimes Against Property

In 2012, hate crime offences against property totaled 2,547. Approximately 74.8 percent of offenses involved destruction/damage or vandalism. The remaining 25.2 percent of crimes against property consisted of robbery, burglary, larceny-theft, motor vehicle theft, arson, and other crimes. (Table 83)

Table 82. Incidents, Offenses, Victims, and Known Offenders, by Bias Motivation, 2012

(Number)

Bias motivation	Incidents	Offenses	Victims[1]	Known offenders[2]
Total	5,796	6,718	7,164	5,331
Single-Bias Incidents	5,790	6,705	7,151	5,322
Race	2,797	3,297	3,467	2,822
Anti-White	657	739	763	756
Anti-Black	1,805	2,180	2,295	1,771
Anti-American Indian/Alaskan Native	101	109	115	92
Anti-Asian/Pacific Islander	121	134	143	119
Anti-multiple races, group	113	135	151	84
Religion	1,099	1,166	1,340	484
Anti-Jewish	674	696	836	232
Anti-Catholic	70	79	86	27
Anti-Protestant	33	34	35	24
Anti-Islamic	130	149	155	110
Anti-other religion	92	107	115	36
Anti-multiple religions, group	88	89	101	44
Anti-atheism/agnosticism/etc.	12	12	12	11
Sexual Orientation	1,135	1,318	1,376	1,281
Anti-male homosexual	605	720	741	754
Anti-female homosexual	146	162	175	116
Anti-homosexual	321	369	393	358
Anti-heterosexual	24	26	26	20
Anti-bisexual	39	41	41	33
Ethnicity/National Origin	667	822	866	639
Anti-Hispanic	384	488	514	393
Anti-other ethnicity/national origin	283	334	352	246
Disability	92	102	102	96
Anti-physical	18	20	20	16
Anti-mental	74	82	82	80
Multiple-Bias Incidents[3]	6	13	13	9

1 The term *victim* may refer to a person, business, institution, or society as a whole. 2 The term *known offender* does not imply that the identity of the suspect is known, but only that an attribute of the suspect has been identified, which distinguishes him/her from an unknown offender. 3 In a *multiple-bias* incident, two conditions must be met: (a) more than one offense type must occur in the incident and (b) at least two offense types must be motivated by different biases.

Table 83. Incidents, Offenses, Victims, and Known Offenders, by Offense Type, 2012

(Number)

Offense type	Incidents[1]	Offenses	Victims[2]	Known offenders[3]
Total	5,796	6,718	7,164	5,331
Crimes Against Persons	3,258	3,968	3,968	3,948
Murder and nonnegligent manslaughter	5	10	10	5
Forcible rape	15	15	15	18
Aggravated assault	644	854	854	1,011
Simple assault	1,336	1,570	1,570	1,697
Intimidation	1,230	1,489	1,489	1,182
Other[4]	28	30	30	35
Crimes Against Property	2,547	2,547	2,993	1,413
Robbery	126	126	149	251
Burglary	142	142	174	145
Larceny-theft	258	258	281	166
Motor vehicle theft	23	23	24	8
Arson	38	38	46	37
Destruction/damage/vandalism	1,906	1,906	2,263	757
Other[4]	54	54	56	49
Crimes Against Society[4]	203	203	203	243

1 The actual number of incidents is 5,796. However, the column figures will not sum to the total because incidents may include more than one offense type, and these are counted in each appropriate offense type category. 2 The term *victim* may refer to a person, business, institution, or society as a whole. 3 The term *known offender* does not imply that the identity of the suspect is known, but only that an attribute of the suspect has been identified, which distinguishes him/her from an unknown offender. The actual number of known offenders is 5,331. However, the column figures will not sum to the total because some offenders are responsible for more than one offense type; and are, therefore, counted more than once in this table. 4 Includes additional offenses collected in the National Incident-Based Reporting System.

Table 84. Offenses, Known Offender's Race, by Offense Type, 2012

(Number)

Offense type	Total offenses	Known offender's race						Unknown offender
		White	Black	American Indian/ Alaskan Native	Asian/Pacific Islander	Multiple races, group	Unknown race	
Total	6,718	2,793	992	51	40	229	571	2,042
Crimes against Persons	3,968	2,257	739	40	34	183	248	467
Murder and nonnegligent manslaughter	10	8	1	0	0	0	1	0
Forcible rape	15	6	2	0	0	1	4	2
Aggravated assault	854	533	186	13	2	37	46	37
Simple assault	1,570	834	360	20	19	124	75	138
Intimidation	1,489	857	184	7	13	20	119	289
Other[1]	30	19	6	0	0	1	3	1
Crimes against Property	2,547	456	159	10	4	39	314	1,565
Robbery	126	42	55	1	0	10	7	11
Burglary	142	30	16	0	0	8	24	64
Larceny-theft	258	79	22	1	1	2	36	117
Motor vehicle theft	23	5	0	0	0	0	2	16
Arson	38	12	4	1	3	1	7	10
Destruction/damage/vandalism	1,906	260	57	5	0	18	231	1,335
Other[1]	54	28	5	2	0	0	7	12
Crimes against Society [1]	203	80	94	1	2	7	9	10

1 Includes additional offenses collected in the National Incident-Based Reporting System.

Table 85. Offenses, Offense Type, by Bias Motivation, 2012

(Number)

Bias motivation	Total offenses	Crimes against persons						Crimes against property							Crimes against society[1]
		Murder and nonnegligent manslaughter	Forcible rape	Aggravated assault	Simple assault	Intimidation	Other[1]	Robbery	Burglary	Larceny-theft	Motor vehicle theft	Arson	Destruction/damage/vandalism	Other[1]	
Total	6,718	10	15	854	1,570	1,489	30	126	142	258	23	38	1,906	54	203
Single-Bias Incidents	6,705	10	15	853	1,564	1,487	30	126	141	258	23	37	1,904	54	203
Race	3,297	1	4	448	754	829	10	50	69	136	13	14	787	25	157
Anti-White	739	1	1	95	199	121	6	23	29	85	10	3	94	20	52
Anti-Black	2,180	0	0	317	481	635	1	20	28	22	2	8	574	0	92
Anti-American Indian/Alaskan Native	109	0	3	10	22	8	3	3	6	21	1	0	18	4	10
Anti-Asian/Pacific Islander	134	0	0	18	29	33	0	3	3	6	0	3	38	1	0
Anti-multiple races, group	135	0	0	8	23	32	0	1	3	2	0	0	63	0	3
Religion	1,166	8	0	44	128	158	3	4	18	64	4	14	692	14	15
Anti-Jewish	696	0	0	11	72	87	1	2	10	17	1	2	486	5	2
Anti-Catholic	79	0	0	10	4	7	1	0	0	11	0	2	38	3	3
Anti-Protestant	34	0	0	0	1	1	0	1	1	9	1	2	16	1	1
Anti-Islamic	149	2	0	14	41	43	1	0	1	4	0	4	39	0	0
Anti-other religion	107	6	0	8	4	16	0	0	2	2	1	2	63	1	2
Anti-multiple religions, group	89	0	0	1	4	4	0	1	3	18	0	2	48	4	4
Anti-atheism/agnosticism/etc.	12	0	0	0	2	0	0	0	1	3	1	0	2	0	3
Sexual Orientation	1,318	1	10	211	453	262	11	50	23	24	3	6	249	5	10
Anti-male homosexual	720	1	4	114	285	141	4	39	8	5	1	4	112	2	0
Anti-female homosexual	162	0	4	14	45	43	1	1	2	5	2	0	43	0	2
Anti-homosexual	369	0	1	75	111	70	0	10	8	6	0	1	84	1	2
Anti-heterosexual	26	0	0	1	3	3	6	0	1	2	0	1	6	1	2
Anti-bisexual	41	0	1	7	9	5	0	0	4	6	0	0	4	1	4
Ethnicity/National Origin	822	0	1	131	196	230	5	21	28	21	2	3	165	4	15
Anti-Hispanic	488	0	1	89	127	127	3	16	15	13	2	1	81	2	11
Anti-other ethnicity/national origin	334	0	0	42	69	103	2	5	13	8	0	2	84	2	4
Disability	102	0	0	19	33	8	1	1	3	13	1	0	11	6	6
Anti-physical	20	0	0	4	9	3	0	0	0	1	1	0	0	1	1
Anti-mental	82	0	0	15	24	5	1	1	3	12	0	0	11	5	5
Multiple-Bias Incidents[2]	13	0	0	1	6	2	0	0	1	0	0	1	2	0	0

1 Includes additional offenses collected in the National Incident-Based Reporting System. 2 In a multiple-bias incident, two conditions must be met: (a) more than one offense type must occur in the incident and (b) at least two offense types must be motivated by different biases.

Table 86. Offenses, Known Offender's Race, by Bias Motivation, 2012

(Number)

Bias motivation	Total offenses	Known offender's race						Unknown offender
		White	Black	American Indian/Alaskan Native	Asian/Pacific Islander	Multipleraces, group	Unknown race	
Total	6,718	2,793	992	51	40	229	571	2,042
Single-Bias Incidents	6,705	2,786	990	49	40	227	571	2,042
Race	3,297	1,572	492	37	18	103	274	801
Anti-White	739	209	305	21	3	20	58	123
Anti-Black	2,180	1,206	141	12	10	70	173	568
Anti-American Indian/Alaskan Native	109	47	14	3	3	3	13	26
Anti-Asian/Pacific Islander	134	64	18	0	1	2	17	32
Anti-multiple races, group	135	46	14	1	1	8	13	52
Religion	1,166	245	46	2	7	34	103	729
Anti-Jewish	696	101	20	0	4	20	45	506
Anti-Catholic	79	23	1	1	0	0	9	45
Anti-Protestant	34	10	4	1	0	1	5	13
Anti-Islamic	149	61	10	0	2	8	19	49
Anti-other religion	107	31	2	0	0	1	12	61
Anti-multiple religions, group	89	14	8	0	1	3	11	52
Anti-atheism/agnosticism/etc.	12	5	1	0	0	1	2	3
Sexual Orientation	1,318	506	315	5	9	70	116	297
Anti-male homosexual	720	277	193	4	5	53	46	142
Anti-female homosexual	162	52	38	0	2	3	14	53
Anti-homosexual	369	148	73	1	2	11	52	82
Anti-heterosexual	26	11	5	0	0	0	3	7
Anti-bisexual	41	18	6	0	0	3	1	13
Ethnicity/National Origin	822	413	117	4	6	17	71	194
Anti-Hispanic	488	278	67	2	3	9	31	98
Anti-other ethnicity/national origin	334	135	50	2	3	8	40	96
Disability	102	50	20	1	0	3	7	21
Anti-physical	20	12	3	0	0	0	1	4
Anti-mental	82	38	17	1	0	3	6	17
Multiple-Bias Incidents [1]	13	7	2	2	0	2	0	0

1 In a multiple-bias incident, two conditions must be met: (a) more than one offense type must occur in the incident and (b) at least two offense types must be motivated by different biases.

Table 87. Offenses, Victim Type, by Offense Type, 2012

(Number)

Offense type	Total offenses	Victim type					
		Individual	Business/ financial institution	Government	Religious organization	Society/ public[1]	Other/unknown/ multiple
Total	6,718	5,350	310	193	181	203	481
Crimes against Persons [2]	3,968	3,968	n.a.	n.a.	n.a.	n.a.	n.a.
Crimes against Property	2,547	1,382	310	193	181	0	481
Robbery	126	118	1	0	0	0	7
Burglary	142	103	12	1	4	0	22
Larceny-theft	258	174	61	2	8	0	13
Motor vehicle theft	23	19	2	0	0	0	2
Arson	38	22	2	1	8	0	5
Destruction/damage/vandalism	1,906	904	222	187	161	0	432
Other[2]	54	42	10	2	0	0	0
Crimes Against Society [2]	203	n.a.	n.a.	n.a.	n.a.	203	n.a.

1 The victim type society/public is collected only in the National Incident-Based Reporting System (NIBRS). 2 Includes additional offenses collected in the NIBRS. n.a. = not available

Table 88. Victims, Offense Type, by Bias Motivation, 2012

(Number)

Bias motivation	Total victims	Crimes against persons						Crimes against property							Crimes against society[1]
		Murder and nonnegligent manslaughter	Forcible rape	Aggravated assault	Simple assault	Intimidation	Other[1]	Robbery	Burglary	Larceny-theft	Motor vehicle theft	Arson	Destruction/damage/vandalism	Other[1]	
Total	7,164	10	15	854	1,570	1,489	30	149	174	281	24	46	2,263	56	203
Single-Bias Incidents	7,151	10	15	853	1,564	1,487	30	149	173	281	24	45	2,261	56	203
Race	3,467	1	4	448	754	829	10	61	85	140	13	19	919	27	157
Anti-White	763	1	1	95	199	121	6	31	34	88	10	4	99	22	52
Anti-Black	2,295	0	0	317	481	635	1	22	37	22	2	12	674	0	92
Anti-American Indian/Alaskan Native	115	0	3	10	22	8	3	4	8	22	1	0	20	4	10
Anti-Asian/Pacific Islander	143	0	0	18	29	33	0	3	3	6	0	3	47	1	0
Anti-multiple races, group	151	0	0	8	23	32	0	1	3	2	0	0	79	0	3
Religion	1,340	8	0	44	128	158	3	4	19	80	5	16	846	14	15
Anti-Jewish	836	0	0	11	72	87	1	2	10	30	1	2	613	5	2
Anti-Catholic	86	0	0	10	4	7	1	0	0	14	0	2	42	3	3
Anti-Protestant	35	0	0	0	1	1	0	1	1	9	2	2	16	1	1
Anti-Islamic	155	2	0	14	41	43	1	0	1	4	0	5	44	0	0
Anti-other religion	115	6	0	8	4	16	0	0	3	2	1	3	69	1	2
Anti-multiple religions, group	101	0	0	1	4	4	0	1	3	18	0	2	60	4	4
Anti-atheism/agnosticism/etc.	12	0	0	0	2	0	0	0	1	3	1	0	2	0	3
Sexual Orientation	1,376	1	10	211	453	262	11	57	26	25	3	6	296	5	10
Anti-male homosexual	741	1	4	114	285	141	4	42	10	5	1	4	128	2	0
Anti-female homosexual	175	0	4	14	45	43	1	1	3	6	2	0	54	0	2
Anti-homosexual	393	0	1	75	111	70	0	14	8	6	0	1	104	1	2
Anti-heterosexual	26	0	0	1	3	3	6	0	1	2	0	1	6	1	2
Anti-bisexual	41	0	1	7	9	5	0	0	4	6	0	0	4	1	4
Ethnicity/National Origin	866	0	1	131	196	230	5	26	40	23	2	4	189	4	15
Anti-Hispanic	514	0	1	89	127	127	3	19	24	14	2	1	94	2	11
Anti-other ethnicity/national origin	352	0	0	42	69	103	2	7	16	9	0	3	95	2	4
Disability	102	0	0	19	33	8	1	1	3	13	1	0	11	6	6
Anti-physical	20	0	0	4	9	3	0	0	0	1	1	0	0	1	1
Anti-mental	82	0	0	15	24	5	1	1	3	12	0	0	11	5	5
Multiple-Bias Incidents[2]	13	0	0	1	6	2	0	0	1	0	0	1	2	0	0

1 Includes additional offenses collected in the National Incident-Based Reporting System. 2 In a multiple-bias incident, two conditions must be met: (a) more than one offense type must occur in the incident and (b) at least two offense types must be motivated by different biases.

Table 89. Incidents, Victim Type, by Bias Motivation, 2012

(Number)

Bias motivation	Total incidents	Victim type					
		Individual	Business/ financial institution	Government	Religious organization	Society/ public[1]	Other/unknown/ multiple
Total	5,796	4,444	295	190	178	107	492
Single-Bias Incidents	5,790	4,439	295	190	177	197	492
Race	2,797	2,240	146	105	12	152	142
Religion	1,099	489	92	52	154	15	297
Sexual orientation	1,135	1,050	26	22	4	10	23
Ethnicity/national origin	667	578	27	11	7	14	30
Disability	92	82	4	0	0	6	0
Multiple-Bias Incidents [2]	6	5	0	0	1	0	0

1 The victim type society/public is collected only in the National Incident-Based Reporting System. 2 In a multiple-bias incident, two conditions must be met: (a) more than one offense type must occur in the incident and (b) at least two offense types must be motivated by different biases.

Table 90. Known Offenders, by Known Offender's Race, 2012[1]

(Number)

Race	Number
Total	5,331
White	2,909
Black	1,242
American Indian/Alaskan Native	49
Asian/Pacific Islander	47
Multiple races, group[2]	471
Unknown race	613

1 The term *known offender* does not imply that the identity of the suspect is known, but only that an attribute of the suspect has been identified, which distinguishes him/her from an unknown offender. 2 The term *multiple races*, group is used to describe a group of offenders of varying races.

Table 91. Incidents, Bias Motivation, by Location, 2012

(Number)

Location	Total incidents	Bias motivation					Multiple-bias incidents[1]
		Race	Religion	Sexual orientation	Ethnicity/ national origin	Disability	
Total	5,796	2,797	1,099	1,135	667	92	6
Abandoned/condemned structure	4	2	0	0	2	0	0
Air/bus/train terminal	75	40	2	22	6	5	0
Amusement park	2	2	0	0	0	0	0
ATM separate from bank	1	1	0	0	0	0	0
Auto dealership new/used	2	1	1	0	0	0	0
Bank/savings and loan	15	7	4	1	2	1	0
Bar/nightclub	105	46	1	41	14	3	0
Camp/campground	4	0	2	1	1	0	0
Church/synagogue/temple/mosque	235	20	200	5	9	0	1
Commercial office building	95	40	14	28	13	0	0
Construction site	12	8	1	1	2	0	0
Convenience store	72	35	9	14	14	0	0
Daycare facility	3	1	2	0	0	0	0
Department/discount store	51	30	6	10	3	2	0
Dock/wharf/freight/modal terminal	1	1	0	0	0	0	0
Drug store/Doctor's office/hospital	44	27	7	1	7	1	1
Farm facility	3	3	0	0	0	0	0
Field/woods	48	21	11	10	4	2	0
Gambling facility/casino/race track	3	2	1	0	0	0	0
Government/public building	66	47	9	5	4	1	0
Grocery/supermarket	52	39	2	6	4	1	0
Highway/road/alley/street/sidewalk	1,058	556	78	268	140	15	1
Hotel/motel/etc.	39	17	4	8	10	0	0
Industrial site	5	1	3	0	1	0	0
Jail/prison/penitentiary/corrections facility	46	25	5	7	9	0	0
Lake/waterway/beach	10	4	2	4	0	0	0
Liquor store	10	6	1	1	2	0	0
Park/playground	53	36	8	4	5	0	0
Parking/drop lot/garage	330	191	24	67	46	2	0
Rental storage facility	5	2	1	0	1	1	0
Residence/home	1,887	978	293	355	213	45	3
Rest area	7	6	0	1	0	0	0
Restaurant	103	53	9	26	14	1	0
School/college[2]	222	118	36	52	15	1	0
School—college/university	76	29	19	15	12	1	0
School—elementary/secondary	185	104	26	31	22	2	0
Service/gas station	39	18	6	5	9	1	0
Shelter—mission/homeless	1	1	0	0	0	0	0
Shopping mall	27	10	6	8	3	0	0
Specialty store (TV, fur, etc.)	51	24	11	3	12	1	0
Other/unknown	743	243	293	133	68	6	0
Multiple locations	6	2	2	2	0	0	0

1 In a multiple-bias incident, two conditions must be met: (a) more than one offense type must occur in the incident and (b) at least two offense types must be motivated by different biases. 2 The location designation School/college has been retained for agencies that have not updated their records management systems to include the new location designations of School—college/university and School—elementary/secondary, which allow for more specificity in reporting.

Table 92. Offenses, Offense Type, by Participating State, 2012

(Number)

Participating state	Total offenses	Crimes against persons						Crimes against property							Crimes against society[1]
		Murder and nonnegligent manslaughter	Forcible rape	Aggravated assault	Simple assault	Intimidation	Other[1]	Robbery	Burglary	Larceny-theft	Motor-vehicle-theft	Arson	Destruction/damage/vandalism	Other[1]	
Total	6,718	10	15	854	1,570	1,489	30	126	142	258	23	38	1,906	54	203
Alabama	6	0	0	0	1	1	0	0	0	1	0	0	2	0	1
Alaska	6	1	0	1	3	0	0	0	0	0	0	0	1	0	0
Arizona	209	0	0	43	35	75	0	5	4	4	0	0	43	0	0
Arkansas	30	0	0	3	6	5	1	0	0	2	0	0	8	1	4
California	1,089	0	2	226	237	245	0	29	11	3	2	10	324	0	0
Colorado	233	0	1	37	55	49	0	9	7	19	4	1	48	3	0
Connecticut	176	0	0	8	46	66	0	1	2	7	1	0	44	1	0
Delaware	11	0	0	0	1	5	0	1	0	0	0	0	4	0	0
District of Columbia	81	0	0	8	35	14	0	14	0	1	0	0	9	0	0
Florida	166	1	0	42	43	23	0	4	3	0	0	1	49	0	0
Georgia	21	0	0	2	6	8	0	0	0	0	0	0	5	0	0
Idaho	39	0	0	3	9	13	1	1	1	1	0	0	10	0	0
Illinois	101	0	1	24	27	14	0	3	1	0	0	2	29	0	0
Indiana	38	0	0	5	7	2	0	1	1	0	0	0	22	0	0
Iowa	8	0	0	1	0	3	0	0	0	0	0	0	4	0	0
Kansas	97	0	0	7	26	26	1	0	4	6	0	0	24	3	0
Kentucky	230	0	0	12	51	66	6	10	12	14	1	1	43	8	6
Louisiana	4	0	0	1	1	1	0	0	0	0	0	0	1	0	0
Maine	61	0	0	2	13	27	1	0	0	0	0	0	18	0	0
Maryland	45	0	0	14	11	0	0	1	0	0	0	1	18	0	0
Massachusetts	190	0	1	31	34	39	2	1	3	14	1	0	60	3	1
Michigan	718	0	0	86	161	213	0	5	10	19	3	2	113	5	101
Minnesota	83	0	0	7	14	34	0	4	0	1	0	2	21	0	0
Mississippi	19	0	0	0	5	1	1	0	0	5	0	0	2	2	3
Missouri	121	0	0	20	25	28	0	3	6	3	0	2	33	1	0
Montana	39	0	0	6	8	0	2	0	1	6	1	0	13	1	1
Nebraska	10	0	0	1	4	1	0	0	1	1	0	0	2	0	0
Nevada	113	0	0	30	26	18	0	5	4	2	0	2	26	0	0
New Hampshire	34	0	0	2	8	11	0	0	0	1	0	0	12	0	0
New Mexico	4	0	0	3	0	0	0	0	0	1	0	0	0	0	0
New York	741	1	4	18	251	40	0	5	15	12	0	6	389	0	0
North Carolina	140	0	0	12	35	33	0	1	2	3	0	3	51	0	0
North Dakota	52	0	0	2	17	12	0	2	2	7	0	0	7	3	0
Ohio	296	0	0	13	47	112	2	4	11	11	1	2	87	2	4
Oklahoma	26	0	0	2	8	11	0	0	2	2	0	0	1	0	0
Oregon	64	0	0	6	7	22	0	1	0	2	0	0	24	1	1
Pennsylvania	42	0	0	7	9	15	0	0	1	1	0	0	9	0	0
Rhode Island	15	0	0	2	1	2	0	0	2	0	0	0	8	0	0
South Carolina	172	0	0	21	34	24	2	1	11	31	2	0	28	5	13
South Dakota	37	0	1	8	10	4	0	0	0	0	0	0	14	0	0
Tennessee	367	0	2	44	93	80	6	6	12	27	2	2	48	6	39
Texas	60	0	0	7	18	10	0	0	1	2	0	1	21	0	0
Utah	113	0	0	4	22	12	4	0	3	8	1	0	36	2	21
Vermont	14	0	0	0	5	1	0	0	0	1	0	0	7	0	0
Virginia	152	0	0	16	36	25	0	1	0	1	0	0	73	0	0
Washington	323	1	3	40	64	84	1	5	5	28	3	0	85	3	1
West Virginia	29	0	0	2	6	1	0	0	2	6	1	0	4	3	4
Wisconsin	91	6	0	24	8	13	0	3	2	5	0	0	26	1	3
Wyoming	2	0	0	1	1	0	0	0	0	0	0	0	0	0	0

1 Includes additional offenses collected in the National Incident-Based Reporting System.

SECTION VII

APPENDIXES

APPENDIX I: CRIME TRENDS

In 2012, crime in the United States did not consistently continue its trend of decline. Violent crimes rose by a rate of 0.7 percent, while property crime fell by 0.9 percent. (Table 1B) The violent crime category includes murder, forcible rape, robbery, and aggravated assault, while property crimes include burglary, larceny-theft, and motor vehicle theft. Arson is also a property crime, but data for arson are not included in property crime totals due to variable participation from the reporting agencies.

Types of Crimes in 2012

The trend and the types of crimes committed in the United States not only continues to cover the main categories of murder, forcible rape, robbery, aggravated assault, burglary, larceny-theft, motor vehicle theft, and arson described in this publication's earlier chapters, but we are also facing an continuous increase in crimes committed through cyberspace and the Internet. These crimes are classified as scams or Internet fraud.

As Internet use has become a mainstay in our society and the world, the occurrence and development of Internet-based crimes has become widespread. As individuals, businesses, and organizations look for and implement efficient and effective ways to deter the ability of criminals to attack through cyberspace, new ways of victimizing Internet users continue to evolve.

Internet Fraud

The Internet Fraud Complaint Center—a partnership between the National White Collar Crime Center (NW3C), the Bureau of Justice Assistance (BJA), and the Federal Bureau of Investigation (FBI)—was established May 8, 2000, to address the ever-increasing incidence of online fraud. Just three years later, in response to the exponential increase in cyber crime of all types, the center changed its name to the Internet Crime Complaint Center (IC3®). With more than two million complaints received since its inception, IC3 serves as the nation's portal for reporting Internet crime and suspicious activity.

In 2012, the Internet Crime Complaint Center (IC3) actively pursued its mission to address crimes committed using the Internet, providing services to both victims of online crimes and to law enforcement. IC3 received 289,874 complaints. The adjusted dollar loss of complaints was $525.4 million, and 8.3 percent increase from 2011.[1]

The 2012 IC3 Internet Crime Report reveals both the scope of online crime and IC3's battle against it. Some of the most common victim complaints included FBI-related scams, identity theft, and advance fee fraud.[2] IC3 received and processed more than 24,000 complaints per month. Based on victim complaints, the top five states were California (13.41 percent), Florida (7.98 percent), Texas (7.22 percent), New York (5.70 percent) and New Jersey (3.81 percent). Victims in California reported the highest dollar losses with a total of nearly $68.2 million. The average financial loss for reporting victims was $4,573.

IC3 serves as a powerful conduit for law enforcement to share information and pursue cases that often span jurisdictional boundaries. Collaboration within this partnership has produced a number of technological advancements to streamline the way complaints are processed and referred to investigators. Initially established as simply a convenient method for citizens to report Internet crime information, IC3 has evolved into a vital resource for both victims of online crime and for law enforcement across the country that investigate and prosecute a wide range of cases.

Below are recent scams and cyber crimes reported by the IC3 and the FBI in recent FBI press releases, and tips on ways to avoid becoming a victim of these crimes. Any type of cyber attack should be immediately reported to the local FBI office as well as to the IC3's Web site at www.IC3.gov. The IC3's complaint database links complaints together to refer them to the appropriate law enforcement agency for case consideration. The complaint information is also used to identify emerging trends and patterns. Information about recent Internet and cyber crime can be found at http://www.fbi.gov/scams-safety/e-scams.

Mystery/Secret Shopper Schemes

The IC3 has been alerted to an increase in employment schemes pertaining to mystery/secret shopper positions. Many retail and service corporations hire evaluators to perform secret or random checks on themselves or their competitors, and fraudsters are capitalizing on this employment opportunity. Victims have reported to the IC3 that they were contacted via e-mail message and U.S. mail to apply to be a mystery shopper. Applicants are asked to send a résumé and are purportedly subject to an extensive background check before being accepted as a mystery shopper. The employees are sent a check with instructions to shop at a specified retailer for a specific length of time and spend a specific amount on merchandise from the store. The employees receive instructions to take note of the store's environment, color, payment procedures, gift items, and shopping/carrier bags and report back to the employer. The second evaluation is the ease and accuracy of wiring money from the retail location. The money to be wired is also included in the check sent to the employee. The remaining balance is the employee's payment for the completion of the assignment. After merchandise is purchased and money is wired, the employees are advised by the bank the check cashed was counterfeit, and they are responsible for the money lost in addition to bank fees incurred.

In other versions of the scheme, applicants are requested to provide bank account information to have money directly deposited into their accounts. The fraudster then has acquired access to these victims' accounts and can withdraw money, which makes the applicant a victim of identity theft.

Tips

The IC3 provides tips to help users avoid becoming a victim of employment schemes associated with mystery/secret shopping. They can also be found at http://www.ic3.gov/media/2010/100120.aspx:

- Do not respond to unsolicited (spam) e-mail messages
- Do not open links contained within an unsolicited e-mail message
- Be cautious of e-mail messages claiming to contain pictures in attached files, as the files may contain viruses. Only open attachments from known senders. Scan all attachments for viruses, if possible
- Avoid filling out forms contained in e-mail messages that ask for personal information
- Always compare the link in the e-mail message to the link you are actually directed to and determine if they match and will lead you to a legitimate site
- There are legitimate mystery/secret shopper programs available. Research the legitimacy on companies hiring mystery shoppers. Legitimate companies will not charge an application fee and will accept applications online
- No legitimate mystery/secret shopper program will send payment in advance and ask the employee to send a portion of it back

Work from Home Scams

Consumers continue to lose money from work-from-home scams that assist cyber criminals to move stolen funds. Worse yet, due to their deliberate or unknowing participation in the scams, these individuals may face criminal charges. Work-from-home scam victims are often recruited by organized cyber criminals through newspaper ads, online employment services, unsolicited e-mail messages or "spam," online and social networking sites advertising work-from-home opportunities. Once recruited, however, rather than becoming an employee of a legitimate business, the consumer is actually a "mule" for cyber criminals who use the consumer's or other victim's accounts to steal and launder money.

Fraudulent Classified Ads and Auction Sales

Internet criminals post classified ads and auctions for products they do not have and make the scam work by using stolen credit cards. Fraudsters receive an order from a victim, charge the victim's credit card for the amount of the order, then use a separate stolen credit card for the actual purchase. They pocket the purchase price obtained from the victim's credit card and have the merchant ship the item directly to the victim. Consequently, an item purchased from an online auction but received directly from the merchant is a strong indication of fraud. Victims of such a scam not only lose the money paid to the fraudster, but may be liable for receiving stolen goods.

Shoppers may help avoid these scams by using caution and not providing financial information directly to the seller, as fraudulent sellers will use this information to purchase items for their schemes. Always use a legitimate payment service to ensure a safe, legitimate purchase.

Diligently check each seller's rating and feedback along with their number of sales and the dates on which feedback was posted. Be wary of a seller with 100 percent positive feedback, with a low total number of feedback postings, or with all feedback posted around the same date and time.

Phishing and Smishing Schemes

In phishing schemes, the fraudster poses as a legitimate entity and uses e-mail messages and scam Web sites to obtain victims' personal information, such as account numbers, user names, passwords, and so on. Smishing is the act of sending fraudulent text messages to bait a victim into revealing personal information.

Be leery of e-mail messages or text messages that indicate a problem or question regarding your financial accounts. In this scam, fraudsters direct victims to follow a link or call a number to update an account or correct a purported problem. The link directs the victim to a fraudulent Web site or message that appears legitimate. Instead, the site allows the fraudster to steal any personal information the victim provides.

Smishing schemes involve fraudsters calling victims' cell phones and offering to lower the interest rates for credit cards the victims do not even possess. If a victim asserts that they do not own the credit card, the caller hangs up. These fraudsters call from TRAC cell phones that do not have voice-mail, or the phone provides a constant busy signal when called, rendering these calls virtually untraceable.

Another scam involves fraudsters directing victims, via e-mail, to a spoofed Web site. A spoofed Web site is a fake site that misleads the victim into providing personal information, which is routed to the scammer's computer.

Tips to avoid becoming a victim of cyber fraud. These can be found at http://www.fbi.gov/scams-safety/e-scams:

- Do not respond to unsolicited (spam) e-mail messages
- Do not open links contained within an unsolicited e-mail messages
- Be cautious of e-mail messages claiming to contain pictures in attached files, as the files may contain viruses. Only open attachments from known senders. Scan the attachments for viruses, if possible
- Avoid filling out forms contained in e-mail messages that ask for personal information.
- Always compare the link in the e-mail message with the link to which you are directed and determine whether they match and will lead you to a legitimate site.
- Log directly onto the official Web site for the business identified in the e-mail message, instead of "linking" to it from an unsolicited e-mail message. If the e-mail message appears to be from you bank, credit card issuer, or other company you deal with frequently, your statements or official correspondence from the business will provide the proper contact information
- Contact the actual business that supposedly sent the e-mail message to verify whether the e-mail message is genuine
- If you are asked to act quickly, or there is an emergency, it may be a scam. Fraudsters create a sense of urgency to get you to act quickly
- Verify any requests for personal information from any business or financial institution by contacting them using the main contact information
- Remember, if it looks too good to be true, it probably is

Prize Sweepstakes or Lottery Schemes

Prize sweepstakes or lottery scheme perpetrators use counterfeit checks that bear legitimate-looking logos of various financial institutions to fool victims into sending money to the fraudsters.

Fraudsters tell victims they've won a sweepstakes or lottery, but to receive a lump sum payout, they must pay the taxes and processing fees up front. Fraudsters direct individuals to call a telephone number to initiate a letter of instructions. The letter alleges that the victim may elect to take an advance on the winnings to make the required up-front payment. The letter includes a check in the amount of the alleged taxes and fees along with processing instructions. Ultimately, victims believe they are using the advance to make the required up-front payment, but in reality they are falling prey to the scheme.

The victim deposits the check into their own bank, which credits the account for the amount of the check before the check clears. The victim immediately withdraws the money and wires it to the fraudsters. Afterwards, the check proves to be counterfeit and the bank pulls the respective funds from the victim's account, leaving the victim liable for the amount of the counterfeit check plus any additional fees the bank may charge.

Persons may fall victim to this scheme due to the allure of easy money and the apparent legitimacy of the check the fraudsters included in the letter of instruction. The alleged cash prizes and locations of the financial institutions vary.

Tips to avoid being scammed (from http://www.ic3.gov/preventiontips.aspx#item-11):

- Be cautious when dealing with individuals outside of your own country
- Be leery if you do not remember entering a lottery or sweepstakes
- Beware of lotteries or sweepstakes that charge a fee prior to delivering your prize

- Be wary of demands to send additional money as a requirement to be eligible for future winnings
- It is a violation of federal law to play a foreign lottery via mail or phone

Charitable Contribution Schemes

The FBI warns the public to be aware of and report any instances of alleged fraudulent activity related to relief operations and funding for victims. Criminals exploit these tragedies by sending fraudulent e-mail messages and creating phony Web sites designed to solicit contributions.

The National Center for Disaster Fraud was created by the Department of Justice to investigate, prosecute, and deter fraud in the wake of Hurricane Katrina, when billions of dollars in federal disaster relief poured into the Gulf Cost region. Its mission has expanded to include suspected fraud from any natural or manmade disaster. More than 20 federal agencies, including the FBI, participate in the National Center for Disaster Fraud, which allows the center to act as a centralized clearinghouse of information related to disaster relief fraud.

Use due diligence before giving contributions to anyone soliciting donations or individuals offering to provide assistance to those affected by the tornadoes. Solicitations can originate from e-mail messages, Web sites, door-to-door collections, flyers, mailings, telephone calls, and other similar methods.

Before making a donation of any kind, consumers should adhere to the following guidelines (from http://www.fbi.gov/sandiego/press-releases/2012/tips-on-avoiding-fraudulent-charitable-contribution-schemes):

- Do not respond to any unsolicited (spam) incoming e-mail messages, including requests to open links contained within those messages, because they may contain computer viruses
- Be skeptical of individuals representing themselves as members of charitable organizations or officials asking for donations via e-mail messages or social networking sites
- Beware of organizations with copycat names similar to but not exactly the same as those of reputable charities
- Be cautious of e-mail messages that claim to show pictures of the disaster areas in attached files because the files may contain viruses. Only open attachments from known senders
- Ensure that contributions are received and used for intended purposes by making contributions directly to known organizations rather than relying on others to make the donation on your behalf
- Do not be pressured into making contributions; reputable charities do not use such tactics
- Be aware of whom you are dealing with when providing your personal and financial information. Providing such information may compromise your identity and make you vulnerable to identity theft
- Avoid cash donations if possible. Pay by credit card or write a check directly to the charity. Do not make checks payable to individuals.
- Verify Web sites. Legitimate charities do not normally solicit donations via money transfer services. Most legitimate charities' Web sites end in .org rather than .com.

Scareware

Scareware is malicious software that poses as legitimate computer security software and purports to detect a variety of threats on the affected computer that do not actually exist. Users are then informed they must purchase what they are told is anti-virus software to repair their computers. The users are then barraged with aggressive and disruptive notifications until they supply their credit card number and pay for the worthless "anti-virus" product. The product is, in fact, fake.

The FBI has seized more than 40 computers, servers, and bank accounts linked to scareware schemes.

The scareware scheme used a variety of ruses to trick consumers into infecting their computers with the malicious scareware products, including web pages featuring fake computer scans. Once the scareware was downloaded, victims were notified that their computers were infected with a range of malicious software, such as viruses and Trojans, and badgered into purchasing the fake anti-virus software to resolve the non-existent problem at a cost of up to $129. In one scheme, which was based in Kyiv, Ukraine, an estimated 960,000 users were victimized by this scareware scheme, leading to $72 million in actual losses.

In 2012, almost 2,000 scareware victims had lost over $134,000.[3]

Online Vehicle Shopping Scams

Online vehicle shoppers are being victimized by fraudulent vehicle sales and false claims of vehicle protection programs (VPP). In fraudulent vehicle sales, criminals attempt to sell vehicles they do not own. They create an attractive deal by advertising vehicles for sale at prices below book value. Often sellers state that they need to sell the vehicle because they are moving for work, to include military deployments.

Because of the alleged pending move, criminals refuse to meet the victim in person or allow a vehicle inspection, and they often attempt to rush the sale. To make the deal appear legitimate, the criminal instructs the victim to send full or partial payment to a third-party agent via a wire transfer payment service and to fax the payment receipt to the seller as proof of payment.

The criminal pockets the payment but does not deliver the vehicle. Criminals also attempt to make their scams appear valid by misusing the names of reputable companies and programs.

In a new twist, criminals use a live-chat feature in e-mail correspondence and electronic invoices. As live-chat assistants, the criminals answer victims' questions and assure them the deals are safe, claiming that safeguards are in place to reimburse buyers for any loss. The criminals falsely assert that their sales are protected by liability insurance coverage up to $50,000.

Automotive shoppers should exercise due diligence before engaging in transactions to purchase vehicles advertised online. In particular, shoppers should be cautious of the following situations (from http://www.ic3.gov/media/2011/110815.aspx):

- Sellers who want to move the transaction from one platform to another (for example, from Craigslist to eBay Motors)
- Sellers who claim that a buyer protection program offered by a major Internet company covers an auto transaction conducted outside that company's site
- Sellers who push for speedy completion of the transaction and request payments via quick wire transfer payment systems
- Sellers who refuse to meet in person, or refuse to allow the buyer to physically inspect the vehicle before the purchase
- Transactions in which the seller and vehicle are in different locations. Criminals often claim to have been transferred for work reasons, deployed by the military, or moved because of a family circumstance, and could not take the vehicle with them
- Vehicles advertised at well below their market value. Remember, if it looks too good to be true, it probably is

Timeshare Marketing Scams

Timeshare owners across the country are being scammed out of millions of dollars by unscrupulous companies that promise to sell or rent the unsuspecting victim; timeshares. In the typical scam, timeshare owners receive unexpected or uninvited telephone calls or e-mail messages from criminals posing as sales representatives for a timeshare resale company. The representative promises a quick sale, often within 60 to 90 days. The sales representatives often use high-pressure sales tactics to add a sense of urgency to the deal. Some victims have reported that sales representatives pressured them by claiming there was a buyer waiting in the wings, either on the other line or present in the office.

Timeshare owners who agree to sell are told that they must pay an upfront fee to cover anything from listing and advertising fees to closing costs. Many victims have provided credit cards to pay the fees ranging from a few hundred to a few thousand dollars. Once the fee is paid, timeshare owners report that the company becomes evasive—calls go unanswered, numbers are disconnected, and Web sites are inaccessible.

In some cases, timeshare owners who have been defrauded by a timeshare sales scheme have been subsequently contacted by an unscrupulous timeshare fraud recovery company as well. The representative from the recovery company promises assistance in recovering money lost in the sales scam. Some recovery companies require an up-front fee for services rendered, while other promise no fees will be paid unless a refund is obtained for the timeshare owner. The IC3 has identified some instances where people involved with the recovery company also have a connection to the resale company, raising the possibility that timeshare owners are being scammed twice by the same people.

If you are contacted by someone offering to sell or rent your timeshare, the IC3 recommends using caution. Listed below are tips you can use to avoid becoming a victim of a timeshare scheme (from http://www.ic3.gov/media/2012/120125.aspx):

- Be wary if a company asks you for up-front fees to sell or rent your timeshare
- Read the fine print of any sales contract or rental agreement provided
- Check with the Better Business Bureau to ensure the company is reputable

To obtain more information on Internet schemes, visit www.LooksTooGoodToBeTrue.com. Also, anyone who believes they have been a victim of this type of scam should promptly report it to the IC3's Web site at www.IC3.gov.

Payday Loan Telephone Collection Scams

The typical payday loan scam involves a caller who claims that the victim is delinquent on a payday loan and must make payment to avoid legal consequences. Callers pose as representatives of the FBI, "Federal Legislative Department," various law firms, or other legitimate-sounding agencies and claim to be collecting debt for companies such as United Cash Advance, U.S. Cash Advance, U.S. Cash Net, or other Internet check-cashing services. The fraudsters relentlessly call the victim's home, cell phone, and place of employment in attempts to obtain payment. The callers refuse to provide information regarding the alleged payday loan or any documentation and become verbally abusive when questioned.

One of the most insidious aspects of this scam is that the callers have accurate information about the victims, including Social Security numbers, dates of birth, addresses, employer information, bank account numbers, and names and telephone numbers of relatives and friends. The method by which the fraudsters obtained the personal information is unclear, but victims often relay that they had completed online applications for other loans or credit cards before the calls began.

The Internet Crime Complaint Center has observed variations of the scam in which the caller tells the victim that there are outstanding warrants for the victim's arrest. The caller claims that the basis of the warrants is non-payment of the underlying loan and/or hacking; if it's the latter, the caller tells the victim that he or she is wanted for hacking into a business" computer system to steal customer information. The caller will then demand payment via debit/credit card; in other cases, the caller further instructs victims to obtain a prepaid card to cover the payment.

The high-pressure collection tactics used by the fraudsters have also evolved. In one complaint, a person posed as a process server and appeared at the victim's job. In another instance, a phony process server came to a victim's home. In both cases, after claiming to be serving a court summons, the alleged process server said the victim could avoid going to court if he or she provided a debit card number for repayment of the loan.

If you are contacted by someone who is trying to collect a debt that you do not owe, you should take the following steps (from http://www.ic3.gov/media/2012/120221.aspx).

- Contact your local law enforcement agencies if you feel you are in immediate danger
- Contact your bank(s) and credit card companies
- Contact the three major credit bureaus and request an alert be put on your file
- If you have received a legitimate loan and want to verify that you do not have any outstanding obligation, contact the loan company directly
- File a complaint at www.IC3.gov

Malware Installed on Travelers' Laptops Through Software Updates on Hotel Internet Connections

Analysis from the FBI and other government agencies demonstrates that malicious actors are targeting travelers abroad through pop-up windows while they are establishing an Internet connection in their hotel rooms.

Travelers' laptops are being infected with malicious software when using hotel Internet connections abroad. In this attack, the traveler attempts to set up the hotel room Internet connection and is presented with a pop-up window notifying the traveler to update a widely used software product. If the traveler selects to accept and install the update, malicious software is installed on the laptop. The pop-up window appears to be offering a routine update to a legitimate software product for which updates are frequently available.

The FBI recommends that all government, private industry, and academic personnel who travel abroad take extra caution before updating software products through their hotel Internet connection. Checking the author or digital certificate of any prompted update to see if it corresponds to the software vendor may reveal an attempted attack. The FBI also recommends that travelers perform software updates on laptops immediately before traveling, and that they download software updates directly from the software vendor's Web site if updates are necessary while abroad.

Tips for Online Shopping

As more and more individuals purchase merchandise online via company Web sites or auction sites, users need to take precautions to ensure safe and reliable transactions. Safeguard online purchases by following these general tips to protect you on auction sites and to avoid credit card fraud.

Tips to Avoid Internet Auction Fraud (from http://www.fbi.gov/scams-safety/fraud/internet_fraud)

- Understand as much as possible about how the auction works, what your obligations are as a buyer, and what the seller's obligations are before you bid
- Find out what actions the Web site/company takes if a problem occurs and consider insuring the transaction and shipment
- Learn as much as possible about the seller, especially if the only information you have is an e-mail address. If it is a business, check the Better Business Bureau where the seller/business is located
- Examine the feedback on the seller
- Determine what method of payment the seller is asking from the buyer and where he/she is asking to send payment
- If possible, purchase items online using your credit card, because you can often dispute the charges if something goes wrong
- Be cautious when dealing with sellers outside the United States. If a problem occurs with the auction transaction, it could be much more difficult to rectify
- Ask the seller about when delivery can be expected and whether the merchandise is covered by a warranty or can be exchanged if there is a problem
- Make sure there are no unexpected costs, including whether shipping and handling is included in the auction price
- There should be no reason to give out your social security number or driver's license number to the seller

Tips to Avoid Credit Card Fraud

- Ensure a site is secure and reputable before providing your credit card number online
- Don't trust a site just because it claims to be secure
- If purchasing merchandise, ensure it is from a reputable source
- Promptly reconcile credit card statements to avoid unauthorized charges
- Do your research to ensure legitimacy of the individual or company
- Beware of providing credit card information when requested through unsolicited e-mails

The FBI warns to be cautious when making transactions over the Internet—making purchases, investments, doing business with unknown Internet companies, or doing business with foreign countries (419 fraud—a letter from a foreign country or government asking for your cooperation with moving large sums of money to overseas bank accounts). Some of these sites could be fraudulent or be scams to get access to your bank accounts and money. The FBI advises us to do our homework and confirm the legitimacy of any business or site that we contemplate transacting business with over the Internet.

1. iC3 Internet Crime Complaint Center, 2012 Internet Crime Report, http://www.ic3.gov/media/annualreport/2012_IC3Report.pdf. Methodology of evaluating loss amounts: FBI IC3 Unit staff reviewed for validity all complaints that reported a loss of more than $100,000. Analysts also converted losses reported in foreign currencies to dollars. The final amounts of all reported losses above $100,000 for which the complaint information did not support the loss amount were excluded from the statistics.
2. Complaint category statistics that are based on the perceptions of the complaints are not typically accurate for statistical purposes. The statistics pulled from the complaints themselves, however, are considerably more accurate as they are categorized and grouped through the IC3 automated system. IC3 does not verify complaint data.
3. http://www.ic3.gov/media/annualreport/2012_IC3Report.pdf

APPENDIX II: METHODOLOGY

Submitting Uniform Crime Reporting (UCR) program data to the Federal Bureau of Investigation (FBI) is a collective effort on the part of city, county, state, tribal, and federal law enforcement agencies to present a nationwide view of crime. Law enforcement agencies in 47 states and the District of Columbia voluntarily contribute crime data to the UCR program through their respective state UCR programs. For those states that do not have a state program, local agencies submit crime statistics directly to the FBI. The state UCR programs function as liaisons between local agencies and the FBI. Many states have mandatory reporting requirements, and many state programs collect data beyond the scope of the UCR program to address crime problems specific to their particular jurisdictions. In most cases, state programs also provide direct and frequent service to participating law enforcement agencies, make information readily available for statewide use, and help streamline the national program's operations.

Criteria for State UCR programs

The criteria established for state programs ensure consistency and comparability in the data submitted to the national program, as well as regular and timely reporting. These criteria are:

1. The state program must conform to the national UCR program standards, definitions, and information required.
2. The state criminal justice agency must have a proven, effective, statewide program and have instituted acceptable quality control procedures.
3. The state crime reporting must cover a percentage of the population at least equal to that covered by the national UCR program through direct reporting.
4. The state program must have adequate field staff assigned to conduct audits and to assist contributing agencies in record-keeping practices and crime-reporting procedures.
5. The state program must furnish the FBI with all of the detailed data regularly collected by the FBI from individual agencies that report to the state program in the form of duplicate returns, computer printouts, and/or appropriate electronic media.
6. The state program must have the proven capability (tested over a period of time) to supply all the statistical data required in time to meet publication deadlines of the national UCR program.

Data Completeness and Quality

National program staff members contact the state UCR program in connection with crime-reporting matters and, when necessary and approved by the state, they contact individual contributors within the state. To fulfill its responsibilities in connection with the UCR program, the FBI reviews and edits individual agency reports for completeness and quality. Upon request, they conduct training programs within the state on law enforcement record-keeping and crime-reporting procedures. The FBI conducts an audit of each state's UCR data collection procedures once every three years, in accordance with audit standards established by the federal government. Should circumstances develop in which the state program does not comply with the aforementioned requirements, the national program may institute a direct collection of data from law enforcement agencies within the state.

Reporting Procedures

Offenses known and value of property–Law enforcement agencies tabulate the number of Part I offenses reported based on records of all reports of crime received from victims, officers who discover infractions, or other sources, and submit these reports each month to the FBI directly or through their state UCR programs. Part I offenses include murder and nonnegligent manslaughter, forcible rape, robbery, aggravated assault, burglary, larceny-theft, motor vehicle theft, and arson. Each month, law enforcement agencies also submit to the FBI the value of property stolen and recovered in connection with the offenses and detailed information pertaining to criminal homicide.

Unfounded offenses and clearances—When, through investigation, an agency determines that complaints of crimes are unfounded or false, the agency eliminates that offense from its crime tally through an entry on the monthly report. The report also provides the total number of actual Part I offenses, the number of offenses cleared, and the number of clearances that involve only offenders under the age of 18. (Law enforcement can clear crimes in one of two ways: by the arrest of at least one person who is charged and turned over to the court for prosecution or by exceptional means—when some element beyond law enforcement's control precludes the arrest of a known offender.)

Persons arrested—In addition to reporting Part I offenses each month, law enforcement agencies also provide data on the age, sex, and race of persons arrested for Part I and Part II offenses. Part II offenses encompass all crimes, except traffic violations, that are not classified as Part I offenses.

Officers killed or assaulted—Each month, law enforcement agencies also report information to the UCR program regarding law enforcement officers killed or assaulted, and each year they report the number of full-time sworn and civilian law enforcement personnel employed as of October 31.

Hate crimes—At the end of each quarter, law enforcement agencies report summarized data on hate crimes; that is specific offenses that were motivated by an offender's bias against the perceived race, religion, ethnic or national origin, sexual orientation, or physical or mental disability of the victim. Those agencies participating in the UCR program's National Incident-Based Reporting System (NIBRS) submit hate crime data monthly.

Editing Procedures

The UCR program thoroughly examines each report it receives for arithmetical accuracy and for deviations in crime data from month to month and from present to past years that may indicate errors. UCR staff members compare an agency's monthly reports with its previous submissions and with reports from similar agencies to identify any unusual fluctuations in the agency's crime count. Considerable variations in crime levels may indicate modified records procedures, incomplete reporting, or changes in the jurisdiction's geopolitical structure.

Evaluation of trends—Data reliability is a high priority of the FBI, which brings any deviations or arithmetical adjustments to the attention of state UCR programs or the submitting agencies. Typically, FBI staff members study the monthly reports to evaluate periodic trends prepared for individual reporting units. Any significant increase or decrease becomes the subject of a special inquiry. Changes in crime reporting procedures or annexations that affect an agency's jurisdiction can influence the level of reported crime. When this occurs, the FBI excludes the figures for specific crime categories or totals, if necessary, from the trend tabulations.

Training for contributors—In addition to the evaluation of trends, the FBI provides training seminars and instructional materials on crime reporting procedures to assist contributors in complying with UCR standards. Throughout the country, representatives from the national program coordinate with representatives of state programs and law enforcement personnel and hold training sessions to explain the purpose of the program, the rules of uniform classification and scoring, and the methods of assembling the information for reporting. When an individual agency has specific problems with compiling its crime statistics and its remedial efforts are unsuccessful, personnel from the FBI's Criminal Justice Information Services Division may visit the contributor to aid in resolving the problems.

UCR Handbook—The national UCR program publishes the *Uniform Crime Reporting (UCR) Handbook* (revised 2004), which details procedures for classifying and scoring offenses and serves as the contributing agencies' basic resource for preparing reports. The national staff also produces letters to UCR contributors, state program bulletins, and UCR newsletters as needed. These publications provide policy updates and new information, as well as clarification of reporting issues.

The final responsibility for data submissions rests with the individual contributing law enforcement agency. Although the FBI makes every effort through its editing procedures, training practices, and correspondence to ensure the validity of the data it receives, the accuracy of the statistics depends primarily on the adherence of each contributor to the established standards of reporting. Deviations from these established standards that cannot be resolved by the national UCR program may be brought to the attention of the Criminal Justice Information Systems Committees of the International Association of Chiefs of Police and the National Sheriffs' Association.

Population Estimation

The FBI calculated 2012 state growth rates using the U.S. Census Bureau's 2011 and 2012 provisional state/national population estimates. The FBI then estimated population figures for city jurisdictions by applying the 2012 state growth rate to the updated 2011 U.S. Census Bureau data.

Population totals for 2000 and 2010 are from the decennial U.S. Census Bureau population counts.

NIBRS Conversion

Thirty-two state programs are certified to provide their UCR data in the expanded National Incident-Based Reporting System (NIBRS) format. For presentation in this book, the NIBRS data were converted to the historical Summary Reporting System data. The UCR program staff constructed the NIBRS database to allow for such conversion so that UCR's long-running time series could continue.

Crime Trends

By showing fluctuations from year to year, trend statistics offer the data user an added perspective from which to study crime. Percent change tabulations in this publication are computed only for reporting agencies that provided comparable data for the periods under consideration. The FBI excludes from the trend calculations all figures except those received for common months from common agencies. Also excluded are unusual fluctuations of data that the FBI determines are the result of such variables as improved records procedures, annexations, and so on.

Caution to Users

Data users should exercise care in making any direct comparison between data in this publication and those in prior issues of *Crime in the United States*. Because of differing levels of participation from year to year and reporting problems that require the FBI to estimate crime counts for certain contributors, some data may not be comparable. In addition, this publication may contain updates to data provided in prior years' publications.

For information about the FBI's caution against ranking, including warnings about variables affecting crime and characteristics of jurisdictions, please see http://www.fbi.gov/about-us/cjis/ucr/crime-in-the-u.s/2012/crime-in-the-u.s.-2012/resource-pages/caution-against-ranking/cautionagainstranking.

Offense Estimation

Some tables in this publication contain statistics for the entire United States. Because not all law enforcement agencies provide data for complete reporting periods, the FBI includes estimated crime numbers in these presentations. The FBI estimates data for three areas: Metropolitan Statistical Areas (MSAs), cities outside MSAs, and nonmetropolitan counties; and computes estimates for participating agencies that do not provide 12 months of complete data. For agencies supplying 3 to 11 months of data, the national UCR program estimates for the missing data by following a standard estimation procedure using the data provided by the agency. If an agency has supplied less than 3 months of data, the FBI computes estimates by using the known crime figures of similar areas within a state and assigning the same proportion of crime volumes to nonreporting agencies. The estimation process considers the following: population size covered by the agency; type of jurisdiction; for example, police department versus sheriff's office; and geographic location.

Estimation of State-Level Data

In response to various circumstances, the FBI calculates estimated offense totals for certain states. For example, some states do not provide forcible rape figures in accordance with UCR guidelines. In addition, problems at the state level have, at times, resulted in no useable data. Also, the conversion of the National Incident-Based Reporting System (NIBRS) data to Summary data has contributed to the need for unique estimation procedures. A summary of state-specific and offense-specific estimation procedures can be found online at http://www.fbi.gov/about-us/cjis/ucr/crime-in-the-u.s/2012/crime-in-the-u.s.-2012/methodology.

APPENDIX III: OFFENSE DEFINITIONS

The Uniform Crime Reporting (UCR) program divides offenses into two groups. Contributing agencies submit information on the number of Part I offenses known to law enforcement; those offenses cleared by arrest or exceptional means; and the age, sex, and race of persons arrested for each of thse offenses. Contributors provide only arrest data for Part II offenses. These are definitions of offenses set forth by the UCR.

The UCR program collects data on Part I offenses to measure the level and scope of crime occurring throughout the nation. The program's founders chose these offenses because (1) they are serious crimes, (2) they occur with regularity in all areas of the country, and (3) they are likely to be reported to police.

Part I offenses include criminal homicide, forcible rape, robbery, aggravated assault, burglary, larceny-theft, motor vehicle theft, and arson.

Criminal homicide—a.) Murder and nonnegligent manslaughter: the willful (nonnegligent) killing of one human being by another. Deaths caused by negligence, attempts to kill, assaults to kill, suicides, and accidental deaths are excluded. The program classifies justifiable homicides separately and limits the definition to (1) the killing of a felon by a law enforcement officer in the line of duty; or (2) the killing of a felon, during the commission of a felony, by a private citizen. b. Manslaughter by negligence: the killing of another person through gross negligence. Deaths of persons due to their own negligence, accidental deaths not resulting from gross negligence, and traffic fatalities are excluded.

Forcible rape—The carnal knowledge of a female forcibly and against her will. Assaults and attempts to commit rape by force or threat of force are also included. Statutory rape (no force used—female victim is under the age of consent) and other sex offenses are excluded. Sexual attacks on males are counted as aggravated assaults or sex offenses, depending on the circumstances and the extent of any injuries.

Robbery—The taking or attempted taking of anything of value from the care, custody, or control of a person or persons by force or threat of force or violence and/or by putting the victim in fear.

Aggravated assault—An unlawful attack by one person upon another for the purpose of inflicting severe or aggravated bodily injury. This type of assault usually is accompanied by the use of a weapon or by means likely to produce death or great bodily harm. Simple assaults are excluded.

Burglary (breaking or entering)—The unlawful entry of a structure to commit a felony or a theft. Attempted forcible entry is included.

Larceny-theft (except motor vehicle theft)—The unlawful taking, carrying, leading, or riding away of property from the possession or constructive possession of another. Examples are thefts of bicycles or automobile parts and accessories, shoplifting, pocket-picking, or the stealing of any property or article that is not taken by force and violence or by fraud. Attempted larcenies are included. Embezzlement, confidence games, forgery, worthless checks, and the like, are excluded.

Motor vehicle theft—The theft or attempted theft of a motor vehicle. A motor vehicle is self-propelled and runs on land surface and not on rails. Motorboats, construction equipment, airplanes, and farming equipment are specifically excluded from this category.

Arson—Any willful or malicious burning or attempt to burn, with or without intent to defraud, a dwelling house, public building, motor vehicle, aircraft, personal property of another, and the like.

The **Part II** offenses for which only arrest data are collected, are:

Other assaults, also known as other assaults (simple)—Assaults and attempted assaults that are not of an aggravated nature and do not result in serious injury to the victim. Included in this category are stalking, intimidation, coercion, and hazing.

Forgery and counterfeiting—The altering, copying, or imitating of something, without authority or right, with the intent to deceive or defraud by passing the copy or thing altered or imitated as that which is original or genuine; or the selling, buying, or possession of an altered, copied, or imitated thing with the intent to deceive or defraud. Attempts are included.

Fraud—The intentional perversion of the truth for the purpose of inducing another person or other entity in reliance upon it to part with something of value or to surrender a legal right. Fraudulent conversion and obtaining of money or property by false pretenses. Confidence games and bad checks, except forgeries and counterfeiting, are included.

Embezzlement—The unlawful misappropriation or misapplication by an offender of money, property, or some other thing of value entrusted to that offender's care, custody, or control.

Stolen property; buying, receiving, possessing—Buying, receiving, possessing, selling, concealing, or transporting any property with the knowledge that it has been unlawfully taken, as by burglary, embezzlement, fraud, larceny, robbery, and the like. Attempts are included.

Vandalism—To willfully or maliciously destroy, injure, disfigure, or deface any public or private property, real or personal, without the consent of the owner or person having custody or control by cutting, tearing, breaking, marking, painting, drawing, covering with filth, or any other such means as may be specified by local law. Attempts are included.

Weapons; carrying, possessing, and the like—The violation of laws or ordinances prohibiting the manufacture, sale, purchase, transportation, possession, concealment, or use of firearms, cutting instruments, explosives, incendiary devices, or other deadly weapons. Attempts are included.

Prostitution and commercialized vice—The unlawful promotion of or participation in sexual activities for profit, including attempts. To solicit customers or transport persons for prostitution purposes; to own, manage, or operate a dwelling or other establishment for the purposes of providing a place where prostitution is performed; or to otherwise assist or promote prostitution.

Sex offenses (except forcible rape, prostitution, and commercialized vice)—Offenses against chastity, common decency, morals, and the like. Incest, indecent exposure, and statutory rape, as well as attempts are included.

Drug abuse violations—The violation of laws prohibiting the production, distribution, and/or use of certain controlled substances. The unlawful cultivation, manufacture, distribution, sale, purchase, use, possession, transportation, or importation of any controlled drug or narcotic substance. Arrests for violations of state and local laws, specifically those relating to the unlawful possession, sale, use, growing, manufacturing, and making of narcotic drugs. The following drug categories are specified: opium or cocaine and their derivatives (morphine, heroin, codeine); marijuana; synthetic narcotics—manufactured narcotics that can cause true addiction (demerol, methadone); and dangerous nonnarcotic drugs (barbiturates, benzedrine).

Gambling—To unlawfully bet or wager money or something else of value; assist, promote, or operate a game of chance for money or some other stake; possess or transmit wagering information; manufacture, sell, purchase, possess, or transport gambling equipment, devices, or goods; or tamper with the outcome of a sporting event or contest to gain a gambling advantage.

Offenses against the family and children—Unlawful nonviolent acts by a family member (or legal guardian) that threaten the physical, mental, or economic well-being or morals of another family member and that are not classifiable as other offenses, such as assault or sex offenses. Attempts are included.

Driving under the influence—Driving or operating a motor vehicle or common carrier while mentally or physically impaired as the result of consuming an alcoholic beverage or using a drug or narcotic.

Liquor laws—The violation of state or local laws or ordinances prohibiting the manufacture, sale, purchase, transportation, possession, or use of alcoholic beverages, not including driving under the influence and drunkenness. Federal violations are excluded.

Drunkenness—To drink alcoholic beverages to the extent that one's mental faculties and physical coordination are substantially impaired. Excludes driving under the influence.

Disorderly conduct—Any behavior that tends to disturb the public peace or decorum, scandalize the community, or shock the public sense of morality.

Vagrancy—The violation of a court order, regulation, ordinance, or law requiring the withdrawal of persons from the streets or other specified areas; prohibiting persons from remaining in an area or place in an idle or aimless manner; or prohibiting persons from going from place to place without visible means of support.

All other offenses—All violations of state or local laws not specifically identified as Part I or Part II offenses, except traffic violations.

Suspicion—Arrested for no specific offense and released without formal charges being placed.

Curfew and loitering laws (persons under 18 years of age)—Violations by juveniles of local curfew or loitering ordinances.

APPENDIX IV: GEOGRAPHIC AREA DEFINITIONS

The program collects crime data and supplemental information that make it possible to generate a variety of statistical compilations, including data presented by reporting areas. These statistics enable data users to analyze local crime data in conjunction with those for areas of similar geographic location or population size. The reporting areas that the program uses in its data breakdowns include community types, population groups, and regions and divisions. For community types, the program considers proximity to metropolitan areas using the designations established by the U.S. Office of Management and Budget (OMB). (Generally, sheriffs, county police, and state police report crimes within counties but outside of cities; local police report crimes within city limits.) The number of inhabitants living in a locale (based on the U.S. Census Bureau's figures) determines the population group into which the program places it. For its geographic breakdowns, the program divides the United States into regions and divisions.

Regions and Divisions

The map below illustrates the nine divisions that make up the four regions of the United States. The program uses this widely recognized geographic organization when compiling the nation's crime data. The regions and divisions are as follows:

Northeast

New England—Connecticut, Maine, Massachusetts, New Hampshire, Rhode Island, and Vermont

Middle Atlantic—New York, New Jersey, and Pennsylvania

Midwest

East North Central—Illinois, Indiana, Michigan, Ohio, and Wisconsin

West North Central—Iowa, Kansas, Minnesota, Missouri, Nebraska, North Dakota, and South Dakota

South

South Atlantic—Delaware, District of Columbia, Florida, Georgia, Maryland, North Carolina, South Carolina, Virginia, and West Virginia

East South Central—Alabama, Kentucky, Mississippi, and Tennessee

West South Central—Arkansas, Louisiana, Oklahoma, and Texas

West

Mountain—Arizona, Colorado, Idaho, Montana, Nevada, New Mexico, Utah, and Wyoming

Pacific—Alaska, California, Hawaii, Oregon, and Washington

United States Regions and Divisions

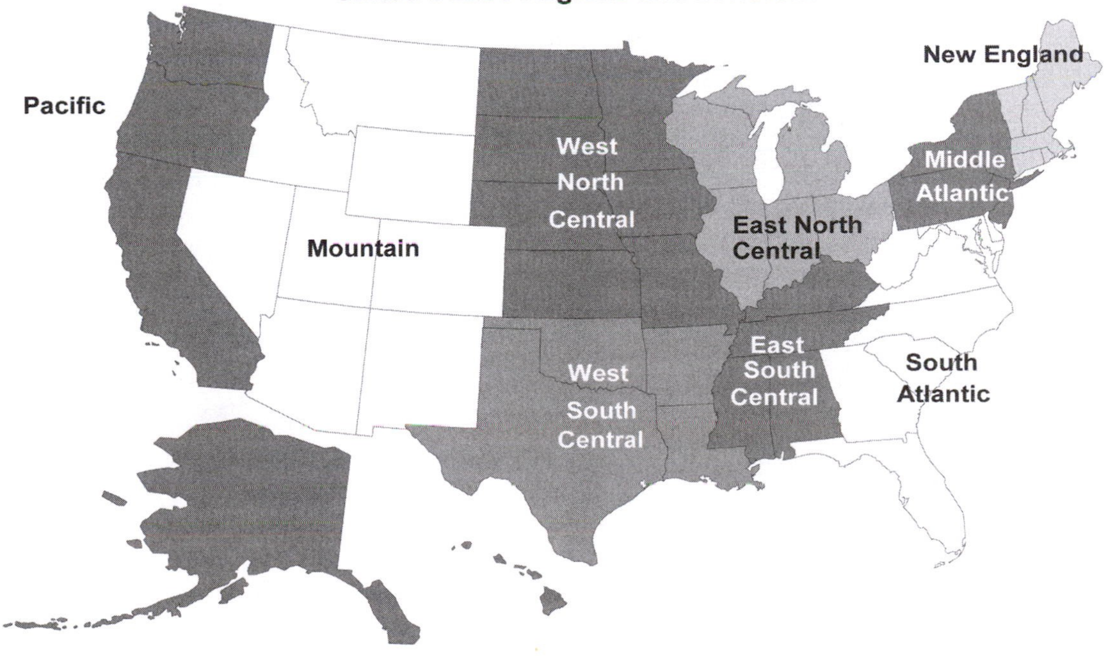

Community Types

To assist data users who wish to analyze and present uniform statistical data about metropolitan areas, the program uses reporting units that represent major population centers. The program compiles data for the following three types of communities:

Metropolitan Statistical Areas (MSAs)—Each MSA contains a principal city or urbanized area with a population of at least 50,000 inhabitants. MSAs include the principal city, the county in which the city is located, and other adjacent counties that have a high degree of economic and social integration with the principal city and county (as defined by the OMB), which is measured through commuting. In the program, counties within an MSA are considered metropolitan counties. In addition, MSAs may cross state boundaries.

Some presentations in this publication refer to Metropolitan Divisions, which are subdivisions of an MSA that consists of a core with "a population of at least 2.5 million persons. A Metropolitan Division consists of one or more main/secondary counties that represent an employment center or centers, plus adjacent counties associated with the main county or counties through commuting ties," (Federal Register 65 [249]). Also, some tables reference suburban areas, which are subdivisions of MSAs that exclude the principal cities but include all the remaining cities (those having fewer than 50,000 inhabitants) and the unincorporated areas of the MSAs.

Because the elements that comprise MSAs, particularly the geographic compositions, are subject to change, the program discourages data users from making year-to-year comparisons of MSA data.

Cities Outside MSAs—Ordinarily, cities outside MSAs are incorporated areas. In 2010, cities outside MSAs made up 6.5 percent of the nation's population.

Nonmetropolitan Counties Outside MSAs—Most nonmetropolitan counties are composed of unincorporated areas.

Metropolitan and nonmetropolitan community types are further illustrated in the following table:

Metropolitan	Nonmetropolitan
Principal cities (50,000+ inhabitants) Suburban cities	Cities outside metropolitan areas
Metropolitan counties	Nonmetropolitan counties

Population Groups

The program uses the following population group designations:

Population Group	Political Label	Population Range
I	City	250,000 or more
II	City	100,000 to 249,999
III	City	50,000 to 99,999
IV	City	25,000 to 49,999
V	City	10,000 to 24,999
VI [1,2]	City	Fewer than 10,000
VIII (Nonmetropolitan county)[2]	County	N/A
IX (Metropolitan county)[2]	County	N/A

[1]Includes universities and colleges to which no population is attributed. [2]Includes state police agencies to which no population is attributed.

Individual law enforcement agencies are the source of UCR data. The number of agencies included in each population group may vary from year to year because of population growth, geopolitical consolidation, municipal incorporation, and so on. In noncensus years, the program estimates population figures for individual jurisdictions. (A more comprehensive explanation of population estimations can be found in Appendix II.)

The categories below show the number of agencies contributing to the program within each population group for 2012:

Population Group	**Number of Agencies**	**Population Covered**
I	76	57,282,509
II	215	32,127,222
III	477	32,968,839
IV	890	30,799,296
V	1,923	30,520,288
VI[1,2]	9,514	26,643,643
VIII (Nonmetropolitan county)[2]	2.922	28,098,639
IX (Metropolitan county)[2]	2.273	75,473,604
Total	**18,290**	**313,914,040**

[1]Includes universities and colleges to which no population is attributed. [2]Includes state police to which no population is attributed.

APPENDIX V: THE NATION'S TWO CRIME MEASURES

The Department of Justice administers two statistical programs to measure the magnitude, nature, and impact of crime in the nation: the Uniform Crime Reporting (UCR) program and the National Crime Victimization Survey (NCVS). Each of these programs produces valuable information about aspects of the nation's crime problem. Because the UCR and NCVS programs are conducted for different purposes, use different methods, and focus on somewhat different aspects of crime, the information they produce together provides a more comprehensive panorama of the nation's crime problem than either could produce alone.

Uniform Crime Reporting (UCR) program

The UCR program, administered by the Federal Bureau of Investigation (FBI), was created in 1929 and collects information on the following crimes reported to law enforcement authorities: murder and nonnegligent manslaughter, forcible rape, robbery, aggravated assault, burglary, larceny-theft, motor vehicle theft, and arson. Law enforcement agencies also report arrest data for 20 additional crime categories.

The UCR program compiles data from monthly law enforcement reports and from individual crime incident records transmitted directly to the FBI or to centralized state agencies that report to the FBI. The program thoroughly examines each report it receives for reasonableness, accuracy, and deviations that may indicate errors. Large variations in crime levels may indicate modified records procedures, incomplete reporting, or changes in a jurisdiction's boundaries. To identify any unusual fluctuations in an agency's crime counts, the program compares monthly reports to previous submissions of the agency and to those for similar agencies.

The FBI annually publishes its findings in a preliminary release in the spring of the following calendar year, followed by a detailed annual report, Crime in the United States , issued in the fall. (The printed copy of *Crime in the United States* is now published by Bernan.) In addition to crime counts and trends, this report includes data on crimes cleared, persons arrested (age, sex, and race), law enforcement personnel (including the number of sworn officers killed or assaulted), and the characteristics of homicides (including age, sex, and race of victims and offenders; victim-offender relationships; weapons used; and circumstances surrounding the homicides). Other periodic reports are also available from the UCR program.

The state and local law enforcement agencies participating in the UCR program are continually converting to the more comprehensive and detailed National Incident-Based Reporting System (NIBRS). The NIBRS provides detailed information about each criminal incident in 22 broad categories of offenses.

The UCR program presents crime counts for the nation as a whole, as well as for regions, states, counties, cities, towns, tribal law enforcement areas, and colleges and universities. This allows for studies among neighboring jurisdictions and among those with similar populations and other common characteristics.

National Crime Victimization Survey

The NCVS, conducted by the Bureau of Justice Statistics (BJS), began in 1973. It provides a detailed picture of crime incidents, victims, and trends. After a substantial period of research, the BJS completed an intensive methodological redesign of the survey in 1993. It conducted this redesign to improve the questions used to uncover crime, update the survey methods, and broaden the scope of crimes measured. The redesigned survey collects detailed information on the frequency and nature of the crimes of rape, sexual assault, personal robbery, aggravated and simple assault, household burglary, theft, and motor vehicle theft. It does not measure homicide or commercial crimes (such as burglaries of stores).

Twice a year, Census Bureau personnel interview household members in a nationally representative sample of approximately 40,000 households (about 75,000 people). Approximately 150,000 interviews of individuals 12 years of age and over are conducted annually. Households stay in the sample for 3 years, and new households rotate into the sample on an ongoing basis.

The NCVS collects information on crimes suffered by individuals and households, whether or not those crimes were reported to law enforcement. It estimates the proportion of each crime type reported to law enforcement, and it summarizes the reasons that victims give for reporting or not reporting.

The survey provides information about victims (age, sex, race, ethnicity, marital status, income, and educational level); offenders (sex, race, approximate age, and victim-offender relationship); and crimes (time and place of occurrence, use of weapons, nature of injury, and economic consequences). Questions also cover victims' experiences with the criminal justice system, self-protective measures used by victims, and possible substance abuse by offenders. Supplements are added to the survey periodically to obtain detailed information on specific topics, such as school crime.

The BJS published the first data from the redesigned NCVS in a June 1995 bulletin. The publication of NCVS data includes *Criminal Victimization in the United States*, an annual report that covers the broad range of detailed information collected by the NCVS. The bureau also publishes detailed reports on topics such as crime against women, urban crime, and gun use in crime. The National Archive of Criminal Justice Data at the University of Michigan archives the NCVS data files to help researchers perform independent analyses.

Comparing the UCR program and the NCVS

Because the BJS designed the NCVS to complement the UCR program, the two programs share many similarities. As much as their different collection methods permit, the two measure the same subset of serious crimes with the same definitions. Both programs cover rape, robbery, aggravated assault, burglary, theft, and motor vehicle theft; both define rape, robbery, theft, and motor vehicle theft virtually identically. (Although rape is defined analogously, the UCR program measures the crime against women only, and the NCVS measures it against both sexes.)

There are also significant differences between the two programs. First, the two programs were created to serve different purposes. The UCR program's primary objective is to provide a reliable set of criminal justice statistics for law enforcement administration, operation, and management. The BJS established the NCVS to provide previously unavailable information about crime (including crime not reported to police), victims, and offenders.

Second, the two programs measure an overlapping but nonidentical set of crimes. The NCVS includes crimes both reported and not reported to law enforcement. The NCVS excludes—but the UCR program includes—homicide, arson, commercial crimes, and crimes committed against children under 12 years of age. The UCR program captures crimes reported to law enforcement but collects only arrest data for simple assaults and sexual assaults other than forcible rape.

Third, because of methodology, the NCVS and UCR have different definitions of some crimes. For example, the UCR defines burglary as the unlawful entry or attempted entry of a structure to commit a felony or theft. The NCVS, not wanting to ask victims to ascertain offender motives, defines burglary as the entry or attempted entry of a residence by a person who had no right to be there.

Fourth, for property crimes (burglary, theft, and motor vehicle theft), the two programs calculate crime rates using different bases. The UCR program rates for these crimes are per capita (number of crimes per 100,000 persons), whereas the NCVS rates for these crimes are per household (number of crimes per 1,000 households).

Because the number of households may not grow at the same annual rate as the total population, trend data for rates of property crimes measured by the two programs may not be comparable. In addition, some differences in the data from the two programs may result from sampling variation in the NCVS and from estimating for nonresponsiveness in the UCR program.

The BJS derives the NCVS estimates from interviewing a sample and are, therefore, subject to a margin of error. The bureau uses rigorous statistical methods to calculate confidence intervals around all survey estimates, and describes trend data in the NCVS reports as genuine only if there is at least a 90-percent certainty that the measured changes are not the result of sampling variation. The UCR program bases its data on the actual counts of offenses reported by law enforcement agencies. In some circumstances, the UCR program estimates its data for nonparticipating agencies or those reporting partial data. Apparent discrepancies between statistics from the two programs can usually be accounted for by their definitional and procedural differences, or resolved by comparing NCVS sampling variations (confidence intervals) of crimes said to have been reported to police with UCR program statistics.

For most types of crimes measured by both the UCR program and the NCVS, analysts familiar with the programs can exclude those aspects of crime not common to both from analysis. Resulting long-term trend lines can be brought into close concordance. The impact of such adjustments is most striking for robbery, burglary, and motor vehicle theft, whose definitions most closely coincide.

With robbery, the BJS bases the NCVS victimization rates on only those robberies reported to the police. It is also possible to remove UCR program robberies of commercial establishments, such as gas stations, convenience stores, and banks, from analysis. When users compare the resulting NCVS police-reported robbery rates and the UCR program noncommercial robbery rates, the results reveal closely corresponding long-term trends.

Conclusion

Each program has unique strengths. The UCR program provides a measure of the number of crimes reported to law enforcement agencies throughout the country. The program's Supplementary Homicide Reports provide the most reliable, timely data on the extent and nature of homicides in the nation. The NCVS is the primary source of information on the characteristics of criminal victimization and on the number and types of crimes not reported to law enforcement authorities.

By understanding the strengths and limitations of each program, it is possible to use the UCR program and NCVS to achieve a greater understanding of crime trends and the nature of crime in the United States. For example, changes in police procedures, shifting attitudes towards crime and police, and other societal changes can affect the extent to which people report and law enforcement agencies record crime. NCVS and UCR program data can be used in concert to explore why trends in reported and police-recorded crime may differ.

INDEX

N